SEVASTOPOL'S WARS

OSPREY
PUBLISHING

MUNGO MELVIN

SEVASTOPOL'S WARS

CRIMEA FROM POTEMKIN TO PUTIN

First published in Great Britain in 2017 by Osprey Publishing,
PO Box 883, Oxford, OX1 9PL, UK
1385 Broadway, 5th Floor, New York, NY 10018, USA

E-mail: info@ospreypublishing.com

Osprey Publishing, part of Bloomsbury Publishing Plc

ISBN: 978 1 4728 0794 6
PDF e-book ISBN: 978 1 4728 2228 4
ePub e-book ISBN: 978 1 4728 2227 7

Index by Zoe Ross
Cartography © Barbara Taylor
Typeset in Garamond Premier Pro and Adobe Garamond Pro
Originated by PDQ Media, Bungay, UK
Printed in China through World Print Ltd.

17 18 19 20 21 10 9 8 7 6 5 4 3 2 1

Back cover image: The 'Soldier and Sailor' monument overlooking Sevastopol Bay.
(©RIA Novosti/TopFoto)
Back flap image: Mungo Melvin (Author's Collection)

Osprey Publishing supports the Woodland Trust, the UK's leading woodland conservation
charity. Between 2014 and 2018 our donations will be spent on their Centenary Woods project
in the UK.

To find out more about our authors and books, visit **www.ospreypublishing.com**. Here you will find
extracts, author interviews, details of forthcoming events and the option to sign up for our newsletters.

CONTENTS

PART THREE: CITY OF REVOLUTION

PART FOUR: MODERN WAR

LIST OF MAPS

LIST OF ILLUSTRATIONS

BETWEEN PAGES 256 AND 257

1. The Basilica of Ancient Chersonesos. (Vladimir Zizak)
2. St Vladimir Cathedral in Ancient Chersonesos. (Vladimir Zizak)
3. Prince Grigory Aleksandrovich Potemkin. (Photo by Hulton Archive/Getty Images)
4. Russian Empress Catherine II ('the Great'). (Fine Art Images/Heritage Images/Getty Images)
5. Monument to the foundation of Sevastopol. (Vladimir Zizak)
6. Monument to Kazarsky and the sailors of the brig *Merkurii*. (Vladimir Zizak)
7. Admiral Mikhail Petrovich Lazarev. (Fine Art Images/Heritage Images/Getty Images)
8. Vice Admiral Vladimir Alekseyevich Kornilov. (SCRSS/TopFoto)
9. Rear Admiral Vladimir Ivanovich Istomin. (New York Public Library)
10. Vice Admiral Pavel Stepanovich. (Popperfoto/Getty Images)
11. 'Russian Squadron on the Sevastopol Roadstead' by Ivan Aivazovsky. (Fine Art Images/Heritage Images/Getty Images)
12. 'View of Sevastopol' by Carlo Bossoli. (Fine Art Images/Heritage Images/Getty Images)
13. 'Docks at Sevastopol' by William Simpson. (Hulton Archive/Getty Images)
14. 'Hot Day in the Batteries' by William Simpson. (Universal History Archive/Getty Images)
15. Emperor Nicholas I. (Fine Art Images/Heritage Images/Getty Images)
16. Emperor Alexander II. (Hulton Archive/Getty Images)
17. Prince Alexander Sergeyevich Menshikov. (Fine Art Images/Heritage Images/Getty Images)
18. Professor Nikolay Ivanovich Pirogov. (Universal History Archive/UIG via Getty Images)
19. Lord Raglan, Omar Pasha and Marshal Pélissier, 7 June 1855. (Library of Congress)
20. Lieutenant General Sir John Fox Burgoyne. (Universal History Archive/Getty Images)
21. Count Lev (Leo) Nikolayevich Tolstoy. (Universal History Archive/UIG via Getty Images)
22. Charles George Gordon. (Photo by Hulton Archive/Getty Images)
23. The Fourth Battery at Sevastopol's Fourth Bastion, 1920. (© IWM Q 37442)
24. Monument to General Eduard Ivanovich Todleben. (Vladimir Zizak)
25. The Malakhov Tower depicted after the withdrawal of troops in 1855. (RIA Novosti/TopFoto)
26. The reconstructed Malakhov Tower today. (Vladimir Zizak)
27. 'Huts and Warm Clothing for the Army' by William Simpson. (Fine Art Images/Heritage Images/Getty Images)
28. 'Railway at Balaklava' by William Simpson. (Oxford Science Archive/Print Collector/Getty Images)
29. View of Balaklava, photographed by James Robertson. (Public domain)
30. The Black Sea Fleet Museum. (Vladimir Zizak)
31. Detail of 'The Defence of Sevastopol 1854–1855' by Franz Rubo. (Author's collection)
32. The Panorama, the Defence of Sevastopol 1854–1855 Museum. (Author's collection)
33. The Monument to the Scuttled Ships. (Vladimir Zizak)
34. Impounded Russian warships during the German occupation of Sevastopol, 1918. (Bundesarchiv)
35. The mutinous Russian battleship *Prince Potemkin*, 1905. (Hulton Archive/Getty Images)
36. Lieutenant Pyotr Petrovich Schmidt, leader of the *Ochakov* mutiny. (© TASS/TopFoto)
37. The Monument to Lieutenant P. P. Schmidt. (Vladimir Zizak)
38. The German battlecruiser SMS *Goeben*, 1914. (Bundesarchiv)
39. Rear Admiral Wilhelm Anton Souchon. (ullstein bild/ullstein bild via Getty Images)
40. General Robert Paul Theodor Kosch. (Library of Congress)
41. Emperor Nicholas II. (The Print Collector/Getty Images)
42. Vladimir Ilyich Ulyanov, alias Lenin. (Sputnik/TopFoto)
43. Pyotr Nikolayevich, Baron Wrangel. (Fine Art Images/Heritage Images/Getty Images)
44. Mikhail Vasilyevich Frunze. (RIA Novosti/Sputnik/ TopFoto)

BETWEEN PAGES 480 AND 481

LIST OF TABLES

AUTHOR'S NOTE

Any book that concerns itself with Russian history or language presents a number of challenges to English-speakers. This note seeks to explain the different systems of dates in use until 1918; the conventions adopted in the transliteration of the Russian Cyrillic alphabet; how the names of individuals and places may change according to historical period and language; and what units of measurement are used. The note concludes with a summary of military terminology, together with comparative tables of army and naval ranks, and a general key to the colour maps.

DATES AND CHRONOLOGY

Until the Bolsheviks adopted the Western (Gregorian) calendar on 31 January 1918, Russia had followed the Julian calendar. This dating system lagged eleven days behind the Gregorian in the eighteenth century, twelve days in the nineteenth century and thirteen days in the twentieth century. Where 'Old-Style' Russian dates of the Julian calendar are quoted, these are annotated as: [OS]. Where both the Julian and Gregorian dates need to be shown together, such as when referring to documents or key historical events, the day concerned is rendered as '3 (14) June 1783', where 3 is the Julian and 14 the Gregorian date – this example is the foundation date of Sevastopol. These exceptions apart, all other dates given in this book, including the Chronology, follow the 'New Style' of the Gregorian calendar.

Readers may find the Chronology a useful guide to the most important events that have affected Crimea and Sevastopol, either directly or indirectly, from the foundation of the Greek colony of Chersonesos in 422–421 BC (near which site modern Sevastopol was established) to the seventieth anniversary of the liberation of Sevastopol celebrated on 9 May 2014.

SPELLINGS AND PLACE NAMES

This book adopts a simplified British Standard system of transliterating Cyrillic Russian text into the Latin alphabet. This method of transliteration, as opposed to the alternative United States Library of Congress system, is largely intuitive in so far as the English spelling mirrors both Russian and English pronunciation closely. So the Russian letter 'я' becomes 'ya' as in the Crimean coastal city of Yalta; and 'ю' becomes 'yu' as in the common Russian female name of Yuliya, which, just to complicate matters, is often rendered as the more familiar 'Julia'.[1] The Russian letter 'e' presents more difficulties in that it can be transliterated either as 'ye' or remain 'e', depending on its position in a word, and after which letter it stands. At the beginning of a word it becomes 'ye' as in the western Crimean port of Yevpatoriya; it is likewise pronounced and transliterated as 'ye' following vowels, as in the name of the legendary Red Army Chapayev Rifle Division[2], and after the Russian soft ь and hard ъ signs. The Russian 'ё' presents a particular difficulty in that it is usually spelt in English without an umlaut as in familiar Russian surnames such as Gorbachev, Khrushchev and Potemkin. In each case, however, the pronunciation of 'e' in these names is 'yo'. To simplify matters elsewhere, 'yo' is generally used rather than 'ё', so the Russian city name (and word for eagle) becomes Oryol.[3] Exceptionally, I spell the river that feeds into Sevastopol Bay as Chernaya (its familiar form in Crimean histories) rather than Chërnaya or Chyornaya.

The names of Russian tsarinas and tsars are given in their conventional forms such as Catherine II (usually referred to as Catherine the Great), Nicholas I and II, Alexanders I–III. Generally Russian first (given) names have been transliterated more closely, such as Nikolay and Aleksandr, or Aleksey and Sergey. Ukrainian forms are similar but follow different spelling. The 'ii' and 'iy' endings in many Russian names (both first and family) have been simplified to 'y' as in Dmitry and Trotsky. There are exceptions, however, not least in the citing of individuals or names of ships, when either common convention differs or where another usage is directly quoted. It is impossible to be entirely consistent in such matters, as personal preferences play a part. In most cases, the female version of a Russian family name ends with an 'a'; hence Vorontsov becomes Vorontsova. Russians have three names: given, patronymic and family. The patronymic is derived from the father's given name, so the son of an Ivan has Ivanovich as his second name; in turn, his daughter's patronymic would be Ivanovna.

Place names offer many pitfalls to the unwary. Over the period of this book, political events have forced not only changes in borders, but also shifted linguistic boundaries, custom and practice. I have chosen, at the risk of upsetting my Ukrainian friends, to retain the more familiar Russian spelling of Kharkov

12

(Kharkiv in Ukrainian), Kiev (Kyiv), Lvov (Lviv), Nikolayev (Mykolaiv) and Odessa (Odesa). For the sake of simplicity, I have dropped the Russian soft sign ь (transliterated as ') throughout the main text of the book so Sevastopol, for example, is not spelt Sevastopol', and Kharkov is not Khar'kov. The former, erroneous, British use of 'Sebastopol' and 'Balaclava' in place of Sevastopol and Balaklava has not been followed in this book. I have used the more familiar Dnieper rather than the Russian Dnepr or Ukrainian Dnipro for the great river that bisects Ukraine.

Within Crimea, many names of villages were changed in 1945 following the expulsion of the Tatar population the year before and to commemorate the victory won in the Second World War. Thus Kamara (near the Balaklava battlefield of 1854) was renamed Oboronnoye and Chorgun became Chernorechye. The Tatar hamlet of Yukhary Karalez, where Field Marshal Erich von Manstein sited his forward headquarters during the final Axis assault on Sevastopol in 1942, was renamed Zalesnoye. Wherever possible, both old and new names have been given on the maps to assist readers in tracing past events across modern terrain.

MEASUREMENTS

The metric system of measurement, which was adopted by the Soviet Union in 1924, is used throughout with some important exceptions. British imperial system units are used when directly or indirectly quoted, and in referring to specific calibres of artillery weapons such as '12-inch guns', according to the country of origin and period concerned. To enable comparisons to be made between certain distances and calibres, in some instances both units of measurement are shown. Two obsolete Russian units of measurement are quoted. The first is the 'verst', a unit of distance that corresponds to 1.0668 kilometres; the second is the 'pood', a unit of weight, corresponding to 16.3807 kilogrammes.

MILITARY TERMINOLOGY

Those not familiar with military terminology may find the following details helpful. Although weapons technologies have evolved significantly since the Crimean War, a considerable degree of continuity existed in army structures until the First and Second World Wars. The basic tactical building block of the French, German and Russian Armies (and later the Red Army), was the infantry regiment, composed of three or four battalions.[4] In most continental armies, two regiments formed a brigade, and two brigades a division.[5] Two to three divisions were grouped into an army corps. Several such corps formed an army. By the time of

Formation/ Unit/Sub Unit	Typically Commanded By			
	American Army	British Army	German Army	Soviet Army
Army Group/*Front*	General of the Army or General	Field Marshal or General	Generalfeldmarschall (Field Marshal) or Generaloberst (Colonel General)	Marshal Sovetskogo Soyuza (Marshal of the Soviet Union) or General armii (General of the Army)
Army	General or Lieutenant General	General or Lieutenant General	Generaloberst (Colonel General) or General der Infanterie (General of Infantry)	General armii (General of the Army) or General-Polkovnik (Colonel General)
Army Corps/Corps	Lieutenant General or Major General	Lieutenant General	General der Infanterie (General of Infantry) or Generalleutnant (Lieutenant General)	General-Leytenant (Lieutenant General)
Division	Major General	Major General	Generalleutnant (Lieutenant General) or Generalmajor (Major General)	General-Major (Major General)
Brigade	Brigadier General	Brigadier	Generalmajor (Major General)	General-Major (Major General) or Polkovnik (Colonel)
Regiment	Colonel	Lieutenant Colonel	Oberst (Colonel)	Polkovnik (Colonel)
Battalion	Lieutenant Colonel	Lieutenant Colonel	Oberstleutnant (Lieutenant Colonel) or Major	Podpolkovnik (Lieutenant Colonel)
Company	Captain	Major or Captain	Hauptmann (Captain)	Kapitan (Captain)
Platoon	1st Lieutenant	Lieutenant or Second Lieutenant	Leutnant (Lieutenant)	Starshiy Leytenant (Senior Lieutenant); Leytenant (Lieutenant); Mladshiy Leytenant (Junior Lieutenant)

Table 0.1 – Officer Army Ranks used during the Second World War

the First World War, with the huge expansion of the numbers of troops employed, a force of several armies was called an 'army group' – the equivalent of a Russian '*front*'. The terminology of the British Army, by comparison, differs to this day in one important respect: the term 'regiment' is often used interchangeably with battalion. The British cavalry consists of battalion-sized regiments. Infantry battalions and cavalry, and later, armoured (tank), regiments were grouped together in brigades.

To aid comparison between the German and Soviet formations during the Second World War, German armies are numbered in full as 'Eleventh', while a Soviet one is abbreviated to '51st'. By convention, German corps are given Roman numbers such as 'XXX', while a Soviet (or an earlier Imperial Russian) one is referred to by an Arabic number such as '19th'.

Military ranks for the most part are standardised between armies. During the Second World War, German and Soviet Army ranks were broadly similar, as were American and British ones. The principal differences arose in the level of command of a regiment, in which British practice differed as explained above, and in the rank of Brigadier (General). This rank did not exist in the German and Soviet Armies. Army and navy ranks are compared in the following tables, together with a general key to the colour maps (2–17) that describes the military symbols employed. Please note that British ranks such as Major General used to be hyphenated and Soviet ones such as General-Major remained so.

US Navy	Royal Navy	German Navy	Soviet Navy
Fleet Admiral	Admiral of the Fleet	Großadmiral	Admiral-flota Sovetskogo Soyuza; Admiral-flota
Admiral	Admiral	Generaladmiral	Admiral
Vice Admiral	Vice-Admiral	Admiral	Vitse-admiral
Rear Admiral	Rear-Admiral	Vizeadmiral/ Konteradmiral	Kontr-admiral
Commodore	Commodore	Konteradmiral/ Kommodore	
Captain	Captain	Kapitän zur See	Kapitan 1. ranga
Commander	Commander	Fregattenkapitän	Kapitan 2. ranga
Lieutenant Commander	Lieutenant Commander	Korvettenkapitän	Kapitan 3. ranga
Lieutenant	Lieutenant	Kapitänleutnant	Kapitan-leytenant
Lieutenant (Junior Grade)	Sub-Lieutenant	Oberleutnant zur See	Leytenant
Ensign	Midshipman	Leutnant zur See	Mladshiy Leytenant

Table 0.2 – Officer Naval Ranks used during the Second World War

MAPS

xxxxx ☐	Army Group or *Front* (Russian/Soviet)	◪	Cavalry	—xxx—	Inter-formation Boundary (in this case between corps)	
xxxx ☐	Army	⬭	Armoured	➤	Attack	
xxx ☐	Corps	⊠	Infantry	↩☐	Withdrawal/Delaying action	
xx ☐	Division	⊠	Mountain Infantry	⚓	Naval Anchorage or Port	

Colour Codes Used on Maps		
Colour	Maps 5–10	Maps 11–17
Blue	French	German
Brown	Turkish/ Sardinian	Romanian
Green	Russian	White Russian
Purple	Allied	–
Red	British	Soviet

x ☐	Brigade	⊠ sss	Marine or Naval Infantry
III ☐	Regiment (not British)	◉	Assault Gun or Anti-Tank Gun (Armoured)
II ☐	Battalion	ı|ı	Towed Artillery

Table 0.3 – General Key to the Colour Maps 2–17

Other symbols used, such as those for roads, railways and the front lines of armies, whether in attack or defence, should be self-evident. To save space in the maps, some dates have been abbreviated in the form of '5 Nov 55' in the case of 5 November 1855, for example. To avoid any ambiguity, the year concerned is given in full in the map title.

PROLOGUE

*'Every day the main city clock plays "Legendary Sevastopol".
While listening to this melody, remember everything this
glorious city [has] survived and look at its sights attentively
and respectfully.'*

From a Sevastopol guidebook (2003)[1]

Brass bands playing, drums beating, crowds cheering and flags fluttering in the light spring breeze – a richly-medalled Red Army veteran, retired marine plant engineer and noted local historian, Vladimir Stepanovich Usoltsev, takes stock of the scene around him. Although eighty-eight years old, and getting frail, he remains determined to join the parade this year. From the forming-up point on Sevastopol's Suvorov Square, down the gradual gradient of Lenin Street to the special veterans' viewing stand at the war memorial on Nakhimov Square is relatively easy going (see Map 2). Many friends and members of his family are present specially to support him. Sadly, his dear wife, Antonina Terentyevna, passed away some eight years before. He can surely make the distance today, perhaps for the last time. He steps off at a careful, measured pace: the veterans are on the march again! Every now and then he recognises an old colleague in the crowd beckoning to him. Vladimir Stepanovich waves back happily. With pride he reflects on the fact that he has taken part in this annual march at Sevastopol for over fifty years.

It is Friday, 9 May 2014 – 'Victory Day', which is a double commemoration in the Crimean port and main base of the Russian Black Sea Fleet. Soviet forces liberated this 'city of glory' from its German and Romanian occupiers on

17

9 May 1944. Exactly one year later, on 9 May 1945, victory in Europe was declared by the Soviet Union over Nazi Germany. Since the end of the Second World War, both events have been celebrated together in Sevastopol by parades and displays of military and naval hardware. Following the break-up of the Soviet Union in 1991, the armed forces of both the Russian Federation and Ukraine took part, often parading side by side in a demonstration of fraternal unity.

Victory Day is the most important event in Sevastopol's calendar, closely followed by Navy Day. For many of the elder residents, including former naval and military personnel, such as Vladimir Stepanovich, it serves as a reminder of the 'good old days' of Soviet power and influence. For the vast majority of Sevastopol's population and its many visitors on the day, the parade remains a fitting and poignant tribute to the enormous losses and suffering endured by the Soviet peoples during the 'Great Patriotic War', some 29 million.

Yet today is a very special Victory Day, and the procedure will differ from previous years. It is rumoured that none other than Vladimir Vladimirovich Putin, President of the Russian Federation, will be present. Another victory celebration is in the air. As he marches, Vladimir Stepanovich thinks about this remarkable turn of events. The Ukrainian military is no longer present. 'Crimea is at last fully Russian,' he muses, 'and Sevastopol has been liberated again!' The Crimean Spring has become the Russian Spring. What has occurred has exceeded the veteran's wildest dreams. Only recently, on 18 March 2014, the city of Sevastopol and the Republic of Crimea were reunited with Russia. Usoltsev himself had written a book about Sevastopol's founder, Rear Admiral Thomas Mackenzie.[2] In 1783, the Russo-Scot had built the first modern city here during the reign of Empress Catherine the Great. Sevastopol was, and remains, as Russian as the great northern port of Arkhangelsk (Archangel), where Mackenzie reputedly was born in 1740.

After half an hour, the veterans reach Nakhimov Square. On gaining their reserved seats, Vladimir Stepanovich turns briefly to his sister, Valentina Fedorovna. He smiles to her and opens his lips to speak, but no words are needed for his bright eyes say it all: 'joy!' The siblings then watch the military bands, honour guards and marchers pass, contingents of sailors of the Black Sea Fleet, soldiers, airmen, younger veterans, re-enactors, various groups of workers, young people and school children in their thousands. The procession of smart uniforms, colourful flowers and stirring music appears endless. All are happy. It is such a wonderful, splendid occasion for them and countless other spectators. Yet perhaps a silent minority of Ukrainians in this arch pro-Russian city mourn the manner in which Russia has recently annexed Crimea and Sevastopol.

Overhead, modern Russian fighter jets streak over Sevastopol Bay. In the grand harbour below, naval vessels, headed by the flagship of the Black Sea Fleet, the guided missile cruiser *Moskva*, put on a dramatic display. The delighted crowds cannot recall such a powerful demonstration of Russian military capabilities for many years, perhaps the grandest such occasion since Soviet days.

The greatest cheer of the day comes when the President, hot foot from Moscow's Red Square parade, flies into Crimea during the afternoon. He crosses Sevastopol Bay by naval cutter. Walking up the noble steps of the *Grafskaya Pristan*, the Count's Landing Stage, he then crosses Nakhimov Square, mobbed by the crowd. A chanting chorus of *'spasibo, spasibo'* (thank you, thank you) greets him. At the vast monument to the fallen of the Great Patriotic War, flanked by veterans of the Black Sea Fleet, the President lays a wreath. It is a moment of both personal and national triumph.

Not far away, the end of an apartment block has been freshly painted with a giant mural of Vladimir Putin in naval uniform. In bold letters is written: 'Welcome home to the native harbour'. The President of the Russian Federation does not need to read these words: he senses the same message from the jubilant masses in front of him. Instead he tells his ecstatic audience, many with tears in their eyes: 'We are proud of your courage and bravery, and we respect the way you have kept your love of the Fatherland through the years and generations. And now, the Fatherland is embracing you once again as family, as daughters and sons.'[3]

As they prepare to leave their seats at the end of a glorious day, Valentina Fedorovna quietly says to her brother, 'I can die now, for I have lived this day'. Vladimir Stepanovich feels exactly the same way. It is indeed the last time that the proud veteran marches on the Victory Day parade.[4]

Seven years before, almost to the day, a middle-aged British visitor and a Crimean guide approach the city of Sevastopol from the north. A new day in early May brightens as the morning fog swiftly clears. It rolls back towards a sandy, deserted beach only a kilometre away, and then drifts further out over an uninviting, silver-grey sea. Thankfully, the drizzle has now stopped. A warming sun revives the pair, along with the infusion of clear fresh air. A small Russian Orthodox chapel emerges into view; its golden onion dome glistens brightly. All is perfectly still in the old settlement of Lyubimovka to their front.

Abruptly a dog barks and scampers into sight. Precisely at this moment, my companion Eduard whispers: 'Look: do you see it?' Scarcely masking my irritation, I respond: 'What's there? What do you mean? It's just an animal!' But all of a sudden, without further prompting, something extraordinary catches my eye. A time-frozen image fixes my attention.

Two hundred metres beyond the chapel, and only just discernible against a dark-green grassy bank, I detect two armoured turrets lurking under low camouflage nets. These formidable armaments look as if they once belonged to a battleship. Peering more closely through my binoculars as the visibility steadily improves, I observe six long barrels poking out menacingly towards the Crimean shore. Their intimidating appearance – such an unambiguous symbol of military power – both surprises and shocks me. I ask myself whether these are some old museum pieces, or could they still be serviceable weapons of war?

My guide, a former Sevastopol city police inspector and now keen military enthusiast, quickly enlightens me. Eduard proclaims the guns are none other than those of the legendary Coastal Battery No. 30. With obvious pride, he tells me that during the Second World War the devastating fire of their equally formidable predecessors broke up countless German attacks towards Sevastopol. Throughout the 250-day siege of the city in 1941–42, the battery proved a tough, tiresome thorn in the side of the Axis forces under General Erich von Manstein's command. The Germans grudgingly respected the brave soldiers of the battery they called 'Fort Maxim Gorky I'. After many attempts, they eventually destroyed it by a lethal cocktail of ferocious air, artillery and ground attack. The Soviets' valiant resistance here – against all the odds – became one of the defining tales of the heroic defence of Sevastopol.

My discovery of this famous city – its notable characters and chronicles, defences and defenders – had barely begun. Back in 2007, I was writing a biography of Manstein, and planning a battlefield tour of his Crimean campaign of 1941–42. A few years later, following the completion of that study, my interest in Sevastopol increased. I resolved to research deeper into the city's past, and so reveal its wider military history.

Apart from dimly remembered episodes in the histories of the Crimean and Second World Wars, or as an occasional tourist destination (along with Yalta, Sevastopol used to be one of the routine stops during Black Sea cruises), the city was little known outside the former Soviet Union until the events of 2014. Its origins and enduring purpose lie in its commanding strategic position as the most important naval anchorage in the Black Sea. While nature has been kind to Sevastopol, history has proved less so: the city has been fought over several times, involving two great sieges. Twice it has been almost completely destroyed. Yet twice it has risen, phoenix-like, from the ashes. On both occasions, its combatants and builders, whether naval, military or civilian, have shown remarkable resilience. Not just for the citizens of the former Soviet Union, do their displays of courage, fortitude and grit continue to astound.

Sevastopol leaves a lifelong impression on any visitor. A young and feckless Count Leo Tolstoy served here as a junior artillery officer during the Crimean War. As he expressed so timelessly in his sketch of the city then under siege by British and French forces (1854–55):

> The principal, joyous, thought you have brought away with you is a conviction of
> the strength of the Russian people; and the conviction you gained, not by looking

at all those traverses, breastworks, cunningly interlaced trenches, mines, cannon, one on top of the other, of which you could make nothing; but you have received it from the eyes, words, and actions—in short, from seeing what is called the 'spirit'—of the defenders of Sevastopol.[5]

In Britain we rarely dwell on this 'War with Russia', which subsequently became known as the Crimean War. This mid-nineteenth-century conflict – and one much larger in locus than the Crimean peninsula – was widely regarded as an unfortunate aberration. The naval campaigns of the Baltic and Far East were overshadowed by the Crimean land battles of Alma, Balaklava and Inkerman.

The trials and tribulations of the British Army 'before Sevastopol' became the subject of an immediate parliamentary inquiry, which found significant weaknesses in various aspects of command, organisation, supply and medical support.[6] So in many respects, the war represented a failure best quickly forgotten, except for the individual gallantry shown on the battlefield. Outstanding bravery was recognised by the institution of the Victoria Cross in 1856. Made from the bronze of captured Sevastopol cannon, it is conferred for 'most conspicuous bravery, or some daring or pre-eminent act of valour or self-sacrifice, or extreme devotion to duty in the presence of the enemy'. No fewer than 111 VCs were awarded to members of the British armed forces as a result of the Crimean War.

The cannon from Sevastopol provide an important clue as to the subject of this book. When the Minister of Defence of the Soviet Union, Marshal D. T. Yazov, visited the Royal Military Academy Sandhurst, England, in the late 1980s, a bumptious British Army officer (of a type now fortunately almost extinct) intervened. He remarked that several of the guns in front of the Old College were captured at Sevastopol, and that 'we still had them'. The very senior Soviet officer, a veteran of the Great Patriotic War (as the Second World War is still described in Russia), put him down brilliantly – 'But we still have Ukraine'.[7] His confidence, however, proved misplaced. Yazov, in common with many millions of disillusioned Russians, was forced to witness the abrupt break-up of the Soviet Union and emergence of Ukraine as an independent, sovereign state, Crimea included.

Yazov was involved in the 1991 coup against President Mikhail Gorbachev and suffered a spell of imprisonment.[8] With the incorporation of Crimea, and not least Sevastopol, into the Russian Federation in March 2014, however, the last laugh in this story – for now at least – goes to Yazov. In November that year, President Vladimir Putin cordially greeted him on his ninetieth birthday. Although Yazov's rehabilitation had preceded Sevastopol's reunification with Russia, no doubt he felt vindicated by his action twenty-three years before. For him and like-minded people, Crimea and Sevastopol, only nominally 'Ukrainian', were worth fighting for.

During the Second World War, the German and Romanian forces under Manstein's command eventually captured the Black Sea fortress of Sevastopol on 1 July 1942. Manstein's success prompted the rare thanks of a grateful Adolf Hitler and earned him a field marshal's baton in the process. Despite this accolade, the 250-day-long struggle for the city proved to be a Pyrrhic victory. On both sides, the death toll was staggering.[9] The stoic Soviet defence had imposed considerable distraction, dissipation and delay on German forces. The battle for Sevastopol contributed to the failure of the *Wehrmacht*'s summer offensive. Operation BLAU (BLUE) culminated four months later in the northern Caucasus and at Stalingrad. Despite their defeat in Crimea, Soviet forces drew considerable satisfaction from the battle of Sevastopol. Although soon over-shadowed by their subsequent victory at Stalingrad, the defence of the Crimean city provided much inspiration to the Soviet people and to the country's armed forces.

The endurance and heroism demonstrated at Sevastopol yielded welcome grist to the Soviet propaganda mill. Unsurprisingly, one of the Red Army's most notable war correspondents, Ilya Ehrenburg, described Sevastopol as a 'city of courage'. He penned further: 'it has become a symbol of resistance ... The heroes of Sevastopol will travel throughout the length and breadth of liberated Russia. Flowers will blossom for them.'[10] There is no doubt that the prolonged defence of Sevastopol, although ultimately doomed, was a considerable Soviet military achievement.[11]

The city and the main base of the Black Sea Fleet were totally reconstructed after the Second World War. So too was Battery 30 in 1954. In that same year, Nikita Khrushchev, First Secretary of the Communist Party of the Soviet Union, graciously 'gifted' Crimea to the Soviet Socialist Republic of Ukraine to mark the 300th anniversary of the union of Russia and Ukraine. Throughout the post-Soviet period, the coastal battery at Lyubimovka has remained manned, supplied and held in readiness by Russian Federation troops; the Cold War does not seem to have ended here. Perhaps this should not surprise us, for Sevastopol and its fleet together hold a unique, special place in both Russian imperial and Soviet history.

As I was to learn, the story of Sevastopol displays a captivating combination of contrast and paradox, much still entwined with myth and propaganda. Reminders of Sevastopol's harsh realities forged by war remain very evident. Its true history comes to life not only from reading the accounts of its citizens and defenders, but equally from exploring the city's noble boulevards, mighty bastions and pretty parks. Monuments appear round every corner: former sons and daughters, admirals and generals, and Red revolutionaries aplenty, all provide honorific watch. More than 2,000 memorials stand within this city of cenotaphs and commemorative plaques. No fewer than three eternal flames burn here. Sevastopol prides itself on recording its eventful past and so preserving its unique heritage.

Yet Sevastopol is no historical theme park. People still live here and are fiercely proud to do so. The modern city is not only an important naval base, but also a bustling industrial centre of over 400,000 inhabitants. Tooting taxis and *Topik* mini-buses race swishing electric trolley buses up and down Sevastopol's wide thoroughfares. If not a local, confront these vehicles on Lenin Street, Nakhimov Prospekt or Ushakov Square at your peril.

Throughout the city's rich past one detects strong evidence of a patriotic and zealous revolutionary spirit. Sevastopol has energised and enthused its garrison, fleet and citizens alike for over two centuries: it survives today. The city dominates geographically and historically. Likewise, its place in literature is secure, not least through the writing of Tolstoy. This study traces the major threads that provide context and continuity. These include the enduring strategic significance of Sevastopol and the projection of Russian maritime power in the Black Sea (and further afield) from its naval base and through the eponymous fleet. Sevastopol's story is a complex and moving tale of war and peace; of industrial and social change; of episodic destruction, revolution and reconstruction. These broad themes permeate the contents of this book. After an introductory chapter describing Crimea's geography, ancient history and the Crimean Khanate, *Sevastopol's Wars* describes the city's military and naval development from its modern founding in 1783 by Thomas Mackenzie at the orders of the Catherine the Great to the events of 2014.

Two caveats are perhaps necessary. First, in painting such a wide canvas, there is always the danger of gaps appearing in the narrative, if not perspectives overlooked in the analysis of events. I regret, for example, there was not enough space in the book to include more of the extensive historiography of the city. Secondly, the annexation (or reunification) of Crimea by Russia has changed attitudes in the West. As Andrew Monaghan has pointed out, recent discussion about Russia 'has become more partisan as a result of the war in Ukraine'.[12] This point was brought home to me forcibly when giving a lecture at the Royal United Services Institute, London, in 2014. As I finished my talk, a distinguished retired senior officer stood up and accused me of 'excusing President Putin'. I replied then, as I appeal to my readers now: 'to explain is not to accommodate'. Yet I cannot deny, as the biographer of Sevastopol, a certain admiration for, if not empathy with, my subject.

Those who have lived and served in Sevastopol, or have visited the city down the centuries, help retell its dramatic story from Potemkin to Putin, including veterans from the Second World War. These few surviving old sailors, soldiers and airmen, the womenfolk of that generation, and the vast majority of Sevastopol's population today, consider themselves to be Russian. Since 1991, there has been little affinity, let alone loyalty, to the Ukrainian state. As one embittered Russian veteran complained to me in 2012, 'we feel, and are treated like, foreigners in our own country'.[13] One seemingly trivial example may illustrate the prevailing mood of Sevastopol. On a fine summer's day that year, my interpreter and I encountered three young children playing on the pedestal of Lenin's statue in the city centre. Tanya asked the eldest, a ten-year-old girl: 'Are you from Sevastopol?' Quick as a flash, she replied: 'I'm Russian!'[14]

On 21 February 2014, a pro-Western people's revolution took place in Kiev, Ukraine's capital city, and President Viktor Yanukovych's pro-Russian administration was overturned. Two days later, 'self-defence' units appeared in Sevastopol ostensibly to protect the city from Ukrainian nationalists. They established a ring of seven checkpoints on its approach roads.[15] This action became known as Sevastopol's 'third defence'. Meanwhile, Russian Federation forces, many stationed on Crimea, intervened. Within a month, the Crimean peninsula and Sevastopol were both in Russian hands again following a controversial referendum. The world, and particularly the West, looked on – amazed by the audacity of the Russian action, deemed by many as unwarranted aggression. The final chapter of this book helps to explain why, with Russian encouragement and support, a counter-coup in Crimea and Sevastopol occurred.

This historical study of Sevastopol offers no judgements as to the rights and wrongs of either the current dispute between the Russian Federation and the West, or of the fraternal conflict between Ukraine and Russia. As opinions are so sharply divided on such matters, no doubt some perspectives presented in this book may please some, but equally offend others. But what this book does attempt to show is that the events of 2014 in Crimea can be traced to those of decades and centuries before. On the basis that such understanding may provide the best prospect for wise policy in the future, I trust that *Sevastopol's Wars* may both inform discussion and provoke some new thinking about Russia.[16]

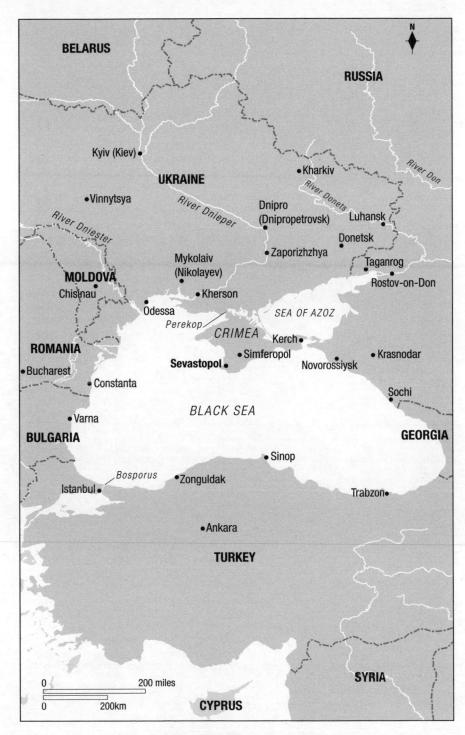

BELARUS

RUSSIA

Kyiv (Kiev) •

UKRAINE

Kharkiv •

• Vinnytsya

River Dnieper

River Donets

Dnipro
(Dnipropetrovsk)

Luhansk •

River Dniester

Donetsk •

Mykolaiv
(Nikolayev)

• Zaporizhzhya

Taganrog •

MOLDOVA

Chisinau •

• Kherson

Rostov-on-Don •

Odessa •

Perekop

SEA OF AZOZ

ROMANIA

CRIMEA

Kerch •

• Krasnodar

• Bucharest

Sevastopol •

• Simferopol

Novorossiysk •

• Constanta

Sochi •

BLACK SEA

• Varna

BULGARIA

GEORGIA

• Sinop

Bosporus

• Zonguldak

Istanbul •

Trabzon •

• Ankara

TURKEY

| 0 | 200 miles |
| 0 | 200km |

SYRIA

CYPRUS

1. Sevastopol and the Black Sea Region

PART ONE

EARLY SEVASTOPOL

CHAPTER I

CRUCIBLE OF CONFLICT

'How beautiful, when day is dawning,
To see you, shores of Tauris ...'

Pushkin[1]

AN ANCIENT LAND

In former times, the gently undulating grasslands of the Pontic steppe stretched from the Carpathian Mountains over 1,200 kilometres eastwards to the river Volga, and from the southern Black Sea shore some 300 kilometres or so north to a temperate, mixed forest zone.[2] Nomad Nogai horsemen and other, older tribes once roamed across this vast lowland plain. The old Slavonic name for this steppe, formerly a wild, frontier region, was *Ukraina*, meaning 'on the edge'. This area now lies within Ukraine, a territory also once known as 'Little Russia'; fatefully, the future of this country now hangs in the balance, lying awkwardly between east and west. Although heavily industrialised during late tsarist and Soviet times, particularly in its now disputed east, Ukraine is still famous for its bounteous black soils which make its farmland so rich: aptly, its national flag of a blue stripe above one of yellow signifies golden wheat fields ripening under huge open skies.

The mighty river Dnieper bisects Ukraine (see Map 1). From its source in distant Russian marshes, it flows south through Belarus and Smolensk via Ukraine's capital Kiev towards the Black Sea. Today, it carries commercial and tourist traffic. Downstream lie a number of modern industrial cities, dams, reservoirs and hydroelectric plants. In ancient times, the Dnieper, known to the Greeks as the Borysthenes, served as an important trade link, part of the 'Amber Route', which linked the Baltic shore to the Black Sea. The once impressive fortress of Ochakov (now Ochakiv), bitterly contested by the Russian and Ottoman Empires during the latter half of the eighteenth century, guarded its *liman* (estuary).

To the south-east, a prominent land mass projects into the northern reaches of the Black Sea. This is the Crimean peninsula. Depending on one's taste, its shape resembles a lozenge, a diamond pendant or a malformed, old-fashioned child's kite. In area, Crimea is a little smaller than Belgium and a touch larger than the American state of Maryland.[3] Since Neolithic times successive peoples have sought this special place, drawn by its position, climate, hunting, grazing and agricultural potential, and not least by the rich fisheries of the Black Sea.[4] The name 'Crimea' stems from the Turkish word *kerim*, meaning fortress, as in the Tatar town of Qırım (now Stary Krym). This old settlement once served as the Crimean capital of the 'Golden Horde' – those Tatars descended from the terrifying Mongols led by Genghis Khan.

Any land is only as secure as its borders and entry points: Crimea proves no exception to this rule. At its north-western corner, the Perekop isthmus links the peninsula to Ukraine. Only 5–7 kilometres wide, this narrow neck of vital ground has long served as the principal gateway to Crimea. For many centuries, the 'Turkish Wall', which straddles the Perekop, formed the peninsula's main line of defence. Fighting to secure this strategically vital portal has featured prominently in many of the military campaigns associated with the region's past. The land bridge is washed on its eastern shore by a shallow expanse of water and salt marsh known as the 'lazy sea', the Syvash. Towards its eastern end, stretching towards the Sea of Azov, lies the Chongar peninsula, which acts as an alternative entry route. Nowadays, in a similar manner to the Perekop, it carries both road and rail links between the peninsula and Ukraine.[5] Further east still, there extends a perilously slender land bar, the Arabat Spit, which is far too narrow to serve as a reliable line of communication.

Crimea's geography can be divided simply into three fairly distinct zones: the northern and central steppe, which occupies about three-quarters of the peninsula; the high mountains of the south-east; and the narrow coastal southern strip. An extension of the steppe, the Kerch peninsula, about 100 kilometres long, forms Crimea's eastern extremity. The narrow straits of Kerch – in ancient times known as the Cimmerian Bosporus – separate Crimea from the Taman peninsula of Russia, linking the Sea of Azov to the Black Sea. Thus Crimea is almost completely surrounded by sea, a largely self-contained geophysical entity.

François, Baron de Tott, the resident French consul to Crimea during the 1760s, explained that the peninsula's 'vast plenty of waters do not form there any remarkable river', for 'the proximity of the shore attracts every rivulet to the sea'. Yet, he opined, 'the greatest heats never dry up the springs, and the inhabitants find in every hollow the most delicious water, which by running alternately through agreeable meadows, and falling amongst rocks, is beautifully limpid'.[6] His description of rural Crimea holds true today.

As a French visitor, Jean Racault, Baron de Reuilly, commented at the beginning of the nineteenth century, 'nature has not refused the Crimea any of the advantages that may be derived from its position; ... [its] plants are as various ... as the districts which compose it are by their situation, the qualities of their soil, and the nature of the air.'[7] Long have the most fertile parts of the steppe been irrigated and cultivated: cereal production has featured prominently since the arrival of the first Greek colonists. This bounteous breadbasket supplied grain to many Greek cities. Much of the landscape, however, remained wild and unexploited. The lower and middle slopes of the limestone Crimean Mountains that rise up to 1,545 metres in elevation are still swathed in verdant forests of pine, yew, juniper, oak, beech, black locusts and strawberry trees. The last wolves here were killed only after the Russian Civil War in the 1920s when large-scale logging was undertaken. Deer, wild boar and fox remain, as do the many species of birds, including the Short-toed Eagle, Eastern Steppe Buzzard and Peregrine that soar above mountain top and steppe. In early spring, fed by the melting snow, Ukraine's longest waterfall, the Uchan Su near Yalta, crashes down over a near-vertical cliff almost 100 metres high.

De Tott observed throughout Crimea 'an astonishing quantity of flowers', with 'whole fields, covered with tulips', which formed, 'from the variety of their colours, the most pleasing picture'.[8] Along the spectacular southern shore, with lofty mountain sentinels arrayed in dramatic, scenic backdrop, extends a lush, narrow strip of land: Crimea's 'Riviera', which enjoys a Mediterranean sub-climate. A later British traveller of the mid-nineteenth century, Mrs Kate Guthrie, noted that 'this scenery has been compared to that of Amalfi, and the Maritime Alps near Salerno; but the Crimean coast, from Aloushta [sic] to Balaclava, we thought much finer'.[9] In spring, this whole area – the 'garden of Russia' – bursts into a sea of colour with snowdrops, crocuses, primulas and peonies all to the fore, complemented by almond, apple and cherry blossom on the lower mountain slopes, country roadsides and city streets, Sevastopol's boulevards and parks included, enchanting inhabitants and visitors alike.

With the construction of the railway from Moscow via Kharkov in the late nineteenth century, fresh flowers from Crimea were swiftly transported to the markets of these cities and of St Petersburg, and used to decorate the homes and palaces of the rich and the royal.[10] The peninsula's vineyards have been famous since Greek colonial times. At the turn of the twentieth century, it could be fairly said that 'no grand-ducal or princely table anywhere in Russia' would be set 'without bottles of red and white wine from the host's Crimean estate'.[11] Inkerman and Massandra wines may not enjoy the international reputations of those of Bordeaux or Tuscany, but their quality is more than local: they deserve to be far better known and more widely drunk.

Crimea's captivating natural beauty and agricultural bounty, however, mask the turbulent history this land has long endured. A closer examination of the peninsula and particularly of its south-western extent soon reveals the abundant signs of ancient peoples and the scars of modern wars. Of all the localities of Crimea, Sevastopol – both city and wider region, where the southern mountain chain meets the western Black Sea shore – can make a credible, if not compelling, claim to holding one of Europe's greatest concentrations of significant archaeological and historic sites.

BEACON OF CIVILISATION

It is hard to identify the original inhabitants of Crimea: the peninsula drew successive waves of migrant tribes, becoming a melting pot of various peoples down the ages. Archaeologists have dated bones of Crimean cave dwellers to over 30,000 years ago, among the oldest human remains identified in Europe. Numerous *kurgans* (burial mounds) testify to the presence of the Scythians, a powerful tribe that populated the Pontic and Crimean steppes during the Bronze and Iron Ages. They had largely displaced the former rulers of these lands, the Cimmerians.

During the seventh to fifth centuries BC, Milesian Greeks established a series of towns on the Black Sea's western and northern littoral, including Crimea. This programme of colonisation was driven by a combination of demographic pressures and agricultural shortages at home and of mercantile enterprise – a burning desire to explore and to expand trade whenever and wherever an opportunity beckoned. The new pioneers were attracted by 'an abundant and accessible supply of food-stuffs, especially fish and grain'. Meanwhile, the Scythian 'masters of the steppes' originally gave the newcomers their 'consent and blessing', no doubt wishing to trade with the Greeks bearing useful gifts such as metals and pottery.[12]

The Milesians called the people they encountered in the southern part of Crimea the 'Tauri' and their new homeland 'Taurike Chersonesos'. A prominent triangular-shaped peninsula, named Heraklion or Chersonesos, the latter an ancient Greek word for such a geographical feature, forms the south-western tip of Crimea (see Map 3).[13] This area possesses some useful natural defences. While the heavily indented northern shore is generally gently sloping, the southern is characterised by high cliffs. A ridgeline, the Sapun Gora, forms the eastern base of the peninsula. This steep escarpment runs between Sevastopol Bay (in classical times known as the *Ctenus Limen*) and a narrow inlet on the southern coast, the *Symbolon Limen*, now the present port of Balaklava.[14]

Near Balaklava, now lying within the municipality of greater Sevastopol, several Taurian settlements existed. Legend has it that the religious customs of the terrible Tauri – as bloodthirsty as the savage Scythians – included human sacrifice to a deity. Euripides modelled his famous tragedy *Iphigenia in Tauris* on the unfortunate princess, daughter of Agamemnon, who, on being sacrificed to the goddess Artemis, was instead taken by her to be 'set down ... in the land of the Tauri to be her priestess'. Apparently, the Tauri 'possessed an image of Artemis which had fallen from heaven' and their religion involved keeping up 'a savage rite of sacrificing to it all strangers who were cast on their shores'.[15]

For it was here – on a remote corner of the Crimean peninsula, on the ethnic fault-line between those who spoke their tongue and those who did not – that the Milesians founded in 422–421 BC the city of Chersonesos of Tauride (see the larger inset of Map 3). It was so named because of its commanding position on a narrow neck of land between two bays now known as Karantinnaya (Quarantine) and Pesochnaya (Sandy), a promontory that could be secured from landward attack by a stone wall linking these two sea inlets.[16]

Beyond the defences of their 'Peninsular City', the Greek colonists cleared and cultivated their *chora*, the local countryside, embracing much of the south-western tip of Crimea.[17] They divided up the ground into a grid pattern, tilling and farming the land. Some of these plots were large enough to be considered rural estates. Chersonites from ancient times to the Middle Ages grew wheat, barley and rye, and cultivated grapes, fruit and vegetables. They also fished and extracted sea salt. South-western Crimea, where Chersonesos was built, and much later Sevastopol founded, receives relatively little rain, about 350mm a year. Therefore the inhabitants of this area have always had to conserve water carefully: farmers, whether ancient or modern, must irrigate their fields patiently throughout long, hot summers when temperatures can approach nearly 40°C in the shade. In contrast, winters can be surprisingly cold. Although it is uncommon for snow to lie for any time on the coastal area, temperatures can plunge on rare occasions in winter to -20°C. But in comparison with the bulk of Russian and Ukrainian lands, the Crimean weather is mild, albeit displaying a great deal of local variation.

Down the centuries, the citizen farmers, tradesmen and soldiers of the garrison housed in Chersonesos had to defend their precious city numerous times. Despite a series of barbarian attacks, the city held firm against successive waves of invaders – surviving, as a modern guidebook puts it, as a 'beacon of civilisation in a turbulent world'.[18] Specifically:

> The mighty walls [of Chersonesos] span nearly the whole city's history from the fourth century BC to the fourteenth or fifteenth century AD. They were constantly being repaired and modified as methods of siege warfare changed and in response to the attacks by practically every barbarian (literally 'non-Greek speaking') group whose name has left its mark on history. Chersonesos was the ultimate prize and the key to control of the northern Black Sea coast.[19]

Hence ancient Chersonesos and modern Sevastopol share an enduring strategic role: as a firm bastion and safe haven from which to secure and to project economic and naval power. Despite the presence of equally fearsome and bloodthirsty local Tauri and regional Scythians, the early history of Chersonesos was not persistently violent. Largely through their diplomatic and mercantile skills the Greek colonists managed to forge pragmatic accords with their Crimean neighbours and with other nearby states. Economic interdependence led to peace much of the time.

Expert academic opinion holds that Chersonesos distinguished itself from other Greek colonies by its 'unique ability to survive and prosper long after its neighbours and rivals ceased to exist'.[20] Through the centuries, the city maintained close links with the prominent powers of the Black Sea region. While mighty states such as Athens, Macedonia, the Bosporan kingdom, and not least Rome, all rose and fell, plucky Chersonesos outlived them all save for the Byzantine Empire, which collapsed with the Ottomans' capture of Constantinople in 1453. Furthermore, the Crimean city managed 'no less adroitly' its affairs with the 'ever-present barbarians, the indigenous Taurians, the late Scythians and Sarmatians'; and later, with the Huns and the Goths.[21]

The consecutive Greek, Roman and Byzantine incarnations of Chersonesos would have looked extremely impressive to inhabitants and local tribesmen alike. If arriving by sea, visitors and traders would have landed on the beach at Quarantine Bay, lying next to the south-eastern sector of the city. On approaching this shore, the city's massively constructed walls with its series of flanking towers would have looked unassailable, surely deterring all but the most confident attacker equipped with powerful engines of war. Long stretches (over 900 metres) of the curtain walls survive to heights of up to 10 metres, the masonry of their successive Greek, Roman and Byzantine builders remaining visible in distinctive strata. The most notable structure – then as now – is the formidable round Tower of Zeno, which stands at the south-eastern corner of the wall circuit. Progressively rebuilt and reinforced from the third century BC to the tenth century AD, it stands proudly today 9 metres tall and 23 metres in diameter as a potent reminder of the once formidable strength of the city's fortifications.

Having passed through the city's main gate on the southern, landward side, an ancient traveller or merchant would have soon made his way to the mid-point of the busy main street of Chersonesos that runs on a south-west to north-east axis, some 900 metres long and 6.5 metres wide. On both sides stood neat blocks of houses, hotels, shops, small factories and public buildings, all laid out in a regular, symmetrical fashion. Our visitor would not have gone thirsty: wine could be cheaply purchased while fresh water was freely available. The city, originally fed by wells and rainwater captured from roofs, was supplied in Roman times by underground aqueducts that brought water from springs as far as 10 kilometres away into a central city storage cistern, from which it was further distributed. A sophisticated system of supply and drainage served not only the military barracks, businesses and private residences of the city, but also the public toilets and baths. Chersonesos was indeed an oasis of civilised comfort on the Crimea.[22]

Based on its enduring security and stability, Chersonesos prospered. Its lifeblood was its trade. So much so that the ninth-century Byzantine Emperor Constantine VII *Porphyrogennetos* (the purple-born) is said to have advised his son: 'If the Chersonites do not journey to Byzantium and do not sell the hides and wax that they can get by trade from the Perchenegs [a semi-nomadic Turkic tribe], they cannot live. If grain does not pass across [from the cities and provinces of Asia Minor], the Chersonites cannot live.'[23] In fact, Constantine VII was doing down the sophisticated craftsmen of Chersonesos. The city grew rich not only through its farming and fishing, but also on also on account of its fine workmanship, including pottery and intricate metal working in copper, bronze and gold. Its artefacts and artistry were to be found all across the ancient world. The first coins were struck in Chersonesos during the fourth century BC: this practice continued for a further 1,500 years; the city's mint is one of the most remarkable ancient ruins.

Chersonesos thrived culturally too: the striking remains of the Greek theatre (the only one discovered on the territory of the former Soviet Union) attract tens of thousands of tourists today. When first built in the Hellenistic period, it could have seated up to 2,000 of the city's inhabitants, between a fifth and a tenth of the estimated population.[24] The theatre is still used for performances, both Greek tragedies and comedies, and various modern works.

During a considerable part of the city's Greek period, democracy also flourished. One of the most famous treasures uncovered during the excavations of Chersonesos during the late nineteenth century is a marble stele, on which a civic oath was inscribed in the late fourth or early third century BC. Its wording is quite remarkable as it represents one of the world's very first written sources of civic pride and democratic sentiment. A short extract reveals the common duties and responsibilities avowed of all citizens, illuminating ideals that should still resonate:

> I swear ... I shall act in concord with my fellow citizens on behalf of the protection and freedom of the polis[25] and its citizens. I shall not betray to anyone whomsoever, whether Greek or barbarian, Chersonesos, ... the other forts, and the rest of the chora, which the people of Chersonesos inhabit.... But I shall carefully guard all of these for the demos of the people of Chersonesos. I shall not put down the democracy ... I shall neither offer nor accept a gift to harm the polis and its citizens.[26]

With the decline of Greek influence, Chersonesos was absorbed into the 'Kingdom of the Bosphorus' during the second century BC, a power based on the city of Panticapaeum (now Kerch). Its people, the Sarmatians, an immigrant tribe of the steppe, blended with the Greek colonists to create 'a brilliant new synthesis', whose goldsmiths 'produced some of the most magnificent artistic jewellery of the ancient world'.[27] Later, facing new barbarian threats, the citizens of Chersonesos requested Rome's protection.

During the early second century AD, corresponding to the reorganisation of the Empire's frontiers under Emperor Hadrian, a strong military presence was established along the south-western coast of Crimea. It included vexillations (detachments) from three legions: I Italica, V Macedonia and XI Claudia.[28] A garrison of unknown size was based within the citadel of Chersonesos, in which were erected barracks, a headquarters building and, unusually for Roman practice, baths, which were normally established outside the walls of a fort or civil cantonment. Across the Empire, towns and cities were being increasingly fortified to counter a growing barbarian threat. As one strategic analyst of the Roman Empire has highlighted, 'In the East, garrisons had long been housed in cities, or rather, in specific areas of cities. Now the pattern became more general, extending from London to Chersonesos on the Black Sea ...'.[29]

Following the division of the Roman Empire by Emperor Diocletian (AD 284–305) shortly before the turn of the third century AD, Chersonesos was administered by the eastern part. In AD 324, Emperor Constantine founded his new capital, Constantinopolis. Thus it was to this new centre of power – Constantinople (now Istanbul) – that Chersonesos would turn in times of trouble. The benefit was to prove mutual. During the early fourth century Constantine battled with the barbarian Goths, whose invasions threatened to destroy Roman civilisation. In launching offensive operations on the Danube in

AD 332 against this fearsome foe, he appealed to the 'free and warlike people' of Chersonesos for assistance. Gibbon described their cause and campaign:

> The Chersonites were animated against the Goths by the memory of the wars which, in the preceding century, they had maintained with unequal forces against the invaders of their country.... Obedient to the requisition of Constantine, they prepared, under the conduct of their magistrate Diogenes, a considerable army, of which the principal strength consisted in crossbows and military chariots. The speedy march and intrepid attack of the Chersonites, by diverting the attention of the Goths, assisted the operations of the imperial generals. The Goths, vanquished on every side, were driven into the mountains.

A very grateful Constantine rewarded the 'faithful Chersonites' with a 'perpetual exemption from all duties ... for their vessels which traded to the ports of the Black Sea'.[30] Constantinople and Chersonesos remained interdependent thereafter, as a modern history of the latter explains:

> Chersonesos served Constantinople as an outpost in the midst of a predominantly barbarian world, as an invaluable trading port, as a lookout for the movement of barbarians from the east and north who threatened the borders, as a staging area to proselytize for political and religious ends, and as a convenient place to deposit political undesirables. The area was still within Byzantine authority, but far enough away to ensure that the exiles could do little damage. These included Pope Martin I and the emperor Justinian II.[31]

Justinian II spent the first three years of his ten-year exile (AD 695–705) in the Crimean city. When he was restored to the imperial throne, Chersonesos was fortunate to escape the retribution of a vengeful emperor who fostered 'an implacable hatred' towards the place and people. In his view, its hostile inhabitants had 'insulted his exile and violated the laws of hospitality'. Determining darkly that 'all are guilty, and all must perish', he ordered the city's destruction in AD 710. The brave Chersonites, however, were spared extinction when Justinian's fleet and troops proved 'unwilling and unable to perpetrate' his revenge and mutinied. Failing to escape many a brutal tyrant's fate, the Emperor was later assassinated and little mourned.[32]

While it is hard to imagine ancient Chersonesos as Byzantium's distant 'Siberia', its far-flung position on the edge of civilisation became increasingly one of frontier outpost. Against the odds, the beleaguered city withstood further barbarian attacks by the Huns in the fourth century. It remained the principal Byzantine bastion in Crimea until the thirteenth century. Its survival for nearly two millennia depended not only on its formidable defences and doughty defenders, but also on its largely peaceful co-existence with neighbouring peoples. Contemporary historians of Chersonesos, perhaps exhibiting some undue idealism in the light of more recent world history, have declared:

> The city ... and its hinterland shared a history with other groups from the beginning: indigenous Taurians, Scythians, Sarmatians, Goths, Huns, Khazars, Rus', and finally the Genoese. All these cultures left behind conspicuous monuments of their presence. Chersonesos, multi-ethnic in every period, set an example for the modern world of how such a heterogeneous society can not only succeed but also prosper.[33]

In many ways the survival of Chersonesos depended on the application of a subtle form of statecraft that had long sustained the Byzantine Empire as a whole. The rulers of Constantinople developed a grand strategy that 'relied less on military strength and more on all forms of persuasion—to recruit allies, dissuade enemies, and induce potential enemies to attack one another', based on superior 'diplomacy and intelligence'.[34] Modern soldiers, statesmen and strategists would do well to reflect on the need for the latter, as such understanding forms the basis of pragmatic if not principled action.

Ancient Chersonesos remains a fascinating place. Its fine ruins evoke images of the power and splendour of times past, reminding one of the fragility of civilisation. Cities, as in the destiny of empires, rise and fall. Sometimes inaccurately described as an eastern Pompeii, or a Russian Troy, Chersonesos boasts none the less a set of quite remarkable archaeological remains. As the site has not been fully excavated, many exciting finds and unknown treasures may yet lie undiscovered. The once powerful city state died a slow death of unrelenting, dismal decay during the Middle Ages; it never fully revived under a century of Genoese control, during which the eastern port of Caffa (now Feodosiya) became Genoa's Crimean centre of trade and influence. Chersonesos then lapsed into total obscurity as an unremarkable fishing village during the Tatar Khanate. In direct consequence of imperial Russia's quest to establish a naval base on Crimea, Chersonesos was 'rediscovered' through the foundation of nearby Sevastopol (3 kilometres to the east) towards the end of the eighteenth century. As one of the first foreign tourists of modern times to visit, a Mrs Maria Guthrie, perceptively recorded in the 1790s, 'nothing can facilitate the destruction of any antient city so much as building a new one near it'. Furthermore, she noted, 'this has been so much the case with the Grecian Cherson, that many remains of antique edifices seen within these 20 years, ... have been swallowed up by Russian Sebastopol to the great regret of the curious traveller who now visits the desolate and abandoned spot'.[35]

Old Chersonesos, despite the neglect and depravations suffered since its demise under Tatar rule and the arrival of the Russian fleet, remains as a cultural and religious site of enduring importance to Russia and Ukraine. Christianity first came to Chersonesos in the sixth century. Saints Cyril and Methodius visited in the ninth: these two monks introduced the Cyrillic script to the Slavic peoples. As significantly, it was here that Volodymyr (Vladimir), the leader of the Kievan Rus, was baptised on Easter Day in AD 988 (or, more likely, 990), which led to the introduction of Orthodox Christianity to the lands of Rus. How this remarkable event came about represents a common, founding, chapter of the histories of Russia, Ukraine and Sevastopol. Facing a rebellion he could not handle alone, Emperor Basil II turned to Prince Vladimir for assistance, who duly sent a well-armed force of 6,000 troops to Byzantium. In return, once the rebellion had been crushed, the Prince requested the hand of the Emperor's sister, Anna, a marriage that would further raise his international prestige and influence. While Basil II was in no position to refuse Vladimir's demand, he made the wedding conditional on the Kievan prince becoming a Christian. In typical Byzantine fashion, however, the Emperor schemed and prevaricated, making the prospective groom wait in vain for the arrival of his bride. Vladimir was not amused, to say the least, and resolved to punish Basil II for failing to meet his obligations. Consequently, he besieged Chersonesos. True to past form, the city's defenders stoutly resisted. But when Vladimir learned of the underground water supply, he gave orders for it to be dug out and blocked. It was then only a matter of time before the parched inhabitants surrendered. This great misfortune for both the city and the empire coincided with a spectacular stellar happening – probably the arrival of Halley's comet in 989 (its next return in 1066 was recorded in the Bayeux Tapestry), which was deemed a bad omen. In any event, a much-chastened Basil II sent his sister to Chersonesos, where Vladimir was duly baptised and happily married to Anna.

Handing back the captured city with magnanimity – for he could have razed it to the ground – the Slav prince triumphantly returned to Kiev with his new bride. Thereafter he dedicated his life to the adoption of his people to Christianity with all the devotion and energy of one recently converted.[36] The Tithe Church of Kiev became the religious centre of Rus, 'the greatest structure yet seen so far east and north in the European landscape'. At the same time, Vladimir turned his vast kingdom, stretching from Kiev in the south to Novgorod in the north, and from the Dnieper in the west to the Volga in the east, into a 'fully-fledged early medieval state' – one 'ready to join the club of Christian European polities'.[37] Such is the historic and religious significance of Vladimir to Russia, Ukraine and Sevastopol.

Ancient Chersonesos, for decades a convenient source of building stone for Sevastopol, by the late nineteenth century became an object of tourism and site of archaeological investigation. Miraculously, the ancient ruins largely survived the ravages of both the Crimean War (the French Army was based nearby) and the Second World War. Ironically, the archaeological park and its immediate environs, the former now a 'National Preserve' and UNESCO world heritage site, are endangered today not only by sea erosion, but rather more so by inadequate control of Sevastopol's creeping urban expansion.[38] Encroachment by local developers threatens to spoil the conservation and exhibition of a site that should be attracting growing numbers of international tourists. Whether Russian-controlled Sevastopol will now balance these competing demands better than the previous administration appointed by Ukraine remains to be seen.

THE CRIMEAN KHANATE

In the wake of the Mongol invasion of Russia, the Tatars occupied Crimea during the thirteenth century. The Tatar Khanate of Crimea, also known as the Krym Tatary, was founded in 1441. For centuries, however, it extended north, east and westwards along the Black Sea coast well beyond the boundaries of modern Crimea. At first the Khanate was allied, but not directly subject, to Ottoman Constantinople. Recognising Ottoman suzerainty in 1475, Khan Mengli Giray declared his fidelity to the Sultan: 'we are the enemy of your enemy, the friend of your friend'.[39] The Tatars not only defended the Ottomans' borders along the Black Sea's northern littoral, but also from their near-impregnable Crimean base boldly raided neighbouring lands such as the Grand Duchy of Lithuania with formidable bodies of horsemen. Even for the early Russian state of Muscovy, lying to the north and north-east of the Grand Duchy, the Tatars represented a persistent danger that needed to be eliminated – and their lands brought under control.

The pitiless destruction wreaked by the Tatar horsemen left a fearful impression on Muscovite Russia that endured to the time of Catherine the Great and beyond. So much so that the 'Muslim warlords', according to a modern history, became 'the bogeymen of the Russian psyche; the south was a source of menace, terror and death'.[40] The Russian quest for revenge against the Tatars, however, was as much religious as revanchist. Following the fall of Constantinople, Moscow became the 'capital of the Orthodox Church and its dukes heirs of the Byzantine Caesars'. Ivan III (1462–1505), who in 1472 had married Sophia, niece of Constantine XI, the last eastern Roman Emperor, 'devoted his reign to [the] emancipation of Russia from the slackening yoke' of the infidel Tatars.[41] He strove to extend Muscovite rule southwards, a tradition followed by his successors in the wake of perpetual Tatar hostility.

Russian histories record a long series of major Tatar incursions from the sixteenth to the eighteenth centuries and tit-for-tat military actions in response. There were diplomatic, political, economic and military grounds for these campaigns. The Crimean Tatars had sacked Kiev in the Grand Duchy in 1483, while in 1515, and again in 1521, they had penetrated as far north as Moscow, approximately 1,500 kilometres from Crimea. Such was the long reach of their raiding forces. This flexing of military power, however, was no one-way affair. The steady advance of Muscovy in the mid-sixteenth century south-east towards the Caucasus and the Caspian Sea, and southwards to Crimea and the Black Sea, provoked a vigorous Tatar reaction. Khan Devlet Giray refused to accept the Muscovite conquests of Kazan in 1552 and Astrakhan in 1556, which undermined the Khanate's wider sphere of regional influence. More acutely, the appearance of a Muscovite army under Ivan IV, 'the Terrible', in 1554 at the Perekop directly threatened its security.

In 1558 the Khanate launched a major counter-offensive against Moscow. It was defeated with a reaction of sufficient vigour that Russian forces again reached the Crimean peninsula in 1559 and 1560, but failed to conquer it. Even such limited success proved only ephemeral, as Crimea lay well beyond Muscovy's grasp.[42] Taking full advantage of the internal confusion generated by Ivan the Terrible's *oprichnina* – his internal reign of terror against the rising *boyar* aristocracy – the Crimean Tatars in 1571 under Devlet Giray launched a major expedition deep into Muscovy. This time, their long raid north brought them right up to the walls of Moscow's mighty citadel, the Kremlin. Unable to prise open the *kreml* ('fortress' in old Russian), they burned 'much of the city, withdrawing from the Muscovite state after laying waste a large area and capturing an enormous booty and 100,000 prisoners'. If that was not enough suffering, then 'famine and plague added to the horror of the Tatar devastation.'[43] All this death and destruction was very much in the campaigning mould of Genghis Khan. His ferocious Mongol horde had shattered Russian armies one after another in 1238, sweeping through the countryside, burning villages and towns in their path, and either killing or driving away the population, leaving alive 'neither a cat nor a dog'.[44]

The German adventurer Heinrich von Staden, who had become one of Ivan's *oprichniki*, his feared secret police and personal guard, described the nature of the Tatar menace that posed an existential threat to Muscovy's rule:

> ... the Crimean Khan now strives to conquer Russia with the support and assistance of the Turkish Sultan—who does not deny him this support—to carry the Grand Prince and his two sons, bound, into captivity, and to seize the great treasure that has taken many centuries to collect. From this the Turkish Sultan would receive an especially large sum.[45]

Although the Crimean Tatars, either supported by, or on behalf of the Turks, never managed to conquer either the Grand Duchy of Lithuania or Muscovy, they renewed their campaigns and sorties against their northern neighbours for much of the rest of the sixteenth century and the early seventeenth. In turn, successive Muscovite rulers invested in establishing lines of fortifications to defend their southern frontiers, which none the less were breached on numerous occasions by Tatar marauders. Such actions merely added to the Russians' longstanding grudge against the Crimean Tatars, which would one day be avenged. Muscovites, who viewed the Muslim Tatars as alien usurpers in historic Slavic – Russian – lands, looked forward to when their traditional enemy could be driven back into the Black Sea. The dream of gaining unhindered access to its warm waters, however, remained just that for a century and more. With such fundamental tensions, establishing any form of peace and stability in this troubled, hotly contested region would prove most elusive.

The armies of the Crimean Khanate were not always on the offensive. They also had to repel raids by an equally combative and daring foe, which struck across the thinly inhabited 'wild fields' or border wasteland of southern Ukraine. This persistent opponent was the fearsome 'host' or '*sech*' of Dnieper Cossacks, based on an island in that river 'beyond the rapids', Zaporizhia (now the site of the modern city of Zaporizhzhya).[46] In common with other Cossack groups, including that of the river Don further to the east, the Dnieper Host was a fiercely independent and closely integrated military society, which displayed many similarities to that of ancient Sparta. The Cossacks got their name from the Turkish word *kozak*, meaning 'adventurer', which they were by tradition and inclination. From the sixteenth to the eighteenth centuries the Dnieper Host (the Zaporozhian Sech) fought alternately Lithuanians and Poles, Ukrainians, Russians, Ottomans and Tatars in a bewildering series of shifting alliances of convenience. As one modern historian has rather quaintly put it, in this unruly frontier land, the Cossacks and Tatars represented 'Europe's "cowboys and Indians"'.[47]

As Russian power and influence spread southwards in the latter half of the eighteenth century, the Cossacks had increasingly become an obstacle in the development of the empire's latest domain, *Novorossiya* (new Russia).[48] Unwisely, many groups had linked themselves to the Pugachev rebellion (a serf uprising under a false claimant to the throne) of 1773 against Catherine the Great. Acting on the orders of Prince Grigory Potemkin, in June 1775 Russian troops threatened to destroy the Dnieper Cossacks. Facing an attack of overwhelming odds, the Zaporozhian Sech wisely surrendered. Luck, however, was still on their side. Potemkin, who had a 'passion for the Cossacks', realised the combat potential of these irregular light horsemen. Ideally suited by technique, temperament and tradition to patrol Russia's far-flung frontier regions, they soon provided some of the most effective and loyal troops under imperial command.[49]

Since the fifteenth century, the Crimean Tatars had sallied north into Muscovite and Russian lands in the pursuit of income. They supplied the Ottoman Empire with a very valuable commodity: a steady source of strong, mostly blonde, Slavic slaves. One estimate has it that over 150,000 men, women and children were kidnapped from southern Russia – modern Ukraine – during the period 1601–55 to 'sell to the fleshpots and rowing-galleys of Constantinople'.[50] Those who were lucky enough to escape such cruel fates were sold for ransom-money. The Tatars' barbaric practice was euphemistically termed 'harvesting the steppe'. There seemed to be no limit to their shamelessness and savagery. In 1662, for example, the Crimean Tatars captured the town of Putivl, in today's north-eastern Ukraine, carrying off 'all the 20,000 inhabitants into slavery'.[51] This assault, however, marked one of the last great raids, for between 1635 and 1653 Muscovy's forces had worked tirelessly to construct new border defence lines to prevent the Tatars making such bold penetrations.[52]

RUSSIAN MILITARY EXPEDITIONS TO CRIMEA

In the late seventeenth century, both the Regent Princess Sophia (half-sister of Peter the Great) and later the young Tsar himself tried to rid Russia of the Tatars' marauding menace and standing affront to national honour by offensive as well as defensive means. Eradication of this running sore was certainly an immediate aim. Yet much wider geopolitical, existential considerations entered Russian decision-making too: this was not some minor border dispute or abstract religious quarrel. The causes of conflict ran much deeper, resulting in a clash of empires that would grate and grind over successive wars for two centuries and more, in which Sevastopol would ultimately play a most significant role as Russia's most important southern naval base.

Muscovite – later imperial – Russia looked in other directions as well as southwards: it advanced aggressively not only to secure its frontiers, but also to grow its economy and to gain international influence and prestige. In so doing it would fight against some neighbours or near-neighbours (such as Sweden and the Ottoman Empire) while allying with others (such as Poland and Austria) in temporary coalitions of political expediency. Since the late fifteenth century, the main threat to the survival of Christian eastern and central Europe emanated from Constantinople. The Ottoman Empire's expansion culminated in the failed Turkish siege of Vienna in 1683, in which Crimean Tatars fought loyally for the Sultan. Poland and Austria managed to contain, then defeat, the Ottoman threat, driving the Turkish army back down the Danube. These powers then sought

Russian assistance in the continuation of their war. For a promise of help from Moscow, a hefty price had to be paid. From this position of advantage, Sophia's favourite, Prince Vasily Vasilyevich Golitsyn (1643–1714), negotiated a treaty of 'eternal peace' with Poland in 1686. He scored a handsome gain: the incorporation of former Polish Kiev into the Muscovite domain. In return, the Russians pledged to declare war on the Ottoman Empire and attack its vassal, the Crimean Khanate.[53] This alliance set the scene for the first major Russian campaigns against Crimea for over a century: both were to expose the limitations of Russian military expertise.

For all Golitsyn's diplomatic skills, success deserted him when he attempted to engage the Tatars in battle. More a capable statesman than a competent military commander, in both 1687 and 1689 he directed abortive expeditions against the Crimean Khanate. On the first, he led his army across the wide southern steppe towards the Perekop. Golitsyn's operation badly miscarried – 'to suffer heavy losses and defeat as the lack of water and the huge distances exhausted his troops, while the Tatars set the grass on fire'.[54] Without adequate food or forage, and in the burning summer heat, Russian troops, horses and oxen all perished while the nimble Tatar horsemen fell back on to their own safe pastures. As many Russian generals, and, later, French and German commanders, were to ignore at their peril, the provision of adequate logistics was vitally important when campaigning over such large expanses of distant, hostile terrain. If history does not exactly repeat itself, unfortunately it seems that military commanders, and equally their political masters, regardless of nationality or era, are prone to neglect the lessons of past wars. Truly great generals such as Marlborough, Frederick the Great and Suvorov not only knew their history, but were also able to adapt to meet changed circumstances and to learn from their mistakes. Of course, they also enjoyed a fair degree of good fortune, which Golitsyn and many others painfully did not.

Golitsyn's first campaign proved an expensive embarrassment. His army of 100,000 men had not even reached the Perekop before having to turn back 100 kilometres north. He lost 45,000 men, returning to Moscow 'without ever sighting, much less engaging, the main Tatar army'.[55] At this time, Russia faced the possibility of its alliance with Poland dissolving if it did not meet its treaty obligations and resume operations against the Crimean Khanate. But in 1688, the Tatars struck first – and most audaciously so. In their inimitable style, they raided and ravaged a vast area of Ukraine, threatening the cities of Poltava and Kiev. They captured 60,000 prisoners before returning triumphantly to their Crimean stronghold. With diplomatic and domestic pressures mounting, there was no alternative but for Russia to mount a fresh campaign in an effort to eradicate this persistent Tatar threat, once and for all.

In 1689, Golitsyn launched his second offensive with a still larger army of 112,000 men. Significantly, it was supported by an enormous park of 450 cannon – an early example of the Russian military's predilection for employing huge quantities of artillery, which was later formidably manifest in the Soviet Red Army. Although the Tatars repeated their scorched-earth tactics, the Russians made better progress across the southern steppe than in their previous campaign. Fighting off cavalry attacks with massed cannon fire, and despite their lines of communication remaining under continual threat of interdiction, Golitsyn's army struggled forward and managed this time to reach the Perekop. There, the apparently impregnable fortification of the Turkish Wall blocked any further progress. Military wisdom has it that an obstacle must be covered by observed and accurate fire if it is to prove effective in battle, and so it proved in this case. The Tatars under Khan Selim Giray I certainly knew their craft: they concentrated their troops on a narrow front of 7 kilometres with both flanks securely protected by the sea. Immediately behind the ditch stood an earthen berm, a high rampart, which was lined with a wall of serried cannon and infantry. Further in depth, the remainder of the Khan's army, including a strong reserve of cavalry, was held ready in a protected citadel. The odds for the Russians, whether tactical or operational, did not look at all promising, to say the least.

Having advanced so far, and despite his lack of military experience, credit must be given to Golitsyn for not making a futile military gesture at this juncture. As one historian aptly observes, he 'was in no mood to launch an assault. His men were tired, his water short, he lacked the necessary siege equipment.'[56] In such unfavourable circumstances, the Russian commander attempted to apply his proven diplomatic skills. But he was in no position to bring, let alone force, Selim Giray I to come to terms. The Crimean ruler indignantly refused Golitsyn's peremptory demands including a promise never to attack Ukraine again and the abolition of the Russian tribute. Unable to reach an agreement or to storm the Perekop, Golitsyn was forced to turn tail and conduct an ignominious retreat. His second campaign had yielded another humiliating disaster, involving the loss of 35,000 men – 20,000 killed and 15,000 taken prisoner.[57]

The marked failure of Golitsyn's operations severely reduced the influence of Regent Sophia, which in turn facilitated her subsequent overthrow by her brother Peter in September 1689. He assumed control of Russia alongside his feeble half-brother Ivan, as co-tsar. One consequence of the exchange of power in the Kremlin was the scapegoating and exile of Golitsyn, stripped of noble rank and all privileges, to a remote Siberian village, where he lived in a 'wretched existence' until he died in 1714.[58] His misfortune was not only to fail militarily against the Tatars, but as much to pitch himself on the losing side of an unforgiving Russian dynastic conflict. Vasily Golitsyn cuts a typically tragic figure in Russian history:

although lucky to escape with his head, had Peter trusted and re-employed him, he might well have contributed further to Russia's much needed development as an accomplished statesman and moderniser.[59]

In the far north, Russia's sole seaport, Archangel, was frozen for half the year. The harbour at ice-free Murmansk was not constructed until 1915–16 during the First World War to compensate for the Turkish closure of the Bosporus, which had denied Russian and Allied passage to and from the Black Sea. In the latter part of the seventeenth century, moreover, Sweden dominated the Baltic, thwarting Russian expansion until Peter's military success on land led to the founding of St Petersburg in 1703. Meanwhile, within six years of coming to power, Peter was drawn into campaigning in the south, opening a 'new era in Russo-Turkish relations as well as in Russian history'.[60] The warm waters of the Black Sea proved an alluring alternative avenue for imperial acquisition and trade. There were other factors at play too. Once again, a combination of renewed Tatar raids in Ukraine and international diplomatic pressure prompted Russian military action in this theatre.

Observing that Russia had failed to bring any effective pressure to bear against Turkey, Poland threatened to make a separate peace with the Sublime Porte – the central government of the Ottoman Empire. This calculated ploy triggered a powerful Russian response. Her strategy had three inter-related objectives: first, to maintain the alliance with its western ally; secondly, to humble Constantinople; and thirdly, to punish the Crimean Khanate. The latter two goals, elegantly encapsulated by a modern biographer of Peter the Great as 'to harry the Turk and to suppress the Tatar', matched the young Tsar's desire to bring his beloved army into action, to build a fleet which would sail freely in the Black Sea, and to open up new trade routes.[61]

In contrast with Golitsyn's unfortunate expeditions, Peter designed a novel scheme of deployment and system of supply, adopting an indirect approach. Rather than heading straight for Perekop and Crimea in the manner of previous Russian campaigns, he aimed to unlock Ottoman power in the region by twin offensives designed to capture the Turkish fortresses guarding the mouths of the rivers Don and Dnieper. Success in both locations would permit Russian access to the Black Sea, and yield operating space for a new fleet. Rather than being laboriously carried over the steppe by ox-cart, munitions and provisions for both armies would be transported far more efficiently by river barges. Peter's main focus was the fortress of Azov, which stood on the southernmost branch of the Don, about 24 kilometres upstream of its mouth.

Still, the Russian leader's first attempt in 1695 to seize the Turkish strongpoint failed. Supplied by sea, it proved impervious to the attacks of the Muscovite army. The siege dragged on from June to October despite Peter's undoubted energy in directing operations as sovereign and general, including his misdirected enthusiasm in personally firing mortars as artilleryman 'Peter Alekseyev' during the Russian bombardments. Deficiencies in command and in tactics, and not least in the quality of engineer and artillery support, all undermined the effectiveness of the Russian military effort. Following a final, failed assault, Peter lifted the siege and turned about, retiring up the Don on 12 October. The autumnal retreat to the north over seven weeks in heavy rains and swollen rivers turned into a catastrophe. Harassed by the Tatars, and with supplies fast running out, the Russians lost more 'in lives and equipment than in the entire summer siege'.[62]

Peter, worthy of his later sobriquet, drew the appropriate conclusions and learnt from his disappointing experience at Azov and its even more disastrous aftermath. Over the winter 1695/96 he ordered and supervised the construction of a new fleet of ships at Voronezh on the upper Don, 'displaying his tremendous energy everywhere'.[63] By May 1696 he had assembled a flotilla of thirty sea-going naval craft and upwards of 1,000 barges to transport his troops. For the second assault on Azov, the Russian army was not only twice as strong as that of 1695, but also far more technically competent. It possessed another advantage too: a significantly weakened opponent. Astonishingly, the Turkish garrison had failed to repair the damage to the stronghold's defences from the previous year before the second Russian siege started. Such unforgivable military negligence was duly identified and punished. Well supported on this occasion on both land and sea, and with their opponents' defences breached, the Russians carried the fortress in a lightning, storm attack, forcing the Turks to capitulate in July 1696. The fortress of Azov, however, was not deemed suitable as a naval base. Peter established a shipbuilding yard at Taganrog on the northern coast of the Sea of Azov, where fourteen ships of the line were constructed within three years. Although the Azov Flotilla could not be described as a fleet, its establishment represented none the less a significant step in the projection of Russian maritime power towards Crimea and the Black Sea.

While Peter had scored a notable operational success at Azov, the first by Russia against the Ottoman Empire, the war against Turkey was by no means won strategically. This was not the moment to triumph: the wise Tsar recognised that he did not yet possess the necessary allies or national resources to fight and win a wider war against the Ottoman Empire. For the meantime, a policy of consolidation as opposed to further expansion was called for on Russia's southern front. Furthermore, the necessary naval capacity and expertise were lacking. Accordingly, Peter despatched a large-scale fact-finding mission, known as the 'Grand Embassy', to Italy, Holland and England in order to win friends and to assimilate technical knowledge. Over the period 1697–98, Peter spent eighteen months abroad learning the modern ways of Western European states, including Prussia, the Hapsburg Empire, Holland and England. Throughout he travelled anonymously as Pyotr Mikhailov, and worked as a shipwright in both Dutch and English yards.[64]

The results of Peter's protracted foreign sojourn were mixed. Although he failed to build a new coalition against the Ottoman Empire, he had learnt much from his experiences, not least on administrative and naval technical matters. During his period abroad, negotiations with Turkey had dragged on. Eventually, on 14 July 1700 a peace treaty was signed in Constantinople, by which Russia retained Azov and Taganrog. Perhaps as significantly, the Turks renounced the Crimean Khanate's claim to its annual tribute, so much and so long resented by Muscovy's rulers. The Russians also gained access to the Holy Land for pilgrimage, which represented a highly significant religious concession by the Ottoman Empire. Defending their special 'rights and privileges' would later trigger a dispute over the control of the Holy Places by the Christian churches that helped lead to the Crimean War. Events, meanwhile, were moving rapidly elsewhere.

In 1700, Peter, now allied with the states of Saxony–Poland and Denmark, declared war on Sweden under the young Charles XII, so entering the Great Northern War. For nearly a decade when Swedes and Poles (under King Stanislaus, now fighting against Russia) combined to fight a series of inconclusive and costly campaigns conducted deep inside Russian territory. By early summer of 1709, however, Charles had over-reached himself: his much-diminished army was fast running out of supplies. The Swedish leader – with the support of Cossacks of the Ukrainian Hetmanate under Ivan Mazepa and those of Zaporizhia – decided to besiege Poltava, a small fortified town and depot on the Kiev–Kharkov road in left-bank Ukraine.[65] Not only did the town's Russian garrison and townsfolk resist, but also a Russian field army closed in and built counter-entrenchments on the nearby river Vorskla, thus partly isolating the Swedes.

On 27 June (8 July) 1709, St Sampson's Day, a greatly superior Russian army under Peter the Great met Charles XII's depleted force. The Swedish King's plan of attack miscarried when his advancing force got lost in the woods – reflecting the ever-present 'friction of war'. In the first hours of the morning light, the Russians' massed artillery blew away swathes of Swedish infantrymen. In a brisk counterattack led by the Russian Tsar in person, the Swedes and their allies were routed. The battle marked a strategic turning point. In the assessment of a leading twentieth-century military historian, J.F.C. Fuller, it represented 'one of the most portentous events in the modern history of the western world'. In terms that still echo today, he noted: 'By wresting the hegemony of the north from Sweden; by putting an end to Ukrainian independence, and by ruining the cause of Stanislaus in Poland, Russia, an essentially Asiatic power, gained a foothold on the counterscarp of eastern Europe.'[66] For Ukraine, the Russian victory extinguished hopes of a national revival until its brief resurgence in 1918 in the wake of the Russian revolution of 1917 and the end of the First World War.

Despite his great triumph of Poltava, the Russian Tsar's position was not as secure as he might have supposed. Sensing an opportunity to reverse the disgrace of the treaty signed a decade before, Turkey intervened against Russia in 1710. Peter, flushed with his recent success against the Swedes and ignoring the lessons of his previous campaigns, led a poorly prepared army against the Turks in Moldova, plunging 'deep into an enemy country in defiance of communications and supply', repeating in the process the recent mistakes of Charles XII.[67] Inadequate leadership, ineffective planning, insufficient logistics and, above all, over-confidence let the Russians down – reversing all the martial qualities they had displayed so notably at Poltava. The price of such hubris and neglect in war is typically humiliation and dishonour. Thus Peter's army was very fortunate to avoid annihilation in July 1711 at the hands of a superior Turkish force near the river Prut (approximately midway between the Danube and the Dniester).

By skilful diplomacy if not through blatant bribery, Peter negotiated peace terms with the Ottoman Empire, managing to extricate his army largely unscathed. He thus snatched a battlefield 'draw' from near certain defeat and destruction. The strategic penalties contained in the resultant Treaty of the Prut, however, were severe. Russia was forced to abandon her newly acquired possessions on the Azovian littoral and to remove her newly established flotilla from that sea. Having secured peace – albeit at a high price of lost terrain and tarnished reputation – in the south, Peter was able to refocus his military effort once more in the Great Northern War against Sweden, and to fight on for a further decade.

Peace with Sweden was finally concluded on favourable terms at the Treaty of Nystadt on 30 August 1721. Russia gained the Baltic provinces and the southern extremity of Finland, so securing the strategically important approaches to the Gulf of Finland that protected her new capital near the mouth of the river Neva, St Petersburg, which Peter had founded in 1703. Despite having made significant gains in the north, Russia was understandably weary of war. A resumption of hostilities against the Ottoman Empire in an effort to wrest control of the Black Sea was beyond her existing economic and military capabilities and the prevalent political realities. In consequence, Crimea remained an independent Khanate stronghold. Yet Russia had emerged from the Great Northern War measurably stronger, not only in terms of newly acquired territory but also in international prestige. Furthermore, Peter, now officially termed 'the Great' and Emperor, reformed much of the administration of the state and modernised many of Russia's institutions. These included the Orthodox Church, her armed forces and shipbuilding industry. It is widely considered that the 'modern Russian navy was the creation of Peter the Great'.[68] Although Russia's maritime focus remained in the Baltic, her new navy, built and run largely on British and Dutch lines, would provide a foundation of expertise and tradition of service for subsequent employment in the Black Sea. Although Russia is typically deemed to be a great continental heartland and land-based power, Peter fully recognised the value of a navy, declaring in his naval regulations of 1720 that the 'state possessing an army has got one hand, but possessing a navy also, has got both hands'.[69]

Throughout the course of the eighteenth century, Russia never abandoned her enduring geostrategic ambition to gain permanent access to the warm waters of the Black Sea and beyond, to secure control of Crimea, and to reduce if not eliminate Ottoman – Muslim – influence in Europe. The Russo-Turkish War of 1735–39 under the reign of Empress Anna provided the first opportunity for a renewed Russian attempt to conquer Crimea since the tsardom of Peter the Great. Existing tensions between the empires were exacerbated by the Crimean Khan's campaign in the Caucasus that had undermined Russian influence. Tatar raids on Russia's southern vassal, the Cossack Hetmanate (corresponding to much of modern Ukraine), in 1735 provided a suitable *casus belli*. Russia opened operations against the Ottoman Empire the following year.

Several of the many famous foreigners – mercenaries in all but name – in Russia's imperial service now enter our story. The first is Field Marshal Count Burkhard Cristoph von Münnich, a military engineer and army reformer of Danish-German extraction. On 20 May 1736, he led the Russian Dnieper Army, some 62,000 men strong, into Crimea. He forced the Turkish Wall, overwhelming the Turkish defences at the Perekop, later to feature more famously in battles of both the Russian Civil War and the Second World War. In one of those remarkable coincidences of military history, a certain Christof Hermann von Manstein took a leading part in Münnich's Russian operations in 1736, while one of his descendants, Erich von Manstein, commanded the German forces that defeated Crimea's Soviet defenders in 1941–42. The storming of the Perekop was common to both these wars and the Russian Civil War. We are fortunate that the eighteenth-century German soldier left a detailed memoir of his seventeen years in Russian service, including an account of the campaign of 1736.

In stark contrast to Golitsyn's limp-wristed gambit half a century before, it would appear that Münnich attempted to negotiate a peaceful settlement from a position of strength. Manstein describes the situation:

> As soon as the [Russian] army had arrived near the lines, Münnich sent a letter to
> the Khan, acquainting him that he was sent on the part of the empress, to punish

the Tatars for the frequent incursions they had made into the Ukraine, that he was proceeding to execute this order, and lay all the Crimea waste; but nevertheless if the Khan would put himself under the protection of her imperial majesty, receive a Russian garrison in Perekop, and bind himself to acknowledge the sovereignty of Russia, he would enter into a negotiation, and cease from all hostilities ...[70]

Unsurprisingly, yet unwisely in this case, Khan Feti Giray refused Münnich's terms. Battle was then joined. According to Manstein, the 'Russian troops marched with a proud bearing to the attack'. He then paints a heroic picture of the successful assault of the Perekop defences:

> The fire of the enemy was at first extremely brisk; and the soldiers were a little astonished on coming to the side of the ditch, to find it so deep and so broad; but as it was dry they threw themselves into it, and, pressing on, assisted one another to clamber with their pikes and bayonets; the artillery, in the meanwhile, keeping up a constant fire against the parapet. The Tatars, seeing how serious the affair began to be, did not wait for the soldiers mounting to the top, but betook themselves to flight, abandoning their camp, which indeed was poorly enough provided. There did not then remain any the least impediment to the troops passing the lines, which are extraordinary works ...[71]

Exploiting the momentum of this attack, Münnich's powerful offensive brought him to the Khanate capital at Bakhchisaray (meaning 'garden palace'), which he occupied on 17 June 1736. Carrying out his threat to the full, he set the Khan's exquisite palace on fire and destroyed the town and other Tatar settlements. Despite such apparent success, Münnich was soon in deep trouble. Once again major inadequacies in supply and medical support left a Russian Army unable to cope with hunger and disease. Without reinforcements on land or any significant naval support in the Black Sea, Münnich was forced to withdraw from Crimea and turn back to Ukraine, an ever familiar and ultimately dismal outcome for Russian arms.[72] He was also forced to give up the Dnieper fortress of Ochakov. Meanwhile, Münnich's colleague Field Marshal Count Peter Lacy, an Irishman, led the Don Army to spectacular success in seizing the Ottoman fortress of Azov on 19 June 1736, reprising Peter the Great's triumph of 1696. On this occasion, the limited but effective support of the Russian maritime forces in the Sea of Azov proved decisive. Lacy's partner in arms was a Norwegian, Vice Admiral Peter Bredal, who skilfully employed the Don Flotilla.

Despite their mixed record of success in 1736, the Russians returned to the offensive in the next campaigning season. With 40,000 men under command, Lacy struck into the Crimean peninsula. He neatly bypassed the Perekop fortifications by using shallow-draught boats to cross the saltmarshes of the Sea of Syvash. Routing an inferior army of the Khanate in the field in two battles in June 1737, he seized Crimea's former commercial centre at Karasubazar (since 1945, Belogorsk), also seat of the principal Jewish community, razing it to the ground. Notwithstanding this initially successful campaign, the Russian Army was forced to withdraw, once again owing to a lack of supplies. Lacy returned the next year and ravaged Crimea once more, but by winter had returned to Ukraine. Hence the peninsula remained under Khanate rule.

During the Russo-Turkish War of 1735–39, Russian forces had managed on three occasions to penetrate or outflank the Turkish defences of Crimea, to forge southwards into its interior, encounter and defeat Tatar armies, and then to capture and destroy major Khanate towns and strongholds. But on each campaign, they were unable to hold seized terrain for more than a few months at a time. Logistical difficulties, arising from a flawed organisation of supply, exacerbated by poor lines of communication, disease and almost non-existent medical care, severely restricted Russia's ability to sustain military power in Crimea. More akin to large-scale raids than properly resourced invasions, let alone serious attempts to incorporate territory, neither Münnich nor Lacy's efforts succeeded in occupying the peninsula. Why, one might ask, did the Russians repeat the same old mistakes time and time again? It is one thing to identify lessons, but quite another to learn and apply them in any given strategic context. It would take bold political leadership, linked to improved military organisation and logistics, and, crucially, the application of maritime power, if Russia were to achieve its historic, strategic goal of annexing Crimea and establishing a major naval base on the peninsula. By the end of the century, all this would be achieved by a combination of diplomacy, force and subterfuge, not least at a time when two of Europe's major powers, Britain and France, were distracted by their involvement in the American Revolutionary War of 1775–83.

POTEMKIN AND THE RUSSIAN ANNEXATION OF CRIMEA

Prince Grigory Potemkin (1739–91), foremost favourite and lover of Empress Catherine II, called 'the Great', can lay good claim to being the initiator of Russian dominion over Crimea, founder of modern Sevastopol and father of the Black Sea Fleet. As a young horse guards officer, he had come to Catherine's attention in the summer of 1762, the year of her accession. Later that year he became her protégé and was appointed to her court as a 'gentleman-of-the-bedchamber'. Thanks to her patronage he rose rapidly both at court and in the army, gaining within six years the ranks of chamberlain and of major general of cavalry respectively. A man of undoubted talents, however, he also distinguished himself on active service during the Russo-Turkish war of 1768–74. Becoming Catherine's favourite and lover in the period 1774–76, he remained her closest confidante to the end of his life in 1791. In this process, he acquired 'both unrivalled official, bureaucratic power connected with the numerous titles and offices he held and the intimate, personal power that came with his singular relationship with Catherine'.[73]

Appointed by his sovereign in 1776 as commander-in-chief and governor-general of the newly established province of *Novorossiya*, Potemkin masterminded and drove energetically, if not frantically, Russia's southward expansion in the late eighteenth century towards the Black Sea. Although his most ambitious grand design – the beloved 'Greek project',[74] which he shared with his Empress – of establishing a new Russian Byzantium in Constantinople was never fulfilled, Potemkin had already become a legend in his own lifetime. He was famed for his many military and organisational achievements, and not least on account of his especially close and influential bond with Catherine. An extraordinarily dynamic individual, he has been aptly described as 'unique in combining the ideas of an entrepreneur with the force of a soldier and the foresight of a statesman'.[75]

With such a potent mix of abilities and connections, Potemkin attracted approbation and opprobrium in equal measure. Senior military subordinates such as General Alexander Suvorov, one of Russia's most famous soldiers, revered him, writing in obsequious awe: 'Illustrious Prince! Father! ... My life is yours to the very end'.[76] While Potemkin is still ridiculed in popular Western literature for allegedly constructing false-fronted villages to give an illusion of economic progress, his achievements made over two centuries ago in the name of his sovereign lady – his 'little mother', or darling *Matushka* – were real enough. Although neither a Marlborough nor a Napoleon, Potemkin surely deserves greater recognition for his many accomplishments than he receives. Modern cities such as Dnipro (formerly Dnipropetrovsk, and earlier, Yekaterinoslav), Kherson, where he is buried, and not least Sevastopol, are all living testament to his strategic vision, organisational skills and willpower.

For generations before Catherine the Great and Potemkin, a succession of Russian rulers had harboured political and economic ambitions in the south. They wished not only to secure their vulnerable southern frontier, a vast open steppe that could not easily be defended, but also to incorporate new agricultural lands, exploiting the fertile soils of Ukraine. Furthermore, Russia needed a warm-water port and access to new markets for her goods, particularly her highly valuable exports of grain. Any durable solution lay in eliminating the chain of Ottoman fortresses strung along the northern shore of the Black Sea, in occupying the Crimean peninsula, and not least in establishing new centres of commerce and citadels of military and naval power. Ultimately, the long-standing goal was seizing Constantinople (significantly described as the city of Caesar – Tsargrad – in old Russian) and in opening the Bosporus and Dardanelles, known collectively as the Turkish Straits. Moreover, religion played an important part in this expansionist policy. Russian strategic ambitions were underpinned by a burning desire to re-establish Orthodox Christianity in the Balkans and Black Sea lands, sweeping back in the process Islam from the European continent and from the Caucasus. It cannot be emphasised enough that religion, a vital element of Russia's governance and national consciousness (and arguably so today in Putin's Russia), was an important if not driving factor in many of her political considerations in the eighteenth and nineteenth centuries.[77] Significantly, Catherine had made her dream personal, having named her second grandson, born in 1779, Constantine. She had commemorated his birth with the provocative issue of silver coins bearing an image of Constantinople's great Byzantine church of St Sophia with an Orthodox cross crowning the cupola of the mighty basilica, which had become a mosque (the Hagia Sophia) following the Ottoman capture of the city in 1453.[78]

Conversely, the Ottoman Empire had for centuries sustained its hegemony over the region by denying Russia access to the Black Sea. One of its principal agents in containing Russian expansion was the Crimean Khanate. It acted not only as a military buffer state, protecting the Ottoman Empire, and providing a most valuable recruiting ground of *akincis* (raiders – light cavalrymen) for her army, but also acted as an important trading hub and source of revenue.[79] Furthermore, Crimea – along with the Balkans – was a significant stronghold of Ottoman power and centre of Islamic teaching and influence on the European continent, which would not be conceded without a determined struggle. Hence the contest for control of Crimea became an enduring element of Russo-Turkish wars over four centuries, including the Crimean War. It became a central battleground of a persistent round of conflicts that reflected deep divisions in political, economic and religious interests that could rarely be compromised. Against this backcloth, the central themes of nationalism, religion and war run through Sevastopol's story.

Russia could not attempt to seize and hold the Crimean peninsula in perpetuity without controlling the Black Sea. It would require a more capable, sea-going, fleet and a secure harbour on the peninsula, at which to berth, victual, repair and build ships. Hence the founding of Sevastopol would be intimately linked to the Russian annexation of Crimea, and become an essential part of this long-anticipated, grand enterprise. Forcing the Perekop isthmus, achieved in earlier campaigns, was but a necessary, yet insufficient, operational condition. It was Potemkin who first realised the decisive, strategic importance of Russia possessing both a powerful Black Sea Fleet and an associated naval base and arsenal on Crimea. He understood that ships sailing from Kherson on the Dnieper remained vulnerable to interdiction as long as the estuary fortress of Ochakov remained in Turkish hands. Although Sevastopol was established five years beforehand, the capture of Ochakov in 1788 would provide for the enduring security of southern Russia, including Crimea and its new naval base. Potemkin generated the political leverage and military resources to mount the annexation of the peninsula on a long-term basis, and possessed the necessary drive and statecraft to carry it off. His burning ambition was also assisted by the increasing political instability of the Khanate, weakened by internal dissent and division, and by the concomitant decline of Ottoman power in the region. Within just over a decade, Russia's grand strategy of political persuasion, underwritten by economic subsidies, and armed with growing military and naval power would bear fruit: the incorporation of Crimea into Russia would become Potemkin's prime legacy and Sevastopol his proud monument.

Despite the lack of substantive progress towards seizing Crimea during the first three-quarters of the eighteenth century, the peninsula had captured popular imagination in Russia long before her fleet entered Akhtiar (soon to be named Sevastopol) harbour in May 1783. After all, as we have seen, the city of Chersonesos was the birthplace of the Russian Orthodox Church in 988. No doubt this deeply symbolic, historically significant, religious connection inspired Potemkin, when corresponding with Catherine the Great in the autumn of 1782, to declare: 'Kherson of Tauris!! Piety streamed to us from you: behold, how Catherine the Second now brings you afresh the meekness of Christian rule.'[80] Hence possession of Crimea was not only a just cause to be supported, but also a rightful crusade.

Furthermore, Potemkin remained in no doubt as to the peninsula's geostrategic value to Russia in relation to the Ottoman Empire. He argued to his sovereign:

> If you do not seize [Crimea] right now there will come a time when everything that we might now receive free [might cost us dear]... Now imagine that Crimea is yours and that wart on our nose is no more. The state of our borders suddenly becomes excellent: along the [river] Bug the Turks share a border with us, and must conduct business directly with us themselves, and not through others. Their every step will be visible. In the Kuban lands, in addition to the local fortresses supplied with troops, the Don Host, with its large numbers, is always at the ready there.[81]

Catherine, however, did not pursue, initially at least, a policy of outright annexation of Crimea. Shortly after her accession in July 1762, she had rejected the recommendation of her chancellor and political adviser, Count Mikhail Vorontsov, to bring the Crimean peninsula under Russian control forthwith. Fostering diplomatic influence over the Khanate, rather than bringing direct military action against it, was Catherine's preferred course of action at first. Hence a Russian consulate was established in Bakhchisaray. But within a decade, the overall political situation had changed. By the time of the Russo-Turkish War of 1768–74, during which the Tatars failed to support the Ottoman Empire as wholeheartedly as in previous conflicts, it was clear that the Sublime Porte's influence on Crimean affairs was waning. Internal political disputes within the Khanate also marked this period. A combination of Ottoman weakness and Crimean division emboldened Russian foreign policy, which, in turn, became increasingly assertive in relation to Constantinople.[82]

In contrast to previous Russo-Turkish wars and campaigns against the Crimean Tatars, the strategic conditions had turned considerably to Russia's advantage. Since the time of Peter the Great, Russia had edged her southern border ever closer to the Crimean peninsula; her economic resources and military potential – not least her maritime power – had likewise grown significantly. More particularly, the Russian Navy had inflicted a crushing defeat on the Ottoman fleet at the battle of Chesma on 5–7 July 1770 in the Aegean Sea. Thus there was now a much-diminished risk of an effective Turkish response in the Black Sea. As one historian of the Crimean Tatars has observed, if the 'Ottomans could no longer protect the Crimeans against Russian expansion', the opportunity was ripe for 'an arrangement with the tsarina'.[83]

An impudent Tatar attack on a Russian garrison on the lower Dnieper in early 1771 provided the necessary rationale for a forthright rejoinder in Crimea. A military intervention later that year led to the installation of Sahib Giray as Khan of a semi-independent Crimea. His regime was backed by heavy Russian subsidies. In so doing, Catherine the Great attempted to lure the Khanate away from Ottoman influence. In 1774, a rival Tatar leader, Devlet Giray, mounted a coup that ousted Sahib. A second Russian invasion in November 1776 propelled Shagin Giray, pro-Russian Tatar and protégé of Catherine, to power at the beginning of 1777.[84] Later that year, there was a revolt against Shagin's unpopular and corrupt rule, which was only put down in February 1778 with further Russian military assistance. By the time new unrest broke out in Crimea in 1782, triggering a fourth Russian military intervention, Catherine and Potemkin were tiring of propping up an expensive and unreliable puppet state.

The long-term future of Crimea, however, including the foundation of Sevastopol, was largely decided by events elsewhere – principally through the outcomes of battle in the Danubian theatre of war against the Ottoman Empire – and influenced by European great power politics, including the partition of

Poland. While the Ottoman army suffered from feeble leadership, poorly trained troops and inadequate supply, the conflict demonstrated Russian military prowess in the ascendant. In 1769, Russian forces captured the major Turkish fortress of Khotyn on the Dniester. The next year, Field Marshal Count Pyotr Rumyantsev fought a brilliant campaign down the river Prut in 1770, winning a string of victories against superior Ottoman forces, including his great triumph at Kartal, all achieved at relatively little cost. Following this success, Rumyantsev advanced to the lower Danube where he captured the Turkish fortresses of Izmail, Kilia and Braila. Clearly, Russian military leadership and tactics had become more effective since Peter the Great's inglorious performance of 1711.[85] While Crimea was temporarily overrun by Russian troops in 1771, a combination of the First Partition of Poland in 1772 and the Pugachev rebellion in 1773 diverted Russian strategic attention away from the Ottoman Empire for the time being.

Decisive results against the Turks were again achieved in the summer of 1774 by Russian troops under aggressive command. Having crossed the Danube in early July with 50,000 men, Rumyantsev adeptly deployed a powerful forward detachment of 8,000 men under the energetic leadership of Alexander Suvorov. The latter grouping broke through the Turkish lines at Kozludzhi, 80 kilometres south of the river, by means of a surprise night attack expertly conducted against vastly superior Turkish forces (40,000 men). As in 1770, Russian innovation and initiative were much in evidence, as was the demoralising shock effect of the fearsome Russian bayonet charge.[86] While Suvorov may be remembered for his famous watchword 'the bullet is a fool, but the bayonet is a fine fellow', his military legacy was far more significant.[87] The strategic impact of the Russians' tactical and operational level successes on the Ottoman high command was equally important. The Turkish commander-in-chief, the Grand Vizier Muhsinzade Mehmed, who feared that nothing now could prevent the Russian Army from advancing all the way to Constantinople, sued for peace. Rumyantsev, a soldier-statesman, demonstrating his powers of diplomacy as well as those of generalship, sensed a critical moment of psychological advantage over the Turks. He pressed for, and gained, the very best of strategic terms for Russia on the field of battle.

This remarkable turn of events is highly significant to Sevastopol's history. The ensuing Treaty of Kuchuk Kainardzhi[88] (in Turkish: Küçük Kaynarca), signed on 10 (21) July 1774 in an obscure Bulgarian village, the location of Rumyantsev's headquarters, helped set the conditions for Russia's annexation of Crimea nine years later. Russia gained immensely from the treaty, receiving more than compensation for the humiliating concessions made at the Prut in 1711. In exchange for the conquered Danubian provinces of Moldavia and Wallachia, restored to Ottoman rule, Russia won strategically significant stretches of the Black Sea littoral. These included the restoration of Azov and Taganrog in the Sea of Azov, the acquisition of Kerch on Crimea, and, crucially, the surrender of the Dnieper delta including the land between the rivers Bug and Dnieper, less the fortress of Ochakov. These territorial advances provided Russia with two routes of access to the Black Sea, at last realising Peter the Great's grand dream in the south. Furthermore, freedom of navigation was assured for Russian merchant ships to transit the Turkish Straits. Crucially, the peace also included the cessation of Ottoman sovereignty over Crimea. A khanate independent of Constantinople would prove far more susceptible to Russian influence. Additionally, Turkish reparations to the tune of 4.5 million roubles represented the icing on the cake.

Overall, as a modern biographer of Catherine the Great concludes, 'the war had tipped the balance of power in the region in Russia's favour; Europe was now aware that predominance in the Black Sea had passed to Russia'.[89] On this basis, the annexation of Crimea was surely now only a matter of time. Catherine hesitated, however, for the political conditions were not yet quite right. While she waited for Khanate affairs to unravel further, she consolidated Russian power in the region with Potemkin at the lead. Furthermore, this step-by-step approach would require the construction and deployment of a new fleet capable of operating in the Black Sea, and an associated operating base.

Meanwhile, Russian colonisation of Crimea took place as if Catherine had been pursuing a strategy of assimilation as opposed to annexation. Yet the reverse process also happened. Aiming to destabilise the Crimean economy and thereby to undermine the Khanate leadership, in 1779 Potemkin ordered the evacuation of over 30,000 individuals of the Christian merchant class (principally Greeks but a good number of German colonists too), who had been settled in Crimea. Suvorov supervised this mass exodus, a distasteful task for any general, which caused much suffering.[90] By 1782, it appeared that Shagin Giray's days were numbered: without further Russian military support and extensive subsidies he could not hope to cling to power. So the stage seemed set for the irrevocable end of Crimean Tatar rule. Why Catherine delayed her decision to annex the peninsula until 1783 remains 'one of the major questions of Crimean history'.[91]

For Crimea's predominantly Tatar population, the period between the peace of Kuchuk Kainardzhi and the Russian annexation in 1783 was unstable and unsatisfactory all round. The nine years of nominal independence marked an unhappy episode of troublesome transition from Khanate to Russian rule: one of intra-Tatar rebellion, associated Turkish meddling in Khanate affairs and, in turn, a series of Russian military interventions. This twisting course of events has led to historians claiming that an immediate annexation of Crimea in 1771–72, or following the Treaty of Kuchuk Kainardzhi in 1774, rather than that realised in 1783 would have caused overall 'much less bloodshed, destruction, and turmoil'.[92] The fact that Crimea was finally occupied with minimal loss might suggest it could have been incorporated into the Russian Empire a decade earlier. Although this contention has merit in hindsight, it ignores the self-imposed political restraint that Catherine had applied: she wished to portray Russia as the protector of Crimea rather than as its predator. It has been ever thus in international affairs, as President Putin was keen to demonstrate in 2014. Opportunity and context proved equally crucial in the eighteenth century. During the period of 1771–82, Russia intervened in Crimea four times. The first three campaigns were designed to maintain in power a khan of Russian choosing; the last aimed to shake away the final vestiges of Crimean Tatar power. So when the time appeared opportune for Russia to annex Crimea, Potemkin achieved this goal in 1783 on behalf of his grateful empress without battle.[93]

Towards the end of 1782, Potemkin had argued the case for the final act of conquest in a century-long drama with an impassioned letter to Catherine:

> Acquiring the Crimea can neither strengthen nor enrich you. It can only secure peace. This would be a powerful blow – against whom? The Turks. And this obliges you even more to do it. Believe me, with this acquisition you will achieve immortal glory such that no other Sovereign in Russia has ever had. The glory will pave the way to still another even greater glory: with the Crimea will also come supremacy over the Black Sea. Upon you depends whether the path of the Turks is to be blocked and whether they are to survive or to perish.[94]

Catherine, however, had still not ordered the annexation of Crimea. 'After weighing up all the pros and cons', however, she 'launched intensive diplomatic and military preparations' for this final act. Specifically, on 8 December [OS], she issued a secret decree to her College (Ministry) of Foreign Affairs to study the issue and to wrap up dealings with the Porte, as well as reviewing Russia's relations and 'reasoning with all other powers'.[95]

Less than a week later, on 14 December 1782 [OS], she instructed Potemkin to appropriate Crimea, that 'nest of pirates and mutineers', for Russia 'at the first opportunity'. Both the conditions and others' perceptions had to be right. The rationale for such a step could be, for example, the 'death or captivity of the current Khan, his betrayal of Russia or creation of obstacles in the occupation of Akhtiar (later, Sevastopol) harbour'.[96] In the international sphere, moreover, she wished to avoid any impression of conquest. Hence she desired that the Tatars would consent to the incorporation of their lands into Russia, and publicly so. Furthermore, she wanted the Tatar leadership to swear an oath of allegiance to her in an act of submission. Potemkin was left to mastermind these details in the first half of 1783. The correspondence of the period between sovereign and plenipotentiary indicates how tense the situation had become for both. Potemkin pressed Catherine again on the strategic benefits to Russia if Crimea were to be annexed:

> The allegiance of the inhabitants of the New Russia province will then be beyond doubt. Navigation upon the Black Sea will be unrestricted. Pray note that otherwise your ships will find it difficult to leave port, and even more difficult to return. And what is more, we shall rid ourselves of the difficulties of maintaining fortresses now located at distant points in the Crimea.[97]

Catherine and Potemkin realised that there was a window of opportunity in 1783 to annex the peninsula while Britain and France were negotiating a peace on the conclusion of the American War of Independence, and when neither Prussia nor Austria would intervene to assist the Porte. When Crimea was finally annexed, and a naval base established at Akhtiar in May 1783, as described in the next chapter, it fundamentally shifted the balance of power in the Black Sea region. Not a single European state, however, directly opposed Russia's action – as was the case in 2014. The Ottoman Empire was condemned to look on helplessly, nursing its pride and biding its time to mount a military challenge, which indeed would soon come.

From the moment she established her naval base in Crimea, Russia was able to curb the Turks' remaining power in the Black Sea region even further. Sevastopol provided a vital naval base in this strategy of containment, whose warships could threaten Constantinople. In modern military terminology Sevastopol would be described as a strategic centre of gravity, a hub of maritime power. This explains why the city, its fleet, dockyards and arsenal attracted so much British and French attention immediately prior to, and during, the Crimean War (1854–56). It not only accounts for the fact that Sevastopol became the focus of the German campaign in Crimea during the Second World War (1941–42), but also provides the principal rationale underpinning Russia's actions over Crimea more than seventy years later.

CHAPTER 2

THE FOUNDING OF SEVASTOPOL

'Here on 3 (14) June 1783 was founded the city of Sevastopol – the naval fortress of South Russia'[1]

THE FOUNDER

In the early 1780s, a long-forgotten Scottish soldier of fortune travelled to the Russian imperial court at St Petersburg. Variously described as a 'military adventurer of dubious character' and 'the Northern Imposter', James George Semple Lisle sought a commission in the Russian Army.[2] While awaiting an audience with Prince Grigory Potemkin, quite by chance he met a certain Thomas Mackenzie. In his memoirs, Semple Lisle described the latter as a 'Captain of the Russian navy, an officer who, both as a private gentleman and a soldier, has ever held the highest esteem of all that have the happiness to know him'.[3] Recognised as an unconventional fighting sailor and energetic organiser, Mackenzie was soon to be promoted to rear admiral and specially selected – although happenstance also intervened – to play a pivotal role in the founding of Sevastopol. This event was his crowning achievement, an act that Semple Lisle claimed to have witnessed.

Mackenzie, of Scottish stock, was born on 18 February 1740 [OS]: the only son of Rear Admiral Thomas Mackenzie and Ann Young, granddaughter of Admiral Thomas Gordon, who had joined the Russian Navy in 1717 during the time of Peter the Great.[4] His birthplace is believed to be Archangel, northern Russia. One of several experienced British, and particularly Scottish, naval officers who entered Russian employment, in 1736 Mackenzie senior had transferred from the Royal Navy as a shipmaster to the Russian Navy, serving his new country with distinction for thirty years. As Catherine the Great strove to improve her fleet's effectiveness in the latter half of the eighteenth century, many more British officers were tempted to follow this career path, induced by a doubling of pay.[5] Such individuals included John Elphinstone and not least Samuel Greig, who rose to the rank of grand admiral, becoming widely recognised as the 'father of the Russian navy'.[6] Nothing is known of Thomas Mackenzie's childhood and schooling until 1759, when, observing family tradition, he entered the Royal Navy as an able seaman. Having learnt the basics of seamanship, he left as a midshipman in 1765. In that year he returned to his family and, retaining his rank, joined the Russian Navy, in which he was known as 'Foma Fomich (Thomas son of Thomas) Mekenzi'. Honing his leadership and navigational skills, he sailed in various ships across the Baltic, Norwegian and Northern Seas. His career developed rapidly, based on a mixture of personal drive, nautical expertise and an uncanny ability to seize an opportunity – a combination of qualities that ran in the family. In professional and personal terms, however, Thomas Mackenzie was on occasion to sail perilously 'close to the wind'.

During the war with Turkey (1768–74), Russia projected her growing maritime power into the Mediterranean for the first time. The principal focus of Russian operations in that conflict was the struggle for control of the provinces of the lower Danube, Wallachia and Moldavia, together with a subsidiary campaign in Crimea. Yet Catherine the Great's council of war sought other ways to weaken the Ottoman Empire. Her then favourite and advisor, Prince Grigory Orlov, suggested the Russian Navy should enter the Mediterranean. A Greek nationalist revolt in Morea (the Peloponnese) provided a promising opening.[7] Abetted by Russian agents and supported with arms, the Greeks' insurrection against Ottoman rule could be supported further by Russian naval forces, which had grown in quantity and quality under the energetic direction of Catherine. Moreover, there would surely be opportunities to engage and defeat the Turkish fleet, thereby diminishing the Ottoman Empire's international prestige. Catherine was attracted to this bold strategy of the indirect approach. At that time, however, the only seagoing fleet of any offensive capability Russia possessed was based in the Baltic; the small flotilla of minor vessels in the Sea of Azov was in no position to force the Turkish Straits to reach the Mediterranean Sea. Thus the Russians had to deploy their warships via the North Sea, the English Channel and the Eastern Atlantic. Although carried out with critical British naval logistical support, such a distant and daring deployment was none the less a hugely challenging undertaking for the Russian Navy.[8] The conflict provided the young, ambitious Mackenzie, newly promoted to lieutenant, with his first taste of action at sea.

In November 1769 the leading squadron of Russian warships from the Baltic under Admiral Grigory Spiridov entered the Western Mediterranean, wintering at the British base of Port Mahon on Minorca. Meanwhile, on 20 October 1769 Mackenzie sailed from Kronstadt (the Russian Navy's main base in the Baltic) for the Mediterranean with a second battle squadron commanded by Rear Admiral Elphinstone. After a long 145-day voyage, excluding an extended, three-month stop for repairs and to winter at Spithead, off Portsmouth, Elphinstone's ships passed Gibraltar on 3 May 1770 and arrived off the southern tip of the Peloponnese peninsula, Cape Matapan, on 20 May. Within a week, Elphinstone's squadron sighted and engaged a superior Turkish fleet, forcing it to retreat eastwards into the Aegean Sea.

A brief pause in the fighting then ensued. Meanwhile, both Russian squadrons were united under the overall command of Count Alexey Orlov (brother of Grigory), with Commodore Samuel Greig acting as his technical adviser. On 5 July 1770, the enemy fleet was found lying at anchor in the strait between the island of Chios and the Turkish coast, near modern Izmir. Although having only nine ships of the line to the Turkish sixteen, the Russian fleet attacked the next day. Spiridov's flagship, the *Sviatoi Yevstafiy*, engaged the Turkish flagship, the *Real Mustafa*, which caught fire and exploded – destroying both ships in the process. Despite this loss, the Russians were able to force their opponents into the narrow Bay of Chesma. Mackenzie, then serving on Elphinstone's flagship, the 80-gun *Sviatoslav*, fought with particular valour during the following action. During the night of 6/7 July 1770, sailing in a formation of vessels commanded by Greig, Mackenzie commanded one of four fireships that helped bring about the destruction of the Turkish fleet.[9] In his own words:

> [Having made] for the centre of the enemy's ships, my grapplings at my fore-yard arm caught the bob-stay of one of their largest ships of war, and to my good fortune I set my vessel on fire, and in about five minutes the Turkish ship was all in a blaze. I got off, thank God, without fear or wound, and brought all my men safe off, though closely pursued by the enemy. The moment I came on board the Lord High Admiral I was congratulated on my being made a Captain.[10]

For his gallant deed, Mackenzie was decorated with the Order of St George (Fourth Class).

Strategically, the Russians had won a decisive victory at negligible loss – the greatest defeat inflicted on the seemingly omnipotent Ottoman naval forces since the battle of Lepanto in 1571. No fewer than fifteen Turkish ships of the line had been destroyed in the conflagration of Chesma; approximately 9,000 Turkish sailors perished in the battle as a whole.[11] This astonishing, one-sided, achievement demonstrated not only that the Russian Navy had come of age, but also placed it firmly in the first division of European navies. The early reforms of Peter the Great and the subsequent recovery of naval investment and expertise under Catherine the Great had paid off handsomely. Furthermore, a significant element of the Russian success was down to the skilled and audacious actions of British naval officers who served under the Russian flag.

Following the cessation of hostilities with Turkey, Mackenzie returned to the Baltic, where he continued to serve with merit, going on to command various vessels. Notwithstanding his promotion to captain second rank (the equivalent of commander) in December 1775, he courted controversy and censure. It arose from his tenure in command of the 66-gun ship of the line *Deris,* then a unit of the Russian squadron operating off Portugal. In Lisbon, several British nationals, formerly prisoners of Spain, had joined the ship. During a voyage to Kronstadt during the winter of 1780–81, having battered against a violent storm in the English Channel, Mackenzie had diverted his ship into Portsmouth for repairs without authorisation. This incident occurred during the time of the 'League of Armed Neutrality' (1780–83), by which Catherine the Great intended to protect neutral (such as Russian) shipping from interception and search by Royal Navy ships looking for French contraband. In this delicate diplomatic context, the Russian Admiralty had expressly prohibited Russian warships from entering British ports. So Mackenzie's action was highly embarrassing, and all the more exacerbated by British newspaper reports implying that the *Deris* had sailed to Portsmouth through the promise, or even the exchange, of money. Mackenzie's personal role in the affair remained ambiguous. Furthermore, he had intensely annoyed the Russian naval leadership by failing to submit regular reports. Condemning his conduct, the College of Admiralty pronounced: 'Keep Mackenzie under suspicion until he has redeemed himself through assiduous service, and for this reason he can no longer be considered so dependable, distinguished and knowledgeable in maritime affairs as he was previously held to be.'[12]

Under this cloud, Mackenzie was forced to leave the service for a short time. Fortunately for him and the Russian Navy, he was rehabilitated on the express order of Catherine the Great because she needed to retain such experienced officers with manifest potential. Mackenzie's career revived within a couple of years. On 12 January 1783 [OS], the Russian Admiralty promulgated his promotion to rear admiral for service in the Azov and Black Seas.[13] He was directed to join Vice Admiral Fedot Klokachev, a more senior and distinguished veteran of Chesma, who had recently been recalled from protracted sick leave and warned to command the Azov Flotilla.

AKHTIAR HARBOUR

During the intervening period, Prince Potemkin as governor-general of *Novorossiya* had steadily increased Russian influence and activity in the south. Only a month before Mackenzie's advancement, as we have seen, Catherine the Great had issued a secret edict on 14 December 1782 [OS] to her plenipotentiary to seize Crimea and to undertake immediate preparations accordingly. In her judgement, it was imperative to build up Russia's naval presence in the Black Sea as quickly as possible in order to deter and, if necessary, to defeat any Turkish intervention in response.

The Russian Admiralty, based on General Suvorov's advice, had already identified the grand natural harbour of Akhtiar Bay (named after the small Crimean Tatar shoreline settlement of Ak Yar, meaning 'white cliff') as a potential naval base.[14] Preliminary measures to reconnoitre and secure the habour had been put in hand. The Tatar Khanate had even considered that year ceding Akhtiar Bay to Russia, perhaps believing it to be the lesser of two evils – the greater being the loss of Crimea. Yet Potemkin had continued to press hard for the annexation of the entire peninsula, so the 'offer' had been refused. None the less, in November 1782, Potemkin had ordered two frigates of the Azov Flotilla, the *Khabar* and *Ostorozhniy*, under the command of Captain First Rank I. M. Odintsov, to winter at Akhtiar. In his survey report, Odintsov declared: 'I have the honour to recommend a chart of Akhtiar harbour with its inlets, soundings and shorelines marked, suitable for fifty warships and other vessels.'[15]

Events for Russia, Potemkin and Mackenzie then moved fast. On 22 January 1783, Catherine the Great had appointed Klokachev to command the Azov Flotilla. The next day he departed St Petersburg for Kremenchug on the Dnieper to confer with Potemkin, from whom he received further instructions. He then hoisted his flag at his new Azov command at the naval port of Taganrog. In March, Klokachev ordered a second reconnaissance of the southern shores of Crimea, and particularly of Akhtiar, to confirm its suitability as a base. Captain-Lieutenant Bersenev duly sailed forth. Arriving at Akhtiar in April to carry out a detailed survey, he found it to be a large, deep and safe anchorage. His encouraging report described 'four bays, protected from winds by the mountains and a fifth, a roadstead, stretching in length to seven, and in width to one and a half versts,[16] with a depth of ten fathoms, with a silty bed'.[17] Together with Odintsov's earlier report, Berensev confirmed Akhtiar as an excellent harbour for a fleet, one that would allow ships to be anchored in safety close inshore. Furthermore, the land around the bay also had the precious advantages of being both largely uninhabited and undisputed at that time. In all respects, therefore, the location seemed ideal for the construction of a base for a Black Sea squadron with all the necessary on-shore facilities. It would soon form a vibrant hub of maritime power from which the Russian Navy could cruise and dominate the region's waters.

In parallel with Berensev's reconnaissance, on 8 April 1783 [OS], Catherine signed a decree 'to take under our power the Crimean peninsula, the Taman peninsula and all the Kuban lands'.[18] The annexation was only to be made public once Potemkin had completed his mission. By the time that the Ottoman Empire and Western Europe's major powers had woken up to the fact that something significant was under way, Russian troops were already on the march. By mid-month, under the direction of Lieutenant General Count Anton de Balmen, commander-in-chief of Russian forces in Crimea, a grenadier battalion had secured the shoreline of Akhtiar harbour. It was subsequently reinforced on 1 May 1783 by the Kaporsky and Dneprovsky infantry regiments, together with batteries of field artillery.[19] This prudent pre-emptive measure reprised that of Suvorov, whose timely action at Akhtiar in 1778 had thwarted a Turkish landing at the bay. On Balmen's advice, Klokachev ordered to sea two armed schooners and a frigate to patrol off the Crimean coast to give early warning of any possible Turkish naval incursion. Yet the only way to secure Crimea on an enduring basis in accordance with the Empress's intent was to sail in strength to Akhtiar and to build a permanent port infrastructure there, a task which Klokachev now proceeded to carry out. Under his command were three 44-gun frigates, two 16-gun vessels, three armed schooners, and other small craft.

Klokachev's small flotilla departed Kerch on 5 May 1783. Despite it being a relatively short sea passage around the Crimean eastern and southern seaboard, his ships did not sail into Akhtiar harbour until 13 May. Presumably the Russian vessels had been delayed by bad weather for there are no accounts of any engagements with the Ottoman Navy. Gunners of the Russian shore batteries fired a salute of honour to welcome the safe arrival of what would become the new Black Sea Fleet. Without delay, reconnaissance of the new harbour and base area commenced. Mackenzie's biographer, Vladimir Usoltsev, captures the scene as Admirals Klokachev and Mackenzie toured the bay in a 12-gun brig, the *Bityug*:

> They were intrigued as they looked over the steep, wooded, southern shores of the
> bay, the ruins of Inkerman [lying at the eastern end] and the deserted shore on the
> northern side.... They visited the [firing] positions the gunners had set up on the
> northern promontory at the entrance to the bay. The beauty and splendour of the
> coastline caught their imagination.... When the admirals alighted on a flat
> headland the other side of the first inlet after the entrance to the bay, they
> immediately decided to establish the port here.[20]

The admirals' point of disembarkation on the southern shore lies at the heart of the modern city of Sevastopol, only a short walk from Nakhimov Square and the Count's Landing Stage.

On 17 May 1783, Klokachev sent two despatches to the College of Admiralty. The first confirmed the safe arrival of his squadron at Akhtiar, and that he had taken under his command two frigates from Kherson under the command of Captain First Rank Odintsov, which were already lying in the roadstead at anchor.[21] Of the new harbour, the Russian admiral was full of praise:

> I shall not omit to convey hereby to Your Excellency that even upon entering the haven of Akhtiar I was struck by its good position from seaward and, having gone in and looked round, I am able to say that in all Europe there is no harbour like it for position, size and depth. A fleet of up to 100 vessels of war may be kept in the harbour. Furthermore, the limans [inlets] are so arranged that they naturally divide into different harbours, that is – naval and merchant.[22]

In his second report Klokachev recorded that he had received orders from Potemkin to proceed without delay to Kherson to take over command of the Dnieper Flotilla and the 'admiralty', or naval shipyard, there.[23] The city's governor, General Quartermaster Ivan Hannibal, a veteran of Chesma and principal builder of the new city of Kherson, had recently fallen out with Potemkin over an argument about the construction costs and bills. Hence he had been recalled to St Petersburg. Now Klokachev relieved him: one of the admiral's main tasks was to revive the stalled shipbuilding effort in the Kherson yards. Before Klokachev departed for Kherson on 19 May 1783, when writing to an army colleague, he extolled further the merits of Akhtiar's fine natural harbour: '[I've] not seen better in the whole of Europe and it's impossible to find a finer place for keeping a fleet.'[24] He was not alone in this glowing assessment.

With Klokachev's reassignment to Kherson, consistent with his appointment as overall commander-in-chief of the Black Sea and Azov Fleet, responsible for both ships and infrastructure, Rear Admiral Thomas Mackenzie was left in command of the squadron at Akhtiar. As such he was charged with constructing a new, permanent naval base. In this monumental task, his flag lieutenant, Lieutenant Dimitry Nikolayevich Senyavin, ably assisted him. Senyavin later rose to the rank of admiral: he would become commander-in-chief of the Black Sea Fleet and consequently governor of Sevastopol.[25]

Russian sailors soon began to find their bearings at Akhtiar harbour and to identify the most suitable anchorages and moorings. In order to orient themselves initially, they relied on the local Tatar names for geographical features. Soon, however, they began to use their own, which have stuck. Akhtiar (now Sevastopol) harbour is a veritable 'bay of bays': there are approximately thirty of them – hence the 'comb' appellation of ancient times (see Map 4). Klokachev's and Mackenzie's crews named the principal bays that first summer. Sailing eastwards along the southern shore of the main bay, the first inlet they encountered was that which the Tatars called 'Kadi-liman' (Judge's Bay). When the Russians disembarked guns from ships to store them here during refits or over winter, this little inlet became known as 'Artilleriysky'. Nowadays the bustling Artillery Bay is one of modern Sevastopol's main ferry terminals – a loud siren warns passengers that the ferry is just about to depart for the short crossing to the 'northern side'. The next inlet is far bigger, the largest in the main bay of Sevastopol. Although the Tatars called it 'Chaban-liman' (Shepherds' Bay), it has always been known in Russian as the 'Yuzhnaya', or Southern, Bay. It was here that Mackenzie allocated berths for his squadron, with his flagship the frigate *Krym* being given hers first.

At the Southern Bay's entrance, leading off eastwards, there is a smaller inlet where ships of the line were also anchored. As a result, it was called 'Korabelnaya' (Warship) Bay and remains so-called. Today, however, it is in the much larger Southern Bay where modern Russian warships are berthed. Further east along the main bay there is a cove where a team from the first two ships that overwintered in 1782–83 established a careening wharf – a jetty for scraping clean, caulking and repairing the part of a ship normally under water. As a result, it became known as 'Kilenbukhta' (Keel) Bay, described in British accounts as Careening Bay. Ships are still repaired here. Opposite this site lies Holland Bay on the northern shore. As a modern Sevastopol guidebook explains, it got its name not because there were any Dutch sailors present in Russia's first Black Sea Fleet, but rather from the name given to a gully leading up from the shore, which was used for the storage of planks, ropes and other pieces of ships' equipment. A similar storage site at St Petersburg was known as 'Holland' after the Dutch sailors who had established it during the reign of Peter the Great. Thus sailors from the Russian Baltic Fleet who were involved in the construction of Sevastopol simply 'used the name they had become accustomed to' for the same purpose. On the northern shore, the two major inlets opposite the Southern Bay are still known today as 'Severnaya' (Northern) Bay and Old Northern Bay.[26] At the former is a vehicle ferry terminal for the passage to Artillery Bay on the southern side; to the west of Old Northern Bay lies the Michael Battery; further west still is Matyushenko Bay with a landing stage for the passenger ferry across Sevastopol Bay.[27]

BUILDING THE CITY

On 23 May 1783, Mackenzie sent a despatch to St Petersburg confirming the departure of Klokachev and giving the detailed deployment of the vessels under his new flag which he had hoisted in the frigate *Krym*.[28] His main fighting force was a squadron of five frigates stationed at Akhtiar harbour, cruising near the Crimean shore.[29] Klokachev had already identified the need for a major depot and strong coastal fortress that would match the mighty Kronstadt in the Baltic. This would entail building a complete naval infrastructure from scratch. It would need to include: alongside berthing; a careening yard; a magazine for powder, shot and shell; a biscuit factory and provision stores; barracks for the garrison and ships' companies; and a civilian settlement.[30] Fixed shore defences would have to follow soon. All this was no simple undertaking: at first, Mackenzie had only his own sailors to call on, together with some soldiers of the garrison and limited numbers of tradesmen. A lack of skilled people, provisions, construction tools and building materials presented very significant challenges in the founding of Sevastopol.

Under Mackenzie's good management and energetic supervision, however, these obstacles were overcome and building work soon commenced. This activity was initially concentrated on the western side of the southern harbour. The area here was cleared of shrubs and trees, and, in early June 1783, the foundations of the first masonry buildings were laid down.[31]

The first constructions in stone comprised a house for the admiral, a chapel, a 'smithery' for the future shipyard, not far from the entrance to the southern harbour, and a pier. Senyavin described the rate and style of the overall building effort:

> The speed at which these constructions were carried out was extraordinary: each ship's captain hurried to build a house for himself and a barracks for his crew. Of course these houses were of unpretentious architecture ... [simple buildings] that were reminiscent of Novorossiysk huts, but nevertheless they allowed the officers and crews to take shelter from the impending winter cold. However, not one wattle construction was erected in the newly-founded town of Sevastopol; the solicitous Mackenzie began to burn lime, make bricks and build stone buildings.[32]

In fact, the Russians had easy access to some very suitable building stone nearby: they could simply rob the ruins of ancient Chersonesos. According to Senyavin, this act of expediency (there was no thought then for any conservation) 'greatly contributed to the speedy construction of barracks for naval personnel, port workshops, shops and residents' houses'. Such was the frenetic pace of work, in order to complete as much as possible before the onset of winter storms and snows, that 'a dock was built in little over a month, and the forge in almost three weeks'.[33] On 13 July 1783, Mackenzie reported to the vice president of the College of Admiralty, Count Ivan Chernyshev, that he had completed the small dockyard and was continuing with the construction of the barracks. Moreover, 'ship repair work had already begun in the harbour'. So progress all round seemed excellent.[34]

During that first summer at Sevastopol, Senyavin recorded Mackenzie's style of leadership, which combined succinct direction with convivial distraction:

> Before lunch, when the commanders were all assembling, the admiral, announcing the order of the commander-in chief said: 'gentlemen, here we shall stay for winter, try each to build for yourself something, I will help you with timber, as much as I can to distribute, besides you know yourself what to do; nothing more, let's go and eat'. The captains bowed to him and realized that his speech was short, clear and substantial. They sat at the table, had a good lunch; … in the evening they finished up drinking, and were dancing on the quarterdeck.

Senyavin added rather cryptically that 'Miss Sally played her role here very well, and by midnight the ball was over and everyone left' – but left no clue either to the identity of the lady or her relationship to Mackenzie.[35]

The spiritual needs of the garrison and fleet also received due priority: the chapel of St Nikolay Chudotvorets (St Nicholas the Miracle-worker) was consecrated on 6 (17) August 1783. Just eight weeks had passed since Klokachev's and Mackenzie's arrival at Akhtiar. It was some time that month, during the first hectic summer of Russia's new Crimean naval base, when 'Major' Semple Lisle visited on official business. By then he had been admitted into Russian military service and was now acting as an aide-de-camp to Potemkin.[36] On arrival, he met his 'old friend Admiral Mackenzie, with his little fleet'. Impressed by what had already been accomplished, Semple penned: '[the] fortifications and other works were in great forwardness, and every thing bore the aspect of improvement'.[37]

The pair then went by boat to 'visit an antient building', which Semple Lisle recalled as 'antient Chersonese' that lay in an 'almost inaccessible' cove. After failing to reach it by sea, they scrambled over the rocks 'from the land side'. They found there a building 'if it can be so called … almost cut out of the rock; but it is uninhabited except by one man'. From this scant description one cannot be sure whether Mackenzie and his visitor actually visited the main part of the old city of Chersonesos. The individual they encountered was perhaps a hermit or holy man. As Semple Lisle recalled: 'whether he lived there from motives of religion, or of concealment, I cannot say. The few remaining natives however showed him much respect, and supplied him with necessaries'. Admiral Mackenzie, for whom Semple Lisle's admiration was clearly evident, 'gave strict orders that [the man] should not be molested'.[38]

Semple Lisle's account reminds us that although Akhtiar was sparsely inhabited at the time, and ancient Chersonesos deserted, save for one solitary individual, the rest of Crimea was not. During Semple Lisle's stay at Akhtiar, he and Mackenzie received a visitation from a number of the 'native' Tatar chiefs, attempting to ingratiate themselves with their new 'Russian' masters. Each of the pair was presented with a horse. Mackenzie's was richly decorated with ornamental leatherwork and silver stirrups. Semple Lisle recorded the amusing, if not embarrassing, scene that then ensued: 'Mackenzie eyed the gawky beast with much pleasure, and in the presence of the whole company jogged my elbow, and, poising a stirrup in his hand said, "Take you the horse, I will have the stirrups by G[o]D – each of them will make a pair of candlesticks"'. 'Had he said two pair[s]', Semple Lisle noted further, 'I do not think his calculation would have been extravagant'.[39] Although there is some doubt as to the authenticity of Semple Lisle's autobiography, or at least to parts of it, his pen-portrait of his Crimean host and his domain rings true:

> Admiral Mackenzie, whose name may truly be said to have graced an early part of this narrative, had gone round to the harbour of Actiare, now called Sebastopole; he had there, with the rapidity which distinguished all his movements, begun to build a house for himself, marine barracks, hospital, store-houses, erect batteries, and put the harbour into a respectable state of defence.[40]

Semple Lisle then took ill at Akhtiar and, still weak, journeyed to Karazubazar in the Crimean peninsula to re-join his master, Prince Potemkin, who was suffering from a severe fever himself, probably malaria. The Scotsman's Crimean sickness was more likely to have been the plague, which he noted had broken out 'among us'. This disease took a heavy and steady toll of the Russian sailors, soldiers and settlers stationed in Crimea and southern Ukraine, including the ports of Kherson and Taganrog.

Semple Lisle was lucky even to survive and to tell the tale. Indeed, Klokachev reported to the College of Admiralty that at Akhtiar alone no fewer than thirty-nine men had died during the last three weeks of September, while a further seventy had perished in Kherson during the first week of October.[41] Shortly afterwards, the vice admiral (aged fifty-one) himself succumbed to the plague in November 1783, and was buried in a common grave in the outskirts of the city. The harsh reality of military and naval duty, let alone the arduous construction effort at Akhtiar, meant that life was tough, dangerous and, in many cases, short. Injury, sickness and death were constant companions: rank carried no privileges in this regard. Earlier that year a lonely Catherine had been particularly concerned about Potemkin's absence and the risks to his health in South Russia. Writing to him on 9 June 1783 [OS], she opened her heart:

Not only do I often remember you, but often regret and grieve as well that you're there and not here with me, for I'm lost without you. I beg you in every possible way: don't tarry over the occupation of the Crimea. I am now frightened by the threat the plague poses to you and everyone else. For God's sake, do be careful and order all measures be taken against it.[42]

In a letter of 13 June [OS] that had crossed with that of his Empress, Potemkin had shown he was well aware of the dangers posed by the disease, observing:

The most alarming aspects of this plague are the reports coming out of the Crimea, where it has appeared in different districts and in our hospitals. I rushed there as soon as I learned of this and took measures to separate the sick from the uninfected, and saw to it that all their clothing was fumigated and washed. I divided the sick according to their illnesses; thank God there are only five as of now.[43]

Sadly, Potemkin's optimism that the plague had been curbed was mistaken, as Klokachev's reports and his own ultimate demise in the autumn make clear. Despite the practical measures undertaken to minimise the spread of the plague, medical science had yet to determine the causes of this deadly disease and how best to counter it.[44] Effective antibiotics were not introduced until over a century later. Constantinople was a known centre of frequent outbreaks of the plague during both the eighteenth and nineteenth centuries. Any trade with that city – or stationing of troops there – brought with it the risk of infection, as the British Army was to find to its cost during the Crimean War, at its hospital at Scutari (now Üsküdar, a municipality of Istanbul) of Florence Nightingale fame.

Meanwhile, work at Akhtiar had continued apace throughout the summer, as reflected in both Senyavin's and Semple Lisle's enthusiastic accounts. In his despatch of 20 November 1783 [OS] to the College of Admiralty, Mackenzie had reported good progress at Akhtiar: 'The building [of] houses, headquarters, officers' accommodation, sailors' barracks, local material and provision stores', he wrote, 'is coming to completion'.[45] Yet he also felt bound to temper undue expectations of what more could be achieved in the short term, raising the 'extreme shortage' of materials. Furthermore, due to the onset of winter, he explained that transport vessels could no longer sail safely, nor could rowing boats be risked on the passage to Kherson. Mackenzie had been forced to send a frigate there in order to maintain communications with his superior headquarters.

Since the city's foundation, Catherine had been kept well informed about progress made in establishing the new naval base. Writing on 13 June 1783 [OS], less than six weeks after the arrival of Admirals Klokachev and

Mackenzie and their modest fleet, Potemkin had recorded his impressions of the new anchorage to Catherine. He could scarcely disguise his passion for the place:

> I shan't describe the beauty of the Crimea, which would take much time, leaving this for another occasion. I shall only say that Akhtiar is the best harbour in the world. Petersburg, situated upon the Baltic, is Russia's northern capital; Moscow is its central, and may Kherson of Akhtiar be my sovereign's southern capital. Let them see which sovereign made the best selection.[46]

Completing one of those intriguing full circles of history, President Putin accorded Sevastopol 'federal city' status on 18 March 2014, the two others of the Russian Federation being Moscow and St Petersburg.[47]

Potemkin's description may have prompted Catherine in April 1784 to rename Akhtiar as Kherson, linking it to the ancient ruins of Chersonesos that lay close nearby. Meanwhile, according to some historians, she had already decided that 'Sevastopol' would be the name of another new city – one already well under construction near the mouth of the Dnieper river, where, a few years before, Potemkin had already established a Russian garrison, naval base and shipyard. Accidentally, the envelopes with Catherine's decrees were mixed up. By default, Sevastopol became today's Kherson and the intended Kherson was called Sevastopol.[48]

In the event, both Potemkin and Catherine were delighted with the new name of their Crimean foundation and so it stuck. Derived from the Greek words 'Sebastos' and 'polis', Sevastopol means 'venerable' or 'holy' city.[49] After the death of the Empress, her successor, Tsar Paul I, in an act of pique on 12 December 1796 [OS] ordered the reversion of Sevastopol to Akhtiar as he tried to rid Russia of all traces of Potemkin, whom he had so detested. Catherine's wishes appeared to prevail, however, when Akhtiar was once again renamed Sevastopol on the order of her grandson, Alexander I, in 1801. In some official correspondence, nevertheless, the city was still called by its old Tatar name. Only following an order issued by Tsar Nicholas I in March 1826, that Russians were 'not to call the city Akhtiar anymore, but always Sevastopol', was Catherine's (and Potemkin's) name for the place secured for posterity.[50]

The official decision to erect a fortress at Sevastopol only followed the initial work on the sailors' settlement and the port infrastructure. The name 'Sevastopol' first appeared in an imperial decree of 10 February 1784 [OS], in which Catherine had commanded that 'a large fortress at Sevastopol with an admiralty and wharf for first-rate ships' be constructed.[51] The Empress also took the opportunity to honour the foundation of the city by ordering a medal to be struck with the inscription 'The Advance of Russia'. Shortly before, another medal had been issued celebrating the establishment of the Black Sea Fleet with the words 'The Glory of Russia' – an act of faith that would be more than redeemed in the future.[52] Detailed proposals for the development of Sevastopol (beyond that which Mackenzie had already put in hand, largely on his own initiative) would have to wait for a couple of years. To obtain the necessary professional technical advice, Potemkin turned to Colonel of Engineers Nikolay Ivanovich Korsakov. He was an up-and-coming officer, who had visited Britain in 1776–77 to complete his education and to study canal building.[53] Potemkin had praised him highly in a letter to Catherine in July 1783: 'Matushka, we've never had such an engineer as Korsakov. The way he finished off [the fortress of] Kinburn, it looks really grand. We need to hold on to this man.'[54] Accordingly, Potemkin soon entrusted him with the refinement of Kherson's docks and fortifications. But the budding engineer was to take on wider responsibilities, including surveying Sevastopol and designing its longer-term development.

In a report for Potemkin dated 14 February 1786 [OS], Korsakov set out a ten-year plan for the construction of the Crimean city, its defences and naval infrastructure. The first priority that year was to increase the provision of supplies and tools, and 'to prepare for the next summer with sufficient quantities of bricks, tiles and lime'. Within five years, the engineer envisaged that Sevastopol would be turned into a 'defensive state', with 'stone fortress lines, parapets and glacis protected with turf'. In addition, by this year (1791), all the necessary permanent barracks for the soldiers of the garrison and for the ships' crews of the fleet would be constructed, along with warehouses, powder magazines, a jetty and a lighthouse. Over the next five years of the planned period of construction, forts guarding the sea approaches to the harbour would be built, together with docks and other facilities required for the Admiralty. Finally, 'public buildings such as churches, coaching inns and the governor's house' would all need to be completed.[55]

Sadly, Korsakov died a tragic and quite unnecessary death during the siege of Ochakov in early October 1788, when he impaled himself on his own sword having accidentally fallen into a deep ditch while visiting the Russian batteries.[56] 'Russia', as one expert of the period has noted, 'certainly lost what it could ill afford—an enlightened and experienced officer and a highly skilled and resourceful engineer'.[57] Had Korsakov not slipped so unluckily, not only would he have witnessed the fall of the Turkish fortress on 17 December 1788, but also it can be reasonably assumed that he would have lived to supervise his grand plan of defence for Sevastopol. Korsakov was buried in the graveyard of St Catherine's Cathedral at Kherson, in which building Potemkin's body was interred in 1791. In the meantime, progress at Sevastopol during would turn out much slower than originally planned.

Returning to Sevastopol during its foundation year, 1783–84, Mackenzie's difficulties over materials and weather were compounded by a lack of cash and delegated authority to deal directly with local officials, such as were accessible. He was forced to ask the College of Admiralty in St Petersburg, for example, to demand 'woodland of suitable trees' from local Tatar sources and to cover 'the expense at fair cost'. Mackenzie went on to complain bitterly: 'In the absence of permission of the College I have not taken the liberty myself of procuring timber. At present I have no money for my squadron, let alone for anything else.'[58] Such were – and remain in the world today – the challenges confronting an independent, pioneering spirit frustrated and thwarted by the dead hand of remote officialdom. The ingenious Mackenzie, however, seems to have found an alternative source of liquid funds. Seven months later, on 12 (23) June 1784, for example, he reported to Count Chernyshev about a recent visit by Potemkin to Crimea. 'I met His Highness', he wrote, 'at Sevastopol':

> ... where he was pleased to stay two days examining in detail the buildings on the shore and the arrangement of the fleet, and he departed from here greatly pleased. Being here, I took the liberty of reporting to him the spending of much money on various civilian buildings and other requirements, which he was pleased to promise to pay, and I hope Your Excellency and the College will forgive me for my audacity for that which I have done.[59]

Apparently, permission from the Russian College of Admiralty was not forthcoming. There could well have been several reasons for this frustrating state of affairs – at least from Mackenzie's perspective. First of all, personal relations between Potemkin and Chernyshev were poor as the latter resented the Prince's establishment of the Black Sea Fleet, which increasingly lay outside the purview of the Admiralty in St Petersburg.[60] Secondly, the Portsmouth incident of 1781 was probably not forgotten, and there may indeed have been grounds for suspicion of embezzlement or fraud in Sevastopol. Mackenzie's Russian biographer concurs with this judgement, observing: 'Those who possess much power and have disposal of great resources in terms of material, labour and finance often confuse the public purse with their own. Mackenzie was not immune to this'.[61] It would appear that a disciplinary case was brought against him in 1785 for the unauthorised expenditure of treasury monies. Any proceedings, however, were forestalled by Mackenzie's untimely death – probably from the plague – on 10 January 1786 [OS].

Looking back, despite the suspicion that he was 'flexible' with government funds, Mackenzie's accomplishments in just over two and a half years at Sevastopol were remarkable. To put his misdemeanours into context, Mackenzie's attitude to government money was pretty much universal in this period, in Britain let alone Russia. Otherwise his record is exemplary. Under his direct supervision, Russian ships' crews and tradesmen had founded a city and constructed a naval port, which in time would become a worthy counterpart to Kronstadt in the Baltic. The admiral's drive, determination and energy had been an example to all. Mackenzie remained true to his independent, kind-hearted and amusing character, which had earned him the admiration and loyalty of his subordinates, including Senyavin. Evidently, he was a gregarious and jolly soul, and hence never one to miss a party.

Writing about the events of 31 December 1785 [OS], Senyavin recorded Mackenzie's last revelries. It was a familiar scene of convivial carousing that took an unfortunate, morbid turn:

> ... there were celebrations all day at Admiral Mackenzie's home. After a sumptuous dinner everyone immediately started playing cards and dancing; everyone took part, there were no spectators and anyone who wished joined in the fun. Half an hour before midnight they were invited to supper; at the last minute before the New Year all the glasses were filled with champagne, the clock struck twelve, everyone stood up and congratulated the Admiral and one other on the New Year. But our Admiral quickly sat down on a chair.[62]

Something was clearly wrong. Mackenzie, quite removed from his usual ebullient state, was downcast. His guests asked: 'What's the matter with you? What's happened to you?' The admiral responded gravely, 'I shall die this year: there are thirteen of us sitting at the table.' It is said that naval men are superstitious: but his comrades tried to dispel such depressing thoughts in him. Mackenzie then attempted to put a brave face on the occasion, even 'putting on a woman's dress and pretending to be an old Englishwoman dancing a minuet'. This strange behaviour, apparently, 'was his favourite joke whenever he made merry.' Such levity, however, proved short-lived. As his loyal flag lieutenant recalled further, 'Suddenly, during the evening of the 7th [January], the Admiral fell ill and on the morning of the 10th he passed away; I pitied him deeply.'[63]

There is little doubt that Senyavin and the other officers and sailors of Russia's first Black Sea Fleet greatly respected their beloved admiral and deeply mourned his loss. Thomas Mackenzie had proved himself early in his career as a brave and intrepid officer in assisting with the destruction of the Turkish fleet at Chesma: during his final years in the Russian Navy he had overseen the construction of a new city and port. He had achieved much through his professional expertise, personal energy and, not least, charm and dint of character.

Mackenzie was interred with full military honours in a mound overlooking the Southern Bay. Below lay his own creation – Sevastopol, the new naval base built with the sweat and toil of his Russian ships' companies. As Usoltsev's investigations have revealed, the admiral's place of burial 'was known for a long time as Mackenzie's Kurgan, but after the Crimean War the name was changed to Zelyoniy Kholm, Green Hill and after that to Krasnaya Gorka, or Red Hillock'.[64] Today an old T-34 tank, a monument to the fighting there during the Second World War, is set on a plinth close to this spot. No sign, however, of Mackenzie's precise burial place remains in Sevastopol: neither is there any important memorial to the city's founder. This omission is probably due to his foreign, Scots name. Russian nationalism and Sevastopol's pride have always been closely intertwined. Soviet historians (and even some contemporary local Russian sources) have falsely ascribed Mackenzie's role and achievements to his subordinate Senyavin.[65] The former's house, which was developed into the governor's residence, survived the Crimean War but was levelled in the early 1900s to make way for improvements to the area around Nakhimov Square.

The only significant reminders of Mackenzie's name today are the range of wooded hills, *Mekenzievy Gory*, the Mackenzie Heights, that lie to the east of the city, and a 'Mackenzie Boulevard' situated in a new housing estate near the Mackenzievy Gory railway station on the northern side of the city, not far from Inkerman. One day, the omission of any fitting memorial to Thomas Mackenzie in Sevastopol may be corrected if the late Vladimir Usoltsev's campaign to gain the founder of the city due recognition were ever to be revived.[66]

The inventory of the late Mackenzie's estate at Sevastopol provides some remarkable insights into the lifestyle of this extraordinary Russian of Scots parentage. According to one Russian historian, he enjoyed a 'laird's taste and means for comfort, verging on luxury in [contrast to the] squalid conditions of early Sevastopol'. Where he obtained such wealth amongst such impoverished surroundings can only be supposed: embezzlement, however, cannot be ruled out. Apparently, Mackenzie lived the good life, owning:

> ... several farms well-stocked with beast and fowl, a doocot, a stable with twelve horses, and seven different carriages for travel. His house, by far the grandest in the town, with gilden railings, tiled fireplaces and silken curtains, teemed with fancy furniture, crystal, porcelain, silverware and paintings, and later served as a residence for the Empress [Catherine the Great]. The admiral left eight hem-studded rings and 2,213 roubles in cash as well as sixteen decks of cards and 56 books.[67]

It is also clear that Thomas Mackenzie had a keen eye for the ladies. At the time of his death, he left a widow without issue in Kronstadt and a five-year-old son (Thomas Henry Mackenzie) with Mrs Maria Bryne from Portsmouth, presumably conceived during his sojourn in that city during the winter of 1780/81. There was also an unnamed 'poor English girl' reported living with him in Sevastopol, who apparently survived him, but was left 'destitute', presumably the 'Miss Sally' mentioned by Senyavin in 1783.[68] Mackenzie's wife, likewise, lived in poverty. After she petitioned Admiral Greig for assistance, 'her house in Kronstadt was made over to her for the duration of her lifetime by order of Catherine II'.[69] Until his untimely demise, Mackenzie, aged 45 years, had enjoyed his food, drink and national dress in common with many of his expatriate landsmen. Apparently, the admiral's personality stood out best 'in the contents of his cellar and wardrobe'. More specifically:

> [Mackenzie's] sweet tooth is conspicuous: 60 pounds of treacle, 45 of sugar, 45 of honey, seven of raisins and nineteen forms of pastry. The thirst is there too: 554 empty and 374 full bottles of assorted wines plus six measures of vodka and three casks of French brandy. Finally, among his thirty coats and uniforms is listed a kilt in green and blue, a tartan plaid, a velvet bonnet, a Scots broadsword, a dirk and other items of Highland apparel.[70]

Mackenzie's name lived on to the Crimean War. As we shall see later, British troops encountered Mackenzie's Farm on the march from the Alma battlefield to Balaklava in late September 1854. Earlier visitors to Sevastopol were certainly aware of his role. As with Semple Lisle, the place seemed to attract colourful characters. Another would soon follow.

Shortly after Mackenzie's death, a certain Elizabeth, Lady Craven, a 'seductive and pushy' beauty, who had scandalised London with her immodest dress and various brazen affairs, arrived at the new Russian base.[71] Carrying Potemkin's warm blessing, it would appear that she was given the red-carpet treatment in Sevastopol.[72] In a letter of 12 April 1786 to her lover and future husband, the Margrave of Brandebourg, the travel-writer confided:

> I have the whole house to myself, where the architecture and furniture are English; it belonged to an Admiral Mackenzie, who is just dead – I crossed an arm of the sea ... to arrive here – and upon landing, at the bottom of a flight of several steps, I was surprised by two or three voices, who said, we are your countrymen, my Lady – and in fact, there are several of my country men as captains or lieutenants in this navy – The Admiral's house is just above this landing-place and makes a fine appearance.[73]

Returning to Lady Craven's account, she reminds us why the Crimean base became so important to the Russian Navy, and remains critically so today:

From the singularity of the coast, the harbour is unlike any other I ever saw; it is a long creek that is formed by the Black Sea and between two ridges of land, so high that *The Glory of Catherine*,[74] one of the largest of the Russian navy, which is at anchor here, cannot be seen, as the shore is above the pendant[75]—The water is so deep that this touches the land—All the fleets in Europe would be safe from storms or enemies in these creeks and harbours, for there are many. —Batteries at the entrance to them, on one side, would be sufficient effectually to destroy any ships that would venture in, and placed towards the sea must even prevent the entrance of a fleet.[76]

Despite the mild exaggeration in her description, the English traveller was highly perceptive in her analysis of Sevastopol's defences. For the fortifications she envisioned were precisely those that would be constructed over the subsequent fifty years or so, notably Fort Constantine on the 'northern side' that continues to guard the entrance to Sevastopol Bay. These defences would be first tested in combat during the Crimean War. Perhaps in her analysis of Sevastopol's defences and potential Lady Craven had been schooled – if not charmed – by Nikolay Korsakov, whom she had met in Kherson a month earlier. Evidently, she had been greatly impressed by the young engineer, writing about 'a very civil spirited young man', and predicting that he would 'make a distinguished figure in the military annals of Russia'.[77] In describing his work in renewing Kherson's fortifications, she declared, 'by [his] active and studious spirit, I have no doubt that they will be executed in a masterly manner'. As we have seen, the governor of *Novorossiya* shared her faith in him. Potemkin would surely have warmly approved of Craven's concluding assessment of Korsakov: '[He] seems to have the welfare of this place and the honour of his nation very much at heart…. I can conceive of nothing so pleasant to a young soldier, as to be employed in places where his talents must create the defence and stability of newly acquired possessions'.[78] With such patriots of perspicacity and purpose serving their countries, new empires are deftly designed, built and defended.

IMPERIAL TRIUMPH TO SEVASTOPOL

Potemkin was so proud of his achievements in New Russia that he wished to display them personally to Catherine. The Empress, too, was anxious to observe at first hand what had been undertaken and accomplished in her name. Her interest particularly applied to the incorporation of Crimea into Russia and the establishment of Sevastopol as a principal port of the new southern fleet. By mutual desire, a plan emerged for an expedition to review the newly won domains in the south. The year set for this processional journey (1787), four years after the founding of Sevastopol, was both significant and symbolic – it marked the silver jubilee of Catherine's accession in 1762. Such was the complexity of the enterprise, it required four years in the planning. The grand tour would become the 'longest journey of her life and the most spectacular of her reign'.[79] Involving a winter sleigh ride from St Petersburg to Kiev, and thence, following the ice-melt, a procession down the river Dnieper in the spring, it became the 'longest, most lavish, expensive boating party in world history'.[80] Foreign ambassadors were invited to meet the Empress at Kiev. After joining the festivities there, they would then accompany her by galley on a resplendent journey downstream to Kherson, and onwards by carriage to Crimea and Sevastopol.

It was this imperial triumph of Catherine the Great that established the famous legend of the 'Potemkin villages'. Contrary to this and other myths, however, the grand tour was not merely some flamboyant, vainglorious extravagance – despite its unprecedented expense.[81] Above all, it served an earnest diplomatic purpose. Catherine and Potemkin wished to demonstrate to the crowned heads of Europe that the Russian Empire, with her recent territorial expansions and growing maritime power, was a state of substance to be reckoned with. Furthermore, it would signal to the world that the Ottoman Empire and particularly Constantinople, only a couple of days' sailing from Sevastopol, was now well within their sights. Such ambition reflected their joint and 'glorious dream of recreating the Greek Empire, with Constantinople as its capital, and Catherine's grandson Constantine as its Emperor'.[82] In sum, the royal journey of 1787 was far more than some voyage of pleasure, or stately visit. Designed to 'impress Europe and to intimidate the Turks', it was an unambiguous statement of strategic intent.[83] Sevastopol with its new Black Sea Fleet was the final station of the tour: it would prove a very fitting and impressive climax.

Meanwhile, in 1783 Potemkin was already preparing for Catherine's eventual visit. In his eyes this occasion would seal Sevastopol's foundation, blessing the new city with the sovereign's presence and granting it imperial patronage. Accordingly, under his direction the grand tour of the south was planned with consummate care: neither important details nor impressive displays were spared. For the Empress and her entourage, a special gazetteer, describing the principal places that they would visit, was prepared. The entry for Sevastopol, presumably drawing on earlier naval reports, confirmed the suitability of the harbour, declaring it to be 'one of the best havens in the world'.[84] Rear Admiral Thomas Mackenzie had already proved the merit of Sevastopol as a secure anchorage for the Black Sea Fleet over three winters. 'The town of Sevastopol', continued the gazetteer, 'which is currently under construction, is situated in one of the bays – the closest to the sea, on a flat terrace of the shore and area surrounded by the mountain ridge.' No doubt readers and visitors alike would have been impressed by the rate of its construction, for 'judging by the short period of time [elapsed]', the town already 'has many buildings, and is supplied with all necessities for the vessels berthed and naval personnel lodged there'.[85]

In planning the tour, Potemkin desired not only to commemorate the destination but also to honour the royal route to Sevastopol. Reflecting Russia's ultimate objective, Constantinople, he erected along the way a series of decorative arches under which the imperial party would pass, inscribed provocatively with the words 'The Road to Byzantium'.[86] The message could not have been clearer, whether to friend or foe. Unfortunately, none of these arches survives today. On taking up the suggestion of the imperial governor of Taurida, Vasily Kohovsky, Potemkin ordained that the processional way should also be marked by a series of decorative limestone columns, set at intervals of 10 versts (equating to 10.67 kilometres).[87] Their legacy, however, was not as lasting as Potemkin would have wished. As unwanted symbols of tsarist rule, most of the surviving memorials were demolished during Soviet times. Four remain in Crimea. These include the final one of the imperial route that stands on the north side of Sevastopol at the edge of the small park of Uchkuyevka. Until recently, the surviving milestone provided the only reminder of Catherine the Great's triumphant visit to the city in 1787. Curiously, it was falsely re-engraved in the 1860s, stating that the Empress visited in 1887 rather than 1787!

The former Catherine's Square was renamed Nakhimov Square after the Crimean War in honour of the famous admiral, who had fallen in the heroic defence of the city, and Catherine Street became Lenin Street after the Bolshevik revolution and the subsequent Civil War. The first modern memorial to Catherine the Great in Sevastopol was not unveiled until the 225th anniversary of the foundation of the city in 2008. Funded through public subscription, the monument symbolically faces the Officers' Club of the Russian Federation's Black Sea Fleet on Lenin Street (significantly not re-named), a stone's throw away from the fleet museum in central Sevastopol. This belated recognition of the Empress is historically significant, marking the rehabilitation of Russia's Romanov legacy in the city.

Such was the importance of Catherine's visit to Sevastopol, Potemkin brooked no risk to the success of this event, designed to gratify his Empress and to astound her foreign guests. Accordingly, in January 1787 he conducted a formal preliminary inspection of the new base. Accompanied by the Venezuelan adventurer and future revolutionary, Francisco de Miranda, with whom he had been recently acquainted, Potemkin ensured that all was either ready or in an advanced state of preparation. His South American companion recorded visiting Mackenzie's former house, which had been 'sold for 4,000 roubles', and then ˙ning in the barracks with the captain of the warship *Count Voinovich*.[88] This same modest dwelling, suitably adorned and appointed, was used five months later to accommodate Catherine on her imperial visit. Despite its humble origins, Mackenzie's house then became known as a palace, and, suitably adorned and extended, was used as the governor's residence in Sevastopol for many decades.

Meanwhile, Catherine soon commenced her long journey. Departing St Petersburg in the bitter cold on 14 (25) January 1787, she rode across the snowy wastes in a massive sleigh, 'containing a drawing room, library and bedroom', drawn by thirty horses. Her court followed in nearly two hundred other sleighs, both large and small.[89] This enormous caravan arrived at Kiev twenty-one days later. Then followed an extended, if not frenzied, round of diplomatic activity and entertainment, one of grand assemblies and private audiences, lavish balls and sumptuous banquets. Prominent among the foreign guests in her majesty's close circle were: Prince Charles-Joseph de Ligne, field marshal, confidante and envoy of Joseph II of Austria, who would join later; the British diplomat Alleyne FitzHerbert, Minister Plenipotentiary to Russia; and the Comte de Ségur, the French ambassador, poet and raconteur. While FitzHerbert left no record of the tour (disastrously, all his papers were lost when his London house burnt down in 1797), fortunately the memoirs of both de Ligne and de Ségur have survived. The latter provides both an acute impression of Potemkin (describing him as 'powerful and capricious') and a particularly valuable record of the visit to Crimea and Sevastopol – on which this account draws.

On 12 May 1787 the royal flotilla eventually set off down the Dnieper to great fanfare. Fuelling the legend of Potemkin's infamous achievements, one more modern (American) writer captures the scene:

[The Prince's] wonders unfolded on either hand. His enemies were astounded. The shores of the Dnieper were a vision of Eden. Prairies were covered with grazing herds of cattle and sheep attended by shepherds playing on pipes. Picturesque villages decorated with garlands rose on either bank. Troops of soldiers in magnificent new uniforms manoeuvred in the fields. At dusk happy, carefree bands of young peasants in holiday dress danced and sang at the river's edge. After nightfall there were illuminations and fireworks on the shore.[90]

More importantly, there were urgent affairs of state to be undertaken *en route* to Crimea. Near Kaidak on the Dnieper, Joseph II – travelling incognito as Count Falkenstein – joined the Empress. Catherine was keen to court the Austrian Emperor, as without his assistance any grand move by Russia to further expand her borders at Turkey's expense would be highly problematical. It was a deadly serious business: the two sovereigns had been secretly conferring on this subject since 1781.

Thus the primary object of the imperial journey was to keep Joseph engaged in the 'Greek' project by impressing him with Russia's growing strength, and particularly her maritime capability. Unmasking Sevastopol with its new fleet was the trump card to be played. Previous wars had shown that while Russia could defeat the Ottoman Empire in battle, her advantage, whether on land or sea, was as yet insufficient to conquer European Turkey and to seize Constantinople and the Straits – indeed this remained Russia's ultimate goal up to the First World War.[91] In the late eighteenth century, as throughout the nineteenth and into the early twentieth, Russia needed powerful allies in order to crush Turkish resistance. If Austria and Russia were to combine forces against their common historic foe, then surely the map of Europe could be redrawn to their joint benefit. A new Byzantium beckoned: this bold vision remained the essence of Catherine's and Potemkin's grand design. It would require Joseph's active and sustained support, moreover, if it were ever to be realised.

The next day the two monarchs journeyed together to the newly founded city of 'Catherine's Glory' – Yekaterinoslav. Under Potemkin's ambitious plans, it was intended as the new capital of *Novorossiya* with a grand palace, university, law courts, an academy of music, botanic garden and textile factories.[92] The two heads of state laid the foundation stone of the Transfiguration Cathedral, a design claimed by some to rival St Peter's in Rome. Lack of funds, however, would soon limit the size of both the palace and the cathedral; the university was not founded until 1918. On 26 May, Catherine and Joseph inspected the new fortified city and port of Kherson, another of Potemkin's foundations. There, at the Dnieper shipyards, they launched three warships including a 66-gun and an 80-gun ship of the line, naming the latter the *St Joseph*.[93] Presumably this symbolic gesture of friendship was not lost on the Austrian emperor and his fellow guests.

On arrival in Crimea, Catherine stayed at the former Khan's palace in Bakhchisaray, which, on her orders, had been tastefully restored by her Scottish architect Charles Cameron. Having renovated the 'inner courts and secret gardens enclosed by high walls and hedges of myrtle', he had redecorated 'the cool uncluttered rooms with tiled walls in glowing colours [with] thick carpets [and] elaborate tapestries'.[94] The outstanding features, however, were the marble fountains at the centre of every room; the most impressive of these, the Fountain of Tears, which continues to attract thousands of visitors today, became the inspiration for Pushkin's famous epic poem, *The Fountain of Bakhchisaray* (1823).[95] It was in that old Tatar city, and while absorbing the Islamic atmosphere of the palace and its immediate surroundings, including the tall minarets, bustling bazaars and veiled women, that Catherine composed an evocative poem to her prince, reflecting her vision for Crimea:

I lay at eve in the summer-house of the Khan,
Amidst the infidel and the faith of Mohammedan.
'Cross from the house there stood a mosque most tall,
Whither five times a day an imam the people did call.
I thought to sleep, my eyes barely shut for the night,
When, with ears stopped, he did roar with all his might ...
Oh, miracles of God! Who amongst my kin of yore
Slept calmly, free from the Khans and their hordes?
And disturbed from my sleep amidst Bakhchisaray
By tobacco smoke and cries ... Is this place not paradise?
Praise to you, my friend! This land you did seize,
Secure it now with your vigilance, as you please.[96]

By this time, however, the many foreign observers were getting increasingly impatient to view the new Russian fleet. Throughout the journey to the Crimea, doubts as to its very existence had crept in. Potemkin played on the guests' growing scepticism by refusing to provide any details as to the number of ships or their capabilities, increasing uncertainty as the great journey progressed south. Since their departure from Kiev, Potemkin had shown his flair for the theatrical. Now the time came for his masterstroke. When the imperial party reached the north side of Sevastopol Bay on 2 June 1787, he unveiled a special surprise for his sovereign and her guests.[97] Potemkin had constructed a lavish lunch marquee with a hidden terrace that overlooked the rocky seashore below. De Ségur describes what then unfolded:

During the meal of their imperial majesties, [to the accompaniment of] agreeable harmonious music, suddenly the windows of a great balcony were opened. Then a magnificent spectacle seized our attention: through a line of Tatar horsemen, which parted, we saw behind them a deep bay ... In the middle of this roadstead, bounded by the appearance of a vast sea, a formidable fleet built, armed and equipped in two years, was deployed in battle formation in front of the pavilion where we dined with the Empress. The fleet saluted their sovereign with the fire of all its guns, a thundering sound, which served to proclaim that the Black Sea had a new mistress ...[98]

With a little hyperbole, the French nobleman surmised that Catherine's fleet could reach Constantinople within thirty hours and plant their pennants on its walls. The ships of the line were real enough: at a stroke, the misgivings of her amazed foreign guests evaporated. Although de Ségur omits this specific detail, it is credible – as other accounts suggest – that the party was served champagne at this sweet moment of triumph and that Catherine, at the very apex of her power, proudly proposed a toast: 'Let us drink to the Black Sea Fleet of Russia!'[99] The Empress then drove down to the shore to board a boat, and toured the harbour to inspect her new fleet. Her senior travelling companion and ally, Emperor Joseph II of Austria, declared it to be 'the most beautiful port I have ever seen'. Of the Russian warships lying at anchor he noted that 'The truth is that it is necessary to be here and to believe what I see'.[100] Ségur left a vivid description of the new city on that memorable day:

> [Having admired] the wide and deep coves that nature seems to have eroded into the two sides of this natural harbour, ... we disembarked at the foot of a mountain, on which rose the new Sevastopol.... Already several shops, an admiralty, entrenchments, 400 buildings, that were in the midst of construction, a mass of workers, a strong garrison, two hospitals, several ports for careening, for trade and for quarantine, gave this fledgling creation the appearance of an imposing city. It seemed inconceivable to us that at 800 leagues from the capital, in a region so recently conquered, Prince Potemkin had achieved in [just] two years ... the building of a city, constructing a fleet, erecting forts, and bringing together so large a number of inhabitants.[101]

Sevastopol had developed quickly, and would soon assume growing importance. A combination of Mackenzie's work from 1783, the initial stages of Korsakov's plan of 1786 and Potemkin's direction throughout had ensured that the royal visitors of 1787 were suitably impressed. A significant development was the construction of a magnificent stone landing stage, dubbed 'Catherine's' in that year, on the site of the former wooden one. Although not necessarily as spectacular, other works had been more urgent. In 1784, for example, construction of the city's water supply had commenced, as it was soon found that local wells provided insufficient water for the growing number of residents, which in those early years were primarily naval and military. Typically it was none other than Potemkin who had ordered the search for a new water supply. A suitable source was found 8 kilometres away at Captain E. P. Sarandinaki's country dacha, and the first water pipe to Sevastopol was then laid. Construction of a fully adequate water supply system, however, was not completed until the 1820s, to be supplemented a decade later by an aqueduct for the new docks.[102]

The future development of the city rested firmly on the presence of the Black Sea Fleet: this symbiotic relationship would prove enduring. By imperial order of 13 August 1785 [OS], Catherine confirmed the status of the Admiralty and naval staff at Sevastopol. The Russian Navy's growing importance in Crimea can be demonstrated by the numbers involved: while at Kherson and Nikolayev

4,104 sailors were established, a total of 9,584 men in ships companies and in shore functions was required at Kerch and Sevastopol, with the majority based at the latter port. Thus the preponderant basing of the Russian Navy at Sevastopol had a major influence on the city's livelihood and future.[103] Furthermore, the importance of trade had not been forgotten. In an edict of 22 February 1784 [OS], Catherine had declared the city to be a free port, and soon the first commercial vessels arrived from Kerch, Taganrog, Kherson and Nikolayev. Within three months, no fewer than twenty foreign ships had moored in Sevastopol harbour.[104] The foundation of the city was one of the most impressive achievements of Catherine's reign: the fleet berthed in the Sevastopol roadstead and associated harbours became a potent symbol of Russian maritime power in the Black Sea and beyond for two centuries and more. It remains so today.

THE GROWING SIGNIFICANCE OF SEVASTOPOL AND THE BLACK SEA FLEET

While Catherine's imperial tour culminated in Sevastopol, though a magnificent success in advertising at home and abroad the extent of Russia's recent acquisitions and the reality of her new Black Sea Fleet, it did not fulfil all her strategic intentions. In the short term, the event rebounded dramatically in relation to Turkey. Catherine's flamboyant, provocative visit to Crimea in May 1787 and associated demonstration of naval capability at Sevastopol alarmed the Ottoman Empire to such an extent that the Porte, outraged, declared war on Russia within three months on 13 August. This outcome was surely not intended, for rather than Turkey being intimidated by this show of force, Russia found herself initially on the back foot. She was poorly prepared for so sudden a conflict with Turkey. Potemkin had reckoned with several years' preparation time, which was in the event denied to Russia. Such is the unrelenting law of unintended strategic consequences. Indeed, in a letter to Potemkin dated 24 August 1787 [OS], Catherine had asked, 'what is to be done if the bubble has burst ahead of time? ... If the Turks have declared war, then I suppose they have left the fleet in Ochakov in order to prevent [our] ships built in Kherson from reaching Sevastopol.'[105] Thus, for all their recent triumphs, Catherine's and Potemkin's statecraft had been found wanting. Russia had been surprised by the lack of sufficient diplomatic warnings and military indicators. This shortcoming reflected a remarkable institutional deficiency in Russia's intelligence about, and understanding of, its longstanding opponent (Turkey) that future leaders in St Petersburg (and subsequently in Moscow) would need to address.

In the ensuing conflict with the Ottoman Empire, Catherine provided political oversight to Potemkin's military strategy but did not attempt to micromanage him. While she offered frequent advice, she would also on occasion need to steady his nerve and to deliver the odd admonishment. A frequent theme of her correspondence was not only the state of affairs in Sevastopol, but also inquiries as to his health (and that of her armed forces at land and sea), for Potemkin had been weakened by his attack of malaria in Crimea in 1783. Shortly after the war had broken out, for example, she wrote:

> I rely upon your fervent care that you will keep the Sevastopol harbour and fleet free from harm; in winter a fleet in the harbour is always in danger. Of course, Sevastopol is not Chesme [Chesma]. I admit that only one thing that frightens me, namely, the plague. For the sake of God Himself, I beg you – in your three provinces, in the army and in the fleet take all possible measures in a timely manner so that this evil doesn't steal into us again as a result of carelessness. I know that in Tsargrad itself there is now no word of the plague, but as it is for ever present there, so their troops spread it wherever they go. Send me (and for me alone) your plan for how you intend to fight the war in order that I may know it and then might judge you according to your very own ideas.[106]

Five days later Catherine wrote again, stressing that she would 'not miss a single opportunity to lend help wherever it may be required of me'. But she added an important codicil: 'I beg you in every possible way that in the future you continue to notify me of the true state of affairs with the same exact trust. I know that in difficult and dangerous circumstances one must not be dejected, and so I remain toward you ever friendly and benevolent.'[107] Soon came, however, a severe test of their relationship. A much alarmed Potemkin wrote on 24 September [OS], declaring:

> Your Majesty, I've become despondent. Though I've taken every possible measure, still everything is topsy-turvy. The Sevastopol fleet has been smashed to pieces by storm; its remains are in Sevastopol—all the small and unreliable vessels, or, to put it better, the useless ones. The ships and large frigates have been lost. God strikes us, not the Turks. On top of my illness, this has struck me an extreme blow; my spirit's broken, I'm at my wits end. I have requested that command to be entrusted to another.[108]

Fortunately for Russia, although badly battered, the entire fleet had not been destroyed. In a second letter written that day, however, still in extreme despair and ignorant of the true state of affairs, Potemkin even suggested to Catherine that Russia should withdraw from Sevastopol and the Crimean peninsula. It drew a stiff response from the Empress:

> We occupied the Crimea in former times in order to strengthen our defences, and now the Crimea is in our hands. Once the fleet is repaired, I hope this notion will completely vanish, and I hope it appeared only when you thought that the fleet had been lost. But if you want, I shall order you to construct a nice little dozen frigates on the Don. Why, the Sevastopol fleet uses them even now.[109]

That dealt with the military question, but as to the attitude of her dear Prince, Catherine remonstrated with him: 'You are as impatient as a five-year-old child, whereas the affairs you have been entrusted at this moment demand an unshakeable patience'.[110]

Suitably rebuked, Potemkin soon came to his senses. The immediate object of the campaign was to eliminate the great Turkish fortress of Ochakov, in so doing largely eliminating the possibility of the mouth of the Dnieper being blocked by a hostile power. While Potemkin provided the operational direction and the resources, Suvorov led at the battlefront. Following a series of typically valiant but costly attacks by Russian forces, the Turkish strongpoint fell in December 1788. It had been a gruelling six-month siege: the capture of Ochakov removed the last remaining Ottoman threat to Russian commercial and naval traffic in transit to and from the Black Sea. Meanwhile, the Black Sea Fleet under the inspiring command of Admiral Fyodor Ushakov – the Russian Nelson – scored a series of stunning victories against inferior Turkish opponents. At the battles of Fidonisi (1788), Kerch Strait and Tendra (both 1790), and Cape Kaliakra (1791), Russian naval prowess was demonstrably in the ascendant.

During the war against Turkey, Austria had come to Russia's aid, as Joseph II had promised. This was just as well, for Russia had to deal simultaneously with an internal revolt and a foreign war on two other fronts. To the west, Polish nationalists tried to exploit Russia's distraction in the south in an attempt to reduce her influence on Polish affairs. Unfortunately for the Poles, the reverse came about with the Second Partition of Poland in 1793, in which Prussia and Russia annexed historic Polish lands. With the Third Partition in 1795, all that remained of an independent Poland disappeared as Prussia, Russia and Austria divided the spoils. Sweden had also declared war against Russia in a highly opportunistic manner, but the fighting in the north had ended inconclusively. Although Constantinople and the Straits were not secured (partially due to Austria making an early peace with the Porte before its ally), Russia emerged from the war against Turkey considerably stronger, having humbled the Ottoman Empire on land and at sea. Through the Treaty of Jassy (1792), Russia consolidated her grip of the Black Sea region. Most crucially for the development of Sevastopol and the Black Sea Fleet, the Ottoman Empire finally recognised the Russian annexation of Crimea. While the 'liberation' of Constantinople would remain a distant dream, the capabilities of the fleet continued to grow in the following brief period of peace that lasted until the next round of conflict with Turkey, which commenced in 1806.

The port of Sevastopol provided the logistic and training base that supported Ushakov's run of successes. From its central location, the Crimean citadel acted as the vital hub – or dynamo – for the generation of Russia's burgeoning maritime power, which, weather permitting, could be projected at will across the Black Sea. In this manner, Sevastopol had become Russia's strategic centre of gravity in the south, a jewel in the imperial crown. That is why its destruction was later to become the primary objective of France and Britain during the Crimean War.

In 1795 Mrs Maria Guthrie (in Russian imperial service) visited Sevastopol. Her record of observations contained in letters to her husband working in St Petersburg is remarkable in both its geographical detail and associated analysis, of which the Russian Navy would have been proud, if not concerned about the disclosure of sensitive information. The 'Euxine Portsmouth', she remarked, is 'one of the finest and most secure ports in the world, while for size it might contain all the fleets that Russia has on the Baltic, the White Sea, the Caspian, and the Euxine.'[111] She next described the buildings of Sevastopol:

> The new city is seated, in form of an amphitheatre, on the side of the hill, which divides two of its fine basins, one of which serves for the port, and the other for performing quarantine; a precaution very necessary to guard against the plague when a direct communication with Constantinople is kept open. The old Tatar houses here, as well as everywhere else in the peninsula, are small and ill-built; but we find along the quay some new buildings in a much better taste, the natural consequence of it being the station of the great Euxine fleet, and of course, the chief residence of flag and other naval officers ...[112]

Turning to the rationale for Sevastopol's founding, she considered that the 'fleet of large ships lying in this port ... constitutes the naval force of the Euxine; and we have seen by the result of the last war, that it is fully adequate to vanquish that of the Turks, which, although strong in ships, is weak in naval skill.' Furthermore, she estimated that:

> The Russian navy ... will be well entitled to rank high, and even to give laws to the Euxine, when its establishment shall be complete, which is settled at 15 ships of the line and 20 frigates, beside the necessary complement of smaller vessels of war

to attend to it; indeed, even the force that we found here is very respectable for such a sea, viz.—three ships of the line from 80 to 90 guns; six from 70 to 76; one of 54; eleven of 40 to 48 ...[113]

In this manner, the Black Sea Fleet was set to become an important instrument of Russian power. It was to remain so for two centuries and more. Sevastopol would gain significant defences too. The city, meanwhile, did not neglect to honour its great naval hero Ushakov: one of its busiest central squares continues to bear his illustrious name.

Within twenty years of its foundation, Sevastopol had become well established. De Reuilly, for example, noted its emerging form:

> The town, built in streets parallel to each other, is on an ascent, and is divided into quarters by some other streets at right angles; ... immediately after the admiralty, [lie] the arsenal, and the houses of the officers of the marines; higher, the houses of the inhabitants, the market, and the Greek church; the hospitals, and the barracks for the seamen. The magazines are chiefly on the other side of the lesser port [the Southern Bay], and form a sort of suburbs, as well as the barracks of the garrison, built some distance in the upper part.[114]

All this development, however, had come at a price. Crimea generally, and particularly the area close to Sevastopol, had once been full of timber. As a result of widespread deforestation, supplies were becoming scarce. De Reuilly observed critically that the 'Russians seem desirous to outdo the Tartars in the art of devastation.... [Although] the mountains which surround the port of Sevastopol were covered with young trees, [these] have been torn up by the sailors and the soldiers.'[115] The reason was simple enough: they took the wood for fuel to cook and to keep warm. At least some in Russia realised that such destruction of natural resources could not continue. When the French statesman visited the Tsar, Alexander I, he was asked what he 'thought of the Crimea', to which he replied: 'Sire, nature had done everything for it'. The Emperor's response was revealing: 'You are right, but we have done nothing as yet to assist nature'.[116] While Sevastopol would see many man-made changes to the terrain in the course of its history, not least in the development of its naval infrastructure, the ground surrounding the city would still shape the battles to come.

CHAPTER 3

BASTION OF
MARITIME POWER

*'I reiterate the urgent necessity of paying attention to this ...
wonderful port [of Sevastopol]. Its fortifications should be as
impregnable as those of Gibraltar and Malta.'*

Admiral Mikhail Petrovich Lazarev (1834)[1]

STRATEGIC CONTEXT

By the end of the Napoleonic Wars, Russia's geostrategic position in northern
Europe had been greatly enhanced by her victory during the Finnish War of
1808–09. Notwithstanding considerable assistance from the British navy, Sweden
had been defeated on land by Russia. In the process she lost Finland, which
became a Russian grand duchy. Thereafter, Sweden fell into comparative decline
and was no longer either willing or able to challenge Russia's dominance of the
Baltic. In the Black Sea region, however, the Ottoman Empire remained a power
to be reckoned with. Britain with her unrivalled navy of global reach could seek
to constrain many Russian ambitions, but not, for instance, hinder her expansion
through central Asia. Meanwhile, Sevastopol's purpose remained to provide a
safe haven and a protected arsenal for Russia's southern fleet. '[Its] object',
concluded a mid-nineteenth-century German expert on Russian life and

institutions, Baron August von Haxthausen, 'is to secure the dominion of Russia in the Black Sea, and this is still further assured by the construction at Sevastopol ... of a fortified port of war, which, according to the accounts of competent persons, will not have its equal in the world'. Besides, he wrote, the establishment of Sevastopol 'will allow this power to take the offensive against Constantinople'.[2] Britain not only feared such a development, but was equally concerned that, should the Black Sea Fleet obtain free passage of the Turkish Straits, Russian warships would then cruise the Mediterranean.

Although it lay far away from the seat of Russian imperial power and the College of Admirals in St Petersburg, successive tsars took a keen interest in their growing Black Sea domain, and particularly in its naval development. During the reigns of Alexander I (1815–24) and Nicholas I (1825–55), and particularly under the enthusiastic direction of the latter, Russia increased its investment both in the ships of the Black Sea Fleet and in the supporting facilities and defences of Sevastopol. Maritime strength, however, is not just a matter of providing the necessary warships. The fighting power of the Russian fleet in the closing years of sail was greatly enhanced by the innovative and inspirational leadership of two exceptional, long-serving commanders-in-chief: Aleksey Samuilovich Greig and Mikhail Petrovich Lazarev. These individuals held this post during the periods 1816–1833 and 1834–1851 respectively.

Greig, son of the Admiral Samuel Greig, was a fighting sailor first and foremost. Following his father's footsteps, he had been educated in Scotland (in his case, at the Royal High School in Edinburgh), and had served as a midshipman and junior officer in the Royal Navy from 1785 to 1796. In Russian naval service he quickly distinguished himself, coming to particular prominence in the wars against revolutionary France, and in the Napoleonic Wars, including the Russo-Turkish War of 1806–12. Most notably, under the overall command of Vice Admiral Dmitry Senyavin (Thomas Mackenzie's flag lieutenant in 1783–86), Greig took part as a rear admiral in the naval battles of the Dardanelles (11 May 1807) and Athos (16 June 1807), which resulted in severe defeats of the Turkish Navy. Appointed to command the Black Sea Fleet in 1816, he remained in post for seventeen years, during which time he distinguished himself again in combat during the next war with Turkey in 1828–29. He introduced many naval reforms, both in tactics and administration. As commander-in-chief of the fleet he was also military governor of Nikolayev (now Mykolaiv in Ukraine) and Sevastopol. In the former city on the river Southern Bug, at which the headquarters of the fleet was then established, he was particularly revered for his various works. For the fleet these included the development of shipyards, and for commerce the construction of various port facilities.[3]

In parallel, Sevastopol – both as a city and as a naval base – experienced a steady growth in the second quarter of the nineteenth century until the eve of the Crimean War in 1853. Its expansion reflected the growing importance of the Black Sea Fleet as a strategic instrument of power in Russia's increasingly assertive foreign policy. In this formative period, three men played significant roles in Sevastopol's story: Nicholas I; Admiral Lazarev; and John Upton, a British civil engineer, who was active in the city from the 1830s until his death in 1851. The combined efforts of emperor, admiral and engineer did much to shape and determine the development of Sevastopol and the Black Sea Fleet for nearly two decades. In early 1854 a fourth man with an equally prominent historical role came to Sevastopol: Lieutenant Colonel Eduard Ivanovich Todleben. He masterminded the Russian defence of Sevastopol during the war. Subsequently, he wrote the first detailed, if not definitive, official military history of that operation.[4] The six Allied bombardments of Sevastopol (October 1854 – September 1855) and the subsequent demolitions of its naval infrastructure, however, brought about the destruction of most of their collective achievement. None the less, the various contributions of these four individuals to Sevastopol's history and heritage remain important.

Theorists of maritime strategy have long recognised the various roles of navies. Potential tasks in peace and war are many and complementary. They include: showing the flag; safeguarding commerce; blockading enemy countries, providing protection, transport and supply to land forces; bombarding shore targets; deterring other navies from intervening; and not least seeking out and engaging an opponent's fleet. The ultimate aim of any navy is to secure command of the sea. As the latter state can seldom be established absolutely, 'maritime preponderance' may represent a better description. Furthermore, there is also considerable scope for co-operation between land and sea forces in 'joint' operations.[5] The deterrent role of one navy against another is reflected in a 'fleet in being', a term that came into widespread use in naval circles towards the end of the nineteenth century.[6]

This diverse range of naval tasks was amply illustrated during the Russo-Turkish War of 1828–29. In that conflict Russia enjoyed maritime preponderance in, if not command of, the Black Sea due to the damage inflicted on the Turkish–Egyptian navy at Navarino on 20 October 1827. This one-sided battle in the Eastern Mediterranean – fought in support of the Greeks' struggle for independence from the Ottoman Empire – marked the spectacular destruction of a Turco-Egyptian fleet by a combined Russian, French and British force under the command of Vice Admiral Sir Edward Codrington, Royal Navy. As the Turkish Straits were closed to Russian vessels, the Russian warships involved in this engagement (four ships of the line and four frigates) came from the Baltic rather than the Black Sea Fleet. Whereas France and Britain made peace with the Porte, Russia seized the opportunity presented by Turkish weakness and declared war again in April 1828. In the ensuing conflict, as a result of its losses at Navarino, the Ottoman Navy had been reduced to just six ships of the line and three frigates. The Russian Black Sea Fleet now enjoyed a numerical advantage with nine ships of the line and four frigates.[7] For the first time since the foundation of Sevastopol in 1783, therefore, Russia could exercise its maritime power in the Black Sea with little risk of effective restraint by an opposing state. Maintaining a substantial naval presence in the region mattered to Russia then as now.

Perhaps the most striking example of naval combat during the war of 1828–29 was one of asymmetry rather than of scale. It involved the fight of the 20-gun brig *Merkurii*, a 445-ton vessel launched in 1820 at Sevastopol.[8] Under the command of Captain-Lieutenant Alexander Kazarsky, she fought single-handedly against two much larger Turkish ships on 14 May 1829 and, against all odds, won. This celebrated engagement took place when a group of three Russian warships encountered a much stronger Turkish squadron near the Bosporus. While the two faster Russian ships, the frigate *Shtandart* and the brig *Orfei*, made good their escape, the *Merkurii* was pursued and trapped in light winds between the 110-gun *Selimye* and the 74-gun *Real-Bei*. The situation seemed hopeless with a Turkish numerical superiority of firepower of over nine to one. Yet quantity is rarely the sole determinant of war, whether on land or sea. Considered to be one of the bravest and most resourceful young officers of the Black Sea Fleet, Kazarsky decided to stand and fight rather than strike his flag. Through a combination of skilled manoeuvring by sail and oar, and with precise cannon fire, he managed to disable his opponents' ships by damaging their rigging. Despite the *Merkurii's* hull being holed no fewer than twenty-two times, and receiving nearly 300 hits on her sails and rigging, the indomitable little ship escaped, a testament to the strength of its construction and a tribute to the proficiency of its captain and crew. The Russian casualties were surprisingly light: only four killed and six wounded. Kazarsky and many of his crew were decorated and promoted for their exceptional valour while all were rewarded with a doubling of pay for life.

Whereas the *Merkurii's* action that day is still fondly remembered by the Russian Navy, and a model of possibly 'the most heroic Russian warship during the Age of Sail'[9] is displayed proudly in Sevastopol's museum of the Black Sea Fleet, some naval commentators expressed doubts as to the standard (Russian) version of events. Fred T. Jane, author of such works as *All the World's Fighting Ships* (1898) and *The Imperial Russian Navy* (1899), for example, considered it a 'moral impossibility that so small a craft as the Mercury could have disabled two ships-of-the-line in four hours, even if they had done no shooting'. On that basis, he concluded: 'the most natural assumption is that the Turks were frigates, that have grown to ships-of-the-line since'.[10] Whatever the truth of the matter, one suspects that had a similar action involved a British warship rather than a Russian one, then Jane might have been less sceptical and rather more generous in his praise.

The principal role of the Black Sea Fleet during the war, and more generally during the first half of the nineteenth century, however, was to support the Russian Army's campaigns on the Sea's western and eastern littorals. The fleet played a major role of the Russian siege of Varna (now in Bulgaria) in the autumn of 1828. In the spirit of his illustrious predecessor Peter the Great, Nicholas I had personally directed the bombardment of the city from aboard the ship of the line *Parizh*, a 110-gun three-decker and flagship of the Black Sea Fleet, commanded by Admiral Greig.[11] Following the fall of Varna on 10 October 1828, there was a pause in operations as the Russians, having taken heavy losses in their land operations, consolidated their gains in the Danubian provinces, and winter approached. During the following spring and summer, the Black Sea Fleet supported and supplied the Russian Army in its march southwards towards Constantinople.

Switching to the opposite end of the Black Sea, earlier in 1828 another major Russian expeditionary campaign had been launched from Sevastopol. Field Marshal Ivan Fydorovich Paskevich was the overall commander, with the Black Sea Fleet under Greig providing support. Their first major success was the capture of the Ottoman fortress of Anapa, where the Caucasus and the southern base of the Taman peninsula meet, in Turkish-controlled Circassia on 12 July. Russian forces were then able to extend their operations southwards along the Black Sea coast to seize the city of Poti, and with other forces approaching from inland Georgia, to converge on the north-eastern shores of Turkey in 1829. Russian naval preponderance in the Black Sea throughout prevented the Ottoman Navy from either interdicting the Russians' sea lines of communication or reinforcing its remaining coastal fortresses such as Trebizond (now Trabzon) by ship. Before Paskevich's army was able to assault that city, the conflict ended with the Treaty of Adrianople on 14 September 1829. As the British soldier-scholar Charles Callwell observed, 'But for the reinforcements and supplies and warlike stores which [Paskevich] was able to draw direct across the Black Sea from the magazines and arsenals of Odessa and Sebastopol, his genius for war alone would not have enabled him to fight so successful a campaign against very superior forces'.[12]

As we shall see, however, the boot was to turn largely on to the other foot during the Crimean War of 1854–56, when the British and French navies were able to exercise almost uncontested command of the Black Sea. Before that conflict, the Russian 'fleet in being' based in Sevastopol had compelled Britain and France to station more ships in the Eastern Mediterranean than might otherwise have been justified. When war came, however, the presence of the Black Sea Fleet failed to deter the Allies from transporting their armies by sea from Varna to land on the Crimean shore near Yevpatoriya in September 1854. Nor did the Russians risk a major fleet engagement with the more powerful British and French combined naval force.[13]

The employment of the Black Sea Fleet in the 1830s and 1840s was largely dependent on Russian relations with the Ottoman Empire, which veered from enmity to a temporary friendship, and then hauled back to the historical norm of rivalry if not outright hostility. The cause of the brief amity between the Turks and the Russians was the rebellion in 1831 of the Egyptian Pasha, Mehemet Ali, against the Ottoman Sultan, Mahmud II. While the Egyptians advanced northwards through the Levant towards Asia Minor, the wider international situation was complex to say the least. Whereas the French supported Mehemet Ali's forces in the Eastern Mediterranean, the British were co-operating with their traditional European foe in operations off the coasts of Portugal and the Netherlands. Unwilling to get involved in a war against France, the British Foreign Secretary, Lord Palmerston, turned down the Porte's requests for naval support. In desperation, Mahmud II turned to the Russian Tsar for assistance.

In March 1833, Nicholas I, not one to miss such an opportunity, sent Admiral Mikhail Lazarev with the mass of the Black Sea Fleet to the Bosporus. The Russian Navy's impressive show of force, comprising no fewer than ten ships of the line, four frigates and transports carrying 11,000 troops, duly deterred Mehemet Ali from advancing on Constantinople. Russia, however, extracted a substantial reward for its supportive action. The resulting eight-year Treaty of Unkiar-Skelessi (in Turkish: Hünkâr İskelesi) signed on 8 July 1833 by Lazarev, publically concluded peace and friendship between the two states and a commitment to mutual assistance in time of war. More specifically, a secret article provided for the closing of the Dardanelles to 'any foreign vessels of war ... on any pretext whatever'. As one scholar of the period has observed, the Treaty 'could only be legitimately said to be directed against England and France if Turkey opened the Bosphorous to Russia and closed the Dardanelles to all warships except Russian ones'.[14] For Russia, the treaty was seen as defensive: being more concerned at the time about the vulnerability of her southern coast, including Sevastopol, she had little interest in projecting power into the Mediterranean.[15] None the less, to other states it appeared that Turkey was 'conferring substantial benefits to Russia' despite Turkey denying that Unkiar-Skelessi had secured for Russia a 'right to pass her fleet through the Dardanelles'.[16] Whatever had actually been agreed between the two parties to the treaty, whether openly or behind closed doors, foreign perceptions counted.

Lord Palmerston, for example, objected to what he saw as the subjugation of Turkey to Russia, breeding in him, it is claimed, 'a fatal hostility to Russia'.[17] In turn, such an attitude would help frame official policy and fuel popular opinion in Britain against Russia for two decades until the Crimean War.

Although Russia had secured the Ottoman Empire as a dependent state for the time being, she was increasingly concerned about the possibility of war with Britain, who, in turn, feared Russian influence spreading into the Balkans, the Mediterranean, the Caucasus and, ultimately, towards India. Thus international peace was threatened by an imperial rivalry where 'expanding spheres of influence in Asia and the Near East intersected'.[18] It was not that conflict between the powers was necessarily inevitable, but in both Russia and Britain the rhetoric of war was burgeoning from the mid-1830s. One incident illustrated all too well the dangers of escalating tensions leading to armed confrontation. In late November 1836, a Russian warship, the *Ajax*, intercepted the British commercial schooner *Vixen* off the Circassian coast near Sudjuk Kale (modern Novorossiysk). It was alleged that the British vessel was carrying not only a cargo of salt, but also arms for the Murid mountain tribesmen, who were then fighting a bitter insurgency against the Russian Empire. By the time of the incident at sea, however, the British crew had already unloaded the supplies of gunpowder for the insurgents and had only salt in the hold. Nevertheless, the Russians confiscated the *Vixen* for breach of customs laws, and then took her to Sevastopol, returning the crew to Constantinople. In the event, Britain was not prepared to challenge the loss of the *Vixen* with any military or naval response, tacitly acknowledging the provocation – if not the blockade running – involved.[19] According to a British visitor to the Crimean city some years later (1844), Henry Danby Seymour, the *Vixen* lay in the harbour as a trophy – 'the Russians were very proud of having taken an English ship, while the English there told me they could never see her without a feeling of shame'.[20]

Nicholas I's director of the College of Foreign Affairs, Count Karl Vasilyevich Nesselrode, was well aware of British concerns as to Russian ambitions and aggrandisement, and the associated potential for Russia to become internationally isolated. In consequence, he steered skilfully a rapprochement with Britain that led to the London Straits Convention of 1841. This international agreement recognised the Ottoman Sultan's right to prevent warships of any nation passing through the Straits, thus anticipating some aspects of the Montreux Convention of 1936, which continues in force today. While Montreux would safeguard the rights of Black Sea states such as the Soviet Union – and its successors, Ukraine and the Russian Federation – for their ships to transit the Straits in peacetime (echoing the provisions of Unkiar-Skelessi), the London Convention barred all warships from transiting the Dardanelles and the Bosporus. It not only prevented the Russian Black Sea Fleet from operating freely in the Mediterranean, but also served to exacerbate Russian fears of a British naval foray into the Black Sea should the Ottoman Empire collude. Unsurprisingly, Palmerston regarded the Straits Convention as a minor triumph: he had worked at getting rid of the Treaty of Unkiar-Skelessi for nearly a decade.[21] In contrast, the Russian Navy, including Lazarev, felt aggrieved by the London Convention for it effectively reversed the terms of the much more beneficial treaty.

Overall, the agreement made in London appeared to favour the British at the expense of the Russians, and hastened the latter's naval and military demands to strengthen Sevastopol's fortifications. Nicholas I had only agreed to the Straits Convention of 1841 for overarching political as opposed to practical strategic reasons. Under Nesselrode's influence he feared that too close an alliance between Russia and the Ottoman Empire might turn the European great powers against him. The Tsar, who did not want war, resolved to seek an accommodation, if not friendship, with Britain, as demonstrated in his official visit to Britain in 1844, accompanied by Nesselrode. His goal was 'to discover what prospect, if any, existed of detaching England from her alliance with France' and to deny France from 'securing a footing on Turkish territory'.[22] Unfortunately, the Russian Emperor confused Queen Victoria's charm and hospitality with her government's caution and latent hostility: no binding, long-term alliance resulted between Britain and Russia.[23] Had Nicholas I imagined that Britain and France would one day ally with the Turks against Russia in war, as was to happen within a dozen years, it is highly unlikely that Russia would ever have agreed to the Straits Convention.

A late eighteenth-century British observer of maritime affairs, Sir John Sinclair, noted perceptively that 'Naval strength is not the growth of a day, nor is it possible to retain it, when once acquired, without the utmost difficulty, and the most unwearied attention'.[24] What applied to the Royal Navy related equally well to the Russian, including its Black Sea Fleet. During the second quarter of the nineteenth century, Sevastopol underwent a remarkable growth as the training and basing needs of its host fleet were progressively addressed, and its shore defences were expensively enhanced. At first, the Russian government's investment was modest and expansion was correspondingly slow. From the mid-1830s onwards, however, the pace of development picked up considerably with significant increases in military and naval expenditure. The primary source of this rise in Sevastopol's significance lay in the perceived risk of attack by Britain and her navy as opposed to the Ottoman threat, which had diminished since the end of the Russo-Turkish War in 1829 and the subsequent treaty of Unkiar-Skelessi.

ADMIRAL LAZAREV AND THE BLACK SEA FLEET
OF NICHOLAS I

At the end of the eighteenth century, and well into the early part of the nineteenth, the Black Sea Fleet had very much been the poor relation of its older, larger and better-established sister in the Baltic. Quite apart from the fewer numbers of warships and support vessels involved, the southern fleet, initially only about a fifth in size, was also severely disadvantaged by the lack of supporting naval infrastructure.[25] With growing Russian emphasis on projecting maritime power in the south, the Black Sea Fleet grew relatively. Between 1826 and 1858, for example, eight 'first rates' (ships of 110–135 guns) were constructed for the Black Sea Fleet while only five were laid down for the Baltic.[26] By the eve of the Crimean War, the Black Sea Fleet had not only expanded to about two-thirds the size of its Baltic counterpart (35 as opposed to 53 combatants of corvette and larger),[27] but it also now benefited from much-improved basing support, training and leadership. Much of this progress can be attributed to Mikhail Lazarev, building on his predecessor's work.

While Aleksey Greig bequeathed much to Nikolayev, the name of Lazarev will forever be associated with the development of Sevastopol. Having joined the Russian Naval College at St Petersburg aged twelve, in 1803 young Mikhail Petrovich was one of the thirty best cadets who had volunteered, and been selected, for a period of extended overseas training with the Royal Navy. It is said that he was present as a midshipman at the battle of Trafalgar in 1805.[28] On returning to the Russian fold three years later, Lazarev served on the ship of the line *Vsevolod*. He fought against his erstwhile comrades-in-arms in an engagement against two 74-gun warships of the British Baltic Fleet (HMS *Centaur* and *Implacable*) in the Gulf of Finland on 26 August 1808. Captured aboard the *Vsevolod*, which was subsequently destroyed, Lazarev was detained by the Royal Navy for a brief period.[29] Notwithstanding this minor embarrassment, his subsequent naval career in Russian service blossomed. Soon recognised as one of the most talented sailors of his generation, he undertook no fewer than three circumnavigations of the globe (1813–16, 1819–21 and 1822–25); the second of which included the co-discovery of the Antarctic continent in 1820.[30] He proved himself equally proficient in war. As captain of the *Azov*, the flagship of Rear Admiral Login Petrovich Geiden, commanding a Baltic Fleet squadron, he served with distinction at the battle of Navarino. Amongst the crew of the *Azov* were none other than Lieutenant Pavel Nakhimov, Midshipman Vladimir Kornilov and Cadet Vladimir Istomin, who all served as famous admirals during the Crimean War. Promoted to rear admiral on account of his assured performance at Navarino, Lazarev went on to command the Russian blockade of the Dardanelles in 1828–29, and, as we have seen, the demonstration to the Straits in 1833.

Appointed as chief of staff of the Black Sea Fleet in 1832, and assuming the post of commander-in-chief and governor of Sevastopol in 1834, Lazarev demonstrated his abilities as both dynamic trainer and energetic reformer. He continued to groom and mentor Nakhimov, Kornilov and Istomin. This trio collectively epitomised the high standards of leadership, technical seamanship and aggressive style of naval combat he had demanded amongst his subordinates in the manner of Ushakov. All three officers were to fall heroically during the defence of Sevastopol in 1854–55. Joining Lazarev in the burial vault of the St Vladimir Cathedral in the heart of the city, the four admirals remain treasured heroes of the Russian Navy.

For all that could be achieved at sea, there was much to be undertaken ashore. Despite the best efforts of his predecessor, Russian naval historians describe Lazarev as a 'ruthless critic of what he considered to have been the shoddy construction standards of Russian Black Sea warships'. Likewise, they note that he 'did much to upgrade infrastructure and quality control' during his tenure in command, and to embrace technical innovation.[31] Specifically, Lazarev was keen to incorporate steam power into the fleet. In 1815 Russia had built its first steam-powered craft, a small, unarmed boat called the *Elizaveta*, in St Petersburg. The launch in 1836 of her first paddle steam frigate, the *Bogatyr*, armed with twenty-eight 24-pounder guns, put the Russians temporarily ahead of the Royal Navy, whose equivalent, HMS *Gorgon*, followed a year later.[32] Russia lacked the industrial base of either Britain or France, moreover, to sustain rapid progress in this field. While British and French yards stepped up the rate of launches of both naval and commercial steam vessels, Russia concentrated her modest home-built steam assets in the Baltic.

While the first steamboat constructed at a Black Sea yard, the *Vesuvy*, was launched at Nikolayev in 1820, the southern fleet's first steam warship, the paddle-powered *Inkerman*, which entered into service in 1838, was built in Britain.[33] The number of naval steam vessels employed in the Black Sea remained relatively few: six British-built steam paddle frigates (five of the Krym class and one larger type, the *Vladimir*) were introduced during the 1840s. The latter was of 1,751 tons displacement, armed with eleven guns; it could make 11 knots, equalling the speed of the largest sailing ships, but independent of wind. None, however, was a capital ship. In 1852, the principal warships of the Black Sea Fleet all remained of sail: three modern first rates (three-deckers) of the Dvenadtsat Apostolov (Twelve Apostles) class, armed with 120–130 guns; seven second rates (two-deckers) of the Sultan Makhmud class (84/90 guns); three second rates of the Khrabryi class (84/96 guns); six heavy frigates (four of 60 and two of 44 guns).[34] By 1854, the fleet included sixteen ships of the line, seven frigates, eight steam-powered paddle frigates and four corvettes, mounting altogether no fewer than 2,181 guns. The Baltic Fleet possessed the only Russian screw-propelled combatants: three ships of the line and two frigates.[35]

Lazarev handed over to his successors a predominantly sail-powered Black Sea Fleet at the apogee of its tactical and technical development. It was not as far behind the British and French navies as might be supposed, but the differential in supporting steam-powered capability was soon to prove significant. In Britain the decision to construct a steam battlefleet had been taken only in December 1852: it was designed to meet a perceived French plan to match, if not overtake, the Royal Navy.[36] As new wooden ships would take between three and four years to build, if the limitations of seasoning timber were taken into account, conversions of existing or partly completed sailing ships would have to provide an interim steam capability. In the coming war this approach would prove adequate as the Russians had insufficient capacity, not least in modern methods of fabrication and steam engine works, to counter the combined British and French naval threat. As naval historian Andrew Lambert has concluded, 'second class, converted ships would be sufficient to keep the Russians in check'. Meanwhile, from a British Admiralty perspective, 'new ships could be prepared to meet the long-term threat from France'.[37]

The Russian Black Sea Fleet held a trump card, however, against its Turkish rival. At Lazarev's urging, the main armament of the ships of the line now included the latest 'shell' cannon that fired exploding projectiles rather than solid round shot, the invention of the French general Henri-Joseph Paixhains in 1822–23. Some authorities argue that it was these new weapons that caused such devastation and havoc in a flotilla of the Ottoman Navy harbouring at Sinope on the northern Anatolian coast, which was destroyed by a Russian squadron at Sinope on 30 November 1853.[38]

Nicholas I was very proud of his navy and visited his warships regularly. Formal inspections of the Black Sea Fleet were undertaken every seven years, usually in association with the reviews of cavalry formations in southern Russia. Previous inspections had taken place in 1837 (which also involved a review of Sevastopol's fortifications) and 1845: the next, due in 1852, proved to be the Emperor's final opportunity to review his southern fleet before the Crimean War. In that year, the fleet had been strengthened by the arrival of the newly completed *Parizh,* the second ship of the Twelve Apostles class.[39]

On 14 October 1852, the tall ships of the fleet, the very last of the line of sail, were assembled on the Sevastopol roadstead. To the west, the telltale trail of smoke of the *Vladimir* with Nicholas I on board appeared. As soon as its imperial pennant came into full view, the *Parizh* fired a welcoming salute. For some unexplained reason, her crew fired a live round, which completely shot away the flagship's decorative ceremonial gangway. To everyone's dismay, its smashed smithereens were swept away by the sea below. As a result, the Emperor could no longer gracefully step on board.[40]

Through the presence of mind of certain officers aboard the *Parizh*, however, this event resulted in a major triumph for the Black Sea Fleet. For 'Lazarev's pupils were different', as one eyewitness recalled, as they 'would not allow themselves to be lost by such an incident'. Instead, they ordered the construction of a makeshift ladder, which duly proved itself. Once safely aboard the *Parizh*, the Emperor dispensed with the usual formalities of inspecting a guard on the quarterdeck. Looking around at the assembled crew, 1,000 young sailors, he asked Captain First Rank Vladimir Istomin, 'where did you obtain such brave young men?' Then Nicholas I addressed the ship's company with a loud 'Hello lads'. A 'mighty and joyful *zdraviya zhelayem*' (we wish you health) boomed the reply.[41] 'Show me what you can do,' the Emperor commanded.

A faultless inspection then ensued, including a practice gun drill. At its conclusion, Nicholas I asked his chief of the navy, Prince Aleksandr Sergeyevich Menshikov, why he had not been shown ships of the Baltic Fleet in the same manner. An embarrassed Menshikov explained that there were no similar ships in the Baltic. Unimpressed by such a lame response, the Emperor bestowed on the *Parizh*'s captain a neck award of the Order of St Vladimir, Istomin's namesake.[42] Thus ended the Emperor's visit. Lazarev would have been justifiably proud of his highly capable successors.

On shore, a Scottish visitor, 'unlawful' by his own admission, Laurence Oliphant, had managed to slip into Sevastopol without permission. He described the preparations for the imperial visit:

> The greatest excitement prevailed during our stay [in the city]; crowds of people had been attracted from all parts of the south of Russia to receive the Emperor; the garrison had been whitewashing their barracks, and drilling themselves with praiseworthy perseverance; while the whole dockyard force had been engaged for months past in getting the ships into the presentable condition they now exhibited.[43]

Oliphant did not remain long enough to witness Nicholas I's review of the fleet, thinking it 'prudent to beat a timely retreat', and so escaped 'from Sevastopol the day before the great event was to take place'.[44]

A lack of personal observation, however, did not prevent Oliphant from making a series of scathing condemnations of the Russian Navy. For example, he recorded 'it is maliciously said, that upon the few occasions that the Russian fleet in the Black Sea have encountered a gale of wind, the greater part of the officers and men were always sea-sick'. Piling on the scorn, Oliphant maintained that it was 'certain that [the Russian sailors] have sometimes been unable to tell whereabouts they were on their extensive cruising ground; and once between Sevastopol and Odessa, it is currently and libellously reported that the admiral was so utterly at a loss, that the flag lieutenant, observing a village on shore, proposed to land and ask the way.'[45] In direct contradiction of the Russian account of the imperial review, Oliphant wrote, 'as we afterwards heard', apparently the Emperor 'did not accompany the fleet on their short cruise outside the port, but expressed himself very much dissatisfied with their performances'. The fact remains that the Russian Black Sea Fleet proved devastatingly competent at the battle of Sinope on 30 November 1853; all Lazarev's training had not been in vain.

Oliphant provided another anecdote of his interrupted sojourn in Sevastopol, which if true, casts a revealing perspective on Nicholas I's unforgiving style of command:

> When we returned to Sevastopol not long afterwards, we heard that the Emperor had left the military proportion of the community a reminiscence that was calculated to produce a deep impression. He had scarcely terminated his flying visit, and the smoke of the steamer by which he had returned to Odessa still hung upon the horizon, when, in a smothered whisper, one soldier confided to another that their ranks had received an addition; ... it was said that the late governor, in a significant white costume, was employed with the rest of the gang upon the streets he had a fortnight before rolled proudly through, with all the pomp and circumstance befitting his high position.

In such a manner, the 'general commanding' had become unceremoniously the 'convict sweeping'.[46] As for the unfortunate's crime, which had deserved so severe a punishment and humiliation, nobody knew precisely, but it would appear that the appropriation of bribes was the most likely cause. Corruption by state officials was endemic then in imperial Russia; as is widely reported, the same cancer of civilised life remains prevalent today in the Russian Federation.[47] The work of the Black Sea Fleet and of Sevastopol's garrison, however, carried on in 1852 despite such frictions and foibles.

Apart from the economic stimulus given by the presence of the Black Sea Fleet, the navy provided the main impetus for the educational and cultural life of the city: Lazarev played a key role in both. In 1826, the first school had opened in Sevastopol for the education of naval cadets, mainly the children of officers and sailors of the fleet.[48] Two years later, a civilian establishment was opened for the offspring of the local nobility, government officials and merchants, while a further – church – school was established in 1833. Nor did the Russian Navy neglect the education of its serving officers. In June 1822 the first fleet library was opened, funded through a subscription of one kopek per rouble of pay, representing a 1 per cent levy. Originally a small store of books was housed in a dwelling owned by a certain Mr Tisdale, an Englishman who had once served in the Black Sea Fleet. Under the energetic direction and support of Lazarev, construction of a proper library started in 1837. Unluckily, it burnt down only eight months following its opening on 14 November 1844.[49] History does not record the fate of the books. Undeterred, the fleet's commander-in-chief and governor of Sevastopol raised new funds. Within two years, construction of a completely new building on the city's central hill was under way, opening in November 1849 to great ceremony. According to a British resident of Crimea and frequent visitor to Sevastopol during the early 1850s, a certain Mrs Andrew Neilson, this impressive building was 'furnished very handsomely with sofas, carpets, and other articles from England, and contains an immense collection of books in all languages'.[50]

Misfortune was again to strike the Black Sea Fleet library when it was badly damaged during the Allied bombardments of the Crimean War. During this conflict the dignified building had done serious military duty, serving as one of Sevastopol's advanced dressing stations for the many Russian wounded, in which toiled the famous Russian surgeon Nikolay Ivanovich Pirogov. Today only a remnant of the old library survives on Frunze Street, namely the beautiful octagonal Tower of the Winds, supposed to be modelled on the ancient Athens Marble Tower. Each of the eight friezes of Sevastopol's copy features a bas-relief of a mythological figure, including Boreas for the northern winds and Zephyrus for the western. Following the Crimean War, the library was re-established in Nikolayev and remained there for thirty-five years. In 1890 an entirely new Black Sea Fleet library was opened in central Sevastopol at a fresh site on Nakhimov Prospekt, only for it to be almost completely destroyed during the Second World War. Rebuilt in the same fine neo-classical style, the 'Maritime Library of Admiral M. P. Lazarev' remains an important educational and historical research institution of the Russian Federation in Sevastopol. Along with the square named after him, this fine building (and the professional study undertaken within it) provides a richly fitting memorial for a man, patriot and sailor, who devoted his life to the Russian Navy, its Black Sea Fleet and the city of Sevastopol. In his extensive, semi-official history, *The Invasion of the Crimea*, Alexander William Kinglake generously wrote of 'the love and reverence with which the seamen [of the Black Sea Fleet] clung to the memory of the commander [Admiral Lazarev].[51]

Lazarev also commissioned the city's first naval or military monument. On his instigation, a fine stone memorial recording the action of the *Merkurii* was built between 1834 and 1839, just off Sevastopol's main shore promenade, near the present-day Nakhimov Square. A stone plinth is surmounted by a bronze model of a Greek trireme, and flanked by reliefs of Nike, goddess of victory, of Mercury, god of navigation and trade, and of Neptune, god of water and the sea. The fourth face features a portrait of the captain of the *Merkurii*. The principal inscription is simply worded: 'To Kazarsky. To posterity as an example.'[52] Over the subsequent years, in the course of the city's proximate association with – if not pivotal roles in – the Crimean War, Bolshevik revolution and the Second World War, many hundreds more memorials would be added.

JOHN UPTON AND THE DEVELOPMENT OF SEVASTOPOL'S NAVAL INFRASTRUCTURE

Notwithstanding the wider political context, the development of the Black Sea Fleet and its host city, Sevastopol, reflected a number of fundamental requirements of maritime power. While nature had bequeathed the Russian Navy a superb sheltered anchorage in the Sevastopol roadstead and in its series of lesser bays and harbours, without the necessary administrative and technical support on shore, a fleet could neither be put to, nor kept at, sea whether in war or peace. Any naval commander worth his salt knows that the efficiency of fleet personnel from admirals to ships' hands 'can only be ensured by evolutions at sea'. Such exercising inevitably generates wear and tear on ships' fabric, machinery and armament. Furthermore, the sea is a persistently hostile environment: 'winds and the waves beat on the battleship and on the gunboat when they are on cruise in time of peace, just as relentlessly as they do in time of war'.[53] So any fleet composed of complex fighting vessels depends on an equally intricate system and base of maintenance and supply: that of the Black Sea was no exception.

Sevastopol's essential port infrastructure included: docks and slipways required for the upkeep and repair of ships; an arsenal in which to hold and maintain weapons of war; magazines to store gunpowder, shot and shell; victualling stores for holding supplies of food; and, critically, a secure source of potable water. In addition, a fleet of the first half of the nineteenth century needed specialist stores in its dockyards to keep sails, spare spars, and cordage, all in good working condition. Ships' navigators depended on accurate charts for sailing, leading to the establishment of a hydrographical department. Navigation lights were required for passages into and out of harbour at night. Additionally, following Russian naval practice in which crews were not kept aboard when held in harbour, and particularly during the winter months when ships were as a rule laid up, barracks were required. The steady toll of sickness – as much as the treatment of wounds of war – demanded a permanent hospital and nursing facilities. At the same time, all contained within a naval base (both personnel and materiel) needed to be protected, leading to the construction of extensive fortifications. All these diverse requirements demanded very considerable investment in financial resources, in technical means and in human design and leadership to conceive, plan and carry out such work.

Sevastopol's old admiralty on the western side of the Southern Bay, first built by Thomas Mackenzie, had for two generations supported ship supply, repair and maintenance. The life of Russian sailing ships and boats constructed of wood was limited due to rot, often to less than twenty years. Worse still, the vessels of the Black Sea Fleet, and particularly those warships and other craft harboured at Sevastopol, suffered particularly from the attacks of a highly damaging shipworm, which bores into and devours submerged timber.[54] As Mrs Guthrie noted in the late 1790s, notwithstanding all the advantages that Sevastopol possessed as a fine and secure port, 'there is nothing perfect in this world, [for] the destructive worm (the *Tredo navalis*, or *calamitas navium* of Linnaeus) seems to have taken up its favourite abode [here]'.[55] Thus the Russian Navy needed a steady supply of new ships if it were to remain a capable and credible maritime force. Securing supplies of good quality timber, and particularly of oak, was not easy.[56] The Russians, presumably on expense grounds, had been slow to adopt the practice of copper-bottoming warships, pioneered by the Royal Navy in the late 1770s. Writing of his visit of 1803, de Reuilly remarked in apparent contradiction that it was 'not yet thought of to copper the vessels bound to the Black Sea, but orders have been given, that henceforth that they should be built with that regulation'.[57]

In stark contrast to the major shipbuilding effort at Kherson, and subsequently at Nikolayev, at which seventy-four major warships were launched during the seventy-year period of 1788–1858, shipbuilding was only intermittently undertaken in Sevastopol in the first half of the nineteenth century. The first such vessel was the corvette *Krym*, armed with 18 guns, built in the summer of 1810.[58] Thereafter, apart from the 20-gun brig *Merkurii*, the most notable ships constructed were four 36–60-gun frigates built between 1828 and 1845.[59] Sevastopol was destined to remain the operational hub of the Black Sea Fleet with its safe haven, naval arsenal and training establishment, exactly as Potemkin had planned over half a century before. Its grand harbour, 'one of the most remarkable in Europe ... a repetition of Malta upon a larger scale, and of Sydney upon a smaller',[60] however, possessed only a fraction of the shore facilities of the much better endowed naval fortress and dockyards of Kronstadt in the Gulf of Finland. Until such basic inadequacies were addressed, the Russian Black Sea Fleet could only operate at a sub-optimal capacity. Lazarev, writing in the early 1830s, complained bitterly that 'the [Sevastopol] admiralty is in a very poor state, consisting mainly of huts – not a kopek has been spent on it'.[61] The establishment of a new admiralty, along with the building of modern dry docks and their associated water supply, on the eastern side of the Southern Bay, were to become his two main construction projects at Sevastopol when he assumed command of the Black Sea Fleet in 1833.

Although Admiral Aleksey Greig had first suggested in 1818 that dry docks should be constructed at Sevastopol, nothing had been done to advance the idea. Several more proposals followed over the years; it was not until early 1831 that such a project was finally approved. Although a Frenchman, Antoine Raucourt de Charleville, had drawn up the original design, the task of developing and executing the work was entrusted to a British engineer called John Upton (c. 1774–1851).[62] His story, as one of Sevastopol's many illustrious characters, is among the most remarkable of the city's history. An English-born civil engineer with a background in canal and road construction, and pupil of Thomas Telford, he came into disrepute in his home country. Accused of defrauding a road company of over £1,000, in July 1826 he jumped bail and escaped trial at the Northampton Assizes. Avoiding arrest, he offered his services to the Russian legation in London, who, at that time, were recruiting engineers to work in modernising southern Russia, including the new cities of Odessa and Sevastopol. Somehow Upton, 'a man of talent, but devoid of integrity', to quote a pithy nineteenth-century British source, made his escape to Russia, even securing the passage of his large family – a wife with four sons and four daughters.[63] He soon established himself as a highly successful architect and engineer. In Odessa, for example, he designed and built the Potemkin steps, which featured nearly a century later in the famous film by Eisenstein of the *Potemkin* mutiny.

In Sevastopol, Upton was responsible for several major projects, including the the Count's Landing Stage, which has survived all the wars visited on the city, and the set of five great dry or graving docks, with their dedicated water supply, destroyed in the wake of the Crimean War. In addition, Upton also designed the Tower of the Winds of the old naval library, and contributed to the plans of Sevastopol's forts.[64] Upton's sons joined their father in serving the Russian Empire, notably William as an engineer and Samuel as an architect. Although Upton senior died in 1851, members of his family, for all their achievements, would later become embroiled in the war that came to Crimea, and would come under the suspicion of the British Army.[65]

The most detailed of several contemporary descriptions of Upton's dry docks and their associated system of water supply comes from a mysterious British visitor, one William Jesse, who travelled Crimea in 1839 as but one station on a much longer tour of Russia.[66] The first impressions of Sevastopol by this British Army captain on half-pay, were not at all complimentary. 'The entrance to the town was most offensive and disgusting, a disgrace to those in command', he complained, 'and quite enough to counter-act all the benefit of a quarantine establishment.'[67] The Briton's troubles, however, were not yet over. As there was no room available at the inn he had been recommended, Jesse was forced to bunk down in a billiard-hall. 'The noise of the balls, as large as nine-pound shot', he recorded, 'together with my usual bed-fellows [presumably lice], kept me awake all night'. Fortuitously for him, however, assistance and sustenance were soon forthcoming in the morning. An invitation had arrived from Colonel Upton, which 'prevented the necessity of returning to this kennel, which [was] frequented by all the riff-raff of the town.'[68] Jesse then experienced 'no little pleasure' in receiving a hearty breakfast from Mrs Mary Upton, a lady, he observed quaintly, 'with all her English habits and feelings unimpaired by a long residence in Russia'.[69] There is little doubt that the Uptons were glad to welcome visitors from the old country. Jesse's warm reception, notwithstanding his first disturbed night in Sevastopol, was not exceptional. Later British travellers such as Charles Henry Scott (in 1844) commented on 'the sense of obligation we labour under to Colonel Upton and his amiable family for their extreme kindness to us during a ten days' sojourn' in the city, affording 'a great deal of interesting information', and by 'accompanying us to see everything worthy of admiration in the neighbourhood'.[70] Visiting in the same year, Seymour was equally impressed: 'I was shown over Sevastopol by Colonel Upton and his sons, who received me very kindly and showed me everything I wished to see'.[71]

Meanwhile, later on his first morning in Sevastopol, Jesse, under the guiding hand of one of Upton's sons (unnamed, but the most likely candidate is William as his father's deputy engineer), viewed the dry docks then under construction in the 'Men of War' harbour, and inspected John Upton's detailed plans. Although the building of the water supply aqueduct had started in 1831, construction was not finally completed until 1852 with the docks only being opened to shipping in 1850. Thus Jesse saw the work at approximately the halfway stage. 'The docks, five in number', he wrote, 'are placed on two sides of a quadrilateral basin'. More specifically, 'the centre one in the rear is capable of receiving a first-rate of the largest size; two are for seventy-four gun ships, and the remaining two for frigates'. Jesse then explained that as there was 'no tide' in the Black Sea, 'the lock principle has been adopted'. A series of three locks, each with a rise of 10 feet (3 metres), enabled ships to be lifted from sea level to the dock basin, and in turn, to the selected dock; and, by the reverse procedure, let down back to sea. Such was the sophistication of the design, each dock could be drained individually by means of a sluice; therefore 'a ship [could be] taken in or out without interfering with the others'.[72] At the time of Jesse's visit, however, it would appear that the locks' and docks' great iron gates, nine pairs of which had been manufactured by the engineering firm of Sir John and George Rennie in London, had yet to be delivered.[73] So important were these to the grand design that Upton's son,

William Upton, the 'Assistant to the Constructor of the Sevastopol Dry Docks', travelled to London to oversee their construction.[74]

The docks would have been of no use whatsoever unless they could be re-filled with adequate supplies of water. The primary source selected was a point in the Chernaya Rechka (the Black River) near a small village, Chorgun (now Chernorechye), lying to the south-east of Inkerman. Jesse noted its elevation 'of about sixty-two feet above the level of the sea'. To transport the water to the docks, under Upton's supervision the Russians had already completed a canal of 'about ten feet wide, and eighteen versts (twelve miles) long with a fall of a foot and a half in each verst'.[75] As deep ravines convoluted the ground between the water source and the docks, the construction of the canal also involved the boring of three tunnels and the building of six aqueducts. This was a considerable project in its own right. Although the water supply canal was destroyed during the course of the Crimean War, a number of impressive series of stone arches of the aqueducts remains to this day.[76] Jesse was particularly impressed by the tunnel near Inkerman, 'about three hundred yards along, and cut through a mass of freestone'. According to another account, 'gangs of labourers working day and night, and relieving each other every four hours, were employed fifteen months upon this part of the work, from July 1832 to October of the following year'.[77] The completion of this 3-metre-high structure, built sufficiently wide to allow footways on either side of the canal, was a highly creditable achievement by Upton and his workforce, one worthy of an engineer such as Brunel and his bands of Irish navvies. Overall, the building of the canal, which was protected by eleven octagonal defended pavilions, lasted ten years and cost 10 million roubles, twice as long in duration, and four times the price, of the initial estimate.[78] Such inflation is often the case for naval and military infrastructure.

Jesse much admired the manner in which the locks and docks at Sevastopol had been constructed. The 'masonry is beautifully fitted', he observed, adding, to his evident national pride, 'the whole of the capstans and machinery of the locks are of English manufacture.[79] Notwithstanding the building of two storage reservoirs, the river Chernaya could still run short, or even dry, during a typically hot Crimean summer, and hence the water supply to the docks could fail.[80] As he does not mention any back-up device, it would appear that Jesse visited before the installation of a steam-powered engine supplied by Messrs Maudsley and Field of London, designed to pump an assured amount of water from the sea.[81] Oliphant recorded Upton's great achievement, noting 'the celebrated docks which have been constructed at an enormous expense under the able superintendence of Col. Upton'.[82]

Upton's other big project at Sevastopol undertaken on behalf of Lazarev and the Russian Navy was the construction of a new admiralty, which had been finally approved in 1835. Preparing the sites required for the erection of both the dry docks and the admiralty involved the removal of a rocky headland between the Southern and Warship Bays. It was a monumental undertaking that involved the shifting by hand of over 2 million cubic metres of earth and stone. This material was not wasted: it was used to reclaim part of the south-eastern portion of the Southern Bay, where the new admiralty was to be built, and subsequently where Sevastopol's main railway station was erected in the 1870s, with a bus station being added after the Second World War. Initially, on the Emperor's orders, soldiers and sailors had been given this backbreaking task. Later Nicholas I changed his mind during his visit to Sevastopol in 1837, considering such employment an inappropriate use of valuable military and naval manpower, quite aside from putting his men's health unnecessarily at risk. Therefore he ordered that convicts should be used instead.[83] Progress, however, was painfully slow: no mechanical means were available to assist construction and the workforce's morale and motivation were low. Jesse's observation that 'upwards of 4,000 men taken from the garrison were at work' indicates that Nicholas I's express orders forbidding the use of troops for construction tasks had been ignored. The British visitor was highly critical of their low productivity, noting that 'very few [of the men] had even hand-barrows; the majority were carrying away the earth in their coat-tails, and in bags about as large as those used by hackney-coachmen in feeding their horses'. Furthermore, as the individuals involved received such minimal bonuses for their efforts, 'the want of common energy exhibited by these men' could be 'easily understood'.[84] Thus it is hardly surprising that in 1841, after six years' work, it was estimated that the overly ambitious project was only one-sixth completed. In fact, although the dry docks had been finished by 1852, the new admiralty was still incomplete when war came to Sevastopol in the early autumn of 1854.

Apart from the time-consuming and very expensive solution of building dry docks, there was another method available to lift smaller craft from the sea for repair, or, conversely, to launch them from land. In the 1840s a British engineer called Morton had invented his patent 'slip', which incorporated a steam-powered marine railway on which ships and boats could be hoisted and lowered. In 1845 Lazarev ordered the testing of one of these new devices at Sevastopol. Notwithstanding interruptions of use during the Crimean War and the Second World Wars, it operated for 120 years until 1965.[85] Other contemporary harbour installations have enjoyed even longer lives. The two Inkerman lighthouses, for example, completed in 1820, and reinstated in 1859 following the Crimean War, remain in use today having been progressively updated over nearly two centuries of operation. From inception, they have been designed to act as a pair of aligned lights. Mariners entering the Sevastopol roadstead by night still follow the course indicated by the upper white light appearing directly above the lower red.[86]

Nicholas I, educated as a military engineer, and one extremely keen on naval affairs, valued especially the new Sevastopol docks for the Black Sea Fleet. Accordingly, he held Upton in high esteem. Although a British-born and trained civilian with no previous military experience, the Tsar had granted him the Russian rank of *podpolkovnik* (lieutenant colonel) so that he could wear a uniform, and thereby be recognised publically as an important imperial official in Sevastopol. Rank and associated dress etiquette mattered then hugely in Russia, and this continues, albeit to a more limited extent, today. Nicholas I remained impatient with the slow rate of progress at Sevastopol. On 25 October (6 November) 1844, Prince Menshikov reported on the state of construction projects in the Crimean city and in Nikolayev. The Emperor, for once reassured by what had been achieved recently, replied succinctly: 'The work proceeds in the correct manner: one may thank Lazarev and promote Upton'.[87] The latter would now be accorded the rank, privileges and accoutrements of a *polkovnik* or full colonel. Moreover, John Upton received prestigious awards in two Russian Imperial orders of chivalry: in 1842, of St Stanislaus, and in 1847, of St Anna.[88] Although he had absconded in disgrace from his mother country, the renegade British engineer had certainly made his mark in Russia: commended as a distinguished engineer, he and the members of his family were welcomed into society. Yet, as with Thomas Mackenzie, Upton's name is scarcely mentioned in popular Russian accounts of Sevastopol. In this, perhaps the most Russian of Russian cities, the role of foreigners in its historic development tends to be suppressed.

SEVASTOPOL'S FORTIFICATIONS

Well before the Crimean War, there was little secret about the possibility of an enemy (read British) attack on Sevastopol. A writer of the 1850s claimed that Sevastopol's defences were 'erected soon after the revolution of 1831 [sic] in Paris, in consequence of an article in a London journal on the Black Sea, in which it was stated, that nothing could be easier, than for a few well-appointed vessels to force the passage of the Sebastopol roads, and set fire to the imperial fleet'.[89] As to which major power might perpetrate such a bold coup, the author left no direct clue: his British readers would have presumed such derring-do to be the preserve of the Royal Navy. From a Russian perspective, and well prior to the Straits Convention of 1841, there was substance in this assumption and growing acknowledgement of the potential British threat to their national interests in the Black Sea region. Such a notion was not far-fetched.

In early 1791, for instance, the British government under Pitt's leadership had considered mounting an expedition to attack the Dnieper fortress of

Ochakov, which, it may be recalled, had fallen to Potemkin and Suvorov in December 1788. Designed to counter Russian expansion at the expense of the Ottoman Empire, the scheme came to nothing. It had been abandoned for the lack of a clear strategy, and most crucially, on account of the failure of the British parliament to vote the necessary funds.[90] Whether the new base at Sevastopol had been identified as a putative objective is not known: the fact remains that war with Russia was averted. While Russia and Britain had become allies of convenience during the French Revolutionary Wars and the Napoleonic Wars, excluding the period 1807–12 (from the Treaty of Tilsit to Napoleon's march into Russia), no lasting friendship emerged. Following the post-war settlement made at the Congress of Vienna, mutual suspicions remained and associated tensions arose, particularly during the 1830s, based, amongst other matters, on the 'Eastern Question' over the future fate of the Ottoman Empire, and the rivalry between the Russian and British Empires for influence in, if not control of, Persia and Afghanistan – known as the 'Great Game'.

In 1828 the Russian ambassador in Paris, Count Carlo Andrea Pozzo di Borgo, had warned Nicholas I that 'although it may not be probable that we shall see an English fleet in the Black Sea, it will be prudent to make Sevastopol very secure against attacks from the sea'. What is more, he declared, 'If ever England were to come to a rupture with us, this is the point to which she would direct her attacks, if only she believed them possible'.[91] Such prescient thinking was not confined to this Russian diplomat. Since his appointment Lazarev had been in no doubt as to the potential threat posed to Sevastopol by a hostile navy. Although he was most hospitable to individual visiting Britons, and notwithstanding his formative years in the Royal Navy, he was wary of Britain's hostile intentions. Writing to Prince Menshikov in 1834, he warned of the possibility of a British attack 'with a navy far stronger than the Black Sea Fleet'. [Therefore] 'I cannot keep silence; I reiterate the urgent necessity of paying attention to this wonderful port. Its fortifications should be as impregnable as those of Gibraltar and Malta'.[92]

Foreign powers, particularly Britain, took a keen interest in the development of Sevastopol, and thus were keen to gather intelligence on it. In 1834, an outline of the planned defences on the southern side of Sevastopol had appeared on Russian surveys of the city. One such document accompanied a report by Lieutenant Colonel A. E. Macintosh, who had visited the city, to the British ambassador in Constantinople in December of that year.[93] Further British 'special investigators' appeared in a series of military and naval missions to the Black Sea region and Sevastopol.[94] These included the Royal Navy officer Adolphus Slade in the summer of 1835, followed by Lieutenant Colonel William Lennox Lascelles Fitzgerald de Ros and Captain Charles Ramsay Drinkwater Bethune, who together went to Sevastopol on two occasions (3–5 and 12–14 November 1835) in the course of an extensive tour of the Danubian Principalities (which we now call Romania and Moldova) and southern Russia. De Ros's journal reveals many fascinating anecdotes about meeting Nicholas I, Count Mikhail Vorontsov, the governor of New Russia, and Admiral Lazarev. It also provides much useful information about the Crimean city, not least the 'general plan of the land fortification'.[95] These visits were overt and official, having been approved by Nicholas I, in return for a Russian inspection of British naval installations.[96] None the less, and despite such confidence-building measures, suspicions between Britain and Russia were set to remain.

It is highly likely that the *Vixen* affair of late 1836, and the associated heightened tensions (and growing dangers of war breaking out) between Britain and Russia in early 1837, prompted Nicholas I and his admirals to review the security of Sevastopol.[97] During his early tenure in command Lazarev had in any case continued to warn of the risk of the naval threat to Sevastopol. Reporting to Prince Menshikov in 1837, for example, he had urged the landing of Russian troops at the Bosporus in order to block the Straits to the British. 'But if they break through to the Black Sea', he concluded, 'the best way to counter them is to protect the fleet at Sevastopol under the guns of its defences, then deploy the fleet to engage the enemy when already damaged by coastal gunfire.'[98] For all the sense in such arguments, there was none the less a hidden, paradoxical, danger that Lazarev never alluded to: Sevastopol might become the object of an enemy attack precisely because of the presence of the Black Sea Fleet, whether it had a protective function or not. Callwell highlighted this issue two generations later. 'Inasmuch as the mobile naval forces of the enemy form the primary objective in warfare afloat', he surmised, 'the fact that hostile fighting-vessels have taken refuge in the fortress offers a strong inducement for undertaking operations against it'.[99] There is no evidence, however, that either Lazarev or Nicholas I ever regarded Sevastopol in such terms. Certainly they viewed the defence of Sevastopol as an entirely legitimate and necessarily expensive project. Whatever the politics and the practicalities, the Russian Emperor in 1837 confirmed his decision to continue fortifying the city on the landward side. It would appear, moreover, that the construction of the docks and admiralty was given priority over any new defences. So work on these proceeded very slowly. The Russians were to pay the price for such neglect in 1854–55.

In his published account of 1841 Jesse underscored the obvious threat to Sevastopol's security. Although its defences were considered 'impregnable' by the Russians, and notwithstanding that it 'may be a long time before that question is decided', he observed: 'if we [the British] should ever contemplate the destruction of the admiralty and fleet ... I have not the least doubt that there are many admirals in our service who would be ready enough to make the experiment'.[100] Jesse returned to this theme in his later work of 1854: 'Sevastopol must be either strictly and securely blockaded, or the fleet within its harbours destroyed. That task would be one from which the heart shrinks, and which dire necessity alone would justify. There can be no doubt [however] that its complete destruction would be a great blow to the Russians.'[101] In fact, the major attack would come soon enough on 17 October 1854 with the first Allied bombardment of Sevastopol by land and sea.

The Russian military engineer Eduard Todleben proved to be one of Sevastopol's heroes of the Crimean War. His professional expertise, innovation and improvisation, and energetic leadership turned the city – virtually defenceless against land attack – into a formidable fortress. Of Baltic German stock, he was born in 1818 in Courland (now a province of western Latvia). Joining the Russian Army in 1836, he trained as a military engineer at St Petersburg and saw active service in the Caucasus in the 1840s. Todleben's growing reputation as an engineer had reached the attention of Nicholas I, who sent him on his mission to advise on the strengthening of Sevastopol's fortifications. Despite some initial difficulties with Menshikov, Todleben would be entrusted with the supervision of erecting the new defensive works, in which earth, as opposed to stone, became the main fabric of improvised construction.

In his authoritative account of the defence of Sevastopol during the Crimean War, Todleben described the city's fortifications in great detail. He narrated their development from the founding of the city in 1783 to 1853, then explained how the defences were reinforced as war approached, and finally documented how frantic attempts were made to strengthen them further as the Allies threatened to seize Sevastopol after the battle of the Alma on 20 September 1854. This is a story of incremental construction of various schemes of defence designed to meet changing perceptions of the threat to port and city, all undertaken within tight constraints on resources. While Sevastopol would eventually be guarded by a formidable series of shore batteries, in stark contrast, the city's defences to landward remained very much weaker until the Crimean War was in progress. Todleben was only able to complete and reinforce them in time by a brilliant series of expedients.

As we have seen, three years after Rear Admiral Thomas Mackenzie founded the city, Colonel of Engineers Korsakov had drawn up a ten-year plan for the defence of Sevastopol from both land and sea attack. Little major work of fortification, however, was undertaken in 1786 or for much of the decade thereafter, notwithstanding the grand imperial visit of 1787. It was not until 1794, following the Russo-Turkish War of 1787–92, that the field batteries erected by Suvorov and Mackenzie a decade before to guard the northern and southern shores of the roadstead were finally replaced with five more permanent fortifications – in earth, and not yet in stone. Although they were armed with about 100 guns between them, these defences were soon considered inadequate. From his visit to Sevastopol in 1803, de Reuilly recalled:

> It is in agitation to add a new battery to those which are already raised, and which seem insufficient; at least I have heard the officers of the [fleet] say, that with a fair wind, a ship in full sail might enter the port without suffering from the cannon of the batteries, and a landing might be easily made on the flat shore that surrounds Sevastopol.[102]

Unsurprisingly, the Russians were not willing to leave their major new naval base so vulnerable to attack. In 1805, the commander-in-chief of the Black Sea Fleet, Admiral Jean Baptiste, the Marquis of Traversay (known in Russia as Ivan Ivanovich de Traversay), an illustrious French naval officer who had served with distinction during the American War of Independence but was now in Russian service, ordered the reinforcement of the shore defences with seven new batteries. With a total of about 200 guns, the Sevastopol roadstead was then protected, according to Todleben, with a 'fairly formidable defence'.[103]

At the same time, the Russian government determined that Sevastopol should also be defended from landward attack, or, better, that any plan to assault the city should be deterred in the first place. In consequence, the construction of two great polygonal forts was planned – one on each of the northern and southern sides of the roadstead. In the event, only the North Fort (later to be known to the Allies as the Star Fort) was built, completed in 1818. On paper, it appeared to be an impressive fortification with walls, according to Todleben, '14 feet high and 10 feet in thickness', and 'surrounded by a ditch of 12 feet in depth and 18 feet in width'.[104] Three great gates guarded its entry points: 'Simferopol' to the north; 'Inkerman' to the east; and a third, 'Sevastopol', opening out to the south towards the roadstead and the city. Such was the enduring focus on denying an attack from the sea, however, that the Russians neglected the maintenance, development and armament of the North Fort prior to the Crimean War. Todleben admitted as much: by 1853 apparently, the 'fort had fallen into ruins' – the urgent repair work recommended by the department of engineers had not been undertaken.[105] A Polish officer in Russian service, Captain Robert Chodasiewicz (Hodasevich), confirmed that even immediately prior to the Allied siege of Sevastopol in September 1854, the North Fort remained 'useless, or worse than useless' as it was 'not properly commanded by other works, but by the high ground around it'. More specifically, 'the citadel of the fort was in a state of neglect; not a single gun was mounted; [and altogether] there were not more than eight guns, and these in a very dilapidated state'.[106] On the conclusion of hostilities in the spring of 1856, a young British Royal Engineer, Charles Gordon (later of Khartoum fame), inspected the fortification, confirming it as 'a tumbledown affair, and not at all formidable'.[107] Ironically, it was this very vulnerability in Sevastopol's defences that the Allies chose to ignore after their victory at the battle of the Alma on 20 September 1854.

Unsurprisingly, Russian admirals took the threat of a naval attack much more seriously than one from land. In 1822 a committee under the chairmanship of Aleksey Greig directed the strengthening of the shore batteries on the southern side. It was not until 1834, the year after he handed over command to Lazarev, that attention was again paid to Sevastopol's landward defences – albeit they were never taken as seriously as those facing to sea. A proposal of that year foresaw the construction on the southern side of the city of seven major bastions made of earth, with stone barracks each housing a company of infantry (250 men) built on their inner faces. While work soon started, initial progress was slow. In November 1835, for example, de Ros had observed a plan which was designed to: 'embrace with a single line of entrenchment, with redoubts at seven or eight of the most commanding angles, the great ridge of land upon which Sebastopol is built, together with the adjacent harbour, barracks, and public works!' He noted, however, 'as far as it has yet advanced the execution of the lines is excellent, but it must have proceeded very slowly, for some of the bastions are unfinished'.[108] Following the inspection of Sevastopol's defences by Nicholas I in 1837, this scheme was extended, no doubt reflecting the rising tensions with Britain at the time. The Emperor directed that the defences on the left (western) flank should be reinforced and an additional bastion on the right (eastern) flank constructed. This planned half-ring of bastions and interconnecting curtain walls would extend for approximately 7 *versts* – approximately 7 kilometres. Despite the imperial intervention, priority was again given to completing the construction of Sevastopol's formidable shore batteries. In any case, the fortification of Sevastopol – whether against sea or land attack – did not receive the highest priority of governmental funding. Coastal defences in the Baltic (such as Kronstadt) and the fortification of Kiev received the lion's share of government funds.[109] The reduction of planned effort at Sevastopol may have reflected a presumption of the waning threat of a British attack, and a higher priority being given to the defences of Kiev and St Petersburg. In any event, the landward defences of Sevastopol remained weak, to the north or south alike, until the Allied armies landed on the Crimean shore in September 1854.

Any description of Sevastopol's fortifications, whether facing the sea or the land, is complicated by their nomenclature. While the Russians *numbered* the secondary batteries guarding the roadstead as well as the bastions protecting the southern side of the city, they *named* their principal stone 'casemented' coastal defences erected on the shores of Sevastopol Bay. The latter comprised Forts Alexander, Constantine and Paul and the Michael Battery. In addition, one major bastion on the southern landward side, the Malakhov Tower, broke the sequence of numbered bastions. This present account provides a summary of Sevastopol's principal fortifications and armaments in order to highlight their significance to the Russian defence of the city, and not least to indicate how they influenced both the Allies' planning and conduct of their assaults. The planned bastions on the southern side of Sevastopol were numbered in a clockwise sequence and positioned as shown in Table 3.1. In addition, a crenellated wall, 17½ feet high, was erected between Bastions 5, 6 and 7 on the western side. Excepting the Malakhov Tower, completed in 1854, the fortifications on the eastern side of the town had hardly been started before war came to Sevastopol.

Russian Bastion	Later Allied Name	Location	State of Construction prior to the Crimean War
No. 1.		Close to the shore, next to Careening Bay overlooking the main roadstead of Sevastopol Bay.	Barracks completed.
No. 2.	Little Redan	*c.* 500m to the south of Bastion No. 1.	
Malakhov	The Tower or the Round Tower	Further to the south, on the Malakhov Hill.	Only the stone Round Tower completed. With supporting earthworks and batteries, later known as the Kornilov Bastion.
No. 3.	Redan or Great Redan	Between the Dock and the Laboratory Ravines, on the Bambor Heights, and in front of the naval hospital.	
No. 4.	Flagstaff (Bastion du Mât)	Opposite the end of the Southern Bay on the Boulevard Heights.	
No. 5.	Central	On the crest of the heights between the Town and Zagoronoy Ravines.	Barracks completed.
No. 6.	Quarantine	On the same elevation, *c.*1,000m to the north of Bastion No. 5.	Barracks completed.
No. 7.	Artillery Fort	On the shore of the roadstead, linked to Shore Battery No. 8.	

**Table 3.1 – Sevastopol's Landward Defences
(Southern Side) prior to the Crimean War**

Apart from the dilapidated North Fort, the Russians had only completed the coastal defences of Sevastopol, consisting of eight forts or batteries, by the end of 1852 (see Map 9). On the southern shore, running from west to east, were: Battery No. 10, Fort Alexander, Bastion No. 7 with Battery No. 8 (a combined land and shore fortification), Fort Nicholas and Fort Paul. The latter two guarded not only the roadstead but also the mouth of the Southern Bay – known to the Allies as the 'Military Harbour'. On the northern side were Fort Constantine, the Michael Battery and Battery No. 4. While Batteries 4, 8 and 10 were constructed of earth, the remaining fortifications were built in dressed stone. Of these constructions, both the sparkling cream-white Fort Constantine and the buff-yellow Michael Battery remain today as potent reminders of the former strength of Sevastopol's mid-nineteenth-century coastal defences.

An enemy fleet attempting to force the Sevastopol roadstead during this period would have been engaged successively by five lines of mostly interlocking fire: (1) from Battery No. 10; (2) from Forts Alexander and Constantine; (3) from Battery No. 8 and Bastion No. 7; (4) from Fort Nicholas and Michael Battery; (5) from Fort Paul and Battery No. 4. It would require a very strong and skilfully directed attacking force indeed to overcome such powerful, layered defences. The spectacular failure of the Allies' naval bombardment of 17 October 1854 would demonstrate just how effective the fire of Sevastopol's batteries (whether made of earth or those encased in stone) would prove against that of wooden ships. It would result in an uneven contest that the Allies would lose and have much cause to regret, notwithstanding the success achieved in the bombardment of the Russian Baltic fortress of Bomarsund in August 1854. With the smooth-bore, low-velocity, flat-trajectory naval guns of the day, even with relatively heavy weapons such as the British 32-pounder, ships had to come in close (500 metres or less) to a stone fort if they were to inflict any serious damage with their round shot. The wooden ships of the time were also highly vulnerable to artillery returning fire with either red-hot shot or explosive shells. The restricted entrance to the Sevastopol roadstead, and particularly the presence of treacherous shoals just offshore, made it very difficult for the Allied ships to engage the forts at sufficiently close range.

For the Russian defenders, however, it was insufficient merely to construct the batteries and wait, relying on their physical presence alone. To have any credible deterrent effect or defensive capability, the forts had to be continually manned and supplied, and their gun crews trained and held at appropriate readiness. This state of affairs had to be monitored closely to ensure military efficiency. In early 1853, Sevastopol's defences were inspected by a high level team sent by Nicholas I from St Petersburg, consisting of General Aleksandr Pavlovich Bezak, chief of staff of the Imperial Artillery, and Major General

Aleksandr Alekseyevich Barantsov, an aide-de-camp of his majesty. The pair was supported by Colonel of Artillery Kartachevsky, who was made responsible for the detailed implementation of all measures required to ensure the effectiveness of Sevastopol's defences.

In his report of 17 February 1853 [OS], Barantsov itemised a total of 451 guns of different types and calibres that armed the eight shore batteries of Sevastopol. Crucially, however, only eight of those listed (on Bastion 7) were positioned to defend against an attack from landward while 'approximately 300' were aligned for defensive counter-fire on to the roadstead.[110] In 1853, Prince Menshikov ordered tests of the batteries' guns and crews, involving the firing of all available types of ammunition, to ensure that if an attack from the sea were to arise, it would be resisted in a most determined and effective manner. To further enhance the defensive power of the guns, furnaces were installed in the batteries to provide a ready supply of red-hot shot. This munition was to prove highly effective against the Allied fleet during its bombardment of the forts. Significantly, little was done to address the deficiencies in the defences to landward, whether in construct or in armament. As opposed to the perceived threat from the sea, the dangers to landward appeared minimal.

By the autumn of 1853 Sevastopol's holdings of coastal artillery had been increased. Now comprising a total of 533 guns of all types, these included: cannon, which fired principally solid iron round shot; 'bombes', which fired exploding shell; 'licornes' (a Russian invention, a hybrid cannon, howitzer and mortar, rated in *poods*) and mortars, as shown in Table 3.2 (overleaf). The heaviest guns and mortars had extreme ranges of up to 3,000 metres, but their effective ranges with any accuracy were less than half of that. Although they had greater destructive power due to their explosive projectiles, the shell guns of the period had lesser range and penetration than guns firing heavy solid shot. None the less, the combined firepower of the various types of gun on the shore forts and batteries made the naval fortress of Sevastopol a particularly hard nut to crack.

Manning the weapons of war mounted in the eight shore batteries required no fewer than 2,708 men, based on gun crews of either five or six. While army artillerymen were responsible for the outer defences of Battery No. 10 and Forts Alexander and Constantine, naval gunners manned the remaining five batteries that dominated the roadstead. Artillery pieces of all types were provisioned with 160 rounds each.[111]

Sevastopol's defences were further strengthened in January 1854 as war with Britain and France approached. Menshikov decided to reinforce the shore fortifications with three new batteries. Two of them (named the Twelve Apostles and the Paris) were positioned on the northern shore; the third (Sviatoslav) on the southern. These batteries were armed with a total of 59 guns. In addition,

Sevastopol Bay Shore Batteries			Guns (Cannon)						'Licornes'			Mortars (5-pood)	Totals
Russian Name or Number	Type	Shore of Bay	'Bombes', 3-pood	36-pdr	30-pdr	24-pdr	18-pdr	12-pdr	Long 1-pood	Short 1-pood	Long 0.5-pood		
No. 10	Earth	South	2	29					12		9	6	58
Alexander	Stone	South	2	11		16	4		19			4	56
Constantine	Stone	North				50			34		4	6	94
Bastion No. 7 with Battery No. 8	Stone/Earth	South	2	9		22		4	11		4	10	62
Michael	Stone	North	8	16		12			28		13		77
Nicholas	Stone	South	10			63			32				105
No. 4	Earth	North			16	15	4		9		3		47
Paul	Stone	South	4		4		11			15			34
Totals			28	65	20	178	19	4	145	15	33	26	533

Table 3.2 – Sevastopol's Shore Defences, Autumn 1853
(after Todleben, *Defence of Sevastopol*, vol. i, pt 1, p. 103)

the ships of the Black Sea Fleet were allocated tasks in defence of their home port. At that time, the fleet comprised fourteen sailing ships of the line, seven frigates, eleven steamships and a number of lesser combatants – adding a further 2,000 guns to the defence, according to Todleben.[112] Vice Admiral Nakhimov's squadron of eight ships of line, six frigates and a number of steamships guarded the entrance of the roadstead, while Vice Admiral Kornilov's squadron of four ships of the line, one frigate and four steamships guarded the Southern Bay, ready to attack the flank of any enemy fleet attempting to force the roadstead.

In April 1854, Menshikov realised belatedly that the fortifications on the northern shore were still vulnerable to sea and land attack from the flanks and rear. Accordingly, he directed the erection of two new batteries. The first of these, the Kartaschevsky (later to be named by the Allies as the Telegraph Battery), was built to the north of Fort Constantine. The second was established further north, near the mouth of the river Belbek. Of circular construction, it was named the Volokhov Tower after its builder. Confusingly, the Allies called this defensive work the Wasp Battery. In addition, Menshikov placed a battery of six heavy (5-*pood*) mortars on the upper platform of Fort Constantine, bringing its total armament to nearly 100 guns of all types.[113] The North Fort, however, remained neglected. By mid May 1854, the shore defences of Sevastopol had been reinforced with five new batteries while existing ones such as Fort Constantine received new armaments. Table 3.3 (overleaf) gives Todleben's summary, which, significantly, omits the North Fort.

Of these 610 guns and mortars, no fewer than 571 were able to fire out to sea and to engage targets on the roadstead, while the remaining thirty-nine weapons, mostly of smaller calibre, served to defend the shore forts from attack by land. The strengthening of the main landward fortifications on the southern side of Sevastopol, however, did not receive the same attention. Menshikov did not believe that the Allies had the means to mount a major invasion of Crimea. Reflecting an assessment that the principal threat of an enemy *raid*, if one were to occur, would be directed from the Black Sea towards the west of the city, this flank of Sevastopol's defences was reinforced on the 'town' side as a first priority. Little thought at this stage had been given to the possibility of a major enemy attack from the north, east (the 'ship' side) or south, let alone that Sevastopol might be invested and would have to withstand a protracted siege. The only exception was the construction of the Malakhov Tower on the eastern side of the city: it would prove itself soon enough as a hotly-contested bulwark of the Russian defence.

Sevastopol Shore Batteries			Guns (Cannon)						'Licornes'			Carronades (all types)	Mortars (all types)	Totals
Name or Number	Type	Shore	'Bombes', 3-pood	36-pdr	30-pdr	24-pdr	18-pdr	12-pdr	1-pood Long	1-pood Short	0.5-pood (all types)			
No. 10	Earth	South	2	29					12		9		6	58
Alexander	Stone	South	2	11		16	4		19				4	56
Constantine	Stone	North				50			34		4	1	8	97
Kartachevsky	Earth	North		1					3		1			5
Volokhov Tower	Stone?	North		8								2		10
Bastion No. 7 with Battery No. 8	Stone/ Earth	South	2	9		22		4	11		4		10	62
Michael	Stone	North	8	16		12			28		13			77
Nicholas	Stone	South	10			63			32					105
No. 4	Earth	North			16	15	4		9		3			47
Paul	Stone	South	4		4		11			15				34
Twelve Apostles	Earth	North		18								2		20
Paris	Earth	North		17								4	1	22
Sviatoslav	Earth	South		14					3					17
Totals			28	123	20	178	19	4	151	15	34	9	29	610

Table 3.3 – Sevastopol's Shore Defences, May 1854
(after Todleben, *Defence of Sevastopol*, vol. i, pt 1, p. 120)

ECONOMIC AND SOCIAL DEVELOPMENTS

It is tempting to view Sevastopol's development in the first half of the nineteenth century being driven purely through its fleet and associated naval infrastructure. Wider economic goals, including supporting trade tempered by security considerations, however, also spurred the city's expansion. In 1820, following an imperial decree, the port was reopened to commercial traffic, but only to merchant vessels and boats arriving from Russian ports. By that time the city embraced: 1,106 houses, three tanneries, three wax and lard works; a brewery and a distillery; a windmill; two smithies and not least four churches.[114] Apart from the ships' crews, the population was now over 3,000, including many retired officers and sailors, setting a trend of local settlement that would continue until the present day. Russia's very first commercial passenger shipping line was established in 1828 between Odessa and Yalta, with a stop at Sevastopol, powered by a British-built paddle-steamer. This was the very same route that the first foreign visitors and tourists would take to the city before and following the Crimean War.

Economic activity within Sevastopol and its population was given further boosts with the publication of an imperial decree in January 1836, which offered incentives to attract newcomers to set up business. Artisans and merchants from other parts of Russia who took up residence in the city were offered tax-free status for their first three years of the ten-year period of 1838–48, then 50 per cent of normal tax rates for the remaining seven. There is little doubt that this measure was highly successful. Together, the expansion of commerce and the parallel development of the Black Sea Fleet with its associated construction of port infrastructure and defences led to a phase of unprecedented growth in Sevastopol. By 1853 the population had soared to nearly 50,000: no less than a sixteen-fold expansion in three decades. Quite apart from the burgeoning naval and military infrastructure, including the dockyard, hospital and barracks, the city now boasted forty-three streets, 2,810 houses, eight churches and four colleges with 500 students enrolled.[115] Commerce in Sevastopol had also greatly expanded. Alongside Yevpatoriya, Feodosiya and Kerch, it had become a major Crimean port for Russian coasting trade, much of it involving the resupply of the fleet and garrison. Foreign vessels visited the other three ports, of which Kerch handled the most goods.[116]

In this period, however, there had been one major interruption to Sevastopol's smooth progress – a popular revolt, which provided a forerunner of the Russian revolution of 1905 and the associated naval mutinies in the Black Sea Fleet. The ostensible cause of the unrest was an outbreak of bubonic plague in March 1830. It led to an insurrection by sailors, soldiers and townspeople in the early summer. It was to be one of the first of a series of major, violent protests that took place

123

throughout Russia that year and during the following, collectively termed the 'cholera riots'. The turn of events in the Black Sea city proved amongst the most serious breakdowns in civil order and military discipline during the first half of nineteenth-century Russia. For a few days, imperial rule was directly threatened. With the detection of the first cases of the outbreak of the plague, the town and naval authorities fully isolated Sevastopol from the outside world in March 1830. As a result, the city's population felt imprisoned. This very strict quarantine measure soon caused hardship amongst the townsfolk and members of the garrison and fleet. Little food or fuel, let alone other provisions, was allowed into the city. In consequence, local prices soared enormously; cold and hunger weakened all but the rich.

By the beginning of June 1830, matters came to a head when groups of dissatisfied sailors and workers prepared to march against the rapidly deteriorating conditions in Sevastopol.[117] The ringing of a church bell sounded the start of the revolt at 7pm on 15 June. According to contemporary police reports, the majority of the protesters came from the Artillery and Korabelnaya districts of the cities, mostly angry sailors armed with wooden staves, accompanied by their equally querulous wives. Within three hours, they had seized most of the town. The rioters ransacked the dwellings and offices of senior army and naval officers, government officials and merchants, leaving many houses 'ravaged to such an extent that only the damaged walls and roofs were left'. Amongst the killed were the acting city military governor, Stolypin, who had been dragged from his house and brutally stoned and beaten, a brigade commander, Colonel Vorobev, and Commissar Second Class Stepanov. Many other residents narrowly escaped being beaten to death, including a staff doctor called Galushevsky. This opening phase of Sevastopol's first insurrection lasted until 0600 hours the next morning when it was held in check by the arrival of armed troops, who faced the crowd down by dint of threatening to shoot them. The local police, however, conceded on 18 June that order in the city was still in doubt.[118]

The mutineers' success proved short-lived. Apart from airing their grievances and demanding that the quarantine should be lifted, they had neither a coherent plan of action nor a competent leader. Meanwhile, the governor of South Russia, Count Mikhail Vorontsov, took expeditious action. He ordered fresh troops from other Crimean cities, including Simferopol, to enter Sevastopol. By the close of 19 June, these forces had not only contained but also crushed the revolt. Thereafter, Russian imperial justice was swift and exemplary. No fewer than 1,500 people were brought to trial for their alleged participation in the riots. Seven mutineers sentenced to death were given public executions on 23 August 1830 in three different parts of Sevastopol to reinforce in the public eye the restoration of law and order. Many others received long terms of imprisonment. By later standards of tsarist, Bolshevik and Soviet reaction to such disorder, however, the authorities were relatively lenient. Harsh naval discipline was restored: the next significant mutinies in the Black Sea Fleet would occur sixty-five years later as part of the first Bolshevik revolution of 1905.

SEVASTOPOL ON THE EVE OF WAR

Within a year or so following the revolt of 1830, Sevastopol was well back on the road to economic recovery. Within another twenty years it had become a handsome and prosperous city. 'A Lady Resident near the Alma', whom the British Library reveals to be Mrs Andrew Neilson, wrote a vivid portrait of the city prior to the Crimean War. On passing the 'northern fort, close to one side of which the road passes, ... enclosed by a deep ditch, lined with stone, and surmounted by an earthen embankment of great thickness', the visitor soon arrives arrived at the shore of the roadstead. There, she recorded, 'Boats of all sizes are in constant attendance to convey goods and passengers across the bay, which is here about a mile broad'. Having boarded a suitable vessel, the following vista unfolded:

> During the passage across, we have a good view of the white stone batteries which are built at short distances from the other, on both sides of the bay, nearly on a level with the water; and further up to the left is a handsome aqueduct, which conveys across a small valley the water required for the docks.[119]

Traversing the roadstead, 'we shape our course towards the Count's [*Grafskaya*] landing-place', the imposing edifice, the inspiration of Lazarev and design of Upton. On reaching that point, Mrs Neilson continued, 'we step on shore, at a well-built quay, from which rises a broad, handsome flight of steps, having at the top a double row of columns, and on each side terraces well supplied with benches for the use of the public'.[120] This imposing portico remains Sevastopol's calling card: few cities enjoy such a grand shore-side entrance.

Within Sevastopol, Mrs Neilson recorded that 'A band of music plays almost every day upon those terraces, which contributes much to enliven the scene. Uniforms alone are visible; and everything around shows that we are now in a military as well as naval town'. Further enriching the city's cultural life, she declared, was a 'very good theatre, with two tiers of boxes'. 'In the winter', she continued, 'besides the Russian company of actors, several very good Italian singers are often engaged, who, with the assistance of the soldiers or sailors to fill up the stage, manage to get up an Italian opera very creditably'.[121]

'Passing through the colonnade, on our right, extending along the water's edge, is the three-tiered battery named Fort Nicholas, close to which is a plain-looking building, called a palace'. Our observer, of course, is referring to Thomas Mackenzie's original house, which had served as a residence for Catherine the Great on her visit to Sevastopol in 1787 and had been extended since. Yet there was another – less pleasant – aspect to the daily life of the city and port, the details of which Mrs Neilson did not spare her readers. As she explained, 'At the head of the inner [southern, military] harbour, to which the main street runs parallel for about half a mile, are hulks used as prison ships, containing many hundreds of unfortunate creatures, loaded with chains, and clad in a motley prison dress to prevent escape'. It was these prisoners, she then recorded pitifully, that were 'employed in the public works; and truly painful it was to see them, and hear the clanking of their chains, as they passed along the street morning and evening'.[122] Sevastopol's defences prior to the Crimean War were the products of such forced hard labour. As previously noted, convicts were also employed in the construction of the dry docks.

Despite the chilling presence of the chain-gangs, Mrs Neilson paints a picture of a largely serene Sevastopol at peace, and not one much preparing, let alone prepared for war. It was a fine city, with many grand buildings such as the assembly rooms, theatre and library; all constructed in the fine Inkerman stone, as were the formidable forts defending its very heart, the roadstead or grand harbour of Sevastopol Bay. On passing Fort Nicholas, Mrs Neilson described the opening vista: 'the street leads to the Artillery bay, the Market-Place, and the worst part of the town, while to the left', she noted, 'passing the Admiralty, is the principal or main street, in which all the best shops, the cathedral, and the residence of the admiral of the port and [houses] of many of the chief families lie'.[123]

Notwithstanding how impressive and effective Sevastopol's coastal defences would appear and prove, the Russian port, in a similar fashion to the British base at Singapore prior to Japan's opening of hostilities in December 1941, suffered from a serious flaw. No one, whether in the Russian government, army or navy, perhaps with the honourable exception of Todleben, and despite the various plans drawn up, would appear to have taken seriously enough the threat of a determined attack from the landward side. Sevastopol's isolated position appeared to offer it passive protection. Lying far away from the main garrisons of the Russian Army stationed to protect Russian Poland and the Caucasus, however, made the naval base vulnerable to any major power which could assemble, protect and transport a large landing force across the Black Sea.

Crimea prior to the eponymous war was a peripheral, far-flung province of Russia without railways (there were none south of Moscow) or well-paved roads connecting the peninsula to the country's heart. Even using her main water highways, such as the river arteries Volga, Don and Dnieper, Russian communications were painfully slow, no faster than in the days of Peter the Great. Any reinforcements of troops, therefore, would have to arrive slowly on foot, with wagon trains trundling across the vast, southern steppes in support. It is a matter of hindsight to speculate whether Nicholas I, who was increasingly concerned about the security of Crimea and Sevastopol as war approached in 1853–54, should have ordered further reinforcements be sent to Menshikov's command, and whether in consequence the Russians could have overwhelmed the Allies in fighting on, or close to, their landing. The Tsar did not. Consequently the Russians were unable to defeat the British and French forces in battle. A 349-day-long siege of Sevastopol ensued, extremely costly to all sides. The Black Sea would become an Allied lake: theoretically, the British–French–Turkish coalition, which would form, could mount an expedition to Crimea whenever they wished. New technology was on their side, for steam power had changed the calculus of war. The age-old limitations of wind and weather on movement by sea, if not eliminated, had been reduced significantly. Armies could now be relatively easily transported, supported and protected across considerable distances with greater certainty, provided no hostile navy intervened or great storm broke (as one famously did on 14 November 1854). With command of the sea and with steam-powered transports, the Allies could reinforce and supply troops on Crimea faster than the Russians could by land. The Russians were slow to comprehend this dawning technical revolution in warfare.

For all the impressive forts and batteries that protected Sevastopol's grand harbour from attack by sea, as we have seen, the city was very poorly fortified against an attack from the landward side. This grave deficiency compounded Menshikov's difficulties. Luckily for him and Sevastopol, however, the Allies had only patchy intelligence as to the weak state of the city's landward defences, and, for this and other reasons, were unable to exploit its vulnerabilities in time. The feeble fortifications facing the interior of Crimea had long been recognised as inadequate, but insufficient resources had been allocated for their development. Even given enough money, materials and manpower, it still would have taken several years to design, build and arm a new series of sophisticated forts of stone to guard Sevastopol from attack by land.[124] This was not the sort of undertaking that could be accomplished in haste.

When Nicholas I had belatedly recognised the growing threat to Sevastopol in 1854, he ordered the despatch of Colonel Eduard Todleben, a leading military specialist with long experience in building field fortifications from earth and timber, to report on the city's defences. The engineer's notes of mid-August that year made depressing reading. While Todleben praised the heavily armed seaward defences, to land he observed that: 'These fortifications consist of several batteries armed with guns of a very small calibre, which could only give some opposition to Tatars'.[125] The professional sapper's sarcasm was not out of place. After the Allied landing, Sevastopol's exposure to enemy attack would soon become clear enough to all thinking soldiers, sailors and citizens. Todleben was indeed the right man to address the deficiencies in the city's defences. The question was whether he would be given the necessary authority, resources and time to make up for years of past neglect.

PART TWO

THE CRIMEAN WAR

CHAPTER 4

THE EASTERN WAR

*'No operation is of such doubtful issue as the
landing in an enemy's country for the purpose of conquest.'*

Field Marshal Sir John Burgoyne[1]

A CONTROVERSIAL CONFLICT

In central London, at the junction of Lower Regent Street and Pall Mall in
Waterloo Place, stands a frequently overlooked object, some way off the normal
the tourist trail. Unveiled in 1861, it consists of a trio of bear-skinned Guardsmen,
and, towering high above them, a bronze female figure with her arms proudly
outstretched, originally known as Honour (later, Victory).[2] This remarkable
memorial commemorates the lives of the 2,162 officers, non-commissioned
officers and men of the Brigade of Guards, who fell either in battle or to disease
during the campaign against Russia in Crimea in 1854–56. One of the most
striking memorials in the United Kingdom to the Crimean War, it recalls a
conflict that became caricatured on account of political misdirection, military
incompetence and unnecessary sacrifice.[3]

If remembered at all, the most enduring and evocative images of the distant
war in Crimea are of the 93rd Highlanders' rock-solid stand at Balaklava (later
immortalised as the 'Thin Red Line') and, more prominently in British national
folklore, the vainglorious charge of the Light Brigade shortly thereafter.[4] Not to
be forgotten is a Victorian icon – the 'lady with the lamp' – nurse Florence

Nightingale. When one wanders around the backstreets of many of Britain's towns today, good numbers of Alma, Balaclava and Inkerman roads or streets appear, with Alma being the most prevalent: in contrast, either 'Sebastopol' or 'Sevastopol' occurs but very rarely.[5] These names mark four dimly recalled battles of over 160 years ago, whose relevance has been lost. The wider 'Eastern' War against Russia, which involved naval campaigns in the Baltic and in the Far East, and the rivalling grand strategic ambitions that brought about the conflict in the first place, remain likewise cloaked in historical obscurity.[6]

Although no fewer than fifty-nine British Army regiments were awarded the battle honour 'Sevastopol', in London – unlike in Paris – there is no grand boulevard of that name commemorating the siege of the city, the capture of which was the very object of the ill-fated Allied expedition to Crimea in the summer of 1854.[7] The resulting, first great struggle for that city remains a testament and tribute to the heroism and valour displayed on both sides, Russian and Allied alike. Its eventual fall in September 1855, however, was predominantly a French affair: a triumph that eclipsed, with some notable exceptions, the comparatively lacklustre performance of the British Army. Although the Royal Navy had not been able to reduce Sevastopol's forts, it had none the less done its traditional job of transporting and sustaining a British expeditionary force extraordinarily well. Despite the huge resources committed in both blood and treasure, the conflict with Russia was regarded in Britain as an unfortunate aberration. The British Army's generalship and systems of supply and medical support in Crimea had been found seriously wanting. Newspaper reports of failure, hardship and sickness fed a national outcry.

The campaign in Crimea became the object of a parliamentary inquiry. Under the energetic chairmanship of the Liberal MP, John Roebuck, a select committee sat nearly every day for four months in 1855.[8] Its report was bitterly critical of the former Prime Minister, Lord Aberdeen. His coalition administration had already fallen with the passing of a parliamentary motion on 26 January earlier that year: 'That a Select Committee be appointed to inquire into the condition of our Army before Sebastopol, and into the conduct of those Departments of the Government whose duty it has been to minister to the wants of that Army.'[9]

After the war's end, France, then but a temporary, expedient ally against Russia, returned to its historic role of being perceived as the main threat to Britain. With splendid irony, the nation's premier naval base of Portsmouth was protected at great expense from an envisaged French attack by a ring of new defences incorporating the lessons from the siege of Sevastopol. Impressive examples of these 'Palmerston's follies' remain today. Fort Nelson, for example, demonstrates well the state of mid-nineteenth-century fortification and armament, where engineers and artillerymen competed for military advantage.

The only shots of anger the British forts witnessed, however, were the air battles over Portsmouth during the Second World War. In the late 1850s, with memories of the Crimean War still fresh, the threat of being 'Sevastopoled' on the south coast of England appeared real enough to the British Prime Minister, Lord Palmerston, and to the British public. The threat arose from the introduction of steam power, which made a surprise dash across the Channel possible in a way undreamed of in the age of sail.

Whatever the associated martial endeavour and glory, the causes and consequences of war, whether political, economic or social, must never be ignored: the Crimean War is no exception to that rule. Russia, in particular, was profoundly affected by its outcome. Within five years of the war's end, Tsar Alexander II had abolished serfdom and implemented the far-reaching military reforms of his Minister of War, Dmitry Alekseyevich Milyutin, in his attempts to modernise Russia. For Sevastopol, the physical results of war were catastrophic. It took nearly two decades to rebuild the ruined city and to re-establish the demolished port and naval base. The defiant spirit of this 'city of sacrifice', as many Russians were to call it, never faded. The Russian blood shed there during the siege of 1854–55, and again during the Second World War, have immortalised the city in that nation's story.[10]

THE ROAD TO WAR

If there were ever a war that would appear to have started on the flimsiest of pretexts then the so-called Crimean War would be a prime candidate. Its causes had little directly to do with Crimea at all. The 'reason why' the war came about – as famously asked of the Charge of the Light Brigade – hardly seems credible.[11] Ostensibly, the origin of the conflict lay in an argument over control of the keys to the Church of the Nativity in Bethlehem between the Armenian, Orthodox and Roman Catholic clergies. The row over the Holy Places extended as to who had the right to rebuild the Church of the Holy Sepulchre in Jerusalem, and who should be allowed to 'restore' the Tomb of the Virgin at Gethsemane. In simple terms, France backed the Catholic position while Russia supported the Orthodox claim. The Ottoman Empire, although trying to keep its distance, soon found itself enmeshed in a ridiculous dispute between 'infidels' that reverberated throughout the late 1840s and into the early 1850s.[12] The discord and distrust between the Russian and Ottoman Empires was longstanding: following the war of 1686–1700, there had been no fewer than six further conflicts during the eighteenth and in the first half of the nineteenth century. The brief interlude of peaceful relations following the Treaty of Unkiar-Skelessi in 1833 was the exception to this norm. Indeed, it would require only a small spark to reignite the historic struggle between Russians and Turks for hegemony of the Black Sea region.

Beyond the religious dispute and the longstanding tensions between the participants, there was a much wider European context to the conflict. The profound and increasingly bitter disagreements between the Christian churches set the scene for equally acrimonious arguments between the leading European powers. They vied amongst each other for geostrategic and influential advantage in what became termed the 'Eastern Question', how to deal with (or to 'exploit' the weakness of, in most cases) the failing Ottoman Empire, the 'Sick Man of Europe'.[13] These 'big power' politics, which dominated the diplomatic manoeuvring, eventually brought Europe to a major war for the first time in forty years since the fall of Napoleon Bonaparte. Apart from the Sultan Abdul Mejid of the Ottoman Empire, who was supported by the British for fear of Russian expansion, the principal actors in this drama were Tsar Nicholas I of Russia and the new French Emperor, Napoleon III. The last of these schemed to break the 'Concert of Europe', a loose coalition of Austria, Prussia and Russia. These conservative, autocratic states strove to maintain the political status quo following the Congress of Vienna in 1815, which had imposed a victors' peace on France. Suppressing the threatening liberalism that had erupted in the 'Year of Revolutions' of 1848, the three states' shared imperative of maintaining royal power and stability had trumped popular calls for democracy.

France, or more accurately its leader, wished to reassert itself in the name of power and glory – and, if necessary, was willing to do so at the expense of others. Napoleon III, in the manner of his more illustrious namesake (his uncle), desired nothing less than to restore France's national grandeur and reputation as the leading European state. The now rapidly industrialising Britain, which had been allied with Prussia and Russia against France for much of the Napoleonic Wars, feared Moscow's expansion towards Persia, the Gulf and Afghanistan, and its clear attempts to undermine the Ottoman Empire.[14] Thus the two traditional enemies France and Britain became increasingly drawn to make common cause with the Ottoman Empire in resisting Russian territorial ambitions, and particularly her claims over the Danubian Principalities.

Russia made the first military move on 2 July 1853, declining a diplomatic solution to the crisis. An army of 50,000 troops breached the Ottoman frontier, invaded the Principalities and advanced as far as Bucharest. In response, the Porte produced a demand for the withdrawal of forces, known as the Turkish Ultimatum. Although this document purported to meet Russian concerns about the rights of Christians, Russia ignored it. A hectic round of diplomatic activity, already in progress in the Austrian capital in an attempt to solve the crisis, culminated in the 'Vienna Note', drafted by the Austrian Foreign Minister, Count Karl von Buol-Schauenstein, at the end of July 1853. Amongst its stipulations, it promised to honour the treaties of Kuchuk Kainardzhi (1774) and Adrianople (1829) with respect to previous agreements between Russia and the Ottoman Empire, including the protection of Christians in the latter. It further stated that the Sublime Porte would not make any adjustments to the settlement of the Holy Places 'without a previous understanding with the governments of Russia and of France'.[15] Russia accepted the Note; but as it appeared to be too pro-Russian in tone and object, it was summarily rejected by the Ottoman Empire. As a result, by the end of October 1853 these two empires were in a state of war. Turkish land forces were successful on the Danube front, pushing back the Russians. Their navy, however, suffered a catastrophic defeat on 30 November 1853, when Vice Admiral Nakhimov's squadron of the Black Sea Fleet trapped and destroyed a flotilla of Ottoman ships in the harbour of Sinope, a port on the northern Anatolian shore.

What, then, of France and Britain? In these two countries there was a sense of public outrage at the 'merciless' destruction of the Ottoman fleet, in which 3,000 Turkish sailors were either killed or wounded for minimal Russian loss. It provided the two allies with a final justification for declaring war on Russia in early 1854. At the end of March, the Earl of Clarendon, Secretary of State for Foreign Affairs, summed up the British war objectives as 'to check and to repel the unjust aggression of Russia ... and to secure a peace honourable to Turkey'.[16] The British government's strategic imperative was to block any Russian attempt to seize the capital of the Ottoman Empire, Constantinople, and so prevent the projection of Russian power into the Mediterranean and her influence beyond. Ever since the days of Catherine the Great and Prince Grigory Potemkin, Russia had held such objectives with a remarkable clarity of aim and consistency of purpose. Such an enduring policy was entirely transparent to Europe's leading powers.

Skipping over the frequently ignored yet strategically significant British naval campaign in the Baltic, which is well beyond the scope of this military history of Sevastopol, it is necessary to review British strategy-making prior to the deployment of the British and French fleets and armies to secure Constantinople and the surrounding area in the summer of 1854. The Black Sea port of Varna, the 'sea capital' of modern-day Bulgaria, was selected as the initial base for British and French forces. Options as to how offensive operations might be developed thereafter remained open. Since the beginning of 1854, however, professional naval advice had maintained that the Russian Black Sea Fleet, based in Sevastopol, had to be eliminated. The First Lord of the Admiralty, Sir James Graham, declared:

A war between Russia and England must necessarily assume a Naval Character: and the principal Theatre of such War may be considered as confined to the Euxine [Black Sea] and the Baltic. It is not in the power of England to strike a decisive blow to the heart of Russia in either of these seas. But Sebastopol is the key of the Black Sea: it is the Center of all Naval Operations within it: it lies to Windward and covers the Russian fleet with perfect security ... and while the Russians hold Sebastopol, the British Naval Supremacy in the Black Sea must be regarded as a temporary and unstable advantage.[17]

In a note to Clarendon on 1 March 1854, Graham developed his arguments for Sevastopol becoming the primary objective of Allied operations if Constantinople were ever to remain safe from Russian threat:

The Dardanelles must be secured; a position in front of Constantinople fortified covering both the city and the Bosphorus; but *the* operation which will be ever memorable and decisive, is the capture and destruction of Sebastopol. On this my heart is set: the eye tooth of the Bear must be drawn: and 'til his fleet and naval arsenal in the Black Sea are destroyed there is no safety for Constantinople, no security for the peace of Europe.[18]

Yet the Russian Bear would fight back, and fiercely oppose any Allied intervention. Significantly, Graham's copy of this letter was annotated '*delenda est Sevastopol*', recalling Cato the Elder's famous advocacy in the Roman Senate for the obliteration of Carthage above all else in the second century BC. A famous and typically contrarian Royal Engineer, Lieutenant General [later Field Marshal] Sir John Fox Burgoyne, now enters our story. Appointed as strategic advisor to the designated British commander, Lord Raglan, he considered (correctly, as it turned out) that Ottoman forces would be able to check any Russian offensive on the Danube. He proffered a stern warning about the risks of an expedition to the Crimea:

With regard to any attack on Sevastopol, it can have little strength as a fortress, and its fate will depend on the power of obtaining firm possession of the Crimea, an attack on which must be well considered before it is undertaken. No operation is of such doubtful issue as the landing in an enemy's country for the purpose of conquest. Modern, and British history in particular, is full of disastrous failures in the attempt, and those which have succeeded have been, generally, most hazardous.[19]

Although Burgoyne was to be proved wrong about Sevastopol's fortifications, which were to be reinforced vigorously by the Russians, his general counsel about the wisdom of any operation in Crimea was ignored with near-calamitous consequences. The British and French governments pressed for prompt military action. Specific direction came from the Duke of Newcastle, the British Secretary of State for War. Writing to Raglan on 28 June 1854, he stated that the British cabinet unanimously favoured an expedition to Sevastopol. At an Allied council of war held on 18 July 1854, both the French and British naval commanders – in common with Burgoyne's advice – urged strongly against an attack on the Crimean naval base.

Raglan and his French colleague, Marshal Achille Le Roy de St Arnaud, nevertheless overruled their subordinates for the lack of any competing alternative course of action. Hardly the product of profound strategic thinking, their decision was based on the political imperative (reflecting mounting public pressure) for a firm warlike measure whatever its chance of success and incalculable cost. Thus the die was cast for a landing on the Crimean shore. Raglan, however, retained his professional doubts. With remarkable candour, he had replied to Newcastle's directive:

> The descent on the Crimea is decided upon more in deference to the views of the British government than to any information in the possession of the naval and military authorities, either as to the extent of the enemy's forces, or to their state of preparation.[20]

There are uncanny parallels here in the British government's impatience for swift, bold action during the early stages of the Falklands War of 1982, and the associated decision to assault Goose Green on 28–29 May. Without a comprehensive plan of campaign other than to capture Sevastopol, the Allies would simply land on Russian territory at a convenient point, aiming to destroy the Black Sea Fleet and to demolish its supporting naval installations.

Within Raglan's army there were misgivings as to the wisdom of attacking Sevastopol. For example, Brigadier General William Tylden, Commanding Royal Engineers, on 10 August 1854 had perceptively pointed out to Lord Raglan the risks of insufficient forces being available for such an operation. 'It is an established fact ... in war', he argued, 'that a weak fortress, which from its extent or other causes, cannot be invested, is much more difficult, and takes longer time to capture than one of much greater artificial strength which can be invested'. Moreover, the time available for the operation was 'necessarily very short' as 'winter in this climate [begins] in November'. Tylden observed additionally that it was unlikely that the Russians would have neglected to reinforce Sevastopol's fortifications, as it was 'well known that many thousand men have been employed in adding to, and perfecting the land defences during the last two years'. Although

Tylden was largely mistaken in this latter regard, he warned ominously that the 'projected attack ... with our present resources at command ... is eminently hazardous, and will at best, require a longer time to effect, than the present advanced season will allow'.[21] Furthermore, the strategic questions of 'what next?', let alone 'to what overall end?', remained unanswered. These matters notwithstanding, practical operational considerations as to whether these objectives were viable, or if the Crimean peninsula as a whole should not be secured first, including the need to block the Russian lines of communication at Perekop and Kerch, had yet to be examined in any detail. Historians today are still divided over whether the original operational idea was anything more than a hasty 'grand raid' as opposed to a more protracted, deliberate plan of campaign.[22] The weight of evidence, on balance, points to the former interpretation.

As in the ill-fated Dardanelles campaign of the First World War some sixty-one years later, there proved to be a huge difference between political expectation and military achievement. Crimean weather and winter, and not least good luck, would come to the aid of the Russian defender in this instance. So neither the raid on Sevastopol nor the wider war with Russia would be over by Christmas. Confusion as to the mission and difficulties in its execution soon multiplied as the Allied troops went ashore. For all these challenges, however, the British and French forces possessed a number of technical and tactical advantages over their opponents that to some extent should have compensated for their lack of a coherent strategy. Steam-powered ships would assist the Allied fleets to attain and maintain maritime supremacy in the Black Sea, providing a secure line of communications and a steady flow of logistic support. On the battlefield, new rifle technology gave British and French infantrymen a significant edge over their Russian counterparts. As in most conflicts, moreover, the margin between success and failure proved slender. As ever, much would depend on the quality of the senior commanders' judgement and decision-making, and not least on the supporting, co-ordinating staff work, liaison and consultation. It was to be found wanting on both sides.

Unsurprisingly, popular British accounts of the Crimean campaign, whether contemporary or modern, tend to focus on the achievements and anguish of the British Army before Sevastopol. If insufficient emphasis is given to the French contribution – which quickly became predominant in the Allied cause – even less attention is given to the Russian perspective.[23] The Allied expedition on the Crimea is seen as a succession of heroic battles with the eventual fall of Sevastopol being regarded as a necessary consequence of superior force being brought to bear. It was an outcome marred by woeful inadequacies of military leadership and administration, characterised by the terrible suffering and sickness of the troops involved. In contrast, there is typically little analysis of the particular circumstances the Russian commanders faced, the choices open to them, the opportunities they either took or missed, and the fate of their valiant men who fought and died in great numbers defending their country.[24]

It was the Duke of Wellington who famously counselled 'guessing the other side of the hill'.[25] Within the inherent uncertainty of war, this superficially simple piece of guidance holds an enduring acumen. Wellington advised looking at a forthcoming battle from the enemy's perspective: analysing the ground and potential courses of action through *his* eyes – and not solely through your own. It is a therefore a great irony that the gallant Lord Raglan, who had served on the staff of the Iron Duke during the Peninsular War and had lost his right arm at his general's side at the battle of Waterloo, failed to follow Wellington's eminent dictum during the Crimean War. His stoicism about his wounding at Waterloo, as did his gentlemanly demeanour, commanded great respect throughout the army; his intellect and powers of command in the years to come impressed rather less. Sadly for the British, Raglan was no second Wellington, and his expeditionary force of 1854–55 was no Peninsular army. Still, when he succumbed to disease in Crimea, he was widely mourned by his troops.

Both Raglan and his French counterparts missed a series of 'openings' generated by the mistakes of the Russian high command. In so doing, the initiative not infrequently passed backed to the Russians. Furthermore, often the defenders of Sevastopol had an uncanny sense of anticipating Allied intentions and then undertaking sensible military measures to thwart their opponent's actions. While none of their achievements prevented eventual failure, the Russians made the Allies pay a high – if not inordinate – price in time, blood and treasure, whether in open battle or during the siege of the city. Although the Allies won the war, theirs was a Pyrrhic victory. Excepting Sevastopol, each of the four major battles of the campaign – Alma (20 September), Balaklava (25 October), Inkerman (5 November 1854) and Chernaya (16 August 1855) – took place on ground that the Russians had chosen, and when they were confident about the outcome. On each occasion, however, they failed to achieve their objectives. In turn, the Allies were unable to exploit their successes. The inability of either side to win a *decisive* battlefield victory condemned Sevastopol to endure a near yearlong gruesome siege – or a heroic, ultimately doomed, 'defence' from a Russian perspective.

Any army is only as good as its officers, whatever the quality of the men under command. In this respect it is useful to examine and contrast Russian and Allied generalship, and the background, purpose and results of the senior commanders' principal decisions. Between the strategy of war and the tactics employed on the battlefield lies the operational level, which provides the essential gearing between the two. Formerly described as 'grand tactics', outside specialist academia and the professional military elite, it remains a dimly understood element in the science of war. Although neither side used 'operational' terminology during the Crimean War, it provides a useful methodology in which to explore the planning, sequencing and outcomes of battle within an overall context of campaign. This is the essence of 'operational art', which we shall encounter later during the Second World War on both the Soviet and Axis sides in the battles for Sevastopol. It was, after all, the brilliant military theorist, Aleksandr Andreyevich Svechin (1878–1938), the 'Russian Clausewitz',[26] who succinctly described the links between the three levels of war in 1927: 'Tactics form the steps from which operational leaps are assembled: strategy points the path'.[27] This alluringly simple description remains valuable today.

During the Crimean War, in defending Crimea generally and Sevastopol specifically against Allied attack, the Russians faced a number of operational-level dilemmas; so too did their opponents hoping to seize the city. Examining these problems helps explain why Sevastopol was besieged for so long and at such great cost. Whether either side could have made the necessary 'operational leaps' to address these challenges in order to bring the campaign to a swift, successful conclusion depended as much on the quality of decision-making by the commanders and their staffs as on the ardour and skill of the fighting troops. Sadly, professional competence in command was found to be lacking on both sides throughout the war, and largely in equal measure. If, with the benefit of hindsight, there was a failing shared by the Russian and the Allied generals, it was an inability to imagine and plan the move after next, and so adeptly convert any tactical success scored into an operational one to best overall strategic effect. Equally, the quality of the associated staff work was poor, and particularly weak in both the British and Russian armies. Headquarters functioned inefficiently; orders often went missing, were unclear or arrived late – resulting in various combinations of confusion, misdirection and delay. The misguided charge of the Light Brigade at Balaklava was but one of many examples of ineptitude. Initially, both British and Russian administration and medical support were largely ineffective too. While the Russian Army possessed a general staff on the Prussian model, the British did not – and were not to institute one until 1905 following the set backs of the Boer War. At least the experience of the Crimean War prompted the creation of a British Army staff college in 1858.

The fundamental basic operational problem facing the Russian commander-in-chief (a joint commander of both naval and land forces) in the western Crimea, Prince Admiral Aleksandr Sergeyevich Menshikov, was *how* to resist the anticipated Allied invasion. Since the Russian Black Sea Fleet was in no position to engage the combined might of the modern British and French, partially steam-powered, navies, the Allies enjoyed command of the sea. Menshikov's more competent naval subordinates certainly appreciated this reality. So Russia's enemies held the strategic and operational initiative: they could determine the time and place of their invasion, subject to what might oppose them on land. Ideally, a defender in such circumstances would hold sufficient forces both to disrupt an opponent's landing operation and then to defeat him on, or near, the shoreline. Had Menshikov tried to defend all the possible landing sites along the Crimean shore, however, he would have spread his limited forces far too thinly. If, on the other hand, he had declined to offer battle on the coast, and allowed the Allies to establish a bridgehead unimpeded and to build up their forces, there was no guarantee that a Russian field army would have been strong enough to meet them in a pitched battle.

The second, and closely related, problem for Menshikov was how to safeguard Sevastopol. Was it best to conserve his forces for the defence of the city, or should he deploy the maximum number of troops available to engage the Allies in battle before they could advance on their objective? It was no secret that the capture of Sevastopol and the destruction of the Black Sea Fleet was their prime aim, for Allied intentions had been openly discussed in London, not least in the newspapers. Such was the lack of Allied operations security that the Russians were able to exploit readily this 'open-source' intelligence. 'We have no need of any spies', a Russian once declared, for 'we have *The Times*'.[28] In ideal circumstances, the Russians would have possessed sufficient numbers of troops both to guard Sevastopol adequately and to defeat the Allies in battle – if not during their landings – but certainly well before they were in a position to mount a hasty raid or to commence deliberate siege operations. The harsh reality, however, was that the Russians had inadequate forces. Menshikov, although parodied in one British history of the war for his 'fatuous and aimless behaviour' on account of his lamentable performance at the Alma, was not a complete fool.[29] In a report sent to St Petersburg on 20 June 1854 [OS], he accurately predicted that the Allies would land in the vicinity of the western Crimean port of Yevpatoriya, and then mount an attack on Sevastopol overland, approximately 100 kilometres by road and track to the south. Bearing in mind that in mid-summer 1854 Menshikov held only twenty-six battalions of infantry and thirty-six light guns, on 30 June [OS], he sensibly called for reinforcements.[30]

By the time fresh troops (principally the 16th Division from Odessa) arrived at the end of August, bringing up his strength to approximately 35,000 men, the Allies had yet to land. Menshikov mistakenly assumed that the imminent danger to Sevastopol had now passed. Only two days before the Allied invasion on 14 September 1854, for example, he wrote confidently: 'My suppositions have been completely borne out; the enemy could never dare to make a landing, and because of the present late season a descent [Russian: *desant*] is impossible'.[31] The

Russian commander-in-chief, however, had overlooked the political pressures on the Allied naval and army leaders that would force them to risk a landing on Crimea in the early autumn, despite the growing hazard of seasonal storms and the short time to campaign before the onset of winter. He was not alone in this miscalculation: the Tsar himself considered that any Allied invasion, if it were to come at all, would now take place in the spring. Unfortunately, time was not on the Russians' side.

Urgent repairs to existing forts and brand new structures were required to protect both the northern and southern 'sides' of Sevastopol. The old 'Star Fort' on the northern, for example, was found to be in state of disrepair. On the southern, progress in constructing a semi-circular ring of fortifications was slow, as was the supply of further reinforcements. Two Russian divisions placed on the march from Bessarabia (now Moldova) following the Allied landings on the Crimean shore in mid-September only arrived just in time to take part in the battle of Inkerman on 5 November 1854. The long march, with no railways available, must have been about 500 kilometres. Thus Menshikov would have to fight the forthcoming battle of the Alma on 20 September not as he might have liked, but as he must. Unfortunately for the Russian cause, however, he was singularly ill-equipped for this vital task by dint of lack of professional experience and personal disposition. Furthermore, Sevastopol, despite the limited reinforcements Menshikov received, and those deployed subsequently, was by no means secure. The outcome of this first battle in Crimea between Russia and the Allies would shape, yet not determine, the campaign to come.[32] Many critical moments would depend on the personalities and policies of the commanders, the fighting spirit and endurance of the combatants, and not least in the realm of friction, error and chance.

THE BATTLE OF THE ALMA

Land warfare, for all the developments in military technology and battlefield tactics over the centuries, is still hugely influenced by terrain, and by the operational factors of forces, time and space.[33] Menshikov, although sensing that the Allies might land in the vicinity of Yevpatoriya, could not be sure that they would not also attempt to come ashore elsewhere. Indeed, any first landing might prove to be either a feint or a supporting attack, rather than the main event. Allied forces might then converge either on the city of Simferopol, the peninsula's administrative centre, or, far more likely, on the naval base of Sevastopol, the declared Allied objective. So Russian troops had to perform four tasks: to defend Sevastopol; to guard the southern and eastern coasts, including the Kerch peninsula; to secure the supply routes across Crimea; and, finally, to oppose the anticipated main Allied landing on the western shore.

Together with the Black Sea Fleet based at Sevastopol, Russian land forces stationed on Crimea in the summer of 1854 consisted of three main groupings: the garrison of Sevastopol, which was soon to be reinforced by the crews and convicts of the fleet; the troops guarding the interior of Crimea and its lines of communication; and the formations of the field army. There was a complicated command structure for these, involving two separate commanders-in-chief and a number of senior naval and military subordinates who enjoyed considerable autonomy. Menshikov had no authority over General P. F. Khomutov, for example, who led about 12,000 troops in the eastern Crimea and the north-western Caucasus. Amongst the latter's responsibilities lay the protection of the vital, main supply route from the Sea of Azov to Sevastopol, via Kerch and Feodosiya. Within Menshikov's own command, there was a distinct lack of unity within his land and naval forces. While he commanded the Black Sea Fleet himself, in practice his chief of staff, Vice Admiral Kornilov, controlled this naval formation. Kornilov, as the governor of Sevastopol, also commanded the city's garrison. To complicate the chain of command, Kornilov was assisted by the deputy commander of the fleet, Vice Admiral Nakhimov (nominally his senior), and Menshikov by Lieutenant General F. F. von Moeller. Furthermore, the majority – but by no means all – of the troops available to take the field to fight the Allied invasion force were grouped within 6th Army Corps under General of Infantry Pyotr Dmitrievich [P. D.] Gorchakov. Of the three divisions in this corps, only two (the 16th, complete; and the 17th, less one regiment), commanded by Lieutenant Generals O. A. Kvintsinsky and V. Ia. Kiriakov respectively, were already present in the Crimea.

With so many 'chiefs', it is surprising that the Russian command system functioned at all – but at least the senior commanders enjoyed common bonds of language, tradition and patriotism. The same advantages could not be said for the Allied high command, which did not exist in any unified sense. This was a campaign planned and conducted by French and British army and naval leaders (and for members of the older generation, former enemies) acting in close concert, with the Turks, and later, the Piedmont–Sardinians, performing supporting roles. Campaigning by coalition committee rarely results in either a coherent plan or cohesive action. The inherent weakness of the Allied command structure, lacking an overall commander-in-chief with a supporting, combined staff, was soon evident when battle was joined. In the Crimean campaign, however, there were significant shortcomings in the command of forces on all sides. For the Russians, the first challenge was how to react when firm intelligence of an Allied invasion fleet was received. The quality of Menshikov's decision-making then and subsequently, for good or ill, would do much to determine the resulting campaign on the Russian side.

Amphibious operations, requiring the seamless synchronisation of armies and navies (and, later, air forces), are inherently complex, risky and prone to failure unless well planned, prepared and led. In the late eighteenth and early nineteenth centuries, for example, the British had a poor run of such operations. The failures of the British–Russian invasion of Holland in 1799 (despite some initial progress) and of the British Walcheren expedition (a complete disaster) a decade later, were pertinent reminders of the challenges involved. In the twentieth century, it would take the successes of the Sicily and Normandy campaigns of 1943 and 1944 respectively to remove the stigma of failure at Gallipoli in 1915.

Commanders can be simply surprised by events, or otherwise caught out by being at the wrong place and time: Menshikov was no exception. There is a parallel to the events of the Waterloo campaign of 1815, thirty-nine years before the Allied landing on the Crimean coast. Menshikov happened to be attending the Borodino Regimental ball in Sevastopol on the evening of 11 September 1854 when he first heard that the Allies were steaming towards Crimea. Unlike Wellington at the Duchess of Richmond's ball in Brussels, who subsequently rushed to the battlefield of Quatre Bras during the early hours of 16 June 1815, Menshikov remained surprisingly inactive. On 13 September 1854, the Allies raided Yevpatoriya and then, seizing their opportunity, captured the largely undefended town without a fight. It was only when news of this shocking event were announced in Sevastopol, allegedly interrupting an evening performance of Gogol's play [the] *Government Inspector* [Russian: *Revizor*], did the reality of impending war on Crimea sink home to all in the city.[34] The Allies' main landing was surely imminent; when, wondered many citizens, would they hear the sound of gunfire nearing their noble city?

At last Menshikov had to act, and to commit his army to battle. His forecast of a landing south of Yevpatoriya was confirmed when the Allies came ashore at Kalamita Bay on 14 September. He had failed, however, to make any adequate preparations for this eventuality, not wishing to commit any forces to the town's security. Decide he must immediately: in deploying his forces to meet the enemy, he had to determine where and how to make his stand. The Russian commander was sufficiently tactically aware to realise that it would be best to site any defensive position to take best advantage of any natural obstacles such as watercourses and ridges to enhance the fighting power of his troops. Between Yevpatoriya and Sevastopol four minor rivers run into the Black Sea: the Bulganek, Alma, Kacha and Belbek. Menshikov decided to fight behind the Alma, which lies approximately 25 kilometres north of Sevastopol.

Menshikov had the following forces at his disposal: the 16th Infantry Division with two brigades each of two regiments; the 17th Infantry Division with a brigade of two regiments and a brigade of one regiment only; a weak reserve brigade from 13th Division with two regiments each of two battalions (instead of the usual four apiece); a brigade from 14th Division with two regiments; three separate infantry battalions (one rifle and two naval); an engineer battalion; the 6th Cavalry Division with a hussar brigade; and two regiments of Don Cossack cavalry. In sum, he had forty-three infantry battalions, sixteen squadrons of light cavalry, eleven squadrons of Cossacks and 84 guns.[35]

The position Menshikov selected appeared to be sound (see Map 5). From his perspective, the left, sea flank, appeared secure with cliffs over 20 metres high rising up from the shore. Across the centre, to the north of the river Alma, the ground slopes gently down to the river, while to its south, the terrain is steeper, climbing up to a ridge that runs up west to east-southeast at elevations between 60 and 120 metres.[36] From this higher ground – open downland – the Russians could observe and dominate with artillery fire both the approaches and exits to the river. Their right, inland flank, however, benefited from no particular protecting terrain feature except its steep and broken slopes. Therefore it was vulnerable to being 'turned', although such a manoeuvre of envelopment could be observed unless carried out on a very wide arc. Two main routes crossed the Alma: the river was forded by a wagon track at the village of Alma Tamak (now named Peschanoye), 1.5 kilometres inland, and bridged 3.5 kilometres further upstream by the post road at Burlyuk. In British accounts of the battle, this road is described as the 'Causeway' and as being flanked on its eastern side by 'Kourgane Hill', and to its west by the 'Telegraph Height', a hillock on which stood an unfinished signal-tower.[37] Neither of these terrain features, moreover, is as prominent on the ground as the names might evoke on paper. The high ground to the south of the Alma resembles more of a plateau, gently sloping towards the sea, indented by an oblique depression up which the old post road climbed.

Menshikov's overall plan of campaign, let alone his design for battle at the Alma, is obscure, for no detailed records remain of any orders he may have given. Russian sources reveal his actions rather than his intentions. Other than deciding to let the Allies fight him on ground of his choosing, he appeared blissfully content in his self-assured assumption that a defensive battle on the Alma, successfully conducted, would be sufficient to defeat the Allies and cause them to abandon their expedition. Menshikov's confident claim to Nicholas I (discovered in a despatch seized after the battle) that the Russians could hold the Alma position for 'at least three weeks', betrays some contradiction in his thinking. Was his real purpose to *delay* the Allies' advance on Sevastopol, buying precious time for the strengthening of the city's defences, rather than to *defeat* his opponents? And if so, where and how would he next engage the Allies, at the city's edge or at some intermediate line such as the river Belbek to the Mackenzie Heights? Or could he draw the Allies even closer in towards Sevastopol Bay, and attack them on their exposed inland flank? We do not know the answers to these questions. We can only surmise that Menshikov – lacking the requisite military experience or training – was not clear in his own mind as to what he could realistically achieve with the limited forces at his disposal. Under his leadership, furthermore, the Russian Army was not one to conduct elaborate manoeuvres. It would fight and die at the Alma for 'God, Tsar and Motherland', confident of victory against the foreign aggressors. Whether it would succeed would depend not only on Menshikov's tactical dispositions before the battle, but also on his handling of his army, and, of course, on the plans and actions of the Allied forces. Back in Sevastopol, Kornilov confirmed in a diary entry the optimism the Russians felt: 'The [Alma] position selected by the prince is particularly strong and we are therefore quite content ... God does not abandon the righteous and we therefore await the outcome calmly and with patience'.[38] Such optimism by senior officers, and equally of their troops, in the ability of the Russian high command and their trust in the Lord, however, was sadly misjudged.

Menshikov, while carelessly discounting the threats to both his flanks, positioned the main weight of his force astride the post road from Yevpatoriya to Sevastopol, which he identified as the Allies' main axis of advance. Accordingly, he established his principal defensive positions on the northern, forward slopes of the Telegraph Height and Kourgane Hill, fortifying the latter with two redoubts, later named the 'Great' and 'Lesser' by the British. Although armed with twelve and nine cannon respectively, sited behind low breastworks, these were not formidable positions.[39] They were exposed, difficult to reinforce and vulnerable to flanking fire and manoeuvre. But if subjected to frontal attack, as they were in the ensuing battle, their Russian defenders could give a good account of themselves. Apart from the construction of the two redoubts, some sensible further preparations for battle had been made. Russian soldiers cleared some of the vineyards on the slopes down to the Alma river, opening up their observation of the battlefield and their fields of fire; artillerymen placed wooden poles near the Alma to give them their ranges. But much more could have been done within the time available. With secured flanks, a fully fortified Alma position would have offered excellent defensive potential. Various options for the deployment of these reserves could have been practised.[40] Such an approach, resting on sound generalship, would have represented a neat 'staff college' solution. Even so, the Russians were holding a solid piece of ground for defence; their troops were brave and hardy. The fundamental weaknesses in their deployment and in Menshikov's leadership had yet to be revealed. Hence the coming Allied victory at the Alma was by no means assured.

Menshikov deployed his army at the Alma as follows. On his extreme left rear, he positioned a battalion of the Minsk Regiment[41] near the coast in the vicinity of the village of Ulkul Akles, approximately 1,500 metres south of the Alma, believing that the Allies would not ascend easily the heights here and attack on this axis. A rough track leading up from the sea, used by the Tatars, was neither blocked nor covered by fire. The Russians' elementary failure here was not only the result of poor reconnaissance by a staff officer, but also the consequence of Menshikov's carelessness in not thoroughly familiarising himself with the forthcoming field of battle.[42] Equally surprisingly, only a lone infantry company was positioned forward in an old Tatar fort that overlooked the mouth of the Alma. Had this been turned into a strongpoint, and defended by sufficient, stalwart troops with artillery, this potential bastion could have greatly impeded an Allied attack, notwithstanding naval gunfire support. So the Russian left was very weakly guarded, a vulnerability that the French were quick to identify and exploit.

The Russians' main line of defence, overlooking the southern bank of the river, only started 2 kilometres inland a little to the east and south of the village of Alma Tamak. Here Menshikov positioned on an over-extended front four reserve battalions drawn from the Brest and Belostok Regiments of the 13th Infantry Division, with the Tarutin Regiment of the 17th Division held ready behind in a second echelon of defence. Further east, in the centre left of the Russian front, two further regiments of this division were deployed: the Borodino Regiment, supported by two batteries of field artillery, blocked the post road while the Moscow Regiment was positioned to its left rear. To the right of this force, the Kazan Regiment occupied the Great Redoubt, with the Vladimir and Uglitz Regiments positioned further up the slopes in second and third echelons respectively, with two Don Cossack field batteries in support. This strong grouping of twelve battalions (three-quarters of 16th Infantry Division) formed the main effort of the defence. On the extreme right of the front, the Suzdal Regiment (from the same division) manned the Lesser Redoubt, with two Don Cossack cavalry regiments held to the rear. Significantly, there was no tactical grouping dedicated to guard the Russian Army's right rear flank other than these forces and two naval battalions. Menshikov's general reserves, positioned 2 kilometres to the south of the Alma astride the post road, consisted of the Volyn Regiment and the remainder of the Minsk Regiment of the 14th Division (all together seven infantry battalions), a hussar brigade and a light horse battery.

Although the overall width of the Russian position at the Alma was approximately 10 kilometres, far less than this frontage was defended in any strength or depth. It is estimated that Menshikov positioned 13,000 men and 36 guns between the sea and Telegraph Height, with 20,000 men and eighty guns covering the post road and stationed on the slopes of Kourgane Hill. With the exception of the forces deployed on this latter, main feature, control of the army was confused in that the deployment of individual regiments did not always

149

match those of their parent formations. This arrangement led to difficult, if not confused, command and control during the battle.

On the morning of 14 September 1854, French and British forces began their landing on the western Crimean coast. No Russian troops were to be seen: only a few bemused Tatar peasant folk looked on. The Allies' chosen point of disembarkation was the unfortunately named Kalamita Bay, approximately 20 kilometres south of the port of Yevpatoriya and 60 kilometres north of Sevastopol. Although interrupted by bad weather, the well-organised French were soon established on land with supplies and tents. Their British compatriots did not fare so well: they slept wet and hungry under the stars. This initial setback did not augur well for the campaign: many bad practices of poor administration in the British Army were to persist for much of the war.

On 17 September, St Arnaud's personal physician and confidante, Dr Cabrol, caustically wrote in his journal: 'We are all ready to march, but the English, established on our left, have yet not disembarked their horses and their siege materiel; the Marshal has decided to place at their disposal all our means of disembarkation.'[43] The French commander, too, became increasingly becoming critical of his ally. Writing in a letter the same day, he complained that 'the English are still not ready, and they keep me here, waiting. I am furious! Finally their landing will end tonight, we have been finished since yesterday evening'. As for the future, St Arnaud declared: 'Tomorrow I will cross the Bulganech and on the 19th I hope to drub the Russians as we ought; I want to push on forward as quickly as possible'.[44] These were confident words of a man who was already very sick with cholera, and would barely outlive the coming battle.

The British, unfortunately but typically, were still not ready to march on the 18th. The absence of a proper field general staff and the lack of efficient 'battle procedure' – involving the execution of set drills including the timely passage of warning orders to generate concurrent activity at all levels – was to plague not only this battle, but also the campaign as a whole, severely reducing the tempo of decision-making and action. Only on the morning of 19 September, when the British were at last ready to move, could the Allies begin their grand advance to the south. Time waits for no soldier in war: every hour lost to the Allies in failing to exploit the unopposed landing was one gained commensurately by their opponents. Hence there was ample opportunity for the Russians to establish themselves on the Alma, to reconnoitre their positions fully, to construct mutually supporting positions and field defences, to practise their battle drills and to rehearse the deployment of reserves. Whether they would make best use of this 'gift horse' of time remained to be seen.

In hot sunshine the Allied march across the open steppe towards Sevastopol at long last commenced. With colours unfurled and bands playing, the French and the Turks stepped off on the right; the British on the left. This vast Allied formation of approximately 60,000 men was protected by an advance guard of the British Light Brigade, who also screened the left, inland, flank. The Allies were untroubled by enemy action until the afternoon. At the river Bulganek, a large mass of Russian cavalry – some twenty squadrons – suddenly appeared. What ensued was more a desultory skirmish than a chance battle of encounter. Neither side was able to engage effectively as the Russians promptly withdrew.

The Allied plan for the attack at Alma is mired in controversy and doubt. Most British accounts underplay the fact that St Arnaud had devised an elegant scheme of manoeuvre, one designed not only to defeat the Russians, but also to crush them. On the evening of 19 September 1854, the French commander-in-chief recorded his intentions as follows:

> The plan of the Battle of the Alma is this. The fleet should protect ... the right;
> General Bosquet will attack the enemy to turn his flank, who is far from expecting
> a surprise such as this. The three other [French] divisions will attack the centre,
> whilst the English, on the extreme left, will make a flanking movement to turn
> the enemy and converge, to fully envelope the enemy, who will be engaged in the
> centre on a cross-fire.... The arc of the circle, which is to be executed by the
> English, is very long but that also describes the Division of Bosquet.... the
> Cavalry will be provided by the English.[45]

However elegant in operational design, there were inherent flaws within this plan of a double envelopment, or pincer movement. It is a complex manoeuvre for any army to conduct: one that requires careful planning and demands tight control in execution. For an allied army, as yet untested in battle, with limited intelligence, scant knowledge of the terrain, poor communications and weak mutual understanding, it represented a tall order. Furthermore, would Raglan comprehend the plan; and even if he agreed it, would the British Army be capable of carrying out the role envisaged by St Arnaud? Before the coming battle, Burgoyne, a veteran of the Peninsular War, held some misgivings. In a letter of 18 September, he reflected: 'Our people are in good spirits at the facility of the landing, but we have a very strong country to force, and where the enemy by a little judgment, with a moderate army in strength comparatively with ours, may give us much trouble'.[46]

The record of the council of war between the two Allied commanders held at a post station on the Sevastopol road during the evening of 19 September 1854 is disputed. It would appear that Raglan neither agreed to, nor disagreed with, St Arnaud's proposals. More particularly, however, the British commander failed to inform his own subordinates precisely as to his intentions for the next day.

Without a detailed reconnaissance and hence knowledge of the Russian position, perhaps Raglan was wise to keep his options open. Furthermore, he knew the limitations of the troops under his command. Due to his lack of experience in handling an army in the field, matching Menshikov's weakness, he might have failed to grasp the full potential of St Arnaud's concept. In consequence, the Allies were to fight the battle without an agreed joint plan, merely fighting alongside each other: moreover, the British divisional commanders remained largely in the dark as to their tasks. Effective orders and tactical ingenuity during the battle were the exception. Captain James Brodie Pattullo of the 30th Regiment of Foot, for example, recorded after the battle:

> ... we deployed into line from the right of the whole English force ... & as each Regt deployed we advanced straight on the enemy's batteries & during the day we received no more instructions.... Our men behaved most gallantly & advanced in perfect parade order to the last moment.[47]

Such a brave but simple approach to the conduct of war was hardly a recipe for success: had Menshikov been more competent in handling his troops, then the outcome of the battle might have been far different.

Russian, French and British descriptions of the battle vary in certain respects. With a few exceptions, however, the armies' orders of battle are generally agreed. The Allies enjoyed a clear yet not an overwhelming numerical superiority of forces over the Russians in infantry of approximately one and a half to one, but were weaker relatively both in cavalry and artillery. The French army of 30,000 men consisted of four infantry divisions, with a Turkish contingent of 7,000 men in support. The 1st and 2nd Divisions, commanded by Generals Pierre Bosquet and François Certain de Canrobert respectively, comprised two brigades apiece, each of three regiments. The 3rd and 4th Divisions under Generals Prince Napoleon and Forey had five regiments each. Apart from a squadron of Spahis, which guarded St Arnaud and his headquarters, the French cavalry had yet to be transported to Crimea. The British under Lord Raglan fielded five infantry divisions, the 1st to the 4th and the 'Light', together with an incomplete cavalry division (commanded by Lord Lucan) including, at this stage only, the Light Brigade (Lord Cardigan). The British infantry divisions – with two brigades apiece – were much smaller than their French or Russian counterparts as all the brigades (except one) consisted of three battalions only.[48]

For the French, St Arnaud's bold scheme of manoeuvre depended on the right arm of envelopment turning the Russians' left (sea) flank. This crucial task was entrusted to Bosquet. When he had achieved this objective, Canrobert and Prince Napoleon were required to mount an attack against the centre left of the Russian position in the vicinity of the Telegraph Height, presumably *after* the British had engaged the Russians' right flank. This desired synchronisation was achieved neither in time nor space. Although St Arnaud did not request the British to attack the Russian centre right – its most heavily fortified and held sector – in a frontal assault, this is exactly what happened. Some accounts indicate that Raglan, when observing the ground on the morning of 20 September with his field glasses (conveniently mounted on a stock so he could use them one-handed), decided against enveloping the Russian position, fearing that it would both exhaust his troops and leave them open to enemy cavalry attack.[49] Furthermore, he had determined that he would attack *after* the French main assault rather than before. In any event, he did not appear to have communicated his intentions to the French who were to wait impatiently for their allies to advance.

According to French narratives of the battle, the timing of their initial assault had to be progressively put back from 0600 to 1200 hours on account of British indecision and delay. Carbol relates, for example, that 'the Marshal sent officer after officer to Lord Raglan' to enquire as to his intentions, but the reply came back, each time, that the British Army would not be ready to move for two hours.[50] As noon approached, St Arnaud could not afford to wait any longer so he ordered Bosquet to launch his attack near the coast. With supporting fire from the Allied fleet, by about 1300 hours, Bosquet's force – led by the nimble North African light infantry (the Zouaves) – crossed the Alma at its mouth and stormed the heights, the Russians having abandoned the Tatar fort without a fight. Bosquet's division, supported by Turkish infantry, and, crucially, by artillery, on reaching the plateau succeeded in turning the Russian position on the Alma.

Before this decisive stage in the battle, however, the Russians on the heights had observed with some astonishment the approaching mass of French, British and Turkish troops, in total about 60,000 men strong. Captain Hodasevich, serving in the Tarutin Regiment, recalled the unfolding scene:

> At 12 A.M. the whole of the allied armies were in full view, and a more magnificent sight man never saw than when, at the distance of about two cannon-shots from us, they began to deploy from marching columns. To the right, as we stood, went the red jackets, and I asked our Colonel who they were, and he informed me that they were the English. Upon hearing this many of the officers and most of the men expressed their regret that the English army was going to attack the right and centre. "It would be good fun to fight with them, as, though they may be good sailors, they must be bad soldiers; why, they would have had no chance with us on dry land!"[51]

Why the Russians were so scornful of the British soldiers' fighting qualities remains unexplained, for Britain and Russia had never gone to war on land before.[52] There were other Russians spectating, including a party of citizens of Sevastopol. Amongst their number were several of the finest ladies of the city, who had ridden out in their carriages to observe the coming battle, allegedly at the invitation of Menshikov. Stands had even been erected to improve their view. Interestingly, a similar event occurred seven years later at the battle of First Bull Run on 21 July 1861, the first major land engagement of the American Civil War. Many of Washington's civilian elite, expecting an easy Union victory, turned up to picnic and witness the unfolding action. As at the Alma, however, the sorely disappointed spectators had to flee the field in confusion and disarray.

Raglan deployed his army off the line of march into two assault echelons, each consisting of a pair of divisions in line, with the remainder of the infantry held back in reserve to the left rear (Sir George Cathcart's weaker 4th Division). Meanwhile, the Light Brigade of cavalry was required to protect the open, inland, flank. The first formations to attack were the Light Division (Sir George Brown) *left*; and the 2nd Division (Sir George de Lacy Evans) *right*. Behind them in a second echelon were the 1st Division (His Royal Highness the Duke of Cambridge) *left*; and the 3rd Division (Sir Richard England) *right*. The reputation of the British Army, in its first major engagement on European soil since Waterloo, now rested on the performance of the officers and men of the twenty-four infantry battalions in these four divisions. It would be a test not only of their steadiness under fire, but also of the manner in which they returned it – for this would be the first major action in which the troops would employ their new Minié rifled muskets.[53] In all, Raglan fielded 26,000 men and sixty guns.

The battle now turned into a series of piecemeal assaults on the Russian positions by French and British forces; the exact timings of these are disputed but the general sequence is as follows. Next to attack was the French 1st Division followed by the 2nd. Under heavy Russian artillery fire Canrobert's and Prince Napoleon's formations made slow progress advancing up the western flanks of Telegraph Height, having failed to establish their artillery in suitable positions either to provide covering fire for their own troops or to neutralise the guns of their opponents. The Russians also started to react, shifting infantry and artillery to block the French attacks on their left flank and centre left. In total, Menshikov ordered seven battalions of infantry, four squadrons of cavalry and four batteries of guns to meet this threat, thus committing almost his entire reserve.

Meanwhile, the British divisions, patiently awaiting orders to move off, remained immobile and exposed in their assault formations, albeit lying down, taking an increasing number of casualties from Russian artillery fire and hidden riflemen. The French desperately needed their ally to take up the fight, as their own attacks appeared to have run out of steam. Consequently, St Arnaud again sent messengers to Raglan urging him to advance. About 1500 hours, Raglan, perhaps more concerned for the plight of his own troops than the stalled French assault, finally ordered the 2nd and Light Divisions to attack – frontally over the Alma, the 2nd on axis astride Burlyuk and the Light directly towards the Great Redoubt. Then, in one of the most curious incidents of the day, Raglan, accompanied by his staff, crossed over the river just to the west of Burlyuk, moving up well in front of his own troops to a knoll where he could view the battlefield better. Utterly unperturbed by harassing enemy rifle and artillery fire, Raglan realised that the Russians holding Kourgane Hill could be enfiladed from this location. So he ordered a couple of field guns and a brigade of the 2nd Division to be brought up.

The Light Division, having advanced through the burning village of Burlyuk and taken considerable numbers of casualties from Russian sharpshooters and artillery fire on approaching the Alma, became fully disorganised in crossing the river. In consequence, the fine parade ground order of the division's attack was broken. Seizing this opportunity, the Russians began to advance down the slope of Kourgane Hill towards them. At this critical juncture, Major General William Codrington, commanding the 1st Brigade of the division, rallied his men, who charged up to the Great Redoubt more as a jumbled, cheering mob than as a drilled formation. A confused melée at bayonet point ensued in the entrenchments, and the Russians began to pull back their endangered guns. At this moment of crisis for the defenders, the Vladimir Regiment then mounted a spirited counter-attack to recapture the Great Redoubt. As the soldiers of Codrington's brigade were tumbled out by the Russians' ferocious charge, allegedly a mysterious bugle call prompted the British to cease firing. An unknown officer had ordered a withdrawal (rather incredibly, it is said that he mistook the advancing Russians for French), which then under Russian pressure turned into a rout.[54] So might have ended the battle as a worthy Russian victory, had not the 1st, 3rd and 4th British Divisions been ready to enter the fray while the Russians lost their nerve.

Events moved quickly. At about 1540 hours, two 9-pounder field gun teams from Turner's Battery had reached Raglan and their crews started to engage effectively the Russian artillery and infantry above on Kourgane Hill.[55] Around the same time, the 1st Division, in following up the Light, finally attacked with its two brigades in line. The Duke of Cambridge had hesitated, waiting in vain for a confirmatory order from Lord Raglan to advance. Only the intervention of an exasperated de Lacy Evans, who informed the Duke that Raglan had passed such an order (he had not), got the Guards Brigade finally advancing towards the Great Redoubt. To its left, under the personal initiative of Major General Sir Colin Campbell, who needed no further direction, the Highland Brigade was already making for the Lesser Redoubt and the Russian right flank. Exhorting his men forward, Campbell spoke:

Now, men, you are going into action. Remember this; whoever is wounded – I don't care what his rank is – whoever is wounded must lie where he falls till the bandsmen come to attend him ... Don't be in a hurry about firing, your officers will tell you when it is time to open fire. Be steady, keep silence, fire low. Now men, the army will watch us; make me proud of the Highland Brigade.[56]

Campbell, a veteran of the Peninsular War with a good eye for the ground and fingertip feel for battle, was probably the most proficient British general of the war. Able to act on his own initiative, he exercised 'mission command' to the full. His brigade would soon show what a well-trained and expertly led formation could achieve. Alone, it neatly performed the role that St Arnaud had intended for the mass of the British Army – turning the Russians' weakly defended right flank.

As the Highland Brigade manoeuvred, there followed an episode involving the Guards Brigade advancing and the remnants of Codrington's brigade rebounding from its debacle at the Great Redoubt, which brought out the worst and best of the British Army's performance in the battle of the Alma. Confusion and disorder were to be redeemed by cool leadership and tactical agility found within the Guards Brigade while exploiting new rifle technology. The Guards had attacked with three battalions in line – Grenadiers on the left, Scots Fusiliers in the centre, the Coldstream on the right. For some unexplained reason, the Scots, who had crossed the Alma before their neighbouring battalions, and without waiting for these units to conform, advanced and ran straight into the retreating elements of the Light Division. Out of this mighty collision, a good number of the Scots Fusiliers emerged to approach the Great Redoubt, only to be cut down by massed Russian musket fire. On the order to retire, the Scots Fusiliers withdrew to the riverbank to reorganise and played no further part in the battle, despite the entreaties of their surviving officers to resume the fight. The two other battalions, however, quickly restored the reputation of the Guards. Declining to conduct a bayonet charge, they relied on their firepower, pouring volley after volley from their Minié rifles into the massed ranks of Russian infantry. The intensity of their shooting was much enhanced by the Grenadiers, who adroitly bent in their line to fire into the Russians' flank, reminiscent of the 52nd Regiment's famous manoeuvre against Napoleon's Middle Guard at Waterloo.

To the Guards' right, riflemen of the 2nd Division joined in this action, engaging both Russian infantry and artillerymen at long range. As the battered Russians began to withdraw up the slopes of Kourgane Hill, the infantry of three British divisions, 1st, Light and 2nd, began a steady advance. Shooting then moving, their practised fire and manoeuvre outclassed their opponents. Meanwhile, on the far left, the Highlanders converged on the summit of the hill, blasting away at the Russian infantry, and closing in with the bayonet. By 1600 hours, as Kourgane Hill and the post road to Sevastopol were cleared, the Russian withdrawal, initially conducted in good order, turned into a panicked flight from the battlefield. It was all too evident that the Allies had prevailed. The power of the new Minié rifle, combined with some tactical common sense at battalion and brigade level, had redeemed many failures of British higher-level command. In contrast, the brave Russians lost their battlefield discipline as defeat beckoned.[57] Menshikov was lucky to escape the field without his army being completely destroyed around him.

Descriptions of the battle of the Alma usually conclude with a debate as to whether the British cavalry should have been unleashed to pursue the fleeing Russians, some of whom were acting 'like a flock of sheep without a shepherd', and whether an immediate advance on Sevastopol could have been mounted. Far less attention is paid as to why the Russians lost the battle. The first question is easily dealt with. The only cavalry formation available to the Allies was the Light Brigade, approximately 1,000 horsemen. As this force was insufficient to do anything more than harry the withdrawing Russians, it is unlikely it would have been able to turn the Russian retreat into a rout. It certainly would not have been able to threaten, let alone carry the city. Had it been immediately deployed towards Sevastopol following the battle, it would have become far detached from the Allies' forward divisions, still licking their wounds after a costly day's fighting. As a result, it would have run the risk of running into a superior Russian rearguard and being destroyed in turn. This was not an empty threat: the Russian cavalry and horse artillery, which had remained very largely uncommitted in the battle, could have engaged and potentially overwhelmed the Light Brigade. On this occasion Raglan's hesitation and caution in forbidding his ever-eager cavalry, much to their chagrin, to pursue the Russians served the British Army well. The Brigade was to prove but a one-shot weapon: its infamous moment in history would come soon enough at the battle of Balaklava, just over a month later.

The Allies were unable to mount a speedy advance towards Sevastopol on the late afternoon of 20 September 1854. The failure to exploit was not the matter of the French needing to pick up their packs left on the north bank of the Alma. Far more fundamental logistic and tactical constraints pertained, as did inadequacies of intelligence and command. Although the Allies had won a victory, which was to be much celebrated in London and Paris, they were not able to translate it quickly into a decisive outcome – the swift capture of Sevastopol and destruction of the Black Sea Fleet as intended. The battle had unfolded in a jumbled, disorganised way. In the planning of the attack, no thought appeared to have been given as to how any success achieved could be quickly exploited. No force was allocated this subsequent mission although the British 3rd and 4th Divisions had remained uncommitted throughout the battle. Their sole task on its conclusion was to bury the dead and to assist with the evacuation of the wounded.

It was one thing to break into and through the Russian defences at the Alma, but quite another to break out from them rapidly towards Sevastopol. The lack of good routes other than the sole firm post road compounded the problem. In simple terms of time and space, other than a sufficiently large force of pursuing cavalry, a suitably powerful force of at least one infantry division would have been hard pressed to catch up the retreating Russians, let alone cut them off. On the battlefield, tired troops had to be reorganised, resupplied and eventually fed. Apart from dealing with the dead and the wounded, prisoners of war had to be guarded and taken away under escort. Above all, there was a lack of transport and organisation. Without proper administrative staffs and troops, the majority of these tasks fell on the exhausted officers and men of the French and British units engaged in the battle. Those who had not fought that day assisted those who had as best they could. Perhaps after a well-earned night's reorganisation and rest, the next day would herald a triumphant advance towards Sevastopol. Yet it was not to be.

Why were the Russians defeated on what appeared to be such a strong defensive position? Hamley was in little doubt, giving full credit to the Allies: 'The Russian general did not overrate the strength of his position; his mistake was in his estimate of the troops who were to assail it.'[58] There was surely more to the Russian defeat, however: one of poor generalship. To his credit, Menshikov's devotion to duty and steadiness under fire were not in dispute. When Allied artillery rounds hit four officers of his escort party riding next to him, he 'remained unmoved', according to Hodasevich. In his account of the battle, the Pole acknowledged that the Russian commander-in-chief 'showed a great deal of personal courage', but added that this attribute was 'not the only quality required' in such a leader.[59] Indeed, the reasons for the Russians' failure at the Alma were many: most resulted from Menshikov's poor decision-making both prior to and during the battle. Hodasevich offered two main reasons for the defeat. First, 'the troops were badly disposed upon the position'; and secondly, 'during the action nobody gave any directions what to do, and everyone acted as he thought fit'.[60] These are grave charges against the Russian command and its formations. Modern Russian military historical research confirms and amplifies Hodasevich's contemporary analysis.

According to the Crimean military historian Sergey Chennyk, there were no fewer than eight components of the Russian defeat: most of them he attributes to Menshikov. The Russian commander-in-chief (and this applies surely as well for the bulk of the Russian officer corps) underestimated the tactical and technical superiority of the Allies.[61] The French showed they were capable of manoeuvring well, while the British were particularly accomplished in bringing the firepower of their new rifled muskets to bear. Conversely, the Russians were poor at manoeuvring on the battlefield, and failed to concentrate their fire, whether artillery or small arms. Too much reliance was placed on the stoicism and staying power of the Russian infantry and their ability to conduct close combat. Other than employing crude bayonet-charges, their tactics were both unsophisticated and unimaginative. Chennyk condemns the Russian generals for exhibiting 'complete tactical ignorance'.[62] Hodasevich gives a graphic example of this lack of professional expertise. He describes the attack of the Vladimir Regiment, which charged with the bayonet British troops without any 'assistance from artillery, though there were still two batteries in reserve that had not fired a shot'. 'This proves', he stresses, 'that our Generals had a very poor notion of military tactics, for to send a regiment to the charge without previously having weakened the enemy by artillery is contrary to all rule'.[63]

It is clear that the Russian commander-in-chief staked far too much on the inaccessibility of his left flank, and in consequence took completely inadequate measures to defend it. Neither he nor his staff had reconnoitred the ground properly: therefore this critical vulnerability in the Russian dispositions was a completely unnecessary 'own goal'. The Russian left centre was also dangerously weak. The over-extended, poorly trained and badly led reserve battalions of the Belostok and Brest Regiments – deployed closest to the river Alma – were threatened from the beginning of the battle. When forced to retreat following determined Allied infantry attacks, their retirement adversely influenced the behaviour of other units. Hodasevich also stressed this psychological factor. He observed that 'the battalions of reserve began to retreat without orders; our battalion [a unit of the Tarutin Regiment] also began to retire, following [their] example'.[64]

The powerful Russian cavalry was a passive observer throughout the battle, as was its much weaker British counterpart. There was an opportunity for the Russian cavalry to turn and attack the British left (eastern) flank but no orders for such a manoeuvre were given either before or during the battle. Furthermore, it would appear that Menshikov and his staff completely ignored administrative and logistical matters. Troops were not resupplied with ammunition and official medical cover was almost non-existent, except for a few regimental doctors and a Russian woman from Sevastopol called Darya, who tended and recovered the wounded on her own initiative. Menshikov's principal failing, however, was that he assumed that the Allies would mount a frontal attack on his position, and all that he and his troops needed to do was to stand their ground. From the evidence available, it seems certain that he had developed no overall concept or scheme of manoeuvre for the battle, and, even if he had, he neglected to communicate his intentions to his subordinates. In sum, the Russian commander's over-confidence, based on holding a good, but by no means solid, over-extended defensive position, exacerbated by his inability to direct purposefully his forces during battle, proved his and his army's undoing. As Chennyk has simply put it, 'Menshikov confused everyone, but most of all he confused himself'.[65]

Subsequent events proved that neither side's commanders exercised a monopoly of hubris or aptitude. The battle of the Alma on 20 September 1854 was a bitterly contested affair: French tactical prowess on the right, shore-side, flank was complemented by British bulldog bravery and musketry in the centre and inland left. The deadly effectiveness of the British and French modern Minié rifles in combat became all too apparent against an enemy still largely armed with smoothbore muskets. The significance of the Allies' superiority in small arms was clear enough to the Russians. Eduard Todleben, for one, noted:

> The sharpshooting of the English caused our troops terrible losses, and, above all, did great mischief to the two light batteries placed in front of the Borodino Regiment on the left of the high road [to Sevastopol]. The situation of these batteries became more difficult still, when after some time, two English guns succeeded in crossing the Alma by the fords below [Burlyuk], and, having ascended a rise of the hill, got into position, and took our two batteries in enfilade. A hail of rifle-balls committed great ravages among the gunners of the artillery, and among the columns of the Regiment of Borodino ...[66]

The Allied victory, however, was neither expertly nor cheaply won. Pattullo summed up the engagement in a revealing letter to his mother, written a couple of days after the battle:

> I hope this may reach you before the official Despatches & assure you of my perfect safety. We have had an action with the enemy & signally defeated them, but I am sorry to say that our loss has been very great.... We (the actors in this horrid business, for I can call it nothing else though a victory) think that there was a great want of generalship & much loss of life in consequence.[67]

With a few exceptions, such as Campbell's Highlanders, British battle drills were lacking and command from Raglan downwards was confused. Casualties had been heavy, particularly within the Fusilier Brigade of the Light Division and within the Guards Brigade of the 1st Division. Yet, for the loss of just over 3,000 men killed, wounded and missing, the Allies had inflicted nearly 7,000 casualties on their Russian opponents.[68]

The Allies, however, made no effort to pursue their weakened foes to Sevastopol, let alone attempt to seize a virtually open city off the line of march in the days following their victory at the river Alma. While an immediate follow-up towards the city during the afternoon of 20 September was impracticable, there was nothing to stop an attempt being made after a short operational pause (perhaps of 24–48 hours) after the battle. The Allies had triumphed in combat but failed conspicuously thereafter to exploit their success. As we have seen, many factors were involved, including an over-estimation of the Russians' ability to fight again in front of the city, the lack of available cavalry, and not least the fatigue of the Allied troops after a hard-fought battle save, of course, the elements that had not been committed. The prime reason, however, was a failure of generalship exacerbated by poor intelligence. A combination of Marshal St Arnaud's worsening illness and Lord Raglan's inability to force a decision stymied any bold advance on Sevastopol, gifting their Russian opponents a welcome opportunity to recover.

ALMA: THE AFTERMATH

While doubt and hesitation prevailed within the Allied command following the battle at the Alma, the Russians had not been idle in Sevastopol. Under the energetic direction of Kornilov, and supervised by Todleben, a combined force of garrison troops, marines, sailors, convicts, workmen and ordinary townsfolk had worked tirelessly night and day since 13 September to extend and reinforce Sevastopol's incomplete defences. During the course of 20 September, the outcome of the battle was eagerly awaited. All hoped that the invaders would be defeated and that the city would be spared an onslaught. When Menshikov rode back into the city late that evening, the painful news of the Russian debacle spread fast. Then disorganised columns of sailors, soldiers, stragglers and the wounded streamed back into the city reinforcing the grim reality of the situation. Of the latter, Hodasevich recalled, 'these unfortunate men arrived in the town, for the most part with their wounds undressed. Few of them were lucky enough to ride, but [the remainder] dragged their mutilated limbs in the greatest agony on foot'. While the city had been organised for defence, nothing had been done to prepare for treating the casualties of war. Over the next day, 'these poor remnants of humanity' continued to arrive.[69] Many more would die in the weeks and months to come.

In Sevastopol, members of the fleet, garrison and residents alike expected the Allies to arrive before the city at daylight on the 21st: a heavy bombardment from land and sea would surely swiftly follow. The Russian commanders now debated what could best be done, fearing the worst. Menshikov, who had seemed paralysed by indecision at the Alma, was now galvanised by events into giving some sensible direction. He determined that it would be futile to attempt to hold the Allies at either the Kacha or Belbek rivers; nor would he attempt to mount a last-ditch defence on the northern side of Sevastopol. As for the fleet in the harbour, he ordered that a number of old men-of-war be scuttled to block the entrance of the roadstead, so denying the Allied warships an opportunity to bombard Sevastopol at short range. Kornilov violently disagreed with his superior's command, believing that the fleet should be put to sea and then closely engage the enemy, evoking the aggressive fighting spirit of Admiral Ushakov. Concealing the direction he had just received from the commander-in-chief, Kornilov convened a naval council of war on the morning of 21 September to outline his plan. His subordinates, however, did not support him: one of them, Captain Zorin, proposed a similar idea to Menshikov in that part of the fleet be sunk and ships' crews should man their cannon on Sevastopol's land defences. Kornilov ignored this advice as well as Menshikov's orders until later in the afternoon of the 22nd, when forced by Menshikov to resign or to obey. Eventually, the order was given for seven vessels – five ships of the line and two frigates – to be sunk on a line between Forts Constantine and Alexander.[70] Unsurprisingly, neither the ships' captains nor their crews welcomed this most drastic decision. Todleben poignantly recorded the Russians' reaction:

> Tears, till then restrained, ran down the bronzed cheeks of our brave sailors. It was thus that the excellent and celebrated road of Sevastopol was transformed for a time into a sterile lake, and the sailors of the Black Sea Fleet forced to abandon their original destination [of battle at sea], engaged in a conflict altogether novel to them, in a military life on shore.[71]

By the morning of 23 September 1854 all the warships less *The Three Bishops* were resting on their bottoms. This sturdy three-decker had to be despatched by gunfire during the early afternoon.

In Sevastopol's harbour, lying just off shore on the southern side of the bay stands perhaps the city's most inspected and photographed tourist attraction. It is the monument to the scuttled ships, consisting of a bronze eagle perched on top of a Corinthian column. Erected in 1904 to mark the fiftieth anniversary of the first defence of the city, it has become an emblem of Sevastopol. Whether the Russian ships should have been sunk remains a matter of debate. As previously indicated, the combined Allied fleet enjoyed an overwhelming quantitative and qualitative superiority over the Russian Navy. The British and French had eighty-nine warships, of which fifty were steam-powered and screw-propelled. In contrast, the Black Sea Fleet could only muster forty-five vessels, of which eleven were paddle steamers.[72] Hence the chances for the Russians to prevail against their enemies at sea were low, to say the least. On the other hand, as events during the first bombardment on 17 October 1854 would show, the Russian coastal defence batteries were able to inflict significant damage on the Allied ships, and hence would probably have prevented any significant incursion into Sevastopol's harbour. Thus there might not have been an imperative to scuttle the Russian ships in the first place. Such a view, however, rests on hindsight and ignores the fact that the released crews and guns provided a very valuable – if not vital – augmentation to Sevastopol's land defences. On balance, therefore, it would appear that Menshikov's decision in this instance was correct. Kornilov, for all his valiant actions in the defence of Sevastopol, perhaps had allowed his personal pride for his Service to triumph over professional judgement.

Notwithstanding Menshikov's direction over the ships, his next decision over the fate of his army reflects the very challenging dilemma he continued to face. Should he concentrate all his efforts on defending Sevastopol, so securing the fleet and its base, or should he move his field force away from the city so that it could threaten the Allies and protect his lines of communication and supply? Could he risk dividing his force to meet both tasks? He knew that powerful Russian reinforcements were on the march so it was vital for him to hold Sevastopol and to secure at least one route to the city. His operational intelligence was good enough to tell him that the Allies were only making a slow advance towards Sevastopol. Thus there appeared to be a window of opportunity for him to extract his army from the city before the British and French closed up and commenced siege operations. Not unreasonably, Kornilov protested, pointing out the severe risks if the garrison and the fleet were forced to defend Sevastopol unaided. Menshikov argued, however, that the enemy 'would not undertake an attack of any vigour, even on the *Servernaya* [the northern side], if it had an army on its flank and rear'.[73]

There might also have been personal factors that impinged on Menshikov's decision. After the defeat at the Alma, military order and discipline had broken down in Sevastopol: the general atmosphere was febrile and mutiny was in the air. 'On the morning of the 21st', narrated Hodasevich, 'a perfect chaos reigned throughout the town; drunken sailors wandered riotously about the streets'. More unnerving perhaps were the calls that 'Menshikov had sold the place to the English, and that he had purposely been beaten at the Alma, where he had caused confusion by giving no directions during the battle'. No commander-in-chief would wish to be called a traitor, and Menshikov lacked the self-assurance and stature to show himself amongst the troops and the townsfolk. According to Hodasevich, in stark contrast, Kornilov 'alone endeavoured to restore order and confidence among the inhabitants'.[74] The situation called for urgent measures: bars and taverns were closed, and all stocks of alcohol were ordered to be destroyed. Albert Seaton has postulated that Menshikov might have reasoned that 'military discipline could only be restored by removing the Russian soldier from shelter and inactivity and making him march in the presence of the enemy.'[75] This argument, however, may overstate the case, as there was no lack of work to be done. All soldiers, sailors, convicts and civilian inhabitants were being formed into parties to build up the city's defences, and were to toil thereafter 'like ants'.

Menshikov left no written record of his decisions. Nor did he explain the rationale for them either to his staff or his subordinates, none of whom he appeared to trust. In any event, the Russian commander-in-chief ordered the bulk of the field army to vacate the city on the night of 24/25 September 1854. This was a calculated risk rather than a gamble because Russian outposts had observed at sunset that the Allies were still camped in the Belbek valley; their fires continued to glow through the night. Other than that, Russian intelligence as to Allied dispositions and likely intentions was extremely patchy. The Russian force consisted of an advance guard of 13,000 troops, followed by the main body of 6th Corps under Gorchakov with Kiriakov's 17th Division in the lead. The troops marched eastwards out of Sevastopol, crossed the river Chernaya near Inkerman and then moved up on to the Mackenzie Heights to join the Bakhchisaray road. Hodasevich's regiment took part on a hazardous night march through difficult terrain. He described its perils as his men approached Mackenzie's Farm: 'Here the road is narrow, with a precipice on one side; and, as the night was dark, several men fell over and were dashed to pieces'.[76]

Who was left to defend Sevastopol? With the vast bulk of the field army gone, apart from the fleet and its crews, only a motley collection of Russian Army units remained in the city. These comprised four reserve battalions of the 13th Division that had 'suffered considerably at the Alma', together with 'four depot battalions of the same division' and a battalion of the Tarutin Regiment.[77] In addition to this list given by Hodasevich, it seems likely that the two marine infantry battalions and an engineer battalion that had been deployed to, and returned from, the Alma remained in Sevastopol. In total, most accounts indicate about 6,000 men bearing arms. The Russian defences immediately after the Alma remained weak. On the northern side, the fortifications, including the crumbling Star Fort, were initially manned only by a reserve battalion, a company of engineers and an 'ill-armed and disorganized body of sailors'.[78] This sector was in fact far more exposed to attack than the defences on the southern side of Sevastopol Bay, protecting the military harbour and the city. Amazingly, this critical vulnerability remained unknown to the Allies. Such a lack of intelligence is remarkable bearing in mind the capture of the Star Fort had played such a prominent part in Allied planning prior to the landings on the Crimean shore. Confusion and disagreement as to both object and method now plagued Allied considerations and decision-making after the Alma. The results would shape the outcome of the campaign in Crimea and the wider war. Paradoxically, the ensuing prolonged siege (from October 1854 to September 1855) of Sevastopol – which was never the Allies' intended plan – resulted in weakening Russia far more than the grand raid originally conceived. By accident, rather than by design, therefore, the Allies pursued a course of action that would bleed their enemy white, albeit at great cost to themselves. Superficially it might appear that the battle for Sevastopol serves as an example of strategic attrition triumphing over operational manoeuvre, yet these aspects of war complement each other.

CHAPTER 5

THE FIRST DEFENCE OF SEVASTOPOL

'Uphold Sevastopol!'

Last words of Vice Admiral V. A. Kornilov

BURGOYNE AND THE ALLIES' FATEFUL FLANK MARCH

The decision not to advance directly on Sevastopol after the victory at the Alma was hotly disputed within the Allied command at the time, and remains a moot point of historical debate. According to the original intention set out by Graham, First Lord of the Admiralty, British and French forces should have mounted a *coup de main* to seize the city, destroy its naval installations and sink the ships of the Black Sea Fleet.[1] Implicit within this plan was the capture of the Star Fort on the northern shore, seen as the key to unlocking Sevastopol's defences. As originally conceived, this operation had more the nature of a 'grand raid' rather than an extended campaign on the Crimea.[2] It reflected the reality that the Allies only possessed limited time and resources to achieve their objective at Sevastopol before the arrival of significant Russian reinforcements and the onset of winter. Abandoning the *coup de main*, an operational approach that rested on speed and boldness, and one which should have exploited the confusion and disorder in the Russian Army immediately following the Alma, risked changing both the course and duration of the operation into a protracted campaign. Although a *coup de main* represented, as the naval historian Andrew Lambert has perceptively observed, 'the only viable method of attempting Sevastopol with the available forces', Burgoyne never had any faith in such a scheme. In so far that the Allies never captured the whole of Sevastopol, notwithstanding a siege of 349 days, Lambert's conclusion that the 'clash of [Burgoyne's] plans with the grand raid ensured the failure of both' is surely correct.[3]

On the morning of 21 September 1854, Raglan was minded to press ahead with the original plan and to assault Sevastopol as quickly as possible from the north (see Map 6). According to Woodham-Smith, however, the 'French had doubts ... the fortifications would prove too strong'.[4] This view is based on Kinglake, who pins much of the failure of the Allies to retain their original plan on the unfortunate St Arnaud. He narrates that the French commander-in-chief had declined to move forward from the Alma battlefield because his troops needed time to rest and reorganise; and that he feared that the Russians would make a determined stand at the Belbek river, and that the French could not 'afford the loss that would be entailed'.[5] This British account would suggest that the dying French commander-in-chief had become unduly cautious, in effect making him the scapegoat for the failure to seize Sevastopol off the line of march. Such an interpretation, moreover, suppresses the fact that it was none other than an impatient St Arnaud who had exhorted the sluggish British to move off the beaches at Kalamita Bay and to advance swiftly towards Sevastopol, as he was to urge again after the Alma.[6] Moreover, it was St Arnaud who had proposed a bold scheme of manoeuvre to destroy the Russian Army at the Alma, one that Raglan had undermined through his habitual insouciance, if not indecision in command. Although experienced in war, Raglan had never led a formation, let alone an army, in the field. The British commander also harboured doubts as to the wisdom of attacking Sevastopol from the north. Kinglake suggests that Raglan had been influenced by Oliphant's description of the poor state of the defences on the southern side.[7] If so, this may have made Raglan more amenable to a change of plan.

A failure of accurate and timely intelligence led the Allied commanders to pay far too much attention to dubious reports (allegedly from Tatar informers) that the northern shore was better protected than the southern one.[8] Surprisingly, there is little evidence of any confirmatory reconnaissance being conducted to confirm the facts of the matter. Meanwhile, on 21 September Todleben and his motley force of soldiers, sailors and townsfolk were hard at work in improving Sevastopol's defences. The Allied decision not to attack Sevastopol from the north, however, was heavily influenced, if not determined, by the advice of Burgoyne to both Raglan and St Arnaud. While the latter may have had his doubts, the French as a whole were not to blame. The father of the ensuing 'flank march' to Balaklava was none other than the grand old Royal Engineer, Raglan's *de facto* strategic advisor. Its adoption meant the abandonment of the *coup de main* and its conversion into a deliberate siege operation.[9] Burgoyne's persuasive role in this matter cannot be over-stated: equally, the consequences of the change of plan were to have a profound impact on the campaign, condemning the Allies to a bitter, costly and protracted struggle for Sevastopol. After the conflict, he was not to escape criticism for his persuasive advice. Kinglake, while acknowledging Burgoyne's long record of meritorious military service, stated that 'he was liable perhaps to be drawn into error by the cogency of his own arguments'. Furthermore, in observing 'it was in the nature of things that the judgment of a man deeply versed in the business of sieges should be more or less warped by his science', Kinglake perhaps verged on the unfair.[10]

Notwithstanding Kinglake's critique, Burgoyne's rationale is worth examining in detail as it displays the operational logic and strategic weakness that underpinned the remainder of the campaign on the Allied side. In a written memorandum composed during the morning of 21 September 1854 at the Alma camp, he offered five reasons for a move to the south of Sevastopol as opposed to attacking the Star (North) Fort on the northern side, together with one piece of reassurance about his proposed course of action.[11] First, echoing the perceived wisdom, he surmised that the defences to the south were weaker and 'would probably be forced rapidly'; secondly, as 'the advance is from the north', he presumed, 'our attack will rather be expected on that side'. Thirdly, even if the northern side were to be taken, 'although it will open the shipping, dockyard etc. to cannonading, it does not insure the entire possession of the important establishments until after a second operation, which may still require us to move round to the south'. Burgoyne's fourth reason for such a manoeuvre rested on securing the ground 'between the sea at Balaklava and along the valley of the Tchernaya'. This point was linked to his final and most important consideration – that of 'communication with the fleet, which is, in fact, our base of operations'. This connection would be best effected by gaining 'the small harbour of Balaklava and the bays near Cape Chersonese [rather] than on the open coast to the north'. As to the risk in 'exposing the communications of the army to [being] cut off', Burgoyne countered this problem by stating that the 'idea is to abandon the communication from the north altogether and establish a new one to the shipping in the south, which would be moved around for that purpose'.[12]

It would appear that Burgoyne had for some time pondered the requirement for a long siege, and the associated need to prepare for one by securing the best ground and base of operations from which to prosecute it. Within his correspondence there is confirmation that the idea of attacking Sevastopol on its southern side had been taking shape well before the Allies had even landed on

Crimea. There is evidence too that that the Royal Engineers had begun the necessary preparations for a siege by collecting materials such as timber in the area of Varna prior to shipping them to Crimea.[13] On 29 August 1854, Burgoyne had written: 'an attack on Sebastopol at the present time must be considered a most desperate undertaking'.[14] But assuming that such an operation would be carried out, he considered that 'a prodigious advantage will be gained by obtaining the use of the little harbour of Balaklava, and perhaps one of the bays round Cape Chersonese, for landing siege trains and stores to far more advantage than on the open beach on the north'. Just as crucially, he opined, 'from [the southern side], it is also not improbable that sites may be obtained for batteries, from whence, at long ranges, the enemy's ships, in their men-of-war harbour and the docks, may be most seriously injured'. 'On every account', he concluded, 'it would seem to be advisable to push across to that side, if possible, instead of stopping on the north to besiege Fort Constantine'.[15] Although we do not know to whom, if anyone, Burgoyne circulated this memorandum, none the less it is clear that his proposal for the flank march was formulated *before* the battle of the Alma, rather than in its immediate aftermath.

The official history of the Royal Engineers states that 'Lord Raglan saw the soundness of the arguments and the value of [Burgoyne's] advice [of 21 September], but was anxious that Marshal St Arnaud should give his opinion on it before he would commit himself'.[16] Although the French Marshal concurred with Burgoyne, members of both the French and British staffs disagreed, reminding their respective commanders-in-chief that the 'general scheme of the campaign was a sudden landing, a pitched battle, and following that, if successful, a *coup de main* to seize the fortress'.[17] They saw the dangers of abandoning the concept of a grand raid in favour of longer campaign.[18] Kinglake takes a subtly different view in suggesting that St Arnaud's criticism was primarily against attempting to assault the Star Fort off the line of march rather than by formal siege. His concern was 'treated as negativing all further idea of attacking Sebastopol from the north'.[19] If this interpretation of events is correct, then the Allied commanders-in-chief took their decision to abandon their original plan of a grand raid by default. The potential consequences, however, were not lost on those present. Sir Edmund Lyons is recorded as stating that Burgoyne's proposal represented 'strategy, but we are in no condition for a strategical operation. We came here for a *coup de main*, but this is strategy'.[20]

Strategy today may be defined as 'a course of action that integrates ends, ways and means to meet policy objectives'.[21] By this terminology, the Allies in September 1854 possessed neither the ways nor the necessary means to conduct a long siege, let alone one undertaken so late in the year. Thus the adopted operational approach (essentially Burgoyne's plan) was fundamentally unsound unless the Allies received very soon major reinforcements of men and materiel. As these were not yet readily available, they could not be counted on in the planning. At the time, however, the Allies presumed Sevastopol would fall following a short bombardment; hence they were not overly concerned about the time constraints on their action. After the victory at the Alma, misplaced optimism infected the troops. Writing home on 28 September, James Pattullo trusted 'that a few days will settle the whole business and my next [letter] may be from Sebastopol'.[22]

Burgoyne's argumentation presumed that a concentric attack on the city was not possible. This assessment was mirrored in other contemporary sources, including that offered by Captain H. C. Elphinstone, who wrote the first part of the narrative of operations conducted by the Royal Engineers in the campaign. He maintained that the separation of the two sides of Sevastopol Bay was 'so complete, that a force investing the one side would find it impossible to render ready assistance to a force besieging the other'; and further, that 'a capture of either side by no means necessitated the fall of the other'.[23] Raglan and St Arnaud, however, had been under considerable political pressure to mount the expedition to Crimea as soon as possible, an operation that assumed no more than a swift *coup de main* against Sevastopol. Notwithstanding Burgoyne's and Tylden's prescient objections voiced *prior* to the siege of the city, Elphinstone stressed the crucial constraint that pertained from the landing until the end of the campaign – a lack of ground forces, a situation that particularly affected the British. 'To undertake simultaneously the attacks on both sides [of Sevastopol]', he declared, 'required far more than the allies had at their disposal'. Thus, only 'the choice of either the one or the other was open to them'.[24] Burgoyne was a sufficiently experienced soldier to understand this issue. Therefore he did not recommend the lazy option of dividing the Allied forces between north and south. Instead, he proposed that the Allies should concentrate all their limited resources in attacking Sevastopol from the south. In adopting his plan, for which he argued persuasively, both St Arnaud and Raglan lost sight of the original strategic idea. They overlooked the desired outcome and timescale of the expedition, a campaign that the British government had hoped would be successfully concluded in six weeks. Such a short period of operations on Crimea may have been wishful thinking, but it is surprising that the Allies did not even attempt to mount a hasty attack off the line of march on the northern side of Sevastopol before committing themselves to the flank march and ensuing siege. As nothing was ventured, nothing was either gained or lost in consequence.

Elphinstone gave further grounds for the decision over the march that expose some fallacious thinking on his part, even if written with the benefit of hindsight. He claimed that to 'assail [the northern position] by a "coup de main" with an army but little superior to the defenders with nothing but field pieces at its command, and with its flanks and retreat quite insecure, would have been a most desperate undertaking'.[25] Reflecting their poor intelligence, however, the Allies were unaware that the fortifications on the northern side of Sevastopol were in disrepair and thinly defended. Furthermore, they did not realise that Menshikov was in the process of sending the bulk of his army out of the city to avoid entrapment, leaving Sevastopol highly vulnerable to an attack off the line of march. Moreover, the Allies falsely presumed that 'no fortification of any importance defended [the southern] side; that the enemy was taking no steps to strengthen it, but devoted all his energies to the north front'. Anticipating that the Russians would be 'quite unprepared to receive them' in the south, the fateful decision was made to attack Sevastopol here – driven largely by the need to establish ports on the Chersonese peninsula to support such an operation.[26] In this manner, the logistical cart was placed ahead of the operational horse.

Failing to attack Sevastopol's weak northern defences without delay proved more than a mere error of tactical judgement.[27] This mistake could not be redeemed during the remainder of the campaign: thus the overall ramifications were strategic. The northern side of Sevastopol remained firmly in Russian hands throughout the war. It provided a secure line of communications to the Crimean hinterland and back to the Russian heartland. More proximately, it functioned as a secure place of refuge for the garrison, which was to be evacuated from the southern side on the night of 8/9 September 1855. Significantly, Field Marshal Manstein was not to repeat the same error in June 1942 during his third assault on Sevastopol. As we shall see, he determined that the northern side had to be cleared before the final attack on the city.

Leaving the Belbek valley on 25 September 1854, the Allies embarked on the so-called 'flank march' to the east of Sevastopol, striking out through difficult country. British troops nearly collided with Menshikov's rear guard in the area of Mackenzie's Farm, the property of the descendants of the Russo-Scottish admiral. While the British secured the port of Balaklava, south-east of Sevastopol, a harbour that was too small for their needs, the French made for the larger and far better suited Kamiesh Bay on the north-western shore of the Chersonese peninsula, to the west of the city. The infantry and engineers of both armies erected camps on the plateau to the west, south and south-east of Sevastopol, with the city in sight but lying outside the beaten zone of the Russian artillery.

Writing at Balaklava on 28 September 1854, Burgoyne justified his advice for the Flank March. In criticising the 'French idea ... to have attacked the North Fort by regular siege', he considered such an approach erroneous as it would have been 'a work of time and difficulty, and would have led to no decisive result'.[28] His assertion, however, remained untested. Although Burgoyne's advice helped condemn the Allies to an extremely costly siege of 349 days, history has been kind to him and to the Allied commanders-in-chief for their collective misjudgement of the situation. As the great Russian surgeon, Nikolay Ivanovich Pirogov (1810–81), who was to lead the Russian medical effort in the city, considered:

> ... all understood well that Sevastopol would have been in trouble had our enemies seized the northern fortifications. All ... agree that if our enemies had stayed in the northern side, they could have entered the city in ceremonial march without a single obstacle. If we look at Sevastopol from the northern hills we can have a plain view almost of all the harbour, with the navy in front of us and the entire city. Rome was saved thanks to foolish geese, and Sevastopol – thanks to a foolish French-British march.[29]

The failure to attack Sevastopol from the north was criticised in Britain. Military experts such as the retired general and colonial governor Sir Howard Douglas (also an international authority on naval gunnery) considered the Northern Fort to be 'the key to Sevastopol'. Until this place were secured, he argued, there could be no hope of capturing the city. Once taken, however, he postulated that the 'Telegraph and Wasp batteries on the northern heights, Fort Constantine and the forts below, being commanded and attacked in reverse, must soon fall'. Then, he surmised, 'the town, docks, arsenal and the barracks on the south side of the harbour would be at the mercy of the Allies'. In contrast, by attacking from the south, the southern part of the town, even if captured, would not be tenable with the Russians still holding the northern side.[30] Yet such was the view of a distant 'armchair' general and not the advice of the man on the spot, General Burgoyne, who had Raglan's ear. In sum, taking all factors into account, it is hard to disagree with Andrew Lambert's damning criticisms:

> The real failure was one of staff work and consultation. There was never any fixed plan of operations on which Raglan could base his opposition to delays and cautious measures, and in the interests of allied harmony he sacrificed his options. Avoiding the north side was an absurd decision.[31]

As the Allies conducted their flank march, the Russians in Sevastopol recovered quickly from the shock of the defeat at the Alma and strengthened the city's defences most expeditiously. What they were able to achieve in a little over three weeks, turning a line of largely unconnected and incomplete works into a formidable set of mutually supported fortifications bristling with cannon, over 7 kilometres long, was nothing less than remarkable. The main credit for directing and organising this supreme effort goes to two enterprising and energetic individuals: Vice Admiral Kornilov and Lieutenant Colonel Todleben. While the former gave the inspirational leadership, the latter provided the technical expertise. Both men were to become heroes of the defence of Sevastopol. Kornilov toured the fortified line on horseback at least once a day. Not only did he inspect the state of progress in the new defences, but he also stopped regularly to converse with the workforce, exhorting them to strive all the harder. Above all, he stressed: 'we must fight against the enemy until the last extremity; each of us must die on the spot rather than retreat. Kill the one who dares to speak of retreat! Kill me myself, if I order you to do so.'[32] On a separate occasion, he had spoken to the men of the Moscow Regiment, which had marched into Sevastopol on 1 October. 'You are here on the frontiers of Russia', he declared; 'you are defending [here] a precious corner of the Russian Empire. The Tsar and all Russia have their eyes upon you. If you do not fulfil your duty to the utmost, Moscow will not receive you as her sons'.[33] So spoke the Hector of Sevastopol, who would lay down his life for his beloved city. In turn, it would fall, as did Troy, albeit the latter to a ruse swallowed by its gullible defenders.

In developing the southern perimeter into a state of adequate defence, there was neither the time nor resources available for adopting any grand or sophisticated designs of fortification. Pragmatism ruled accordingly. Although Todleben was forced to conform to, and to reinforce, the far from completed line of existing bastions and batteries, his experienced eye allowed him to make best use of the intervening ground and the limited means – both in materiel and personnel – that lay at his disposal. The principles on which he proceeded were:

> ... to occupy the least extended position, and the nearest to the city, which would satisfy the necessary conditions, to arm the principal points of the line so selected with the most formidable artillery which could be procured from the fleet, to connect those points with trenches for musketry, and to enable the separate batteries to concentrate a powerful fire on the front and flanks, to sweep the sinuosities of the ground as much as possible.[34]

In so doing, many compromises had to be made between what would have been ideally constructed and what could be achieved in the circumstances, not least in the erection of new batteries and inter-connecting trench lines. 'Rarely' could the Russians 'dig as deep as two-and-a half feet, without coming on the stony subsoil' of the Chersonese peninsula. This difficulty, of course, they shared with their British and French enemies, who would soon be hard at work constructing similar field fortifications.

THE FIRST BOMBARDMENT

While the bulk of Russian field army remained largely inactive, strung out from Inkerman and the Mackenzie Heights back to Bakhchisaray and even further north to Simferopol, the garrison in Sevastopol continued to reinforce the city's defences at a feverish pace. At the same time, the British and French established themselves at Balaklava and Kamiesh Bay respectively, and completed their arc of camps on the Chersonese plateau. In effect a three-week pause in combat operations ensued prior to the first bombardment and potential assault of the city. On the Allied side, the delay and difficulties lay not only in landing men, equipment and supplies, but also involved moving the heavy guns and the ammunition of the siege train from the two harbours up to the firing batteries and ammunition depots, in constructing the artillery batteries and in digging lines of entrenchment. All this work took considerable time and huge effort by all parts of the Allied armies. The challenge in establishing the British gun line before any bombardment could commence is illustrative of the problems faced by the army before Sevastopol.

The British Army's initial siege train of heavy ordnance consisted of: twenty 8-inch shell guns; thirty 24-pounders; ten 10-inch mortars and five 5½-inch mortars – in total 65 weapons with about 520 rounds apiece. With the assistance of the Royal Navy, but 'in the absence of proper wharfage to receive the guns, shot, and shell', it took five days to unload all this equipment and materiel at Balaklava.[35] This small harbour soon proved to be a cramped and thoroughly disorganised place, the poor management of which was to attract much criticism during the campaign, and for long after the conflict. The gunners' problems, however, were only beginning. The planned line of British batteries and trenches lay on the eastern segment of the Allies' partial investment of Sevastopol. These positions were divided into a 'Left Attack', roughly covering the Russian defences from the Fourth (Flagstaff) to the Third (Redan) Bastions, and a 'Right Attack', overlooking the sector from the Redan via the Malakhov to the Second (Little Redan) Bastion.[36] These two 'attacks' were divided by a deep gorge, down which the metalled Vorontsov highway from Yalta ran into the city. Because of this unforgiving terrain feature (which became known soon enough to the British and French as the Vorontsov Ravine), it became necessary to establish a depot at each end of the British position. These were named as the Right and Left Siege Train parks, supporting the batteries in the British Right and Left Attacks. These parks lay 14.5 and 11 kilometres respectively from Balaklava.

As explained in the British artillery's narrative of operations, the only road connecting the port to the camps, batteries, parks and trench lines tracing round the southern rim of Sevastopol represented nothing more than a 'farm track'.

174

Level from Balaklava to the village of Kadikoi,[37] thereafter it climbed steeply up to the plateau. Although 'tolerably good during the weather with which [the army was] at first favoured', its condition soon deteriorated with the coming of the seasonal heavy rains, the infamous Russian *rasputitsa* that turns unpaved roads into muddy obstacles each autumn and spring.[38] As events were soon to demonstrate, it was a major mistake not to construct a new metalled road from Balaklava to the camps, batteries and trench lines established on the plateau. The scarce British military engineer effort then available, however, was focused on the construction of the batteries. In the following year French sappers built a connecting road between Balaklava and the plateau, and a British civilian contractor established a railway line – the first constructed in war.

In the meantime, the siege train had no transportation means of its own – the result of a typical false economy of peacetime.[39] This deficiency was duly resolved by improvisation. In such circumstances, an expeditionary army of limited means traditionally learns to beg, steal and borrow, and quickly so.[40] Unsurprisingly, therefore, the 'horses of the Royal Artillery and Field Batteries' were pressed into service. These beasts of burden were 'unsparingly used to accomplish the task and suffered much'. In addition, 'every vehicle that could be obtained was put in requisition for carrying stores'. Supplementing the Royal Artillery effort, 732 sailors and thirty-five officers of the Royal Navy were landed with fifty guns, of which only twelve 'were at first got up to the front'.[41] Thus began the close co-operation between the Royal Artillery and the Royal Naval Brigade during the campaign. The latter force eventually grew to 'over 2,400 sailors, 2,000 marines and nearly 160 guns'.[42]

While the French siege artillery was ranged against the Russian Sixth, Fifth and Fourth Bastions, the British batteries were directed (from left to right) towards the Barrack Battery, the Third Bastion and the Malakhov Tower. Warships in the harbour and unspecified objects in the town were also targeted. Preparing and arming the batteries continued until 15 October, two days before the intended opening of the attack on the morning of the 17th. A total of seventy-two guns and mortars were readied in the British batteries, forty-nine in the French.

The interval between the battle of the Alma and the commencement of the first bombardment amounted to twenty-six days. This gift of time had been used to very good, disproportionate effect by the Russians. Working like frenzied beavers under Kornilov's and Todleben's direction, they had steadily reinforced the defences of Sevastopol by throwing up great earthworks (redoubts) containing protected gun positions. All of the city's garrison and population was mobilised for this purpose. As Todleben proudly recalled: 'The works were carried out day and night without a break; all the troops of the garrison, artisans and workers of all professions, town inhabitants, wives and their children took part'. He noted that the majority of the women involved were the wives and daughters of sailors of the Black Sea Fleet.[43] Meanwhile, the wasted opportunity in failing to attack was not lost on the Allied troops. Pattullo, writing to his sister Annie on 7 October, observed:

It is a great pity that so much delay is unavoidable as the enemy have been able to throw up formidable batteries on points where they were quite defenceless. Had we been able to bring up only a few guns when we first arrived I feel confident we could have carried the place by assault in a few hours.[44]

For counter-bombardment duties against the French batteries, the Russians held ready sixty-four guns, carronades, licornes and mortars; and fifty-four weapons of all types against the British, making a total of 118. While there would appear to have been a rough parity of artillery at the beginning of the first bombardment, this was not really the case. The Russians possessed a further 123 guns, which were sited in enfilade fire positions to protect their fortifications from any enemy assaults.[45] Both sides would considerably reinforce their artillery batteries during the course of the siege.[46] The Russians, however, were also able to strengthen their garrison significantly in the period immediately before the first bombardment. A week after the battle of Alma, on 27 September 1854, for example, just under twenty-four battalions, amounting to 16,000 men, held the southern side of Sevastopol. Only five days' later, the defending force had increased in numbers by 50 per cent to thirty-six battalions and 24,000 men. By 12 October, the Russians had at least 32,000 men in arms, incorporating regular army and irregular Cossack units, and not least ships' crews from the Black Sea Fleet.[47] With each passing day, Russian strength and resolve grew accordingly. For the Allied armies, however, the period before the first bombardment proved a hugely frustrating time, a circumstance to which Burgoyne admitted readily enough on 6 October in a letter home to his Royal Engineers colleague, Colonel Matson:

Up to our arrival before Sebastopol, everything has prospered to our cause; but here we are in [such] difficulties that I do not see what prospect we have of getting out of. We found the place surrounded by detached loopholed towers, crenelled walls, and earth bastions, with a good many guns mounted, and a tolerable garrison, said to be 20,000. We began, and have continued landing and getting-up siege-guns and train, a most laborious operation, not yet complete ...[48]

It was now clear that the Russians had every intention of contesting Sevastopol, and were preparing for the long haul: Burgoyne's initial hopes of a Russian surrender 'on summoning' without a fight had proved groundless. His growing unease at this turn of events was reflected in a letter written the next day (the

7th). He confided to Matson: 'I was much elated by the success at the Alma and its immediate results, and am grievously disappointed at this bad prospect after it. This is one of the contingencies which made the whole undertaking a desperate one from the commencement.' To his credit, however, Burgoyne conceded some self-criticism on this point, for he confessed he 'did not anticipate the danger to be in this shape.' Clearly downcast if not depressed, he also warned his correspondent: 'I do not spread these cheerless opinions around, but our position is one of extreme difficulty, and I do not perceive how we are to extricate ourselves'. The general then instructed, thus no doubt reflecting on his negativity: 'Do not promulgate these opinions to any but those on whom you can depend, as they would be considered very unseemly in me'.[49] Pattullo and many others, one suspects, would not have been impressed.

Over the next few days, Burgoyne's correspondence continued to display his lack of faith in the enterprise. It betrayed both his growing gloom and sensitivity to the relative success the French were scoring in sapping steadily towards the Fourth Bastion. On 8 October 1854, for example, he remarked that the 'French seem more confident on [their progress], and if a good opening can be made there, we will join them in the assault'. For him, the fundamental problem lay, however, in the British Army having 'half the front of the fortress to attack, and under the most disadvantages, while we have not one half of their force!' Not for the first time, and certainly not for the last, would a British expeditionary force be over-stretched by a mismatch between mission and means. To be fair, however, the discrepancy on this occasion only arose when the *coup de main* gave way to a siege. Furthermore, because of the British supply base lying at Balaklava, Burgoyne complained, 'We have a little mountain to get our guns and siege equipments up, while [the French] are on a plain'. Although he was an extremely experienced soldier and engineer, and had taken part in four great sieges[50] of the Peninsular War as a young officer, as had Raglan, it was clear that he had taken counsel of his fears at Sevastopol. Pattullo's contemporary critique of British leadership and method is revealing:

> I believe ... our directing man Sir J. Burgoyne speaks of confidence of reducing [Sevastopol] in 24 hours after the opening of our fire. At present he will not permit a single gun to be put in position to annoy or prevent the enemy throwing up their works. It seems to a non-engineer singular tactics, but he talks of placing the whole of our guns in position in one night and making one grand simultaneous attack. We can see with the naked eye their daily work and they are most industrious.[51]

While the Allies made ready to mount a deliberate siege operation, bringing up their artillery and digging trenches ('parallels') facing the Russian bastions, the city's defenders were emboldened and encouraged by this development. As Todleben recorded:

> It now became evident to us that the Allies had rejected the idea of an immediate assault, and that they intended first to establish batteries for the purpose of dismounting our artillery: thus we could gain a few days more. All in Sevastopol congratulated each other on this circumstance; all saw in it an important guarantee that the town might yet be saved.[52]

As the painstaking preparations of the British and French continued into the second week of October, 'there remained no doubt whatever' to Todleben 'that the Allies had decided on making no direct attack on Sevastopol, but preferred resorting to the slower process of constructing batteries, in order, first of all, to weaken or silence our artillery'.[53] Hence it became increasingly unlikely that there would be a quick end to the conflict: a long, drawn-out siege would condemn the Allies and Russians alike to a bitter winter and nearly a year of bloody attrition unless, of course, the city could be stormed in one swift violent assault.

Raglan issued orders to the British Army before Sevastopol on 16 October 1854. In the days before any effective general staff training or standard operating procedures had been introduced, there was no fixed format of written orders. Raglan merely provided a list of seventeen short instructions in no particularly logical sequence. These included not only essential details such as the intended time of commencement of fire ('about half past six o'clock from the French and English batteries, in co-operation with the combined fleets'), but also the apparently superfluous such as the 'meat for the men's dinners will be cooked as early as possible tomorrow morning, in case of the army having to move forward'.[54] To modern eyes, Raglan's orders strangely omit what would now be mandatory information such as the overall situation (describing both enemy and friendly forces), the aim or mission of the force under command, his intent and the overall method in a concept of operations or scheme of manoeuvre. One can only deduce that Raglan envisaged that the bombardment could be followed by an infantry assault, and perhaps on that very first day of the attack, but not necessarily so. Specifically, divisions were ordered to have 'parties of Sappers ... ready to carry picks and shovels, crowbars and sledges, bags of powder prepared, felling axes and ladders'. Perhaps more intriguingly, he wrote: 'in the event of an advance [sic], the Commander of the Forces particularly requests the general officers commanding divisions and brigades, the commanding officers of regiments and the officers commanding companies, to impress upon the men the urgent necessity of maintaining their formation, and keeping their order' – as if this event were some grand ceremonial parade on London's Horse Guards rather than an assault on an enemy city.[55] This sort of concern had inhibited the constructive use of ground at the Alma.

Raglan did not describe the necessary conditions that would trigger an assault: presumably it would have depended on the Russian guns being fully silenced, if not a significant breach in the defences being achieved. By any perspective, the British commander-in-chief's intentions were far from clear. Specifically, in his orders there is no mention of any co-operation between the French and the British forces on either land or sea, other than stating General Canrobert's intended location on the battlefield – at the 'Maison d'Eau, on the left of the British line, and on the right of the French position'.[56] In sum, Raglan instructed his army principally on what should have been matters of simple battle procedure prior to an assault, while failing to explain the operational purpose and necessary synchronisation of sea and land forces, artillery, engineers and infantry. This document, however, was not to be his most badly worded order of the campaign: that would follow nine days later at the battle of Balaklava.

A 'combined' or joint operation, bringing together the actions of two or more armed services to a common purpose, is one of the most challenging and complicated acts of war. It is all the more so at, or near, the beginning of a conflict when the diverse forces involved may be both unpractised in their duties and unfamiliar with one another. Such problems are compounded if different nations are involved. Thus the flawed planning and miscarried execution of the first bombardment of Sevastopol exhibited many of the profound difficulties the Allies laboured under during the course of the Crimean campaign. Not only would the British and French have to co-operate closely, but also the activities of the troops ashore, whether in the preparatory bombardment or in the assault of the city, would need to be very carefully co-ordinated with those of the fleets. Within the British and French navies, however, there was no consensus as to the best method of attacking the Russian shore defences – whether at anchor or when under way. Furthermore, experienced sailors knew that the ships' guns of the day had limited effectiveness against well-constructed shore forts made of either stone or earth and the vulnerability of their ships to red-hot shot. The closer the engagement range, the greater the destructive force, albeit at increasing commensurate risk of damage from the Russian guns. More fundamentally, what would be the object of any shore bombardment: were the British and French ships to provide a demonstration to divert the Russian defenders from an Allied land attack, or to assist in a more decisive manner, and if the latter, how best should it be conducted? Hence reaching the necessary agreement and subsequent integration of naval gunfire in time and space – and not least in desired operational effect – proved very difficult to achieve.

Unsurprisingly, the commanders on land would have preferred their naval colleagues to perform as many supporting roles as they could, and as for as long as possible. Yet the Allied fleets, having already landed numbers of guns and correspondingly large amounts of ammunition ashore, were not able to fire for extended periods; nor did their guns have either the elevation or the range to engage anything other than the coastal batteries closest to the entrance to the Sevastopol roadstead. Moreover, there were profound disagreements as to both the wisdom and the method of attack within the naval hierarchy. Vice Admiral Sir James Dundas, the British naval commander-in-chief, was reluctant to get involved in an unequal struggle between wooden ships and stone forts, fearing that if his fleet were to be too badly smashed up, the Allies might lose control of the Black Sea. In contrast, his subordinate Rear Admiral Edmund Lyons, commanding the 'inshore' squadron of British ships, and perhaps closer to Lord Raglan's thinking and wishes, was less concerned about the safety of his ships and considerably more enthusiastic about a combined bombardment and assault of Sevastopol.[57] Vice Admiral Ferdinand-Alphonse Hamelin, in contrast, wished to decrease the vulnerability of his ships by firing at the forts whilst under way. On 16 October 1854, the day before the planned attack, Canrobert, the French Army commander, overruled Hamelin, reasoning that such a cautious approach would hardly convince the Russians that it was a serious attack, let alone cause much damage. In consequence, both Hamelin and Dundas at short notice ordered their ships to fire at anchor, forcing a late change of plans. As the French in particular were short of ammunition, it had already been decided that the ships' bombardment would not start until the late morning, when it was hoped that the naval gunfire support might coincide with the Allied armies' infantry assault of Sevastopol. As a result, the chances of a properly synchronised attack by land and sea were slim at best, given the unpredictability of the timing concerned. But one matter was at least agreed: the British fleet would engage targets on the northern shore of Sevastopol Bay and the French ships the southern.

The bombardment of Sevastopol from the Allied batteries on land started at 0630 hours on 17 October with a total of 121 British and French guns and mortars employed. The time of the infantry's assault, however, had not been determined beforehand. In the event, with the destruction of a French magazine by effective Russian counter-battery fire, the French artillery preparation fizzled out at about 1000 hours. Occasionally such a shot can produce a disproportionate outcome.[58] As the British guns continued to fire, they drew an increasing proportion of Russian guns in response. The circumstances looked hardly propitious for launching an assault: neither Raglan nor Canrobert was minded to give such an order. With the effective cancellation of any attempt to storm the city, and thus a land operation to support, there was little point in carrying out the naval bombardment. Furthermore, as Dundas did not weigh anchor until about 1050 hours, theoretically there could have been time to call off the attack.

Bearing in mind his concerns as to the 'cost–benefit' of any naval bombardment, and that it now made little sense to proceed, some historians have doubted why this 'entirely futile operation' was carried out.[59]

A number of explanations may be offered. First, there was no Allied supreme commander (such as Eisenhower at D-Day), supported by a joint staff, empowered to give the senior army and naval commanders concerned executive orders. Secondly, there were no fast shore–ship communications other than signal flags to effect any sudden change of plan. Thirdly, and perhaps most importantly, there was no desire to call off the naval bombardment. To the contrary, it was prosecuted with great determination and vigour, and accompanied by considerable numbers of casualties, with the British and French navies keen to demonstrate what they could contribute to the campaign. None the less, with the advantage of hindsight, one writer, Peter Duckers, has even described the 'whole thing (in the grand tradition of the Crimea)' as 'something of a farce'.[60] In doing so, and notwithstanding the inherently flawed planning and limitations of the naval artillery attack on the Allied side, he does the Allied ships' crews and Russian defenders alike a disservice, for their artillery duels were both bloody and courageous.

In the evening before the naval attack, the surveying officer of the British fleet, Captain Pratt, had sounded a channel near the entrance of Sevastopol Bay that would allow warships to moor within 800 yards of the main fortification of the northern shore, Fort Constantine. The next afternoon, Lyons' squadron was to make this close approach while the majority of the British and French ships opened fire at much longer ranges between 1,500 and 2,000 yards. There was not a common time to open the bombardment: whereas the French started to engage at 1230 hours, Lyons only opened fire at 1400 hours with the rest of the British ships about twenty minutes later. The principal problem, however, was not of time but rather one of space. Even at the closest ranges achieved on the day, the combined guns of Lyons' squadron, comprising the screw steamers *Agamemnon* (flagship) and *Sans Pareil* with the sailing ships *Albion* and *London*, together with the sailing frigate *Arethusa*, could only make a limited impression on Fort Constantine and the nearby Wasp Battery. In contrast, the Russian gunners manning their coastal defence forts and batteries were able to inflict considerable damage on the British ships. The plunging fire from the Telegraph and Wasp batteries high up on the cliff tops on the vessels below was particularly effective, as were red-hot shot and exploding shell. *Albion* suffered three fires and had to withdraw from the action with eleven killed and seventy-one wounded, as did the *Arethusa*, her rigging cut to pieces, her decks set on fire and her planking badly blown in. Twenty-three of her crew were either killed or wounded. Having fired off their ammunition allowance of seventy rounds per gun, *London* and

Sans Pareil also left the scene. *Agamemnon* valiantly remained in place until 1715 hours, having taken no fewer than 240 hits and been set on fire twice. On account of her proximity to Fort Constantine, she was spared fatal damage as not all of the Russian guns could be directed or depressed against her hull. Within the British fleet alone there were forty-four killed and 266 wounded: the French suffered equally badly. The total of Allied killed or wounded was reported as 520, while the Russians claimed to have lost only about a quarter of that – 138 men *hors de combat*.[61]

Of all the Russian batteries, Fort Constantine suffered the most damage thanks to the weight of fire of the British warships. Of the twenty-seven guns on its upper platform, twenty-two were silenced; their crews were forced to seek cover below. The fort's outer face was 'riddled with rounds' and ten gun embrasures were damaged in consequence. While the artillery pieces in the casements remained intact, of the six furnaces that heated shot, only one escaped destruction. Todleben attributed some of the disarray on the platform to the explosion of three ammunition boxes, placed in the battery's courtyard. Fifty-five men of the fort's company became casualties with five killed and fifty either wounded or injured.[62] Inspecting the site eighteen months later, Charles Gordon confirmed: 'Fort Constantine is well built, and has suffered very little by the fire of the shipping on October 17 [1854]. [The Russians] told us that they could not fight the guns on the top after the first two hours, but the guns were serviceable in casement until the last. There were seven guns lying disabled lying in the courtyard.'[63]

The Allied bombardment from the landward side produced mixed results. British gunners scored the greatest success of the day on the Redan. At 1500 hours its magazine exploded: as a result its guns were temporarily silenced. Of this feat, the British artillery narrative recorded: 'the Right and Left Attacks dispute the credit of sending the successful shell. The gunners and sailors gave loud cheers, and fired shot and shell into the damaged work, which for the remainder of the day feebly replied from one or two guns.' This was indeed the critical moment of the day: as the record continued, 'for some minutes at the period of the day we appeared to have got the Russian fire under [control], opposite our Attacks'. Yet such success was local, for 'opposite the French, the enemy remained unsubdued'.[64]

In his detailed account of the battle of Sevastopol, Todleben reveals how another great opportunity for the Allies (the second on the campaign so far) to seize the city was in fact lost, and ironically at the very place where British troops were to fail miserably during the assaults of both June and September 1855. The Russian engineer makes clear that on 17 October 1854, the British bombardment had indeed demolished a considerable part of the Third Bastion and inflicted significant casualties on its Russian defenders. Todleben claims that the Allies 'ought to have immediately ordered the assault' on that bastion. 'Taking advantage of the smoke which masked the ground', he suggests that the Allies 'might, with impunity, have pushed forward their attacking columns and have occupied the summit of the 3rd Bastion before our troops, obliged momentarily to fall back towards the Naval Hospital and behind the steep coast of the South Bay, could have arrived in sufficient numbers ...'.[65] It was not to be. Despite high hopes of a speedy destruction of the Russian fortifications and subsequent easy capture of the city, the initial day of the Allies' first bombardment proved a combination of a damp squib and a profound disappointment. The British and French had not only failed to observe the true level of damage they had inflicted on the Russian positions, but also missed the brief window in time and space to mount a determined assault on Sevastopol. Apart from the momentary success scored at the Redan, virtually nothing appeared to have been achieved in reducing the Russians' batteries, let alone diminishing the defenders' will to fight. A significant measure of the defenders' success, however, was due to an elaborate bluff, a typical example of Russian concealment and deception – *maskirovka* (little masquerade).

British and Russian gunners continued to exchange fire until dusk. Thereafter, there was no time to rest. Allied engineers strove to repair the damaged British and French batteries, the result of the Russians' tremendous weight of fire returned during the day. Meanwhile, British and French gunners replenished their magazines and replaced disabled ordnance. Their Russian counterparts worked even more feverishly. Sappers and artillerymen, soldiers and sailors alike, rebuilt and re-armed the smashed portions of the bastions and batteries. 'It was determined that not only on the following day no traces of the bombardment should be visible', recorded Todleben, but also that 'a more imposing force than before should appear, so as to upset, on the very first day, all the calculations of the enemy'. Furthermore, he noted:

> During that night attention was especially given to the re-establishment of the 3rd Bastion, which had been nearly annihilated. The most prodigious activity was displayed upon this point; guns and gun-carriages were dug up, platforms were reconstructed, pieces of artillery were conveyed to the bastion and placed in position, while that portion of the bastion which had been destroyed by the explosion was cleared of the rubbish; the embrasures were traced and cleared, the moat which had been filled up was cleaned out and the powder magazines established.[66]

Todleben's analysis after the Crimean War, of course, was based on his defender's perspective and on a good deal of hindsight. On the day in question, however, there is little evidence to show that the Allies either knew about the Russians' relative weakness or, as Raglan's imprecise orders betray, had even prepared for an immediate assault. Although significant failures in intelligence and command were to prove recurring themes on the Allied side, they were also to be replicated by the Russians when they attempted shortly later to lift the siege.

The greatest blow to Russian morale on 17 October 1854, and one that dulled the shine of their defensive success that day, was the untimely death of Kornilov. Viewing the intense artillery duel from the vantage point of the Malakhov Tower, bravely but recklessly he exposed himself to fire. Struck mortally by a cannon ball in the leg, his famous last words as he was carried away from the scene, were: *'Otstaivayte zhe Sevastopol!'* – 'Uphold Sevastopol!' This cry is immortalised on his monument, which was erected on the Malakhov Hill as recently as 7 September 1983. Following Lazarev, Kornilov was the second of the four admirals to be buried in the crypt of St Vladimir's Cathedral in central Sevastopol; in his honour Nicholas I ordered that the defences of the Malakhov Tower were henceforth to be known as the Kornilov Bastion. In a letter to Kornilov's wife, the Emperor paid grateful tribute to the fallen hero:

> Elizabeth Vasilevna. The glorious death of your husband has deprived our fleet of one of its most distinguished admirals and me of one of my dear colleagues, who has continued the excellent tradition of Mikhail Petrovich Lazarev. The whole fleet grieves deeply with you in all your sorrow ... Russia will not forget his [dying] words and your children will bear a name most distinguished in the history of the Russian Fleet.[67]

With the passing of Kornilov, Sevastopol may have lost the leading soul of its defence but the defiant spirit of its garrison and fleet remained undaunted.

Allied doubt and indecision as to mounting a determined assault on the city during the afternoon of 17 October 1854 was in part based on the disappointing results of the naval bombardment. It had neither distracted nor diminished the Russian defensive effort to landward. Despite the combined strength of the Allied fleets that pounded Fort Constantine on the northern shore and Forts Quarantine and Alexander on the southern, the Russian gunners inflicted far more casualties and damage than they received. Every British ship involved, for example, was hit badly.[68] Unless positioned at very close, near-suicidal, range, wooden ships with the ordnance of the day could not render stone fortifications ineffective. Quite the contrary, the bombardment from ship and shore only provoked the Russians into redoubling their efforts to defend their city. With the death of Kornilov, Nakhimov and Todleben deserve most of the credit for energising and leading this stupendous effort rather than Menshikov, who remained an aloof, distant commander.

The first Allied bombardment of Sevastopol continued at various intervals and intensities until 6 November 1854. On the second day, for example, the British artillery narrative recorded: 'the bombardment [on 18 October] was continued at daylight; the enemy, having repaired his works and remounted the guns in the Redan, replied with a formidable fire'. On that date, the British artillerymen were unsupported, having to 'bear the brunt of this day's cannonade, the French being silent'.[69] Initial British confidence ebbed commensurately. While on 18 October, Pattullo was inviting his mother to 'look with confidence to the next mail for the account of the fall of Sebastopol' and even 'the withdrawal of the troops to winter quarters and perhaps to England', five days later (the 22nd), he was forced to admit that '[we are] still diligently digging and hammering our way into the tough stronghold of the Czars, but to a mere observer we seem to make but little progress'.[70] The day before, according to the Royal Artillery's record, the British fire had been 'considerably reduced' as 'ammunition was running low'. In contrast, the French, who 'had been labouring with energy to reconstruct and re-arm their batteries' were able to open fire that morning 'with success' – the 'Russian fire' being 'very slack in return'. Estimates as to what the Allies had achieved in the first week of their bombardment varied. While the Royal Artillery recorded on the 21st that the 'enemy's works at dusk appeared to have been very much damaged, and many guns were silent', Lord Raglan was of a less optimistic view.[71] Perhaps another opportunity to mount an attack had passed. Two days later (23 October) he reported to the Duke of Newcastle:

> Our fire has ... been constant and effective; but the enemy having at their disposal large bodies of men, and the resources of the fleet and arsenal at their command, have been enabled by unceasing exertions to repair the redoubts to a certain extent, and to replace many of the guns that have been destroyed in a very short space of time, and to resume their fire from works which we have succeeded in silencing.
>
> This facility of repairing and re-arming the defences naturally renders the progress of the assailants slower than could be wished; and I have it not in my power to inform your Grace, with anything like certainty, when it may be expected that ulterior measures may be undertaken.[72]

In other words, while Raglan recognised the remarkable powers of recovery of the Russian defenders, he was not prepared to forecast when an Allied assault of Sevastopol could begin.

In retrospect, it is all too easy to criticise the Allies' performance during the first critical weeks of their campaign in Crimea. After all, the last time the British and French armies had been involved in a major European war, they had fought against each other during the Waterloo campaign of 1815. Now they were new allies learning how to combine their efforts to best effect in order to defeat a common, and extremely determined, foe. In the month following the Allied landings, however, two great opportunities to assault and capture Sevastopol had been missed: the first, following the defeat of the Russians at the Alma; the second, when British artillery had all but neutralised the defences of the Great Redan and the Malakhov during the afternoon of 17 October 1854. The operational initiative then passed to the Russians: two famous battles ensued, those of Balaklava (25 October) and Inkerman (5 November 1854). In both actions, the Russians failed in their attempts to break the siege by engaging the Allied rear and flanks.

THE BATTLE OF BALAKLAVA: BRAVERY AND BLUNDER

A noted British historian of the Crimean War, Baring Pemberton, when comparing the charges of the Light and Heavy Brigades at Balaklava, keenly observed that 'to the unexcitable Anglo-Saxon mind glorious failure had a greater sentimental appeal than meritorious success.'[73] In popular British history, therefore, the battle of Balaklava is remembered chiefly for its high drama of the daring death-ride of the Light Brigade. In contrast, the success of the Heavy Brigade that fateful day is long forgotten. In any serious analysis, however, Lord Cardigan's rash rush of the Russian guns – triggered by a fatally badly-worded order from Lord Raglan via Lord Lucan – soon became the byword for the serial incompetence displayed by the British Army's leadership in Crimea. This penultimate engagement within the battle of Balaklava has been not only exhaustively studied by historians, but also narrated by poets and filmmakers alike.[74] Alfred, Lord Tennyson may have made a memorable contribution to English literature – and hence strongly influenced the popular narrative of the war – with his immortal lines 'Into the valley of Death rode the six hundred', but he adds little to our understanding of the wider events of 25 October 1854.[75] The poet also distorted the ground by describing a slight depression between two low ridges as a 'valley'. Furthermore, the disproportionate attention paid to the charge of the Light Brigade has largely obscured the true nature of the battle. What the Russians set out to achieve, and how the Allies, largely by happenstance, thwarted their opponent, remains often overlooked.

At first sight, the operational rationale for the battle would appear clear enough. It is generally supposed, as a result of the first Allied bombardment, that the Russians sought to raise the siege of Sevastopol by seizing Balaklava – the 'sole lifeline of the British Army'.[76] Such an act would have not only crippled the Army's logistics, but also enabled the Russians to threaten critically the Allied lines arrayed around the southern side of the city. Contrary to this received wisdom, however, the port of Balaklava was never the Russians' main objective. Their more limited aims were twofold. First, they sought to seize the Allied line of fortified redoubts astride the Kadikoi Heights, known to the Allies as the Causeway Heights, which secured the Vorontsov Road and formed the outer belt of Balaklava's defences. Secondly, they wished to attack the British camps and gun-parks in the vicinity of the village of Kadikoi to the immediate north of Balaklava, and so restrict – if not cut – the lines of communication between the port and the main Allied camps on the Chersonese plateau. For this operation, the Russians assembled a force insufficiently capable of conducting a decisive battle against the Allies: it was a strictly limited manoeuvre in time, space and resources. The prime reasons for these constraints lay in the incoherence and indecisiveness of the Russian command. During the first bombardment, which rumbled on and off for nearly three weeks, a combination of heavy Allied artillery fire and French entrenching operations closing in on the Fourth Bastion increasingly threatened the security of Sevastopol. If this fortification were to fall, then the rest of the city's southern perimeter would be imperilled. Later in the siege the extensively fortified Malakhov Tower would assume the status of being key to the Russian defence, recognised by all sides. In the meantime, the Russians held on to the Fourth Bastion, which was to remain in their hands until their withdrawal from the southern side of Sevastopol, eleven months later. Within the garrison in October 1854, however, there were growing doubts as to how much powder there remained for the guns, firing over 10,000 rounds a day, and hence how long such resistance could be sustained at this rate of expenditure.[77]

The future prospects for the Russians appeared mixed. On the positive side, significant reinforcements were on the way: the first major formation to arrive, following a series of forced marches from Bessarabia (now modern Moldova), was the 12th Division of 4th Army Corps on 16 October 1854. Yet morale in Sevastopol had been particularly dented by the untimely death of Kornilov on 17 October at the Malakhov. Furthermore, casualties from Allied fire (over 1,000 on the first day of the bombardment, falling to 250 per day thereafter) and disease, chiefly from diarrhoea, according to Hodasevich, were beginning to exact a rising toll on the Russian defenders.[78] The paucity of supplies and not least the onset of hunger were concerns that were set to mount. In addition to the heavy punishment inflicted on the bastions and batteries, many buildings in the city had been either burnt or badly smashed up during the weeklong bombardment. But all was by no means lost: Todleben continued to work wonders in repairing and extending Sevastopol's defences by night after the artillery attacks of the day.

On 23 October, Menshikov brought his commanders together to discuss the worsening situation and, in response, to consider how to break the Allied siege by counter-attack. Colonel A. E. Popov, the recently appointed chief of staff of the Sevastopol garrison, suggested an assault of the British battery on Green Hill. Once secured, Russian artillery fire could then be directed on to other British positions and the Allied line broken. While Menshikov was attracted to Popov's idea, Lieutenant General Pavel Petrovich Liprandi, commanding the 12th Division, disagreed, believing it too costly for the effort involved. He favoured instead an attack on a much larger scale launched from the east flank to threaten the security of the entire Allied force. Surprisingly, although the British port of Balaklava was probably the most vulnerable point in the Allied position, it did not feature as a specific objective in Liprandi's plan. Praised in one Russian account for 'his energy and coolness as well as being a good tactician', and a 'good general to command troops',[79] Liprandi recommended an ambitious multi-pronged attack up and over the Sapun escarpment to seriously disrupt, if not to defeat, the Allied siege operation.

According to Liprandi's proposal, on the first day of the intended attack, the Russians advancing from the village of Chorgun would seize the redoubts on the Kadikoi Heights (see Map 7). On the second day, leaving a strong force of infantry and artillery to secure these captured positions, the Russians would storm the Sapun feature in three divisional columns, exploiting the Allies' weak defences on this open flank, and assault the dispersed encampments around Sevastopol. To conduct this major offensive operation, Liprandi calculated that the attackers would need three, preferably four, strong infantry divisions together with powerful artillery and cavalry support. Thus in his estimation it would require 4th Corps complete (10th, 11th and 12th Divisions) and an unspecified further division, each with integral artillery; a rifle battalion; three regiments of dragoons, two regiments of hussars and three Cossack regiments; and reinforcing batteries of horse artillery. In total, this force would amount to sixty-five infantry battalions, fifty-two squadrons of regular cavalry, eighteen detachments (*sotni*) of irregular Cossack cavalry and almost 200 guns.[80]

Although a recent arrival in Crimea, Liprandi knew the ground in question. His division had occupied the village of Chorgun in the upper valley of the river Chernaya on 18 October. On his own initiative, he had already conducted with his principal subordinates a detailed reconnaissance of the Allied defences of Balaklava and the Sapun escarpment over a three-day period (19–21 October). So he was in a good position to advise Menshikov of the practicalities of mounting an attack in this area. Liprandi argued that success would be achieved not only on account of the Russians' superior numbers, but also in exploiting the Allies' mistakes in failing to adequately defend their open, eastern, flank running along the Sapun escarpment. General P. D. Gorchakov, the commanding general of 6th Army Corps, supported Liprandi's proposed course of action.[81] As the bulk of 4th Corps was still on the march to Crimea, however, insufficient forces were currently available, a fundamental flaw that could only be addressed by postponing such an attack.

In light of the doubt and dissension amongst his principal advisers and subordinates, and probably wary of making such a big decision, Menshikov wavered. Perhaps mindful of Liprandi's reputation as a high-flying officer, who had fought with distinction during the war in Poland of 1830–31, in the suppression of the Hungarian rebellion in 1848–49, and in the recent campaign of 1853 against the Turks in Wallachia, he was tempted to agree with his forceful subordinate. Despite it being his suggestion, however, Liprandi already had growing doubts as to the viability of his own plan if it were to be executed too early. He warned Menshikov that with 'his limited forces he would have no real chance of success and that the attack would awaken the Allies to the weakness of their flank'.[82] With this in mind, the Russian commander-in-chief could have wisely delayed the operation until the balance of 4th Corps arrived with the 10th and 11th Divisions at the end of October. Yet he did not – yielding to pressure from Nicholas I to take swift, resolute action. Furthermore, Menshikov made no attempt to combine Liprandi's operation with any powerful sortie from Sevastopol – perhaps one based on Popov's suggestion – designed to confront the Allies with two simultaneous attacks. What makes this deficiency all the more surprising is that such an operation (to be named by the Allies as 'Little Inkerman') was mounted on 26 October, the day *after* the battle of Balaklava.

Menshikov, whose generalship had already been found wanting at the Alma, seemed incapable of designing a decisive battle to defeat the Allies on Crimea. As Liprandi wrote laconically in his journal, 'The only wish of Menshikov was to do something to divert the enemy's attention away from Sevastopol'.[83] Hence Liprandi was authorised to launch only a limited operation to seize the Kadikoi Heights and to attack the camps and parks behind them, and crucially to conduct these tasks with the forces immediately available. Ironically, a much more ambitious course of action would be attempted nearly two weeks later on 5 November 1854, which became known as the battle of Inkerman, by which time the balance of 4th Corps had arrived. Nevertheless, Liprandi's attack at Balaklava on 25 October was far more than a 'reconnaissance in force' as claimed by one historian.[84] His substantially reinforced division, known as the 'Detachment of Chorgun', comprised twenty-five battalions of infantry, thirty-four squadrons (or equivalent Cossack *sotni*) of cavalry and seventy-eight guns.[85] To put this force into perspective, it represented in total about 25,000 men, not far off the strength of the entire British Army at the time on Crimea. Sickness had already begun to take a steady toll of casualties on the Allied side, and particularly among the British.

Notwithstanding his misgivings about whether he had sufficient troops for the task at hand, Liprandi had a good chance of success in the forthcoming action. His British and Turkish opponents were very much weaker in numbers and, in the case of the redoubts, defending poorly prepared and badly supported positions. Luck and skill, however, would intervene on the Allied side, largely eclipsed by the tragic loss of the Light Brigade as a fighting body. The majority of the Allied forces present in Crimea were committed to the investment of Sevastopol. Two French brigades under Bosquet, forming the *Corps d'Observation*, about 4,000 men in total, encamped on the Sapun escarpment between the Col de Balaklava and the Vorontsov Road, provided the principal infantry force to protect the Allies' eastern flank. Further north lay the tented camps of the British 1st and 2nd Divisions, whose tasks were split between manning the trenches around Sevastopol and, in the case of the latter, in guarding the extreme right of the Allied line near Inkerman.

In contrast, the protection of Balaklava was very much made an 'economy of effort' task. The port's outer defences consisted of a series of six redoubts strung along the line of the Vorontsov Road, which ran between the North and South Valleys of Balaklava. By the time of the battle, only four of these positions (1–4) had been completed and manned. The easternmost First Redoubt, positioned on Canrobert's Hill a short way to the south of the road, was armed with three 12-pounder naval guns brought ashore from HMS *Diamond* and defended by about 600 Turkish troops. The Second, Third and Fourth Redoubts each contained two such guns and about 300 Turks. Nearer to the port a small Allied force manned an inner line of defence. It consisted of six companies of the 93rd Highlanders and a battalion of Turks together with a field battery (Barker's), positioned near Kadikoi. About 1,200 Royal Marines, reinforced by two companies of the Highlanders, with six batteries of naval guns, held the Balaklava Heights. Altogether, this grouping of about 2,500 men would be reinforced by two further companies of Highlanders in Balaklava, and by whatever 'odds and sods', including the sick and the convalescents, could be brought up from the port area in the case of emergency. Sir Colin Campbell commanded this mixed bag. He was also nominally responsible for the redoubts, although their vulnerability to Russian attack was all too clear to him. Critically, he had no means to direct the Turks in action.

Both the Heavy and Light Cavalry Brigades of Lord Lucan's Cavalry Division were encamped at the end of the South Valley to the north-west of Kadikoi. Hardly befitting the title of a division, this force only amounted to about 1,500 cavalrymen with six field guns (Maude's Battery) in support. Widely acknowledged as the 'finest administrator and soldier since Wellington', Campbell had more combat experience than any other serving officer in the

Army.[86] He had commanded a division at the battle of Chillianwalla in 1849 during the Second Anglo-Sikh War, and, most recently, had displayed great tactical acumen at the Alma. Yet, as a man without social rank or influence, he was still only a brigade commander in Crimea. Thus he was junior to Lucan, whose status as a divisional commander and personal feelings Raglan had no wish to undermine. As a result, command in the coming battle was divided with no overall commander 'on the spot'.[87] Other than Raglan himself, there was no one else to direct and co-ordinate the actions of Campbell's and Lucan's forces. This severe shortcoming in the system of command soon became all too apparent. In total, the Allies possessed about 4,000 men with thirty-five guns in the defence of Balaklava and Kadikoi, discounting the *Corps d'Observation* and other elements of the French and British armies encamped on the Chersonese plateau that could be quickly called up should the need arise.

Liprandi deployed his forces as follows. The left attack column, under Major General Nikolay Karlovich Gribbe, comprised: the Dnieper Regiment (less one battalion) and a company of riflemen; with ten guns, a squadron of Uhlans (lancers) and a *sotnya* of Don Cossacks in support. This group was required to advance from the Baidar valley and secure the small village of Kamara (now named Oboronnoye), thereby securing the Russians' left flank. From this position, it would then support the attack on the redoubts. Liprandi's main effort, led by Major General Konstantin Romanovich Semyakin, commander of the 12th Division's 1st Brigade, consisted of two echelons, which, on crossing the river Chernaya, would deploy to mount two parallel attacks. The left centre attack column was formed by the Azov Regiment, reinforced by a battalion of the Dnieper Regiment and a rifle company, supported by ten guns. This regimental group, containing the most experienced and reliable elements of Liprandi's force, was tasked with the capture of the First Redoubt. Behind them, but swinging to their right, forming the right centre attack column, was the Ukraine Chasseur Regiment (three battalions) with eight guns under command of Major General Fedor Grigorivich Levutski, the 2nd Brigade commander in the division. His objective was the Second Redoubt.

Meanwhile, Colonel Aleksandr Petrovich Skuderi, commander of the Odessa Chasseurs Regiment, led the right attack column. A rifle company, three *sotni* of the 53rd Don Cossack Regiment and eight guns supported his regiment of four battalions. On crossing the Chernaya by way of the Traktir Bridge, his task was to cross the North Valley and take the Third Redoubt. Liprandi ordered Skuderi to be 'energetic' in his assault so as to give the Allies the impression that his was the main axis of the attack.[88] Liprandi designed his attack on a broad front in order to overwhelm the enemy in the first three redoubts as quickly as possible and to prevent their mutual support.

Further to the right, according to Liprandi, but far more likely to have been held between the centre and right infantry attack columns, lay the main body of cavalry under the command of Lieutenant General Ivan Ivanovich Ryzhov. It comprised the 2nd Brigade of Hussars from the 6th Light Cavalry Division, reinforced by two recently arrived composite 'march' regiments (formed into the united Uhlan Regiment) and *sotni* of the 53rd Don and 1st Ural Cossack Regiments, together with two batteries of horse artillery (a total of twenty-four guns). Ryzhov's task was to exploit the anticipated success of the infantry against the redoubts and to press on towards Kadikoi, although some doubts remain as to what he thought he was required to do.

Finally, there was a supporting force under the command of Major General Osip (Josef) Petrovich Zhabokritskiy, a composite column comprising the Suzdal and Vladimir Regiments (the latter less one battalion) with fourteen guns, two companies of rifles, two hussar squadrons and two *sotni* of Don Cossacks. Zhabokritskiy, not renowned for his initiative according to one modern Crimean historian, was tasked with seizing the Fedyukhin Heights and protecting the right flank of the Russian attack. In general reserve stood a very modest force consisting of a battalion of the Ukraine Regiment, a rifle company and two batteries of artillery held back in the vicinity of the Traktir Bridge.[89]

There is little doubt that Liprandi had planned his operation well; his subordinate commanders were confident in his leadership. Ryzhov, for one, declared – admittedly well after the battle – that 'full justice must be done to General Liprandi, whose orders, including the most trivial, were the most well thought out and sensible. Each commander was given clear, well-founded, and detailed measures to be taken in every situation that could possibly arise.'[90] The Russian troops were more sanguine about the outcome of the battle than their senior commanders. A participating junior artillery officer, Stefan Kozhukhov, summed up the emotions of many in his detailed commentary on Balaklava:

> The eve of just about any battle, especially at the beginning of a war when an army is not yet used to dangers, gives rise to much emotion, and this instance of 13 [25] October was no exception. We spent the whole day in the most animated discussions involving extremely varied predictions for the next day's results. Everyone spoke of difficulties, but no one mentioned failure. I think that this was not because everyone was certain of success, but because before a battle it was somehow not only uncomfortable to speak of defeat, but even to think of it.[91]

Nevertheless, the Russian commander at Balaklava evidently inspired his troops as a squadron commander of the Composite Uhlan Regiment, Lieutenant Koribut-Kubitovich, recalled:

When everything was ready for battle, General Liprandi rode along the troops with his suite. He turned toward his division and expressed his hope that it would fight as courageously as on the Danube. He added that he had no doubt of the success of our arms…. With his few words, General Liprandi completely electrified his force. The soldiers answered the words of their beloved commander with a tremendous 'Ura!'. And this was not that response which is given so languidly and calmly on exercises; it was a cry foretelling victory, unaffectedly rising from the mighty chests of our soldier heroes.[92]

The unfolding battle can be broken down into three main elements (or phases in retrospect), each of which needs to be studied in turn and related to each other if a true understanding of the battle, including its dynamics and outcome, is to be derived.[93] In the opening phase, Gribbe's column took Kamara unopposed in stark contrast to the ferocious periods of fighting the settlement was to endure in 1941–42 during the Second World War. The battle of Balaklava proper opened at about 0600 hours with a powerful bombardment by Russian artillery of the First Redoubt. Thereafter followed an unequal artillery duel. By 0730 hours, the redoubt on Canrobert's Hill, the eastern anchor to the outer belt of Balaklava's defences, had fallen to a well-conducted attack by the Azov Regiment. Initially, the Turks in this position resisted stoutly but they were then overwhelmed by force of numbers. The main body of the Russian infantry pressed on to the Second, Third and Fourth Redoubts; the Turks fled from these, hardly firing a shot. By this stage Raglan, already alerted to the fighting, was observing the battle from a vantage point on the Sapun escarpment. Sensing the growing risk to Balaklava, he prudently ordered the British 1st and 4th Divisions to march from their camps and to be prepared to engage the Russian Army in order to regain the lost positions. Their response that day would be painfully slow, and especially that of Cathcart's division, whose commander and men insisted on breakfasting before moving towards the Balaklava battlefield. The French commander, General Canrobert, equally aware of the threat to the Allies' eastern flank, also brought up his 1st Infantry Division and the 1st Cavalry Division.

Meanwhile, the operational initiative remained firmly in the hands of Liprandi. Now, in the second phase of the battle, came the opportunity for the Russian cavalry to show its mettle. In his account of the action, Ryzhov recalled:

My work began once the last redoubt was taken—work that incontrovertibly was the most difficult of that whole affair. I fully understood the task laid on me: with the 6th Division's hussar regiments, in a weakened state though they were [to] ascend a slope on which were all the English cavalry and even some of his infantry, in a fortified position. But it was not mine to reason why. It was enough that

I received an order and I considered it a sacred duty to carry out what I had been charged with as best I understood it, placing my trust in God's help.[94]

The forces Ryzhov had observed on reaching the heights of the Vorontsov Road were the Heavy Brigade of Brigadier-General James Scarlett 'no more than 500 yards from me', and a 'rather strong battery emplaced in Kadikoi village', which was defended by Campbell's Highlanders, to the south-west and south respectively. The Russian cavalry commander captured the scene thus:

... the enemy stood calmly and waited as by agreement. The silence on each side was surprising; only the Cossacks were shouting, but that was far off and no one paid them any attention. Only an enemy battery's heavy fire from the direction of Kadikoi reminded us where we were and why we had come. Finally my entire line flew quickly at the enemy's front.[95]

What then followed, however, was a rather confused action, which did not show the Russian cavalry in best light. Ryzhov's description is self-serving, not least because he claims his enemy to have been 'superior in numbers', which was manifestly not the case. Excluding the Light Brigade, he outnumbered Scarlett and Campbell; furthermore, the Russian cavalry had the significant tactical advantage of charging downhill towards the enemy to their front. Ryzhov, however, divided his force, sending four squadrons of the Ingermanland hussars to attack the British infantry, while his main body strangely stood firm, rather than attacking the British cavalry.

Very soon Colin Campbell's little band would enter the fray. By now it had been reinforced by numbers of Turks, who had withdrawn from the redoubts and formed up on the left and right of the 93rd Highlanders. A hundred invalids brought up from Balaklava by Lieutenant Colonel Daveney further supported the Scots infantry. Russian artillery fire had caused some casualties to his men, so Campbell prudently drew them back from a slight crest in front of No. 4 Battery. In his after-action report, he described the ensuing action:

During this period our batteries on the heights, manned by the Royal Marine Artillery and the Royal Marines, made most excellent practice on the enemy's Cavalry, which came over the hill in our front. One body of them, amounting to about 400, turned to their left, separating themselves from those who attacked Lord Lucan's Division, and charged the 93rd Highlanders, who immediately advanced to the crest of the hill, on which they stood and opened their fire.[96]

In trusting the firepower of their Minié rifles, the Highlanders rejected the previous military convention of forming a square to face attacking cavalry. So unlike their forbears at Waterloo, they were formed up in two long ranks. In this formation, the Highlanders fired three volleys against the Russian hussars. The first, which probably went high, failed to have any discernible effect. The second, however, forced the Russian cavalry to swerve and 'turn to their left'. Campbell's (and not forgetting that of the commanding officer of the 93rd, Lieutenant Colonel Ainslie) steadiness and tactical poise was evident when the enemy 'made an attempt to turn the right flank of the 93rd, having observed the flight of the Turks, who were placed there'. In response, the 'Grenadiers of the 93rd, under Captain Ross, were wheeled up to their right and fired [the third volley] on the enemy, which manoeuvre completely discomfited them'.[97] Prior to, and during this engagement, the Royal Marine batteries had kept up a good rate of longer-range fire: their 8-inch shell guns in particular caused many casualties amongst the Russians, 'bowling over horses and riders'.[98]

Meanwhile, according to Lucan's report, the Heavy Brigade was 'fortunate enough in being at hand when a large force of Russian cavalry was descending the hill'. Ryzhov's force was in fact now static. The commander of the Cavalry Division then 'ordered Brigadier-General Scarlett to attack with the Scots Greys and Enniskillen Dragoons, and had his attack supported in second line by the 5th Dragoon Guards, and by a flank attack of the 4th Dragoon Guards.'[99] Ryzhov recalled what ensued:

> I had served for 42 years, taken part in 10 campaigns, been in many great battles such as Kulm, Leipzig, Paris, and others, but never had I seen a cavalry attack in which both sides, with equal ferocity, steadfastness, and—it may be said— stubbornness, cut and slashed in place for such a long time, and even in the whole history of cavalry attacks we do not find many such instances.[100]

Despite the fact that his attack had failed to destroy either the British cavalry or infantry, let alone capture the guns at Kadikoi, Ryzhov, whose horse was killed under him during the action, claimed a magnificent success:

> Even those most ill-disposed to us cannot call this fight anything but most daring, decisive, and exemplary, and in its own time it will take its place in the history of cavalry actions. I do not know why, in the report of this notable day, this attack was not written about in detail, unless, as it seems to me, it is not appropriate for such a weak unit to ascend uphill and attack a strong enemy in a fortified position.[101]

The balance of evidence points to a completely opposite interpretation. As Lucan was far more accurately to report two days after the battle, 'Under every disadvantage of ground, ... eight small squadrons succeeded in defeating and dispersing a body of cavalry estimated at three times their number and more'.[102] The Russians received the charge of the British 'Heavies' at the halt, always a mistake. Apart from this circumstance, the Heavy Brigade's success was based on good timing, shock effect and, above all, tight control – an imperative that had been famously ignored at its charge at Waterloo on 18 June 1815. In addition, the guns of Barker's and Maude's batteries had poured fire on to the retreating Russians until they disappeared from view over the Causeway Heights.

On re-crossing the line of redoubts, the Russian hussars and Cossacks descended into the North Valley in considerable confusion to seek the protection of their own artillery, hardly the action of a victorious force. Lord Cardigan's Light Brigade, however, had failed to support the Heavy Brigade, remaining passive throughout their sister formation's action. In this manner, an opportunity to harry if not strike the retreating Russians was lost in consequence. Nevertheless, the British Army during this second phase of the battle had repulsed a superior force of Russian cavalry through a combination of the sound leadership of Campbell and Scarlett and the tactical skill of their commands.

Had the battle of Balaklava been concluded at this point then it would probably have gone down in the history of the Crimean War as a relatively minor engagement, an honourable draw in which the failure of the Russian cavalry largely negated the success of their infantry. Yet the Russians had seized not only the Turkish-manned redoubts but also taken away the British guns positioned there. This embarrassing affront was to lead to the climactic phase of the battle, involving the charge of the Light Brigade and the much overlooked, and successful, supporting action by the French *Chasseurs d'Afrique*.

Unsurprisingly, the armies and senior commanders involved in the battle of Balaklava drew quite different conclusions from the action, depending on their nationalities and personal axes to grind. Lord Raglan received a great deal of criticism for his conduct of operations during the Crimean War, but nothing was to prove more controversial than the series of orders he gave to Lord Lucan on 25 October 1854 from the Sapun escarpment, culminating in the charge of the Light Brigade. So much has been written about this single event, it is hard to add anything new from a British perspective.[103] From a Russian viewpoint, however, the battle and the final British charge remain equally controversial – but for quite different reasons. The overall failure of Liprandi's operation, although it was immediately celebrated as a great success, led to later recrimination within the Russian Army. Above all, the poor performance of the Russian cavalry attracted wide condemnation, as did Ryzhov's own role in squandering the initiative gained by the infantry.

During the course of the battle thus far, Raglan had become progressively concerned about the fate of the British guns in the four seized redoubts on the

Causeway Heights. It would appear that he formulated in his own mind a plan to recapture them once both his infantry divisions were ready to attack. At no stage, however, did he design either a coherent course of action to achieve this objective or communicate one to his subordinates. Yet where was the British infantry? While the 1st Division was now approaching the battlefield via the Col de Balaklava, there was no sign of the 'laggard' 4th.[104] Becoming increasingly impatient about the delayed assembly of his infantry, Raglan dictated an order to Lucan (his third of the day): 'Cavalry to advance and take advantage of any opportunity to recover the heights. They will be supported by the infantry which have been ordered to advance on two fronts.'[105] This particular command, although not as celebrated as Raglan's next, which launched the charge of the Light Brigade, is equally ambiguous. Quite apart from some doubt in Lucan's mind as to which cavalry brigade was to advance, on which fronts were the infantry to advance since, so far, only the 1st Division had arrived? So Lucan waited impassively, taking no further action other than redeploying the Light Brigade to the head of the North Valley.

Meanwhile, the head of Cathcart's 4th Division – with full stomachs if not itching for a fight – finally arrived in the South Valley. Ordered to assault the Third Redoubt, Cathcart prevaricated, believing his men to be in no fit state to launch an attack immediately off the line of march. Why could not the Guards and Highlanders of the 1st Division mount the operation? The passivity of both his infantry and cavalry hugely vexed Raglan, whose patience then broke on hearing an alarming report that the British guns were now being towed away by the Russians. While it is not known whether this claim was true or not, it certainly jolted him into action. Immediately, he dictated an order to Major General Richard Airey – the Quartermaster General and his nominal 'chief of staff' – to write for the benefit of Lucan: 'Lord Raglan wishes the cavalry to advance rapidly to the front, follow the enemy, and try to prevent the enemy carrying away the guns. Troop horse artillery may accompany. French cavalry is on your left. Immediate.'[106]

A century and a half later, this infamous (fourth) order to Lucan on 25 October 1854 featured in the British Army's new doctrine of 'mission command' as an example of how *not* to give direction in battle, and to provide a memorable caution of the perils of miscommunication and poor staffwork.[107] At Balaklava, however, what might have been self-evident to Raglan high up on the crest of the Sapun escarpment (at approximately 230 metres elevation) was not at all clear to Lucan below. From his position approximately 100 metres lower than the escarpment near the head of the North Valley, he had not observed the Russians removing the guns from the redoubts; their action lay in his 'dead' ground. Hence Lucan was uncertain as to which enemy force Raglan was concerned about. His confusion was compounded by the actions of Raglan's impetuous aide-de-camp and cavalry enthusiast, Captain Louis Edward Nolan, who, on passing Raglan's written order to Lucan, stressed on his own authority that the cavalry was to attack 'immediately'.

Lucan, unsure as to which guns the order referred and hence on which axis he should order an advance, asked for clarification. It is said that Nolan indicated with his sword not in the direction of the Causeway Heights (as Raglan had intended), but rather pointed down the North Valley, where a battery of Russian guns had been established. Reluctantly, Lucan directed Cardigan to advance, who sensibly protested about the wisdom of the order.[108] None the less, he obeyed, leading the Light Brigade into a killing zone with enemy shot and shell pouring in from three sides. Russian artillery batteries and riflemen delivered enfilading fire from the Fedyukhin and Causeway Heights. In addition, there came the frontal fire of the eight guns of the 3rd Don Cossack Battery in the well of the valley. Spectators on the Sapun escarpment watched the unfolding scene with a combination of admiration and horror. Famously Bosquet was heard to remark, '*C'est magnifique, mais ce n'est pas la guerre. C'est de la folie.*' (It's magnificent, but it isn't war. It's madness'.)[109]

The rest, as they say, is history for the Light Brigade charged, not only reaching the Russian artillery in the valley, but also engaging with some success a superior force of Russian cavalry positioned behind the Don gunners. Some of the British riders even pursued their foe as far as the river Chernaya. The surviving, isolated remnants then withdrew, returning back up the North Valley, taking further losses in the process. According to Liprandi's account (which, despite its exaggeration and distortion, is rather more reliable than Ryzhov's):

> The enemy made a most obstinate charge, and, notwithstanding the well-directed fire of grape [*kartechnyi*, canister] from six guns of the light battery No. 7, and that of the men armed with carbines [*shtutserniki*, riflemen] of the regiment of chasseurs of Odessa, and a company of the 4th battalion of riflemen at the right wing, as well as the fire of a part of the artillery of the detachment of Major-General Jabrokritsky, he rushed upon our cavalry; but at this moment three squadrons of the combined regiment of lancers attacked him in [the] flank. This unexpected charge, executed with precision and vigour, was attended with brilliant success. The whole of the enemy's cavalry in disorder precipitated itself in retreat, pursued by our lancers and by the fire from our batteries.[110]

During this stage of the battle, it had been the Heavy Brigade's turn to spectate. Although Lucan had followed the Light Brigade with the Heavy Brigade, after it too came under fire, he stopped its advance. Had it not been for the timely charge of the *Chasseurs d'Afrique* on to the Fedyukhin Heights, which eliminated the Russian fire from this position and covered the Light Brigade's withdrawal, it is likely that the British light horse would have suffered far more than their 278 casualties, of whom 156 were killed and missing, and 122 wounded, out of a mounted strength of 673 all ranks. Yet it was not quite the complete disaster that is commonly supposed. Fortunately for them, the Russian lancers, completely contrary to Ryzhov's account, had failed to block the retirement of the Light Brigade and to inflict serious casualties. Had it been so engaged, then the British brigade's losses might have been much higher. Another Russian source explains:

> [The British] escaped really because there was no effective pursuit on the part of the hussars or the lancers. They withdrew along their original fatal route and almost all of them were subject to the canister fire of the 7th Light Battery and the bullets of the Odessa Regiment, untouched by hussar sabres and not pierced by lancer spear points.[111]

Furthermore, it would appear that the failures in the British system of command that led to the misdirected charge of the Light Brigade at Balaklava were evenly matched by the less memorable errors of the Russian commanders. Neither Ryzhov nor Liprandi was able to seize the opportunity presented by the British action. The fact remains that the Russian cavalry also withdrew in disorder – returning to its line of departure at the beginning of the battle. Overall, it may be suspected that the combined efforts of the 93rd Highlanders' defence, and the charges of the British Heavy and Light Brigades, and not least that of the French *Chasseurs d'Afrique*, unnerved Ryzhov in particular, and perhaps Liprandi too. It would appear that the shock actions of the Allied cavalry at Balaklava might have induced a psychological effect amongst Russian cavalry quite disproportionate to the numbers involved. We do not know what was discussed between the Russian commanders after the battle, but it is hard to imagine that Liprandi would have been particularly complimentary to his comrade-in-arms Ryzhov. After all, he had devised a good plan but it had not been executed as well as he might have anticipated. Liprandi surely must have been disappointed. The battle of Balaklava serves as a useful reminder of the realm of chance and the significance of human factors in war. It warns us of the critical importance, if not fallibility, of commanders' decision-making in the heat of battle, when the situation is confused and uncertain. It was found wanting in both the British and Russian armies, but neither Raglan nor Menshikov was to acknowledge any such shortcomings after either this battle or the next. Both 'talked up' the success of their armies, as many senior commanders are wont to do. It takes great moral courage to acknowledge any failures; and rather more so to address them effectively, especially if their source lies in either personal or systemic institutional weaknesses.

Following the battle Raglan sent an after-action report to London. After describing the general situation, he praised the defence of the 93rd Highlanders and highlighted the charge of the Heavy Brigade. Raglan described the latter action as 'one of the most successful I ever witnessed, [it] was never for a moment doubtful, and is in the highest degree creditable to Brigadier-General Scarlett and the officers and men engaged in it'. In his despatch the British commander-in-chief then had to account for the charge of the Light Brigade, the context of which Raglan explained as follows:

> As the enemy withdrew from the ground which they had momentarily occupied, I directed the cavalry, supported by the Fourth Division, under Lieutenant-General Sir George Cathcart, to move forward, and take advantage of any opportunity to regain the heights; and, not having been able to accomplish this immediately, and it appearing that an attempt was making to remove the captured guns, the Earl of Lucan was desired to advance rapidly, follow the enemy in their retreat, and try to prevent them from effecting their objects. In the meanwhile the Russians had time to reform on their own ground, with artillery in front and upon their flanks.[112]

Omitting any reference to the lack of clarity in his orders, Raglan attempted to shift the blame for what happened next on to Lucan, alluding to 'some misconception of the instruction to advance', and writing that 'the Lieutenant-General considered that he was bound to attack at all hazards, and he accordingly ordered Major-General the Earl of Cardigan to move forward with the Light Brigade.' Spinning the outcome of the consequent charge, Raglan drew attention to the fact that the 'order was obeyed in a most spirited and gallant manner'. Furthermore:

> Lord Cardigan charged with the utmost vigour, attacked a battery which was firing upon the advancing squadrons, and, having passed beyond it, engaged the Russian cavalry in its rear; but there his troops were assailed by artillery and infantry as well as cavalry, and necessarily retired, after having committed much havoc upon the enemy.[113]

Raglan then conceded that the losses sustained by the brigade had been 'very severe in officers, men, and horses'. Yet these had been 'only counterbalanced by the brilliancy of the attack and the gallantry, order, and discipline which distinguished it, forming a striking contrast to the conduct of the enemy's cavalry which had previously been engaged with the heavy brigade'.[114] While there is more than an element of truth in Raglan's account, it masks the fact that the already under-strength Light Brigade had ceased to be an effective fighting formation, and that this circumstance had resulted largely from *his* indecisive decision-making and incoherent orders. None the less, and contrary to popular supposition, the charge of the Light Brigade, and more particularly that of the *Chasseurs d'Afrique* (whose action Raglan had rightly commended) caused considerable confusion amongst the Russians and tempered their initiative during this final phase of the battle. It is significant that Liprandi declined to continue the action despite having considerable uncommitted forces at hand, including most of his infantry. He was a wise enough general, however, to see that the growing presence of the British and French infantry would soon tilt the scales in the Allies' favour. Although he had not taken Kadikoi, let alone struck Balaklava, Liprandi had garnered a modest success in seizing the redoubts. At any rate this modest achievement would dangerously shrink the narrow lines of communication between the British port and their camps on the Chersonese plateau.

Menshikov, however, was soon to claim a big victory: in his immediate report to Nicholas I, written on the evening of the battle, he stressed:

> ... our offensive operations began against the besiegers and were crowned with success. Lieutenant General Liprandi was given the task of using his division to attack the detached fortified enemy encampment covering the road from Sevastopol to Balaklava. He carried out this undertaking this morning in a brilliant manner. In our hands there are now 4 redoubts in which 11 guns were taken.[115]

In turn, Liprandi, in his detailed, rather more factual report to Menshikov written in the immediate aftermath of battle on 14 (26) October 1854 declared:

> I owe the success of the day to the zeal and excellent arrangements of the respective chiefs, and the courage and ardour of all the troops; more particularly Major-General Semyakin, commander of the 1st brigade of the division entrusted to my command, and under his orders Colonel Krüdener, in command of the regiment of infantry of Azov, who were ordered to attack the strongest redoubt, No. 1, situated upon a [large and] very steep height, personally exhibited an example of courage and judicious arrangements. The attack of the regiment of infantry of Azov was executed with boldness, celerity, and decision.[116]

Yet what had the Russians actually achieved? Although the Allies' outer defences, the line of redoubts, had been captured, the villages of Balaklava and Kadikoi remained in British hands. The Allied half-ring of circumvallation around the southern side of Sevastopol was unaffected by the battle. More significantly, the Russian threat to the Allies' eastern, open flank had been recognised: it would be reinforced accordingly. The limited Russian success would soon be overshadowed by their costly defeat two weeks later at Inkerman.

CHAPTER 6

INKERMAN AND THE SPIRIT OF SEVASTOPOL

'[Resisting the] bombardment ... will remain as the most brilliant and glorious feat not only in Russian history but [also] in the history of the world.'

Leo Tolstoy[1]

PRELUDE TO THE INKERMAN BATTLES

Other than raising the morale of the troops, sailors and the remaining townsfolk of Sevastopol, the battle of Balaklava achieved little of consequence for the Russians. From their viewpoint, the British and French invaders remained on sacred Russian soil and the defence of the city continued. Quite apart from the poor performance of the cavalry, Liprandi's operation had been conducted prematurely with insufficient forces. As he had forecast, it had merely alerted the Allies as to the danger on their eastern flank. Moreover, Menshikov knew that it was highly likely that the French and British would soon expand their efforts in Crimea. At the same time, Nicholas I had pressed him for more decisive results:

I hope you will find an opportunity to attack the enemy and uphold the honour of our arms when the 10th and 11th Divisions reach you. It is extremely desirable to prove to our foreign enemy, and even Russia itself, that we are still the same Russians of 1812 – Borodino and Paris Russians! God will help you, amen![2]

With the onset of winter fast approaching, both sides sought to achieve a quick decision in the campaign: the key questions were who would act first, how, and to what effect.

The arrival of the remaining divisions of 4th Corps on 3 and 4 November 1854 gave Menshikov a temporary numerical advantage, with 107,000 men to the 70,000 of the Allies.[3] While the Russians considered various options to break the siege, French troops were pushing hard towards the Fourth Bastion, sapping to within 150 metres of this major fortification. As historian Albert Seaton has summarised, the Russian Emperor was 'convinced that Menshikov must at all costs exploit his superiority in numbers before the enemy should redress the balance'. Thus Nicholas I 'believed it to be imperative that the Russian[s] should attack before the French broke into Sevastopol'.[4] In fact, the French were planning a major assault on the city on 18 November 1854. The Russians sensed correctly that there was little time available in order to seek the initiative again before the Allies attacked. Furthermore, on the arrival of the two remaining divisions of 4th Corps, Menshikov would have no excuse but to mount a major attack in line with the Emperor's increasingly impatient demands.

The Russians undertook two offensive operations against the Allies in the aftermath of Balaklava. A limited sortie towards the camp of the British 2nd Division on 26 October, which became known as 'Little Inkerman', was the first. Ten days later, it was followed by a very much more powerful and ambitious attack on 5 November 1854, which became the main battle of Inkerman. Both actions were fought over the same piece of ground, the north-eastern outliers of the Sapun escarpment – the Inkerman Heights – overlooking Sevastopol to the west, the roadstead to the north, and the small settlement of Inkerman lying across the Chernaya river valley to the east. In hindsight, therefore, it is tempting to view the engagement of Little Inkerman as either a reconnaissance in force or as a 'dress-rehearsal' for the subsequent battle.[5] Although there is merit in both descriptions, the timing of the smaller operation is highly significant. As originally conceived, Little Inkerman was not envisaged as an essential preliminary to a subsequent operation. Rather, it was conducted to exploit the assumed British disorder after the battle of Balaklava. Apart from this opportunistic element, both the 'Little' and 'Big' battles of Inkerman can be best regarded as spoiling attacks to forestall a major Allied assault on Sevastopol. Whether the Russians could achieve more, and break the siege altogether by inflicting a serious blow on the Allies, remained to be seen. Certainly Nicholas I, if not Menshikov, desired and anticipated a decisive result for Russian arms. Before we look at either action in any detail, however, it is necessary first to review the state of Russian ambition, planning and organisation, and then to describe the field of battle.

In response to the Emperor's direction, Menshikov initially considered mounting another major operation from the vicinity of Chorgun, exploiting the Russians' exterior lines. Had it been conducted, it would have given the Russians an opportunity to reprise Liprandi's original grand plan of attack on to the Sapun escarpment rather than mount a second battle of Balaklava. Yet Nicholas I intervened, ordering an operation instead against the British Army's exposed right flank on the Inkerman Heights. Why the Emperor gave such specific instructions, rather than trusting the judgement of his commanders on the spot, is unknown. Perhaps he thought another operation in the vicinity of Chorgun would either be too risky or too obvious in the wake of Balaklava. It had long been Nicholas's habit, however, to interfere in the detailed running of the Army by sending a flood of detailed missives to his generals. Throughout his reign, he 'completely dominated' the Russian military system and discouraged new ideas, preventing 'the staff from performing any but the most routine service functions for the Army'.[6] The Russian General Staff therefore could not function effectively along the lines of its Prussian counterpart. Furthermore, the penalty of such micro-management and the stifling of initiative was not only a reduction of personal initiative but also, and equally damaging, a marked deficit in honesty amongst many of his senior soldiers. In consequence, subservient and weak-minded commanders such as Menshikov were at pains to paint events in the best available light and to withhold bad news from their Emperor.

Whereas the Russian commander-in-chief in Crimea was a brave man, as displayed by his indifference to danger at the Alma, in failing to tell truth unto power, Menshikov's moral courage and powers of leadership were sorely lacking. Criticism of him is a persistent theme of Russian accounts of the war and the defence of Sevastopol, whether from the soldier Hodasevich or from the surgeon Nikolay Pirogov. The latter was particularly disparaging of the Russian commander:

> I saw in the Caucasus that [Count Mikhail] Vorontsov himself visited the wounded, distributed money and medals; but Menshikov only once came to the hospital to visit General Vilboa and didn't bother to take a look at the packed, dirty, half-rotten legions, who were condemned to death. Time will show how he will be regarded as a military leader; even if he defends Sevastopol, I will never attribute to him this achievement. He is unable, or does not wish, to empathise with soldiers – he is a poor Caesar.[7]

In Russian popular history, the main action above Inkerman is known as the battle 'without a map', in which valiant but poorly led Russian troops blundered about in night marches and in the early morning mist. Thus it was hardly surprising that they were unable to prevail against the Allies despite their ardour and superior numbers. As in most military myths, however, there is more than a fragment of truth in this account as maps were indeed in very short supply on the Russian side, and the battlefield was unfamiliar to most of the commanders and troops involved.[8]

Any good soldier, regardless of rank, knows that the lie of the land is one of the most important determinants of battle. Therefore in planning any operation, or describing one in retrospect, terrain is usually the first factor to be considered. Generally, the ground, rather like the weather, can be regarded as 'neutral': it may offer certain advantages and disadvantages to both sides in any engagement. It is up to the combatants involved to exploit or to mitigate these to best effect. On balance, however, the broken ground of Inkerman favoured the defence; the local British troops already knew the terrain better than the Russians, who were mostly new to Crimea. Yet the Allies would not have it all their own way. Rolling ground not only breaks up lines of sight, thereby reducing commanders' overall vision and understanding of events, it can also divide forces into isolated pockets, both physically and psychologically, so hindering effective mutual support. Inkerman, which was fought over rough, heavily convoluted, terrain – and for much of the time in the mist – is a prime example of how geography and meteorology weigh heavily on land combat.

The ground, on which both 'Little Inkerman' and the subsequent main battle took place, is not as easily describable as some have claimed.[9] The intricate topography (see Map 8) needs to be viewed from both the defenders' and attackers' perspectives if it is to be understood. Just to complicate things a little further, the majority of the local place names in British accounts of the battle appear neither in Russian histories nor in their maps of whatever period or scale. Abutting Sevastopol Bay at its eastern end, the area's principal geographical feature is a triangular-shaped, convex-sloped tip of the Sapun escarpment. Known initially to the British as 'Cossack Mountain' or 'Mount Inkerman', it became known during the battle as 'Shell Hill', the scene of an intense artillery duel at the height of the engagement. The Russians were to commemorate this otherwise unremarkable hump of 189 metres elevation as 'Mount Suzdal', named after one of the regiments that participated in the battle of 5 November 1854. Returning to the British terminology of the Crimean War, this height had two shoulders, the 'East' and 'West Juts'. A short neck of land known as 'The Saddle', at its narrowest point about 400 metres wide, connected Shell Hill to the 'Home Ridge', just over a kilometre to the south. On the southern folds of this latter feature lay the 2nd British Division's camp, approximately 190–200 metres in elevation. Thus while Home Ridge was slightly higher (10 metres at most) than Shell Hill, it certainly did not dominate it.[10] Deep re-entries (*balki*) cut into this whole area. On its western extremity is the Careening Ravine, which runs up from the eponymous bay south-eastwards towards the main Sapun Ridge with Shell Hill on its left and 'Victoria Ridge' on its right. Running off this ravine on its eastern side are two gullies, the Mikriakov, which led up to The Saddle, and 'The Wellway' leading directly to the 2nd Division's camp. A newly completed Russian military way linked the First Redoubt of Sevastopol's southern defences to the destroyed bridge over the river Chernaya, sited near its mouth and downstream from the ruins of Inkerman. This road ran for the most part parallel to the shore of Sevastopol Bay, as did John Upton's aqueduct, which supplied water to the town and its new dockyards. Constructed by the Russian 6th Engineer Battalion in the summer of 1854, this coastal route was known as the 'Sapper Road' to both sides. From its base, two ravines offered approaches up the northern slopes of Shell Hill, the Georgievsky and the Volovia.

On the north-eastern side of Shell Hill, overlooking the Chernaya river valley and the old monastery and castle at Inkerman, were three further possible routes up on to the heights. The first was the post road, which ran from Simferopol via Bakhchisaray to Sevastopol. Looping up from the river crossing at Inkerman, it climbed under the lee of the East Jut on the northern flank of the Quarry Ravine before levelling out on Home Ridge, and linking to the Vorontsov Road further south at a windmill. The more difficult second and third approaches to Shell Hill were by way of the Quarry Ravine – on an older track of the post road – and by the St Clement's Ravine. A spur of Home Ridge, known as 'Fore Ridge', ran north-north-eastwards towards the latter ravine. The whole area was covered with stunted oak, which severely reduced movement, observation and fields of fire. Critically, the Russians would need to repair the bridge at Inkerman if this northern axis of approach were to be used.

There were only three British defences of any note in the Inkerman area. The first was 'The Barrier', which blocked the old post road to the north of the 2nd Division's area. A low breastwork protected the camp itself. To the north-east, on a spur of Fore Ridge lay No. 1 Redoubt – also known as the Sandbag Battery. It no longer contained the two guns that had been temporarily established there to counter a Russian gun on the opposite heights across the Chernaya river valley. The British defence of the area rested solely on a small force of 'picquets'. Their task was to observe likely enemy axes of approach and to provide early warning of any Russian threat to the troops stationed in the camps.[11]

LITTLE INKERMAN

The engagement known as 'Little Inkerman' on 26 October 1854 can be told briefly. Designed to divert Allied attention from Liprandi's force lying close to the north of Balaklava, and to distract the British and French from their siege operations, the Russian sortie amounted to a determined probe of the Allies' exposed right (north-eastern) flank above Inkerman. Colonel Dimitry Petrovich Federov led a force of six battalions drawn from the Borodino and Butyrsk Regiments supported by four light guns – altogether around 4,300 men. The fact that the Russian troops were equipped with entrenching tools suggests there might have been an intention to establish a forward position on the Inkerman Heights, not only to threaten the British flank, but perhaps also to act as a base or secured line of departure of a future attack.[12]

Leaving Sevastopol at noon by way of the Sapper road, Federov led his men across the Careenage Ravine and, unobserved, clambered up the north-western and northern slopes of Shell Hill. On his right (western) flank, a protecting column of 700 marines advanced up the Careenage Ravine. At about 1300 hours, the British screen of picquets (principally of the 49th Regiment) on Shell Hill was first engaged. Rather than falling back as would be expected, the picquets, although greatly outnumbered, fought back determinedly. Although this vigorous action bought time for the 2nd Division to stand to and move up, it also prevented the division's guns from effectively engaging the Russians. De Lacy Evans, the general officer commanding, resisted the temptation to mount an immediate counter-attack on ground of the Russians' choosing. Instead, he ordered forward two companies to assist with the withdrawal of the picquets, which were now being forced back under weight of enemy numbers. From about 1415 hours, the British artillery and riflemen on Home Ridge poured a furious fire on to the Russian troops on Shell Hill and on those who sought to take cover in the Quarry Ravine. Meanwhile, the Russian marines in the narrow confines of the Careenage Ravine were blocked by a plucky band of sixty sharpshooters under Captain Gerald Goodlake, who won a Victoria Cross for his spirited action. Back on Shell Hill, Federov was badly wounded; when their commander was evacuated from the battlefield, the steam went out of the Russians. By 1445 hours, they had turned tail and begun to retire towards Sevastopol. At this juncture, de Lacy Evans ordered three battalions (the 30th, 41st and the 95th) to pursue the Russians off Shell Hill. Their advance was only brought to a halt by cannon fire from Sevastopol and from warships in the roadstead.[13]

The Russians lost about 270 men in their venture; the British could be pleased with the relatively light losses of only twelve men killed and seventy-two wounded. The overall results of the action were paradoxical. Although the Russians appeared to have lost, their armed reconnaissance had not only revealed quite a lot of useful information about the terrain, but also, and more importantly, provided a good understanding as to how the British protected their camp, how lightly it was defended, and not least the time taken to bring up reinforcements. The Allies, who should have been energised into swiftly strengthening their exposed flank, instead undertook very little. After the successful defensive action on 26 October, an astonishing complacency, if not hubris, brought about a false sense of security, particularly within the British Army. The Allies were soon to be tested in perhaps the most hard-fought single action of the entire Crimean campaign. Whether 'Little Inkerman' was originally designed as a sortie aimed at merely disrupting the British, or perhaps more seriously as a reconnaissance for a subsequent major operation, it should have been studied far more closely in the interim and counter-measures planned.

THE BATTLE OF INKERMAN

At the battle of the Alma the Allies attacked the Russians occupying the higher ground: at Inkerman the situation was reversed. But any such simple comparison must end here. The Russians at the Alma, although poorly prepared, had expected an Allied attack, and viewed it steadily unfolding hour by hour, beneath them. In contrast, despite the warning given by 'Little Inkerman', the British at Inkerman were surprised by the timing, axes and power of their opponent's assaults. The Russian plan which finally emerged, though superficially simple, challenged those forces required to execute it, demanding close co-ordination. Requiring an 'attack on the English position', without specifying this objective in any further detail, the overall design for battle would depend on the timely actions of four distinct forces, of which two were destined to assault directly the exposed British positions at Inkerman.

The first attack grouping, under the command of Lieutenant General F. I. Soimonov, consisted of seven infantry regiments[14] (approximately 19,000 men) drawn from the 10th, 16th and 17th Divisions with a *sotnya* of Don Cossacks, two companies of riflemen, nearly 300 sappers and thirty-eight guns in support. This composite force was composed of two echelons. The first, commanded by Major General Vilboi, was to march out of Sevastopol and to ascend Shell Hill in a south-easterly direction to the left (north and east) of the Careening Ravine. There it was to join a second attack column of five regiments[15] drawn from the 11th and 17th Divisions with ninety-seven guns under Lieutenant General P. Ia. Pavlov, a force of just under 16,000 men. Approaching from the north, this force was required to cross the Chernaya by the bridge site at Inkerman and would then, via the Sapper road, climb up on to the Inkerman Heights by way of the Georgievsky and Volovia Ravines, the post road and the Quarry Ravine. Once Vilboi's and Pavlov's march groups united, they would come under command of General of Infantry P. A. Dannenberg, the commanding general of 4th Corps. His combined force of about 35,000 men would then attack the British positions, rolling up the Allied camps from north to south. Dannenberg left six battalions (approximately 4,000 men) and thirty-six guns on the Mackenzie Heights to guard his rear, the post road to Bakhchisaray.

Meanwhile, the 'Detachment of Chorgun' of about 20,000 men, nominally under the direction of the elderly General of Infantry Prince P. D. Gorchakov, but consisting in the main of Liprandi's 12th Division (four regiments) with the mass of the Russian cavalry (fifty-two cavalry squadrons and ten Cossack *sotni*), supported by eighty-eight guns, was required to 'distract' the Observation Corps rather than 'attack' the Allied positions on the Sapun escarpment. The fourth, and much smaller, group of about 5,000 men, a regiment under command of Major General N. D. Timofeev with twelve light guns, was to launch a sortie from the Sixth Bastion of Sevastopol to engage and distract the French siege corps. Remaining on guard duties in Sevastopol were a regiment apiece from the 10th, 14th and 17th Divisions, two battalions of Cossacks and some remnants of the 13th Division. Together with the disembarked naval crews manning many of the city's guns, about 20,000 men were left to defend Sevastopol. Menshikov had not specified a general reserve for the engagement. The main 'reserves' that existed on the day at Inkerman lay principally in the four regiments contained within the second echelon of Soimonov's attack group under the command of Major General O. P. Zhabokritskiy. Excluding the force guarding his line of communications to Bakhchisaray, Menshikov had committed the vast majority of his forces – 60,000 men and 234 guns – to the Inkerman operation.[16] Although his heart may not have been it, the battle enshrined Menshikov's last-ditch effort to end the siege of Sevastopol before winter. While the Emperor had not journeyed in person to supervise the attack, holding high hopes of its success, he had despatched his two younger sons, the Great Grand-Dukes Michael and Nicholas. On his behalf they were tasked to inspect the Russian troops and to witness the coming attack – not only to provide a fillip to Russian morale, but also to report back to their concerned father on the true state of military affairs in Crimea. They were to prove themselves as critical observers of Menshikov's poor generalship. Whatever effect they had on the Russian Army, the presence of the royal princes at Inkerman would provide some comic relief for a critical British press: they were to be lampooned in London's *Punch* magazine as the 'Russian bear's cubs'. Their bite, however, soon came – and Menshikov would prove to be the telling target of their criticism.

The Russian planning for Inkerman was optimistic, to say the least. In the days before effective battlefield communications based on field telegraph, telephone or radio, a multi-directional offensive operation of this scale and scope needed more than a degree of good luck if it were to succeed. In stark contrast to the period before Balaklava under Liprandi's direction, there had been precious little time for the passage of orders, let alone for adequate reconnaissance and preparation. Menshikov's instructions to Soimonov, for example, were passed via Colonel Popov only during the night before the battle. Furthermore, in a misguided attempt to clarify these 'sketchy' orders, Dannenberg had changed a number of critical details of timing and location. Specifically, he ordered Soimonov to attack at 0500 instead of 0600 hours, and approach the British positions via Victoria Ridge, in other words to the right of the Careenage Ravine rather than to its left as Menshikov had intended. There was some sense in this amendment: Shell Hill was too small for the assembly of twelve infantry regiments; and a determined assault from Victoria Ridge could have fatally divided the British Army. In the event, Soimonov chose to ignore Dannenberg's late intervention and followed the original direction of Menshikov. The all-too-likely congestion of troops on Shell Hill was alleviated by the late arrival of Pavlov's force. For this and for a variety of other reasons, including ineffectual command throughout, Russian attacks during the battle were launched sequentially in a piecemeal manner. The late changes in Russian tactical planning resulted in considerable confusion within their chain of command, which was exacerbated by poor co-ordination between the commanders involved on the day.

The Allied defences within the immediate area of the Russian assault were thin: a lack of numbers, made worse by sickness, had ruled out the guarding of the Heights of Inkerman in any strength. The British Army's main effort lay in the trench lines and batteries directed towards the Redan and the Malakhov. So only light forces were available to screen the heights and to provide an alert of any Russian attack. Other than a few isolated positions, there were no properly defended localities with the exception of the Sandbag Battery, the brutal fight for which was to form an important part of the battle. The British plan of defence, such as one existed, rested on troops being brought up from their camps as quickly as possible in order to meet the threat, dependent on where it would manifest itself. Despite the recent engagement at Balaklava, and the sortie of 'Little Inkerman' (so-called, of course, after the main battle), there would appear to have been no prior co-ordination between the British and French commanders in the event of a strong Russian attack requiring a combined response. Fortunately for the Allies, however, the personal initiative of General Bosquet would do much to save the day for the hard-pressed British when his forces arrived as much-needed reinforcements.

If the ground of Inkerman is difficult to describe, then the battle is all the more so. The action ebbed and flowed across the Inkerman Heights for nearly seven hours, involving a multitude of actions by Russian, British and French regiments, battalions and companies in a bewildering sequence of local attacks and counter-attacks. This account only gives a summary of the main events, more to indicate the character of the battle rather than attempting to describe the detail of the combat involved.

The opening scene of that fateful day of battle is well captured by Todleben, who wrote:

> The night was still dark when our troops quitted their bivouacs. The English, without the least suspicion of the danger to which they were about to be exposed, were sleeping peaceably in their camps. Their outposts, soaked in rain, shivered at the cold blast of an icy wind, and half stupid with fatigue and inanition, did not lend much attention to what passed in our camp.... At four o'clock a.m. they heard the sound of a church bell, which roused the attention of the enemy, but did not attract it long. The 5th of November fell on a Sunday, and the English outposts took the ringing of the bells to be the call to morning prayers.[17]

The tolling bell was the call to assemble Lieutenant General Soimonov's force near the Second Bastion. At 0500 hours, his first assault echelon of three regiments commenced their march. Despite the rain and poor visibility, and getting lost briefly, his men reached the crest of Shell Hill by 0600 hours, achieving surprise. The British, however, reacted vigorously. In the coming morning light, notwithstanding the mist, they were able to engage the Russians successfully, relying greatly on the superior firepower of their rifled muskets. At this stage of the action, artillery had yet to play a significant role on either side. Both Soimonov and his deputy were killed during this initial stage of the battle, not only depriving his force of the vital command and control it required in the heat of battle, but also resulting in a critical delay of the order reaching Zhabokritskiy to bring up his regiments.

Meanwhile, the arrival of Pavlov's force had been hindered by the time required to reconstruct the bridge at Inkerman (completed at about 0700 hours), the bad weather and the steep climb up multiple tracks to the heights above Inkerman. As a result, before Pavlov arrived, Soimonov's men had already been in action for over two hours and taken heavy casualties. Tellingly, British troops had begun to push them back. The committal of Pavlov's and Zhabokritskiy's troops, however, tilted the balance again in favour of the Russians. To his credit, Dannenberg had energetically brought up most of Pavlov's artillery. Massed on Shell Hill the grand Russian battery of twenty-four heavy and sixteen light guns, together with three further batteries firing from positions above the Kilen Balka and naval gunfire support from two frigates *Chersonese* and *Vladimir* in Sevastopol Bay, produced a 'terrible carronade', which caused many losses within the British infantry.

The Russians proceeded to bring up further artillery during the morning: Edward Hamley estimated that no fewer than sixty Russian guns, including heavy 'guns of position' were sited on Shell Hill, against which six British batteries, each of six 9-pounders, could not hope to prevail.[18] In this unequal artillery duel, conducted at ranges of less than 1,000 metres across the Saddle, the Russian superiority of fire was all too evident. It was not countered effectively until two long 18-pounder naval guns were brought up on Raglan's orders, coming into action about 0930 hours, together with reinforcing French field artillery. Remarkably similar to his decision to bring up field artillery at the Alma, this deployment was the British commander-in-chief's main contribution to the battle. Although taking heavy losses to the Russian guns, the combined Allied counter-battery fire neutralised much of the Russian artillery assembled on Shell Hill.[19] Yet it was not only the Allied guns that inflicted the damage. According to Todleben, 'A perfect cloud of riflemen, hid in thick brushwood, opened a very violent and very accurate fire against our artillery at the distance of 800 paces'. Furthermore, 'although the 'English artillery hurled shrapnel on our artillery and infantry', it was 'more the fire of rifled small arms which reached our artillerymen, of whom the greater part were killed or wounded'.[20] Whatever the prime cause, the fact remains that the Russians could not sustain their static artillery effort on Shell Hill. This state of affairs, combined with the pressure exerted by the timely arrival of French reinforcements, and not least their most effective field artillery, caused the Russian attack to lose momentum and, finally, to break their troops' resolve.

For most of the battle, apart from the artillery, the Allied defence rested on the isolated spirited actions of various units and sub-units, acting largely on their own initiative, giving rise to the appellation of Inkerman as the 'Soldiers' Battle'. As Hamley stated graphically:

> On our part it was a confused and desperate struggle. Colonels of regiments led on small parties, and fought like subalterns, captains like privates. Once engaged, every man was his own general. The enemy was in front, advancing, and must be beaten back. The tide of battle ebbed and flowed, not in wide waves, but in broken tumultuous billows.[21]

The fight of the Coldstream and Grenadier Guards, and of soldiers of the 41st (Welch) Regiment, locked in gruelling combat at the Sandbag Battery, is but one example of many such celebrated small unit actions that took place that day.[22] Bosquet, ever capable of a memorable line, called it appropriately '*quel abattoir*'. Hodasevich, a company commander in the attacking Tarutin Regiment, offers a Russian perspective of this ferocious engagement at the height of the battle:

> I brought my company to within forty yards of the battery ... with a loud hurrah my company of about 120 men rushed at the battery; ... I scrambled up the

barbette of the battery, and saw by the red coats that we were engaged with Englishmen ...; they retired about 400 yards, and opened a fire of rifles upon us.[23]

But rather than exploiting their local success, confusion then reigned amongst the Russian troops: Hodasevich's sub-unit then 'became mixed up with the crowd [of other units], so that it was impossible to restore order'.[24] Worse was soon to come when the Yekaterinburg Regiment below engaged the men of the Tarutin fighting above, mistaking them for their enemy; this was but one of the friendly fire incidents of the battle. Such was the chaos ruling 'something extraordinary around the battery', Hodasevich continued, while 'some of the men were grumbling at the regiment of Yekaterinburg, others were shouting for the artillery to come up'. Confusion soon turned to paralysis: while the Russian buglers 'constantly played the signal to advance, ... nobody thought of moving; there we stood like a flock of sheep'.[25]

Raglan desperately needed fresh forces in order to withstand Russian attacks elsewhere. The only source of troops in adequate numbers, however, lay in Bosquet's *Corps d'Observation*. During the initial course of battle, Bosquet had offered General Cathcart, commanding the British 4th Division, a number of battalions as reinforcements.[26] Although these were initially refused, elements of Bourbaki's brigade (a light and a line battalion, together with four companies of *chasseurs* and twelve guns) were subsequently fed into the battle. This force was no 'mere handful' as the Russians were contemptuously to observe.[27] Bosquet's ability to provide more substantial forces for the seesaw fight over the Inkerman Heights, however, depended on the actions of the Russian Detachment of Chorgun. If P. D. Gorchakov had seriously engaged the French, so preventing their assistance to the British, then it is highly likely that the Allies would have been threatened with defeat at Inkerman. But the Russian commander, completely out of touch with both Menshikov and Dannenberg, had little clue as to the severity of the combat waging nearby, and no inkling whatsoever as to how close the Russians were to overpowering the British defence. Now the time had surely arrived for the Detachment of Chorgun to march to the sound of the guns: to assault the French positions on the Sapun escarpment, and so link up with Dannenberg's force. The opportunity was missed by a small margin. If there was perhaps one event that could have turned the campaign, if not the war, decisively in the Russians' favour, this was it. Yet Gorchakov remained entirely passive, save for conducting an ineffectual artillery exchange. Bosquet saw the demonstration for what it was and rushed the majority of his force towards the Inkerman battlefield. By 1100 hours or so only 3,000 French soldiers were left to face P. D. Gorchakov's detachment on a strict 'economy of effort' mission.[28] One of the most competent Allied commanders of the war, Bosquet wisely applied the complementary principle of 'concentration of force'. He hurried reinforcements amounting to 8,000 infantry and cavalry, some ten infantry battalions, four squadrons of the *Chasseurs d'Afrique*, two field and two horse artillery batteries to fight at Inkerman. This considerable grouping arrived just in time: large enough to prevent the Russians winning, but would it be sufficient to defeat them comprehensively? It proved not to be the case as the battle neared its final stages.

At around 1300 hours, Dannenberg, quite unexpectedly and entirely without reference to Menshikov, took the decision to quit the field. The move came as a complete surprise to all involved in the battle. When the Russians withdrew off Shell Hill there was considerable disorder. In some regiments, officers lost control of their men, as was the case in Hodasevich's:

> During the retreat, or rather flight, from the two-gun battery, we lost a great many men from our ignorance of the ground; everyone ran according to his own judgement, and many found themselves at the top of high precipitous rocks or the quarries, and such was the panic that had taken possession of the men that many of them, making the sign of the cross, threw themselves over and were dashed to pieces.[29]

On nearing the bridge at Inkerman, mercifully now out of range of Allied artillery and rifle-fire Hodasevich recalled, 'we could no longer hear the sound of the whistling bullets'. But there had been severe losses during his company's engagement. On mustering his troops, he found 'only forty-five men left out of one hundred and twenty, the number with which I had left the bivouac that morning'. Such was the severity of the Russian losses.[30] Hodasevich's portrait of this fearful flight from the field of battle contrasts starkly with an upbeat eyewitness account by a reporter of Sevastopol's *Morning Chronicle*, who wrote:

> It is difficult to believe that there are troops in the world, which can retreat in such a brilliant manner as the Russians did. This retreat Homer could have compared with the withdrawal of a lion being encircled by his hunters. He steps back shaking his mane, looking bravely in the face of his enemies, and then again fearlessly continues his way back, bleeding from the many wounds inflicted on him, but remaining undefeated and heroic.[31]

Somewhere between these two views of the Russian retreat – one inglorious, the other indefatigable – lies the truth of the matter: although severely damaged, the Russian Army was not destroyed. As at the Alma, the Allied armies were in no position to exploit their success and to assault Sevastopol immediately after the battle. The city remained besieged for another eight months.

For all engaged, Inkerman had proved a most bitterly fought battle in a very confined area, most of the fighting taking place within a square mile or so. Two days after the battle Pattullo wrote home to his mother, stating the 'Almighty has mercifully brought me uninjured through another day of frightful carnage'.[32] Sadly, as we shall see, his luck would run out later in the campaign. The casualty figures for the battle remain disputed. Of the 40,210 Russians who had participated, no fewer than 10,729 had been killed, gone missing or were wounded, representing a casualty rate of approximately 27 per cent. Proportionately, the British losses were even worse with 2,357 casualties out of 7,464 engaged, or 32 per cent. In comparison, the French had come off relatively lightly with only 929 casualties from 8,219, or 11 per cent.[33] Yet these stark figures do not fully demonstrate the impact on the units involved for such casualties were not uniformly distributed across the forces that fought. Within the Russian field army, for example, of the forty-eight battalions committed, sixteen (four regiments) remained unscathed, but twelve were 'utterly ruined'; a further twelve 'had to be withdrawn from the order of battle'; and ten 'were deemed for duty at reduced strength'.[34]

Although the losses were fewer in number within the British Army, they were equally crippling. For many of the units engaged at Inkerman the numbers of casualties were approaching the order of the first day of the Somme on 1 July 1916, albeit the total figures in the latter engagement were many times greater. In Pattullo's battalion, for example, he lists the loss of '3 officers & ... 4 wounded, 27 men killed & missing & about 95 wounded, which now leaves our unfortunate Regt with only 4 duty officers & 248 men'.[35] Put another way, of the 850 men who had commenced the campaign, only 30 per cent remained fit to fight. Today, such a unit would be declared non-operational. Although the battle had been won, the Pyrrhic price of victory was even higher than the raw casualty figures reveal. The 2nd and 4th Divisions and the Guards Brigade of the 1st had taken the brunt of the losses. Overall, officers, regardless of rank, had been struck down disproportionately. For example, out of the ten general officers involved at Inkerman, all were either killed or wounded. Thus there was no case of 'château-generalship' – the misdirected criticism of senior officers during the First World War – as the senior officers often fell at the head of their troops. This pattern of loss was similar on the Russian side: six general officers and six regimental commanders became casualties.[36] In consequence of the battle of Inkerman, the fighting power of the British Army in Crimea was greatly reduced since no strong drafts immediately arrived to make up the losses. Just as critically, many experienced old non-commissioned officers and men had fallen or been invalided. One military historian, a veteran of the Second World War, narrates poignantly,

Their replacements were never again to capture the spirit which had driven their predecessors up the heights of the Alma, and which had enabled the few to stand against the many in the scrub at Inkerman. In the 'Soldier's Battle' not all had been heroic; in battle the cowards often survive, perhaps eventually to out-number the fearless.[37]

This acerbic assessment has evidential merit: a combination of the losses incurred at Inkerman and the deprivations of a harsh Crimean winter robbed the British Army of much of its former élan and fighting power. As British officers were to discover to their horror later in the campaign during the final assault on Sevastopol's Third Bastion (the Great Redan) on 8 September 1855, their men, many of them young and inexperienced recruits, would 'not necessarily follow them against the enemy'.[38] While there may have been some isolated cases of a lack of courage at Inkerman, the bravery of the British Army overall at this action has never been questioned. No fewer than thirty-one regiments were awarded the battle honour of Inkerman. The Royal Military Academy at Sandhurst still includes an Inkerman Company; significantly, the only Crimean War battle so honoured.

INKERMAN: POST-MORTEM AND AFTERMATH

The consequences of Inkerman were many. First, it resulted in a stalemate around Sevastopol over the next three months, which were cold and wet; the inhospitable conditions made life a misery for most combatants in the British Army. In comparison, over that first Crimean winter the French were better founded in their camps and kept well supplied. There was no question, however, of suspending the conflict in the time-honoured eighteenth-century tradition of returning to 'winter quarters'. The most serious shortcomings of the British Army remained at command level – with Raglan and his headquarters staff – and in both administration and medical support. Meanwhile, the Army's logistical problems were to be compounded by the seasonal bad weather, heralded by the 'Great Storm' of 14 November 1854, which left many ships both in Balaklava harbour and lying close off shore either sunk or disabled. No fewer than twenty-two vessels were lost: fifteen transports and five steam corvettes. Perhaps the most severe loss was that of the steamship *Prince*, which was carrying the bulk of the winter clothing for the Army. New stores were ordered and supplied, but they would take some months before arriving in Crimea. Another significant aspect of the disaster was the deficit of twenty days' supply of forage for the Army's horses: this setback compounded the lack of transportation between Balaklava and the camps.[39]

While the Allies were no longer in a position to mount a fresh bombardment and an associated assault on Sevastopol until the spring, the Russians could not risk fighting another major battle without further reinforcements. Secondly, as a result of battle losses and an inability to send out new formations – brigades or divisions – as opposed to a trickle of individual units (battalions) and drafts of replacements, the British became very much the junior partner to the French. Such was the lack of troops, a situation soon to be made even worse through the inadequacies of shelter, heating and food supplies, and associated sickness, that the French had to take over Inkerman sector from the British. In illustration of the British Army's manpower problem, although the nominal size of the force under Lord Raglan's command had increased from 35,643 officers and men on 1 October 1854 to 43,005 three months later, over the same period the number 'present under arms' had fallen from 23,040 to 21, 973.[40] For the rest of the campaign, the French were responsible for about four-fifths of the siege lines at Sevastopol, including those facing the Malakhov Tower, the eventual principal objective of the Allied attack. Thirdly, the Russians began to see that the campaign in Crimea was unlikely to be won: their army was unable to defeat the Allies in a pitched battle, while their enemies were still very much able to continue prosecuting their siege. Even without another major bombardment (the second would follow on 9 April 1855), the lack of success slowly sapped away at Russian national morale. This phenomenon was more evident at the imperial court in St Petersburg than at Sevastopol, whose defenders still fought with plenty of grit and determination.

In a similar manner to Balaklava, the 'blame game' within the Russian Army soon began following the battle of Inkerman. Unsurprisingly, charges of incompetence were to be levelled at Menshikov. A day after the action, in an attempt to ward off such criticism, he had written a characteristically misleading if not mendacious report to Nicholas I, in which he claimed:

Our first attack was entirely successful and the English fortifications were taken and 11 guns spiked. Then French reinforcements arrived and the English brought up their siege artillery which our field guns could not engage. The enemy won the battle on account of his numerical superiority and the effect of his rifle fire.[41]

Two days later, on 8 November 1854, Dannenberg, whom Menshikov had blamed in a private letter to the Emperor, conveniently passed the buck to the deceased Soimonov, pinning on him much of the responsibility for the failure:

Unfortunately, [he], instead of taking the direction ordered, crossed on to the right [east] bank of the Kilen-balka and, without waiting for the appearance of the left [Pavlov's] column, quickly went forward at dawn until he was engaged by heavy rifle fire. The enemy, not being threatened on the left flank [the Victoria Ridge] was able to concentrate all his forces between the upper Kilen-balka and the Inkerman [Chernaya] valley, on broken ground highly suitable for defence.[42]

As might be expected, Todleben provided a more balanced – if not politically correct – view in his account of the defence of Sevastopol, albeit written with the hindsight of subsequent events, not least the outcome of the war. Of the Russian troops, he had no doubts as to their qualities despite the confusion and disorder that had accompanied their fight and flight. 'If self-denial, enthusiasm and courage are enough to insure victory', he enthused, 'assuredly it would have been on the side of the Russians'. Yet the British had also made their mark during this hard-fought battle. Todleben gave his opponents due credit, noting generously that 'it is only just to recognise the fact that in valour and in tenacity [the Russians] encountered worthy rivals in the English'.[43] The equilibrium of fighting spirit between the armies, however, could not account for the Russian defeat. Todleben attempted to explain away this outcome principally in terms of unfavourable terrain and inferior armament, while only hinting at the grave weaknesses in command and tactics.

Despite the ground being chosen by the Russian high command, Todleben drew attention to the 'narrowness of the field of battle', which 'paralyzed the movements of our troops'. Identifying that the confined area between the Careening Ravine and the river Chernaya did not allow the Russians to deploy more of their forces simultaneously, he noted that this constraint prevented them from taking advantage of their numerical superiority. Thus, 'we had to bring our troops into action by piecemeal'. What Todleben failed to point out, however, was the fact that had strong Russian columns attacked from elsewhere other than the vicinity of Shell Hill, they might have converged to engulf and overwhelm the Allied defence.

As at the Alma, Todleben highlighted the superiority of the 'English troops, armed with rifles', who 'opened fire at long range and did great mischief to our troops, before the latter could approach the enemy near enough to use their muskets'. Yet many of the engagements were conducted at much closer range in close country, where the Russians were not so disadvantaged. None the less, it is clear that Allied rifle power at battalion and company level dominated the firefights. The precision of such small-arms fire also caused the loss of a 'great number' of Russian officers, which not only weakened the 'energy' (presumably the resolve) of the troops, but also 'disturbed the unity of action'. In other words, the losses disrupted Russian leadership and decision-making in battle; presumably, the loss of British senior officers such as Cathcart had no such detrimental effect. Todleben's final criticism was directed against the Russian artillery. Despite acting at Inkerman with 'great art and coolness against the artillery of the enemy', it 'scarcely gave any assistance to our infantry'. In stark contrast, he claimed that 'the English artillery always came to the assistance of their infantry, mowing down the Russian columns and skirmishers with a fire of grape. But our troops were deprived [of] the support of their artillery.'[44]

Although the factors Todleben listed certainly contributed to the Russians' lack of success, he omitted to state the more profound reason: the deep deficits in generalship, which adversely affected both the planning and the execution of the operation. The root causes of the Russian Army's failure at Inkerman were first an inability to sufficiently concentrate forces in time and space to achieve decisive effect, reflecting shortcomings in command and supporting staff work; and secondly, a distinct lack of firm direction during the battle. While this latter failing also afflicted the British Army, it did not affect the outcome of the battle in the same way. Largely speaking, all the British (and later, the French) units had to do was to stand and fight in a more or less static manner, while the Russians not only needed to regroup and to attack again, but also to manoeuvre, if they were to prevail. It did not help that there was such animosity between commanders such as Menshikov and Dannenberg, with the former set on denying the latter a major role in the battle for as long as possible, and the latter attempting to modify his superior's plan. In writing to his elder brother Alexander (the successor to Nicholas I), Grand Duke Nicholas was in little doubt as to the prime source of the disaster. It was not that the 'troops would not fight' – to repudiate one of Menshikov's outrageous claims – rather, the 'disorder originated from [the commander-in-chief]'. Indeed, the royal prince continued disparagingly,

Staggering though it is to relate, Menshikov had no headquarters at all, just three people who work at those duties in such a fashion that if you want to know something you are at a loss to know whom to ask. Yesterday, for the first time, Menshikov went among the troops to thank them for what they had done, and when he returned he remarked to me on the fine morale of the Vladimirsky, who said they were ready to give battle again. The Vladimirsky was one of the regiments he had just been cursing.[45]

Quite apart from Menshikov's individual failings, the Russians laboured under institutional weaknesses. Although the Russian Army possessed a general staff, it was a very poorly established and under-manned organisation: a pale shadow of the Prussian system (*Grosser Generalstab*) on which it had been modelled. Although charged with 'the general distribution, quartering, movement, and activity of the military land forces', together with higher military education and military survey, its influence on the planning and conduct of war at the strategic and operational levels respectively was minimal.[46] Neither was there any effective counterpart of the Prussian Field General Staff (*Truppengeneralstab*) in advising formation commanders whilst on campaign. Hence both personal and procedural deficiencies in the chain of command from the Emperor downwards to theatre commanders such as Menshikov (and thence to his principal field subordinates, Generals Dannenberg and P. D. Gorchakov) could not be compensated for by outstanding general staff work. As at the Alma, the battle of Inkerman was to show up severe shortcomings in Russian tactics, technology and training, all matters which an authoritative and efficient general staff should have addressed before the war.

What made the Russian defeat at Inkerman all the more galling was the enforced inactivity of about two-thirds of Menshikov's force: P. D. Gorchakov's troops, for example, never even came into action. Albert Seaton's critical conclusions about the Russian conduct of the battle neatly say it all: 'Menshikov's manoeuvre had involved the movement without maps, reconnaissance or proper preparation, of a large body of troops on concentric axes, over difficult and unknown ground during mist and darkness, on to a plateau too small to allow deployment.'[47] Thereafter, 'as on the Alma' the Russian commander-in-chief 'did not display those qualities of generalship needed to direct and co-ordinate [the] forces under his command'. Overall, Seaton observed that 'there was an almost total lack of control over operations'. Thus a potential victory 'fell from the grasp of a commander who lacked any powers of decision'.[48] Unsurprisingly, following the defeat at the Alma, the ephemeral 'victory' at Balaklava, and now the crushing disappointment at Inkerman, Menshikov's days as commander-in-chief were numbered. Nicholas I would need to find a considerably more competent leader, a new strategy and far more effectively conducted operations if the campaign were to be won. Such was the Emperor's misplaced faith in Menshikov, however, it would take another failure of Russian arms before his long-overdue dismissal took place. The Allies, although weakened by the battle of Inkerman, were none the less able to continue besieging Sevastopol. For the Russians, meantime, no early relief was in prospect.

At the grand strategic level too, the odds were beginning to turn against the Russian cause. In December 1854, Austria had formed an alliance with Britain and France. Although Austrian troops were not to become engaged in the conflict, Russia feared that the war might well be widened with the opening of a new front in Eastern Europe – an attack on its soil in the manner of Napoleon's campaign of 1812. In the event, such a massive undertaking was never on the cards. The main focus in both Paris and London remained achieving victory in Crimea, not least to assuage dimming public confidence in the campaign during the winter, despite the welcome defensive success at Inkerman. Piedmont–Sardinia had joined the anti-Russian coalition in January 1855, despatching an expeditionary corps of 15,000 men under General Alfonso La Marmora to Crimea. This force was to play an important role in the battle of the Chernaya river of 16 August 1855, the Russians' final, futile attempt at lifting the siege of Sevastopol. In Britain, following the fall of Lord Aberdeen's coalition government on 30 January 1855 as a result of mounting criticism of the poor conditions endured by the British Army facing Sevastopol, Lord Palmerston became Prime Minister. He and his Whig ministry were determined to bring the Russian Emperor to account. Although Britain did not possess a large army in Crimea, there was always the Royal Navy to carry the fight into the Baltic again and to the Far East.

Nicholas I was not prepared to let either Menshikov or his army remain idle. Although the Russian commander-in-chief was spared his post for the present, the elderly General-Adjutant Dmitry Yerofeyevich Osten-Saken relieved Dannenberg as the commanding general of 4th Corps, and became the commander of the Sevastopol garrison. Yet the prime problem lay with Menshikov. Very rarely to be seen south of the roadstead, he possessed neither much faith in the defence of Sevastopol nor any obvious empathy with its defenders. Largely indifferent to the fate of his men, he whiled away his time either in his main headquarters on the Belbek river nearly 20 kilometres distant, or, less frequently, in his forward headquarters on the northern side. There was nothing in his limited officer qualities to compare him with either Nakhimov or Istomin, both heroic admirals who would fight and fall in the defence of Sevastopol, following the same fate as Kornilov. Although a cultured, well-read man, Menshikov's 'aristocratic demeanour, and intolerance of those he considered his inferior' hardly endeared him to his command.[49] The soldiers and sailors manning the city's defences hardly knew their commander-in-chief: their disrespect for him was all too evident in their insolent nickname, 'Prince Izmenshchikov', a play on the Russian word *izmena*, which means treason.

Meanwhile, the chances of recovery and survival for the thousands of Russian wounded after Inkerman were low, as was the case following the Alma. Pirogov, who arrived in Sevastopol eighteen days after the latest blood-letting, found

... more than 2000 wounded, packed together lying on dirty mattresses, all mixed up, and for almost ten days in a row from morning to evening I had to operate on such wounded who should have been treated immediately after the battle. Only on the 24th November appeared the chief of staff and a general staff doctor, as if there were no war in progress. They neither provided linen nor means of transport.

In the same letter home, the great surgeon could not conceal his contempt for the Russian high command's maladministration and brazen neglect of the troops.

'Whom do [they] take a soldier for?' he asked; and 'Who will fight boldly when he's convinced on being wounded, he'll be abandoned like a dog?'[50] Despite Pirogov's entreaties to the Russian chain of command, conditions within the improvised hospitals of Sevastopol remained deplorable. 'Only a few wounded lie on mattresses', he complained, the 'majority ... lie on boards'. Furthermore, 'because of a lack of linen and straw', the wounded 'have to stay for four or five days on mattresses which are soaked with pus and blood'.[51] Such were the appalling deficiencies in the Russian Army that led to so many deaths through wounding, sickness and disease.

ALLIED DISCORD AND THE RECALL OF BURGOYNE

By the beginning of 1855, despite the defensive success at Inkerman, concerns were growing amongst the Allied commanders, and not least amongst their senior artillery and engineer advisers, as to how best to conclude the siege. The principal question was where to focus the next bombardment and assault on Sevastopol. Burgoyne, the Allied general officer present most experienced in siege warfare, had urged since November 1854 that the main effort should be made against the Malakhov Tower, rather than the Bastion du Mât (the Fourth Bastion), which hitherto had been the French Army's preferred objective. Rather bizarrely, Burgoyne fell unwittingly into a bitter dispute with the French, who complained about his conduct, which in turn led to his recall home. For those interested in the personal dynamics of coalition operations, Burgoyne's downfall is a cautionary tale of the perils of misunderstanding between allies within a theatre of war and of pernicious political opportunism at home. Equally, military decisions amongst coalitions are often made on the basis of which national commander brings the most forces to bear, and not necessarily on the one who gives the best advice.[52]

Burgoyne first argued for an attack towards the Malakhov and 'the more complete occupation of the Inkerman Ridge' in a memorandum of 23 November 1854. He had identified (quite rightly, as it was to turn out on 8 September 1855) that this Russian position formed the key to the southern defences of Sevastopol, and that 'renewed efforts should be made against the Tower front [rather] than on the Redan'.[53] In order to achieve this desired action he suggested, in a further memorandum two days later, that the French should relieve the British Army from its Left Attack so the latter could concentrate on prosecuting an assault against the Malakhov Tower. He noted that the transport of the required 'additional artillery from Balaklava' would be 'greatly impeded by the dreadful state of the country', so this operation would take much effort to prepare.[54] At the time, however, the French were still firmly wedded to the plan of mounting their main attack against the Bastion du Mât, and not inclined to spread their effort elsewhere. Although Burgoyne conceded a lack of Allied agreement in another memorandum of 11 December 1854, he again made the case for the British to extend their positions at Inkerman, and not least to 'make advances towards the little height in front of the Tower' – by which he meant the 'Mamelon' (which was later to feature in a number of bitter engagements).[55] In a subsequent note of 20 December, Burgoyne submitted to Lord Raglan that the French be requested either to take over the British Left Attack or to assist elsewhere. 'Operations on the Right now undertaken by the British', he observed, 'are quite paralyzed for want of an adequate force'. In promoting his case, he claimed that General Canrobert was 'willing to reinforce the Right, so as to enable the British to take more active measures in the general proceedings'.[56] Although the French were subsequently to adopt the plan he had been recommending over recent weeks, Burgoyne was quite mistaken in believing that he had already gained the support of either the French commander or his chief engineer, General Michel Bizot. Far from it, in a letter of 28 December 1854 to Raglan, Canrobert, as Burgoyne reported home nearly a month later (22 January 1855) while arguments between the Allies rumbled on, had made 'accusations against the British proceedings, and of me in particular'. The causes of the French objections were twofold: first, the British were imposing on the French 'an undue share of the general operations'; and secondly, the British had receded 'from the plans originally laid down for the attack', to which they 'had fully assented'.[57] In consequence, Burgoyne admitted on 26 January 1855 that the French were still 'very angry with us'.[58]

The dispute between Bizot and Burgoyne was more than a professional disagreement between two senior engineers about the best methods of prosecuting the siege: it had become national and personal. Such differences can easily come to the fore in coalition operations, even among close allies. Bizot had formulated the original complaint, considering Burgoyne to be obstructive by trying to effect a major change in plan, and so delaying operations until the spring. Matters, however, did not rest in Crimea. Canrobert had sent a copy of his letter to Napoleon III, who, in turn, sent out his trusted military adviser and aide-de-camp, General Adolphe Niel, to investigate.[59] The letter was also passed to the British ambassador in Paris, and sent onwards to London. Niel arrived in Crimea at the end of January 1855, consulting Burgoyne on the 29th. Although there would appear to have been a meeting of minds, the exchange was not assisted by a mutual lack of proficiency in foreign languages. Hence Burgoyne sent a long memorandum the next day to Major General Rose (but intended as much for Niel) at the French Army's headquarters in which, having apologised for the 'very imperfect way' in which he could express himself in French, argued again for operations being directed towards the Malakhov as opposed to 'assaults on the

Redan and the Bastion du Mât.'[60] It would seem that Burgoyne's persistent advocacy of the Malakhov, long opposed by Bizot, had made a much better impression on Niel. At an Allied council of war held on 1 February 1855, it was decided that the Malakhov should be included in the scheme of attack. Writing home to Colonel Matson on the 5th, Burgoyne noted with obvious pride:

> The French are, I think, beginning to perceive that they were proposing to make too confined an attack against a great place, and are coming round to my wish of extending it.... They profess that they will have 250 guns in battery: and [with] the presence of General Niel, and my explanatory letters for him ... have led to their full adoption of the project for extending the attacks on the right all round the Tower of Malakoff.[61]

Although personally and professionally vindicated, Burgoyne could not afford to be triumphant about this abrupt change of French heart. While military decisions were being made in Crimea, the British government in London had come under increasing public and parliamentary pressure on account of the reported inadequacies of the British Army before Sevastopol. From the letters and press reports he received from Britain, Burgoyne could not ignore the rising tide of criticism and clamour for change. 'The consequences', he concluded on 9 February, 'may very likely reach *me*, and may send me home in disgrace!' Furthermore, he presumed he would be 'kicked out'.[62] His prognostication was entirely accurate – and already unfolding. Without waiting for General Niel to report back to Paris, the British government had secretly decided to replace Burgoyne. A suitable relief was conveniently at hand in the theatre of war. Major-General H. D. Jones, originally appointed as Commanding Royal Engineer in Constantinople, was re-directed to Crimea. On 10 February he joined Raglan's staff in command of the Royal Engineer Department.[63] Although Burgoyne had been appointed originally as a *strategic* adviser to the British commander, rather than as the Royal Engineers' commander, the writing was clearly on the wall. Six days later, the newly appointed Secretary of State for War in Palmerston's administration, Lord Panmure, announced in the House of Lords:

> [There being] no longer any occasion for the services of Sir John Burgoyne in the camp—General Harry Jones having now gone out there to take the command of the Engineer department—I have thought it my duty to recall Sir John Burgoyne to the office which he before filled with so much public advantage in this country—that of Inspector General of Fortifications, attached to the Ordnance Department.[64]

Burgoyne's family and friends sensed he had been made a politically convenient scapegoat for others' inadequacies. According to Wrottesley, the editor of Burgoyne's letters, Panmure wrote to Burgoyne on 23 February to 'assure him that there was no intention of casting any slur upon him by his recall from the seat of war'. The next day Panmure felt obliged to offer an explanation to the House of Lords. Burgoyne had been recalled 'not from any fault found with him by the Government', but rather that 'a younger officer' had been sent out 'to assume the duties of Commander of the Royal Engineers', not least to spare 'a man now far advanced in years ... from the sufferings of a Crimean winter'.[65] Indeed, as in all good spin there was some truth in the explanation – Burgoyne, while still sprightly for his age, had been born in 1782.

Raglan, who had done nothing to contest Burgoyne's dismissal, when writing on 19 March, professed his 'deep regret' about his imminent departure; and in thanking him for his assistance, declared his 'sincere conviction' that Burgoyne's 'conduct of operations of the siege of Sebastopol affords abundant proof' of his 'great ability and experience'.[66] Burgoyne showed great grace over the whole business, admitting to Matson on the 15th, 'whatever it may be to my own personal feelings, it will be quite as well for the public service that I should hasten home'.[67] His final duty before leaving Crimea was to issue a laudatory order of the day to the Royal Engineers, in which he expressed his 'strong testimony to the exemplary manner' in which all ranks had 'performed under his own eye their arduous duties before Sebastopol'.[68] So ended Burgoyne's direct involvement in the siege: on return home he continued to advise the government from time to time about the conduct of the Crimean War and to offer advice to his successor in theatre. Later he was to provide critical reviews of historians' accounts of the conflict, British and Russian alike.

RUSSIAN FAILURE AT YEVPATORIYA

While the French and British debated how to prosecute the siege of Sevastopol, Nicholas I continued to press Menshikov for decisive results in Crimea. Rather than making another attempt to attack the main Allied armies, thoughts turned to the port of Yevpatoriya, which had remained in Allied hands since the initial landings of mid-September 1854. In early 1855, its tiny French garrison of about 300 hundred troops had been relieved by a very much stronger Turkish contingent of 20,000 men under Omar Pasha. The Russians feared that this large force might be reinforced. According to reports, two new French divisions were being despatched to Crimea, and possibly a Piedmont–Sardinian contingent of 15,000 might join them. In a 'worst case' scenario, the Russians feared that this powerful Allied grouping might strike through the heartland of the peninsula to capture the Perekop. In this manner, the Allies could cut one of the Russians' principal lines of communications with Crimea – the other lying via the river Don and the Sea of Azov. Although this ambitious course of action was never attempted, there was some truth in this supposition: Napoleon III was already looking at ways at bringing the Crimean campaign to a fitting victorious close without the need for a potentially very costly assault on Sevastopol.

The prospects for the Russian attack on Yevpatoriya were poor from the outset: the opportunity to seize the port when it was weakly defended had been lost. The Turkish-led defence was based on strong fieldworks and thirty-four pieces of heavy artillery. Further support was available from British, French and Turkish warships lying close off shore. For their attack, the Russians assembled a force of twenty-two infantry battalions, twenty-four cavalry squadrons and 108 guns – altogether about 19,000 men – under the command of Lieutenant General Stepan Aleksandrovich Khrulev. Although he was openly confident of success, and had been selected by Menshikov precisely for his optimism, privately he harboured doubts as to the sense of any attempt to seize Yevpatoriya. Khrulev's attack on the morning of 17 February 1855 was badly conceived and executed. Allied naval guns installed on the town's defences made short work of the Russian artillery. A deep ditch filled with water hindered the Russian infantry assault, and the defenders were able to repel the Russian attack with ease. The fighting had lasted barely three hours: Russian casualties amounted to '768 men killed, missing, and wounded' while the Allies suffered fewer in comparison.[69] After this setback, Khrulev declined to continue the operation, wisely cutting his losses.

The Russians had precisely nothing to show for their abortive attempt to capture Yevpatoriya. In contrast, Allied options for various operations in Crimea, including the interdiction of the Perekop or the investment of the northern side of Sevastopol, remained open. Not only did the Russian Army's faith in its senior leadership take another serious blow, but also Nicholas I finally saw the need to remove Menshikov. Worse still, the shock of yet another defeat hit the Emperor hard physically and psychologically. He had already gone down with a bout of influenza the day before the attempt to seize Yevpatoriya. But when Nicholas I heard of its failure on 23 February, according to Dr Mandt, his personal physician, 'the news of the reverses ... stunned him and struck the final blow'. Thus the Emperor's condition took an immediate turn for the worst. From his deathbed four days later he instructed his son Alexander, the Crown Prince, to send Menshikov a letter of dismissal. It recorded the fact that 'His Majesty was most grieved by the unsuccessful attack on Yevpatoriya undertaken by General Khrulev at your order, and by the considerable losses which our brave troops have suffered yet again – without any profit whatsoever'.[70] Nicholas I died a broken man on 2 March 1855. While much of Russia mourned his passing and greeted his successor, there remained no end in sight for a conflict that was consuming so much of the nation's scarce resources. Whether Alexander II would continue the war with renewed vigour or seek an acceptable peace had yet to be seen.

Menshikov's temporary replacement was the sixty-five year-old Osten-Saken until the nominated permanent relief, General of Artillery Prince Mikhail Dmitrievich [M. D.] Gorchakov (the brother of P. D. Gorchakov) arrived from the Danube front. While neither of these individuals inspired much confidence in Sevastopol, none was vilified to the same extent as Menshikov. Osten-Saken, however, was not keen to get involved in the minutiae of the defence of the city, and, by official order, on 18 February 1855 [OS] he appointed Admiral Nakhimov to command the garrison, normalising the *de facto* arrangements already existing. M. D. Gorchakov's arrival on 19 March did not affect the situation in Sevastopol to any marked degree. One critical contemporary account referred to him as 'an ancient old man, disoriented, lost in words and thoughts – not resembling at all a commander-in-chief'.[71] He would not prove to be an energetic individual, and in terms of professional competence, despite his illustrious early military career, he proved hardly more effective than the disgraced Menshikov. On the same day, Rear Admiral Vladimir Istomin was struck by a cannon ball at the Kamchatka Lunette; so fell one of the most 'talented organisers of the defence'.[72] Istomin was buried next to Lazarev and Kornilov in the vault of the still incomplete St Vladimir's Cathedral.

LEO TOLSTOY AND THE DEFENCE OF SEVASTOPOL

Lev (Leo) Nikolayevich Tolstoy enters Sevastopol's story a few weeks after Inkerman. Some years before, as a feckless young man of noble origins, he had deserted his university studies in Kazan and dissipated his time thereafter in the gambling rooms, drinking dens and whorehouses of Moscow and St Petersburg. In 1851, aged twenty-three, having lost heavily both his money and reputation, Tolstoy travelled to the Caucasus and joined his brother to serve in the Russian Imperial Army. On the outbreak of war with the Ottoman Empire in 1853, he applied to enter the staff of his uncle, General M. D. Gorchakov, then serving as commander-in-chief of the Army of the Danube. Following the cessation of hostilities in the Principalities and the associated Russian withdrawal to their own territory by August 1854, Tolstoy grew restless, bored by the tedium of life in a headquarters. Writing to his aunt, T. A. Yergolskaya, from the 'pretty, provincial town' of Kishinyov[73] in late October 1854, Tolstoy welcomed the reports from Crimea, which had been 'cheering of late', for 'today we learned the news of Liprandi's victory' – the battle of Balaklava. Not wishing to miss the main action, he dreamt of 'camp life' and was 'envious of those who follow it.'[74]

Tolstoy reached Sevastopol towards the end of November 1854. Remaining on and off duty in the city for the next nine months, he wrote about his experiences of war in a semi-autobiographical manner. He captures his first impressions in the opening pages of the first of his three *Sevastopol Sketches* ('In December 1854'):

A cold mist blows in from the bay; there is no snow—all is black—but the sharp morning frost creaks underfoot and makes the face tingle, while only the distant murmur of the sea, now and then overpowered by the thunder of the cannons in Sevastopol, breaks the stillness of the morning. All is quiet on the ships. It strikes eight bells.[75]

On crossing the roadstead from the northern side, the visitor hears 'the steady murmur of voices which reaches you across the water, and ... the majestic sounds of the firing which, it seems to you, now grows stronger in Sevastopol'. Then, in a manner felt by so many when entering the city for the first time, some 'feeling of courage or pride surely enters your soul, and the blood flows faster in your veins, at the thought that you, too, are in Sevastopol'.[76] When disembarking at the Grafskaya landing place, Tolstoy observes:

On the quay, soldiers in grey, sailors in black, and women in many colours throng noisily. Women are selling rolls, peasants with samovars are calling 'hot [drinks,]' and here, on the very first steps, lie rusty cannon-balls, bombs, grape-shot, and cast-iron cannons of various calibres. A little beyond is a large open space where huge beams, gun-carriages, and sleeping soldiers are lying; ... To the right the street is blocked by a barricade with small cannon mounted in embrasures.... To the left is a handsome building ..., and near it stand soldiers with blood-stained stretchers — everywhere you see unpleasant indications of a war camp.[77]

Tolstoy's imaginary visitor is confronted soon enough by the grim realities of war. On entering the large Assembly Hall that served as a field hospital, he observes 'the sight and smell of forty or fifty of the amputated and the most severely wounded, some in beds but most on the floor'. Then he views the surgeons 'engaged on the horrible but beneficent work of amputation'. On 'coming out of this house of pain', he notes that 'you will be sure to experience a sense of relief', but you will also 'realise your own insignificance, and you will go to the bastions calmly and without hesitation'.[78] In such cameos, Tolstoy revealed to Russia the battle for Sevastopol in all its horrific reality, a far cry from the tales of heroism that had hitherto reached the public.

On picking his way carefully through the city up to the central, exposed Fourth Bastion, known to the British as the Flagstaff Battery, the visitor experiences:

The whiz of cannon ball or bomb near by, impresses you unpleasantly as you ascend the hill, and you at once understand the meaning of the sounds very differently from when they reached you in the town. Some peaceful and joyous memory will suddenly flash through your mind; consciousness of your own personality begins to supersede the activity of your observation; you are less attentive to all that is around you, and a disagreeable feeling of indecision suddenly seizes you.[79]

Tolstoy skilfully paints a picture of mounting danger for his readers. 'You seem to hear the different sounds of bullets all around,' he writes, 'some humming like bees, some whistling, and some rapidly flying past with a shrill screech like the string of some instrument. You hear the awful boom of a shot which sends a shock all through you and seems most dreadful'.[80] For anyone who has been under fire this is a very realistic portrayal of combat.

Proceeding along a narrow trench, eventually the Fourth Bastion is gained. 'You will come out at ... a flat space with many holes, surrounded with gabions filled with earth, and cannons on platforms, and the whole walled in with earthworks.'[81] Tolstoy then directs attention to the gun crews:

Quickly and cheerfully [they] man the gun and begin loading. Look well into their faces, and note the bearing and carriage of these men. In every wrinkle, every muscle, in the breadth of their shoulders, the thickness of these legs in enormous boots: in every movement, quiet, firm, and deliberate, are seen the distinctive traits of that which forms the strength of the Russian—his simplicity and obstinacy.[82]

In this manner, Tolstoy pays handsome tribute to his Russian countrymen. His reader's thoughts are abruptly broken as the eyewitness tugs a literary lanyard:

Suddenly the most fearful roar strikes not only your ears but your whole being, and makes you shudder all over. It is followed by the whistle of the departing ball, and a thick cloud of powder-smoke envelops you, the platform, and the moving black figures of the sailors.[83]

Tolstoy describes a classic artillery duel between opposing batteries, where fire is exchanged on a deadly tit-for-tat basis. At the Fourth Battery, the Russian gun crews calmly await incoming shot or shell. A mortar bomb explodes amongst them. Tolstoy's observer is 'startled by the groans of a man'. To the stretcher-bearers who have come to his aid, the mortally wounded man utters his last farewell 'with an effort in a trembling voice, "Forgive me, brothers!"'

Now comes a precious moment for Tolstoy to reflect on the meaning of it all. Perhaps written in some dark, dank dug-out under flickering candlelight, he penned: 'The principal, joyous, thought you have brought away with you is a conviction of the strength of the Russian people'. This view is gained 'not by looking at all those traverses, breastworks, cunningly interlaced trenches, mines, cannon', but one received 'from the eyes, words, and actions—in short, from seeing what is called the 'spirit'—of the defenders of Sevastopol'.[84] The consummate – romanticising – skill of his writing is reflected in the final lyrical lines of his opening Sketch, concluding a first day spent in Sevastopol: 'The evening closes in…. The sound of some old [waltz] played by a military band on the boulevard is borne along the water, and seems, in some strange way, answered by the firing from the bastions.[85]

While Tolstoy's first piece of writing about Sevastopol stems from his experiences of December 1854, conditions inside the city remained much the same for the remainder of the Allied siege until September 1855. The Russians, however, were not passive. In contrast with the British, who were largely content to build up supplies, re-equip and wait after Inkerman, the defenders of Sevastopol were very active in attempting to disrupt the Allies. Apart from the violent artillery exchanges that took place during the major bombardments, they undertook a series of daring sorties and raids on the Allied trench lines and batteries; furthermore, a vicious fight developed between French and Russian engineers below ground level.

One of the most effective operations mounted by Russian troops from Sevastopol's defences took place during the night of 10/11 March 1855. It involved the seizure and fortification of a small mound, Green Hill, known to the French as the 'Mamelon Vert' situated in No Man's Land between the Malakhov and the French siege lines.[86] The French, as had Burgoyne well beforehand, had already identified the feature's tactical importance. The Russians' erection of the powerful Kamchatka Lunette with ten cannon on top of the Mamelon would not only make the French assault on the Malakhov very much more difficult, but also impede any British advance towards the Redan.

Twelve days later, during the night of 22/23 March, the defenders of Sevastopol launched an ambitious series of sorties against numerous sectors of the British and French lines. Under the command of Lieutenant General Khrulev – perhaps attempting to salvage his damaged reputation following the debacle at Yevpatoriya – no fewer than eleven Russian battalions were involved. Although some damage was done to the Allied positions, the Russians were beaten off in savage fighting. In comparison with the losses of the great battles, the casualty toll might appear light, but none the less a few hours of night combat had cost the Russians 1,300 men, the French 642 and the British eighty-five.[87] Not only was the lack of vigilance on the part of the Allies disturbing (the British were probably more to blame here than the French), but the spirited action also showed, as had the recent capture of the Mamelon, that the Russians were far from a spent, demoralised force. Consequently, the morale of the defenders of Sevastopol was boosted from such operations, and suitable heroes were identified for propaganda purposes. One such individual was a Ukrainian sailor, Piotr Koshka. His speciality was raiding Allied batteries and trenches, and in taking enemy officers prisoner. This man of 'rare daring' took part in eighteen such sorties, including Khrulev's operation. His valour was recognised in a battlefield commission to quartermaster. On his final action he was seriously injured. Despite receiving a bayonet wound in his stomach, which normally would have been fatal, Pirogov decided to operate on him. Thanks to the skill of the gifted surgeon, Koshka survived: his name became legendary in the defence of Sevastopol.[88] Today his statue flanks that of Admiral Kornilov on the Malakhov Hill.

In siege operations, mining to bring down an enemy's castle towers or town walls had been a well-practised method of attack since the Middle Ages, and in ancient times before that. Although British engineers had undertaken limited mining operations during the Peninsular War, it was the French who tunnelled under the Russian defences of Sevastopol. Their principal target was the Fourth Bastion; work began in October 1854. The Russians, however, were quick to respond in counter-mine operations, in many ways presaging the bitterly contested underground warfare on the Western Front of the First World War. The basic technique involved the construction of a gallery over a calculated distance to a point where a charge of black powder explosives would be laid in a chamber, tamped (constrained with sand bags and timber to maximise the blast or lifting effect in the desired direction) and then detonated at a desired time. Russian counter-miners used the same technique except that their object was to destroy the French shafts and the engineers digging them. The scope of this underground war at Sevastopol was unprecedented in nineteenth-century warfare. By way of illustration, the Russian official account listed that in the vicinity of the Fourth Bastion over the period 3 February to 5 September 1855, there were 107 French and eighty-three Russian detonations. The quantities of explosive involved might have been small in contrast to the hundreds of tonnes used during the First World War, but nevertheless the French expended nearly 60,000 pounds of gun powder, about six times the quantity employed by the Russians. Inevitably there were many casualties: nine Frenchmen were killed (including by asphyxiation) and ninety-four wounded; Russian losses were higher with fifty-four killed and 137 wounded.[89] An entrance to a surviving Crimean War tunnel is still visible at Sevastopol's Fourth Bastion.

CHARLES GORDON AND ALLIED TECHNICAL DEVELOPMENTS

Charles George Gordon, a Victorian national hero, was killed at Khartoum, Sudan, in 1885.[90] Thirty years before, the young Royal Engineers officer disembarked at Balaklava on 1 January 1855, a month short of his twenty-second birthday. Before embarking for Crimea he had informed his parents that 'I go out in charge of the huts'.[91] The flat-packed structures were probably the first examples of the British Army's expeditionary camp infrastructure, which are taken for granted in much more recent operations in the Balkans, Iraq or Afghanistan.

Gordon's first recorded impressions of Crimea, written two days after his arrival, were not particularly positive:

> The roads are bad beyond description, being quite a morass the whole way up. I have not yet seen Sevastopol, and do not hear anything about the siege. We hear a gun now and then, but they are generally fired by the Russians at the French. No one seems to interest himself about the siege, but all appear to be engaged in foraging for grub…. The weather continues very mild, with rain and few showers of snow.[92]

In the same letter, Gordon noted that he had seen 'Mr. Russell, the *Times* correspondent'. It had been William Howard Russell's critical reporting of the war during the late autumn of 1854 that had aroused public indignation at home and placed so much pressure on the British government to improve supplies and soldiers' conditions, culminating in John Roebuck's parliamentary motion.

The lack of adequate winter shelter and warm clothing for the British Army before Sevastopol took its grim toll. On 8 January 1855, when the weather took a severe turn for the worse, Gordon noted that two infantry officers had 'frozen to death'.[93] Captain Henry Clifford, subsequently to be awarded a Victoria Cross for his gallantry at the battle of Inkerman, recorded on the 12th that there were '999 sick in Camp, of the Light Division', and complained that 'we have no Huts up here yet'.[94] A week later, Clifford wrote that the 'poor men are certainly suffering more than human nature can stand. They are dying off fast every day'.[95] Gordon, however, had noted on the 3rd that 'about 300 huts are here'. Understandably, with the mounting rates of death, sickness and frostbite, the delay in the erection of the huts caused considerable anger within the British Army.[96] Yet a lack of suitable roads and transport precluded them being put up swiftly where they were needed – in the camps on the Chersonese plateau that overlooked Sevastopol. A recent technological innovation brought much-needed respite. The Grand Crimean Central Railway, as it was rather pretentiously to be called, owed its existence to the public clamour in Britain for 'something to be done' in order to address the logistic difficulties faced by the British Army before Sevastopol.

The inspiration for the Crimean railway came from Samuel Morton Peto, a railway entrepreneur and Liberal MP, partnered with Edward Ladd Betts and Thomas Brassey. In early November 1854, Peto had approached the Duke of Newcastle with a plan to construct a very basic, just fit-for-purpose railway. A month later, the Secretary of State for War informed Raglan that the contractors would 'have the railroad at work three weeks after landing at Balaklava'.[97] Although the challenges in meeting this urgent operational requirement were enormous, the drive and determination of the Victorian railwaymen were soon evident. Quickly and efficiently, the necessary materiel and steam winding-engines (at this stage no locomotives were envisaged) were assembled, and the shipping hired to transport the equipment to Crimea. A bespoke labour force comprised 250 'platelayers, navvies and miners', with additional craftsmen such as 'masons, bricklayers, carpenters, blacksmiths, enginemen and fitters'.[98]

When Gordon arrived in Crimea, construction of the railway had yet to start. When opened in stages from the end of February, the railway proved to be an absolutely essential lifeline to the Allied troops besieging Sevastopol. It was a highly impressive achievement: within three weeks of arrival of the equipment, materials and men at Balaklava, a wharf and sidings at the port had been constructed and the first, short section of the railway had started to run. British navvies, supported by a group of 200 Croat labourers, were hard at work.[99] At its peak, the railway's workforce grew to over 1,000 men. While Clifford was 'astonished to see the progress of the Railway in Balaklava' (as noted on 12 February), he observed acerbically that the 'Navvies ... do more work in a day than a Regiment of English soldiers do in a week.' Yet the huts were by then 'springing up in every direction'.[100] On 23 February, the first trainload of supplies reached Kadikoi. Onwards and upwards the navvies pushed, the line soon ascending the Col de Balaklava to surmount the southern end of the Sapun escarpment. On 26 March, 'the first load of shot and shell was carried right through to the headquarters depot' on the Chersonese plateau.[101] In just under seven weeks, 11 kilometres of track had been completed, linking Balaklava and the British lines.

In the interim, the logistical and organisational problems at Balaklava had been compounded by the need to support a proportion of the French Army as well. As Gordon observed, 'Through our smallness of numbers, we have given up the Inkerman batteries to the French, who will for the future victual a division from this place, which will add to the confusion, and that is now pretty considerable.'[102]

The young engineer officer quickly became bored at Balaklava: 'there is not much doing here at present. The Russians and French keep up a little fire, but our trenches are silent.'[103] On 18 January 1855 Gordon recorded his first glimpse of Sevastopol: 'I do not think I ever saw a prettier city; ... the surrounding country is a beautiful one and very picturesque.'[104] On 2 February 1855, Gordon wrote 'I am making lots of sketches and will send some home soon,' adding that the 'health of the men has improved greatly; the wet is what makes them ill'.[105] Ten days later, he observed critically, 'Nothing much is doing, except repairing our batteries and getting ready for our second siege', by which he meant the second bombardment of Sevastopol that in fact did not commence until 9 April 1855.[106]

Gordon proved no idle camp-wallah, although he did enjoy the comfort of a 'quite warm' double-lined tent. As an officer of energy and enterprise, he served regular turns of duty in the trenches, supervising sapper working parties and leading night-time reconnaissance patrols out into the No Man's Land between the Allied and Russian lines. The British trenches, which zigzagged their way towards the Russian defences in a number of 'parallels' and branches, were hard to navigate at night without lights. Engineer officers and non-commissioned officers became the most reliable guides – it is said that the British Army's exhortation 'Follow the Sapper!' stems from this period.[107] Gordon's first taste of combat was a friendly fire incident during one of these night patrols, when two of his own sentries mistakenly fired at his working party, immediately provoking in turn 'a shower of bullets' from the Russians.[108] The ever-resourceful Russians established a series of 'rifle pits', another of Todleben's innovations, which they pushed out towards the French and British trenches and batteries. These outposts proved difficult to dislodge: the Russian sharpshooters who manned them proved highly dangerous to Allied troops. Gordon was extremely lucky to survive a sniping incident at the end of February, in which he gave due credit to the high standard of Russian skill at arms: 'A shot ... nearly as possible did for me; the bullet was fired not 180 yards off, and passed an inch above my nut into a bank I was passing'.[109]

Towards the end of March 1855, Gordon made some positive comments on the progress of the siege:

> The Russians are said to be short of ammunition, which seems likely, as they do not fire very much. Our artillery does great damage to a new work they have just erected on the Mamelon; the practice is capital. The railway is progressing rapidly. It is not very far from this spot.... We are very well off, and the men look first-rate.[110]

Gordon's impressions contrast greatly with the depressing reports of the British Army that had so inflamed popular opinion at home at the turn of the year. As he remarked caustically, 'If people here knew what trash appears in the papers, they would stare. Everyone out here is sick and tired of the bygone grievances.

Nothing is easier than to find fault.'[111] In fact, the British Army was fast recovering from the winter malaise of illness and inactivity. Plentiful ammunition, food and other stores were now being brought up from Balaklava efficiently by rail. Gordon recorded that 'More than 500 rounds per gun are up in the batteries.'[112]

Towards the end of April, Gordon provided a further indication of the changing character of warfare. '[The] electric telegraph is complete ... we can hear London in twelve hours, and it is to be thrown open to officers, at £1 12s. 6d. per message.'[113] Because this novel method of communication was expensive, Gordon does not appear to have used it. Yet the telegraph represented a significant technological achievement. In consequence, the Allied commanders on Crimea were tied much closer to their governments in Paris and London. Written orders, which had until recently taken weeks or even months to reach the theatre of war, could now be supplemented by telegraphic communications that would take a few hours (or a day or so at worst) to transmit and decode on receipt. Hence the days of unfettered expeditionary warfare were over. A decentralised *laissez-faire* approach, long practised in navies, and much later codified in some armies as 'mission command', would hereafter be constrained by frequent political inquiry or, from a military standpoint, over-direction and interference in the conduct of war. The commanding generals would soon have to come to terms with this new state of affairs. Politico-military relations would never be the same again.

CHAPTER 7

DEFEAT AND DEFIANCE

'Bravery in the soldiers and mediocrity in the generals are the chief characteristics, on both sides, of the present war.'

Friedrich Engels[1]

THE SECOND BOMBARDMENT AND NIKOLAY PIROGOV

As Engels's acerbic assessment reveals, all sides in Crimea displayed plenty of courage but rather less generalship, whether in Allied siegecraft or in Russian battlefield manoeuvre. The battles of Alma, Balaklava and Inkerman had demonstrated the growing effectiveness of modern weapons, which outpaced the ability of the generals to adjust their tactics in response. In presaging developments subsequently shown in the American Civil War, the Franco-Prussian and Russo-Japanese Wars, and the First World War, the increasing power of the defence relative to the offence was becoming all too evident, whether on a Russian bastion at Sevastopol or at a French entrenchment on the Fedyukhin Heights facing the Chernaya river.

While the campaign on Crimea approached its climax at Sevastopol, largely ineffectual Allied naval operations in the Baltic, and the Russo-Turkish fighting in the Caucasus, including the Russian siege of the Turkish fortress of Kars, remained under way. Meanwhile, diplomatic efforts to end the war continued in Vienna. The new Tsar, Emperor Alexander II, wished the conflict to be concluded as quickly as possible. Naturally enough, he desired the best possible terms available to Russia, and ideally with the minimum loss of both territory and international reputation. With so much national blood spilt and treasure expended, however, a resolution that satisfied all parties to the conflict would take time to cement. Hence the Russians and the Allies both sought in the interim to win an elusive, strategically decisive, victory, and thereby bring the maximum possible advantage to the conference table. Whereas the Allies prepared for a second major bombardment of Sevastopol, the city's hard-pressed defenders realised that time was not on their side. Sooner rather than later, therefore, another major effort to raise the siege would be required.

Industrial war, of which Crimea was perhaps the first in many respects, is as much a matter of massing sufficient quantities of matierel as of concentrating the required numbers of men. The completion of the railway from Balaklava to the Chersonese plateau made an enormous difference to the British logistic situation before Sevastopol. Now supplies and particularly artillery ammunition could be brought up with comparative ease. As a result, large quantities of powder, shot and shell were deposited in the forward magazines ready for the next major bombardment of the city. Likewise the French prepared and readied their batteries.

The second bombardment finally commenced on 9 April 1855. After a few days, it prompted Charles Gordon to compare the effects of the Allied and Russian artillery. Writing on 13 April 1855, he recorded:

> We re-opened fire last Monday, ... and took our friends the Russians by surprise. The fire still continues, and the enemy's works are very much injured.... The Russian fire, although good, is not nearly as brisk as it used to be, which may be on account of shortness of ammunition, or from want of gunners, their old ones being dead. Our batteries are a little knocked about, but there are not more than two guns disabled by the enemy's shot.

A week later, he noted the 'French keep up their fire very well, and have reduced that of the Russians very much. Our 13" mortars do a great deal of harm to the Russians.... There are frequent fires in the town from the shells.[2]

Within the battered defences of Sevastopol, Pirogov observed the shattering impact of the Allied bombardment:

> On Monday of Holy Week on 29 March [OS] at 5 a.m. we were awoken by a strong cannonade – the windows of my room were rattled as if hundreds of blacksmiths were striking at the walls with their hammers. We quickly dressed ... bombs and rockets were flying; we ran at full speed to the dressing station and soon a huge hall was filling up with the wounded with terrible injuries: severed hands, legs torn off at the knees or the waist.

The consequences for members of the Russian garrison were severe: 'We received over 400 wounded within the [first] 24 hours', the surgeon noted, 'and carried out more than 30 amputations. From this day on, the bombardment continued every day and night to 6 April [OS]'.[3] It was estimated that the Allies fired 168,700 rounds of shot and shell into Sevastopol during their nine-day bombardment, and the Russians responded with just under half that number. The ever-resourceful Russians, however, albeit at heavy cost in men and materiel, were able to repair at night the damage inflicted by day, following Todleben's direction and improvisational talent.

In the event, the second Allied bombardment failed to bring about a decision in the campaign, as had the first. As in October 1854, there was no general attack on the city. Yet it was becoming clear in this war of attrition that the Allies were slowly but surely gaining an advantage in the longer term, particularly in their ability to reinforce their forces besieging Sevastopol, and to keep them well supplied. Inside the city, morale began to drop again, and doubts as to the viability of its defence began to resurface. In a letter of 30 April 1855 [OS], Pirogov captured the prevailing mood – one more of frustration than of fear:

> Neither the work nor labour frightens us – we're trying our best – but the obstacles which have taken root [here] impede us from making improvements. The challenges grow like hydra's heads: you cut off one and another one appears.... Various rumours are spreading about the possibility of Sevastopol either falling or standing: some are confident that it cannot fall as an army of 120,000 lies inside it. Others say that [the city] is in great danger and will not withstand [an enemy attack]. In any case, I'm sure that the matter won't be resolved soon.[4]

A week later, the surgeon returned to one of his main themes of his correspondence with his wife: his despair at the Russian senior leadership in Crimea and Sevastopol. Fed up with 'military intrigues', he observed caustically:

> One does not need to be a great strategist to understand the manner in which vulgarity and stupidity are demonstrated here: headquarters consist of worthless people; the most competent of military men do not conceal rude mistakes, indecisiveness and nonsense, which prevail here in military affairs. Many even wish Menshikov to be back. If God does not help us, we cannot count on anyone, and need to leave this place on our own accord.[5]

For the first time an evidently fatigued and intensely frustrated Pirogov betrayed his own misgivings about the wisdom of prolonging the defence of Sevastopol. Perhaps speaking for many, he declared privately: 'In St. Petersburg I am sure they have no idea as to what's going on here'. More glumly he recorded: 'The best thing now is to move into the middle of nowhere, to see nothing but the surroundings and to hear nothing.' Then came the crunch: 'Today I am sending a request to Gorchakov to transfer me and the other doctors who escorted me here to St. Petersburg'.[6] Unsurprisingly, his application was turned down.

Pirogov remained in Crimea until the end of 1855, serving in Sevastopol, Bakhchisaray and Simferopol – the latter city representing the Russian's main centre of medical care and convalescence. Altogether he spent seven months in Sevastopol and another seven elsewhere in the peninsula during the war. His medical achievements during the war were many and significant. In Eastern Europe and in the states of the former Soviet Union, Pirogov is remembered, honoured and treasured.[7] Without exaggeration, both civilian and military medicine today owe much to his pioneering methods. First, he was an early advocate of preventative medicine and cleanliness. He organised voluntary female nurses to take care of the injured; he introduced a series of fundamental practices, including anaesthesia (using both ether and chloroform) to military surgery and the use of plaster to stabilise and set fractures. He streamlined operating procedures by teams of surgeons working together; and established a system of triage to prioritise and regulate the treatment of the wounded whether at the dressing station, field or base hospital. In many respects he was well ahead of his time.

The triage system, which Pirogov adopted in Sevastopol, was a model of pragmatism that dealt with both the steady flow and the inevitable surges of wounded after battle or a heavy bombardment that threatened to overwhelm the medical system. On expert inspection by members of the medical staff, the newly arrived were divided into four basic categories. Those with slight injuries, including many of the 'walking wounded', were sent to dressing stations, many of which were located in the shore batteries, before being returned to their units for front-line duty. More serious cases needing surgical treatment were held ready for operations within the next twenty-four hours or so. The most urgent cases, however, were dealt with as quickly as possible in the main operating theatre established within the Assembly Rooms for Nobles at Catherine's (now Nakhimov) Square. The remainder, the mortally wounded or dying, were entrusted to the care of nurses and priests in places such as Gushchin House, situated on Morskaya Street.[8]

Apart from his duties as the senior Russian surgeon in the besieged city, Pirogov was responsible for the 'Sisters of Mercy' – the nurses who had journeyed from St Petersburg and Moscow to Sevastopol to tender whatever assistance they could to the growing numbers of Russian military sick and wounded. On 6 December 1854 [OS], a little under a month after he arrived in Sevastopol, he wrote:

About five days ago the Community of the Holy Cross of [Grand Duchess] Helena Pavlovna arrived here, about 30 of them, setting zealously to work; if they continue in such a manner, undoubtedly it will bring a lot of good. They serve alternately day and night in the hospitals, assist with the dressing of the wounds and in operations, hand out tea and wine to the wounded, and watch over the servants, ward-keepers and even the doctors.[9]

This group, the first of several to reach the Crimean theatre of operations, was mainly of noble origin. These ladies, however, were not the first nurses to work in the city. Local women drawn from the townsfolk and the families of the garrison had assisted the Russian Army since the battle of the Alma. In an earlier letter, Pirogov had recorded that 'during the bandaging of the wounded, one can see every day three or four women; the first is the famous Darya; another is an officer's daughter, a girl of seventeen; another is a soldier's wife'.[10] The woman he named specifically was a local heroine, Darya Lavrentevna Mikhailova, an eighteen-year-old whose father, a Russian sailor, had died during the battle of Sinope. She later became better known as Dasha Sevastopolskaya (Dasha of Sevastopol). Completely on her own initiative, she had nursed the Russian wounded on the Alma battlefield and thereafter tended them within Sevastopol. Her selfless and inspiring commitment in the city amongst eventually 120 female nurses acting in various capacities became legendary across Russia: so much so, Nicholas I rewarded her with 500 silver roubles with a promise of 1,000 if she were to marry, and a gold medal 'For Zeal' in November 1854.[11] As Pirogov observed, Darya proudly wore her award as she tended the men under her care. The surgeon also noted her 'prettiness', which would have made her a welcome sight in the wards of the wounded.[12] Although her accomplishments were real enough, her humble, working-class, origins made her subsequently a suitable heroine of the Soviet propaganda machine.[13]

There is little doubt, had it not been for the work of Pirogov, of the likes of Darya, and of the Sisters of Mercy, the immense suffering endured by the Russian wounded and dying during the campaign as a whole and siege of Sevastopol specifically would have been far worse. Pirogov later drew together the learning he had gained from the two conflicts in which he had served during the 1840s and 1850s. Published in 1864, his monumental *Basics of General Military Surgery* became a standard textbook in the German-speaking world, as did its translation in Russian within his homeland.[14] His treatise contained many hard-won lessons about the need for cleanliness and the prevention of disease in military hospitals. In particular, he was convinced that 'efficient administration' formed the bedrock of effective military medical practice in wartime – 'not the medicine [and] not the surgery'.[15]

Pirogov described how hard pressed the Russians were in finding suitable locations for the care and treatment of their wounded in Sevastopol, an aspect of the siege that finds little attention in most Allied accounts. Following the battle of the Alma, the main naval hospital on the eastern, 'ship', side of Sevastopol (the Korabelnaya suburb) was soon overflowing. Once the Allied bombardment started, it became increasingly untenable. Whether this institution was specifically targeted is not clear, but Pirogov recorded that it had to be abandoned in March 1855. By this time, many other buildings were being used as makeshift dressing stations and hospitals, including the Nicholas and Paul Batteries on the southern side of Sevastopol and the Michael Battery on the northern.[16] Although these fortifications offered better protection than the private houses and officers' messes pressed into service, they were hardly ideal with their congestion, limited light and poor ventilation.

One passage in Pirogov's tract on military surgery probably did not endear him to his former employer, the Russian Army. Recalling no doubt all the intense frustrations he had experienced in Sevastopol, he gave full vent to his concerns:

> The aspiring military physician has a moral obligation not to be indifferent to all administrative abuses – for their consequences are more harmful than the blunders of medicine and surgery. [Any] military surgical respect for superiors, fear or narrow-chested egotism should not stop him from speaking the truth and so exposing evil where it concerns the welfare of thousands.[17]

Perhaps significantly, Pirogov's professional association with military medicine paused for many years following the Crimean War.[18]

THE SIEGE CONTINUES

By April 1855, an expanding French Army of 110,000 men dwarfed the British contingent in Crimea, mustering about 30,000. Frustration, if not a little envy, about the French began to creep into Gordon's correspondence. His commentary became highly critical:

> I cannot say much for the enterprise of our allies. They are afraid to do anything, and consequently, quite cramp our movements, as you will easily understand that if one part of the trenches is pushed on before the other parts, the advanced sections will be liable to be attacked and outflanked by the Russians. I think we might have assaulted on the Monday, but the French do not seem to care about it.

If Gordon's criticisms of the French appear to be unfair, he is similarly critical about his own high command and about his opponents. His impatience, if not youthful impetuosity, is revealed in another letter:

> We are pushing forward our batteries as fast as possible, but cannot advance our trenches until the French take the Mamelon, as it would enfilade our advance works. We are very comfortable as far as grub, etc., is concerned; but want to see some result in our work, as the summer is very near, and we ought to be doing something. I do not think the Russians can do us any harm, but unless we take the place we can do them as little.... I must conclude this very stupid letter (which is not my fault as none of the three nations—French, English, or Russians—will do anything).[19]

From the late autumn of 1854, and until the end of the Crimean campaign, the French remained the dominant partner in the coalition as far as land forces were concerned, and were able to influence its strategy accordingly. By the early summer of 1855, with 120,000 men now deployed, the French could call the shots. The British Army was no longer the second largest force: that belonged to the Ottoman Empire, which had sent about 55,000 Ottoman troops under Omar Pasha. Meanwhile, the newly arrived Piedmont–Sardinian contingent mustered 17,000.

Both the Allies and the Russians proved more enterprising than Gordon's complaints reveal. The French and the British held the operational level initiative, seeking ways to increase the pressure on Sevastopol and so break the stalemate that the siege had become. A major weakness in their campaign remained, however: the failure to seize the northern side of the city. Although there was never any attempt to mount such an operation, the Allies undertook another, less direct one in order to reduce the flow of Russian supplies to Sevastopol. The objective chosen was the town of Kerch on the eastern tip of Crimea, at the entrance to the Sea of Azov. Neither its capture on 25 May 1855 nor the subsequent naval operations in that sea, however, reduced significantly the ability of Russian forces in Sevastopol to resist. When the Allies finally entered the city in September they found vast quantities of foodstuffs. The defenders' principal shortage lay in ammunition and gunpowder, the supply of which was largely unaffected by the loss of Kerch.

Meanwhile, under continuing heavy pressure from Paris and London, Allied commanders renewed offensive operations towards and around Sevastopol. As ever, the French were in the lead. Their forces cleared the Fedyukhin Hills north of the North Valley, along which the Light Brigade had charged on 25 October 1854. In consequence, the Russians evacuated the redoubts along the Causeway

Heights (on the line of the Vorontsov Road) they had captured at the beginning of the battle of Balaklava six months before. The Sardinians secured the French right by occupying dominating positions on Gasfort Hill. The French also stormed Russian trenches in front of the Quarantine and Central Bastions to the west and south of Sevastopol respectively.

In June 1855 Russian forces in and around Sevastopol totalled about 75,000 men. While the city was defended by seventy-eight battalions of infantry (45,000 men) and 9,000 naval gunners, a small field army of thirty-nine battalions (21,000 men), with 100 field guns positioned in the Belbek valley and on the Mackenzie Heights, both secured the line of communications to inland Crimea and acted as a threat to the Allied besieging troops. According to Russian estimates, the Allies outnumbered them by about 2.25:1 with about 170,000 men at their disposal: approximately 100,000 French (an under-estimate), 45,000 British (an over-estimate), 15,000 Sardinian and 10,000 Turkish troops.[20] Despite this apparent numerical preponderance, any Allied offensive operation aimed at concluding the siege would depend on concentrating in time and space sufficient artillery, infantry and engineer assault forces to wear down Russian resistance and to break though their powerful defences. In terms of operational planning, the outstanding questions remained: where to focus that effort; how best to sequence and synchronise artillery support and infantry attack; and how to unite the disparate Allied forces in a commonly agreed course of action. Without an over-arching Allied command, the answers lay primarily with the majority shareholder, the French.

In early June, the new French commander-in-chief, the veteran of the Algerian conquest General Aimable-Jean-Jaques Pélissier, who had succeeded Canrobert on 16 May 1855, determined that the Allied main attack – conducted by his army – should be directed at the Malakhov (see Map 9). He had correctly identified this position as the key to unlocking the Russian defences of Sevastopol, confirming Burgoyne's assessment, which had proved so controversial earlier in the year. As one perceptive historian of the war has observed, once the Malakhov was held by the Allies, 'the Redan and the entire quadrant from the Point Battery [the First Bastion] on the harbour's edge to the north-east round to the Barrack Battery to the south could be taken in reverse'. Furthermore, the 'main anchorage in the harbour from which [the Malakhov] was only 2,000 yards [distant] would become unusable'. Hence the Korabelnaya suburb 'must be abandoned', which meant the fall of Sevastopol.[21] And so it would duly prove: not only as a result of the successful French attack of September 1855, but also during the second siege of Sevastopol in early July 1942 during the German final assault on the city.

Acutely aware of the vital importance of the Malakhov, over the past eight months the Russians under Todleben's painstaking direction had steadily strengthened their defences in this sector. These measures included not only the establishment of new redoubts such as the Mamelon and the 'White Works', but also the novel employment of land mines known as *fougasses*, an early form of improvised explosive device. These lethal contraptions could be either initiated by the defender or set off by an unwitting attacker. Writing home to his sister Georgina on 14 June 1855, a British officer, Hugh Robert Hibbert, complained about the 'wretched Russians', who had 'discovered a new system of annoyance ... which consists of a series of small mines or barrels of gunpowder let into the ground between our works and theirs.' These weapons proved deadly effective. Hibbert noted the gruesome details: 'any unfortunate meandering along the grass without knowing why, suddenly finds himself going up in the air like a squib with his legs and arms flying in different directions'. As a result, 'we have had many men blown up by these things'.[22] Interestingly, none other than Charles Gordon employed such mines when he defended Khartoum against the besieging Mahdi in 1885, although many proved less effective than those used by the Russians at Sevastopol. As Gordon's biographer noted humorously, some of the devices were 'more terrifying than lethal: a donkey trod on one and walked away looking angry.'[23]

FIRST ASSAULTS ON THE MALAKHOV AND THE REDAN

Before a decisive attack on the Malakhov could be undertaken, the Allies had determined that its outposts had to be eliminated. The third bombardment commenced on the afternoon of 6 June with the fire of nearly 550 Allied guns and mortars. Awaiting an imminent assault, the Russians brought up fresh reserves to counter it, reinforcing their most threatened eastern sector. Meanwhile, while the French assembled a considerable force of four brigades, the British chose to commit only a couple of battalions to this preliminary attack. On the night of 6–7 June, under heavy Russian fire, the French seized the Mamelon and a couple of other redoubts, incurring heavy losses in the process (roughly 5,500 men).

Tolstoy noted laconically in his diary, 'on the 26th [May], the Selenginsk, Volynsk, and Kamchatka Redoubts were captured. I was in Sevastopol the next day and convinced myself that it would not fall.'[24] By this time, he had finished his tour of duty in the Fourth Battery and was now commander of a mountain battery stationed in Belbek, about 20 kilometres north of Sevastopol. His posting had been made on the orders of Alexander II, who wished that the young writer be removed from danger. Tolstoy, however, was not happy with his lot. Confiding to his diary, he confessed he was 'ill-qualified for practical activity, or if I am capable of it, it costs me a great deal of effort, which is not worth applying since my career is not a practical one'.[25] Apart from his writing, Tolstoy continued to drink, gamble and womanise. For the majority of the men either defending or preparing to attack Sevastopol, however, fighting (or waiting to fight) remained uppermost in their daily lives.

While the French had stormed *en masse* the Mamelon, the British had managed to raid into Sevastopol's south-eastern suburbs for little gain and captured the 'Quarries', a position which lay to the front of the Redan. Although this was greeted as a welcome success in an army that had fought no major engagements since the battle of Inkerman, the losses of 671 men killed and wounded – about half the number of troops engaged – were grossly disproportionate to the small pocket of terrain secured. Not only were the excessive numbers of officer casualties worrying, but also the staff work involved in the operation had been poor, if not, according to Baring Pemberton, 'wretched'. It was more of the same old, sad story of the British Army of the Crimea: the necessary 'orders received had been confused and sometimes contradictory'. Some very basic errors had compounded the problem. According to the same critical historian, 'Headquarters who did the planning had miscalculated not merely the strength needed to occupy the Quarries but also to repel counter-attacks. Reserves had been too few and too distant.'[26] Such deficiencies appeared to anticipate many of the shortcomings that were to be suffered by the British Army on the Western Front of the First World War, not least in the battles of Loos of 1915 and the Somme in 1916.

According to Pattullo, the value of the Allies' operational approach, let alone in gaining this minor objective such as the Quarries, was doubtful. In a letter home of 11 June, he questioned the wisdom of attacking in the manner of a 'bit by bit system rather than hazard the success of the siege on an assault', feeling convinced that 'prudent delays will cost us more than a bold dash'. Moreover, in his view, taking the Quarries represented 'a step too far' as it was 'commanded by many Russian works' and hence could 'never be converted into an offensive work'. Pattullo considered that 'it would have been soon enough to have taken [the Quarries] the day before we assault the Redan'.[27] That the British would be required to mount a major attack on the Redan appeared to be in no doubt despite the fact that this position would become untenable to its Russian defenders once the Malakhov had fallen. Not for the first time in the campaign or, for that matter, in many wars thereafter would national pride and coalition dynamics triumph over operational logic. The sad fact remains that the two British assaults on the Redan in June and September 1855 both proved largely unnecessary and highly costly failures, exhibiting both futility in concept and incompetence in execution. The only redeeming feature of the second attack is that it probably assisted the French in resisting the inevitable Russian attempts to regain the Malakhov.

After the successful preliminary operations in early June, opinions differed as to how soon Sevastopol could be taken and the siege successfully concluded. Gordon for one wrote optimistically on 8 June 1855 that 'I do not think the place will hold out another ten days; and once taken, the Crimea is ours'.[28] Such confidence, although widespread, was greatly mistaken. The great Allied attack on 18 June, symbolically chosen since it was the 40th anniversary of the battle of Waterloo, was defeated with heavy losses on both sides. Pélissier's plan, agreed by a feeble Raglan (probably already sick with cholera), at a council of war held on the 16th, was the most ambitious Allied operation to date. It foresaw no fewer than 44 French battalions (30,000 men) attack across a broad zone to capture the First and Second Bastions, as well as the Malakhov. Of the forces to be committed, the French main effort (two out of three divisions) was directed at the latter objective. Once the Malakhov was taken, the British with a composite force of about 14,000 men drawn from the Second and Light Divisions were required to assault the Third Bastion – the Redan – and the Péressip at the head of the Southern Bay. After a day-long bombardment on the 17th (the fourth of the siege), the French attack was timed for 0300 hours, an hour before dawn on the 18th.

Such was the undue haste in mounting the Allied operation that it was badly planned and prepared. As in all combat, the devil lay in the detail, not least in the lie of the land and the distances the infantry and engineers would have to cover in their assaults under fire across open terrain. Whereas the French had advanced their trenches to about 400 metres in front of the Malakhov, their troops had over 600 metres to cross in attacking the Second Bastion – the Little Redan. Meanwhile, the British would need to storm across about 400 metres of open ground to reach the Third Bastion – the Redan. Although the Allied bombardment on the 17th appeared to have inflicted great damage on their enemy's defences, disastrously for the British and French the next day, their artillery preparation lifted that evening allowing the Russians a God-sent opportunity to repair their positions overnight and to ready themselves for a major assault in the morning. Furthermore, the Allies' opportunity for mounting a surprise attack was lost when Russian listening posts at about 0200 hours detected large bodies of troops assembling in the Careening Ravine. Duly warned, Lieutenant General S. A. Khrulev, appointed overall commander of the forces in the Korabelnaya, alerted all his troops in anticipation of an imminent attack. Russian fighting patrols soon confirmed the presence of the French troops.[29] The ever-present friction of war intervened when General Joseph-Décius-Nicolas Mayran, commanding the French right, mistook a rocket for Pélissier's signal to launch the operation. Thus he began his attack about fifteen minutes before the agreed time of 0300 hours. Control of the battle broke down thereafter with other French troops launching too late, and the British attacked the Redan without waiting for the Malakhov to be captured first. In this manner, the disaster unfolded in utter confusion.

Everywhere the Russians were ready and successful in repulsing the Allied attacks. In the north, the Kremenchug Regiment, supported by naval gunfire, beat off the assault on the First Bastion. The Vladimir Regiment defended the Second Bastion equally successfully with artillery and musket fire; although the Poltava Regiment at the Malakhov was hard pressed for a time, reinforcements under Khrulev's personal command helped drive off the French. Meanwhile at the southern side of the Malakhov, while the French had captured the Gervais Battery, they were not able to hold it when further Russian troops intervened. It was this resulting fierce action that triggered the premature British assault on the Redan, made in the laudable attempt to assist their ally. Yet the attack was not pressed home with either much skill or vigour. The next day, in a letter to Lord Panmure, Raglan justified his decision to launch the British attack: 'if the troops had remained in our trenches, the French would have attributed their non-success to our refusal to participate in the operation'.[30]

By 0600 hours on 18 June, the fighting was over. Neither the Malakhov nor the Redan was taken since the Russians, despite the heavy preparatory bombardment, were still able to engage the Allied attackers with a very high volume of effective artillery and musket fire. The fundamental flaws in the Allied planning and execution were threefold: first, the lack of time for adequate preparation; secondly, the failure to maintain and focus the artillery bombardment until the infantry assault was launched; and, thirdly, to direct other artillery support in an attempt to delay and disrupt the move of Russian reinforcements. In their failed attacks, the French lost 3,553 and the British 1,728 men. In contrast, although the Russians suffered 3,950 casualties, the majority of these were sustained in the bombardment of the 17th rather than in the combat of the 18th. Furthermore, the small proportion of the Allied assault troops who managed to reach their objectives were outnumbered and outfought. As Albert Seaton has pointed out, 'in close quarter fighting, the Russian musket was in no way inferior to the British [and French] rifle'.[31] Whether the Allies could address their deficiencies and find a more promising method of attack in some future operation remained to be seen.

In the immediate aftermath, there was no doubt that the action had proved a great defensive victory for the Russians, and one which did wonders for their morale. While Tolstoy, who was not involved in the action, merely recorded 'yesterday morning an assault was repulsed',[32] the Russian high command was jubilant. Within Sevastopol, unsurprisingly, the 'spirits of the Russian defenders rose enormously'. Confidence in the ability of the city to maintain its defence rose accordingly, although the numbers of men lost and the quantity of ammunition expended could not be made up so easily. The senior officers involved were showered with awards, and in some cases, increases in pay, from a delighted Tsar Alexander II, who tasted the first military success in his reign as Emperor. Further afield, there were also positive diplomatic consequences. The mood in Vienna changed following the recent Allied failures at Sevastopol.

After the futile attempt to storm the Redan, Gordon, who had taken part in the British attack, was very critical of his army's performance:

> [The Russians] opened with a fire of grape which was terrific. They mowed down our men in dozens, and the trenches being confined, were crowded with men, who foolishly kept in them, instead of rushing over the parapet of our trenches....
> Our men dribbled out of the ends of the trenches ten and twenty at a time, and as soon as they appeared they were cleared away.[33]

It was clear that the distance between the British trenches and the Russian fortifications was too great, and the interval of time between the lifting of artillery fire and the ensuing infantry assault was too long. There were also familiar problems in the command and co-ordination of the attack, and not least the worrying breakdown in fighting spirit and cohesion amongst the troops involved. Pattullo, who had watched the miserable affair from a trench close by, commented that 'the reverse we have this day sustained will ever be a sad blot on the ever memorable day'. Once again, British staff work and battle procedures had proved inadequate as 'dawn [had] found us far from prepared ... from a want of previous arrangement and an ignorance of whom we were immediately acting under' prior to the assault on the Redan. 'Each Brigadier', maintained Pattullo, seemed to have 'a different and vague idea of the general operation'. Such confusion reflected the lack of clear orders within an ineffective chain of command. Bearing in mind the French failure to secure the Malakhov, in his opinion, the attack 'should never have been made'.[34]

Pattullo reviewed the failed assault on the Redan in successive letters home. While on the evening of the abortive attack of 18 June he had written 'I hardly think that Lord Raglan will again attempt storming [it]', he admitted 'it is impossible to form any opinion of future operations'. Five days later, however, he now 'felt confident that we could succeed in an assault if well arranged, of course at great sacrifice of life, but it is too bad to lead men to slaughter without a prospect of success'.[35] Writing to his sister on 13 July, Pattullo then appeared to change his mind, commenting 'I begin to think another assault on the Malakoff Hill will be the first operation but the Redan will not be attempted I think again'. Although he was right about the sequencing of the attacks, unfortunately for him and the British Army, the Redan was indeed assaulted for a second time and sadly the British failed to profit from the experience of their first attempt. As a result, many officers and men, including Pattullo, died in the process. Similar difficulties in assault technique and in command were encountered during the second assault, and on a much greater scale on the Western Front, 1914–18, not least at the first day of the Somme on 1 July 1916. While the French were able to advance their trenches much closer to the Malakhov in the late summer of 1855, the British were not able to make such progress. Rocky ground made entrenching difficult, but surely a greater effort should have been made. In consequence, the beaten – 'killing' – zone the British infantry and sappers had to storm across under fearsome Russian fire remained substantial (over 150 metres) during the subsequent, and equally disastrous, attack on the Redan in September. Both assaults reflected a failure to synchronise the preparatory and covering artillery fire and the infantry assaults; equally, the inability to mass a sufficiently large attacking force and to reinforce it expeditiously reduced the chances of success greatly. What made the failures at the Redan within the British Army particularly galling, however, was the disturbing fact that some of the men – many inexperienced young recruits – had refused to follow their officers and senior non-commissioned officers into pressing home their attack. The British chain of command cannot be absolved from this breakdown in unit cohesion: the lack of training and preparation for the assaults on the Redan characterised many of the shortcomings of the army of the East.

Gordon, intriguingly, remained excessively optimistic following the debacle of the first Redan assault. Writing on 21 June, he stressed 'I am confident that if we had left the trenches in a mass some of us would have survived and reached the Redan, which, once reached, the Highland Brigade and Guards would have carried all before them, and the place would have fallen.'[36] It is said that Lord Raglan died of a broken heart following the disaster at the Redan. In fact, he succumbed to cholera on 28 June 1855. A modern British historian of the Crimean War summed him up as follows:

> He was decent and gentlemanly and kind to his personal staff, but utterly out of his depth in commanding a field army in mid-nineteenth-century warfare. He was responsible for many of the failures in the Crimean campaign and [had] shown a lamentable lack of leadership qualities.[37]

British participants of the war, however, displayed rather more sympathy towards their fallen commander. Gordon, for example, for all his previous criticisms of the conduct of the siege, noted generously: 'Lord Raglan died ... of wear and tear and general debility. He is universally regretted, as he was so kind. His body will be taken to England. I am really sorry for him. His life has been entirely spent in the service of his country.'[38] Pattullo echoed Gordon's sentiments almost word for word. In his opinion, the British commander had 'sunk from sheer debility' for 'his age was too great for such a wear and tear of responsibility as he bore'.[39]

Any critique of Raglan must face the fact that, such was the paucity of talent, there were few suitable and available to assume command with the possible honourable exception of Sir Colin Campbell, who had proved himself tactically adept at the Alma and Balaklava. Whether he would have proved a better commander-in-chief of an expeditionary army (by now, a minor partner to the French) remains a matter of conjecture: his solid performance during the Indian Mutiny of 1857 suggests that he might well have galvanised and focused the British military effort on Crimea. His loyal staff officer, Lieutenant Colonel Anthony Sterling, however, was in no doubt as to his superior's ability: 'C[ampbell] is so capital a commander, that they think him equal to three or four battalions'.[40]

Lord Raglan's successor, General Sir James Simpson, recently sent out to Crimea to act as chief of staff, was another Peninsular veteran. Aged sixty-three years, he was 'a very good old man'. Yet he proved even less effective than Raglan: according to Baring Pemberton's scathing critique, the new commander-in-chief 'gave no orders, ... devised no plan [and] left everything to the Staff'.[41] The trouble was that there was no properly trained and organised staff to rely on in the British headquarters. Thus the weaknesses in the British high command were institutional as much as individual: with no effective general staff to assist senior commanders in exercising the functions of command, control and communications the set-up was amateur to say the least.[42] Simply put, no army can function effectively on operations without adequate training, administration, supply and effective battle procedures. All were singularly lacking on the British side during the Crimean War.

Meanwhile, the Russian command suffered a similar loss and severe blow to morale with the untimely death of Nakhimov on the morning of 10 July 1855. As was his routine, he had ridden out to tour the fortifications with a couple of his aides-de-camp. Inspecting the Third Bastion his party came under heavy fire. Displaying his usual sangfroid, he ignored his subordinates' entreaties to take immediate cover. One of his aides recalled that Nakhimov, who was normally a taciturn individual, was unusually cheerful and talkative that day. 'Whether or not one is going to be hit', the admiral maintained, 'is God's will, but not to brave the fire would show a weakness of character'. Furthermore, he declared, 'one should always be ready for death and meet it calmly when it comes, for only a coward fears death'.[43] Thus it would appear that Nakhimov had experienced some sort of premonition of his fate that morning. Soon thereafter, on reaching the defences at the Kornilov Bastion on the Malakhov Hill, the admiral recklessly climbed up on to the fire-step and exposed himself to enemy view. 'Immediately', his aide recounted, 'a bullet struck the sandbag at his elbow'. Undeterred, the Russian admiral observed that 'Their shooting is pretty good today'. Indeed it was, for 'a moment afterwards there was a second shot' that hit him on the face.[44]

Mortally wounded, Nakhimov was carried back to his quarters; without regaining consciousness, he died two days later on 12 July 1855. The hero of Sinope and Sevastopol, one of Russia's most illustrious naval leaders, was buried in the admirals' crypt of St Vladimir alongside Lazarev, Kornilov and Istomin. His name will forever be associated with Sevastopol – his proud statue in the centre of Nakhimov Square serves as permanent reminder to city resident and visitor alike of his selfless service and sacrifice to Russia.

THE BATTLE OF THE CHERNAYA RIVER

After their success in fending off the Allied attacks against the Malakhov and Redan on 18 June 1855, The Russians' euphoria proved short-lived. Although their enemies had suffered a severe setback, the strategic calculus of the war as a whole and the logistic advantage the Allies enjoyed in Crimea had not changed. The empire's resources were being stretched to the limit, as forces that guarded Russian Poland, and particularly the Baltic under Allied naval threat, could not be stripped to feed the war in the south. Russian joy turned into despair when they realised that they could not sustain their defence of Sevastopol indefinitely as daily losses continued, up to 250 men through death, wounding and illness. With Nakhimov dead, and Todleben recovering in a Belbek hospital from severe wounds he experienced on 18 June, the leading, confident lights of the Russian military effort were no longer present. Although brave hearts wished to fight to the last man, more sober minds pointed to the wisdom of withdrawing from the southern side of the city in order to reduce the casualty rate caused by the Allied artillery bombardment. As long as the northern side were held, it would still be able to deny Sevastopol to the enemy. Indeed, preparations for the construction of a floating bridge over the roadstead were well advanced under the direction of Gorchakov's chief engineer, Lieutenant General Aleksandr Vasilyevich Bukhmeier.

Alexander II, meanwhile, wished to end the war. To him, raising the siege of Sevastopol by an offensive battle remained the only politically acceptable course of action other than an incurring an ignominious surrender. His commander on the spot, Prince M. D. Gorchakov, however, was unwilling to risk such an action against superior Allied forces. Writing to the Russian Minister of War, Prince Vasily Andreyevich Dolgorukov, on 8 July [OS], Gorchakov's concerns betrayed both realism and defeatism. 'If I were to attack the enemy', as instructed, he declared: 'I would be smashed by the third day with a loss of between 10,000 –

15,000 men. On the fourth day Sevastopol would be lost'. Yet the alternative represented a Hobson's choice, for 'if I do not attack, the enemy will take Sevastopol anyway within the course of the next few months'.[45]

Alexander II was singularly unimpressed by such abject argumentation. In order to stiffen Gorchakov's resolve he despatched General-Adjutant Baron Pavel Alexandrovich Vrevsky to Crimea. As a trusted confidant of the Tsar, Vrevsky acted as his representative in Gorchakov's headquarters and soon became the commander-in-chief's 'guide and mentor'.[46] As Seaton has observed, the Emperor 'kept up a relentless pressure' on the hapless Gorchakov. Russian intelligence had picked up that the French were preparing to send another 24,000 men to Crimea, and there remained a distinct risk that the Allies might attempt to block the Perekop – a concern, it will be recalled, that had prompted the abortive operation against Yevpatoriya earlier in the year. On the Tsar's orders, the Russian Army had mobilised further forces for Crimea, including 2nd Corps (4th, 5th and 7th Reserve Infantry Divisions), and even called up elements of the people's militia or home guard, the *Narodnoe Opolcheniye*, such was the shortage of manpower. These reinforcements – vital to any new Russian offensive operation – were already on the march and due to arrive about the beginning of August. With these troops approaching their destination, on 30 July (OS), Alexander wrote to Gorchakov, stressing: 'I am convinced of the necessity that we should attack; otherwise all the reinforcements recently sent to you, as has happened in the past, will be sucked into Sevastopol, that bottomless pit'. Four days later, the Emperor emphasised yet again 'the necessity' [of doing] something decisive in order to bring this frightful massacre to a close.'[47]

M. D. Gorchakov found himself in an impossible position: while he had no faith in any attack, he could not ignore the Emperor's direction. Furthermore, he was being pulled in two directions. His effective deputy, the commander of the Sevastopol's garrison, Osten-Saken, to whom he turned for advice, thought that the limited offensive, which Gorchakov had reluctantly conceived against the Fedyukhin and Gasfort Heights, 'absurd'.[48] Unwilling to risk his army in an all-out attack against the Allies on the Chersonese plateau, the Russian commander-in-chief had resolved, if battle must be done, to engage his enemies on the left (western) bank of the Chernaya River. It was clear even to him that such an operation could not represent a simple re-run of the Balaklava operation with its opening attacks on the weakly held redoubts astride the Vorontsov Road. Strong French and Sardinian forces now held the Fedyukhin and Gasfort Heights respectively.

Well aware of Gorchakov's vacillating character and manifest indecision, but not prepared to sack him, Alexander II suggested that his subordinate should convene a council of war to determine the best course of action. Under

Gorchakov's chairmanship, the military council duly sat on 28 July (9 August) to consider whether to remain on the defensive or to undertake an offensive, and if the latter, to determine its object, scope and date. The next day the council reconvened and its members gave their views. While Osten-Saken maintained his opposition to any offensive, arguing instead for an evacuation of the southern side of Sevastopol, significantly a majority of the generals, including the experienced Khrulev and Liprandi, agreed to some form of attack without directly endorsing Gorchakov's proposals.

In the event, Gorchakov made the worst possible decision on the common but calamitous basis of 'something must be done'. Although unconvinced as to the prospects of its success, and failing to win the confidence of his subordinates, he ordered an attack on the Fedyukhin and Gasfort Heights to be mounted on 4 (16) August. His own nagging doubts and Osten-Saken's earlier critique were to be reinforced by Todleben. When consulted at his hospital bed on the 2nd (14th), the gallant engineer could not discern the underpinning aim of the offensive Gorchakov outlined to him, and, doubting that the Fedyukhin Heights could be taken by storm attack, argued strongly against the operation. None the less, under Vrevsky's overbearing influence, Gorchakov confirmed that the attack would go ahead. One can surely agree with Seaton's damning assessment: 'Rarely can a commander-in-chief have attacked with so little confidence in the outcome of his undertaking.'[49] Alexander II must also bear some responsibility for this parlous state of affairs: knowing that Gorchakov was so weak as a commander-in-chief, he should either have given him direct orders to attack or have replaced him. Yet the whole idea of the attack was fundamentally flawed.

The ground on which the battle was fought and the dispositions of the Allied defending forces can be described as follows by imagining a pair of intersecting diagonal crosses (see Map 10). From bottom-right (south-east) to top-left (north-west) ran the narrow river Chernaya of 5–7 metres in width and 1–2 metres in depth when full. Parallel to it for the most part on the southern and western side lay the aqueduct that supplied water from the vicinity of the village of Chorgun to Upton's dry docks in Sevastopol. From the bottom-left (south-west) to the top-right (north-east) ran the road from Balaklava, which crossed the North Valley (of Light Brigade fame) and through a gorge in the Fedyukhin Heights led on towards the Mackenzie Heights. At the point of intersection of the Chernaya river and this road lay a stone bridge, known as the Traktir.

The French 1st, 2nd and 3rd Divisions (of Generals Herbillon, Camou and Faucheux respectively) held the Allied left and centre on the Fedyukhin Heights, which run parallel to the Chernaya with the aqueduct in between. The French also defended a small bridgehead forward of the Traktir. Under overall command of an Algerian veteran, the sixty-one-year-old Émile Herbillon, commonly known to the French Army as 'Le père Herbillon', this force comprised 18,111 men and sixty-six guns. On the right flank stood 9,000 Sardinians with thirty-six guns under General Alfonso La Mamora. They defended a main position on the isolated Gasfort Height, lying between the Chernaya and the Vorontsov Road, with outposts positioned to the north of the river on another solitary feature, Telegraph Hill. Broadly speaking, the country was open with scant natural vegetation and cultivation. Both the French and Sardinian contingents were well dug in, with carefully sited batteries and prepared entrenchments and good fields of fire for their artillery and riflemen. Behind these forces, considerable further Allied troops were available in depth as general reserves: thirty squadrons of British cavalry at Kadikoi; twenty squadrons of French cavalry, two battalions and twelve guns in the Baidar valley; and 10,000 Turkish infantry with thirty-six guns at Kamara. In sum, without having to call up reinforcements from the camps on the Chersonese plateau, the Allies could muster over 40,000 men and nearly 100 field guns, with further horse artillery available.

Gorchakov's plan of attack did not get much further in conception beyond an order of deployment, or an advance to contact. On the Russian right, opposing the French, General-Adjutant N. A. Read, commanding 3rd Corps, on orders, was to cross the river with two infantry divisions in line: the 7th on the far right, and the 12th (minus one regiment) in the vicinity of the Traktir Bridge. On his left, Liprandi, responsible for 6th Corps, was to clear the Sardinians off Telegraph Hill with the 17th Division, but not cross the river Chernaya to attack Gasfort without express orders from the commander-in-chief. Liprandi's other division, the 6th (of only two regiments), was required to advance on the far Russian left towards Chorgun, and be prepared to support the 17th Division's attacks with covering artillery fire. Behind the 3rd and 6th Corps came Gorchakov's main reserve under General Shepelev of the 4th and 5th Infantry Divisions, together with further artillery and cavalry. In total, the Russian offensive grouping comprised 47,622 infantry, 10,263 cavalry, 224 field guns and 48 horse artillery guns.[50] In view of the strength of the Allied positions in terrain that was well suited for defence, the Russians – despite their superiority in artillery – were insufficient in numbers to outfight let alone overwhelm and defeat their opponents, whatever the quality of their generalship, which, in the event, was to be found wanting yet again.

Allied intelligence about the impending operation was good: there would be no surprise as at Inkerman. On 14 August, General Simpson reported to Lord Panmure: 'from the information we have received from the country as well as the examination of deserters, I have reason to believe that the Russians may attempt to forces us to raise the Siege by a vigorous attack from without'.[51] Furthermore, as might have been predicted, the initial moves and assembly of such large bodies of

Russian troops had not gone unnoticed, and by the evening of the 15th, the French and Sardinians were on high alert and ready to receive the anticipated Russian attack. The Russian operation of the next day developed in a chaotic, poorly co-ordinated manner in the early morning mist. There was next to no proper synchronisation of corps, divisions and regiments, which in the main were committed piecemeal, or integration of artillery support with infantry attacks. The doubt and disorder with the Russian chain of command compounded the inevitable friction of war to lamentable effect. Apart from Gorchakov, Read must bear a lot of responsibility for the confusion in the battle. His glib executive order, for example, to the general officer commanding the 7th Division, Lieutenant-General N. I. Ushakov, was far from clear: merely *pora nachinat*, or 'time to begin'![52] Unsure precisely what action to take, the divisional commander sought clarification. On hearing firing to his left, the 12th Division in action around the Traktir Bridge, Ushakov decided to advance across the river and canal with three regiments but forgoing any artillery support. Although the mist had hidden the Russians' approach, the French had still heard them, and on coming into sight, unleashed such a heavy weight of artillery case shot and rifle fire that Ushakov lost over 2,000 men within twenty minutes.[53] Under pressure from French counter-attack at the bayonet, his men broke and ran, retreating across the two water obstacles. Lieutenant-General K-M. A. Martinau's 12th Division had not fared much better. Although his regiments had taken the French position forward of the Chernaya with relative ease through weight of numbers, on advancing up the slopes of the Fedyukhin Heights in column, his troops were beaten back in a murderous fire. Thus by 0730 hours, Read's corps had been defeated and the French had regained their bridge. Gorchakov was not wise enough to call off the battle, presumably as he still had two-thirds of his force (four out of six divisions) unengaged except for some elements of the 17th Division.

The only glimmer of hope in the battle so far had occurred earlier in the morning on the Russian left: Liprandi's 17th Division had swiftly swept the Sardinian outposts off Telegraph Hill, and awaited orders to attack their opponents' main position on Gasfort. Gorchakov could have released the 6th Division to advance in support, but chose instead to bring up the 5th Division. At this stage of the action, it appeared that he had concluded belatedly that his main effort – where he sought a decision through concentration of force – should be on the left, exploiting the minor gain already scored. Yet when Read called for reinforcements, Gorchakov changed his mind and issued new orders to the 5th Division, redirecting this formation to the area of the Traktir Bridge. So there was the inevitable order and counter-order: march and counter-march. As a result, Gorchakov reinforced failure as opposed to success, breaking one of the most elementary maxims of war. On receiving the 5th Division, Read compounded

1. In 422–421 BC, Greek settlers founded a colony on south-western Crimea and named it the peninsular city – Chersonesos. Against all odds, their prosperous city survived for nearly 2000 years. The '1935 Basilica', depicted here, is but one of its famous ancient remains. (Vladimir Zizak)

2. St Vladimir Cathedral, built amidst the ruins of Ancient Chersonesos during the latter half of the nineteenth century, was destroyed during the Second World War. Painstakingly rebuilt, it was re-consecrated in 2004 in the presence of the presidents of Russia and Ukraine. (Vladimir Zizak)

3. Prince Grigory Aleksandrovich Potemkin (1739–91), confidant of Catherine the Great and governor of *Novorossiya* (New Russia), urged his Empress to annex Crimea and to establish a major naval base at the fine harbour of Akhtiar – renamed Sevastopol. (Photo by Hulton Archive/Getty Images)

4. Russian Empress Catherine II ('the Great') (1729–96), aided by Potemkin, expanded her empire to the shores of the Black Sea at the expense of the Ottoman Empire and the Crimean Khanate. She inspected the newly founded city of Sevastopol in May 1787. (Photo by Fine Art Images/Heritage Images/ Getty Images)

5. In 1983 this monument was erected on Sevastopol's central Nakhimov Square to commemorate the site 'of the foundation on 3 (14) June 1783 of the city of Sevastopol and naval fortress of South Russia'. Sadly, it fails to mention Rear Admiral Thomas Mackenzie. (Vladimir Zizak)

6. Erected in 1839, the Monument to Kazarsky commemorates the spirited action of the brig *Merkurii* against two Turkish warships at the Bosporus on 14 May 1829. An inscription on the monument reads: 'To Kazarsky. To posterity as an example.' (Vladimir Zizak)

7. Admiral Mikhail Petrovich Lazarev (1788–1851), who trained in the Royal Navy, as commander-in-chief of the Black Sea Fleet and governor of Sevastopol (1834–51) did much to modernise and train the Black Sea Fleet, and to develop the city's naval and civil infrastructure. (Photo by Fine Art Images/ Heritage Images/Getty Images)

8. Vice Admiral Vladimir Alekseyevich Kornilov (1806–54), a most talented officer, provided inspirational leadership during the early days of the defence of Sevastopol until struck down at the Malakhov Tower during the first Allied bombardment on 17 October 1854. (SCRSS/TopFoto)

9. Rear Admiral Vladimir Ivanovich Istomin (1810–55), alongside his colleagues Kornilov and Nakhimov, was the youngest of the three officers mentored by Lazarev. All three fell at Sevastopol, and were interred in the Admirals' Vault of the city's St Vladimir Cathedral. (New York Public Library)

10. Vice Admiral Pavel Stepanovich Nakhimov (1802–55) led the Russian squadron on 30 November 1853, which destroyed the Turkish fleet at Sinope. His fine monument on Nakhimov Square recognises his outstanding leadership during the defence of Sevastopol. (Photo by Popperfoto/Getty Images)

11. This fine painting of 1844, the 'Russian Squadron on the Sevastopol Roadstead' (Ivan Aivazovsky), depicts the tall sailing warships of the Black Sea Fleet, together with one of its first steam ships, in their secure natural harbour of Sevastopol. (Photo by Fine Art Images/Heritage Images/Getty Images)

12. This 'General View of Sevastopol, 1856' (Carlo Bossoli) shows a beautiful city as it was on the eve of the Crimean War. It was soon to be destroyed during a 349-day siege, including six bombardments, by British and French forces (1854–55). (Photo by Fine Art Images/Heritage Images/Getty Images)

13. The 'Docks at Sevastopol' (William Simpson) shows the principal achievement of the renegade British civil engineer John Upton (*c.* 1774–1851). Assisted by his son William, Upton did much to improve the infrastructure of the naval base, including a new Admiralty. (Photo by Hulton Archive/Getty Images)

14. A 'Hot Day in the Batteries' during the Siege of Sevastopol 1854–55 (William Simpson) shows a small detail of the action during one of the Allied bombardments of Russian Sevastopol during the Crimean War, which finally fell on 8/9 September 1855. (Photo by Universal History Archive/Getty Images)

15. Emperor Nicholas I (Nikolay Pavlovich Romanov, 1796–1855) ruled Russia autocratically from 1825. Although he had authorised the strengthening of the Black Sea Fleet and the fortification of Sevastopol, Russia was ill prepared for the Crimean War. (Photo by Fine Art Images/Heritage Images/Getty Images)

16. On his accession in 1855, Emperor Alexander II (Aleksandr Nikolayevich Romanov, 1818–81), wished to conclude the Crimean War on favourable terms, but was forced to accept the demilitarisation of the Black Sea. He is remembered as the 'Tsar Liberator' for his abolition of serfdom. (Photo by Hulton Archive/Getty Images)

17. Prince Alexander Sergeyevich Menshikov (1787–1869), commander-in-chief of land and naval forces in Crimea. His inadequacies at the Alma (20 September 1854) and in subsequent battles led to his dismissal in February 1855 and relief by Prince M. D. Gorchakov. (Photo by Fine Art Images/Heritage Images/Getty Images)

18. Professor Nikolay Ivanovich Pirogov (1810–81), one of the leading military surgeons of the nineteenth century, practised many new methods when serving as a senior surgeon during the defence of Sevastopol. He was very critical of both Menshikov and M. D. Gorchakov. (Photo by Universal History Archive/UIG via Getty Images)

19. The 'Council of War' of Lord Raglan, Omar Pasha and Marshal Pélissier (the British, Turkish and French commanders-in-chief), photographed by Roger Fenton on 7 June 1855. Lord Raglan, who succumbed to cholera on 29 June, died allegedly broken-hearted because of the failure of the Allied attacks on 18 June 1855. (Library of Congress)

20. Lieutenant General Sir John Fox Burgoyne was one of the leading Royal Engineers of the nineteenth century. Appointed to advise Lord Raglan, he recommended the 'flank march' in September 1854 that resulted in the prolonged siege of Sevastopol as opposed to an attack off the line of march. (Photo by Universal History Archive/Getty Images)

21. Count Lev (Leo) Nikolayevich Tolstoy (1828–1910) not only fought during the defence of Sevastopol (1854–55), but also wrote a series of brilliant Sketches that vividly portrayed military duty and daily life in the besieged city, highlighting its irrepressible spirit. (Photo by Universal History Archive/ UIG via Getty Images)

22. Charles George Gordon (1833–85) served as a young Royal Engineer officer at Sevastopol. His letters home provide a compelling narrative of events. He subsequently became famous for his martial exploits in China and died a martyr's death at Khartoum in Sudan. (Photo by Hulton Archive/Getty Images)

23. This image from 1920 shows the Fourth Battery at Sevastopol's Fourth Bastion, near which the Panorama Museum was opened in 1905. Leo Tolstoy served at the battery for a short period in 1855, which provided inspiration for his semi-biographical account of the defence of the city. (© IWM Q 37442)

1854 ОБОРОНА СЕВАСТОПОЛЯ 1855

24. This magnificent monument to the celebrated Russian engineer, General Eduard Ivanovich Todleben (1818–84), who masterminded the defence of Sevastopol, 1854–55, was erected at the northern end of Sevastopol's Historic Boulevard in 1909. (Vladimir Zizak)

25. During the siege of Sevastopol, the Malakhov Tower proved to be the principal bastion of the Russian defence. Its eventual fall to a successful French attack on 8 September 1855 precipitated the Russian withdrawal from the city to the northern side of Sevastopol Bay. (RIA Novosti/TopFoto)

26. The reconstructed Malakhov Tower today serves as a museum and poignant reminder of the First Defence of Sevastopol during the Crimean War. When Vice Admiral Kornilov fell here in 1854 it was renamed the Kornilov Bastion. A monument to him stands nearby. (Vladimir Zizak)

27. This picture of 'Huts and Warm Clothing for the Army' (William Simpson) depicts the challenges faced by the British Army during the terrible winter of 1854–55, during which thousands perished to sickness – exacerbated by inadequate clothing, hygiene and shelter. (Photo by Fine Art Images/Heritage Images/Getty Images)

28. The 'Railway at Balaklava' (William Simpson) shows the port terminal of the Grand Central Crimean Railway constructed by contractors in early 1855 to provide a vital lifeline to the troops and batteries on the Chersonese plateau above besieged Sevastopol. (Photo by Oxford Science Archive/Print Collector/Getty Images)

29. The 'View of Balaklava with [the] Genoese fort, from the Guards' camp' (James Robertson) shows some of the huts constructed by Royal Engineers in early 1855. This early example of prefabricated expeditionary campaign infrastructure, however, came too late for the many who had perished over the winter. (©2006 Alinari / TopFoto)

30. The Black Sea Fleet Museum, Lenin Street, Sevastopol, was opened in 1869 to commemorate the actions of the fleet since its foundation in 1783 and its exploits during the Crimean War. It now contains an impressive collection of Second World War materials. (Vladimir Zizak)

31. Detail of the Panorama's circular canvas, 115 metres long and 14 metres high, 'The Defence of Sevastopol 1854–1855' by Franz Rubo, which depicts the defence of the city at the Malakhov Tower on 18 June 1855, when its Russian defenders repulsed a major French attack. (Author's collection)

32. The Panorama, the Defence of Sevastopol 1854–55 Museum, designed by V. A. Feldman, architect, and constructed by O. I. Anberg, military engineer, to hold the great canvas of the Defence of Sevastopol, was opened on 26 May 1905. It remains a favourite tourist site. (Author's collection)

33. The Monument to the Scuttled Ships, Sevastopol Bay, erected in 1904, commemorates the sacrificial sinking of Russian warships of the Black Sea Fleet to block the entrance of the harbour to Allied ships following the battle of the Alma on 20 September 1854. (Vladimir Zizak)

34. Sevastopol's Southern Bay in 1918 during the German occupation contained many impounded warships of the Russian Black Sea Fleet, including the former *Prince Potemkin*. Allied forces then took over the ships in November 1918 at the end of the First World War. (Bundesarchiv)

35. The mutinous Russian battleship *Prince Potemkin* (1905), which became the subject of a famous film by Sergei Eisenstein in 1925. (Photo by Hulton Archive/Getty Images)

36. Pyotr Petrovich Schmidt (1867–1906), led the mutiny aboard the armoured cruiser *Ochakov* in November 1905 at Sevastopol. Suppressed by forces loyal to Emperor Nicholas II, it proved to be one of the most violent episodes of the 1905 Russian revolution. (© TASS/TopFoto)

37. The 'Monument to Lieutenant P. P. Schmidt', erected by the Soviet administration in 1923, which stands in the Communards Cemetery, Sevastopol, was designed by Schmidt himself before he was shot by firing squad on 19 March 1906 for leading the failed *Ochakov* mutiny. (Vladimir Zizak)

38. The German battlecruiser SMS *Goeben* (1914) evaded interdiction by the Royal Navy in the Mediterranean in August 1914 and fled to Constantinople. Under a Turkish flag, it bombarded Sevastopol on 29 October 1914, which provoked Russia into declaring war against Turkey. (Bundesarchiv)

39. Rear Admiral Wilhelm Anton Souchon (1864–1946) commanded the German Navy's *Mittelmeerdivision* (comprising the *Goeben* and the light cruiser *Breslau*) in 1914 and then assumed command of the Turkish fleet. He planned the bombardment of Russian ports on 29 October 1914 and on subsequent occasions. (Photo by ullstein bild/ullstein bild via Getty Images)

40. General Robert Paul Theodor Kosch (1856–1942) commanded the German forces that occupied Crimea in April 1918 against light opposition from Bolshevik forces, and entered Sevastopol unopposed on 1 May 1918. Life in the revolutionary city was relatively peaceful. (Library of Congress)

41. Emperor Nicholas II (Nikolay Aleksandrovich Romanov, 1868–1918), the last Russian tsar, was a frequent visitor to Sevastopol, where he routinely inspected units of the Black Sea Fleet and the garrison. Following his abdication on 15 March 1917, the Bolsheviks were to murder him and his family. (Photo by The Print Collector/Getty Images)

42. Vladimir Ilyich Ulyanov, alias Lenin (1870–1924), led the Bolshevik revolution in November 1917, overthrowing the Provisional Government which had assumed power following Nicholas II's abdication. Lenin was the architect of the modern Soviet state. (Sputnik/TopFoto)

43. Pyotr Nikolayevich, Baron Wrangel (1878–1928), a professional army officer who fought in the First World War and the Civil War, commanded the Whites' Russian Army (April – November 1920) and enjoyed brief success before being defeated by superior Red forces. (Photo by Fine Art Images/Heritage Images/Getty Images)

44. Mikhail Vasilyevich Frunze (1885–1925), as commander-in-chief of the Red Army's Southern *Front*, defeated the Whites' Russian Army on Crimea in November 1920, thus bringing the Civil War in southern Russia to a close. It was followed by the Red Terror. (RIA Novosti/Sputnik/ TopFoto)

the error by committing its four regiments into the attack one after another rather than massing them. Gorchakov then intervened and ordered the division to attack the Fedyukhin Heights as a concentrated force. Under overwhelming pressure, the French were forced off the Traktir Bridge again, but the Russian division, assaulting in three great columns, soon suffered the same fate as that of the 7th and 12th Divisions earlier in the morning. Concentrated French artillery and rifle fire destroyed Read's final attack in a manner similar to the Union Army's destruction of the Confederates' vainglorious attack on Cemetery Ridge (popularly known as Pickett's Charge) at Gettysburg on 3 July 1863 or the disastrous Union assault at Cold Harbor almost a year later. The Russians fell back across the Chernaya and the French followed up, regaining Traktir Bridge yet again. Within the 5th Division, the losses, particularly amongst the officers, were very severe, almost entirely eliminating the formation's senior leadership. The divisional commander, the two brigade commanders, the four regimental commanders and nine out of sixteen battalion commanders were either killed or wounded. The corps commander, Read, had also fallen, struck by a shell splinter.[54]

After the failure of the 5th Infantry Division's attack, Gorchakov should have been wise enough to admit defeat and to withdraw. Taking over command of Read's corps, he determined to continue the engagement. Following his orders, the Russians then made one final, fruitless effort to attack the French on the Fedyukhin Heights. Gorchakov ordered two regiments (eight battalions) of the largely uncommitted 17th Division to attack *westwards* from Telegraph Hill. Caught in a killing zone beaten by heavy fire from both the French and the Sardinian defended positions, the attempt failed with great losses as in all previous attacks. By 1000 hours the battle appeared to be all but over when the Russians began a general withdrawal from the Chernaya towards the Mackenzie Heights. Then they stopped, turned about and re-formed, and the onlooking Allies wondered whether the action would be resumed. It was not and the Russians finally left the battlefield full of their dead and dying. Excepting Inkerman, the battle of the Chernaya river was the costliest of the war. Whereas the Allies (chiefly the French) suffered about 1,800 men killed and wounded, the Russians lost 2,273 dead, 1,742 missing and 3,995 wounded, just over 8,000 men in total.[55] Bearing in mind that only three and a half of the six Russian divisions (the 12th, 7th, 5th and half of the 17th in that order) were fully committed during the battle, the casualty rate of the forces engaged approached 30 per cent.[56]

Although Tolstoy took part in the battle, he did not incorporate a pen-portrait of the engagement in his *Sketches*. In his private diary, however, he recorded briefly on 4 August [OS], 'On the 3rd and 4th I went on an expedition and was in a terrible and disastrous action'.[57] Although Tolstoy's mountain battery was not committed during the battle, it is safe to presume he observed the unfolding disaster, which further reduced his confidence in the Russian high command. So much so, that his subsequent satirical verse (with its first line ''Twas in August, on the Fourth' – relating to the date of the battle according to the old Russian calendar) about the events of the Chernaya got him into deep trouble. Parts of it have been translated thus:

> So they pondered, racked their brains,
> Drew up plans with care and pains!
> On a large white sheet.
> All so smooth without a blot—
> But some ravines they clean forgot
> Which we had to cross!
> But while General—you know—
> With long prayers made great ado
> We had to retreat.[58]

Tolstoy's scathing critique, which became immediately popular in the Russian Army and widely sung, was surely justified but it hastened the end of his military career. The absence of detailed planning and the general lack of clarity about Gorchakov's intentions before and during the engagement constituted only two of several reasons for the Russian defeat. As already indicated, there was also faulty co-ordination between the formations involved, and in the integration of artillery support. As a result of these multiple failings, as Sergey Chennyk has highlighted, the battle was divided into 'separate episodes, which were connected neither in time nor space'. Thus unity of purpose was not achieved. Other errors compounded this problem, not least the poor organisation of the march and the series of tactical mistakes made during the course of the divisional and regimental attacks. Chennyk blames the 'late appearance of the reserves', which remains a matter of dispute. In addition, he criticises the decentralisation of command within the Russian forces for some of the difficulties encountered. To other interpretations, such empowerment – fostering tactical initiative within an overall framework of operational intent – would seem as a positive rather than a negative (or would be if the commanders had been educated and trained in 'mission command'). Yet Chennyk surely puts his finger on a key issue when he complains about the complete lack of Russian operations security.[59] Consequently, no surprise was scored: the Allies were ready for the Russian attack, and soundly defeated it.

Although British troops were not directly involved at the Chernaya, some were close at hand, including Sterling, now a staff officer of the newly constituted Highland Division under the command of Sir Colin Campbell.[60] Writing the day after the engagement, he stated that 'I feel sure that I saw 2,000 dead Russians in the plain beyond the Chernaya', an estimate which he confirmed the next day, having walked the ground. Charitably, he considered that the Russian troops who had made the attack, 'seem to have behaved with uncommon courage'. He also added that the Sardinians had 'behaved very well', a sentiment echoed by Pattullo, who observed that the battle was a 'most brilliant and successful affair & has proved the Sardinians to be good soldiers'.[61] A participant of the action, Lieutenant Giuseppe Francesco Ceresa di Bonvillaret, commented in his diary about the general joy after the battle, adding 'by the evening, the champagne had arrived'.[62] Members of the Sardinian contingent had good reason to celebrate. Praised by the French and British alike for their 'stoicism and bravery', it sealed a close bond of trust and friendship that not only held fast during the remainder of the campaign, but also later helped cement French support for the cause of Sardinia–Piedmont in the Second Italian War of Independence of 1859. Sadly, the Sardinian memorial chapel on the summit of the Gasfort Hill was destroyed during the fighting of the Second World War.[63]

After the Russian failure at the Chernaya, both Pattullo and Sterling understood that it was now only a matter of time before the Allies attacked Sevastopol. Noting that we 'shall do nothing against the place till the new mortars arrive', the latter observed that there was 'a regular drain in the trenches, which is very annoying'. By this Sterling meant the steady trickle of losses on the Allied side. 'Every day', he narrated on 17 August, '2,800 go into the right attack, out of which twenty are usually hurt'. He added, 'the enemy, of course, lose many also; it is said, near 300 a day'. Within Sevastopol, Sterling believed that 'all the inhabitants' had been 'sent away', and that their houses had been 'turned into hospitals'. Contemplating the losses on both sides, he concluded that 'humanity is paying pretty dearly for the fancies of Peter and Catherine'.[64] In other words, the Russian foundation and subsequent defence of Sevastopol was proving very costly for all sides involved. Sterling had hit upon a serious point: was the blood-price already incurred for the city worth it?

The initial Russian reaction to the result of the battle of Chernaya, meanwhile, was one of disappointment rather than despair. Yet when the enormity of the defeat sank in, 'despondency and grief' became widespread amongst Sevastopol's defenders. As an eyewitness, M. A. Vrochenskiy, recorded, 'everyone realised from now on that the destiny of Sevastopol was settled ... [all] became depressed about the forthcoming destruction of the city and fleet'.[65] The Russians could soon expect the resumption of the bombardment and a following assault on the city's fortifications, perhaps repeating the attempts of 18 June. But such was the overall Allied strength (and particularly of the French) that no sector of the defensive system could be put at risk.

THE FINAL ALLIED ASSAULT, 8 SEPTEMBER 1855

By the time of the battle of Chernaya, developments in Sevastopol were beginning to indicate Russian intentions. For example, construction of the Russian pontoon bridge across the roadstead from Fort Nicholas to Fort Michael was now well under way. On 17 August, Sterling commented that the Russians had built '200 metres' of its eventual 900 metres length, and that it was '10 metres broad'. But he also expressed the hope that 'we shall be able to destroy it before its completion', which, in the event, proved to be wishful thinking.[66] The bridge, a triumph of Russian military engineering, escaped effective Allied artillery and mortar fire. On 28 August, Simpson reported to Panmure that it had been completed, and was 'actually in use by the enemy', noting further that 'a considerable increase of troops, with a great deal of movement' was 'observable in the Town'.[67] The floating bridge would provide, as the Russians had prudently planned many months before, a vital withdrawal route.

The most significant event following the battle of the Chernaya was the opening of the fifth Allied bombardment on 17 August. Coming immediately on the morning after the lost battle, it had considerable psychological effect, exacerbating the Russian decline in morale. Yet in a curious way, Russian spirits within Sevastopol began to rise as they braced themselves for the inevitable Allied assault. Perhaps some had some an inkling of Todleben's plans for strengthening the defences, others for his contingency plan for an evacuation. Obvious to all, however, whether friend or foe, was the new bridge across the roadstead. So when the attack came, the doughty defenders of the redoubts, bastions and batteries would fight as stubbornly as on previous engagements. Their commander-in-chief, M. D. Gorchakov, however, remained unconvinced as to the wisdom of continuing the defence and doubted his army's ability to repulse the enemy. Unable to bring himself to order a withdrawal to the northern side unless expressly approved by Alexander II, he determined to make a final stand in Sevastopol despite fearing heavy losses. Even if privately the Emperor may have feared the worst, he hastened the despatch of reinforcements to the south and ordered Gorchakov to prepare for a winter campaign. At the same time, he tired at the relentlessly growing cost of the war: 'when I think of the heroic garrison of Sevastopol and the dear blood that is shed every minute in defence of our native land, my heart is drenched with this blood.'[68] Alexander II's determination to continue the war at such high cost, of course, prolonged the agony. Yet, as historian Cecil Woodham-Smith has wisely observed, although the decision to prolong the defence of Sevastopol 'was as useless as heroic, ... there are moments in war, ... when the effect on morale not only for the present but [also] the future, makes the sacrifice worthwhile'.[69]

The Allies remained equally determined to capture Sevastopol. British artillery fire was concentrated against the Redan and the Malakhov again, 'to enable the saps to advance'. As an example of excellent co-operation between the Allies, the chronicler of *Artillery Operations* noted: 'We obtained a decided superiority over the Malakoff at an early period of the day, and enabled the French working parties to push their approaches'. Such support proved to be a crucial element in facilitating the French Army's eventual success in storming this objective. Learning from past mistakes, 'a heavy fire from the mortars was kept up on the Malakoff and Redan' during the night.[70] Hence the Russians would not have it so easy as in previous bombardments in making good the daytime destruction during the short hours of darkness. The furious bombardment by overwhelming artillery and mortar fire cost the defenders of Sevastopol over 1,000 men a day, an attritional battle that could not be sustained.

Without an overall Allied supreme commander and a supporting general staff, the separate British and French Army commanders-in-chief, Generals Simpson and Pélissier respectively, depended to large extent on the professional advice from their respective artillery and engineer commanders.[71] On 3 September 1855, these specialist officers were 'once more summoned to assemble', having already met beforehand to determine a joint course of action. The 'principal Officers of Artillery and Engineers' duly reported: 'the labours of the Siege have reached a point that the Assault should take place without delay'. In their joint note to the Allied commanders-in-chief, they observed that while the 'approaches' to the Malakhov had 'arrived to about twenty-five yards of the place', the works before the Redan 'cannot be pushed further without great difficulties, which would entail serious impediments to the attack'. Reprising the previous arguments of Burgoyne and Pélissier, they recommended that 'the principal attack should be directed against the works of the Malakoff; if we succeed in scaling it and making a solid lodgement, the fall of the Karabelnaia suburb will be inevitable'. This operation would form the main attack, to be launched by the French, and would include within its scope an assault on the Little Redan. Such was the importance of the Malakhov, it was recognised that 'the enemy will make every effort to regain it'. Thus, in their opinion, it was necessary 'to preserve that separation of the enemy's forces which results from the great extent of the fortifications of Sebastopol'. Hence there needed to be supporting operations elsewhere in order to fix Russian reinforcements rather than to obscure the location of the main attack. Russians and Allies alike knew where that would appear. 'When the success of the attack on the Malakoff shall be certain', the report stated, 'at an agreed signal the English will assault the Redan, and the French the works of the Town at the same time'.[72] These latter attacks were to be directed against the Second 'Quarantine' and, more particularly, towards the Fifth 'Central' Bastion.

Significantly, the intervening Fourth 'Flagstaff' Bastion (lying between the Redan and the Fifth) would not be assaulted in order to 'avoid the obstacles which the enemy has accumulated at the salient of [this fortification]'. Although not specifically mentioned, there was also a concern that the bastion had been heavily mined, and would be blown up when attacked. The authors of the report, however, failed to acknowledge one of the consequences of failing to assault this part of Sevastopol's defences: it would mean that the left flank of the British attack on the Redan, which would have to cover more than 150 metres of open ground, would be highly vulnerable to enfilading Russian fire. The senior artillerymen and engineers concluded by proposing that the 'cannonade' should be resumed 'with great vigour for three days, at the expiration of which' Sevastopol should assaulted 'on the three points indicated, by day, but an hour to be named hereafter'.[73] Simpson and Pélissier accepted this plan without any variation, directing that the bombardment (the sixth and last) would commence on the morning of 5 September 1855. The final detail of the timing of the assault on the 8th was soon identified, reflecting some cunning in the plan for attacking the Malakhov. The French had observed that the Russians routinely changed over their forces at midday. As the old guard marched out, the new one waited patiently to enter the Malakhov. At precisely this moment of weakness, during a relief in place, the French would attack, and the final battle for Sevastopol would begin. Another advantage of this timing lay in the habit of the Russian garrison as a whole to eat their main meal of the day around noon, and hence positions would only be weakly manned.

The Royal Artillery's narrative of the campaign listed 197 British guns and mortars being held ready in position on 3 September. The French armament was three times larger with a total of 627 pieces in seventy-two batteries, a very significant proportion of which, however, was directed against the Malakhov and the Little Redan – 267 guns and mortars in thirty-four batteries.[74] Thus over half the available Allied artillery was able to engage the main French and British objectives. In comparison, the Russian forces possessed a total of '1,200 guns and mortars', but in most cases these weapons were of 'inferior calibre and range'. Furthermore, the defending gunners of Sevastopol 'suffered from a grave shortage of shells and powder'. On 5 September, the Russian garrison within Sevastopol comprised '96 battalions of infantry, three of *opolcheniye* [militia] and one rifle battalion', which together with engineers, naval and army artillerymen, made a total of 49,000 men. General Khrulev continued to command the crucial eastern half of Sevastopol, the Korabelnaya, including the Great Redan, Malakhov and Little Redan, roughly corresponding to the Third, Fourth and Fifth Sectors of the Russian defences.[75] By now Russian battalion strengths averaged fewer than 500 men; such were the recent losses that many units could only muster 350–400 soldiers apiece on this final defence of the city.

An anonymous British account of the final bombardment and the fall of Sevastopol, which claimed to be compiled from 'authentic correspondence and reports of eye-witnesses' painted the unfolding scene on 5 September 1855 in purple prose:

> The day on which the deadly carronade opened against the doomed fortress was one of the loveliest ever witnessed in the Crimea. The air was pure and light, and a gentle breeze from the south-east, which continued all day, drifted over the steppe, and blew gently into Sebastopol. The sun shone serenely through the vapours of early morning and wreaths of snowy clouds on the long lines of white houses inside those rugged defences of earth and gabionade which had so long kept our armies gazing in vain on the 'august city'.[76]

When the Allied guns opened fire at about 0430 hours, according to the same journalistic source, an 'iron storm tore over the Russian lines, tossing up, as in sport, jets of earth and dust, rendering asunder gabions, and "squelching" the parapets, or bounding over among the houses and ruins in their rear'. Allegedly, the 'Russians seemed for a while utterly paralysed; their batteries were not manned with strength enough to reply to such an overlapping and crushing fire'. Yet soon enough the brave gunners of Sevastopol returned fire, as they had done during each of the previous five bombardments. As ever, the Russians made 'good practice', but on this occasion they fired 'slowly and with precision, as if they could not afford to throw away an ounce of powder'. When darkness fell on this opening day of the bombardment, the fire and counter-fire thundered into the night. As one witness described it: 'There was not one instant in which the shells did not whistle through the air—not a moment in which the sky was not seamed by their fiery curves or illuminated by their explosion'. Such was the intensity of the pyrotechnics, 'the lines of the Russian earthworks of the Redan, Malakhoff, and all their batteries were rendered plainly visible by the constant light of the bursting shells.'[77]

The bombardment continued for another two and a half days until noon of Saturday, 8 September. The Allies had caused great devastation within Sevastopol's defences, particularly around the Malakhov and the Second Bastion, but also within the town. During the first two days of this final artillery preparation, the Allies fired over 52,000 rounds while the Russians returned 'with about 20,000'. In three days, the Russians had 'lost 89 guns and 113 carriages to enemy fire', mainly in the eastern sector of their defences. Even Todleben's massive earthen fortifications crumbled under this unprecedented weight of fire. For the first time during the defence, the repair teams could not keep pace. As a result, Russian personnel and materiel losses accelerated. By noon of the day of the

French and British attacks, 8 September, there were already 2,000 casualties.[78] The open question remained, however, mindful of the events of 18th June, whether on this occasion the Allied bombardment had been sufficiently successful at degrading the Russian's defences, enabling the Allies' assaults to succeed and so end the siege.

The French Army's main attack was planned and conducted by Bosquet's II Corps, and consisted of three assaults. While General Dulac's division attacked the Little Redan, La Motterouge's division would attempt to pierce the curtain wall midway between the Little Redan and the Malakhov. The corps (and army) main effort would lie with General MacMahon's divisional attack on the latter objective. Each of Bosquet's three divisions held considerable further reserves in support of at least two regiments apiece. Meanwhile, the British plan of attack was in essence a re-run of that of 18 June, albeit with some minor refinements. Codrington, assisted by Markham, was placed in overall command. Two assault columns of 1,000 men each drawn from the 2nd and Light Divisions, commanded by Colonel Windham and Brigadier Shirley respectively, were chosen supposedly as a recompense for the troops' long service in the trenches. Fresher, and arguably more capable, divisions, the Highland and the 3rd, were to remain as reserves, a matter which was to attract considerable debate after the attack.

Amongst the British assault force on 8 September was James Pattullo, who wrote on the eve of battle: 'At last there is no longer any doubt that we are going to make another assault on Sebastopol'. Even though he was the commanding officer of the 30th Foot, part of the column drawn from the 2nd Division, he declared he was 'totally ignorant' of 'the general arrangements'. Sensibly he believed that 'the French must be really settled' in the Malakhov 'before we advance to the attack'. Yet he also betrayed some foreboding as to the results of the day ahead, admitting he was 'very sanguine'. Although he anticipated 'success', he declared: 'I have never been an advocate of the assault system over the investment'. In what would prove to be his final letter home, his concluding lines reflected a sense that they might indeed be his last:

> One of God's greatest blessings is hope & I am full of it. It has pleased him to spare me through many dangers & I earnestly pray that He will yet spare me once more to revisit all those I hold dear on earth. Should I be fated to fall, I trust I have a higher hope that we may meet in heaven, dear Mother, y[ou]r affect[ionat]e Son James.[79]

There is no doubt that the Allies achieved a considerable surprise in the timing of the first assaults. The Russians expected them to be made at either dawn or dusk. Although there had been warnings from listening posts before dawn of enemy

(French) movement in front of the Second Bastion and the Malakhov, no attack transpired and the defenders, which had been duly 'stood-to', were then quietly 'stood-down'. A further warning of enemy troops massing came about 1100 hours from Russian observation posts on the Inkerman Heights. Delays and confusion, however, in the transmission of this critical, time-sensitive, information ensured that neither the Russian commanders within Sevastopol nor their troops manning the defences were ready for the noon attack of the French. Within minutes, MacMahon's men had stormed into the Malakhov, and by 1230 hours the key to the defence of Sevastopol was fully in their hands. They then resisted all Russian attempts to recover their lost position. What made the Russians' task more difficult was the fact that the Malakhov, unlike the other bastions, was designed and built for all-round defence with a deep surrounding ditch traversed only by a narrow bridge on the inner, north-western, side. Once the French had firmly established themselves, it proved impossible to eject them. As fate would have it, the Russian mine under the Malakhov, designed to be blown if enemy troops managed to penetrate its defences, was not quite ready with the main shaft requiring a couple of days' further work.[80]

In his semi-autobiographical account, Tolstoy describes the unfolding Allied assault on Sevastopol from a commanding viewpoint – the Telegraph Mound at the Star Fort – on the northern side of the city. As noon on that fateful day approached:

> The sun stood high and bright above the Roadstead, which, in the glad, warm light, was playing with its ships at anchor, with their sails and with the boats.... Sevastopol—still the same: with its unfinished church, its column, its quay, its green boulevard on the hill, its elegant library building, its azure creeks filled with masts, its picturesque aqueduct arches, and with blue clouds of powder-smoke now and then lit up by the blood-red flame of cannon; ... Along the whole line of fortifications, but especially on the left side, appeared, several at a time, with lightnings that at time flashed bright even in the noonday sun, puffs of thick, dense, white smoke.... The reports of explosions never ceased, but rolled together and rent the air.[81]

Tolstoy's fellow observers (a naval officer and a seaman) then spied the movement of troops from the Allied entrenchments, remarking that 'thick columns [are] advancing'. The French storm of the Malakhov was by now in full swing. Tolstoy captures this decisive action with a wonderfully rich and evocative piece of prose:

> And really, with the naked eye one could see what looked like dark spots moving down the hill from the French batteries across the valley to the bastions. In front

of these spots dark stripes were already visibly approaching our line. On the bastions white cloudlets burst in succession as if chasing one another. The wind brought a sound of rapid small-arm firing like the beating of the rain against a window. The dark stripes were moving in the midst of the smoke and came nearer and nearer. The sounds of firing, growing stronger and stronger, mingled in a prolonged, rumbling peal.

The skilled narrator then switches deftly to dialogue to enhance the dramatic effect:

"An assault!" said the naval officer, turning pale and letting the seaman look though the telescope. Cossacks galloped along the road, some officers rode by, the Commander-in-Chief passed in a carriage with his suite. Every face showed painful excitement and expectation. "It's impossible they can have taken it," said the mounted officer. "By God, a standard! ... Look! Look!" said the other, panting, and walked away from the telescope: "A French standard on the Malakhov!" "It can't be!"[82]

All this, of course, represented a work of semi-fiction, but it surely echoed well the events and emotions of the day. By a magnificent feat of arms the French had indeed captured the Malakhov, and continued to hold it despite all the Russians' valiant and costly attempts to regain this vital citadel on the eponymous *kurgan* that dominated Sevastopol. But everywhere else bitter failure prevailed. Although the French managed to penetrate the Second Bastion, the Russians drove out the attackers. In contrast, Bosquet's third main assault on the Korabelnaya almost succeeded: the French stormed over the curtain wall between the Second Bastion and the Malakhov, and broke through the defensive lines behind it, only to be forced back by vigorous Russian counter-attacks. In fact, the Russians' success here, and failure at the Malakhov, can be explained in part by Khrulev's immediate response to the French assault. Judging that the Malakhov would hold out, he instead rushed his reinforcements to the more weakly defended Second Bastion, and then diverted them to block and defeat the French penetration in the area of the Curtain Wall and its battery. It proved to be a fatal command decision made in the heat of battle.

The raising of the *Tricolore* high on the Malakhov, as famously depicted by the war artist, William Simpson, signalled the British assault on the Redan. Designed primarily as supporting effort to restrict the ability of the Russians to contest the Malakhov, following the debacle of 18 June, mounting the attack had become a matter of national honour. It might have been expected that the British high command would have designed a new plan for the assault, and trained for it. Yet it was not to be. Gordon now picks up the story:

> Our men went forward well, losing apparently few, put ladders in the ditch, and mounted on the salient of the Redan; but though they stayed there five minutes or more, they did not advance, and tremendous reserves coming up drove them out. They retired well and without disorder, losing in all 150 officers, 2400 men killed and wounded. We should have carried everything before us if the men had only advanced.[83]

He alludes here to one of the most disturbing episodes of the British Army's history. Large numbers of troops simply refused to obey the orders of their officers and to attack. True, the assault was made in the teeth of murderous fire, but was this disaster not also a failure of tactics and command, as well as a lack of collective courage? Another British soldier, Henry Clifford, observed: 'What almost breaks my heart and nearly drove me mad, was to see our soldiers, our English soldiers that I was so proud of, run away ... was it right to send any men two hundred yards in the open against a place like the Redan, with guns vomiting forth grape?'[84] Notwithstanding this bitter critique, there was also great valour and determination shown that day. In all, the British made three attempts to seize the Third Bastion. Each, however, was driven off: Russian accounts state their 'troops excelled themselves' in its defence.[85]

In contrast, the French had been able to drive their trenches much nearer to the Malakhov and had suppressed its defenders' fire far more effectively. The fact remains that the complete reverse at the Great Redan is one of the few occasions when the British Army failed to live up to its historic reputation for bravery if not for skill. It left a very sour note of shame in Crimea, and explains in part why the Redan was never made a battle honour. A renewed assault on this bastion was planned for the next day: the Highlanders would storm it and hopefully redeem the Army's shattered reputation.

While the French had succeeded at the Malakhov, their further three attempts to capture the Second Bastion and another assault on the Curtain Wall all failed. So too did all the assaults on the other side of the city, mounted at 1400 hours and focused on the Fifth Bastion and the associated Shvarts and Belkin Lunettes. Altogether, the Allies mounted attacks on seven different localities on Sevastopol's southern ring of defences, some of these several times. While Todleben lists twelve assaults, Vrochenskiy suggests thirteen in total, of which all but one were repulsed.[86] In view of this defensive success, it is unsurprising that the Russians were by no means ready to concede defeat. Gorchakov steadily fed in reinforcements from the northern side as the battle for Sevastopol approached its climax. During the course of the afternoon the Russians made repeated attempts to dislodge the French from the Malakhov. Khrulev led one attack himself, and was wounded. More junior commanders then took over, each in turn to be either wounded or killed in this decisive action to retake the vital terrain of the Malakhov. As the casualty list steadily mounted, the commander-in-chief appeared on the scene at about 1730 hours to assess the situation, which had become critical.

THE RUSSIAN EVACUATION

Looking up towards the battered Malakhov, now very firmly in French hands, General Prince Gorchakov faced the most difficult decision of his career: to continue the fight or to withdraw. Not known for his military acuity, he none the less quickly resolved that it was not possible to recover the lost position and to sustain the defence of the southern side. He considered it now opportune to withdraw across to the northern side of Sevastopol – exploiting, as he declared in his subsequent despatch to the Emperor, the exhaustion of the Allies, who 'were in no condition to interfere with the evacuation'.[87] In making this judgement, whether contemporaneously or retrospectively, Gorchakov was undoubtedly correct in stark contrast to many of his previous decisions. He sensed rightly that the Allies' caution would delay any immediate follow-up: British and French troops, fearing that the enemy's fortifications were mined, would later enter the city very carefully. Returning to his forward command post in Fort Nicholas, Gorchakov gave orders at about 1800 hours for the evacuation to commence.

From 1900 hours until the next morning at about 0800 hours, Russian forces conducted a very well planned and orchestrated operation. It included not only the establishment of rearguards guarding road-blocks and the ordered movement of the garrison across the roadstead by ship, boat and the floating bridge, but also the denial – through an extensive series of demolitions – of much of southern Sevastopol. Todleben credits Major General Prince V. I. Vasilchikov, the chief of the general staff of the garrison, as the mastermind of the evacuation, though it would appear that the great engineer had been involved.[88] For much of the Crimean campaign, Russian staff work had been lamentable. But the orders for the evacuation, including detailed tables of march, betray a very professional guiding hand. By and large, the troops defending the western 'Town' side withdrew across the floating bridge while those who had defended the Korabelnaya district were evacuated by steamer. Although the crossings were packed, strict march discipline was kept throughout. An eyewitness, A. N. Suponev, described the crossing thus:

> It's hard to describe what the Sevastopol defenders experienced in their souls in those moments. [For some,] unwillingly, tears were welling in their eyes. Others, especially old sailors, were sobbing like children.... Cannon balls and bombs were

falling in the water every now and then on both sides of the bridge; the weather was calm, the stars were shining in the sky, but they were dim against the background of burning houses and fortifications and even brighter flaming shells, which were piercing the sky in different directions…. Quietly, without noise and any crushing, moved the mass onward: so silenced they were by these dramatic events. What grandiosity and striking inner tragedy this scene conveyed.[89]

Tolstoy's fiction would then have us believe that 'on reaching the North Side and leaving the bridge, almost every man took off his cap and crossed himself. But behind this feeling there was another, a sad, gnawing, and deeper feeling, which seemed like remorse, shame, and anger.'[90] Yet, whatever the truth of this particular matter, for once in the campaign, a Russian military plan had been executed in time and space to near-perfect precision. As a result, a mini-Dunkirk was achieved: all those involved in the evacuation could be proud of such a success snatched from failure.

How was it all accomplished? It is clear from the records that each regiment was allocated its place in the order of march, with specific rallying points and places of embarkation as required.[91] Pre-designated signal rockets regulated the rearward movement stage by stage: the operation proceeded remarkably slickly with minimal losses, save for the most serious, immobile wounded, who were left to their own devices, many to perish. Todleben states that the vast majority of the Russian wounded were transported across the roadstead, and only about 500 men were left to their fate. The true number of these unfortunate soldiers and sailors, however, was many times more, which took away some of the shine from the otherwise successful withdrawal. A sole doctor, bearing a letter from Gorchakov to Pélissier requesting medical aid on the grounds of humanity, was left to care for them.[92] On 10 September, Charles Gordon recorded that Russians came back to the city under a flag of truce to remove their wounded from the hospital, noting:

We had only found out that day [that it] contained 3000 wounded men. These unfortunate men had been for a day and a half without attendance. A fourth of them were dead, and the rest were in a bad way. I will not dwell any more on it, but could not imagine a more dreadful sight.[93]

Meanwhile, the detonation of thirty-five powder magazines within the fortifications led to a general conflagration of the city. During the night of 8/9 September and in the coming day, Gordon had observed:

… terrible explosions, and going down to the trenches at four a.m., I saw a splendid sight, the whole town in flames, and every now and then a terrific explosion. The rising sun shining on the scene of destruction produced a beautiful effect. The last of the Russians were leaving the town over the bridge. All the three-deckers, etc., were sunk, the steamers alone remaining. Tons and tons of powder must have been blown up.[94]

Returning to the Russian perspective of events, Tolstoy pictures a gunner (it could have been the author himself) who had survived the carnage at the Malakhov, and then managed to cross over to the north side. This anonymous individual now looks back at the city, observing:

Along the whole line of the Sevastopol bastions, which for so many months had been seething with such amazingly energetic life, for so many months had seen heroes relieved by death as they fell one after another, and for so many months had aroused the fear, the hatred, and at last the admiration of the enemy—on these bastions no one was now to be seen. All was dead, ghastly, terrible but not silent: the destruction still went on.[95]

Tolstoy then conjectures the impressions made on the Allied side:

The enemy saw that something incomprehensible was happening in awe-inspiring Sevastopol. The explosions and the deathly stillnesses on the bastions made them shudder; but still, under the influence of the strong and firm resistance of that day, they dared not yet believe that their unflinching foe had vanished; and silently, and anxiously immovable, they awaited the end of the sombre night.[96]

By 0800 hours on 9 September, the main evacuation operation had been completed. The commander of the garrison, Count Osten-Saken, together with Vasilchikov, then crossed over to the northern side. Bukhmeier immediately ordered the destruction of the floating bridge: any demolition parties left on the southern side would have to cross the roadstead by boat. During the course of the morning, unmolested by the Allied troops, volunteer Russian engineer and infantrymen proceeded to blow up the magazines of Coastal Batteries 7, 8 and 9, and of Forts Nicholas and Paul. At the same time, six of the fleet's remaining men-of-war were scuttled, including the *Parizh*, which Nicholas I had so proudly inspected a few years before, together with seven other small naval vessels. Six steamships that played such a vital part in the evacuation survived only for another couple of days. The burning of Sevastopol 'lasted two days and two nights', during which time a heavy pall of smoke lay of the city.[97]

Gordon entered the Redan that morning, where a 'dreadful sight was presented. The dead were buried in the ditch, the Russians with the English'. He went on to record that 'We now got into the town, ... and it seems quite strange to hear no firing. It has been a splendid city, and the harbour is magnificent'.[98] A few days later, Pirogov reflected on the news of the Russian evacuation: 'One act of the tragedy finishes; another begins, which will be surely not long lasting'.[99] One wonders whether he would have chosen to remain with the Russian wounded had he still been serving in the city. On 8 September 1855 alone, Russian losses amounted to nearly 13,000 men while the Allies suffered just over 10,000, the vast majority of the latter falling in the attacks on the Second Bastion, the Malakhov and the Great Redan.[100] At enormous cost, the Allies had gained the southern side of Sevastopol. But what next, and was it all worth it? Recriminations and reflections on both sides would soon begin.

PART THREE

CITY OF REVOLUTION

CHAPTER 8

RUIN, PEACE AND RECOVERY

'Ruined Pompeii is in good condition compared to Sebastopol.
Here, you may look in whatsoever direction you please, and
your eye encounters scarcely any thing but ruin, ruin, ruin!'

Mark Twain[1]

REFLECTIONS

Under conditions of great hardship, Russian forces had resolutely defended the southern side of Sevastopol for 349 days. Having repulsed all but one of the Allied attacks on 8 September 1855, the garrison withdrew in good order by bridge and boat across the roadstead. An independent commentator, albeit not an eyewitness, Major Richard Delafield of the United States Army, described this operation as a 'masterly retreat that does great credit to Russian military genius and discipline'.[2] Nearly 1,000 metres of water now separated the opposing forces. There is little merit in exploring in detail what might have happened had Gorchakov decided to continue contesting Sevastopol. Suffice it to say that the Allies would have renewed their intense bombardment and mounted a series of powerful attacks with fresh formations. Indeed, Sir Colin Campbell's Highland Division had prepared to assault the Great Redan on the morning of the 9th. The casualty toll on both sides might have been very high, but the result would hardly have been in doubt: the Allies would have succeeded in penetrating Sevastopol's defences at several places sooner or later.

When British and French troops occupied the city centre and secured its naval installations they could not easily exploit the situation. There was no simple way to storm the opposite shore, which was very strongly defended. The Russians continued to hold the northern side in force until the end of the war. None the less, the British and French forces (and more particularly the latter) had scored a notable success. In the eyes of their governments and publics, it hardly mattered whether Sevastopol was usable as a port or not. That it remained denied to the Russians counted far more. In any case, following the final scuttling of the remaining Russian ships in September, the Black Sea Fleet no longer existed. That result, after all, had realised the original object of the campaign.

Unsurprisingly, in view of the sacrifice and valour shown, there was a concerted attempt by the senior Russian figures involved to glorify the defence and to gloss over the need for the evacuation. They aimed not only to thank the soldiers and sailors concerned and to boost their morale, but also to justify their own actions and to describe the outcome in a positive light. A series of defiant orders of the day portrayed the defeat in grandiloquent terms – designed, as Todleben proudly observed, 'to strike at the heart of each defender of Sevastopol'.[3] The target audience of such documents included not only the participants of the siege, but also Russia's armed forces and the nation as a whole. After such a prolonged defence, the sudden loss of the city touched all parts of society, even those living far from the centres of power in St Petersburg and Moscow. For example, a friend of the deceased Admiral Nakhimov, the former naval cadet M. A. Bestuzhev, residing in the remote Siberian town of Selenginsk, declared: 'Sevastopol fell, but fell with such glory that every Russian, and especially every sailor, should be proud of such a defeat that represents a brilliant victory'.[4] Such a paradoxical perception reflected the national honour generated by the steadfast defenders of Sevastopol.

Giving the lead, Alexander II was the first to reflect publically on the loss of Sevastopol. On 30 August (11 September) 1855, the Emperor wrote to the 'Armies of Russia', expressing his 'profound gratitude for the tireless efforts' of the garrison and paying tribute to the sacrifice made in terms of 'the blood shed for nearly a year'. His imperial edict concluded with a stirring patriotic appeal, which would set the tone of Russian historiography of the defence of the city thereafter. Citing the exemplar battles of Poltava (1709) and Borodino (1812), the Tsar declared that 'the name of Sevastopol, which has acquired immortal glory by so much suffering, ... will remain forever etched in the memory and hearts of all Russians'.[5]

Prince M. D. Gorchakov's order of the day to the land and maritime forces of Crimea, dated 31 August (12 September), appealed to his 'valiant comrades-in-arms'. In justifying his decision to evacuate the southern side, he compared the loss of the city with the decision to abandon Moscow in 1812, and suggested that the defence of Sevastopol could be likened to the battle of Borodino. Whether such historical examples lifted the spirits of the tens of thousands of exhausted sailors and soldiers under his command is unknown. His next claim, nevertheless, might have stretched their credulity. Putting a brave face on the situation, if not entirely ignoring its realities, Gorchakov maintained: 'Sevastopol truly tied us to its walls. By its fall [however], we have regained our freedom of action: a new [type of] war beckons, a campaign in open country, for which the Russian soldier has a particular aptitude.'[6] The survivors of the battles of Alma, Balaklava, Inkerman and Chernaya, of course, probably had different memories and perceptions.

It is questionable whether the Russian commander-in-chief was sufficiently professionally competent, let alone psychologically fit enough, to fight a new campaign of any sort. After all, he had departed the blazing southern side of Sevastopol a broken man. On reaching the pier prior to crossing the roadstead, apparently he had 'tried to keep up a cheerful manner, but as he climbed down the ladder, his optimism was disappearing'. When he reached his boat, 'he looked up at the clear night sky, and said in French (lest he be understood by the sailors present): "*je vois mon étoile de malheur* [I see my star of woe]"'.[7] Gorchakov was not only an unlucky general, but also one who failed to inspire optimism in others. Shortly after the fall of the city, one of his most ardent critics, Pirogov, visited the northern side. Viewing for a long time – both by eye and telescope – the Malakhov Hill and other fortifications lying across the roadstead, he commented: 'These days, I saw two famous shattered ruins: Sevastopol and Gorchakov. The harbour divides one from the other.'[8]

Amongst the troops, the state of morale, both during and following the evacuation, was mixed. The prevailing mood reflected a combination of anger, pride and sadness. Tolstoy would have us believe that 'almost every soldier, looking back from the North Side at the abandoned town, sighed with inexpressible bitterness in his heart, and menaced the enemy.'[9] In his memoirs, Valerian Zarubaev, a Sevastopol resident and the officer commanding the 1st Carabineers Company of the Aleksopol Light Infantry Regiment reflected: 'So, Sevastopol fell. Our unparalleled toil, an eleven-month-long defence, resulted in a lamentable outcome. But our conscience, the one of little men, is clear in the face of the Emperor and the Motherland. All, whatever depended on us, we performed immaculately.'[10] Not all involved, however, were quite so ebullient: other accounts suggest rather different reactions. It would appear that the decision to abandon the southern side was taken badly by some of the sailors, who wished to continue defending their home port and naval arsenal. Nakhimov's fearless example had cast a long shadow. 'We cannot leave, we did not receive any order', they complained. 'The Army may leave, but we've got our own commanders; as we did not receive any orders from them, how can we leave Sevastopol? How is it possible? The assault was repulsed everywhere; the French are left only on the Malakhov, but they will be chased away tomorrow! ... We must die here, rather than leave. What will people in Russia say about us?'[11]

Of all the senior officers, Osten-Saken, closest to the troops involved, probably struck the most resonant chord in his proclamation to the garrison of Sevastopol: 'Brave warriors! Until the very end, you have done your duty ... your contemporaries and future generations will treat you virtuously; your motherland will boast of your exploits. Peace be with our valiant brothers-in-arms who have fallen in the defence of this city.'[12] The combined sentiments of Alexander II, Gorchakov and Osten-Saken, and of many of their subordinates, provided the foundations of an enduringly defiant historical narrative, one which Tolstoy had already skilfully captured in his opening Sketch: the indomitable 'spirit of Sevastopol'. Despite describing in captivating detail the events of 8 September in his final essay, he merely commented in his diary on 2 (14) September that 'Sevastopol has surrendered!'[13] Although technically this was not the case, the city had none the less been abandoned to the Allies. The Emperor of All the Russias (as the Tsar was titled formally) and the Russian nation were spared such a humiliation. During the long siege and throughout the major battles of the Crimean War, Russian sailors and soldiers had fought bravely, patriotically and tenaciously. They had done their duty, and died in their tens, if not hundreds, of thousands. Notwithstanding the loss of the city, the defence of Sevastopol would enter the annals of the Russian nation as a stirring heroic deed.

British reactions to the fall of Sevastopol were varied, depending on position and perspective. Sterling, for example, combined bitter disappointment at the failure at the Great Redan with an admiration of the French and Russian armies' performance during the battle. Writing at length on 10 September 1855, he compared the success of the 'French rush' at the Malakhov with 'the sad catastrophe of the English attack on the Redan'. 'Sad', he remonstrated, 'not merely from our loss of life, but from the palpable inexperience of the General [Codrington], who did not understand his métier, and from the misbehaviour of the reserves with him, who ought to have followed the first assaulting columns'. On the other hand, the French 'have performed a marvellous feat of arms; they were lucky as well as brave'. He noted that the Russians before abandoning the Redan 'dressed our wounded, and they did not blow up the magazine [there], which was very humane on their part'. More particularly, they had 'made a magnificent retreat; carrying off their whole garrison intact over the bridge, ... leaving us in quiet possession of the ruins of the town'.[14] In so doing, he pre-empted Gorchakov's claim in his order of the day that the Russians had left their opponents not the noble city of Sevastopol, but rather a 'pile of smoking ruins'.[15] Sterling, however, was mistaken in his overly optimistic belief that the Russians would abandon Crimea after the fall of Sevastopol. He concluded his long letter home in emphasising:

> ... if the Russians quietly go away, we shall occupy both sides of the harbour, clear
> it out, fill [it] with our ships, and wait for spring. We all feel intensely the disgrace
> of our failure, and also feel sure, if our Highlanders had assaulted instead of the
> others, that we should have taken the place.

Once again he criticised the British command, complaining that 'The crack young Generals Codrington and Markham had the entire management of it; and what a pretty mess they made! Codrington, who was with the front Division, ought to have rushed up to the Redan when he found men wavering.'[16]

The artilleryman Edward Bruce Hamley attributed the cause of the great conflagration that engulfed Sevastopol to a combination of 'the results of shells from our 13-inch mortars' and the Russians' own efforts made 'all for destruction'. Unsure as to the enemy's motives in setting fire to the city, and bearing in mind that the Russians might wish to return one day, he declared piquantly that:

> ... their traditionary stroke of policy in burning Moscow seems to have impressed
> on the national mind a general idea of the virtue of incendiarism; and the
> catastrophe of Russian towns and fortresses, like that of a Vauxhall entertainment,
> would appear incomplete without a general conflagration.[17]

As an aide-de-camp to the British Army's senior Royal Artillery officer in Crimea, Sir Richard Dacres, Hamley accompanied his principal on a tour of the town on 10 September. They first entered the Central (Fifth) Bastion, and from that vantage point, viewed the now derelict, burnt-out, Sevastopol below. Observing a 'suburb of ruined hovels, roofless and windowless', Hamley reported that '[we] looked across the ravine to the best-built portion of the skeleton city'. There, 'some houses were still smoking, and one or two were in flames, especially near Fort Nicholas'. Venturing into the city centre and passing 'down a road parallel to the Inner Harbour', the two gunner officers encountered neither Russian soldiers nor townsfolk, but rather 'a great many cats and a few dogs ... the latter skulking and downcast, the former making for their retreats in a great hurry'. Yet they were soon to make a macabre discovery, one already referred to in Gordon's account. 'Along the water's edge', Hamley narrated, 'was a very spacious well-built barrack left unconsumed amid the surrounding flames'. On inspecting the interior of this building, it was 'scarcely possible to conceive a situation more horrible than theirs ... [Russians] lying helpless, and tortured by wounds, without assistance, and without nourishment, surrounded by flaming buildings and exploding mines'.

The next night (the 11th), the remaining vessels of the Black Sea Fleet, the six British-built paddle steamers, including the *Vladimir*, whose pugnacious captain had boasted that he would make a dash for Odessa, were burned and scuttled by their crews in the roadstead. This final act of defiant demolition prompted Hamley to observe:

> So ended amid death and destruction the great siege of Sevastopol. The drama, with its many dull tedious passages, and its many scenes of intense and painful interest, extending over nearly a year, had for actors the three greatest nations of the earth, and all the world for an audience. The catastrophe solved many difficulties, quieted many doubts, and falsified many prophecies.[18]

The fighting had more or less ceased. Notwithstanding that there was no armistice agreed, let alone a peace signed, there was a widespread sense that the campaign was almost over. This belief, however, was premature as the Allies were to mount an expedition to bombard and raid the Russian forts at Kinburn at the mouth of the river Dnieper on 17 October 1855. Meanwhile, reflecting on the dénouement at Sevastopol, Hamley lifted his literary gaze from the city to the 'barren plateau, with which the army of the East is now so wearily familiar'. On this hallowed ground were scattered the 'bones of a mighty host ... Russian and Turk, Frenchman and Englishman'. With a final flourish, Hamley concluded:

> When these great armies have departed, when the cities of tents have vanished, and the last echoes of the tramp of troops, the hum of camps, and the roll of artillery, have died away, these solitudes, tenanted only by the fox and the eagle, will continue for us and our descendants a colony of the dead.[19]

Hamley's accounts of the siege of Sevastopol were published contemporaneously in *Blackwood's Magazine*. His literary as well as military ability marked him out for advancement in the years following the Crimean War, not least in his appointment as professor of military history at the newly founded British Staff College in 1859. Notably, his major work, *The Operations of War*, published in 1866, would become a standard text at that institution.

The official British view of the fall of Sevastopol was expressed in General Simpson's despatch to Lord Panmure of the 9th September, in which he reported on 'the glorious results of the attack of yesterday, which has ended in the possession of the Town, Dockyards, and Public Buildings, and the destruction of the last three Ships of the Russian Fleet in the Black Sea'. Having paid due tribute to his ally's success in carrying 'the apparently impregnable defences' of the Malakhov with 'that impetuous valour which characterizes the French attack', the commander-in-chief then painted a heroic picture of the abortive British operation:

> [The columns of assault] left the trenches at the preconcerted signal, and moved across the ground, preceded by a covering party of 200 men, and a ladder party of 320. On arriving at the crest of the ditch, and the ladders placed, the men immediately stormed the parapet of the Redan, and penetrated into salient angle. A most determined and bloody contest was here maintained for nearly an hour, and, although supported to the utmost, and the greatest bravery displayed, it was found impossible to maintain the position.

Furthermore, Simpson highlighted the 'conduct and gallantry exhibited by the troops, though their devotion was not rewarded by the success which they so well merited'.[20]

Rear Admiral Sir Edmund Lyons, commanding the Royal Navy's Mediterranean Fleet and ships in the Black Sea, in his own despatch to the Secretary of the Admiralty of 10 September, confirmed that a 'north-west gale and heavy sea rendered it impossible for any vessel to act upon the batteries situated on the lee shore of this exposed Roadstead'. So there was no repeat of the artillery duel between Allied wooden warships and Russian stone shore forts that had occurred on 17 October 1854, and no opportunity for the newer British vessels such as Lyons' flagship, the screw-propelled steamship, HMS *Royal Albert*, to show their mettle. But one technical innovation did figure in the events of 8 September 1855: 'the French and British mortar vessels attached to the Fleets kept up a very effective fire from their position in the Bay of Strelitzka [Arrow Bay]'. Lyons concluded his report by commending the harmonious relations with the French fleet, writing of his 'gallant colleague, Vice Admiral Bruat' and their 'most perfect understanding and hearty co-operation in the great cause of humanity in which we are all engaged'.[21]

Naturally, French views on the fall of the Sevastopol were more upbeat than the British. As Napoleon III had wished, the siege had been concluded with a demonstrably French military success if not a triumph. The campaign in Crimea had reached its desired strategic and political objective. Now was the time for the granting of national honours in grateful recognition. Pélissier, for example, was promoted to the rank of Marshal of France on 12 September 1855, and following his return to France was created the 'Duke of Malakoff' on 22 July 1856. His principal subordinates, Bosquet and Canrobert, were also advanced to marshal.

Meanwhile, Alexander II, having accepted the finality of the fall of Sevastopol, resolved to travel from St Petersburg to southern Russia in order to visit his troops. This was more than a mere morale-raising trip: the Emperor, no doubt, wished to ascertain from his commanders on the spot their views as to how the campaign might be progressed, and bearing in mind his concerns about the commander-in-chief, decide on M. D. Gorchakov's future. Arriving at Nikolayev in mid-September, he spent six weeks there and in Odessa, a period which coincided with the Allied attack on Kinburn. Eventually, he travelled to Crimea and was met by Gorchakov at Simferopol on 28 October (9 November) 1855. The same day, he inspected the 4th and 5th Infantry Divisions near Bakhchisaray and then reviewed troops of 4th Corps in the vicinity of the river Kacha. Accompanied by his brothers, Grand Dukes Nicholas and Michael, the next day he inspected soldiers of 5th Corps in the Belbek valley; visited the fortifications on the northern side of Sevastopol; and then reviewed troops encamped close to their positions at Inkerman and on the Mackenzie Heights. Over two successive days, the Emperor rounded off his busy tour of inspection with rides to the Russians' advanced posts before departing Crimea on 1 (13) November 1855.[22] His visit to the Russian Crimean Army is remembered today. A commemorative plaque at the village of Topoli, in the Alma valley midway between Simferopol and Bakhchisaray, records his inspection of 2nd Corps on 28 October (9 November); another memorial tablet can be seen at Yukhary Karalez (now Zalesnoye), a former Tatar settlement lying 20 kilometres east of Sevastopol, where the Emperor reviewed troops of 3rd Corps on 30 October (11 November) 1855.[23]

Throughout his visit to his army before Sevastopol, Alexander II, according to Todleben's flattering account, 'deigned to speak in the most graceful manner, affirming to the troops his expression of gratitude for their service and heroism they had shown during the defence of Sevastopol'. In the manner of any interested, if not enlightened, head of state, the Tsar visited the wounded and thanked them personally for the sacrifices they had made. He also 'spoke to the men awarded with the Military Cross about the fighting in which they had participated, and which had earned them this decoration, and listened attentively to these brave soldiers'. In turn, while Russian troops proclaimed their loyalty to their sovereign by shouting compliments of 'loud Hurrahs', their officers ingratiated themselves by 'protesting their inviolable devotion in attesting that they were, at all times, ready to shed their blood for the Emperor and Motherland'.[24] Before he departed Crimea, Alexander II issued an imperial decree, which awarded all participants of the heroic defence of Sevastopol a silver medal, attached to the ribbon of St George. This commemorative act was of enormous historical significance: the black and orange colours of this ribbon have since that day signified Sevastopol's pivotal place in Russia's national story. Citizens of the city still proudly display these proud symbols of St George, as do Russians across the world every year on 9 May, celebrated as the Victory Day of the Second World War.

While Todleben failed, disappointingly, to document any of the military discussions between Alexander II and Gorchakov as to future intentions, he did include the Emperor's personal letter of thanks to the commander-in-chief of the Russian land and maritime forces in Crimea. His words represent an astonishing tribute entirely free from any recriminations, in which he praises Gorchakov in fulsome terms for his conduct of the defence of Sevastopol:

> ... you ceded the terrain [of the city] foot by foot; by strengthening your resolve with the sound principles worthy of an experienced leader such as yourself, you have abandoned to the enemy the ruins purchased by him at the price of precious blood; and, after making a glorious withdrawal by unusual means ... , you are ready to meet the enemy again with the same courage...

Evidently, if the Tsar had harboured any doubts as to Gorchakov's suitability, these were swiftly cast away during the course of the visit: he had been impressed by the 'joyous and martial air' displayed by the troops, and by the good order and discipline that prevailed in the army. Having thanked the commander-in-chief for his intelligence and courage, Alexander II concluded his letter by confirming: 'It is particularly pleasing for me to repeat here the expression of sincere gratitude that I have already had the opportunity to personally assure you of. I beg you, Prince, to appreciate the permanent goodwill that I bear you'.[25]

M. D. Gorchakov's unlucky star, like a rapidly receding comet, had quickly faded from sight. Now honoured by the Emperor as a conquering hero rather than castigated as an inadequate general, his position as commander-in-chief was safe. Alexander II conveniently forgot his subordinate's indecision prior to the battle of the Chernaya river and his failures in command during that action. Fortunately for Gorchakov, and perhaps for Russia, he was not to be further tested during the remainder of the campaign. As the Allies proceeded to demolish what was left standing in Sevastopol on the southern shore, the main events over the next few months would be diplomatic rather than military. Hence the Emperor would now look for news from Vienna rather than Sevastopol. The diplomat responsible for negotiating a suitable peace was the Russian ambassador to Austria, Prince Aleksandr Mikhailovich [A. M.] Gorchakov – none other than the cousin of the two Gorchakov brothers who had both served in Crimea.

THE DEMOLITION OF SEVASTOPOL'S NAVAL AND MILITARY INFRASTRUCTURE

It will be recalled that the prime object of the Allied expedition to Crimea was the destruction of the Russian Black Sea Fleet and its associated supporting infrastructure in Sevastopol. In September 1854, the Russians had sunk many of their warships in the roadstead to block its entrance to Allied warships. Later, many other vessels, including further sailing ships of the line and steamers, were scuttled to deny their use to the Allies. In his despatch of 15 September 1855, Rear Admiral Lyons reported: 'The bottom of the splendid harbour is now encumbered with more than 50 sunken vessels, including 18 sail of the line and several frigates and steamers, whose menacing attitude but a short time ago materially contributed to bring on the war in which we are now engaged'.[26]

With the Russians having done a large part of their demolition work for them, Allied engineers could turn their attention to Sevastopol's 'military-maritime' infrastructure, including their largest object of destruction – the newly completed dry docks. The result of the millions of man-hours, let alone of roubles, invested in this grandiose project, which had become for Nicholas I as much an object of prestige as one of naval utility, would be blown up. The intrinsic value to the Russians of Upton's work, however, was clear to the Allies, not least to Lyons. In the same despatch he observed:

> The five docks and the adjoining basins are magnificent, and together with the steam machinery for filling them up from the Tchernaya and for pumping them out, are in excellent order; and the resources of all kinds still remaining after the enormous expenditure during the siege, showed very plainly the importance the enemy attached to having a large depot at the threshold of the Bosphorus.[27]

The magnitude of the Allied demolition task was daunting. Nothing in the history of warfare had been attempted on this scale before. Prior to the introduction of high explosives such as dynamite (patented by Alfred Noble in 1867), huge quantities of gunpowder would be required. Whatever the explosive means, deep shafts and extensive galleries would need to be constructed to hold the necessary demolition charges, which then would have to be 'tamped' (packed) in order to direct and maximise the explosive effect. All such effort required considerable engineer resources and expertise, and a great deal of additional labour supplied by the infantry. According to the British official report, apart from the supervising Royal Engineer officers, the demolition task involved 'a party of 350 [men] of the 18th and 48th Regiments, in addition to the Royal Sappers and Miners, amounting to 85'.

These soldiers and engineers worked 'for the greater part of the time, day and night during the severest weather'.[28]

Preparatory work on the demolitions started on 13 September 1855, within five days of the Russian evacuation of the southern side of Sevastopol. The operation, which was to take over five months, became a model scheme of collaboration between French and British sappers. For the latter, it was also a testing ground for the employment of a new 'galvanic' – electrical – system of initiating charges, a technology brought out to Crimea by the submarine engineer John Deane, and one originally intended for the demolition of the sunken ships. This civilian diver was to work closely with the Royal Engineer demolition parties.[29] It was agreed that the French would be responsible for the three access locks and two dry docks on the northern, 'sea', side, while the British would focus on the inner three dry docks on the southern side. The destruction of the central basin was a shared task. Ensconced on the northern shore, the Russians could have seriously interfered with the Allied demolition effort by firing at the British and French sappers, who were well within the range of their artillery and mortars. But they chose not to, sending over instead a few rounds from time to time to remind their opponents that a state of conflict still pertained. Fortunately, such incidents cost few casualties.

Apart from the official Royal Engineers' report on the demolition of the docks, a number of personal accounts of the work undertaken reveal its extraordinary scope and complexity. These include not only Deane's correspondence, but also a series of detailed letters by Charles Gordon, who was based in Sevastopol's dockyard from December 1855 to March 1856. Writing on 4 December 1855, for example, the intrepid Royal Engineer officer recorded that the 'quantity of powder we shall use is 45,000 lbs., in charges varying from 80 lbs. to 8000 lbs.'. The French, he explained, 'do not sink their shafts so deep as we do, but use heavier charges'. Several of the British shafts were 'very deep', and 'in others there is from eight to ten feet of water'. Gordon also commented on the construction of the docks, which were 'very well made', noting that the 'gates alone cost £23,000'. Indeed, at some considerable time and trouble, these massive items were salvaged as trophies of war, a task in which the chief and assistant Engineer of HMS *Royal Albert* assisted. In the same letter, Gordon opined that 'there is not much prospect of the Russians leaving the north side. We can see them hutting themselves'. Perhaps more crucially for the supply and welfare of the Allied troops over the coming winter, he added, 'we have now got locomotives on the [railway] line [from Balaklava], which is a great improvement'.[30] Until then, a rather inefficient combination of horse power and a static steam engine pulling wagons up the Sapun escarpment by cable had been used.

On 27 December 1855, Gordon noted that 'Our works at the docks approach completion, and we hope to blow up some portion of them on Saturday next....

The powder for our demolition will be upwards of twenty-two tons.' The French engineers, however, had been quicker off the mark, having already initiated their first charges the previous Saturday. Gordon was generous in his praise of his Allied colleagues: 'the explosion presented a splendid appearance, and succeeded admirably, not a stone being left standing'.[31] British and French engineers combined their efforts to shatter the relative peace and tranquillity of the last day of the year with a series of deafening blasts. William Howard Russell provided a vivid pen-picture of the unfolding dockyard scene:

On the 31st ult, it was at six minutes to one that the drum was beaten by the French Sapper for the 39 French and four English engineers to light their port-fires ... the charges in the side and bottom of the French dock exploded almost simultaneously. Shortly afterwards the large charges in the piers of the entrance and behind the steps leading down to the dock blew up. These three charges shook the ground terribly, and propelled large stones perpendicularly into the air to the height of at least 900 feet. In 9½ minutes the English charges exploded, causing a very neat demolition of half the side wall of the basin.... There is every reason to expect that in another fortnight the whole of the Sebastopol docks will be totally worthless for any purpose whatsoever.[32]

Demolition work continued apace throughout January. On the 20th, Gordon wrote 'we have blown up our part of the docks, and are very busy with the remainder, which we hope to get over by the end of the month.[33] Five days later, Deane, in charge of the electrical detonation system, informed his sister, Sarah Ann, in Whitstable: 'We are getting on very well with the destruction of the Docks, frequently discharging several thousand pounds of gunpowder every day, and the havoc, as you may imagine, is frightfully grand'.[34]

On 3 February 1856, Gordon wrote his most detailed account of the Allied demolitions, both completed and forecast, including not only a commentary on the technical aspects concerned, but also an assessment of the quality of the French engineers. There is little doubt that, as a young, energetic and aspiring professional officer, he was consumed by his important task:

We all of us have been extremely busy in loading and firing our mines in the docks, which required all our time, as were so very short of officers, having only three, while the French have twelve. Our force of sappers was only 150, and the French had 600. We have now finished the demolition, which is satisfactory, as far as the effects produced are concerned; but having used the voltaic battery instead of the old-fashioned [gun-powder] hose, we have found that electricity will not succeed in large operations like this ...[35]

As for the French, they had 'done their work very well, using more powder than we, and firing all their mines with hose'. His Allied counterparts had evidently impressed him: 'We have seen a great deal of the French engineers; they are older men than ours, and seem well educated'. Tellingly, he added, 'The non-commissioned officers are much more intelligent than our men. With us, although our men are not stupid, the officers have to do a good deal of work which the French sapper non-commissioned officer does'.[36] In later years, Gordon was to complain of the poor quality of the British demolition work at Sevastopol. Writing from the Sudan in 1877, he commented 'what a mess we made of that dock'; and in another letter of the same period, 'miserable is the only term which could be applied to your dock demolition'.[37]

If the construction of Sevastopol's docks had been unprecedented in its ambition and expense, requiring much ingenuity and innovation in the process of their building, their destruction had proved similarly demanding in a technical sense. Significantly, the Russians never attempted to repair or reconstruct the docks, such was the comprehensive extent of the Allied demolitions. Furthermore, by the time a new shipbuilding plan for the Black Sea Fleet was adopted in 1881, and the Russian Navy re-established its base at Sevastopol in 1890, warship design had evolved greatly since the 1830s. Now much larger ironclads were required as capital ships, and Upton's docks, even if rebuilt, would not have been big enough to accommodate any but the smallest of modern naval vessels.

Having completed their work of destruction in the dockyard, the French turned their attention to Fort Nicholas; Gordon was party to their plans for a hasty demolition. Although the Russians had mined their 'splendid fort, mounting 128 guns, and capitally finished for barracks', they had not had time to lay their charges before their evacuation. The French engineers would complete the task with '105,000 lbs. of powder in the demolition', or nearly 50 metric tonnes, representing over twice the total quantity of explosives used by the British in the dockyard. According to Gordon, the French intended to place 'charges of 2500 lbs. each in every alternate casement and will tamp up all the orifices'.[38] Although Gordon did not describe the ensuing demolition of the fort, there is no doubt that the French sappers knew their business. While Fort Constantine and the Michael Battery remain today on the northern side of Sevastopol as striking monuments of nineteenth-century coastal fortifications, Fort Nicholas (and later Fort Paul) was erased efficiently from the southern shore. There are no vestiges of these once mighty bastions of Russian power today.

From their secure batteries on the northern shore of the roadstead, it might be presumed that the Russians would have tried to interfere with the Allied programme of demolitions – what remained of their noble city after the Allied bombardments was being scientifically removed in their direct view. Gordon's account provides valuable insights into the Russian demeanour in the early months of 1856. In essence, a regime of 'live and let live, but attack us at your peril' prevailed – one, in practice, adopted by the Allies. 'The Russians do not molest us now', he observed. Further, 'We can hear them call out and sing, especially on Sundays. We see them drill, which they do every day'. More remarkably, 'They even have the coolness to fish in the harbour'. Fortunately, for the Russians concerned, 'We never fire, [and] neither do the French'. If provoked, however, the Russians would react vigorously. In illustration of this posture, Gordon described a recent, confused incident. Presumably on his own initiative a French Navy captain with a small team of sailors had rowed over by night to the northern side of the roadstead, and tried to set fire to a Russian steamer lying on its side. The French were soon detected. In response, the Russians 'fired into the boat, and then continued the fire from all their guns, expecting a grand attack'. In turn, their 'tremendous fire' put the Allies on the southern side 'under arms, expecting an attack by boats'. 'After an hour of shelling', Gordon continued, 'the Russians left off, and all again was silent'.[39] Such an event, however, proved a violent exception to a pragmatic, pacific rule.

Gordon also drew attention to the mining and counter-mining operations undertaken by French and Russian engineers respectively. Because the British were not involved in this particular branch of land warfare, many historians of the Crimean War have overlooked this aspect of the siege of Sevastopol. The French and the Russians took these operations very seriously and expended much effort in them. So much so, Todleben considered the 'underground war' sufficiently important to devote a special volume of his history of the defence of Sevastopol to the subject. In many ways this special niche of combat practised at Sevastopol was to presage the much better known tunnelling and counter-tunnelling operations on the Western Front of the First World War. The locus of most of the French and Russian mining was the Fourth Bastion, which from the first bombardment onwards, had been singled out for particular attention and attack by the French. 'We had seven French engineers to dine with us the other day', Gordon narrated; 'they were very agreeable and we learnt a great deal about their mining'. Apparently, the French engineers used to hear the Russians tunnelling, and would attempt to blow in their mineshafts. On gaining access to the Bastion du Mât after the Russian withdrawal from the southern side of Sevastopol, the French found, to their amazement, 'two systems or layers of mines, one about ten feet below the surface of the ground, and the other about forty foot'. Until they occupied the bastion, the French sappers were unaware of the Russians' lower set of mines, and not amused to detect that 'their [own] advanced trenches were quite mined and loaded in the lower tier'.[40] At the Fourth Bastion alone, the French found no fewer than thirty-six mines ready with charges laid and tamped. Modern visitors to this bastion – famed for the partially reconstructed Fourth Battery, temporarily commanded by Leo Tolstoy – can still view an entrance to a Russian engineers' tunnel.

Having destroyed the docks and the shore forts on the southern side, the Allies looked for further demolition targets in Sevastopol. By this time, an informal truce prevailed in Crimea. Although a peace was in the offing, it made sense in the interim to complete the denial of the city for any further military or naval purpose by the Russians, destroying anything useful. Thus notwithstanding the signing of an armistice in Paris on 26 February 1856, the Allies at Sevastopol pressed on with their demolitions. The next site chosen was the complex of 'White Barracks' (also known as the 'White Buildings') on the eastern side of the South Bay. The work there was to demonstrate the inherent risks involved in demolitions. On 9 March 1856, Gordon recorded:

> We had a sad accident the other day. An officer of ours, Major Rankin, was setting light to a line of mines under the wall of the White Barracks, and it is supposed the fuse was bad, as, instead of its burning as long as it ought to enable him to get it away, the charges of powder went off instantaneously, and he was buried in the ruins. We got his body out after considerable trouble.[41]

What made this incident particularly poignant for Gordon, a fellow Royal Engineer, was the fact that Rankin had not only 'got his majority and company about two months ago', but also he had been the 'engineer who went with the ladders' at the abortive attack on the Redan on 8 September 1855.[42]

Meanwhile, the Allies' destruction of the Russian barracks continued. *The Times* reported in London on 13 March 1856, 'as if to celebrate the armistice, the so-called "White Buildings" were blown up this afternoon'. Another demolition target, a brig in the dockyard, was also 'to be blown up by way of experiment', and so the paper claimed, 'for the particular gratification of Mr Deane, the "infernal diver"'... '[However, his] experiment with the brig failed; the reason why has yet to be ascertained'. The news report then explained that 'Mr Deane attributes his occasional failures to the state of the wires'. As the Royal Engineers had observed, Gordon included, the novel electrical means of initiation of demolition charges had yet to be perfected. Deane, the newspaper noted, appeared to be 'indefatigable in his endeavours to overcome difficulties and perfect his apparatus'.[43]

Following the signing of the Treaty of Paris on 30 March 1856, demolition works at Sevastopol finally ceased. A degree of informal contact had already been established between the Allies and the Russians, with the river Chernaya acting as the mutually agreed boundary. Gordon noted that the 'Russians make a good business out of selling crosses and other things to our officers'.[44] Deane also recorded this trade, an early example of battlefield tourism: 'we can walk along the line of demarcation and exchange civilities and talk to the Russians within 20 feet. Numbers of them flock down to the edge of the river ... and we the allies meet them all along its bank, and exchange purses, handkerchiefs, coin for coin'.[45]

Charles Gordon had spent four busy months working on the destruction of Sevastopol's naval and military infrastructure, demolishing its dockyard, quays, forts, barracks and storehouses. He departed Crimea in February 1856, a wiser man who impressed his comrades-in-arms. In a report written on 1 February for General Sir William Codrington, Lieutenant Colonel Edward Lloyd, commanding the Royal Engineers, acknowledged the 'very valuable assistance' he had received from a number of individuals, including 'Colonel [John William] Gordon, C.B., the Executive Officer, Major Nicholson, ... the Resident Engineer, and Lieutenants Cumberland, Graham and C. Gordon, Royal Engineers'. He praised these sapper officers for their 'unremitting zeal, attention, and devotion to the work'. Lloyd also took the opportunity to thank John Deane, to whom he was 'much indebted'.[46]

The two Gordons, who were unrelated, made their names at Sevastopol; and both were scarred by their experiences. The elder Gordon (1814–70), nicknamed 'Old Fireworks' for his coolness under fire during the siege, was subsequently promoted to major general and knighted. By this time, however, Sir William Gordon was 'a sick man, largely because of the wound to his right hand and arm received outside Sevastopol. The pain never left him and worsened with the years.' Most probably he was also suffering from what we describe today as post-traumatic stress disorder: during his later career, his 'behaviour became more and more irrational.' On a joint trip together, his Crimean comrade, close friend and younger namesake, fearing the worst, had confiscated his razors but William took them back in a brief struggle and committed suicide.[47] Charles Gordon, who also became a major general, was equally renowned for his courage and bravado at Sevastopol. A fellow Royal Engineer and noted military historian, [later Colonel] C. C. Chesney, wrote of him as follows:

[He] had first seen war in the hard school of the 'black winter' of the Crimea. In his humble position as an engineer subaltern he attracted the notice of his superiors, not merely by his energy and activity ..., but by a special aptitude for war, developing itself amid the trench-work before Sebastopol in a personal knowledge of the enemy's movements such as no other officer attained. 'We used to send him to find out what new move the Russians were making' was the testimony given years since to his genius by one of the most distinguished of the officers he served under.[48]

Young Gordon had certainly made his mark with his particular brand of valour and professional expertise. He was decorated with the French Legion of Honour, a special distinction for such a junior officer.

As many other visitors following the Crimean War would testify, Sevastopol was utterly wrecked: its reconstruction would take several decades to complete. The city's birth in 1783 was the direct result of Catherine the Great's decision to found and base a Russian Black Sea Fleet on the Crimean peninsula. Apart from a few dogs and cats, and the Allied troops of occupation, the city was essentially dead. The question now arose whether Alexander II would be in a position to direct its renaissance: the terms of any peace settlement would provide the answer.

THE TREATY OF PARIS (30 MARCH 1856)

During the Crimean War, the path to peace, as has so often been the case in other conflicts, proved as rocky as the road to war. What made the peace-making so complicated and uneven in this instance was not only the number of powers involved, but also the divisions that emerged between the Allies, and principally those which opened up between Britain and France. In addition to the five direct parties to the conflict (Russia, France, Britain, Turkey and Piedmont–Sardinia), both Austria and Prussia were involved in the discussions. Russia was particularly sensitive to the attitude of Austria, as she could ill afford to fight another major European power on her western border. Turkey desired to be recognised as an independent, sovereign state, free from interference from powers such as Russia, and to be admitted to the Concert of Europe as an equal member. Hence the Ottomans wished a clean break from the previous bilateral treaties with individual European states, the majority of which were termed (and not just regarded as) 'capitulations'. Britain and France supported Turkey's aspirations, not only out of historic goodwill, but as much to contain Russian might and ambition.

Amongst the Allies, the extent to which Russia's wings should be clipped marked a point of divergence between British and French views – a fissure which, of course, the Russians would seek to exploit. In broad terms, Britain rigorously demanded more concessions from her opponent, maintaining – to Russian eyes at least – its traditional role of belligerence. At the same time, Napoleon III wished to re-establish France as the leading continental power, and to that end, he steered negotiations as independently as possible from Britain. Furthermore, he desired that any peace conference be held in Paris rather than in Vienna, so as to mark the centrality of his nation's resurgent role in world affairs. In this matter, Alexander II would support him. Russia wished to restore good relations with France as quickly as possible.

So the war, and in turn the peace, were not just about solving the 'Eastern Question': they had as much to do with the rebalancing of power within Europe. Thus there was a great deal of realpolitik being undertaken far from the battlefronts, as states jostled for position and influence, both military and economic, in the greatest round of European diplomacy since the Congress of Vienna of 1814–15. The main contextual differences, however, rested not only in the reversal of the roles of Russia and France, but also in the lack of a decisive, war-ending battle that forged the peace. As grievously as Russia had suffered, her army had not been vanquished in a titanic battle similar to Napoleon's defeats at Leipzig (1813) or at Waterloo (1815); nor had she been humiliated by an enemy occupation of her capital.

The foundations of the peace eventually brokered rested on a development of the 'Four Points', based on the 'Vienna Note', which, it will be recalled, Britain, France, Austria and Prussia had drawn up in August 1853. As the fighting proceeded in various theatres of operations, whether on land or sea in Crimea, Caucasus, Baltic or in the Far East, protracted negotiations continued in parallel in Vienna; their pace and direction would be affected by the vicissitudes of war, and not least the outcomes of battle. While the numerous twists and turns of these peace negotiations are beyond the scope of this military history, the outcome, enshrined in the Treaty of Paris, signed on 30 March 1856, is not: after all, Sevastopol's future, and that of the Black Sea Fleet, was so determined. None the less, it is useful to summarise the diplomatic process involved in advancing towards a final treaty.

In November 1854, the Russian cabinet had accepted the Four Points, namely: '(1) abolition of the Russian protectorate over the Principalities [of Moldovia and Wallachia, parts of the future Romania]; (2) freedom of navigation of the Danube; (3) revision of the Treaty of 1841, so as to eliminate Russian preponderance in the Black Sea; and (4) general European supervision over the carrying out of the [Turkish] Sultan's pledges of rights and immunities to his Greek Orthodox subjects'.[49] The latter provision would replace the previous Russian guarantee vested in Article VII of the Treaty of Kuchuk Kainardzhi of 1774. As far as the Allies were concerned in the midst of the Crimean campaign, the time was not yet ripe for peace. Having decided to eradicate Russia's principal naval base on the Black Sea, the task was incomplete until Sevastopol fell on 8/9 September 1855. When the Crimean campaign was in progress, the Allies resolved further to curb Russian power on a more permanent basis by the neutralisation of the Black Sea.[50] For Britain, however, that represented a necessary but none the less insufficient condition for peace to be made. Palmerston, true to his colours, opposed any moderation with Russia. Viewing the war in a wider geostrategic context, as befitting the world's leading naval power of the period, the British government determined to mount an expedition to the Baltic in 1856 with overwhelming force – based on the new naval technology of ironclad bombarding vessels – in order to dictate harsher terms to Russia. The principal objective would be the destruction of Kronstadt, so eliminating the base of the Russian Baltic Fleet. With both this port and Sevastopol denied, the Russian Navy would retain only Archangel, reversing the gains made over 150 years.

Against this background, it is surprising that any peace was agreed so quickly. The principal impetus came from Vienna. Acting also on behalf of Britain and France, the Austrian government drew up an ultimatum to be sent to Russia. Termed the 'Memorandum on the Preliminaries of Peace' and adopted in Vienna on 14 November 1855, it contained five key provisions. In brief summary, there was to be a 'complete abolition of the Russian protectorate over the Principalities'; secondly, 'the freedom of the Danube would be assured'; thirdly, 'the Black Sea would be neutralised and forbidden to warships'; fourthly, 'the rights of the Christian subjects of the Porte should be consecrated'; and fifthly, 'the belligerent powers' reserved 'the right to bring forward, in the interest of Europe, special conditions over and above the four [aforementioned] guarantees'.[51] Both Britain (which had not been involved in the drafting of the ultimatum) and Russia found these terms initially hard to accept, but for quite opposite reasons. While the former found them insufficiently robust, the latter felt them too harsh to stomach: the main sticking point was the future of the Black Sea Fleet. Although the situation appeared to have changed fundamentally with the fall of Sevastopol, in so far as the objective of the Crimean campaign had been met, Allied cohesion was strained with regard to future policy.

In terms of land forces, the coalition was not evenly balanced as France had fielded nearly four times as many troops as Britain. Not unnaturally, Napoleon III felt he should have a major stake in determining how best to conclude the war and make the peace. There appeared to be three options open: first, to widen the war to increase the pressure on Russia, perhaps by encouraging the Poles to rise up, or by involving Austria, Prussia and Sweden militarily (along the lines of Palmerston's wishes); secondly, to reduce the war to a naval blockade in the Baltic and Black Seas; thirdly, to end it as quickly as possible through diplomacy. Believing that he had largely achieved his war aims, including breaking the conservative, Russian-dominated Holy Alliance, the French Emperor backed the last approach, and strongly supported the Austrian mediation. As Britain could not continue prosecuting the war without the French, reluctantly it had to follow its ally.

The outstanding question was whether an isolated Russia would agree to the Austrian ultimatum; Alexander II called an imperial council to debate the matter.

Held on the evening of 3 (15) January 1856 in the Winter Palace at St Petersburg, the meeting proved controversial. The longstanding Minister of Foreign Affairs, Count Nesselrode, urged acceptance of the Austrian terms, arguing, as Curtiss has neatly summarised, 'for they were not extremely severe, and there was no prospect of better ones, for the longer the war lasted, the worse the peace terms would be, with Russia's resources draining and no hope for the future'.[52] The Soviet historian Yevgeniy Viktorovich Tarle summarised Nesselrode's position as 'the longer the war goes on, the more enemies will unite against Russia'. Mikhail Vorontsov (now a prince) considered that although the conditions of the peace constituted a burden to Russia, there was no chance of securing a more favourable settlement if Russia were to continue the war. Not only would further casualties and expenses result, but also Finland and Poland might be lost and the state would experience complete financial exhaustion. These stark assessments represented the reality of the situation, which the other members of the state council, whether responsible for military, diplomatic or economic affairs, could only confirm. The former Ambassador Extraordinary and Plenipotentiary of Russia in Vienna, Baron Peter Kazimirovich Meyendorf, for example, held that 'the war inevitably brings us to bankruptcy'; and if Russia were to continue the war, she would become 'as weak as Austria after the Napoleonic Wars and Sweden after the wars of Charles XII'.[53] When a vote was taken, 'all were in favour of accepting' the Austrian ultimatum. With the endorsement of the Emperor, the next day Nesselrode telegraphed Prince A. M. Gorchakov in Vienna, instructing him to accept the ultimatum unconditionally. On 1 February 1856, a protocol accepting the terms was signed, and an agreement made to hold peace talks in Paris in March in order to compose a treaty to conclude the war. The location signified Napoleon III's restoration of France's international prestige. In the meantime, an armistice would be put in place.

The work of the Paris peace conference was not only undertaken expeditiously, but also conducted in cordial terms, a tone set by the warm hospitality of the French hosts – and not least that afforded to the Russian delegation. As Napoleon III took a major hand in the negotiations, it was clear that France and Russia would largely settle the future of continental Europe. Prussia was not yet strong enough, and Austria, for all her diplomatic prowess, was no longer a military power of the first rank. Britain, for all her naval might, could not influence affairs on land without strong military allies. Her army had not distinguished itself in Crimea; her diplomatic lead, represented by Lord Clarendon in Paris, was not supported as Castlereagh had been in Vienna in 1814–15 by an internationally prominent figure such as Wellington.

On 30 March 1856, a general treaty of peace was signed in Paris between Great Britain, Austria, France, Prussia, Russia, Sardinia and Turkey. Its first article proclaimed 'Peace and Friendship'; the second required the reciprocal evacuation of territories 'conquered or occupied'. While Article III dealt with the Russian restoration of Kars to the Turks, Article IV required the restoration to Russia of 'the Towns and Ports of Sebastopol, Balaklava, Kamiesch, Eupatoria, Kertch, Jenikale, as well as all other Territories occupied by Allied Troops'. Addressing the causes as opposed to the results of the war, Article VII admitted the Sublime Porte to the 'System (Concert) of Europe' and required the other signatories to 'respect the Independence and the Territorial Integrity of the Ottoman Empire'. Addressing both French and Russian antebellum concerns, Article IX recorded the Sultan's 'generous intentions towards the Christian population of his Empire'. Additionally, the same article stated that other powers had neither the right 'to interfere, either collectively or separately, in the relations of [the Sultan] with his subjects, nor [to meddle] in the Internal Administration of this Empire'.[54]

Five of the Treaty's articles affected Sevastopol through the regulation of naval and commercial traffic in the Black Sea and the Turkish Straits. Article X dealt with the latter, revising the convention of 1841 by means of a new act, which formed an annex to the Treaty with the 'same force and validity as if it formed an integral part thereof'. Reaffirming the historic norm, the Dardanelles and the Bosporus would be closed to foreign warships when the Porte was at peace. While this provision prevented Russia from sending her ships through the Straits to the Mediterranean, it also prohibited other powers' ships from entering the Black Sea. In many ways, the following four articles (XI–XIV) flowed from this new Straits convention.

Article XI 'neutralised' the Black Sea. Specifically, its 'Waters and its Ports, thrown open to the Mercantile Marine of every nation', were 'formally and in perpetuity interdicted to the Flag of War, either of the Powers possessing its Coasts, or of any other Power'. The associated Article XII declared that 'Commerce in the Ports and Waters of the Black Sea' should be 'free from any impediment' and subject 'only to the Regulations of Health, Customs, and Police'. Article XIII had the most direct bearing on Sevastopol in that, following the neutralisation of the Black Sea under Article X, Russia and the Ottoman Empire engaged 'not to establish or to maintain upon that Coast' any 'Military-Maritime Arsenal'. Hence neither a fleet nor the necessary naval infrastructure and depot for one could any longer be maintained at Sevastopol or at any other Russian Black Sea port, negating at a stroke the grand designs of the Russian emperors from Catherine the Great to Nicholas I. There was a minor consolation contained in Article XIV that allowed Russia and Turkey to agree to a number of 'Light Vessels, necessary for the service of their Coasts, which they reserve to themselves to maintain in the Black Sea'.[55] A convention of the same date of the Treaty provided that each of these two powers could retain ten light steamships for policing purposes.

Many of the Treaty's provisions concerned the Danubian Principalities. While Articles XV–XIX dealt with the regulation of the river Danube, including the establishment of a commission to promote its navigation and commerce, Article XX concerned the 'rectification' of the Russian frontier in Bessarabia in exchange for the towns and ports specified in Article IV, including Sevastopol. In mid-May 1856, Charles Gordon left Crimea to join the international boundary commission charged with tracing the new frontier line – designed, in his words, 'to eloign [to remove to a distance] the Russians from the Danube and its tributary lakes and streams'.[56] Taken together, Articles X–XIV effectively proscribed Russia from rebuilding her fleet in the Black Sea and projecting maritime power to the Bosporus and beyond into the Mediterranean. Thus the Treaty severely curtailed Russia's longstanding grand strategic ambitions, matching Great Britain's and France's original war aims. The encouragement of commerce for all would hardly recompense Russia for the loss of her southern fleet and its home base at Sevastopol. Unsurprisingly, Russia would view the Treaty, and specifically the articles affecting the Black Sea, as an unfair victors' peace, and seek opportunities in the years to come to abrogate its provisions.

Russian, and later Soviet, historians of the Crimean War were bound to highlight the disappointment and division that came with the peace. Tarle, for example, documents the immediate reaction to Alexander II's decision to agree to the Austrian ultimatum. 'Very soon the upper circles of the public were informed about the historical meeting in the Winter Palace', he noted. Specifically, 'Slavophiles were irritated to their limits, blaming Nesselrode and all the Court aristocracy for their cowardice and betrayal'. Vorontsov, with his strong British connections (his sister was the Countess of Pembroke) became a particular target of their scorn, based on the supposition that any continuation of the war 'would affect his pocket both in Russia and England, which was his "soulmate" in money, spirit and blood'. Furthermore, 'other voices were heard in Court'. Tarle cited 'an influential lady-in-waiting, A. F. Tutcheva, who wrote in her diary "yesterday rumours were circulating in the city that we had agreed to make peace [meeting the] Austrian conditions so humiliating to Russia. [As a result,] men were crying from shame".'[57] After the Treaty was signed, reaction in Russia was muted and sombre. The great military historian and army reformer, Major General D. A. Milyutin, summed up the mood. Writing of the proclamation in St Petersburg, being 'announced to the city by gun shots from the St. Peter and St. Paul fortress and accompanied by a Te Deum, it could not represent good news'. Reflecting on the results achieved in Paris, he considered that while 'the miseries of war had came to an end, the peace was bought at an expensive price. Russian national feelings were insulted. The young Emperor had to pay for failures of the war, which he did not start.'[58]

So the Crimean War had ended. An absurd dispute about access to a number of religious sites in the Holy Land, which turned into a mighty struggle for power and position in Europe, had cost all the nations involved dearly, but none more so than Russia. The wider international consequences of the war were equally profound. By removing Russia, the principal opponent of change between 1815 and 1850, as a dominant force in the European arena, the conflict made possible the later unification of Italy and Germany, and the consequent relegation of Austria to the position of a second-rate power.

AMERICANS IN SEVASTOPOL: THE RAISING OF THE SUNKEN SHIPS

Following the signing of the Treaty of Paris, and the evacuation of Allied forces from Crimea in the early summer of 1856, the Russian government was faced with a quandary: what to do about Sevastopol, when its *raison d'être*, the Black Sea Fleet, no longer existed? With the neutralisation of the Black Sea and the prohibition of 'military-maritime arsenals' under Articles XI and XIII respectively, it made no sense – in the short term at least – to attempt to rebuild a fleet, let alone reconstruct the port infrastructure for one. Yet the Russian Navy had other fleets (such as the Baltic) and it urgently needed ships; a great deal of national maritime investment lay submerged, lying on the mud of the Sevastopol roadstead. The total number of vessels involved was about 100, in other words nearly double the estimate given by Admiral Lyons in September 1855. According to the listing made by the United States naval historian Chuck Veit, the sunken ships included forty-two naval vessels: sixteen sailing ships of the line; six frigates; five corvettes; at least six other armed vessels (schooners, cutters and brigs); and nine steamers. The balance was made up with a wide range of transports, merchant vessels and sundry other craft.[59]

The sunken ships were distributed in six main areas, reflecting the series of Russian scuttling operations during the defence of Sevastopol. At the roadstead's mouth between Forts Alexander and Constantine remained the original line of ten ships sunk in September 1854, when the Russians feared an immediate Allied attack following the battle of the Alma. Next came a double line of vessels scuttled in February 1855 between Fort Nicholas and the Michael Battery. Behind these obstacles were further warships and merchant vessels sunk in September 1855 between Fort Paul and the Fourth Battery (Fort Catherine). These included the precious steamers sacrificed on the 11th following the fall of the southern side, such as the *Vladimir*. At various times, but principally in September 1855, other vessels were scuttled in the Southern Bay, including transports and prison hulks. Approximately half way up the roadstead, between Fort Paul and Careening Bay, lay a group of three merchant ships; and, finally, at the far, eastern end of the roadstead, near Inkerman and the mouth of the river Chernaya, were ten further such vessels.

Within the Russian government, thoughts turned to an ambitious salvage operation in Sevastopol's waters with the aim of achieving two objectives: first, to recover as much of the fleet as possible, including its armaments and machinery; and secondly, to open the harbour for commercial traffic. In time, it was hoped, a new Russian Black Sea Fleet would return to its home port. Nothing like this had been attempted before; its planning and execution (let alone the technical means) was well beyond the capability of the Russian Navy to conduct, assuming, of course, the victorious Allies would permit such a task. The Treaty of Paris, however, had made no such provision. In the absence of any specific prohibition, the Russians felt it well within their rights to recover their own property, whether on land or on the seabed. Calling on their former enemies – either French or British experts – to assist in this project was politically out of the question. Furthermore, despite their best efforts, British demolition and diving teams had made little impression on either removing or raising the sunken ships prior to the Allied evacuation of Sevastopol. For that matter, it had suited the Allies' strategic purpose to leave the roadstead in a blocked condition. That left only one power in the running – the United States of America, which had, in many respects, proved a passive ally during the Crimean War, and shared an historic hostility to Britain. In any case, there was a considerable mutual desire to improve economic relations between Russia and the United States. As a report in the New York *Herald* of March 1857 declared: '[The Russian] government and people prefer to trade with this country in preference to England, for their hatred of the English is as intense as ever.'[60]

Although the United States officially remained neutral throughout the Crimean War, the Americans had supplied Russia with weapons of war and even a ship, the SS *America*. Additionally, about thirty American surgeons and physicians served in various positions on the medical staff of the Russian Army.[61] Of these, however, only a handful or so worked at any one time in the main hospitals of Crimea. One such individual was William Riddick Whitehead of Virginia, who served under Pirogov in Sevastopol from February 1855. As the individuals concerned were civilian volunteers rather than uniformed members of the United States Army or Navy, their presence did not constitute any breaking of neutrality. Those involved were acting in purely private, humanitarian, capacities, albeit being paid handsomely for their professional services – about double what they would have received at home. Yet such high adventure and surgical experience came at a very high price: almost half of the Americans succumbed to epidemic diseases such as typhus fever, cholera and smallpox. By way of example, of the two American colleagues who were meant to meet Whitehead in Sevastopol, one was already dead and the other dying.[62] Many of the survivors, however, were soon to put their practical experience to intensive use during the American Civil War (1861–65).

In the spring of 1855, the United States government established a military commission to report on the 'Art of War in Europe'. Under the direction of the engineer Major Richard Delafield, the team included another engineer, Major Alfred Mordecai, a specialist in ordnance, and a rising star of the cavalry, Captain George B. McClellan. As McClellan's biographer has narrated, their trip had begun well in London, where the commissioners were promised 'full cooperation in any inspection of the British forces besieging Sevastopol', but in Paris, permission to visit French forces on Crimea was made conditional on not visiting the Russians subsequently. Delafield felt unable to accept this limitation. Another disappointing bureaucratic hurdle confronted them in St Petersburg, which the team reached in mid-June. Although they were 'granted an audience by Alexander II readily enough, ... their application to visit Sevastopol disappeared into the Russian labyrinth'.[63] Otherwise, the Russian authorities appeared keen to show their guests a number of installations, including the naval base of Kronstadt and several other military establishments.

A short conversation with the Emperor following a review of troops on 26 June concluded 'with a declaration on his part of the hope that the United States and Russia would continue always in peace and in friendship.'[64] Their raised spirits, however, were quickly dashed: much to their annoyance, the Americans received no reply about inspecting either Sevastopol, or the Russian Baltic forts of Sveaborg (now Finnish Suomenlinna) and Reval (Tallinn, Estonia). Finally, on 13 July they were informed by Baron Lieven, the Russian Adjutant General, that 'although his country had no secrets or information on military science to withhold ... the commanding officers of these places had requested that strangers or other persons not concerned in the operations should not be permitted to visit them, as such visits occasioned them a great deal of embarrassment ...' Further, although the Emperor 'might, of course, overrule such objections', in the meantime, the Americans' 'request could *not be granted*'.[65] Such was the ingenious, if not disingenuous, wording of the Russian rebuff. While Delafield offered no opinion about this disappointing outturn, the unwillingness of the Russians to show Sveaborg was perhaps due to the fact that an Allied fleet had shelled it in August 1854. Their apprehension about Sevastopol might simply have reflected fears about a possibly imminent fall of the fortress.

After visiting Kronstadt twice, offered as a compensation for not being permitted to view the Russian defence of Sevastopol, and Moscow, Delafield and his colleagues travelled on to Prussia, Austria and Turkey. By courtesy of a Royal

Navy steamer from Constantinople to Balaklava in early October, the Americans eventually reached Crimea, where they remained for nearly a month. With the personal interest and support of General Simpson, 'every official and personal facility and kindness was extended ... by the officers of the English army'.[66] In contrast, Delafield's team did not feel able to visit French facilities as the same conditionality on any visit still applied. On the southern side of Sevastopol the American officers were able to observe the strength of the Russian field defences and note the comprehensive nature of the British system of logistics, the latter much improved over the last twelve months. For all its impressive detail, however, Delafield's subsequent comprehensive report – which reflected a close study of the Austrian, British, French, Prussian and Russian armies – missed two important matters. The first was the necessary modernisation of an army's high command, which now required a general staff to plan and execute operations; the second was the impact of the new rifled musket on the battlefield, which would render traditional, Napoleonic-style, infantry tactics obsolete.[67] The officers and soldiers of McClellan, ironically termed the 'Young Napoleon', who later commanded the Union Army of the Potomac in 1861–62, would have to learn these painful lessons during the American Civil War. Antietam (17 September 1862), for example, proved the bloodiest single-day of battle in American history.[68]

Prior to, during, and following the Crimean War, many influential Russians (including the Tsar, as already noted) had pro-American feelings, or saw the United States as a counter-weight to France, and especially to Britain. Tolstoy touches on such sentiments in his Sketch *In August 1855*: 'One of [the soldiers] explained that the siege of Sevastopol would not last much longer, because a reliable fellow in the fleet had told him that Constantine, the Tsar's brother, was coming with the 'Merican fleet to help us'.[69] While there was no foundation in this typical sailor's rumour, the possibility of a Russian request for American support was not as far-fetched at the time as it might appear today. The United States Minister to Russia, Thomas Seymour, had reported home shortly after his appointment in March 1854 that the 'Russian government had an "ardent desire for the friendship of the U. S. and ... still closer bonds of political and commercial intercourse"'.[70] Seymour, who had facilitated Delafield's visit to Russia, enjoyed good relations with Admiral Grand Duke Konstantin Nikolayevich, the brother of Emperor Alexander II. In September 1855, Seymour informed the United States government that the Grand Duke wished to 'draw to some extent on American genius and enterprise' in his plans to modernise the Russian fleet.[71] Clearing Sevastopol's grand harbour would prove a major test of Russo-American co-operation.

As Veit's investigations have revealed, it would appear that at some time in late 1855 or early 1856, a Russian official or member of the military recalled that an American named John Gowen had been involved four years previously in the recovery of a United States warship that had sunk in Gibraltar harbour eight years before, and had at the same time rendered a damaged Russian warship some welcome assistance. Via the Russian ambassador in Washington, Gowen received 'at some point in the first half of 1856' a request from Grand Duke Konstantin to assist in the raising of the Black Sea Fleet at Sevastopol. Bitten by the idea, and not least by its commercial opportunities, Gowen travelled to Russia over the period August–December 1856, completing a detailed reconnaissance of the Sevastopol roadstead. News of the intended salvage operation soon spread. Charles Gordon, for example, writing from Moldovan Chișinău (Kishinev) on 6 December, related that William Russell, the *Times* correspondent, had called in at the Bessarabian boundary commission on his way back to London from Sevastopol. His visitor revealed that 'Nothing [in Sevastopol] has yet been done, and it will remain untouched for two years. The American engineers in the Russia service hoped to be able to get the sunken vessels (seventy-seven in number) up again.'[72]

Returning home to Lynn, Massachusetts, Gowen spent the first half of 1857 preparing for the salvage operation; and establishing for this purpose on 20 April a new concern, registered in Philadelphia, the 'Marine Exploring Company'. The necessary capital had to be raised; men, machinery and other necessary materiel had to be assembled. All this essential preliminary activity was accomplished in a relatively short time.[73] By June, Gowen was back in Sevastopol, 'setting up shop'. One of his first visitors was an extraordinary British character, a biblical and oriental lecturer, John Gadsby, who travelled to Crimea with his eighteen-year-old nephew on a grand tour of education and edification.

Gadsby's record of his visit to Sevastopol and its environs in July 1857 is useful in recording the city's military history for a number of reasons, not least in commenting on the early stages of Gowen's enterprise.[74] In a similar manner to William Jesse's initial experiences of Sevastopol nearly thirty years earlier, Gadsby's first impressions of the city were not positive, and were equally affected by the lack of suitable hotel accommodation. Recalling his arrival at Sevastopol during the afternoon of 17 July 1857, Gadsby wrote: 'what a scene did the city present! As soon as I had arrived at the top of the steps leading from the harbour, I felt my heart sink'. More specifically:

> I could have imagined I was amongst the death-like ruins of Pompeii. There was
> not a whole house to be seen, except the Americans', and that only on the ground
> floor; ... Nothing but skeleton walls, standing like so many tall, shattered, and
> perforated grave-stones! On our right, as we passed up the main street, were a
> number of one-storey wooden cottages, new; and nothing but these, and the
> ruined houses on our left were to be seen until we arrived at our hotel.

Sevastopol, in his opinion, 'must, before the war, have been one of the finest cities in the world'.[75] The Briton's feelings chimed with those of the American Delafield, who had reported from his tour of inspection two years earlier: 'Not a habitable building was seen over the entire surface of what was once a very handsomely built city.... [Only] blood-stained ruins were left to the victors as the fruits of this siege'.[76] Such was the devastation of the Sevastopol, it would have resembled a city of the mid-twentieth century obliterated by a combination of aerial bombing and artillery bombardment, much like Stalingrad in 1942–43.

Sadly, Gadsby's hotel was not world class: in fact, quite the opposite. 'We had been recommended to the Hotel Schneider', he complained, but 'we found that the Americans had taken entire possession of it for some time'. Denied accommodation within what remained of a former centre of Sevastopol's social life, where Russian officers used to entertain and make merry, the British duo were forced to lodge in Sevastopol's only other functioning guesthouse – the squalid 'Sebastopol', which Gadsby described as a 'most miserable place, more like an Asiatic caravanserai than a European hotel'. The visitors' sangfroid was sorely tested by the 'dirt in abundance', a bed 'almost hard as a plank', and 'both fleas and flies being as troublesome as in Egypt'.[77] The notorious bed-bugs of Sevastopol had also attracted the attention of the Americans (or perhaps more the other way about), who had protested about the 'curse of this country—fleas, fleas, O Lord! the fleas! ... You can form no idea of the wretched nights we spend fighting them.'[78]

Gadsby's subsequent tour of the city included the dockyard, where he found the 'dry docks all in ruins'. Having seen the British equivalent in Malta, he noted 'it sinks into nothing compared with what these Sebastopol docks must have been'. Although the Russians 'had made no attempt to restore the docks, ... the bakery, wharves, and warehouses' had been rebuilt. Furthermore, Gadsby observed 'large quantities of the *matériel* of war lying about, having been collected by the Russians'.[79] This account suggests that the Allies had not completed clearing the city before their evacuation in the early summer of 1856. It would also appear that Sevastopol – contrary to the provisions of the Treaty of Paris – had not been completely demilitarised by the Russians.

In his description of his visit to the northern side on 24 July 1857, Gadsby relates that Fort Constantine was still manned. Although refused permission to enter the installation, he and his British companions, including a rather mysterious Russian-speaking individual called 'Mr. C.', took shelter at its outer gate during a heavy rainstorm. Chancing their luck, they rushed past the bemused sentries through the inner gate to the fort's central courtyard, the *place d'armes*, where they were apprehended and unceremoniously escorted to the exit.[80] The following (and rather inevitable) exchange then resulted when 'Mr. C.' demanded to speak with the commanding officer. 'He was sent for, and came. "What do you want?" he asked. "We wish to see the fort," replied Mr. C. "Are you foreigners?" "Yes." "Americans?" "No." "What then are you?" "English." "Then I cannot admit you without the permission of the general." We therefore bowed, and compulsorily, but not less politely retired.' Nationals of the former enemy were clearly far from welcome. None the less Gadsby's little group had observed what Sevastopol's military administration and the fort's guard force had tried to deny them seeing: 'the Russians still had the fort armed, and that they had no intention of disarming it'. The fact that military objects on the northern side of Sevastopol had not been decommissioned was soon confirmed elsewhere. On continuing their informal tour of inspection, Gadsby noted the Star and Wasp Batteries 'with their guns still mounted'. When the Britons reached the Michael Battery, which had been converted into a hospital, cheekily they asked permission to enter. 'But the officer in command was so long in making his experience, and the stench was so intolerable,' Gadsby related contemptuously, '[that] we left before he arrived'.[81]

In his memoir, the British traveller also mentioned an amusing but telling incident concerning Gowen's team in Sevastopol – presumably narrated by one of the Americans he had met. When celebrating Independence Day on the 4th of July, apparently a number of Russian officers had joined in, 'who enjoyed themselves greatly, heartily joining in [the Americans'] cheers'. There was, nevertheless, a surprise in store: on being 'told the next day that they had been shouting "The Republic for ever!", [the Russians] were perfectly horrified, and expressed a hope that it would not reach the emperor's ears'.[82] More detailed American accounts of this event describe it as a grand, 'handsomely decorated' occasion, decked out with American and Russian flags and portraits of George Washington and Alexander II. Thirty uniformed Russian officers attended, including an admiral; two Russian bands provided music over a lavish dinner.[83] The senior Russian involved was probably Rear Admiral Butakov, hero of the fight of the *Vladimir* against the Turkish steamship *Pervaz-i Bahri* in 1853 and of the defence of Sevastopol, who had been appointed naval governor of Nikolayev and Sevastopol in 1856. The Americans had serious work to do rather than party: the challenges they faced, however, were considerable. Not only did Gowen and his men have to build their own houses to live in, they also had to construct suitable craft to operate in Sevastopol's waters. Their main salvage task, though, remained at the roadstead, where ships lay 'in every direction; some with their masts only sticking up, and some with the hull partly exposed'.[84]

By the time Gowen's workforce arrived in Sevastopol, the Russians had already managed to salvage a number of sunken ships from the harbour, including four transports and the steamer *Khersones*.[85] Such vessels, most probably, were the most accessible and structurally sound. After repairs, these ships were then used in the salvage operation. Raising the large number of remaining vessels, or clearing them by demolition, now lay ahead: it would prove a most time-consuming and demanding task. With his long experience of salvage work, Gowen had already determined the required methods during his reconnaissance. On return to the United States, he had ordered the construction of four large caissons in a Philadelphia shipyard to provide suitable platforms for raising the ships. Each of these semi-submersible structures (sized approximately 15 x 15 x 4 metres) was equipped with a 40-horsepower steam engine for pumping out the water and driving a lifting chain attached to a sunken vessel. As Veit has described, the chain mechanism had 'an estimated lifting power of 500 tons, and the caissons themselves were believed capable of raising 700 tons dead weight through the displacement of water'. Having raised the ships to the surface in this manner, Gowen's plan was for his team then to 'plug the holes drilled in the hulls by the Russians, insert hoses into the holds, and the pumps would empty the vessel of water'.[86] Another technique was also available: using divers to patch the holes underwater, and then to pump out the water within the hull, allowing a ship's own natural buoyancy to provide the necessary upwards lifting force. Whatever the methods employed, the Americans were operating at the extreme limits of diving and salvage technology at the time: thus there was a great deal of trial and error involved until they developed a reliable system.

Gowen's team would meet, and eventually overcome, many administrative and technical challenges during the course of their operations in Sevastopol's roadstead and Southern Bay. Russian red tape, for example, delayed the arrival of essential stores and machinery in the summer of 1857. Once the salvage operations started in earnest, lifting chains would either break, or be too strong for the rotten ships' structure to bear; throughout, divers would have to work in almost zero visibility. The greatest difficulty appeared to be caused by the attacks on the wooden ships through the dreaded worm *Teredo navalis*, which had reduced the life of successive generations of ships of the Black Sea Fleet since they had first anchored in Sevastopol harbour in 1783. On account of this and other problems, Gadsby was highly pessimistic regarding the Americans' chances of success: 'As to the ships,' he observed, 'they must now be so embedded in mud and barnacles, that no human power can move them, except by blowing them up'. Quoting a contemporary London *Times* newspaper report, which had described the teredo as having 'eaten the body of the Russian fleet, leaving only the outer shell', Gadsby, on completing his book on 31 March 1858, remained convinced that the 'Americans would not be able to raise the sunken ships'.[87] Yet he, and other like-minded gainsayers, had grossly underestimated the stubborn perseverance and technical ingenuity of Gowen, who had invested so much time, effort and resources into the salvage project.

Veit's detailed research shows that Gowen's team made steady, albeit slow, progress. By the end of their first season at Sevastopol, however, the Americans had only scored very modest results. Although they blasted a few ships, requiring enormous amounts of gunpowder in the process, not one vessel had been raised. The attempt to lift the 84-gun ship of the line *Chesma*, for example, had failed miserably. As Veit has explained, 'Her timbers were so riven with shipworm chambers that, no matter how fast [the] pump was run, water percolated through the sides of the ship just as quickly; what appeared to be solid bulwarks were, in fact, mere shells.'[88] Notwithstanding these difficulties, the Russian authorities were not impressed by the poor rate of work. Undaunted, over successive years Gowen and his team built larger and more reliable caissons, modified their techniques to lift the ships, and blew apart the vessels that could not be raised economically once they had been stripped of any valuable items.

The incremental gains made during 1858 proved gradual. By September of that year, only six vessels had been raised (excluding any major warship), and one ship had been completely removed through blasting. Demolition operations, meanwhile, were under way on a further ten vessels, including the former flagship of the Black Sea Fleet, the 120-gun *Parizh*.[89] A breakthrough came in late 1859 or in early 1860 following Gowen's introduction of two larger, and fundamentally redesigned, caissons; and the modification of the associated lifting techniques, incorporating stronger chains.[90] The raising of the 6-gun paddle steamer *Krym* on 20 December 1859 before winter closed down operations on the roadstead proved significant because the Russians had placed a premium on the raising of the scuttled steamers. Having failed to lift three ships of the same class by the contracted date of 1 November 1859, Gowen was forced to pay monthly penalties to the Russian government.[91] Gowen's new methods, however, were beginning to demonstrate their potential; he must have hoped that the pace of salvage operations would steadily increase in the New Year – the fluidity and hence the future of his company depended on it.

Perhaps it was money pressures that forced Gowen back to operations at the height of winter: he raised ships from the bottom of Sevastopol's harbour in February and March 1860, including the steamers *Bessarabia* and *Gromonsets*. These were valuable ships of the Krym class, whose salvage reduced the level of Russian fines.[92] Of the sail warships that formed the vast majority of the three lines blocking the entrance and first section of the roadstead, none was raised intact. All were removed through demolition. One big prize remained to be raised: the famous 11-gun steamship *Vladimir*, which lay – at ten fathoms – in the deepest waters of the roadstead. As we have seen, this fast little warship had carried Nicholas I on his final inspection of the Black Sea Fleet before the Crimean War; under Butakov's command, it had forced the surrender of the

Turkish paddle frigate *Pervaz-i Bahri* in the first engagement between steamships; together with the *Khersones*, its long-range naval gunfire support had covered the withdrawal of Russian troops after the battle of Inkerman on 5 November 1854. Prior to the closure of the roadstead, it had also proved an effective blockade runner, harrying Turkish merchant ships along the Anatolian coast. Significantly, the precious *Vladimir* was the last vessel that the Russians scuttled, and the final ship Gowen managed to raise. He achieved this feat on 17 August 1860.[93] Thereafter, the remaining ships were all cleared through demolition.

By the end of 1860, it is estimated that seventeen warships and thirteen merchant ships remained to be dealt with.[94] The salvage operation continued well into 1862, by which time the American Civil War was in progress. Russia proved to be a staunch supporter of the Union cause, repaying the assistance given by the United States during the Crimean War. Both Russia and the Northern States feared Britain would take advantage of American division: in the event, the United Kingdom remained neutral despite widespread sympathies for the Confederate South. Equally, the North and Russia shared a belief in abolitionism: respectively, the end of black slavery and the freeing of the serfs. In June 1861, when Alexander II greeted the Union Minister, Cassius Clay of Kentucky, in St Petersburg, the Russian Tsar declared that the two nations were 'bound together by a common sympathy in the common cause of emancipation'.[95] Hence despite the petty bureaucratic difficulties John Gowen experienced in Sevastopol, Russo-American political relations in the middle of the nineteenth century were positively warm in stark contrast to most of the twentieth, and the first decades of the twenty-first.

Meanwhile, both the blasting and the raising of ships at Sevastopol proved a very time-consuming process due to the difficulties in either placing charges under water or placing lifting chains under the hulls; mud on the harbour bottom and the effects of the shipworm delayed and complicated both tasks. Once Gowen had finished his work in the summer of 1862, Sevastopol was honoured by a visit of Alexander II and the Grand Duke Konstantin, who viewed the cleared roadstead and its lesser bays. Although the Emperor thanked Gowen for his services, the Russian government never paid him, and all his property in Russia was confiscated. It represented a gross injustice; despite many years of attempting to obtain any redress from the Russians, he was unsuccessful.[96] In what proved to be the 'largest maritime salvage operation in history' in terms of the number of ships removed, Veit has summed up Gowen's admirable achievements:

> The fact that John Gowen was cheated of the financial reward of his labours did
> nothing to tarnish his reputation as an engineer. In the space of five years, he had

cleared the harbour of Sevastopol of seventy-four ships. Of these, thirteen (all merchantmen) had been broken up and left on the bottom for the *teredos*; thirty-nine had been blasted into manageable pieces and brought up; and twenty-two had been raised whole.[97]

REBUILDING AND REGENERATING THE CITY

Rebuilding and regenerating Sevastopol was an enormous task, which would take several decades. Progress, initially at least, was slow. Charles Gordon made a brief return to the city while *en route* to a new military survey mission in Armenia to mark the frontier between Russia and Turkey. In a letter home dated 3 June 1858, he observed:

> The place is still an utter ruin, scarcely anything has been done to restore it.... About 8000 or 9000 people are in the town. They are miserably poor, and most of them live in the cellars of the houses. Some wooden huts have been erected in the streets; but generally speaking, the place is deserted and looks very gloomy.[98]

Interestingly, Gordon failed to mention Gowen's salvage operation, although he knew of its existence. Later visitors, including many famous, also remarked on Sevastopol's desolate and dilapidated condition. The Russian playwright, Alexander Ostrovskiy, came in the summer of 1860. Writing to his actor friends P. M. Sadovskiy and S. S. Kosheverov on 19 June, he mused: 'One cannot view this town without tears; definitely not a stone was left here untouched. When you approach Sevastopol from the sea, you anticipate viewing a big stone-built city in perfect surroundings, but as you come closer, [all] you can see is a lifeless corpse'.[99] Over the years, a steady stream of foreign visitors followed, including Mark Twain in 1867. In his highly popular travelogue of his extensive journey to Europe and the Holy Land, *The Innocents Abroad*, he recalled observing:

> ... [only] fragments of houses, crumbled walls, torn and ragged hills, devastation every where! ... For eighteen long months the storms of war beat upon the helpless town, and left it at last the saddest wreck that ever the sun has looked upon. Not one solitary house escaped unscathed – not one remained habitable, even. Such utter and complete ruin one could hardly conceive of.[100]

Within ten years of Twain's visit, Sevastopol was well on the road to recovery, albeit it remained demilitarised for the present. Apart from Gowen's salvage work, there were three main drivers of economic and social development: the activities of a Russian shipping company, the arrival of the railway and the reopening of the port to international trade. Local manufacturing industries returned, such as brick and tile factories, together with soap and wax works, and breweries. When the naval shipbuilding and the Black Sea Fleet eventually returned to Sevastopol, its expansion accelerated accordingly. These events, however, lay towards the end of the century. In the meantime, it appeared that neither the Russian government nor the Naval Department appeared to be interested in rebuilding the city and its port infrastructure, as there was insufficient will yet to challenge the Treaty of Paris directly. The renaissance of Sevastopol, however, was greatly boosted by an indirect, camouflaged, approach – a typical example of the celebrated Russian *maskirovka*.

In the immediate aftermath of the Crimean War, the Russian government sought not only to promote commerce in the Black Sea, but also to find a way as quickly as possible to circumvent the limits imposed under the Treaty of Paris on its southern fleet: only six corvettes of 800 tonnes and four lighter vessels of 200 tonnes were allowed. In an attempt to meet both objectives in one initiative, the clever idea arose to establish a state-sponsored fleet of civilian steamers, which in time of war could be converted into armed merchantmen and transport ships. In order to avoid Allied objections, the potential naval use of the new vessels was not advertised. On 3 (15) August 1856, Alexander II approved the charter of a joint stock shipping company, the Russian Steam Navigation and Trading Company (ROPiT)[101]; its main office and operating base was established in Odessa. The firm developed very rapidly. Government start-up capital and substantial annual subsidies allowed it to finance the acquisition of new steamships to complement those raised from Sevastopol's roadstead, including the *Khersones*, *Danube*, *Prut* and *Reni*. By the end of 1857, the company had ordered five new ships from Britain and already had seventeen steamers in service. These included the 3,900-tonne *Crown Prince* and the 3,600-tonne *Kornilov*, which could double up as cruisers.[102]

ROPiT devoted a lot of attention and effort to Sevastopol. It took over the old Lazarev admiralty site, cleared the detritus of the recent war, and built a repair yard. Warehouses, workshops and foundries soon followed, as did a new ship lift. As a result, the civilian workforce expanded, and dockyard skills were in high demand. Consequently, in 1866 the company opened the first technical school in Sevastopol: forty boys were the first students, the children of ROPiT officers. Two years later commercial shipbuilding began. Altogether, ROPiT made a most crucial contribution to the revival of trade and to the rejuvenation of port infrastructure in Sevastopol; it also made the city more easily accessible to businessmen, imperial officials and travellers alike. ROPiT's vessels not only plied the waters of the Black Sea, maintaining important national links between Odessa, Nikolayev and Sevastopol for example, but also ran international routes to Constanza, Constantinople, Alexandria and Marseilles.

Major military and diplomatic developments in the early 1870s changed the status of the Black Sea and its littoral, including Sevastopol. Since the end of the Crimean War, under Alexander II's benign leadership, Russian had been undergoing a period of domestic reform, most notably the emancipation of the serfs in 1861. Renewed confidence and stability at home generated demands for greater assertiveness abroad. Prince A. M. Gorchakov, who had succeeded Count Karl Nesselrode as Foreign Minister in April 1856, had long wished to restore Russia's stature and influence. In August 1856, for example, he famously sent a circular to Russia's diplomatic missions abroad stating: 'Russia is accused of getting isolated and keeping silence in the face of facts that are neither in harmony with law, nor with justice. They say that Russia is sulking. Russia is not sulking, she is composing herself.'[103] In other words, under his guidance, Russia was determined over time to recover her position as a leading European if not world power.[104] To do so, she needed allies. Significantly, throughout his career, Gorchakov had made a point of cultivating Otto von Bismarck, who had been the Prussian ambassador in St Petersburg over the period 1858–62, prior to being appointed Minister President by Wilhelm I.

Largely on Gorchakov's personal initiative, Russia repudiated the neutralisation of the Black Sea on 31 October 1870, taking advantage of the plight of one of the main upholders of the Treaty of Paris, France, then embroiled in a major war against Prussia. Gorchakov's timing was immaculate: the date of his circular to the powers of Europe was dated just four days after the French Army's ignominious capitulation at Metz. Most importantly, he knew that he could count on the support of Bismarck in any confrontation over the issue. Equally, the rapprochement between Russia and Prussia helped ensure the neutrality of Austria. Italy was in no position to assist France, notwithstanding the fact that her emergence as a unified state had been greatly assisted by Napoleon III's intervention against Austrian forces in 1859. Thus the French Emperor was not only defeated on the battlefield (notably at Sedan as well as Metz), but also isolated internationally. His erstwhile ally Britain offered no more than a diplomatic protest on 10 November 1870 against Russia.[105]

The reasoning contained in the Russian denunciation was blunt: other provisions of the Treaty had already been broken; and the neutralisation was in any case 'unreasonable'. Although his first point had little validity, Gorchakov argued the second point skilfully, stressing the unfairness of the situation facing his nation:

> ... while Russia was disarming in the Black Sea, ... and likewise loyally deprived herself of the possibility of taking measures for an effectual Maritime Defence in the adjoining Seas and Ports, Turkey preserved her privilege of maintaining

unlimited Naval Forces in the Archipelago and the Straits; France and England preserved their power in the Mediterranean.[106]

Furthermore, in time of war, Turkey could allow foreign ships into the 'unguarded' Black Sea and the 'undefended' southern coast of Russia. In an age of steam, a swift sortie against Russia's coastal cities and ports could be mounted very quickly, increasing her vulnerability to attack.

The unilateral abrogation of one of the treaty's most important articles, the acceptance of which had caused Russia so much humiliation, was strongly opposed by Great Britain. Although unwilling to enforce the treaty by military means, she felt that the 'right of releasing a party to a treaty belonged only to the governments which had been parties to the original instrument', and invited these to a conference in London to discuss both the breach and the precedent it set. Consequently, the relevant powers signed a declaration on 17 January 1871, recognising 'that it is an essential principle of the Law of Nations that no Power can liberate itself from the engagements of a Treaty, nor modify the stipulations thereof, unless with the consent of the Contracting Powers by means of an amicable arrangement'. In turn, the Black Sea articles of the Treaty of Paris were amended in a new treaty signed on 13 March 1871, effectively rewarding Russia for her temerity. Specifically, Articles XI, XIII and XIV of the 1856 Treaty were annulled, as was the associated Straits convention. Most importantly, the new treaty made no mention of the neutralisation of the Black Sea.[107] Although Russian honour was restored quickly, rebuilding the requisite fleet and the necessary port infrastructure would take much more time and investment.

The Russo-Turkish War of 1877–78 need not detain us with any detail here. Notwithstanding the setbacks incurred in the very costly, but ultimately successful, siege of Plevna (20 July – 10 December 1877), of which Todleben masterminded the final stages, Russia liberated Bulgaria from the Ottoman Empire. Russia's victory might have been swifter, with considerable grand strategic consequences, had she possessed a modern, steam-powered Black Sea Fleet and an associated amphibious capability. None the less, an advantageous Treaty of San Stefano was signed with Turkey in March 1878. Europe's great powers, however, alarmed by Russia's gains, subsequently watered down this settlement at the Congress of Berlin held that summer, presided over by Bismarck. As a result, the boundaries of the Balkans were drawn less beneficially to Russian interests.[108]

Although the naval actions of the war of 1877–78 were minor in both scale and outcome, they were none the less noteworthy for the Russians' pioneering use of the torpedo. The introduction of this new weapon illustrated the technical renaissance of the Russian Navy that took place during the final quarter of the century. Sevastopol-based ships and establishments would later make significant contributions to a revival of Russia's maritime power in the Black Sea, powered by increasing government investment in the naval arm.

The Crimean campaign had shown the immense difficulties that Russia had faced without efficient strategic rail lines of communication. Moving men and materiel across vast distances proved a slow and tedious business. Prior to the war, there was only the 600-kilometre double track main line that connected St Petersburg with Moscow. Following the conflict, Sevastopol desperately needed a connection to Russia's rail network in order to drive commerce, let alone to provide an important military link in due course. Although a concession to build a railway line between Moscow and Sevastopol had been awarded in 1856, insufficient investors' funds were forthcoming. Russia's rail network developed slowly until a boom in the late 1860s and early 1870s, facilitated by government intervention, from which Sevastopol benefited greatly. Work began on the state-financed line between Moscow and Kursk in 1865. Following its completion in 1868, the line was extended successively to Kharkov, Lozovaya, Alexandrovsk,[109] Melitopol and Simferopol, finally reaching Sevastopol, where the first goods train arrived on 27 October 1875. Passenger trains soon followed. In contrast to the relatively easy going across the Ukrainian steppe, construction of the railway in the final approaches to Sevastopol had been complicated by the Mackenzie Heights and the northern flanks of the Sapun escarpment; the negotiation of these natural barriers required no fewer than two substantial bridges and six tunnels of various lengths.[110]

The coming of the railway in 1875 unlocked the city's economic and industrial potential and accelerated its reconstruction. Businessmen, state officials and the imperial royal family – the latter in transit to their summer palace at Yalta – could now travel in relative speed and comfort from St Petersburg to Sevastopol, completing a journey of 2,200 kilometres within three days. In the twenty-first century, until the breaking of rail links between Ukraine and Crimea following the Russian annexation in 2014, the same trip was undertaken in under thirty hours. The celebrated author Anton Chekhov delighted in his arrival by train at Sevastopol one bright summer morning in 1888, declaring: 'The city is beautiful both as it is, and also because it sits near a most beautiful sea'.[111] A decade later, the playwright would make frequent use of the railway connection to Crimea on his journeys to and from his Yalta home. One of his younger friends, Alexei Maximovich Peshkov, was another famous rail traveller. Arriving for medical treatment in Crimea in January 1897, he visited Sevastopol and the ancient ruins of Chersonesos. Under the penname Maxim Gorky, this prolific writer and devoted Marxist would later become a political activist and leading follower of the Bolsheviks.

1875 also saw the opening of Sevastopol as an international port. Commerce developed relatively rapidly despite the interruption imposed by the Russo-Turkish War of 1877–78. In 1888, for example, 384 foreign ships entered the harbour and 380 left. Yet the probable expansion of such traffic was cut short when the Russian government decided in 1890 to re-establish Sevastopol as the main base of the Black Sea Fleet and as a military fortress. Warships, naval crews and training establishments were moved from Nikolayev to Sevastopol, along with the Black Sea library. As an expanding and modernising navy, together with its associated shipbuilding effort, required all of the port's facilities, commercial shipping was transferred to Feodosiya in 1894.[112]

By the early 1890s, Sevastopol had become a centre of naval ship construction, albeit remaining second in importance to Nikolayev. In his history of the Russian Imperial Navy, Fred Jane noted that three gunboats were launched in 1887; these were followed by the 'second-class' battleships *Chesma* and *Sinop* in 1886 and 1887 respectively; and the 'first-class' battleship *Georgii Pobedonosets* (George the Victorious) in 1892. All four battleships were of the Ekaterina II class, the lead vessel of which was built at the Nikolayev admiralty dockyard. A further battleship, the larger (13,000 tonnes) and more heavily armoured *Tri Svyatitelya* (The Three Holy Hierarchs), launched at Nikolayev in 1893 but completed at Sevastopol in 1895, soon joined the fleet. ROPiT continued to run the shipbuilding and repair facilities in Sevastopol: while the gunboats were built 'on small slips intended for the construction of merchant vessels', the larger warships were constructed in two large docks, about 'four hundred feet long and twenty-seven feet deep'.[113] By the turn of the twentieth century the Black Sea Fleet contained a broad mix of ironclad ships of the line, armoured cruisers, destroyers and minelayers. The five battleships based in Sevastopol, each armed with either six or four (in the case of *Tri Svyatitelya*) 12-inch (305mm) guns, formed the main striking power of the fleet.

The Russian Navy was at the forefront of bringing new communications technology to Sevastopol. The city's (and Crimea's) first telephone exchange, operated by the Naval Department, opened in 1894. Five years later a more startling development occurred. Soviet and Russian historians claim that radio communications were established between *Georgii Pobedonosets* and *Tri Svyatitelya* on 25 August (6 September) 1899, representing a 'first' in both world and naval history. The Russian 'father of radio', the physicist Alexander Stepanovich Popov, had developed the novel transmitting and receiving equipment. Tests later in September recorded wireless communications between ships at ranges of over 'tens of kilometres'.[114] Meanwhile, the Italian radio pioneer Guglielmo Marconi had been conducting similar tests over land and water in Europe and North America.

The number of the city's inhabitants, including its naval and army personnel, more than quintupled between 1874 (11,000) and 1900 (58,000). Of this latter total, 8,700 were workers who laboured either in the dockyard or in the many factories and industrial plants that were springing up. Sevastopol's recovery had proved a long haul: it had taken over forty years to restore the population level last seen immediately prior to the Crimean War. Local transportation links were greatly improved through the inauguration of a steam ferry service between Artillery Bay and the north side in 1897, and in the opening the following year of a tramline from the main railway station to Nakhimov Prospekt.[115]

CHAPTER 9

THE 1905 REVOLUTION

*'Today you judge and execute us by firing squad, but
tomorrow, or may be in a year, we will do the same to you,
[or] even worse.'*

S. P. Chastnik, a ringleader of the *Ochakov* mutiny[1]

REFLECTION AND COMMEMORATION OF THE CRIMEAN WAR

It would take a long time for Russia to come to terms with her defeat during the Crimean War. As an essentially pre-industrial state, she had found to her cost that she could not compete effectively with the rising industrial powers of Britain and France. The loss of Sevastopol and the constraining terms of the Treaty of Paris, and those regarding the Black Sea in particular, had added to her humiliation. Russia needed to modernise if she were to catch up, prompting Alexander II to initiate an internal reform programme, which culminated with the abolition of serfdom in 1861. There were no future steps, however, towards democracy. On the military front, there was much cause for concern in the Army's performance and equipment, illustrated by its obsolescent small arms in the face of Allied rifle power.

With the passage of time, Alexander II had reflected on the wisdom and course of the Crimean campaign. As Tarle records, when travelling from Paris to Nice in 1865, the Emperor stopped for a few hours in Lyon, where he met

314

Marshal Canrobert. What he told the former French commander-in-chief of the French Army at Sevastopol from October 1854 to May 1855, was extraordinary: 'it had been pointless for the Russians to defend Sevastopol so fiercely because if they had ceded [the city] immediately, they would have preserved their forces completely intact, and [in any case], the capture of Sevastopol would not have brought the French and British closer to victory'.[2] Alexander II's explanation to Canrobert as to the reasons for his nation's defeat was equally revealing. Apparently, he 'attributed the Russians' failure in the main to the difficulties of supplying food and ammunition from the centre of the Empire to Sevastopol through the terrible mud and snow-drifts during the *bezdorozhe* [the 'roadless' season]'. In contrast, 'the Allies, thanks to their naval superiority, enjoyed uninterrupted and abundant supplies'.[3] While there was clearly some evidential merit to this argument, notwithstanding the fact that the Russians were relatively well supplied in September 1855, Allied materiel advantage was not the only important factor in the loss of Sevastopol. Grave Russian mistakes also contributed to their defeat, such as the misdirection that occurred during each of the battles of Alma, Balaklava, Inkerman and Chernaya river.

The Russian Emperor, however, could not admit to errors or inadequacies in either his own leadership or that of his principal subordinates. Thus any notion of futility within the failure was suppressed in historical accounts of the sacrifice borne by Sevastopol's defenders. From a Russian perspective, therefore, Tolstoy's famous 'spirit' would triumph over the apparent senselessness of the defence, and gloss over the undistinguished roles played by many of the senior Russian commanders involved, excepting the likes of Admirals Kornilov and Nakhimov. No paradox is involved here: once the defence of Sevastopol had commenced, the city's retention had become a matter of national prestige, if not one necessarily of military logic. Thus the Russians had determined to fight on, almost regardless of the human cost involved. The battles of Verdun and the Somme of 1916 in the First World War would assume a similar dynamic.

Meantime, commercial life returned slowly to Sevastopol in the 1860s, as did the rebuilding of the city. The first tourists following the Crimean War provided a welcome boost to the fragile local economy. When Mrs Kate Guthrie, a British traveller, visited the city during the middle of the decade, she stayed at the Hotel Vetzel, which had opened on Catherine Street.[4] Built from the shattered remains of Admiral Nakhimov's house, the establishment had been recommended to her by none other than Mrs John Gowen, who had resided there some time during her husband's salvage operation. Close to her hotel, Mrs Guthrie observed a structure in the 'course of erection, the only sign of activity we ever saw in this ruined town'. With this remark, she was probably exaggerating, for by that time ROPiT had conducted a lot of reconstruction in the dockyard, and rebuilding was going on elsewhere. None the less, what the British lady observed was of historical significance. She had heard that 'the work was being carried on at the expense of Baron Todleben, and was intended, some said, for a museum; others, for a private residence'.[5]

In fact, both versions given to Mrs Guthrie were true. Fine houses were being built in Catherine (now Lenin) Street, restoring one of Sevastopol's main thoroughfares to its former grandeur. On 14 September 1869, the first Sevastopol military museum opened on the ground floor of Todleben's house at Number 18. Its foundation existed not only with the support of the great engineer, but also as a result of an initiative of Sevastopol's residents and former members of the Black Sea Fleet. An organising committee had raised funds from all over Russia towards the establishment of the museum. Such was the museum's popularity, a larger building dedicated to the history of the Russian Navy, including its vital contribution to the defence of Sevastopol during the Crimean War, opened its doors in 1895. Restored after suffering damage during the Second World War, the Black Sea Fleet museum remains one of Sevastopol's most important tourist attractions. Poignantly, the building's imposing façade, made of Inkerman stone, is decorated with the number 349, commemorating the number of days of the first siege of Sevastopol.[6] Various cannon and mortars from the Crimean War are preserved at the museum's entrance, all expressive reminders of the city's violent history.

In due course, the principal heroes (the 'great men') of the defence of Sevastopol each received their monuments – indeed, so many, that memorials of one type or another dominate the most important vistas of the city. The first admiral to be honoured was Kornilov, whose statue was unveiled on the Malakhov Hill on 5 (17) October 1895, the forty-first anniversary of his death. Destroyed during the fighting of the Second World War during the second siege of the city, a replacement monument was erected in 1983. On 18 (30) November 1898, the forty-fifth anniversary of the battle of Sinope, a statue to Nakhimov was dedicated on Sevastopol's main square near the Count's Landing Stage. Originally known as Catherine's Square, in Soviet times Sevastopol's central meeting place was re-named Nakhimov Square, but not before the eponymous memorial was removed in 1928 and replaced with one of Lenin in 1932. Such iconoclasm was a common occurrence in the Soviet Union when statues of the tsars and members of the imperial royal family, and of the admirals, generals and other figures who supported the old regime, were torn down in their hundreds across the land. When Nakhimov was rehabilitated as a national hero, an imposing new figure of him, telescope in hand, was returned to its rightful place in 1959. Significantly, it was positioned to face a vast new war memorial, which had been erected to commemorate the second defence of Sevastopol and the dead of the Second

World War. Three bas-reliefs on the statue's pedestal depict Nakhimov amongst sailors of the Black Sea Fleet; on the bastions of Sevastopol; and on the deck of the ship of the line *Empress Maria*. An inscription on the fourth face records 'Glory to the Russian Fleet'.[7]

Todleben's grand memorial lies at the top of steps that lead up from Sevastopol's other great square – that of Ushakov. Unveiled in 1909, this imposing monument consists of a bronze representation of the great engineer inspecting the fortifications, whose construction and repair he had so energetically supervised during the first defence of the city. His statue stands on a massive granite pedestal, richly decorated with depictions of infantrymen, artillerymen and engineers, and showing part of a bastion, and an entrance to an underground mine – all participants and elements of the siege he described in his history. Within the town below, the building of St Vladimir's Cathedral, which had begun on 27 July 1854, had only just got under way when war came to Sevastopol. Although work recommenced in 1858, progress was slow. Mrs Guthrie, for example, observed it 'still in the course of construction ... its cupolas had not yet been spread with flashing gold or enlivening green'.[8] Sevastopol's first cathedral was finally opened for worship in October 1888, a significant milestone in the rebuilding of the city following the Crimean War.

Todleben's burial vault lies not in the city, but rather on the northern side of Sevastopol in the 'Common' or Fraternal Cemetery, so called on account of the number of common graves it holds. Earlier this large burial ground had been known as the '100-thousand Cemetery', signifying the approximate number of Sevastopol defenders of the Crimean War interred there. There are 472 mass graves here, each with tens or hundreds of nameless men, as well as 130 individual graves of officers and generals. A most striking monument to the Crimean War lies at the cemetery's heart. Overlooking the roadstead, the prominent pyramidal-shaped Church of St Nicholas was consecrated in 1870. Its outside faces are mounted with large stone plaques listing the Russian regiments that fought in the war, together with a record of their losses. The interior of the church contains the names of the officers who fell during the Crimean campaign. Elsewhere one can find the tombs of Prince M. D. Gorchakov, of General K. A. Khrulev and of many other leading commanders involved in the first defence of Sevastopol.[9] The cemetery has remained much in use since the Crimean War: there are not only memorials to the dead of the Second World War, but also to the 600 sailors who died in the unexplained massive explosion of the *Novorossiysk* battleship in Sevastopol harbour in 1955, and to the submariners from Sevastopol who perished in the *Kursk* disaster of 2000 in the Barents Sea.

Away from this haunting place, lying on the opposite side of the roadstead in the sea just off Primorsky Boulevard, stands perhaps the most famous memorial to the

Crimean War – the Monument to the Scuttled Ships. Erected in 1904, it commemorates the Russian vessels sunk at the entrance to the roadstead in September 1854 and February 1855. If not as famous as the Little Mermaid on Copenhagen's waterfront, Sevastopol's sea monument deserves greater historical and architectural recognition: standing atop a soaring Corinthian column, a bronze eagle with a wreath of laurels in its beak extols the sad sacrifice of the Black Sea Fleet to the greater good of Sevastopol's defence.[10] Surprisingly, a few scratches apart, this memorial survived the city's destruction during the Second World War. Such is its historical significance to the Russian Federation, the monument to the sunken ships is featured on a 100-rouble banknote brought into circulation in early 2016.

All over Europe, as towns and cities expanded rapidly in the nineteenth century, old confining defensive walls and more modern fortifications such as bastions and redoubts were torn down. The resulting spaces were often filled with either grand boulevards or green parks. Sevastopol also benefited from this trend. As early as 1881, groves of trees had been planted in the area of the former Fourth Bastion of the Crimean War defences. Over the years, a picturesque park was established in a kite-shaped parcel of land about 800 metres long overlooking Sevastopol's Southern Bay. Within this area, the Sevastopol municipal authorities laid out in 1904–05 an 'Historic Boulevard' astride the park's major north-south axis. It was designed to provide a fitting memorial and museum to the defence of the city.

At the park's south-eastern face, looking out across eastwards to the Redan (the Third Bastion) and the Malakhov Hill, the city fathers reconstructed a defensive gun position from the siege of 1854–55. The Fourth Battery remains today as one of the most redolent reminders of the Crimean War, particularly due to its special connection to Leo Tolstoy. Close by stands a white bas-relief memorial to the artillery officer and writer. The battery's seven cast-iron, muzzle-loading cannon, originally taken from the scuttled ships, were set in restored fortifications. Their embrasures are lined with earth and rock-filled gabions, which were such a notable feature of the military engineering of the time and have since been returned to in the guise of defensive 'blast' walls in today's counter-insurgency operations. The Fourth Battery's gun positions are linked together by a memorial wall 80 metres long and 2 metres high. For contemporary battlefield and other tours of Sevastopol and the Crimean War, this is one of the 'essential' viewpoints, for it is at this location where Tolstoy's epic accounts of the defence of Sevastopol can be recounted to best dramatic effect. Moving down the historic boulevard, other monuments of the siege appear. These include an obelisk that commemorates the defenders of the Fourth Bastion; another, beyond the central fountain of the park, remembers those who bravely held the nearby Yazon Redoubt. Todleben's monument marks the northern end, completing a short walk embracing so much of Sevastopol's rich Crimean War history.

The principal monument of the park and most famous city landmark, apart from the monument to the scuttled ships, is the Museum of Panorama, 'The Defence of Sevastopol in 1854–55', opened in 1905. This highly impressive building houses a foreground of accurately reconstructed fortifications and guns, which lies immediately in front of a circular vertical canvas, 115 metres long and 14 metres high. So skilfully is the whole battle scene designed and presented that it is extremely difficult for a viewer, standing on a raised platform in the middle of the building, to discern where the figures of the foreground end, and where the individual portraits on the canvas begin. For those who have witnessed a similar construction at the Waterloo battlefield in Belgium, the Sevastopol model is far grander and several times more effective, such is the meticulous attention to detail and perspective. The snapshot of battle, so accurately and vividly depicted in the Panorama, represents the high point of the Russian defence on 6 (18) June 1855 with the repulse of the Allied attacks on the Malakhov and the Great Redan. Visitors observe the scene as if they were standing that day at a central point on the summit of the Malakhov Hill, one now occupied by the monument to Admiral Kornilov. Franz Rubo was the principal artist of the Panorama. Born in Odessa of French origin, he lived for most of his working life (1856–1928) in Germany. Assisted by two other painters and twenty students of the Bavarian Academy of Arts in Munich, Rubo took three years (1902–04) to complete the work. In parallel, V. A. Feldman, architect, and O. I. Anberg, military engineer, designed and constructed the building to hold the great canvas.

On 26 May 1905 a religious service was held in the Panorama, involving senior military and naval commanders, civil leaders and surviving veterans of the Crimean War, to commemorate the completion of the building. The next day, the Panorama was opened to the public. Although the museum attracted great numbers of visitors, their initial reaction was mixed. A local newspaper reported a range of views, particularly amongst the elderly veterans of the defence of Sevastopol. One queried why a number of the soldiers portrayed were 'sitting quietly as if nothing has happened'; another asked 'why don't the soldiers look scared?'. On the other hand, a visitor (presumably, but not necessarily, a civilian) complained about a 'dead body exhibited covered in a greatcoat but exposing a bandaged wounded foot ... we don't need this.'[11] For all the Panorama's great artistic and historical qualities, there was no pleasing some.

CIVIL AND NAVAL UNREST

The rapid economic recovery of Sevastopol in the final decades of the nineteenth century was accompanied by the first significant outbreak of civil unrest since the cholera riots of 1830. Paradoxically, this incident occurred in connection with the building of the railway, a development that soon brought much progress and prosperity to the city. Approximately 500 railway navvies involved in the construction of the Inkerman tunnels downed tools on 14 May 1873 for ten days, one of the first big strikes in the city's turbulent history.[12] Significantly, the workers not only protested about their poor pay, but also on account of their passports (internal identification documents) being retained against their wishes by the railway contractor. Even after the arrest of six of the ringleaders, the strikers refused to go to back to work, sensing public sympathy for their cause. Rather surprisingly, both their employer and the local authorities backed down, acceding to the tunnellers' demands: the latter could claim a rare victory in the fight for Russian workers' rights and conditions.[13]

The withdrawal of labour by the men at Inkerman was but a local warning sign of the much wider political and social discord that emerged in Russia following the stalled programme of legal and social reform instituted by Alexander II. Despite the abolition of serfdom by the 'Tsar Liberator', no real progress had been made towards creating a modern democracy on Western European or American lines: the gap between the largely aristocratic governing elite and the mass of the population, whether of the growing numbers of intelligentsia or of industrial workers, remained as large as ever. Eschewing non-violent protest, the opposition movement of student radicals called *Narodnaya Volya* (People's Will) aimed to overturn the ruling system by eliminating its head. Thus 'hunting the Tsar' became their prime objective. After six failed attempts, the group succeeded in assassinating Alexander II by bomb attack in St Petersburg on 13 March 1881. That act of terror was not the end of the struggle: other groups soon followed in its wake, and many more attacks against other figures took place. Exactly six years later, an effort to kill the new Emperor, Alexander III, failed. One of the executed perpetrators was none other than Alexander Ulyanov, Vladimir Lenin's elder brother.[14]

On Sevastopol's northern outskirts there exists a close connection to People's Will. In the vicinity of Lyubimovka lies the former Alkadar state farm. It is now one of Crimea's most famous wineries, named after Sophia Perovskaya, a young lady of aristocratic stock, who was brought up on her mother's estate here in the 1850s. Early in the following decade her family moved to St Petersburg, at that time Russia's capital city. When a teenager she controversially embraced revolutionary ideas, mixed with the 'wrong sort' and in consequence fell out with her parents. She became a leading member of People's Will, and was directly implicated in the assassination of the Emperor. Shortly afterwards she was arrested, convicted and sentenced to death by hanging. Executed on 15 April 1881, aged only 27, along with four other co-conspirators, she subsequently became an icon of Soviet propaganda, which exploited her memory as a tragic revolutionary figure. In the 1920s the Soviet authorities opened a museum dedicated to Sophia Perovskaya in her childhood home at Lyubimovka. Today it is open to the public, a pertinent reminder of Russia's past, and of her volatile and violent politics.

Although People's Will groups appeared in Sevastopol in the 1870s, they found little local support and soon disintegrated. The city authorities, however, were always on the look out for subversive activity during this increasingly troubled period. Foreign ships were often targets of their suspicions. On 27 May 1883, for example, Sevastopol police searched the steamship *Medusa*, which had arrived from Marseilles. On board they found a sailor called Mattee in possession of a box of banned literature, including a biography of Perovskaya. When a Sevastopol resident, Ivan Nikolaivich Telepnev, visited him aboard, both were arrested. On searching Telepnev's home, police found more than 'seventy items of forbidden publication'.[15] Although such incidents remained comparatively rare, they represented a sign of the times. Efficient train communications between the rapidly expanding industrial centre of St Petersburg and the Crimean city facilitated the spread of popular literature. Examples included pamphlets issued by the 'League of Struggle for the Emancipation of the Working Class' founded by Lenin in 1895, which promoted the emergence of social-democratic and revolutionary groups.

Local histories of Sevastopol record a spike of political activity, civil unrest and doubts about the loyalty of the fleet in the early 1900s prior to the revolution of 1905. In March 1902, for example, a Sevastopol Workers' League was founded. The following year, 3,000 dockyard workers went on strike during July in protest about the sudden imposition of a 'non-working day' without payment. Crowds of citizens joined the workers in solidarity. Although the arrival of a company of armed sailors led to the dispersal of the strikers and their supporters, the naval authorities began to worry about the reliability of their crews, since some were known to be sympathetic to the workers. Such was the concern that the commander-in-chief of the Black Sea Fleet, Admiral N. I. Scrydlov, called a special meeting on 16 December 1903 to discuss counter-revolutionary measures. In his report, he requested the Russian Navy headquarters to send officers to 'enforce discipline within ships' crews' and to be given the authority to 'exile politically active lower-rank sailors to the Caspian Flotilla and the Pacific Fleet'.[16] Little did he know how prescient his warning would prove: over the next two years there would be not only violent agitation but also two major mutinies within his command.

In 1904, the tempo of political developments and associated unrest increased. The first congress of the Russian Social Democratic Labour Party (RSDLP)[17] had been held in Minsk in 1898. Its second party congress in Brussels of 1903 led to a split between those who followed Lenin's centralist, revolutionary approach, and those in favour of a more liberal, democratic way of thinking. Those who supported Lenin had a slender majority, and were later termed 'Bolsheviks', over the minority 'Menshiviks'.[18] Within a year, the impact of this ideological division was felt in Sevastopol. In July 1904, the local Bolshevik-leaning committee of the RSDLP turned to the central committee, requesting permission to leave the Menshivik-led Crimean Union of the party, which allegedly had deprived them of the right to have a direct line of communication to central party organs, to print their own leaflets and to plan their own political activities.[19] Although the result of this application has not been found, its posting was significant. Neither for the first nor the last time did those in Sevastopol seek an independent, special, political status from the remainder of Crimea, seeing themselves as the true guardians of the Bolshevik (and later Communist) movement.

Notwithstanding the internal wrangling within the RSDLP, and other differences across Russia between the more pacific 'social democrats' and more violent 'social revolutionaries', protests within the Black Sea Fleet were mounting. Sailors' 'agitations' took place in the Lazarev naval barracks in early November 1904. The ostensible cause was a botched attempt by the newly appointed autocratic commander-in-chief, Vice Admiral G. P. Chukhnin, to stop the circulation of social-democratic literature amongst the crews. His order prohibiting any 'walking out' into the town – in other words, a collective confinement to barracks – and the threat of severe punishment to those who either offended, or protested, was met with a mass outbreak of violence. The sailors destroyed much of the barracks, tore down its gates and started marching into the city. This mutinous commotion was only contained by the deployment of the armed marine guard company, which remained loyal to the naval chain of command. Several hundred men were arrested, thirty-five of whom were brought to court and punished. In turn, this event generated further political activity: the Sevastopol committee of the RSDLP – presumably now acting independently – issued leaflets throughout the city demanding the immediate release of the sailors concerned.[20] It would appear that agitation had become part of the body politic of Sevastopol: on this basis, it hardly surprises that it soon became a centre of revolution.

THE 1905 REVOLUTION

Excepting possibly the Pugachev rebellion of 1773–75, which was the largest peasants' revolt in Russia's history, the revolution of 1905 proved to be the biggest threat to tsarist control of the Russian Empire since the Romanovs came to power in 1613. Although the events of 1905 led to the promise of a limited form of constitutional monarchy, the wave of political agitation, social unrest, industrial strife and naval mutiny fundamentally undermined respect for, and trust in, the Tsar and his government. It proved a harbinger of the revolutions of 1917 during the First World War, which ultimately led to the Civil War, the deaths of Nicholas II and his family, and the establishment of the Communist Soviet Union. The sailors' mutinies and workers' protests that led to an armed uprising in Sevastopol in 1905 subsequently became totemic events in the Bolshevik narrative of the establishment of the Soviet state. Sevastopol's sailors and townsfolk were united once again, not in the defence of their city as in 1854–55, but rather in marching together in the van of revolution. It is an extraordinary story.

The origins of the naval mutiny aboard the Russian Black Sea battleship *Knyaz Potemkin Tavricheskiy* are relatively easy to trace. Only commissioned in 1904, with 13,500 tonnes full displacement and 18 knots top speed, the *Potemkin* was the newest of seven pre-Dreadnought-class ships of the line based in Sevastopol.[21] Although these warships had not been deployed to the Far East, unrest in the Black Sea Fleet had spread during the Russo-Japanese War (1904–05). Many of the best officers and crews had been transferred to ships in the Pacific and Baltic squadrons; many friends and former colleagues had perished in these units.

The war had started with a surprise Japanese naval attack by night on the Russian naval base at Port Arthur, Manchuria, on 8/9 February 1904. Following this action and subsequent engagements, a Japanese blockade and a prolonged siege ensued. In mid-August 1904, the Russian Navy in the Far East had suffered a series of further defeats at the skilled hands of the Imperial Japanese Navy. In response, the Russian government decided to send the Baltic Fleet under command of Admiral Zinovy Rozhestvensky to reinforce its naval presence in the Far East. The omens for the Russian force against the Japanese fleet were poor to say the least. On 22 October 1904, at an early stage of its ill-fated voyage to the Pacific Ocean, Russian warships opened fire on a group of fishing trawlers from Hull off the Dogger Bank, believing them to be Japanese torpedo boats; they sank one and damaged six. Incredible as this incident in the North Sea might appear in retrospect, there was some risk of an accidental British–Russian war resulting at the time. Although Britain was not bound by the Anglo-Japanese Treaty of 1902 to enter the conflict on Japan's side, her sympathies were not with Russia. Fortunately, French diplomatic efforts eased tensions.[22] As a result of this incident, however, the British government determined to oppose any attempt by units of the Black Sea Fleet to pass through the Turkish Straits to join their Baltic counterparts (by this stage described in the British military and naval press as a 'fleet of lunatics') in the Eastern Mediterranean.[23]

The tragic end to the Russian's unfortunate naval deployment to the Far East came seven months later. Nearing the end of its long voyage to Vladivostok (the

Russian battleships having sailed round the Cape of Good Hope while smaller units used the Suez Canal), the united Russian force was intercepted by the Imperial Japanese Navy in the Straits of Tsushima off Korea on 27–28 May 1905. Admiral Togo Heihachiro handled his forces with consummate skill, matched by his crews' fine gunnery. In the resulting action, the Russian fleet was almost totally destroyed. It was the greatest naval engagement since the battle of Trafalgar, one hundred years before, and equally decisive.

Russian naval leadership and technique had proved not only reckless but also thoroughly incompetent – a far cry from the exemplary actions of Admirals Ushakov, Lazarev, Kornilov and Nakhimov. For the loss of only 110 men killed, the much younger Japanese Navy, modelled largely on British Royal Navy lines, inflicted horrendous casualties: 4,830 men killed and 5,917 captured.[24] In the action's one-sided losses, it represented the reverse of Nakhimov's stunning success against the Ottoman fleet at Sinope in 1853. Only one Russian warship, the armed yacht *Almaz*, reached Vladivostok. The disaster of Tsushima brought about a humiliating conclusion of the war for Russia. Under the mediation of the United States, ably facilitated by President Teddy Roosevelt, peace with Japan was signed under the Treaty of Portsmouth (New Hampshire) on 5 September 1905. As a result, Russia gave up her Far Eastern base at Port Arthur, which by then had been captured by the Japanese, and conceded the southern half of Sakhalin Island, which was recovered by Stalin at the end of the Second World War. Russia's international prestige sank accordingly, as did the defeat undermine domestic confidence in tsarist rule and damage the fragile, if not febrile, morale in her navy, not least amongst the sailors stationed at Sevastopol.

Well before the disaster at Tsushima and the end of the war, there had been revolutionary stirrings within the Black Sea Fleet that reflected widespread unrest and upheaval across Russia. The catalyst for this protest movement was the infamous 'Bloody Sunday' of 9 (22) January 1905. When a mass of unarmed workers marched on the Winter Palace in St Petersburg to present a petition to Nicholas II, the Russian Imperial Guard opened fire into the crowd. Over 100 protesters were killed and many more injured.[25] Within days, industrial action brought a million workers out on to the streets in St Petersburg and other cities. For a generation, Russia's rulers had been in denial about the need for fundamental political reform. Tsars Alexander III and Nicholas II clung to the inward-looking mantra of Nicholas I: Russia needed orthodoxy, autocracy and nationality rather than democratic ideas imported from Western Europe. In such conditions, the domestic pressures for measured, if not revolutionary, change could only mount. Within the innately conservative hierarchy of Russia's armed forces, moreover, there remained trenchant opposition to any liberal, let alone humanising, adjustment to the terms and conditions of service.

Life for ordinary sailors was harsh: they were under-paid, badly led, poorly administered and inadequately fed. Discipline was oppressive and ruthlessly enforced. Equally damning, civil liberties were strictly curtailed; when granted, their time off duty was restricted to only six hours a month. As the author of a study of the *Potemkin* mutiny notes, sailors were 'forbidden to smoke in public, eat in restaurants, attend the theatre, ride a tram, or sit in any train compartment other than third-class'.[26] A warning sign at the entrance of Sevastopol's Primorsky Boulevard, 'no dogs and lower ranks allowed', typified this form of social apartheid.[27] Unsurprisingly, within the Black Sea Fleet there was a growing sense of grievance that would soon erupt into violent protest. In such circumstances, the emergence in Sevastopol of a sailors' revolutionary group, the 'Tsentralka', which called for nothing less than the end of tsarism, seemed inevitable. Its members had planned a mass mutiny across the fleet on 4 July 1905, but circumstances brought forward the insurrection to an earlier date on the battleship *Potemkin*.

The scene of the crucial Tsentralka meeting before the mutiny could not have been more symbolic: it took place on the Malakhov Hill, where so many Russian sailors had fought and died in the defence of Sevastopol fifty years before. One of the Tsentralka's leaders was Afansy Nikolayevich Matyushenko, a torpedo quartermaster of the *Potemkin*. During the afternoon of 25 June, *Potemkin* slipped her moorings in Sevastopol harbour and steamed towards Tendra Island off the Ukrainian coast in order to test-fire her 12-inch guns. The following day the warship arrived off Tendra, and was met by the torpedo boat *Ismail* that brought supplies from Odessa. In the early hours of 27 June, the crew of the *Potemkin* discovered maggots in rotten meat and refused the soup made from this source. When ordered to consume the disgusting broth against their wishes, the crew declined. In turn, the ship's second-in-command, Ippolit I. Gilyarovsky, allegedly threatened to execute the crewmen involved. This incident provided the last straw for the mutineers led by Grigory N. Vakulinchuk and Matyushenko. In the resulting struggle for control of the *Potemkin*, eight out of eighteen ship's officers were killed; Vakulinchuk was mortally wounded. Under Matyushenko's command, *Potemkin* made for Odessa, arriving at the port that evening (see Map 11).[28]

At that time Odessa was experiencing a general strike so the circumstances appeared opportune for combined revolutionary action between sailors and workers. Yet the social democrats of the city and the crew of the *Potemkin* could not agree on an effective course of action. On 29 June the funeral of Vakulinchuk turned into a political demonstration gone ugly. Despite the memorable portrayal in Sergei Eisenstein's revolutionary film of 1925, *Battleship Potemkin*, there was no shooting on the famous steps that led up from the port. None the less, there were a great many casualties in Odessa, possibly reaching the thousands. The city, however, did not fall to the revolutionaries. Meanwhile, ostensibly loyal units of the Black Sea Fleet were closing in, concentrated at Tendra Island. Still under Matyushenko's rebel command, the *Potemkin* departed Odessa and with much bravado steamed through the middle of the opposing squadron, whose crews refused to open fire. Temporary rebellions had broken out on *Potemkin's* sister ships, the *Tri Svyatitelya*, the *Dvenadtsat Apostolov* and *Georgii Pobedonosets*. Meanwhile, a fifth mutiny took place on the *Prut*, a minelayer and training ship, but it failed to rendezvous with the *Potemkin* at Odessa.[29]

The rebellion, however, proved short-lived and ineffective – at least in the short term. *Potemkin* proceeded to the Romanian port of Constanza (Constanta), where it was refused supplies. It then sailed for the eastern Crimean port of Feodosiya before returning to Constanza, where the crew surrendered to the Romanian authorities on 8 July 1905. Matyushenko escaped to Switzerland where he met exiled Russian revolutionary leaders including Lenin, but grew homesick. When he re-entered Russia in 1907, his recklessness was awarded with arrest, trial and execution. Meantime, the *Potemkin*, which had been scuttled by its mutinous crew in Constanza's harbour, had been quickly salvaged by the Russian Navy and towed back to Sevastopol. On 27 July (9 August) 1905, St Panteleimon's feast day, when the Russian Navy commemorates its major victory over the Swedish fleet at the battle of Gangut on 27 July (7 August) 1714, the *Potemkin* was re-commissioned and renamed as the *Panteleimon*.[30]

Although government control was forcibly restored, the *Potemkin* mutiny was not the end of disobedience and disorder in the Black Sea Fleet. Political protests soon spilled over on to the streets of Sevastopol. Local newspapers were full of articles documenting the disorder affecting the city during the summer and autumn of 1905. *Krymskiy Vestnik* (Crimean Herald) reported, for example, that on Friday 14 (27) October, 'a crowd of 400–500 men marched up and down Nakhimov Prospekt distributing flyers ... Cossacks and infantry arrived and order was re-established. All shops in the town were closed.[31]

As civil unrest in both towns and in the countryside spread across Russia throughout the year, matters had come to a head in October with strikes that paralysed the national railway network. On the advice of the reformer Sergey Witte, chairman of the Council of Ministers, who had skilfully negotiated the Treaty of Portsmouth, the government responded. The Tsar's 'October Manifesto', published on 17 (30) October 1905, 'guaranteed civil liberties to all Russians, announced a Duma [assembly] with the true legislative function of passing or rejecting all proposed laws, and promised a further expansion of the new order in Russia'.[32] This brief document put Russia on the path to becoming a constitutional monarchy. Unsurprisingly, Sevastopol's citizens were anxious to learn about such a potentially groundbreaking document. A local report proclaimed: 'Today we received news that freedom will be given to the Russian people. At last liberty is coming – freedom of expression in spoken word and in print'. The same newspaper article recorded that the Tsar's manifesto had been 'received like thunder across the city'. As the citizens of Sevastopol 'did not trust rumours, they wanted to see telegrams and newspapers. People hugged and kissed each other – there was great joy'.[33]

The political concessions of the October Manifesto, although initially welcomed as in Sevastopol, proved too little and too late. Its publication failed to stem the mounting civil unrest, mutinous activities and increasing violent agitation across Russia. In Sevastopol strikes broke out again across the city as bitterness about poor pay and conditions intensified. Above all, the increasingly politicised sailors and workers of Sevastopol were disappointed in the slow pace of the reforms promised in the Manifesto, and demanded an immediate stake in the running of the country. In the aftermath of the *Potemkin* mutiny, rebellious sentiments had remained strong within the Black Sea Fleet. Sevastopol provided a melting point of radical views, where militant sailors, dockyard workers and factory employees all mixed and shared their grievances.

A remarkable individual, Pyotr Petrovich Schmidt, now enters the history and mythology of Sevastopol and of the Russian 1905 revolution. A career officer of the Imperial Russian Navy, and in the rank of senior lieutenant, Schmidt captained minelayer No. 253. Although not a member of any political party, when on shore he acted well out of his naval sphere. In a declaration of 31 October 1905, he called on citizens to stand up for their rights and demanded that the authorities free political prisoners. Responding to Schmidt's passionate language and stirring rhetoric, and in a manner reminiscent of the Parisian mob's storming of the Bastille of 14 July 1789, an angry crowd marched towards the city prison. Troops blocking their path opened fire with machine guns. Surprisingly, only a few demonstrators were killed in the ensuing mêlée. Schmidt continued his protest at Sevastopol's official town council, and two days later spoke at the funeral of the shot demonstrators, which attracted a crowd of several thousand mourning sympathisers.

Schmidt's speech on 2 November 1905, made in the form of a solemn oath to the fallen protestors, became a clarion call of the revolutionary movement in Sevastopol and beyond. Repeated by all present, he declared:

> Next to a coffin one should say only prayers. Let words of love and a sacred oath become a prayer, which we now all offer. We avow that we'll never surrender even the smallest portion of our hard-won rights. We affirm that we shall sacrifice all our work, soul, and lives to preserve our freedom. This we hereby swear.[34]

At the cemetery, Schmidt was promptly arrested by the authorities and taken to the battleship *Tri Svyatitelya*. In response, violent protests broke out in the city and across the fleet, shaking the confidence of Sevastopol's civic and naval leaders. In an effort to calm tensions and to bring an end to the matter, on 20 November, Schmidt was forcibly retired from the Russian Navy as a captain of second rank (equivalent to an American or British naval commander), a promotion designed to buy his silence. Yet revolutionary feeling in Sevastopol, and across Russia, was far from over. A major armed confrontation in Sevastopol soon ensued. Although eclipsed in history by the preceding *Potemkin* mutiny, the second event was much larger in scale, and in many ways more significant for the city, Black Sea Fleet and the Russian revolutionary armed struggle.

On 24 November a mutiny broke out quite suddenly in the Lazarev naval barracks. Soon embracing a couple of thousand sailors, it caught the Black Sea Fleet command and the city by surprise despite the growing discontent. Other acts of disobedience took place in other parts of the Sevastopol fortress and associated coastal defence batteries. It was clearly a much better organised event than the *Potemkin* incident: sailors, soldiers and civilians, including militant dockyard workers, closely co-operated in their armed protests across the city.[35] The local military and naval authorities appeared powerless to contain, let alone counter effectively, what was rapidly becoming a major insurrection. The following day, Vice Admiral Chukhnin telegraphed Nicholas II in St Petersburg, reporting that 'sailors are in charge here' and that 'workers of the dockyard are joining the Socialist Party'. Warning of the gravity of the situation in Sevastopol, the admiral advised: 'in order to suppress this movement, a great number of troops with artillery will need to be sent here – otherwise [we'll be forced to] submit to the sailors' demands'.[36] Events had taken a political turn for that same day (25 November), Sevastopol's various revolutionaries elected a *soviet* (council) of sailors', soldiers', and workers' deputies under the chairmanship of I. P. Voronitsyn. Their demands went well beyond the city, calling for nothing less than the creation of a constituent assembly; the establishment of a republic; the introduction of an eight-hour workday; and not least agreement to a shorter period and better conditions of military and naval service. The local revolt continued to gather momentum: the Sevastopol Soviet, which Schmidt had joined, established a 'Sailors' Commission', charging it with the 'organisation of order within the city' and with the 'provision and distribution of food and fuel'.[37] Hence the revolutionaries' immediate objective was nothing less than to seize and exercise full control over the city, fortress and port.

There were few immediate options open to the government in curbing the revolt other than its suppression with armed force. When such a response was mounted, it proved swift and decisive. Locally, there had been recent concerns that Sevastopol's Russian Army garrison could not be fully relied on: according to some, its two infantry regiments, the 49th Brest and the 50th Belostok,[38] were both on the verge of mutinying. As a result, these formations had already been marched out of the city as their officers wished to distance the men from local agitators (both sailors and townsfolk), who had been sneaking revolutionary manifestos into the soldiers' barracks. Meantime, the majority of the military engineers of the fortress were siding with the naval mutineers. A large body of armed sappers under the leadership of Under Officer Barishev had marched into the barracks of the 28th Naval Crew on 26 November. Sailors greeted their army comrades with loud 'hurrahs'.[39] The same day martial law was declared in Sevastopol, loyal troops were already being assembled in Crimea to crush this revolutionary activity.

The centre of the mutiny now moved to a 'protected' (lightly armoured) cruiser, the 6,645-tonne *Ochakov*, equipped with twelve 152mm (6-inch) guns. A modern ship, built in Sevastopol and launched in 1902, she had yet to be fully accepted into service by the time of the events of 1905. Moored at Sevastopol in November of that year she was not yet fully operational. When a number of her officers went ashore, members of the ship's company had seized control over the vessel. The mutineers elected a thirty-one-year-old ship's storeman, Sergey Petrovich Chastnik, as their captain, and raised the red flag of the revolution on the *Ochakov's* mast. A day later (27 November), members of the Sailors' Commission called on Schmidt at his flat in Sobornaya (Cathedral) Street, and invited him to become their head. So ended his very brief enforced retirement. Accompanied by his sixteen-year-old son, Yevgeniy, Schmidt boarded the *Ochakov* to become the leader of the second Black Sea Fleet mutiny. On the 15th (28th), the following signal was hoisted on the warship's mast: 'I command the fleet. Schmidt'. In fact, the naval vessels based at Sevastopol were roughly equally divided between those crews who supported the mutiny and those which remained loyal to the Tsar.

Red flags appeared on the following warships: the destroyers *Zavetny*, *Zorkiy* and *Svirepy*; minelayers No. 265, 268 and 270; and other vessels moored in the Southern Bay. To these were added the battleship *Panteleimon*, the cruiser *Griden*, the mine transport *Bug*, the gunboat *Uralets*, and the training vessels *Dnestr* and *Prut*. Roughly 2,200 sailors on ships took part in the mutiny, together with about 6,000 men from various shore establishments.[40] According to a subsequent press report, based on the prosecution case made at his eventual court martial, Schmidt blamed all the present troubles on the government, alleging that 'Russia is flooded in blood, it is humiliated, deprived of dignity'. In his view, only the immediate establishment of a Constituent Assembly would save the nation. In the meantime, Schmidt required his officers to 'enforce the agitation ashore', and demanded that the remainder of the fleet's ships at Sevastopol join the mutiny. Yet by no means were all the sailors of the Black Sea Fleet so persuaded: on the

Sinop, no more than a quarter were sympathetic, and on the *Tri Svyatitelya* perhaps a fifth.[41] When Schmidt shouted to the captain of the *Mercury*, 'join us, the Russian people are with us', the prompt reply was unequivocal: 'We serve the Tsar and the Motherland, while you are a pirate and force people to serve you!'.[42]

Schmidt gave a highly provocative speech on the morning of 28 November. He declared that he had been 'engaged in revolutionary activity' since his young days. With 'all the troops' being at his side, he had decided, 'with the support of the navy and the fortress', to demand from the Tsar the immediate calling of a Constituent Assembly. If this plea were to be refused, he would 'cut Crimea off and send [his] sappers to the Perekop Isthmus to construct batteries'. Furthermore, anticipating that workers across Russia would strike in support, he would then make the following demands: that Crimea should form a republic with him becoming 'president and commander of the Black Sea Fleet'. Threateningly, he pronounced that 'only the Cossacks represent an obstacle to me…. For every crack of a Cossack's whip, I will hang one of you, my hostages, who make up over a hundred people'. At the end of his speech, he warned those he held: 'If your life is precious to you, write to your relations and acquaintances to solicit support of my terms – the removal of troops from this besieged state'. The *Sevastopol Gazette* then reminded its readers that Schmidt's actions could be characterised as 'if he were trying to suffocate the authorities at their throat'. Yet in response, 'he would have to realise that if these same authorities had any real power, they would suffocate Schmidt themselves'.[43]

Stirred into decisive action by this revolutionary event, the tsarist government hurriedly concentrated troops from Crimea and neighbouring provinces to crush the mutiny in Sevastopol. The commander of 7th Army Corps, Lieutenant General Baron A. N. Meller-Zakomelskiy, based in Simferopol, and the commander-in-chief of the Black Sea Fleet, Vice Admiral G. P. Chukhnin, were given the task of restoring imperial law and order. Both were granted dictatorial powers. Quickly they deployed infantry and artillery units to confront and engage the rebels. Chukhnin could also count on the predominantly loyal crews of the battleships *Rostislav* and *Tri Svyatitelya*, and of other vessels of the fleet in the coming fight. The government's suppression of the naval mutiny was uncompromising and resolute. After an ultimatum to surrender had been ignored, Meller-Zakomelskiy and Chukhnin gave the order to open fire at 1530 hours on 28 November. The coastal defence guns of the fortress and of the fleet were directed against the *Ochakov* and the smaller destroyer *Svirepiy*. At the same time, army field artillery batteries located on the Malakhov Hill and on the Historic Boulevard bombarded the naval division barracks.[44] Any visitors to the Panorama museum that day might have reflected on the extreme irony of the situation: fifty years after the defence of Sevastopol, Russian sailors and soldiers were now shelling ships of the fleet and their installations ashore, killing their own comrades-in-arms and shipmates.

In his memoirs of his father, entitled *Red Admiral*, Yevgeniy Schmidt described how the mutineers' flagship came under fire at point-blank range:

> The guns of the *Rostislav* fired at the *Ochakov* ... and from the north the second blow came from the fortress artillery. Salvo followed salvo every five to ten seconds. *Rostislav* fired constantly and without missing (it was difficult to miss at a range of 200 *sazhen* [427 metres]) from guns of different calibres mounted on its port side. The fortress artillery fired with their 10-inch and 11-inch guns.... During the fight, *Ochakov* received fifty-two hits from large calibre guns.... [Additionally,] machine guns on the Grafskaya quay swept our decks.[45]

The mutineers' reaction was one of immediate panic. As soon as the *Rostislav* fired its first salvo, sailors on the *Ochakov* fled their posts. Young Schmidt compared them to a 'herd of mad animals', whom his father vainly tried to control. 'Amid the running and roaring mass', he recalled, 'I saw [him] with his hands outstretched. He grabbed sailors, blocked their way, trying to re-establish order. [But] his words "God is with us, the Russian people are with us" had no more effect.' Meanwhile, other sailors were jumping into the water to escape the ferocious fire on the *Ochakov* only to be machine-gunned 'mercilessly'. Those who managed 'to reach the shore by some miracle' were finished off by 'soldiers of the punishment detachment' lining the harbour wall. Residents watching the tragedy from Primorsky Boulevard saved a lucky few of the sailors by giving them civilian dress and sending them into the town.[46]

Yevgeniy Schmidt affirms that the mutinous crew of the *Ochakov* returned not a single shot throughout the one-sided engagement. He estimated that the firing lasted about an hour and a quarter. Its results were catastrophic: 'chaos and destruction reigned ... the decks were stained in blood ... the upper part of the ship was turned into shapeless pieces of debris'. As the *Ochakov* burned, the end seemed near. Schmidt spoke to his son: 'Give me your hand! If we die, we die together'. The only chance in survival lay in abandoning ship and attempting to swim unobserved to a friendly vessel as darkness now fell. Pyotr Schmidt lowered the red flag on the *Ochakov*; then father and son slipped down a cable on to a nearby barge and jumped into the icy water. Swimming towards Minelayer No. 270, the sixteen year old noticed the water was covered by 'hundreds of floating heads ... but head after head quickly disappeared under water, leaving only a brief red stain'. Other mutineers, although not wounded, drowned through cold and exhaustion. Both the Schmidts were strong swimmers, however, and were plucked out of the water.[47]

Once safely on board the minelayer, Pyotr Schmidt again took charge. According to his son's account, its crew and a small group of survivors of the *Ochakov*, together numbering about thirty to forty men, agreed to his plan – to head out to sea and to steer towards either Romanian or Bulgarian shores, where they could seek political asylum. The mutineers' last bid for freedom proved short-lived. 'Full steam ahead', shouted Schmidt to the engine room and soon the minelayer 'flew like a bird at a speed of 30 knots'. Yet it was not fast enough to make good their escape. As they reached the beam of the Chersonesos lighthouse, the first shell of the *Rostislav* flew overhead. The second missed as well, but the third struck the engine room, killing the crew serving there and destroying the machinery. Only when the minelayer slowed and drifted did Schmidt, his son and the mutineers finally realise 'that the game was up, and that [their] last card had been played'.[48] Any further resistance would have been futile.

Boarding crews from the *Rostislav* promptly arrested the surviving mutineers on the minelayer. Although some 2,000 mutineers were taken prisoner in Sevastopol, it was not possible to establish the full casualty toll. According to a subsequent newspaper report, Sevastopol's naval hospital treated twenty-nine seriously wounded, thirty-two slightly wounded and nineteen with burn injuries. While fifteen burnt corpses were removed from the damaged *Ochakov*, fifty members of the crew remained unaccounted for, presumed dead, many by drowning. Given the intensity of the bombardment and the resultant fires, and not least the machine-gunning by troops on shore, however, these figures look suspiciously low. Similarly, by 'some miracle', the forty naval officers 'arrested' by Schmidt were all released unscathed. Both phenomena remain unexplained.[49]

In the aftermath of the mutiny, up to 6,000 men were prosecuted and imprisoned, many serving long sentences of penal servitude. By coincidence, or more likely by design, the court martial of the main ringleaders took place on 16 February 1906 [OS] at the fortress of Ochakov at the mouth of the river Dnieper, where the mutineers were imprisoned. Their trial was widely reported: the press commentary – no doubt under the threat of censorship – remained strictly loyal to the government's position. Seeking ways to denigrate the mutineers, *Sevastopol Gazette* asked: 'how can Schmidt affirm that he did it all on behalf of the Russian people? Where is his letter of authority, and who signed it? ... If [he] was fighting for the Russian people, he would have died on the *Ochakov*, rather than fleeing from the ship'. The same critical report quoted the naval prosecutor who stated 'the current case is hugely significant both for the public and the service'. 'One can estimate the material damage', he maintained, 'but the moral and ethical harm is beyond evaluation. The wrongdoing is grandiose both in its insolence and criminal design.'[50]

The outcome of the Ochakov court martial was in little doubt: the main leaders of the mutiny, including Schmidt, Chastnik and two others, were condemned to death by firing squad. Throughout his incarceration in the Ochakov fortress, Schmidt had been reconciled as to his inevitable fate since mutiny was a capital offence; clemency was most unlikely given the fact that he was the leader of the rebellion. At the end of December 1905, well before the opening of his court martial, he had written a letter detailing his desired burial arrangements. In this testament he made a number of requests designed to perpetuate his memory and the revolutionary struggle he represented. First, he asked that his body be handed over to Sevastopol workers for burial, and that they should be 'full masters of the ceremony', as he was 'their deputy and carried this title with honour'. Secondly, he wished that 'representatives of all Sevastopol's educational establishments' be present at his funeral, as 'children trusted me greatly', together with a plea for a school orchestra. Thirdly, he desired to be 'buried next to the common grave of the unlucky victims of the executions during the night of 18/19 October near the prison building', as he had made an oath to them and wished his body to be put to rest at that place. Fourthly, he wished that 'everything should be in red, including the coffin shroud; nothing should be in black'. Finally, and most defiantly, Schmidt requested that if the city of Sevastopol should allocate money for a monument, then it should follow his design. Specifically, he desired that it should form a rock inscribed with his oath, on which should be placed an anchor and a flagstaff with a red flag made of tin. 'I raised the banner of revolution of the Russian fleet, who stayed loyal to the people', he declared, 'let this flag of freedom fly at my grave'. In conclusion, he modestly observed that 'such a monument won't cost much'.[51]

At the end of his court martial, having received his sentence of execution by firing squad, Schmidt summed up his final thoughts. He wrote them down for his defence counsel to preserve for posterity:

In my last minute I shall think:
Long live the Russian Tsar!
Long live the coming people's representatives.
Long live rejuvenated, mighty, happy and free Russia![52]

The executions of the mutineers took place at 0845 hours on 19 March 1906 on the small Black Sea island of Berezan opposite the fortress of Ochakov, a location chosen presumably to preclude any mass demonstrations of protest taking place. Unsurprisingly, the authorities ignored every aspect of Schmidt's letter regarding his funeral arrangements. He and his co-mutineers were buried without ceremony in unmarked graves on the island – a Soviet-era monument now marks the isolated spot.

The reaction to news of the executions was mixed. Certainly the authorities feared protests, and warned that strikes, demonstrations or even church services about Schmidt would be stopped, and any participants would be taken to court. Yet newspaper accounts confirm that some demonstrations linked to the execution of Schmidt did take place, together with calls for the abolition of the death penalty. Other papers in the immediate aftermath of the executions questioned whether Schmidt, as a 'mentally sick person' – he had indeed a history of mental illness – would have been executed in 'normal times'.[53] Opinions seemed to harden, however, as the months wore on. Significantly, the *Sevastopol Gazette* quoted a critical opinion piece from the Simferopol newspaper *Trud* (Work) in August 1906:

> Many heroes were born in the revolution. But we cannot call the traitor Schmidt a hero – he spoilt the lives of hundreds of people. He ran away from the *Ochakov* when under shellfire, leaving those whom he had initially led. Revolution gives birth to heroes but this is how she prepares for death.[54]

Soviet writers would later claim that had it not been for the solidarity of Sevastopol's sailors, soldiers and workers with the arrested mutineers, together with the agitation of the RSDLP, the courts of the tsarist government would have awarded a much larger number of death penalties. According to a modern account sympathetic to Schmidt, the authorities cracked down on the mutineers 'brutally'.[55] This assertion warrants challenge. Had the boot been on the other foot, then one might suppose that a revolutionary government would have treated the mutineers equally, if not far more, severely. The evidence for such a supposition lies in the much more pitiless manner in which the Bolsheviks suppressed the Kronstadt mutiny of March 1921 – ironically one in which the crew of the battleship *Sevastopol* took part against the Red government. While historians argue over the exact number of captured sailors executed after the fall of Kronstadt to the Bolsheviks, it is probably safe to state that some five hundred rebels were shot without trial immediately, and 2,000 more subsequently. To put this into context, over 10,000 Red troops had been killed in assaulting the Baltic fortress.[56]

The 1905 revolutionaries sought to avenge the prosecution of the *Ochakov* mutineers. Even before the execution of the ringleaders, they tried to kill Chukhnin. Although he survived a first, fumbled, assassination attempt by the female socialist E. A. Izmailovich (whom he ordered to be shot on the spot) on 9 February 1906, his luck ran out six months later. A sailor, Ya. C. Akimov (assisted by the admiral's gardener, F. G. Shatenko) shot and mortally wounded Chukhnin at his dacha at Holland Bay, on Sevastopol's northern side, on 11 July

1906. He succumbed to his wounds that night in the naval hospital situated at St Paul's Cape on the other side of the roadstead. Chukhnin, the ruthless suppressor of both the *Potemkin* and *Ochakov* mutinies, was buried with full naval honours at St Vladimir's Cathedral on 14 July 1906, being laid to rest not far from the crypt of his far more illustrious predecessors – Admirals Lazarev, Kornilov, Istomin and Nakhimov.[57]

In some ways, the Russian Navy formed the vanguard of the 1905 revolution. In the period 1905–07, no fewer than sixty ships were involved in various mutinous activities. Of these, those relating to the *Potemkin* and *Ochakov* are the most famous. Less well known is the mutiny aboard the armoured cruiser *Pamyat Azova* of the Baltic Fleet, whose crew rebelled off Reval (Tallinn) in 1906. Mutinies affected virtually all the fleets and major bases of the navy: Kronstadt, Sevastopol, Sveaborg and Vladivostok. That no fewer than '36,736 predominantly revolutionary-minded sailors were discharged from all fleets' in the years 1905–06 illustrates the scale of the problem facing the Russian Navy.[58] With such a statistic in mind, it is tempting to exaggerate the importance of the navy's contribution to the revolution, particularly if too much reliance is based on Soviet, or Soviet-leaning, historical sources. Many ships' crews in Sevastopol and in other naval bases remained throughout this period steadfastly loyal to the government and their Tsar. Specifically, when the obedience of local army units was put to the test during the *Ochakov* mutiny, most soldiers fought for the Tsar rather than joining the mutineers. Nicholas II acknowledged this fact in a telegram he sent to the commander of 7th Army Corps on 19 November (2 December) 1905, in which he expressed his 'gratitude for the energetic and swift suppression of the mutiny'. More particularly, he ordered Baron A. N. Meller-Zakomelskiy to inform the Belostok Regiment, 'who had sealed with blood their loyalty to duty' that the Tsar returned to them his 'confidence and goodwill', and that the unit could 'retain its colours'. Further, he instructed, 'pass it on to all the units [concerned], who remained loyal to their oath and duty to their superiors, my sincere gratitude for their glorious service'.[59]

Both the *Potemkin* and *Ochakov* mutinies are highlighted in the museum of the Black Sea Fleet in Sevastopol: models of the two famous warships are accorded a place of honour. In accordance with the Bolshevik (later Communist) practice of singling out leading revolutionaries, their heroic deeds would become instruments of propaganda. Hence many towns across the former Soviet Union have streets named after Schmidt, including Sevastopol. The Ulitsa Schmidta runs off the north-western corner of Ushakov Square at the junction with one of the city's main thoroughfares, the Bolshaya Morskaya. Meanwhile, Schmidt's old family home in the Ukrainian coastal city of Berdyansk on the Sea of Azov, houses a museum still open to the public. Hence notwithstanding the end of the

Soviet Union, Schmidt is still remembered as a martyr and revolutionary hero.

The 1905 revolution constituted in many ways a dress rehearsal for the twin revolutions of 1917 that would remove the Russian monarchy, subsequently end Russia's involvement in the First World War and lead to the establishment of the Soviet State.[60] As might be expected, Lenin commentated on the *Ochakov* mutiny as it was unfolding. In an article entitled 'The Armed Forces and the Revolution', which appeared on 16 (29) November 1905 in the Bolshevik newspaper *Novaya Zhizn* (New Life), he observed:

> The insurrection at Sevastopol continues to spread. Things are coming to a head. The sailors and soldiers who are fighting for freedom are removing their officers.... The squadron has refused to put to sea and threatens to shell the town if any attempt is made to suppress the insurgents ... the term fixed for the sailors' surrender expires today, the 15th. We are thus on the eve of the decisive moment. The next few days— perhaps hours—will show whether the insurgents will win a complete victory, whether they will be defeated, or whether a bargain will be struck.

Lenin then emphasised the wider importance of the events occurring in Sevastopol for Russia's armed forces, including those protesting in St Petersburg, as they signified:

> the complete collapse of the old slavish order ... the system which transformed soldiers into armed machines and made them instruments for the suppression of the slightest striving after freedom.... [Thus] the Sevastopol events are neither isolated nor accidental. Let us not speak of former attempts at open insurrection in the Navy and in the Army. Let us compare the sparks at St. Petersburg with the fire at Sevastopol.... The soldiers stationed in St. Petersburg want better rations, better clothing, better quarters, higher pay, a reduction in the term of service and shorter daily drill.

Lenin was equally keen to stress the more fundamental struggle to achieve greater respect for soldiers (and by extension, to sailors), and that they should be afforded basic human rights. Hence he highlighted that the 'more prominent' among the demands of the protestors in St Petersburg were none other than 'those which could be presented only by the civic-minded soldier'. These included:

> ... the right to attend in uniform at all meetings, 'on an equal footing with all other citizens', the right to read *all* newspapers and keep them in the barracks, freedom of conscience, equal rights for all nationalities, complete abolition of all deference to rank outside the barracks, the abolition of officers' batmen, the

abolition of courts martial, jurisdiction for the civil courts over all military offences, the right to present complaints collectively, the right to defend oneself against any attempt on the part of a superior to strike a subordinate. Such are the principal demands of the soldiers in St. Petersburg.

'These demands', he concluded, showed 'that a great part of the Army is already at one with the men of Sevastopol who have risen for liberty'.[61] Although Lenin's hopes for 1905 were dashed, they were to be realised in full measure in 1917.

Violent mutiny and civic unrest, whether on the ships of the Black Sea Fleet, in Sevastopol's army barracks or on the city's streets, had turned into an armed uprising. While they were unsuccessful, as were other mutinies at Kronstadt and elsewhere, the *Potemkin* and *Ochakov* mutinies would provide inspiration for the second Bolshevik revolution of twelve years later. Although the forward march of revolutionary socialism had been checked in 1905, the course of Russian history was being changed irrevocably. It would require the particular military stresses and economic strains of the First World War to bring about the final break with the old Russian tsarist order; economic, political and social life across the nation would never be the same again.

Several prominent reminders of this tumultuous period remain: various monuments in Sevastopol commemorate the naval mutiny and associated revolutionary action in 1905. A fisherman discovered the site of Schmidt's burial place on Berezan Island some years after his execution. In May 1917, in the wake of the Russian 'February' revolution, as discipline in the Black Sea Fleet once more began to break down, sailors demanded that the remains of the executed ringleaders of the *Ochakov* be laid to rest in the crypt of St Vladimir's Cathedral in the place of the famous nineteenth-century admirals. Without acceding directly to this demand, the beleaguered commander-in-chief, Vice Admiral A. V. Kolchak, ordered that the reinterment should instead take place in the Cathedral of the Intercession of the Holy Virgin. Ironically, Sevastopol's second cathedral had only been consecrated in the revolutionary year of 1905. Kolchak would shortly become one of the main leaders of the 'White', anti-Bolshevik, cause during the Russian Civil War.

Schmidt's remains were to be moved yet again as a result of the 'October' revolution of 1917. On 14 November 1923, the Soviet authorities finally laid Schmidt to rest in Sevastopol's Communards Cemetery. In accordance with his wishes, a monument 'to the Leaders of the Armed Uprising in November 1905', marks his grave, which matches his desired design. The other leaders of the mutiny are buried elsewhere in the same cemetery. Memorial plaques to Schmidt and to the mutiny he led are to be found on the site of his former house, and on the embankment of Primorsky Boulevard opposite the Monument to the

Scuttled Ships. The latter states: 'Here on 28 November 1905, tsarist troops brutally shot the revolutionary sailors of the "Ochakov" cruiser'. A much larger bronze bas-relief commemorating the armed uprising in November 1905 stands in the Korabelnaya district of Sevastopol near the Lazarev naval barracks at the edge of the main road leading down to the Southern Bay and main railway station. Its motifs represent the main participants of the revolutionary activity in Sevastopol: a 'soldier, a worker and three sailors standing up in arms under a waving flag'.[62]

Although the naval mutiny was over, civil unrest and rebellious activity remained. The Tsar's prestige had been undermined, as had his government's control been weakened. Despite a widespread crackdown by the authorities, acts of disobedience and terror continued all over Russia: the streets of Sevastopol were not immune from these after-shocks of revolution. On 27 May 1906, for example, two individuals associated with the Revolutionary Socialist Party tried to murder Lieutenant General V. S. Nepliuev, the commander of Sevastopol fortress, at a military parade marking the tenth anniversary of the Nicholas II's coronation. Although the bomb thrown at the general's feet by the sixteen-year-old Nikolay Makorov failed to explode, that of his accomplice, Ivan Frolov, did, killing the general and six bystanders, and injuring thirty-seven others.[63]

ON THE EVE OF THE FIRST WORLD WAR

In addition to its historic role as the main base of the Black Sea Fleet, by 1914 Sevastopol had become a major Russian military town with a considerable army garrison. The principal fighting formations remained the 49th (Brest) and the 50th (Belostok) Infantry Regiments, each of four battalions, which together comprised the 1st Brigade of the 13th Infantry Division. Also stationed in Sevastopol were the divisional headquarters and the 13th Artillery Brigade, which provided fire support to the division. The 13th Infantry was one of the two divisions of 7th Army Corps, which was subordinated in peacetime to Headquarters Odessa Military District. The fighting strength of this division was 14,180 rifles, forty-eight field guns and thirty-two machine guns (equating to two per battalion).

In time of war, 7th Corps with its divisions would be grouped together into numbered field armies. According to Russia's latest mobilisation scheme in 1914 (Plan No. 19A), 7th Corps was destined for the newly designated Eighth Army under the command of General A. A. Brusilov that would be deployed as part of the South-Western Front.[64] Following the outbreak of the First World War, 7th Corps would take a prominent role in the Russian Army's advance into Austro-Hungarian Galicia.

As a 'second class' fortress, Sevastopol was also home to several units of static fortress troops. These comprised: two artillery battalions; a sapper company; two submarine mining companies; a military telegraph company; a pigeon station and an engineer depot.[65] The city also contained a number of other miscellaneous units and organisations, including an army gymnastics and fencing school, a marine battalion and the 24th Crimea Frontier Brigade – the latter a formation of the Special Corps of Frontier Guards subordinated to the Finance Ministry in St Petersburg.[66]

A new fighting service was also being founded in the years immediately before the First World War. Sevastopol became one of Russia's centres for the development of army and naval aviation. A flying school was opened at Kacha, to the north of the city, which was also the base of the army's 2nd Aviation Company. The Russian Navy also started experimenting with seaplanes, including those of American (Curtiss) design and Russian models developed by Grigorovich, which were soon to become very useful to the Black Sea Fleet.

Notwithstanding the considerable army presence, Sevastopol remained first and foremost one of Russia's principal naval bases and the main arsenal of the Black Sea Fleet. After the profound shocks of 1905, the Russian Navy enjoyed a brief renaissance. The investment made particularly in the five years immediately preceding the First World War was remarkable. Whereas routine government spending on the army increased by 25 per cent between 1909 and 1914, the navy budget multiplied by over two and a half times. Very significant additional grants of money were also made to the navy during this period. In comparison to Germany, Russia was becoming a significant naval power again. As historian Norman Stone has noted, 'in 1907–8 she had spent £9,000,000 on her navy, to the Germans' £14,000,000; but by 1913–14 she was spending £24,000,000 to the Germans' £23,000,000'.[67] Thus Germany was not only fighting a naval race against Britain, but also one with Russia.

Although the bulk of Russian naval spending was directed to the Baltic, the Black Sea Fleet also greatly benefited from this pre-war surge of investment. The goal for the southern fleet was that it should become 'half as strong again as the combined fleets of the neighbouring states of Turkey, Bulgaria and Romania'.[68] There was also the risk of Austrian ships supporting the Turkish fleet, should both countries be in a state of war with Russia. Against this strategic requirement, Stone (in his otherwise masterly study of the Eastern Front of the First World War) is surely mistaken in asserting that the Russian naval authorities 'blundered between the Baltic and the Black Sea, ending up with two half-navies'.[69] Geographic and political realities compelled Russia to divide her naval effort in this manner and to maintain two major fleets. Furthermore, as Stone states, 'plans were going ahead for seizure by naval coup of Constantinople and the

Straits'.[70] Russia therefore desired to increase her offensive naval power in the Black Sea, so re-establishing the maritime preponderance she had last enjoyed in the decades before the Crimean War.

Turkey did not remain passive as Russia steadily increased her naval presence in the Black Sea: a naval race between these powers then ensued. Attempting to steal a march on the Russians, in 1911 the Ottoman government ordered a dreadnought from a British shipyard. At that time, the Russian Navy had yet to receive in service any examples of this new type of battleship, which took its name from HMS *Dreadnought* of 1906. This revolutionary vessel was the first all 'big gun' battleship, which, together with its steam turbine propulsion, gave it impressive advantages of firepower and speed over all previous designs. Russia's first four dreadnoughts, laid down in June 1909, were all destined for her Baltic Fleet. The first of that class, the *Gangut*, launched in 1911, did not enter service until 1915. Meanwhile, Turkey had procured a 'super-dreadnought' of the latest British type, armed with ten 13.5-inch (340mm) guns. Launched at the Vickers yard at Barrow-in-Furness in 1913, she was named the *Reşadiye (Reshadieh)*. At a stroke, therefore, the Russian Black Sea Fleet's warships would be outclassed. Her three most modern pre-dreadnoughts were not only under-armed in comparison with only four 12-inch (305mm) guns apiece, but also were insufficiently armoured to prevent penetration by 13.5-inch shells.[71] The Russians' disadvantage was set to increase in 1914 when Turkey purchased a second dreadnought from Brazil, then nearing completion at the Armstrong Whitworth yard at Newcastle-upon-Tyne. Although smaller than the *Reshadieh*, the newly acquired *Sultan Osman I* was still a very strongly armed ship, equipped with fourteen 12-inch guns. Both battleships were due to enter service in the Turkish Navy during the second half of 1914.[72]

Responding to the challenges presented by both Germany and Turkey, new leadership, and above all, fresh investment in materiel, was soon making its mark within the Russian Navy. As the British *Navy Annual* of 1913 proclaimed, its 'progress during the past twelve months is probably more worthy of notice than that of any other foreign navy'. On the eve of the First World War, the Russian Navy was on the road to recovery but had yet to achieve full efficiency. An ambitious new shipbuilding programme, supported by a 'complete reorganisation of the national resources for naval construction' was put under way. 'Equally sound' were 'the changes which are being introduced in the training and organisation of the *personnel*'.[73] Although the Russian Baltic Fleet was due to receive its first dreadnoughts in 1914, the next batch of modern battleships was destined for the Black Sea. At the outbreak of the First World War, however, the *Imperatritsa Mariya*, *Imperator Alexander III* and *Ekaterina II*[74], each to be armed with twelve 12-inch guns in comparison with *Potemkin*'s four, were still under construction in the new yards specially built for them at Nikolayev. Laid down in 1911–12, these powerful warships of 22,960-tonne displacement apiece were not due to join the fleet at Sevastopol until 1915, and might not be fully operational until early 1916.[75] As we shall see, the Russians' lack of modern capital ships in the Black Sea was to prove a critical shortcoming at the start of the coming war.

A balanced fleet required more types of vessel than battleships alone. In the 1900s, the Nikolayev yards were also very busy building cruisers and destroyers for service in the Black Sea; in addition, the first classes of submarines appeared, including a novel type of submersible minelayer – the *Krab* launched in 1912. In the summer of 1914, the Black Sea Fleet comprised: six battleships (*Evstafi* (1911), *Ioann Zlatoust* (1910), *Georgii Pobedonosets* (1893), *Panteleimon* (1902), *Rostislav* (1900) and *Sinop* (1890)); two cruisers (*Kagul*, the former *Ochakov* (1905), and its sister ship *Pamyat Merkuriya* (1907)); eighteen destroyers and seven submarines.[76]

Regardless of all the material investment being injected, all was not well within the Russian Navy's personnel despite the reforms made following the 1905 *Potemkin* and *Ochakov* mutinies. As the *Navy Annual* of 1913 revealed, 'trouble [has] recurred in the Black Sea, where a mutinous spirit was disclosed, and stringent measures were adopted'.[77] This comment understates the extent to which subversive activity existed in the fleet during 1912, in which a planned mutiny was 'forestalled only by hours, and several instigators, after trial by court martial, faced the firing squad'.[78] Two years before, Sevastopol's sailors had gone on strike in solidarity with dockyard workers, who had downed tools when repairing the battleship *Rostislav*. In response, the authorities had satisfied the workers' demands for better pay and improved the diet of naval crews. Headquarters Black Sea Fleet determined, however, that a much firmer response would be needed in the face of any future unrest. In the spring of 1912, Bolshevik elements within the ships harboured at Sevastopol had started plotting an armed mutiny, which was due to break out on the *Ioann Zlatoust*. Somehow word got out: naval police acted immediately to forestall any insurrection. Thirty-six sailors were arrested on this battleship alone while approximately 500 men were rounded up on other ships. Six of the ringleaders were executed by firing squad.[79] As ensuing events would soon demonstrate, the Black Sea Fleet would need to be at the top of its professional game in the forthcoming war and could ill afford such indiscipline and dissipation of fighting power.

A brief interlude of sunny calm in Sevastopol preceded the coming storm. Since the arrival of the railway, the tsars were frequent visitors to the city, not least to inspect its military facilities and the fleet's ships of the line before cruising round Crimea's beautiful southern coast to stay in their summer palaces at Yalta. The city's newspapers describe one such four-day event in mid-August 1913, a highlight of the imperial tour of Russia to commemorate the 300th anniversary of the Romanovs. It proved a glorious episode in the royal family's last golden summer from the moment the imperial train arrived on the 9th until the party departed Sevastopol harbour for Yalta aboard the royal yacht *Standart* on the 13th.

The Black Sea Fleet and the army garrison on shore fired a series of salutes in honour of their sovereign. Overhead, pilots in their brand new flying machines provided a spectacular air display. Nicholas II visited the Fraternal Cemetery on the northern side and Sevastopol's naval hospital; he reviewed the battleships and cruisers of the fleet, and inspected the troops of the Brest Regiment and the 13th Artillery Brigade, all smartly arrayed. The Emperor also took the opportunity to see the sights at Balaklava, Inkerman and Chersonesos. Members of the family took in other destinations: young Alexey (Nicholas II's heir) was shown round the Malakhov while Grand Duchess Olga visited the Panorama museum.[80] Sevastopol put on the best possible show for the Russian sovereign: as the Emperor himself recalled, 'the city drowned in flowers, bunting and flags; in the evening, fireworks illuminated the sky'.[81]

Despite the violent unrest associated with the revolution of 1905 and its aftermath, the celebrations in 1913 in Sevastopol and across Russia reflected a genuine, popular devotion to the Russian crown. There had been some political progress and the economy was booming. Thus there was no certainty of another revolution occurring. Tragically, this public rejoicing happened just a year before the onset of the First World War. Widespread disillusionment over the heavy losses and incompetent war management led to the revolutions of 1917. Under extreme shock, the foundations of Russia's imperial power proved insufficiently deep to prevent the collapse of the tsarist government, and the subsequent murder of the royal family in the summer of 1918. By then a devastating civil war, which lasted until 1921, was already in full swing.

CHAPTER 10

WORLD WAR TO CIVIL WAR

'[The Goeben*] was steaming on an unobstructed course for the Dardanelles, carrying with her for the peoples of the Near and Middle East more slaughter, more misery and more ruin than has ever before been borne within the compass of one ship.'*

Winston Churchill[1]

THE *GOEBEN* AND THE START OF THE FIRST WORLD WAR

Winston Churchill's remarks about this infamous German battlecruiser, although crowned with his habitual hyperbole, contained a certain irony. The shelling of Sevastopol by the warship *Goeben* under a Turkish flag on 29 October 1914 triggered a chain of events that affected the scale and course of the First World War. It provoked, as intended in Berlin, Emperor Nicholas II into declaring war on the Ottoman Empire. It led to the associated dissipation of Russian military effort in the Caucasus towards her traditional enemy, which otherwise would have been available, at least in part, to fight German and Austro-Hungarian forces on Russia's Western Front.[2] Additionally, the Ottoman government's closure of the Turkish Straits, which blocked immensely valuable grain exports from Black Sea ports such as Odessa, wreaked enormous economic damage in Russia.

Although Turkey had signed a secret treaty of defensive alliance with Germany on 2 August 1914, she was not in a rush to join the Central Powers in any war against the Triple Entente of Britain, France and Russia.[3] The unexpected appearance of the *Goeben* at Constantinople on 16 August 1914 following its dramatic flight from the Royal Navy in the Mediterranean, however, provided a powerful stimulus to the pro-German war lobby in Turkey at a critical moment. This act, and not least the subsequent bombardment of Sevastopol, cannot be entirely divorced from the deeds of the British First Lord of the Admiralty – Winston Churchill. His decision on 28 July 1914 to requisition two Turkish battleships nearing completion in British shipyards, the *Reshadieh* and the *Sultan Osman I*, enraged the Turkish government and nation, whose people had paid dearly for these dreadnoughts through public subscription. While the Royal Navy had gained in the process two further warships (renamed HMS *Erin* and HMS *Agincourt* respectively), this painful affront to Turkish pride and sensibility helped sway the Ottoman government into actively supporting Germany as opposed to remaining passive at the beginning of the First World War.

The *Goeben*, commissioned in 1912 and displacing 22,976 tonnes formed the mainstay of the German Navy's *Mittelmeerdivision* (Mediterranean division), in which she was supported by the light cruiser *Breslau* (4,570 tonnes). In fact, the *Goeben* represented the sole capital ship of the *Kaiserliche Marine* (German Imperial Navy) in the region, albeit a very powerful one. A modern Moltke-class battlecruiser, she was armed with ten 280mm (11-inch) guns, benefited from very good armour protection and compartmentalisation, and enjoyed a top speed exceeding 25 knots – indeed, she had achieved 28 knots on her sea trials. With these characteristics the *Goeben* was superior in both speed and survivability to the three 12-inch gun British battlecruisers that formed the main striking power of the Mediterranean Fleet: *Indefatigable* (18,800 tonnes); *Indomitable* and *Inflexible* (each of 17,652 tonnes displacement).[4]

Goeben's task before the First World War had been to fly the German flag at various Mediterranean ports, exercising naval diplomacy through the very visible demonstration of maritime power. Her war role, however, appeared clear enough. On the outset of any hostilities between France and Germany, it was presumed that the *Goeben* would attempt to interdict French transports carrying the XIX (Colonial) Corps of three divisions from North Africa to France. Equally, it was the principal task of the British and French Mediterranean Fleets to protect them. As Barbara Tuchman noted in her classic study of the opening phase of the First World War, *The Guns of August*, 'the presence or absence of an entire army corps from its designated place in the line could be decisive upon the French plan of battle, and the war, as both sides believed, would be determined by the fate of France in the opening clash with Germany.' German priorities for the *Goeben*, however, would later change when Berlin determined 'the need to bring every possible pressure upon the reluctant Turks to declare war'.[5]

The escape of the *Goeben* during the opening days of the First World War, which was to have such disastrous cumulative consequences for the Allied cause in that conflict, is mired in controversy. Notwithstanding the assassination of the Austrian Archduke Franz Ferdinand at Sarajevo at the hands of the Serb terrorist Gavrilo Princip on 28 June 1914, and the resultant gathering storm of war that spread from the Balkans across Europe, all seemed quiet in the Mediterranean and Black Seas that high summer. Routine naval training and port visits continued: the Austrian, British, French and Italian fleets remained on a peace footing, as did the *Mittelmeerdivision* under the command of Rear Admiral Wilhelm Souchon. During the second half of July 1914 *Goeben* underwent essential maintenance to her troublesome boilers in the friendly Austro-Hungarian naval port of Pola (now Croatian Pula), near the head of the Adriatic.[6]

The rush to war took place in the last few days of July and the first days of August 1914, driven by a series of mobilisations and counter-mobilisations, whose combined momentum proved unstoppable. In brief summary, Austria–Hungary started the process with its mobilisation against Serbia on 25 July, and declared war on the 28th. In response, Russia ordered a partial ('precautionary') mobilisation of its south-western military districts against the Hapsburg Empire on the 29th. On the same day, Germany started mobilising her army, and on the 31st Russia began her full mobilisation. The slide towards a general European war accelerated on 1 August when Germany declared war on Russia while both France and Belgium began to mobilise.

Following the declaration of war by Germany on France on 3 August, Souchon bombarded the French North African ports of Bône and Phillippeville the following day. It might have been expected (and this was certainly Churchill's wish) that the powerful British Mediterranean Fleet under command of Sir Archibald Berkeley ('Arky-Barky') Milne would have engaged and sunk the *Goeben* and *Breslau* once Britain and Germany were at war. Yet Churchill's ambiguous directions to the British Mediterranean Fleet – over the head of the First Sea Lord and Chief of Naval Staff, Prince Louis of Battenberg – only added confusion to an already unclear and delicate situation. Churchill's instruction of 30 July 1914, written five days *before* Britain declared war on Germany, typifies his meddling approach:

> Your first task should be to aid the French in transportation of their African army corps by covering and if possible bringing into action individual fast German ships, particularly the Goeben, which may interfere with that transportation.... Except in combination with the French as part of general battle, do not at this

stage be brought to action against superior forces. The speed of your squadrons is sufficient to enable you to choose your moment. You must husband your force at the outset and we shall hope later to reinforce the Mediterranean.[7]

In the event, Souchon's plucky leadership and guile in deceiving his opponents as to his intentions as to both course and purpose outclassed the hesitant response by Milne, whose force included the three I-class battlecruisers. Although he enjoyed an overall superiority in available firepower, no opportunity arose for the British admiral to engage his German foes in a decisive action. The outcome of such a battle, however, would not necessarily have been a foregone conclusion. At the battle of Jutland on 31 May 1916, the fight between the German battlecruiser SMS *Von Der Tann* (a sister ship of the *Goeben*) and HMS *Indefatigable* resulted in the latter vessel being sunk by shellfire within fourteen minutes and without having inflicted any damage on her opponent.[8]

The details of the dramatic flight of the *Goeben* and *Breslau* to the Dardanelles can be briefly told. Having left Pola, Souchon sailed down the Adriatic with the *Goeben* on 30 July, anchoring off Brindisi on 1 August, where the battlecruiser was joined by the *Breslau*. Refused coal there, the German ships made for Messina, where German merchant ships could supply them with the much-needed fuel. Partially re-fuelled, after midnight on the 2nd, Souchon quitted the Sicilian port and headed for the French Algerian ports of embarkation on the North African coast. While the *Goeben* shelled Philippeville and the *Breslau* struck Bône on the morning of the 4th, two of Milne's battlecruisers, the *Indefatigable* and *Indomitable*, were steaming westwards in an effort to intercept the German ships. When *Indomitable* sighted the *Goeben* at 1034 hours, the latter and the *Breslau* were already sailing *eastwards* following their brief bombardment actions. So the British and German warships passed each other in opposite directions; with no state of war yet existing between the two nations, fire was not opened on this last day of peace. As quickly as possible, the British ships turned about and a chase ensued.[9]

Although none of the battlecruisers involved could achieve her best speed, *Goeben* made good use of her 2–3-knot advantage while thrashing her delicate boilers in the process. During the afternoon of the 4th, Churchill had confusingly cancelled the authorisation he had given the day before allowing the engagement of the *Goeben* should she attack French transports. Yet the French ships were not yet at sea. By 2100 hours on the 4th, the Royal Navy ships lost sight of the *Goeben* and *Breslau* and the pursuit was broken off. The British ships returned to Malta to refuel. At midnight, Britain declared war against Germany on account of its violation of Belgian neutrality. Now the constraints on Milne's force were lifted. Naval aviation being in its infancy, however, the Mediterranean Fleet lacked the necessary means either to spot or to slow the evading German ships from the air, let alone undertake such an operation at night. Thus no attempt could have been made to bomb or torpedo the *Goeben* in a manner similar to the disabling of the *Bismarck* by a Swordfish from the aircraft carrier HMS *Ark Royal* on 26 May 1941. In August 1914, the only reliable way to stop the *Goeben* and *Breslau* was by resolute surface action. Meanwhile, because the German ships had been steaming so fast, they already required more coal: accordingly, Souchon returned to Messina to refuel on the 5th.

The German admiral needed to be informed of his next destination urgently, as every hour's delay would benefit the Royal Navy, who were surely converging on Sicily. The news from the Naval General Staff in Berlin on the morning of the 6th, however, was doubly discouraging. First, his intended port of call at Constantinople was 'not yet possible for various reasons'; secondly, Austria, despite declaring war on Russia that day, would not commit to supporting Souchon in the Mediterranean for risk of an engagement with the Italian, French or British navies – states with whom she was not yet in conflict. France and Great Britain declared war on Austria–Hungary on 12 August 1914. In a remarkable example of decentralised 'mission command', Berlin allowed Souchon to decide for himself where to head. He determined to set course for Constantinople, arguing:

> It was impossible for me to remain in the Mediterranean in face of the crushing superiority of the enemy and total lack of means of subsistence.... I did not want to enter the Adriatic and be dependent on the Austrians. Thus, I firmly decided to enter the Dardanelles, if necessary against the will of the Turks, to carry the war into the Black Sea. I hope to carry the Turks with me in a war against their traditional enemy, the Muscovites.[10]

While Souchon's force took on coal, the Royal Navy missed a golden opportunity to bottle up the *Goeben* and *Breslau* in Messina's harbour. Although Milne's battlecruisers were not permitted to engage their opponents in neutral Italian waters, they could have attempted to block both ends of the Messina Straits in an effort to prevent the German force from escaping. Yet other than the cruiser HMS *Gloucester* guarding the southern exit, no British ships were lying in wait. Milne's three battlecruisers remained uncommitted at Malta: the decisive moment had passed. As a result, Souchon was able to head into the Eastern Mediterranean during the morning of 6 August unmolested, with the *Gloucester* shadowing but safely out of range of the *Goeben*'s guns.[11]

On 7 August, a British cruiser squadron under the command of Rear Admiral Ernest Troubridge, steaming near the mouth of the Adriatic, located but failed to engage the *Goeben* on its flight towards the Dardanelles. As well as being slower and less well protected, his four ships (the 9.2-inch gun armoured cruisers HMS *Defence*, *Duke of Edinburgh*, *Black Prince* and *Warrior*) were out-gunned and out-ranged by the German battlecruiser. While strictly speaking Troubridge followed Churchill's orders in 'avoiding a superior force', he was later to be court-martialled for his decision not to attack the *Goeben*. In similar circumstances during the Second World War a force of three British cruisers took on the German pocket battleship the *Admiral Graf Spee* at the battle of the river Plate on 13 December 1939. Ironically, twenty-five years before, and far less benignly, news of Troubridge's passivity in the Mediterranean is said to have urged Rear Admiral Sir Christopher Craddock to take undue risks at the battle of the Coronel on 1 November 1914, when he engaged a superior German squadron commanded by none other than Vice Admiral Graf Maximilian von Spee. The honour of the Royal Navy was to some extent restored when the captain of the *Gloucester*, Howard Kelly, briefly engaged the *Breslau* at long range during the afternoon of the 7th. But when the much more powerful *Goeben* opened fire, the lone British cruiser fell back to a safe distance. By the time the German ships rounded Cape Matapan and entered the Aegean, Kelly, with his ship running short on fuel and with strict orders from Milne not to proceed beyond Matapan, broke off the pursuit.[12]

The Royal Navy had fumbled embarrassingly in the opening days of the First World War at a most critical juncture. As a result, the *Goeben* and *Breslau* reached the safety of the Dardanelles unscathed on 10 August 1914. Their flight into the 'welcoming arms of neutral Turkey' constituted a major setback to the Royal Navy and to the British government, including the First Lord of the Admiralty, Winston Churchill. It led directly to Turkey's entry into the First World War and the ill-fated British–French expedition to Gallipoli in 1915.[13] Souchon's bold (and it must be stressed, lucky) handling of just two warships, the *Goeben* and *Breslau*, in the Mediterranean and Black Seas in 1914 demonstrates the extraordinary strategic leverage of seapower.[14]

Shortly following his arrival at Constantinople, Souchon, acting under orders of the German government, handed over his two ships to the Ottoman Empire. The symbolic transfer on 16 August 1914 was not quite as it seemed: although the *Goeben* became the nominal flagship of the Turkish Navy as the reflagged *Yavuz Sultan Selim*, it retained its German crew and command. Staged propaganda pictures showing German sailors happily wearing Turkish uniforms and fezzes did not fool anyone as to who commanded and crewed the *Goeben* and *Breslau*. Souchon, now the newly appointed commander-in-chief of the Turkish Navy, and fully in accordance with the momentous decision he had made at Messina, launched an audacious raid – under the cover of 'manoeuvres' – on 27 October 1914 into the Black Sea. This time, however, his decision was fully in line with Berlin's intent. Just prior to setting sail from Constantinople, Souchon had boasted to the Turkish Minister of War, Enver Pasha, that he 'would smash the Black Sea Fleet' – 'Ich werde die Schwarzseeflotte zerschmettern!'.[15] On 29 October, Souchon's two German warships, supported by several Turkish units, bombarded the Russian ports of Odessa, Sevastopol, Yalta, Feodosiya and Novorossiysk (see Map 11).

Souchon's operation was well planned.[16] Its successful execution, however, would depend on whether he could surprise the Russians sufficiently, and inflict a sufficient amount of damage, before his opponents could respond effectively. While there was always a risk that he might meet the Russian fleet at sea, Souchon was confident that the speed, gunnery and protection of the *Goeben* would give him a marked advantage in any engagement. He was less sanguine, perhaps, about the effectiveness of the Russian shore defences. Sevastopol, for example, was protected at the beginning of the First World War against naval attack by multiple coastal artillery batteries and minefields at sea. From Cape Lukul in the north to Cape Sarych in the south there were no fewer than twenty-nine stationary batteries armed with guns from 75 to 280mm calibre, thirty-six machine-gun nests and thirteen searchlight stations. Apart from the minefields already laid, there was a plan to lay a considerable number of electrically detonated mines on the approaches to Sevastopol.[17] The outcome of war, however, depends as much as on the decisions of men and women in the chain of command as on the capabilities of the machines and weapons they control. Souchon's opponent was Vice Admiral Andrey Eberhardt, who had commanded the Black Sea Fleet since 1911. He had not only successfully suppressed the mutiny of 1912, but also trained his crews hard in the immediate pre-war years, introducing new battle drills for the engagement of enemy ships. Despite criticism from some naval quarters on account of indecisiveness, he was soon to distinguish himself as one of the more competent Russian naval leaders during the First World War. The defence of Sevastopol and the future of the Black Sea Fleet rested in Eberhardt's hands.

While the German and Turkish warships were setting out on their mission, the Black Sea Fleet was also preparing for war. During the evening of 27 October and in the course of the next day, Eberhardt had received reports from commercial shipping that the *Goeben* was at sea accompanied by a number of smaller vessels. With the exception of a number of minelayers *en route* to Yevpatoriya, and the *Prut* – another minelayer – heading for Yalta, the warships of the Black Sea Fleet were all moored in Sevastopol harbour. At 1730 hours on 28 October, Eberhardt received information from the Naval General Staff that Turkey – according to reliable sources – 'has decided to go to war immediately'. A half-flotilla of the remaining minelayers was placed at two hours' notice to go to sea; the battleships and cruisers were placed at three hours' notice; and all remaining ships at ten hours'. Command of the fleet was established on board the old battleship *Georgii Pobedonosets*. Coaling of the ships in harbour was completed by 2200 hours.[18]

The first hostile act of the conflict between Russia and Turkey took place at Odessa harbour in the early hours of 29 October 1914 when two Turkish destroyers, the *Muavenet* and the *Gairet*, torpedoed and sank the *Donets*, a Russian gunboat. Another such vessel, the *Kubanets*, was damaged by gunfire while the *Beshtau*, a minelayer, was set on fire. Eberhardt, awaiting details of enemy ship movements in his headquarters in Sevastopol, heard the news at 0415 hours by means of a radiogram sent from the duty ROPiT steamship in Odessa. Within an hour, his staff had alerted all the Russian naval installations and fortresses of the Black Sea Fleet command that the war had started. Meantime, the *Breslau* was already in action, laying a minefield in the Kerch Strait before joining the Turkish gunboat *Berk* in bombarding Novorossiysk harbour, sinking fourteen steamers and setting ablaze sixteen oil tanks. On the Crimean peninsula, a heavily armed Turkish light cruiser, the *Hamidiye*, shelled Feodosiya and Yalta harbours on the eastern coast, sinking a few commercial vessels and causing some damage to the ports.[19]

What then of the *Goeben*? Souchon had reserved his flagship, accompanied by two Turkish torpedo boats, the *Tashoz* and the *Samsun*, for the main attack on Sevastopol. As a preliminary measure, under cover of darkness the Turkish minelayer *Nilufer* dropped mines in the approaches to the main base of the Black Sea Fleet.[20] Yet by the time Souchon's striking force neared its objective in the first light of day, the Russians were on high alert and ready to engage on sight any approaching enemy warships. While there had been some confusion by the defenders as to the arming of the mine defences that protected the approaches to the Sevastopol roadstead, Souchon had already lost the vital element of surprise. In addition to the earlier warnings from Odessa, Russian coastal observation and communication posts strung along the Crimean coast had provided a series of sightings of a 'large vessel with multiple gun turrets' looming out through the morning mist. At 0612 hours, Russian minesweepers positively identified the ship as the *Goeben*, which was steaming directly towards Sevastopol 'at a distance of 35 cables' – approximately 6.5 kilometres. Sixteen minutes later (0628 hours), the coastal defence batteries on Sevastopol's northern side opened fire, together with one (No. 12) on the southern. In total, eight batteries with forty-four guns ranging in calibre from 152 mm to 280 mm engaged the German warships.[21]

Two minutes later, *Goeben* quickly returned fire with a series of five-gun salvoes from her main armament. The first fell in front of Battery No. 4; the second near the shore line; the third behind the battery, while the fourth landed even further behind without causing any damage. The *Goeben* then increased its range and shelled the main harbour and the infrastructure immediately adjoining the roadstead. Although no ships were sunk, one salvo splashed the *Panteleimon*. Russian luck held out when another salvo landed amongst a flotilla of minesweepers, but struck no vessel. If the Black Sea Fleet was not surprised by the German attack, the citizens of Sevastopol certainly were: no one in authority had thought of warning them. Contemporary accounts tell how 'suddenly shells were heard, window glass rattled and the residents awoke ... nobody had expected an enemy to appear; initially, all thought it was a mere training shoot, but the fire became more frequent and the sounds of the heavy guns grew louder and louder'. Other reports recorded that 'dockyard employees on their way to work in the port were frightened and rushed about the promenade', while 'women shrieked hysterically and were running around in different directions with fear in their eyes'.[22]

Several of *Goeben*'s shells exploded well ashore. One hit a coal store; another struck a railway embankment, destroying some track; a third burst on the hill above a dry dock showering debris on to the minelayer *Velikiy Knyaz Aleksey*. When a fourth round exploded on the promenade of the naval hospital near the venereal ward, it hit a number of unlucky patients who were viewing the bombardment – of these reckless spectators, two were killed and eight badly wounded. This last strike represented the *Goeben*'s most lethal result in its shelling of Sevastopol. Other reports of the bombardment refer to a shell hitting a school, destroying a classroom. Although no children were hurt (presumably because the shelling occurred before school started), a teacher who lived in the building was traumatised.[23]

At 0648 hours, Souchon decided to call off his bombardment on account of the mist still impeding visibility, and not least because of the intensive fire of the Russian shore batteries. He had made his point in attacking Sevastopol and striking at Russia's main base in the Black Sea. Altogether, the *Goeben* had expended forty-seven rounds of its main armament and twelve rounds of its secondary for little immediate, tangible effect other than to terrorise the inhabitants of Sevastopol and to give its defenders some useful target practice. Within a couple of minutes the German battlecruiser turned away, and slipped out of sight. The Russian shore batteries had fired off no fewer than 360 shells.[24] One of the batteries on the northern side managed to land three rounds on the *Goeben*; a shell that hit its funnel failed to explode. So the damage received on the German warship was only superficial. Likewise, there was little harm done to the Russian shore defences. An exception occurred at Battery No. 16, 'General Khrulev', located between the village of Uchkuyevka and the mouth of the river Belbek. During the course of the engagement with the *Goeben* an internal explosion destroyed one of the four 10-inch 1895 model guns of this battery, killing six and injuring eleven men, one of whom subsequently died of his wounds. Had it not been for the energetic efforts of Staff Captain Mironovich and his men, who extinguished the fire that threatened to engulf nearby ammunition, the casualty toll would have been much higher.[25] Other than the *Georgii Pobedonosets*, the Sevastopol's harbour guard ship, no warship of the Black Sea Fleet had opened fire during the action. As the *Goeben* quickly disappeared from view, the crew of this veteran battleship optimistically fired three rounds from her 6-inch bow guns; yet the range by then was far too great and the Russian shooting fell well short.[26]

Wisely, Eberhardt decided not to set his fleet immediately to sea and to pursue the *Goeben* – it would not only have proved a hopeless chase on account of the Russians' disadvantage in speed, but also an un-reconnoitred sortie out of Sevastopol might have run into a recently laid German minefield – perhaps as Souchon had intended. Later that day, however, a brief engagement did occur. Quite by chance, the *Goeben* met a small group of Russian ships including the *Prut* and three destroyers (large torpedo boats) led by the *Leitenant Pushchin*. When the *Goeben* opened fire, the commanding officer of the *Prut* proceeded to scuttle his ship – a prudent decision on account of her load of 110 mines. Surprisingly, rather than turning tail, the *Leitenant Pushchin* and the other two destroyers made an audacious torpedo run against the *Goeben* despite the great weight of fire being directed towards them. This seemingly suicidal attack was only broken off when two 150mm shells of *Goeben's* secondary armament scored direct hits on the *Leitenant Pushchin*. Yet the brief engagement had shown, as the Russian naval historian Nekrasov has stressed, 'the aggressive attitude of the Black Sea Fleet', an operational approach which Admiral Eberhardt was to demonstrate in ample quality during the months to come.[27]

While the physical damage inflicted on the Russian Black Sea Fleet and its base infrastructure at Sevastopol was insignificant, setting aside the more substantive destruction achieved at Novorossiysk, the slight to Russian national honour and reputation was immense. In response, Russia declared war on the Ottoman Empire on 2 November 1914. France and Britain followed suit on the 5th. In his report of 3 November to Kaiser Wilhelm II, Souchon proudly explained how he had convinced Enver Pasha to approve the operation against the Russian ports. He had gained the agreement, should the Turkish Minister of War be forced to state that the German admiral had conducted the bombardments purely on his own initiative, that the Bosporus would remain open to allow a withdrawal of the German ships. In describing the action, Souchon made a point of being highly disparaging of the performance of the Turkish ships involved, expressing contempt for their crews who had, 'almost without exception, shamefully failed'. A 'sufficient improvement' in performance, Souchon claimed, could not be achieved because the idleness of the Turkish sailors 'was too great'.

In stark contrast, he praised the 'professional joy, self-sacrifice, iron will and toughness of the trained German officers and men'.[28] Souchon's crews, yet to face the Russian Navy at sea, would soon be tested in action again.

MILITARY OPERATIONS AND IMPERIAL VISITS

Although Germany brought the war directly to Sevastopol's doorstep with the *Goeben's* bombardment on 29 October 1914, the city had already witnessed the departure of most of its army formations three months earlier, following the Russian mobilisation at the end of July. In accordance with the General Staff's initial deployment plans, the 13th Division of 7th Corps joined Brusilov's Eighth Army that was concentrated in the vicinity of Proskurov (now Khmelnytskyi), in western Ukraine. This was the southern-most of the four Russian armies deployed to face Austro-Hungarian forces. On the onset of active operations, as the right-hand formation of Eighth Army, 7th Corps took part in the rapid Russian advance over the river Gnila Lipa that forced the collapsing Austro-Hungarian Third Army on 2 September 1914 to abandon the city of Lemberg, which became Russian Lvov (and later, Ukrainian Lviv).[29] By this time, however, it was evident that a great many of Sevastopol's sons in the Brest and Belostok Regiments and the 13th Artillery Brigade would not return. Losses on this 'Eastern' Front (as in the West) during the opening period of war proved extraordinarily high: modern field artillery and machine guns broke up infantry formations neither organised nor trained to deal with such firepower.[30]

Following Russia's declaration of war on Turkey, the Black Sea Fleet was now free to conduct offensive operations. On 4 November, Eberhardt sortied out from Sevastopol. He planned to engage the *Goeben* by luring it on to a newly laid minefield off the Bosporus and by damaging Turkish installations at Zonguldak on the northern Anatolian coast. As coal from this port not only fuelled the Turkish Navy but also the city of Constantinople, it was to remain an important strategic target during the war and would be blockaded in due course. Meantime, although no major fleet action ensued, Russian warships sank three Turkish transports. On the same day Eberhardt's battle squadron returned to Sevastopol, the 7th, the *Breslau* bombarded the port of Poti on the Caucasian coast, an event which infuriated the Russian supreme headquarters, the *Stavka*, who deemed the protection of the Russian coastline to be Eberhardt's top priority. The commander-in-chief of the Black Sea Fleet, however, remained adamant that this task could only be met by the elimination of the most potent threat to Russian security – the *Goeben*.[31] The opportunity to achieve this goal came soon enough. On 15 November, Eberhardt steamed from Sevastopol bound for the Turkish port of Trebizond (Trabzon); having shelled this important supply base on the 16th, he set course back to Crimea. The following day Souchon departed Constantinople with the *Goeben* and *Breslau* and steered to intercept the Russian fleet south of Crimea. The clash desired by both sides took place just after noon on 18 November 1914 in bad weather about 30 kilometres south of Cape Sarych.

The sea battle off Cape Sarych is now an almost completely forgotten episode of the First World War's naval history.[32] Eberhardt's formation consisted of the *Evstafi*, on which he flew his flag, followed by his other pre-dreadnought battleships: *Ioann Zlatoust*, *Panteleimon*, *Tri Svyatitelya* and *Rostislav*. Very poor visibility impaired the firing of both sides, preventing at least two of the Russian ships from engaging. Notwithstanding this limitation, however, the very first salvo of the *Evstafi* struck the *Goeben*. The German ship concentrated her return fire on the Russian flagship, damaging it with four shells. The results of this brief engagement, which had lasted only fourteen minutes, were mixed. While the Russians had managed by a combination of superb gunnery and a measure of good luck to inflict considerable damage and casualties (thirteen killed and three wounded) on the *Goeben*, they had failed to bring more than a fraction of the firepower of the Black Sea's battleships to bear, largely down to the poor weather and a breakdown of communications. As a result, the German battlecruiser escaped to fight another day, but from then on Souchon would have to reckon with a Russian fleet that would be handled with audacity and competence. When the new Russian 'Empress' class dreadnoughts came into service in 1915, moreover, the tables would surely be turned decisively. Rather than the Black Sea Fleet being 'crushed', as the German admiral had idly boasted, the appropriate question was now: when would the *Goeben* and *Breslau* be sent to the bottom? In the meantime, the action off Cape Sarych provided a much needed 'tonic not only for the morale of the Black Sea Fleet but [also] for the Russian Navy'.[33] While the bombardment of Sevastopol on 29 October 1914 had been suitably avenged, with the recovery of professional confidence in the fleet could the mutinies and other revolutionary activities of 1905 and 1912 now be safely forgotten?

As the war dragged on the Eastern Front, Russian troops were also heavily engaged against Turkish forces in the Caucasus. Sevastopol's naval base remained very active as Admiral Eberhardt continued offensive operations to attack Turkish shipping in the Black Sea, along with continuing efforts to blockade the vital port of Zonguldak, and not least to seek a decisive engagement with the elusive *Goeben*. At the same time, Eberhardt's German counterpart, Souchon, attempted to find ways to harm Russian interests, by bombarding her ports such as Odessa again, and by seeking to locate and sink units of the Black Sea Fleet. These cat and mouse operations continued throughout 1915 and 1916 because neither force was strong enough to deny the Black Sea to the other. The scope of the Russian fleet's activities widened in the first part of 1915 with a series of diversionary bombardments of the Bosporus, designed to draw off Turkish effort from engaging the Allies in the Dardanelles, including the landings at Gallipoli on 25 April.

The entry into service of the *Imperatritsa Mariya* in the summer and her sister ship the *Imperatritsa Ekaterina Velikaya* at the end of 1915 increased the striking power of the fleet nand allowed the formation of two balanced task groups, each formed of a modern battleship, a cruiser and a squadron of new destroyers, together with a seaplane carrier. This novel type of ship had been introduced at the beginning of the year: the *Imperator Aleksandr I* and *Imperator Nikolay I* were converted cargo steamers that could carry each eight to nine aircraft. In addition, the light cruiser *Almaz* was converted to carry four seaplanes. A third task group contained the latest pre-dreadnoughts, supported by destroyers and a seaplane carrier.[34] The value of the new dreadnoughts was demonstrated on 9 January 1916 when the more heavily armed *Imperatritsa Ekaterina Velikaya* engaged and out-ranged the *Goeben*, which was forced to withdraw under the weight of the Russian battleship's fire – some '96 rounds from her 12-inch/52 calibre guns [which] achieved several straddles'.[35] There is little doubt that the success of the Black Sea Fleet and its arsenal at Sevastopol demonstrated good returns on Russia's considerable pre-war investment.

In recognition of the fleet's important contribution to the Russian war effort, Tsar Nicholas II visited Sevastopol in 1915 and again in 1916. He narrated both occasions in his personal diary, in which he rarely offered any colour as to either people or event. On the morning of 30 April 1915, for example, following a briefing on board the *Georgii Pobedonosets* by Admiral Eberhardt, he noted succinctly that he 'visited a brand-new dock, almost completed, and sailed around the squadron by cutter'. He then 'inspected the hospital ship *Pyotr Velikiy*', aboard which he met two wounded men from the *Almaz*. Army units, however, were not forgotten. By the length of his detailed description, the Tsar obviously took great pride in awarding the officers and men of 'his' 6th Plastun (Cossack infantry) Battalion with decorations for their conduct in battle. The following day Nicholas II inspected further Cossack units, and at the front of the 3rd Plastun, announced that the Tsarevich, his son Alexey, would become its *Shef* (honorary colonel).[36]

Nicholas II's visit to Sevastopol in May 1916 turned out to be the last time a Russian emperor would grace the city, for the tsarist days were now quickly numbered. At that time, however, there was little clue as to how and when imperial rule would be so rudely and devastatingly cut short. True to form, local dignitaries loyally welcomed the arrival of the Tsar in their midst. A. F. Yeratsev, the head of the Sevastopol city administration, declared grandiloquently: 'at a time of unprecedented war, great Emperor, you lead valorous troops, evoking everywhere feelings of reverential adoration. On behalf of all the faithful population of Sevastopol, who are blessed again by your imperial visit, I dare to proffer our heartfelt affection'.[37] The official's rich flattery, however, left not even a fleeting impression on Nicholas II: the speech failed to score a mention in the Tsar's diary, presumably because he would have heard such sycophancy all the time. As in the previous year's visit, while the Emperor's main objective in Sevastopol remained to reassure himself as to the condition of the Black Sea Fleet, it also provided some welcome family time with the Tsarina and their four adolescent daughters and young son.[38] His tour of inspection on Thursday, 25 May, which included the two new Empress-class battleships, evidently got off to a good start. Writing up his diary on the imperial train that night, he confided 'all ships are in great order and offer a mighty impression'.[39]

The following day, accompanied by Alexey, Nicholas II inspected no fewer than twenty-five navy vessels, ranging from further ships of the line to the cruisers, destroyers and minelayers of the fleet. Saturday, 27 May, contained another equally busy programme with morning mass on the *Imperatritsa Mariya* followed by a situation update from Admiral Eberhardt on the headquarters ship *Georgii Pobedonosets*. The afternoon, which started 'with all the children' viewing the new naval cadet school under construction near Holland Bay on the northern side, was rounded off with an inspection of a seaplane station in Sevastopol harbour. On the final day of the imperial visit, Sunday, 28 May, the family attended mass in St Vladimir's Cathedral, after which Nicholas II took Alexey to the Panorama museum. Then the royal party inspected new coastal defence batteries near the ruins of the ancient city of Chersonesos.[40] During the course of the four-day visit, members of the royal family also took the opportunity to visit the war wounded being treated in Sevastopol's hospitals and medical institutes.

Despite the success of the imperial visits to Sevastopol, and the growing strength and confidence of the Black Sea Fleet, nothing could escape the fact that the First World War as a whole was going badly. During the course of 1915, Russian Poland had been abandoned under pressure of a powerful and skilfully conducted German offensive, while the accumulated losses of 1914 and 1915 in killed, missing, wounded and prisoners of war had already grown into the millions. The year 1916, however, provided two brief rays of hope. The first was the success of the Russian offensive in the Caucasus, involving a major operation to seize the Turkish supply base of Trebizond at the beginning of the year, in which the Black Sea Fleet played a prominent role. Eberhardt had proposed that the port be captured in a large-scale amphibious operation, so cutting off elements of the Turkish Army defending to the east in the province of Lazistan. The newly appointed commander of the Caucasian *Front*, Grand Duke Nikolay Nikolayevich, whom Nicholas II had relieved of overall command of the Russian Army, however, turned down this operational idea, favouring an advance along the Anatolian coast. In arbitrating between the two commanders-in-chief in the Black Sea region, *Stavka* (the Russian high command) provided a compromise course of action. It directed that the Russian Army's advance be 'supplemented by tactical envelopments, using assault landings in the immediate rear of Turkish positions'; and in order to speed up the advance, as many army units as possible should be redeployed by sea while the fleet provided the maximum amount of naval gunfire support.[41] In the event, three tactical assault landings conducted in March proved successful, as was the transport of land forces over the Black Sea during April to reinforce and support the advancing Caucasian Army. This successful co-operation between Russian army and naval units contributed significantly to the capture of Trebizond on 1 May 1916.[42]

In many ways, such joint operations on the Black Sea littoral mirrored the successes of 1828–29 in an earlier Russo-Turkish war. Although the Russian fleet could not prevent the two German warships, or the odd Turkish unit for that matter, from making occasional sorties, the Russian Navy was able to enjoy maritime preponderance in the Black Sea for the most part. Critics of Eberhardt, however, took advantage of the fact that the *Goeben* and *Breslau* had managed to shell Tuapse and Sochi respectively on 17 July and to return to Constantinople unmolested. A critical report of the handling of the Black Sea Fleet led to Eberhardt's dismissal and his replacement by the forty-two-year-old Aleksandr Vasilyevich Kolchak.[43] Eberhardt departed a disappointed and frustrated man. Although neither a Lazarev nor a Nakhimov, he had achieved much during his appointment, not least in rebuilding a mutinous fleet, in suppressing Turkish trade and in supporting the Russian Army in its recent campaign. Whether his successor would manage to remove the thorn of the *Goeben* remained to be seen.

Towards the end of 1916, a mysterious event in Sevastopol harbour cast a long shadow over the revival of the Black Sea Fleet and Kolchak's assumption of command. Quite suddenly, during the early evening of 22 November, a massive explosion erupted in the forward part of the *Imperatritsa Mariya*. The immense structural damage, along with the subsequent fire and multiple secondary explosions, led to the ship going down with the loss of 216 men and 232 wounded. There remains no satisfactory explanation for one of the ship's magazines exploding with such catastrophic results. One theory suggests that it was the work of sabotage; another argues that the self-ignition of faulty cordite was to blame.[44] Fortunately for the Black Sea Fleet, its third dreadnought, the *Imperator Alexander III*, was just about to enter service. Hence the balance of naval power in the Black Sea was unaffected by the tragedy of the *Imperatritsa Mariya*. Kolchak, however, was severely depressed by the incident. In a letter to his beloved friend, Anna Vasilievna Timireva, he confided: 'As soon as I returned to my cabin, I realised what despair and grief really mean. I regretted that I didn't prevent the explosion of the propellant magazine ... I loved this ship as a living creature'.[45]

Elsewhere during the year, an event in Russia's main theatre of war, the 'Eastern' Front, had provided a second fillip to the nation's morale. General Brusilov, by then commander of the Russian Army's South-Western Front, scored a great success over Austro-Hungarian forces. Launched on 4 June 1916 in present-day western Ukraine, the Brusilov offensive met Russia's commitment made at the inter-Allied Chantilly conference of December 1915 to undertake a series of simultaneous attacks against the Central Powers in the summer of 1916. The British–French offensive at the Somme on the Western Front was but one of these. By the time Brusilov's operations were closed down on 20 September, Russia had not only inflicted, albeit at very great cost to herself, a heavy defeat on Austria–Hungary, but had also forced the Hapsburg Empire to withdraw forces from the Italian front, and prompted Germany to divert forces from the Western Front. Yet in many other respects Brusilov's victory proved Pyrrhic. Although his success encouraged Romania to enter the Entente's cause on 27 August 1916, the subsequent defeat of that country and its occupation by German forces not only extended Russia's land front but also worsened her maritime position in the Black Sea. Germany was also to extract considerable quantities of valuable oil and grain from Romania, which helped sustain her war economy into 1917 and 1918. Above all, the huge number of Russian casualties involved (up to 1.4 million) significantly contributed to the growing war weariness amongst her armies at the front and population at home.

THE REVOLUTIONS OF 1917

Readers must turn to other texts to learn in any detail of the origins and course of the Russian revolutions of 1917. It is tempting to simplify an immensely complex situation along the lines that tsarist Russia had lost not only public respect, but also the authority and will to govern. The defeats and losses of 1914–16 on the Eastern Front had been too great. Notwithstanding the false dawn of the Brusilov offensive, there was a widespread suspicion that either stupidity or treachery lay at the root cause of Russia's ills. The Tsar had done himself no favours in assuming the mantle of commander-in-chief of the army. By distancing himself at his supreme military headquarters, the *Stavka*, at Mogilev, far away from the politicking, rumours and intrigues of St Petersburg, Nicholas II had not appreciated the extent to which his German-born wife, Alexandra Fedorovna, had undermined faith in the Russian monarchy through her dubious dealings with the highly controversial spiritualist Rasputin. After three years of war, Russia found herself in an extremely exhausted and volatile condition.

Yet perhaps the biggest contributory cause of Russia's fragility was economic rather than military. Intense industrial mobilisation had brought about an overheated domestic economy, which could not balance supply and demand. As peasants deserted the land for the towns and cities seeking far better paid employment in munitions factories, agricultural production slumped. The railways could not cope with both military and civil requirements. As food and fuel became short, particularly in highly industrial centres such as in Petrograd (St Petersburg had been so renamed in 1914), inflation soared as did widespread deprivation and disaffection. When the troubles reached breaking point, Russia's brittle institutions of state possessed little resistance to the combined shock of mass unrest and military rebellion.[46]

In late February 1917, protests on Petrograd's streets attracted 200,000 striking workers. As the police and gendarmerie attempted to break up such demonstrations, matters became increasingly violent. When the garrison of Russia's capital city joined – rather than shooting at – the populace (there would be no repeat of the Bloody Sunday of January 1905), what had started as dissension, born largely of economic and social distress, became political and revolutionary. When it became clear that the imperial government had lost control of the streets, and could no longer rely on the army, Nicholas II abdicated on 15 March 1917. The popular revolution resulted in the establishment of the Provisional Government, consisting of a motley collection of Radical Democrats, People's Socialists, Social Revolutionaries, Mensheviks and Kadets (Constitutional Democratic Party). Although the Bolsheviks were not represented in this administration they dominated the Petrograd Soviet, which consisted of sailors', soldiers' and workers' delegates. This organisation exercised much of the real power of the land, such was embodied in the military, factories, telegraphs and railways – the means of force, production and communications. Similar soviets were established across Russia.

During the first few months following the revolution an uneasy truce existed between the Provisional Government and the Petrograd Soviet. As spring turned into summer, however, it became all too evident that the Bolsheviks had little interest either in supporting the government or in helping to guide Russia towards a liberal democracy. Vladimir Lenin, who returned in April 1917 from exile in Switzerland to Russia in a sealed German military train, had no truck with liberalism, preferring to stir up a class war between the bourgeoisie and the proletariat. Popular support for the Bolsheviks, which had started from a low base, steadily increased as disappointment with the Provisional Government grew as its impotence became all too obvious, a sentiment expertly fuelled by Lenin's alluring demands for 'peace, land and bread'. Division rather than unity dominated Russian politics, as the Provisional Government attempted to continue prosecuting the war – a policy energetically driven by its Minister of War and subsequent chairman, Alexander Kerensky. The so-called Kerensky offensive of June 1917 faltered after a couple of days: the troops involved began to melt away from the front as German and Austro-Hungarian forces counter-attacked. Meanwhile, economic activity declined and civil law and order increasingly broke down across the country. Discipline collapsed amongst its war-weary armed forces with many soldiers and sailors becoming disaffected through German propaganda. Sevastopol and the Black Sea Fleet were not spared these phenomena, which would lead within months to a second revolution – a Bolshevik coup.[47]

Wartime Sevastopol was a busy male-dominated military–industrial city, whose prime purpose remained the support of the Black Sea Fleet. On 30 December 1914, its recorded population of 102,572 included 54,858 men directly connected with either the navy or the army and 12,664 workers, of whom 4,196 were employed in the port facilities. A year later, there were thirty-nine factories and other plants operating in the city producing goods to the value of 15,611,755 roubles. Significantly, the naval dockyard's share of the output amounted to nearly 94 per cent of this total. Unsurprisingly, as in 1905, the mix of sailors and dockyard workers provided a fertile breeding ground for industrial unrest and political agitation. The impetus for the start of revolutionary activity came with the news of 17 March 1917 concerning the abdication of Nicholas II. Two days later elections to a soviet of working deputies took place in Sevastopol, in which – it should be stressed at this early stage of political developments in the city – only two Bolsheviks were represented. Simultaneously, a number of sailors' committees were formed on the ships of the Black Sea Fleet and an overarching 'United Central Military-Executive Committee' was established in Sevastopol.

Following the dissolution of governmental authority, Admiral Kolchak had written despairingly in March that 'catastrophe is coming closer ... only my conditional authority and influence, which may disappear at any minute, prevents a complete break-down ... and then I will have to deal with the historical disgrace of a senseless mutiny in the fleet during wartime'.[48] His dire predictions were to prove uncannily accurate. On 22 April, thousands of people took to the streets of the city in demonstrations. They welcomed home the return of sailors, who, benefiting from a national amnesty, had been recently released from either exile or prison resulting from their participation in the mutinies of 1905 and 1912. Buckling under the pressure of sailors' protests, on 13 May, Kolchak reluctantly ordered the renaming of warships bearing imperial names. Thus the *Imperator Alexander III*, *Imperatritsa Ekaterina Velikaya* and *Nikolay I* became the *Volya* (Will), *Svobodnaya Rossiya* (Free Russia), and *Demokratiya* (Democracy) respectively. By this time, serious political developments were already under way:

Sevastopol's Bolsheviks had created the first autonomous Bolshevik organisation in Crimea, which was connected to other similar groups in the Donets Basin (Donbas) industrial region. On 14 June, the Sevastopol committee of the Russian Socialist Democratic Labour Party (RSDLP) was established.

Sevastopol was not only proving to be a centre of political change, its cultural life was evolving too in response. In June 1917, the great Russian opera singer Fyodor Ivanovich Shalyapin, who was holidaying in Crimea, came to the city to give a concert for wounded officers and men. Having heard sailors singing in a church choir, he was impressed by the quality of their voices and resolved to train them further for public recitals, recruiting a sailors' brass orchestra to provide the accompanying music. On an open stage set up on Primorsky Boulevard, Shalyapin appeared in a sailor's uniform and carrying a red banner. Together singer and choir sang to great acclaim 'A Song of Revolution' written by the great man, followed by a number of traditional Ukrainian and Russian folk songs and more classical works of Schubert and other composers.[49]

By the early summer it had become increasingly evident that the efficiency and readiness of the Black Sea Fleet were fast evaporating as 'supplies were no longer forthcoming' while dockyard workers and sailors alike took 'more and more time off to attend various meetings' called by Bolshevik organisers.[50] A remarkable foreign visitor to Sevastopol during these troubled times confirmed the worst fears of Admiral Kolchak earlier in the year. Rear Admiral James H. Glennon represented the United States Navy Department in a special mission sent to Russia by President Woodrow Wilson under the leadership of the former Secretary of War (and of State), Senator Elihu Root. The Americans' task was to determine how best to assist the Provisional Government in continuing the war effort against Germany and Austria–Hungary. While Root remained in Petrograd, Glennon and his personal staff journeyed to several Russian Navy bases including Archangel and Vladivostok. Their brief sojourn in Sevastopol probably represented the first visit by an official American military or naval delegation to the city since the Delafield Commission of 1855. Arriving on 20 June 1917, Glennon inspected several ships, submarines and destroyers of the Black Sea Fleet and a number of coastal defence batteries. His aide, Lieutenant Alva D. Bernhard, recalled their experience on going aboard the fleet headquarters ship, the *Georgii Pobedonosets*. To the Americans' surprise, there was not a single officer in sight: the quarterdeck was 'full of idle sailors in dirty white uniforms milling aimlessly around'. It turned out that almost all of the officers had left the ship the previous night. Those who had remained were confined to their quarters: the arrested officers feared for their lives every time someone knocked at their cabin door.[51]

The explanation for this complete breakdown in naval discipline was simple enough: a mutiny had taken place on board the previous day. Members of the sailors' committee on the *Georgii Pobedonosets* had confronted Kolchak, insisting that he hand over his personal weapons – and specifically his finely decorated, gilded Sword of the Order of St George, which he had been awarded for gallantry at Port Arthur in 1904 during the Russo-Japanese War. Rather than acceding to this demand, the admiral declared, 'You did not award it to me. I won it at sea— and I give it back to the sea!' as he threw his prized possession into the waters of the Sevastopol roadstead.[52] Miraculously, Kolchak survived this incident. No longer enjoying a command to speak of, he was immediately summoned to report to *Stavka*. In a strange combination of defiance and defeatism, he issued his final order of the day to the Black Sea Fleet:

> I believe the resolution of the delegates' meeting concerning the disarmament of officers to be disgraceful to the command, officers, fleet and me…. [But] I call on officers, in order to prevent possible incidents, to voluntarily obey the demands of the crews and to hand over all weapons…. [While] I consider it to be harmful if I remain as commander-in-chief of the fleet, I await with calmness the decision of the government.[53]

Shocked by what he and Bernhard observed on the *Georgii Pobedonosets* and elsewhere at Sevastopol, 'at the risk of his own life', Glennon resolved to confront the Sevastopol Soviet of sailors, soldiers and workers. He urged the mutinous Russian sailors, who had taken over the warships moored in the harbour, to 'restore authority' to their officers.[54] Glennon departed Sevastopol on the evening train of 22 June bound for Petrograd: on the very same train sat none other than a downcast Admiral Kolchak, who had just handed over his disintegrated 'command' to Rear Admiral V. K. Lukin. In turn, Kolchak's recall turned into a dismissal: Kerensky fired him 'for failing to maintain discipline'.[55]

Meantime, Glennon's brave appeal to the mutineers in Sevastopol appeared to have proved an extraordinary success, but one too late to save Kolchak. On 24 June, the American ambassador in Russia, David R. Francis, wired Robert Lansing, the Secretary of State in Washington:

> Glennon returned from Sevastopol where arrived when mutiny incited by Kronstadt sailors was at its height. All officers were deprived of swords and side arms. Glennon made two speeches which had excellent effect. Subsequently mutineers rescinded objectionable resolutions, restored all officers except Admiral Kolchak who came here on order Minister of War to explain why needless loss. Discipline restored in Black Sea Fleet …[56]

Events, however, were to prove that the restoration of normal command arrangements within the Black Sea Fleet was but temporary. By a sequence of curious twists of fate, Kolchak headed for the United States in September 1917 on a mission on behalf of the Provisional Government. While he was serving abroad, the Bolsheviks seized power in Russia. Kolchak eventually returned to his homeland to become one of the leading figures of the White cause during the Civil War, for which he fought and died.

For all the mutinous activity within the Black Sea Fleet, the Bolsheviks were experiencing a hard time in Sevastopol in advancing their case. In August 1917, a Bolshevik propagandist called Nadezhda Ostrovskaya came to the city in order to spread revolutionary disaffection within the Black Sea Fleet. In 1907, her earlier attempt to achieve this kind of subversion had failed; she had narrowly escaped arrest by fleeing to Geneva. Returning ten years later to Sevastopol, she found widespread indifference to the Bolshevik movement. Writing to the Central Committee in Petrograd she complained, 'It is difficult here. No one listens to [us]'. A month later, her growing frustration was evident: 'The masses here are politically uneducated. There is no literature.... Either you send two more Bolshevik agitators and make the Black Sea Bolshevik, or again your indifference and silence will result in Kerensky rule and anarchy'.[57]

During the early autumn of 1917, paralleling developments in Petrograd and elsewhere in Russia, the influence of the Bolsheviks rose in Sevastopol. Whereas on 24 July only eleven out of 455 deputies of the Sevastopol Soviet were Bolshevik, by 2 November, there were fifty-eight, now outnumbering the forty Mensheviks. Although the Social Revolutionaries still formed the majority party, the Bolsheviks were benefiting from an increased investment in their movement. Some of the credit for this change of fortunes goes to two agitators sent from Petrograd in consequence of Ostrovskaya's rebuke of the Central Committee: Nikolay Pozharov and Yuri Gaven. Although Gaven confirmed that the Bolsheviks' standing was steadily improving in the fleet, he found Sevastopol's dockyard workers to be 'abnormally conservative'. Events in Petrograd, however, rapidly overtook such local concerns. On 6 November a message was received in Sevastopol stating that the October socialist revolution inspired by Lenin had taken place in Petrograd. The Sevastopol Soviet of Military and Workers Deputies decided the same day to take power into their own hands, and sent to the Petrograd Soviet and All-Russia Congress of Soviets a telegram proclaiming 'We welcome the victorious revolution. Soviet has taken power. Waiting for instructions. Sevastopol.'[58]

While the Bolsheviks had seized power in Petrograd, they remained a minority element within the Sevastopol Soviet. That was not the case, however, within the Black Sea Fleet, which held its first congress in the period 19 November to 2 December 1917. The twelfth anniversary of the *Ochakov* mutiny of 28 November 1905 provided a suitable rallying point. Comparing the events of 1905 and 1917, Sevastopol's *Izvestiya* (News) noted:

Twelve years ago, on this day ... the Black Sea Fleet raised the red banner of mutiny, headed by its Red Admiral, P. P. Schmidt ... Today we agree that this mutiny was premature: the rest of Russia was not ready to support it ... [and] even if that mutiny had been successful, our comrades [elsewhere] would not have been able to exploit it, as we lacked the necessary means of communications, such as telegraphs and railways.[59]

In contrast, the Black Sea Fleet sailors in November 1917 were in a much stronger position as the telegraphs and railways across Russia came increasingly under Bolshevik control. Sevastopol's sailors assumed a militant position in support of the revolution, which was threatened by a backlash in southern Russia. In late October, the Cossack Ataman, General Aleksey Maksimovich Kaledin, based in the city of Novocherkassk, had announced martial law within the Don district. When he set about suppressing the soviets that had sprung up locally, Bolshevik leaders in nearby Rostov-on-Don appealed for armed assistance from the sailors of the Black Sea Fleet. In Sevastopol, Pozharov insisted armed groups be despatched immediately to assist their fellow Bolsheviks. Within days, a 2,500-man-strong 'revolutionary detachment' was formed under Aleksey Vasilievich Mokrousov, a former sailor and longstanding member of the Bolshevik movement. On 7 December Mokrousov's force entered Rostov-on-Don where it was heavily engaged and beaten by a combined group of Cossacks and soldiers of the newly founded anti-revolutionary Volunteer Army.

When the bloodied sailors of the Black Sea Fleet returned to Sevastopol later in the month, they sought vengeance for their defeat and losses at Rostov-on-Don in murdering at least thirty naval officers in Sevastopol on 28 December. In one particularly notorious incident, a 'group of thirty' sailors took six senior officers, including three admirals, to the Malakhov Hill. There, in accordance with the resolution of the crew of the destroyer *Gadzhibey*, they were shot on account of their involvement in 'the suppression of the revolutionary movement'.[60] The murders on the Malakhov, 'which soon became a favourite spot for execution', typified the spate of violence that swept across Sevastopol. This bloodlust had been fuelled by the exhortations of the sailors' commissar, Vasily Vasilievich Romanets, who had received instructions from the Central Committee in Petrograd to 'act with all determination against the enemies of the people. Don't wait for any order from above'.[61] From now on, there would be no turning back in the Bolsheviks' use of extreme means in pursuit of their political aims.

By 16 (29) December, sailors had seized control of both the fleet and the city. Under the shadow of their weapons, a new military–revolutionary committee was formed with eighteen Bolsheviks and two left-leaning Social Revolutionaries. Three days later, 'Revcom' published the first edition of its own *Izvestiya*.

According to a Soviet-era account of the 1917 revolution in Sevastopol, the original soviet dominated by the Socialist Revolutionaries was 'liquidated'.[62] By the end of 1917, the fleet 'ceased to exist as a fighting force': German and Turkish naval units could now operate with impunity in the Black Sea. In bitter consequence, all Eberhardt's and Kolchak's efforts in countering the German–Turkish maritime presence during nearly three years of war appeared to have been in vain.

Although Bolshevik control had yet to be consolidated in the remainder of Crimea, Sevastopol became its bulwark on the peninsula. Simferopol, on the other hand, had become a centre of anti-Bolshevik sentiment and action. In particular, the Crimean Tatars were flexing their muscles. During the summer of 1917, the Milli Firka (National Party) had been founded: this popular movement rapidly took hold as its message was spread in the Tatar newspaper *Golos Kryma* (Voice of Crimea). In the power vacuum then existing, the Tatars assumed control of their towns and villages and grew more confident in their aspirations. On 9 December 1917 Crimean Tatar nationalists held their first Kurultay (constituent assembly) at the historically symbolic Khan's palace in Bakhchisaray. The thirty-three-year-old Tatar leader, Noman Celebi Cihan, became the first head of government of the newly proclaimed Crimean People's Republic. As a modern historian of the Crimean Tatars, Brian Glyn Williams, has observed, the 'Tatar leadership had come to demand not just cultural autonomy for Crimea, but [also] territorial autonomy'. In this struggle, however, sailors of the Bolshevik-dominated Black Sea Fleet, who were 'disinclined to acknowledge the Tatar Kurultay's authority', vehemently opposed the creation of an independent Muslim Crimea. Hence a 'show-down' between the two centres of competing power on the peninsula – Simferopol and Sevastopol – became 'inevitable'.[63]

Any description of political change during this tumultuous episode in Sevastopol's history would be far from complete without mentioning the violence and extreme human cost involved. The transition from tsarist to Bolshevik rule over the years 1917–20 proved far from peaceful: the inhabitants of Russia and Crimea generally, and Sevastopol more specifically, suffered extreme deprivations and losses caused by successive phases of 'Red Terror' perpetrated by the Bolsheviks, and by the atrocities of their opponents. Crimean cities witnessed horrifying scenes in which many of those who opposed Bolshevik rule, or were merely representatives of former imperial authority, were cruelly eliminated. On the nights of 21/22 and 22/23 February 1918, for example, Sevastopol's sailors murdered over 100 officers and citizens, a bloodbath which became known as the Bartholomew's Nights – recalling the St Bartholomew's massacre of the Huguenots in France on 23–24 August 1572.[64]

The experience of General Baron Pyotr Nikolayevich Wrangel, an aristocrat of German Baltic extraction, who had fought with distinction for the Russian Imperial Army during the First World War, is illustrative of this wave of terror. Following the October Revolution of 1917, and the resultant dissolution of Russia's army as a fighting force, Wrangel took refuge in his mother-in-law's estate near Yalta. Life in rural Crimea appeared peaceful enough initially, but one day his 'explosive temper' caught up with him. Hearing a gardener insulting his wife, Wrangel forcibly ejected the man concerned by the 'scruff of the neck'. In response, the gardener denounced him as 'an enemy of the people.' Wrangel's son captures the bitter consequences:

> Retaliation was prompt: that night a band of Red sailors broke into the house and [my father] was hauled out of bed under the menace of a revolver…. [He] and his brother-in-law, a captain of the hussars, were bundled into a car…. They were driven to the harbour, now crowded with a bloodthirsty throng…. As they got out they saw a horrible sight; bodies torn limb from limb were strewn about. Howling for blood, the mob of sailors and dishevelled civilians screamed: 'Here come the blood-suckers. To the water with them!' … Besides the bodies on the pier, several people had been thrown alive into the water with weights attached to their feet.[65]

Much to their shock and surprise, Wrangel and his brother-in-law were among the lucky ones to survive this murderous incident: they were imprisoned instead. Their good fortune continued with their subsequent release from captivity, following the brave intervention of Wrangel's mother-in-law and wife.

Wrangel and his family then hid among the friendly Tatar population, devout Muslims, who opposed the Bolsheviks at that time for good reason. The brief period of Tatar rule in central Crimea had been violently brought to an end by sailors from Sevastopol. A force of nearly 3,000 men, equipped with machine guns and artillery, commanded by Mokrousov, had confronted a Tatar political and military gathering on 14 January 1918. Several hundred were killed in the vicinity of Suren (now Siren) railway station, 8 kilometres south of Bakhchisaray. Celebi Cihan was amongst the prisoners: taken to Sevastopol and imprisoned, he was one of the victims of the Bartholomew Nights. The arrival of German troops in late April 1918 ended this episode of Bolshevik rule in Crimea: a period of German occupation began.

THE GERMAN MILITARY INTERVENTION AND OCCUPATION OF 1918

Following the Bolshevik assumption of power in Russia through the October Revolution of 1917, its leaders determined that they needed to conclude participation in the First World War as quickly as possible if their regime were to take hold domestically. The emergence of the Volunteer Army indicated that counter-revolutionary forces would oppose them, and that a civil war would ensue. Accordingly, Lenin despatched Leon Trotsky in December 1917 to conduct peace negotiations with German representatives at Brest-Litovsk. These talks proved to be very one-sided as the Germans imposed, rather than discussed, terms; so much so, that Trotsky stormed out in protest in February 1918.

Meanwhile, events in Ukraine were influencing Germany's position with regard to Bolshevik Russia. One of the consequences of the February Revolution was a reawakening of Ukrainian nationalism, a development which was to be paralleled seventy years later as the Soviet Union dissolved. While the Ukrainian Central Rada (Council) had claimed national autonomy in March, on 20 November 1917 it asserted Ukraine's independence from Russia. The declaration of a Ukrainian People's Republic incited a violent Bolshevik backlash. Ukraine quickly descended into chaos. It became quickly evident, as historian Dominic Lieven has remarked, that no 'Ukrainian regime on its own could mobilize sufficient resources or loyalty to defend itself against Russia'.[66] The threats to Ukrainian nationalism were as much internal as external: a civil war resulted.

On 8 February 1918, the Bolsheviks seized control of Kiev, overthrew the Rada, and imposed a regime of Red Terror throughout much of the city and more widely across Ukraine – many scenes of which are graphically described in Mikhail Bulgakov's seminal novel, *The White Guard*.[67] Atrocities included the shooting of 1,000 former tsarist officers. In response, representatives of the Rada fled to Brest-Litovsk and signed there on 8/9 February a peace treaty with Germany, requesting military assistance to re-establish their authority. Thus the stage was set for a military intervention that would ultimately lead to German troops entering Sevastopol on 1 May 1918. Then, as in 2014, a bitter dispute between Russia and Ukraine over which political orientation Kiev should take would spill over to Crimea and Sevastopol with wider international consequences.

Germany's strategic goals in Ukraine were twofold: first, to force Russia to sign the terms that would be incorporated in the Treaty of Brest-Litovsk; and secondly, to establish a sphere of influence in the East. There were also thoughts of colonisation, particularly in Crimea, where German settlers were already well established. In effect, Ukraine would become a satellite state, providing Germany with valuable economic resources to be exploited. Indeed, a specific condition of the treaty with Ukraine required that it provide Germany with 1 million tonnes of grain over a six-month period. Within the wider context of the First World War, however, every German military formation retained on the Eastern Front, including Ukraine, would be at the expense of reinforcing the West, where Germany was soon to launch major operations against the British and French armies in an attempt to win the war before the arrival of sufficient American troops decisively tilted the balance of forces to Allied advantage. The enforcement of peace in the East, however, involved establishing control not only over the vast expanse of Ukraine, but also over Russia's Polish and Baltic provinces. It would require no fewer than a million men to achieve this goal, albeit most were in the older age classes, and manning lower-grade formations such as *Landwehr* divisions.

Impatient to conclude a peace with Russia and to re-establish Ukrainian nationalist authority in Kiev, on 16 February 1918 the German high command in the East set out the rationale for a renewed campaign in the East, Operation FAUSTSCHLAG (PUNCH):

> The resumption of ... military operations does not aim at the Russian people, but the Bolsheviks, the enemies of all state order, who prevent peace and declared war on the Ukraine which had concluded peace. The purpose of the operation is to topple the Bolshevik government and hence to bring us peace with Russia.[68]

On 18 February 1918, German forces starting pushing eastwards on a wide front towards Narva in the north and Kiev in the south. Ten days later, Austro-Hungarian forces joined the offensive and pressed into southern Ukraine, heading towards Odessa. Opposition by disorganised and ill-disciplined Bolshevik military units proved only slight. The speed of advance is illustrated by the fact that German troops entered Kiev on 2–3 March, having covered over 500 kilometres in under three weeks, exploiting railway lines to best advantage.

Faced with overwhelming external pressure from the Baltic to the Black Sea, the Bolshevik leadership in Petrograd realised that Russia would lose even more land, population and economic resources if she did not return to the negotiating table. In directing such expediency, Lenin was clear enough: 'This peace must be accepted as a respite enabling us to prepare a decisive resistance to the bourgeoisie and imperialists'.[69] On 3 March, the Treaty of Brest-Litovsk was signed. The settlement represented to Russia nothing less than an abject humiliation, 'without precedent or equal in modern history', involving the loss of: 'territory nearly as large as Austria-Hungary and Turkey combined; fifty-six million inhabitants, or 32 per cent of the whole population of the country; ... 73 per cent of her total iron and 89 per cent of her total coal production'.[70] Such harsh terms did not go unnoticed amongst the Western Allies, who realised that the war had to be won against Germany, whatever the cost.

Within Ukraine, the Rada was soon returned to power, but its authority and reach proved nominal. As Bolshevik forces withdrew, many of their activists stayed put and armed groups melted away into the civilian population of urban centres. An economically impoverished and politically divided Ukraine remained

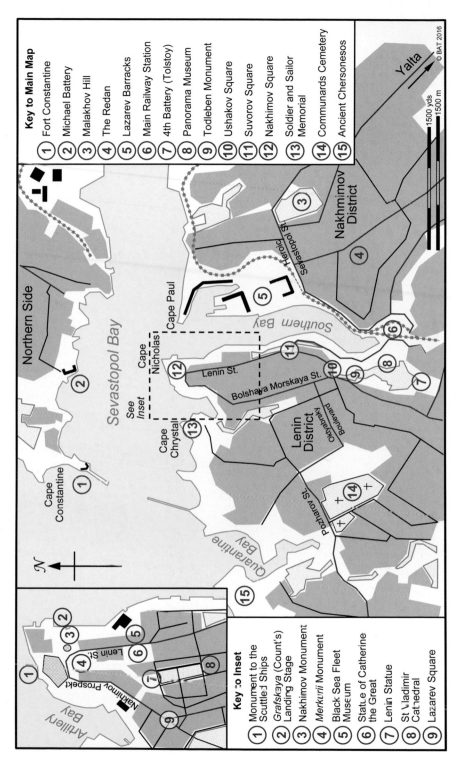

© BAT 2016

Northern Side

Sevastopol Bay

Cape Constantine

Cape Nicholas

Cape Paul

Cape Chrystal

Quarantine Bay

Southern Bay

Nakhimov District

Lenin District

Lenin St.

Bolshaya Morskaya St.

Heroic St.

Sevastopol St.

Okryabrsky

Bolshaya

Pozharov St.

Yalta

1500 yds
1500 m

See Inset

Artillery Bay

Nakhimov Prospekt

Lenin St.

2. Central Sevastopol's Historic Locations and Monuments

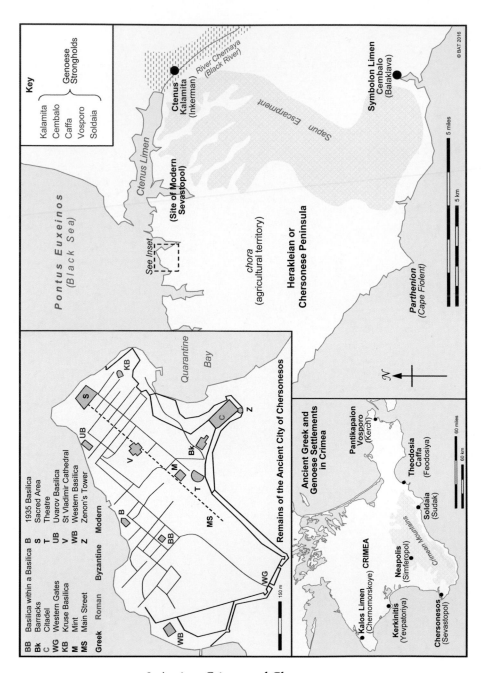

Key

Kalamita
Cembalo
Caffa }
Vosporo
Soldaia } Genoese Strongholds

Pontus Euxeinos
(Black Sea)

Ctenus Limen

Ctenus
Kalamita
(Inkerman)

River Chernaya
(Black River)

Sapun Escarpment

Symbolon Limen
Cembalo
(Balaklava)

(Site of Modern
Sevastopol)

See Inset

chora
(agricultural territory)

Herakleian or
Chersonese Peninsula

Parthenion
(Cape Fiolent)

5 miles

5 km

© BAT 2016

Quarantine Bay

Remains of the Ancient City of Chersonesos

KB

S

T

UB

V

M

Bk

C

Z

B

BB

MS

WG

WB

150 m

BB	Basilica within a Basilica	B	1935 Basilica
Bk	Barracks	S	Sacred Area
C	Citadel	T	Theatre
WG	Western Gates	UB	Uvarov Basilica
KB	Kruse Basilica	V	St Vladimir Cathedral
M	Mint	WB	Western Basilica
MS	Main Street	Z	Zenon's Tower

Greek   Roman   Byzantine   Modern

N

Ancient Greek and
Genoese Settlements
in Crimea

Pantikapaion
Vosporo
(Kerch)

Theodosia
Caffa
(Feodosiya)

Soldaia
(Sudak)

Crimean Mountains

CRIMEA

Kalos Limen
(Chernomorskoye)

Neapolis
(Simferopol)

Kerkinitis
(Yevpatoriya)

Chersonesos
(Sevastopol)

60 miles

60 km

3. Ancient Crimea and Chersonesos

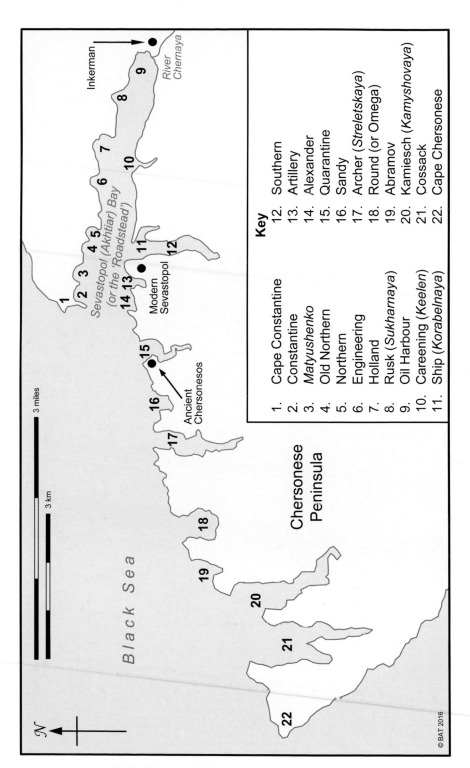

Black Sea

3 miles

3 km

N

Inkerman

River Chernaya

9

8

7

10

6

Sevastopol (Akhtiar) Bay (or the 'Roadstead')

5
4
3
11
12

2
14 13
1

Modern Sevastopol

15

16

Ancient Chersonesos

17

Chersonese Peninsula

18

19

20

21

22

© BAT 2016

Key

1.	Cape Constantine
2.	Constantine
3.	*Matyushenko*
4.	Old Northern
5.	Northern
6.	Engineering
7.	Holland
8.	Rusk (*Sukharnaya*)
9.	Oil Harbour
10.	Careening (*Keelen*)
11.	Ship (*Korabelnaya*)
12.	Southern
13.	Artillery
14.	Alexander
15.	Quarantine
16.	Sandy
17.	Archer (*Streletskaya*)
18.	Round (or Omega)
19.	Abramov
20.	Kamiesch (*Kamyshovaya*)
21.	Cossack
22.	Cape Chersonese

4. The Principal Bays and Capes of Sevastopol

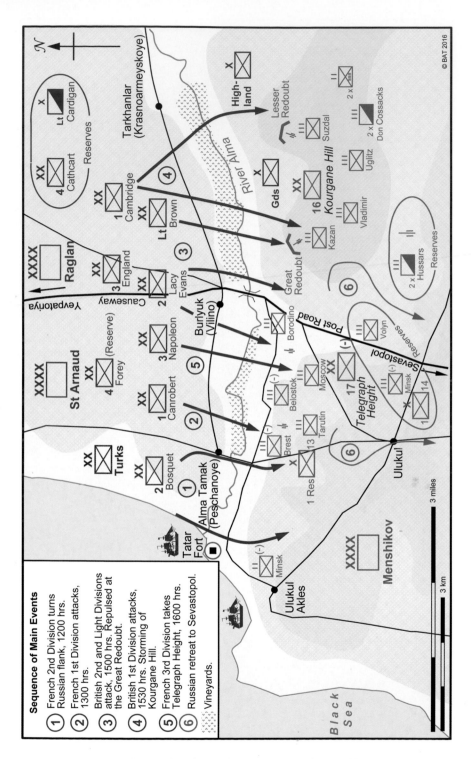

© BAT 2016

Sequence of Main Events

1. French 2nd Division turns Russian flank, 1200 hrs.
2. French 1st Division attacks, 1300 hrs.
3. British 2nd and Light Divisions attack, 1500 hrs. Repulsed at the Great Redoubt.
4. British 1st Division attacks, 1530 hrs. Storming of Kourgane Hill.
5. French 3rd Division takes Telegraph Height, 1600 hrs.
6. Russian retreat to Sevastopol.

⣿⣿ Vineyards.

5. The Battle of the Alma, 20 September 1854

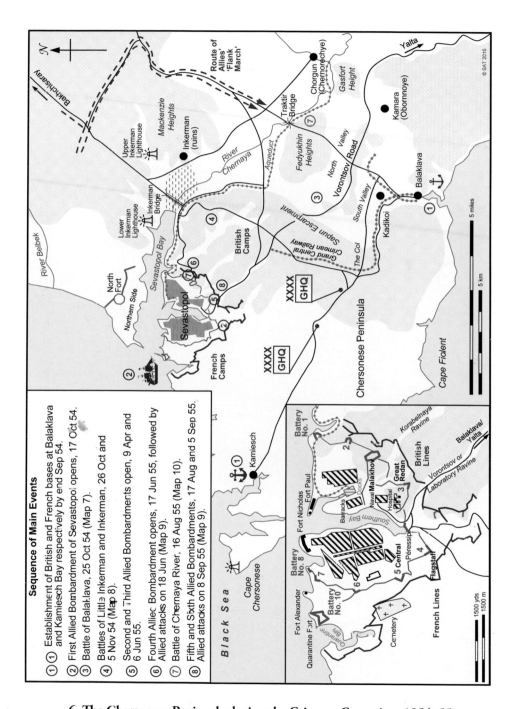

Sequence of Main Events

1. Establishment of British and French bases at Balaklava and Kamiesch Bay respectively by end Sep 54.
2. First Allied Bombardment of Sevastopol opens, 17 Oct 54.
3. Battle of Balaklava, 25 Oct 54 (Map 7).
4. Battles of Little Inkerman and Inkerman, 26 Oct and 5 Nov 54 (Map 8).
5. Second and Third Allied Bombardments open, 9 Apr and 6 Jun 55.
6. Fourth Allied Bombardment opens, 17 Jun 55, followed by Allied attacks on 18 Jun (Map 9).
7. Battle of Chernaya River, 16 Aug 55 (Map 10).
8. Fifth and Sixth Allied Bombardments, 17 Aug and 5 Sep 55. Allied attacks on 8 Sep 55 (Map 9).

6. The Chersonese Peninsula during the Crimean Campaign, 1854–55

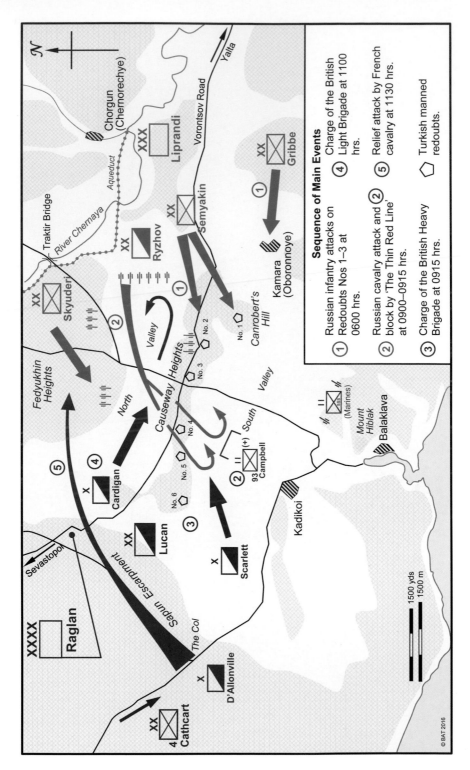

Sequence of Main Events

① Russian infantry attacks on Redoubts Nos 1–3 at 0600 hrs.

② Russian cavalry attack and block by 'The Thin Red Line' at 0900–0915 hrs.

③ Charge of the British Heavy Brigade at 0915 hrs.

④ Charge of the British Light Brigade at 1100 hrs.

⑤ Relief attack by French cavalry at 1130 hrs.

⬠ Turkish manned redoubts.

7. The Battle of Balaklava, 25 October 1854

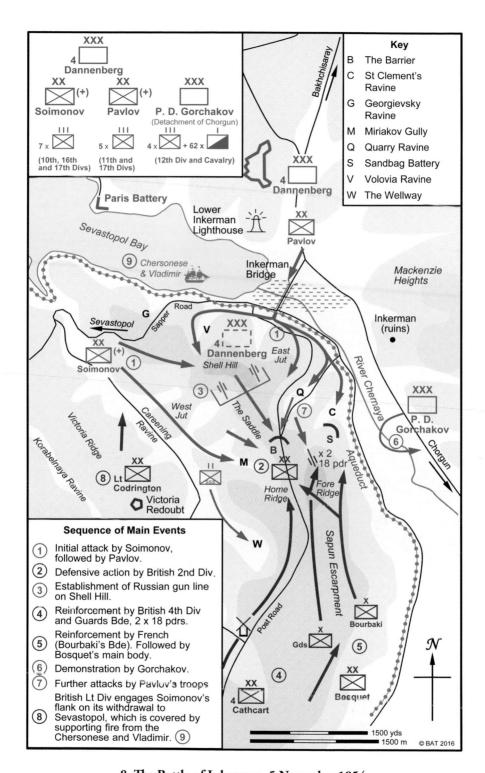

Key

B	The Barrier
C	St Clement's Ravine
G	Georgievsky Ravine
M	Miriakov Gully
Q	Quarry Ravine
S	Sandbag Battery
V	Volovia Ravine
W	The Wellway

XXX
4
Dannenberg

XX
Soimonov (+)

XX
Pavlov (+)

XXX
P. D. Gorchakov
(Detachment of Chorgun)

7 x ||| (10th, 16th and 17th Divs)

5 x ||| (11th and 17th Divs)

4 x ||| + 62 x | (12th Div and Cavalry)

Bakhchisaray

XXX
4
Dannenberg

Paris Battery

Sevastopol Bay

Lower Inkerman Lighthouse

XX
Pavlov

9 Chersonese & Vladimir

Inkerman Bridge

Mackenzie Heights

Road
Sapper

G

Sevastopol ←

XX
Soimonov (+)
1

V
XXX
4
Dannenberg
Shell Hill
1

East Jut

Inkerman (ruins) ●

River Chernaya

XXX
P. D. Gorchakov

3

West Jut

The Saddle

Q
7

C

S

6

Chorgun

Careening Ravine

Victoria Ridge

Korabelnaya Ravine

XX
8 Lt **Codrington**

Victoria Redoubt

|| SSS

M
2

B

XX

× 2
18 pdr

Aqueduct

Fore Ridge

Home Ridge

W

Sapun Escarpment

Post Road

4

x
Bourbaki

Gds
x

5

XX
Cathcart
4

XX
Bosquet

Sequence of Main Events

1. Initial attack by Soimonov, followed by Pavlov.
2. Defensive action by British 2nd Div.
3. Establishment of Russian gun line on Shell Hill.
4. Reinforcement by British 4th Div and Guards Bde, 2 x 18 pdrs.
5. Reinforcement by French (Bourbaki's Bde). Followed by Bosquet's main body.
6. Demonstration by Gorchakov.
7. Further attacks by Pavlov's troops
8. British Lt Div engages Soimonov's flank on its withdrawal to Sevastopol, which is covered by supporting fire from the Chersonese and Vladimir. 9

1500 yds
1500 m
© BAT 2016

N

8. The Battle of Inkerman, 5 November 1854

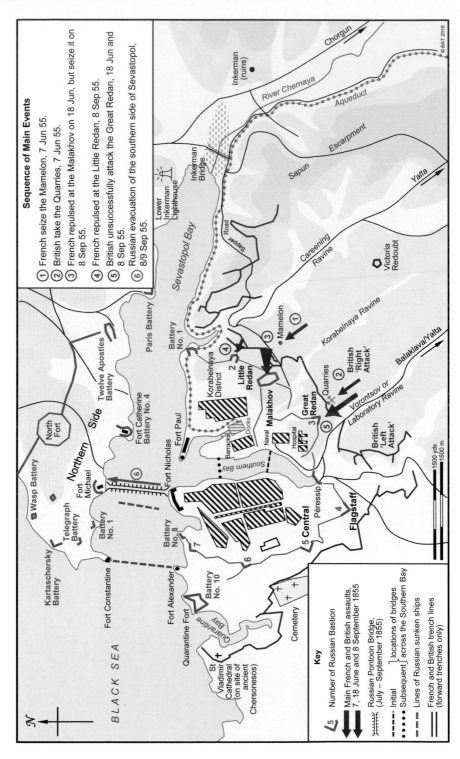

Sequence of Main Events

1. French seize the Mamelon, 7 Jun 55.
2. British take the Quarries, 7 Jun 55.
3. French repulsed at the Malakhov on 18 Jun, but seize it on 8 Sep 55.
4. French repulsed at the Little Redan, 8 Sep 55.
5. British unsuccessfully attack the Great Redan, 18 Jun and 8 Sep 55.
6. Russian evacuation of the southern side of Sevastopol, 8/9 Sep 55.

© BAT 2016

Key

L5 Number of Russian Bastion

Main French and British assaults, 7, 18 June and 8 September 1855

Russian Pontoon Bridge, (July – September 1855)

Initial ⎫ locations of bridges
Subsequent ⎭ across the Southern Bay

Lines of Russian sunken ships

French and British trench lines (forward trenches only)

1500 yds
1500 m

BLACK SEA

Kartaschersky Battery

Telegraph Battery

Wasp Battery

North Fort

Twelve Apostles Battery

Northern Side

Fort Michael

Battery No. 1

Fort Nicholas

Fort Constantine

Fort Alexander

Quarantine Fort

St Vladimir Cathedral (on site of ancient Chersonesos)

Quarantine Bay

Battery No. 10

Battery No. 8

Cemetery

Péressip

Flagstaff

5 Central

Fort Catherine Battery No. 4

Fort Paul

Paris Battery

Battery No. 1

Korabelnaya District

Little Redan

Malakhov

Great Redan

Quarries

Naval Hospital

Barracks

Docks

Southern Bay

Sevastopol Bay

Mamelon

British 'Right Attack'

British 'Left Attack'

Balaklava/Yalta

Korabelnaya Ravine

Vorontsov or Laboratory Ravine

Sapper Road

Lower Inkerman Lighthouse

Inkerman Bridge

River Chernaya

Aqueduct

Chorgun

Inkerman (ruins)

Careening Ravine

Sapun Escarpment

Victoria Redoubt

Yalta

9. The Allied Assaults on Sevastopol, 7 and 8 June and 8 September 1855

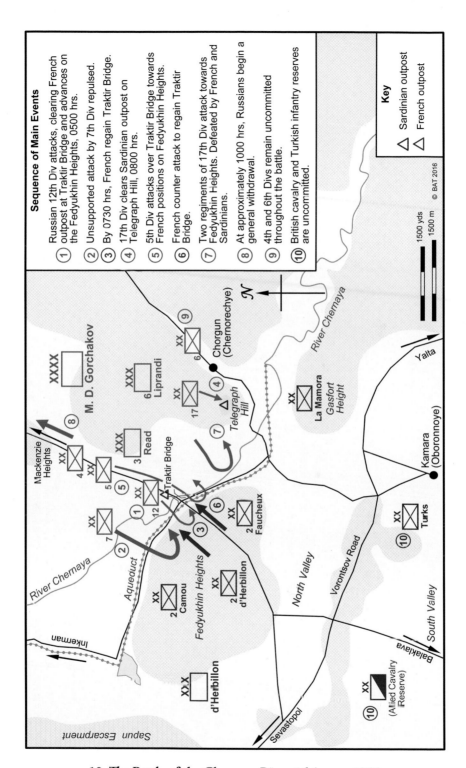

Sequence of Main Events

1. Russian 12th Div attacks, clearing French outpost at Traktir Bridge and advances on the Fedyukhin Heights, 0500 hrs.
2. Unsupported attack by 7th Div repulsed.
3. By 0730 hrs, French regain Traktir Bridge.
4. 17th Div clears Sardinian outpost on Telegraph Hill, 0800 hrs.
5. 5th Div attacks over Traktir Bridge towards French positions on Fedyukhin Heights.
6. French counter attack to regain Traktir Bridge.
7. Two regiments of 17th Div attack towards Fedyukhin Heights. Defeated by French and Sardinians.
8. At approximately 1000 hrs, Russians begin a general withdrawal.
9. 4th and 6th Divs remain uncommitted throughout the battle.
10. British cavalry and Turkish infantry reserves are uncommitted.

© BAT 2016

Key

△ Sardinian outpost

△ French outpost

1500 yds

1500 m

10. The Battle of the Chernaya River, 16 August 1855

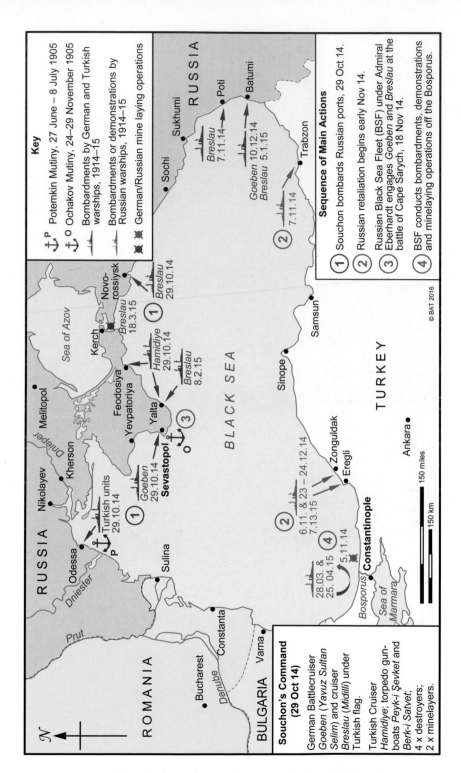

Key

⚓ᴾ Potemkin Mutiny, 27 June – 8 July 1905

⚓º Ochakov Mutiny, 24–29 November 1905

╫ Bombardments by German and Turkish warships, 1914–15

╫ Bombardments or demonstrations by Russian warships, 1914–15

⚫ᴸ German/Russian mine laying operations

Sequence of Main Actions

① Souchon bombards Russian ports, 29 Oct 14.

② Russian retaliation begins early Nov 14.

③ Russian Black Sea Fleet (BSF) under Admiral Eberhardt engages *Goeben* and *Breslau* at the battle of Cape Sarych, 18 Nov 14.

④ BSF conducts bombardments, demonstrations and minelaying operations off the Bosporus.

Souchon's Command (29 Oct 14)

German Battlecruiser *Goeben* (*Yavuz Sultan Selim*) and cruiser *Breslau* (*Midilli*) under Turkish flag.

Turkish Cruiser *Hamidiye*; torpedo gunboats *Peyk-i Şevket* and *Berk-i Satvet*;
4 x destroyers;
2 x minelayers.

RUSSIA

Sea of Azov

Novo-rossiysk
Breslau 29.10.14
Breslau 18.3.15 ①
Kerch

Feodosiya
Yevpatoriya
Yalta
Hamidiye 29.10.14
Breslau 8.2.15
③

Sevastopol ⚓º
Goeben 29.10.14 ①

Melitopol
Dnieper
Kherson
Nikolayev

Odessa ⚓ᴾ
Turkish units 29.10.14 ①

Dniester

RUSSIA

Sochi
Sukhumi
Poti
Breslau 7.11.14
Batumi
Goeben 10.12.14
Breslau 5.1.15
Trabzon
7.11.14 ②

BLACK SEA

Samsun
Sinope

Zonguldak
Eregli
6.11. & 23 – 24.12.14 ②
7.13.15

TURKEY

Ankara

Constantinople
28.03. & 25.04.15
5.11.14 ④

Bosporus
Sea of Marmara

Sulina

Bucharest
Danube
ROMANIA

Constanta

BULGARIA
Varna

Prut

N

© BAT 2016

150 miles
150 km

11. The Black Sea in Revolution and War, 1905–15

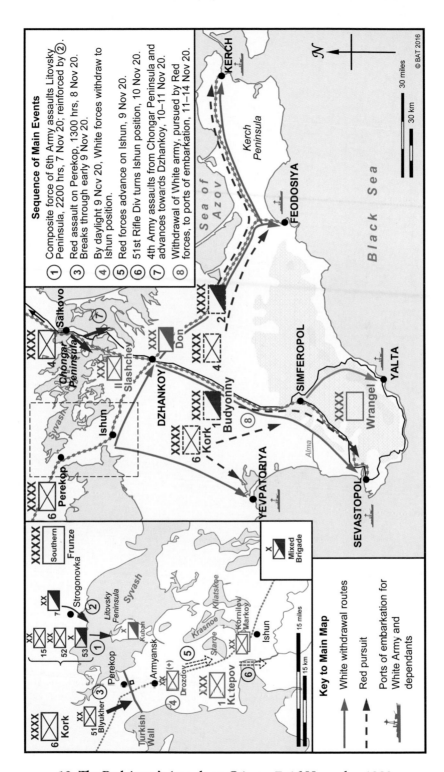

Sequence of Main Events

1. Composite force of 6th Army assaults Litovsky Peninsula, 2200 hrs, 7 Nov 20; reinforced by 2.
2. Red assault on Perekop, 1300 hrs, 8 Nov 20. Breaks through early 9 Nov 20.
3. By daylight 9 Nov 20, White forces withdraw to Ishun position.
4. Red forces advance on Ishun, 9 Nov 20.
5. 51st Rifle Div turns Ishun position, 10 Nov 20.
6. 4th Army assaults from Chongar Peninsula and advances towards Dzhankoy, 10–11 Nov 20.
7. Withdrawal of White army, pursued by Red forces, to ports of embarkation, 11–14 Nov 20.

KERCH

Kerch Peninsula

Sea of Azov

FEODOSIYA

Black Sea

30 miles

30 km

© BAT 2016

Salkovo

Chongar Peninsula

XXXX 4

Syvash

XXX II Slashchev

Ishun

Perekop

XXXX 6

DZHANKOY

XXX Don

XXXX 4

Budyonny

XXXX 1

SIMFEROPOL

XXXX Wrangel

YALTA

Alma

XXXX 6 Kork

YEVPATORIYA

SEVASTOPOL

Southern XXXXX Frunze

XX 7
Strogonovka

Litovsky Peninsula

Syvash

XX 15 XX 52 X 53
XXXX 6 Kork
XX 51 Blyukher
Perekop
Turkish Wall
Armyansk
Kuban x
Krasnoe Kliatskoe
Starye
Drozdov XX(+)
Kornilov Markov
XX 1
Kt tepov
Ishun

X Mixed Brigade

Key to Main Map

White withdrawal routes

Red pursuit

Ports of embarkation for White Army and dependants

15 miles

15 km

---

12. The Red Army's Assault on Crimea, 7–16 November 1920

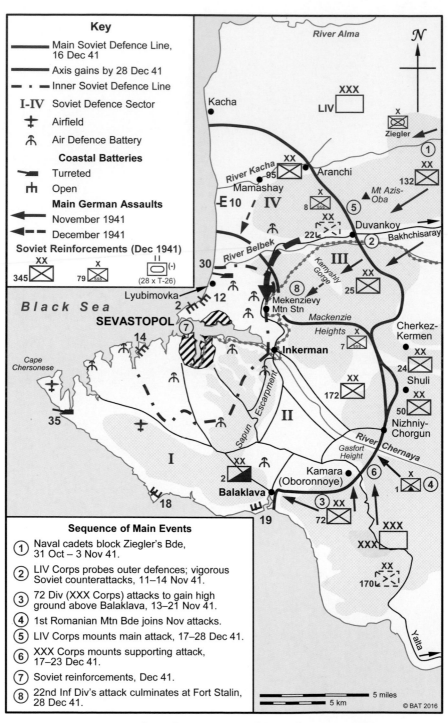

Key

— Main Soviet Defence Line, 16 Dec 41

— Axis gains by 28 Dec 41

–·– Inner Soviet Defence Line

I-IV Soviet Defence Sector

Airfield

Air Defence Battery

Coastal Batteries

Turreted

Open

Main German Assaults

⟵ November 1941

⟵– December 1941

Soviet Reinforcements (Dec 1941)

345 | 79 | (28 x T-26)

River Alma

Kacha

XXX
LIV

X
Ziegler ①

River Kacha

XX
95 Aranchi

Mamashay

E 10 IV

X
8 ② Mt Azis-Oba

XX
132

⑤

Duvankoy

Bakhchisaray

②

XX
22

River Belbek

30

III

XX
25

Kamyshly Gorge

⑧

Mekenzievy Mtn Stn

Black Sea

SEVASTOPOL

⑦

2

12

Mackenzie Heights

X
7

Cherkez-Kermen

XX
24 Shuli

14

Inkerman

35

Cape Chersonese

Sapun Escarpment

II

XX
172

XX
50

Nizhniy-Chorgun

I

River Chernaya

Gasfort Height

XX
2 Balaklava

Kamara (Oboronnoye)

⑥

X
1 ④

18

19

③ XX
72

XXX

XXX

XX
170

Sequence of Main Events

① Naval cadets block Ziegler's Bde, 31 Oct – 3 Nov 41.

② LIV Corps probes outer defences; vigorous Soviet counterattacks, 11–14 Nov 41.

③ 72 Div (XXX Corps) attacks to gain high ground above Balaklava, 13–21 Nov 41.

④ 1st Romanian Mtn Bde joins Nov attacks.

⑤ LIV Corps mounts main attack, 17–28 Dec 41.

⑥ XXX Corps mounts supporting attack, 17–23 Dec 41.

⑦ Soviet reinforcements, Dec 41.

⑧ 22nd Inf Div's attack culminates at Fort Stalin, 28 Dec 41.

5 miles

5 km

© BAT 2016

**13. Sevastopol's Defences: First and Second Axis Assaults,
October – December 1941**

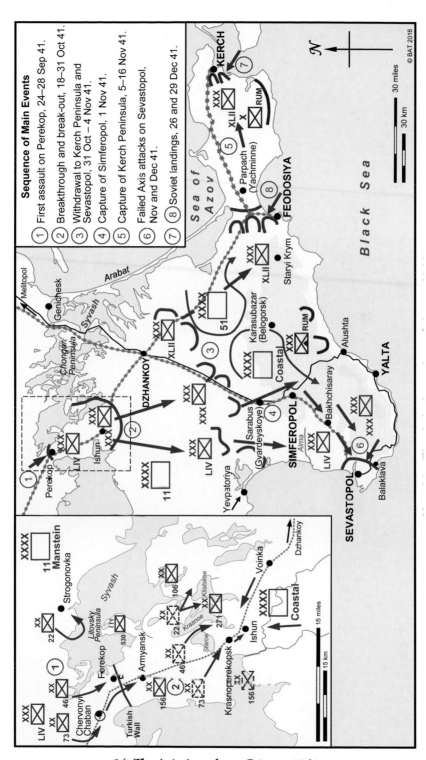

Sequence of Main Events

1. First assault on Perekop, 24–28 Sep 41.
2. Breakthrough and break-out, 18–31 Oct 41.
3. Withdrawal to Kerch Peninsula and Sevastopol, 31 Oct – 4 Nov 41.
4. Capture of Simferopol, 1 Nov 41.
5. Capture of Kerch Peninsula, 5–16 Nov 41.
6. Failed Axis attacks on Sevastopol, Nov and Dec 41.
7. 8. Soviet landings, 26 and 29 Dec 41.

© BAT 2016

14. The Axis Assault on Crimea, 1941

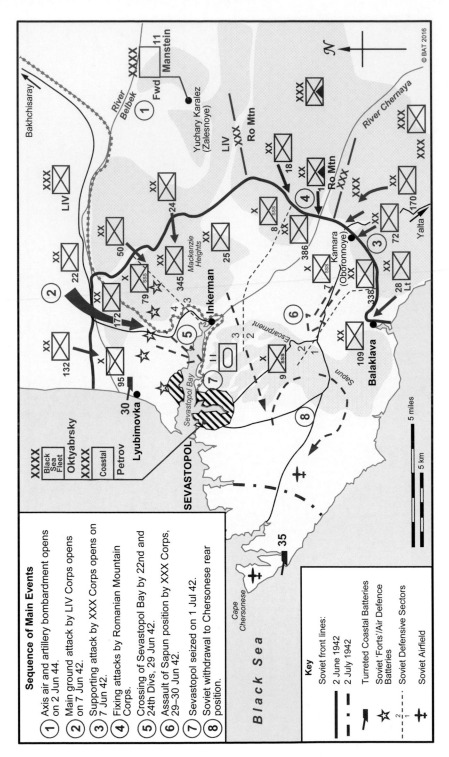

Sequence of Main Events

1. Axis air and artillery bombardment opens on 2 Jun 44.
2. Main ground attack by LIV Corps opens on 7 Jun 42.
3. Supporting attack by XXX Corps opens on 7 Jun 42.
4. Fixing attacks by Romanian Mountain Corps.
5. Crossing of Sevastopol Bay by 22nd and 24th Divs, 29 Jun 42.
6. Assault of Sapun position by XXX Corps, 29–30 Jun 42.
7. Sevastopol seized on 1 Jul 42.
8. Soviet withdrawal to Chersonese rear position.

Key

Soviet front lines:
- 2 June 1942
- 2 July 1942

Turreted Coastal Batteries

Soviet 'Forts'/Air Defence Batteries

Soviet Defensive Sectors

Soviet Airfield

15. Sevastopol: The Third Axis Assault on Sevastopol, 2 June – 4 July 1942

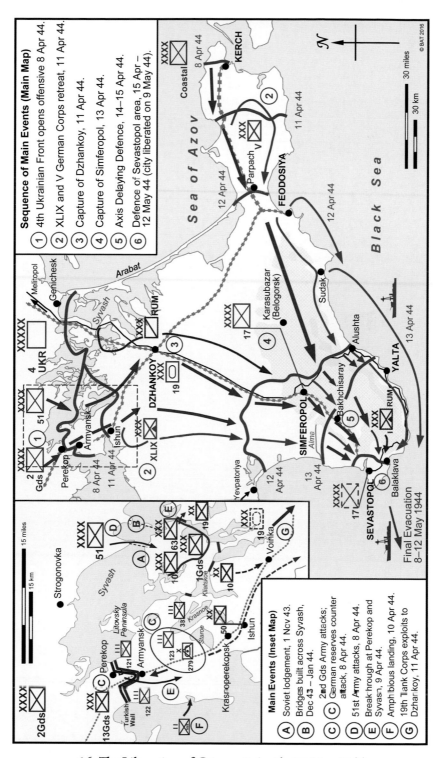

Sequence of Main Events (Main Map)

① 4th Ukrainian Front opens offensive 8 Apr 44.
② XLIX and V German Corps retreat, 11 Apr 44.
③ Capture of Dzhankoy, 11 Apr 44.
④ Capture of Simferopol, 13 Apr 44.
⑤ Axis Delaying Defence, 14–15 Apr 44.
⑥ Defence of Sevastopol area, 15 Apr –
   12 May 44 (city liberated on 9 May 44).

© BAT 2016

Sea of Azov

Black Sea

KERCH
8 Apr 44
②
11 Apr 44
Parpach
FEODOSIYA
Coastal
XXXX
V
XXX
12 Apr 44
Sudak
12 Apr 44
Arabat
Genichesk
Melitopol
Sivash
RUM
XXX
Karasubazar
(Belogorsk)
④
17
XXXX
Alushta
13 Apr 44
YALTA
5
RUM
XXX
I
Bakhchisaray
③
DZHANKOY
19
XX
Armyansk
Ishun
XXX
XLIX
②
8 Apr 44
11 Apr 44
1
51
XXXX
2 Gds
XXXX
Perekop
4
UKR
XXXXX
SIMFEROPOL
Alma
12 Apr 44
13 Apr 44
Yevpatoriya
Balaklava
6
SEVASTOPOL
17
XXXX
Final Evacuation
8–12 May 1944

30 miles
30 km

15 miles
15 km

Strogonovka
Sivash
Litovsky Peninsula
Perekop
Armyansk
III 121
III 122
Turkish Wall
13Gds
XXX
2Gds
XXXX
C
E
F
2Gds
XXXX
13Gds
XXX

51
XXXX
D
B
A
XX 19
XXX
63
XX
10
1Gds
XXX
XX
10
Kiatskoe
Ishun
Krasnoperekopsk
Krasnoe
Staroe
XXX 33
III 123
X
279
50
XX
19
G
Voihka

Main Events (Inset Map)

Ⓐ Soviet lodgement, 1 Nov 43.
Ⓑ Bridges built across Sivash,
   Dec 43 – Jan 44.
Ⓒ 2nd Gds Army attacks;
   German reserves counter
   attack, 8 Apr 44.
Ⓓ 51st Army attacks, 8 Apr 44.
Ⓔ Break through at Perekop and
   Sivash, 9 Apr 44.
Ⓕ Amph bious landing, 10 Apr 44.
Ⓖ 19th Tank Corps exploits to
   Dzhankoy, 11 Apr 44.

16. The Liberation of Crimea, 8 April –12 May 1944

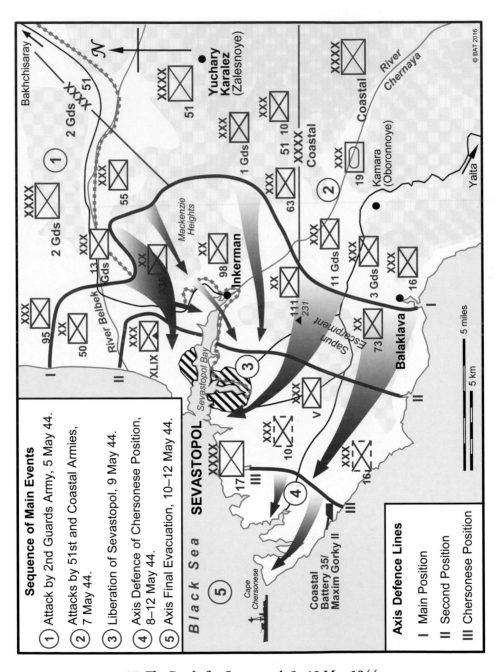

Sequence of Main Events

1. Attack by 2nd Guards Army, 5 May 44.
2. Attacks by 51st and Coastal Armies, 7 May 44.
3. Liberation of Sevastopol, 9 May 44.
4. Axis Defence of Chersonese Position, 8–12 May 44.
5. Axis Final Evacuation, 10–12 May 44.

Axis Defence Lines

I   Main Position
II Second Position
III Chersonese Position

© BAT 2016

17. The Battle for Sevastopol, 5–12 May 1944

in a chaotic, anarchic condition. It soon became clear that the Rada would be unable to exercise control without German forces occupying the remainder of the country. What had started as a strict 'economy of effort' operation suffered mission creep on a very large scale in time, space and forces. Rather than occupying only western Ukraine as originally intended, the Germans were now drawn much further eastwards to Kharkov, the Donbas industrial region and Rostov-on-Don. Ukraine, as Peter Lieb has pointed out in his illuminating description of the German campaign, had 'turned out to become [a] Pandora's Box', and an expensive one too.[71]

In late March 1918, Headquarters Army Group Eichhorn-Kiew was established in Kiev, reflecting the name of its commander-in-chief, General Field Marshal Hermann von Eichhorn. Amongst the major reinforcements already deployed to Ukraine were four divisions of Generalkommando zbV Nr. 52, commanded by General of Infantry Robert Kosch.[72] Drawn primarily from occupation duties in Romania, his command consisted of the 212nd and 217th Infantry Divisions, the 15th Landwehr Division and the Bavarian Cavalry Division.[73] As documented in the official German history of the First World War, in mid-April German forces under Kosch struck into Crimea to seize the '*Kriegshafen* (naval port) of Sevastopol', and so 'secure the ships of the Black Sea Fleet'.[74]

Bolshevik forces blocked the Perekop. They were to meet their match in Kosch, a very experienced Prussian soldier.[75] From his personal papers of the period, it is clear that he understood his role to be as much political as military, evidenced by the manner in which he negotiated his way through a web of problems in southern Ukraine and Crimea. Hence Kosch had not only to fight the Bolsheviks, but also to deal with the various competing demands of German colonists, Tatars, Ukrainians and anti-revolutionary Russians. At the same time, he managed to correspond daily with his wife, sending detailed accounts that often read as if they were designed for publication in a post-war travel guide.

In a letter of 17 April 1918, after describing at some length a local vineyard, and recounting the tasting of its best bottle, which compared well to the finest of Rhine wines, Kosch turned to the prevailing military situation. Noting laconically that 'several thousand men under the commander of the Black Sea Fleet, a sailor, are said to be gathered at the Perekop', he mused that it would be 'all the better, if they stand and fight here rather than in Sevastopol'.[76] Returning to the same theme the next day, as the German assault on the Perekop by the Bavarian Cavalry Division (reinforced by an infantry regiment of the 217th Division) was under way, Kosch opined, 'Hopefully all will work out easily and quickly here, so that resistance in Sevastopol will not be too strong'.[77] By the following day (the 19th), it was clear that the enemy defence at the Perekop had crumbled, and the Bavarian cavalry were in fast pursuit of the fleeing Bolsheviks.

By 21 April, German troops were plunging deep into Crimea on two convergent axes towards the provincial capital, Simferopol. Members of the Bolshevik government of the Soviet Tauride Republic had already fled the city the day before, aiming to sail to Novorossiysk. Their luck ran out when a Tatar band intercepted them at the Crimean coastal town of Alushta, where they were tortured and shot, avenging the murder of Celabi Cihan. At the same time, anti-Bolshevik rioting began to spread along the coast from Yalta to Feodosiya.[78] Sevastopol sailors and Red Army Guards attempted to suppress these disturbances, but such diversion dissipated the forces available to oppose the German forces. While the Bavarians continued their advance from the Perekop in the north-west, from the north-east, elements of the 15th Landwehr Division were pressing down the main railway line from Ukraine. The latter German formation had encountered a body of 2,000 men calling itself a 'Ukrainian brigade', which was likewise trying to press south as quickly as possible by train, aiming for Sevastopol. The situation was proving complex enough for Kosch without the entry of a third party. The German commander regretted that his troops had not stopped the Ukrainians, being deeply sceptical as to their composition and intentions, declaring: 'I consider this band to be fleeing Bolshevists. If it turns out that they really are Ukrainians, then they have no reason to be in the Crimea; and their presence could lead to serious developments. But in all the confusion here one cannot easily distinguish friend from foe'.[79] Unbeknown to Kosch, in fact this force belonged to the Ukrainian Pyotr Fedorovich Bolbochan, the general officer commanding of the 1st Division of the Zaporizhian Corps.

Meanwhile, matters were coming to a head in Sevastopol. As it became increasingly evident that there was little that could be done to prevent the Germans from entering the city, the question as to the future of the Black Sea Fleet became ever more urgent. Because of its strategic value, this was much more than a local issue. For months past, the ownership of the fleet had been a major concern in Petrograd, Kiev and Berlin. Whereas the Soviet government desired that the ships be evacuated as soon as possible to the safe Bolshevik harbour of Novorossiysk, the Rada maintained that the fleet ought to become the property of the Ukrainian People's Republic, and that it should be 'cleansed of any Bolshevik elements'. The German high command, though not publically contradicting the Ukrainian claim, determined that her forces – meaning Kosch's troops – should secure the fleet for the German Empire. Such was the situation, however, that notwithstanding any deliberations made in capitals, the sailors of the Black Sea Fleet were determined they would decide. At a delegates' meeting of soldiers and sailors in Sevastopol held on 21 April, it was resolved, bearing in mind that the 'Black Sea Fleet acted as the vanguard of the revolution ... and that it should never lower that banner', that the ships should be sailed to Novorossiysk.[80]

During the night of 21/22 April, the Bolshevik leader Gaven met with the commanders of local Red Army units, representatives of the fleet and the port workers, and informed them that any prolonged defence of Sevastopol would be futile. Sufficient time, however, needed to be bought in order to organise the evacuation of the Black Sea Fleet. Although no final decision had yet been made to mount this operation, additional Red forces were sent from Yevpatoriya and Sevastopol to stiffen up the imperilled battlefront along the Alma river.

As the debate about the future of the Black Sea Fleet rumbled on, German troops and, quite independently, the Ukrainians continued their advance southwards. Kosch wrote on 23 April that 'we are already in the middle of Simferopol'. Curious as to how matters would develop, he noted that in the meantime the 'Bolshevists have dug in along the historic Alma river', alluding to the Crimean War battlefield. Again, he expressed the hope that his opponent would stand and fight rather than withdraw to the 'fortress' – meaning Sevastopol.[81] On the 24th, matters in Simferopol became very confused. Kosch now accepted that the Ukrainians were legitimate in so far as they were serving in a military formation raised by the Kiev government, and conceded that they were well organised. None the less, in his opinion, 'they had no reason to be in the Crimea'.[82] Evidently, it had not yet occurred to him (or Eichhorn had failed to inform him) that the Ukrainians had exactly the same intentions as he – to capture Sevastopol and to seize as much of the Black Sea Fleet as possible. While Headquarters Army Group Eichhorn attempted to establish from the Kiev government what their forces were up to, the Germans in Simferopol – at that time inferior in numbers to the Ukrainians – were hardly in a position to do anything but wait for further direction. In the midst of this uncertain situation, the Bolsheviks had mounted a counter-attack into the city. Although it had been repulsed, it represented 'an unbelievable cheek', in Kosch's opinion, while demonstrating to him that the Germans would have to reckon with 'considerable resistance both in front of, and within, Sevastopol'.[83]

On the very same day, yet another complicating factor entered Kosch's considerations. He received a delegation from the Crimean Kurultay, which the Bolsheviks had bloodily smashed in mid-January 1918. The Tatar representatives explained to Kosch their aspirations for the foundation of a Tatar Crimean republic. Realising the importance of his visitors' message, Kosch passed on immediately the contents of their discussions to General Field Marshal Eichhorn. On 25 April, he drove forward to join his troops in Simferopol, and, appropriately enough, was quartered in the residence of a former commanding general of the Russian 7th Army Corps, General of Infantry Eck. In conversation, Kosch learned that Eck and his wife, who both spoke 'near perfect German', had been robbed by the Bolshevists – the old general's medals had been ripped off his chest. The elderly couple had lost their only son at the battle of Tannenberg in 1914; now they were living in poverty, and fearing for their lives.[84]

Within Sevastopol, opinions differed widely as to what to do about the warships in the harbour. On 25 April, the Central Committee of the Black Sea Fleet (Tsentroflot) wrote to Kiev requesting a truce, and if this were agreed, promised to hand over the fleet.[85] That same day, a delegation left for Simferopol in order to start negotiations with the German command on the basis that if the fleet were to become Ukrainian, then the occupying power would no longer require to seize Sevastopol. Taking a completely contrary position, the Sevastopol Soviet decided to evacuate the fleet, army and as much as possible of the population to Novorossiysk.[86]

By the 27th, Kosch had learned a little more about the Ukrainian contingent in Simferopol, 'with whom he hoped to avoid any serious conflict'. Apparently the 2,000–3,000 men were 'mostly officers, who were serving as soldiers'. In his opinion, in breaking all agreements made between General Field Marshal Eichhorn and the Ukrainian government, this group was 'attempting to secure the Crimea for Ukraine'. As this intention did not correspond to German wishes, Kosch was ordered to take the Ukrainians under his command, and not to involve them in any further operations beyond Simferopol. Anticipating what the Ukrainian reaction would be, he ordered his troops at 1000 hours on the 26th to surround them with heavy arms, and at the very same time required the local Ukrainian commander, Ataman Zurab Natiev of Bobochan's division, to report to him in person. Whilst all this was going on, Kosch's troops were repelling another attack on Simferopol and attacking the Bolshevists at Feodosiya, which was eventually taken on the 30th. Bowing to *force majeure*, and much to their anger, on the evening of the 27th the Ukrainian troops returned northwards by train back up the line to Dzhankoy.[87] Although there would be no Ukrainian liberation of Sevastopol, Kiev's troops had none the less played a small part in applying pressure on the Bolshevik forces in the Crimea.

During the course of 27 April, Kosch and his corps staff issued orders for the continuation of operations towards Sevastopol. His plan was simple enough. On the 28th, a combined arms detachment from the 15th Landwehr Division would conduct a flank march from Simferopol to the towns of Alushta and Yalta, and advance along Crimea's southern coast towards Balaklava, rounding up Bolshevik troops on the way, including those trying to escape from Sevastopol. The following day, the remainder of the 15th Division (deployed on the left) and the 217th Infantry Division (on the right) would undertake the main advance towards Sevastopol on the axis of the principal highway to the city. Simultaneously, the Bavarian Cavalry Division would continue to secure the eastern part of Crimea and reconnoitre towards Kerch.[88]

As Kosch did not believe that the Bolsheviks would give up Sevastopol easily, he planned a deliberate plan of attack to seize the fortress city. Quite out of the blue he received some welcome reinforcements. An Imperial Russian Army officer called Major-General Remischen appeared with a small corps of Tatar volunteers he had raised, requesting weapons and ammunition. Kosch willingly supplied these arms, as he needed all the men he could muster. Remischen also informed his German host that the Dowager Empress, Maria Feodorovna, and the Grand Duke Nikolay Nikolayevich were living under house arrest 'in a Yalta palace' (probably the Dulber at that time), guarded by Bolshevists. In response, Kosch explained that his troops would free them, but he could not promise to do anything more, as 'members of the imperial family from now on could only be treated as private persons'. In a rather spiteful remark for his wife (and probably not, for obvious reasons, shared with the Russian general), Kosch, observed that if 'they got a hungry a little, then that would be a very modest punishment for their warmongering'. Clearly no fan of the Russian monarchy, he added wistfully, 'sic transit gloria mundi' – thus passes the glory of the world.[89]

Meanwhile, German troops had captured the Russian flying school at Kacha, north of Sevastopol, seizing thirty-six aircraft, and a number of motorcars and unspecified armoured vehicles. Corps intelligence staff confirmed that the Bolshevists were preparing to defend Sevastopol, and that several warships in the harbour were under steam. Air reconnaissance photographs revealed that some were flying Ukrainian flags. Kosch interpreted this act as an attempt of the crews to avoid German attack – but it 'wouldn't help them much', he noted.[90] Unbeknown to the German commander, however, the issue of the flags was being hotly contested in Sevastopol, not only exposing the rift between pro-Ukrainian and pro-Soviet groups, but also revealing the continuing indecision as to whether the ships of the Black Sea Fleet should set sail or remain in harbour. Whereas the crews of the battleship *Volya* and the cruiser *Pamyat Merkuriya* proposed to hoist Ukrainian ensigns, and to hand over their vessels to the Ukrainian state, the majority of the other crews refused to do so. The leading Ukrainian elements within Sevastopol proposed that not only should the ships fly the blue and yellow colours of Ukraine, but the city as a whole should do so as well. Sensing which way the wind was blowing, many inhabitants of the city decided to register as Ukrainian subjects at the Ukrainian Commissariat on Nakhimov Prospekt.[91]

Confusion continued within the Black Sea Fleet when ships' crews received a succession of conflicting orders. Whereas on the 27th ships were ordered to make ready for the evacuation, two days later they were told to raise Ukrainian flags. For the revolutionary-minded, this proved an insult too far. In response, the crew of the destroyer *Kerch* signalled 'Disgrace. Sell-out of the Fleet', and then set sail for Novorossiysk. Yet this unilateral act might have provided the impetus for the execution of a much larger operation. During the night of 29/30 April, fourteen destroyers escorted a number of transports carrying Red Army troops from Sevastopol to Novorossiysk. While the Bolsheviks were abandoning the Crimean naval base, Rear Admiral M. P. Sablin (who had expediently sided with the Bolsheviks at the beginning of the year) decided to order the lowering of both Ukrainian and Red flags on the ships of the fleet. In their place, the Russian Navy's ensign, the blue on white St Andrew's Cross, was to be raised: all ships were warned to make ready for a departure to sea at 2200 hours.[92]

Also on the 30th, Kosch received a Ukrainian deputation from Sevastopol, who informed him that not only were the ships in the harbour flying their national flags, but these had been hoisted in the city as well. His visitors argued that as Ukraine and Germany were allies, there would be no purpose whatsoever in attacking Sevastopol. Sensing a trick, Kosch resolved to refer the matter to his superior, General Field Marshal Eichhorn. He anticipated that the direction he would receive would confirm his intention not to recognise the Ukrainian flags, and, above all, that he should continue with his operation to storm the fortress. As his troops seized the heights around Sevastopol, another delegation appeared from the encircled city. This party consisted of the mayor and representatives from the city *duma*, workers' soviets, dockyard workers and Ukrainian inhabitants of the city. These individuals were worried that any fighting for Sevastopol would bring about considerable suffering, and asked Kosch how he might induce the Bolsheviks to surrender. The German corps commander replied that he would guarantee their lives if they handed over the fortress without a fight. Kosch confided to his wife that he could make this offer, as 'it would be impossible for him to order the execution of 5–8000 Bolsheviks'.[93] In contrast, it must be noted, commanders of the German *Einsatzkommandos* during the Second World War had far fewer scruples. Simply said, the 'Germans of 1941 bore no semblance' to their counterparts of 1918, whose occupation had been relatively benign.[94] Kosch urged the members of the delegation from Sevastopol to take written copies of this offer and distribute them in the city, thus increasing the psychological pressure on the Bolshevist defenders.

Realising that his opponents were divided and possessed little will to fight, on 30 April Kosch ordered that Balaklava and the northern side of Sevastopol should be secured immediately. Meanwhile, the situation of the Black Sea Fleet grew ever more perilous. By the evening, lead elements of the 217th Infantry Division had entered the undefended northern side of Sevastopol, setting up machine-gun posts and field artillery positions along the shore, including Fort Constantine at the mouth of the roadstead. At the very last opportunity, for Sevastopol was bound to fall the following day, a number of ships of the Black Sea Fleet attempted to escape during the night, led by the battleship *Volya* – in contradiction of her crew's earlier intentions. Despite the complete darkness, there was no way the Russian vessels could avoid detection; soon they came under German fire. Prohibited from replying, so as not to break the terms of the Treaty of Brest-Litovsk, somehow four Russian warships managed to slip out of the roadstead and made their way safely to Novorossiysk. Apart from the *Volya*, these were her sister ship, the *Svobodnaya Rossiya* (which had suffered some damage from German artillery fire), and the destroyers *Derzkiy* and *Bespokoinyi*. The remaining naval vessels should have been scuttled in the harbour, but their crews had mysteriously 'disappeared'.[95] The *Goeben*, which was intended to appear off Sevastopol during the afternoon of the 30th, arrived late at 0200 hours on the 1st, and so failed to intercept the departing Russian ships.[96]

Notwithstanding the escape of a small part of the Black Sea Fleet, a combination of Kosch's information operations and direct military action generated the desired result of an unopposed entry into the city. At 0700 hours on 1 May, Kosch drove from Simferopol to Inkerman. His forward troops reported that there had been little resistance so far, and no serious opposition appeared forthcoming. Judging that the moment had to be seized immediately, Kosch ordered the advance to continue forthwith with three battalions, a cavalry regiment and a field artillery detachment – the only forces he had to hand. These units reached the city's outskirts without experiencing any fighting at about 1430 hours. Moving in towards the centre of Sevastopol, the Germans met silent crowds, who watched them march by. Not all the onlookers were necessarily sullen. Russian sources suggest that some city residents felt a certain relief as their occupiers arrived. 'We could have been killed by "our own"', they said, '... but now we can sigh quietly, because "our" people have left, and our enemies have come'. There was grudging respect too. Their new occupiers made a good visual impression, being 'clean, smartly uniformed and well shod ... their artillery guns glisten in the sun and their wagons are pulled by strong, well-fed horses'. Evidently a good number of citizens, 'exhausted by anarchy', sensed reluctantly in their German conquerors 'power and order'.[97] According to one authority of the period, the Bolshevik regime, just overturned, had been 'remarkable only for its senseless cruelty'; no one had been able to 'control the looting and sadism of the sailors'.[98]

At Nakhimov Square, Kosch treated himself and the spectating population of Sevastopol to a ceremonial march past with military music – he failed to explain how a band was immediately available. Yet, 'it would have been more interesting and more glorious', he commented later that day, 'had we had to fight our way in'. As to whether such a bloodless victory was any less valuable to Germany than a costly, contested, one he left no comment. Looking around the city centre and the harbour, he observed that practically all the public buildings, naval ships and commercial vessels were flying Ukrainian flags, as previously reported. Kosch was unimpressed, deeming that German emblems should be raised in their place the following day. But recognising the political sensitivity of this measure, he wisely referred any such decision to Eichhorn. Indeed, the German high command had signalled that any final settlement of the future of Crimea would be a matter reserved for negotiation between Russia and Ukraine.

Having savoured the capture of Sevastopol, and having ensured that all the important locations in the city were being suitably secured by his troops, the German commander returned with his staff to Simferopol. After stopping off at a telephone station to report the good news to army group headquarters in Kiev, he and his team celebrated their success with a bottle of *Sekt* (sparkling wine). Tired from the 'experiences of a significant day', Kosch mused in his letter home whether this would mean the end of his war, as 'fighting here is no longer likely, if no insurgency arises'. Notwithstanding that important caveat, the important work of occupation now beckoned, bringing 'a host of very political tasks'.[99]

Meanwhile, as Sevastopol was occupied by German troops, significant changes had already taken place in Kiev. The German military command consisting of General Field Marshal Eichhorn and his chief of staff, Lieutenant General Wilhelm Groener, had become increasingly unhappy in the manner in which the predominantly socialist Ukrainian government was attempting to exercise its power. On 29 April 1918, German forces sanctioned a *coup d'état*, which installed the former guards cavalry general of the Imperial Russian Army, the aristocrat Pavlo Skoropadsky, as Hetman of Ukraine. He promised to restore peace and order, and to return the country to the rule of law. Although his dictatorship proved very controversial and short-lived, Skoropadsky's contribution to his fledgling nation cannot be under-estimated. A leading Canadian–Ukrainian historian, Serhii Plokhy, credits this period of rule as a 'great boon for Ukrainian state and institution building'.[100]

The seizure of Kerch on 2 May completed the German quest for control over the entire Crimean peninsula. With the arrival of the *Goeben* and the Turkish cruiser *Hamidiye* in Sevastopol the same day, Kosch felt confident enough to declare that 'all is now secure in our hands'. He wondered, however, if it was now just a matter of a peaceful occupation, or whether future operations would extend to the Caucasus in order to secure the Bolsheviks' last harbour of refuge at Novorossiysk, and perhaps to link up with the Turks at Batum.[101] Whatever, more local affairs in Simferopol and Sevastopol demanded his attention. Kosch appointed the commander of his cavalry division, Major General Moritz, Graf von und zu Egolffstein, as military governor of Sevastopol. The Bavarian aristocrat established his headquarters in the noble Hotel Kist (now the Moscow House) on Nakhimov Square, with his staff conveniently quartered in nearby apartment blocks. At the same time, Kosch pondered on the possibility of establishing his corps headquarters some time soon in the Livadia Palace at Yalta, the former summer residence of the tsars.[102]

In Sevastopol's great harbour the remaining ships of the Black Sea Fleet were moored, consisting of seven ships of the line (all pre-dreadnoughts), three cruisers, twelve destroyers and fifteen submarines, together with a host of support vessels.[103] The occupying forces needed professional naval expertise to take charge of this considerable prize. A vice admiral of the German Navy, Albert Hopman, now enters the history of Sevastopol. Then chairman of the international Naval-Technical Commission (Nateko) in German-occupied Odessa, Hopman was appointed at the beginning of May 1918, at his own suggestion, commander-in-chief of German naval forces on land and at sea in the Black Sea area. Before he even reached Sevastopol, he had learned of the controversial flagging of the former Russian ships. Fulfilling Kosch's wishes, all these now flew the German imperial war flag. Hopman was horrified by this development, noting in his diary on 7 May: 'Instead of binding Ukraine, and later the whole of Russia, to us economically and politically, we have turned everything on its head and support the Turkish policy of robbery and murder'.[104]

In Petrograd, Russia's new leaders were aghast at the German occupation of Crimea and the takeover of the portion of the Black Sea Fleet moored in Sevastopol, which had not escaped to Novorossiysk, as 'war booty'. Lenin's formal protest to the German government of 11 May 1918 set out an angry list of denials and complaints, including:

3. If part of the [Black Sea] fleet considered itself attached to the Ukrainian fleet, it remained in Sevastopol. If our fleet left Sevastopol this only happened after the Germans' offensive and the attack on Sevastopol; consequently, in this case the Brest Treaty was violated by the Germans and not by us.
4. The facts prove, therefore, that we firmly stand by the Brest Treaty, but the Germans have violated it by occupying the entire Crimea. ...
6. They have occupied the Crimea after the German Government ... had quite precisely stated that it considered the Crimea not being part of the territory of Ukraine.

Lenin's argumentation makes it quite clear that, to Russian eyes, whether imperial or Bolshevik, the fate of Crimea remained inextricably wound up with that of Sevastopol, whose enduring importance as the arsenal of the Black Sea Fleet should never be under-emphasised. With regard to the warships then in Russian hands at Novorossiysk, Lenin offered an olive branch: 'Nor do we in any way refuse to return the fleet to Sevastopol if this port ... is not annexed in one form or another and is not occupied by Germany, and a clearly defined peace with the Germans, ... is concluded'.[105] Yet Germany's overwhelming military power at the time could not be challenged. Accordingly, the Bolshevik leader's fine rhetoric was ignored and German demands for the surrender of the ships in Novorossiysk intensified.

Arriving at Sevastopol on 9 May, Hopman quickly made contact with his colleague, Vice Admiral Hubert von Rebeur-Paschwitz, who had succeeded Souchon in July 1917 as commander of the German Mittelmeerdivision and senior officer of the Ottoman and Bulgarian naval forces allied to Germany. Hopman's two liaison officers with General Kosch, Captain Georg Wodarz and Korvettenkapitän (Lieutenant Commander) Eric Schlubach, then briefed him on the local situation. 'Conditions in Sevastopol remain very unclear', they stressed. While 'the workers had little enthusiasm', the city 'was full of sailors'. Furthermore, Major General von Egloffstein had only 'four battalions, three field artillery batteries and a cavalry squadron' at his disposal – a rather small force to control a city as large as Sevastopol. The following morning the two admirals met on the *Goeben* to discuss the situation further. Rebeur-Paschwitz reported that the Turkish government would support the establishment of a Tatar republic of the Crimea, and aim to draw this new political entity into its sphere of influence.[106] Against this complex political background, it was becoming clear to Hopman that he would have his hands full in extracting as much as possible of the Black Sea Fleet, infrastructure and valuable war materiel in Sevastopol on behalf of the German government.

Hopman was not just a leading technician of the German Imperial Navy, he was also an astute strategic thinker blessed with an uncanny feel for the politics of the confusing and volatile state of affairs now pertaining between Germany, Ukraine, Russia and Crimea. In a detailed memorandum sent to Berlin on 27 May 1918, for example, he offered a broad survey of the international situation. He criticised the view that Russia must first be broken apart and then dominated by Germany. Respecting the intrinsic strength of that nation based on a 'common language, church and culture', he regarded Russia not as a 'dying old man', but much more a 'strong young man' (*ein kräftiger Bursche*), who was currently laid low by a strong fever and thereby fully defenceless, but would 'recover'. Specifically, 'we cannot chop up the Russian nationhood'. But he was surely wrong to observe that 'Ukraine and Great Russia will always strive with elemental force to come together'.[107]

Moving away from the political sphere to the practical challenges facing the German occupiers in Sevastopol, a couple of weeks later Hopman recorded that the workers in the dockyard 'went on strike immediately after our arrival;

protracted negotiations have led to its official closure'. While a proportion of the men wanted to go back to work, others, 'under Bolshevik influence', did not. As a repair yard, the dockyard was potentially very productive, and was better suited than Nikolayev, which was optimised for shipbuilding. Furthermore, vast quantities of materiel urgently required by the German Navy lay in Sevastopol, including 'copper, bronze, asbestos packing and hemp rope'. Industrial problems apart, in this first month of occupation in Sevastopol, the Germans were enjoying a honeymoon period. 'Life [here]', observed Hopman, 'is completely peaceful. Until now there have been no disturbances, and the streets are teeming with loafers of both sexes'. Despite prices being very high, 'all the places of amusement, hotels and theatres are overflowing'.[108] For the time being, although there was no love lost between them, Russians and Germans co-existed courteously if not curiously, as exemplified within the Naval Club in which the 'German Army took over the ground floor and left the first floor to the Russian Navy' and 'coldly exchanged salutes' at the common entrance.[109] It was an extraordinary time.

Although the local situation in Sevastopol in mid-June 1918 appeared stable enough except for a rising number of strikes, the wider political arena was anything but. While tensions rose between Ukraine and Crimea, the Bolsheviks continued to boost their arms and influence within the region. As we have seen, General Kosch had met with representatives of the Tatar Kurultay in Simferopol in late April before the occupation of Sevastopol. His attempts at gaining the agreement of the former head of the Tatar assembly, Cafer Seydamet Qırımer, to form a Crimean government acceptable to Germany had failed: the latter's demands for the foundation of an independent Khanate had proved excessive. Instead, an apparently more compliant individual, a Lithuanian Tatar and former Russian Army lieutenant general, Matvei Sulkevich, was appointed to form a new provincial administration. Yet Kiev wished to interfere, and on 12 June Skoropadsky's government informed the German ambassador, Alfons, Baron Mumm von Schwarzenstein, of the necessity of Crimea joining Ukraine. Sulkevich would have none of this: on 25 June his new Crimean government not only announced the autonomy of the peninsula from Russia and Ukraine, but also introduced Crimean citizenship.[110]

A bizarre customs dispute then arose between Ukraine and Crimea, despite both jurisdictions being under German occupation. In September, Skoropadsky escalated the situation by blockading the Crimean peninsula, which forced the Crimean government to join the state of Ukraine as an autonomous region.[111] In part consequence (for there were other factors at play, notably the imminent end of the German occupation following its defeat on the Western Front and signing of the armistice on 11 November 1918), on 16 November a new anti-Soviet and anti-separatist government headed by the liberal politician of Jewish Karaite origin, Solomon Krym, replaced Sulkevich's administration.[112]

Throughout this unstable period of Crimean governance, however, Tatar nationalists had not given up their claims for complete independence. On 21 July they submitted to the German Supreme Command a letter in which they stated, 'The Crimean Tatar people who, owing to the fall of the Crimean Khanate 135 years ago, fell under [the] Russian yoke', [are fortunate in having this opportunity] to report their political aspirations to the attention of the German government'.[113] Claiming to represent the majority of the population (a deliberate exaggeration as the true proportion was nearer 30 per cent), they demanded 'the transformation of Crimea into an independent neutral Khanate, but supporting German and Turkish policies; recognition of independence by Germany and her allies; creation of a Tatar government with the aim of liberating Crimea from Russian domination and Russian political influence'. Significantly, while stressing their ambition for independence, the Tatars expressed their support for the Central Rada of Ukraine.[114] Nearly 100 years later, many Tatars and Ukrainians would unite in their common opposition to Russia's re-annexation of Crimea in March 2014.

While Crimea's future was being determined in 1918, on 11/12 June Bolshevik forces had executed a daring amphibious landing west of Taganrog on the Sea of Azov. With about 10,000 men, the Reds had destroyed the city, part of a much wider struggle to undermine and ultimately overthrow an independent Ukrainian state. At the same time, Germany had become increasingly impatient with Bolshevik Russia over her failure to hand over ships of the Black Sea Fleet harbouring in Novorossiysk. On 14 June, Germany demanded that the ships be returned to Sevastopol by no later than 19 June, having guaranteed that after the war the fleet would be returned to Russia. If Russia did not comply, Germany would advance on all fronts. Reacting to this ultimatum, Lenin had directed by secret instruction that the ships should be scuttled. Within the crews, however, opinions were divided. While eight warships, including the *Volya*, sailed for Sevastopol, on 19 June the dreadnought *Svobodnaya Rossiya* and five destroyers were scuttled at Novorossiysk.

Within the German Navy, dissension was also on the increase. On 28 July, a secret meeting was detected on the *Goeben*, then undergoing repairs in Sevastopol's dockyard. Sixty German sailors were arrested: it was believed that Bolshevik thinking had infected the sailors involved. Later Soviet sources would claim that six Germans were executed for their mutinous activity.[115]

The German occupation of Crimea and Sevastopol continued throughout the summer and early autumn of 1918 while the fortunes of the Central Powers declined markedly, as did Hopman's confidence and morale. Ludendorff's series of grand offensives on the Western Front had come to a grinding halt at the Second Battle of the Marne in mid-July. From 8 August onwards, Allied forces had commenced their own offensive operations in what became known as the 'Hundred Days Campaign' that progressively pushed German forces into withdrawing eastwards towards the Rhine. The eventual armistice on 11 November, however, was as much the result of Germany's allies being knocked out of the war, combined with mounting domestic tensions that had led to the announcement on 9 November of the abdication of Kaiser Wilhelm II. Within Russia, the Volunteer Army was fighting the Red Army on the Kuban peninsula: this conflict could soon spread to Crimea. Bad news was coming in fast from all fronts.

Already in mid-October, Hopman faced two parallel challenges in Sevastopol: how to deal with a revitalised local Bolshevik threat, and how to defend Sevastopol against a possible attack by Entente forces. Dealing with the first, Hopman discussed with local leaders the proposed establishment of a *Schutzwache* (local guard force), 'in case of an unexpected withdrawal of German troops to ensure the safety of life and property'. International developments, including Turkey's unilateral peace offer on 18 October 1918, encouraged almost daily 'the wildest rumours of an Entente fleet appearing off Sevastopol'. As the 'end' approached 'ever closer', Hopman grew increasingly concerned about the small number of German troops available to defend Sevastopol and the parlous state of the coastal defence batteries, many of which had been looted and vandalised. While he noted hopefully the return into service of the *Volya* and the announcement that *Kagul* was partially operational on 15 October, Hopman was surely naïve in thinking that their crews would fight anyone, let alone an Allied fleet.[116]

Hopman described the armistice of 11 November as the 'blackest day in all German history'. Within a couple of weeks, British, French and Italian ships would be welcomed on their entry into Sevastopol. The next day (the 12th), he received orders that German forces in Crimea were to be evacuated. This complex task, Hopman realised immediately, would require discussion and agreement with the Entente's naval authorities. In a surprising development, the former tsarist commander-in-chief of the Black Sea Fleet, Kolchak, offered his services to help negotiate the necessary arrangements. His offer was not taken up. Kolchak was soon commanding White forces in Siberia.

CHAPTER 11

ALLIED INTERVENTION AND THE RUSSIAN CIVIL WAR

'People of Russia! Alone in its struggle against the oppressor, the Russian Army has been maintaining an unequal contest in its defence of the last strip of Russian territory on which law and truth hold sway.'

Proclamation of General Wrangel, 1920[1]

The Entente Powers and the Russian Civil War

Many of the world's most bloody and brutal of conflicts are civil wars: the bitter experience of Russia, Ukraine, Crimea and Sevastopol over the period 1918–20 proved no exception. As a leading historian of the Russian Civil War has observed, such conflicts 'are tragedies that shape the histories of nations…. [They] leave lasting scars, for defeat in civil war obliterates the principles for which the vanquished fought, just as victory elevates the beliefs of the victors into new, self-evident truths that reshape a nation's destiny'.[2] The war brought widespread destruction and the deaths of many tens of thousands – sailors, soldiers and civilians alike – to Crimea and Sevastopol. The struggle between the Red

Bolsheviks and the White counter-revolutionaries for the peninsula and southern Russia's main naval base served as the main epilogue of that terrible conflict.

Although the fate of Crimea and Sevastopol is accorded only relatively minor status in some accounts of the Russian Civil War, their experiences are in many ways characteristic of other parts of the former Russian Empire. The conflict was not merely an internecine affair between Russians of different ideological and political persuasions. Allied – *Entente* – intervention in Russia, originally designed to prevent critical war materiel from falling into the hands of the Germans, evolved into attempts to limit the spread of Bolshevik rule through active support to the White cause.[3] Thus it played a significant part in determining the intensity and duration of the conflict.

At times it suited the eventual winner, Soviet Russia, to exaggerate the impact of foreign intervention, for how else could corrupt and incompetent White forces have fought for so long? Conversely, Soviet historians also downplayed the impact of Allied intervention, wishing to portray the Bolshevik forces as more than strong enough to prevail and their victory in the Civil War as just and inevitable. The intervening powers not only underestimated the complexity of the situation in revolutionary Russia, but also were inconsistent in their approach and often incoherent in co-ordinating their actions.[4] More damningly, their incongruent efforts proved ultimately futile as poor policies, the results of meagre understanding, were undermined by bad strategy, in which the desired ends, appropriate ways and available means never balanced.[5]

The Entente's support to the White armies on Russian soil left a legacy of bitterness in the Soviet Union that lasted at least a generation. The series of interventions confirmed the correctness of the Marxist–Leninist belief that the 'capitalist–imperialists' would not, indeed could not, allow the socialist revolution to survive. Such perceptions of an inevitable struggle underpinned Soviet domestic and foreign policy decisions for decades.

The presence of foreign forces did not decide the Russian Civil War: it merely prolonged the agony on all sides. According to one recent interpretation, 'although it may not have prevented a White defeat', Allied intervention might possibly have represented 'the key factor in forestalling the sort of Europe-wide "Red victory" that Lenin had envisioned'.[6] While this intriguing view remains open to academic debate, there is little doubt that intervention proved unpopular at home. The British and French governments found it difficult to justify and sustain expensive foreign deployments when there were so many other matters to attend to in the wake of a crippling world war and consequent economic dislocation. Military resources were also stretched as both nations demobilised their armed forces rapidly. On account of the war weariness of the troops, and the risks of exposing them to Bolshevik subversion, many senior French officers and officials were sceptical of intervention.[7] Such feeling was mirrored in Britain, where domestic political hostility, such as manifest in the 'Hands Off Russia' campaign, eventually put paid to interventions.[8]

Following the Russian October Revolution, Britain and France had agreed on 23 December 1917 to allocate areas of responsibility in operations against the Bolsheviks in southern Russia and Turkish forces in the Caucasus. According to this convention, France would assume a zone along the western and northern shores of the Black Sea encompassing Bessarabia (Romania), Ukraine and Crimea. Britain would focus on the south-eastern Black Sea region, including 'the Cossack territories of the Caucasus, Armenia, Georgia and Kurdistan.'[9] Sevastopol, at the centre of the Black Sea and lying at the intersection of both spheres, was equally important to both Britain and France. Critically, the security of the region could not be guaranteed without exercising control over the Russian Black Sea Fleet.

In any military or naval endeavour involving allies or coalition partners, integrated action is best achieved through unified command. Despite the creation of a Supreme War Council in November 1917, the combined command of Allied forces remained a contentious issue, not least in maritime affairs. In October 1918, for example, there had been an angry exchange of letters between the British Prime Minister, Lloyd George, and his French counterpart, Clémenceau, with regard to the command of naval forces acting against Turkey. As each nation claimed overall command, professional rivalry and personal bad blood between the admirals concerned further undermined Allied cohesion. Captain George Chetwode, the commanding officer of HMS *Blenheim*, reported from the Aegean naval base of Mudros on 20 October 1918 that: 'Our C.-in-C [Vice Admiral Sir Somerset Gough-Calthorpe] is here and is not at present in command of the allied forces'. At the time, that responsibility was vested in the French Vice Admiral Jean-François Amet. Chetwode noted that Gough-Calthorpe's subordinate, Rear Admiral Michael Culme-Seymour, commanding the British Aegean Squadron, appeared 'to try to run the show and doesn't hit it off at all with Amet'. Furthermore, Gough-Calthorpe 'has applied to the Admiralty to be placed in command but I believe the French are objecting which makes the position rather odd, as at present Calthorpe is only here in a sort of advisory capacity'.[10] For some reason, the British then proceeded to exclude Amet from the armistice negotiations with Turkey, signed at Mudros on 30 October – hardly a good instance of Allied co-operation.

Meanwhile, within South Russia, the White 'Volunteer Army' had grown in strength and confidence. At the same time as Kosch had advanced into Crimea, other German forces made for Rostov-on-Don, who entered the city during the first week of 1918. This move provided support to the Don Cossacks, who had previously ejected Red forces from the Host's centre of Novocherkassk. Hence the Whites were able to establish a secure base of operations with Cossack support. Over the period June–August 1918, White troops under the command of General Anton Ivanovich Denikin (a former lieutenant general in the Imperial Russian Army) conducted a successful campaign to capture the Kuban peninsula.[11] Critically, they also seized the port of Novorossiysk on 26 August 1918, which facilitated the passage of reinforcements from Crimea, including Wrangel, who had emerged from hiding. Denikin assumed overall command of the White cause in South Russia when the leader of the Volunteer Army, Mikhail Vasiliyevich Alekseyev, died on 8 October 1918.[12] From then on, the fate of Crimea and Sevastopol during the Russian Civil War was to be inextricably linked to the varying fortunes of Denikin, and of his most able subordinate and successor, Wrangel.

ALLIED INTERVENTION AND THE BATTLE FOR SEVASTOPOL, NOVEMBER 1918 – APRIL 1919

Sevastopol's population eagerly awaited the arrival of the Allied fleet in late November 1918: the occasion promised to be a great celebration of Allied–Russian friendship. Naturally there would be rejoicing about the imminent repatriation of the German occupiers. Perhaps more fundamentally, it was generally held that Allied forces would bring peace and stability in troubled times. Subsequent events would demonstrate that neither the British nor the French fully comprehended the risks, or grasped the opportunities, of supporting the anti-Bolshevik, obstensibly liberal government in Crimea, and elsewhere in southern Russia and Ukraine. The failure to invest sufficient understanding and resources in the task of intervention severely reduced its chances of success from the very start. There is surely a simple lesson here: half-thought-through and half-hearted measures may often result in complete failures. Yet our recent history is replete with apparently unlearned lessons.

'In wonderful sunny weather', at 1030 hours on Sunday, 24 November 1918, the British cruiser HMS *Canterbury*, together with an escorting destroyer, steamed into Sevastopol's harbour. The arrival of the two Royal Navy warships finally signalled to the people of Sevastopol and their erstwhile German occupiers that the Great War was over. While it represented a 'bitter moment' for Hopman, the city's population streamed to the quayside to witness this happy event. Flying proudly their St Andrew's Cross ensigns, the ships of the Black Sea Fleet, led by the *Volya*, paid their due naval respects. At noon, the commanding officer of the *Canterbury*, Captain Percy Royds, accompanied by his interpreter, Lieutenant William Hozier, came ashore to hold discussions with Hopman. Their purpose was to make arrangements for the forthcoming arrival of the main Allied battle squadron. Although Hopman recorded a number of technical details involved, what seemed to impress him most was the agreeable manner in which the whole conversation (conducted primarily in English) had proceeded: 'very smoothly and without severity, thanks to the amicable and humorous nature of Royds'.[13]

Significantly, the Royal Naval captain carried an urgent special task from none other than the British monarch, George V. Required without delay to establish contact with the Dowager Empress, the King's aunt, Royds sent her a letter by motorcycle despatch rider that very first afternoon in Sevastopol.[14] In subsequent days, the commanding officer of the *Canterbury* paid a number of visits on Maria Feodorovna.[15] She resisted all attempts at rescue from an increasingly dangerous situation in Crimea, and more locally for her in Yalta, until she boarded HMS *Marlborough* very reluctantly on 7 April 1919. So started the exile of the surviving members of the Russian royal family.

The morning of Tuesday, 26 November 1918 marked the entry of the Allied squadron into Sevastopol. Again, unseasonably warm and sunny weather blessed the occasion. Large cheering crowds welcomed the succession of battleships dropping anchor in the roadstead. First, the Italian *Roma*, followed by the French *Justice* and *Démocratie*, and completed by the British dreadnoughts *Temeraire* and *Superb*, the latter flying the flag of Vice Admiral Sir Somerset Gough-Calthorpe, commander-in-chief of the Mediterranean Fleet. The small 'scout' cruiser HMS *Skirmisher* and about twelve destroyers escorted these ships of the line. Hopman regarded the spectacle as 'a terrible moment'. While he could grudgingly respect and accept the presence of the British ships, he felt that the Italians and French were just enjoying a 'cheap triumph'. He poured scorn on the latter's ships that looked 'unsightly and dirty'. Reflecting on his discussions with the British and French naval senior officers later that day, Hopman again praised the attitude of the former at the expense of their continental allies. He described the senior French naval officer, Rear Admiral Gustav Lejay, as 'old, really fat ... [and] bad-looking', who 'injected poison and venom' into the discussions. 'What a pity that we are in dispute with the British world', he wrote, for the English 'were and remain our best and only comrades in the world'.[16] Yet such sentiments could not change the bitter reality facing him: a disillusioned Hopman would soon leave Sevastopol for a defeated if not humbled Germany.

The evacuation of the German military garrison of Sevastopol and naval teams had already started on 15 November: the waiting sailors and soldiers demanded impatiently to be sent home as soon as possible. According to a Russian eyewitness, the 'Germans were losing their iron discipline'. Order broke down as 'meetings and assemblies occurred in various places – in the former Army and Navy Club, in the Navy Assembly Hall, in units and on the ships'. While German troops had 'entered the Crimea during the Spring almost on a ceremonial march', in the autumn they departed the peninsula 'nibbling sunflower seeds' in an undisciplined, dishevelled state.[17] As Allied forces supervised the evacuation of the remaining German forces, the burghers of Sevastopol were not slow in presenting claims for damages resulting from the German occupation. 'Hotels, schools, shops and private persons' all made applications for recompense, which amounted to an 'astronomic number, namely 2,563,235,505 roubles'. The people of Sevastopol, many of whom may have lodged either fallacious or inflated claims, were to be disappointed: the Allies did not consider it their duty to provide any reimbursement whatsoever for the enemy's actions.[18]

In his first report from Sevastopol of 12 December 1918, Vice Admiral Gough-Calthorpe informed the British Admiralty that he had received a series of senior visitors, all competing for attention and assistance. These included Rear Admiral Vyacheslav Klochkovsky 'of the Russian navy' and Lieutenant General Nikolay Baron de Bode, 'Chief Military representative in the Crimea of General Denikin', as well as Vice Admiral Hopman and Lieutenant General Georg Graf von Waldersee, the German governor of Sevastopol since October.[19] Deputations also came from the Ukrainian and Crimean governments, the mayor and town council of Sevastopol and the Polish inhabitants of the city. From these various conversations, Gough-Calthorpe learned that following the evacuation of the German garrison, it was 'generally anticipated' that 'the Bolshevist element ... would reassert itself with all its attendant horrors, unless the Germans were replaced by Allied forces'. The Bolsheviks were said to have 'large quantities of arms in concealment and to be only awaiting their opportunity'. In contrast, the 'Volunteer Army' existed 'almost only in name'. The latter had fewer 'than 1,000 men in the whole of the Crimea' and these were 'ill armed' and lacked 'equipment and stores'. Noting the stark realities facing him and his Allied squadron, Gough-Calthorpe remarked:

> The Crimean Government appears to be composed of men of little influence, and has no armed forces nor police at its disposal. Its main desire is to obtain the assistance of anyone who is likely to afford protection to the Crimea, and therefore it looks to the army of General Denikin and also to the Allies for salvation from the Bolshevists. It has hitherto been entirely amenable to German control for the same reasons.

While the British admiral might have sensed a coming showdown between the Bolsheviks and their diverse opponents in Crimea and Sevastopol, he observed that as the 'whole political and security situation in the Ukraine is so complex, and changes with such rapidity', it was 'impossible to foresee what developments may occur'.[20] According to other sources, Gough-Calthorpe had insulted the Russian guests aboard his flagship by making them 'wait for hours without even being able to sit down', and by refusing to go ashore to 'receive the traditional bread and salt' of welcome. Whether he knew 'nothing about the political situation in the Crimea' seems unlikely in the light of the discussions he had held with Hopman and Waldersee and the reports he sent home.[21] None the less, if such incidents are to be believed, it would suggest that Gough-Calthorpe had a poor feel for Russian sensitivities: some of his subsequent actions would only make matters worse.

In the meantime, assessing that the departure of the Germans would create a power vacuum in Sevastopol, Gough-Calthorpe considered it necessary to 'make provision for a minimum force' to replace them pending the arrival of the French division which was due to be ordered to the Ukraine. Hence the British admiral, exercising the freedom of command which he then enjoyed, redeployed '500 British marines from the Dardanelles and Bosphorus forts' to Sevastopol in order to provide 'proper protection of the magazines and dockyard against pillage and arson'.[22] The arrival of the Royal Marines contingent on 1 December 1918 marked the presence of the first British armed force in the city since the Allied evacuation in the early summer of 1856 following the end of the Crimean War.

Unsurprisingly, the future of the Russian warships in Sevastopol's harbour did not escape Gough-Calthorpe's close attention. In the same report he recorded that the battleship *Volya* and two destroyers had been taken over by Royal Navy crews and were carrying out trials under their own power. He determined that these vessels should be sent to the port of Ismid, in the Sea of Marmara, for care and maintenance – a pronouncement, which he admitted, had caused 'considerable feeling amongst the Officers of the Russian Navy and the local population'.[23] He justified his decision on the grounds that it would provide 'a salutary and desirable object lesson of the consequences of allowing their ships to fall into German hands and to be manned by them with the clear intention of using them against the Allies'.[24] In this judgement, which smacks of retribution rather than of necessity, Gough-Calthorpe may have made the mistake of looking back rather than forwards. His chief concern was dealing with the complexities of the fast evolving conflict in Russia rather than re-fighting the war with Germany. In the prevailing situation he was badly served by the lack of clear strategic direction from London as to what his role might be or which side, if any, he should take in the conflict. In a report home two months later, for example, on 18 February 1919, he noted that British forces were now 'operating with Admiral Kolchak's anti-Bolshevik Army at Omsk' (in Siberia) and that 'anti-Bolshevik operations appear to be taking place in the North of Russia'. The commander-in-chief of the Mediterranean Fleet then requested that 'active assistance may be given to the Volunteer Army in South Russia when it appears desirable by H.M. ships observing that our present indefinite policy is creating an unfavourable impression in the Volunteer Army'.[25] The telegrammed reply from London was clear enough in this instance: 'War Cabinet have approved that active assistance may be given to the Volunteer Army provided that no Naval forces are landed without reference to and permission from England'.[26]

By the turn of the year, the security situation in Ukraine, South Russia and Crimea was fast unravelling as the fighting between the Bolsheviks and their opponents intensified. On the departure of the Royal Marines in late December, the French 176th Infantry Regiment took over as the main Allied contingent in Crimea, which was supplemented by a Greek infantry regiment in January 1919. Altogether, this combined force of about 4,000 men was never able to establish its influence or control much beyond the boundaries of Sevastopol, let alone protect Crimea and its liberal government from any Bolshevik incursion or insurrection.

Within the city, the French and Greek troops found themselves in the position of progressively beleaguered and incompetent bystanders as Red and White elements vied for power. At first, the struggle between the two factions was largely peaceful, but it became increasingly violent. Bolshevik proclamations calling for opposition to the imposition of a mobilisation law for the Volunteer Army and for the overthrow of the Crimean government appeared on 20 February. Within a month, confidence in that administration had slumped. Metal workers within Sevastopol held a protest meeting, demanding the removal of the Volunteer Army, the freeing of political prisoners and the establishment of control by the Sevastopol Soviet of Workers and Peasants' deputies. Matters deteriorated rapidly when a detachment of the Whites attacked and killed a number of the meeting's organisers, not only alienating many of Sevastopol's population, but also prompting the withdrawal of labour of much of Sevastopol's workforce. Furthermore, Mensheviks and Socialist Revolutionaries threatened to leave the government, whose days were now numbered, its authority being undermined by the actions of Reds and Whites alike.[27]

Elsewhere, as French and Greek forces were already engaged in southern Ukraine, it was becoming increasingly evident that the White Army – unless heavily reinforced – was not in a position to prevent the Bolshevik advance. Crimea's (and thus Sevastopol's) survival as a liberal, counter-revolutionary province, would depend on the ability of the Allies to provide forces for its defence. Yet when the French commander-in-chief, Louis Franchet d'Espèrey (the former commander of the Allied Army of the Orient at Salonika, disparagingly nicknamed by British troops as 'Desperate Frankie'), visited Sevastopol on 25 March 1919 he brought remonstrations rather than resources to bear. Criticising the Crimean government and the Volunteer naval command, he 'denounced as shameful the behaviour of Russian officers, intelligentsia, and bourgeoisie in trying to hide behind the back of the Allies, expecting others to do the fighting'.[28] The French senior officer knew only too well that there was little prospect of the Allies committing sufficient forces to tilt the balance in support of the Whites.

At the end of March 1919, Gough-Calthorpe submitted a most gloomy report. He documented the loss of the city of Kherson on the 11th following an attack by 'superior Bolshevik forces and after heavy fighting'. Notwithstanding the fact that the Greeks had done 'good work with the bayonet', the evacuation of the town's French and Greek defenders ensued. In turn, this setback triggered the French evacuation of Nikolayev. In this matter, the British admiral severely criticised his unreliable ally, and more specifically the local commander concerned, General Philippe Henri d'Anselme, for 'losing his head'. Illustrating just how complicated matters were at the time, about 5,000 German troops still waiting to go home had been 'ordered to cover the evacuation, being warned that their own evacuation depended on their so doing'.[29] Gough-Calthorpe highlighted in a disparaging manner the temporary cease-fire arranged between the Bolsheviks and the French high command, which was to set a pattern in future evacuations. The British admiral, however, was probably not fully aware of the weak, if not wobbly, condition of the French Army at the time. The Allies' units were undermanned with soldiers returning home and not being replaced, and undermined by the 'corrosive effects of Bolshevik propaganda'. In mid-March d'Anselme had warned Franchet d'Espèrey that 'French troops have become unemployable. Entire companies refuse to march even under fire and even to support their comrades'.[30] There was little doubt that both French political will and military morale were sinking fast.

While Odessa seemed set to be the next city to fall to the Bolsheviks, the situation in Crimea also proved 'very unsatisfactory'. Although a weak Volunteer Army garrison at the Perekop had been reinforced from troops from Simferopol, who had been relieved by Greek forces from Sevastopol, Gough-Calthorpe considered the condition of the Volunteer Army 'as bad as it can be'. In his view, it was improbable that tired troops, 'short of food and clothing, and low in morale' would 'long resist any determined attack against either the Perekop or the Simferopol railway' – the latter offering an approach route over the Chongar peninsula. Gough-Calthorpe might not have been a political genius, but forthcoming events would prove the uncanny accuracy of his professional assessment as to how matters would unfold:

[The White forces] are thoroughly disliked by both Bolsheviks and Bourgeoisie and the first news of a Bolshevik success in the north is almost certain to provoke a general Bolshevik outbreak in the Crimea, accompanied by more than the usual list of outrages and massacres, for the Bolsheviks will fall upon the Russian aristocracy, so many of whom have taken refuge in the Crimea, with particular fury.

In vain, he pleaded for the deployment of sufficient forces to hold Crimea. 'A month ago', in his opinion, 'even a comparatively small Allied force would probably have prevented any attack on the Crimea'. Moreover, its presence 'would have restored confidence in, and encouraged, the Volunteer Army'. It was 'now too late for any half measures'. Taking a swipe at the government in Whitehall, and exposing all his frustration, Gough-Calthorpe observed that 'when the massacre has taken place the blame will undoubtedly be apportioned to the Allies, and perhaps more particularly to the British – in whom, at the beginning, so much confidence was placed – for their lack of policy and general indecision'.[31] Such a description of the debacle could easily have been applied seventy years later when European forces (British, French and Dutch), operating under a United Nations peacekeeping mandate, found themselves in similarly complex conditions during the brutal civil war then raging in Bosnia–Herzegovina.

It was not long until the whole pack of weak White cards tumbled in Crimea: the Bolsheviks re-established power ruthlessly throughout the peninsula and threatened Sevastopol. Despite Gough-Calthorpe's dire warnings, no Allied troops blocked the Perekop and the other entrances to Crimea. On 3 April 1919, the 14th Red Army brushed aside the feeble elements of the Volunteer Army, which guarded the Turkish Wall. It had been planned that this ancient fortification would be strengthened in anticipation of an attack, but such was the disorganisation of the Whites, nothing substantial had been undertaken. Within a week, Bolshevik forces had occupied Simferopol, forcing Solomon Krym's ineffective government and the remaining White troops to flee. The latter withdrew eastwards to the Kerch peninsula, where they dug in. Soon Red forces advanced on Sevastopol, their principal objective, and seized the outskirts of the town at the Malakhov Hill on 15 April.

By this time, the Allied garrison had been reinforced by French colonial troops, battalions of Senegalese and Algerian infantry on 12 and 14 April. The addition of these units brought up the Allied force on land to about 7,000 men. Theoretically, taking into account the massive firepower of the Allied naval squadron, the recently appointed local French commander, Colonel Eugène Gervais Trousson, probably had just sufficient strength to mount a determined defence of the city. He failed, however, to co-operate closely with the local Russian authorities and forces. No diplomat, Trousson ignored the wishes of Crimean officials, peremptorily declared martial law, and effectively demoted General Subbotin, the commander of the Volunteer Army forces in Sevastopol, to act as his assistant. While the combative Trousson was certainly ready to fight, the sailors of the French Black Sea Fleet were less so. It soon became evident that the French, as in Nikolayev, and most recently in Odessa, which had fallen to the Bolsheviks without a struggle on the 7 April 1920, had little stomach to spill much blood for Sevastopol.

Amongst this chaotic situation, the Red Army was not able simply to march into the city as Kosch's German troops had done just under a year before. Although the account given in one major text about the Russian Civil War in southern Russia suggests there was only 'a brief exchange of fire' between the Allies and the Red Army, the records of the Royal Navy indicate otherwise.[32] The first battle for Sevastopol since the Crimean War took place over the period 15–17 April 1919. While a relatively minor affair in comparison with the great sieges of 1854–55 and 1941–42, it deserves more than a passing reference in Sevastopol's military history.

We are fortunate that Culme-Seymour, who by this time commanded the British Black Sea and Caspian Squadron, left a detailed account of the action at Sevastopol and the associated French mutiny. His first report regarding the situation at the Crimean naval base was compiled as at 1800 hours, 18 April. Flying his flag on the battleship HMS *Emperor of India*, he arrived at the city during the evening of 17 April. Although he missed the main period of fighting, he consulted the commanding officer of the British light cruiser HMS *Calypso*, Captain Bertram Thesinger, and was further updated by the commander of the French naval forces in the Black Sea, Vice Admiral Amet, on board his flagship, the battleship *Jean Bart*. Both individuals he spoke to had witnessed at first hand combat and diplomacy with the Bolsheviks.

Events had unfolded very quickly on the 15th. At 1330 hours local time, the British monitor *M.17*, positioned at the head of the harbour, reported firing from the south-east. On going forward to investigate, Thesinger encountered a group of Bolshevik cavalry, which had 'come down to the shore with a white flag'. While three Bolshevik representatives were permitted to board the *Jean Bart* to meet Admiral Amet in order to discuss possible terms for a truce, Thesinger was held as a hostage. Rather surprisingly, despite the fact that he was the senior Allied officer present in Sevastopol, Amet 'decided that the terms of the Armistice were for the Military to decide and turned the delegation over to Colonel Trousson'. The Bolsheviks demanded that the Allies evacuate Sevastopol within seven days, while the Red Army would 'immediately appoint a Revolutionary Committee and a Workmen's Soviet'. In response, although the French were prepared to allow the establishment of a Soviet Municipal Government, no Red Army troops would be permitted to enter the city. As this reply did not satisfy the Bolsheviks, 'hostilities recommenced at 16:00'. Presumably Thesinger was released beforehand as he lived to tell the tale to his British superior.[33]

All the Royal Navy warships, including the *Calypso*, were moved to positions outside the roadstead, where they had already come under fire from Bolshevik artillery. At 1600 hours the Allied guns, predominantly French, 'opened a heavy bombardment on the Bolshevik troops and headquarters'. In his report, Culme-Seymour noted that it was 'much regretted that the enemy made their headquarters in the English Cemetery and the French found themselves compelled to bombard this [locality]'. There were other echoes from the previous war: the Allied main defence line in 1919 ran 'from the west side of Careening Bay' and followed 'the line of bastions to Quarantine Bay'. In other words, there was almost a complete reversal of the situation of the siege of 1854–55 when the British and French attacked, and the Russians defended, the very same positions.

During the night of 15th/16th, the Bolsheviks made a strong assault, surprising a French outpost at the Mamelon, and 'driving out the defenders'. The following morning, 'detachments of the Senegalese recaptured it at the point of the bayonet' – echoing an engagement of an earlier conflict. Yet the similarities with the Crimean War can be taken too far. In 1919 nothing like the force densities of 1854–55 pertained; the old fortifications were run-down, and no modern ones had been erected in their place to face an attack to landward. French and Greek soldiers hurriedly erected barbed wire entanglements across the city streets to impede Red Army attacks and established machine-gun nests to cover them. While the French held the eastern sector of Sevastopol's perimeter as far as the head of the Southern Bay, the Greeks were responsible for the remainder of the southern circuit of the city. Although neither British soldiers nor marines were landed, Royal Navy seaplanes 'did good work with bombs and machine guns' during the course of 16 and 17 April, attacking 'enemy batteries and troops on the Balaklava road'. Apparently, the combination of naval gunfire and close air support had 'great moral effect'; the Bolsheviks asked again for a conference to discuss terms late on the 17th. In the event, a suspension of hostilities until midnight on the 25th was agreed.

Fearing that the Bolsheviks, 'not yet in force outside the town', would 'probably use the armistice to bring up considerable reinforcements from outside the Crimea', Culme-Seymour was unconvinced as to the wisdom of agreeing to this accord. Yet he could only advise his French allies, rather than prevail on them to fight on and retain Sevastopol. While only holding the rank of a colonel, Trousson held the inter-Allied appointment of 'Senior Commander of Allied Troops on the Crimea', and enjoyed the 'prerogatives of a major-general'. Thus he was equal in status to the Royal Navy rear admiral. A particular point of disagreement between the Allies arose over the British wish to disable or sink as many as possible of the Russian vessels in the harbour, and to destroy the considerable stocks of ammunition and mines in Sevastopol's arsenals. While the French were concerned that were these to be blown up, the resulting explosion would 'destroy the town', the British were adamant that as much war materiel as possible should be destroyed.[34]

Unimpressed by the accommodation reached between the French and the Bolsheviks, Gough-Calthorpe sent his naval counterpart a stiff, uncompromising rejoinder:

> ... we are definitely committed to afford support to General Denikin and the Russian Volunteer Army. This being so any compromise with their enemies, unless dictated by absolute military necessity, would in my opinion, be detrimental to their interests and therefore wrong.
>
> Although the Allies have been unable to prevent the invasion of the Crimea by Bolshevist forces it is in the highest degree important that the latter should be prevented from acquiring the valuable resources of Sevastopol. Their possession of that base would constitute an ever present menace to our sea communications in the Black Sea, with the liability of our being compelled to resume anti-submarine warfare and the protection of merchant vessels against raiders.

Gough-Calthorpe made it very clear to Amet that 'if the evacuation of Sevastopol becomes a military necessity', it would be 'a matter of supreme importance to destroy beyond possibility of repair all vessels or war material ... which are capable of being in any way employed against the Allies'. Furthermore, he warned, 'the previous record of the Bolshevists gives no reason to suppose that we could rely on their strictly carrying out undertakings they entered into by convention with us'.[35]

Such were his responsibilities, Culme-Seymour could not solely concentrate on affairs in Sevastopol. He was also required to support the troops of the Volunteer Army and the elements of the British mission, which were assisting them. At the same time as the Red Army was closing in on Sevastopol, the remnants of the Volunteer Army on Crimea were defending the Kerch peninsula, holding a defensive line across the isthmus just to the east of Parpach. Allied warships (British, French and Greek) positioned to the north (Arabat Bay) and south (Kaffa Bay) of the peninsula stood by to provide naval gunfire support.[36] On 19 April, Culme-Seymour had departed Sevastopol for Novorossiysk, where he intended to meet General Sir George Milne, Commander-in-Chief Armies of the Black Sea, and then to proceed together with Milne to meet Denikin in Ekaterinodar (now Krasnodar) on the Kuban peninsula. The British admiral never reached his destination. While *en route*, he received a most disturbing report from HMS *Calypso* that the French fleet had mutinied, and that it had been decided to evacuate Sevastopol. Culme-Seymour returned immediately to the city during the night of the 20th/21st. On arrival at 1100 hours on the 21st, the trusty Captain Thesinger briefed him as to what had occurred in his absence.

Disturbances had broken out on the battleship *Jean Bart* during the evening of 19 April, which then spread to the *France*. On 20 April, the crews of the battleships *Justice*, *Mirabeau* and *Verginaud* joined the protest. On the *France* and *Jean Bart*, at the heart of the mutiny, red flags were hoisted and sailors boisterously sang the '*Internationale*'. Rather rashly, in order to undermine the mutiny, shore leave had been at first refused, then granted, on these two battleships.[37] About 500 men landed from these two French ships proceeded to form 'a procession with some local Bolsheviks', who were parading Sevastopol's streets with red flags. In an attempt to stop them, first a patrol from *Jean Bart* fired a few rounds over the demonstrators' heads; then Greek troops fired directly into the crowd. Matters escalated sharply when Colonel Trousson 'sounded the General Alarm and fired three rounds of shrapnel at the procession'. As a result, there were 'about forty French and Russian casualties'. Although the demonstration was dispersed and the French sailors returned to their ships, the mutiny spread to the remainder of the French vessels harbouring at Sevastopol. The mutineers demanded that the French squadron return to France as soon as possible, and insisted that the ships' crews should not do any more work 'until a date of sailing was fixed'. They also required that their delegates be given the right to communicate with each other on various ships. Most critically, French sailors 'refused to fire on the Bolshevists'.[38]

Having been appraised of the basic facts of the mutiny, Culme-Seymour visited Admiral Amet. Unsurprisingly, he found his French colleague 'very much distressed at the state of affairs'. Although he was taking sensible steps to restore discipline within his command, the French admiral had resolved to evacuate Sevastopol since it was 'quite impossible to hold it with his ships in a state of mutiny'. Culme-Seymour then consulted the Greek Admiral Kokoloudis on board his flagship the *Kilkis*, and spoke to Colonel Smyth, a senior liaison officer with the British military liaison mission to the French. Both officers argued against the evacuation. Smyth reported that 'the feeling among the French and Greek troops was also most strongly against the evacuation' and that 'their morale had been much improved by the marked effects of the heavy gunfire from the ships against the Bolsheviks, and the recapture of the Mamelon'. Furthermore, Allied soldiers were 'most anxious to retain' Sevastopol, and 'were extremely angry with the French Navy for letting them down'.[39]

On 21 April, Admiral Amet had reported to Paris the 'gravity of the situation' at Sevastopol, warning of a more serious rebellion. 'Unruly elements' within the French squadron had contacts with Bolshevik groups in the city. The centre of the mutiny lay on board the *France*, whose crew had demanded an end to the war. It was difficult, however, to isolate this warship as crews on other vessels insisted that the complete squadron should sail home.[40]

On further investigation, Culme-Seymour learned from a senior British signal rating, who had served on one of the French ships, about the disaffection amongst the French squadron. It transpired that many of the mutineers' gripes were based on the quality and length of their service. In a striking similarity to the Russian *Potemkin* mutiny of 1905, the French sailors complained about receiving 'bad food' and being 'fed up'.[41] But in view of the widespread nature of the protest and associated anger engendered by the bloody violence on Sevastopol's streets, the French mutiny of 1919 was fast becoming a serious affair. Although Culme-Seymour failed to highlight its significance, Bolshevik propaganda, which exploited the war weariness of the French sailors, represented a major contributory cause of the mutiny. Red propagandists, active amongst French ships in both Odessa and Sevastopol, had promulgated the fact that the 'war was over', and spread the alluring message that capitalism and the bourgeoisie represented common enemies to the peoples of both France and Russia.[42]

Culme-Seymour observed that 'discipline in the French squadron was never very good and now it is practically non-existent'. Hence he grew increasingly worried about the prospect of the Russian ships falling into Bolshevik hands if the French Navy were to leave the city in a precipitate, disordered fashion. Thus on the 21st he made an offer to Admiral Amet to 'hold the town with the assistance of British and Greek vessels only thus leaving you free to sail with your squadron', provided the French and Greek troops on land remained. The next day the French admiral informed Culme-Seymour that the French government had ordered him to evacuate Sevastopol. As this meant the troops as well, the British offer lapsed. Considering the 'evacuation as unnecessary and deplorable', Culme-Seymour telegraphed the commander-in-chief of the Mediterranean Fleet requesting his presence in Sevastopol. Admiral Gough-Calthorpe duly arrived on the battleship HMS *Iron Duke* during the morning of the 24th.[43]

In the meantime, demolition parties of the Royal Navy worked feverishly in the harbour and dockyard preparing Russian ships and war materiel for destruction. On the 23rd, for example, 'three large submarines were taken out and sunk'. Culme-Seymour refused to join Admiral Amet in a meeting with a Bolshevik delegation that afternoon on the grounds that it was not only 'contrary to General Denikin's interests', but also because the 'Bolshevists are not the sort of people with whom arrangements can be made'. On the morning of the 25th, following confirmatory orders of the British naval commander-in-chief, 'the remainder of the submarines were towed out ... and sunk, the cylinders of the remaining destroyers, cruisers, and battleships were destroyed by explosion'.[44] In this manner, the proud Russian Black Sea Fleet was not defeated by enemy action, but rather rendered inoperable by a former allied power bent on denying it to the Bolshevik government. That afternoon, the armistice was extended until the 29th, which gave the British fortuitously more time to complete further demolitions. By the evening of 28 April, the Allies had completed their evacuation of Sevastopol. True to their word on this occasion, the troops of the Red Army had held back from attacking the city since the suspension of hostilities on the 17th. Meantime, the Bolshevik Revolutionary Committee began its work on the 25th. On the morning of the 29th, the 4th Regiment of the Red Army's Zadneprovskaya Division entered Sevastopol to be received – according to a Soviet-era account – 'by a joyous population'.[45]

Culme-Seymour was in no doubt as to who was responsible for the loss of the city. 'The effect of this deplorable evacuation', he noted, 'will be far-reaching and a great encouragement to the Bolsheviks. It was entirely unnecessary and due to French ineptness and incompetence'. With the benefit of hindsight this judgement appears harsh. Apart from the Royal Navy's involvement, British troops were neither engaged nor risked at Sevastopol: the lead nation in the city was France. Considering the wider political context, there were clear limits on the Allies' liability in southern Russia, and not least questions arising about the desirability and affordability of any prolonged intervention. None the less, Gough-Calthorpe's condemning assessment, contained in a report to the British Admiralty on 1 May 1919, said it all: 'With the French evacuation of Sevastopol a first-class naval base is at the enemy's disposal in the centre of the Black Sea'.[46]

A number of French ships remained off Sevastopol for a number of days; at French request, HMS *Calypso* stayed behind as well until the night of 2/3 May. Culme-Seymour explained her presence on the grounds that the French had wished to present an 'Allied' rather than a solely French evacuation; and, secondly, that their officers 'were quite unable to rely on their men and preferred to have a British ship handy in case of trouble'. Bearing in mind that the Royal Navy was not immune from indiscipline during this post-war period, Culme-Seymour's observation appears a trifle unfair. On 25 May 1919, for example, Gough-Calthorpe reported to the Admiralty that '57 stokers' and '76 seamen' of the cruiser HMS *Europa* stationed off the island of Mudros 'had refused duty and been placed under arrest'. All were 'demobilisable or time expired ratings'.[47] Hence war weariness was not the sole preserve of the French Navy.

The Bolshevik takeover of Sevastopol at the end of April 1919 proved short-lived. When Kolchak's forces advanced within 650 kilometres of Moscow in June, the Red Army on that most endangered front urgently needed reinforcements. Trotsky took them from the quieter sector of South Russia. As a result, Denikin was able to break out of the Kerch peninsula. Soon White forces were recovering Crimea. On the 13th, the city and fortress of Sevastopol were declared to be under a state of siege. Sevastopol was reported clear of Bolshevik troops on 25 June. With their evacuation in April fresh in mind, the Allies were cautious about returning to the city. On the 29th, Gough-Calthorpe informed the British Admiralty that he was reluctant to send any vessel larger than a destroyer to Sevastopol for four reasons: it would set a precedent, requiring the Royal Navy to 'to keep a ship there more or less permanently'; it would be embarrassing if the 'Volunteer Army undertakes reprisals against suspects'; he was unsure whether Crimea would be 'recognised as a French zone'; and, finally, he considered that support to the Volunteer Army 'should be especially confined to active operations only'.[48]

On Gough-Calthorpe's instructions, the first vessel to enter Sevastopol harbour was a White Russian destroyer, the *Zhivoi*, on the 26th. According to reports Culme-Seymour received, red flags 'were hauled down and replaced by Volunteer colours, and the old naval ensign was hoisted in ships'. The unnamed commanding officer of the *Zhivoi* 'took complete charge of the town and appointed various of his officers in positions of authority'. HMS *Sportive*, a destroyer, joined the Russians the next day, and confirmed Sevastopol 'to be perfectly quiet'. On 6 July 1919, Culme-Seymour reported to Gough-Calthorpe that the Volunteer Army was undertaking 'up to the present no reprisals'. Yet he added ominously, 'ex-officers who remained during the Bolshevik occupation and who are known to have assisted the Bolsheviks will be tried by Court-Martial'. There was little quarter given during the Russian Civil War. In the same report, Culme-Seymour had recorded that Bolshevik troops had 'committed considerable excesses' before leaving Yalta; 'about 40 people were shot on the breakwater on Monday 23rd June'.[49]

By July the Royal Navy was planning to support White forces in the capture of Kherson by opening up the river Dnieper. In a manner reminiscent of the Crimean War this operation required the reduction of the forts at the mouth of the river, including Ochakov. The necessary naval forces assembled at Sevastopol and at Tendra Bay included cruisers, destroyers, monitors, a seaplane carrier and a minesweeper. 'Combined naval and military operations off Ochakov', reported Culme-Seymour on 19 August 1919, 'have continued successfully', contributing to the capture of Kherson on 14 August.[50] Whether Sevastopol would become an operating base for British warships again remained to be seen in view of Gough-Calthorpe's concerns; he was also short of ships.

CRIMEAN FINALE: FRUNZE VS. WRANGEL

Along with France, the United States and Japan, the United Kingdom was one of the major powers that vainly attempted to support the White cause in defeating the Bolshevik government of Russia.[51] Although the British military and naval involvement in the Civil War is relatively well documented, the fact that British armed forces were employed in Crimea and Sevastopol is often overlooked.

Winston Churchill, holding twin appointments as Secretary of State for War and Air, had a very large hand in promoting and directing the British effort during the conflict. In a speech given at London's Mansion House on 19 February 1919, he criticised the 'foul baboonery of Bolshevism'.[52] Laying bare again his manifest hostility to the Russian revolutionary cause at the Aldwych Club on 11 April 1919, Churchill proclaimed: 'Of all the tyrannies in history the Bolshevist tyranny is the worst, the most destructive, and the most degrading.... The miseries of the Russian people under the Bolsheviks far surpass anything they suffered even under the Tsar'. He reminded his audience that 'there are still Russian Armies in the field, under Admiral Koltchak and General Deniken, who have never wavered in their faith and loyalty to the Allied cause, and who are fighting valiantly and by no means unsuccessfully against that foul combination of criminality and animalism which constitutes the Bolshevist *régime*'. Thus 'we are helping these men, within the limits which are assigned to us, and to the very best of our ability'.[53]

While the British contribution of arms, munitions and technical expertise was substantial, it proved increasingly unpopular. Termed by a critical national press as 'Churchill's private war', the intervention was opposed not only by elements of the Labour Party and the trades union movement sympathetic to the Bolshevik cause, but also by wide sections of the Liberal and Conservative Parties. The Liberal British Prime Minister, Lloyd George, was keen to curb Churchill's enthusiasm. In a statement to the House of Commons on 16 April 1919, he declared 'that to attempt [further] military intervention in Russia would be the greatest act of stupidity that any Government could possibly commit'.[54]

By the time of the Treaty of Versailles of 28 June 1919, which concluded the war with Germany (and of which Russia was not a signatory), British forces had been deployed to no fewer than five theatres at the extremities of the former Russian Empire. In the far north, from their bases in Archangel and Murmansk, British troops, and the armed groups that Britain had helped found, train, equip and supply, had penetrated several hundred kilometres south. In the Far East, a much smaller British contingent supported White forces pressing westwards along the axis of the trans-Siberian railway. A military mission was also stationed in the Baltic states, preparing to support White forces in an offensive towards Petrograd. In the south, a small body of troops from India had been deployed in Transcaspia, the region east of the Caspian Sea, to support local anti-Bolshevik forces. By the summer, the deployments in the latter area and in North Russia were being wound down.

The fifth and perhaps most effective British military mission supported the 'Armed Forces of South Russia' commanded by Denikin. At the height of his success in the summer of 1919, Denikin's troops, ably assisted by British-manned aircraft and tanks, captured the city of Tsaritysn (later Stalingrad, now Volgograd) and Kharkov (now Kharkiv), the main industrial centre of Ukraine, in late June.[55] The White offensive culminated with the seizure of Oryol (Orel), only 400 kilometres south of Moscow, in October 1919. Despite making such spectacular gains, Denikin's army was for the most part badly led and was plagued by inefficient logistics and insecure rear areas. Wrangel's assured leadership was an exception, as demonstrated in the successful Tsaritsyn operation. Neither White politics nor their poorly disciplined forces evinced much support from local populations. While much is made of the Red Terror, there were also significant numbers of Russians who fell to the Whites' atrocities. Hence the Whites' control of recently seized areas often proved only nominal. The Bolshevik partisan activity in Crimea was but a case in point.

In the autumn of 1919, Denikin's army was defeated at Oryol by a powerful, skilfully co-ordinated counter-offensive of the Red Army, which could exploit interior lines of communication to bring up men and materiel. Fortunately for the Whites, the Crimean Corps of the Volunteer Army commanded by Yakov Aleksandrovich Slashchov held the Perekop against Red attacks in December 1919. Crimea would prove to be the Whites' last safe haven in southern Russia. Meantime, the bulk of Denikin's force retreated south of the river Don to the Kuban peninsula. Eventually, the remaining Armed Forces of South Russia were evacuated in March 1920 from Novorossiysk to Crimea with considerable British naval assistance. Shortly afterwards, Denikin was forced to resign and his command was offered to Wrangel, whom he had exiled previously to Constantinople over disagreements in strategy.

Sevastopol's future was inextricably bound up with the Whites' ability to retain control of Crimea. As a political settlement in the Civil War was not in sight, and in the face of vastly superior Red forces that could eventually be brought to bear, Wrangel's future military options were limited, to say the least. Having been given sight in Constantinople of a secret communication sent from the British High Commission to Denikin dated 2 April 1920, he already knew that the Allies no longer supported any prolongation of the Civil War. The blunt note stated that the British government was 'absolutely convinced that the abandonment of this unequal struggle will be the best thing for Russia'. Should Denikin refuse, 'and continue a manifestly hopeless struggle', then the British government would 'find itself obliged to renounce all responsibility for his actions, and cease to furnish him with any help or subvention of any kind from that time on'. The sole sweetener was the offer of 'hospitality and refuge in Great Britain' for Denikin and 'his principal supporters'.[56]

Wrangel travelled from Constantinople to Sevastopol on the British battleship HMS *Emperor of India*, arriving during the morning of 24 April 1920. Fine spring weather provided an auspicious start to his new mission. 'The blue sky was reflected in the calm sea', he recalled in his memoirs. Sevastopol, 'bathed in sunshine, lay white and glittering on the hills that surround the bay'. Detailing the idyllic scene further, he observed people 'moving busily about the quays in all directions ... the atmosphere was so normal that it was quite impossible to realise that this beautiful town was on the verge of ruin'. Such was the weakness of the White forces at that time he mused whether 'in a few days perhaps, the Red waves would submerge [the city], and Red agents execute bloody reprisals there'.[57] These atrocities were to occur in their multitude during the final weeks of the year. In the meantime, Wrangel understood that while he could probably delay a major Red offensive to recover Crimea, he would not be able to defeat it. So Sevastopol's survival as a White city remained only a question of time.

Having ordered his baggage to be transferred to the cruiser *General Kornilov* (the former *Kagul*), aboard which he been offered a cabin suite, Wrangel went ashore to join a meeting of the Russian Army Military Council. It had been in session since midday in Sevastopol's Grand Palace. Wrangel's realism was particularly evident when he was offered the post of 'Commander-in-Chief of the Armed Forces of South Russia'. Before accepting the appointment, he gained an understanding from the senior White leadership present that the most likely outcome of his tenure was none other than the final evacuation of their remaining forces rather than winning the war. In considering the offer, he declared to the Council that he 'could not see any hope of a successful struggle'. The 'English Ultimatum', he explained, 'had destroyed our last hope'. Thus there was nothing left to accomplish other than to 'drain the bitter cup to the dregs'. Pondering over the weight of the responsibility he was to assume, Wrangel took some time off to wander about Sevastopol to reflect on the decision he had to make. He called into the cathedral and spoke to Benjamin, Bishop of Sevastopol. The cleric encouraged him to assume the post and blessed him with him an icon of the Holy Virgin. With his mind put at rest, and resolved to accept the appointment, Wrangel returned to the Grand Palace. During his absence, the Military Council had already unanimously elected him as Denikin's successor. Wrangel counter-signed the Council's record of decision, adding an extraordinary note: 'I have shared the honour of its victories with the Army, and cannot refuse to drink the cup of humiliation with it now. Drawing strength from the trust which my comrades-in-arms place in me, I consent to accept the post of Commander in Chief'.[58]

Wrangel was a remarkable individual, in both ambition and appearance. He exhibited a steely confidence that impressed friend and foe alike during the final period of counter-revolutionary Russia. The fact that he became lampooned in Red propaganda as a fearsome, twisted and malicious 'Black Baron' is a tribute to his standing and reputation. A member of the British military mission in Crimea, Captain Ashton Wade, recalled:

> His tall slim figure, always impeccably clothed in Cossack uniform, ... always commanded respect. Not only was he a leader in the military sphere, but, unlike other White Russian commanders, he had the political sense to realise that without a stable base from which to operate and restore order, both civil and military, his efforts would be in vain.[59]

Despite being given a breathing space during the spring and early summer of 1920 to consolidate his position through the Bolsheviks' temporary inactivity in southern Russia as the Red Army advanced westwards into Poland, Wrangel had little time to galvanise substantive political and military support for the Whites' cause. The simple but long overdue step of renaming the 'Volunteer Army' to the 'Russian Army' would hardly improve its chances of success on the battlefield. The army, after all, had arrived in its final Crimean bastion in a miserable state, 'low in morale'. It had left behind its 'baggage trains, machine guns and artillery'. Quartered mainly around Simferopol, 'some units were no longer in hand. The cavalry regiments were horseless'. The vessels of the White navy had neither coal nor oil. 'Not one ship had the capability to leave port'.[60] To his immense credit, and against all odds, Wrangel not only rebuilt his army and secured the means of its eventual evacuation, but also turned his mind to political requirements. He established a new government of South Russia, which included at its head the former tsarist Minister of Agriculture in Pyotr Stolypin's administration, the moderate Alexander Vasilyevich Krivoshein. Wrangel also tried to establish good relations with the Tatars, and made 'conciliatory approaches to the Ukrainians, Georgians, and other nationalities that Denikin had offended'.[61]

Despite Wrangel's and Krivoshein's best efforts, the well-intended promises of land reform proved too little and too late to make any impact on the political scene. Although the peninsula remained in a state of acute economic hardship, there were some modest signs of betterment during the brief period of White rule. Wrangel's son painted a rosy picture of life in Sevastopol during the spring and summer of 1920. 'The city', he wrote, 'was hardly recognizable'. Specifically:

> From a harassed port where the remnant of Denikin's army had landed—bewildered, angry, and in state bordering on revolt—the town had almost acquired again the looks of its peacetime prosperity. Cinemas and theatres were open again; shops displayed even imported wares; army personnel on duty or on leave were disciplined and in uniform. Schools, hospitals, and government offices functioned normally.[62]

A British eyewitness was of a similar impression. On 7 June 1920, the commanding officer of the battleship HMS *Ajax*, Captain V. H. S. Haggard, reported to Vice Admiral Sir John de Robeck, the commander-in-chief of the Mediterranean Fleet since July 1919, about the situation in Sevastopol. 'Good order is maintained', he wrote. Although 'prices are high and the food scarce ... the population seems well fed and well clothed'. He also noted less positively that 'without being actually hostile, the attitude of officials and the people is cold and even resentful towards the British'. Furthermore, Haggard complained that the citizens of Sevastopol 'cannot understand the half-hearted support of what they consider to be a fight against a danger to the world in general and Great Britain in particular'.

Haggard should not have been surprised by the negative attitude he encountered in the Crimean city. In the very same report, he had recorded that, on 30 May, 'General Percy presented to Baron Wrangel the letter informing him he could expect no assistance in offensive operations and inviting him to negotiate with the Bolshevists'.[63] Disagreeing with Churchill's bellicose warnings about Bolshevist Russia, Lloyd George's government remained firm in its policy of limited liability in the Russian Civil War. In one of his memorable rhetorical flourishes, the increasingly isolated Churchill asked his audience in Sunderland on 3 January 1920: 'Was there ever a more awful spectacle in the whole history of the world than is unfolded by the agony of Russia?' In another speech, given in Dundee on 14 February, he declared 'My regret is we have not got a Russia with whom we can make a real peace. I do not believe [that] the despotism of Lenin and Trotsky ... is fit for a democratic government like ours'.[64]

Notwithstanding Wrangel's political activities in Crimea, his main effort was the regeneration of the Russian Army into a well-disciplined, effective fighting force. He described its parlous state:

> The Army had more than one hundred and fifty thousand mouths to feed, of which scarcely one-sixth could be considered as combatants; the rest were the wounded, the sick, all kinds of invalids, the pupils at the important and less important military schools, a large number of reservists of different ranks—most of them old men—and the employees at many institutions behind-the-lines.

The Army lacked both clothing and munitions; vast stocks of both (mainly British) had been lost in the Kuban. 'Nearly all the tanks, armoured cars, and aeroplanes had been abandoned or had fallen into the hands of the enemy'.[65] Although many of these deficiencies were to be made up, Wrangel suffered from having too many staffs and officers, and insufficient men to man the battalions, regiments and divisions required to defend Crimea.

During the summer of 1920, Ashton Wade was serving at Dzhankoy, a key railway junction 93 kilometres north of Simferopol, in an outstation of the British Military Mission based in Feodosiya. Since his arrival in South Russia in the autumn of 1919, Wade had 'witnessed human distress and suffering daily'. Now he observed further scenes of provincial work and life, confirming some return to normalcy for the people:

> ... the huddled bodies of refugees – men, women and children – dying or already dead from typhus were a common feature of railway stations and other centres of travel. In the Crimea things were different. Although the towns were over-crowded with refugees, a semblance of law and order appeared and was gradually reinforced; trains started to run on time, shops and markets operated more or less normally, as did the postal and other services.

Yet Wade also detected a less pleasing side to Crimea. 'But when one day I saw a body strung up by the neck from a lamppost', he wrote, 'I was sharply reminded that one was mixed up in a revolution infinitely more cruel and bloody than the French Revolution'.[66]

The Russian revolution and associated Civil War would demand yet more blood. The Whites achieved their last hurrah in the conflict when Wrangel's forces stormed the Red defences of the Perekop on 7 June 1920. Breaking out of Crimea into Northern Tauridia, the Russian Army pushed on to the lower Dnieper within a week. This final White offensive operation not only proved a false dawn, but also terminated British assistance. The British Cabinet was not impressed: it considered that Wrangel's action in launching the offensive released Britain from her responsibilities towards him. Thus the Admiralty instructed de Robeck on 11 June: 'British Naval forces are therefore to be strictly neutral and are to afford no repeat no support to Wrangel in offence or defence'.[67] In a report of 19 June to the British Admiralty, Admiral de Robeck demonstrated his sympathy to the White cause. 'Wrangel has acquired new territory from which he can feed the Crimea. Retention of this and maintenance of the morale in rear will be gravely affected by the withdrawal of our support and mission'. Then he observed critically: 'Reason for our withdrawal understood to be due to Wrangel taking offensive. His offensive forestalled Red offensive by 48 hours'.[68]

The Reds' not very skilfully executed counter-attack was defeated, but significantly the Bolsheviks retained a valuable foothold over the Dnieper at Kakhovka, approximately 80 kilometres north of Perekop. Determined attempts to eliminate this bridgehead by attacks with tanks and aircraft all failed, leading to the resignation of Slashchov. While Wrangel had gained some valuable territory, time and food supplies in southern Ukraine, he was not in a position to exploit the situation operationally, let alone strategically. There was no realistic prospect of linking up with Polish forces advancing from the west in order to effect a combined offensive to defeat the Red Army decisively.

The brief revival of White fortunes in Northern Tauridia, coincident with the contemporaneous Russo-Polish war in the summer of 1920, was illusory. With the cessation of hostilities between Poland and Bolshevik Russia on 12 October 1920, the Bolshevik high command was able to turn its attention to Crimea again and focus on eliminating the last remaining White bulwark of any real significance. Trotsky had already entrusted his most able field commander, Mikhail Vasilyevich Frunze, with the co-ordination of the Red Army's operation designed to eradicate White Crimea once and for all. The 'Crimean ulcer', a continual thorn in the side of the Bolsheviks, would need to be cut off at a stroke.

Frunze, born in 1885, a bright and talented school pupil, had been a Bolshevist and propagandist–agitator since attending St Petersburg's Polytechnical Institute in 1904–05. He neglected his academic studies in economics in favour of his revolutionary interests and activities. Invited to the Fourth Congress of the RSDLP held at Stockholm in 1906 in the aftermath of the 1905 revolution, the precocious, twenty-one-year-old Frunze met many delegates including Lenin, Stalin, Trotsky and Voroshilov, all of whom were to become famous figures in the Bolshevist struggle. It is said that, with no military background whatsoever, he remarked to Lenin that the Bolsheviks 'must know military affairs and must have their own officers who are superior to the servitors of the Tsar in military matters'. Frunze, however, would not receive an opportunity to observe an army in action for a decade. Sentenced to penal servitude in 1910 for his complicity in the killing of a policeman, he was imprisoned until 1916. On his release, he made 'frequent trips to the front lines'. In the October Revolution of 1917, he took part in the Bolshevik *coup d'état* and the storming of the Kremlin in Moscow. He then rose quickly within the Red Army, honing his military skills in organisation and combat during the Civil War.[69]

As commander-in-chief of the Bolsheviks' Southern Army Group, Frunze won a spectacular victory against the forces of Admiral Kolchak at Ufa (lying 100 kilometres west of the southern Ural mountains) in the early summer of 1919. The 25th Chapayev Rifle Division spearheaded the Red Army's advance into the city, which was occupied on 9 June. For his efforts, Frunze was awarded the Order of the Red Banner for this successful operation.[70] Although not a professional soldier, he had proved himself as an extremely energetic and enterprising commander, a brilliant auto-didact. His reputation was to be put under greatest test in the forthcoming operation against Wrangel's Russian Army, a more competent and worthy opponent than Kolchak's forces, with some much better trained and equipped troops. In mid-September 1920, Frunze reported to

Lenin in Moscow before assuming command of the Red Army's Southern *Front*. The Soviet leader, concerned about another winter of war, asked him when Wrangel would be defeated. Frunze, confidently but rather impetuously, promised 'by December'.[71] Assuming command of the Southern *Front* on 27 September 1920, he had only two months available.

A brief excursion into the final campaign in southern Russia and Crimea during the Civil War provides an interesting rehearsal of the problems facing the German conquest of Crimea in the autumn of 1941 and in the subsequent Soviet liberation in April–May 1944. Including the German intervention of April 1918, all four cases illustrate that the occupation of Crimea, and the fate of Sevastopol, would be determined by the outcome of operations at the northern gates of the peninsula.

Discounting a major amphibious operation across the Black Sea, for which the Red Army was not equipped, from west to east there were four potential approaches to northern Crimea: forcing the Perekop isthmus; crossing the shallow Syvash Sea; penetrating the Chongar peninsula and narrows; and advancing down the narrow Arabat Spit. Although Frunze's operational problem was simple to expound, it proved more difficult to solve in practice. The ideal solution would have been to defeat Wrangel's forces north of Crimea and deny them the possibility of any withdrawal to the gates, let alone into the depth, of the peninsula. So there was an operational premium on Red forces achieving a rapid penetration to reach the Perekop and Chongar positions *before* White forces could retire behind them. If this gambit could not be achieved, then Crimea would have to be prised open and fought for as well, a 'partial' solution all costing more time, troops and trouble. As is in all military activities, Clausewitzian friction and chance all played their unavoidable parts on both sides. Frunze, bearing in mind his rash promise to Lenin, was in a hurry. He also had General Sergey Sergeyevich Kamenev, the Red Army's commander-in-chief (*Glavkom*) on his back, directing him to liquidate Wrangel 'in the shortest possible time'.[72]

By October 1920, Frunze's Southern *Front*, comprising 133,000 men in total, was pitched against a much smaller White Russian Army of 37,000. By this late stage of the Civil War, Britain had abandoned the Whites, leaving behind in August 1920 only a couple of Russian-speaking officers to man its once strong military mission. There would no longer be any tactically significant air or tank support forthcoming. Wrangel had received a clear warning that to extend operations out of Crimea would lead to a cessation of military aid, which he had chosen to ignore. Ashton Wade noted, 'Whitehall, in its wisdom, [had] decided that enough public money had been wasted in supporting a lost cause'.[73] Yet the truth was more complex. It was simply an example of realpolitik for the British cabinet, who wished to conclude a trade deal with the Soviet government and recognise it diplomatically – however distasteful its origins and policies. As in the past, and as will no doubt represent the case in the future, military advisory and training missions can be equally inserted or withdrawn on grounds of political gesture and expediency. Although the French had yet to remove their support to Wrangel, they were not in a position to reinforce his army effectively to face Frunze's coming offensive. They, unlike their former interventionist ally, would provide the necessary naval support when the time came for an evacuation. The United States Navy also made a very honourable contribution to this operation.

At the beginning of October 1920, Frunze's Southern *Front* consisted of the 2nd Cavalry Army and the 4th, 6th and 13th Armies. The armistice with Poland signed on 12 October freed Semyon Budyonny's 1st Cavalry Army, which soon joined. Frunze received a further reinforcement in the 'Insurgent Army' of about 6,000 men commanded by Nestor Ivanovich Makhno.[74] Frunze's plan of 19 October to trap White forces north of the Crimean peninsula failed when Wrangel skilfully conducted a fighting withdrawal to positions behind Perekop and Chongar by the beginning of November. Budyonny's cavalrymen failed to reach Crimea first. By a whisker, they missed a golden opportunity to seize the Salkovo pass, the northern entrance to the Chongar peninsula (see Map 12). This vital piece of ground was weakly guarded by White forces: had it been breached, a main entrance to Crimea would have been wide open. As Wrangel described, on 30 October, he had 'sent everyone who could bear arms to Salkovo—the Simferopol Military School, the Artillery School and my own escort'.[75] Had either Frunze or Budyonny reacted swiftly to exploit this weakness, then the Russian Army might well have been trapped north of the Crimea.[76] Wrangel's scratch force arrived just in time to hold Salkovo until the main body of his troops had made good their retirement, with the Red cavalry following closely on their heels.

By 2 November 1920, the battle of Northern Tauridia was over. Not only was all the territory gained by Wrangel during the summer lost, but the Red victory had also cost the Whites 20,000 prisoners-of-war. Yet it had been a tough fight. As Frunze reported to Kamenev: 'There is no doubt that [the enemy] fought more fiercely and stubbornly than any other army would have'.[77] Although the White forces had been defeated, Frunze would be forced to undertake deliberate, and potentially very costly, operations to penetrate the Perekop and Chongar defences. The victors' spoils were considerable. The Red Army seized a vast amount of booty, including 'five armoured trains, eighteen guns, nearly a hundred wagon-loads of shells, ten million cartridges, twenty-five locomotive engines, ... and nearly two million *pouds* of corn'. Ominously for the White cause, the Russian Army had not only suffered serious losses, but there were also 'several cases of wholesale surrender ... including a whole battalion in Drozkovsky's division'. Perhaps the bitterly cold weather had lowered morale and combat effectiveness during the battle – during the course of the morning of 29 October, the temperature had fallen to 'fourteen degrees below zero'. A lack of warm clothing and suitable shelter had tested the resilience of the troops. Although the 'Army as a whole was still intact,' Wrangel was forced to accept that 'its fighting power was no longer what it had been'.[78] The question now facing him and his opponent, Frunze, was whether the Whites would be able to repel the Red Army's inevitable offensive into Crimea.

As in previous conflicts, the most suitable, and hence most likely, avenue of approach to Crimea was the Perekop isthmus. The Russian Army's main defence line here was based on the old Turkish Wall, with a ditch 10 metres deep and 20 metres wide and an earthen rampart rising up to 5 metres. In addition to this fortified position, White forces (1st Corps, commanded by Lieutenant General Aleksandr Pavlovich Kutepov) had erected a line of emplacements about 2 kilometres to the north of the ditch, and a further outpost line beyond that. The main defence was allocated to the 1st and 4th Drozdovsy Regiments and the Composite Infantry Guard Regiment, equating to about a division. In immediate local, tactical reserve were the 2nd and 3rd Regiments of the Drozdov Division, assembled in the area of the Armenian Bazaar, next to the town of Armiansk, 4 kilometres south of the main defence line. In depth, about 20 kilometres south of the Turkish Wall, lay the Ishun (then called Yushun) position, which made good use of the obstacle power of a series of inland lakes. Wrangel's veteran Kornilov and Markov infantry divisions were digging in here. The term 'division' here, however, is misleading as these formations were only of regimental strength: the whole corps responsible for the defence of Perekop–Ishun had only about 10,000 men under arms.

Although the positions of Perekop and Ishun looked impressive on paper, they possessed a geographical vulnerability. About midway between Perekop and Ishun, on the eastern shore of the isthmus, lies a small peninsula that juts out into the Syvash Sea. Since ancient times this piece of land (later named the Litovsky (Lithuanian) peninsula) had served as the southern point of a shortcut of 4–5 kilometres' length across the sea to the mainland. In certain weather conditions parts of the route could even be waded, which exacerbated the risk. The Whites' Kuban Brigade under the command of Lieutenant General Mikhail Arkhipovich Fostikov held this critical position.

Fifty kilometres to the east another finger of land, the mainland Chongar peninsula, almost touches Crimea. The bridges carrying the Melitopol–Chongar–Toganash–Dzhankoy–Simferopol railway and the main highway to the peninsula had been destroyed by Wrangel's troops. The 7th and 34th Infantry 'Divisions' held positions facing Chongar, together with the 42nd Don Regiment and a para-military regiment of German colonists. A final avenue of approach for Frunze's forces lay still further east in the form of the Arabat Spit, a slender neck of land that extends almost as far south as the Kerch peninsula. Well-armed White naval vessels patrolled its eastern shore, washed by the Sea of Azov. Only a single regiment was allocated for the defence of the Spit. If Red forces were able to advance down it, potentially they could turn the Russian Army's whole defensive scheme.

Frunze set out his detailed orders to the Southern *Front* for the 'delivery of a decisive blow to the enemy and battles to possess the Crimea' on 5 November 1920. His intent was to mount an energetic attack to the south in order to 'destroy the last shelter of the counter-revolution'.[79] Originally he had intended that the main axis of the operation would follow the Chongar peninsula, with a supporting attack down the Arabat Spit. The secondary axis was designated as the Perekop isthmus. Realising belatedly that it would not be possible to provide any effective support from the sea to forces on the Spit, at the last minute Frunze made the assault on the Perekop and associated attack on the Litovsky peninsula the *front*'s main effort. In practice, he did not reallocate the forces already designated for the attack planned on the 7th.

Whereas the 6th Army, the 2nd Cavalry Army and the Makhno Insurgent Army would force the Perekop and Ishun positions, the 4th Army and the 1st Cavalry Army would breach the defences facing the Chongar peninsula. The 13th Army and elements of 3rd Cavalry Corps formed the *front*'s general reserve. Altogether, this force represented over 100,000 infantry and nearly 40,000 cavalry. In contrast, the White Russian Army, with only 25,000–28,000 combat troops, was outnumbered by about five to one although that advantage was never realised in battle. Although the Red Army possessed about three times as many guns as its opponent, artillery played a relatively insignificant part in the forthcoming battle.

The Red Army's Perekop–Chongar offensive operation opened about 2200 hours on 7 November 1920 when formations of the 6th Army, including the 15th and 52nd Rifle Divisions and the 53rd Mixed [infantry/cavalry] Brigade, crossed the Syvash and advanced towards the Litovsky peninsula. Their progress was facilitated by a combination of fords, which engineers had improved under cover of darkness and daytime fog. Moreover, a strong wind from the west blew the waters of Syvash toward the east and made wading across the shallows quite feasible.[80] Fostikov's outposts, observing their enemy at a kilometre's distance about 0200 hours, brought the Red forces under machine-gun and artillery fire. None the less, the 6th Army had scored a good deal of tactical surprise here, and pushed the defending White forces back. By 0900 hours, the Red attack grouping had gained a 'reasonably secure' bridgehead.

For unexplained reasons, 6th Army had mysteriously failed to mount a simultaneous attack on the Perekop main defences. The lack of any fighting here allowed White troops to launch repeated counter-attacks against the Red bridgehead on the Litovsky peninsula. As a result, Frunze had to reinforce it with the 7th Cavalry Division. It was not until about 1300 hours that the Perekop was assaulted. This attack by Blyukher's 51st Rifle Division, and a series of subsequent attempts to storm the White defences during the course of the afternoon of the 8th, were easily repulsed. Shortages in heavy artillery and poor co-ordination between that arm and the infantry had led to woefully prepared and badly conducted attacks. As a result, the defenders inflicted crippling losses of up to 60 per cent on several Red regiments. It was a critical moment for Frunze as his offensive was stalling. Undaunted, he called up reserves and smashed through the Perekop in the early hours of 9 November. By daylight the Whites had stepped back to their Ishun position.

Elsewhere, Red preparations were in hand for the attacks at Chongar. An advance guard moving down the Arabat Spit had already been halted by the White naval flotilla. Although staff work and communications were primitive, it remains surprising that Frunze did not manage to synchronise an attack from the Chongar peninsula with the assault on the Perekop – a combined operation would have divided the Russian Army's reserves. In fact, the 4th Army's attack did not get under way until midnight on 10–11 November. The delay at Chongar allowed White forces to concentrate on defending the Ishun position.

When the Red offensive broke, Wrangel found himself nowhere near the front. As both a political leader in his capacity as the 'Regent of South Russia' and a military commander-in-chief, his headquarters was in Sevastopol. For the final act of the Civil War, he had vested field command of the Russian Army in Lieutenant General Kutepov. During the evening of the 8th/9th, some twenty-four hours after the opening of the battle, Wrangel was presiding over a meeting of the Crimean government. His chief of staff, Lieutenant General Pavel Nikolayevich Shatilov, handed him an urgent signal from Kutepov. Its stark contents made bleak reading: the Perekop position had been breached, Red forces threatened to surround his troops, and he had been compelled to order a 'general retreat' to the second line of fortifications – at Ishun. The dire news came as a complete shock. At this point, it would appear that the ever-so-calm Wrangel momentarily lost his nerve, if not will to fight. In his memoirs, he freely states that 'we were on the brink of disaster', and admits that it 'was clear ... that the troops were incapable of offering any further resistance'. Although 200 kilometres or so distant from the scene of the action, Wrangel recognised that the 'Army's stock of endurance was already overdrawn, and no fortifications could check the enemy any longer'. Yet he was a good enough soldier to regain his composure quickly: he resolved to 'set out for the front and take stock of the situation', departing for Simferopol at 0300 hours on the 9th.[81]

As Wrangel travelled north from Sevastopol by slow military train on the worn-out railway line, events were unfolding at the front. There was no apparent cause for any panic within the Russian Army: although the principal fortifications at Perekop had fallen, all was not yet obviously lost. During the course of the 9th, Frunze pushed his forces towards the Ishun lakes and then halted them. While this stage of the battle was developing, the closest Wrangel got to the front was the railway junction at Dzhankoy. Kutepov briefed him there during the late afternoon of the 9th. He explained that the 'sprit of the troops was broken ... and the best of the superior commanders were out of action, and [so] it was impossible to count on success'. Although the Ishun position had yet to be attacked in any force, it was clear to Wrangel that it was only a matter of time before it too fell. The two senior officers agreed that they needed to fight on for at least 'five or six days' in order to buy sufficient time to enable the final preparations for the evacuation from Crimea. As Wrangel reflected vividly in his autobiographical account, the 'storm was approaching; our fate was hanging by a thread; we had [now] to strain every moral and intellectual force'.[82]

One of the most important decisions of a military commander in battle is to determine where best to position himself in relation to his mission and role. It would have been tempting for Wrangel to accompany Kutepov and to visit the Ishun front on the morrow, where perhaps his presence would have lifted the sinking morale of his troops. But he wisely decided to follow his head rather than his heart, keenly aware that the fate of his entire army rested in his hands. Thus Wrangel identified that it was essential to maintain good order in Sevastopol: otherwise there would be no hope of any evacuation; and secondly, that he needed to galvanise efforts there. Unfortunately, there were 'almost no troops stationed' in the city. Wrangel's own escort, which had been on guard in Sevastopol (presumably returned from the defence of Salkovo), had been deployed a few days previously to Yalta to confront the 'Green' (anarchist) partisans in the southern mountains. The life of a military under-dog is one of expediency, of which Wrangel proved himself time and time again as master. On this occasion, he 'telegraphed for a company of military pupils from [a] military school to be sent to Simferopol station' to meet his train and join him on his return journey to Sevastopol. In this simple manner, he arranged a new rear area security force for the city, which would be reinforced.

About the same time Wrangel arrived back in Sevastopol at 0900 hours on the 10th, Blyukher's replenished 51st Division had penetrated the western end of the White line of defence at Ishun. At the eastern (Syvash) flank, however, the 15th and 52nd Divisions were pushed back by determined counter-attacks, as Kutepov had planned. Yet the Red Army was composed of stern stuff and could more easily absorb losses at a rate at which the Russian Army could not. Frunze brought up the fresh forces of the 2nd Cavalry Army to counter the attacks of White Cossack units. The more that Kutepov expended forces here, the fewer were available to be employed elsewhere. As his tactical reserves were being consumed rapidly, he possessed no mobile operational grouping ready to counter another major thrust. Moreover, it was only a matter of time before Frunze's next major blow struck.

The 4th Red Army now entered the offensive. Its lead assault division was the 30th Rifle. Realising that time was of the essence, as he had a deadline to meet, the *front* commander paid a personal visit to the divisional command post during the 10th in order to get the attack in this sector moving as quickly as possible. In 30th Rifle Division's first echelon were the 266th Rifle Regiment directed towards the settlement of Tyup-Dhzankoy (now Predmostnoe), and on its right (west), the 268th towards Toganash (now Solenoe Ozero). From the Chongar peninsula, the former unit followed the main road route into Crimea while the latter followed the railway line. The Whites had destroyed both the road and rail bridges over the Syvash just in time at the end of the previous battle for North Tauridia. By the morning of the 11th, although the Red Army's 268th Regiment had bitten into Crimea, it had won no more than a 'most insecure toe-hold'. In contrast, its sister regiment, the 266th, scored a notable success in seizing Tyup-Dzhankoy, driving back the 42nd Don Infantry and the German colonists in the process. It was thus poised to break through the White defences completely and drive south to the vital rail junction and logistics hub of Dzhankoy.[83] The 11th had proved the tipping-point of the battle. Frunze, sensing growing success, exhorted his troops to sustain the fight in an order of the day. 'Soldiers of the Red Army!', he wrote. 'Our valorous forces, having broken through the enemy's fortifications, have stormed into the Crimea. One more blow, and only nasty memories of the White Guards in the Crimea will remain'.[84]

Meanwhile back in Sevastopol, Wrangel, ably supported by his general and administrative staffs, worked frenetically throughout the 10th in issuing the preliminary orders for the evacuation. The necessary preparations had already been made. Now the enabling action, not least the coaling of the shipping already identified, was efficiently executed. The initial instructions envisaged 20,000 men embarking at Kerch; 13,000 at Feodosiya; 10,000 at Yalta; 20,000 at Sevastopol; and 4,000 at Yevpatoriya: in all, some 67,000. In the event, more than double that number would be lifted from these five Crimean ports. As if managing such an ambitious operation were not enough, somehow the White leader found the time for political matters both to support and to explain the evacuation. He 'begged' the French High Commissioner, Count Damien de Martel and the representatives of the other Allied missions, for assistance in providing ships 'if it came to an evacuation and we were obliged to leave the

Crimea'. Having already decided that one would need to take place, Wrangel turned his attention to the Russian and foreign press. In dramatic terms he described the predicament of the Russian Army:

> ... which was fighting not only for the honour and liberty of its own country, but for the common cause of culture and civilization throughout the world, the Army which had just stayed the bloody hand which the butchers of Moscow had raised against Europe, was now abandoned by everyone and at the end of its tether.[85]

There is little doubt that Wrangel's ire was especially directed at the British government, which had proved unflinching in its policy of strict neutrality. On 11 November, the Admiralty had reminded de Robeck that 'no action is to be taken by H.M. Ships to evacuate refugees with the exception of those of British nationality'. In return, the commander-in-chief of the Mediterranean Fleet replied: 'if Red conquest [of] Crimea is inevitable, ... will not repeat not send H.M. ships to Crimea especially to bring away refugees'.[86] Wrangel was fortunate enough, however, to enjoy the support of the French and United States navies.[87]

As 11 November unfolded, the Russian Army's position in northern Crimea crumbled quickly. Red forces were now breaking through across the front: the Latvian Division attacking at Ishun, the 30th Rifle Division converging on Dzhankoy (from Toganash railway station and Tyup-Dzhankoy) and the 9th Rifle Division heading down the Arabat Spit, having crossed the Genichesk Strait. The time to order the necessary evacuation from Crimea was fast approaching. During the afternoon Wrangel received de Martel and the temporary commander of the French Mediterranean Fleet, Vice Admiral Charles Henri Dumesnil, who had just arrived at Sevastopol from Constantinople on the armoured cruiser *Waldeck-Rousseau*. Their discussions lasted for over a couple of hours as Wrangel requested concrete assurances from the French government and navy that his evacuation would receive vital assistance.

The protocol of the meeting recorded that the Wrangel saw 'no other solution than to evacuate the whole of the civil population desirous of fleeing from Bolshevist reprisals, together with the remnants of the White Army, wounded or able-bodied'. Without waiting for formal confirmation that help would be forthcoming from the French, Wrangel issued orders to his troops, by this time withdrawing in contact, to break clean from the enemy. They were to march immediately to the following ports of embarkation: 1st and 2nd Army Corps to Yevpatoriya and Sevastopol; Barbovich's cavalry to Yalta; Fostikov's Kubans to Feodosiya; the Don troops and the Terek–Astrakhan brigade to Kerch. All 'heavy transport was to be abandoned; the infantry was to pack into the wagons; the cavalry was to cover its retreat'.[88]

Wrangel received yet another visitor on the 11th. It says much for his composure and diplomatic skill that he did, bearing in mind the nationality of the officer concerned. Rear Admiral George Hope, commanding the 3rd Light Cruiser Squadron, arrived on HMS *Centaur*. Having been briefed by the head of the skeletal British Military Mission, Colonel Walshe, he then went to see Wrangel. The White commander appeared 'quite calm and determined; but obviously a little wearied and worn'. Wrangel announced that 'only a miracle could hold the front'. Specifically, he explained that 'all his Divisional Generals or Commanding Officers were killed or wounded'. Although 'his troops were fighting well', they had 'suffered heavy losses and were exhausted'. As a result, Wrangel had been forced 'to dismount his cavalry and put them in the trenches'. He informed Hope that the evacuation of the wounded had already commenced; the women and children would follow on the 12th. Wrangel then advised that the evacuation of all British subjects should commence 'at once'. Hope expressed his sympathy and left. The British completed the evacuation of 102 British and Russian men, women and children that same day.[89]

Wrangel had also informed Hope that he intended to issue an order of the day. Its defiant tone and rousing rhetoric could not mask the fact that the Whites' final hour had come:

> People of Russia! Alone in its struggle against the oppressor, the Russian Army has been maintaining an unequal contest in its defence of the last strip of Russian territory on which law and truth hold sway.
>
> ... I now order the evacuation and embarkation at the Crimean ports of all those who are following the Russian Army on its road to Calvary; that is to say, the families of the soldiers, the officials of the civil administration and their families, and anyone else who would be in danger if they fell into the hands of the enemy.
>
> ... May God grant us strength and wisdom to endure this period of Russian misery, and to survive it.

At the same time, a government communiqué warned the population of the 'severe ordeals which await those who are about to leave Russia', and explained that the 'future fate of the evacuated is quite uncertain' because none of the foreign powers had up to this point had promised to receive them. Designed to reduced the demand on the ships, the note advised 'all those who will not suffer directly from the violence of the enemy to remain in the Crimea'.[90] Exactly how people were meant to know beforehand who would be targeted in Bolshevik reprisals was not explained. Many tens of thousands decided to join the evacuation at the very last moment; the tens of thousands who did not awaited a probably cruel fate.

At midnight on 11–12 November, Frunze sent Wrangel a radio message in which he demanded the surrender of all White forces in Crimea. While a number of versions exist of what was stated, it seems clear that Frunze was offering those who surrendered their weapons a 'full pardon for all delinquencies connected with the civil struggle', which went well beyond what Lenin would have authorised. Indeed, the Soviet leader criticised the Southern *Front* commander heavily for the generosity of the terms he offered, stressing 'if the opponent does not accept these conditions, in my opinion they should not be repeated and he should be finished off without mercy'.[91] Wrangel's response, other than ordering all the wireless stations to be closed down, excepting 'one where the officers were running the service', was simply to ignore the message and to intensify his efforts to evacuate as many people as possible from the Crimea.[92]

As Wrangel's troops headed towards their designated ports of embarkation, Red forces followed them. While the 6th Army made for Yevpatoriya and Simferopol, the 1st Cavalry Army struck south to Sevastopol; 4th Army was directed to Feodosiya as 2nd Cavalry Army exploited to Kerch. Despite Frunze's exhortations, the Red Army was surprisingly slow in its pursuit, never able to cut off more than small groups of the retreating White forces. The Russian Army's rearguards were harassed rather then harried: there were no major engagements on the crowded roads leading to the ports. There were no Red air attacks. According to Wrangel, 'we scarcely came into contact with the enemy'. The Whites' luck held.

In describing events in Sevastopol during the last couple of days of White rule, Wrangel portrays a picture of an evacuation proceeding in 'perfect order'. Those 'attempting to create disorder by anarchistic acts' were 'immediately arrested'. One soldier was 'court-martialled and shot two hours later'. No doubt such exemplary justice did help maintain discipline at a very hectic and vulnerable time. Those wishing to embark had exceeded the General Staff's calculations 'by large numbers'.[93]

Other reports of Sevastopol's last few days under White rule provide a complementary perspective. 'The city was seething. Crowds of people were concentrated on the quays with bundles of clothes. Both civilians and military were boarding the ships'. Meanwhile, in the city centre, 'the shops were open, selling goods at sky-rocketing prices'. Although the banknotes of the Chief [Military] Command were still accepted, they lost their value very quickly. Sensing a worsening of shortages, the population stocked up. 'Outside the bakeries, enormous crowds were awaiting freshly-baked bread.' The pressure among people at the quays grew: some present remembered the experiences in Odessa and Novorossiysk and 'nearly assaulted the waiting ships'. During the afternoon of the 12th, more and more refugees on carts arrived in Sevastopol from central Crimea. By the morning of the next day, the log-jam of people, animals and vehicles extended all the way from the Grafskaya pier back up Catherine Street, down the Station Descent (Vokzalnyy Spusk), and past the main railway station as far as the Vorontsov Road on the outskirts of the city. During the night of 12th/13th Wrangel transferred his headquarters to the Hotel Kist on Nakhimov Square. In the Grand Palace, orderlies were burning military papers and maps.[94] As night fell, an eerie calm descended over the city.

By the morning of 13 November 1920, the advance guards of the Red Army had only reached Sarabus (now Gvardeyskoye, about 24 kilometres north of Simferopol). For the first time in many days, Wrangel could afford to relax just a little. He took a stroll around central Sevastopol with his aide-de-camp. 'The streets were almost deserted', he recorded, 'and most of the shops were shut'. The last commander of the White Army became 'more and more convinced that the embarkation would be accomplished smoothly and that everyone would get away in time'. Due to the lack of pressure by Frunze's forces, it certainly looked that way. Kutepov, with his General Staff, arrived in Sevastopol 'at twilight'. He informed his commander-in-chief that the embarkation of his troops would be 'finished by about ten o'clock in the morning'. Wrangel ordered the remaining rearguard in Sevastopol to man the line of fortifications from the Crimean War. Yet there would be no great, climatic assault on the city as had occurred in September 1855. He was confident enough to order the completion of evacuation operations from the city for midday on 14 November.[95]

During the course of the 13th, the embarkation in Sevastopol, despite the huge pressure of numbers, proceeded smoothly. 'The flood of refugees had faded by the evening'. Catherine Street, one of the most noble of the city, then looked 'unrecognizable'. According to an eyewitness, 'torn paper, rags, manure, abandoned carts were scattered all about; hungry horses were nibbling at the bark of broken trees'. In the centre, 'the shops were now closed'. According to another report, the 'turmoil was not now at the quays, but rather in the cafes and restaurants'. The explanation was simple enough: the old sweats in an army always sense an opportunity for a final drink and meal before any new journey. Russian Army volunteers, 'seasoned and experienced men, knew that the enemy was still far away, so for a few hours they could afford to wait for their embarkation'.[96]

A fourteen-year-old youth named Aleksey Sapozhnikov left a particularly poignant account of an incident during the penultimate day of White rule in Sevastopol. 'Suddenly a large squadron of Don Cossacks entered Nakhimov Square ... and dismounted', he recalled. A Cossack general spoke to his men. 'His words were like this: "We are leaving the Motherland. Who knows, may be for ever. Those who wish, may stay".' The vast majority of the cavalrymen took off their saddlebags, and formed up to march away to the waiting ships. 'Some fifteen men, on the contrary, mounted their horses ... and slowly moved off'. 'We came closer', continued Sapozhnikov, observing 'the Cossacks saying farewell to their horses. One elderly sergeant-major, embracing his horse with tears in his eyes, asked us to take his horse and pass her into good hands'.[97] Then the Cossacks were taken by naval cutters and barges to the mass of transports and naval ships moored in Sevastopol's spacious harbours.

On the morning of the 14th Wrangel toured the roadstead in a motorboat, viewing the over-laden ships just before they departed Sevastopol. Then he came back on shore at the Count's Landing Stage, and addressed a small party of students from a military school on Nakhimov Square. In his final rousing speech on Russian soil, Wrangel proclaimed:

> The Army, which has shed its blood in great torrents in fighting not only for the
> Russian cause but for the whole world, is now leaving its native shores, abandoned
> by everybody. We are going into exile; we are not going as beggars with outstretched
> hands, but with our heads

At 1340 hours, he returned to his motorboat and made for the cruiser *General Kornilov*. 'A tumult of cheers', Wrangel proudly recalled, 'went up from the crowded ships'.

Having left the roadstead, the *General Kornilov* proceeded a short distance along the coast to Arrow Bay, where the final stages of the embarkation were still underway. Once all the Russian ships had left the vicinity of Sevastopol at about 0230 hours on the 15th, Wrangel steamed for Yalta on his flagship. On arrival there at 0900 hours, he found the embarkation completed. He went ashore for the very last time in Crimea, finding 'everything was quiet in the town'. Then he made 'a round of the ships, chatting to the officers and soldiers'. His men confirmed that the White cavalry had covered their retreat well, and by dint of forced marches, they had managed to break clean away from the pursuing Red Army units. The enemy were not expected to reach Yalta before the 'next day at the earliest'. Returning to the *General Kornilov*, Wrangel witnessed the White Russian transport ships passing out to sea. Again, loud cheers greeted him as his troops voyaged into the unknown. 'The Russian spirit is great', he reflected, 'and the Russian soul unfathomable'.

Escorted by the *Waldeck-Rousseau* and a destroyer, the *General Kornilov* made for Feodosiya at 1400 hours. While at sea they met the transport *Don*, aboard which was General Fostikov. Wrangel transferred by ship's boat, and conferred with his subordinate. Because there had been insufficient transport capacity to lift all the troops, the embarkation at Feodosiya had not gone so well as in Sevastopol and Yalta. A Kuban division had been diverted to Kerch. Wrangel signalled to General Abramov at the latter port to wait for, and to 'embark the Kubanians at all costs'. The evacuation was not yet completed. While anchored in the roadstead off Feodosiya, at 0900 hours on 16 November, Wrangel received the welcoming news from Kerch that 'Kubanian and Terek troops have arrived; the embarkation is proceeding smoothly'. On his final day off the Crimean coast, the weather mirrored his arrival at Sevastopol in early April: 'the recent cold spell had broken. [It] was fine once again ... even quite hot in the sun. The sea was as clear as a mirror and reflected the transparent blue sky'.

At 1400 hours on the 16th, Vice Admiral Dumesnil and the French Navy afforded Wrangel and his men one closing, fitting honour. The *Waldeck-Rousseau* fired a twenty-one-gun salute – the 'last salute to the Russian flag in Russian territorial waters', which the *General Kornilov* returned in grateful thanks. Shortly afterwards, Wrangel received a radio report from the chief of staff of the fleet, who had made his way to Kerch: 'Embarkation finished. Everyone on board to the last soldier'.[99] At Kerch the evacuation proved a close-run affair. On the 16th, Frunze telegraphed Lenin from Dzhankoy: 'Today our cavalry occupied Kerch. The Southern Front is liquidated'.[100] In this he meant, of course, that Wrangel's army had been destroyed and not his own force.

Although the campaign in Crimea was over, and the White Army expelled from Russia, the evacuation proved successful. Some 145,693 men, women and children, not counting the crews of the ships, had been embarked on 126 ships, employing 'every vessel that was watertight'. By then, Wrangel and his motley armada of Russian and French ships were underway for Constantinople. All apart from the Russian destroyer *Zhivoi*, which foundered in a storm, arrived safely at their destination.[101]

Frunze had literally missed the boat. Arriving just too late at an unnamed Crimean port, he was able to observe through binoculars a number of the ships of Wrangel's Armed Forces of South Russia fading away into the distance. 'It's a pity that we don't have a fleet here', he fumed, 'so we could not finish him off once and for all'.[102] Yet neither Wrangel nor his army was destined ever to return to Crimea. On 16 November, Dumesnil, aboard the *Waldeck-Rousseau*, sent Wrangel a supportive radio message, highlighting: 'Your struggle has not been in vain; the population of South Russia will soon begin to compare your just and beneficent rule with the vile government of the Soviets.... The Admiral, the officers, and the sailors of the French Fleet do reverence to General Wrangel and pay homage to his valour'.[103] So concluded the final major campaign of the Civil War.

As night fell, while the *General Kornilov* made its way from Feodosiya to Constantinople following the Crimea's eastern and southern coasts, Wrangel looked back forlornly towards his departed land. His final words of eulogy sum up the pathos of the scene: 'The stars are gleaming in the darkening sky; the sea is all a-twinkle. The lonely lights on my native shore grow fainter, and then vanish altogether, one after the other. And now the last one fades from my sight. Farewell, my country!'[104]

PART FOUR

MODERN WAR

CHAPTER 12

RED TERROR TO PATRIOTIC WAR

'The principles of Communism are the establishment
of the dictatorship of the proletariat and the
employment of state coercion in the transition period.'

V. I. Lenin[1]

RED TERROR

On the Crimean peninsula, Red power superseded White control within twenty-four hours. Wrangel's fleet departed the Sevastopol roadstead on 14 November 1920; Red Army troops occupied the undefended city on the following day. Leading elements of Budyonny's 1st Cavalry Army and soldiers of Blyukher's 51st Rifle Division received the honour of entering the Whites' last main stronghold. Eyewitnesses recalled that a huge armoured car, bristling with machine guns, represented the first sign of Bolshevik troops. Not only was it decorated with several five-pointed red stars, but it was also festooned with the word 'Antichrist'. According to a modern Sevastopol historian, Dmitry Sokolov, this provocative motto became an 'omen of impending misfortune' to many people remaining in Sevastopol. 'No-one could have imagined', he observed, 'that the reality would be a hundred times worse and more terrible than any misgivings' at the time.[2] Although the Bolsheviks had come and gone before, this time, the Red Army, and the revolutionary government it represented, were here to stay. There would be no escape from its vengeful rule.

The dénouement of Wrangel's regime, if long expected, had proved quite sudden in the event. Following the departure of the Whites' ships, Sevastopol's citizens were dazed and uncertain. Many, and rightly so, were fearful of what would befall them. At least one semblance of normality remained. As there had been no fighting for the city, essential public utilities such as electricity and water were still functioning normally. Shops and restaurants, however, were closed until further notice. Abandoned carts, household belongings, and the sundry impedimenta of a defeated army cluttered the streets and squares of the city centre. All the White Army's heavy weapons such as artillery pieces had been left behind. In the waters of the roadstead and its many harbours only rusting hulks, half-sunken ships and unserviceable craft remained.

Although Frunze informed Lenin on 16 November that Kerch had been occupied, the 'Lion of the Revolution' had proclaimed his main triumph on the 15th. 'Today our units entered Sevastopol', he reported. 'With powerful blows the Red regiments have finally crushed the south Russian counter-revolution'. Optimistically, he added that 'the tortured country now has the chance to begin to heal the wounds inflicted by the imperialist and civil wars'.[3] In fact, the torture had yet to begin. The executions of the Whites who remained, and of anybody suspected of either sympathising with, or supporting, them, assumed such numbers that the waves of 'liquidation' became widespread. Sokolov has described the killings as the 'Revenge of the Winners' in the Russian Civil War, which manifested itself in an unparalleled 'orgy of red terror' in Crimea.[4]

The killings came in apparent contradiction of Frunze's stated intentions of five days before. In his order of the day of 11 November 1920, he had expressly instructed 'all troops of the Red Army to show clemency to those who surrender and to those who have been taken captive'. Furthermore, he stated that the 'Soldier of the Red Army ... is a knight in the treatment of prisoners'. Even more ironically in view of past actions elsewhere and the imminent bloodbath in Crimea, Frunze had emphasised that the 'Red Army is not willing to take revenge. We shed blood only because we are forced to do so by our enemies'. Yet there remained a very big catch in his proclamation: the Revolutionary Military Council of the Southern *Front* had only guaranteed the lives of those 'who had surrendered'. Specifically, 'in the case of refusal, all the blame for the bloodshed will be placed on the officers of the White Army'.[5] Thus there appears to be solid case for suggesting that Frunze's offer of surrender terms, which had been radioed to Wrangel's forces on 11 November, was nothing more than a cynical ploy. Whatever the subsequent course of the Red revenge, there was a considerable degree of premeditation by the Red Army's senior leadership in the treatment of the Whites remaining in Crimea. Thereafter, in the wake of the Red assumption of control over the peninsula, the promise of forgiveness was forgotten and no quarter given to the vanquished.

Although the Red Army's victory in Crimea proved decisive in strategic and political outcomes, it did not represent the stunning military success that Frunze, and later Soviet propagandists, would claim. Despite his overwhelming superiority in numbers (about 4.5 to 1), Frunze had bungled significant parts of the operation.[6] Notwithstanding the successful landing on the Litovsky peninsula, the assaults on the Perekop and Ishun positions were unduly costly (Blyukher's 51st Rifle Division alone lost over 3,000 men), badly supported and poorly co-ordinated. Brute force rather than its tactical skill had characterised the Red Army's triumph over its opponent.

Wrangel's Russian Army remained a well-ordered body to the end. Its ability to conduct a timely withdrawal to five designated ports of embarkation provides due testament to its cohesion and leadership. Hence credit must be given here to Wrangel and his principal subordinates, who maintained the discipline of their force under the most testing operation of war: retreat. Frunze's cavalry armies were unable to exploit quickly enough into the operational depth of Crimea in order to cut off the main bodies of their opponent's infantry. There were times when Wrangel and his men could not believe their luck in being able to break contact, and to mount their evacuation – over three days and more – largely unmolested. For the Russian Army, it represented an inevitable, yet fitting, coda to the Civil War.

Unlike the evacuation of the British and French forces at Dunkirk in 1940, which was followed four years later by the successful Normandy landings of D-Day in 1944, the ejection of the White Army from Crimea in November 1920 proved final. Had Wrangel been able to buy more time, and scraped together further shipping space, perhaps many more opponents of Red rule might have been brought away. Additionally, the British government could have ordered the Royal Navy to assist, as it had done in the evacuation from Novorossiysk earlier in the year. Such an action on strictly humanitarian grounds might have saved another few thousands of White soldiers and their dependants. It would have been a more honourable course than the imposition of 'strict neutrality'. None the less, the end result in Crimea would have been the same: Red victory, revenge and terror.

On the arrival of the Red Army in Sevastopol, there was neither a power vacuum nor civil disorder. The transition from White to Red rule took place almost seamlessly. Even before the final White troops had departed the city, an *ad hoc* revolutionary committee of Social Revolutionaries and Anarchists came together on 13 November. Three days later, within twenty-four hours of the occupation of the city by Red forces, a joint meeting of the Revolutionary Military Councils of the 1st Cavalry, 2nd Cavalry and 6th Armies took place. A number of prominent officers of the Red Army attended, including Budyonny, Blyukher and Kliment Voroshilov. Politely they thanked the members of the Sevastopol Revolutionary Committee 'for their work', and promptly 'replaced them with members of the Red Army'. A new, largely civilian, revolutionary committee, however, was established on 23 November. Its members pledged that 'an iron hand would impose strict revolutionary order in the city entrusted to them'.[7] Obedience would be imposed by the power of the guns of the Red Army. Special detachments were formed to enforce order and to conduct the executions.

Frunze published another order of the day on 17 November 1920. In this lengthy document, he narrated the exploits of the Red Army's Southern *Front*, highlighting what had been achieved in the fifty days since its establishment. In particular, he stressed the fact that the 'last stronghold and hope of the Russian bourgeoisie, their accomplices and foreign capitalists' had been destroyed. The *front* commander proclaimed 'eternal glory to the creators of the revolution and to the liberators of the working people'. Turning his attention to the Red Army formations involved, who had given 'a great new victory' to the Soviet Republic, Frunze commended 'the extraordinary valour of the 51st and 15th Rifle Divisions in the intense battle for Yushun [Ishun]; the heroic attack of the 30th Rifle Division at the Chongar crossing; and the daring work of the 1st and 2nd Cavalry Armies'. All their deeds had been accomplished 'twice as fast as planned'. Not forgetting the propaganda aspect, Frunze turned the knife in his opponent, declaring that the 'adventurer Baron had fled to Constantinople, having abandoned his troops, and leaving them to their own devices'. Wrangel's army, in his opinion, which had 'served foreign interests', had 'disintegrated in the same way as Kolchak's, Denikin's and Yudenich's hordes'. Alluding to the bloodletting that was likely to follow, Frunze expounded the role of the 'Red Banner'. This symbol of 'struggle and victory' would now 'pursue the remnants of the enemy seeking rescue by ship' in the manner of a 'threatening phantom'. He concluded his order with the obligatory Bolshevik party slogans: 'Long live the victorious Red Army' and 'Long live the final world victory of communism'.[8] Although that global ideological objective was never to be achieved, the retribution of the victorious on the defeated in Crimea was only just beginning.

Lenin appeared to give retrospective blessing to the horrors of the Red Terror in Crimea during a speech given to activists of the Russian Communist Party (Bolsheviks) in Moscow on 6 December 1920.[9] Highlighting that there were 'at present 300,000 bourgeois in Crimea', he stated, 'these [people] are a source of future profiteering, espionage and every kind of aid to the capitalists. However, we are not afraid of them. We say that we shall take and distribute them, make them submit, and assimilate them.'[10] The Bolsheviks had just the tool available to achieve this objective. One of the most bloodthirsty and frightening manifestations of the Russian revolution was the 'All Russian Extraordinary Commission to Combat Counter-revolution and Sabotage' – popularly known from its partial Russian acronym as 'Cheka'.[11] Established on the decree of Lenin on 20 December 1917, it was soon to be controlled by Feliks Edmundovich Dzerzhinsky, nicknamed 'Iron Felix'. It was the first of a series of notorious Soviet state security organisations, followed most famously by the NKVD and KGB.[12] Its ruthlessness, cruelty and associated methods of torture appeared to be limitless.

When the Whites lost Crimea, the Cheka retribution was fast, furious and utterly relentless. Although about 100,000 civilians had been evacuated, it is estimated that no fewer than 2,009 officers and 52,687 soldiers of the former Russian Army were left in Crimea. In addition, there were 'about 15,000 wounded and sick in Crimean hospitals'. Despite Wrangel's best planning, not all the Whites could be evacuated; indeed, not all those remaining wished to be. Some had recklessly decided to stay put and risk their fate, perhaps influenced by the White Government's communiqués utterly erroneous and irresponsible reassurances about no harm coming to them. For various reasons, about 200,000 former government officials, journalists, actors, doctors, and other members of the intelligentsia such as teachers, were left behind to face a merciless blood quest. Thus Lenin's figure of 300,000 seems little exaggerated if all former White officers and soldiers were classed as 'members of the bourgeoisie', 'counter-revolutionaries' and 'enemies of workers' power', or any combination thereof.[13] Not all the Whites were entirely innocent victims: during the Civil War there had been many incidents of 'White Terror'. Many Red commissars and Communist activists were shot out of hand, for example, pre-dating the German policy of the Second World War encapsulated in the notorious *Kommissarbefehl* (Commissar Order) of 6 June 1941.[14] In terms of scale, however, the Red Terror of 1920–21 in Crimea was unprecedented.

It was not long before the reckoning began. In Feodosiya, for example, during the night of 16–17 November 1920, about 100 wounded White officers of the Vilna Regiment were shot out of hand at the railway station. Taking the whole of Russia into consideration, it is estimated that the largest concentration of killings in the Reds' reign of terror overall occurred in Crimea, where at least 15,000, and perhaps up to 100,000, people perished. While the numbers involved remain hotly disputed, the balance of historical analysis suggests that at least 50,000 were killed.[15] The Chekist methods of execution varied according to the proclivities of their local leaders and activists – numbers of whom had marked psychopathic tendencies. In Yalta, many of the Whites, their families and suspected sympathisers had heavy stones attached to their bound feet, and were subsequently shot in the back of the neck. Their bodies were then dumped unceremoniously into the sea. In Simferopol, over 20,000 were executed; their bodies were piled on top of each other in the wooded ravines of the Maryno district, now covered by a reservoir.[16] The German mass murders of Jews in Kiev and Simferopol during the Second World War would follow a similar pattern. Whether the executions took place in 1920–21 or in 1941–42, and whatever the nationality or motives of the executors, the killings were none the less heinous crimes against humanity.

In Sevastopol, it is claimed that 'close to thirty thousand people' died in the greater city area, including Balaklava. According to one account, as the Cheka proceeded to hang suspected Whites wherever they found them, Sevastopol's main streets became 'richly garnished with wind-swayed corpses'.[17] A particularly vicious and notorious member of the Cheka involved in the executions in Sevastopol and elsewhere in Crimea was Rozalia Zalkind, also known as Zemliachka. She had served as a commissar in the 8th and 13th Red Armies. In the Bolshevik newspaper *Krasny Krym* (Red Crimea), published after Simferopol fell on 13 November 1920, she wrote: 'We need [a] pitiless, unceasing struggle against the snakes who are hiding in secret... We must annihilate [the Whites, and] sweep them out with an iron broom from everywhere.'[18] She was not alone amongst her Red compatriots. The merciless Zalkind was but one of three individuals at the head of the Revolutionary Committee of Crimea (Krymrevkom). The other two in this troika of terror were her lover, a Hungarian revolutionary and Jew called Béla Kun, and Georgy Leonidovich Pyatakov, a member of the Revolutionary Military Council of the 6th Red Army and close associate of Trotsky.[19] On behalf of the Soviet leadership, these hardened Communists directed a campaign against 'counter-revolutionaries' and 'class enemies'. Driven by a savage cocktail of ambition, hatred and ideology, if not sadism, they took Trotsky's mantra that he would 'not visit Crimea until there was but one White Guard remaining' all too literally.

The task of eliminating the 'enemies of the people' was conducted most zealously in a series of mass arrests and executions across the width and length of the Crimean peninsula. The inevitable Bolshevik bureaucracy assisted the process, which one modern historian has described as a 'conveyor-belt of death'. Orders for the compulsory registration of all inhabitants of Crimea were issued as early as 17 November 1920. Members of the population were required to complete detailed questionnaires that in due course facilitated the rounding up of anyone suspected of being a White soldier or sympathiser. The Bolsheviks who undertook the work of suppressing the phantom of counter-revolution – as there was no credible source of any White opposition let alone possibility of insurrection –

were bloodthirsty, uncompromising and candid. One declared: 'With the punishing, merciless sword of Red Terror, we shall go over all Crimea and clear it of all the hangmen, enslavers, and tormentors of the working class'. In recognition of her efforts, Zemliachka received the Order of the Red Banner from a grateful Bolshevik regime at the beginning of 1921 for her 'tireless, selfless, and energetic organizational and political work', which had 'helped bring about the final victory of the Red Army'.[20] Such was the reality of the fledgling but brutal Soviet state, driven by an ideology that justified its actions on behalf of the proletariat.

By the spring of 1921, however, it was becoming evident that the havoc created by the Red Terror had gone too far. The fear of Red Army soldiers and government officials had grown to such extent that it undermined attempts to get the local economy moving again. Eventually the Soviet leadership put a stop to it and the temporary troika was dissolved. While the honoured Zemliachka lived to the ripe age of seventy and died a natural death in 1947, Béla Kun and Georgy Pyatakov received their richly deserved comeuppances. Both were arrested, condemned and executed during Stalin's purges in the late 1930s for alleged conspiracies against the state. It remains a moot point whether the inhumane methods of what later became known as the Red Terror contributed to the success of the Red Army during the Civil War. But there can be no doubt that the Red retribution following three years of conflict in places such as Crimea was unnecessarily harsh, as so often is the case in civil wars. The enormity of the crimes committed by Russians against Russians in the name of Bolshevik revolution was only to be acknowledged after the dissolution of the Soviet Union.

CRIMEA AND SEVASTOPOL DURING THE INTER-WAR YEARS

After the Russian Civil War and its bloody aftermath, Crimea and Sevastopol were economically and socially devastated. Natural disaster soon followed, which compounded the calamity of conflict and the effects of the Red Terror. According to the census of 1921, Crimea's population stood at 719,531 men, women and children.[21] An extraordinary drought led to the catastrophic famine of 1921–23, in which 100,000 Crimean inhabitants lost their lives, and about 50,000 may have emigrated or disappeared. Hence by 1923, the population was reported as amounting to only 569,500, representing a net loss of 21 per cent.[22] Hunger and need had affected townspeople and country folk alike, of all nationalities. Sevastopol's population in 1923 was recorded as 63,461, with a marked disparity between men (29,325) and women (34,136), no doubt reflecting the recent losses of the First World War and Civil War.[23]

Crimea then, as now, was demographically diverse although the distribution of ethnic groups has changed considerably over the last hundred years. There was no love lost between the two principal ethnic and linguistic communities of Crimea: Russian (including Ukrainian and Belorussian) and Tatar, representing approximately 51 and 26 per cent of the population respectively. Their enmity was historical and contemporary. During the recent period of revolution and civil war, both Reds and Whites had alternatively condemned and courted the Tatars on an opportunistic basis. Although Wrangel was no supporter of Tatar autonomy, he had authorised the assembly of a Tatar congress in Simferopol on 16 May 1920. In a speech to the delegates, he pledged that his government would 'realise cultural-educative, spiritual-religious, and some economic needs of the Tatar population' if the Tatars supported the activities of the Russian Army.[24] In his approach, Wrangel differed from Denikin who had been the most reactionary opponent of Tatar aspirations, pushing not only the left but also the mainstream Milli Firka into the arms of the Bolsheviks. Yet Wrangel's offer fell far short of the desired self-government and it did little to improve relations between the Whites and the Tatars. In any case, the period of Wrangel's rule was too brief to change Tatar perceptions; the Milli Firka hoped to put good relations with the Reds on a permanent footing by stressing their left-wing credentials.

Following the evacuation of the Whites six months later, the Red Terror struck not only the 'White Guardists', but also the 'Tatar Nationalists', despite the fact that some Tatars had fought against Wrangel's troops. Memories of the Bolshevik suppression in 1918–19 of the Milli Firka, which had been outlawed as a 'counter-revolutionary party', were still very fresh. Compounding the problem of the famine were the failures of land reform. Collectivisation – the creation of large state farms (*sovkhozes*) – had left many peasant Tatars dispossessed and impoverished.[25] Many of the landless remained so. The Tatars' response to a new wave of arrests and killings and to economic distress was to take to the Crimean Mountains and to launch an insurgency against the new Communist administration in Simferopol.

In response to a worsening crisis in Crimea during the course of 1921, Lenin's reaction was, for once, enlightened and not repressive. He despatched a trusted Bolshevik Volga Tatar, Mir Said Sultan Galiev, to the peninsula. His task was to establish the causes of the Crimean Tatars' campaign against the new Red government, and to suggest a solution. Galiev recommended not only halting the hated land reforms, but also giving the Tatars a sense of ethnic identity and degree of autonomy, which hitherto had been denied to them. In this manner, it was hoped that they would be attracted to the Communist Party, and would work together with the majority Russian population to build a new socialist republic. Lenin accepted Galiev's advice.[26]

On 18 October 1921, the All-Russia Central Executive Committee and Council of People's Commissars, chaired by Lenin, agreed to establish the

Crimean Autonomous Socialist Soviet Republic (ASSR). This political entity became a 'territorial multinational unit within the Russian Soviet Federative Socialist Republic', whose constitution was adopted on 10 November 1921 by the First All-Crimean Constituent Congress of Soviets. Significantly, a key article in that document declared that the republic established 'equality and right to free development for all the nationalities in Crimea, [and] rejects all the national and national-religious privileges and restrictions that existed before'. So from the very start, the Crimean ASSR was designed as multi-cultural. The new republic's coats of arms included the slogan 'Proletarians of all states unite!' written in both Russian and Crimean Tatar – the latter in Arabic script.[27]

Efforts to give the Tatars administrative, educational and social autonomy in Crimea – the process of 'Tatarisation' – were given a huge boost by the adoption of a new state-wide policy of *korenizatsiya* (rooting) in 1923, which followed the establishment of the Soviet Union in December 1922. Derived from the Russian word *koren* (root), this tool of political management involved positive discrimination on behalf of a certain native people (*korennoy narod*), which was designated as 'rooted' in a particular area or region.[28] In Crimea, it resulted in the appointment of Tatars to senior political and administrative positions. The Milli Firka leader turned Bolshevik Veli Ibahimov, for example, was made chairman of the Crimean Central Committee and of the Crimean Council of People's Commissars. Throughout the new autonomous republic, Tatars were put in charge of municipal administrations, factories, *sovkhozes* and *kolkhozes* (state and collective farms respectively).[29]

Historians differ as to the motives of *korenizatsiya*. On the one hand it can be regarded as a cynical move to divide and rule, and to buy off opposition to the new Soviet state. Alternatively, it can be seen as a genuine, enlightened attempt to spread the fruits of the revolution amongst all the peoples that made up the Soviet Union. Whatever the ulterior or declared purposes, there is little doubt that the policy of *korenizatsiya* brought considerable betterment to Crimean Tatars in the 1920s. During this decade, Tatar culture, language and publications all flourished. The city of Simferopol, for example, reverted to its old Tatar name of Ak Mecit – White Mosque. At primary and secondary schools across Crimea and at the Tauride University in the republic's capital, the study of the Tatar history and heritage were strongly encouraged. There was little place, however, for support to the Tatars' religion in an officially atheist Soviet Union. When Stalin later curbed national identities in the 1930s, including that of the Tatars, Crimea's mosques were progressively shut. The revival of the Tatar culture proved short-lived: and many of its leaders were 'eliminated'.

Since its foundation in 1783, Sevastopol had never had a significant Tatar population. Its citizens throughout the nineteenth century were predominantly Russian and secondly Ukrainian in origin. The Soviet government in Moscow, in a similar manner to the previous Tsarist administration in St Petersburg, viewed Sevastopol as a vital operating base and arsenal for its navy. The condition of the city after the Civil War was fragile: industrial production had all but stopped, and there was no functioning Black Sea Fleet present to support. Therefore one of the first tasks, echoing the aftermath of the Crimean War, was to clear the roadstead of the sunken ships, open the harbour and dockyard for commerce and naval purposes as quickly as possible, and to restart ship repair.

Output in Sevastopol's naval dockyard and life in the city as a whole were much improved through significant enhancements to infrastructure that took place in the early 1920s. One of Lenin's main domestic initiatives was to introduce widespread electrification to Russia (and later the Soviet Union).[30] Sevastopol was chosen as one of the first major projects; a new power station opened in the city in 1923. Local communications were enhanced with the opening of an electric tramline to Balaklava in 1924, approximately 15 kilometres long. Such was the progress made in Sevastopol that foreign visitors were invited to show off the model city's advances made under Soviet rule. On 8 May 1926, for example, a delegation of British railway workers came to Sevastopol and viewed its various sites, both historical and modern, including the Panorama and Naval museums, the dockyard and the fleet. What the visitors made of the trip, having missed Britain's General Strike (4–13 May) during their absence, is not recorded.[31] During 11–12 September 1927, a very strong earthquake (8 on the Richter scale) and a series of after-shocks hit Crimea. While much of Yalta was devastated with about 70 per cent of its buildings damaged, the impact on Sevastopol was also serious. No fewer than 1,140 buildings were affected, including the naval observatory.[32] The repair task was yet another challenge met by the city authorities, but quite modest in scale in comparison to the complete rebuilding of Sevastopol required following the ravages of the Second World War.

During the 1930s, the Soviet Union under an increasingly suspicious and distrustful Stalin witnessed a tightening of the hold that the government and local administrations enjoyed over the population and workforce. Although no obvious external threat existed, an internal one could easily be conjured up and measures adopted to counter it. In this manner, paranoia was institutionalised. On 22 February 1933, for example, the Sevastopol city council adopted a special resolution which required all public organisations to offer 'greater assistance to army and navy units', and to provide 'defensive work' – a blend of civil defence and home guard duties – 'in all enterprises and collective farms in the Sevastopol area, and to sustain the 'high quality of repairs to the ships of the navy'.[33] Little did the city councillors imagine at the time that, within nine years, war would return in a devastating fashion to Sevastopol. Yet the threat from a Fascist Germany under Hitler, who had just been appointed Chancellor on 30 January 1933, would soon become real enough. Reports by a strictly controlled press fuelled concerns as to the dangers faced by the Soviet Union as well as highlighting the state's achievements. On 12 June 1935, a regular airline service opened between Moscow and Sevastopol. One of its main tasks was to bring a thousand copies of the newspaper *Pravda* (Truth) daily to Sevastopol. Because of its strategic importance, the city continued to attract high-ranking visitors. In the same year, on 16 November, S. M. Budyonny, recently appointed as one of the first five Marshals of the Soviet Union, inspected the naval dockyard.[34] Significantly, it was exactly fifteen years since he had attended the Red Army's revolutionary committee in Sevastopol at the conclusion of its successful campaign in Crimea.

In 1936, the French writer, André Gide (the Nobel Prize laureate for literature in 1947), visited the USSR at the invitation of the Soviet Union of Writers. Although sympathetic to Communism, he became increasingly disillusioned with the ideology and political system represented by the Soviet state. In his book *Retour de l'U.R.S.S.* [*Back to the U.S.S.R.*], Gide expressed contradictory views on Sevastopol, 'the last stage of our journey'. Although he considered it 'without doubt one of the more interesting and more beautiful cities of the U.S.S.R.', he also observed 'Russian society, the entire Russian way of life, with its shortcomings, its wants, its sufferings, alas, less select, less intact than in Soukhoumi or Sochi, alongside its triumphs [and] its successes, which allow or promise mankind greater happiness'.[35] Gide's expectations of encountering a sort of socialist utopia appear to have been dashed on meeting the reality. His trip was in any case overshadowed by the death in Sevastopol of his companion, Eugène Dabit, to whom he dedicated the account of the visit.

By 1941, Sevastopol's population amounted to 114,000. Apart from service in the Black Sea Fleet and in the army garrison, work was plentiful in the dockyard, and in other naval and military facilities and factories. The city boasted a couple of internationally renowned medical and biological institutes, three technical colleges and twenty-eight schools. Cultural life was catered to with a theatre, three cinemas, two museums and an art gallery. Soviet records listed meticulously no fewer than seventy-six works canteens and 274 shops.[36] On the eve of war, Sevastopol was a bustling, lively and hard-working place. As the main base of the Black Sea Fleet, it would become a prime target in Germany's intervention against the Soviet Union, as it had been for Britain and France during the Crimean War.

The Development of the Black Sea Fleet and Sevastopol's Coastal Defences

The First World War, Civil War and associated foreign intervention had proved catastrophic to the Russian (now Red) Navy.[37] It is estimated that no fewer than 416 vessels, of which 174 were warships and 242 auxiliaries, were lost during the course of these conflicts.[38] The White Navy had pressed all seaworthy vessels of the Black Sea Fleet from the old to the new into service to effect the evacuation of November 1920. Among these were the modern battleship *General Alekseev* (the former *Volya*, which had been returned by the Royal Navy to Sevastopol and White command in October 1919) and the obsolete pre-dreadnought *Georgii Pobedonosets*, which had made her way to Constantinople under tow. After a period at anchor in the Bosporus, these capital ships and the remaining units of the White fleet steamed into the Mediterranean, where they were interned at the French Algerian port of Bizerte.[39] This naval force was considerable: apart from the two battleships, there were two cruisers (the *General Kornilov* and the *Almaz*), ten destroyers, four submarines, five gunboats, and ten transports or other vessels.[40] Despite protracted negotiations between the French and Soviet authorities, no ship or boat was returned to the Black Sea Fleet.

The various warships that the British had disabled at Sevastopol in April 1919 had not been repaired in the interim. The rusting squadron of pre-dreadnoughts, including the *Evstafi*, *Ioann Zlatoust*, *Sinop* and *Tri Svyatitelya*, and the cruiser *Pamyat Merkuriya*, had all been stripped of their guns, steering mechanisms and electrical systems, and their engines damaged.[41] Below the surface rested the sunken destroyers and submarines. The 'massively damaged' *Imperatritsa Mariya*, which had been raised and re-floated in May 1918, still lay upside down in Sevastopol's northern dry dock.[42] As a result, there was no serviceable Black Sea Fleet to be captured by the victorious Red Army.

The Soviet government placed a high priority in building a new navy, including the re-establishment of the Black Sea Fleet. Since laying down brand new ships would take much time and effort, the most economical way to regenerate maritime power was to repair and renew damaged ships, and to complete any unfinished ones. Reflecting the strategic importance of the task of resurrecting the navy and Sevastopol as its main base in the Black Sea, on 28 June 1922, Sevastopol received a very important visitor, M. I. Kalinin. As chairman of the Central Executive Committee of the All-Russian Congress of Soviets, and hence titular head of state, he was second only in the land to Lenin. Kalinin inspected the naval dockyard, met the crews of the embryonic fleet, viewed the refurbished coastal defence batteries on the southern side of Sevastopol roadstead and watched live firing exercises.[43]

One of the first major warships to be returned to service to the Black Sea Fleet was the *Pamyat Merkuriya* (the former *Kagul*), which was renamed again as the *Komintern* in 1922. On 19 November 1923, Sevastopol's naval dockyard was awarded the 'Red Banner for Work' for the 'extraordinary energy' shown in the restoration and refitting of this cruiser.[44] By 1924, the Black Sea Fleet could muster the *Komintern*, two destroyers, two submarines and twelve other vessels. Although this represented a small start, further warships would follow, including the light cruisers *Admiral Nakhimov* and *Admiral Lazarev*, both laid down in 1913 in Nikolayev. Launched in 1915 and 1916 respectively, construction on both had stopped in 1917. The White forces had attempted unsuccessfully to complete the *Admiral Nakhimov* and bring it into service. Work was resumed on both ships in the 1920s. While the *Admiral Nakhimov* joined the Black Sea Fleet in 1927 as the *Chernova Ukraina*, its sister ship, renamed the *Krasny Kavkaz*, was modernised further and followed four years later. Meanwhile, the *Komintern* served as the mutineers' ship during the filming of the *Battleship Potemkin* in 1925. The dreadnought *Imperatritsa Mariya*, which lay beyond economic repair, was scrapped in the same year. It was also beyond the Soviet Navy's capability to raise the scuttled *Svobodnaya Rossiya* (the former *Imperatritsa Ekaterina Velikaya*) from Novorossiysk's harbour bottom.[45] The Soviet Black Sea Fleet received its first battleship in early 1930, when the *Parizhskaya Kommuna* (the former *Sevastopol*) was transferred from the Baltic, along with the light cruiser *Profintern* (the former *Svetlana*, renamed in 1939 as the *Krasny Krym*). Both vessels, which had been seriously damaged in a storm in the Bay of Biscay in December 1929, were repaired and modernised in Sevastopol.[46] Later these warships were to play prominent roles in the defence of the city in 1941–42.

Although priority was given to modernising the Workers' and Peasants' Red Army and its air force – the Voyenno-Vozdushnye Sily (VVS) – during the Soviet government's Five-Year Plans for expanding the economy, a naval building programme benefited the Black Sea Fleet. At the end of the first plan, which began in 1928, two modern destroyer leaders were laid down in Nikolayev in 1932: the *Kharkov* and the *Moskva*. These Leningrad-class vessels of Italian design were very fast (40 knots) and well armed (with five 130mm guns). Further investment continued in the second plan (1933–37) and its foreshortened successor (1938–41), which allowed the progressive build up of the Black Sea Fleet. While Sevastopol retained its role as headquarters, main base (*glavnaya baza*) and arsenal, naval vessels were also stationed at Odessa, Ochakov and Novorossiysk, and in the two Georgian ports of Poti and Batumi. Nikolayev remained the main shipbuilding and repair yard.

Stalin's ambitions for the development of the Russian Navy rose during the late 1930s. The Soviet Union planned to build no fewer than sixteen super-Dreadnoughts over the period of the third and fourth Five-Year Plans. Under Project 23, the first four Sovyetskiy Soyuz-class battleships, each to be armed with nine 405mm guns and displacing over 60,000 tonnes, were laid down in 1938. Construction of the second of the class, the *Sovyetskaya Ukraina*, in the Andre Marti (South) Yard (Soviet Shipyard No. 198) at Nikolayev, however, was far from complete when the Germans occupied the port in August 1941. Thus the Black Sea Fleet lacked a fully modern battleship during the Second World War. Building of the *Sovetskaya Ukraina* was never resumed.[47]

Immediately prior to the outbreak of war with Germany on 22 June 1941, the following warships were based in Sevastopol: the obsolescent battleship *Parizhskaya Kommuna*; the old cruisers *Krasny Kavkaz*, *Chernova Ukraina* and *Krasny Krym*; the recently commissioned modern Kirov class cruisers *Voroshilov* and *Molotov*; the *Moskva* and the *Kharkov*; and nine other destroyers. Additionally, there were two brigades of submarines (with a total of twenty-one boats in service, and ten under repair), a brigade of ten torpedo boats, and a brigade of minesweeping trawlers that guarded the waters of the main base. Altogether, in just over twenty years since the end of the Civil War, the Soviet Black Sea Fleet had grown from almost nothing to a strong, balanced force of one battleship, five cruisers, seventeen destroyers (including the third leader, *Tashkent*), two guard ships, forty-four submarines, four gun-boats, two minelayers, twelve trawlers, seventy-eight torpedo boats and twenty-four mine hunters.[48]

The Black Sea Fleet included a naval air arm, part of the Soviet Navy's Aviastiya Voyenno-Morskogo Flota (VMF) – the 'aviation of the military maritime fleet'. This integral air force of the Black Sea Fleet (ChF), abbreviated as VVS-ChF, contained: Beriev MBR-2 flying boats for maritime patrol tasks; mostly outdated fighters (Polikarpov biplanes (I-153s) and monoplanes (I-16s)) to provide air defence; and medium bombers. The latter, including Illyushin DB-3s/3Fs and Tupolev SBs, had the range to attack targets on the Romanian coastline. Stationed across eight aerodromes on Crimea (Sevastopol, Karagoz (now Pervomayskoe), Sarabuz (now Gvardeyskoye), Yevpatoriya, Kacha, Belbek, Dzhankoy and Kerch) on 22 June 1941 were 129 bombers, 175 fighters (of which only sixteen were the modern MiG-3s), and sixty maritime reconnaissance aircraft.[49] Complementing the surface and sub-surface capabilities of the Black Sea Fleet, the stationing of medium bombers on the peninsula had turned Crimea into a giant aircraft carrier.

Sevastopol between the wars saw a considerable investment in its coastal defences and dockyard. Before the shells of the German battlecruiser *Goeben* struck Sevastopol on 29 October 1914, it had already been recognised that the city's coastal defences were obsolescent. The range of naval guns had greatly increased, as had the thickness of armour on battleships. The old style of open battery armed with exposed guns of short range and slow rate of fire was no longer adequate to meet the latest threat of ship-to-shore bombardment. The experience of the Russo-Japanese War, not least the siege of Port Arthur, had reinforced such concerns. Before the First World War, the tsarist government decided to protect Sevastopol with new coastal defences. This modernisation programme, however, was far from complete by the outbreak of war in 1914.

The most striking feature of the development plan was two armoured turreted batteries, each of four 12-inch (305mm) guns, to provide the principal defence against naval and amphibious attack. As introduced in the Prologue, the site chosen for the first battery was near the village of Lyubimovka, just south of the Belbek river approximately 5 kilometres north of Sevastopol and lying a kilometre from the coastline (see Map 13). Two great Russian military engineers were responsible for its design: General of Engineers César Antonovich Cui (of French and Lithuanian descent) and Major General Nestor Aloizevich Buynitsky. The former was not only an expert in military fortifications, but also a composer and music critic of equal distinction. Both were professors of fortification at the prestigious Nikolaevsky Engineering Academy in St Petersburg.

In 1913 construction started at Lyubimovka of an underground structure some 130 by 50 metres in size, containing ammunition stores, electrical plant, living and sleeping quarters and a command post – all protected by 4 metres of reinforced concrete. The only exposed elements would be two heavily armoured turrets, each able to rotate 360 degrees, and equipped with two 52-calibre, 305mm naval guns, capable of firing a 471-kilogramme shell to nearly 30 kilometres, and later extended to over 40.[50] When Souchon's force attacked Sevastopol on 29 October 1914, work at the battery at Lyubimovka, however, was only just under way; the turrets were being fabricated in St Petersburg. Had the battery been completed in time to engage the *Goeben*, it remains a matter of conjecture as to whether the attacker or the defender would have won the artillery duel. A critical task for coastal defence gunners is the timely acquisition of the target and, once engaged, spotting the fall of shot to adjust their shooting. A network of observation posts, including one on the Inkerman Heights, provided the necessary firing data to the battery command post. Construction at Lyubimovka halted in 1915 when its designated turrets were diverted to coastal defence batteries in the Baltic. The 1917 revolutions and Civil War precluded the resumption of work. Construction of what became known as Battery 30 was only re-started in 1928 and completed in 1934, over twenty years following the inception of the project.

Battery No.	Location	No. of Guns and Calibre (mm)	Completed	Remarks
	North of Sevastopol Bay			
54	Nikolaevka	4 x 102		Opened fire on 30 October 1941.
10	Mamaschay	4 x 203	1920	Guns from the *Evstafi* pre-dreadnought.
30	Lyubimovka	4 x 305	1934	Two armoured turrets each of two guns.
12	Cape Constantine	4 x 152		
2	Cape Constantine	4 x 100		
	South of Sevastopol Bay			
8	Cape Alexander	4 x 45		Located between Alexander and Martynov Bays in the north-western suburbs of Sevastopol.
14	Cape Streletskaya	3 x 130		Replacing the 4 x 152mm guns removed to reinforce the defences of northern Crimea.
	Southern Coast of the Chersonese peninsula			
35	Cape Chersonese	4 x 305	1927	Two armoured turrets each of two guns
18	Cape Fiolent	4 x 152	1917	
19	Cape Balaklava	4 x 152	1924	
	Mobile Batteries			
724		4 x 152		
725		4 x 152		

**Table 12.1 – Sevastopol's Coastal Defence Batteries (mid-November 1941)
Data from P. A. Morgunov, *Geroycheskiy Sevastopol* (1979)[53]**

A second such modern battery (No. 35) of similar design was constructed on the southern shore of Cape Chersonesos in a much more expeditious manner. Covering the western and southern approaches to Sevastopol, work on this site was resumed in 1924. While the main construction was completed three years later, the essential range-finding and fire control equipment was not installed until the mid-1930s. In July 1929, Battery No. 35 was inspected by none other than Stalin, together with an important German guest, Major General Werner von Blomberg, chief of the *Truppenamt* – the thinly disguised office of the German General Staff, which had been banned in the Treaty of Versailles of 1919. Guides at the battery today tell an improbable story that Stalin intended that the guns be fired in a demonstration shoot, but when he heard that the cost of a shell was the 'equivalent of two tractors', he forbade the firing.[51] Together, both Batteries 30 and 35 could dominate not only the sea approaches to Sevastopol, but also those on land.

Apart from these two heavy armoured turreted batteries, there were eight main coastal defence batteries defending Sevastopol (see Table 12.1).[52] Four were sited to the north of the city: No. 54, 40 kilometres to the north at Nikolaevka; No. 10, just south of the Kacha river at Mamaschay; and Nos. 12 and 2, guarding the entrance to the roadstead at Cape Constantine. On the opposite shore, Batteries 8 and 14 (further to the west) guarded the mouth of Sevastopol Bay. Covering the southern coast of the Chersonese peninsula were Batteries 18 and 19 at Capes Fiolent and Balaklava respectively.

Two mobile batteries reinforced the fixed defences. Meanwhile, several pre-First World War batteries had been taken out of use. These included the former Battery No. 16, 4 kilometres north of Sevastopol Bay, about a kilometre to the south of Lyubimovka and south-west of Battery No. 30, which originally held four 120mm guns. During the Second World War this became a defended locality armed with field artillery known to the Germans as Fort Shishkov. On the southern side of Sevastopol near Arrow Bay lay the old casemated Streletskaya Battery No. 15, previously armed with six 254mm guns. In the 1930s the disarmed battery was used for workshops and storage space. It became a strongpoint again during the second defence of the city in 1941–42.[54]

THE COMING OF WAR

The Soviet Union was spared the first two years of the Second World War, during which Hitler's Germany attacked and conquered most of Western Europe from Norway in the north to Yugoslavia in the south, from Poland in the east to France in the west. Although Stalin believed he had secured peace with Nazi Germany through the Molotov–Ribbentrop Pact of 23 August 1939, he continued to view Germany with growing suspicion as Hitler's victorious armed forces humbled Europe.

The division of Poland in September 1939 (one of the secret provisions of the Pact) had not made Germany and the Soviet Union any less belligerent towards each other. During the ensuing brief period of uneasy peace – in effect an armed truce – between the two states, Stalin did everything he could to prevent any provocation of Germany, and continued exporting supplies of oil and minerals to Germany until the very day war broke out. Although the Soviet Union achieved massive increases in industrial production, notably in armaments, during the Five-Year Plans of the 1930s, and had transformed itself into a war economy, it was not yet ready for a full-scale war against Germany. This may appear surprising if one bears in mind that the Red Army had doubled in size from 1939 to 1941, and that it was already part mobilised when the German attack struck on 22 June 1941. Within the armed forces of the Soviet Union, however, there were shortages everywhere, both deficiencies of materiel (such as modern fighters, radio equipment and vehicles for logistic support), and, perhaps as crucially, significant gaps in the practice of modern war. Although the theory was basically sound, and in many ways more advanced than Germany's, the Red Army was in the throes of a second major restructuring in three years. New doctrine, the brainchild of purged generals such as Tukhachevsky, had been banned. In contrast, the Soviets' experienced and optimistic (if not opportunistic) opponent, the German *Wehrmacht*, stood at the height of its powers.

Stalin's purges of the officer corps during 1937–39 had much more than decimated the senior leadership of the state's armed forces.[55] Among those accused and culled on a variety of trumped-up charges were Marshals of the Soviet Union V. K. Blyukher (Civil War hero), M. N. Tukachevsky (one of the greatest military theorists of all time) and A. I. Yegerov (Chief of the Red Army's General Staff). As a result, many lesser figures rose to prominence during the Second World War. The axe had fallen not only within the land forces (thirteen out of fifteen army commanders eliminated), but also in the navy with only one out of nine admirals remaining. One survivor was Filipp Sergeyevich Ivanov, who changed his surname to Oktyabrsky in 1924.[56] He assumed command of the Black Sea Fleet in March 1939 in the rank of vice admiral. Coming from peasant stock from the Tver region, north-west of Moscow, he had served in the Red Baltic Fleet during the Civil War. He graduated from Petrograd's Communist University in 1922, and from the Frunze Higher Naval School in Leningrad in 1928. The 1930s saw him rise up the naval ladder through various appointments in the Baltic, Black Sea and Pacific fleets. Much of his career at sea was involved in torpedo boats. There was nothing to single him out as particularly suited for fleet command, or indeed, when war came to Crimea, to assume responsibility for the Sevastopol Defence Region in a joint, inter-Service, environment.

Oktyabrsky received his first hint of war when summoned urgently to Moscow in mid-June 1940. At that time, Germany was completing her stunning victory over France, which signed an armistice on the 22nd. When the world's attention was focused on Western Europe, Stalin thought the moment opportune to advance Soviet interests in south-eastern Europe. The purpose of the secret meeting in the Kremlin was soon revealed when the Soviet leader discussed the impending occupation of Romanian Bessarabia (now Moldova) with his senior military advisers. These included the People's Commissar for Defence (Minister), Marshal of the Soviet Union Semyon Timoshenko, the People's Commissar for the Navy, Admiral Nikolay Kuznetsov, the Chief of the General Staff, Marshal of the Soviet Union Boris Shaposhnikov, and a rising star of the Red Army, General Georgy Zhukov. Apart from Kuznetsov, Oktyabrsky was the only senior naval officer present. All these individuals would assume prominent roles in the coming world war. When Timoshenko rejected Oktyabrsky's considered advice about the strength of Romanian naval forces on the Danube, Stalin backed the commander of the Black Sea Fleet. He then ordered Oktyabrsky to make his ships ready for operations against Romanian forces if it came to hostilities.[57] In this manner, Oktyabrsky came to the attention of Stalin, who by and large admired men who stood their ground. Another such individual was Zhukov, who became the Soviet Union's most famous military leader during the Second World War.

In the event, on 26 June 1940, the Soviet government sent an ultimatum to Romania, demanding the evacuation of Bessarabia and of Northern Bukovina (now in south-western Ukraine). Under threat of armed attack by much superior Soviet forces, the Romanians conceded these territories over the period 28 June – 3 July. As this region lay within the Soviet zone of interest designated in a secret annex to the Molotov–Ribbentrop Pact, Hitler declined to provide any assistance to Romania. Yet such was the popular determination to recover the occupied lands, together with the seizure of power by the German-leaning Marshal Ion Antonescu, that Romania joined Germany's war against the Soviet Union, which opened on 22 June 1941. The alliance proved an unequal and unhappy marriage of convenience: Germany desired Romanian oil (its military was a bonus of doubtful quality) while Romania sought an ally, under whose protection she could expand territorially. None the less, Romanian forces, trained and equipped on French lines, while less well equipped and tactically skilled than their German counterparts, occasionally proved doughty opponents of the Soviet Union during the Second World War. They fought in the offensive battles for Odessa, Crimea and Sevastopol in 1941–42. Although mauled in defensive combat associated with the German loss of Stalingrad, they stayed in the fight, garrisoning and feebly contesting Crimea in 1943–44. When the Red Army invaded Romania in August 1944, the Romanian Army quickly collapsed and Antonescu was deposed in a coup; his country switched sides to fight against Germany.[58]

A brief survey of the Soviet military preparations against Germany and the latter's offensive plans for the invasion of the USSR helps explain how the war came to Crimea and Sevastopol in the late summer of 1941.[59] Despite the introduction of new technologies such as the aircraft, tank and radio in the twentieth century, the planning and conduct of operations on land today is still heavily influenced by terrain and the associated infrastructure of human settlement, railways and roads. The German–Soviet war of 1941–45 proved no exception. Geographically, the western part of the USSR was divided by the vast Pripyat forested marshlands, which sit astride the common border of the present states of Belorussia and Ukraine. The Soviet General Staff anticipated (rightly as it turned out) that the German main effort would lie to the north of this major obstacle, and develop in two strategic axes towards Leningrad, and especially, towards Moscow. Stalin, however, was unconvinced. He forecast that the German priority would lie to the south in order to seize the rich farmlands of Ukraine and the industrial zones of Kiev, Kharkov and particularly the Donets Basin, which had become the Soviet 'Ruhr'. In line with Stalin's direction, the preponderance of Soviet strength, particularly in mechanised and armoured formations, lay in Ukraine.

The Soviet mobilisation plan of 1941 required the deployment of three successive strategic echelons. The first comprised the forces of the border military districts, which would become the fighting *fronts* (army groups). In turn, these *fronts* were organised into two operational echelons: a covering force to guard the frontier and to delay the opponent; and the main defence forces, including the mass of the mechanised corps, to defeat it. Behind this, a second strategic echelon would be established along the line of the Dvina–Dnieper rivers. A third strategic echelon would be drawn from forces in the Far East – taking a risk against any resumption of hostilities with Japan – and formations mobilised from internal military districts. The role of the second and third strategic echelons would complete the defeat of the aggressor, drive him back to the frontier and so restore Soviet sovereignty.

The mobilisation potential of the Soviet Union, which was able to raise (excluding separate brigades that amounted to 133 division equivalents) no fewer than 483 rifle, 73 tank, 31 motorised and 101 cavalry divisions by 1 December 1941, was grossly underestimated by German intelligence. As Lenin had remarked, 'quantity has a quality all of its own', an enduring truism ignored by European defence planners since the end of the Cold War, anxious to redeem a perpetual peace dividend regardless of increasing strategic risk. During the initial period of the German–Soviet war, the *Wehrmacht* scored a string of spectacular operational successes, inflicting over 11 million casualties between 22 June 1941 and 18 November 1942. Yet the Germans repeatedly failed to exploit these victories to achieve decisive strategic effect. Ultimately, the Red Army (supported by air and naval forces) outfought its opponent, based not only on a superiority of numbers, but also on its increasing quality and sophistication. German commanders were slow to realise this development.

The German high command, buoyed by its triumphs in Poland, Norway, the Low Countries and France, drew the wrong conclusions about the difficulties Soviet forces had encountered in the winter war against Finland. In consequence, when it came to Operation BARBAROSSA, the invasion of the Soviet Union, German planners over-estimated their forces' capabilities and under-estimated the capacities of men and materiel required to sustain a campaign in the East. Hitler's Directive No. 21, issued on 18 December 1940, required that the 'German Armed Forces must be prepared, even before the conclusion of the war against England, to crush Soviet Russia in a rapid campaign'. The general intention demanded that the 'bulk of the Russian Army stationed in Western Russia ... be destroyed by daring operations led by deeply penetrating armoured spearheads', adding that 'Russian forces still capable of giving battle will be prevented from withdrawing into the depths of Russia'. The final, and as it turned out, wildly ambitious, objective of the offensive was 'to erect a barrier against Asiatic Russia on the general line Volga–Archangel'.[60]

Germany's mechanised and motorised forces, some nineteen panzer and fifteen motorised among a total of 152 divisions, which provided the principal striking power of the offensive, were spread thinly across four panzer groups (later termed panzer armies). One would support Army Group North on its north-easterly strategic axis through the Baltic states to Leningrad. Two would support Army Group Centre (ostensibly the main effort) on its easterly axis through Minsk and Smolensk to Moscow. Only one, however, remained for Army Group South, which developed two axes on a much broader front than the other two army groups. Its main attack would be launched from the Lublin area (Poland) 'in the general direction of Kiev', while further south, forces from Romania would 'carry out a wide enclosing movement'. Pursuit operations would seek the 'early capture of the Donets Basin, important for the war industry' towards the city of Rostov-on-Don.[61]

PREPARATIONS FOR WAR IN CRIMEA AND SEVASTOPOL

On Crimea, far away from the Soviet Union's western European borders and the initial battles, the Soviet 9th Army Corps was based, along with considerable numbers of militia and self-defence units. This corps, initially comprising the 106th and 156th Rifle Divisions and the 32nd Cavalry Division, provided the main fighting power (about 30,000 men) of the 51st Army, which was mobilised in August 1941. Its task was to defend Crimea.

Alongside Oktyabrsky, the second senior officer who played a major role in the defence of Sevastopol was Major General Pyotr Alekseyevich Morgunov. A specialist in coastal artillery, he had spent most of his service in Sevastopol. As a junior officer during the 1920s, he had served in the city's coastal defence batteries. Following various specialist artillery and naval courses, he had commanded Battery No. 35 in the early 1930s. In 1939 Morgunov was appointed commandant of the coastal defence of Crimea and of the main base of the Black Sea Fleet at Sevastopol.

In the years prior to the outbreak of the Second World War in September 1939, the Soviet military and naval authorities had given little thought as to how Sevastopol could be protected to landward. The only measure adopted was to ensure that the long-range 305mm guns of the newly installed Batteries 30 and 35 were capable of engaging land targets with high-explosive shells. In this manner, the fundamental mistake of the British in the defence of Singapore against Japanese attack in February 1942 in not supplying such ammunition for its powerful 15-inch coastal defence guns was not repeated. As war approached in 1940–41, however, the main threats to the Black Sea Fleet at Sevastopol appeared to be either from the air or by airborne assault. German air landing operations in the Low Countries in May 1940 and the British attack by carrier-borne aircraft on the Italian naval base at Taranto in November 1940 provided timely reminders of the need to improve anti-aircraft defences. The successful, albeit costly, German airborne assault on Crete (Operation MERKUR, 20 May – 1 June 1941), which routed a numerically superior British Commonwealth and Greek force, underlined the necessity of bolstering ground forces to defeat any enemy *desant* (landing), whether from the air or from the sea.

On 16 December 1940, People's Naval Commissar Kuznetsov took the initiative in ordering a major inspection of Sevastopol's defences to air and amphibious attack with a view to their urgent upgrading. Morgunov was given responsibility for this task. During the course of late February to early April 1941, he and his team surveyed and planned a series of new defences, which included not only air defence batteries but also a series of minefields, trench lines and reinforced concrete bunkers armed with artillery (incorporating many naval guns), anti-tank guns and machine guns which guarded the railway line from Bakhchisaray and the main roads that led towards Sevastopol.[62] Preliminary work was already under way when the war started on 22 June 1941. The shock of the surprise air attack on the city spurred construction efforts: already during the first days of July some 1,500–2,000 servicemen of the garrison and 2,000 members of the local population were hard at work.[63]

Plans evolved over the period of construction. The initial concept foresaw a ring of defences – rather than a continuous line of fortifications – about 20 kilometres distant from the city centre. As the possibility of a German amphibious or airborne assault much closer to the city became apparent, priority was given to constructing an inner ring of defences. When German forces started to assault the Perekop isthmus in September 1941, the threat of a major ground attack on Sevastopol became all too evident and construction effort was switched back to the outer defences. By 1 November 1941 three lines of defences – none continuous – had been established, incorporating forward observation and command posts, with anti-tank ditches, field fortifications of earth and timber and barbed wire obstacles to complement the minefields laid and concrete gun emplacements. These outer and rear lines are shown on Map 13 and details of the defences are given in Table 12.2 overleaf.

Of particular importance in the Outer Line were the four main fortified areas or strongholds (*opornymi punktami*) built around the villages of Kamary and Chorgun, Shuli and Cherkez-Kermen, Duvankoy and Aranchi. Gorges and ravines along the line of the outer defences were equipped with seventeen so-called 'fire curtains' – perforated pipes or troughs filled with fuel mixture at pressure that would be ignited in the event of an enemy attack.[64] Similar improvised flame traps had been devised for the defence of Britain by the Petroleum Warfare Department in 1940.

The protection of Sevastopol's coastal defence batteries was also enhanced during this period with the erection of machine-gun nests and pill-boxes. Figures vary as to the total numbers of bunkers and pill-boxes constructed. Suffice it to say, however, that notwithstanding the huge efforts made to defend the city from land attack, particularly during the period July–October 1941, none of the lines of defence was yet adequate to block a determined German assault. Much of the strength of Sevastopol's defence was derived from the eighty-two naval guns (45–130mm calibre) incorporated into the inner, main and outer lines, together with many of the thirty-nine guns of Sevastopol's coastal defence batteries.

Additional fire support came from an armoured train and from the warships of the Black Sea Fleet. The train, named after Anatoly Zheleznyakov, a Bolshevik hero who commanded an armoured train during the Russian Civil War, was armed with three 76mm naval guns.[65] The Germans christened this stealthy weapon, which was hidden from view in the railway tunnels near Sevastopol before darting out to open fire, the 'Green Ghost'. Today, the restored *Zheleznyakov* train stands as a proud memorial of the war near Sevastopol's railway and bus stations: a sign on the tender of its locomotive proclaims 'Death to Fascism'. Heavy bombardments were delivered by the battleship *Parizhskaya Kommuna* and by cruisers such as the *Krasny Kavkaz* and the *Krasny Krym*, whose salvoes broke up numerous German assaults on the city.

The anti-aircraft defences of Sevastopol were considerable. They included no fewer than '160 medium calibre guns grouped in 40 batteries, 34 guns of small calibres grouped in seven batteries, and a couple of hundred anti-aircraft machine guns as well as numerous searchlights'.[66] Many of these batteries provided an additional element of the ground defence. Their reinforced concrete underground command posts, ammunition stores and barbed wire defences made them ideal strongpoints: so much so that when the Germans attacked Sevastopol, they identified several anti-aircraft batteries as 'forts' – most notably naming Battery No. 365 as 'Fort Stalin'. This locality witnessed ferocious fighting in both

Line	Distance from city (km)	Length (km)	Depth (m)	Location	Numbers of Bunkers Artillery and A/Tank	Machine-Gun	Other Defences
Outer	15–17	46	Not stated	Eastern flank of fortified port of Balaklava – Kamara – Upper and lower Chorgun – Cherkez-Kermen – Shuli – Duvankoy – Azis-Oba Hill – Aranchi – 1.5km north of the mouth of the river Kacha	29	92	8km barbed wire; 1.7km anti-tank ditch; 9,605 anti-tank and anti-personnel mines.
Main	8–12	35	300	Pt 145.1 – Kadykovka – Pt 74.0 – Eastern slopes Sapun escarpment – Sakharnaya Golovka Hill – Southern and eastern slopes Pt 120.1 – Western slope Kamyshlov Gully – Benchmark 71.9 – Southern and western slopes Barak Gully – along Kacha river to Tyulku-Oba Hill	25	57	13km barbed wire.
Rear	3–6	19	300–600	Arrow Bay – Commune Farm – Pt 60.5 – English Cemetery – Pt 77.4 – Victoria Redoubt – Suzdal Hill – Pt 67.7 – Grafskaya gully – Mekenzievy Gory Station – Pt 42.7 – Pt 36.1 – South of Lyubimovka	28	71	40km barbed wire; 31.5km anti-tank ditch.

Table 12.2 – Sevastopol's Defence Lines (as at 1 November 1941)
Data from P. A. Morgunov, *Geroycheskiy Sevastopol* (1979)[67]

December 1941 and June 1942. Although the fighter defences of Sevastopol were less formidable, German planners could not discount them. Major General Nikolay Alekseyevich Ostriakov commanded an air group based in aerodromes around the city, which included 41 fighters, 31 seaplanes and ten ground attack aircraft.[68] He proved himself as a most resourceful leader.

THE GREAT PATRIOTIC WAR STARTS IN SEVASTOPOL

As far as the Soviet Union was concerned, the Second World War started on 22 June 1941. In Soviet and Russian historiography, the conflict is termed as the 'Great Patriotic War', echoing the terminology used in 1812 to foster national cohesion in countering Napoleon's invasion. The defence of the Motherland in 1941 very quickly became seen as a 'sacred war', reflected in the title of one of the most popular songs of the period – *Svyashchennaya Voyna*. First performed on 26 June 1941 in Moscow, it was sung throughout the war. Its moving music by Alexander Aleksandrov and stirring lyrics by Vasily Lebedev-Kumach, with an evocative chorus that closes with 'This is a sacred war we wage, a people's sacred war', ensure that it remains a favourite choice on Victory Day (9 May) celebrations.[69]

Sevastopol was one of the very first targets German aircraft attacked on the onset of war. The ships of the Black Sea Fleet had just returned to port following several days of intense exercises. Operationally, all was quiet during the evening of Saturday, 21 June. The squares and streets of the city centre, however, were full of the sounds and sights of off-duty sailors and young people enjoying themselves. In a manner reminiscent of A. S. Menshikov visiting a theatre on 13 September 1854 on the eve of the Allied landings, the commander of the Black Sea Fleet attended a concert performance with his wife in the House of the Red Army and Fleet. Then Oktyabrsky took a group of visiting friends from Leningrad back home. After a meal, the admiral retired to bed. Awakened by a call from his headquarters, his staff reported the receipt of a flash signal from Moscow. At 0055 hours, People's Commissar Admiral Kuznetsov ordered the adoption of Operational Readiness State No. 1 – imminent hostilities. The Black Sea Fleet headquarters received this message at 0103 hours and relayed it twelve minutes later to the ships of the fleet and to the coastal defence and air defence commands.[70]

At 0115 hours sirens sounded across the slumbering city and signal flares lit up the sky above. In his memoirs, Zhukov recalled how he was informed in Moscow of the imminent attack on Sevastopol:

> At 0307 hours I was called over the HF [radio] by Admiral F.S. Oktyabrsky, Commander of the Black Sea Fleet, who said that the fleet's aircraft warning

system had reported the approach from the sea of large numbers of unidentified aircraft. The fleet was on full alert. The admiral requested instructions.

"What have you decided to do?" I asked him.

"There is only one thing to do: fire on the planes with the fleet's anti-aircraft batteries."

After a brief exchange with Timoshenko, I said to Oktyabrsky: "Act and report to your People's Commissar."[71]

The first bombs fell on the Primorsky Boulevard and nearby streets at 0348 hours. A local resident, Georgy Zadorozhnikov, then an eight-year-old boy living in Podgornaya Street only six houses away from where an aerial mine landed, recalled the event. 'When the explosion broke the night sleep, window glass from the veranda splashed on our beds. Mother shouted with indignation "Why we were made to glue the windows up, as everything is broken into pieces!"' He and his family shook themselves and ventured out into the street. 'Everything was grey because of the dust.... Part of the house with the sign "Dom Diko" was still standing.... [We saw] a fire engine, an ambulance and stretchers. People were working at the ruins. We could hear crying, moans and wailing'.[72] And so the war began.

Sevastopol had received just over ninety minutes' warning of the German raid. Searchlights picked out the enemy raiders, which were engaged by ship- and shore-based anti-aircraft guns. Three aircraft were shot down: two over the city and one out to sea.

A military history of Sevastopol describes the aim and results of the German attack:

> It turned out that the German aircraft, having accomplished their surprise raid, had dropped sea mines. The German commanders had decided to mine the bays and waterways of Sevastopol in the first hours [of war] with new and to us unknown non-contact magnetic and magnetic-acoustic mines so as to bottle up the ships of the fleet in the bays and then to destroy them from the air. That was the plan which had been thought up for the destruction of the main forces of the Black Sea Fleet.[73]

The German raid did not succeed for a number of reasons. First, the number of the German aircraft (Heinkel He-111) flying from their base in Romania was too few, and only eight mines were dropped. Secondly, the air defences of the city and naval base were on full alert, and met the enemy aircraft with accurate and intense fire. None the less, although minimal damage to the ships of the Black Sea Fleet and its infrastructure ashore resulted, thirty people were killed and two hundred wounded amongst the townsfolk. By committing an insufficient weight of effort, the Germans had failed to emulate the British success at Taranto and squandered the opportunity to deliver a crippling blow. The Japanese did not repeat this mistake at Pearl Harbor on 6 December 1941. The Soviet Union was now at war; within six months, the United States of America would follow.

Returning to the early hours of 22 June 1941, Zhukov received an update on the situation at Sevastopol. 'At 4 a.m.', he recorded, 'I had another talk with Admiral Oktyabrsky. In a calm voice he reported: "The enemy attack has been beaten off. The attempted strike has failed. There has been some damage in the city, however".' In his memoirs, Zhukov emphasised that 'the Black Sea Fleet under Admiral Oktyabrsky was one our first formations to put up organized resistance to the enemy'.[74] Yet the attack on the Crimean city was significant in other respects too. For the Soviet Union, the Great Patriotic War started here: the population of Sevastopol suffered the very first casualties of the 27 million endured by the Soviet people during that conflict. A monument on the former Podgornaya Street now records the names of twenty-one 'victims of war', who lost their lives on that fateful morning.

Immediately following 22 June 1941, daily life went on as normal for the majority of the city's citizens. The women and children of bombed out families, including the Zadorozhnikovs, however, were evacuated to Simferopol, which was not regarded as a likely German target. Although the main areas of fighting still lay far away, the realities of war began to sink in as the Soviet authorities placed Sevastopol on a war footing. Navy, army and air force units received their reservists and made ready. Although warships of the Black Sea Fleet were soon in action off the Romanian coast, the first results of naval operations were inauspicious. When the destroyer leaders *Kharkov* and *Moskva* bombarded the port of Constanta on 26 June 1941, disaster struck. The Romanian destroyer *Regina Maria* intercepted the *Moskva*, and after a brief engagement, hit and sank the Soviet warship. Although the *Kharkov* was damaged by air attack, she was able to make her escape and was soon under repair at Sevastopol.

Oktyabrsky spent the remainder of June and July juggling scarce resources of the fleet to meet the various demands placed on it in maintaining sea control and supporting land forces along the Black Sea's littoral. A host of deficiencies concerned him. These included: poor anti-submarine defences (such as primitive sonar equipment); a lack of escort ships to protect convoys (and a headquarters branch to control convoys was likewise missing); insufficient anti-aircraft defences; and not least inadequate search and rescue capabilities – downed aircraft crews were lost at sea. Many warships were still under repair. German magnetic mines had yet to be mastered. Greater numbers of naval infantry were needed to protect the main base at Sevastopol from attack.[75] While the pre-war neglect would take considerable time, resources and effort to redress, Oktyabrsky and his staff were pragmatic in their approach. Where necessary, ships would need to be cannibalised to provide spares and weapons. 'Necessity is the mother of invention' became his watchword. On occasion, Oktyabrsky found the time to note in his diary events other than pressing naval matters. A comment of 13 July 1941 stands out: 'Today it was announced on the radio that our government has signed an agreement between the USSR and Great Britain regarding a common war against fascism. A bear and a lion against the brown plague! This is brilliant: it's victory!'[76] Sadly for Sevastopol and the Soviet Union, however, that victory lay far off.

Meantime, the war was approaching ever closer. Morgunov issued orders on 12 July 1941 for the organisation of the 'defence of the Main Base and the repulsion of the immediate threat from an enemy assault overland and from the air'. Those with an understanding of the conduct of the defensive battle at the tactical level would recognise that his detailed direction was very thorough. Amongst many other tasks, he required the commanders of designated defence sectors to:

> Conduct reconnaissance of localities in their sectors and sub-sectors on receipt of this present order. Allocate zones for day and night conditions, compile range cards, measure distances to principal boundaries and landmarks; select a command post, designate main and reserve strongpoints; site artillery observation posts and ammunition points. Plan locations for battle outposts, movement routes, communications and a system of signals for day-time and night-time.[77]

Whatever the foresight involved and the quality of the planning of the defensive measures, it would take much time and effort to complete the required works. On 17 July, Oktyabrsky complained that 'Crimea is further being weakened by the deployment of the few well-trained troops on the peninsula to the front. The situation in the south is further complicated by reports of yesterday's abandonment of Kishinev'. In the same diary entry, he noted that the 'entire Danube flotilla has set sail for Odessa'.[78] Sustaining the defence of that city (the siege by the Romanian Fourth Army opened on 14 August) was to become his prime concern, followed by the organisation of its evacuation during the first two weeks of October 1941.[79]

As the battle for Odessa raged, construction continued day and night on improving Sevastopol's defences against air, amphibious and land attack. On 31 July, Oktyabrsky recorded that the Crimean city had 'finally been turned into a virtual naval bastion'.[80] That statement, however, represented a curious piece of self-deception, as the required measures were then far from completed.

Less than a month later, on 23 August, Morgunov issued orders for the 'accelerated construction of defensive installations of the Main Fleet Naval Base'. Specifically, the Military Committee of the Black Sea Fleet, having 'recognized that the anti-tank defences of the Main Base are insufficiently effective,' required that these were to be 'strengthened by the construction of all possible anti-tank obstacles' and of 'artillery underground shelters (casemates) of the enclosed type'. Furthermore, sector commanders were to continue training their personnel 'at an accelerated pace', including learning how to 'use Molotov cocktails, throw grenades under tank tracks, and [practise] concealment in fire-trenches from tanks'.[81]

THE BATTLE FOR CRIMEA, SEPTEMBER–OCTOBER 1941

The German plan for the invasion of the Soviet Union contained a number of fatal flaws. Ignoring the constraints imposed by geography on strategy proved most critical. As the three army groups advanced on divergent axes, the width of their frontages increased. The distances covered by their armoured spearheads, and by the infantry formations that marched behind them, rose commensurately. As the German lines of communication lengthened, their logistic system became increasingly strained. All this led to a dispersion and dilution of fighting power, not least in the vast expanse and depth of Ukraine. Furthermore, Soviet forces resisted fiercely and German losses in both men and materiel mounted alarmingly. There was no second German operational, let alone strategic, echelon of attack. Insufficient numbers of battle casualty replacements and stocks of equipment were available to keep German units in action up to strength. These deficiencies and difficulties unbalanced, if not condemned, the whole campaign from the start. In consequence, the German high command was forced to rob Peter to pay Paul once Operation BARBAROSSA was under way.

When Hitler directed the switch of an armoured group from Army Group Centre to reinforce Army Group South (Directive No. 33, 19 July 1941) in order to complete the encirclement of a Soviet operational grouping at Kiev, it delayed, and thereby prejudiced, the main strategic attack on the Soviet Union's political centre of gravity, Moscow. Well before Operation TAIFUN (TYPHOON) was eventually launched against the capital city on 2 October, however, Hitler had amended fundamentally the military aim of the campaign, which hitherto had concentrated on the defeat of the Red Army. On 21 August 1941, the Führer directed:

> The principal objective that must be achieved before the onset of winter is not the capture of Moscow, but rather in the south – the occupation of the Crimea and the industrial and coal region of the Donets, together with the isolation of the

Russian oil region on the Caucasus. In the north, the encirclement of Leningrad and the union with the Finns.[82]

This was the not the first occasion on which Crimea had featured in Hitler's military considerations. On 12 August, he had ordered Army Group South to 'occupy the Crimean Peninsula, which is particularly dangerous as an enemy air base against the Romanian oilfields'.[83] The series of largely ineffective Soviet air attacks conducted by the VVS bombers had provoked an inflated response. In consequence, the capture of Sevastopol, although not included as a specific objective in Hitler's directive, would become an important, and costly, diversion of scarce Axis effort.

Crimea had another, far more fanciful, place in Hitler's thinking. The peninsula was intended as the Third Reich's province in the southern sun, linked to Berlin by a 3,000-kilometre-long autobahn and a wide-gauge railway. Yalta's Livadia Palace would become a fitting summer residence and retirement home for the Führer. Crimea, which had proved such an attractive location for German colonists in the past, would be cleansed of ethnic Russians, Ukrainians and Tatars and settled by 'pure' Aryan Germans.[84] Significant topographic changes would also be made: the new German Crimea would become Gotenland in memory of the German Ostrogoths who had 'first civilized this great land'. In turn, 'the city of Sevastopol was to be renamed Theoderichshafen and, and Simferopol was to be called Gotenburg'.[85] Although all these dreams came to nought, a much darker reality appeared that would soon afflict the various peoples of Crimea.

The notorious SS death squads of the *Einsatzgruppen* (special action groups) followed closely the advancing formations of the conquering German Army. In Crimea's case, Einsatzgruppe D, under the command of Hans Oldendorf, sought out and murdered the Jewish population. Such action confirmed that an integral part of Hitler's total war against the Soviet Union was the destruction of the 'Jewish-Bolshevistic' system. The resultant genocide reflected a racist ideology that was both anti-Semitic and anti-Slav by design. It involved the liquidation of Jews, partisans and politically active Communists, not least the political commissars in the Red Army and civilian officials working in town administrations.

Army Group South, commanded by Field Marshal Gerd Rundstedt, consisted of the First Panzer Group, the Sixth, Eleventh and Seventeenth Armies, reinforced by the Romanian Third and Fourth Armies (which were not as strong as their German counterparts) and a Hungarian corps. Despite its impressive paper strength, in comparison with the other two army groups, Rundstedt's command made relatively slower progress at first in toughly fought border battles, which allowed time for the Soviet forces to mass further forces to contest Ukraine. Thereafter, Army Group South's armies, with First Panzer

Group in the van, advanced more quickly, encircling three Soviet armies at Uman west of the Dnieper and reaching the outskirts of Kiev and the west bank of the river by 30 August.

Meanwhile, the resolute Soviet defence of the city of Odessa against the Romanian Fourth Army, supported by elements of the German Eleventh Army, would last seventy-three days from 5 August to 16 October 1941. The siege provided a bitter foretaste of what was to come in the protracted battles for Leningrad, Sevastopol and Stalingrad. In due course, all these urban centres were awarded the status of 'Hero Cities' of the Soviet Union. The third important Soviet leader in the defence of Sevastopol in 1941–42 was Ivan Yefimovich Petrov, who had first made his name in Odessa. He had joined the Red Army in 1918, participated in the Civil War as a cavalry officer, and taken part in the war against Poland in 1920. In the opening months of the Great Patriotic War he commanded in turn the 27th Mechanised Corps, the 1st Cavalry Division and the 25th Chapayev Division in Odessa from 20 August 1941. In that capacity he distinguished himself as a courageous and competent front-line commander, beating off numerous Romanian attacks. He assumed command of the Separate Coastal Army on 5 October 1941.[86] Although never seen as a potential senior leader within the Red Army, having attended neither the Frunze Military Academy nor the Voroshilov General Staff Academy, fate brought Petrov to one of the most testing positions during the opening period of the war. The experience he gained in the defence of Odessa would prove invaluable at Sevastopol. Petrov, Oktyabrsky, Morgunov and Ostriakov formed an effective partnership of arms in Sevastopol.

During the ongoing siege of Odessa, German and Romanian forces continued their advance along the coastal regions of Ukraine, paralleling the Black Sea. The German Eleventh Army, supported by the Romanian Third Army, formed the southernmost Axis force. It is at this stage that one of the *Wehrmacht's* ablest, if not most controversial, military leaders enters the story of Sevastopol.[87] As so often happens, it was a matter of pure chance. Following the unlucky death on 12 September 1941 of Colonel General Eugen Ritter von Schobert, commander-in-chief of the Eleventh Army, whose Fieseler *Storch* liaison aircraft had crashed and exploded in a Soviet minefield, General of Infantry Erich von Manstein was appointed in his place. Manstein, one of the rising stars of the German Army between the wars, was a highly talented and ambitious officer. Probably unsurpassed in the German Army at the operational level of war, he had conceived the audacious Operation YELLOW, the German attack on France and the Low Countries in May 1940. It resulted in the stunning Blitzkrieg victory of Germany over the Allied armies, and the resultant evacuation of British and French forces at Dunkirk. Falling out of favour beforehand with the Chief of the General Staff, General of Artillery Franz Halder, he had been appointed commanding general of a second echelon infantry corps in February 1940. During the second phase of the battle for France, Operation RED, in June 1940 Manstein had showed great dash, driving his corps from the river Somme to the Loire as if it were an armoured force. In the opening months of Operation BARBAROSSA he had commanded a motorised corps in Army Group North, where he demonstrated considerable resolution and tactical aptitude. Yet he had also experienced a number of lucky close shaves at the hands of the Red Army, which was far from beaten. Manstein's undoubted professional competence masked one significant weakness: his underestimation of the resilience of his Soviet opponents and their capability to recover from setback, to learn and to adapt.[88]

On assuming his new appointment at Nikolayev on 17 September 1941, Manstein was confronted with an operational dilemma. Reflecting the over-confidence and over-stretch of the German Army in 1941, his army headquarters had been given a 'double mission'. On the one hand he was ordered to seize Crimea, and on the other, to continue the advance eastwards parallel to the northern shore of the Sea of Azov, towards Rostov-on-Don. In breaking the German doctrine of designating a clear main effort, the result was the inevitable dissipation of force, and the risk of delay, if not defeat in piecemeal, by numerically superior Soviet forces. Concluding that he could not attempt both tasks simultaneously, Manstein determined that the conquest of Crimea was the more important of the two on the following grounds. The Soviet air threat to the Romanian oilfields required the elimination of the Soviet airfields. Bypassing the peninsula would expose the southern flank and lines of communication of the army group to attack by Soviet forces remaining unmolested. A further advantage in a campaign in Crimea lay in the possibility of crossing forces over the Kerch Straits to the Kuban peninsula and thence to the Caucasus – which had become one of Hitler's principal strategic objectives.[89]

To the east, the 9th and 18th Soviet Armies were in retreat; to the south, the 51st Separate Army defended Crimea, soon to be reinforced by elements of Petrov's Coastal Army. Manstein's Eleventh Army and the subordinated Third Romanian Army (the equivalent, however, of only two to three German infantry divisions) faced these Soviet forces. The Eleventh Army comprised XXX Corps under General of Infantry Hans von Salmuth; XXXXIX Mountain Corps under General of Infantry Ludwig Kübler; and LIV Corps commanded by General of Cavalry Erik Hansen.

Colonel General F. I. Kuznetsov commanded the 51st Army. To defend Crimea, he deployed his forces initially as follows: the 276th Rifle Division guarded the Chongar peninsula and Arabat Spit; the 106th covered the southern shore of the Syvash and the 156th defended the Perekop. Three cavalry divisions (the 40th, 42nd and 48th) stood ready to combat air landed troops. As army reserve, the 271st Rifle Division was concentrated in the area of Simferopol.[90] Four lower-grade militia divisions guarded Crimea's long coastlines, largely a waste of time and effort as the Germans did not possess a significant amphibious landing capability.[91] The Soviet forces eventually defending the peninsula would rise to a total of twelve rifle and four cavalry divisions of mixed quality.

Once again the decisive battle for Crimea would take place at the Perekop isthmus, the historic gateway to the peninsula, fortified by the Turkish Wall – described in German accounts as the 'Tatar Ditch' (see Map 14). In 1941, Manstein followed in the footsteps of Münnich in 1736, of Kosch in 1918, and of Frunze in 1920. As in the Russian Civil War, a series of defences including anti-tank ditches lay immediately in front of the Turkish Wall; in depth, a second defensive zone had been built around the Ishun lakes. Manstein's initial operation to break into Crimea was conducted by LIV Corps, comprising the 46th and 73rd Infantry Divisions, to be reinforced by two regiments of the 50th Infantry Division and the SS motorised brigade (shortly to become a division), the *Leibstandarte* SS Adolf Hitler. In addition, all available army artillery, anti-aircraft and engineer units were placed in support. XXXIX Mountain Corps was designated as a follow-on force to complete the conquest of Crimea. Meanwhile, XXX Corps and the Third Romanian Army would transition temporarily to defence on the Azov front.

The Soviet 156th Rifle Division, commanded by Major General P. V. Chernyaev, defended the Perekop. His forces were deployed as follows: the 530th Regiment guarded the Litovsky peninsula on the Syvash Sea; on the main position, the 417th Regiment defended the eastern sector to the centre of the isthmus, while the 316th Regiment was responsible for the western sector to the Karkintsky Bay on the Black Sea. The 2nd Battalion of this formation held a forward outpost at the 'Chervonyi Chaban' state farm next to the Kherson–Armyansk–Dzhankoy railway, about 7.5 kilometres north-west of the Turkish Wall.[92]

LIV Corps attacked on 24 September 1941 with two divisions up, 46th left and the 73rd right in the west (main effort), commanded by Lieutenant Generals Kurt Himer and Bruno Bieler respectively. The latter formation received the vast majority of the available artillery support, together with a battery of assault guns providing close support to the attacking infantry. At considerable cost (over 1,100 casualties), LIV Corps cleared the Soviet defenders out of their strongpoint at Chervonyi Chaban, and penetrated as far as the Turkish Wall. During the early hours of the 26th, the 73rd Division stormed the main obstacle. Whereas it was able to break through the Soviet main defences towards the town of Armyansk, undiminishing enemy resistance in the vicinity of the Old Fort, which formed a strongpoint at the centre of the Wall, held up the 46th Division. Thus the left flank of the 73rd Division was exposed to a Soviet counter-attack on the morning of the 27th. By this time, General P. I. Batov, commanding general of 9th Corps, had assembled an operational group for this purpose, comprising elements of the 172nd and 271st Rifle Divisions and the 42nd Cavalry Division. With the fight for the Perekop hanging in the balance, the first regiment of the German 50th Division entered the battle, which stabilised the situation for LIV Corps.[93]

The operational situation on the Azov front, meanwhile, turned considerably for the worse for the Axis forces. With exquisite timing, the 9th and 18th Soviet Armies had attacked the Third Romanian Army on the 26th, and by the morning of the 27th had achieved an alarming penetration of Manstein's eastern line of defence. The Soviet counter-offensive, involving up to twelve divisions with supporting tank formations, now threatened to envelop XXX Corps. Manstein faced the first crisis of his new command. True to form, he decided that the best form of defence was to counter-attack, employing XXXXIX Mountain Corps, reinforced by the *Leibstandarte* and elements of the 50th and 22nd Infantry Divisions.

The Perekop operation, however, continued on 27 September. LIV Corps pushed forward against heavy resistance, fighting off further Soviet counter-attacks. By this time, Batov's force of three divisions had been reinforced with the 442nd Regiment of the 106th Rifle Division and the 5th Tank Regiment.[94] After bitter fighting on the 28th, Armyansk fell. The next day, despite Soviet air superiority, the German ground attack picked up momentum, particularly in 73rd Division's zone. While LIV Corps had pressed the Soviet forces back to their Ishun position, it could achieve no more. In any case, in order to boost the forces for the Azov counter-attack, the corps had been ordered to hand back to Eleventh Army the reinforcing assault gun, heavy artillery and infantry units it had received. During the night of 29/30 September, LIV Corps assumed a defensive posture. Over the six days of the attack (24–29 September), it had battled forward over 20 kilometres and taken over 10,000 prisoners, but had suffered nearly 3,000 casualties in the process. Such losses were indicative of the intensity of the combat. There was no real pause in the battle. Soviet counter-attacks, and artillery and air strikes, inflicted a steady toll of casualties – so much so, by 17th October, LIV Corps had lost nearly 800 further men in its defensive positions.[95]

On their own, Manstein's forces were insufficiently strong to defeat the Soviet offensive grouping north of the Sea of Azov. It took the committal of First Panzer Group to complete the destruction of the Soviet 9th and 18th Armies. The successful conclusion of the battle of the Sea of Azov earned a special mention in the daily *Wehrmachtsbericht* (German Armed Services Report) on 11 October 1941. A week earlier, Manstein had issued first order of the day to Eleventh Army and Third Romanian Army in which he honoured 'our comrades who gave their lives and blood, whose sacrifice has set us on the path to final victory'.[96] The conquest of Crimea and the eventual capture of Sevastopol would demand a very much larger blood toll.

While Manstein met and mastered the threat on his eastern flank, the Soviet command in Crimea had become increasingly concerned about the situation in Odessa and at the Perekop. As the German attack towards the Turkish Wall went into its second day (25 September), General Kuznetsov requested assistance from the Black Sea Fleet. In response, Oktyabrsky directed 'all Fleet aviation assets to assist' 51st Army.[97] By the 26th, as Soviet air losses over the Perekop mounted, he requested reinforcements from Moscow. On the same day, increasingly alarmed about the prospect of a German break-out into Crimea, Oktyabrsky summoned Morgunov and Colonel E. I. Zhidilov, commander of the 7th Naval Infantry Brigade. He ordered them to 'deploy all units to their defence lines by 1800 hours on the 27th', and to speed up the completion of the lines' construction 'according to plan'.[98]

On the 28th, Oktyabrsky requested guidance from the Soviet high command. The response from Stalin to him and Kuznetsov was simple enough: 'Hold on; I trust that the Turkish Wall will soon be retaken'. While Oktyabrsky noted privately, 'a telegram is one thing, reality is another', he sent a situation update to the Soviet leader, including the following key points:

1. Situation in Crimea is difficult. Our forces, largely inferior to the enemy, are withdrawing to the Ishun positions, where there are few defences. Cannot retake the Turkish Wall. Fleet can detach the last naval infantry brigade, but doing this will leave the Main Base undefended in the event of an enemy air assault.
2. The threat of an enemy breakthrough into Crimea is real. If Crimea is taken, we cannot hold Odessa. The enemy will cut communications with the city.... Imperative we evacuate the Odessa Defence Region and transfer all assets to Crimea.
3. Feodosiya and Kerch ordered to strengthen their defensive efforts in case the enemy breaks through to these areas.

At 2130 hours Stalin accepted Oktyabrsky's recommendation to evacuate Odessa and to reinforce Crimea. Scratch forces were assembled to strengthen the defence of the Ishun position, including some 2,000 men in the '1st and 2nd Perekop Naval Infantry Detachments of the Black Sea Fleet'.[99]

Probably sensing that something was amiss with the command and control of 51st Army, on 30 September Oktyabrsky visited its headquarters in Simferopol. While Kuznetsov's staff confirmed the fragility of the Ishun defences, which represented unexpected news, he was astonished to learn that there were no radio communications to the threatened front. In response, the commander of the Black Sea Fleet ordered immediately that mobile radio detachments be sent to Perekop, Chongar and the headquarters in Simferopol.[100] Presumably, Headquarters 51st Army should already have undertaken such basic measures. Perhaps unsurprisingly, General Kuznetsov's days in command were in any case numbered.

On the following day (1 October), Stalin telegrammed to confirm that the forces in Odessa should be evacuated to Crimea, stressing that the 'brave soldiers and commanders had completed their task'.[101] Oktyabrsky lost no time in implementing this decision: evacuation commenced on the 2nd. Yet on the 5th, Stalin appeared to backtrack. He asked Oktyabrsky whether a couple of divisions could remain in Odessa while allowing for the defence of Crimea. The commander of the Black Sea Fleet replied firmly to the negative.[102] Stalin, trusting the admiral's judgement, did not demur. Oktyabrsky knew it was only a matter of time before the city fell and Manstein would resume his attack on Crimea. If there were any delays to the evacuation of Odessa, and if the Germans reached Sevastopol first, both cities would be lost in a double disaster. On 11 October, Oktyabrsky issued orders for completion of the evacuation during the night of 15/16 October.[103] On the 18th he reported to Stalin that the operation had been conducted in an 'exemplary' manner, claiming that '300,000 people' (military and civilians) had been evacuated, along with valuable equipment.[104] Although this figure represents a considerable exaggeration by nearly a factor of three, the Black Sea Fleet had pulled off a remarkable coup.

Reliable Soviet sources state that the following were transported from Odessa: 16,000 civilians, 462 guns, 1,158 trucks, 163 tractors, 24 tanks, 23 vehicles, 19,103 tonnes of munitions, and finally 86,000 soldiers.[105] Several, albeit depleted, formations evacuated included the 25th, 91st and 421st Rifle Divisions and the 2nd Cavalry Division, all of which would be quickly returned to battle. The success of the operation provided a brief ray of hope for the Soviet Union and its forces on Crimea. At first sight, the defenders of Odessa had done their job – tying down as many Axis forces as possible that otherwise would have been available for the Army Group South's operation to seize Ukraine, and not least the Donbas. The Romanian Fourth Army responsible for conducting the siege of Odessa, however, did not advance much further than Bessarabia. Perceptions of its lacklustre performance during the battle contributed much to the Germans' scepticism as to the fighting qualities of their ally.

The stage was now set for the German attack of the Ishun position, and, if successful, its exploitation into the heart of Crimean peninsula. On 15 October, Manstein sent a detailed analysis of the situation to Headquarters Army Group South, in which he itemised the forces and time required to complete the conquest of Crimea. First, he identified that *der Russe* [meaning the Soviet command] would 'fight for the peninsula with all means in view of its importance as a naval and air base', and, above all, that he would 'defend Sevastopol to the end as a symbol of his resistance'. Forthcoming events would prove these assumptions to be entirely accurate. Secondly, the Eleventh Army estimated that there were six and a half infantry divisions of various quality facing them, and two cavalry divisions, each of regimental strength. He warned of further enemy reinforcements arriving, and particularly those from Odessa, as the Soviets would rather give up that city than Sevastopol.

In his calculations of forces, time and space, Manstein reckoned that the Eleventh Army would take five days to break through Ishun and to defeat any Soviet counter-attacks before going over to the pursuit, and to reach the 'area of Simferopol about the eighth day after the beginning of the attack'. Assuming the attack were to be launched on 18 October, he planned his army would arrive before Sevastopol 'at the beginning of November'. Wisely, he added that the time required to take the city 'could not be estimated in advance'.[106] Although Manstein under-estimated the time required to break the Soviet defence at Ishun (it took nearer ten days than five), the leading elements of his army did approach Sevastopol at the beginning of November. While a number of assaults off the line of march were made, it would take until the middle of the month before sufficient forces could be gathered to seal off the city completely. A further month would follow before Manstein felt able to mount a deliberate attack on Sevastopol on 17 December 1941. The toughness of the terrain facing his army, the mounting logistic difficulties, and not least the tenacity of his opponent slowed down all operations and dashed any hopes of a quick success. Such is the friction of war.

Manstein launched his planned offensive at Ishun on 18 October. In contrast with his previous operation at the Perekop, he could at least concentrate all his forces. The German high command and Headquarters Army Group South also realised the importance of the operation, which should have ensured that satisfactory numbers of German air aircraft were made available. Yet the Luftwaffe was once again being stretched too thinly across the whole Eastern Front: the First Panzer Group in its drive towards Rostov-on-Don also required priority air defence and close support. This deficiency would allow the Soviet air force initially to 'dominate the skies' – in Manstein's description – above Ishun, despite the technical superiority of the German fighters, until further Luftwaffe assets were released.[107] The insufficiency of ground forces also disappointed him. Neither XXXXIX Mountain Corps nor the *Leibstandarte* would be returned. The most that Headquarters Army Group South could offer Manstein was a corps headquarters and the 132nd Infantry Division at some stage. In particular, the failure to allocate the Eleventh Army any mobile troops – whether armoured or motorised – would prove a major weakness in the composition of his forces. It would reduce the pace of any exploitation into Crimea and make it unlikely, for example, that the cities of Simferopol, Kerch or Sevastopol could be assaulted successfully from the line of march. Manstein's improvised forward detachment (*Vorausabteilung*) – the 'Ziegler' Brigade Group composed of various German and Romanian motorised elements – did not have anything like the striking power of the *Leibstandarte*, let alone a fully integrated, combined arms, panzer division.[108] Before Ziegler's force, together with the Romanian motorised detachment led by Colonel Radu Korne, equipped with R1 light tanks, could be unleashed, the Ishun position had to be broken through. It would prove a considerably tougher fight than at the Perekop.

Once again, Headquarters LIV Corps was made responsible for the initial attack. For the Ishun operation it was reinforced with the 22nd and 50th Divisions, together with several heavy artillery units, including 30.5 and 35.5cm mortars and 24cm howitzers. XXX Corps with the remaining two infantry divisions (the 72nd and the 170th) was stood by to sustain the operation as the advance made ground and the width of the frontage increased commensurately. These groupings, however, were not fixed. During the course of the attack, XXX Corps assumed responsibility for the left (eastern) zone with the 22nd, 46th and 72nd Divisions while LIV Corps controlled the right (western) zone of attack with the 50th, 73rd and 170th Divisions. When the 132nd Division was released from the Eleventh Army reserve it was allocated to LIV Corps. These groupings would change again in the exploitation or pursuit phase of the operation with the arrival of Headquarters XXXXII Corps, commanded by Lieutenant General Hans Graf von Sponeck.

In the meantime, the Ishun had to be stormed. As the Eleventh Army lacked any amphibious capability, there was no alternative to a direct assault of the Soviet defences. Further, the longer the operation lasted, the greater the likelihood of formations from Petrov's Coastal Army entering the battle – in fact, the first of these were inserted on 22 October, the fifth day of the German attack.[109] So all in all, the Eleventh Army faced far from ideal conditions in which to launch its operation, the outcome of which was far from certain. Manstein acknowledged some of the difficulties involved: 'The salt steppes of the isthmus ... offered no cover whatsoever to the attacker. Yet the air above them was dominated by the Soviet Air Force, whose fighters and fighter-bombers dived incessantly on any target they could find.'[110] To overturn this highly unfavourable situation, which threatened to prejudice his attack, Manstein pleaded for much greater air support. *Staffeln* (squadrons) of Messerschmitt Bf 109F aircraft drawn from three fighter wings (Jagdgeschwader (JG) 3, 52 and 77) achieved local air superiority over the Ishun battlefield on 26 October. Once this had been achieved, the Junkers Ju 87

Sturzkampfflugzeuge (Stuka dive-bombers) of Sturzkampfgeschwader (StG) 77 could provide very effective close air support to the attacking German formations.

The complex terrain of the Ishun position offered a number of advantages to the Soviet defender. Movement was canalised by the Old (*Staroe*) and Red (*Krasnoe*) Lakes, which constrained LIV Corps to attacking southwards on three narrow axes (from west to east): the 73rd Division between the Black Sea (Karkinitsky Bay) and the Old Lake; the 46th Division between the Old and Red Lakes; and the 22nd Infantry Division between the Red Lake and the Syvash. Broadly speaking, the 156th, 271st and 106th Rifle Divisions blocked each of these narrow corridors, although the latter's frontage extended eastwards towards along the southern shore of the Syvash. The ground battle proved extremely costly as losses, particularly in the assaulting German infantry regiments, mounted daily. German reports spoke of the enemy's extraordinary resistance. The fights for the Krasnoperekopsk Bromide plant, the eponymous settlement nearby, and the village of Ishun proved particularly bitter.

Perhaps for the first time in the campaign, there were signs that the fighting power of Eleventh Army was declining rapidly, and morale was in danger of breaking. Manstein recorded that the commander of the 73rd Division, which had taken more than its fair share of the fighting at both Perekop and Ishun, had reported on two occasions that his formation 'could do no more'.[111] Recently arrived drafts were not up to the intensity of the fight. The commander of the 16th Infantry Regiment of the 22nd Division, Oberst Dietrich von Choltitz, recalled that the newly arrived soldiers, 'lacking battle experience and training', would not 'assault the enemy positions when under fire'.[112] Both sides fed more troops into the Ishun battle to sustain their operations. On the German side, the 50th Division came into action on the 21st, the 72nd on the 23rd and the 170th in the 25th. The 2nd Soviet Cavalry Division of the Coastal Army counter-attacked on 22 October, followed by the 95th Rifle Division and a regiment of the 25th Division on the 23rd. The battle reached its climax on the 27th–28th, when under intense German pressure, Soviet forces began to withdraw to the south and south-east. By 29 October 1941, the German attack, which had broken through and beyond the Soviet Ishun Lakes position, turned into a pursuit into Crimea.

Reflecting *Stavka*'s frustration with the conduct of the defence of Crimea, Soviet command arrangements on the peninsula changed early in the battle. On 21 October, Oktyabrsky recorded Admiral G. I. Levchenko had been appointed as 'Commander Crimean Troops' with General P. I. Batov as his deputy responsible for the 51st Army. The hapless if not inept General Kuznetsov was dismissed. Rear Admiral G. B. Zhukov became Oktyabrsky's deputy, and as commander of the Sevastopol Main Base, made responsible for its defence. As

Petrov's divisions were being committed into the Ishun fight, his brief period of independent command came to an end. On the same day, Oktyabrsky realised that it would be unlikely that the Germans could be held at Ishun, noting in his diary that 'it's now clearly a question of delaying their arrival before Sevastopol'.[113] Such pragmatism characterised his style of command.

As the long-feared threat of a German assault on Sevastopol grew closer, not least through the fighting at Perekop, the mobilisation of the people of Sevastopol for war intensified. On 7 October 1941, the Sevastopol Municipal Committee of the Communist Party issued a report concerning the 'General Compulsory Military Training of City Workers'. It recorded what had already been achieved: 'training of three hours a day and four hours at weekends' had been imposed. At that time, 450 people in the home guard in Sevastopol were undergoing a course of basic training of 110 hours.[114] Many hundreds more – with various levels of military experience and states of training – would soon be incorporated into scratch infantry battalions to defend the city. Control of the population became ever tighter as the battlefront approached. A 'state of siege ... across the entire territory of Crimea' was introduced on 28 October. It forbade 'from 2200–0500 hours all movement of individuals and transport' with the exception of 'transport and personnel holding a special pass from garrison commanders'. Offenders were 'immediately to be brought to account and handed over to a court of the Military Tribunal'. The order warned that 'provocateurs, spies and similar enemies who cause a breakdown in law and order are to be shot on the spot'.[115]

The German Eleventh Army's plans for the exploitation into Crimea foresaw a pursuit on three divergent axes. While LIV Corps would head directly for Sevastopol, XXX Corps would seize Simferopol and press on to the Crimean Mountains and the southern coast. XXXXII Corps would advance south-eastwards to Feodosiya and the Kerch peninsula. Although Manstein decided in principle on 1 November 1941 that both LIV and XXX Corps should attack Sevastopol, he had no firm plan at that time as to how the city should be assaulted. Such was the disarray of Soviet forces after the Ishun battle, it would appear that his overriding concern was to cut off elements of the Coastal Army before they could enter Sevastopol. Hence maintaining the momentum of operations was essential.

The initial results of the Eleventh Army's pursuit proved promising. Within LIV Corps, Ziegler's motorised force punched due south, cutting the Yevpatoriya–Simferopol road by 1300 hours on 30 October, and probing as far forward as the river Bulganek by evening. It had covered 90 kilometres in one day. Even with assembling all available wheeled transport together, however, the infantry regiments of the 50th and 132nd Divisions could not be moved by road and so lagged far behind. At 1520 hours on the 31st, Ziegler reported by radio that he had blocked both the railway and main road between Simferopol and Sevastopol in the vicinity of the Alma river, and that his troops had shot up several convoys of Soviet trucks. At noon on the same day, incredible as it may appear, the fastest element of the 132nd Division, its bicycle detachment, reached Yevpatoriya.

On 1 November, Ziegler aimed to 'bounce' the town of Bakhchisaray and to seize bridgeheads over the Alma and even as far south as the river Kacha. Although Sevastopol appeared enticingly close, Ziegler's force was insufficiently strong to mount an effective assault. Meanwhile, the infantry of the 50th and 132nd Infantry Divisions struggled to catch up by dint of forced marches.[116] The consequences of Manstein's lack of mobile troops were becoming all apparent: if Sevastopol could not be attacked immediately, the risks of a protracted siege – and all the commensurate expenses of both men and materiel consumed in any such operation – rose daily. Given the strength of the city's defences, however, it remains debatable whether the employment of the *Leibstandarte* – or a German Army motorised or panzer division – would have proved sufficient for a successful attack off the line of march and quick capture of Sevastopol. Yet such a fully mobile combined arms formation might well have tilted the odds in Manstein's favour.

The second defence of Sevastopol soon began. It proved an epic struggle between the Axis troops under Manstein's command and the Soviet sailors, soldiers and airmen under Oktyabrsky and his colleagues determined to hold it to the very last. For 250 days, the defenders of Sevastopol – and its citizens too – stoutly resisted their opponents in the spirit of the 'Sacred War' song – fighting 'against the evil powers of night, the fascist hordes accursed'.[117]

CHAPTER 13

CITY OF COURAGE: THE SECOND DEFENCE OF SEVASTOPOL

'Throughout the world the immortal name is repeated: Sevastopol. It has become a symbol of resistance, of the grandeur of human achievement, of proud courage.'

Ilya Ehrenburg[1]

Excepting the minor damage caused by the German battlecruiser *Goeben* on 29 October 1914, Sevastopol had escaped the worst destructive effects of the First World War. Likewise, the German occupation, Allied intervention and the Russian Civil War had left few physical scars. The people of the city, however, had suffered enormously in these conflicts from the human losses on battlefields both distant and much closer to home. The terror and famine of the early years of Soviet rule had compounded the previous grief and hurt. Yet the historic main base and grand arsenal of the Black Sea Fleet, painstakingly rebuilt and expanded between the Crimean and First World Wars, and modernised again during the 1920s and 1930s, stood as a proud monument to Soviet power and progress.

When Manstein's Eleventh Army stormed into Crimea in late October 1941, Sevastopol faced an existential threat for the first time since 1854–55. As the siege began, the city assumed substantial military strategic and psychological significance for the Soviet war effort. Notwithstanding the longer struggle of Leningrad, the Soviet defence of Sevastopol, until overshadowed by the subsequent battle for Stalingrad, captured the imagination of the Soviet people and their allies, as the famous Soviet wartime writer Ilya Ehrenburg described. A clash of wills arose between the respective Axis and Soviet leaders, Manstein and Oktyabrsky. Meantime, those under their command fought day and night in a test of endurance that taxed all to their limits.

In contrast to the first defence of Sevastopol in 1854–55, the city in 1941–42 was completely cut off on land. Only tenuous air and sea lines of communication remained; both vulnerable to German air interdiction. As Soviet soldiers, naval infantrymen (marines) and sailors manned the lines of defences, the city's population anxiously awaited the coming onslaught. Contemporary Soviet war correspondents paint melodramatic scenes of the 'city of courage':

> The people of Sevastopol will forever remember the clear nights of November, 1941, when the autumn stars, high and clear, shone over the blacked-out city, and the buildings shook with a disquieting rumble. It seemed as if this rumble was coming from the very bowels of the earth, and in response to it the window-panes vibrated pitifully. It was the rumble of war. In it resounded the tramp of infantry, the clink of horseshoes, the clatter of tank tracks, the jolting rattle of two-wheeled carts and guns, the groaning roar of overloaded lorries.

These background sounds would be rudely pierced when the 'wail of the siren suddenly drowned out all other noises, and in another two minutes A.A. [anti-aircraft] guns and machine-guns were barking furiously'. Above, the night sky lit up 'with searchlight beams and red, yellow and green tracer bullets and shells'. Over the city 'spread the drone of enemy bombers; it was followed by the whine of high-speed engines as our fighters took off to intercept them'.[2] During the eight-month period of the siege, Sevastopol would endure one of the most intense air bombardments of any city of the Soviet Union.

THE FIRST AXIS ASSAULT ON SEVASTOPOL, 30 OCTOBER – 21 NOVEMBER 1941

As far as Soviet and Russian historiography is concerned, the second defence of Sevastopol began on 30 October 1941. It was on this day, or more precisely at 1635 hours, that the gunners of the 54th Coastal Defence Battery at Nikolaevka, some 40 kilometres north of the city, opened fire on the advancing elements of Ziegler's brigade. For three days, Lieutenant Ivan Zaika and his men then fought off attacks by the following German 132nd Infantry Division. Notwithstanding this action, the mass of Manstein's Eleventh Army lay nowhere near Sevastopol on the 30th: that day, Ziegler's motorised force had only reached and cut the Yevpatoriya–Simferopol road. Within the period accorded to the 'first assault', Soviet histories distinguish between the 'failure of the German attacks off the line of march' (30 October – 9 November) and the 'repulse of the enemy attack' (10–21 November 1941).[3]

Descriptions of German operations, largely influenced by Manstein's biographical account, tend to underrate the serious attempts made by Eleventh Army to seize Sevastopol in early November 1941. Likewise, the more deliberate attacks undertaken in the middle of the month receive scant mention.[4] Whereas Manstein writes of only two German assaults of the city – in December 1941 and in June 1942 – Soviet (and now Russian) historians describe *three*, including November 1941. The latter interpretation explains the depiction of the defence of the city in Sevastopol's monolithic memorial to the Great Patriotic War at Nakhimov Square, which shows a Soviet defender warding off two out of three blows struck by a German attacker. Although German and Soviet narratives of the battle for Sevastopol differ in this important regard, they agree on the severity of the combat and the tenacity of attackers and defenders alike.

There remain other significant differences in the histories of the siege. Whereas German military accounts, not least Manstein's, ignore the impact of the fighting on the local population, Soviet historians, unsurprisingly, do not. In painting a picture of heroic resistance, they not only chronicle the effects of the artillery and aerial bombardment of Sevastopol, but also document the enormous contributions and sacrifices made in the defence of the city by the men, women and children, who lived and worked increasingly in underground shelters and factories. Although the siege was of smaller scale and of shorter duration than Leningrad's, the bravery and resilience exhibited in Sevastopol was unprecedented at this stage of the Second World War.

In his diary, Oktyabrsky does not concern himself with such matters as the starting date of the battle for Sevastopol. Reflecting the pace of unfolding events and associated pressure of work, he only made one entry for 29–31 October and none at all for 1–3 November 1941. On 4 November, however, he filled in the gaps. Revealing the harsh reality of the situation, he stated that responsibility for the defence of the Main Base would fall to the Black Sea Fleet: there were 'few ground troops available and almost no reserves'. The defence of Sevastopol rested on 'the 8th Naval Infantry Brigade, the 3rd Naval Infantry Regiment, the 2nd Perekop Regiment, and units formed from the higher naval academy and various naval infantry battalions formed from various establishments and forces of the Fleet, together with powerful coastal artillery and all available aviation assets'. The scattered formations of Petrov's Coastal Army had yet to arrive. Significantly,

Oktyabrsky recorded that since 31 October, 'fierce battles' had raged around 'Kacha and Duvankoy as the enemy tried to breakthrough to the Main Base'.[5] Yet Manstein's pursuit into Crimea abruptly culminated – grinding to a stop – as his leading troops hit the strongly defended perimeter of Sevastopol. The barriers of the *Festungsvorfeld* (outer fortress zone), the power of the coastal artillery and the steadfastness of Soviet troops all came as unpleasant surprises, stealing any chance of a rapid exploitation into the city.[6] Morgunov's barrier plan had scored its first success: the Russian military's historic talent in artillery, fortifications and improvisation became all too apparent in the Soviet defence of Sevastopol.

One of the very first engagements in the defence of Sevastopol involved a very young participant, Aleksandr Romanovich Glushakov. As an eighteen-and-a-half-year-old naval cadet, he studied at Sevastopol's coastal defence school, named after the Leninist Communist League of Youth of Ukraine.[7] Towards the end of October 1941, along with his classmates he was ordered to join a scratch force. Comprised of five infantry companies with a limited number of mortars and artillery guns in support, his unit mustered 1,117 officer instructors and cadets. Such was the urgency of the situation, the school troops were rushed into the field on the night of 29/30 October, occupying a blocking position on the river Kacha south-west of Bakhchisaray. On the 31st, the town came under German artillery fire and then assault. Soon Glushakov's unit came under attack 'from German motorized forces, supported by tanks and aircraft'. Elements of Ziegler's Brigade had attacked the Cadets' position. Glushakov recounted:

> We fought hard and bravely, and such was the ferocity of the combat that we lost 70 per cent of our numbers over the four days from 31 October to 3 November. We were ordered to move back to the Mackenzie Heights, but the Germans were not able to penetrate as far as Sevastopol. Their advance was blocked. The Black Sea Fleet Command ordered our unit to be withdrawn from the front-line because of the very high casualties. We were returned to our schools with our teachers to study. We also provided patrols in Sevastopol, to ensure the black-out [air-raid precautions] and to help maintain order in the city. Only 300 of us were left alive.[8]

One particular cadet from the same school, Aleksandr Ivanovich Maltsev, gave his life during this engagement. Famous for refusing to surrender when he had run out of ammunition, and for defiantly shouting 'sailors do not give up', he hurled his last grenade at the German troops who were closing in on him. For his valour, Maltsev was posthumously awarded the Order of the Patriotic War (First Class). A monument to the fallen cadets of the LKSMU Coastal Defence School still stands next to the Simferopol road above Inkerman.[9]

Actions such as the one experienced by young Glushakov and his comrades-in-arms were typical of the intense fighting and losses experienced by the Soviet defenders of Sevastopol, many serving in such 'emergency' units without adequate training, sufficient support weapons or a proper command structure. The retreating elements of the Coastal Army were not yet available to assist in the defence of the city. On 31 October Petrov and members of his military council assembled for a conference in the small village of Sarabuz, *north* of Simferopol at the very same time as Glushakov was fighting to the *south-west* of Bakhchisaray, illustrating how fluid the situation appeared at the time with no fixed front lines. The meeting was attended by Major Generals Vasily Vorobyov and Trofim Kolomiyets, and Colonel Ivan Laskin, commanders of the 95th, 25th and 172nd Rifle Divisions respectively; together with the commanders of the 2nd and 40th Cavalry Divisions, Colonels Pyotr Novikov and Philip Kudyurov.[10]

According to eyewitness accounts, Petrov pulled no punches in summarising the seriousness of the situation: 'The enemy has seized Dzhankoy and is in pursuit of units of [the] 51st Army, which are retreating towards the Kerch peninsula'. He then declared: 'German tanks were seen south of Simferopol today. The road to Sevastopol through Bakhchisaray is probably cut'. Accordingly, the Coastal Army was 'outflanked on three sides.... [Only] the Kerch road remains open'. Petrov emphasised that 'Sevastopol is the citadel of the Black Sea Fleet. Holding it is necessary in order not to lose our control of the sea. It's no secret that Sevastopol is defenceless against an overland attack since no field forces are stationed there'. Finally came his indirect recommendation to the council of war: 'If the Coastal Army fails to arrive in Sevastopol before large enemy forces, the fortress may fall'.[11] Petrov then heard the views of his subordinate officers. By the narrowest margin of one, the council opted for marching to Sevastopol as opposed to joining the remnants of the 51st Army on the Kerch peninsula.

Petrov's biographer gives his subject due credit for steering this decision, praising his 'strategic foresight'. Crucially, the commander of the Coastal Army realised that 'if Sevastopol were lost, enemy naval forces might [land on] the Caucasian coast'. By 'holding the [main] Black Sea naval base, Soviet troops would remain at the rear of the enemy and in control of part of the Crimean peninsula'. Yet the principal rationale for the defence of Sevastopol, as had been the case at Odessa, lay in tying down as many enemy forces for as long as possible. Every German or Romanian division 'bogged down in fighting' for Sevastopol 'would deny them a part in any offensive against the Caucasus'.[12] And so it proved to be the case: the second defence of Sevastopol lasted no fewer than 250 days. Soviet resistance fixed in place between five and ten Axis divisions throughout the siege, and demanded the additional resources of many more during the course of the Crimean campaign.

By the end of October 1941, only a handful of vehicles remained at Petrov's disposal. Hence most of his men were compelled to march by foot over the mountains to Sevastopol, avoiding prowling German aircraft and ground reconnaissance units that were already scouting towards the outskirts of the city. Petrov's command group and a number of motorised artillery units, however, managed to evade interdiction on the more circuitous coastal road route via Alushta and Yalta. The difficult terrain, poor un-surfaced roads, and the onset of heavy rain impaired the German pursuit, as did the delaying actions of Soviet rear guards. Although Simferopol fell to advance elements of the German 72nd Infantry Division on 1 November 1941, Yalta was not taken until the early hours of the 8th. On 2 November, Petrov stopped at Alushta to confer with Admiral Levchenko, the commander-in-chief of Crimean Troops. Both officers understood the vital importance of holding Sevastopol. Levchenko's orders were crystal clear: 'Together with the Fleet command, you must organise a secure defence of Sevastopol as soon as possible'.[13]

Rather scathingly (charity was evidently not one of his strengths), Oktyabrsky described the appearance of Petrov – 'another troop commander without troops' – in Sevastopol on 3 November. 'He entered my office and said: "Comrade Commander-in-Chief of the Fleet, allow me to report. I have nothing, no troops. Where am I supposed to serve?" He sat down and began to cry. What should I do?'[14] According to Karpov, who omits the emotional scene with Oktyabrsky, Petrov inspected Sevastopol's defences 'as soon as he arrived, and for checking their state and the morale of the troops', presumably escorted by Morgunov. Petrov, 'convinced that the defence [of the city] would gain "strength and fortitude" with the arrival of the Coastal Army', was soon appointed commander of land forces for the defence of Sevastopol.[15] Having fought a fighting withdrawal, his troops entered the city over the next few days (6–10 November). The Germans had arrived too late to prevent this essential reinforcement of Sevastopol. Petrov's old command, the 25th Chapayev Division, was in the best order, followed by the 95th, 157th and 172nd Rifle Divisions. Soon the exhausted Soviet riflemen were sent to the trenches, where the fighting was already raging in several locations, particularly in the northern and north-eastern sectors of the defence. Many Soviet units, which had fought at both Odessa and Ishun, received no respite. Their hardest test now began.

On 4 November, before the arrival of Petrov's men, Oktyabrsky had sent a stark situation update to Stalin and Admiral Kuznetsov:

The Germans are attacking in strength along the Belbek valley from Duvankoy. In many places the enemy has captured the front line of defence. Only the Black Sea Fleet is now defending Sevastopol. After the breach of the Ishun positions, the

Crimean Troops retreated in disarray towards Feodosiya-Kerch. There are indications that part of a division of the Coastal Army is forcing its way through the mountains to Yalta and to Baidar, but has not yet reached Sevastopol. Enemy had occupied Feodosiya, Yevpatoriya and Alushta. I have been obliged to commit all personnel from training divisions, course members from the Naval College and miscellaneous units including ships' companies and airdrome commands to the defence of the Main Base.[16]

On the same day, in recognition of the proximate threat to the Black Sea's main base, the Sevastopol Defence Region (Sevastopolskogo Oboronitelnogo Raiona) was established. This authority joined all maritime, land and air forces, including coastal and air defence units, and subordinated the civil authorities in Sevastopol to military command.

As Oktyabrsky composed his telegram to Stalin, three German divisions of Manstein's Eleventh Army were closing in on Sevastopol in an effort to reach the city before Petrov's Coastal Army could reinforce the city's defences. In the north, LIV Corps with the 132nd Division on the right slowly advanced in contact towards Sevastopol's northern side. To its left, the 50th Division clambered over and battled through the dense scrubland of the Mackenzie Heights to the east of the city and attempted to press further south towards the Chernaya river. Manstein intended to attack Sevastopol from the east. There were still wide gaps in the mountains between the 50th Division and the nearest formation of XXX Corps, the 72nd. This division, having secured Simferopol, headed for Alushta and Yalta on Crimea's south-eastern shore; then it would advance along the coast road towards Balaklava and Sevastopol. It was on these three divisions, representing less than half of Manstein's command, which any chances of a quick assault of the city rested.

The remaining four infantry divisions of Eleventh Army were not yet available to join the attack on Sevastopol. The closest, the 22nd Division of XXX Corps, originally made for Kuru Uzen (now Solnechnogorskoye) on the Black Sea coast north of Alushta. Shortly afterwards, this formation would be re-directed to Bakhchisaray and inserted into the line on the northern flank of the 132nd Division, coming under the command of LIV Corps. Valuable time and momentum was lost in this redeployment. Meanwhile, the three divisions of XXXXII Corps, the 46th, 73rd and 170th, had pursued the 51st Army on the general axis of Dzhankoy–Feodosiya towards the Kerch peninsula. On 3 November, the advance of the 46th and 73rd Divisions stalled at the 51st Army's hasty defence established on the Parpach position, the 18-kilometre-wide neck of the peninsula. At its northern end lay the settlement of Ak-Monai, now Kamenskoye, and in the centre, Parpach, now Yachmennoye. This isthmus would be fought over again several times during the course of the war on the Crimea.

The following day (the 4th), Feodosiya fell to the 170th Division. Under heavy attack by all three German divisions of XXXXII Corps, the Soviet defence on the Parpach line crumbled on 6 November. Battered and disorganised formations of the 51st Army streamed back towards Kerch: few units paused to halt at their rear line of resistance at the Tatar Ditch, some 30 kilometres to the west of the city. This historic fortification was similar in construction to the Turkish Wall at Perekop – a wide and deep ditch, together with an earthen rampart. If held by determined troops and well covered by observed fire, it should have proved a significant obstacle to the Germans' advance. But the 51st Army was no longer capable of conducting an effective defence. Accordingly, XXX Corps breached the Ditch on 10 November and pushed quickly on. While most Soviet units melted away to the east, other pockets of troops put up a more determined fight. Yet the final issue was not in doubt: the city of Kerch fell on 16 November, by coincidence twenty-one years to the day it had been occupied by Red Army forces under Frunze's command.

Although the German clearance of the Kerch peninsula proved successful, the cost had been high notwithstanding the disorganised state of the Red Army. The casualties of the 213th Regiment of 73rd Infantry Division – 659 all ranks, representing nearly a battalion[17] – in just over ten days of combat are indicative of the intensity of fighting. In stark contrast to the lightning campaigns in Poland, Norway, the Low Countries, France and the Balkans, there were no cheap victories to be scored in the war against the Soviet Union. Manstein's other infantry regiments had suffered similar numbers of losses. Even before the fortress of Sevastopol had been attacked for the first time in any strength, the Crimean peninsula was proving a costly sub-theatre of war for Germany.

The bombers of the Luftwaffe's IV Fliegerkorps (Air Corps) could not easily target Soviet forces withdrawing over the forested, mountainous roads towards Sevastopol. Elsewhere, their operations over the Black Sea and Sevastopol were deadly in their effectiveness. Two examples stand out. In broad daylight, not far off the Crimean shore at Yalta, and in sight of many horrified spectators, a German Heinkel He 111 medium bomber torpedoed a Soviet passenger liner, the *Armeniya*, bound for the eastern Black Sea port of Tuapse. The sinking of this ill-fated hospital ship marked with red crosses, on 7 November 1941, resulted in the loss of at least 5,000 people, including many wounded soldiers, civilians and their families. Only eight people survived. *Stuka* dive-bombers scored a more creditable success against a military target in hitting the cruiser *Chernova Ukraina* in Sevastopol's Southern Bay on 12 November, which sank the next day. However, the ever-resourceful Red Sea Navy recovered her 130mm guns, and incorporated them into the city's defences.

One Yalta resident was particularly lucky not to go down with the *Armeniya*. Eighteen-year-old Yevdokiya Sikorskaya, a pharmaceutical student, had been assigned a berth on the ship at Yalta. On the early morning of 7 November, she arrived just too late to board. Witnessing the *Armeniya* slipping anchor, on impulse she decided to join a group of Soviet troops withdrawing on foot to Sevastopol. Subsequently she served as a stretcher-bearer during the defence of the city, carrying at least sixty-four people off the battlefield. The memories of the wounded crying out 'Girl, please don't abandon me' still haunted her seventy years later. She described her experiences in Sevastopol as a 'real hell'. Yet such frightful recollections were accompanied by happier moments. A few years ago, the late Madame Sikorskaya was singing in a Second World War veterans' choir in Yalta. An elderly man in the audience, all bedecked in medals, appeared quite transfixed by her. After the performance, she asked him 'how do I know you?'. The veteran replied, 'I remember your eyes'. As a young girl she had given him blood, which had saved his life.[18]

Somewhat perversely on the day of the *Armeniya* tragedy, Oktyabrsky noted in his diary a 'double celebration': the twenty-fourth anniversary of the coming of Soviet power and a telegram from Stalin and Shaposhnikov naming him as the 'commander of the defence of Sevastopol'. Moreover, 'Sevastopol is not to be surrendered under any circumstances'. As for the loss of the 'hospital ship', it had been 'moved early (0800 hours), contrary to his personal orders to wait until dark (1900 hours)'.[19] Oktyabrsky omits to mention that the *Armeniya* was never intended to call into Yalta on its passage from Sevastopol. The purpose of its diversion there, and consequent daytime sailing, remain controversial. Some hold today that senior members of the NKVD were anxious to evacuate officials, their families and sensitive documents, and not least to safeguard precious works of art from Yalta's palaces from falling into German hands.[20] Manstein, who visited Bakhchisaray on 7 November 1941, did not mention the ship in his private war diary. Apart from detailing the difficulties his troops were encountering as they approached Sevastopol, he wrote: 'Saw an old Tatar palace. Very picturesque. Museum.'[21] Clearly, the German commander-in-chief retained a weakness for military tourism, demonstrated in June 1940 during his less arduous campaign from the Somme to the Loire in France.[22]

Romanian formations reinforced the German Eleventh Army's Crimean offensive. Apart from Kornu's motorised detachment supporting Ziegler's brigade in LIV Corps, Manstein obtained the Romanian Mountain Corps, regrouped to comprise the 1st Mountain and the 8th Cavalry Brigades, supported by the 19th Artillery Regiment. The initial task of this corps was to fix Soviet troops defending the eastern approaches to Crimea, while the bulk of the Eleventh Army attempted to prise open the Ishun Lakes position. As German forces broke through this location on 28 October 1941, Manstein ordered the Romanians to assault the following day. Their task was to form a secondary axis of advance into Crimea.

The Romanian Corps' operation opened with mixed results. Whereas the 8th Cavalry Brigade was held back at Genichesk, 1st Mountain Brigade made better progress at the Salvoko isthmus until the retreating Soviet forces blew the bridges to the Crimean peninsula. On the 31st, the latter brigade crossed over to the peninsula on a floating bridge constructed by German engineers. The 8th Romanian Cavalry Brigade followed over the same route, and joined XXXXII Corps in its operation to clear the Kerch peninsula.

Meanwhile, the 1st Mountain Brigade pressed south to reach the Black Sea shore near Sudak on 5 November, marching 180 kilometres in four days (no mean feat), and assisted in operations to clear the Crimean Mountains of the remnants of Petrov's Coastal Army. On 10 November, the Romanian Mountain Corps was tasked to defend the coastline between Sudak and Alushta, and to hunt down the recently established partisan groups in the mountains that were beginning to harass the German lines of communication. By the end of November, the 4th Mountain Brigade would reinforce the corps, providing Manstein with an opportunity to use these specialist troops in the deliberate assault on Sevastopol.[23] It appears that Manstein entertained a jaundiced view of his ally's effectiveness. In a formal estimate of the situation composed in mid-October 1941, for example, he had assessed the Romanian Corps as 'only capable for security duties, [and] neither for attack nor for difficult defensive tasks'.[24] In coming to this opinion, he seems to have been influenced by the damning critique of the Romanians he received from his staff on taking over the Eleventh Army, and by the performance of the Romanian Third Army during the defensive and counter-offensive phases of the recent battle of the Sea of Azov.[25]

As the pressure of Axis forces increased around Sevastopol, and Kerch seemed similarly threatened, *Stavka* issued new operational directions on 7 November 1941. Addressed to 'Comrades Levchenko, Oktyabrsky and Batov', the orders concerned were designed to 'tie down the enemy's forces in the Crimea and to prevent them from entering the Caucasus across the Taman peninsula [opposite Kerch]'. Supreme Command Directive No. 1882 specified in detail:

1. The Black Sea Fleet's main task will be the vigorous defence of Sevastopol and the Kerch peninsula.

2. Sevastopol will not be surrendered under any circumstances and will be defended with all forces available.

3. All three old cruisers and old destroyers are to be retained in Sevastopol.

4. The Azov flotilla is to support the defence of the Ak-Monai position from the north.

5. [The] battleship and the new cruisers are to be based at Novorossiysk for employment in operations against the enemy-occupied coast. ...

7. Organise and effect the transfer of troops [currently] withdrawing to Yalta, Alushta and Sudak to Sevastopol and Kerch. ...

9. Evacuate everything of value from Sevastopol and Kerch to the Caucasus which is not necessary for defence.

10. Command of the defence of Sevastopol is vested in the Commander of the Black Sea Fleet, Comrade Oktyabrsky, who is subordinated to you [Levchenko].[26]

Subsequent orders issued by the Sevastopol Defence Region on 9 November 1941 (by which time not all Coastal Army units had been assimilated) confirmed the command arrangements and the composition of forces for the four defensive sectors (see Table 13.1). Many of the regiments, and even the battalions, were *ad hoc* in nature, drawing from various sources, including training schools and coastal defence units. The four sector commanders, all divisional commanders of Petrov's Coastal Army, were to distinguish themselves as particularly resilient and resourceful leaders.

On the same day that the organisation of Sevastopol's defences was confirmed, Manstein signed a detailed appreciation of the situation, in which he conceded that his attempts to attack the city off the line of march had failed.[27] Significantly, the contents of this important document are not reflected in his memoirs, whether in the German or English editions. Although elements of Petrov's Coastal Army had yet to enter the fight, the commander-in-chief of Eleventh Army described the enemy as offering 'tough resistance', crediting the fighting qualities of the Soviet naval infantry brigades and the various 'bundled together' fortress troops encountered so far. Manstein acknowledged that the defenders of Sevastopol were being supported most effectively by a combination of the city's outer defences, and the fortress and ship artillery. Most particularly, the 'difficulties of the terrain' were hampering every movement of the attackers.

Manstein acknowledged that his original intention to mount a quick assault on the city from the south-east, involving the 50th and the 132nd Divisions (and later the 72nd), had not succeeded. In explaining this disappointment he cited problems such as 'missing' roads (those shown on the map but not found on the ground), logistic constraints (a recurring theme) and the rain. The most important reason for effectively pausing operations, however, lay in the condition of his troops, whose ability to attack was almost 'expended'. To underline this point, he tabulated the losses and replacements of his seven infantry divisions to 7 November. These statistics yielded a shortfall of nearly 26,000 men – a quarter of his fighting strength. In summary, he noted that the Eleventh Army was 'confronted by a fact that cannot be ignored, ... these divisions will only be fully ready for difficult offensive operations following rest and the arrival of replacements'.[28] Significantly, he quantified neither the strength nor the utility of

Sector	Commander	Principal Formations	Number of Battalions and Sources	
			Black Sea Fleet	Coastal Army
I	Colonel P. G. Novikov, 2nd Cavalry Division	383rd Rifle Regiment	3, including one from the NKVD School	
II	Colonel I. A. Laskin, 172nd Rifle Division	514th Rifle Regiment		2
		2nd Naval Regiment	3	
		1st Sevastopol Regiment	3 (various sources)	
III	Major General T. K. Kolomiyets, 25th Rifle Division	31st Rifle Regiment	1 (air defence)	1
		287th Rifle Regiment	3 (various sources)	
		3rd Naval Regiment	3	
		7th Naval Infantry Brigade	3	
IV	Major General V. F. Vorobyov, 95th Rifle Division	161st Rifle Regiment	1	2
		90th Rifle Regiment	2	
		Local Rifle Regiment	3	
		8th Naval Infantry Brigade	5	
Reserve			Signal School Battalion	80th Reconnaissance Battalion
Totals			31 battalions	6 battalions

Table 13.1 – Organisation of the Defence and Composition of Forces in the Sevastopol Defence Region (9 November 1941)[29]

the Romanian Mountain Corps, which was dispersed in various supporting tasks across the Crimea.

Although desultory attacks on Sevastopol continued for another week, Manstein's gambit to seize the city off the line of march had miscarried. At least he had made the attempt, unlike the Allies in September 1854 following the battle of the Alma during the Crimean War. But the effort, combined with the casualties lost in the Perekop–Ishun battles and the following pursuit operations, had bled his army white. Not that the Soviet defenders of Crimea were in tip-top condition: they too had suffered grievous losses. For all their sacrifice, they had only retained Sevastopol. Anticipating the rhetoric of Soviet war correspondents, Manstein was correct in his view that the city would be held not only for sound strategic, but also for significant symbolic reasons.

Why did Manstein fail to concentrate sufficient forces against Sevastopol as opposed to diverting nearly half his troops to Kerch? Vasily Fedorovich Eliseev, a Second World War veteran and military historian born in 1922, is critical of the German commander: he argues that Manstein had used 'his palm and not his fist' in striking the city.[30] Although this description has considerable merit, the Eleventh Army was also required to support the main effort of Army Group South – then focused on opening the gates to the northern Caucasus. Hence it was critical to clear the Kerch peninsula as well as seizing Sevastopol. In mid-November, for example, Headquarters Eleventh Army was not only directing attacks on the fortress-city, but also planning Operation WINTERSPORT, the crossing of the Kerch Straits by XXXXII Corps to the Kuban peninsula to enable an advance into the Krasnodar region. Once again, the dissipation of German military effort in attempting to undertake too much at the same time, further constrained by poor logistics, led to indecisive results on the battlefield. Manstein exposed his associated frustration on 16 November, complaining: 'The Russians maintain that we have twelve divisions at Kerch and Sevastopol! If we only had at least nine! Always the one or two divisions that would provide a quick success are lacking – the old misery'.[31] Had the fully motorised *Leibstandarte* remained with the German Eleventh Army, Manstein might just have pulled off storming Sevastopol off the line of march in November 1941. But such speculation masks the multiple challenges he and his troops faced in attempting to attack Sevastopol.

Credit must be given to the manner in which the Soviets galvanised their efforts, both morally and materially, in fortifying Crimea's naval bastion. Although neither the 51st Army nor the Coastal Army had exhibited much tactical prowess in the fighting at Perekop and Ishun, the defence of the city by the combination of units of the Black Sea Fleet, the Coastal Army and reinforcements proved far more skilfully conducted and better led. As a result, notwithstanding the loss of the remainder of Crimea, Sevastopol held on against the Eleventh Army until the beginning of July 1942. Soviet resolve remained strong throughout. Take, for example, the experience of the nineteen-year-old Eliseev, who served as a machine-gunner in the 7th Naval Infantry Brigade. He joined his unit on 1 November 1941, soon going into action in the front-line trenches of the Second Sector at Gasfort. When interviewed in 2012 about the state of morale during the defence of Sevastopol, 1941–42, he declared:

> We were all confident that the Soviet Union would win the war. Defeat was inconceivable. But the situation at Sevastopol at the end became difficult. The Germans were eventually able to block it off by land, sea and air. We realised that Sevastopol would be lost – there were no illusions on that score.[32]

Units such as Eliseev's were not only made up of youngsters like himself, but also included a 'strong core of veterans from the First World War and the Civil War'. The tenacious naval infantry, dressed in their black uniforms, became very respected opponents of the Germans, who called them the 'Black Death'.[33] Sevastopol would indeed fall, but it would take a great deal of German and Romanian blood and effort to seize the city.

The resilience and seemingly inexhaustible resources of the Soviet Union were demonstrated in the manner in which reinforcements were poured into Sevastopol during November and December 1941. These included two naval infantry brigades (the 9th and the 79th) and two rifle divisions (the 388th and the 345th), not counting a host of other 'march' (emergency draft) units and sub-units to regenerate existing formations. On 25 November, for example, Oktyabrsky noted the arrival of fourteen rifle companies from the North Caucasus Military District.[34] Equally impressive was the opposite flow. During the first ten days of November, 5,732 wounded and 14,930 civilians were evacuated to other Black Sea ports, together with 26,600 tonnes of valuable war materiel.[35]

German morale dipped after the brief euphoria of the success at Ishun and the subsequent pursuit, which although costly, had been conducted initially in good weather. For many soldiers, the weeks of waiting until Manstein mounted his first main attack on Sevastopol on 17 December 1941 proved frustrating and equally debilitating. On the evidence of the first engagements in November, it became apparent that the fortress of Sevastopol would prove a very tough nut to crack. Making matters worse, the infamous Russian winter arrived early that year – the first snow fell on Crimea on 9 November, which alternated thereafter with heavy rainfalls. As the historian of the 22nd Infantry Division, Friedrich-August von Metzsch, recalled:

It was not altogether cold, but the storms from the sea and the wet snow made life in the front line a misery. Clothing was completely insufficient: many soldiers did not have a coat; far fewer possessed gloves or head protection. Added to this came the general physical exhaustion, which some times led to death even with light wounds.[36]

The 22nd Infantry Division from Lower Saxony was probably one of the toughest, battle-hardened, formations under Manstein's command. Although its leaders were highly decorated and respected (Manstein described the divisional commander, Ludwig Wolff, as 'excellent', and highly rated the commander of the 16th Infantry Regiment, Dietrich von Choltitz), significantly its battle casualties were disproportionately heavy. By the beginning of 1942, the 22nd Infantry had suffered the highest losses of all the German Army divisions committed since the beginning of the war.[37]

While Metzsch claims that 'faith in victory' remained at the time, notwithstanding the entry of the USA into the war on 6 December 1941, the soldiers of the 22nd Division became 'increasingly concerned about the irresponsible and disastrous underestimation of the enemy'.[38] The ultimately successful battle for Sevastopol in June–July 1942, well before the subsequent disasters of Stalingrad (November 1942 – February 1943) and Kursk (July 1943), would show just how much the German armed forces on the Eastern Front had over-reached themselves in the attempt to defeat an implacable, and increasingly competent, foe. The heroic defence of Sevastopol would become an emblematic struggle in the Soviet Union's resistance to Hitler's Germany.

Oktyabrsky's diary entries for November 1941 confirm the intensity of the fighting at Sevastopol, and how desperate the situation seemed at the time. While Manstein's staff struggled with sorting out countless logistical problems in preparation for the forthcoming assault on the city, the Soviets continued to strengthen their defences, scraping together and equipping units as best as could be done in the circumstances. Although no major German assault was under way, there were few pauses in operations. On 15 November, for example, heavy fighting erupted at Balaklava. Here the German 72nd Infantry Division attempted to secure the high, vital, ground surrounding the port as a preliminary operation prior to the main attack. Although its 105th Regiment managed to seize the Genoese Towers, the port remained in Soviet hands. Petrov, identifying the critical situation at Balaklava, declared on the 15th, 'we must recapture the heights ... and reinforce the defence of the whole southern sector'.[39]

While Oktyabrsky's senior colleagues in the Sevastopol Defence Region were desperately shoring up the defence of the city, including the organisation of underground weapons production facilities, the commander of the Black Sea

Fleet had wider concerns. There came at least one welcome simplification in the chain of command. On 20 November, Stalin removed Levchenko and abolished the ineffective Crimean Troops Command. *Stavka* become increasingly concerned about the threat to the Caucasus as the Germans broke into its gateway at Rostov-on-Don on 23 November. Confusingly, Oktyabrsky was ordered to divert scarce resources from Sevastopol to the Caucasus while receiving other forces in the opposite direction. While he considered that the city should be held 'to the very end', he also recognised that 'all assets superfluous to the functioning of the Main Base should be evacuated'.[40]

Within the city, in response to the heavy German air attacks and seemingly constant enemy artillery fire, activities, whether military or civilian in nature, were increasingly conducted below ground level. Wartime accounts of Sevastopol provide remarkable insights into how the defence of the city was sustained, and how daily life and work, and some much needed relaxation, continued despite all the dangers and hardships. In underground workshops, 'new arms, mortars, mines and shells were made and repaired'.[41] In other 'spacious galleries, that in peace time were used to store young champagne', resounded 'the clatter of shoemakers' hammers and the flowing hum of sewing machines'. Large sections of the local sewing- and shoe-making factories, which 'supplied the front with boots, underwear, and uniforms', were housed underground. This subterranean city not only provided munitions and equipment, but also food, healthcare, entertainment and information. A correspondent described the extensive facilities, which included:

> a communal kitchen, a first-aid post and medical clinic, a crèche, a nursery, a school, a cinema, lecture and games rooms. Flights of stairs lead down to the deep vaults in the huge rock. Every day sailors, soldiers and townspeople flock down to see the latest films and news-reels. After the show, people stop in front of the cinema to have a look at the newssheet.

School children were educated in shifts in underground classrooms. Housewives washed clothes for the men at the front, and knitted socks and gloves for them.[42] By 2 December 1941, members of the townsfolk had sent to the defenders of Sevastopol '35,200 articles of warm clothing, 600 kilogrammes of cotton wool, and no fewer than 25,000 other gifts'.[43]

Step by step, daily life in the city grew harder. As one eyewitness recalled, some basic necessities vanished:

> Matches disappeared very quickly. Despite the flames of war, ... it was a real challenge to get a light for a smoke or to ignite a kerosene lamp. We used an old

479

method – a fire striker to get a spark.... Electricity was supplied to our homes less and less. It was available for the last time on the New Year's Eve of 1942. But at 0030 [hours], artillery fire started and electricity ceased for the next few years.[44]

The struggle for Sevastopol had very much become a 'people's war'.

Meanwhile, the German attacks and Soviet counter-attacks continued in late 1941. The period 20–22 November, for example, witnessed intense combat in the vicinity of the Soviet strongpoint of Kamara near the Yalta road, which changed hands several times. On the 22nd, the Eleventh Army war diary conceded that the Soviet forces had succeeded through 'violent counterattacks' in pushing back the forward positions of the 132nd and 50th Divisions, and those of the 72nd Division at Balaklava.[45] In this manner, the desired lines of departure for the forthcoming main attack would have to be fought for once again, and not least Kamara recaptured. The Soviet defence of Sevastopol was proving very active, inflicting a steady attrition on the hard-pressed front-line German units. In the 72nd Division, for example, rifle company strengths varied between twelve and sixty-one men.[46]

The Soviet armed forces paid a heavy price in resisting Manstein's attacks. Altogether, the losses suffered by the Coastal and 51st Armies and the Black Sea Fleet in what was termed the 'Crimean Defensive Operation' from 18 October to 16 November 1941 amounted to 63,860 men, of which no fewer than 48,438 were classed as 'irrecoverable' – dead, presumed dead or missing.[47]

THE SECOND ASSAULT OF SEVASTOPOL, 17 DECEMBER 1941 – 1 JANUARY 1942

During the last week of November 1941, the Soviet defenders of Sevastopol became increasingly aware of the threat of a major German assault on the city. Ground and air reconnaissance, together with prisoner interrogations, revealed logistic preparations and roads jam-packed with personnel and equipment. Anticipating an imminent attack, and notwithstanding the risk of German air interdiction, Oktyabrsky ordered the battleship *Parizhkaya Kommuna* to arrive at Sevastopol by 27 November. Its mission was to bombard German troop concentrations. On 29 November, Soviet intelligence had confirmed the presence of two regiments of the newly arriving 24th Infantry Division, which now meant that there were five and two-thirds German divisions facing Sevastopol. The Soviet high command, whether in Moscow or in Sevastopol, was everything but passive during this period. On 3 December, Oktyabrsky ordered the preparation of assaults from the sea on Yalta and Yevpatoriya; two days later, *Stavka* required planning to start on a much more ambitious landing on the Kerch peninsula.[48]

45. General of the Army Ivan Yefimovich Petrov (1896–1958), commander-in-chief of the Soviet Coastal Army, 1941–42, during the defences of Odessa and Sevastopol; and in 1943–44 at the Kerch–Eltigen landing operation. He also served as a *front* commander. (SPUTNIK/Alamy Stock Photo)

46. Admiral Filipp Sergeyevich Oktyabrsky (1899–1969), commander-in-chief of the Black Sea Fleet, 1939–43 and 1944–48; and commander of the Sevastopol Defence Region 1941–42 during the Second Defence of the city. Stalin trusted him. (SPUTNIK/Alamy Stock Photo)

47. General Field Marshal Erich von Manstein (1887–1973), commander-in-chief of the German Eleventh Army, 1941–1942, which conducted three assaults on Sevastopol. He subsequently commanded Army Groups Don and South. (Photo by Photo12/UIG via Getty Images)

48. General Field Marshal Wolfram, Freiherr von Richthofen (1895–1945), commander-in-chief of VIII Air Corps, which provided critical support to the Eleventh Army in the battles for the Kerch peninsula and Sevastopol in 1942. He subsequently commanded 4th Air Fleet. (Photo by ullstein bild/ullstein bild via Getty Images)

49. The Soviet battleship *Parizhskaya Kommuna* (*Paris Commune*, formerly the *Sevastopol*), whose twelve 12-in. (305mm) guns provided powerful support to the defence of Sevastopol in late December 1941 and to Soviet amphibious landings on Crimea in early 1942. (Photo by TASS via Getty Images)

50. The destroyed harbour at Sevastopol's Southern Bay, following the Axis capture of the city on 1 July 1942, after a prolonged 250-day siege and heavy artillery and air attacks. (Photo by Horst Grund/Bundesarchiv)

51. 'The Defence of Sevastopol', by Alexander Deyneka (1899–1969). The painting of 1942, which became a famous wartime propaganda poster, portrayed Sevastopol's defiant role in the Great Patriotic War, subsequently honoured in its designation as a 'Hero City' in 1945. (World History Archive/TopFoto)

52. General of Engineers Erwin Jaenecke (1890–1960), commander-in-chief of the German Seventeenth Army, 1943–44. His defence of Crimea (October 1943 – May 1944) succumbed to superior Soviet forces of the 4th Ukrainian Front and the Coastal Army. (Photo by ullstein bild/ullstein bild via Getty Images)

53. Marshal of the Soviet Union Fyodor Ivanovich Tolbukhin, commander-in-chief of the 4th Ukrainian *Front*, whose successful Crimean Strategic Offensive Operation of 8 April – 12 May 1944 resulted in the liberation of Crimea and Sevastopol from German occupation. (Photo by Keystone/Hulton Archive/Getty Images)

54. The Soviet Coastal Battery No. 30 at Lyubimovka, with two armoured turrets each of two 12-in. (305mm) guns, known to the Germans as Fort Maxim Gorky I, was destroyed during the Second Axis assault on Sevastopol. It fired its last rounds on 18 June 1942. (Photo by ullstein bild/ ullstein bild via Getty Images)

55. A modern view (2016) of Coastal Battery No. 30, reconstructed in 1954 with turrets (three 12-in. (305mm) guns apiece) taken from the scrapped Baltic Fleet battleship *Frunze* (former *Poltava*). Russian Federation forces preserve the battery, which could be made active again. (Nikolay Skiba)

56. The *Grafskaya* (Count's) Landing Stage, Sevastopol, showing Soviet naval infantry battling to liberate the city from Nazi occupation on 9 May 1944. (Photo by TASS via Getty Images)

57. The Count's Landing Stage with Russian Federation President Vladimir Putin (right) and his Ukrainian counterpart, Viktor Yanukovych (left) during a joint visit to Sevastopol to celebrate Navy Day on 28 July 2013. The Ukrainian flag no longer flies over the city. (Mikhail Klimentyev/ AFP/Getty Images)

58. Coastal Battery No. 35, Cape Chersonese, similar in design to its sister at Lyubimova, was destroyed in June – July 1942, when it formed the last citadel of Soviet defence on Crimea; and the centre of last resistance by German forces in May 1944. (Public domain)

59. The Pantheon of Memory, opened on 3 July 2011, which contains the names of the last 27,000 defenders of Sevastopol in June – July 1942, is part of the Memorial Complex to the Heroic Defenders of Sevastopol at Coastal Battery No. 35, opened progressively since 2008. (© Ivan Nakonechnyy/iStock)

60. 'The Storming of Sapun Mountain' by Pyotr Tarasovich Maltsev (1907–93) in 1958, which depicts the Soviet assault on the Sapun escarpment on 7 May 1944, two days prior to the liberation of Sevastopol, is the centrepiece of the Diorama Museum opened in 1959. (Photo by Fine Art Images/Heritage Images/Getty Images)

61. The Storming of Sapun Mountain Diorama Museum, lying 6 km to the east of Sevastopol, not only houses the eponymous scene of battle, but also embraces an eternal flame; monuments to the units who fought in 1944; and a collection of vehicles and equipment. (Vladimir Zizak)

62. Joseph Vissarionovich Stalin (1878–1953), Soviet leader from the death of Lenin in 1924 to his own death in 1953, who paid no visits to Sevastopol during the Great Patriotic War (1941–45), accelerated the reconstruction of the city in 1948. (Photo by Universal History Archive/Getty Images)

63. Nikita Sergeyevich Khrushchev (1894–1971), First Secretary of the Communist Party of the Soviet Union (1953–64) and Premier (1958–64), directed the transfer of Crimea in 1954 from the Russian Soviet Federative Socialist Republic to the Ukrainian Soviet Socialist Republic. (Bettmann/Getty Images)

64. Clementine Churchill (1885–1977) visited Sevastopol on 23 April 1945 during a tour of Russia in her capacity as Chairman of the British Red Cross 'Aid to Russia' Fund, which donated medical equipment and supplies to the Soviet Union during the Second World War. (Photo by M. Pokatilo/State Archive of Sevastopol)

65. British Prime Minister Winston Churchill (1874–1965), seen here at the heavily damaged Panorama Museum, visited Sevastopol on 13 February 1945 following the Yalta conference. He appeared to show more interest in the Crimean War battlefields than the most recent ones. (From the archive collection of the State Museum of Heroic Defence and Liberation of Sevastopol)

66. The memorial to the 'Heroes of the Defence of Sevastopol in 1941–42', unveiled at Nakhimov Square in 1967. The bas-relief shows a Soviet defender parrying two blows, but yielding to the third, reflecting the Axis assaults on the city during the Second World War. (imageBROKER/ Alamy Stock Photo)

67. Sevastopol's Bicentenary Arch, erected in 1983 at the south-eastern gateway to the city on General Melnik Street, was embellished in 2014 with fore-standing statues of Prince Grigory Potemkin (left) and Catherine the Great (right). (Vladimir Zizak)

68. Boris Nikolayevich Yeltsin (1931–2007), as the first president of the Russian Federation (1991–99), sought good relations with Ukraine, culminating with a Treaty of Friendship signed in 1997. He did not seek to reverse Khrushchev's transfer of Crimea to Ukraine. (Richard Ellis/Getty Images)

69. Vladimir Vladimirovich Putin (1952–), second (2000–08) and fourth (2012–) president of the Russian Federation, has sought to restore Russia as a major power. The re-annexation of Crimea in early 2014 may prove to be one of his most significant acts. (Photo by Mikhail Svetlov/Getty Images)

70. Leonid Danylovych Kuchma (1938–), second president of independent Ukraine (1994–2005), while maintaining cordial relations with Russia, tried to steer Ukraine towards the West as its economy struggled to modernise and its institutions grappled with corruption. (Sergei Gapon/AFP/Getty Images)

71. Viktor Fedorovych Yanukovych (1950–), fourth president of Ukraine (2010–2014), sought closer relations with Russia rather than with the EU. Violent protests from November 2013 in Kiev (Euromaidan) ultimately led to his flight from office on 22 February 2014. (Photo by Sasha Mordovets/Getty Images)

72. Yury Aleksandrovich Meshkov (1945–) was the co-founder of the Republican Movement of Crimea, which sought reunion with Russia in the early 1990s. His election as Crimea's first president (1994–95) was not recognised by Ukraine, and the post was abolished. (©RIA Novosti/TopFoto)

73. Sergey Valeryevich Aksyonov (1972–) became on 27 February 2014 Chairman of the Council of Ministers of the Republic of Crimea, which since 18 March 2014 has been a 'federal subject' of the Russian Federation, a move which remains internationally disputed. (Photo by Mikhail Svetlov/Getty Images)

74. Mustafa Abduldzhemil Dzhemilev (1943–), former Soviet dissident and Chairman of the Mejlis (parliament) of the Crimean Tatar People (1991–2013), was the leader of the Crimean Tatar movement. He has been refused permission to return to Crimea. (NurPhoto via Getty Images)

75. Aleksey Mikhailovich Chaly (1961–), Sevastopol businessman, who funded the Memorial Complex to the Heroic Defenders of Sevastopol at Coastal Battery No. 35, was the people's choice for mayor on 23 February 2014, and was the city's governor, 1–14 April 2014. (Photo by Sasha Mordovets/Getty Images)

76. 'Welcome home to the native harbour', Sevastopol street art in February 2014, indicating the popular support in the city for President Vladimir Putin and reunification with Russia. (Vladimir Zizak)

77. At a mass pro-Russian demonstration in Nakhimov Square, Sevastopol, on 23 February 2014, by a show of hands the people elected Aleksey Chaly to become mayor of the city. (Sergey Gorbachev)

78. One of seven roadblocks erected around Sevastopol in late February 2014 ostensibly to prevent the entry of Ukrainian nationalists into the city. A colloquial translation of the prominent banner is 'wherever we are, Russia is with us'. (Sergey Gorbachev)

79. Members of the Sevastopol *Berkut* (special riot police), astride a BTR-70 8-wheeled armoured personnel carrier, guarding the Perekop entrance to Crimea in late February 2016, proudly displaying the flag of their home city. (Sergey Gorbachev)

80. The Russian Navy armed auxiliary, the guided missile tender *General Ryabikov*, together with a tug, blocking the entrance and exit to Sevastopol Bay on 4 March 2016, which prevented the movement of Ukrainian Navy vessels. (Sergey Gorbachev)

81. A provocative, pro-Russian, billboard concerning the disputed referendum held in Crimea, including Sevastopol, on 16 March 2014. The main caption reads: '16 March we choose' and the word below is 'or'. (Viktor Drachev/AFP/Getty Images)

82. A Russian Federation military mobile patrol under way in Sevastopol, undated but believed to be late February or early March 2016. (Sergey Gorbachev)

83. Masked Russian Special Operations Forces (*Spetsnaz*) soldiers – referred to by Russians as 'polite people' during Operation RUSSIAN SPRING – on guard in Sevastopol, late February/early March 2016. (Sergey Gorbachev)

84. The controversial 'Soldier and Sailor' monument, at Cape Crystal, overlooking Sevastopol Bay. Although construction started in 1981, the monument was not completed until 2007. (Vladimir Zizak)

85. Vladimir Stepanovich Usoltsev (1926–2016), veteran of the Great Patriotic War, noted Sevastopol historian and biographer of Rear Admiral Thomas Mackenzie, shown here on his last Victory Day parade at Sevastopol on 9 May 2014. (Tanya Bukharina)

86. President Vladimir Putin speaking at Victory Day in Sevastopol on 9 May 2014 told a cheering crowd that 'the Fatherland is embracing you once again as family, as daughters and sons' – reflecting the internationally disputed re-annexation of Crimea into Russia. (Photo by Sasha Mordovets/Getty Images)

Such operations were designed not only to pre-empt and dislocate any German attack on Sevastopol, but also to relieve the city and to recover the entire Crimean peninsula. Such were the operational level stakes.

While *Stavka* planned to assume the initiative, Manstein's preparations for a major attack on the city were subject to further, increasingly frustrating, technical delays. Deficiencies in railway and road capacities, and a lack of serviceable locomotives and trucks, all slowed down the movement of men and materiel to Sevastopol.[49] Poor weather, including heavy frosts and freezing fogs, made matters worse. Without sufficient quantities of fuel, guns and artillery ammunition, there was no prospect of launching a successful attack on Sevastopol. On 18 November, Manstein saw little likelihood of mounting the operation until the 27th/28th. But already by the 22nd, he admitted that an attack was not possible until 'December', without being more precise. Eventually, on 13 December it was announced that the long-anticipated offensive at Sevastopol would start on the 15th, only for it to be delayed again, for the final time, for forty-eight hours.[50] These successive delays gave more time for Oktyabrsky, Petrov and Morgunov to prepare for the German assault on the city, and to make, with *Stavka*, the necessary arrangements for their own offensive operations on the Crimean coast.

Full of confidence, and in anticipation of a quick success, Manstein had issued an order of the day on 15 December 1941:

> Soldiers of the Eleventh Army!
>
> The time of waiting is over! All necessary preparations have been made to ensure the success of the last great attack of the year. Everything has been completed thoroughly.
>
> We [now] attack Sevastopol! I know that I can rely on my infantry, assault engineers and assault artillerymen. You have frequently shown [your prowess] in the past. This time, you will also crush the enemy in the first attack, overrun him and strike into his depth. That's what matters.
>
> Equally, I know that all the other Arms always do their best to pave the way for the infantry. Our artillery is stronger and better. Our air force is again in position.
>
> An unshakable confidence will accompany us during the final passage of arms of this fighting year.
>
> Sevastopol will fall![51]

These fine words of exhortation could not mask the fact that the commander of the Eleventh Army had been unable to assemble an overwhelming force to smash through the very strong Soviet defences. Headquarters Army Group South had demanded that the Eleventh Army release the 73rd and 170th Infantry Divisions. Manstein regarded both formations as critical for his forthcoming attack on Sevastopol. In the event, he was able to retain the 170th, but the 73rd was redeployed. Apart from weaknesses in his infantry, Manstein was relatively light on heavy artillery and armour (assault guns). In the short winter days, often affected by bad weather, effective close air support from the Luftwaffe could not be guaranteed. In an effort to offset these deficiencies, Headquarters Eleventh Army attempted to score a tactical surprise. Forsaking a long period of artillery preparation, there would only be very short three-minute barrage designed to neutralise the front-line enemy positions and supporting gun batteries.

Manstein's scheme of manoeuvre, reflected in Headquarters Eleventh Army's orders for the attack of 9 December 1941, placed the overall main effort to the north-east of Sevastopol. Originally, he had wished to mount his main assault over the Sapun escarpment, but it proved impossible to assemble sufficient forces, and particularly heavy artillery, in the southern sector. So the final plan was based on a frontal attack by LIV Corps designed to push in from east to west the Soviet defensive zone to the north of Sevastopol Bay. If successful, this operation would have the effect of eliminating the Soviet Fourth Sector and much of the Third. Once this phase had been completed, a subsequent attack would be mounted from the south-east directed towards the southern outskirts of the city by breaking through the Soviet Sapun positions.

Once again, Hansen's LIV Corps assumed the lion's share of the assault with four infantry divisions (22nd, 132nd, 24th, 50th) attacking abreast. The intended reserve division (the 73rd) for this corps was no longer available, much to Manstein's and Hansen's regret. Simultaneously, XXX Corps provided a subsidiary attack with only one division (the 72nd) – rising during the course of the battle to two with the arrival of the 170th Division. Once again Romanian units performed supporting roles, with a mountain infantry brigade assisting the 72nd Division.

It could be argued that Manstein's unsophisticated and under-resourced tactical plan of attack of December 1941 represented a gamble, and a pretty poor one at that. In terms of design, it seems a far cry from his carefully crafted and nuanced *Sichelschnitt* (Sickle-Cut) operational plan for the attack on France and the Low Countries, a manoeuvre which achieved such stunning success in May 1940. Yet any such comparison must be seen in its strategic context. Elsewhere on Germany's Eastern Front at the close of 1941, the divisions of the *Ostheer* (the Army of the East) were either retreating in the wake of the Soviet superbly timed counter-offensive in the battle for Moscow launched on 5 December, or hunkering down in defensive positions fighting the cold as much as the enemy. Hitler's Directive No. 39 of 8 December 1941 had expressly required the capture of Sevastopol 'as quickly as possible', while elsewhere operations were to be closed down on account of the 'severe winter weather'.[52]

Hitler's controversial 'stand fast' order (the *Durchhaltebefehl*) of 25 November 1941 forbade any surrender or retreat, which, in the opinion of the Eastern Front expert David Glantz, may have 'forestalled [a] German rout'.[53] In late 1941, Manstein's army was the only substantial German force capable of mounting any form of offensive operation. In addition, the German Army experienced at the time a severe leadership crisis. The roll call of recently sacked senior officers included the commanders-in-chief of the army, Field Marshal Walther von Brauchitsch, of Army Group South, Field Marshal Gerd von Rundstedt and of Second Panzer Group, Colonel General Heinz Guderian. These dismissals shocked the upper echelons of the officer corps. Significantly, Manstein described the departure of his old boss, Rundstedt, as '*niederschmetternd*' – devastating.[54] Thus there is little doubt that Manstein felt compelled under multiple pressures to achieve a notable success before the end of the year – as indicated in his order of the day. If, on the other hand, Eleventh Army remained passive, there was every chance that the Soviet forces would mount their own operation to relieve Sevastopol. Although the December assault proved very expensive in terms of lives lost for little tangible gain, Manstein calculated beforehand that he had little option other than to mount the operation. To dismiss his decision in hindsight is to misunderstand the realities of command generally and the stark situation facing the German *Wehrmacht* at the end of 1941 specifically.

In the race against time in the launching of offensive operations on the Crimean peninsula, the Eleventh Army struck the first blow at 0610 hours on 17 December 1941. Initially, the Soviet defenders were stunned. For once, the winter sun shone over Sevastopol. German hopes were raised. Very disappointingly, however, the promised Stuka support failed to materialise – the dive-bombers that provided such necessary close air support had been grounded due to mist obscuring their fields around Mariupol in south-eastern Ukraine.[55] This setback proved an unfortunate start to the operation. Within LIV Corps, the three regiments of 22nd Infantry Division attacked from Duvankoy in a westerly direction astride the Belbek valley, while other troops, including Kornu's motorised regiment, attacked southwards over the river Kacha on a convergent axis. The 132nd Division attacked south of the Belbek valley westwards over very difficult ground towards the Kamyshly gorge. Further south again, the newly arrived, and thereby freshest division, the 24th, commanded by Major General Hans von Tettau, had been designated as the corps' main effort. Its attack took it over the equally challenging terrain of steeply wooded clefts and hills from the vicinity of Cherkez-Kermen,[56] directly towards the eastern end of Sevastopol Bay. The objective of this cleaving attack was to cut off any lateral movement of Soviet forces between the two sides of the roadstead. On the left-hand, southern, flank of LIV Corps, the 50th Division struck once again from the area of Chorgun. XXX Corps's 72nd Division, reinforced by the 1st Romanian Mountain Brigade, attacked between the Gasfort height (known to the Germans as the Kapellenberg) and Balaklava.

The results of the first day of the German attack were costly, disappointing and indicative of the course and outcome of the battle. By far, the 22nd Division made the best progress with the 2nd Battalion of the 16th Infantry Regiment penetrating 4 kilometres along the Belbek valley, while its sister regiments (the 47th and 65th) achieved half this distance. Although the leading elements of the 132nd Division reached the Kamyshly gorge, elsewhere the formation was held up in the dense mountain scrub. Worse still, the 24th Division made even less impression on the Soviet defences. While the 50th Division in the Chorgun area made some initial progress against the Soviet Second Sector, vigorous counter-attacks neutralised its earlier gains. Underlining the effectiveness of the Soviet defence, on 17 December, LIV Corps lost no fewer than 306 men killed in action, 1,342 wounded and a further fifty missing – in sum, 1,698 men or the equivalent of two complete battalions. Disproportionately heavy were 24th Division's 592 casualties. Unsurprisingly, General Hansen shifted his main effort from the 24th Division to the 22nd, so as to reinforce his gains in the Belbek valley.[57]

The Soviets' relative defensive success, however, had been won at a very high price. At the time of the German attack, Oktyabrsky was not present in Sevastopol, so responsibility for directing the defence of the city fell to General Petrov and his sector commanders. The fighting in the Third and Fourth Sectors (north-east and north respectively) proved particularly fierce in containing the main German attack. On 17 December, the 8th Naval Brigade, the 25th Rifle Division, the 40th Cavalry Division (fighting dismounted!), the 172nd and 95th Rifle Divisions and the 7th Naval Infantry Brigade were all involved in heavy combat. Such intense fighting recurred over the following days. As one Soviet-Russian history has described it, 'the defenders of Sevastopol resisted the enemy's superiority in numbers and equipment by their bravery and stubbornness. Every hundred metres that the enemy advanced was at a cost of valuable and enormous losses, but the ranks of the Black Sea fortress were quickly thinned'. The alarming gaps in the Soviet units were filled with 'personnel from the coastal batteries, sappers and rear echelon units, and workers from city enterprises'.[58] There were no further reserves of manpower available. From the very first hour of battle, Manstein's ambitious attack on Sevastopol had turned into a highly attritional fight – a 'slugfest'. In determining the outcome of the battle, it was fast becoming more a matter of resilience rather than tactical finesse. Both sides were fast running out of resources.

Some Soviet historians claim that Manstein planned to attack in such a way as to occupy Sevastopol in four days, in other words by 21 December and within six months of the opening of Operation BARBAROSSA. Others suggest that he had promised Hitler the capture of Sevastopol as a Christmas present – by the 24th.[59] There is slim evidence for either assertion. What is clear, however, is that both sides faced a crisis around 21/22 December 1941. While the German 22nd Division continued to make progress in the Belbek valley, and the 132nd made some modest gains to the south in the vicinity of Kamyshly, neither the 24th nor the 50th Divisions had achieved much. Already on the third day of the attack (19 December), Manstein had considered redirecting the 24th Division to attack further north, but Hansen convinced him otherwise. In the south, the 72nd Division finally managed to capture the Gasfort feature, but gained nothing more of significance. What the Germans did not realise at the time was just how thin the Soviet lines of defence were becoming, and how critical the battle appeared to the Soviet command. In such knife-edged situations, rhetoric has long been a favourite weapon of war.[60] On 21 December 1941, the Military Council of the Black Sea Fleet issued a defiant proclamation to the defenders of Sevastopol: 'Not a step backwards in the fight for Sevastopol! ... Remember the eyes of the peoples of not just the Motherland, but of the whole world, are on Sevastopol. The Motherland expects us to be victorious over the enemy. Not a step backwards! Victory will be ours!'[61] Despite the immense pressure, the defenders of the city did not break.

In the nick of time, the 79th Naval Infantry Brigade, which had been preparing for an assault of Feodosiya, was landed at Sevastopol on 21 December and rushed into action. Oktyabrsky also returned to the city, delayed by fog. That same day, the Soviet command toyed with the idea of launching a major counter-offensive out of the city. After further reflection, Oktyabrsky and his colleagues considered it preferable to make such an attempt following the intended major *desant* operations – the amphibious landings on the Crimean coast at Kerch and Feodosiya. As a result, Oktyabrsky anticipated that Manstein's assault would 'grind to a halt'.[62] This forecast would prove accurate. In the meantime, however, German pressure to the north of Sevastopol proved relentless. Although the 79th Brigade under the energetic command of Colonel A. S. Potatov mounted a limited counter-attack, the 388th Rifle Division partially disintegrated on 22 December, exposing the flank of the 8th Naval Infantry Brigade. This turn of events forced Oktyabrsky to authorise that evening the withdrawal of all remaining Soviet forces north of the Belbek valley.[63] As the Soviet perimeter shrank particularly in the Fourth and Third Sectors, casualties continued to mount alarmingly while further cracks in the integrity of the defences appeared.

For all the occasional manifestations of chance (or luck) in its various guises, war is conducted predominantly in a hostile environment of friction and uncertainty. In the face of perceived failure, or disappointing progress, pessimism can afflict even the most capable and positive of leaders. While opposing commanders may view the very same facts on the ground, their perceptions of either success or failure may differ markedly. Several hours before Oktyabrsky's decision, matters looked overwhelmingly bleak for the commanding general of LIV Corps. In a telephone call to Manstein during the morning of 22 December, Hansen reported:

> The situation on an over-extended front and with constantly sinking fighting strengths has become very critical. Attempts to straighten out the bend in the front north of the Belbek have failed. The 24th I.D. has lost very much its punch in costly combat in the impenetrable wooded terrain. I must state that clearing the enemy positions north of the Belbek is not possible with the forces at my disposal![64]

During the course of that day and the next, the 22nd Division, supported by the attacks of the 132nd to the south, managed to achieve the impossible. The Soviets stepped back south of the river Belbek, thus abandoning an important segment of their outer defensive perimeter.

Despite the retirement, and the continuing losses (on 22 December, no fewer than 2,500 wounded were evacuated to the Caucasus, and 2,000 followed on the 23rd), Oktyabrsky remained steady in his determination to hold on. Reinforcements continued to flow in. On the 24th, the second half of the 345th Rifle Division disembarked at Sevastopol, together with a battalion of twenty-eight T-26 tanks. Although the admiral described this armoured support as 'feeble', as half were armed with 45mm guns and the remainder with machine guns, the newly arrived troops were none the less most welcome. In contrast, Christmas Eve brought neither rest nor relief to the German attackers. Although the historian of the 22nd Infantry Division recalled that enemy activity that day was 'relatively quiet', the forward troops 'sat freezing in trenches and in Russian bunkers ... and for the first time doubted success because of the recent losses'.[65]

On the 25th, the defenders of Sevastopol repelled German attacks from the direction of Chorgun and Mackenzie Farm in the eastern Second Sector. In the northern Fourth Sector, the 22nd Infantry Division was subjected to heavy artillery bombardment and air attack. In particular, the 305mm guns of Maxim Gorky I (Coastal Battery No. 30) caused 'much damage'.[66] As German morale dropped, Soviet optimism grew. That day, Oktyabrsky noted 'we are feeling more confident now – units are in better order ... and the enemy too is licking his wounds'. More particularly, he took comfort from the impending Soviet counter-offensive, which ushered 'a new stage in the battle for the Crimea'. Indeed, the landings south of Kerch on 26 December promised much, including the relief of Sevastopol. Yet for all his optimism, the defence of the city was taking a steady toll on Soviet forces. On the 27th, Oktyabrsky reported that in the ten days since the start of the German attack, there had been '12,000 wounded, 1,000 killed and 3,000 lost without trace' – in all, some 16,000 casualties.[67] The German pressure continued the next day.

LIV Corps resumed its assault on the fortress area north of Sevastopol Bay on 28 December. Once again, the 22nd Infantry Division was in the lead, supported by artillery and Nebelwerfer rocket strikes – the German soldiers called this weapon the '*Stuka* by foot'.[68] With the 16th Infantry Regiment to the left and the 65th to the right, the division attacked on a narrow axis towards 'Fort Stalin' and 'the Bastion' respectively. The latter objective was a resolutely defended locality on a ridgeline to the east of Battery 30. Although the 65th Regiment gained the Bastion on the 28th, a powerful Soviet counter-attack, supported by tanks, drove the Germans off the following day. That success threatened the exposed right-hand flank of the 16th Regiment, which had penetrated the Soviet defences as far as the Mekenzievy Gory station, only 2 kilometres distant from the shore of Sevastopol Bay. None the less, Colonel Choltitz's men fought off Soviet tank attacks on the 29th and maintained their positions on the 30th. Gathering their strength for one final push, on the night of the 30th/31 December, after three attempts, leading elements of the 16th Infantry Regiment penetrated the wire defences of Fort Stalin. 'Indescribably heavy' Soviet artillery strikes and the rapidly dwindling rifle company strengths (in some cases down to ten to twenty men), however, prevented any further German advance.[69] The abortive attack on Fort Stalin represented the high water mark of Manstein's second attempt to storm Sevastopol. No further progress was made: the burnt-out divisions of his Eleventh Army could do no more.

THE SOVIET KERCH–FEODOSIYA AMPHIBIOUS OPERATION

While Manstein's attack on Sevastopol was in full progress, Soviet forces mounted a major counter-offensive on 26 December 1941. In accordance with *Stavka's* instructions, the 44th and 51st Armies of the Caucasus *Front*, commanded by Major General A. N. Pervushin and Lieutenant General V. N. Lvov respectively, with the close support of the Black Sea Fleet and its Azov Flotilla, launched an ambitious amphibious operation designed to seize the Kerch peninsula and to relieve Sevastopol. The 51st Army landed about 15,000 troops to the north and south of Kerch; the 44th Army provided a supporting attack at Cape Opuk on the north of the peninsula, retaining the bulk of its forces for its subsequent operation at Feodosiya on 29 December.

The Soviet landings in the vicinity of Kerch on the 26 December by elements of the 224th Rifle Division, 2nd Rifle Brigade and 83rd Marine Infantry Brigade were beset by problems. Stormy weather impeded the transfer of troops from ships to shore; insufficient anti-aircraft support and tactical errors gave the defending Luftwaffe and the German 46th Infantry Division some initial success in eliminating a number of beachheads. None the less, the commanding general of XXXXII Corps, Lieutenant General Hans Graf von Sponeck, wished to order a withdrawal. Manstein curtly ordered him to 'hurl [the enemy] back into the sea'.[70] He also placed the Romanian 8th Cavalry and 4th Mountain Brigades, together with the German 213th Infantry Regiment (the remaining regiment of the departed 73rd Division), on the march towards Kerch. Korne's motorised regiment was also warned off. By the 28th, it looked as if the landings at Kerch could be contained, if not eliminated, by the 46th Division before these reinforcements arrived.

During the early hours of 29 December 1941, one of the most critical days of Manstein's military career, the 44th Army landed in strength at Feodosiya and to the north of the town. Fearing being cut off, Sponeck ordered the evacuation of the Kerch peninsula. Reporting his assessment of the situation and decision to Headquarters Eleventh Army at 1025 hours, he then confirmed that the withdrawal was under way at 1102 hours. Sponeck did not receive Manstein's counter-order of 1112 hours, expressly forbidding any such retirement, because Headquarters XXXXII Corps had already packed up its radio station and was already moving westwards. Communications remained broken until 1500 hours. Then Sponeck informed Headquarters Eleventh Army that the withdrawal of the 46th Division was proceeding to plan. In view of the worsening position at Feodosiya as further Soviet forces were landing and throwing back the town's weak German garrison, it made no sense now to turn the division around. Although greatly annoyed by what had happened, not least because his intent had not been followed, Manstein realised he had to accept the *fait accompli*. He relieved Sponeck later that day, replacing him with Lieutenant General Friedrich Mattenklott, who had only just been appointed the acting commander of XXX Corps.[71]

At the height of the crisis on 29 December 1941, Manstein learned from Headquarters Army Group South about Hitler's latest intentions. These were not helpful: oblivious to the facts on the ground, the Führer ordered that the attack on Sevastopol be continued without regard to events unfolding at Kerch. Yet the developing situation at Feodosiya threatened the integrity of Manstein's entire command. By the morning of the 30th, the Soviet 44th Army had established nearly 23,000 men and thirty-four tanks ashore. Such a force was capable of cutting off the withdrawing German 46th Division. If reinforced, and when joined by the 51st Army, it could drive towards the centre of Crimea. If the vital logistics and railway hubs at Simferopol (where 10,000 German wounded lay in hospitals) and Dzhankoy were seized, or the 'lifeline' between the two interdicted, then the game was surely up for the Eleventh Army.[72] On the Sevastopol front, Hansen reported on the evening of the 29th more bad news: his attacks that day had made no substantial progress. Furthermore, widespread mist prevented the Luftwaffe from providing the much-needed close air support over both Sevastopol and Feodosiya. All in all, as Manstein confided to his private diary, it was 'quite a bad situation'.[73] Such understatement in crisis, almost British in tone, could not obscure the reality of the situation. Unless he was able to redeploy forces very quickly from Sevastopol to the eastern Crimea, Manstein faced the possibility of defeat. Significant reinforcements would ease the situation for the Eleventh Army enormously.

The Soviet command, although its landings at Kerch had proved clumsy and disappointing, had achieved a major coup at Feodosiya. It opened the prospect of a serious embarrassment to Manstein's army, if not its destruction. In these circumstances, sheer luck as much as any fine judgement in the execution of command, appeared to benefit the Axis forces on Crimea. On several occasions, grave deficiencies in Soviet generalship saved Manstein's bacon. Neither the 44th Army nor the 51st Army seemed capable of taking the initiative, and thereby exploiting the weaknesses of their opponent. Looking on from Sevastopol, notwithstanding the mounting pressures on Manstein, Oktyabrsky grew increasingly restless as he saw this priceless opportunity to relieve the city being squandered. He had more local problems too.

On 28 December the commander-in-chief of the Black Sea Fleet recorded not only heavy losses at Kerch, but also disappointments at Sevastopol. Oktyabrsky complained that his sector commanders were 'overestimating the enemy: two to three German companies attack with five to seven tanks in support and we commit all our resources against them'. Furthermore, the 'Generals complain that matters are "very difficult"'. The requirement, he concluded, was 'not to underestimate the Germans, but rather to have self-belief'. As German attacks continued on 29 December, Oktyabrsky noted that 'although the enemy had suffered heavy losses, ... they keep coming. [Their] blindness to unreasonably heavy losses has become incomprehensible'. Although the troops of the Caucasus *Front* were fighting to expand their beachheads, the enemy was 'resisting fiercely and is not retreating'. While he observed optimistically that 'our situation at Sevastopol should change', Soviet forces were losing the operational initiative as Manstein assembled his forces to block any enemy moves further west, and eventually to mount a counter-attack to retake Feodosiya.[74] He also decided to continue operations at Sevastopol, informed by Hitler's insistence that the city be captured as soon as possible.

Despite LIV Corps mounting limited attacks on Sevastopol on 30 December, and notwithstanding the local success of the 16th Infantry Regiment, Headquarters Eleventh Army was forced to accept the realities of the situation. Manstein and his senior staff realised that the only way to eliminate the growing Soviet threat to the army's vital lines of communication in Crimea was to close down the attack on Sevastopol and to release forces for this task. Matters in the east of the peninsula had to be stabilised as a matter of urgency. It says something for Manstein's powers of persuasion that he managed to convince Hitler that it was necessary not only to cease offensive operations at Sevastopol, but also to withdraw to positions that could be better – and more economically – defended than the exposed outposts in the midst of the Soviet defences. Although any retrograde move ran counter to the Führer's 'stand and fight' diktat, Hitler acquiesced in this case. Manstein gave the necessary orders on 31 December, permitting the depleted and exhausted divisions of LIV Corps to retire north of the river Belbek.

In this manner, the year ended not with a triumphal German capture of Sevastopol, but rather with a consolidation of the lines of circumvallation around the city. The retirement involved giving up much of the ground captured at great cost by divisions such as the 22nd. Commenting on this retrograde move, Manstein noted in his memoirs that:

> Hitler's disapproval of this decision, which – although he could not change it – clashed with the strict ban he had just placed on any voluntary withdrawals, weighed little in comparison with one's own responsibility to the troops who had sacrificed so much. This decision had to be taken, particularly when thinking of them and their preservation.[75]

Hardly an example of a 'lost victory', the Germans' second assault on Sevastopol (and in Manstein's eyes, it remained strictly the 'first'), on which so much hope had been placed, resulted in a disappointing, if not ignominious, defeat. Contrary to Manstein's and others' claims, it seems improbable that the committal of another infantry division, let alone a single regiment, would have tilted the balance in favour of the attacker.[76] Yet Oktyabrsky and the valiant defenders of Sevastopol could not afford to rest on their laurels. Although they had strenuously resisted the onslaught, and had not succumbed, their casualties had been very heavy. The Axis forces involved now knew the fortress area much better and would draw lessons from the recent operations, and apply them in any subsequent attacks. Meanwhile, the Soviet high command pinned high hopes on developing the Kerch–Feodosiya amphibious operation into a full-blown campaign to rid the enemy from Crimea altogether. Although the plans of the Caucasus *Front* held much promise, the results proved most disappointing.

Blow and Counter-blow: January–April 1942

With the cessation of the German attacks on the city, Sevastopol's fate now rested on the outcome of the fighting on the Eastern Crimea. While Oktyabrsky had his hands full in naval affairs supporting the Caucasus *Front*, Petrov and his colleagues in Sevastopol were relegated to bystander status for much of the following five months. Not that fighting died down completely at Sevastopol: while a general lull pertained, it was rudely interrupted from time to time by powerfully conducted Soviet probing attacks on the German lines, regularly with air support. Typically, these actions were designed to coincide with Soviet attacks elsewhere in an effort to prevent their opponents from redeploying forces away from the Sevastopol front. Trench warfare became the norm around the city, resembling in many ways the siege of 1854–55.

From a Soviet viewpoint, if the Crimean peninsula were to be liberated and Sevastopol relieved, all depended on the rapid exploitation of the successes gained at Kerch and Feodosiya. In his memoirs, Manstein was quick to criticise his opponents for failing to do so, while providing his readers with a master-class in campaign design. In his opinion, the 51st Army had followed the 46th Division 'only hesitatingly'. The 41st Army, rather than attacking to the west, 'to our amazement', had struck 'eastwards with strong forces to meet 51st Army'. In this manner, 'the enemy obviously focussed on the tactical objective of destroying our forces on the Kerch peninsula, and thereby lost sight of the operational level objective of cutting the lifeline of the Eleventh Army'.[77] An inspection of the Soviet records reveals a rather more complex situation, as well as yielding some examples of incoherent leadership. The first days of 1942 witnessed an extraordinary exchange between an impatient *Stavka* and the ponderous headquarters of the Caucasus *Front*, struggling to overcome doubts and delays incurred by poor weather and constrained logistics. It represents an interesting case study in the vast gulf between the theoretical demands of military strategy and of operational art on one hand, and the practical planning and conduct of tactical operations on the other.

On 1 January 1942, the commander of the Caucasus *Front*, Lieutenant General D. T. Kozlov, sent to Moscow his proposals for the liberation of the Crimean peninsula. His concept of operations was 'to encircle fully and isolate enemy units ... by an attack by a motor-mechanised group in the direction of Perekop with a simultaneous attack on Simferopol and along the coast of the Black Sea'. Kozlov foresaw his offensive being launched between 8 and 12 January. Late the following day (the 2nd), *Stavka* sent a directive that not only approved Koslov's plan, but also demanded that he make 'every effort to accelerate the period for the concentration of forces and the commencement of the general offensive'. For that purpose, the Supreme high command 'proposed' (in fact demanded) that Koslov exploited 'all possible means of transferring forces to Crimea both by the military means of the Black Sea and by the civilian fleet'. Optimistically, the *Stavka* directive added: 'In the event you determine an enemy withdrawal from the Crimea, quickly launch a general offensive with all the forces and weapons you have in the Crimea, regardless of whether you have completed the concentration, to reach the Perekop and Chongar regions and cut off the enemy withdrawal'.[78] In the event, Kozlov never came close to achieving this distant objective.

Manstein, although hard-pressed, had no intention of withdrawing from Sevastopol or Crimea as a whole. As *Stavka* realised only too well, every day of hesitation by Kozlov increased the Germans' chances of countering the threat posed by the Caucasus *Front*. By early January, the Eleventh Army had managed to generate sufficient forces to man a thin line of defence from the neck of the Kerch peninsula to Feodosiya, which was sealed off. The next step was to assemble a force capable of recapturing this city. For this purpose, the 132nd and 170th Infantry Divisions were sent on the march from Sevastopol.

As German attention was focused on the east of Crimea, Soviet forces pulled off another surprise – an amphibious landing at Yevpatoriya on the western coast on 5 January 1942. Once again, Manstein had to scrabble around to find sufficient forces to eliminate this new threat. In addition to sending the reconnaissance battalion of the 22nd Infantry Division, the 70th Engineer Battalion (Motorised), and a number of artillery batteries, the 105th Infantry Regiment of the 72nd Division, already being transported by vehicle from Balaklava towards Feodosiya, was diverted to Yevpatoriya. Such a large German grouping might have been an over-reaction had not the battalion-sized landing force (approximately 700 men) from the 2nd Naval Infantry Regiment, deployed by sea from Sevastopol, been joined by several hundreds of local partisans and armed townsfolk. Furthermore, Manstein could not risk further enemy forces being landed and posing a potent threat to his lines of communications. What had been designed as a minor diversion to distract the German command, and to reduce their forces facing Feodosiya, turned into a most brutal fight for Yevpatoriya.

After two days of intense combat, the mixed bag of German units under the overall command of Colonel Friedrich-Wilhelm Müller of the 105th Infantry Regiment gained control of Yevpatoriya. Combat engineers, led by Lieutenant Colonel Hubertus-Maria Ritter von Heigl, were particularly prominent in the fighting. According to one of his junior officers, his commanding officer 'didn't hesitate to deploy immediately flamethrower and demolition teams at crucial points', and to lead his men from the front 'against the strongest nest of resistance of the town, the Crimean hotel'.[79] In the action, the popular commander of the 22nd Division's reconnaissance unit, Lieutenant Colonel Oskar von Boddien, fell during the action. The aftermath showed the *Wehrmacht* at its revengeful worst. While Manstein wrote that '1,200 armed partisans were killed', Soviet accounts state that no fewer than 3,000 people were executed, including civilians and uniformed naval infantrymen, who had been taken as prisoners of war.[80] As elsewhere in the German–Soviet War, little quarter was given. In recognition of his leadership and valour at Yevpatoriya, Ritter von Heigl was awarded the Knight's Cross to the Iron Cross on 13 January 1942, and promoted soon thereafter.

Meanwhile, notwithstanding the initial optimism about the landing at Yevpatoriya, Stalin's frustration about the lack of progress made by Kozlov grew daily. Over a secure communication link, on 5 January Stalin remonstrated with the *front* commander:

> The overall strategic conditions require that the offensive begin no later than the 12th. Otherwise, it will be [too] late, since the situation in the Crimea will worsen for our army. Amass as many forces as you can in Feodosiya and on the Kerch peninsula, bring up your rear services, strengthen your air group, and operate with all decisiveness, without hesitation and without constantly glancing back.

Although Kozlov intended that his offensive would begin with preliminary raiding operations during the night of 11–12 January, in the event he was not ready to launch either these or his main offensive. The Germans struck in force first. (The landing of a Soviet regiment at Sudak on 15/16 January was overtaken by events further north and was aborted.)

On 15 January 1942, the Eleventh Army's attack to recapture Feodosiya opened. Conditions were far from ideal: the best time to attack such a beachhead is as soon as possible – before the landed troops have consolidated and prepared defences against such an operation. In this case, the moment of maximum vulnerability had passed: 44th Army (estimated at a minimum of six divisions) had benefited from over two weeks to make ready for the German response. Several problems, however, had delayed the start of Eleventh Army's attack, including the time required to concentrate the barely sufficient forces (three weakened German divisions and two Romanian brigades) and coping with an unexpected thaw on 9 January that impeded all road movement. Moreover, bad weather had limited support from the Luftwaffe prior to the assault.[81] One positive development was the timely arrival of the Romanian 18th Infantry Division, the first of the reinforcements that Manstein had pleaded for. None the less, the commander-in-chief of the Eleventh Army had considerable doubts about the operation. On 14 January, he noted in his diary that it had been a 'most difficult decision to attack with only three weak divisions, weak artillery, no armour and questionable Stuka support'. But it represented the 'last chance ... one must take the plunge. May God help us!'[82] Although the Germans enjoyed nothing like the three-to-one superiority in numbers typically required by an attacker, the Soviet defence, badly prepared and poorly led, dissolved much quicker than anticipated.

Manstein's simple plan proved effective. While XXXXII Corps would hold the neck of the Kerch peninsula with the Romanians, the German 46th Infantry Division and the separate 213th Infantry Regiment would assist XXX Corps (132nd and 170th Divisions) in mounting the main attack towards Feodosiya. Redeeming its reputation after its unauthorised retirement from Kerch, the 46th Division's attack broke through the Soviet defences on the heights south of Petrovka to the north-west of the city. A German air strike on the command post of the 44th Army seriously wounded its commander, Pervushin, which disabled effective control. Meanwhile, XXX Corps steadily advanced on Feodosiya, clearing the city of Soviet forces by early 18 January. Although the 44th Army had been defeated, many of its troops managed to escape to safety on ground held by the 51st Army on the Kerch peninsula. The Soviet defence and withdrawal proved chaotic. Pervushin's unlucky temporary relief, Major General Ivan Fyodorovich Dashichev, was stripped of command on 21 January. Court-martialled, and found guilty of negligence and indecision, he spent ten years in a gulag.

Wishing to exploit his swift success at Feodosiya as quickly as possible, Manstein planned to continue the attack on to the Kerch peninsula. It was not to be: not only were his troops tired, but also (and more critically) the promised additional air support and a reinforcing panzer battalion were diverted elsewhere within Army Group South's command. The opportunity having passed, Axis and Soviet forces confronted each other across the neck of the Kerch peninsula (the Germans called it the Parpach position, the Soviets the Ak-Monai) for the ensuing four months. Stalin, however, was far from pleased with the resulting situation. He regarded the loss of Feodosiya as but a temporary setback, and remained throughout 'focused on his goal of clearing the Crimea of German forces and relieving the besieged Sevastopol garrison'.[83] Although the recovery of Feodosiya was not decisive for the Eleventh Army, as a strong enemy grouping remained on the Kerch peninsula, its success had certainly stabilised the situation in Crimea. Manstein could afford a sigh of relief: the operation had not only provided a welcome boost to German morale, but also restored his confidence and reputation after the recent disappointments at Sevastopol and Kerch.

After the bitter fighting at Feodosiya, both sides were exhausted and incapable of mounting any major operations. Hence there was no immediate prospect of Sevastopol being relieved by Soviet forces. While Kozlov, under heavy personal pressure from Stalin, prepared to launch a fresh offensive on 31 January (for which he was far from ready), *Stavka* took the opportunity to reorganise the chain of command. The Caucasus *Front* was divided into the Crimean *Front* and the Transcaucasus Military District. The former grouping now included the 44th, 47th and 51st Armies, the forces of the Sevastopol Defence Region, the Black Sea Fleet, the Azov Flotilla and the Kerch Naval Base. Surprisingly, in view of his poor performance to date, Lieutenant General Kozlov was confirmed as the commander-in-chief of the new Crimean *Front*. Yet there was a sting in the tail: *Stavka* sent two representatives to supervise his work and that of his staff. The individuals concerned, both 'close cronies' of Stalin, were Commissar of First Rank L. Z. Mekhlis, the chief of the Red Army's main political directorate, and his assistant, Major General P. P. Vechny, drawn from the General Staff. According to Glantz, 'both were already universally feared and loathed by many in the Red Army officer corps'.[84] The insertion of such long-handled 'screw-drivers' into the chain of command rarely makes for good teamwork, but Kozlov was in no position to protest. *Stavka*'s authority was absolute. Despite his best efforts, and notwithstanding the 'encouragement' of Mekhlis and Vechny, the Crimean *Front*'s long-heralded Kerch operation to 'liquidate the enemy Feodosiya grouping' did not commence until 27 February 1942.

While much attention focused on Kerch and Feodosiya, LIV Corps (22nd, 24th, 50th Infantry Divisions), two regiments of the 72nd Infantry Division and the 1st Romanian Mountain Brigade, continued to man their lines around Sevastopol. Equally, the Soviet defenders (estimated by the Germans as seven rifle divisions, a dismounted cavalry division and three naval infantry brigades) had 'ringed their city with an iron wall'.[85] Petrov's men did all in their power to make life as difficult and dangerous as possible for their opponents. Sevastopol's defences prior to the December 1941 attack had been strengthened considerably by the incorporation of new coastal defence artillery batteries, primarily utilising recovered 130mm naval guns, which could engage inland targets (see Table 13.2 overleaf). Although many of the guns' barrels had been worn out by intensive firing, particularly during December 1941, the Soviet gunners managed to replace these. Thus the weight of artillery fire on the Germans and Romanians was scarcely diminished in 1942.

Apart from the daily disruptive and often deadly shelling, a particularly feared threat came from the band of expert Soviet snipers. These skilled observers, scouts and crack shots picked off many hundreds of careless Axis officers and soldiers going about their duties. One of the most famous sharpshooters, who distinguished herself

Battery No.	Location	No. of Guns and Calibre (mm)	Remarks
19	State Farm No. 10	2 x 130	Additional two guns mounted at Cape Balaklava.
701/111	Malakhov Hill	2 x 130	Eastern suburb of Sevastopol.
702/112	Camp of the Coastal Defence Naval Academy	2 x 130	
703/113	English Cemetery	2 x 130	To the south-east of Sevastopol towards the Sapun escarpment.
704/114	Dergachi village	2 x 130	
705/115	Mekenzievy Gory station	2 x 100	
		2 x 130	
706/116	Dacha Maksimovicha	2 x 130	
2 bis	Cape Constantine	2 x 100	Additional two guns mounted.

Table 13.2 – Sevastopol's Additional Coastal Defence Batteries[86]

at both Odessa and Sevastopol, was a woman. On 6 April 1942, Senior Sergeant Lyudmila Mikhailovna Pavlichenko was awarded a diploma by the Military Council of the Red Army recognising her achievement in 'exterminating 157 German Fascist invaders'.[87] Her final tally was 309. Wounded by mortar fire in June 1942, she was withdrawn from any further combat and awarded as a Heroine of the Soviet Union. Unsurprisingly, much was made of her extraordinary achievement – she was sent on publicity tours to the United Kingdom and the United States of America.[88] She retired as a major and returned to academic life after the war.

During the period February–May 1942, the main locus of the various Soviet offensives and the German counter-attacks on Crimea remained the Kerch peninsula. Until the middle of April, the Crimean *Front* held the initiative. Its commanders squandered their numerical advantage recklessly and wastefully by launching a series of poorly planned and co-ordinated attacks. The Eleventh Army, which was progressively reinforced, managed to repel these with relative ease. On 8 May 1942 Manstein's forces attacked, annihilating the Crimean *Front* and recapturing the Kerch peninsula in a spectacular operation. This German success paved the way for the final assault on Sevastopol, which followed in June. On several occasions, however, the prospects for any Axis victory on Crimea looked remote as the Soviet superiority in numbers, particularly on the Kerch peninsula, was brought to bear.

The Crimean *Front*'s original plan for its February operation involved two armies (the 51st and the 44th) attacking towards the river Biyuk Karasu and Stary Krym respectively in a first operational echelon. The 47th Army, commanded by Major General K. S. Kolganov, ferried over from the North Caucasus was held in the second echelon as a *front* mobile group. Envisaging the complete defeat of Manstein's army, the latter force had been allocated a number of tasks, of which the most ambitious was to 'cut the withdrawal routes of the enemy Crimean grouping with an attack towards Dzhankoy'. By the time planning was completed, however, the operation had been scaled back to 'encircle and destroy the enemy Feodosiya grouping' with more limited army objectives in time and space. When fully concentrated by the end of February, the *front* comprised eleven rifle and cavalry divisions, three rifle brigades, a tank brigade, a motorcycle and a motorised rifle regiment, together with reserve tank and artillery regiments. Soviet sources suggest that the attackers enjoyed a 'two-fold superiority over their opponents in troops and artillery and [an] absolute superiority in tanks', based on Manstein fielding 'five infantry divisions', together with 'three Romanian brigades'.[89] In fact, the Eleventh Army had managed to assemble three German divisions (the 46th, 132nd and the 170th), the Romanian 18th Infantry Division, a Romanian brigade, and the separate German 213rd Infantry Regiment.

Despite the time taken to prepare its offensive, the Crimean *Front* failed to make much initial impression on the Eleventh Army's defences, although the 18th Romanian Division suffered heavy casualties. In support, the Coastal Army in Sevastopol mounted a series of thirty-five attacks over the period 27 February – 2 March, of which 'eleven were at least regimental strength'. Although the 22nd and 24th Divisions were hard hit, the German defences held here as well. Back on the Kerch peninsula, the poor weather (often cited as being militarily advantageous to Soviet forces), as much as indifferent leadership, disrupted Koslov's plans. At 2340 hours on 2 March 1942, he reported pessimistically:

> As a result of the impassable roads and the impossibility of operating off the roads with tanks and infantry, I have decided to halt the offensive temporarily along the lines we have achieved in readiness to resume a decisive offensive once the ground becomes trafficable.[90]

Such a lack of progress and negativity did not go down well with Stalin, whose displeasure was relayed by his *Stavka* colleague Vasilevsky. On behalf of the Soviet leader, he accused Kozlov of failing to employ skilfully the 'supporting rocket artillery, mortars, artillery, tanks and aviation'. None the less, Kozlov's recommendation was accepted and the offensive was 'paused' accordingly on 3 March. Astonishingly, Kozlov kept his post, but his *front* chief of staff, Major General Fyodor Ivanovich Tolbukhin was scapegoated for the highlighted deficiencies.[91] Mekhlis's hands were all over this dismissal. Disastrously for

Kozlov, he lost the trusted general staff officer and gained the suspect Vechny in place as his chief of staff. From now on, the scheming Mekhlis exercised undue power in the *front* headquarters. His misguided influence would contribute considerably to the unfolding catastrophe.

Although the Coastal Army attacked the German line held by the 24th Division at Sevastopol on 6 March, the Crimean *Front*'s offensive on the Eleventh Army's Parpach position did not resume until 13 March. Such a lack of synchronisation typified the Soviet planning of the period. Slowly but surely, however, the weight of Soviet numbers began to push in the northern sector held by XXXXII Corps; it looked for a time that Kozlov would finally achieve his long-awaited success. Manstein's troops were becoming tired, and the Romanians (on which the Soviets applied the maximum pressure) were near to breaking. He urgently requested reinforcements – two panzer divisions and stronger air support – from Army Group South not only to hold his positions, but also then to go over to the offensive. Help, meantime, was already on the way. The German high command had already released the newly formed 22nd Panzer and the 28th Light Infantry Divisions. Manstein was allocated these formations in mid-March on the strict proviso that they were only to be employed in the case of an absolute emergency. These circumstances pertained sooner than anticipated. Although the first counter-attack mounted by the 22nd Panzer Division under the command of Major General Wilhelm von Apell proved disappointing, which Manstein put down to a lack of training, it did manage to disrupt an imminent Soviet attack. By this time, the offensive power of the Crimean *Front* was steadily diminishing. Manstein noted with satisfaction that when the next major blow arrived on 26 March, only four Red Army divisions were employed.[92]

The final Crimean *Front* attack was launched on 9 April 1942. It soon culminated, having made little progress. By the 11th, it was clear that the reinforced German and Romanian defences would hold firm and the operation was called off. By the 15th, the Soviet forces had retired to their initial positions. Kozlov's losses were staggering. According to Glantz's reckoning, these were 'more than 40 per cent of the *front*'s personnel, 52 per cent of its tanks, and 25 per cent of its artillery'. In the four-month period 1 January – 30 April, the total *front* losses amounted to 352,000 men. What had gone so disastrously wrong? Critics of the *front*'s performance highlight many factors, including: poor intelligence; inadequate training; very weak combined arms integration (requiring the close co-operation of infantry, armour and artillery); and not least a failure to exploit the considerable fire support available from the Black Sea Fleet and its Azov Flotilla.[93] Setting aside the failures of Soviet leadership, the net result of the Crimean *Front*'s offensive operations was a severely damaged, disorganised and demoralised force, highly vulnerable to attack. With the failure of the Crimean

Front to make any serious headway, burning itself out in the process, the operational initiative passed to Manstein and his Eleventh Army.

OPERATION BUSTARD HUNT (8–19 MAY 1942)

Manstein's operation to recapture the Kerch peninsula must be seen in its wider context. Hitler's plans for 1942, described in Directive No. 41 of 5 April 1942, foresaw the capture of Leningrad in the north, holding in the centre and concentrating all available forces in the south to secure the economically important oilfields of the Caucasus.[94] The latter represented the primary strategic objective of Operation BLUE. An essential prerequisite of the German summer offensive was the completion of the conquest of Crimea, including the elimination of Soviet forces on the Kerch peninsula and the long-awaited capture of Sevastopol. Having considered the sequencing of these tasks, Manstein concluded that the enemy forces on the Kerch peninsula should be given 'no time to recover from his abortive attacks'.[95] Thus the elimination of the enemy grouping on the peninsula must take priority – the assault on Sevastopol would have to follow.

In designing and conducting the operation, which was to be nicknamed TRAPPEN-JAGD (BUSTARD HUNT), Manstein's difficulties, as ever, largely centred on his deficiencies in resources. Although seriously weakened, Kozlov's Crimean *Front* remained a force to be reckoned with, and was observed to be building up its defences. The Eleventh Army's intelligence staff estimated that the enemy grouping comprised no fewer than seventeen rifle divisions, three rifle brigades, two cavalry divisions and four tank brigades. Therefore Manstein needed to assemble the maximum land and air force available in order to deliver a sufficiently hard knockout blow to conclude the operation as expeditiously as possible. To generate sufficient mass, he needed to rebalance his forces. At his disposal were seven German infantry divisions and a separate infantry regiment, together with the 22nd Panzer Division, although the latter's availability was limited. At least four infantry divisions would be required to hold the half-ring around Sevastopol. In addition to the German 22nd, 24th and 72nd Infantry Divisions deployed here were the 1st and 4th Romanian Mountain Brigades, which had both been designated as 'divisions'. Although these 'new' formations received some additional artillery, their infantry strength remained unchanged. Manstein sent the 18th Romanian Infantry Division to Sevastopol to release his 50th Infantry Division for employment on Operation BUSTARD HUNT. Also made available was the 105th Infantry Regiment released from the 72nd Division.

Once again the Romanians provided reinforcements. VII Corps, commanded by Major General Florea Mitranescu, comprised the 10th and 19th Infantry Divisions, together with the 8th Cavalry Brigade (to be retitled as a division).

Even having assembled all available forces, the Eleventh Army was still outnumbered by at least two to one for its attack, representing a complete inversion of the normal planning assumptions for such an operation. Three significant force multipliers were employed to offset this numerical disadvantage. First, surprise as to the timing, axis, speed and strength of the attack; secondly, the concentrated air power of VIII Air Corps commanded by Colonel General Wolfram, Baron von Richthofen, and particularly its specialist *Stuka* groups; thirdly, the shock effect of armour and mechanised troops. In addition to the 22nd Panzer Division, which had undergone some much-needed combined arms training since its disappointing performance on 20 March, Manstein assembled a further mobile force, a motorised brigade commanded by Colonel Karl-Albrecht Groddeck. This *ad hoc* formation, approaching a division in strength, comprised two groups: 'Kornu' and 'Müller'. German reconnaissance, infantry, artillery, assault gun, anti-tank, anti-aircraft and engineer units reinforced the former, based on the Romanian 3rd Cavalry Regiment. The latter, formed around the truck-mounted 401st Infantry Regiment, was similarly reinforced to make it a combined arms battlegroup.

Headquarters Eleventh Army's orders of 30 April 1942 for the Kerch operation represent a model of brevity and clarity. Manstein's intent encapsulated his shrewd operational idea, which played as much on Kozlov's inability to envisage such an attack as on the imbalance of the Soviet dispositions:

> The Army attacks on X-Day at Y-hour to recapture the Kerch peninsula. The first objective, following breaking through the Parpatsch position in the sector Black Sea – Parpatsch, is the encirclement and destruction of the strong enemy forces facing the front of XXXXII A.K. through envelopment from the south, and later the east. At the same time, this operation is to be protected offensively from enemy reserves [attacking] from the east, thereby initiating the thrust towards the final objective, Kerch.[96]

The supporting scheme of manoeuvre contained an important element of deception. It rested on holding (but portraying this action as preparing for a major attack) in the north of the Parpach isthmus against the 'bulge' of the Soviet forward line – the only tangible legacy of the Crimean *Front*'s successive attacks since the end of February – while developing a powerful strike in the south (the real main effort) with XXX Corps against three divisions of the 44th Army. Once this corps had penetrated the Soviet forward defences, it would be reinforced with the 22nd Panzer Division. This formation would be turned north-eastwards to envelop the northern enemy grouping (the 51st Army, together with elements of both the 44th and 47th Armies) contained within the 'bulge'. When this manoeuvre had been achieved, then the remainder of Eleventh Army, including German and Romanian formations held ready in the centre and northern sectors, would join the attack to complete the destruction of the enemy's forward units. Meanwhile, on the extreme right-hand (southern) flank, Groddeck's brigade would strike due east to pursue and cut off any Soviet forces retreating towards Kerch.

Unwittingly, Kozlov, under the pernicious influence of Mekhlis, played into Manstein's hands by not developing a well prepared, deeply echeloned defence (a mistake significantly not repeated by the Soviet command at the battle of Kursk in July 1943). The formations of the Crimean *Front* were packed too far forward, held ready to mount an attack rather than to parry one. In breach of common sense, let alone tactical doctrine, no central armoured reserve or mobile group was held ready either to block any German penetration or to counter-attack. The 47th Army, although concentrated close behind the 51st Army, was neither configured nor prepared for this range of tasks.

Manstein deployed his forces as follows. The Romanian VII Corps with the 19th Infantry Division forward and the 10th in the rear, held the northern-most sector. In the centre, Mattenklott's XXXXII Corps had placed two divisions in the front, the 170th left and the 46th right. The 170th Infantry Division and the 132nd Infantry Regiment were warned off to redeploy to join XXX Corps, commanded by Lieutenant General Maximilian Fretter-Pico, when the attack was under way. This corps, deployed on the southern flank, comprised the 50th, 28th Light and 132nd Infantry Divisions. These formations were required to breach the 44th Army's defences, so enabling the passage and manoeuvre of the 22nd Panzer Division when released by Headquarters Eleventh Army.

It is a measure of the operational surprise scored by Manstein's offensive on 8 May 1942 that on receiving reports of its opening, Oktyabrsky recorded it was 'strange, but true that the enemy has gone over to the attack on the Kerch peninsula'. His consternation and dismay became all too apparent the following day when he noted 'our troops are running away ... despite a numerical advantage of 5:1'.[97] The Eleventh Army had achieved a significant penetration of the 44th Army's position on the first day of the offensive. Lieutenant General Johann Sinnhuber's 28th Light Division had made particularly good progress, attacking on a narrow front in a north-easterly direction towards the settlement of Arma Eli (now Batalnoye). To its right, the 132nd Division likewise struck hard into, and through, the brittle Soviet defences. Recognising that this success should be exploited expeditiously, at 1000 hours on the morning of the 9th, Fretter-Peco recommended that the 22nd Panzer Division should be unleashed. Headquarters Eleventh Army released it at 1400 hours. That afternoon, having moved through the 132nd Division's zone of attack, von Apell's formation slipped around to the right (east) of the 28th Light Division and slickly attacked off the line of march. Co-operating closely together, both divisions gained the heights north of Arma Eli, beating off local Soviet armoured counter-attacks in the process. Now heading due north, if both formations could continue their advance at same pace, there was every chance of enveloping the main enemy grouping. During the late afternoon, however, the weather broke suddenly. Heavy rainstorms prevented any further vehicle movement across most of the front for the rest of day. The only exception was Groddeck's brigade that was able to start its move east.

When the weather cleared on the morning of the 10th, the German attack resumed. To the left (west) of the 22nd Panzer and 28th Light Divisions, the 50th Infantry Division caught up. Now three German divisions wheeled north together. This manoeuvre proved to be the decisive act of the whole operation. Cutting the Dzhankoy–Kerch railway line, then battling Soviet tank units centred on Oguz Tobe (north-east of the village of Semisotka), the 22nd Panzer Division reached the shore of the Sea of Azov by the evening of the 11th. With XXXXII Corps attacking eastwards that same day, the main Soviet force had been encircled. The Eleventh Army consolidated its impressive gains on the 12th, defeating numerous enemy attempts to break out of the pocket.

In Sevastopol, an exasperated Oktyabrsky, if not Kozlov much nearer to the action, recognised the magnitude of the unfolding crisis. On 12 May he noted 'discomforting news from the Crimean *Front*. Enemy is advancing while our troops withdraw towards the Tatar Ditch. This could turn out to be a real disaster, if not worse'.[98] And so it turned out. In the face of Manstein's manoeuvre, the *front*'s high command proved powerless to respond. The attack had caught them completely off-balance and unprepared, both physically and psychologically. Confirming the old military maxim that a mistake in initial deployment cannot easily be corrected once battle is joined, the *front* was now condemned to destruction in detail.[99] While their soldiers fought and died in their tens of thousands in countless tactical engagements, there would be no redemption for the elementary mistakes made at the *front*'s command level by the incompetent trio of Kozlov, Mekhlis and Vechny.

The pursuit phase of BUSTARD HUNT commenced on 13 May. To effect this, both German corps were reorganised efficiently. In the north, XXXXII Corps advanced eastwards with the 19th Romanian Infantry Division working along the northern coast, and with the 46th and 28th Divisions striking either side of the Kerch railway line towards the Tatar Ditch. None of these formations met any determined resistance. To the south, in XXX Corps, the 170th and 132nd Divisions made similar progress, with the 22nd Panzer Division changing axis to advance rapidly to the south-east in an effort to cut off withdrawing Soviet units. In the extreme south, the Groddeck Brigade continued its drive. By the morning of 14th May, the advancing Romanian and German formations had crossed the

Tatar Ditch, which, in a similar manner to November 1941, had not been robustly defended. The path was now clear for the Eleventh Army's final push towards the city of Kerch and the clearance of the peninsula. Judging that he had more than sufficient forces available to conclude BUSTARD HUNT successfully, on 14 May Manstein pulled the 50th Division out of the attack and placed it on the march back to Sevastopol. These hardened German infantrymen – the *Landser* – received neither rest nor respite.

The capture of Kerch by the 170th Division and the 213rd Infantry Regiment on 16 May did not complete BUSTARD HUNT. Manstein's forces continued to mop up the enemy in the easternmost part of the peninsula until the 19th, defeating miscellaneous pockets of determined Soviet forces. A few hundreds of men, who hid in the subterranean Adzhimushkay quarries near Kerch, fought on until the end of October 1942.

Oktyabrsky was mystified by the course of the battle, even before it concluded. 'How could this have come about', he pondered on 14 May. 'Do the Germans have a new, secret weapon? How could a single German-Romanian army of seven-eight divisions destroy three armies of eighteen–twenty divisions?'[100] The answers to these questions lay in the wide gaps in the competence of commanders, and associated differentials in fighting power, between the Axis and Soviet forces. By 17 May, Oktyabrsky concluded the main reasons for the rout of the Crimean *Front*, 'a terrible defeat', lay in: 'panic ... and loss of direction; carelessness and the resulting lack of defence in depth; and the decision to evacuate rather than organise a defence [at Kerch]'.[101] His stark assessment was surely valid.

Following the Second World War, this disastrous, highly embarrassing episode on the Kerch peninsula, sandwiched between the successful battle of Moscow and the ultimately doomed, but none the less 'heroic', defence of Sevastopol, tended to be neglected by Soviet military historians. There were exceptions. Karpov, for one, was not afraid to praise Manstein's imaginative approach and successful concept of operations, which, in his view, rested on:

> First, the factor of surprise. Confident of its superior strength, the Commander of the Crimean Front did not believe in the possibility of [an] attack on the part of the Germans who had much smaller forces here. Second, ... Manstein ... using an armoured division against the advanced positions of one of the Soviet armies ... ruptured the entire system of Soviet defences as far as the Sea of Azov. Third, Manstein took advantage not only of the surprise factor but also of the manoeuvrability of his troops and their efficient control.[102]

In addition, it must be stressed that Manstein had managed to deceive Kozlov as to where his main blow would land, and furthermore, directed it at the weakest part of the Crimean *Front*'s defences – against the formations of the 44th Army positioned between the Black Sea and Parpach.

War contains its own peculiar paradoxes. Manstein described Operation BUSTARD HUNT as a 'true battle of annihilation', which 'had been fought to the finish'. The relative ease of its success (170,000 prisoners, 1,133 guns and 258 tanks captured), however, did not provide any reliable indication as to how the battle for Sevastopol would develop.[103] The third and final assault on the city would witness a much more effective and better-led Soviet defence. In the meantime, many of the senior officers of the vanquished Crimean *Front* were punished. Despite his closeness to Stalin, Mekhlis could not escape demotion and removal from his post as Deputy Commissar for Defence. Kozlov was dismissed and demoted by one rank; Vechny went at the same time. Chernyak was relieved on 29 May 1942: he along with his fellow army commander, Kolganov, and Major General Nikolayenko, the *front* air commander, were all reduced to the rank of colonel.[104] Lieutenant General Lvov of the 51st Army had escaped such ignominy by being killed in action on 11 May 1942 as a result of a German air attack.

Manstein had already been promoted to colonel general on 7 March 1942. He now faced one of the greatest tests of his career: the assault and capture of Sevastopol – a city that had defied two previous attacks. Success would earn him his field marshal's baton: cometh the hour, cometh the man?

CHAPTER 14

THE END OF THE SECOND DEFENCE AND AXIS OCCUPATION

'Inspired by the heroic example of the Sevastopol people, our Red Army and Navy will deliver more destructive blows against the plundering Fascist Armies.'

Vice Admiral F. S. Oktyabrsky[1]

OPERATION STURGEON CATCH (2 JUNE – 4 JULY 1942): PLANNING AND PREPARATIONS

Following his spectacular success on the Kerch peninsula, a mopping up operation in Hitler's eyes, Manstein could now concentrate on capturing the fortress of Sevastopol. Speed was of the essence as the opening of the main German summer offensive, Operation BLUE, depended on the timely conclusion of operations on Crimea. Only then, in accordance with Führer Directive No. 41 of 5 April 1942, could all available forces be concentrated in the southern sector of the Eastern Front 'with the aim of destroying the enemy before the Don, in order to secure the Caucasian oilfields and the passes through the mountains themselves'.[2] Furthermore, following the fall of Sevastopol the German high command

505

intended that Manstein's Eleventh Army would cross the Straits of Kerch to the Kuban peninsula and 'intercept the enemy forces falling back on the Caucasus from the lower Don'.[3] Therefore, in addition to the imperative of speed, Manstein needed to conduct his attack economically with this future task in mind. Conversely, the Soviet defenders of Sevastopol would perform their duty in thwarting this grand German operational design by prolonging the siege of the city for as long as possible, and in inflicting the maximum number of casualties on their foes.

Bearing in mind his previous two attempts to storm Sevastopol had ended in failure, Manstein had ample reason to deliberate carefully on his plan of attack. He understood that the defenders of the city had used the first half of 1942 to strengthen their fortifications. There was little prospect of achieving more than local surprise. As his forces for the attack were already 'given' (one Romanian and seven German infantry divisions, together with a Romanian mountain division), his two main planning considerations were of time and space: when and where to mount the assault on the city?

Headquarters Eleventh Army's preliminary orders for Operation STURGEON CATCH, the third German assault on Sevastopol, issued on 14 May 1942, required that the initial main attack on the fortress area would again be conducted in the north (see Map 15). As in December 1941, Manstein wished to clear the enemy defences on the northern side of Sevastopol Bay prior to launching an attack on the city. In his memoirs, Manstein justified this apparently unimaginative approach on purely practical grounds:

> ... although the enemy fortifications were undoubtedly stronger and more numerous in the northern area of the fortress ... than in the southern part, the going there was far easier. Above all, the artillery and the Luftwaffe could be used to infinitely greater effect in the north than in the hilly country of the southern sector.[4]

The decision as to when and where to launch a subsequent attack against the 'inner fortress ring and the town of Sevastopol' was reserved for later, dependent on how the situation developed. 'Fundamental to the conduct' of the assault, the orders stressed, was the 'closest concentration in time and place of the artillery and air force action'. Instead of the snap, surprise bombardment of only three minutes that had proved ineffective in December 1941, Manstein planned on no fewer than five days of artillery preparation and intense air attacks before the offensive would be launched.

As Manstein and his subordinate commanders planned their forthcoming offensive, Petrov and his troops prepared to meet it as best they could. From a Soviet perspective, all was not well in Sevastopol. Although the city's fortifications had been developed, *Stavka* and the Caucasus *Front* had concentrated their resources on the Kerch–Feodosiya operation, and in the subsequent attempts to break out of, and then hold, the Kerch peninsula. As a result, Sevastopol had only received a trickle of the much-needed reinforcements, weapons and munitions. Karpov estimated that Soviet units were at a 'maximum of fifty per cent strength'; there were insufficient rifles for the men and not enough ammunition for the artillery. Making matters worse, the Luftwaffe enjoyed air superiority over the Black Sea that imperilled resupply by ship. Yet Oktyabrsky and Petrov played their limited cards carefully. Before the German attack struck, Petrov redeployed Laskin's 172nd Rifle Division from the Second to the Fourth Sector on the northern side of Sevastopol Bay, where he perceived – correctly – the main German blow would land.[5] The deployment of Soviet forces over a defensive frontage of 34 kilometres is shown in Table 14.1 below.

Sector	Frontage	Main Defence Forces	Sector Reserve	Commander
I	7.5km	109th Rifle Division. (456th, 381st and 602nd Rifle Regiments).	773rd Rifle Regiment, 388th Rifle Division.	Major General P. G. Novikov
II	12km	Two battalions, 7th Naval Infantry Brigade. 386th Rifle Division (769th, 775th and 772nd Rifle Regiments) 8th Naval Infantry Brigade.	One battalion, 775th Rifle Regiment.	Colonel N. F. Skutelnik
III	8.5km	3rd Naval Infantry Regiment. 25th Rifle Division (54th, 31st and 287th Rifle Regiments) 2nd Perekop Regiment. 79th Naval Infantry Brigade.	Two battalions, 2nd Perekop Regiment.	Major General T. K. Kolomiyets
IV	6km	172nd Rifle Division (747th and 514th Rifle Regiments) 95th Rifle Division (90th and 161st Rifle Regiments)	214th Rifle Regiment.	Colonel A. G. Kapitokhin (later Colonel I. A. Laskin)
General Reserve, also Guarding the Coast of the Chersonese Peninsula				
		388th Rifle Division (less 773rd Rifle Regiment). Three Battalions, 7th Naval Infantry Brigade. 345th Rifle Division. 383rd Rifle Regiment. 9th Naval Infantry Brigade. 81st and 125th Independent Tank Battalions.		

Table 14.1 – The Deployment of Soviet Forces at Sevastopol, 1 June 1942[6]

In addition, over the period of 13–17 June, the 138th Separate Rifle Brigade, together with over 6,000 individual battle casualty replacements, arrived in Sevastopol to reinforce the hard-pressed garrison.

Within Manstein's concept of operations, Hansen's LIV Corps (comprising the 22nd, 24th, 50th and 132nd Infantry Divisions, commanded by Generals Ludwig Wolff, Baron Hans von Tettau, Friedrich Schmidt and Fritz Lindemann respectively), together with the reinforced 213th Infantry Regiment, was tasked to conduct the main attack in the north. Its mission was to clear the enemy defences as far south as the shore of Sevastopol Bay and to seize the Gaytany (Inkerman) Heights at the eastern end of the roadstead. To its east and south came Major General Gheorghe Avramescu's Romanian Mountain Corps with the 18th Infantry and 1st Mountain Divisions. The Romanians received the limited tasks of fixing the enemy to their front and of supporting the attacks of the German neighbouring divisions on both flanks. Fretter-Pico's XXX Corps (the 72nd and 170th Infantry, and the 28th Light Divisions, commanded by Generals Philipp Müller-Gebhard, Erwin Sander and Johann Sinnhuber), was required to capture the enemy's forward zone of defences, including the strongpoints of Kamara and Chapel Mount, so securing a line of departure for a subsequent attack on the Sapun escarpment. In addition, the threat on the corps' left flank from the Balaklava Heights had to be eliminated.

Contrary to Soviet claims that the Axis forces employed no fewer than 450 tanks, including 300 of the 22nd Panzer Division, Manstein had been forced to hand back to Army Group South the bulk of this formation following the recovery of the Kerch peninsula. The sole remaining tank battalion of its armoured regiment (the 204th), which remained in Crimea, was not initially included in the attack on Sevastopol. Thus apart from a company of captured Soviet tanks (*Beutepanzer*), the only armoured support originally made ready for the offensive was provided by three detachments (battalion equivalents) of assault guns. LIV Corps was allocated two of these units; XXX Corps only one.[7] In addition, Panzer-Abteilung 300 operated *Goliath* radio-controlled tracked land mines, which carried a high-explosive demolition charge used to destroy bunkers.[8]

THE AXIS PRELIMINARY AIR AND ARTILLERY BOMBARDMENT, 2–6 JUNE 1942

Manstein managed to amass the heaviest concentration of German artillery ever achieved during the entire course of the Second World War, as summarised in Table 14.2.

Axis Zone of Attack	Guns and Heavy Mortars				
	Light	Heavy[9]	Heaviest (excepting Karl and Dora)	Total	Percentage
North	154	114	46	314	51
Middle	57	65	-	122	20
South	95	78	2	175	29
Totals	306	257	48	611	
Rocket Launchers (Nebeltruppe)					
Formation	10.5cm	15cm	28/32cm	Total	Percentage
North Corps	22	216	318	556	74
South Corps	-	96	102	198	26
Totals	22	312	420	754	

Table 14.2 – Axis Artillery at the Sevastopol Front, 6 June 1942[10]

In addition to the 'normal' artillery guns and mortars, Eleventh Army employed a number of 'specials'. These included the super-heavy 600mm Karl howitzers and the enormous 800mm Dora gun. The latter, firing giant 7-tonne shells, originally designed for the breaching of the Maginot Line, was first employed at Sevastopol. While Manstein described this 'monster' weapon as a 'miracle of technical achievement', he considered that the 'effectiveness of the cannon bore no real relation to all the effort and expense that had gone into making it'.[11]

Although the numbers of guns, mortars and rocket launchers look impressive, in contrast to its opponents, whether American, British or Soviet, the artillery was the weakest arm of the German Army. Manstein himself conceded that the Axis artillery employed at Sevastopol in June 1942 was 'trifling ... when compared to the masses of guns later considered indispensible by the Russians for a breakthrough in open country'.[12] In comparison with the seventeen Axis guns per kilometre of front at Sevastopol, Soviet tube densities would routinely exceed this density by tenfold and more later in the war. Germany would pay the price for a misplaced faith in the mobility of its armoured forces in fighting a battle of manoeuvre while paying insufficient attention to the requirement for mass artillery.

Overwhelming German strength, however, was very much evident in the skies above Sevastopol. Richthofen's VIII Air Corps supplied an unprecedented amount of air support to Eleventh Army. It also provided a division of air defence artillery (*Flak*) used in the ground role. According to its orders, the Air Corps mission was to 'destroy the morale of the defenders of Sevastopol, and specifically enemy reserves, artillery positions, fortified positions, and command posts throughout the whole enemy territory'. To achieve this bombardment, 'active enemy anti-aircraft batteries and enemy aircraft' were to be 'completely wiped out'. The city of Sevastopol was to be destroyed by rolling attacks throughout the course of the day from 0700 to 1900 hours.[13] Priority targets included the harbour, logistic installations and airfields. Altogether, about 600 aircraft from Stuka-Geschwader 77 and Kampf-Geschwader 51, 76 and 100 were allocated for the air operation.[14] In contrast, Soviet sources state that there were only 116 aircraft available for the defence of Sevastopol.[15] Hence the air battle over Sevastopol proved to be an unequal contest from the outset.

On the evening of 1 June 1942, Oktyabrsky recorded in his diary a radio report of the British bombing of the German city of Cologne, the first raid of the war involving more than 1,000 aircraft.[16] Although Sevastopol had been bombed regularly during the siege, and not least in recent days, little did he imagine that the morning would bring such destruction much closer to home. Colonel Ivan Laskin, who would assume command of the Fourth Sector, recalled the opening of the air and artillery bombardment on 2 June:

> A whirlwind of fire was raging round all our positions. The sky grew dim because of the explosions of thousands of bombs and shells. The aircraft were still coming in – one wave after another – and the bombs were falling incessantly. Enormous lumps of ground and uprooted trees were flying up. Over a thousand guns and mortars were bringing down fire ... and in addition over a hundred bombers were attacking. An immense cloud of dark-grey smoke and dust was rising higher and higher until it screened the sun. The sunny day turned bleak and gloomy as during a solar eclipse.[17]

Yet the casualties amongst the Soviet defenders remained remarkably light. Karpov recounted a revealing exchange between Petrov and Major General T. K. Kolomiyets, commander of the 25th (Chapayev) Rifle Division in the Third Sector, about the losses involved. The latter reported: 'Matusevich has three killed and two wounded soldiers. Antipenko has three wounded'. In view of the intensity of the bombardment, Petrov expressed his doubts about these low numbers, snapping back: 'Is that so? ... Is your information correct?'. After a brief silence, Kolomiyets responded, 'I would not dare to deceive you'. As a rule, Red Army commanders tended to follow Lenin's famous maxim, 'trust is good, but control is better'.[18] Consequently, Petrov verified the numbers of casualties brought into the field hospital by phoning the chief of the Medical Service. As Karpov observed:

> It turned out that during 4 June [1942], in that [bombardment], the hospital admitted only 178 casualties. This information confirmed the reports of the sector commanders. Thus was justified the many months' work of the defenders of Sevastopol, who had created an effective trench system. It now prevented heavy losses from such an unprecedented firestorm.

Although the defenders of Sevastopol had got away comparatively lightly during the first days of the bombardment, the city had not. The fine streets that ran down to the sea were quickly reduced to rubble.[19]

On 4 June, Oktyabrsky recorded some welcome news. At 0200 hours, the cruiser *Krasny Krym* and the destroyer *Soobrazitelny* made it into Sevastopol, bringing 2,600 reinforcements and considerable quantities of munitions. 'The remarkable thing', he remarked, 'is that we've received weapons'. Therefore 'we can now arm the naval infantry regiments and brigades'. After unloading, the two warships took aboard '2,000 women, children, evacuees and many wounded' and quit the main base. During the course of this one day, the Germans flew '400 sorties and dropped over 2,000 bombs', including 'many incendiaries'.[20] During the early hours of the 6th, the destroyer leader *Tashkent* and the destroyer 'BT' (*Bditelniy*) slipped into Sevastopol harbour, unloaded and departed with an undisclosed number of wounded and evacuees (mainly women and children). Soviet forces also used the short period of summer darkness to attack. Oktyabrsky noted that 'our aviation has been bombing the enemy all night, mainly his front line, rear areas and reserves'.[21]

Sevastopol's air defences by day were overwhelmed by force of numbers: the city and its population suffered grievously as a result. Boris Voyetekhov, a Moscow-based Soviet playwright and war correspondent who witnessed the final weeks of the siege, recorded the devastating effects of the Axis bombardment. 'The Luftwaffe', he wrote, 'had divided the city into sections for the purpose of bombing, and systematically reduced each in turn, smashing block after block'. As a result, there was 'no place in the town where instruments of death had not prevailed. No place was safe from bombs, land mines or shellfire from the enemy's siege guns.... Theatre Square, Marine [Primorsky] Boulevard, and Grafskaya Harbour were littered with fragments of shells and bombs'. Voyetekhov alleged that defenceless townspeople were singled out. Specifically, 'enemy squadrons sought out women and children who were sheltering among the rocks while awaiting their turn to be evacuated'. Then 'powerful explosives cleft the ground and buried them in the debris beside the sea'. And 'everything that moved – cutters, cars, and motor-cycles – was pursued and attacked'.[22] Although the truth of this particular claim is unknown, such action was not isolated during the Second World War.

According to Karpov, the concentrations of German air and artillery attacks allowed Petrov to deduce that the enemy's main blow would initially land in the direction of the area defended by Laskin's 172nd Rifle Division and Potapov's 79th Naval Infantry Brigade. Petrov also anticipated a subsequent attack along the axis of the Yalta–Sevastopol highway. With this assumption in mind, on 6 June he set off for a forward observation post overlooking the defences of the

Fourth Sector, summoning the formation commanders of this sector and the neighbouring Third. Laskin recalled his superior's considerations:

> [Petrov] looked at each of us intently and asked, 'Have you noticed that the enemy's fire has been less intensive since 1000 hours? Manstein is giving his artillerymen an opportunity to make thorough preparations for a more intensive fire plan tomorrow. Based on intelligence at Army HQ, we should expect an attack tomorrow.

The commander of the Coastal Army then informed his subordinates that a decision had been made to 'conduct artillery counter-preparation in order to engage the principal enemy formations assembled in forming up places for an assault on the northern axis and along the Yalta–Sevastopol highway in the south'. Accordingly, at 0250 hours on 7 June, Sevastopol's artillerymen shelled the anticipated Axis lines of departure, hitting German and Romanian troops ten minutes before they were due to assault at 0300 hours. Although there was only sufficient ammunition for a twenty-minute fire plan, the disruption caused by the Soviet gunners was significant. According to prisoner of war reports, it had not only delayed the German attack by up to three hours, but also forced the reorganisation of units in order to make good the losses inflicted.[23]

THE INITIAL AXIS ATTACKS, 7–9 JUNE 1942

After five days of intense aerial attack and artillery preparation, the time had at last come for the Axis ground assault on Sevastopol. Manstein did not wish to miss this climactic moment, which he documented in colourful detail in his memoirs. On the evening of 6 June, together with his chief of staff, Major General Friedrich Schulz, his principal general staff officers for operations (the Ia) and intelligence (the Ic), Colonel Theodor Busse and Major Hans-Georg Eismann respectively, and his aide-de-camp, Lieutenant 'Pepo' Specht, Manstein climbed up to a specially prepared observation point. Perched on a cliff top on the southern edge of the wooded El Burun feature near his forward headquarters at the Tatar village of Yukhary Karalez (now Zalesnoye), this lofty vantage point offered him a 'gigantic spectacle' of the opening of the attack. 'As dawn turned the eastern sky to gold and swept the shadows from the valleys' on the morning of 7 June, Manstein witnessed his artillery opening up 'in its full fury by way of prelude to the infantry assault'. At the same time, 'squadrons of the Luftwaffe hurtled down on their allotted targets'.[24]

Manstein claimed the scene unfolding before him as being 'unique in modern warfare for the leader of an army to command a view of his entire battlefield'.

Perhaps he unconsciously compared himself here to Moltke the Great at the battle of Sedan on 1/2 September 1870, who from his famous *Feldherrnhügel* (commander's hill), directed Prussia's crushing defeat over the French Army under Napoleon III. Yet not only was the strategic situation now quite different, but the character and technology of war had evolved considerably over the intervening seventy years. As the following weeks of intensely attritional fighting would show, Manstein at Sevastopol could not hope to replicate Moltke's masterly triumph of manoeuvre at Sedan.

In any event, Manstein's observation post provided him with an unparalleled opportunity to survey the geography of the battle. He recalled:

> To the north-west the eye could range from the woodlands that hid the fierce battles of 54 Corps' left wing from view right over to the heights south of the Belbek valley, for which we work to fight so bitterly. Looking due west, one could see the heights of Gaytany [Inkerman], and behind them, in the far distance, the shimmer of [Sevastopol] bay where it joined the Black Sea. Even the spurs of the [Chersonese] peninsula, on which we were to find vestiges of Hellenic culture, were visible in clear weather. To the south-west there towered the menacing heights of Zapun and the rugged cliffs of the coastal range.

Significantly, Manstein not only described the strength of Sevastopol's fortifications 'embedded in steel, concrete and granite' in his account, but also talked up the qualities of his opponents. He remarked of the 'dogged resistance' of the defenders of the city, 'whose natural elements were the advantage of terrain and the tenacity and steadfastness of the Russian soldier reinforced by the iron compulsion of the Soviet system'. Yet it remained to be seen whether the skill and 'spirit of the German soldier', with all his 'courage, initiative and self-sacrifice', according to the German commander, would prevail over the brave men of the Coastal Army and the Black Sea Fleet defending their native land.[25]

The War Diary of Headquarters Eleventh Army recorded the disappointing results of the first day of battle, during which Sevastopol's spirited defenders had fought stubbornly, blunting or defeating a series of attacks:

> [We had the] impression that the enemy was in no way surprised.... The enemy fought most tenaciously across the whole battlefront. He was supported by accurate fire from his heavy coastal batteries, which could not be engaged effectively either by our artillery or Luftwaffe.... The enemy resistance is tougher than anticipated. Hoped-for objectives for the day were achieved nowhere. Enemy positions in difficult terrain are so favourable that despite the most intense artillery, rocket and air attack, they cannot be destroyed.

With typical German military frankness, the war diarist then highlighted deficiencies in the conduct of friendly force operations. 'The failure in the sector of the 1st Romanian Mountain Division', he concluded, rests 'on the inadequacy of the force and its inability to exploit immediately strong preparatory fire'. Yet the German 28th Light Division did not escape criticism either. Its lack of success could be traced to multiple causes, including 'over-hasty preparation, insufficient reconnaissance and over-tired troops'. Furthermore, even after the first day of assault, many of the divisions of Eleventh Army were experiencing shortages of ammunition. This inauspicious start indicated the enormity of the challenges faced by the attacking Axis forces. Sevastopol would prove again a very tough nut to crack.

As if Manstein were not confronting sufficient difficulties, the dead hand of the Führer soon became apparent. Although Hitler had yet to intervene in the tactical conduct of the battle, he declared that 'the attack on Sevastopol must be fought through quickly enough to allow the Luftwaffe to be freed up for other tasks as planned'. If the attack does not succeed, he stressed, then it must 'be abandoned and the fortress besieged'. This direction was duly logged at Headquarters Eleventh Army during the late afternoon of 7 June. Thus Manstein needed to make demonstrable progress at Sevastopol as fast as possible – the massive air support he was receiving from Richthofen's VIII Air Corps remained on borrowed time.[26] Within a few days, Hitler demanded of his staff a daily update on the attack, with the corresponding tactical details marked up on a large-scale 1:25,000 map.

Oktyabrsky's reaction to the first day of the offensive was remarkably succinct. 'At 1000 hours', he noted, 'it was clear that the enemy had gone over to a general attack ... and that a tough fight for Sevastopol has begun'. This third assault represented 'the decider!' All day, 'fierce battles raged across the whole front from Balaklava to Lyubimovka'.[27]

Fighting the next day proved initially just as difficult for the attackers. By the late afternoon, however, Soviet resistance began to slacken in the north. Accordingly, LIV Corps achieved some penetration, particularly in the 22nd Division's sector, whose regiments battled their way towards the Mekenzievy Gory Station. The pattern of the previous assault in December 1941 appeared to be repeating itself with the greatest inroads in the Soviet defence being made by this elite infantry formation. Meanwhile, Manstein remained acutely aware of his lack of reserves, required to sustain the momentum of the offensive. At the start of the attack, Headquarters Eleventh Army had double-counted the reconnaissance battalion of the 22nd Infantry Division as a reserve although it already had a standing task to guard the coast in the vicinity of Yevpatoriya. This unit was now fed into the all-consuming attack on Sevastopol.

Manstein desperately needed additional troops. Although his request to the German Army High Command (*Oberkommando des Heeres* (OKH)) to redeploy the 46th Division (or elements of it) from the Kerch peninsula had been denied, he was authorised to move the 4th Romanian Mountain Division towards Sevastopol. Additionally, a German armoured battalion (III./Panzer Regiment 204), equipped with Czech-designed Panzer 38 (t) tanks, guarding the Kerch peninsula, was released for eventual employment in the southern (XXX Corps) sector of attack. These units represented the first of a steady stream of Axis reinforcements fed into the cauldron of Sevastopol.

Despite the setback on the northern side, Oktyabrsky appeared remarkably content with the outcome of 8 June, recording that 'life goes on despite the fierce raids'. Ships and submarines continued to bring in the necessary supplies, including fuel. Overall, he observed, 'particularly heavy fighting went on all day'. Against the Soviet positions, the enemy 'squeezes, tears and slashes'. None the less, 'our soldiers are fighting hard and holding out against everything except in the cases of the 79th and 172nd Divisions'. That evening, Oktyabrsky ordered his forces to pull back to the third line of defence in the northern sector.[28]

Within Sevastopol the young Georgy Zadorozhnikov recalled a typical day of this period: 'A sultry and hot day started. The city lies in ruins; there are no people in sight, but the Germans keep on bombarding'. During the final weeks of the battle for the city, life for the population became increasingly difficult. 'There has been no electricity for a long time; the water supply has disappeared ... we now use sea water. We are trying to boil and filter it in order to make it drinkable ... but it still keeps its disgusting nauseating taste'.[29]

On 9 June, both sides still contested Sevastopol's outer line of defence. German air strikes and artillery bombardments continued to soften up Soviet positions and attempted to neutralise, if not destroy, the very troublesome enemy coastal artillery. A significant success had already been achieved before the ground assault. As Oktyabrsky noted on 6 June, one of the turrets of Coastal Battery No. 30 had been put out of action. It had taken a direct hit through the roof from one of the Germans' giant 600mm Thor mortars. Such was the effectiveness of the heavy coastal guns in breaking up the German attacks, Soviet repair teams worked feverishly to keep the remaining turret firing.[30]

As the Axis attacks continued with undiminished intensity, the incremental pressure on the defenders of Sevastopol mounted. 'All day, the fiercest battles have raged', Oktyabrsky commented on the 9th. Specifically, the '79th [Naval Infantry] Brigade has mainly held its line [while] the 345th [Rifle] Division has fought heroically all day'. Yet the four divisions of Hansen's LIV Corps steadily inched their way towards the northern side of Sevastopol Bay. The commander of the Black Sea Fleet noted laconically that the 'Mekenzievy Gory station has changed hands three times. By evening our troops were on the southern edge of the station and the enemy on the northern.' That night, Oktyabrsky received a timely fillip to morale: 'greetings and hopes for victory ... from all the other fleets: Baltic, Northern, Amur and Pacific'.[31] Yet rather than the good wishes, however well intended, he needed many more men and weapons to hold his main base.

On the other side of the battle lines, Manstein grew increasingly concerned about Eleventh Army's failure to make a significant impression on Sevastopol's defences. Finding fault with the tactics employed thus far, on 8 June he issued orders requiring more effective integration of combat arms on the battlefield. He observed that 'the effect of concentrated artillery fire and air power' was not being 'immediately and fully exploited'. Accepting that the enemy's flanking fire and the difficulties of the terrain impeded the infantry regiments' assaults, he directed that a series of corrective measures be adopted. These included ensuring more concentrated artillery fire to either neutralise or destroy enemy objectives, more effective counter-battery fire, and not least the better combat reconnaissance of mines.[32] The mine problem on the northern front (LIV Corps) caused particular concern. According to a report compiled by the Eleventh Army's chief engineer, Major General Gustav Boehringer, while Russian mines were 'spread across the whole terrain', minefields as such were 'less common'. In the first four days of the ground attack, the army suffered 153 mine casualties – not a great number overall, but it required two-thirds of all combat engineer resources to deal with this threat. In four days alone (7–10 June) the German *Pioniere* (sappers) made safe 15,600 mines, representing but a fraction of the total laid by the Soviet defenders.[33]

Apart from improving the integration of his forces, Manstein realised that the only way to sustain his attack was to feed fresh infantry regiments into the assault. In a letter to the German Army Chief of the General Staff, Colonel General Franz Halder, on 9 June 1942, he re-iterated his case for the release of 'at least one regiment' of the 46th Division at Kerch, stressing the fact that each of the four infantry divisions committed to the northern attack had already suffered at least 1,000 casualties.[34]

THE ATTACK CONTINUES, 10–16 JUNE 1942

Despite the ferocity of the fighting over the first three days, and consequent losses, morale held up on both sides as the battle for Sevastopol approached its decisive stage. Across the northern and north-eastern fronts of the city, the Soviet defenders attempted to stabilise the situation as the German maintained their pressure. Lindermann's 132nd Division and Schmidt's 50th Division made only small territorial gains, while Wolff's 22nd Infantry Division continued to make the best progress, battering into the Soviet defences on the northern side. In the centre, the Division's 65th Regiment went over to temporary defence having seized Mekenzievy Gory station, and fought off the numerous Soviet counter-attacks in response. To its east, in reaching the Black Sea Fleet's fuel tank farm, which lay towards the eastern end of Sevastopol Bay, the 47th Regiment achieved on 11 June the deepest penetration of LIV Corps thus far in the battle.

Two days later, on 13 June, the 16th Infantry Regiment on the 22nd Division's right flank stormed Fort Stalin (Anti-Aircraft Battery No. 365). Its commander, First Lieutenant Ivan Semenovich Pyanzin, sent a defiant last radio message: 'We can resist no longer. All personnel ineffective. Open fire on our positions and command post'.[35] For such stoic valour, Pyanzin was posthumously awarded 'Hero of the Soviet Union'. At the site of the battery, a large monument commemorates his sacrifice and that of his men, who fought to the bitter end. Although only a local action with little operational significance, the seizure of this strongpoint was none the less highly symbolic for the Eleventh Army. Having failed in their attempt in the icy snows of December, Dietrich von Choltitz's men were delighted by their hard-won success in the scorching heat of a Crimean summer. Their own sacrifice had at last been rewarded. One seriously wounded German soldier joked: 'It's not so bad – we have the Stalin'.[36]

Meanwhile, the remaining three divisions of LIV Corps (132nd, 50th and 24th) had yet to advance so far. Only when Hansen reorganised his forces, inserting the 24th Division between the 132nd and 22nd, and deploying the Romanian 4th Mountain Division in its wake on his left flank, was LIV Corps able to mount a more effective, concentrated attack on the northern side. This operation followed on 17 June. Having considered this option during the second assault in December 1941, it remains surprising that Hansen did not amend his scheme of manoeuvre for the final attack launched on 7 June 1942.

The defence of Sevastopol continued to be sustained by the Red Navy, whose vessels repeatedly ran the gauntlet of German air attack. In a manner similar to the contemporaneous British defence of Malta, brave Soviet crews manned a succession of cruisers, destroyers and submarines which ferried vital reinforcements, fuel and materiel to the Crimean main base. As the Russian war correspondent Eugene Petrov declared, the strength of the city's defences in the summer of 1942 rested on 'a combination of courage and efficiency'. By way of example, he stressed:

> Before this war no expert in naval warfare would have believed that a warship could unload troops, ammunition and supplies, embark wounded servicemen, women and children for evacuation, all in the space of two hours, and at the same time put up an intensive barrage from all its guns in support of the infantry.[37]

The crew of the cruiser *Molotov* performed this particular feat during the night of 12/13 June. It delivered 2,998 soldiers of the 138th Separate Infantry Brigade, twenty-eight guns, eight mortars, 1,000 and more machine guns and over 100 tonnes of ammunition. While unloading and loading, it fired off fifty-one rounds of its main armament (180mm) and eighty-four of the secondary (100mm) against a range of land targets nominated by the Sevastopol Defence Region. No fewer than 1,065 wounded and 350 women and children were evacuated to the eastern Black Sea port of Tuapse.[38]

Voyetekhov detailed the deadly hectic that ruled the nightly routine at Sevastopol's docks: 'the landing stages were illuminated by parachute flares and searchlights, and as soon as the German gunners got the range the shelling began'. Soon a 'glowing stream of fire poured out upon the narrow target; the sound was unbearable as the dying screamed'. Nearby, 'oil tanks, where submarines unloaded fuel supplies, blazed while cases of ammunition on the quay exploded. Lorry-drivers rushed overloaded machines through the flame and smoke ...'.

Yet for all this vivid imagery, the Soviet reporter reminded his readers that the 'main object [here] was to maintain the tremendous tempo of loading and unloading'. Accordingly, any shirkers were ruthlessly despatched. 'Among the dock labourers', Voyetekhov recounted, 'were a number of convicts'. One of them, 'apparently only too anxious for a German victory, had organised a group of malcontents and the work was going slowly'. The responsible dockyard chief required the convict to open his mouth and to say 'Ah!' When the man failed to respond, the boss 'repeated the order and then shot him in the teeth, spattering those around him with blood and brains'. Turning to the others, the boss demanded 'I want speed'.[39] Such was the rough and ready justice of Stalin's wartime Soviet Union.

On 10 June 1942, the Luftwaffe sank the transport *Abkhaziya*; on the 13th its sister ship *Georgia* suffered the same fate. Both ships had contained vital supplies of ammunition for Sevastopol. As a result, and notwithstanding the arrival of the *Molotov* and the unloading of the majority of its stores, stock levels in the beleaguered city began to run alarmingly short. Despite the risks involved, Oktyabrsky ordered the *Molotov* to return as soon as possible with the maximum possible load of men and munitions. On the night of 15/16 June, the cruiser sailed into the Black Sea Fleet's harbour carrying 3,175 soldiers, 373 tonnes of ammunition and 45 tonnes of food. Again, the cruiser's guns were used to bombard Axis positions. The Germans returned fire as usual with shells exploding amongst the docks and warehouses. Luckily unscathed, the *Molotov* took off 1,625 men and 382 other evacuees. Evading German air attacks, the warship arrived safely at Novorossiysk on the 17th.[40]

On the eastern and south-eastern fronts of Sevastopol, corresponding to the Soviet Second and First Sectors respectively, Romanian and German forces continued to nibble away at the Soviet defences in heavy fighting. On the southern, coastal flank of XXX Corps, the 28th Light Division advanced very slowly towards Balaklava across the convoluted terrain of steep cliffs and deep gullies. Astride the main Yalta–Sevastopol highway, the erstwhile Vorontsov Road, the corps struggled to drive a wedge into the defenders' forward positions. As Manstein described, however, eventually 'the fortified strongpoints of "North Nose" and "Chapel Mount" and "Ruin Hill" fell to 72 Division, while 170 Division took Kamary'.[41] On the northern flank of XXX Corps, the Romanian 1st Mountain Division secured the 'Sugar Loaf'.

Axis airpower continued to make itself felt at Sevastopol. On 14 June Oktyabrsky noted that 'the enemy has again increased his air attacks and increased the size of the bombs being used. Over 700 sorties dropped around 2000 bombs'. In addition, in order to reduce Soviet air action and aerial resupply, German artillery targeted the aerodromes 'with large-calibre weapons', and hit them with 'around 700 shells'. On the 17th, Oktyabrsky complained of a 'really hard day' with over 1,000 enemy sorties, claiming that the Germans only dropped heavy bombs of over 3,500 kilogrammes.[42]

In the meantime, Manstein had finally secured the agreement of OKH to exchange the infantry regiments of the worn-out 132nd Division for those of the fresher 46th Division. Both divisional headquarters remained in place to preserve local situational awareness. While this redeployment was under way, effectively Manstein lost a division's worth of fighting power. The strength of all his infantry divisions, however, was diminishing rapidly. Many regiments were reduced to battalion strength. Without further reinforcements forthcoming, the Axis attempt to storm Sevastopol would surely stall. OKH conceded this point and sent further infantry formations on the march to Crimea – Manstein mentions 'three extra infantry regiments [arriving] in time for the final phase of the struggle'.[43] By 22 June, Soviet intelligence had already identified newly arrived infantry regiments from 'each of the 97th, 125th and 213th Divisions, and a fourth regiment from an as yet unidentified division'.[44] In fact, German records confirm that the Eleventh Army received no fewer than *five* German infantry regiments, nearly equating to two further divisions, during the course of the final assault on Sevastopol.[45]

Concurrently, OKH – presumably under instructions from Hitler – pressed Manstein again for the early release of VIII Air Corps, which was required for the main summer offensive, Operation BLUE.

PRESSING IN THE SOVIET DEFENCE, 17–27 JUNE 1942

Following ten days of Axis ground attack, and renewed air and artillery bombardment, the Soviet defence held, but only just. In the half-ring of strongpoints and trenches around Sevastopol, Petrov's depleted formations struggled to maintain the integrity of their positions.

Soviet Defending Forces		Axis Attacking Forces	
Sector	Forces	Corps	Division
IV (North)	95th Rifle Division 345th Rifle Division	LIV (German)	132nd Infantry 24th Infantry
III (North-East)	25th Rifle Division 79th Naval Infantry Brigade		22nd Infantry 50th Infantry
II (East)	386th Rifle Division 7th and 8th Naval Infantry Brigades	I Mountain (Romanian)	1st Mountain 18th Infantry
I (South-East)	109th Rifle Division 388th Rifle Division	XXX (German)	72nd Infantry 170th Infantry 28th Light
General Reserves/ Uncommitted Forces	138th Rifle Brigade 9th Naval Infantry Brigade		4th (Romanian) Mountain

Table 14.3 – Comparison of Forces at Sevastopol, 17/18 June 1942

Sensing that the fighting power of its opponents was on the wane, Eleventh Army now redoubled its efforts to press on to the inner fortress zone with powerful assaults by each of its corps. At 0245 hours on 17 June, LIV Corps launched a determined attack across its front to gain the northern side of Sevastopol Bay. Overcoming fierce resistance, and notwithstanding its heavy losses, LIV Corps managed to capture several strongpoints of the Soviet second line, such as the 'Cheka', 'GPU', 'Siberia' and 'Volga' forts (all German nicknames). On the corps western flank the 132nd Division, the redeployed 24th Division and the 213th Infantry Regiment attacked parallel to the coast. The latter formation, led by Colonel Otto Hitzfeld, broke through the Soviet defences and seized Coastal Battery 30 at Lyubimovka, or at least its upper part. Its crew under Captain Georgy Alexander continued to resist for several days until German engineers blew in the tunnel system. Meanwhile, the 132nd Division developed its attack towards the old Sishkov Battery, which overlooked the Crimean coast nearer to Sevastopol.

Oktyabrsky described 17 June as particularly 'tough going'. He committed his last reserve, the newly arrived 138th Rifle Brigade, in a fruitless attempt to stem the advance of LIV Corps.[46] The German 24th Division pressed home its attack in a southerly direction until it reached the North Fort and Fort Constantine, both of Crimean War fame, on 21 June. Although small detachments of Soviet troops defended these obsolescent fortifications, their resistance ultimately proved futile in the face of overwhelming odds. None the less, their valour entered the annals of Sevastopol. Seventy-four naval infantrymen under the command of Captain Yevseyev, for example, held off all attacks on Fort Constantine for three days and three nights. 'At dawn of the fourth day', according to Leonid Sobolev, the marines were 'ordered to go on board the last boat'. Carrying their wounded and weapons, the survivors:

> ... went down to the harbourside in silence, without any hurry, uniforms in tatters, covered in dust, wounded; they made a solemn procession of heroes, a terrible and wonderful vision of the Black Sea glory, the great-grandchildren of the Sevastopol sailors who once upon a time built this old fort.[47]

To the 24th Division's left, its rival, the 22nd Division from Lower Saxony, made even faster progress. Its forward elements infiltrated as far as Holland Bay during the night of 18/19 June, thus reaching Sevastopol's harbour area. To Wolff's men, the city centre now lay tantalising close across the water. From his diary record, the normally phlegmatic Oktyabrsky appeared alarmed for the first time during the second defence of Sevastopol. 'The enemy is bursting into the city and has taken [the suburb of] Bartenevka and the Fraternal Cemetery', he wrote on 18 June. Further, the '95th Rifle Division is completely routed and remnants are fighting on the northern fortifications'. As a result, there were no substantial forces remaining to defend the northern side of Sevastopol. By this time, resupply of the city and its defenders had become increasingly reliant on submarines. On 18 June, for example, six boats unloaded and left for the Caucasus. As Oktyabrsky noted optimistically, 'another four were expected for the next day', adding 'the only thing that saves us now is the submarines'.[48]

Over the next couple of days, the German 24th and 22nd Infantry Divisions proceeded to secure the cliff tops along the northern shore of Sevastopol Bay. On the eastern flank of LIV Corps, the 50th Division managed to reach the tank farm and the 'Old Fort' towards Inkerman. To its south, the 1st Romanian Mountain Division also made good progress. In the XXX Corps sector, 16 June, rather than the 17th, had proved a significant day with a penetration of the outer Soviet defences covering the Sapun position. Yet every step forward had come at great cost.

Increasingly frustrated by the difficulties of attacking Sevastopol, German forces attempted to undermine Soviet resolve through propaganda broadcasts. These information operations were directed mainly against the Red Navy and its naval infantry. As Voyetekhov explained, usually their transmissions would begin 'with an appeal to the Marines – of whom the Germans were most afraid'. Typically, the broadcasts contained the following appeal:

> You who bear the name of 'Black Death', awaken from your opium dream of Bolshevist propaganda. A German sailor is talking to you. I have the same feelings as you. If you love the Black Sea, come to us and it will be yours as before. Our Führer will appreciate your action and give each of you a motor launch.

In response to such incredible nonsense, the defenders would 'roar with laughter'. Skilfully, the Soviet commanders exploited this reaction to their own advantage. The mirth was recorded and re-transmitted back by radio and, on occasion, through loudspeakers. Such ridicule only served to rile the Germans, who 'opened up with gunfire and switched on their sirens, trying to drown out the laughter but in vain'.[49]

For all the skills employed in rebuffing the German propaganda, Oktyabrsky's and Petrov's forces were in deep trouble by the last week of June 1942. At 2230 hours on 25 June, for example, Oktyabrsky recorded: 'it has been reported that the 25th Rifle Division, the 3rd Naval Infantry Regiment and the 8th Naval Infantry Brigade ... are being surrounded'. Accordingly, he had given the order for these units to withdraw. Sensing the approaching disaster, he added: 'The situation is getting more and more complicated. There are no reserves, few forces, [but] we'll continue to fight.... Again there were over 500 air sorties. The enemy is hammering our troops and the harbours in the main'. Yet the next day Oktyabrsky struck a more defiant note: 'We've been fighting off rabid attacks for twenty days. Yes, General von Manstein, it's not so simple to overcome the heroic Black Sea Fleet. Let's fight a bit more ...' None the less, there had been 450 Axis air sorties over Sevastopol that day, and 'more than 2,500 bombs' dropped. Such strikes 'continue to decide every question ... smashing and wrecking everything'. As Oktyabrsky conceded, 'the bastards are torturing us'.[50]

By the morning of 26 June, the Eleventh Army had taken possession of Sevastopol's outer defences. Its task now was to break into the inner fortress area, bounded in the north by Sevastopol Bay, and in the east and south-east by the Sapun escarpment running from the Inkerman Heights towards Balaklava. In accordance with timely battle procedure, Headquarters Eleventh Army had already issued a warning order on 20 June, which was followed up by the main set of orders on the 24th. As ever, Manstein's options for the forthcoming final stage of the assault on Sevastopol were limited by the factors of forces, time and space.

Notwithstanding the successes scored so far, the Axis forces' advances towards the centre of Sevastopol had been bought at a high price in men and materiel. Thus the prime difficulty Manstein faced was the diminished fighting power of his infantry, notwithstanding the reinforcements that had either arrived, or were still *en route*. Having regularly visited his units over the previous weeks, he was only too aware of their plummeting offensive capacity, which was 'virtually at an end'. He recalled that 'regiments had dwindled away to a few hundred men each, ... and one company being pulled out of the line with a strength of one officer and eight men'.[51] The defenders of Sevastopol were extracting a heavy toll on their opponents as the final stage of the battle approached.

In deciding where his forces should mount the final attack, Manstein had considered the possibility of launching the main thrust from the south-east, and designating XXX Corps as the Eleventh Army main effort. As he explained in his memoirs, and in reprising earlier considerations, this 'ideal solution' was not practicable for a number of reasons:

> Moving the divisions alone was bound to take several days, and in this time the enemy would have an opportunity to recover his strength. In the frontal area, the two sectors [north and south] were only linked by one narrow road which he had taken immense trouble to build through the mountains the previous winter. In any case, it could not bear the weight of the heavy artillery, and the task of moving that quantity of guns round by way of Yalta and stocking them with ammunition when they reached the southern sector would have taken weeks to complete.[52]

Time was not on his side for this course of action. In any case, the 'Supreme Command' would surely redeploy VIII Air Corps sooner rather than later to support the main German offensive of 1942 directed towards the Caucasus.

With limited forces and time remaining, and much constrained by the terrain, Manstein sought an economic way of attacking Sevastopol. Inspiration came to him when visiting the 22nd Infantry Division's positions above Sevastopol Bay. Looking out over the main harbour area, he realised that an attack across this stretch of water – between 800 and 1,000 metres wide – would turn the Soviet defences on the Inkerman Heights and along the Sapun escarpment. Not only would this manoeuvre open up a direct path to the city centre, such an operation would also come as a complete surprise to the defenders. But was the assault crossing feasible? Manstein discussed his idea with the senior commanders of LIV Corps, who raised a number of valid objections, including how the necessary boats were to be loaded, launched and then steered across to the southern shore within the observation and direct fire of the enemy. Yet Manstein overruled his subordinates' concerns, counting on 'the very reason that it appeared impossible, ... [the attack across Sevastopol Bay] would take the enemy unawares'.[53] In sticking to his plan, Manstein exhibited a great deal of self-confidence and determination. Many leaders would have opted for a less risky course of action, but potentially a more costly one in the longer term.

The day of attack ('U-Tag') was originally foreseen as 27 June. But preparations for LIV Corps' attack were not complete by that date. Therefore the main offensive was postponed to the early morning of 29 June. In a preliminary operation on the 28th, the 50th Division had seized the village of Inkerman in bitter house-to-house fighting. It captured its old monastery, which housed the headquarters of the 25th Rifle Division, and secured the eastern bank of the Chernaya, together with the railway bridge over the river.

Oktyabrsky's account of this period is punctuated by increasing concerns as to the sustainability of the defence. On 27 June, for example, he calculated that the minimum daily requirements were '500 tonnes of ammunition, 200 tonnes of food, 75 tonnes of fuel'. But Sevastopol was only receiving 'about 100 tonnes of ammunition, 40 tonnes of food and 30 tonnes of fuel daily'. The critical manpower situation alarmed him equally. 'We've endured twenty days of merciless siege', he wrote on the 28th, 'in this period we have lost up to 24,000 [wounded] and 9,000 dead. Some 3,000 – 5,000 men are missing – at total of up to 40,000'. Yet the commander of the Black Sea Fleet drew some comfort from asserting that the 'enemy has suffered three if not four times more'.[54] Although Oktyabrsky exaggerated the extent of the Axis losses, German and Romanian casualties were none the less high, as Manstein's concerns demonstrate.

THE FINAL ACT, 28 JUNE – 4 JULY 1942

The final days of Sevastopol before the German occupation proved increasingly chaotic as the integrity of the Soviet defence broke down and confusion reigned. Soviet accounts paint a heroic picture of defiant resistance while German ones tend to gloss over the difficulties Manstein's forces faced in overcoming the defenders' last strongholds. Manstein's attack of 29 June 1942 (Operation FACKELTANZ (TORCH DANCE)) on the inner fortress zone of Sevastopol delivered the fatal blow to the Soviet city, dispelling any hopes of its defenders about the practicality of fighting on. Once the 22nd and 24th Divisions established themselves on the southern shore of Sevastopol Bay, and elements of the 50th and 132nd Divisions attacking from Inkerman had linked up with them, the writing was on the wall for the Soviet troops defending Sevastopol and the remaining civilian population of the city. The assault by XXX Corps up and over the Sapun escarpment, which enveloped Sevastopol from the south-east and thrust westwards into the Chersonese peninsula, delivered the *coup-de-grace* to Petrov's Coastal Army.

The night assault crossing of the 22nd and 24th Infantry Divisions, as intended, caught the Soviet units guarding the southern shore of the bay completely unawares. In the first wave of attack, launched at 0100 hours, the powerful craft of the 902nd and 905th Assault Boat Commandos transported the leading infantry companies of the 16th (left) and 31st (right) Infantry Regiments across Sevastopol Bay. Lodgements were quickly secured. During following hours, the trusty powered boats brought the balance of the two divisions across. The associated attack from Inkerman by the 50th and 132nd Divisions (inserted on this flank) broke through the brittle front of the 386th Rifle Division. During the course of the 29th, another sunny and hot day,

German troops established themselves from Suzdal Hill on the Inkerman Heights westwards towards the Malakhov Hill on Sevastopol's eastern outskirts. LIV Corps had achieved a significant success, matched by XXX Corps' assault astride the Yalta–Sevastopol highway on the Sapun defences.

The 170th Division acted as the main effort of XXX Corps. At 0230 hours on the 29th, it attacked on a narrow frontage of only 800 metres immediately to the north of the Yalta–Sevastopol highway. Its initial assault echelon comprised a battalion apiece from each of its three infantry regiments. The remaining units followed up close behind. The 105th Infantry Regiment from the 72nd Division acted as divisional reserve, ready to exploit the anticipated storming of the Sapun position. Despite the Soviets' mines, field fortifications and intense fire, the 170th Division, supported by assault guns and the Goliath demolition devices, broke through the defences. The German infantrymen succeeded in gaining the crest of the escarpment within eighty minutes. Meanwhile, the associated attacks of the Romanian 1st Mountain Division to the 170th Division's north, and of the 72nd and 28th Light Divisions to its south, made good progress. Already by 0715 hours, in view of the successes scored across the front so far, an increasingly optimistic Headquarters Eleventh Army confirmed that LIV Corps would seize Sevastopol while XXX Corps cleared the Chersonese peninsula. The final attack of the day involved 28th Light Division's assault at 1830 hours on the English Cemetery of the Crimean War. Although this particular operation miscarried, XXX Corps had none the less achieved a significant penetration of the Soviet defences some 5 kilometres wide and 3 deep. As a result, and in complementing the assault of LIV Corps, Axis forces now directly threatened Sevastopol's centre from the east and south-east.

By the end of the day, Oktyabrsky had more or less conceded defeat. His diary entry for 29 June says it all: 'There's a clear threat that [during the course of] tomorrow, the enemy will break through into the city because I don't have any reserves. The situation cannot be changed'. That evening, about 2200 hours, Oktyabrsky quitted his main headquarters in Sevastopol for the final time and made for his reserve command post at Coastal Battery No. 35. He arrived there 'more or less safely ... whistling bombs and shells on the road confirmed gravity of the situation'. There Oktyabrsky' principal subordinates – 'comrades Petrov, Morgunov and Fadeev' – joined him. Petrov then assembled his divisional and brigade commanders and issued orders for a general withdrawal to the Chersonese peninsula. The prospects for continuing the struggle looked bleak: not only were the Red Army troops and naval infantry tired, there were also neither reserves available, nor sufficient ammunition remaining for a protracted fight. Unsurprisingly, morale began to diminish at all levels; some tragic mistakes or errors of judgement were made in the heat of battle.

On the western side of the river Chernaya, just upstream from its opening into Sevastopol Bay, runs a line of white limestone cliffs, long quarried for their fine building stone. Before the Second World War, cavernous galleries had been blasted out of the quarries to store the region's famous sparkling wine. These cellars, belonging to *Spetskombinat* Nr. 2, nicknamed 'Shampan', had since been converted into underground ammunition stores, factories and shelters for the wounded and evacuated members of the city's population. A young resident concerned, Valentina Pavlovna Kutuzova, recalled daily life there:

> It was the champagne, which was kept in the quarries, which saved people's lives during those difficult days. Initially people wanted to pour it out and use the empty bottles for petrol [bombs]. But when it became impossible to go out to fetch water because of the firing, champagne was used to cook food, and boiled for tea.... At the end of the defence, in the hospital, which could accommodate only 500 beds, 2000 wounded were concentrated. Those who could not get a bed, slept on a concrete floor, which was slanted; and in a little gully, blood was running. Not everyone could endure seeing so much blood, and often people who came to provide help fainted.

As leading elements of the German 50th Division approached the underground complex, the Soviet command decided to deny it to the enemy, resulting in the deaths of most inside. Valentina Pavlovna, who was lucky to escape, recalled the unfolding tragedy:

> ... our Red Navy sappers informed us about the forthcoming explosion, but no one believed them as there were so many wounded in the quarries who could not walk themselves. Nevertheless, the explosion came unexpectedly; the blast wave in the neighbouring quarries turned everything upside down, all the separations [between the rooms] were destroyed. The rooms were filled with the smell of smoke. Those who could not walk, stayed in bed; [other] people, burning alive, jumped up and immediately fell down.[55]

'Just as our troops were entering Inkerman', Manstein recorded, 'the whole cliff ... shuddered under the impact of an enormous detonation'. As a result, a 30-metre wall of rock collapsed over a length of some 300 metres, 'burying thousands of people beneath it'.[56] No one knows how many people were entombed in the quarries. The destruction of the underground complex remains one of the great controversies of the defence of Sevastopol – why were they not evacuated in good time?

The Axis attacks continued on 30 June with undiminished vigour. At 0900 hours, men of Colonel Kurt Versock's 31st Infantry Regiment of the 24th

Division managed to break into the defensive complex on the Malakhov Hill, which, as in the Crimean War, represented the last major bastion of the defence of Sevastopol. Within half an hour, it had fallen. Meanwhile, the other divisions of LIV Corps (22nd, 50th and 132nd), together with the Romanian 4th Mountain Division, pressed into the city's eastern and south-eastern outskirts. Within XXX Corps, having received heavy air and artillery support, the 28th Light Division renewed its attack on the English Cemetery, which fell to the recently arrived 420th Infantry Regiment in a dawn assault. The fighting had wrecked the place. As Manstein remarked, 'the Russians had developed [it] into a main strongpoint of their outer ring of fortifications, and the marble monuments once erected to British soldiers were now in ruins'.[57]

At midday, Headquarters Eleventh Army directed XXX Corps to swing one of its divisions to the north-west in order to envelop Sevastopol. Accordingly, the 28th Division was directed to advance towards the Crimean shore between the Quarantine and Strelitskaya Bays. To its south, the 72nd and 170th Divisions pushed into the Chersonese peninsula in order to defeat the remnants of the Coastal Army, who were withdrawing westwards. At the end of 30 June, the war diarist of XXX Corps summed up the situation:

> One gains the impression that a cohesive [Soviet] defence no longer exists. It is abundantly clear that yesterday's breakthough of the Sapun position represented the key to [unlocking] the fortress, and that the defensive power of the Russians is broken. [Our] divisions are rapidly gaining ground to the west.[58]

Boris Voyetekhov, attached to Oktyabrsky's headquarters, witnessed the abandonment of Sevastopol:

> Now we were leaving this town and these ruins. Through demolished streets were coming the survivors, many of them wounded, of the staff of the Black Sea Fleet. Slowly the front was sagging and its valiant defenders falling back among the rubble, the avalanches of shattered bricks, piles of masonry, twisted girders, and festoons of broken cables, towards the Chersonese Peninsula. It was reckoned that at that time only eleven buildings in Sevastopol remained intact.[59]

That same day (the 30th), Oktyabrsky sent a telegram to Stalin in which he described the rapidly deteriorating situation. He claimed that Soviet forces at Sevastopol 'could not hold out for more than two or three days', which turned out to be an optimistic forecast. More controversially, he asked permission to evacuate a number 'of the "responsible commanders" and citizens to the mainland during the night of 30 June/1 July 1942'. At 1800 hours, the commander of the

Black Sea Fleet received a telegram from Kuznetsov, the People's Commissar for the Navy, with *Stavka*'s approval.[60] Oktyabrsky had already organised aircraft and submarines for this purpose, and selected those lucky enough to be given a passage out of Sevastopol.

Although the Soviet public was informed about the struggle for Sevastopol, its imminent fall was not mentioned in the official communiqués. None the less, heavy hints about the outcome, contained in phrases such as 'heavy fighting' in the 'immortal city', had been dropped in the final days of the battle. Ilya Ehrenburg wrote a series of defiant despatches, including one on 30 June 1942 for *Red Star* (the Red Army's newspaper), which both praised the heroism at Sevastopol and tilted against the ignominious surrender of Tobruk by British and Dominion forces on 21 June:

> The Germans boasted: 'We shall drink champagne on June 15 on the Grafsky Embankment.... Experts foretold: 'It's a matter of time of three days, perhaps a week'.... But they forgot one thing: Sevastopol is not merely a city. It is the glory of Russia, the pride of the Soviet Union. We have seen the capitulation of towns, of celebrated fortresses, of States. But Sevastopol is not surrendering. Our soldiers do not play at war. They fight a life-and-death struggle. They do not say 'I surrender' when they see two or more enemy men on the chessboard.[61]

The facts on the ground, however, spoke otherwise. At Battery 35, Oktyabrsky summoned his military council. Both news and mood were grim and gloomy. The exhausted commander of the Black Sea Fleet then gave his final direction on Crimean soil. The remnants of the Coastal Army – the 25th, 109th and 386th Rifle Divisions – would mount a last stand. These formations were required to defend 'for one more day' a line drawn from Strelitskaya Bay to the Turkish Rampart, and then to the sea in the south. Oktyabrsky appointed the unfortunate Major General Novikov, commander of the 109th Division, as the senior officer left behind to lead this rearguard. Between 0100 and 0130 hours on 1 July, all other members of the senior command staff were to leave for the 'mainland' either by submarines or ships. In a concluding note of pathos in his diary, Oktyabrsky admitted, 'The situation is complicated ... there are many people at Battery 35, all of whom wish to fly out or leave by sea ... the hardest question is the evacuation of the wounded. There are very many wounded and no means of evacuating them.'[62]

At this point, Oktyabrsky's diary entries abruptly stopped. There is no indication that he felt guilty about what happened. Seventeen years later, at meeting held at the restored Sevastopol Panorama museum in December 1958, Oktyabrsky described rather than justified his actions during that fateful night on the Chersonese peninsula:

Some of the personnel, very few, left on small boats – tugs and cutters. Some broke out and joined the partisans in the mountains; some were taken prisoner by the Germans and Romanians. Personally, together with several of my comrades ... I was flown away by a special crew in the only aircraft to depart from the Chersonese aerodrome. [The take off took place] at night, under enemy fire, surrounded by explosions, without any illumination of the runway.[63]

Oktyabrsky's PS-84 aircraft (a Soviet version of the famous DC-3 Dakota) flew him and members of his military council to safety in Krasnodar. In this manner, he left in the lurch the vast of majority of his men, who were either killed in action over the final few days or became prisoners of war. Many tens of thousands of them were shot or murdered by their captors in other barbarous ways, or left to starve to death or to succumb from disease.

According to Karpov, Petrov, dismayed by the outcome of the battle, contemplated taking his own life at Battery 35. A member of the Coastal Army's military council, Colonel Ivan Filippovich Chukhnov, dissuaded him from doing so – arguing: 'So you have decided to help the Nazis to get rid of you. But who will come back to liberate Sevastopol? ... It must be your duty'.[64] Shortly after Oktyabrsky's departure, Petrov, accompanied by his deputy, Morgunov, and his chief of staff, Krylov, together with other members of his military council and headquarters staff, made their way down a cliff path to a jetty. There the escape party boarded a tug, which took them out across 200 metres of choppy water to a Shchuka (pike) class submarine, the Shch-209. At 0259 hours the submarine set course for Novorossiysk. Further personnel were evacuated on another PS-84 aircraft and a second submarine that morning. The latter vessel carried Communist party members from Sevastopol's city council. Despite the threat of interdiction, both aircraft and submarines reached their destinations. In this manner, over two hundred people were taken to safety. Yet apart from Novikov, all the senior leaders and functionaries had left Crimea.[65]

Sevastopol endured its final German air bombardment of the war during the early hours of 1 July. Its purpose was demonstrative and coercive. Manstein justified the raid in his memoirs: the 'enemy was to be shown that he could not expect to extract a further toll of blood from us in house-to-house fighting'.[66] Young Zadorozhnikov recalled the 'massive artillery preparation' the evening before, which continued at even fuller intensity the next morning. But by then 'the city was empty'.[67] In the event, the coda of German destruction in Sevastopol had been completely unnecessary. Even Manstein admitted that it 'seemed probable that the enemy had pulled the bulk of his forces out to the west the previous night'.[68] Thus there would be no heroic last stand of Soviet forces in the city centre.

Following the completion of the artillery preparation at 1230 hours, the four German divisions of LIV Corps and the Romanian 4th Mountain Division lost no time in rushing into the now practically undefended Sevastopol. While the 24th Division occupied the Korabelnaya suburb to the east of the Southern Bay, the 132nd Division, advancing from the south-east, struck towards the historic heart of the town. At 1315 hours, men of Lieutenant Colonel Ludwig Kirschner's 72nd Infantry Regiment hoisted the German war flag on the shattered cupola of the burnt-out Panorama, together with the Romanian national flag. For the second time in the history of Sevastopol, the Germans had raised their standard above the city. Zadorozhnikov observed that 'a red flag ... and in its central white circle, a black spider – the swastika – celebrated the [Germans'] victory'. He ran away to tell his shocked mother that 'they too have a red flag ... and if the flags were of similar colour, everything would surely be the same'.[69] Such youthful naivety would very soon evaporate.

During the course of the afternoon, Colonel Ernst Maisel's 42nd Infantry Regiment secured Lenin (now Nakhimov) Square. Manstein could not resist the immediate temptation to enter the ruined city and to congratulate his victorious troops in person. Arriving at Lenin Square in the early evening, he was briefed by Maisel, looked briefly around and then returned to his forward command post at Yukhary Karalez. There could not have been a greater contrast to Koch's bloodless entry into the city on 1 May 1918.

Reflecting with his forward headquarters staff on recent battles and associated lost comrades, Manstein's thoughts were interrupted by a special radio communiqué, which announced the fall of Sevastopol:

> Above the city and port flutter the German and Romanian flags. German and Romanian troops under the command of Colonel General von Manstein, steadfastly supported by Colonel General von Richthofen's battle-hardened air corps, after twenty-five days of fierce battle, have as of midday today, taken the most powerful land and sea fortress of all that have ever existed in the world.

This broadcast was closely followed by a teleprinter message from the Führer:

> To the Commander-in-Chief of the Crimean Army, Colonel-General v. Manstein
> In grateful appreciation of your exceptionally meritorious services in the victorious battles of the Crimea, culminating in the annihilation of the enemy at Kerch and the conquest of the mighty fortress of Sevastopol, I hereby promote you Field-Marshal. By your promotion and the creation of a commemorative shield to be worn by all ranks who took part in the Crimean campaign, I pay

tribute before the whole German people to the heroic achievements of the troops fighting under your command.

Adolf Hitler[70]

The late evening of 1 July 1942 was Manstein's hour of triumph, in many ways the zenith of his career. It also represented a high point in Germany's military fortunes that year, which were soon to be dashed on the snow-topped mountains of the North Caucasus and in the smashed streets of Stalingrad.

Of course, the victory at Sevastopol was not solely a German one. The Romanians took a full part in the battle, not least during its final days. Early on 1 July, for example, as members of the 4th Mountain Division entered the city, their comrades in the 18th Infantry Division cleared Balaklava, taking 10,000 prisoners in the process, eliminating most of the 109th Rifle Division.[71] The 1st Mountain Division then followed up along the southern coast, rooting out elements of the 388th Rifle Division from the batteries at Cape Fiolent.[72]

Although Sevastopol was now firmly in Axis hands, the fighting in Crimea was not quite over. On the western tip of the Chersonese peninsula, Soviet forces continued to fight, centred on Coastal Battery No. 35. By 1800 hours on the 1st, German forces had advanced to within a kilometre of this strongpoint. Soviet troops awaited in vain under heavy shellfire for evacuation by air or sea. Their resistance then stiffened. The battle waged for the following three days with repeated, desperate attempts by Soviet units to break through to the east by night. Attacks and counter-attacks alternated by day, in which fanatic *Komsomol* members took part. In his epic account of the defence of Sevastopol, B. A. Borisov, chairman of the city's defence committee, described the tragic fate of two such individuals – Nadya Krayevaya and Sasha Bagrii – in the last stand:

> [The pair] then joined one of the rearguard units ... Taking rifles and cartridges from dead soldiers, they tried with the others to break through to the Crimean hills to join the partisans. But in the shelling half the brave people were killed ... A second attempt to break through was no more successful, and as the Germans started their final attack, the shots from the Russians became fewer and fewer ... Most of the survivors now counter-attacked with nothing but their bayonets. Nadya was killed. The last thing that was heard of Sasha Bagrii was this: he was seen, scarcely able to move, in a column of prisoners. Then he was seen half-dead and spitting blood at Bakhchisaray and then at Simferopol.[73]

It was not until the 4th that the final Soviet defences on the Chersonese peninsula were crushed, with the German 57th Infantry Regiment of the 9th Division seizing Coastal Battery 35, the last citadel of Soviet power on Crimea. By the end of the main period fighting, the Germans had captured no fewer than 30,000 men, women, girls and boys on the bloody patch of land of the Chersonese peninsula. German air supremacy over Sevastopol and its approaches prevented any evacuation. Hence there was no repeat of the highly successful operation conducted at Odessa in October 1941: only 1,726 individuals were taken off from Sevastopol in all types of vessels in the period 1–10 July 1942.[74] Altogether, Axis forces claim to have taken 97,000 prisoners of war during the third assault on the city in June–July 1942, including 26,000 wounded. By any measure, the outcome of the battle was a significant blow to the Soviet Union.

The final days of the fighting had proved no less intense or brutal than the start of the offensive at the beginning of June. On 4 July, Headquarters Eleventh Army recorded:

> [In Maxim Gorky II] the remnants of the Coastal Army had sought refuge ... and fought to buy time for the hoped-for evacuation. Up to this morning the enemy had conducted numerous counter attacks, involving armed women who fought with exceptional fanaticism. The bloody losses which the enemy suffered by these attacks ... and from our own attacks in the last stage of the fighting are extraordinarily high ... The action was completed during the course of the afternoon.... Thus the battle for Sevastopol has ended.

The War Diary listed the vast amount of booty captured by Manstein's army. It included: '467 guns, 26 tanks, 824 machine guns, 758 mortars, 86 anti-tank guns and 69 anti-aircraft guns'. Furthermore, '3597 bunkers of all type of construction had been seized, including the most modern works of Maxim Gorky I and II'.[75] Axis engineers lifted and made safe 137,000 mines. VIII Air Corps had inflicted a huge amount of damage on the city of Sevastopol, its naval infrastructure and defences, and not least on personnel and materiel. Over the period 2 June to 3 July 1942, Axis aircraft flew 23,751 sorties and dropped 20,529 tonnes of bombs. They destroyed 123 Soviet aircraft for the loss of thirty-one. Out to sea, they sank four destroyers, a submarine, nine smaller craft and four transports, and damaged many more ships.[76]

The defence of Sevastopol had made very great demands on Soviet blood and treasure. Semi-official figures, only released after the end of the Cold War, state that over the period 30 October 1941 to 4 July 1942, the total casualties incurred by the Coastal Army and the Black Sea Fleet amounted to 200,481, including 156,880 'irrecoverable' losses. This total represented an average daily loss of 808 men.[77] The Axis victory, none the less, had been won at considerable cost as well. Unfortunately, comparable statistics for the Eleventh Army's Crimean campaign are not available. Official German figures released on 7 July 1942 refer to 'total losses', presumably referring to the June/July battle, amounting to: '872 officers and 23,239 non-commissioned officers and men, of which 190 and 4147 respectively were killed, and 11 and 1580 missing' in action.[78] The Romanians' losses of all types were 8,454 men.[79] Altogether, the final assault on Sevastopol cost the Germans and their Romanian allies over 32,000 men, of which between a quarter and a third were killed or missing in action.[80]

THE AXIS OCCUPATION, 1 JULY 1942 – 9 MAY 1944

Sevastopol now lay under the eyes, flags and guns of a new order. Oppressive occupation replaced defiant defence; overnight, Fascism swept out Communism. On 2 July, Manstein made the German 50th Infantry Division responsible for the security of the city and appointed its commander, Major General Friedrich Schmidt, as the first German town commandant. Two days later, Schmidt's immediate superior, the commanding general of LIV Corps, General of Cavalry Erik Hansen, held a victory parade at Lenin Square. Although Zadorozhnikov did not mention this particular event in the account of his childhood, he remembered his initial impressions of German troops:

> During the first day of occupation we did not see a single German. At approximately 10 a.m. on the second day, two German officers appeared in the street. It was the first time that I had seen Germans so close. They were strikingly neat and clean: shiny boots, ironed uniforms, snow-white collars ... ordinary young faces with smoothly shaved pink faces.

Shortly afterwards, however, the young citizen of Sevastopol gained a quite different perspective of the new occupiers: 'Soon appeared in our street at different times separate groups of German soldiers. These men were not groomed: they were sloppy, rough and clumsy. Not speaking a word, they confiscated our pillows, pans and various trifling pretty things – boldly they ransacked our belongings'. Then, echoing the Reds' take over of power in the city in November 1920, 'all Sevastopol's men aged sixteen and over had to be registered at the *Komendatura* (the German commandant's office)'. Furthermore, the population left in the town had to pay tribute. As Zadorozhnikov recalled, 'no matter whether they could afford it or not, each family had to provide twenty eggs and sour cream or milk periodically'.[81]

The full registration of the city's inhabitants on 9 July 1942 was conducted with the aim of 'identifying Communists, members of the Communist Youth League (*Komsomol*) and of establishing those members of the population capable of work'. This process helped the Germans 'identify persons willing to co-operate with the new authorities'.[82] Within greater Sevastopol, the population was found to be 36,000, which represented a very significant reduction from the immediate pre-war (1939) total of 114,252. Of the present inhabitants, there were 7,000 Ukrainians and 1,800 Crimean Tatars. In view of the recent fighting, the Russian majority in the city 'was cautious with regard to the Germans, if not hostile'.[83]

Hitler had declared the destruction of Bolshevism as his prime aim in the war against the Soviet Union, the chief symbol of which was Lenin. Almost every city and town in the land contained a street or a statue of the first leader of the Communist state. Sevastopol, a centre of revolution in both 1905 and 1917, had both. Yevgenia Petrovna Baranenko, another wartime child, recalled:

> In July 1942, the Germans drove at gunpoint the remaining Sevastopol residents to the central square where the Lenin monument, miraculously intact, still stood. The [occupiers'] idea was to topple the bronze figure ... and to show in this way the triumph of the new order. However, when the tank, which was connected to the statue by a rope, started with a jerk, the rope broke.... Lenin remained firm on his pedestal. In the square, there was a roll of laughter and giggling. People were broken up immediately, and the monument was destroyed at night, without witnesses.[84]

The new occupiers exercised strict control of Sevastopol through physical checks, psychological pressure and brutal punishment. If, for example, a person was found at home during a document check without a pass, then, shockingly, the whole family was shot. A curfew was soon established within the city: in summer and spring, it ran from 2000 to 0600 hours; in winter, from 1700 to 0600 hours. Citizens stopped by a police patrol without a special night permit were liable to arrest and punishment such as forced labour for up to ten days. Quickly on the heels of Manstein's triumphant Eleventh Army came the dark forces of the *Sicherheitsdienst* (SD – Security Service) of the SS. Other than the liquidation of the Jewish population, their main task was to 'expose communists, state security officials and police, state employees, partisans and members of underground organisations'.[85]

On 10 July 1942, the Simferopol-based newspaper *Voice of Crimea*, now under close German editorial supervision, offered this mixed view of Sevastopol:

> The picture, which is unfolding before us, represents chaos and destruction. We find it very difficult to get through the streets, which are littered with rubble ... and thick smoke [still] shrouds the city. The first inhabitants are beginning to leave the cellars, mainly women and old people. It is clear that they are happy that this horror is ending for them at last.[86]

German troops set to work in clearing the demolished city. Engineers blew up buildings which threatened to collapse, cleared mines, opened up Sevastopol's thoroughfares, and with the help of the local inhabitants, restored the water supply. In the face of such widespread destruction, however, normality could not be returned easily. Because the tram system had suffered so much damage, for instance, it proved impossible to repair during the occupation and later reconstruction of the city. After the war, trolleybuses took over the former tram routes.

Within Sevastopol, disease and starvation threatened following the entry of the Eleventh Army. German sources maintain that the occupiers took important steps to support health in the city. The officer commanding of the 1/150th Medical Company of the 50th Division, Oberstabsarzt (Major) Dr Dohme, was made responsible for the medical care of Sevastopol's local population and the Soviet prisoners of war, of which 5,000 were either injured or wounded. With limited clean water and poor sanitation, there was a high risk of contagion in the summer heat. Yet 'thanks to preventive measures and the active support of Russian doctors, the German medical service was able to quickly localise an outbreak of dysentery in a prisoner of war camp and to prevent its spread'.[87] Such claims nevertheless run counter to the German record of routine mistreatment and abject neglect of their prisoners.

For the victors, there were other distractions. Within days of the city's fall on 1 July 1942, Manstein planned an elaborate celebration and memorial service for the Eleventh Army. Rather than holding the commemoration in Sevastopol, he decided that the park of the former Tsar's palace at Livadia, Yalta, would provide a more fitting venue. All battalion commanders and above, together with the officers, non-commissioned officers and men who been awarded the Knight's Cross or the German Cross in gold, were invited.[88] In his speech, Manstein thanked the soldiers of the Eleventh Army and of the VIII Air Corps for their 'dedication and courage, their steadfastness in often almost desperate situations, and for everything they had done'. Shortly afterwards, matters turned sour. It would appear that the Soviet command got wind of this victory party. The celebrations were broken off prematurely when several Soviet bombers made a surprise raid on Livadia, during which a number of the drivers were either killed or wounded – an unfortunate, if not ominous, end to the commemoration.[89]

Following the fall of Sevastopol, Manstein issued an order of the day to the troops of Eleventh Army, in which he declared:

> In an onslaught of 25 days, your courage has forced the strongest fortress of the enemy and destroyed its army. Even the most dogged resistance of the opponent broke under your will to win. Your guns smashed tanks and rocks. Our air force and artillery prised open breaches, but our infantry regiments and engineer battalions deserve the greatest glory.[90]

Once matters in Sevastopol were settled and the immediate business of his army completed, Manstein departed Crimea to spend a period of happy leave with his wife in Romania. As the personal guests of Marshal Antonescu, they enjoyed lavish hospitality during their sojourn in the Carpathian Mountain resort of Predeal and visits to the ethnic German communities in the Siebenbürgen (Transylvania).[91]

Manstein had much for which to thank his Romanian hosts. As historian Mark Axworthy states, Antonescu had proved 'an impeccable ally'. Since assuming command of the Eleventh Army in September 1941, Manstein had repeatedly requested and received reinforcements from the Romanian leader. Although their fighting power was lower than the equivalent German formations, the Romanians had proved essential to victory. They had often performed supporting, 'economy of force' roles, repeatedly releasing 'scarce German units for decisive attacks which they diligently supported with secondary assaults of their own'.[92] In the recent fight for Sevastopol, moreover, they had taken proportionally heavier casualties. While German officers much criticised the Romanians' technique, they were not as battle shy as many thought. Yet courage could not make up for a lack of heavy arms and tactical competence in many areas.

For the surviving Soviet commanders, who ostensibly had little reason to celebrate other than their own salvation, the ultimately doomed defence of Sevastopol might have triggered some personal reflection. Very soon, however, the defeat was converted into a heroic, commemorative cause in support of the national propaganda effort. Hence Oktyabrsky wrote a defiant despatch, which appeared in *Pravda*, praising the valiant deeds of his men and denigrating the actions of the enemy:

> Following the order of the High Command of the Red Army, our forces abandoned the city of Sevastopol on 3rd July, 1942. For over eight months our heroic marines, infantrymen, pilots, gunners, mortar crews, and tankmen defended the naval fortress with a bravery and endurance unexampled in the history of war. The enemy entered the city over mountains of his own dead. The Germans had to pay dear[ly] for this so-called victory. It was a Pyrrhic victory, and try as they would, they were unable to hide this fact from the world.[93]

Petrov, too, reviewed the outcome of the battle for Sevastopol on his return to Moscow at the end of July 1942. The former commander of the Coastal Army was invited to write an introduction to an account written by a war correspondent, A. M. Khamadan, titled *Sevastopolians*. 'The heroism and valour of the defenders of Sevastopol in the Patriotic War during the years 1941–1942', proclaimed Petrov, 'serves as a guiding star, an example of bravery to all who honestly and sincerely hate Fascist barbarity, who wish people happiness and a cruel death to aggressors, arsonists and murderers on Hitler's side....'.[94]

Oktyabrsky concluded his account of the city's defence with the words: 'The hour is not far off when the bandits will all meet their infamous end on the battlefields of the Patriotic War just as hundreds and thousands of Germans met theirs at the walls of legendary Sevastopol'.[95] Oktyabrsky remained the commander of the Black Sea Fleet until the end of the war, despite the loss of its main base. Petrov's future was less assured. Although he went on to command a succession of armies and fronts during the remainder of the war, he never remained in any post for long. He returned to Crimea as commander-in-chief of the North Caucasus *Front* during the landings on the Kerch peninsula in November 1943.

When Petrov and Oktyabrsky pondered on recent events, the appalling handling of the Soviet personnel left behind at Sevastopol was already under way. The victors' retribution over the vanquished came quickly. Such were the numbers of prisoners of war involved, the Germans established 'more than twenty' camps in and around Sevastopol. Soviet accounts maintain that in July 1942, '450 men were liquidated at Inkerman'; in August, 'there were mass shootings in all the camps'. The occupiers introduced a novel method of disposing of their enemies: 'From November 1942, they began to remove 20–30 prisoners daily from the Lazarev Barracks and bury them alive in bomb craters. After the liberation of Sevastopol, 190 such craters were discovered containing 2,020 bodies'. Yet other cruel ways were found to kill. On one occasion, 'about 2,000 people were loaded on to a barge which was then set out to sea from where it did not return'.[96] This pattern of murderous activity was consistent with the war crimes committed earlier in the campaign during Eleventh Army's period of activity. Of the seventeen charges that Manstein faced at his trial at Hamburg in 1949, it is noteworthy that nine concerned, or related to, the mistreatment of prisoners of war on Crimea. Of these he was found guilty of one without amendment, and four with changes in wording – perhaps unjustified – that had the effect of reducing his culpability from crimes of commission to those of omission.[97]

Although Manstein had won his victory, the German Army desperately needed the forces under his command to meet its many commitments elsewhere on the Eastern Front. The first to be redeployed were the heavy artillery units and the separate infantry regiments, which had reinforced Eleventh Army during its final assault on Sevastopol. Only two German infantry divisions were destined to remain on Crimea: the 46th and the 50th. While the 22nd Division was transferred to Crete and the 72nd Division diverted to Army Group Centre, the remaining formations of XXX and LIV Corps (the 24th, 132nd and 170th Infantry Divisions, together with the newly retitled 28th *Jäger* Division) were redeployed with Headquarters Eleventh Army to participate in the siege of Leningrad in Army Group North's area of operations.

Rather than the whole of Eleventh Army, as originally intended, in early September 1942, only Headquarters XXXXII Corps and the 46th Division crossed the Straits of Kerch (Operation BLÜCHER) to join the offensive of the Seventeenth Army towards the North Caucasus. The 50th Division followed in late October, joining the First Panzer Army, having already detached its engineer battalion (the 71st) for employment in the battle of Stalingrad. That this division returned to Crimea within a year can be traced directly to the Hitler's over-ambitious plans for the summer and autumn of 1942. For the majority of 1943, the peninsula remained garrisoned by various Romanian formations (principally the divisions of I Mountain Corps), together with sundry German replacement and training units.[98]

The breaking up of the Eleventh Army, and the transfer of its remaining resources from south to north, at a time when the *Ostheer*'s main effort was in the south represented one of Hitler's egregious errors of judgement during the Second World War. As Manstein remonstrated in his memoirs, 'this dismemberment of an army in which the same corps and divisions had worked together for so long was deplorable'. Stressing the vital importance of understanding and cohesion, he stated: 'mutual acquaintanceship and the trust that comes of fighting hard battles together are factors of the utmost importance in war and should never be disregarded'. Furthermore, when the Germans sought 'decisive results' in the south of the front, this represented a 'task for which we could never be too strong'.[99] Subsequent events would confirm this line of reasoning – one that Manstein had raised to no avail at the time with Hitler. The Führer, however, believed that the commander-in-chief of the Eleventh Army, on the strength of his crowning success at Sevastopol, was just the man to repeat the same trick at Leningrad. Such hopes proved entirely illusory.

Following its redeployment to the north, completed on 27 August 1942, all Eleventh Army's energies were almost immediately consumed in countering a Soviet counter-offensive at Lake Lagoda in September 1942 rather than attacking the Soviet Union's second city. Dissipating, rather than reinforcing, the fighting power of Eleventh Army in this manner deprived Hitler of a powerful operational level reserve on the Eastern Front, which would have been proved extremely useful in staving off the defeat at Stalingrad. Yet there were simply too few resources available as German forces were vastly over-extended across the 2,000-kilometre-long front from Leningrad to the North Caucasus with contradictory, divergent priorities. When disaster inevitably struck at Stalingrad in early November 1942, Hitler sent for Manstein to rescue the surrounded Sixth

Army.[100] While Headquarters Eleventh Army transformed itself into Headquarters Army Group Don (later South) almost overnight, it lacked the necessary troops to mount an effective relief operation. Without the means, no amount of German will could prevail.

In Sevastopol, the German commandant returned routine administration to the municipal authority, which was headed by P. Supryagin throughout the occupation. Not that the German presence remained any less repressive, but during the autumn of 1942 and in early 1943, life in the city slowly returned to a semblance of normality. As in 1918, one of the first tasks was to clear the harbour and to repair the docks. The relatively junior Korvettenkapitän (Lieutenant Commander) Hans von Richthoven was appointed harbourmaster, and placed in charge of demining operations and in putting the essential port infrastructure back in order.[101] A passenger ferry service across Sevastopol Bay from the Grafskaya Quay to the northern shore resumed in February 1943. Already in September 1942, train services had started again between Sevastopol and Bakhchisaray, and then as far as Simferopol.[102]

In early December 1942, the *Voice of Crimea* reported optimistically the progress made over the last few months:

> Sevastopol is unrecognisable: the streets have been cleared of debris. Children hurry along clear pavements in the morning with their books and jotters; one primary and two middle schools have been opened.... On Sundays, citizens enjoy listening to music and singing in the theatres, which has been organised by the Department for Culture. Food supplies are improving every day: five restaurants and three bakeries ... have been opened. Fishermen are supplying fish to the city.[103]

Within a couple of weeks, the same newspaper announced that the city hospital, two outpatients' departments and three clinics had been reopened. In addition, Sevastopol's industrial enterprises were being 'reborn from the ruins and ash'. Under a decree of the city commandant, all children between eight and sixteen years of age were required to attend school. By January 1943, four schools were functioning in Sevastopol with a total roll of about 2,000 children, supported by forty teachers. Cultural and religious life returned too. Despite the very widespread destruction, in December 1942 a theatre opened in accommodation on Lenin Street alongside the Black Sea Fleet museum. By this time, the Pokrovsky Cathedral, the Kladbishchenskaya Church and Sevastopol's mosque were all functioning.[104]

Any account of improving living conditions in Sevastopol during the occupation cannot obscure the harsh fact that German killings and deportation policies steadily reduced the population of the city to but a small fraction of its pre-war level. As food was in such short supply, widespread starvation threatened. Elsewhere in the southern part of Crimea, it is estimated that approximately 100,000 civilians had died over the previous winter. Now the occupying authorities attempted to solve the problem of insufficient food supplies by simply deporting the population.[105] By way of example, from September 1942 to January 1943, over 30,000 inhabitants were forcibly transported from greater Sevastopol. In fact, a much larger-scale 'clearance' of Crimea had been planned to encompass the entire Slavic population (estimated at about 700,000) prior to the peninsula's settlement by Germans. Only the Crimean Tatars (150,000–200,000) and Germans already present (*c.* 300) would be allowed to remain.

When Manstein learnt of this plan, he objected to it on purely practical rather than moral grounds. On 3 June 1942 he wrote to OKH pointing out that the mass deportation of the majority population would bring about 'the cessation of the commercial, industrial and transport sectors, and the decay or destruction of the mass of the housing stock in both town and country'. Furthermore, he warned that many of the population would attempt to flee to join the partisans. Specifically, he stated that 'German propaganda about "liberation from Bolshevism" would be invalidated'.[106] A month later, immediately after the fall of Sevastopol, the staff of Headquarters Eleventh Army discussed the economic impact of the planned action, including the knock-on consequences for the occupying Axis forces – notably the supply of food. In the event, only the Jewish population was eliminated in 1941–42. Notwithstanding the frequent deportations and killings that followed, no widespread clearance of a further population took place until Stalin expelled the Crimean Tatars in May 1944.

During the twenty-two months of occupation, members of the surviving population in Sevastopol aged between fifteen and sixty years old were required to work directly for the occupiers. Their tasks included 'constructing defensive works, [repairing] roads and railway lines, clearing streets and houses, and picking up metal'. Police 'actively drove people to work and organised round-ups', and those who shunned work 'were subjected to repressive measures'. Inhabitants were at constant risk of being dragged away from their homes for no apparent reason under the infamous *Nacht und Nebel* (darkness and fog) action, and then being despatched to Germany to work as slave labourers.[107]

THE RESISTANCE MOVEMENT IN SEVASTOPOL

In the face of such a regime of fear, opposition to German rule in Sevastopol soon established itself. Within the city, resistance groups sprang up. Unlike their more openly armed counterparts in the largely inaccessible forests of the Crimean Mountains, the underground movement in Sevastopol's urban environment led a more precarious existence. None the less, they made their mark. According to a local history of the resistance, published in 2007, plans had been put in place for up to forty nominated personnel – mainly Communist Party activists and *Komsomol* workers – to remain in Sevastopol in July 1942 in order to organise and conduct resistance against the occupier. But in the confusion of the last few days, many of these individuals were caught up in the fighting and were either killed or taken prisoner, or were evacuated.[108] Therefore any resistance during the occupation had to start spontaneously.

During the late summer and early autumn of 1942, several unconnected groups in Sevastopol began their activities to undermine and obstruct the work of the German authorities. One of their first accomplishments was to assist the escape of Soviet prisoners of war from prisons and camps. While some prisoners of war were led towards the forests to join the partisans, others were given new documentation, accommodation and work so they could remain in the city as civilians. By early 1943, resistance groups had established themselves in Sevastopol's naval dockyard and in the main prisoner of war camp at Lazarev barracks. A third group described itself as the 'Communist Resistance Organisation in the German Rear' (KPOVTN), which by the late summer became the main focus of resistance in Sevastopol and surrounding area. As other groups merged into it, its membership grew from 50 in early 1943 to nearly 200 people by the end of the year.[109] To put this effort into a wider perspective, the latter figure represented about 5 per cent of the total partisan movement in Crimea.[110]

The leader of the unified KPOVTN was Vasily Dmitrievich Revyakin, a former soldier, who used the nickname 'Orlovsky'. In February 1943, he managed to convince officials of Sevastopol's labour exchange that he had never served in the military because of severe tuberculosis, and that he was a biology and chemistry teacher. Fortunately for him, however, his documents had been 'burnt in a fire'. So he managed to bluff his way about his identity. Having acquired legal registration in the occupied city, Revyakin was sent as a teacher to School No. 4 on the northern side of the city. This employment provided him with the ideal cover for his resistance activities.[111]

Revyakin's speciality was propaganda. He and his assistant, G. P. Guzov, first distributed hand-written leaflets made out of school notebooks in March 1943 to local inhabitants. They appealed to the people of Sevastopol, 'moaning under the yoke of Hitler's enslavement', to rise up in a 'mutual fight against the bloody conquerors'.[112] Then the resistance cell used a typewriter (a rebuilt machine from the parts of two salvaged ones) and acquired a printing press to produce leaflets, 100–150 at a time, which were distributed in April and May. On 10 July 1943, they published their first edition of the resistance newspaper

Za Rodinu ('For the Motherland'), which then appeared two to three times a month with up to 600 copies being printed. Revyakin's base was his wife's house at No. 46, Laboratory Road. Under the kitchen floor, he established a secret publishing room in a cellar. German officers were billeted very nearby at No. 48, which provided not only some unlikely protection for the underground activities, but also an electrical supply.[113]

The other main aspect of the resistance movement was 'diversion' – or direct action. N. I. Tereshenko headed a group for this purpose, which became part of the KPOVTN. At any one time, he could count on up to sixty activists to cause damage to the Axis means of transportation. Trains became one of their favourite targets. Adding either sand or water to freight wagons' axle boxes, which would then fail catastrophically, caused derailments. On one occasion, during the night of 23 January 1944, the railway resistance group managed to cause an ammunition train with sixty-three wagons to blow up. More bizarrely, in December 1943, they poisoned 150 pigs, which had been confiscated from the local population to be sent to Germany as Christmas gifts.[114]

Ironically, the resistance movement suffered its greatest losses during the final weeks of the Axis occupation. Having directed their efforts initially towards the local population, by early January 1944 the propagandists' efforts extended to sedition. Leaflets were produced urging German and Romanian officers and soldiers to fight with the Red Army in order to 'demolish the Nazi regime'. Perhaps this agitation provided the impetus for the mass arrests that followed in March and April. 'All investigative forces', including 'German and Romanian gendarmes, Russian police and agents of the security forces' were directed to find the underground printing house. A reward of 50,000 roubles was offered to anyone providing its location. Slowly but surely the net tightened around Revyakin and his colleagues. They produced their last edition of *Za Rodinu* on 8 March 1944.[115]

At 0200 hours on 14 April, No. 46 Laboratory Road was raided – Revyakin and his publishing team had been betrayed. Those arrested including his typist, Zhenia Zakharova. On the 17th, Revyakin's heavily pregnant wife, Lidia Nefedova, was rounded up. In the three days 14–16 April 1944, more than forty active members of the resistance, including Revyakin, his wife and Zakharova, were shot in the Yukharin Ravine, at the 5-kilometre point on the Balaklava road. In a note to her mother, written a few hours before her execution, Zhenia had penned defiantly:

> My dearest Mama! At night we hear the roar in the soil – these are our troops arriving.... Yesterday behind the [window] bars a greyish fluffy little sparrow perched. He was twittering to us for a long time about the spring, snowdrops

blooming and the imminent. It's a pity we won't be here! I am hungry for life! I am only 20. But I don't regret choosing this path. It's better to die standing, rather than to live on one's knees.[116]

In sum, the underground movement in Sevastopol, as in many other places of occupied Europe, caused more annoyance than disruption to the Axis authorities. None the less, the actions taken by the brave members of resistance movement, whether in terms of propaganda, sabotage or subversion, played an important part of the city's wartime history. For the members of the beleaguered civil population, the resistance provided hope – somebody was fighting back on their behalf. For the occupiers, it reminded them that they were just that – and lived on borrowed time as one day Sevastopol would be liberated by Soviet forces. When many of the leaders of the resistance were shot, the city was on the eve of attack by the 4th Ukrainian *Front*. Their contribution to the war effort was not forgotten. After the liberation, the name of Laboratory Road was changed to Revyakin Street; and the resistance fighter's home at No. 46 now houses Sevastopol's resistance museum.

CHAPTER 15

LIBERATION AND RECONSTRUCTION

'Hello, dear Sevastopol! Beloved city of the Soviet people, hero city, mighty city! The whole country is saluting you joyously!'

Pravda, 10 May 1944

THE ISOLATION OF CRIMEA, 1943–44

The future of Crimea under Axis rule remained inextricably linked to events unfolding elsewhere. The German summer offensive of 1942 culminated on the slopes of the North Caucasus and in the city centre of Stalingrad on the Volga. In the second of three great turning points on the Eastern Front, in Operation URANUS, superior Soviet forces encircled the German Sixth Army and elements of the Fourth Panzer Army at Stalingrad in November 1942.[1] Manstein's relief operation in December failed. Following the Sixth Army's capitulation in early February 1943, German forces, together with their Hungarian, Italian and Romanian allies, were pushed back to the river Don. They were then driven further westwards into the Donbas industrial region of eastern Ukraine. Kharkov, the fourth largest city of the Soviet Union, was abandoned on 15 February 1943. Opposite Kerch, the German Seventeenth Army, commanded by General of Engineers Erwin Jaenecke, retained a strong bridgehead on the Kuban peninsula.

544

Manstein effected a temporary reversal of German fortunes with his stunning counter-stroke between the rivers Dnieper and Donets, which resulted in the recapture of Kharkov on 14 March. The tide of war, however, turned once again in mid-summer. Hitler pinned much misplaced faith in inflicting a major blow on the Red Army at Kursk. The Germans' catastrophic defeat at that battle in July 1943 was immediately followed by a series of powerful Soviet offensives. In consequence, Manstein's Army Group South was hounded out of left-bank (eastern) Ukraine as far as the Dnieper. The southern sector of the Eastern Front then stabilised.

Meanwhile, the Soviet advance parallel to the Sea of Avov threatened to isolate Axis forces on the Crimean peninsula, and not least the Seventeenth Army on the Kuban bridgehead. One of the lesser-known Axis operations (KRIMHILD) of the Eastern Front concerns the evacuation of this army to Crimea. Completed over the period 7 September to 9 October 1943, it involved the transport of 177,355 German and 50,139 Romanian troops, together with 55,942 'Russian' *Hilfswillige* (volunteer auxiliary troops) and civilians over the Kerch Straits.[2] Altogether, this represented a fighting force of sixteen German and Romanian divisions. This operation exceeded in scale the evacuation of Axis forces from Sicily to mainland Italy undertaken the previous month. Efficient organisation and, above all, the protective Luftwaffe fighter screen proved essential to the success of KRIMHILD.

At this time, of all the German sectors of the Eastern Front, perhaps none had a greater claim for reinforcements than Army Groups South and A, commanded by Manstein and Field Marshal Ewald von Kleist respectively, which were under increasing pressure from four attacking Soviet *fronts*. Only a minority of the German troops evacuated from the Kuban were retained on Crimea to reinforce the peninsula's defences, the 50th and 98th Infantry Divisions. This compromise solution violated the principle of concentration of force. Had the entire Seventeenth Army (German and Romanian divisions alike) been sent north it might have made some difference to the battle for Ukraine. Had it been retained, however, it would have been to little purpose in the long run as it made little sense to hold on to the peninsula following the loss of Ukraine.

Jaenecke established his headquarters at Simferopol. His subordinate formations were deployed as follows (see Map 16): XLIX Mountain Corps, incorporating the Romanian Cavalry Corps, was dispersed thinly among the western coast, the northern approaches to Crimea and Feodosiya in the east; V Corps defended the Kerch Peninsula; and I Romanian Mountain Corps continued to secure the south and south-east of the peninsula, containing the partisans of the Crimean Mountains. Jaenecke had little time to rest or re-train his troops. He soon faced a powerful concentration of Soviet forces, the 4th

Ukrainian *Front* under the command of General Fyodor Tolbukhin, who had distinguished himself when leading the 58th Army during the battle of Stalingrad. On 23 October 1943, Tolbukhin's troops broke through the *Wotan* position defended by Colonel General Karl-Adolf Hollidt's German Sixth Army (which had been reconstituted with fresh formations following the disaster at Stalingrad). The south-eastern Ukrainian city of Melitopol fell on the 24th; two of Tolbukhin's armies (the 2nd Guards and the 51st) then stormed across the Nogai steppe towards the lower Dnieper, splitting the southernmost corps (XLIV) of the German Sixth Army asunder.

Within a week, on 30 October, the first Red Army armoured spearheads had reached and blocked the Perekop. As a result, Crimea was cut off and the Seventeenth Army trapped. The irony in this situation is that Jaenecke had accurately foretold such an outcome. He had commanded a corps at Stalingrad and been wounded there. As the last general to be flown out of the pocket in late January 1943, he did not wish to be trapped again. Under a study nicknamed 'Michael', he had already planned to withdraw his army by way of the Perekop to Ukraine. Although he had convinced his immediate superior, Kleist, and the Chief of the General Staff, Colonel General Kurt Zeitzler, of the wisdom of abandoning Crimea, he had failed to reckon with the adamant opposition of Hitler. Nor did Jaenecke understand the positions of the heads of the German navy and air force.

While Grand Admiral Dönitz regarded Crimea as an essential base for conducting naval operations in the Black Sea, Reichsmarschall Göring considered the peninsula a hugely important 'aircraft carrier' for supporting the Eastern Front. Both these arguments chimed with Hitler, who wished to deny Crimea to Soviet forces for as long as possible for precisely these reasons. As in 1941, the German leader wished to prevent Soviet aircraft being launched from the peninsula to bomb the Romanian oilfields, which remained vital to Germany's war economy. There were wider political considerations too, not least to dissuade Turkey from joining the Allied cause against the Axis powers. So the Führer disagreed with the professional advice of his senior soldiers (as he had done frequently before), and ordered the despatch of reinforcements to Crimea instead.

Jaenecke signalled the enactment of Plan 'Michael' for the night of the 29th/30th. In response, on the evening of the 28th, Hitler countermanded this move with an unequivocal order: 'The Crimea is to be held under all circumstances and with all means, even if the land line of communications should be broken'.[3] Bearing in mind the Soviets' closure of the Perekop exit on the 30th, it remains debatable whether the Seventeenth Army would have been able to leave Crimea by this route in time. Nevertheless, senior German commanders on the Eastern Front, including Manstein, pleaded for the immediate evacuation of Crimea in order to free up valuable forces for employment elsewhere – 'a particularly painful prospect', he noted, 'for those of us who had conducted Eleventh Army's bitter struggle for the peninsula'.[4] Throughout the winter of 1943/1944 there remained the possibility of an evacuation to Odessa (reversing the Soviet operation of October 1941), which only fell to Soviet forces on 14 April 1944.

THE WINTER BATTLES OF 1943/44 FOR THE KERCH PENINSULA AND PEREKOP–SYVASH

For the Seventeenth Army, the situation took a dramatic turn for the worse when Soviet forces mounted an amphibious landing at Eltigen (now Geroyevskoye) on the Kerch peninsula in the early hours of 1 November 1943. Elements of the 18th Army commanded by Colonel General Konstantin Nikolaevich Leselidze – principally the 318th Rifle Division and the independent 386th Naval Infantry Battalion – secured a precarious toehold on the beach and on the bluffs immediately beyond, approximately 15 kilometres south of the city of Kerch. Two days later, formations of the 56th Army under Lieutenant General Andrey Antonovich Grechko (later a long-serving, post-war Soviet Minister of Defence) stormed ashore at Yenikale to the east of Kerch. The Axis forces guarding the eponymous peninsula were hard pressed by these two landings. Immediately at hand was the 98th Infantry Division of General of Infantry Karl Allmendinger's V Corps, followed by the Romanian 6th Cavalry and 3rd Mountain Divisions.

Whereas German and Romanian troops were able to contain and push in the Eltigen beachhead, and eventually eliminate it on 7 December 1943, the Soviets had concentrated far more troops at Yenikale. By the evening of 3 November, units drawn from the 2nd and 55th Guards Rifle and the 32nd Rifle Divisions had won a bridgehead 8 kilometres wide and 5 kilometres deep, including the village of Baksy (now Glazovka). Massive supporting artillery strikes characterised this operation. By the 11th, the Soviets had landed 27,000 men safely ashore. Under a month later, this total approached 75,000. At these odds, no amount of courage or pressure by the Axis forces could dislodge the heavily reinforced Soviet foothold on Crimea. It appeared only a matter of time before the 56th Army would attempt to break out of this redoubt, most likely in conjunction with a powerful attack at the Perekop.

Overall command of the Soviet Kerch–Eltigen operation rested in General of the Army Ivan Petrov, the commander-in-chief of the North Caucasus *Front*. On 15 November 1943, *Stavka* directed that the separate Coastal Army be reformed from this *front* headquarters and the troops previously assigned to the 18th and 56th Armies. This reorganisation of command put Petrov back in charge of his 'old' army, which he had previously commanded at Odessa and Sevastopol. The forces at his disposal were considerable: nine rifle divisions, which outnumbered the Axis forces on the Kerch peninsula by over three to one.

With heavy fighting continuing on the eastern tip of the Kerch peninsula, Jaenecke renewed his attempts to gain agreement for the evacuation of the Seventeenth Army. Again he obtained the support of Zeitzler. At the beginning of December, the Axis ration strength on Crimea amounted to 270,000 men, of which only 32,293 Germans and 30,218 Romanians – representing only a quarter of the total – were fighting troops manning defensive positions at either Kerch or Perekop/Syvash.[5] The vast majority comprised navy and air force personnel, various army and corps units, rear area troops, coastal batteries, Russian 'volunteers' and labourers. It made eminent sense to start 'thinning out' the non-essential from this mass, and then to commence a staged withdrawal of front-line units from their fronts. Hitler, however, saw things completely differently and confirmed the deployment of two reinforcing infantry divisions to Crimea, the 73rd and the 111th, which arrived in February and March 1944 respectively. Both these formations, though, were not even at half strength.[6]

Over the winter months, the Kerch front remained active with frequent Soviet attacks directed by Petrov that wore down the strength of the hard-pressed 98th Infantry Division in particular. During the three-month period from 1 November 1943 to 31 January 1944, for example, this German formation took over 12,000 casualties while receiving only 6,000 replacements. The commander of the 98th Division, Lieutenant General Martin Gareis, who was highly praised for his competent handling of the Soviet landings in November 1943, fell out with his corps commander, Allmendinger, over the excessive demands placed on his formation. He left Crimea on long-term sick leave in February 1944, never to return.[7] Yet such discord at command level was not restricted to the German Army.

On the Soviet side, Petrov was removed from post in the same month, demoted to colonel general and placed in the reserve pool of officers. The reason given in his personal file – 'high-handedly distancing himself during the conduct of a combat operation, which caused the failure of this operation' – reads as if he did not concern himself with the necessary details.[8] His biographer, Karpov, counters this rationale by stressing that Petrov did quite the opposite. The real answer probably lies in the failure of the Eltigen landing, in Stalin's impatience with the slow progress made in expanding the Kerch bridgehead, and in Petrov's associated inability to inflict a decisive defeat on inferior Axis forces.

By a whisker, elements of the 4th Ukrainian *Front* failed to breach the Perekop–Syvash front at the end of October and beginning of November 1943. The German Seventeenth Army was lucky to block the northern entrances to Crimea just in time, while closing its own escape route to the Dnieper. On 30 and

31 October, Soviet tank units very nearly managed to force a passage down the Perekop isthmus, and to break out into the undefended 'rear' areas of northern Crimea. Had it not been for an *ad hoc* grouping of infantry and construction units under the command of Major General Otto Weber, supported by the powerful 88mm guns of the 9th Flak (Air Defence) Division and an armoured *Flak* train, the result might have been quite different.[9] This improvised force illustrated the German Army's priceless capability in the Second World War to 'battlegroup' under a single commander various units, which previously had no relation to each other, in a very timely and effective fashion. On the evening of the 31st, Lieutenant General Friedrich Sixt, the commander of the 50th Infantry Division, established his headquarters in the town of Armyansk, 4 kilometres south of the Turkish Wall, and assumed overall command.

By 1 November, reinforcements of several assault gun and anti-tank units had strengthened the 'Gruppe Sixt' further. By this time, the assault gun, originally developed to support infantry in the attack (a pre-war initiative of Manstein), had become one of the German Army's most trusted anti-tank weapons with its long-barrelled 75mm gun. Although Soviet attempts to break through at Perekop were thwarted by the solidifying German defence, the attackers managed none the less to force a shallow salient at the Turkish Wall. Despite several German counter-attacks, this breach could only be sealed off and not eradicated. In addition, to the east, Soviet troops crossed the shallow Syvash Sea and established a bridgehead on Crimea at Cape Dzhangar, forcing back elements of the Romanian 10th Infantry Division. This dangerous lodgement, which threatened the towns of Voinka and Ishun on the important line of communication from Dzhankoy to the Perekop, could not be eliminated either.

The fighting on the Perekop–Syvash front continued sporadically until the middle of December. By this time, the reinforced 50th Infantry Division, in a reversal of roles from 1941, held the Perekop isthmus with seventeen battalions, nearly double its normal structure. In stark contrast to Kerch, the northern approaches to Crimea remained quiet for the remainder of December 1943 and January 1944. Both sides dug in and prepared for the next round of fighting for the peninsula.

Within the German high command, concerns about Crimea continued to trouble Hitler and his senior military advisers, exacerbated by a lack of unity of command on the Eastern Front, which was largely the Führer's own making. During a conversation with Zeitzler on 27 December 1943, for example, Hitler declared: 'We've simply got to defend this second Stalingrad if at all possible. We can't just cold bloodedly turn our backs on it because its got nothing to do with Field Marshal von Manstein's Army [Group South]. We can't do that; we must remember there will be men lost here'. The trouble was that operational control of Axis forces in the southern sector of the front was split between Manstein and von Kleist, who commanded Army Group A, which included the German-Romanian Seventeenth Army on Crimea. But Hitler had wider strategic concerns too. 'In Romania it all depends on the Head of State', he continued. 'If [Marshal Antonescu] loses his army here [Crimea] – you must read the letters he's been writing to me'.[10]

Zeitzler responded: 'My only thought is that the disaster might be even greater'. After a discussion about possible troop reinforcements either to the north (to assist the Finns) or to the south (to safeguard Crimea), Hitler concluded: 'I think the loss of the Crimea is the worst thing that could happen. It would have the worst possible effect on Turkey. The Finns can't give up; in the [final] analysis they've got to defend themselves'. The conversation resumed later that day and continued on the next (28 December). Such was the threat to the southern sector of the Eastern Front (which together Manstein and Kleist attempted to hold against superior Soviet forces) that even Hitler conceded: '... if the worst comes to the worst we may lose the Crimea, the iron-ore area of Krivoirog and Nikopol [in Ukraine]. So if we don't clear up this affair!...'.[11] Yet all time *Stavka* was biding its time to mount a major operation to liberate Crimea. So the question was not whether Crimea would fall, but rather when.

THE SOVIET CRIMEAN STRATEGIC OFFENSIVE OPERATION AND THE AXIS RETREAT TO SEVASTOPOL

The Soviet Crimean strategic offensive operation (8 April – 12 May) complimented the Odessa offensive (26 March – 14 April 1944), forming together one of Stalin's famous 'ten blows', a term he coined in early November 1944 to describe the expulsion of Axis forces from the Soviet Union.[12] *Stavka* had been in no hurry to liberate Crimea as prosecuting the battle for Ukraine had been given higher priority. But by the spring of 1944, the time was now ripe to complete unfinished business and to restore Sevastopol as the main base of the Black Sea Fleet.

The German Seventeenth Army awaited the impending Soviet offensive with some trepidation. XLIX Mountain Corps, commanded by General of Mountain Troops Rudolf Konrad, guarded the northern gateways to Crimea. Its defences looked secure – but only superficially so. While the German 50th and 336th Divisions defended the Perekop sector and the eastern Syvash, the Romanian 10th and 19th Infantry Divisions covered the remainder of the Syvash–Chongar front. The 9th Cavalry Division screened the western coast. Two out of the 279th Brigade's three assault gun batteries supported the German formations. Considerable effort had been expended in repairing the former Soviet fortifications breached by Manstein's Eleventh Army in the battles of September and October

1941, and building a deeply echeloned defensive system, including trench lines at Ishun. Yet given enough pressure, the dam of the Perekop would surely burst. A Soviet break-out from the Dzhangar bridgehead towards Ishun would undermine its foundations.

V Corps with the 98th Infantry Division, the recently arrived 73rd Division, the Romanian 3rd Mountain and 6th Cavalry Divisions defended the Kerch peninsula. A second assault gun brigade on Crimea (the 191st) acted as the mobile reserve for this corps. The I Romanian Mountain Corps (two mountain divisions) continued to secure the southern and eastern coastlines and the Crimean Mountains. Until deployed to Ishun, the 111th Infantry Division acted as the Seventeenth Army reserve, a role then taken over by the improvised *Gebirgsjägerregiment Krim* (Mountain Infantry Regiment Crimea). Hence, as shown in Table 15.1, Jaenecke could count on five weak German and seven Romanian Divisions, and two assault gun brigades, which provided the only significant armoured support. In addition, the Luftwaffe's versatile 9th Flak Division (Motorised), commanded by Major General Wolfgang Pickert, provided both anti-aircraft and anti-tank support.

Northern (Perekop–Syvash–Chongar) Front Group Konrad (XLIX Mountain Corps)		Eastern (Kerch) Front V Corps
		73rd Infantry Division
50th Infantry Division	Romanian Cavalry Corps	98th Infantry Division
336th Infantry Division	Romanian 10th and 19th	Romanian 3rd Mountain Division
Romanian 9th Cavalry Division	Infantry Divisions	Romanian 6th Cavalry Division
279th Assault Gun Brigade		191st Assault Gun Brigade
Seventeenth Army Reserves: 111th Infantry Division Mountain Infantry Regiment Crimea		**Crimean Coasts and Southern Mountains:** I Romanian Mountain Corps Romanian 1st and 2nd Mountain Divisions

Table 15.1 – Combat Organisation of the German Seventeenth Army, April 1944[13]

With the abandonment of Kherson on the lower Dnieper by German forces on 13 March 1944, the 4th Ukrainian *Front* could focus on preparing its offensive into northern Crimea. Eighteen rifle divisions of the 2nd Guards and the 51st Armies, commanded by Lieutenant Generals G. F. Zahkarov and Ya. G. Kreizer respectively, were amassed for this purpose. The reinforced 19th Tank Corps, two separate tank brigades and further mechanised units (with over 500 tanks altogether) provided the *front* with considerable striking power. As in all the major Soviet offensives by this final period of the war, the provision of supporting artillery was lavish.

At Kerch, the Coastal Army, now under the command of General of Army Andrey Ivanovich Yeryomenko, comprised three rifle corps with twelve rifle divisions and two naval infantry brigades, supported by over 100 tanks. Around 2,000 aircraft of the 4th and 8th Air Armies supported the Coastal Army and the 4th Ukrainian *Fronts* respectively. The mission of both Soviet groupings was to liberate Crimea. Their concentric attacks would be directed towards Sevastopol, their final, common, objective. Such was the importance of the offensive in Stalin's eyes, that he sent none other than the Chief of the General Staff and *Stavka* representative Marshal of the Soviet Union Aleksandr Mikhaylovich Vasilevsky to coordinate operations at the beginning of April 1944.

Meanwhile, under Jaenecke's leadership, Headquarters Seventeenth Army, together with air and naval staff support, had prepared a detailed study plan entitled 'Eagle' for the withdrawal of all Axis forces on Crimea to Sevastopol and their subsequent evacuation. The envisaged operation comprised five phases:

1. Withdrawal of logistic units and elements not necessary for the battle by rail and air transport to Sevastopol, and then [by sea] to the mainland.
2. Sudden pulling back of motorised combat troops to prepared intermediate positions – for V Corps, the Parpach position; for XLIX Corps, the 'Gneisenau' position [from Yevpatoriya eastwards to the north of Simferopol].
3. Withdrawal of forces on foot in one clean move via the intermediate positions to Sevastopol.
4. Abandonment of the intermediate positions.
5. Holding the fortress of Sevastopol until the evacuation of all troops.[14]

In terms of time and space, it was estimated that the march to Sevastopol (from Perekop, 215 kilometres and from Kerch, 280) would require six to seven days while the evacuation by sea would take about three weeks. Yet all would depend on the ability of Axis forces to: hold and delay the advance of Soviet forces sufficiently to allow the withdrawal from Perekop and Kerch; to defend Sevastopol for the necessary time; and not least, to protect the naval forces required for the evacuation. The loss of Odessa on 8 April 1944 compounded the problem. It meant that a longer sea passage would be required to make Romanian ports such as Constanta (212 as opposed to 158 nautical miles), which, in turn, would decrease the rate of evacuation.[15]

Jaenecke's plan rested on timely authority being given to commence the retirement from the fighting fronts and to initiate the evacuation. In his operational direction for the Eastern Front issued on 2 April 1944, however, Hitler had already confirmed the requirement 'to hold firm on Crimea'. Thus the peninsula was to be defended until further notice. In the same order, the Führer opined that 'the Russian offensive in the south of the Eastern Front has passed its climax. The Russians have exhausted and divided their forces'.[16] Such blind optimism was entirely misplaced: only six days later the storm broke at the Perekop.

The Soviet Crimean strategic offensive operation was launched at 0900 hours on Easter Saturday, 8 April 1944, following an intense, hour-long artillery preparation. As in the previous campaigns for Crimea, whether during the Civil War or the initial period of the Great Patriotic War, the decisive battle took place on the Perekop–Syvash front. While the 2nd Guards Army assaulted the German positions at Perekop, the 51st Army burst out of the Dzhangar bridgehead and attacked the Romanian troops defending the Syvash sector. For two days the German 50th and 336th Divisions, reinforced by the 111th, were able to withstand the Soviet onslaught. The Romanians also fought well initially, but on 9 April their 10th Division was forced back.[17] With neither tactical nor operational reserves available to plug the gap, at 1000 hours on 10 April Headquarters Seventeenth Army initiated the 'Eagle' plan, and ordered XLIX Mountain Corps to pull back to Sevastopol. The withdrawal, which commenced during the night of the 10th/11th, involved a forced march over 160 kilometres of open steppe.

The vanguards of 19th Tank Corps closely pursued the retreating Axis units towards Simferopol. German ground attack aircraft (the Luftwaffe flew 3,796 sorties in the period 2–22 April 1944), the 88mm guns of the 9th Flak Division and the remaining assault guns fought a bitter delaying action, preventing a rout. None the less, the Soviet advance could not be stopped. Sergeant Vladimir Antonovich Kolesnikov, a mine specialist serving in a sapper battalion, took part in the rapid drive towards the south. Often his unit forged in front of the tanks, clearing mines and other obstacles from their path. 'We reached Dzhankoy on the 11th and Simferopol on the 13th', he recalled. 'Although there was not much German resistance, [thereafter] we could not break through their defence lines in front of Sevastopol immediately'.[18]

With the leading elements of the 19th Tank Corps – equipped with the fast T-34 and the slower lend-lease British Mk IX Valentine tanks – snapping hard on their heels, the retreating columns of XLIX Corps covered the march to Sevastopol in three days. Soviet tank units entered Simferopol during the evening of 13 April within twelve hours of Jaenecke and his staff rapidly abandoning their former headquarters. To the south, the main highway to Sevastopol was jam packed with the retreating units of XLIX Corps. There now seemed every prospect of these troops being overrun, and Sevastopol being attacked off the line of march. In contrast to the ground north of Simferopol, however, the wooded hilly terrain between Bakhchisaray and Sevastopol offered opportunities to impose a more effective delay on the advancing Soviet tank units. History repeated itself at the head of the Belbek valley, south of Bakhchisaray. In late October 1941, Manstein's attempt to rush Sevastopol with Ziegler's brigade had been parried by the Black Sea Fleet's naval infantrymen and cadets. Now a scratch German force under the command of Colonel Paul Betz, the recently appointed commandant of the fortress of Sevastopol, blocked the Soviet advance. His battlegroup, which consisted of two infantry battalions, six Flak batteries, a handful of assault guns and an armoured train, held off numerous Soviet tank and infantry attacks for twelve precious hours during the course of 14 April. This effective delaying action saved many elements of XLIX Corps, whose tail elements streamed into Sevastopol later that evening. The retreat to the city had proved a close run and costly affair, reducing the 50th, 336th and 111th Divisions to not much more than regimental strength.

On the Kerch peninsula, V Corps was ordered to commence its withdrawal under the 'Eagle' plan on 10 April, Easter Monday. At 1900 hours, the 73rd and 98th Infantry Divisions and the Romanian 3rd Mountain and 6th Cavalry Divisions started moving back towards Parpach. Immediately, the Coastal Army pursued these retreating formations. As historian Paul Carell narrates, a 'terrible race began between the motorised Soviets and the troops of V Corps who, after prolonged positional warfare, had lost the habit of swift movement and whose transport in any case was largely horse-drawn'.[19] Despite these disadvantages, the bulk of the German and Romanian divisions evaded their pursuers and reached the Parpach position first, albeit taking considerable casualties in the process. Although the quickest route to Sevastopol lay through Simferopol, the rapid advance by the 19th Tank Corps now threatened to interdict it. Therefore Seventeenth Army diverted V Corps to the longer, nominally safer, coastal road via Sudak, Alushta and Yalta.

Conducting a series of relentless forced marches and bitter rearguard actions, the rapidly exhausting troops of V Corps managed to reach Sudak by the evening of 13 April, and Alushta the next morning. Relief came to about 10,000 lucky men, who were evacuated by the German *Kriegsmarine* from Feodosiya on the 12th, and Sudak on the 13th, to Balaklava. Small groups were also picked up from Alushta and Yalta on the 14th and 15th respectively. For the remainder, there was no alternative but to march on, fighting off ambushes by partisans on the way. The divisional history of the 98th Division recounts the desperate nature of this retreat in one action near Sudak:

> It became dark. Firing began. First it was only an anti-tank gun. Shell after shell landed in the village.... [Then] hand grenades came flying down. Submachine-gun fire sprayed from windows and rooftops.... Several trucks drove away, but

became lost in the darkness and became stuck. The columns were close to panic. There were still a few of the 'old warriors' left, however, and they saved the situation by placing well-aimed bursts of fire at the muzzle flashes.... The columns resumed their march at about midnight. This dance was repeated several times before the sun rose again.[20]

On the 15th, the depleted divisions of V Corps reached Yalta and managed to catch a few hours rest before moving off again along the coastal road to Alupka and, much further still, to reach the safety of Sevastopol, now defended by a thin line of Romanian mountain troops. The next day, the final elements of V Corps entered the fortress area. Already, forward elements from the 19th Tank Corps pushed towards the city, but had been blocked by the Romanians.

It had proved a lucky escape for those who survived the gruelling march to Sevastopol. Along with their comrades serving in XLIX Corps, and in the remnants of the Romanian formations, all now dreamt of a timely evacuation from Sevastopol to Romania. For many, however, it was not to be. The Russian inhabitants of Crimea, in contrast, gave the Soviet troops a jubilant welcome as they liberated town after town, and none more so than along the eastern coast as Feodosiya, Sudak, Alushta and Yalta fell successively to the Coastal Army over the period 13–16 April. For them, the hated occupation and oppression of more than two and half years was at last over.

Yalta had survived the occupation relatively unscathed. A wartime resident, the then fourteen-year-old Alla Vasilevna Khanilo, recalled the 'heartfelt joy of the liberation'. She declared that the city had largely 'saved herself'. The Germans had used Yalta – as had the Communists before them – as a location of treating wounded and convalescents in various sanatoria. Soviet bombers, which 'caused more damage than the German ones' did not attack these buildings, focussing instead on the docks and timber yards.[21] In 1946, Alla Vasilevna joined the staff of the Chekhov museum. She found that Germans had respected the great Russian writer's house – in particular, his library had remained unharmed. 'Perhaps it was the presence of so many German works and translations of Chekhov', she opined, 'that helped its survival'. But equally, she stressed, the presence of Chekhov's daughter Maria and the fact that German officers were billeted there, including a certain Major Baake, 'may have had something to do with it'.[22]

The Final Battle for Sevastopol, April–May 1944

Jaenecke had angered Hitler by ordering the withdrawal of Seventeenth Army to Sevastopol without seeking permission. The Führer accused him of disobedience and losing his nerve. Nevertheless, the reality of the situation imposed by the Soviet

Crimean offensive forced Hitler to accept the necessity of the move, albeit under the strict conditions that Sevastopol was to be held until further notice, and hence, 'no combat troops were to be transported away'. Exploiting to the full the flexibility he had received, Jaenecke ordered the evacuation to Constanta to commence on 12 April. In this manner, Wehrmacht personnel, members of the civil and military administrations, rear area services and other staffs were carried to safety in Romania. By the beginning of May approximately 100,000 people had been evacuated. The remainder of the Seventeenth Army, some 125,000 (78,000 Germans and 46,000 Romanians) participated in the defence of Sevastopol. Remarkably, the German official history records that the 'fighting strength' was only 'about 20,000'.[23] This figure, representing about two divisions of combat soldiers, at first sight seems rather low. Yet the majority of the divisions which had fought and marched from either northern or eastern Crimea had suffered a terrible bleeding – the 73rd Infantry, for example, was deficient by no less than 79 per cent of its personnel.[24] Most of the Axis divisions' heavy equipment was lost *en route*. While officially recorded losses over the nine days of fighting amounted to 13,131 Germans and 17,652 Romanians, at least 13,000 men remained unaccounted for.[25]

The title of 'Fortress Sevastopol' was as illusory as the term 'Fortress Crimea'. Since the fall of the city to Manstein in July 1942, limited work had been undertaken to repair and rebuild the former Soviet lines of fortification. Although it would have taken a great deal of additional time, manpower and materiel to have restored them, bearing in mind the level of previous destruction, it remains surprising that Jaenecke, a military engineer by training, had not insisted on much more being done. German coastal artillery faced seaward rather than landward; the powerful Soviet Batteries 30 and 35 had been so badly wrecked that reinstating them would have required a major construction and technical effort, which had not been made available. Frantic attempts made in recent weeks to make up lost ground could not turn Sevastopol into a fortress of anything like the strength of June 1942. Soviet/Russian historical claims that its defences had been considerably augmented prior to the final battle for the city can be dismissed as propaganda designed to magnify the achievement of liberation.[26]

The Luftwaffe, having lost all its main bases on Crimea, was restricted to the small airfield on the Chersonese peninsula. On 25 April, only forty-six combat aircraft remained operational, including sixteen fighters and twenty-one ground attack. The only saving grace lay in the 9th Flak Division, which had retained 73 per cent of its heavy guns and 65 per cent of its lighter weapons. The infantry divisions, however, had lost over two-thirds of their field artillery during the retreat to Sevastopol.[27] Furthermore, the force ratios of attacker to defender in April 1944 were considerably greater to the 4th Ukrainian *Front*'s advantage than to Eleventh Army twenty-two months before. Tolbukhin's *front* now incorporated the Coastal Army, commanded by the newly appointed Lieutenant General Kondrat Semenovich Melnik. In all, the Soviet force assembled for the assault on Sevastopol amounted to 470,000 men in twenty-nine rifle divisions and a reinforced tank corps.

By scraping together all the available men who could bear arms, Seventeenth Army managed to build up its combat strength to approximately 64,000 men. As shown in Table 15.2, this force embraced not only German and Romanian Army troops, but also miscellaneous German navy and air force units. The fifteen grenadier regiments of the five German 'divisions' provided the backbone of the defence of Sevastopol, reinforced by a mix of Romanian and German battalions, including emergency makeshift 'alarm' units. Jaenecke and his subordinate commanders opted to place the vast majority of their forces in the main defence line, which followed the old Soviet outer perimeter in the north and north-east, and then paralleled the eastern face of the Sapun escarpment southwards to Balaklava. There were insufficient forces remaining to form either army or corps reserves at formation level, let alone to man a lightly prepared second position. Wisely, however, the rear position on the Chersonese peninsula, designed to protect any final evacuation, had received some attention. Despite his misgivings about the wisdom of holding Sevastopol other than to enable the evacuation, Jaenecke struck a defiant note in his Army Order No. 3 of 16 April: 'In the defence of the fortress there will be not a step back. Behind us is only the necessary space for ... the fortress and the Black Sea'.[28]

	Northern Front (XLIX Mountain Corps)	North-Eastern and Eastern Front (V Corps)
Principal German Army formations	50th Infantry Division 336th Infantry Division	98th Infantry Division 111th Infantry Division 73rd Infantry Division
Miscellaneous German reinforcing units	Navy 'combat battalions' 81st Field Replacement Battalion 623rd Security Battalion 17th Army Assault Battalion and Weapons School Two 'alarm' battalions One 'alarm' company	Air Force 'combat battalions' 85th Field Replacement Battalion Three 'alarm' battalions Two 'alarm' companies
Reinforcing Romanian formations providing battlegroups	1st Mountain Division 2nd Mountain Division	3rd Mountain Division 19th Infantry Division 6th Cavalry Division 9th Cavalry Division
Other Romanian units	Corps Troops, I Romanian Mountain Corps	Corps Troops, Cavalry Corps

Table 15.2 – Axis Forces Defending Sevastopol, 18 April 1944[29]

By 18 April, the Axis forces had occupied their positions (see Map 17). For the troops who had marched from Perekop or Kerch there had been precious little time available for rest or recuperation, let alone to erect new field defences or to strengthen previous ones. The next day, both the Coastal and the 51st Armies launched probing attacks that were beaten back. On the morning of 23 April, the latter army and the 2nd Guards Army launched a more determined assault on the north-eastern front defended by XLIX Mountain Corps. Although these Soviet attacks continued for several days, they were all repulsed – at the sacrifice of heavy losses to the defender and attacker alike. On the 27th it was the Coastal Army's turn to attack the positions of V Corps. Making best use of the remaining assault guns, the Axis defence held firm on the Sapun position. But this series of preliminary attacks all served to wear the defenders down, and to identify where and how best to mount the next assault. By late April, however, it was evident that it was only a matter of days before the Soviets launched a fully resourced, well co-ordinated and decisive attack designed to destroy the Seventeenth Army and to liberate Sevastopol.

In the meantime, as matters approached the climactic fight for the city, Jaenecke had not given up seeking authority to evacuate the fighting elements of his army. Already his superior, Colonel General Ferdinand Schörner, the recently appointed commander-in-chief of Army Group South Ukraine, accompanied by General Allmendinger, had attempted to wrest a favourable decision from Hitler in person on 21 April. Antonescu too demanded an immediate evacuation. But the Führer had stubbornly turned their entreaties down, demanding – somewhat curiously – that Sevastopol must hold out for at least another eight weeks, by which time the anticipated Western Allied invasion of France would have been beaten back.[30] Undeterred, Jaenecke flew to Hitler's Alpine retreat in southern Germany, the Berghof near Berchtesgaden, on 29 April. His attempt to convince the German leader to authorise the immediate evacuation of Sevastopol was met with a resounding 'Nein! ... Sevastopol must be held to the last man bearing arms'. Hitler promised to send more men and equipment to the Seventeenth Army – thus reinforcing inevitable failure.

Jaenecke did not return to Crimea. During his return via Schörner's headquarters in Galatz (Galati), Romania, he was informed of his removal from army command. Forbidden to fly on to Sevastopol, his relief was none other than Allmendinger, whose corps was taken over on 4 May by Lieutenant General Friedrich Müller, a veteran of Manstein's Crimean campaign as a regimental commander of the 72nd Infantry Division. Another casualty of Hitler's contempt was the commanding general of XLIX Mountain Corps, Konrad, who had not been forgiven for breaking off battle at Perekop–Ishun. General of Artillery Walter Hartmann, who had lost both an arm and a leg earlier in the war, but not his fighting spirit, relieved him.[31]

Although Jaenecke had been dismissed, his chief of staff, Major General Wolfdietrich, Ritter von Xylander, and the naval commander of Crimea, Rear Admiral Otto Schulz, together with Luftwaffe staff support, continued to work up the detailed evacuation plan. A draft of this joint (navy, army and air force) document (Study 'Leopold') had been completed on 22 April 1944. It foresaw first the transport of the remaining unnecessary personnel; then the evacuation of XLIX Corps from Sevastopol, followed by V Corps from the Chersonese peninsula. The last two stages would require fourteen uninterrupted days. Yet nobody knew when the main Soviet assault would hit Sevastopol and whether it would render much, if not all, of the plan irrelevant. Meanwhile, during the last two weeks of April, Seventeenth Army received 2,647 battle casualty replacements while 4,836 wounded German soldiers were evacuated. Of Hitler's much heralded reinforcements, from 1–12 May, only 1,300 men arrived with a small amount of equipment, including fifteen heavy anti-tank guns.[32]

Tolbukhin held the operational initiative. It was up to him to determine the timing, axes and sequencing of his three armies' attacks against Sevastopol, just it had been Manstein's decision to direct his three corps in 1941–42. Acknowledging the dictates of terrain, the Soviet commander-in-chief followed a similar scheme of manoeuvre in 1944 – as depicted on Map 17. He determined that the 2nd Guards Army should first attack the northern front, followed by the 51st Army and the Coastal Army assaulting the eastern front, including the Sapun position, two days later. Following Manstein's method, Tolbukhin sought to fix the enemy's defence in the north, so triggering the committal of his reserves, before switching his main effort to an attack from the east directed at Sevastopol and the Chersonese peninsula.[33]

The 2nd Guards Army launched its supporting, but none the less major, attack in the north at 0900 hours on 5 May. After a two-hour bombardment by 400 guns and 400 rocket launchers, five rifle divisions from the 13th Guards Rifle and the 55th Rifle Corps hit the German 336th Infantry Division hard in the north-eastern sector of the Axis defence. Major General Wolf Hageman's formation, defending the eastern Belbek valley and the Mackenzie Heights, repulsed repeated attacks over the next couple of days. In the process, however, he was severely wounded and evacuated, and his troops were worn down by the intensity of the fighting.

As the 2nd Guards Army continued its attack in the north, the 51st and Coastal Armies launched the main effort of the 4th Ukrainian *Front*'s offensive on the morning of 7 May. In this principal zone of attack, Soviet forces had concentrated 200 guns, rocket launchers and mortars per kilometre of front. In the planned break-through sectors, this number was almost double. The skies above were filled with the fighters and ground attack aircraft of the 8th Air Army, who were to fly 1,460 sorties that day.

The 51st Army attacked with two rifle corps in its first echelon, the 63rd on the left (main effort) assaulting the mid-point of the Sapun escarpment, and the 1st Guards on the right towards Inkerman. Major Generals P. K. Koshevoi and I. I. Missan commanded these two formations. In the army's second echelon, the 10th Rifle Corps (Major General K. P. Neverov) was tasked to support the 63rd Rifle Corps, and building on its anticipated success, to storm into the south-eastern outskirts of Sevastopol. To the south, the Coastal Army attacked with three rifle corps (16th, 3rd Mountain and 11th) abreast, commanded by Major Generals K. I. Provalov, A. A. Luchinsky and S. E. Rozhdestvensky respectively. The 19th Tank Corps formed its second echelon, ready to exploit rapidly into the Chersonese peninsula once a breakthrough of the German main position had been achieved. Thus across these two armies, no fewer than five corps attacked in the first operational echelon, with two in the second. While this force density looks impressive, it should be noted that Soviet rifle corps were typically smaller than their German or Western Allied equivalents by this stage of the war: an average rifle division mustered at best 5,000 infantrymen. At Sevastopol, however, the German and Romanian forces were in even worse shape.

In the limited time available since its arrival from the Kerch peninsula, the German V Corps, reinforced by Romanian units, had strengthened an impressive looking defence on the Sapun escarpment. Its steep slopes were 'completely criss-crossed with trenches, dotted with artillery and machine-gun positions, interlaced with anti-personnel and anti-tank obstacles, and its base was covered in mines'.[34] Yet the odds were at least six to one in favour of the attacker: in some sectors, at least nine to one.

At 0900 hours, the Soviet artillery preparation began: an intense maelstrom of fire – over 80,000 shells – lasted ninety minutes. From north of the 'Serpentine' (switchback) of the Yalta–Sevastopol road to Balaklava Bay in the south, the German 111th and 73rd Infantry Divisions, commanded by Major Generals Erich Gruner and Hermann Böhme, took the full brunt of this barrage and the subsequent mass assault by Soviet tanks and infantry. The anticipated main axes of the Soviet attack were soon confirmed – astride the two principal routes towards Sevastopol over the Sapun escarpment.

The 186th Grenadier Regiment of the 73rd Division defended the critical sector that included the 'Saddle' at the southern end of the escarpment. This feature carried the road from Balaklava and Kadikoy to Sevastopol, precisely where the Coastal Army intended to break through. Taking the main weight of the Coastal Army's attack, with the 83rd Naval Infantry Brigade in the van of the 11th Guards Rifle Corps, the German regiment was torn apart and pushed back. Although a counter-attack by five weak battalions of divisional, corps and army reserves led by Lieutenant Colonel Pflugradt, commander of the 70th Grenadier

Regiment, temporarily restored the situation, relentless Soviet pressure led to a breakthrough at the Saddle at 2145 hours. This was not the only significant penetration of the main position, however.

The 111th Division, also under heavy attack, fought an equally desperate struggle, and nowhere more intensely than at the Serpentine. Here its 50th Grenadier Regiment withstood wave after wave of Soviet troops storming up the steep slopes of the Sapun escarpment astride the main road to Sevastopol. This particular attack has been immortalised in the post-war Diorama museum and memorial to the liberation of Sevastopol, which opened with great ceremony in 1959. Two rifle divisions – fighting side by side here – were particularly involved in the assault here on 7 May 1944: the 33nd Guards Rifle Division (Colonel N. K. Zakurenkov) of the 11th Rifle Corps and 77th Rifle Division (Colonel A. P. Rodionov) of the 63rd Rifle Corps.

Following nine hours of intense combat, at 1930 hours soldiers from both divisions almost simultaneously reached the crest of the escarpment. As the guidebook to the Diorama explains, 'one after another, red flags appeared at the top'. One of the first officers to gain the summit was Lieutenant V. F. Gromakov, who 'picked up a red banner which had fallen from the hand of a dead warrior, and on hoisting it high, led his men forward'. For this courageous feat, he was made a Hero of the Soviet Union.[35] He was but one of many so decorated for outstanding bravery and leadership that day. By nightfall, the Sapun was won: the 10th Rifle Corps had already been moved up to support 63rd Rifle Corps. 19th Tank Corps was readied to join the Coastal Army's battle on the 8th.

The Soviet penetrations at the Saddle and the Serpentine on 7 May, and the associated loss of most of the Sapun position in between, threatened the destruction of the Seventeenth Army, and hence the loss of Sevastopol. Reports of enemy tanks advancing on the main road from the Serpentine towards the English Cemetery only increased concerns as to an imminent collapse of the Axis defence. Yet all was not lost. Headquarters Seventeenth Army had one last trick up its sleeve in order to stabilise the situation, albeit with low-value cards. That night, plans were put in place to launch a counter-attack on the 8th in order to establish a defensive line along the Sapun escarpment. But where were the necessary forces to come from? Fortunately, Operation WILDKATZE (WILD CAT), the withdrawal of XLIX Corps from the northern side over Sevastopol Bay, was already under way. In this manner, units from the 50th Infantry Division became available for redeployment to add to those being extracted from the 98th and 111th Divisions. Battlegroups 'Faulhaber' (four battalions) and 'Marienfeld' (two battalions) were assembled during the early hours of 8 May in the vicinity of the English Cemetery and of the Nikolayevka vineyard to the south-east of Sevastopol. During the same night, the rear, Chersonese, position was occupied by the remnants of the

Romanian 2nd Mountain Division. They were soon joined by elements of the German 50th and 336th Divisions. By 0800 hours, Seventeenth Army established its final headquarters in the ruins of Coastal Battery 35.

Meanwhile, Sevastopol's inhabitants had not remained immune from the fighting. Many were killed or injured as a result of Soviet air raids on the port infrastructure and Axis ships in the city's many inlets and harbours. Once in range, the Red Army's artillery joined in. The German command reacted to the grave threat to the evacuation operation with characteristic ruthlessness. Its response was to round up members of the local population to use as human shields. Valentina Kutuzova remembered the horror of such an action:

> On 1 May 1944, the Germans drove us on lorries to the Streletskaya Harbour and pushed us aboard a transport vessel, in whose hold Germans and Romanians were sitting. [As we got underway,] a bombardment started. Women were standing on the deck, and lifting their children above their heads, shouting and crying. Our vessel was damaged. It began to sink. A wave swept several people into the harbour. Many people fell on their knees and prayed. Mama and I exchanged farewells as we awaited death. The water was reddened by the blood in the harbour; the wounded were crying loudly. The commander of the vessel decided to turn back to the city. We managed to moor near the hospital. People disembarked and ran away in panic from the ship, but the Germans tried to stop us. With difficulties, we broke through and reached our home (Komsomolskaya Street 12). Having hidden ourselves, we waited for liberation.[36]

A week later, the long dreamed-of and much prayed-for day of liberation lay very close. At dawn on 8 May, the three attacking Soviet armies resumed their offensive. Troops of the 2nd Guards Army finally managed to capture the Mackenzie Heights and pressed into the northern side of Sevastopol. On their left, southern, flank the 1st Guards Rifle Corps of the 51st Army captured Inkerman. Already on the 8th, as both the Coastal and 51st Armies exploited their gains made the previous day, the first Soviet tanks neared the city. A vanguard platoon of the 22nd Guards Tank Regiment of the 51st Army neared the Green Hill (where Thomas Mackenzie was buried in 1786) on Sevastopol's eastern outskirts. In an engagement there, the platoon leader, Lieutenant I. I. Revkov, 'destroyed three tanks and four guns' and defeated 'a force of 150 enemy soldiers and officers'. His tank was one of the first to break into Sevastopol, over twenty-four hours before the main body of the 1st Guards Rifle Corps arrived. For this action, Revkov and his driver-mechanic, Senior Guards Sergeant N. S. Vodolazkin, were both awarded the title of Hero of the Soviet Union.[37] Today a T-34 tank still stands above Revyakin Road commemorating this first stage in the liberation of Sevastopol.

The German counter-attacks by the Battlegroups 'Faulhaber' and 'Marienfeld' on the morning of 8 May, which aimed to link up with the 186th Grenadier Regiment at the Saddle and to destroy the wedge of Soviet forces advancing from the Serpentine on the English Cemetery respectively, initially made some progress. One German battalion even managed to fight its way to within 800 metres of the Serpentine, but was beaten back and destroyed in the attempt. Other German units were either cut off by advancing Soviet forces or broken up by ground attack aircraft and artillery strikes. By noon the counter-attacks had petered out. They had proved but a forlorn drop in an ocean of advancing Soviet forces. As a result, the Sapun position was irretrievably lost and the Seventeenth Army's fate sealed. During the course of the day, the 3rd Mountain Rifle Corps and the 16th Rifle Corps broke through towards the German second position and by evening had captured the village of Karan (now Frontskoye) near the southern coast, west of Balaklava.

The Seventeenth Army, with no reserves remaining to counter the gathering momentum of the Soviet attack from north to south, had shot its bolt. Allmendinger reported to Schörner that there was no prospect of holding Sevastopol for more than a day or so. At 2115 hours, Schörner signalled the Führer's headquarters: 'Request evacuation since further defence of Sevastopol no longer possible'.[38] By 0215 hours on 9 May, Allmendinger received the necessary, long-awaited authority from Hitler. Having ordered the withdrawal of the remainder of the army to the Chersonese position, he demanded that an emergency embarkation of the entire force must begin as soon as possible – and no later than the night of 10/11 May. Yet it remained questionable whether sufficient shipping would arrive in time, and whether the Seventeenth Army could hold out long enough. The prognosis was not good.

By 8 May, about 50,000 Axis troops remained on Crimea. During the afternoon of 9 May, Soviet troops broke through in force into Sevastopol. Units of the 2nd Guards Army together with elements of the 1st Guards Rifle Corps (51st Army) cleared the Korabelnaya suburb on the eastern side of the city. By 1900 hours, the 216th and 257th Divisions of 10th Rifle Corps had joined in, advancing from the south-eastern approaches. At the same time, the 11th Guards Rifle Corps (Coastal Army) occupied the south-western outskirts of the city. Thus all three armies of the 4th Ukrainian *Front* participated in Sevastopol's liberation. The majority of the remaining Axis forces had abandoned the city by 1600 hours. Although there was some street fighting, there was to be no desperate battle in the city centre.

News of the success quickly reached Moscow. Stalin and other members of *Stavka* rejoiced. The Soviet leader's congratulatory telegram to the 4th Ukrainian *Front* read: 'In commemoration of the victory won, the formations and units who distinguished themselves in the battle for the liberation of Sevastopol, should be honoured with the title 'Sevastopol', and awarded with decorations.'[39] Anxious to refurbish and redeploy the 2nd Guards and 51st Armies as quickly as possible, *Stavka* (with Stalin at its head) demanded that every remaining German be eliminated within twenty-four hours. Future strategic offensive operations against the main weight of the German Army in the East beckoned.[40]

The fight on the south-western tip of Crimea, meanwhile, was not yet over. German and Romanian troops streamed back in a chaotic retreat to the Seventeenth Army's final redoubt on the western tip of the Chersonese peninsula, closely pursued by the 19th Tank Corps and the forward elements of the 16th and 10th Rifle Corps. History now repeated itself. Although the roles had been reversed, events followed in a similar pattern to those of July 1942. The defenders now fought stubbornly while waiting patiently for evacuation. Then tragedy struck. During the early morning of 10 May two transports, the *Totila* and the *Teja*, moored off the coast – 2 nautical miles north of Cape Chersonese – just out of the range of Soviet artillery. About 5,000 men were ferried out to the *Teja* and 4,000 to the *Totilla*. Both vessels were bombed and torpedoed, and sank during the course of the day. Only 400 men were rescued. All hopes now rested on the evacuation planned for the night of 10/11 May. Although the hours of darkness much reduced the threat of air attack, all the remaining areas held by Axis forces were swept by artillery fire. The last airfield on the peninsula had already been bombed and shelled so much that it appeared unusable. Somehow the brave pilots of fifty Ju-52 transports, much as their colleagues had done at Stalingrad, managed to land and take off heavily over-loaded, picking up 1,000 wounded during the night of 9/10 May. They were the lucky ones, for many more could not be flown out.

By nightfall of 10 May, there were around 30,000 Axis soldiers left on the Chersonese peninsula. In a mass effort to save them, about 190 German and Romanian warships and merchant vessels steamed across the Black Sea. Then fate cruelly intervened. A great storm blew up and severely delayed the convoys. Consequently, the evacuation had to be postponed to the 11th/12th; Seventeenth Army would need to hold on for a further day. The majority of the headquarters personnel were fortunate in being evacuated from Maxim Gorky II during the early hours of the 11th. There were many parallels to Petrov's escape on 1 July 1942. This time, however, a German E-Boat (a motor torpedo boat (MTB)), rather than a submarine provided the means of rescue. A German eyewitness, Captain Hensel, described the escape:

> The fort was under continuous artillery and mortar fire but the subterranean
> passages opened out into the cliff face on the coast. So we climbed down in the

dark on rope ladders, and from 0100 hours onwards waited among the cliffs. Two hours passed without any sign of life. Only the Russian shells whined overhead, towards the sea. We had almost given up hope…. But suddenly … [a] voice called on us to embark. There were two MTBs. Because of the rocky coast they could not come right in. Fortunately, the sea was quite calm. So we rowed out in small boats, eight men to each. It was a slow business and by then it was getting light. But at last we were ready to put out to sea. Each MTB had taken aboard 50 men…. [We set off] at full speed…. Eight hours passed before we entered the calm waters of the port of Constanta. We were saved.[41]

During 11 May, the remaining German and Romanian troops fought off no fewer than seven Soviet attacks, but took considerable numbers of casualties in the process. The underground tunnels and casements of Maxim Gorky II were soon over-filled with the growing numbers of the wounded. The final night of the evacuation proved only partially successful in that thousands were rescued, but many were left behind. All forces had been ordered to retire to their points of embarkation in various bays and coves at 2300 hours, to dig in for local defence, and to await the arrival of their allotted ships. *In extremis*, however, any available vessel could be boarded.

Of the German divisions, the majority of the 98th was evacuated. While only one regiment of the 50th (the 121st) was transported, much of the 111th Division was stranded. The men of the 73rd and 336th Divisions had mixed fortunes. On the orders of Army Group South Ukraine, an E-Boat rescued Generals Allmendinger and Pickert, and the remainder of the Seventeenth Army headquarters staff. Both generals shared the common experience of being flown out of the encircled Stalingrad, and were lucky to escape with their lives again.

At daylight on the 12th, under cover of air bombardment and artillery fire, Soviet forces pushed on towards the cliffs and embarkation beaches. The last ships had left a couple of hours before. By noon it was mostly over: with a few exceptions, the remaining Germans and Romanians surrendered, over 15,000 men. They were marched off in long columns into captivity, many either to die or to serve long years in prison camps. Major General Hermann Böhme, commander of the 73rd Division, was amongst them, taken at his command post. He was only released from the Soviet Union in 1955, one of the 16,000 *Spätheimkehrere* (late home-comers or returnees). His counterpart in the 111th, Erich Gruner, however, was dead. He had tried to give himself up, but was shot. Some scattered elements of the Axis forces fought on until they were either killed or ran out of ammunition. A final lucky few (seven officers and seventy-five men) were taken off by an E-Boat during the night of 12/13 May.

Despite the disasters of the final few days, the majority of the Seventeenth Army's troops – Germans and Romanians alike – were evacuated safely from Crimea. On 12 April, the Army strength was approximately 230,000 men. Of these, 130,000 were transported by sea and a further 21,457 recovered by air – mostly wounded. During the period of the final battle for Crimea and Sevastopol (8 April – 13 May 1944), 57,500 men (31,700 Germans and 25,800 Romanians) were listed as either killed or missing in action.[42] Amongst the latter, the Red Army reported taking 26,000 prisoners of war. That left an unaccounted deficit of over 21,000 men.

Notwithstanding the numbers saved during the course of the evacuation, there was little to celebrate about in the Axis camp. The defeat could not provide a 'Dunkirk' effect that would enter a defiant nation's narrative, and galvanise it to further action. In stark contrast to the Soviet defence of Sevastopol in 1941–42, which had lasted 250 days, the city had been abandoned within five days of the final battle starting on 5 May 1944. Therefore no triumphant legend could be generated. None the less, during the last days, the *Wehrmacht* communiqués put a brave face on the unfolding disaster. On 10 May, for example, it was reported that 'in the Sevastopol bridgehead German and Romanian troops are engaged in further heavy fighting with the advancing enemy. In the course of our withdrawal, the rubble of the city of Sevastopol has been abandoned'. Three days later, as the end approached, it was announced that 'yesterday our rearguards near Sevastopol were still engaged in bitter fighting with numerically far-superior forces, and with exemplary bravery, covered the evacuation of German-Romanian formations'.[43]

No amount of heroic gloss, however, could mask the magnitude of the defeat on the Crimean peninsula, and the directly associated loss of Sevastopol, in which capture so much German and Romanian blood and treasure had been expended. Although it was not on the scale of the twin disasters of Stalingrad and Tunis (in February and May 1943 respectively), or of the destruction of Army Group Centre in June–July 1944, the Seventeenth Army as a fighting force had been eliminated. Four Axis corps were destroyed: the German V and XLIX Mountain; and the Romanian I Mountain and Cavalry.

Once more Hitler had gambled, and in consequence the peoples of Germany and Romania had paid a bitter price. Although the loss of Crimea turned not out to be the 'second Stalingrad' that Hitler had feared in late December 1943, none the less it represented a sobering setback for him and the Axis cause. Yet in a similar manner to the reconstitution of the German Sixth Army after its downfall at Stalingrad, a new Seventeenth Army was raised. It fought in Galicia, the East Carpathian Mountains, and finally in Silesia at the war's close in May 1945 – all further battles lost in the long retreat to Germany's ultimate defeat.

THE IMMEDIATE AFTERMATH OF THE LIBERATION

Liberated Sevastopol received its first very important visitor in mid-May 1944, Marshal Vasilevsky.[44] During his inspection of the victorious troops of the 4th Ukrainian *Front*, his sojourn in the ruined city was rudely cut short when his car hit a mine and rolled over. Receiving a head wound, caused by flying glass from the smashed windscreen, he was evacuated to Moscow for treatment.

The mine threat in and around Sevastopol was omnipresent, whether in urban areas, or in the fields and forest tracks. Combat engineers, including Vladimir Kolesnikov and his men, laboured round the clock to clear the mines and other unexploded ordnance. Shortly after the liberation, an American war correspondent, Eddie Gilmore, described the narrow roads around Sevastopol. Initially, he was puzzled why Soviet drivers drove so carefully. The explanation came soon enough. 'On the other side of the road we could see why', he noted, for there were 'mines, little piles of the flat pancake kind, every fifty yards or so'. As a passenger, he hoped 'as never before for efficiency on the part of the Red Army's de-mining units'.[45] He survived to tell the extraordinary tale of Sevastopol's very first days as a liberated city.

Although Kolesnikov's platoon did not participate in the 'storm' of the Sapun escarpment on the 7th, it was soon employed in this devastated sector of the Sevastopol battlefield. The former sapper sergeant recalled:

> We conducted demining operations on the Sapun escarpment and in the outskirts of the city. We also cleared a massive German mine, a tonne of TNT, from a well near the Sapun position. One day near the end, 11 May, we came under shellfire. I had come to inspect progress in the clearance operation. There was still a German battery firing. In a detonation very close by, my driver was wounded, and our car tyres were damaged and went flat. I was lucky to escape relatively unscathed – but was left practically deaf for two to three days.

Kolesnikov, in common with the vast majority of the members of the 4th Ukrainian *Front*, was not a former inhabitant of Crimea or Sevastopol – he hailed from the Rostov-on-Don region. None the less, he regarded the battle for Sevastopol as the 'greatest test and honour' of his life. When the city was liberated, he and his men 'shouted for joy', but quickly remembered their fallen comrades. 'The sacrifice of so many', the veteran recalled over seventy years later, 'was not in vain'.[46] Although a Yalta resident in his later years, Kolesnikov stressed that his 'deepest feelings remain connected to Sevastopol'. He spoke, no doubt, for thousands.

The statistics of Soviet casualties incurred during the Crimean Strategic Offensive over the period 8 April – 12 May 1944 make sombre reading. From a combined strength of 462,400 (4th Ukrainian *Front*, Coastal Army, 4th Air Army, Black Sea Fleet and Azov Flotilla), there were 84,819 losses. Of these were 17,754 'irrecoverable', with 67,065 'sick and wounded'. This represented an average daily loss rate of 2,423 a day.[47] Taken together, the number of Axis and Soviet military deaths approached 80,000–100,000, excluding many thousands of civilians. But to what end? Hitler's decision to defend for Crimea for as long as possible might have had some remote strategic benefit, but, operationally, in the words of the German official history, it 'blocked for months the personnel and materiel resources that would have better served the stabilisation of the southern part of the Eastern Front'.[48] No wonder, then, why senior German officers such as Kleist, Manstein and Zeitzler were so frustrated by the Führer's decision-making.

From a Soviet perspective, the Crimean offensive eliminated the 'last enemy bridgehead' threatening the rear areas of fronts operating in the right-bank [of] Ukraine'.[49] Although the cost appeared high, in relative manpower terms, Tolbukhin's liberation of Crimea and Sevastopol represented one of the most economical Soviet strategic operations of the Great Patriotic War. Crucially, the offensive enabled the Black Sea Fleet to return to its main base. Moreover, the success at Sevastopol had a symbolic value during the Great Patriotic War perhaps second only to the earlier victory at Stalingrad or the later triumph in Berlin. At 0100 hours on 10 May 1944, the bright flashes and thunderous booms of 342 guns firing twenty-four volleys in honour of the liberation of Sevastopol broke the blackout and relative peace of a Moscow wartime night.

The Soviet authorities were keen to show off the place of victory to Moscow-based foreign war correspondents. Very quickly a flight to Crimea was organised. As Alexander Werth recalled, 'my trip ... on May 14–18 [1944] was perhaps the strangest Crimean holiday anyone ever had'. His vivid account paints a depressing picture of destruction:

> From a distance Sevastopol, with the long and narrow bay beyond, looked like a live city, but it was also dead. Even in the suburbs, at the far end of the valley of Inkerman, there was hardly a house standing. The railway station was a mountain of rubble and twisted metal; on the last day the Germans were at Sevastopol they ran an enormous goods train off the line into a ravine, where it lay smashed, its wheels in the air.

The reporter noted that the city, 'bright and lively before the war', now appeared 'melancholy beyond words'.[50]

The group of foreign correspondents also included Eddy Gilmore, the Moscow correspondent of the Associated Press. Like Werth, he recorded the immediate aftermath of the battle for Sevastopol. In the Belbek valley he found 'evidence of heavy fighting', including 'treads of tanks hurled over the landscape'. Near the Crimean coast north of Sevastopol, he narrated that 'the rank stench of death fouled our nostrils'. The explanation came soon enough from their escorting Red Army officers. It was here, apparently, that a Romanian cavalry regiment had been 'smashed up'; a number of 'dead horses and a few soldiers' still lay about. On reaching the northern shore of Sevastopol Bay, the party overlooked the harbour and city centre beyond. Gilmore was not prepared for what he then saw:

> Before me, across a quarter of mile of water, lay a sight more shocking than the killed soldiers and slaughtered horses—a real dead city. Not a single spiral of smoke rose from the place which once had held more than 100,000 people. The day was quiet and we could hear none of the sounds familiar in a city—blowing of whistles, rumble of street cars, blasts of automobile horns, bells of switching engines in railway yards.

It was an 'awful thing', he noted, 'to look at the corpse of a city, especially one that once had been so beautiful and gay'. The correspondents' conducting officers then explained how Soviet forces – presumably members of the 2nd Guards Army – had crossed the harbour in 'every way' they could. The means found included not only 'craft captured from the enemy, on our own craft, [and] on hurriedly made barges', but also, extraordinarily, 'on coffins which the Germans had arranged here to use for their own dead'.

The deep harbour of Sevastopol's roadstead still bore the macabre marks of recent fighting as well as of the German siege of 1941–42. Gilmore described the water as 'dotted black with many objects'. Some of these could be distinguished as the masts or 'smokestacks of ships'. Coming round the eastern end of the harbour, the team of journalists observed: 'hundreds of shot-up, wrecked, exploded locomotives and freight cars'. These vehicles, according to Gilmore, 'bore the names of many German cities: Berlin, Frankfurt, Hannover, Hamburg, Dresden. There were even some with Paris on them'.[51]

Back in the city, the correspondents wandered around the deserted, ruined streets. The evacuation of many thousands of Sevastopol's population during the defence of 1941–42, and the subsequent crimes of the occupation, explained the lack of people. Not only had 24,600 inhabitants been sent to Germany as slave labour, but also, more shockingly, no fewer than 27,306 civilians had been shot or hanged during German rule in the city. The majority of those killed were either Jews or Communists. Only 3,000 *Sevastopoltsi* (Sevastopolians) survived to witness the liberation.

The war reporters had a discussion with their host, the newly re-appointed mayor of Sevastopol, Vasily Petrovich Yefremov. As chairman of the city council during the defence of 1941–42, he had been 'one of the last Russians to leave, although wounded, and one of the first to re-enter'. Yefremov explained why the city centre was so empty of people – because 'those living in the outskirts had not yet lost the habit of looking upon this [area] as *verboten*' – a territory forbidden to enter on pain of death.[52] Only time would heal this problem. The group visited the Panorama museum. As Gilmore noted, it stood 'virtually in ruins, its roof and sides knocked in and its floor burned out'. Moved by such impressions and other sights, he described the 'deadest city of Russia':

> The once-beautiful Sevastopol of lilac trees, pretty promenades, many trees, classical architecture, warmhearted people, and nightly open-air concerts in summer is like an old, broken, wounded man, not bitter but tired of the cannon's roar and the whine of bombs.[53]

Both Gilmore and Werth visited the Chersonese peninsula, and the cape at its western tip. The former described the scene that confronted him as 'something I'll never forget, even if I cover wars for the rest of my life'. He recalled:

> ... a graveyard of German planes. Every shape and model have been there, burned out, bombed, riddled by Stormoviks [Russian low-altitude strafing planes] and shattered by shells. The Cape itself was bare of trees. The earth was red, almost like that around brickyards. It was hard and firm except where Russian shells had ploughed it up.

Looking down from the cliff tops on to the evacuation beaches that had witnessed such desolation and destruction less than a week before, Gilmore observed:

> ... the Germans. There were lots of them at the water's edge, about 35 feet beneath me. Their bodies, in green-gray, were huddled or heaped around groups of makeshift barges and rafts on which they had tried to get away…. I looked at the rafts closely. They were made of planks, on which desperate men had tied empty gasoline cans and ammunition boxes. Why, they couldn't have got one across the Potomac, the Hudson or the Ohio River.[54]

At the lighthouse on Cape Chersonese, where so recently a final engagement had been fought, Werth noted a skeleton 'with a few rags still clinging to it'. Closer inspection revealed white-and-blue stripes still visible – 'the *telniashka* (singlet) of a Black Sea sailor'. The British reporter mused, 'was he one of those who, nearly two years before, had fought here to the last – just like the Germans – on this very

Chersonese Promontory, and had been left here on this desolate spot, to rot away unburied?' Leaving that question unanswered, on looking out to the calm blue sea beyond, Werth wondered whether there were still:

> ... some rafts ... with desperate men clinging to them, drifting over waters where only three years before the pleasure steamers still cruised between Odessa, Sevastopol and Novorossiysk. Of the three, only Odessa looked like a city. Novorossiysk, like Sevastopol, was also a heap of ruins.[55]

Within eighteen months (1 November 1945) Sevastopol would become one of fifteen cities within the Russian Soviet Federative Socialist Republic (RSFSR) given priority status for reconstruction.[56] Novorossiysk was another.[57] In his study *Russia at War 1941–1945*, Werth pondered on the rapid success of the 4th Ukrainian *Front's* operation to liberate Sevastopol and to defeat the Axis forces:

> It will remain one of the puzzles of the war why, in 1941–42, despite overwhelming German and Romanian superiority in tanks and aircraft, and a substantial superiority in men, Sevastopol succeeded in holding out for 250 days and why, in 1944, the Russians captured it within four days. German authors now explain it simply by the great Russian superiority in effectives, aircraft and all other equipment. But did not the Germans and Romanians enjoy the same kind of superiority in 1941–42? Was there not something lacking in German morale by April 1944 – at least in a remote place like the Crimea? For, as we know, the Germans could still put up suicidal resistance once on German soil.[58]

To a large extent, Werth answered his own question: there can be little doubt that notwithstanding the quantitative advantage enjoyed by the Soviet forces in 1944, their morale (driven by faith in their cause and confidence in a successful outcome) exceeded that of their opponents. After all, the 'fighting power' of a force depends not only on the *conceptual* (how to fight) and *physical* (with what to fight) components, but also on the *moral* – a combination of leadership and motivation. It has a transitory quality – what holds true for one set of operational circumstances may not necessarily apply for the next. There is little doubt that Tolbukhin's Crimean Strategic Offensive was one of the best-led and organised major operations conducted by the Red Army during the Second World War.

THE EXPULSION OF THE TATARS AND OTHER NATIONALITIES

On his final night in Crimea, Werth had a revealing human experience with regard to the local population. Billeted in a Tatar cottage, he recalled:

... there was an old man there, and an old woman, and their son, a boy of fifteen or sixteen. They had, behind the house, a large vegetable garden, all of their own; ... and beyond the vegetable plot were immense fields of green wheat. But the Tatar family were morose and frightened, scarcely said a word, and the woman claimed to be very ill... I remember the look of fear that came over the old man when a Soviet officer knocked on the door in order, as it turned out, merely to billet me on him.[59]

That very same day, on 18 May 1944, the forcible expulsion of the entire Tatar population from Crimea to the Central Asian republics, such as Uzbekistan, commenced.[60] Within Tatar communities and their diaspora, this fateful event is still remembered as the *Kara Gun* (Dark Day). No doubt, the family that Werth stayed with would have been swept up in the merciless work of the NKVD's internal troops. At gunpoint, the populations of entire villages, and sections of heavily Tatar peopled towns such as Simferopol, Bakhchisaray and Stary Krym, were all given short notice to pack up and leave, and herded on to trucks, then trains. Alexander Solzhenitsyn described the mechanics of this action in his famous work, *Gulag Archipelago*:

> The motorized columns did not go right up to the settlements, but stayed at the road junctions while special troops encircled villages. Their orders were to allow the inhabitants an hour and a half to get ready, but political officers cut this down, sometimes to as little as forty minutes, to get it over more quickly and be on time at the assembly point – and so that richer pickings would be left lying around for the detachment of the task force left behind in the village ... which had to be burned to the ground. [The troops] took the Tatars to the stations, and there they went on waiting in their trains for days on end, wailing and singing mourning songs of farewell.[61]

Thus, as Solzhenitsyn noted, Stalin finally achieved what the Russian administrators and landowners of the Taurida Governorate had desired in the 1860s, and that which Alexander II had refused to countenance.[62]

By mid-1944, the Tatars had become a 'nation in exile'. Their supposed crime was collaboration with the Nazi aggressor. The Soviet authorities alleged that their co-operation with the enemy had been widespread: many thousands of villagers or Soviet prisoners of war had either joined police units and 'self-defence' battalions, or been absorbed directly into German infantry formations. Many other thousands of Tatars, however, had fought either as partisans against the German and Romanian occupiers, or had joined units of the Red Army. So the collective punishment swept up many thousands of loyal Tatars who had risked their lives for the Soviet Union, along with their entire families.

The Tatars were not the only people affected by Stalin's punitive exile. In June 1944, the Armenians (9,620), Bulgarians (12,420) and Greeks (15,040) were expelled as well – 2,300 Germans had already been banished in August 1941. Russian records document that no fewer than 228,543 men, women and children were deported from Crimea, 'of whom 191,014 were Crimean Tatars (more than 47,000 families)'. Mixed couples were not spared. If a husband was a Crimean Tatar and his wife Russian, for example, 'both were recorded as Tatars and were subject to deportation'.[63]

A Tatar account of the transportation by train brings the inherent cruelty of Stalin's Soviet Union into sharp relief:

> It was not to be shot. It was a journey of lingering death in cattle cars, crammed with people, like mobile gas chambers. The journey lasted three to four weeks, and took them across the scorching summer steppes of Kazakhstan. They took the Red partisans of the Crimea, the fighters of the Bolshevik underground, the Soviet and Party activists. Also invalids and old men. The remaining men were fighting the Fascists at the front, but deportation awaited them at the end of the war. And in the meantime, they crammed women and children into the trucks, where they constituted the vast majority. Death mowed down the old, the young and the weak. They died of thirst, suffocation, and the stench.... On the long stages, the corpses decomposed in the huddle of the trucks, and at the short halts, where water and food were handed out, the people were not allowed to bury their dead and had to leave them beside the railway track.[64]

It is estimated that at the very least a tenth of the Tatar people perished either on the journey to the 'Stans', or during their wilderness years of hunger, deprivation and disease immediately following the deportation. Some Tatar sources claim that the total loss was much higher, perhaps as much as 50 per cent. The Soviet government justified its actions in the following manner:

> In the period of the Fatherland war many Crimean Tatars betrayed the Motherland, deserted from units of the Red Army defending the Crimea, and turned over the country to the enemy, joined German formed voluntary Tatar military units to fight against the Red Army in the period of occupation of the Crimea by German-Fascist troops and participated in German punitive detachments. Crimean Tatars were particularly noted for their brutal reprisals towards Soviet partisans, and also assisted the German occupiers in organizing the forcible sending to German slavery and mass destruction of Soviet people.[65]

Within the Soviet elite, or amongst Crimea's majority Russian population, there was little sympathy for the fate of the Tatars.

In Sevastopol, for instance, Werth recorded the gist of Yefremov's accusations. The Tatars, he asserted, 'had played a particularly cruel game in hunting down disguised Russian soldiers'. Without raising any doubts as to the veracity of such claims, Werth concluded, 'Altogether, the Tatars' record was as bad as could be. They had formed a police force under German control and had been highly active in the Gestapo ...'[66]

In nineteenth- and early twentieth-century Sevastopol, the Tatars had always formed a small minority of the population. Yet it was significant enough for a district of the city, located on the eastern shore of the Southern Bay between the main railway station and the naval barracks, to be called 'Tatarskaya'. Although the ostensible rationale for the expulsion of the Crimean Tatars was their collaboration with the enemy, nothing in Stalin's world was ever quite what it appeared at the time. The Soviet authorities not only deported the Tatars, but also other Muslim nationalities such as the Chechens, Ingush and Balkars, all of whose homelands were close to, or bordered with, the old enemy Turkey. As one expert author on the subject, J. Otto Pohl, has concluded, the Soviet government held a paranoid fear:

> ... that these nationalities would not be completely loyal to the USSR in the event of a conflict with Turkey. In the minds of Stalin and Beria these ethnic groups represented a potential pro-Turkish fifth column living close to vulnerable Soviet military assets. Thus one of the main reasons for the deportation of these groups was to prevent any espionage, sabotage, diversion, or other assistance to Ankara by their members.

Thus the Soviet leadership believed that military control of the Black Sea region 'depended on a solidly loyal population in the Crimea'.[67] This imperative would not have surprised either Potemkin or Catherine the Great, and would find new resonance in 2014 when Russia re-annexed the peninsula.

The expulsion of the Crimean Tatars in May 1944 led to a change of the status of Crimea. With no Tatar population remaining, by a decree of 20 June 1945 it changed from an autonomous republic of the RSFSR to an *oblast* (an administrative unit equating to a province).[68] Sevastopol, however, received a special status in 1948, which in practice meant that it was treated as a federal city directly administered by Moscow. Unsurprisingly, the exiled Crimean Tatars remained very sore about their treatment at the hands of the Soviet government. One of Gorbachev's most visible reforms under his programme of *perestroika* (restructuring) was to allow the Tatars to return from Uzbekistan and other

Central Asian republics to their former Crimean lands. Following a decree of the Supreme Soviet of the USSR acknowledging the 'illegal and criminal repressive acts against peoples subjected to forcible resettlement' on 14 November 1989, a mass movement commenced.[69] Then only about 20,000 Crimean Tatars lived on the peninsula – but within 'only seven months no fewer than 135,000 Crimean Tatars had availed themselves of this right'.[70] Of course, this policy did nothing for Gorbachev's popularity among the Russian population of Crimea. By 2001, 12 per cent of Crimea's population was Tatar. Disputes over the ownership of land became common, and did little to improve community relations. The exile of the Crimean Tatars (*Surgun*) and memories of their prolonged suffering *en route* to, and in their places of encampment as 'special settlers', continue to cast long shadows, not least following the events of 2014.

In 1944, the Soviet authorities took other measures to erase the Crimean Tatar legacy. Following the deportations, more than 80 per cent of place names of Tatar origin were replaced with Russian ones. A few exceptions were made for major towns such as Bakhchisaray, Dzhankoy, Ishun, Saki and Sudak.[71]

THE IMMEDIATE CHALLENGES OF SEVASTOPOL'S POST-WAR RECONSTRUCTION

The basic essentials for human life are water, food, shelter and fuel: in the ruins of Sevastopol in May 1944, these were scarce commodities. Ravaged by war since the first air raid nearly three years before, it was a city, according to Gilmore, 'without water, electricity, street cars, buses, telephones, movies, theatres, clothing stores, and general food stores'.[72] He failed to mention that the sewage system no longer functioned in most areas. Thus in the immediate aftermath of the liberation, living conditions in Sevastopol, following so much death and destruction, remained difficult if not horrendous. Within days, however, the Red Army had restored a limited water supply and opened bakeries and emergency ration shops. In this manner, the inhabitants' first needs were met: the remaining priorities would have to follow, including housing. Thankfully, winter remained a long way off. The key to a rapid recovery was the reopening of the railway at the beginning of June 1944, followed by the clearance of the harbour and the repair of the docks. Then food and goods for the population, and equipment and materiel for reconstruction, could be brought in much more efficiently by rail or ship, rather than by road. Moreover, the Black Sea Fleet could return, which it did to a rapturous welcome, on 5 November 1944.

In May 1944, Yefremov informed the visiting foreign correspondents that of the '15,000 buildings and houses that stood before the war, fewer than 500' were now habitable.[73] Although these statistics may reflect a modest exaggeration in the extent of the damage – as other official figures state that as much as 16 per cent of residential buildings remained – the very widespread devastation was evident to all.[74] Gilmore compared the obliteration of Sevastopol with what he had observed in the blitzed cities of England. 'Old Plymouth', he stated, 'was the only one I remembered as being so generally wrecked, although the centre of Coventry was most like this'. Yet these two British cities in question had only suffered air attack: they had been spared the intense artillery bombardments and land battles that Sevastopol had endured in both 1941–42 and in 1944.

Sevastopol (as too the Crimea) was resettled surprisingly quickly. On 1 January 1945, for example, 38,753 people were recorded in the city, including many thousands of workers involved in the reconstruction effort. By January 1950, the population of 120,000 exceeded the pre-war figure.[75] Apart from the rebuilding work, a combination of industrial development and investment in the Black Sea Fleet drove this growth. Additionally, many demobilised from the USSR's armed forces opted to settle in the city and make their future in Sevastopol.

'Brigades' of Soviet workers and columns of prisoners of war provided the main manpower for the reconstruction of Sevastopol. But they had to work to agreed architectural plans and approved urban designs: the new city would not be a simple reincarnation of the old. The Soviet Union, whether functioning in war or in peacetime, was highly centralised. Following the victory at Stalingrad, and the rapid recovery of lost territory as far as the river Donets in Ukraine, when it became evident that the Great Patriotic War could, if not would, be won, the Soviet government established a Committee on Architectural Affairs in April 1943. This organisation, a national design bureau in effect, issued authorised reconstruction plans for implementation across the devastated cities and towns of the country. Thus when the initial plans for the rebuilding of Sevastopol emerged in 1945, they emanated from Moscow, and not from the Crimean city. The central question to be addressed, one in common to all destroyed cities across Europe, was whether there should be a restoration of the old buildings and street layout, or a radical redesign on a new pattern. Fortunately, Sevastopol was spared the fate of Plymouth, whose blitzed medieval buildings were replaced with controversial modernist concrete designs on an entirely new road grid.

In a detailed monograph, the American academic Karl D. Qualls has documented the plans for the reconstruction of Sevastopol. He explains that two quite different designs competed for approval. One, inspired by members of the Committee of Architectural Affairs, including the leading Moscow architects Barkhin and Ginzburg, intended to convert the city into a monumental outdoor museum, glorifying the victory of the Great Patriotic War. The other, a local one, was inspired by Sevastopol architect Grigory Lomagin, and later, Yuri Trautman.

Favouring a more conservative rebuilding of the city, retaining its former proportions and resurrecting its memorials to the Crimean War, their proposals received the support of prominent naval figures such as Oktyabrsky and Sevastopol's town council.[76]

In the event, the locals had their way: the Moscow plans were rejected. Thus Sevastopol was to be rebuilt largely preserving the shape and proportions of the pre-war city, and retaining the ensemble of the Panorama and other monuments, including Todleben's, on the Historic Boulevard (see Map 2). Plans to erect a new museum to the Second World War on the site of the Panorama, and to rebuild Sevastopol's principal memorial to the Crimean War on the Malakhov Hill, were rejected. Attempts to rename famous streets and squares similarly failed. While Lenin (the old Catherine) Street remained, as it does today, the other two main streets of the city centre, kept their pre-war names of Bolshaya Morskaya and Nakhimov Prospekt. Lenin (formerly Catherine) Square, however, was renamed Nakhimov in 1959, and a new statue of the famous admiral was erected to replace the one blown up by the Bolsheviks.[77]

Significantly, Lenin retains a special place of honour in post-war Sevastopol. His huge, 7.5-metres-tall statue atop a 13-metre obelisk is sited on the city's central hill below St Vladimir's Cathedral. Four smaller statues adorn the pedestal: a sailor, soldier, worker and peasant – a representative quartet of the founding forces of the revolution. With wonderful historic and geographical juxtaposition, Lenin looks out over Sevastopol Bay in the direction of the nearby headquarters building of the Russian Federation's Black Sea Fleet, with its prominent Russian flag flying proudly. After Stalin's death the central Stalin district was renamed Lenin.

In addition, recent commanders of the Great Patriotic War were added to Sevastopol's topography. Ulitsa Chersonesskaya and Karantinnaya were renamed respectively Admiral Oktyabrsky and General Petrov Streets. Earlier military and naval heroic figures were also honoured. In the bicentenary year, 1983, Pushkin Square was renamed Suvorov. Ten years later, the former Commune Square became Ushakov Square. This merry-go-round of renaming familiar locations in Sevastopol must have confused the local residents. The present Lazarev Square, for example, received no fewer than four different names during the Soviet period.[78]

DISTINGUISHED ALLIED VISITORS

In early 1945, less than a year since its deliverance from German occupation, Sevastopol was still very much a wrecked, desolate city. Yet its surviving population, augmented by the Soviet military, was working hard to restore normality. During this period, the city administration proudly welcomed a number of special foreign visitors. The first was the British Chief of the Imperial

General Staff, Field Marshal Alanbrooke, who accompanied the British Prime Minister, Winston Churchill, to the Yalta conference (4–11 February 1945). The daily routine involved military talks between the uniformed heads of the American, British and Soviet armed forces, followed by the political discussions between Roosevelt, Churchill and Stalin and their foreign ministers. Midway, Alanbrooke was keen to take a break from Yalta and to view the Crimean War battlefields. The field marshal gained Churchill's agreement to take leave of absence on condition that he 'trained some officer to show him the Balaklava battlefields'. The individual selected from the British delegation was Brigadier Roger Peake, Deputy Director of Military Intelligence at the War Office.

Alanbrooke left a detailed description of his tour of 7 February 1945 in his diary. Following the Vorontsov Road from Yalta, the British party of officers, with an 'excellent Russian guide, good cars [and] excellent drivers', arrived at the battlefields of Balaklava. 'There was the port on our extreme left', Alanbrooke wrote, [and] 'on our immediate left the site of the Charge of the Heavy Cav[alry] Brigade, and on our right the site of the memorable Charge of the Light Cav[alry] Brigade!'. Yet he and his colleagues could not ignore the 'ample signs of the vast recent conflicts to capture Sevastopol and then to free it!' There remained, he noted: 'a grave beside a wrecked aeroplane here, a broken-down tank there, rows upon rows of shell and bomb craters, twisted iron cheveaux-de-frise, tangled basket wire, odd graves, and the usual rubbish of a battlefield'. As Alanbrooke remarked, it was 'very strange how history can repeat itself under a different guise'.

Departing the Balaklava battlefields of 1854, 1941–42 and 1944, Alanbrooke's group approached Sevastopol. Shortly, 'the ghost' of the city 'loomed up in front of us'. The scene moved the field marshal in an uncommon way:

> Such a ghost! Hardly a house standing, and those that stood had no roofs, but over the whole port rested that inexplicable atmosphere of pride such as one only feels on rare occasions. Verdun always gave me that feeling. I had it strongly today. If the Russians succeeded in holding out for 11 [sic] months against double their number of Germans, favoured by overwhelming superiority in the air and in armour, whilst suffering great privations on the supply side, then there is no doubt in my mind that the Russian is a very very great fighter.[79]

The British officers continued their day of military tourism with lunch at the 'Russian Admiral's HQ', where they were given 'a wonderful reception' and a briefing on the liberation of Sevastopol, followed by a tour of famous Crimean War sights such as the Flag Staff Hill, the Malakhov Hill, and not least the British military cemetery. The latter place, a cornerstone of the Soviet and German defences in 1942 and 1944 respectively, was 'in a bad way,' recorded Alanbrooke, having been 'heavily shelled'. He added: 'nearly all the memorial chapels and graves have been smashed. A pathetic sight.'[80] The area was never to be restored properly after the war.

The Yalta conference closed shortly after midday on 11 February 1945. Having hosted a farewell luncheon at the Livadia Palace for the British and Soviet leaders, together with their senior advisors, President Franklin D. Roosevelt motored to Sevastopol during the late afternoon. On arrival, he boarded the USS *Catoctin*, the American command and communications ship for the conference. Making a somewhat ungenerous tilt at the culinary skills of their recent hosts at Yalta, the official account refers to the *Catoctin* serving 'a delicious steak dinner ... which was a real treat ... after eight days of Russian fare'. Presumably tired after the meal, the President did not attend a concert given in Sevastopol that evening by members of the band of the Black Sea Fleet. According to the record of the trip, however, the American leader had ample opportunity to witness:

> ... scenes of stark destruction [in Sevastopol] wrought by the Germans. The city was virtually levelled to the ground except for the walls of the houses and other buildings which the mines, bombs and shells in recent battles left standing like billboards – mute testimony of the horrorful wanton Nazi vengeance.[81]

Early the following morning (the 12th), the American delegation proceeded to the airfield at Saki, where they boarded flights to Egypt. Sevastopol had clearly made a deep impression on Roosevelt: it is said that he remarked: 'if I could walk, then I would reach the sacred places of Russia: Leningrad, Stalingrad and Sevastopol. I would kneel and kiss this sacred land.'[82]

The British Prime Minister stayed on in Crimea for a couple of days of rest and recuperation. Quitting the exquisite Vorontsov Palace at Alupka, where he had stayed throughout for the conference sessions at Livadia, he motored to Sevastopol on the 12th. There he went aboard the transatlantic liner *Franconia*, which had been moored in the harbour as a headquarters ship for the British delegation should the accommodation in the Yalta area prove unsuitable. Churchill recalled the scene from Sevastopol's harbour: 'From the deck we looked out over the port, which the Germans had practically destroyed, though now it was full of activity again and in the night-time its ruins blazed with lights'.

On 13 February 1945, Churchill took the opportunity to inspect the Balaklava battlefield, where his Soviet hosts were much keener to describe more recent fighting than to assist their distinguished guest in viewing the site of the infamous charge of 25 October 1854. The Prime Minister recalled:

> I visited the scene, accompanied by ... the Russian admiral commanding the Black Sea Fleet, who had orders from Moscow to be in attendance whenever

> I came ashore…. As Peake pointed to the line on which the Light Brigade had been drawn up the Russian admiral pointed in almost the same direction and exclaimed 'the German tanks came at us from over there'.

When Peake outlined the Russian dispositions at the battle of Balaklava, their Russian host 'intervened with obvious pride', pointing out 'that is where a Russian battery fought and died to the last man'. Churchill replied to explain that the British party was 'studying a different war' – one of 'dynasties, not of peoples'. Although the Russian 'gave no sign of comprehension' the British leader thought that the admiral seemed 'perfectly satisfied' and all 'passed off very pleasantly'.[83]

For reasons that cannot easily be explained, Stalin declined to visit Sevastopol in February 1945; he could easily have accompanied his guests Churchill and Roosevelt, or waited until they had departed Crimea. One can only surmise that the Soviet leader did not wish to identify himself with Sevastopol until the war was concluded, and the reconstruction effort was well under way. Over three years were to pass until the Soviet leader made a fleeting inspection of the city in September 1948, his first visit since 1929.

During the spring of 1945, at the invitation of the Soviet government, Winston Churchill's wife Clementine undertook a tour of Russian hospitals and other facilities in her capacity as chairman of the British Red Cross 'Aid to Russia' Fund. This charitable foundation had provided warm clothing, medical equipment (including X-Ray machines) and supplies throughout the war since 1941. Her visit to Sevastopol on 24 April 1945 proved one of the highlights of her programme in Russia. Olga Dmitrievna Lazarchuk (born 1930) recalled Mrs Churchill visiting 'our half-ruined' School No. 14 that day on Matyushenko Street, one of the first three schools opened in September 1944:

> We were dressed in our winter coats. The [British] delegation came in. An elderly lady and a younger – I had the impression that Mrs Churchill was the elderly lady in a military-style uniform … with a beret on her head…. Next to them were two men in black naval uniforms. We were told if they would treat you with chocolates, take one each, but do not eat immediately…. The chocolate boxes were opened and we were treated with them … we put them next to the ink pots saying 'thank you', … [and later] brought them home to show and share with family members.[84]

Clementine's visit also included a tour of Sevastopol's famous historical locations, including the ancient city of Chersonesos and the Historic Boulevard. At the latter, a cameraman recorded Mrs Churchill in splendid historical juxtaposition, standing in front of Todleben's damaged (headless) monument: an envoy of contemporary Allied friendship next to a former foe. Sevastopol made a poignant impression on Clementine, who wrote: 'It presented so melancholy a spectacle ... Before the Nazis destroyed it in their blind rage, it must have been a dream of beauty, as lovely as a poem, with its many pillared and frescoed houses'.[85]

Clementine Churchill's visit to Sevastopol soon brought material results. Only two months after her visit to Russia, a comprehensive set of equipment and medical supplies for a 500-bed hospital was sent to Crimea. Nearly half of the set (200 beds) was allocated to Sevastopol. At a time of great shortages, the gift of specialist tools, medical clothing and medicine (and many other items) provided a Godsend to the local health care system. For her aid to Russia, Clementine Churchill was awarded the Order of the Red Banner for Labour in Moscow on 7 May 1945. In comparing the two 'Churchill' visits to Sevastopol, a modern archivist of the city has observed that Clementine followed a 'path radically different from the route of Winston Churchill'. In visiting the battlefields of the Crimean War, the British Prime Minister had 'acted as a patriot', and Mrs Churchill – 'primarily as a humanist'.[86]

Clementine Churchill's visit was fondly remembered in Sevastopol for many years. Olga Lazarchuk went to practise in the 1st City Hospital in 1954, where she saw 'patients fashionably dressed in gorgeous robes – thick cotton and dark-ruby velvet', which had been received through the Red Cross Fund. In the 1960s, however, 'there were no robes for patients anymore: only doctors wore them'. Olga proudly told people 'these are Mrs Churchill's presents' – probably the last vestiges of the temporary wartime friendship between Britain and the Soviet Union. Winston Churchill, in contrast, was remembered as the one who kept on delaying the opening of the Second Front – 'people who did not fight at war meant little for us!'[87]

STALIN'S INTERVENTION AND THE MAIN RECONSTRUCTION OF THE CITY

Despite Sevastopol receiving a special status for reconstruction in 1945 as one of the 'fifteen cities', the progress made during the immediate post-war years was disappointingly slow. The symbolic naming by Stalin of Sevastopol as one of the first four 'hero-cities' of the Soviet Union on 1 May 1945 failed to bring any immediate preferential treatment.[88] Little was achieved apart from clearing the streets, reinstating basic utilities, opening schools and providing emergency accommodation. Great housing shortages remained. It took the personal intervention of Stalin in 1948 to accelerate matters, ensuring that the city received a much higher priority for resources.

During his time in office, Stalin's visits to Crimea were rare, and to Sevastopol even less common. Before the war, he had inspected the Black Sea Fleet and Sevastopol's new coastal batteries in 1929. On conclusion of the Yalta conference in February 1945 he chose not to visit. Nor did he visit in the summer of 1947, when he again stayed at the Livadia Palace and enjoyed a voyage across the Black Sea to Sochi aboard the cruiser *Molotov*. Stalin, however, visited Sevastopol in September 1948. By all accounts, this was a very low-key event – some state that he travelled incognito.[89] Yet the consequences proved highly significant for the future of the city.

After seeing for himself that Sevastopol remained far from being reconstructed, notwithstanding the self-congratulatory reports from local administrators, Stalin put new initiatives in train. The Council of Ministers of the USSR discussed the city's needs. On 29 October 1948, the Presidium of the Supreme Council of the RSFSR directed that the city was to be given special status. A bespoke commission, the Directorate for the Restoration of Sevastopol,[90] was created to plan and manage the rebuilding of the city 'within a three- to four-year timetable with the appropriate "monetary resources and construction materials for this task"'.[91]

The special priority given to Sevastopol was not merely symbolic. The measure served to increase military utility and social cohesion concurrently. At a time of rising tensions during the Cold War, Stalin saw the strategic imperative not only of developing Sevastopol as the main base for the Black Sea Fleet, but also in providing naval personnel and the civilian residents a city worthy to live in, and one with which they could identify with pride. Such an approach provided continuity from imperial times. As in the Second World War, however, Sevastopol was much more than a naval base. It airfields, not least the large naval air station at Kacha, became in many ways equally important. With the rapid development of radar, Sevastopol's position on the Black Sea, and on the southern extremity of the Soviet Union, became increasingly useful during the Cold War. Of particular strategic significance was the 'Dnepr' (NATO nickname 'Hen House') phased array radar station at Cape Chersonese, developed in the 1960 and 1970s, which provided early warning of ballistic missile attack.

Meanwhile, Sevastopol's accelerated reconstruction during the period 1949–54 is a testament to the organisers' successful coordination and integration of decision-making, personnel and materiel, and not least to the tens of thousands of individuals who worked on the rebuilding projects and in restoring essential infrastructure. To meet the labour shortages, special construction 'brigades' of expert tradesmen, and those who had general skills in the building trade, were established. Mikhail Gregorievich Molenov, who came from the Penza *oblast* of the Volga region, was one of those called up as a twenty-two-year-old for such labour duty in 1949. As 'one of approximately 30,000', he recalled in 2011,

'I was brought to Sevastopol to work on its reconstruction'. As a civilian in a quasi-military organisation, he served four years in the city: his brigade worked primarily on Primorsky Boulevard. Asked about the role of German prisoners of war, he replied that 'there were still many about, working at clearing the city of its ruins, but they had not done so much rebuilding when we arrived – that was our job'. Mikhail Gregorievich was particularly proud of one task: 'As a mason, I helped reconstruct the commemorative white columns on Nakhimov Square, which we carved out of Inkerman stone'.[92] Then he added quietly in a reverential tone, 'every time I visit the hero-city and see the columns again, I remember those times, over sixty-five years ago. They were hard, at times very hard with not much food to eat and very long hours, but we were all honoured to play our part in rebuilding Sevastopol'.[93]

On 6 November 1950, the first trolley bus ran in the city, and by the end of that year, the new railway station was in operation. But Sevastopol's future also lay in commemorating the recent past. In June 1952, for example, a monument at Cape Paul was erected in memory of the crew of the destroyer *Svobodny*, sunk in 1942 – a 5.5-metre obelisk surmounted with a red star.[94]

Unsurprisingly, the restoration of the world-famous Panorama became one of the top priorities for the Soviet government and Sevastopol's city administration. The building, as one of the principal icons of the city, was faithfully and sensitively restored in the early 1950s. It was decided, however, that the associated canvas needed to be replaced in its entirety. Working in the austere conditions of the immediate post-war era, a team of eighteen Moscow artists under the direction of V. H. Yakovlev and P. P. Sokolov-Skalya drew a brand new canvas, working from old records and the remaining materials, which had been shipped out of Sevastopol in late June 1942 on the *Tashkent*.

The Panorama was reopened with great celebration on 16 November 1954, marking the centenary of the first defence of the city. Nowadays, the museum remains not only on every tourist's route, but also serves as a centre of research for academic studies into the history of Sevastopol and as a classroom for successive generations of Crimean and local schoolchildren. The Panorama dominates much of the city's skyline and landscape: its content conveys the intensely patriotic and proud 'spirit of Sevastopol' – one that is shaped, if not defined, by its dramatic and violent history as an 'eternally Russian city'. The Panorama is but one department of the Museum of the Heroic Defence and Liberation of Sevastopol. The others are: the Diorama complex that commemorates the 'Storming of the Sapun Mountain' on 7 May 1944; the Malakhov Hill, St Vladimir's Cathedral; and the Resistance museum.

The completion of the reconstruction of Sevastopol in 1953–54 coincided with the 100th anniversary of the Crimean War. The city, honoured in 1954 with the Order of the Red Banner, remained highly militarised. By then, however, the new signs of the Cold War had replaced the old scars of the Second World War. Such was the sensitivity and secrecy of Sevastopol's numerous defence industries and bases it became a 'closed city'. The population continued to grow steadily, reaching 393,015 in 1989. Ultimately, Sevastopol's future was bound up with that of Crimea, and its status within the Soviet Union. Although tied geographically to Ukraine by way of the Perekop isthmus, the city remained predominately Russian (74.5 per cent) in language and outlook – the second biggest nationality was Ukrainian (20.6 per cent).[95] While a decision to transfer Crimea to Ukraine in 1954 made hardly any difference to daily life and work during the Soviet period, its consequences following the disintegration of the Soviet Union and the end of the Cold War in 1990–91 were to be profound. The Russian Federation's disputed annexation of Crimea and the March 2014 can only be understood in the context of Sevastopol's enduring importance as the base of the Black Sea Fleet.

CHAPTER 16

FRATERNAL CONFLICT

*'Everything in Crimea speaks of our shared history and pride
...The graves of Russian soldiers whose bravery brought
Crimea into the Russian Empire are also in Crimea...
Sevastopol – a legendary city with an outstanding story, a
fortress that serves as the birthplace of the Black Sea Fleet – [is]
dear to our hearts, symbolizing Russian military glory and
outstanding valour.'*

Vladimir Putin, 18 March 2014[1]

KHRUSHCHEV'S 'GIFT' OF CRIMEA TO UKRAINE

The Soviet leader Nikita Khrushchev is probably best remembered for his
brinkmanship during the Cuban missile crisis of October 1962, if not for the
alleged brandishing of his shoe at the United Nations General Assembly two
years before. That Khrushchev 'gifted' Crimea to Ukraine illegally in 1954 during
a vodka-induced fit of bonhomie or skulduggery is largely a myth.[2] Yet perhaps
of all the matters he is associated with, the Soviet government's decision to
transfer Crimea from Russia to Ukraine probably has the greatest strategic impact
today. Khrushchev had previous designs on Crimea. His biographer William

Taubman records how in 1944, while leader of the Communist Party in Ukraine, Khrushchev had proposed repopulating the Crimean peninsula with Ukrainian peasants following Stalin's expulsion of the Crimean Tatars. Apparently Khrushchev had speculated with a Ukrainian colleague, 'Ukraine is in ruins, but everyone wants something from it. Now what if it received the Crimea in return?'[3]

Although nothing came of this wartime idea, an opportunity appeared a decade later to re-present it. Following Stalin's death on 5 March 1953, the Soviet leader's heir apparent, Georgy Malenkov, assumed the position of chairman of the Council of Ministers. When Malenkov stood down on 14 March 1953 as First Secretary of the Communist Party of the Soviet Union (CPSU), Khrushchev was appointed 'senior secretary' in his place. By the end of the year, however, Khrushchev (now confirmed as 'First Secretary'), ensured that all major decisions went through him. While his rival Malenkov nominally exercised more power, this relationship changed to Khrushchev's advantage during the course of 1954.[4]

Inspection of the protocols of the Soviet, Russian and Ukrainian authorities reveals that the transfer of the Crimean *oblast* of the RSFSR to the Ukrainian Soviet Socialist Republic (UkSSR) was a *collective* decision, and certainly not Khrushchev's alone. Superficially, it would appear that such deliberation satisfied – on narrow technical grounds – Article 18 of the 1936 constitution of the USSR, which stipulated that 'the territory of a Union Republic may not be altered without its consent'.[5] Although the Supreme Soviet of the RSFSR had agreed the transfer, significantly neither the assemblies of the two republics concerned, nor the people of Crimea, had been consulted on the matter. This democratic deficit provided one of the sources of the long-running dispute over Crimea that eventually led to the events of 2014.

The future of Crimea was discussed in a series of choreographed meetings in early 1954, culminating with the Presidium of the USSR Supreme Soviet convening on 19 February. At this session it was agreed, *inter alia*, that:

> The transfer of the Crimean Oblast to the Ukrainian Republic meets the interests of strengthening the friendship of the peoples of the great Soviet Union, and will promote the further strengthening of the fraternal link between the Ukrainian and Russian peoples and the still greater prosperity of Soviet Ukraine, the development to which our Party and government have always devoted great attention.[6]

The official notification (9 March 1954) of the transfer of Crimea to Ukraine, signed by Kliment Voroshilov, chairman of the Supreme Soviet, provided two explanations. The first, historical, referred to a 'noble act on the part of the Russian people' to commemorate the 300th anniversary of the 'reunification of

Ukraine with Russia'. This wording referred to the Treaty of Pereyaslav of 1654 between the representatives of the Ukrainian Cossack Hetmanate and Tsar Alexis I of Russia. The second rationale was geographic and economic: the transfer made sense in terms of the 'territorial proximity of Crimea to Ukraine, the commonalities of their economies, and the close agricultural and cultural ties between the *oblast* and the UkSSR'.[7]

An American academic, Mark Kramer, has argued that 'neither of these ostensible justifications holds up to scrutiny'.[8] His own research reveals a more nuanced interpretation of the motives and consequences of Khrushchev's Crimean initiative. Kramer holds that Khrushchev was motivated by a desire to bolster Soviet control over Ukraine by demographic means. This line of reasoning, however, is questionable. In 1959, according to the first post-war census, just less than three-quarters (71 per cent) of the Crimean population of 1.2 million were ethnically Russian, while the vast majority of the remainder (22 per cent) were Ukrainian. The Tatars, having been expelled in 1944, did not figure. Hence bringing 800,000 or so Russians into Ukraine in 1954 did not fundamentally affect the balance of nationalities in Ukraine, which had a population of nearly 42 million in 1959, of which 32 million were Ukrainian and 7 million Russian.

Kramer also believes that internal politicking played an important role. In his opinion, Khrushchev hoped to enlist Oleksiy Kyrychenko, First Secretary of the Communist Party in Ukraine and a full member of the CPSU Presidium, in his bid to outflank – if not oust – Malenkov. Neil Kent considers that the transfer was in part undertaken 'as a public relations exercise, intended to some degree to lend Khrushchev the image of a Ukrainian patriot'. He also feels that the transfer was 'done as a way of keeping the immediate responsibility for Crimea at arm's length from Moscow, enabling the peninsula to serve as a testing ground for a new initiative to further industrialise it'.[9] This latter judgement chimes with the academic Jeremy Smith, who regards that the move 'signalled an end to the increasingly Russo-centric political, cultural, demographic and ideological shifts of the 1930s and 1940s'.[10]

So it would appear that a number of factors motivated Khrushchev in 1954, not least a desire to expand the borders and to boost the productive capacity of the Ukrainian Soviet Socialist Republic. Little could he anticipate the longer-term consequences of forcing a significant Russian population into Ukraine. The possibility of the Soviet Union breaking up, let alone a fraternal conflict between Russia and Ukraine breaking out some day, would have been quite beyond Khrushchev's imagination, and likewise of tens of millions of his countrymen.

In the Soviet post-war period, such was the integration of the USSR, it scarcely mattered whether Crimea was part of Ukraine or Russia. Most Crimean citizens thought of themselves as Crimean first, then either as Russian or

Ukrainian depending on their nationality. Many families, moreover, were of mixed Slavic parentage: there was a close integration of Russian and Ukrainian speakers. Within Crimea, the culture and language spoken remained predominantly Russian, and no place more so than Sevastopol, which remained the most Soviet of former Soviet cities. The Crimean Tatar heritage was limited to a few historical sites such as the former Khan's palace at Bakhchisaray.

In any event, there were sound, practical economic grounds for uniting Crimea to Ukraine, which stood the test of time for six decades. Until recently (2016), most of the peninsula's water and electricity came from mainland Ukraine. Crimea's primary rail and road links to Russia remain via Ukraine rather than by way of the less convenient ferry route over the Kerch Straits to the Krasnodar region. Only the erection of a 19-kilometre bridge over the Straits, optimistically planned for completion in 2019, will provide a reliable, fixed link to Russia. Crimean agriculture and industry were much enhanced by the construction of the North Crimean Canal (1963–75), which brought irrigation and drinking water from the river Dnieper to near Kerch, with many subsidiary pipelines that fed other parts of Crimea, including the capital Simferopol.[11]

Meanwhile, notwithstanding the transfer of Crimea to Ukraine in 1954, Sevastopol was recognised as a separate entity. It remained an 'object of all-Union significance' throughout the Soviet post-war period.[12] As the main base of the Black Sea Fleet, its strategic importance ensured that it was administered directly by Moscow. The city attracted a growing number of scientific-technical institutes and military-industrial concerns that played vital roles in the Soviet Union's advances in electronics, naval systems, aeronautics and space technology. Significantly, in 1961, Sevastopol made the famous Soviet cosmonaut, Yuri Gagarin, the first man to venture into outer space, an honorary citizen, joining the ranks of Todleben and Tolstoy.[13] The connection was preserved after Gagarin's untimely death in 1968: in 1975 one of the city's districts was named after him.

Balaklava was chosen as the primary submarine base for the Black Sea Fleet. During the 1960s, in the western hillside of the port, an underground, atomic-bomb-proof, resupply and repair facility was constructed. In its long caverns, Kilo-class submarines were berthed, armed and victualled. An extensive stone quarry, noisily still in use today, masked its under-water sea entrance and exit. Decommissioned at the end of the Cold War, the 'Naval Museum Complex', is now open to the public. Far larger than any James Bond film set, this 'object' was a top-secret facility within a restricted zone of a closed city. Local residents, workers and naval personnel all required special passes.

During the 1980s, the local authorities in Sevastopol resumed the memorialisation of the city. To celebrate its bicentenary, in 1983 a monument was erected in Nakhimov Square and a huge triumphal arch was placed over the main highway – General Melnik Street – linking the Sapun escarpment to the city centre.[14] Only twenty-five years later, however, the arch required extensive restoration. Yet this project proved far less contentious than the massive 41-metre-high 'Monument to the Soldier and the Sailor', designed to honour the Soviet forces who had fought in Sevastopol during the Second World War. First proposed in 1972, construction at Cape Crystal, overlooking Sevastopol Bay, finally started in 1981. Mismanagement and a lack of funds slowed, and then stopped, its completion. When work was 'frozen' in 1989, there was even talk of demolishing the incomplete structure. Although construction resumed in 2006, allowing the monument to be opened on 8 May 2007, the planned memorial complex at Cape Crystal remains incomplete.[15]

THE DISSOLUTION OF THE SOVIET UNION

During the Cold War, many former members of the Soviet Navy settled in Sevastopol. With its temperate climate, good infrastructure and rich history, it provided a popular choice for retirees, many of whom were veterans of the Second World War. Over the years, subsequent generations joined them. This group was (and remains) an intensely patriotic community. Towards the end of the Soviet period, however, there were increasing signs of a collapse of the former certainty and order. At a meeting convened in the Veterans' House in Sevastopol (*Dom veteranov*) in December 2012, retired Colonel Genady Nikolayevich Ryzhenok, who commanded the 299th Educational Centre of Naval Infantry, recalled:

> Sevastopol [during the Cold War] was a very active city; it was stable; people believed in the future and trusted the Government. There were no indications of the impending catastrophe. In 1985 the Government changed. As a commander, I noticed the first signs of disturbing change in 1986. During the days of the 27th Congress of the Communist Party of the USSR, it was a custom that officers and enlisted personnel, the sailors, watched together the news on the TV programme *Times* at 9 o'clock in the evening. We heard Gorbachev, who spoke of *perestroika* and the awakening of national self-consciousness. The sailors asked me 'what is Gorbachev talking about?' That was the first signal of misfortune.[16]

Ryzhenok explained that he felt that 'the country would fall apart and people would not be able to travel freely'. For him, there was no doubt that Gorbachev was 'a catastrophe for the USSR. The break-up of our country was criminal'.[17] Two of his Cold War Black Sea Fleet colleagues enthusiastically agreed with him, as did an older veteran of the Great Patriotic War, Rear Admiral Glushkov.

Perhaps the citizens of Sevastopol were reflecting – either consciously or sub-consciously – Vladimir Putin's widely reported remarks of 2005 concerning the collapse of the Soviet Union, which he regarded as the 'greatest geopolitical catastrophe of the century'. Yet an important caution must be applied here. As Andrew Monaghan has argued, it would be erroneous to suggest, as other commentators have done mistakenly, that Putin intended 'to rebuild the USSR', and that his statement represented 'an early indicator of what was to come in 2014'.[18] That said, Putin gave ample warning then and thereafter that he wished to restore Russia as an influential, if not great, power.

The dissolution of the Soviet Union generated not only opportunities for the former socialist republics, such as the Baltic states, but also crisis and confusion in the governance of other constituent parts, including Crimea and Sevastopol. Quite apart from the fall of the Berlin Wall and the subsequent unification of Germany, the rot, as ardent Soviet nationalists still see it, set in with Lithuania's declaration of independence on 11 March 1990. Under the leadership of Boris Yeltsin, Russia followed suit on 12 June (celebrated as 'Russia Day'), effectively igniting a fuse that would see the entire construct of the USSR explode. This led to Ukraine's independence on 24 August 1990, and its declaration in February 1991 that Crimea would become an autonomous republic within Ukraine. This act enraged Russian revanchists, who had long mourned the transfer of Crimea to Ukraine. They redoubled their efforts in seeking the peninsula's return to Russia, propelled by a sense of wider loss with regard to an independent Ukraine. 'Their more than 300-year union', argues Russia expert Bobo Lo, 'ensured that Ukraine 'occupied an important niche in Russia's imperial syndrome or identity'.[19] Yet modern political, economic and security concerns applied in 1991 and in the two decades thereafter as much as any historical sentimentality. Without Ukraine, Russia had lost not only a significant population of 50 million, but also a strategically important bulwark – if not buffer zone – in Eastern Europe.

August 1991 saw a failed coup attempt against Gorbachev, the President of the Soviet Union, which resulted in Yeltsin's position becoming greatly strengthened and Gorbachev's authority seriously undermined. Within Russia, the future of Crimea remained a hot topic of discussion. At a meeting at Belvezha, Belarus, on 8 December 1991, the leaders of Russia, Ukraine (Leonid Kravchuk) and Belarus (Stansilav Shushkevich) agreed to establish the Commonwealth of Independent States (CIS). Sources differ as to what Yeltsin intended and said with regard to Crimea and Sevastopol. The British academic Richard Sakwa argues that although the Russian leader had been urged to seek the re-annexation of Crimea, he declined to do so. As far as Yeltsin was concerned, 'the CIS would effectively mean the continuation of the Soviet community, above all in security and defence matters, and hence it would make little difference to which republic the peninsula belonged'.[20] Other accounts suggest that Yeltsin might not have been in a fit condition to argue the case over Crimea, when his main concern was to reach an accord over the CIS. In his gripping account of the break-up of the Soviet Union, Serhii Plokhy states:

> Yakov Alekseichik, one of the few media representatives in attendance, noticed that Yeltsin was 'not quite in good form'. The 'Soviet'-brand champagne with which Yeltsin had celebrated every article in the agreement was clearly affecting something more than the process of dissolving the Soviet Union. The newspaper reporters were advised not to ask Yeltsin any questions.[21]

If this representation of events is correct, then rather than Crimea being lost to Russia by a drunk Khrushchev in 1954, the opportunity to regain it was forsaken by an inebriated Yeltsin in 1991. Significantly, in his memoirs Kravchuk recorded that Yeltsin, under a lot of stress and worried about Gorbachev's reaction, 'was visibly nervous' that day, perhaps describing not only the physical, but also the mental state of the Russian leader.[22]

Although Crimea remained in Ukraine, it could be argued that the special strategic position of Sevastopol within the Soviet Union, enshrined in 1948, meant that it should have reverted to Russia – as the internationally recognised 'continuer', as opposed to 'successor', state. Had there been greater goodwill between Ukraine and Russia, there might have been scope for some sort of Russian Federation 'sovereign base' on Crimea, analogous to the British facilities established in 1960 on Cyprus at Akrotiri and Dhekelia.[23] In the absence of any formal agreement, the status of Sevastopol and the armed forces stationed on the Crimean peninsula, and most notably the Black Sea Fleet at Sevastopol, remained a bone of contention between Ukraine and Russia.

The 'War of Laws'

During the 1990s, Crimea's status within Ukraine (and in relation to Russia, for that matter) was in a state of flux, reflecting the continuing discord between the government in Kiev and the peninsula's politicians in Simferopol. The dispute revolved around the Crimeans' wish for autonomy, if not independence from Ukraine – 'secession within secession'. On 20 January 1991, a referendum took place on Crimea about the establishment of the Crimean Autonomous Soviet Socialist Republic (ASSR) as part of the USSR. Of the 1,441,019 citizens who participated, an overwhelming 93.26 per cent voted for the restoration of the ASSR. Under a year later, on 1 December 1991, Crimea narrowly voted for independence (54 per cent) from the USSR in stark contrast to Ukraine as a whole (91 per cent).[24]

On 26 February 1992, the Supreme Soviet of Crimea proclaimed the 'Republic of Crimea', declared its independence on 5 May 1992 and adopted its own constitution, which stated that the peninsula was not part of Ukraine. The dispute between Kiev and Simferopol escalated when Yury Meshkov, the Prime Minister, was elected President of Crimea on 4 February 1994. He declared that Crimea's clocks should run on Moscow as opposed to Kiev time, and demanded that all Ukrainian troops should leave the peninsula. Sergey Tsekov, speaker of the parliament and leader of the Crimean Republican Party, pronounced: 'We are not ignoring Kiev, and we are not threatening Ukraine's territorial integrity, [but] we are only realizing the programme of Crimean and Russian reunion'. Although in many ways twenty years ahead of their time, Meshkov and Tsekov embodied a deep-rooted pro-Russian unionist sentiment that ran through much of the population of Crimea and Sevastopol.[25] It was never to be extinguished.

In the early to mid-1990s, Kiev and Simferopol traded denunciations and provocations in a 'war of laws'. According to the Kiev-based think-tank and polling institute, the Razumkov Centre, during the period 1992–95, 'the central authorities of Ukraine took dozens of legislative acts that invalidated more than 40 legislative acts of the Republic of Crimea'. During these years, Kiev 'did not control ... developments on the [Crimean] peninsula; directives of the [weak] central authorities were ignored'.[26] On 17 March 1995, however, Ukraine's parliament, the Verkhovna (Supreme) Rada, took firm action, annulling the Crimean constitution of 1992 and declared the post of Crimean President as void.

For a time, a violent standoff between Crimea and Ukraine appeared inevitable. In the face of a fast-deteriorating situation, international attempts were made to broker a settlement between Kiev and Simferopol. The Organisation for Security and Cooperation in Europe, for instance, held a conference on Crimean problems in Locarno during 11–14 June 1995. Through such diplomacy, conflict was avoided and the basis of a compromise agreement was found, albeit one disappointing to Crimea's pro-Russian leaders. A referendum on secession planned for 25 June 1995 was cancelled. Negotiations continued. Kiev abandoned its plan for direct rule and retained Crimea's parliament.[27] In June 1996, the Ukrainian government confirmed Crimea's status as an autonomous republic and granted it devolved powers under new constitutional arrangements. The peninsula did not secede: despite the differences between Ukraine and Crimea, the military, interior troops and police all remained loyal to Kiev. President Kuchma had maintained close personal relations with the leaders of these security forces. Additionally, Russia stood well back – all critical circumstances that did not pertain in 2014.

The Ukrainian Rada approved a new national constitution on 28 June 1996.[28] In this fundamental law, a number of its chapters ('titles') and specific provisions ('articles') deal with Crimea and Sevastopol. Several of these matters, including the design of the state of Ukraine and the status of its language, bear heavily on subsequent relations between Ukraine and Russia, and not least on the status of Crimea and Sevastopol. Within the 'General Principles' chapter of the Ukrainian Constitution, Article 2 declares that 'Ukraine shall be a unitary state' and that its territory 'within its present borders shall be indivisible and inviolable'. Notwithstanding the size of the state (excepting Russia, Ukraine is the largest land mass in Europe), there is no federation.

There is only one official language: Article 10 sets out that the 'State language of Ukraine shall be the Ukrainian language'. Two specific provisions apply: 'The state shall ensure comprehensive development and functioning of the Ukrainian language in all spheres of social life throughout the entire territory of Ukraine' and the 'free development, use and protection of Russian and other languages of national minorities of Ukraine shall be guaranteed in Ukraine'. The classification of Russian as a minority language as opposed to a second state language provoked dissatisfaction within those central, eastern and southern regions of Ukraine that had a majority Russian-speaking population, including the city of Kiev. That said, Article 11 could be read to provide protection to such populations, not least those of Crimea and Sevastopol. Not only does it require that the State promote 'the consolidation and development of the Ukrainian nation', but also 'the development of ethnic, cultural, linguistic, and religious identity of all indigenous peoples and national minorities of Ukraine'. Such assurances, however, did little to assuage the concerns of the predominantly Russian-speaking east and south.

A complete chapter (Title X) of the Ukrainian constitution is devoted to the former Autonomous Republic of Crimea (ARC). Whereas Article 134 states that the ARC is 'an integral constituent part of Ukraine', and 'resolves issues relegated to its authority' (in other words, decides matters within its competence), the next article authorised a constitution for the ARC, which would require approval by Ukraine's Rada. Article 137 itemises the regulatory powers devolved to Crimea, which include: agriculture and forestry; public works, tourism, culture, transport, hunting and fishing; and hospital services. Perhaps surprisingly, education is not included. Within Article 138's listing of 'issues under the authority' of the ARC, however, lies the requirement to ensure 'the functioning and development of the state language [Ukrainian] and national languages and cultures'. Although Crimea's minority Tatar population receives neither specific mention nor protection in the Constitution, the ARC is required to 'participate in the development and realisation of state programmes for the return of deported peoples'.

Significantly, Sevastopol is not covered in the chapter dealing with the ARC. Article 133 (Title IX) simply states that the 'cities of Kyiv and Sevastopol shall have a special status determined by the law of Ukraine' without giving any further detail. Likewise, Article 118 states no more than 'particular aspects of exercising executive power in the cities of Kyiv and Sevastopol shall be determined by special laws of Ukraine'. Thus Sevastopol remained a separate political entity from Crimea, as in Soviet times. Simferopol retained its status as the Crimean capital city, as in imperial Russia and the Soviet Union.

Following the adoption of Ukraine's constitution, it took nearly two and a half years of deliberation and negotiation before the Ukrainian Rada confirmed the ARC's own constitution on 23 December 1998. Significantly, Article 10 included specific protection for languages other than Ukrainian in the ARC: 'alongside the official language, the application and development, use and protection of Russian, Crimean Tatar and other ethnic groups' languages shall be secured'. Furthermore, the same article emphasised that 'Russian, being the language spoken by the majority of population and the language acceptable for purposes of interethnic communication, shall be used in all spheres of public life'. Articles 11–13 authorised the use of Russian in official documentation, in legal matters and in the post, telegraphs and in the consumer services such as health and transport.[29]

For all the supposed harmony between Kiev and Simferopol over the constitution, one important matter had not been resolved – the status, rights and wellbeing of the returning communities of the nationalities deported by the Soviet government in the 1940s. These 'formerly deported peoples' include Armenians, Bulgarians, Germans and Greeks. The Crimean Tatars and other 'indigenous' peoples, such as the remaining Krymchaks and Karaites of Jewish origin, form the largest group by far. According to the last Soviet census of 1989, there were 38,365 Tatars residing in Crimea: by mid-1995 this number had grown to an estimated 240,000. There have been many obstacles preventing the reintegration of Tatars into the mainstream Crimean political, economic and social life. These include the vexed questions of legal identity; land, housing and property; political participation; socio-economic issues; language, culture and religion; and education.[30]

The Tatars, however, were active in organising themselves in order to improve their lot. On 29 June 1992, the first modern Tatar congress, the *Qurultay* of 250 delegates elected by local communities, was held in Simferopol. In turn, it elected a 33-member Mejlis, an unofficial parliament. Its chairman, and leader of the Crimean Tatars, was Mustafa Dzhemilev (Jemilev), a former Soviet dissident and human rights activist. Born in Crimea in 1943 but brought up in Uzbekistan, he campaigned long on behalf of his people to be allowed to return to Crimea – and was imprisoned in the Soviet Union on several occasions for his efforts.

As a minority, the representation of the Crimean Tatars in the Simferopol parliament depends on the electoral system in force. The initial arrangements were good, if not generous. On 14 October 1993, a special Tatar quota of fourteen out of ninety-six seats was agreed. Yet this arrangement did not survive the annulment of the Crimean constitution on 17 March 1995. With the adoption of a majority voting system for the hundred directly elected members, the quota was not restored. In the 2010 elections to the Crimean parliament, six Tatars appeared on other party lists. Thus the influence of the Tatar community at the heart of Crimean political discourse waned, while their sense of exclusion and grievance, fuelled by economic and social deprivation, increased. Russian Crimeans feared on the one hand Tatar demands for a separate Tatar state of Crimea, and on the other, their consistent preference for Ukrainian as opposed to Russian rule. Thus the Tatars were seen as an obstacle to any reunion with the Russian Federation.

Sevastopol and the Black Sea Fleet

The apparent settlement of the 'Crimean question' through constitutional reform in 1996 and the ending of the 'war of laws' helped effect an accord between Russia and Ukraine. It manifested in a 'Treaty on Friendship, Cooperation and Partnership', signed by Presidents Yeltsin and Kuchma in Kiev on 31 May 1997. Before this document could be finalised, however, there needed to be agreement over the partition of the Black Sea Fleet and its facilities at Sevastopol. For many Russian politicians and their military and naval advisers, safeguarding the main base of the fleet at Sevastopol was of vital strategic importance to the future of Russia. Hence there were attempts to 'lift' Sevastopol out of Crimea and Ukraine. Recognising its value, Ukrainians also made a play for the fleet.

Soon after Ukraine gained its independence, on 3 January 1992 President Kravchuk demanded that members of the Black Sea Fleet take an oath of loyalty to Ukraine. The fleet commander at the time, Admiral Igor Vladimirovich Kasatonov, famously replied: '*nyet!*', and kept the Russian Federation flag flying high above Sevastopol and on his ships. In an interview of 2012, a Sevastopol veteran of this period, retired Colonel Viktor Alekseyevich Potapov, proudly confirmed this defiant stance:

> Yeltsin said 'I don't need revolutionary Sevastopol'. So the city was thrown away to Ukraine. Only the Black Sea Fleet in the south-western *Stavka* direction didn't give an oath of loyalty to the new Ukraine. It remained loyal to the Russian Federation. Out of 5000 men in a naval infantry regiment, for example, only four gave an oath to Ukraine.[31]

Subsequent developments show how post-Soviet Russia exercised calculated pressure on the newly founded state of Ukraine, with the future of the Black Sea Fleet providing a recurring source of profound disagreement and much friction.

Analysis of the Russian–Ukrainian crisis over Sevastopol during the 1990s provides invaluable context for events two decades later.[32]

On 9 July 1993, the Supreme Soviet of the Russian Federation adopted a resolution citing the 'federal status for the city of Sevastopol within the administrative and territorial borders of the city district as of December 1991', and entrusted the Russian government with a programme to safeguard the status of Sevastopol. In response, the Ukrainian government raised a formal protest to the United Nations Security Council. It complained that Russia's 'action was in flagrant disregard of universally recognized principles and norms of international law, in particular Article 2 (4) of the [United Nations] Charter'. As the United Nations' record of the Council's deliberation over the matter makes clear, however, the representative of the Russian Federation emphasised that the decree 'diverged from the policy of the President and the Government of the Russian Federation'. Furthermore, he 'contended that his country remained dedicated to the principle of the inviolability of the borders within the Commonwealth of Independent States and would strictly abide by its obligations under international law'.[33] None the less, on 20 July 1993, the Council issued an official statement, in which it reaffirmed:

> its commitment to the territorial integrity of Ukraine, in accordance with the Charter of the United Nations. The Council recalls that in the Treaty between the Russian Federation and Ukraine, signed at Kiev on 19 November 1990, the High Contracting Parties committed themselves to respect each other's territorial integrity within their currently existing frontiers. The Decree of the Supreme Soviet of the Russian Federation is incompatible with this commitment as well as with the purposes and principles of the Charter, and without effect.

Significantly, the statement concluded by welcoming 'the efforts of the Presidents and the Governments of the Russian Federation and Ukraine to settle any differences between them by peaceful means' and in urging 'that they take all steps to ensure the avoidance of tension'.[34]

Unfortunately for both Russia and Ukraine, the deliberations at the United Nations failed to generate a settlement: the dispute continued to dog mutual relations for another four years. Although Presidents Boris Yeltsin and Leonid Kuchma met on 9 June 1995 at Sochi to discuss how the Black Sea Fleet might be divided, no agreement was found. Moscow and Kiev remained deadlocked over the issue. Apparently, Kuchma refused to agree that the Russian Fleet's headquarters could remain in Sevastopol while the Russians demanded sole use.[35] Statements by senior Russian officers and resolutions by politicians in Moscow during the course of the following year raised further difficulties.

On 14 August 1996, Rear Admiral Aleksandr Grinko of the Black Sea Fleet detailed the enduring importance of Sevastopol and the significant investment made in its naval infrastructure:

> The entire Black Sea has no more convenient, deep, closed and vast bays than the Sevastopol bays. Their advantages are obvious from all standpoints: geopolitical, geostrategic, operational and tactical. In [the] years of the Soviet Union's existence a dock frontage extending over 10 kilometres was built in Sevastopol; a developed system of basing, command and control, defence, operational and combat support and ship repair was created; and the organisation of the base had been worked out. As a main base, Sevastopol [is] framed by a system of defence and protection from the air, from under water, from sea and from land. A system for [target] identification and for issue of target designation and a stable, reliable system of navigation, hydrometeorological and logistic support were developed.

Having highlighted Sevastopol's qualities, Grinko stated the strategic benefit of maintaining Sevastopol as a naval base of the Russian Federation, echoing the argumentation of Potemkin two hundred years before. 'Black Sea Fleet forces', the admiral declared, 'are capable of controlling all main axes of deployment of probable enemy forces, and above all, exits from the Bosporus Strait and the western and central parts of the Black Sea, thereby providing protection for Russia's southern borders'.[36] It cannot be stressed enough that Sevastopol's geographical position and its well-developed defence facilities lend it enormous strategic value. It is no wonder that its ownership has been so long contested.

Notwithstanding the end of the Cold War over five years before, it was significant that Grinko still referred to 'probable enemy forces' – presumably those of the North Atlantic Treaty Organisation (NATO). With its main base at Sevastopol, the Russian Black Sea Fleet could dominate the entire region, including the Sea's southern and eastern parts. Meanwhile, within nationalist circles in Russia a 'Sevastopol' campaign had developed with General Aleksandr Lebed, the chief of the Russian Security Council, and the mayor of Moscow, Yury Luzhkov, among its most prominent protagonists. The latter was particularly active in Sevastopol, establishing a branch of Moscow's state university in the Crimean port. When visiting the city on 23 December 1994, he declared: 'We relate to Sevastopol as to the eleventh district of Moscow, no matter how many customs and border issues there are. The desire of most of its inhabitants to be and feel Russian must not be suppressed'.[37]

Fed by such patriotic demands, on 16 October 1996, the Russian State Duma (parliament) unanimously adopted a draft bill to cease the division of the Black Sea Fleet, the terms of which were still being negotiated at governmental level.

Although an apparent breakthrough in the talks aimed at resolving the fleet question, which would, in turn, pave the way for the signing of the long-awaited Friendship Treaty, appeared on 22 October, the Russian Duma soon put another spanner in the works. On 24 October, it passed a fresh declaration demanding that the 'Ukrainian Supreme Soviet drop its unilateral approach to such issues as dividing the former Soviet Black Sea Fleet, Crimea's arbitrary transfer from Russia to Ukraine in 1954 and the status of Sevastopol'. Unsurprisingly the Ukrainian government reacted angrily to such demands, and on 6 December 1996 the Rada approved a resolution that declared Sevastopol 'has been, and shall remain, Ukrainian territory' and appealed for the support of 'international institutions on grounds of infringement upon our sovereignty'. It then prepared a draft law that required the 'withdrawal of all foreign troops from Ukrainian territory by the year 2000'.[38]

Despite the years of angry rhetoric and rising tensions between Russia and Ukraine over Sevastopol, resolution of the issue appeared on 28 May 1997 when Prime Ministers Viktor Chernomyrdin of Russia and Pavlo Lazernko of Ukraine signed the Black Sea Fleet Agreement. A pragmatic deal was done. Ukraine granted basing rights to Russia for twenty years in return for relief in debt repayments and a leasing fee. Altogether, the Black Sea Fleet consisted of no fewer that 525 combatant, auxiliary and support ships. Presidents Yeltsin and Kuchma had already agreed in principle in 1995 to split this force in half. Now Russia agreed to buy back 117 Ukrainian vessels as part of the debt relief (amounting to $526 million). This arrangement left Ukraine with just under 20 per cent of the fleet, while Russia retained just over 80 per cent. In terms of Sevastopol's maritime estate (see Map 2), Russia would have sole use of the Kazachya and Quarantine Bays, while both nations would share the Sevastopol Bay (including the Southern Bay) and the Streletskaya Bay.

In addition, barracks and support installations ashore were split – the lion's share going to the Russian Federation. These included the fleet's headquarters building and the Pirogov Naval Hospital in central Sevastopol, the 810th Naval Infantry Brigade at Kazachya Bay and the 41st Guided Missile Boat Brigade at Quarantine Bay, and not least the fleet's main ammunition stores and fuel farms. The Russian Federation also retained the naval airfields at Kacha and Gvardeyskoye (4 kilometres to the north of Simferopol's international airport). The Agreement limited the number of Russian Federation personnel based on Crimea to 25,000. In return for the lease of its basing facilities to Russia, Ukraine would be paid $98 million a year for twenty years.[39]

Following the 1997 Agreement, the Russian Black Sea Fleet never gave up its local control of Sevastopol's harbour, maintaining most of its infrastructure and all of its hydrographical and navigational facilities, including the lighthouses. The Ukrainian Navy, whose headquarters was established in Sevastopol, became tolerated 'guests' in their own country. Differences as to which nation should exercise control over the harbour and its approaches were never satisfactorily resolved.

The 'Treaty of Friendship, Cooperation and Partnership' between Ukraine and the Russian Federation, signed by Presidents Kuchma and Yeltsin in Kiev on 31 May 1997, crowned the apparent rapprochement between the two countries. Ukraine's and Russia's actions in 2014 need to be viewed against its provisions. Building on the earlier treaties of 19 November 1990 and 23 June 1992, both 'High Contracting Parties' reaffirmed the need to strengthen fraternal relations and the requirement to adhere to the norms of international law. Specifically, Article 1 set out that the two states, as 'equal and sovereign nations', would 'base their relations on mutual respect and trust, strategic partnership, and collaboration'. The second article required that both parties would 'respect each other's territorial integrity, and confirm the inviolability of the borders existing between them' in accordance with the UN Charter and under the Final Act of the Conference for Security and Collaboration in Europe (1975). Developing the provisions of the first two articles, the third declared that the Russian Federation and Ukraine would:

> ... construct their relations with each other on the basis of principles of mutual respect for sovereign equality, territorial integrity, the inviolability of borders, the peaceful settlement of disputes, the non-application of force, including economic and other means of pressure, the right of peoples to decide their own fates freely, non-intervention in internal affairs, the upholding of human rights and basic freedoms, collaboration among nations, and the conscientious fulfilment of international obligations assumed, as well as other generally accepted norms of international law.[40]

Despite the warm, conciliatory and friendly tone of the treaty, it took a considerable time before it was ratified. While the Ukrainian Rada in Kiev ratified the treaty on 14 January 1998,[41] progress in Moscow was much slower. Unsurprisingly, in view of the previous debates over the Black Sea Fleet, the ratification process caused bitter political divisions within Russia. Opponents, including Lebed, Luzhkov and Sergey Baburin (the leader of the Russian All-People's Union), argued that the treaty confirmed that Crimea and Sevastopol belonged to Ukraine. Advocates, with the Russian Prime Minister Yevgeny Primakov to the fore, held that establishing good, stable relations with Ukraine was ultimately more important.[42] Under Primakov's influence, the Russian State Duma finally passed a decree ratifying the treaty on 25 December 1998. In turn, on 17 February 1999 the Federation Council confirmed this decision.[43] Significantly, in its note about the ratification, the Council expressed its concerns and wishes over Crimea and Sevastopol:

> Members of the Federal Council express the hope that the Ukrainian Party understands the facts, on the basis of historical, economic, ethno-social and similar factors, objectively and properly measured in their particularities, with respect to Russia and Crimea, in which the majority of the inhabitants are Russian.
>
> The legendary hero-city of Sevastopol is dear to Russians. Let us strive to ensure that it remains the symbol of Russian friendship with the Ukrainian people, serving to provide against the dangers aimed at Russia and Ukraine from the south. For this reason, it is absolutely necessary for our two nations to be in complete accord with respect to the implementation of programmes regarding economic and social actions in this city of heroes.[44]

Since the collapse of the Soviet Union, the longstanding quarrel over Crimea and Sevastopol had been the cause of much tension between Ukraine and Russia. While there was now hope in both Kiev and Moscow that this dispute had at last been put to rest, subsequent political developments ensured that the matter returned to haunt both states.

WORSENING RELATIONS BETWEEN RUSSIA AND THE WEST

Many in the West proclaimed the end of the Cold War as a victory. Yet, as Sakwa reminds us, 'Russia did not in the least consider itself as a defeated power'.[45] Likewise, the Russian habit of exerting strong pressure on its neighbours – now comprising the states of the former Soviet Union – did not die in 1991. Former Soviet republics such as the Baltic states and especially Ukraine, only second in importance to Russia in the former Union, were soon described in Moscow as belonging to Russia's 'near abroad'. Already in 1995, David Pryce-Jones, the author of *The War that Never Was: The Fall of the Soviet Empire 1985–1991*, warned that such 'freed satellites' were 'susceptible to being coaxed or bounced into a reconstituted sphere of influence, if not empire'.[46] A year later, the political commentator Anatole Kaletsky observed that 'Russian public opinion would never allow a government to abandon completely its pretensions to influence over Russian-speaking populations in "the near abroad"'. Kaletsky caveated his assertion by stating 'the bleak reality of Russia's economic and military weakness ... would probably rule out a return to the aggression of the Stalin era'.[47] Within little over a decade, however, Russia's fortunes had improved very significantly.

Vladimir Putin, both as President and as Prime Minister, has overseen a remarkable revival of the Russian Federation as a power to be taken seriously, and one prepared to flex its muscles in pursuit of its national interests.

For both strategic and historical reasons Russia never accepted that many states of the former Soviet Union, and Ukraine in particular, should enjoy full national sovereignty and independence as understood in the West. Crimea, however, never fitted in to Russian conceptions of this 'near abroad'. The peninsula represented 'home' territory both psychologically and physically – the latter through the basing of the Black Sea Fleet at Sevastopol. Thus notwithstanding the fine words of the Black Sea Agreement and the Friendship Treaty of 1997, there are good grounds to suppose that many in Russia (not least members of the ruling elite) never accepted the loss of Crimea and Sevastopol following the collapse of the USSR. Had there been a substantial convergence of political orientation and systems between Russia and Ukraine, rather than the opposite, then there might have been a lasting settlement. People, decisions and events in both countries – and elsewhere – conspired both wittingly and unwittingly to undermine it. Furthermore, any chance of sustaining good relations between Russia and Ukraine, and not least maintaining a durable accord over Crimea and Sevastopol, was probably doomed as trust and co-operation between Russia and the West progressively declined from the start of the new century.

The signing of the 'Founding Act on Mutual Relations, Cooperation and Security' between NATO and the Russian Federation in Paris on 27 May 1997 represented the high point of East–West relations since 1991. The agreement's rationale 'to build ... a lasting and inclusive peace in the Euro-Atlantic area on the principles of democracy and cooperative security', rested on constructing 'a stable, peaceful and undivided Europe, whole and free, to the benefit of all its peoples'. Specifically, both parties shared a commitment to refrain 'from the threat or use of force against each other as well as against any other state, its sovereignty, territorial integrity or political independence', and respected 'the inviolability of borders and peoples' rights of self-determination'.[48]

In view of subsequent events, not least the conflicts between Russia in Georgia (2008) and in Ukraine (from 2014 onwards), which are covered later, the Act appears highly idealistic. It made no difference to the 'frozen conflicts' in Moldova/Transnistria, Nagorno-Karabkh and Abkhazia/Ossetia. Although easily stated in hindsight, the deterioration of relations between Russia and NATO from 2007 onwards demonstrates how the best of intentions can be thwarted by subsequent actions with unintended consequences. In this regard, Russian commentators would point out that the progressive eastward expansion of NATO following 1997 threatened *their* legitimate security interests. NATO's actions in places such as Kosovo in 1999 sowed further seeds of mistrust and discord.

Since 1991 Ukraine has reached out towards the West – its sovereign choice albeit in a divided country. On 8 February 1994, Ukraine became the third state of the former Soviet Union to join NATO's Partnership for Peace (PfP) programme – the first two to sign were Lithuania and Estonia on 27 January and 3 February respectively. At that time such an association with NATO could not be interpreted as being anti-Russian for the Russian Federation joined likewise on 22 June 1994.

In Budapest on 5 December 1994, representatives of the Russian Federation, Ukraine, United States of America and the United Kingdom signed a memorandum that provided for Ukraine's nuclear disarmament.[49] In return for giving up the Soviet-era nuclear weapons stored in its territory (although Russia had retained control of these by holding the launching codes), Ukraine believed it had received firm assurances for its future security from key NATO members. These proved to be groundless in 2014. Meanwhile, increasing numbers of PfP countries joined NATO. In 1999, the former Warsaw Pact members Poland, Hungary and the Czech Republic entered the Alliance. A second group in 2004 included the former Soviet Socialist Republics of Estonia, Latvia and Lithuania. All six states joined the European Union as well, reinforcing their 'Western' credentials.

At the 43rd Munich Conference on Security Policy, on 10 February 2007, President Putin delivered a stunning attack on the United States' dominance in a 'unipolar world', which he viewed as 'not only unacceptable, but also impossible'. Next he strongly denounced NATO:

> I think it is obvious that NATO expansion does not have any relation with the modernisation of the Alliance itself or with ensuring security in Europe. On the contrary, it represents a serious provocation that reduces the level of mutual trust. And we have the right to ask: against whom is this expansion intended? And what happened to the assurances our Western partners made after the dissolution of the Warsaw Pact? Where are those declarations today? No one even remembers them.

The Russian President then proceeded to quote from a speech of the NATO General Secretary, Manfred Woerner, in Brussels on 17 May 1990: '... the fact that we are not ready to place a NATO army outside of German territory gives the Soviet Union a firm security guarantee'. More prophetically, or perhaps ominously for some, Putin closed his remarks by reminding his audience that 'Russia is a country with a history that spans more than a thousand years and has practically always used the privilege to carry out an independent foreign policy.

We are not going to change this tradition today. At the same time, we are well aware of how the world has changed and we have a realistic sense of our own opportunities and potential'.[50]

President Putin's speech set a cold chill running throughout the West, whose leaders and commentators were surprised by the vehemence of the Russian leader's views. Although concerned, most Western heads of state at the time failed to realise the implications of Putin's policy announcement. NATO's language in its communiqué following its summit in April 2008 in Bucharest, for example, was muted. Yet Putin's words were far from empty rhetoric: his 2007 Munich speech provided a portent of relations to come. The global community had been warned that Russia was back on the world stage, and that it would flex its muscles in pursuit of its own ambitions as a great power. The West's leaders – whether in Berlin, Paris, London or Washington – failed to appreciate the growing risk of confrontation with an increasingly assertive Russia. The United States and the United Kingdom were particularly distracted by wars in Afghanistan and Iraq: in some cases, international centres of expertise on the Soviet Union and the Russian Federation were wilfully disbanded.[51] The timely wake-up call over the brief Russo-Georgian conflict in 2008 failed to provoke any serious attempts in the West to understand Moscow's concerns and interests, let alone deter Russia from undertaking actions to safeguard her national interests at the expense of others. This is not to excuse President Putin's actions, rather to explain them: to empathise is not to sympathise.

POLITICAL DEVELOPMENTS 2004–12

Since Ukraine's modern foundation, corruption, division and discontinuity have undermined its development. In stark contrast to Poland and the Baltic states, who have prospered following the end of the Cold War, Ukraine has languished demographically, economically and politically. In two decades its population fell by 10 million to 44 million – as a result of emigration and a falling birth rate. Its GDP has yet to recover to the level of 1991.[52] Although its general foreign policy has steered towards the West, contrary pro-Russian shifts also took place in the country's complicated, and at times contradictory, 'multi-vector' foreign relations. Far from being isolated from these swings, often Crimea became a litmus test for the state of Russian–Ukrainian relations. Events and policies in Kiev quickly affected perceptions, and drove reactions, in Simferopol and Sevastopol.

Leonid Kravchuk, a former leader of the Communist Party of Ukraine, became the first President of independent Ukraine. His successor in 1994, Leonid Kuchma, served two five-year terms. Viktor Yanukovych, who served as Prime Minister in 2002–04, put himself forward for President in the 2004 election. Viktor Yushchenko and Yulia Tymoshenko opposed him. When Yanukovych was prematurely announced as the presidential winner against a background of alleged electoral fraud, Tymoshenko called on the population to protest. Hundreds of thousands did so in Kiev and in Ukraine's other major cities in what became known as the 'Orange' revolution. In a re-run of the presidential election on 26 December 2004, Yushchenko won by a narrow margin of just under 4 per cent over Yanukovych.

One man's democratic revolution is another's illegal *coup d'état*. Western governments, and especially the American, welcomed the triumph of 'people power' in Ukraine. In contrast, President Putin, who had publically backed Yanukovych, was appalled. In strongly supporting Ukraine's aspirations towards the membership of both NATO and the European Union, the West became party to her internal politics and associated external relations with Russia. As Sakwa argues, 'democratic protest about electoral fraud was inextricably bound up with geopolitical contestation, a fateful combination that would have devastating consequences in 2014'.[53] While few would have anticipated ten years before that Russia would react so angrily and boldly with regard to Crimea, Moscow gave loud warnings in the intervening period. If heard at all, they were not always accorded the attention demanded by the Russian leadership. Sound statecraft requires an understanding of others' points of view and vital strategic interests – even if these are diametrically opposed to one's own.

Following the Orange revolution of 2004–5, the resulting polity in Ukraine proved highly unstable. Whereas the President is elected by popular mandate every five years, prime ministers, appointed by the head of state, come and go more frequently. Tymoshenko proved a controversial and unpopular prime minister under President Yushchenko. Effective teamwork between them proved impossible. Dismissed in September 2005, Tymoshenko was replaced by Yury Yekhanurov. Yanukovych made an unexpected comeback as Prime Minister in August 2006. In the rapidly spinning carousel of Ukrainian politics, Tymoshenko re-appeared back in her old post in December 2007. Yet nothing really changed for the better: the world economic crisis of 2008 hit Ukraine exceptionally hard.

Ukraine's pro-NATO leaning continued to irritate Moscow. Despite being the first CIS country to join the PfP programme, Ukraine had been kept on the waiting list for membership of the Alliance. No doubt with a view to NATO's Bucharest summit in April 2008, the Russian Ministry for Foreign Affairs warned on 13 January that year that any 'further expansion of NATO could produce a serious political-military upheaval that would affect the interests of Russia'.[54] Unsaid, however, were the vital interests of other states, including Ukraine's. Berlin and Paris, meanwhile, took due note of Moscow's concerns. Their leaders, Chancellor Angela Merkel and French President Nicholas Sarkozy, successfully lobbied the American President, George W. Bush, to delay Ukraine's and Georgia's entry into the Alliance. Although both aspirant states were informed that they would accede to NATO in due course, they were not invited yet to join the Alliance's Membership Action Plan. In many ways, this triumph of prevarication represented the worst possible outcome for Ukraine and Georgia. Although having invested heavily towards NATO accession, not least through deploying forces to Iraq in support of the American-led coalition, Ukraine and Georgia had still gained nothing substantial in return. The distant prospect of membership at some ill-defined future date provided no security guarantees for the present. The Baltic states, in contrast, had benefitted since 2004 from the protection of Article 5 of the Washington Treaty. Yet Russia felt provoked by the Alliance's longer-termed intentions as much of her western and southern frontiers now abutted either NATO or pro-NATO states.

In post Cold War Crimea, NATO remained particularly unpopular. In late May and in early June 2006, for example, violent protests broke out in Feodosiya. Demonstrators objected to the presence of US troops preparing for a Ukrainian–NATO exercise, SEA BREEZE, which had been due to start on 17 July 2006. On 6 June 2006, the Crimean parliament declared Crimea as 'NATO-free territory'. As reported in the *Guardian* newspaper two days later, the Russian parliament, 'often a mouthpiece for the Kremlin', warned Ukraine about joining NATO: 'Ukraine's accession to the military bloc will lead to very negative consequences for relations between our fraternal peoples'.[55] Perhaps this was the first warning of the conflict with Russia to come.

Attitudes on Crimea changed little during the following years. Popular polling results in 2011 indicated that considerably more Crimeans than Ukrainians as a whole viewed NATO as a threat. Whereas 52.8 per cent of Ukrainians and 56.1 per cent of Russians living on the peninsula feared the Alliance, only 13.1 per cent of those polled in central Ukraine were of the same view. These figures and other related statistics remain significant in a number of ways. First, both Ukrainian and Russian nationalities on Crimea held similar opinions over NATO; in contrast, only 18.5 per cent of Crimean Tatars agreed with them. Secondly, within Ukraine's regions there were also marked disparities. While only 10 per cent of western Ukrainians saw NATO as a threat, four times as many (40 per cent) of those living in the east feared the Alliance.[56]

During the late 2000s, pro-Russian sentiments were already stirring again on Crimea. The Russian Society of Crimea, which began its activities in the early 1990s by calling for the preservation of Russian identity, evolved into a popular movement calling for the reintegration of the peninsula into Russia. Historic events provided a useful launching pad for such irredentist demands. On 19 April 2008, for example, members and supporters of the society held a rally and march in Simferopol to celebrate the 225th anniversary of Catherine the Great's Crimean Manifesto. Speakers reminded their audience of Crimea's 'eternal' ties to Russia. Veteran pro-Russian campaigner Sergey Tsekov, the society's leader, expressed confidence that 'Crimea was, is, and always will be Russian land, and that Crimeans of different nationalities are united in Russian language and Russian culture – an integral part of the great Russian world'. The leader of the Crimean Cossack Union, Aleksandr Shevtsov, declared: 'Today we are defending our land and our right to be Russian, to be the people who know their history, who want all the peoples of the Crimea to live in peace and friendship'.[57] With the exception of Moscow, few people in European capitals, took much notice of such agitation.

The world was reminded of the importance of Sevastopol and the Black Sea Fleet during the short war between Georgia and the Russian Federation in August 2008. In the Russian Navy's first offensive combat operation since 1945, units of the Russian Black Sea Fleet, led by the guided missile cruiser *Moskva* and the destroyer *Smetlivy*, were despatched from Sevastopol and Novorossiysk. Two naval infantry battalions were disgorged from three landing ships on the Abkhazian coast, and on 10 August 2008 the Russian guided missile corvette *Mirazh* sunk the Georgian patrol boat *Tbilisi*.[58]

Although the Russian government was annoyed by the President Yushchenko's visit to Tbilisi on 12 August 2008 at the height of the conflict with Georgia, it was more concerned by the Ukrainian leader's declarations regarding the Black Sea Fleet. Not only did Yushchenko try to limit the future deployment of the Russian fleet, but he also announced that the lease for the base at Sevastopol would be terminated in 2017, when the twenty-year term agreed in 1997 concluded.[59] Although the Russian Federation had made some effort to update the Black Sea Fleet's facilities at Novorossiysk, its exposed harbour and limited facilities can never match the quality of Sevastopol's anchorages and infrastructure. For practical reasons, therefore, Moscow remained desperate to maintain its base in Sevastopol. Furthermore, the value of Russia's well-found airfields, radar sites, listening posts and storage facilities on the Crimean peninsula reinforced the imperative of retaining Sevastopol. Yushchenko's policy leading towards Ukraine's eventual membership of NATO placed all those essential bases to Russia at existential risk.

In the meantime, there remained a strong suspicion that Ukraine's recurring problems with Russia over the supply and payment for natural gas, manifested in the 'gas wars' of 2005 and 2008–09, were linked to her foreign policy, which Russia perceived as being hostile. Although Yulia Tymoshenko apparently resolved the matter in making a controversial deal with Prime Minister Putin in January 2009, Russia could always turn off the gas stopcock again. In recent years

(2014–16), Ukraine has attempted to curb its energy demands and reduce its reliance on imported Russian gas.

Ukraine's presidential election in 2010 set the country on a collision course between the executive and the people, ultimately leading to the events of November 2013 – February 2014 and President Viktor Yanukovych's toppling from power. It remains debatable whether such a clash was inevitable. But given the deep political and regional divisions in the country, and the intensifying dissatisfaction about its governance, there was a good chance of protest, if not revolution. While in the first round, Yanukovych of the Party of the Regions enjoyed a handsome lead of 10 per cent over his rival Yulia Tymoshenko of the All-Ukrainian Union, the run-off on 7 February generated a much closer winning margin of just over 3 per cent (48.95 to 45.47 per cent). While Tymoshenko received a majority vote in Kiev and in seventeen western and central *oblasts*, Yanukovych won in Sevastopol, the Autonomous Republic of Crimea and in the more densely populated eight eastern and southern regions. The latter candidate's best results were in the strongly pro-Russian *oblasts* of Donetsk (where he had been a former governor) and Luhansk, followed by the city of Sevastopol and Crimea.[60]

Following his appointment as President on 14 February 2010, Yanukovych lost little time in seeking an accord with Russia. On 21 April 2010 in Kharkov, he met Dmitry Medvedev, who had succeeded as Russian President in 2008. Putin, however, as Prime Minister (2008–12), probably retained ultimate control of the Russian Federation. Echoing the Black Sea Fleet agreement of 1997, another deal was done over gas. In exchange for a 30 per cent discount on the price of imported Russian natural gas, Ukraine allowed the Black Sea Fleet to remain based at Sevastopol for a further twenty-five years from 28 May 2017, with automatic five-year extension periods.[61] All then seemed settled with regard to the Black Sea Fleet and Sevastopol for decades to come.

Yanukovych attempted to resolve the contentious Russian language issue. Although Russian remained the majority language employed in newspapers, journals, books and television programmes in Ukraine, it enjoyed no official status outside Crimea. On 3 July 2012, the Rada passed the 'Kolesnichenko–Kivalov' language law in a stormy, at times violent, session. Within a region, it permitted a local language spoken by at least a 10 per cent minority of the population to be declared official. While this law applied not only to Russian in eastern and southern Ukraine, but also to Romanian and Hungarian in the west, the main desired effect was to promote Russian. In response, nearly half of Ukraine's twenty-seven political entities approved Russian as a second official language. As Sakwa has noted, the more widespread endorsement of Russian did not apply to Ukraine's civil service, military or higher education, where use of the Ukrainian language remained mandatory.[62]

Ukrainian nationalists, however, strongly opposed Russian becoming a 'regional language'. Protesters took to the streets, fearing that 'Russian would become a *de facto* government language for eastern Ukraine'. Further, if Russian speakers were no longer encouraged to learn the Ukrainian language, they argued, the country 'would be even more divided as a result'.[63] For such nationalists, examples of pluralist states with two or more official languages, such as Belgium, Canada and Switzerland, cut little ice. For them, Ukraine's sense of nationhood is defined by its language and separateness from Russian culture and influence. Such distinction is not ephemeral: it remains an emblematic issue for Ukraine and an enduring concern for Russia and pro-Russians.

On 15 July 2010 Yanukovych signed a law on 'the fundamental principles of the country's domestic and foreign policy', which stipulated Ukraine's non-aligned status. As a result, the national objective of joining NATO was abandoned, albeit constructive engagement with the Alliance would continue.[64] Within Ukraine's armed forces, a purge had already taken place of individuals closely associated with NATO. General of Ukraine Ivan Svida, the Chief of the General Staff, and hence Ukraine's senior serving military officer, resigned on 28 May 2010 following unbridgeable policy differences with Yanukovych. The heads of the Ukrainian navy and air force, Admiral Ihor Tenyukh and Colonel General Ivan Rusnak respectively, had already departed in March. Other officers and officials were either summarily dismissed from post or transferred to posts unconnected with NATO.

EUROPEAN ASSOCIATION, KIEVIAN WINTER AND CRIMEAN SPRING, 2013–14

From November 2013 to March 2014 events in Ukraine – principally those in Kiev and on the Crimean peninsula – unfolded at a manner and pace last seen in Europe with the fall of the Berlin Wall and the break-up of the Soviet Union in 1989–91. What transpired in the 'Crimean Spring' of 2014 is directly related to the preceding 'Kievian Winter' of 2013–14 and Ukraine's steps towards signing an association agreement with the European Union (EU). The strategic consequences of Russia's incorporation of Crimea and Sevastopol are hard to understate: relations between West and East undertook a sharp reverse. While both NATO and the EU regard Crimea and Sevastopol as 'illegally annexed', the Russian Federation considers both entities as finally being 'reunified', and therefore beyond any further discussion or renegotiation.

Far from the break-up of the Soviet Union heralding the 'end of history', as controversially proclaimed by the American political scientist Francis Fukuyama in 1989, recent events in Eastern Europe and in other parts of the world remind us that new history is continually being made. More fundamentally, Western liberal democracy is not necessarily the 'final form of human government', as Fukuyama once believed.[65] This system is under constant pressure from a number of sources, whether states or terrorist groups. Contradictions and challenges abound. While other polities, such as in Russia, may have quite different perspectives from those of the West, they may also share views. Meanwhile, unexpected events, such as the '9/11' terrorist attack on New York in 2001, may catch one completely unawares in their timing, proximity, and effect.

Ukraine's westward orientation has not solely been concerned with NATO membership. Since its disappointment at the 2008 Bucharest Summit, approaching the EU appeared an externally more credible, and internally less contentious, path than joining the Alliance. Paradoxically, the far-reaching events of 2013–14 in Kiev and Crimea demonstrated that the EU, rather than NATO, had become the main driver of division within Ukraine, and indeed between that state and the Russian Federation.

In many respects, the recent roots of the eventual crisis over Crimea, Sevastopol and eastern Ukraine in 2014 can be traced back to 2009. That year saw the signing of the EU's Lisbon Treaty, which includes a mutual assistance and a solidarity clause. It also provides the basis for the development of the EU's Common Security and Defence Policy and the EU's foreign policy arm – the European External Action Service. Therefore any association with the EU brings important security as well as economic dimensions. Furthermore, the EU's 'Eastern Partnership', launched in May 2009, is overtly political. Under this initiative, Brussels planned to 'strengthen its ties' with six states: Armenia, Azerbaijan, Belarus, Georgia, Moldova and Ukraine, all former republics of the USSR. The broad objective of this programme, however, was to bind these states into the Western European political and economic system. Notwithstanding the events in Ukraine in 2013–14, this policy remains unchanged.

The immediate goal of the Eastern Partnership is to forge 'association agreements', aiming to achieve not only 'political association and economic integration', but also 'a shared commitment to a close and lasting relationship based on common values'. The agreements also contain provisions towards a 'Deep and Comprehensive Free Trade Area', designed to align the legal systems and key sectors of a partner state's economy to the EU's common standards.[66] Although falling short of 'candidate' status, an association agreement can be regarded as a significant first step in a process designed to bring about EU membership – and the political, economic and security integration that comes with it. Hence it could be argued that the process of assimilation starts with the convergence of association.

Crucially, whether a member of the EU or not, Ukraine's foreign and security policy would increasingly be drawn westward. Article 7 of the EU-Association Agreement with Ukraine, subsequently signed on 21 March 2014, makes this point crystal clear:

> The Parties shall intensify their dialogue and cooperation and promote gradual convergence in the area of foreign and security policy, including the Common Security and Defence Policy (CSDP), and shall address in particular issues of conflict prevention and crisis management, regional stability, disarmament, non-proliferation, arms control and arms export control as well as enhanced mutually-beneficial dialogue in the field of space.[67]

Unsurprisingly, adopting the EU route proved not only contentious in Ukraine, but also in Russia. Moscow now feared an 'EU-orientated Ukraine' as much as a potential NATO member on its western border. The Ukrainian–Russian trade partnership, stemming from the integrated days of the USSR, also remained significant. Russia accounted for 24 per cent of Ukraine's exports and 30 per cent of its imports. Additionally, many of Ukraine's defence industries supplied essential equipment for Russia's armed forces, including engines for helicopters and warships.[68] Furthermore, Ukraine's association with the EU would undermine the Russian Eurasian Economic Union project. Thus it is not hard to see why the Russian Federation saw itself being challenged geopolitically – encircled by hostile economic and military powers. The EU, however, remained confident that Ukraine, along with Georgia and Moldova, would sign an association agreement at the EU's Eastern Partnership summit meeting at Vilnius on 28–29 November 2013. In the event, whereas Georgia and Moldova initialled their respective agreements, Ukraine did not.

On 21 November 2013, the Ukrainian Cabinet of Ministers decided to suspend final preparations towards signing an association agreement at Vilnius. Yanukovych justified this decision by claiming he needed more time to review the matter. He probably did, as the consequences for Ukraine were far-reaching in many spheres of national life and international relations. While there was considerable uncertainty as to the longer-term internal benefits to Ukraine, Russia was vocal as to the immediate threats posed by the association agreement to its economy and security. It would appear that the 'eurocrats' of the EU's External Action Service had not appreciated the difficulties that Ukraine would face either at home or with Russia. In the past, the expansion of the EU had never generated such internal opposition or international tension. Thus its politicians and senior officials alike were ill prepared to deal with such a hotly contested issue. As a Russian International Affairs Council report of 2015 simply concluded: 'Moscow sees the Eastern Partnership as an attempt to weaken Russian influence in the post-Soviet space and offer a different development model to the former Soviet Republics'.[69] No wonder, then, that Russia actively opposed it in 2013, and continues to do so.

The authors of the joint declaration issued after the Vilnius Summit – at which Yanukovych appeared – seemed oblivious of the brewing internal and international crises generated by the association process:

> The participants of the Vilnius Summit take note of the decision by the Ukrainian Government to suspend temporarily the process of preparations for signature of the Association Agreement and Deep and Comprehensive Free Trade Area between the EU and Ukraine. They also take note of the unprecedented public support for Ukraine's political association and economic integration with the EU.

Rather strangely, the EU and Ukraine also agreed 'to reiterate their commitment to the signing of this Agreement on the basis of determined action and tangible progress in the three areas emphasised at the 2013 EU–Ukraine Summit'.[70] In other words, there was some prospect that Yanukovych would some day return to Brussels and seek new terms. Such a prospect failed to mollify the growing number of anti-government, pro-EU, protestors in Kiev. Whatever the EU's and the Ukrainian government's intentions, the Eastern Partnership helped trigger the crisis that led inexorably from the second Maidan in Kiev to the Russian annexation of Crimea and Sevastopol.

The Russian Federation did not waste much time in making Yanukovych an alluring offer before the EU could tempt him again with a revised association agreement or other incentive. In yet another gas deal, cash-strapped Ukraine was offered a $15 billion loan and a one-third discount on the price of Russian natural gas. Although Yanukovych accepted the deal on 17 December 2013, his time in office was now numbered. Almost a month before, pro-European demonstrations erupted in central Kiev on 21 November, which grew in increasing scale and level of violence over the winter months. Anti-government protests spread throughout Ukraine. Meanwhile, the focus of opposition in the capital became termed the 'Euromaidan'.[71] This second protest quickly surpassed in duration the first Maidan protest – the 2004 Orange revolution – of only seventeen days.

It is well beyond the scope of this book to document in any detail the events in Kiev and elsewhere in Ukraine leading up to the 'people's revolution' (or coup, from a Russian perspective) that occurred in February 2014.[72] Its consequences, however, soon rebounded in Crimea and Sevastopol. Although moving pictures of the protest were shown around the world's television screens, the key opinion-forming audiences were those in Ukraine and Russia. Two opposing narratives quickly emerged. In the modern '24/7' information environment, perceptions are shaped not only by television and press reports, but also by social media. Such methods worked both to mobilise anti-government protesters and to inflame views against them. Whereas Ukrainian nationalists saw a valid people's protest in Kiev's Maidan [Independence Square] and on the adjoining streets being violently attacked by the authorities' riot police, reactions in Moscow, Eastern Ukraine, Crimea and Sevastopol were quite different.

Russian and pro-Russian official and unofficial reporting of the Euromaidan focused on Ukraine's far-right activists, including those drawn from the *Svoboda* (Freedom) Party and the militant *Pravy Sektor* (Right Sector) group that emerged from the section of the square it organised. A giant portrait of the Ukrainian nationalist Stepan Bandera and the various flags of the right, including the black and red stripes of the Ukrainian Insurgent Army,[73] proved particularly powerful symbols in portraying the Maidan's demonstrators as either neo-Nazis or fascists. Some undoubtedly were. Yet of the hundreds of thousands of Ukraine's citizens who protested in Kiev and elsewhere, statistically only a small proportion could be ascribed as being members of the far-right. The Ukrainian opposition represented a much broader church, including many liberals, who objected to Yanukovych and the corrupt form of government he represented. None the less, there were many other protestors too: those mainly from eastern and southern Ukraine who campaigned against the EU and NATO, and felt that their voice was being ignored. There had been, after all, neither an election nor referendum on the issue of EU association.

The spilling of blood can easily whip up tensions, converting civil unrest into armed insurrection, and leading to the distortion of history. A hundred protesters were killed on Kiev's streets in January and February 2014, as were eighteen policemen. While the former are portrayed as victims and heroes of the revolution, the latter are largely forgotten, except in their home communities. The bloodshed that occurred outside Kiev attracted less attention. On 2 May 2014, no fewer than forty-two pro-Russian demonstrators perished in an Odessa trade union building, which had been set on fire by pro-Maidan protestors.[74] So the conflict was not wholly a one-sided affair of brutal police murdering innocent demonstrators. These facts need to be remembered when judgements are passed on the rights and wrongs of the Ukraine crisis.

THE ANNEXATION OF CRIMEA: OPERATION RUSSIAN SPRING, FEBRUARY–MARCH 2014

After days of mounting violence in Kiev, on 22 February 2014 the Ukrainian Rada voted President Yanukovych out of office. A last-minute deal brokered the day before by the foreign ministers of France, Germany and Poland (Laurent Fabius, Frank-Walter Steinmeier and Radoslaw Sikorski) between the three principal opposition leaders (Arseny Yatsenyuk, Oleg Tyagnibok and Vitaly Klitschko) and Yanukovych was overtaken by events. A majority of the people on the streets wanted rid of the President. Apart from a small team of bodyguards, the President's security forces melted away. Fearing assassination more than impeachment, Yanukovych fled to Kharkov, and then to Crimea. A Russian military helicopter spirited him away to safety and oblivion. A government under interim President Oleksandr Turchynov and Prime Minister Yatsenyuk established itself in Kiev.

One of its first, and most regrettable acts, was to announce the suspension of Russian being recognised as a regional language. This not only appalled many Russian speakers in Eastern Ukraine and Crimea, but also provided a propaganda gift to the Kremlin and pro-Russian groups. The changeover of power – portrayed as an illegal coup – in Kiev sparked rallies across Eastern Ukraine, Crimea and Sevastopol. The prompt cancellation of the proposed language measure was not believed: it continued to fuel protests. More fundamentally, there were fears of Ukrainian ultra-right nationalism being enforced throughout the whole country. In the eyes of many pro-Russians, the self-appointed Kiev 'junta' had neither legitimacy nor authority. Conversely, pro-Ukrainians, and especially the Tatars, came on to the streets in Crimea to proclaim their loyalty to Kiev. Hence the stage was set for strife, if not secession, on the peninsula.

In 2014, the situation was far different from that which had prevailed twenty years before. Then Russia was weak: now it was far stronger and bolder. Although it is not known in any certainty, President Putin could have taken the decision to annex Crimea as early as the night of 22/23 February. Perhaps the popular calls made on 23 February in Sevastopol for independence from Ukraine may have strengthened his resolve. Without access to the official record of the Russian government's decisions, however, any such presumptions must remain speculative. While Moscow was careful not to hint at any possible intervention at this time, it would appear from subsequent events that some contingency planning for such an operation had already taken place. Preparations for what became popularly known in Russia as Operation RUSSIAN SPRING were in any event swiftly put in hand. Many Russian residents of Crimea, moreover, called the reunification their 'Crimean Spring' to emphasise the spontaneous and self-determined action of local residents, as opposed to what had been ordained and orchestrated elsewhere. Regardless of who ordered whom, what then happened on 26/27 February and the days thereafter on the peninsula surprised the world by its audacity, speed and sophistication.

Unlike the Soviet military interventions in Hungary (1956) and Czechoslovakia (1968), there was no invasion spearheaded by tank columns. In contrast, tightly disciplined, well-armed, uniformed (albeit unmarked) truck-borne groups suddenly appeared from nowhere. Anonymous units of 'little green men' (principally Russian Federation Special Operations Forces (*Spetsnaz*)) mysteriously appeared. These 'polite people' (*vezhlivye lyudi*) facilitated the takeover of power in Simferopol and elsewhere on the peninsula by pro-Russian activists.[75] These groups swiftly secured key government offices and military installations in Crimea, notably the parliament building in Simferopol and its international airport. The nearby Black Sea Fleet naval air base at Gvardeyskoye provided an ideally located point of entry for reinforcements flown in from Russian territory. Ships of the Black Sea Fleet blockaded Ukrainian navy and coast guard units in their bases at Sevastopol, Balaklava, Feodosiya and Kerch.

By treaty, Russia was permitted to station up to 25,000 members of its armed forces on the peninsula. Russian sources indicate, however, that only 16,000 were present in early 2014. In effect, the Russian bases at Sevastopol and in other locations on Crimea acted as Trojan Horses within Ukraine's main gates. It is estimated that at least an additional 6,000 men were flown in by either transport aircraft or helicopters at the end of February 2014. A small but highly proficient number of these troops, both already in place and brought to Crimea, were Russian Federation Special Operations Forces. Ambiguity as to the origin and status of the troops involved characterised this operation.

While expert external observers soon recognised the *Spetsnaz* for what they were, the fiction of only 'self-defence' forces being involved was maintained for a considerable time in the international media. Russian denials were taken at face value by gullible Western broadcasters, apparently ignorant of the deception and disinformation methods inherent in warfare, whether ancient or modern. To be fair, local 'self-defence' militia groups, easily distinguishable by their less disciplined demeanour and indifferent dress, were involved as well. Sometimes professional Russian forces, former Ukrainian *Berkut* riot police and local irregulars were mixed up at the same places or incidents, complicating the identification of those involved. Many of the volunteers signed up in the days immediately following Yanukovych's dramatic departure from Kiev on 22 February. Except in Sevastopol, where their role was highly significant, the local self-defence groups' effort in Crimea was a strictly supporting one – adding to the overall confusion and distraction as to what was under way and by whom.

Russia could not have taken over Crimea without the passivity of Ukraine's armed forces stationed on the peninsula and the strong support of the local population and its leaders. Already in May 2013, six months before the second Maidan protest, members of the Russian Society of Crimea, and its political wing, the United Russia Party, were demonstrating against the growing influence of the Ukraine far-right. In January 2014, the Maidan in Kiev triggered large anti-Maidan protests in Simferopol. These were countered by pro-European ones in early February, which spawned yet greater demonstrations against the Maidan.[76] Their leader was a Crimean businessman, Sergey Aksyonov of Moldovan origin. Known by his critics as the 'Goblin', he had a controversial, allegedly criminal, past. In 2010, as leader of United Russia Party, he had been elected as a deputy of the Crimean parliament. His party won three seats on just 4 per cent of the vote.[77] The vast majority of seats (80 out of 100) was held by Viktor Yanukovych's Ukrainian Party of the Regions. The Prime Minister of Crimea, the chairman of the Council of Ministers, Anatoly Mogilyov, supported an autonomous Crimea within the state of Ukraine. As the protests mounted against the Kiev Maidan in the winter of 2013/2014, Aksyonov rather than Mogilyov caught the mood of the pro-Russian community, which became increasingly alarmed by the reportage of events in Kiev on both Ukrainian and Russian television.

26 February 2014 proved a crucial day in Crimea's secession from Ukraine and eventual incorporation by the Russian Federation. Outside the parliament building in Simferopol, thousands of pro-Russian separatist demonstrators clashed with large numbers of pro-Ukrainian supporters. Inside, members of the parliament met to consider whether a referendum should be held to reduce Crimea's links to Ukraine: union with Russia was not yet tabled. As the meeting was non-quorate, no vote was taken. Before dawn the next morning (the 27th), masked armed men seized the parliament building. Reporters were barred from entering, as was the premier, Mogilyov. A disputed number of parliamentarians, however, made their way into the building to take part in debates as to Crimea's future. By that evening, two results were notified: fifty-three members voted to replace Mogilyov with Aksyonov and sixty-one voted for independence. Some viewed these results as fabrications as it was never clear how many members of parliament were present, and what had been voted for under duress.[78] Throughout this process, the deputy of the United Russia Party, Dmitry Polonsky, assisted Aksyonov. He soon became Crimea's new information minister and deputy prime minister.

Those organising the pro-Russian counter-revolution in Crimea realised that the peninsula needed to be sealed off from mainland Ukraine. Sevastopol journalist Sergey Gorbachev claims that the Sevastopol-based detachment of *Berkut*, recently returned from the Euromaidan in Kiev, undertook the critical role of blocking the Perekop isthmus and the Chongar road and rail crossings on 26/27 February 2014. Gorbachev maintains that the unit performed this duty entirely on its own initiative.[79] The extent to which regular Russian Federation forces took part from the start of this action is disputed, not least whether they wore *Berkut* uniforms. But what is clear is that Kuban Cossacks and Russian Federation troops subsequently reinforced members of the *Berkut*. Thus there was little possibility of armed Ukrainian nationalist amateur forces entering the

Crimean peninsula. The 'defenders' of Crimea claim that their rail and road blocks were put in place only 'just in time' – two hours before a large group of bus-borne *Pravy Sektor* activists arrived at the border. If so, this event represents a considerable irony.

The Ukrainian narrative of the Euromaidan holds that members of the reviled *Berkut* (drawn from many cities, including Donetsk and Sevastopol) were responsible for the brutal murders of the 'holy hundred' of innocent protestors in Kiev. Now members of the *Berkut* had become the vanguard of the defence of Crimea against the same *Pravy Sektor*. In Sevastopol, members of *Berkut* were given flowers, embraced by local residents and treated to heroes' welcomes: it would appear that this event was spontaneous and not staged for the media. At that critical time in late February, Ukraine's armed forces were neither poised nor directed to intervene in the peninsula. The bulk of the Ukrainian Army remained stationed in the west of the country, a legacy of the Soviet Union when Red Army formations of the second operational echelon were held ready to march towards Western Germany.

In Operation RUSSIAN SPRING, apart from the blocking of the Crimea's northern approaches, the decisive acts on 27 February 2014 included the seizure and isolation of the government offices and parliament building in Simferopol, and not least control of the deliberations and decisions within. Without the involvement of Russian Federation Special Operations Forces, it is doubtful whether these actions could have been accomplished. In the process, Ukraine's military power on Crimea had been neutralised without a fight. One of the mysteries of Operation RUSSIAN SPRING is the failure of the Ukrainian armed forces to resist. As the territorial integrity of their country had been violated by an external power, one might have supposed that a more robust response would have resulted. Furthermore, within months there appeared to be a remarkable recovery in Ukrainian military performance, as evidenced in the bitter fighting in Eastern Ukraine. As far as can be established, a number of factors, which remain speculative on account of the lack of corroborating evidence, may have been at work.

Ukrainian forces stationed on Crimea enjoyed close contacts with their Russian counterparts and never envisaged them as opponents. It is also alleged that Russians and pro-Russians had infiltrated the Ukrainian defence intelligence and the internal security service (SBU) at all levels. If this is true, then the Ukrainian military may have received few, or deliberately misguided, warnings as to what was likely to occur and was already under way. With the recent change of government in Kiev, there was a lack of decision-making at the highest level beyond a general will to avoid becoming sucked into an armed conflict with a much superior military power. These three factors combined to produce a passivity, if not paralysis of command, at local levels, resulting in inaction.[80]

The fourth matter, for which there is more substantive evidence, relates to the mass desertions of Ukrainian soldiers, sailors and airmen, many of whose families and friends lived on Crimea. Russian forces induced them to break with Ukraine not only by offers of higher pay, but also by fostering their alienation from the new regime in Kiev. One Russian source indicates that 18,000 of the 22,000 members of the Ukrainian armed forces stationed on Crimea switched their loyalty and gave a new oath to the Russian Federation. 'Deep in their hearts', according to Sergey Gorbachev, 'they realised that Crimea was not part of Ukraine and that the peninsula's population would not follow the Maidan'.[81]

Of course, the matter was not at all one-sided. In the absence of either direction or support from Kiev, some members of the Ukrainian armed forces on the Crimean peninsula put up a spirited non-lethal resistance. Among these were airmen at Belbek to the north of Sevastopol, which resisted Russian attempts to seize the Ukrainian air base until 22 March 2014.[82] Overall, however, Ukraine's long-neglected armed forces on Crimea were neither mentally nor physically prepared for a fraternal conflict. They had both been starved of adequate resources and denied the necessary leadership. The contrasts with the Russian Federation could not have been greater. Yet Ukraine's failure to resist the annexation was probably a mistake – it emboldened Russia and shamed many Ukrainians.

THE 'THIRD DEFENCE' OF SEVASTOPOL

For many of the people of Sevastopol, its 'third defence' began shortly after the break-up of the Soviet Union. The Moscow-based politician, Sergey Baburin, then a member of the Council of the RSFSR Supreme Soviet, first coined the term during a visit to Sevastopol. Addressing officers of the Black Sea Fleet in January 1992, he declared, 'Comrades, the Third Defence of Sevastopol has started'.[83] As a solidly Russophone city, its population had stoutly resisted the attempts of successive governments in Kiev to make it a Ukrainian-run administration. Its treaty port status gave it an autonomy underwritten by the presence of the Black Sea Fleet. No other city in Ukraine enjoyed such a strong Russian heritage and consistent support from Moscow. With the exception of Boris Yeltsin, Russia's political and military leaders alike never lost interest in Sevastopol.

Lenin's statue looks sternly towards the nearby headquarters of the Russian Fleet, one of the most prominent buildings in Sevastopol's city centre. A large Russian flag flies from a tall mast on its roof. Before February 2014, with scarcely concealed pride, Sevastopol citizens used to tell visitors that this flag was always flown higher than Ukrainian national emblems on neighbouring structures. As in other parts of the world, flags are an emotive issue. In late February 2014, Sevastopolians lost no time in tearing down Ukrainian flags from buildings.

As events in Kiev unfolded in early 2014, Sevastopol's citizens, who had minimal trust in the ability of Ukraine's security forces to protect them from extremists of the far-right, became increasingly concerned about the prospect of violence coming to their streets. Although one might doubt the credibility of such threats, local perceptions mattered then, as they do now. Nevertheless, the prospect of large numbers of Maidan protesters being transported to the Crimean peninsula to make serious trouble in Simferopol and Sevastopol appears far-fetched. Yet precisely this was attempted on 27 February 2014. Sevastopolians also remembered the events of 1 March 1992, when a so-called 'Train of Friendship' arrived at Sevastopol. On that occasion, members of the far-right Ukrainian National Assembly – including the Ukrainian People's Self-Defence organisation (reviled by Russians as 'Bandera' nationalists) staged a protest in the city centre and tore down Russian flags from buildings.[84]

On Sunday, 23 February 2014, the day after the take-over of power in Kiev, Sevastopol's residents gathered at their traditional meeting place, Nakhimov Square. Sergey Gorbachev claims that over 30,000 people were present.[85] Various speakers spoke out against the Maidan and the alleged *coup d'état* in Ukraine's capital, but 'avoided direct calls for Russian intervention'. Undeterred, crowds waving Russian flags chanted 'Russia, Russia, Russia', or 'Sevastopol, Crimea, Russia'. Loud calls were made for Sevastopol to declare its independence from Kiev and to determine its own future. A local resident, Anatoly, declared: 'Sevastopol is a Russian town and will always be a Russian town ... we will never surrender to those fascists in Kiev'. Olga, a pensioner, told a British journalist: 'We hoped there wouldn't be a split in the country, but if a fully Bandera regime emerges in Kiev then we will be part of Russia'. Dmitry Sinichkin, president of the Sevastopol branch of the 'Night Wolves' motorcycle group, warned that 'bloodshed is inevitable'.[86] On this occasion, however, there was none. Members of the local police were sympathetic to the crowd, and there was no violence.

The people demanded a new leader. The name of a Sevastapolian businessman and benefactor, Aleksey Chaly, emerged. As the founder and chief executive of Tavrida Electric, he was a well-liked and respected local figure, best known for his expensive development of the ruined Coastal Battery No. 35 as a poignant war memorial. When the Pantheon of Memory in the museum complex opened in 2011, it immediately struck a resonant chord with many sections of Sevastopol's population anxious to learn of their city's wartime past. Chaly also developed a history programme for the city's school children and funded scholarships to support students attending university. The fact that he was not a member of a political party added to his popularity. Holding a Russian as opposed to a Ukrainian passport, Chaly was nominated as mayor on 23 February by a simple show of hands in Nakhimov Square.

At the same time, the people of Sevastopol took the law into their own hands and established self-defence groups. It is claimed that no fewer than 15,000 volunteers were recruited in two days: 23 and 24 February 2014. Many of those who entered this 'home guard' were drawn from retired military and naval personnel. One of their first acts was to establish on 24 February seven checkpoints on the roads leading to Sevastopol.[87] The locations selected were familiar to all older residents: exactly the same ones used in the former Soviet times when access to the 'closed' city was strictly controlled. Now Sevastopol was denied to any possible interference or provocation from Ukrainian nationalists. In the absence of any substantive threat to Sevastopol emerging, the checkpoints assumed a symbolic status of defiance.

As the chairman of the city's administration was an appointee of the President of Ukraine, there was no mechanism for electing a mayor in Sevastopol. The official holder of the office, Volodymyr Yatsuba, resigned on 24 February. Chaly convened the city council and assumed the post of 'people's mayor' the same day. On 26 February he informed the new Ukrainian government that he would not submit to instructions from Kiev, effectively proclaiming the unilateral independence of Sevastopol. Chaly's personal moment of triumph came when he was invited to represent Sevastopol at the signing of the treaty of accession in the Kremlin on 18 March 2014. President Putin appointed him as acting governor of Sevastopol on 1 April 2014. Two weeks later, however, retired Vice Admiral Sergey Menyaylo assumed this position, while Chaly became head of the Sevastopol parliament. The two individuals – quite different in both background and temperament – clashed, and Sevastopol's economic development stalled.[88]

Meantime, participants of the 'defence' of Sevastopol were awarded various 'Third Defence' medals. For the most part, their actions had been confined to manning barricades and roadblocks. None the less, their contribution to Sevastopol's return to Russia was regarded as highly emblematic – one further example of Tolstoy's famous spirit.

THE CRIMEAN REFERENDUM OF 16 MARCH 2014

One of the first votes of the 'new' Supreme Council of Crimea on 27 February 2014 concerned the holding of a referendum on the status of Crimea within Ukraine. The original date set for this plebiscite was 25 May, later amended to 20 March. Presumably, it was brought forward to provide legitimacy for Russia's actions at the bar of world opinion. By 6 March, however, with Russian forces and local 'self defence' groups in full control of the peninsula, save a number of isolated Ukrainian military units, the Supreme Council voted to bring forward the referendum again to 16 March and to change its terms.

On the tri-lingual ballot paper (Russian, Ukrainian and Crimean Tatar), voters were offered two choices. The first read: *'Do you support the reunification of Crimea with Russia with all the rights of the federal subject of the Russian Federation?'* The second was: *'Do you support the restoration of the Constitution of the Republic of Crimea in 1992 and the status of Crimea as part of Ukraine?'* Critics quickly pointed out that there was no choice available to maintain the status quo of the Autonomous Republic of Crimea of Ukraine within the latest (1998) constitution. Furthermore, both the Crimean parliament and the city council of Sevastopol had already voted on 11 March for secession from Ukraine. So in effect voters were asked to endorse a decision already being put in train. Unsurprisingly, Ukraine's new government denounced the referendum, declaring it illegal as it contravened the provisions of its constitution.

According to the official results, there was an overall turnout of 83.1 per cent of the 1,844,589 registered voters. Within Crimea, 97.47 per cent voted to join the Russian Federation; in Sevastopol the figure was 96.59 per cent. International commentators have disputed both the level of turnout and the results over the two choices. Andrew Wilson, for example, considers that while 'Russia was used to such dictator-majorities, ... this one wasn't even ethnically plausible – 24 per cent of the population were Ukrainian and 13 per cent Tatar'.[89] Certainly, large numbers of Tatars boycotted the referendum, and it seems unlikely that the Ukrainian population (although many have been pro-Russian) would have so overwhelmingly voted for secession. There was another odd aspect of the result: it might have been expected that a greater proportion of Sevastopol's residents, living in the strongest bastion of Russia support on the peninsula, would have voted for union with Russia in comparison with their counterparts in Crimea. On 5 May 2014, a Russian report suggested that this was indeed the case, with 'the vast majority of the citizens of Sevastopol [voting] in favour of unification with Russia with a turnout of 50–80 per cent'. Within Crimea, however, on a lower turnout of 30–50 per cent, 'about 50–60 per cent voted for unification with Russia'.[90]

Although official groups of international observers were not present to monitor the vote, there were unofficial monitors drawn from several European states. Notwithstanding considerable doubts as to the legitimacy, legality and results of the referendum, it would appear that a majority of the people of both Sevastopol and Crimea who voted was in favour of the union with Russia. By a very clear margin (100 states for to eleven against, with fifty-eight abstentions), the United Nations General Assembly rejected the unification in its session on 27 March 2014. Before this vote, however, President Putin had lost no time in incorporating Sevastopol and Crimea into the Russian Federation.

On 18 March, Crimean and Sevastopol leaders were invited to the Kremlin to sign a treaty of accession. In his following speech to State Duma deputies,

Federation Council members, heads of Russian regions and civil society representatives in the Kremlin, President Putin declared that the referendum had been held 'in full compliance with democratic procedures and international norms'. He justified the unification on several grounds, not least emotional:

> In people's hearts and minds, Crimea has always been an inseparable part of Russia. This firm conviction is based on truth and justice and was passed from generation to generation, over time, under any circumstances, despite all the dramatic changes our country went through during the entire 20th century.

Putin questioned the legitimacy of the transfer of Crimea to Ukraine in 1954, observing:

> The decision was made behind the scenes. Naturally, in a totalitarian state nobody bothered to ask the citizens of Crimea and Sevastopol. They were faced with the fact. People, of course, wondered why all of a sudden Crimea became part of Ukraine. But on the whole – and we must state this clearly, we all know it – this decision was treated as a formality of sorts because the territory was transferred within the boundaries of a single state. Back then, it was impossible to imagine that Ukraine and Russia may split up and become two separate states.

In this discourse, the Russian President glossed over the fact that Ukraine and Russia were *both* founder states of the United Nations in 1945. But what about the Crimean Tatars, the indigenous population, whose Khanate had been seized by Russia in 1783? Putin gave the following reassurances:

> I believe we should make all the necessary political and legislative decisions to finalise the rehabilitation of Crimean Tatars, restore them in their rights and clear their good name.
> We have great respect for people of all the ethnic groups living in Crimea. This is their common home, their motherland, and it would be right – I know the local population supports this – for Crimea to have three equal national languages: Russian, Ukrainian and Tatar.[91]

Actions, however, speak louder than fine words. In 2014, the two most prominent Crimean Tatar leaders, Mustafa Dzhemilev, and his successor Refat Chubarov, were banned from entering the Russian Federation for five years.[92] More recently (April 2016), a Crimean court banned the Tatar Mejlis, labelling it an 'extremist organisation'.[93] The Crimean Tatar television station had already been taken off the air.

To Putin on 18 March 2014, however, what mattered first and foremost was that the 'outrageous historical injustice' over Crimea had been righted to the benefit of the majority Russian population, and that Sevastopol had been secured. He had declared that Khrushchev's inspired transfer of Crimea from Russia to Ukraine in 1954 as unconstitional: now, to popular national acclamation, he had reversed that move. Crimea, 'historically Russian land', and Sevastopol, 'city of Russia's military glory', had finally been returned home.[94]

EPILOGUE

'Exactly one year ago, Russia ... and the Russian people showed
amazing togetherness and patriotism in supporting
the aspirations of the people of Crimea and Sevastopol to return
to their native shores.'

Vladimir Putin, 18 March 2015[1]

SEVASTOPOL'S WARS REVIEWED

Crimea's enduring strategic importance to the Russian Empire, and later to the Soviet Union and the Russian Federation, has been amply demonstrated in a succession of conflicts fought since the eighteenth century. As we have seen, the peninsula has featured prominently in various Russo-Ottoman wars, the Crimean War, the First and Second World Wars, the Russian Civil War and during the most recent clash between Ukraine and Russia. Possession of the fine natural harbour at Sevastopol from 1783 enabled the establishment of the Russian Black Sea Fleet and the projection of maritime forces throughout the region and well beyond. Therefore it should come as no surprise that Sevastopol has been contested so frequently during the last two centuries and more.

In addition, on account of so much Russian blood spilt and treasure expended, the city has retained a symbolic historical and cultural significance that complements its intrinsic geostrategic value. Any narrative of Sevastopol's wars must also recognise the enduring impact of the battles of 'spirits and souls' as well as those of men and machines. Russia's political leaders, past and present, have sought to legitimise their actions on Crimea by mobilising popular patriotic

623

sentiment. Indeed, in referring back to the events of the previous year, President Putin proclaimed on 18 March 2015 that:

> We understood and felt with our hearts and minds at that moment just how much the links between time and generations matter to us, and how much our heroic forebears have done for our country. We understood that Crimea was much more to us than just a piece of land, even a strategically important piece of land.[2]

Hence spanning across the wide arc of Sevastopol's history from Potemkin to Putin, the promotion of Russia's historic claim to Crimea runs as a second golden thread alongside Tolstoy's famous 'spirit of Sevastopol'.

With the exception of Russia's first and second annexations of Crimea in 1783 and 2014 respectively, Sevastopol's wars have involved a variety of different types of combat – at sea, on land, and in the air. Over the centuries, the character of warfare has evolved steadily with the introduction of new tactics and technologies, accompanying equally profound changes in economic, political and social systems. Sevastopol experienced the dawn of industrial warfare at close quarter during the Crimean War when it was bombarded heavily on six occasions during 1854–55. Steam-powered ships and railways supplied British and French guns, which in density of shot and shell overmatched the Russian defence. Successive Russian attempts to raise the 349-day-long siege – Sevastopol's 'first defence' – proved fruitless, largely due to a combination of inept generalship, technological inferiority, over-stretched logistics and unsustainable casualties.

For twenty years following the Crimean War, Sevastopol lay in ruins. The long-awaited connection of the railway from Moscow and St Petersburg in 1875 provided the necessary stimulus for the city's reconstruction and enabled the reconstitution of the Black Sea Fleet. Meantime, defeat in the war prompted a limited modernisation of Russia, most notably the emancipation of the serfs in 1861 by Alexander II. Although political reforms stalled thereafter, the military reforms of Dmitry Milyutin (Minister of War, 1861–81) corrected many of the failings of the Crimean War. As Russia became increasingly industrialised by the turn of the nineteenth century, popular discontent with the status quo increased. Russia's armed forces, reflecting the society from which they were drawn, were not immune to political agitation. Ironically, the new railways enabled the distribution of subversive literature and the travel of its radical propagandists.

By their very nature, politics and the machinery of war are often closely meshed. The Black Sea Fleet, for example, experienced violent outbursts of mutinous activity in 1905 and 1917 during the Russian revolutions, both momentous events that remain deeply etched into Sevastopol's history and memorialisation. The *Potemkin* and *Ochakov* (Schmidt) mutinies of 1905 yielded much inflammatory material to the Bolshevik cause. Apart from the brief bombardment by the German battlecruiser *Goeben* in late October 1914, the city escaped the worst of the First World War. The German occupation (May–November 1918) provided a brief period of relative calm prior to the tumultuous storms of the Russian Civil War. In this bitter conflict, information activities (including the use of lurid propaganda posters) accompanied more conventional fighting on the battlefield. The widespread murder of civilian populations provided a precursor of even worse death and destruction during the Second World War.

Attempts by British and French 'Entente interventionists' to prop up the White cause during the Civil War not only proved militarily useless, but also did much to poison diplomatic relations with the Communist Soviet Union for decades thereafter. Following the arrival of Allied ships at Sevastopol in late November 1918, a murky episode (documented by Russian historians as 'Muddy Times') began with a succession of Allied contingents trying to maintain order in the city. An incursion into Crimea led to the Red Army's seizure of the peninsula in April 1919. The Bolsheviks' skilful disinformation machine helped undermine the morale and discipline of French forces, which led to a mutiny within the Black Sea squadron and the end to French intervention on land. After a brief revival of White fortunes in the spring and summer of 1920, Red forces triumphed in their operations to recover Crimea. White rule expired in mid-November 1920 with the evacuation of their forces and dependants – nearly 150,000 in number – from Sevastopol and four other Crimean ports. After this mass exodus, a cruel Bolshevik retribution followed for several months. Sevastopol witnessed an orgy of bloodshed during the Red Terror's unbridled liquidations.

The subsequent establishment of a new Red fleet in Sevastopol serves as a pertinent reminder of the significance of Crimea and its premier naval citadel. It also helps explain why Bolshevik forces could not tolerate the Whites retaining even a toehold in southern Russia. Thus there would be no equivalent of Chinese nationalist Formosa (Taiwan) surviving after the Communist takeover in mainland China in 1949.[3] Bolshevik, then Soviet, Russia needed to secure Crimea for sound strategic reasons as well as ideological and political ones.

During the twentieth century, Soviet naval and air bases on Crimea and at Sevastopol helped assure the USSR's dominance of the Black Sea. These facilities were extensively developed both prior to, and following, the Second World War. Sevastopol was fought over twice in that conflict. It first endured a 250-day-long siege in 1941–42 by German and Romanian forces. This abortive 'second defence' of Sevastopol was followed by an oppressive Axis occupation that lasted until the Red Army mounted its Crimean strategic offensive operation in April

1944, culminating in the battle for the city and its liberation on 9 May 1944. The 'information' aspects of this period are noteworthy. They remind us that the morale both of troops at the battlefield and of populations at home matters hugely. In turn, confidence and optimism on both fronts rest largely on the recognition given and news fed (and, in many cases, denied) to both communities. Three examples from 1942 provide evidence of this phenomenon in both victory and defeat.

On 1 July 1942, soldiers of the Eleventh Army raised the German war flag over Sevastopol. Later on this day of triumph or tragedy, depending on one's perspective, Hitler announced Erich von Manstein's promotion to the rank of field marshal in recognition of his and his army's success. Significantly, the Führer also awarded all participants of the campaign the right to wear a 'Crimean Shield' badge on their uniforms. This visual honour was designed as much to recognise the sacrifice of the fallen as to glorify the achievements of the victors.

Strictly speaking, the Soviet leaders of Sevastopol, although defeated, never surrendered during the Second World War. After resisting strenuously Manstein's third and final assault in June 1942, the city's defenders were overwhelmed by sheer weight of force. Having inflicted heavy casualties on their opponents, Soviet troops abandoned the city. Intense fighting continued on the Chersonese peninsula until 4 July, and, sporadically, for a week thereafter. Unsurprisingly, the Soviet press highlighted the outstanding valour displayed during the defence. Commenting after the fall of the city in 1942, a Soviet writer declared triumphantly:

> Having fulfilled its task, Sevastopol lowered its flag, but only to hoist it again soon, very soon – in the hour of victory. The defenders did not surrender the glory and the honour of our Motherland; instead they covered their banners with glory for all time. Sevastopol was, and will always remain, the fortress of the Black Sea Fleet.[4]

Yet there was also an external audience to address – or in this case a requirement to suppress bad news. Seeking to avoid the international humiliation of any publicised ceremony of capitulation, Stalin authorised the evacuation of senior officers and officials of the Sevastopol Defence Region, including Vice Admiral Filipp Oktyabrsky, during the early hours of 1 July 1942. Thus the German propaganda machine was denied any images similar to those recorded by the Japanese at Singapore when the British commander, Lieutenant General Arthur Percival, accompanied by a white-flag bearer, surrendered to his Japanese opponent, Lieutenant General Yamashita Tomoyuki, earlier that same year on 15 February 1942. Stalin also realised that there was little sense in losing valuable commanders who had proved themselves in the battles of Odessa and Sevastopol.

Controversially, however, the troops were left to fend for themselves without their senior leadership – only one general officer stayed with his men to be captured. For the remaining 97,000 officers, soldiers, sailors and airmen, and the surviving local inhabitants, there was no escape.

The full extent of the disaster for Soviet arms at Sevastopol in the summer of 1942 was never revealed at the time either to the Red Army or to the Soviet population. In the modern 'information age' it remains highly unlikely whether the news of such a calamity could be denied for long either at home or abroad. None the less, information can still be manipulated to promote a particular cause: a 'narrative' can be created to mitigate or manage the impact of catastrophic news.

FRATERNAL CONFLICT AND HYBRID WARFARE

Of all Sevastopol's wars, the 'third defence' of the city in February 2014 against an assumed (largely phantom) Ukrainian nationalist threat, and the contemporaneous Russian annexation of Crimea, appears at first sight to be the strangest of them all. For how could the city be 'defended', or the peninsula overrun, with scarcely a shot fired in anger? The world looked on at these events with a mixture of disbelief and misunderstanding. It remained unclear (albeit for a short time) as to who was conducting, let alone masterminding, activities that eliminated Ukrainian power on Crimea. Ambiguity and deniability appeared as the watchwords of the Russian-led operation.[5]

In military circles, limited attention was given in the late 2000s about the supposedly new doctrine of ambiguous or hybrid warfare. When published, Frank Hoffman's ground-breaking study of 2007, *Conflict in the 21st Century: The Rise of Hybrid Wars,* caused a brief stir amongst the military–academic community.[6] The value of the term 'hybrid war' rests in its all-inclusive scope, and variability in intensity and duration, according to the strategic and operational situation. It may encompass a combination of warfighting methods employing a range of conventional and unconventional (including non-military) forces, as well as non-violent methods of modern information and cyber warfare and old-fashioned diplomatic and economic pressure. Insurgents may adopt a confusing mix of terrorist, guerrilla and information practices to oppose nominally more powerful state forces.[7] Thus hybrid warfare is 'multi-dimensional' (and perhaps this is a better term than 'hybrid'): it can be embraced by both the strong and the weak. Neither possesses a monopoly of its goals and techniques.

Since the Russian annexation of Crimea in 2014, hybrid warfare has been widely associated with the Russian Chief of the General Staff, General of the Army Valery Gerasimov. His article of early 2013 in the Russian defence journal

Voyenno-promyshlennyy kuryer (Military–Industrial Courier), entitled 'The Value of Science in Prediction', drew attention to the blurring of war and peace, and to 'measures short of war'. Specifically, Gerasimov mentions the role of 'special operations forces and internal opposition' in creating 'a permanently operating front through the entire territory of the enemy state'.[8] Looking back on the events in Crimea in 2014, one might be tempted to focus on this particular theme to the exclusion of the wider messages contained in Gerasimov's rubric: 'New challenges: the need to rethink the forms and methods of warfare'. Modern multi-dimensional warfare, as practised by Russian armed forces and others, is a fully integrated way of war, and would appear to have become Russia's method of choice resting on a wide spectrum of violent and non-violent capabilities.

On 18 March 2014, just two days following the controversial referendum, the Republic of Crimea and the city of Sevastopol were incorporated into the Russian Federation. Whereas most Russians see this 'reunification' as the righting of an historical injustice, the Ukrainian government and many of its population regard Crimea as being under 'illegal military occupation'.[9] The latter view is reinforced by the continuing violent conflict between Ukraine's security forces, augmented by volunteer units, including some from the Right Sector and other (as seen by Moscow) neo-Nazi organisations such as the 'Azov Battalion', and 'separatist terrorists' (as seen by Kiev). Pro-Russian groups in the Donetsk and Luhansk *oblasts* of eastern Ukraine have proclaimed these regions as independent people's republics. Despite repeated Russian denials, there is strong – if not incontrovertible – evidence to suggest that regular Russian Federation forces, and not just 'volunteers', have been involved in the fighting since August 2014.[10] Notwithstanding ceasefires and de-escalation measures agreed at Minsk on 5 September 2014 and 11 February 2015, the conflict rumbles on: it could expand in intensity at any moment in the absence of a political settlement. Ukraine wishes to see Crimea and Sevastopol returned, and its territorial integrity fully respected by Russia.

For all the innovation in military affairs, armed diplomacy has deep roots. David Glantz, a noted American military historian of Soviet operations during the Great Patriotic War, has pointed out that the contemporary Russian approach to advancing its interests has long antecedents. In a letter to *The Economist* on 20 September 2014, he wrote:

Vladimir Putin is acting in the time-honoured Russian tradition of an opportunistic land grab in Ukraine.... In 1478 Ivan the Great destabilised much of what is now Ukraine, but which at the time was a possession of the Grand Duchy of Lithuania, by the systematic provocation of Lithuania's border lands. Basil Dmytryshyn, a historian, described it as 'a policy designed to demoralise the people living along the frontier and to prompt them to seek Muscovy's protection, thereby moving the frontier west. Ivan publicly disclaimed all responsibility for these tactics, but privately he encouraged them and rewarded the defectors.'

Glantz added perceptively that 'Fourteen years into this strategy Ivan threw away all pretence of non-involvement and invaded Lithuania, occupying key bits of its territory. Mr Putin is indeed playing a long game in Ukraine.'[11]

James Sherr, a leading expert on modern Ukraine, has also explored this theme. In the context of the wider conflict that erupted in Ukraine's eastern *oblasts* during 2014, he characterised hybrid war as follows:

> [It] has caused bewilderment, and it was meant to. For hundreds of years, irregular wars on the fringes of the empire, Tsarist and Soviet, have followed similar principles. The model of warfare is built around informal networks rather than top-down structures; it is untidy and adaptable, covert and vicious, and it is designed to erase the frontier between civil and interstate conflict. Its constituent parts are not only serving officers of Spetsnaz units and the Federal Security Service, but retired servicemen and deserters, the private security forces of oligarchs, Cossacks, Chechen fighters, adventurers and criminals.[12]

Notwithstanding these valuable insights, Sherr penned his article before high-intensity warfare, including the use of mass tanks, heavy field artillery, multiple-launch rocket systems, together with unmanned aerial vehicles (drones) and electronic jammers and detectors, manifested itself in Eastern Ukraine.[13] Russian-backed forces are quite prepared to employ modern forms of 'combined-arms' tactics as well as the techniques of information warfare. Their use of disinformation in Crimea and in this conflict (as in more peaceful political discourse) is as old as the hills: it represents nothing more than the obverse of a coin marked deception. Disinformation, however, is as much a strategic tool as an operational or tactical one. It remains fundamental to Russian political and military effort to confuse, disrupt and delay the response of an opponent.

As Andrew Monaghan has wisely pointed out, use of the 'hybrid label serves to draw a veil over the conventional aspects of the war in Eastern Ukraine'.[14] Therefore one needs to come to careful conclusions from the latest of Crimea's wars, and to take particular care in their future extrapolation. Indeed, Gerasimov was at pains to point out in his article of 2013;

> Each war does present itself as a unique case, demanding the comprehension of its particular logic, its uniqueness. That is why the character of a war that Russia

or its allies might be drawn into is very hard to predict. Nonetheless, we must. Any academic pronouncements in military science are worthless if military theory is not backed by the function of prediction.[15]

Hence perhaps one of the biggest ironies of Operation RUSSIAN SPRING lies in its misinterpretation by some in the West as a novel form of war. It is not a template and should be seen in its proper context: a particular response to a specific set of circumstances, of which the most critical were local military basing and the support of the majority of the local population. In the Donbas, both Ukrainian and Russian armed forces (and their proxies) have acted quite differently. They have fought there an intense type of combat, albeit employing modern technology, much more akin to the fighting last seen between the rivers Don and Dnieper in 1943 during the Second World War. A future conflict will not necessarily resemble Crimea or Eastern Ukraine, let alone Afghanistan, Iraq or Syria. Scrutiny of the operational methods employed by Russian forces on Crimea in February 2014 may have deflected analysis away from understanding the integrated manner in which Russia has mobilised its information, economic and military resources in pursuit of its political objectives.

'Hybrid warfare' is not a term contained in the military lexicon of the Russian Federation. Russian commentators use its direct translation, *Gibridnaya voyna*, to describe 'something that the West is currently waging on Russia'.[16] The greatest prize of *maskirovka* is to induce an opponent to deceive himself as to what your real intentions are by laying an utterly plausible false trail. Hence the great emphasis placed on disinformation, deception and surprise within Soviet and Russian military doctrine still remains worthy of close examination: the annexation of Crimea in 2014 provides a compelling case study.[17]

There would appear to be an important general lesson to draw from the events of 2014 in Sevastopol, Crimea and eastern Ukraine. If 'ambiguous' warfare is to remain true to its name, then it must continue to evolve ambiguously. If its ends, ways and means become all too clear, it no longer deserves such an appellation. Thus attempts to codify it too precisely are probably self-defeating, as is the quest to pin down the start of a crisis involving this form of ambiguous warfare. The potentially decisive hostile act will typically be masked in uncertainty and deniability. Hence a conflict may already be well under way before the defending party realises so. This manifestation of multi-dimensional war is but another extension of political design.

REFLECTIONS ON RUSSIA, UKRAINE AND CRIMEA

Ultimately, the Russian Federation under President Putin acted in Sevastopol, Crimea and Eastern Ukraine because it felt compelled to safeguard its vital national interests. In other words, the ends justified the means whatever the resulting international opprobrium, and the ways adopted were those deemed most appropriate to the situation. More prosaically, one could argue, as Tim Judah states in his compelling study *In Wartime: Stories from Ukraine*, that Putin annexed Crimea 'because he could'. While there is merit in this argument, it belies the strategic imperative from a Russian point of view. Whether the Russian leader annexed Crimea in an unprincipled fashion solely in order to cook a snook at the West in return for its recognition of Kosovo breaking away from Serbia in 2008, remains unlikely, given Sevastopol's long-standing, if not existential, importance to Russia. For his bold, bloodless, action, Putin was awarded with huge popular acclaim all the way from Moscow's Red Square to Sevastopol's Nakhimov Prospekt. The message was clear to all at home and abroad: 'Russia is back!'.[18] Catherine the Great and Potemkin would surely have been delighted.

In response to the Russian annexation of Crimea, Ukraine's position found widespread international support. Following its meeting of 20/21 March 2014, the European Council declared that it 'strongly condemned the annexation of Crimea and Sevastopol to the Russian Federation' and that it would 'not recognise it'.[19] Subsequent EU documentation refers to an 'illegal annexation', confirms the EU's policy of non-recognition and lists the 'substantial restrictions' imposed on 'economic exchanges' with Crimea and Sevastopol.[20] On 27 March 2014, the United Nations General Assembly, by a non-binding majority vote, adopted a resolution calling upon states not to recognise changes in the status of Crimea.[21]

Through the events of early 2014, Crimea and Sevastopol returned briefly to the centre stage of world attention. Until then, the two great sieges of the Crimean War and the Second World War were but dimly remembered events. But for the peoples of Russia, Crimea and Sevastopol, their shared history remained a vital element in their nation's story and sense of self-worth. Ownership of these places matters fundamentally: it is not just a matter of patriotic jingoism: it is as much about the renewed confidence and pride felt in being a member of a strong, assertive country that has risen again from the chaos and confusion of the break-up of the USSR. Vladimir Putin is widely credited with that national renewal. Sevastopol may well prove to be his prime legacy, as it was Potemkin's.

Many warning signs of future dispute or conflict were missed during the period 2008–13. Thus the crisis in 2013–14 came as a surprise to most external observers, particularly to those who had neglected the recent history of Crimea. The squabbling of the early 1990s between Russian and Ukraine, including the 'war of laws' between Kiev and Simferopol when Crimean republicans attempted to claim and exercise independence, had been overlooked if not forgotten. Examination of Sevastopol's long and turbulent story reveals the city's true significance: one far greater than just that of a faraway historic place and erstwhile tourist destination. Sevastopol emerges as a persistent locus of interest in international affairs. For over 230 years it has remained a vital hub – a strategic centre of gravity – of Russian naval and national power, one as important as Portsmouth is to the United Kingdom and Norfolk, Virginia, is to the United States of America. Thus Sevastopol represents not some discretionary overseas base for Russia, but rather an essential bastion of her homeland.

While it is tempting for an historian to narrate and explain events following the end of the Cold War in neat chronological order, the various ups and downs of Russian–Ukrainian relations, and the shifts and reversals of policies, indicate the folly of so doing. Many decisions made prior to the Friendship Treaty of 1997, as much as those taken thereafter, contributed to its disregard and ultimate irrelevance. The wider domestic and international context helped define the paths both countries took. At the risk of generalisation, three main factors appear to be involved. First, many Russians profoundly regret that Ukraine no longer wishes to acknowledge, let alone commemorate, their shared heritage. Ukrainians, however, and increasingly so since 2014, wish to forge their own distinct destiny. Secondly, Ukraine and Russia never were, and never will be, equals. Russia's economic and military superiority over its western neighbour means that it holds the whip hand in any crisis or conflict of interests. Thirdly, Russia restored its position as a world power under Vladimir Putin, its economy and military spending buoyed by increased oil and gas revenues. The collapse of this income, together with Western economic sanctions, meanwhile, has brought increasing hardship to Russia's people and no new political choice.

In contrast, post-Soviet Ukraine has never enjoyed the good times experienced by Russia. It has struggled to develop economically since the end of the Cold War. Staggering levels of corruption and theft on a vast scale have debilitated state governance and strangled its economic development. Equally, Ukraine has found it difficult to find either consensus or continuity in its internal and external politics. Janus-faced, Ukraine looked alternatively east and west for much of the period 1991–2014. It proved an impossible task: a schism between its peoples was probably inevitable with pro-Russian communities, such as in Sevastopol, looking to Moscow for material and moral support.

As far as one can risk looking ahead, it seems inconceivable that Russia, whether led by Vladimir Putin or not, would be prepared to give up either Crimea or Sevastopol. The purpose of significant reinforcements (2014–16) to Russian naval, ground, air and air defence forces (not least the most capable S-400 *Triumf* missile system in August 2016) stationed on the peninsula is abundantly clear.[22] Such deployments confirm Moscow's determination to hold Crimea and Sevastopol in perpetuity in pursuit of Russia's strategic interests, and to deter any attempts to reverse its actions of February–March 2014. Russia remains very much a 'hard power', one not to be messed with, and quite capable of surprising the West again.

In many respects Vladimir Putin's *russkiy mir* (Russian world) has come full circle since the time of Potemkin and Catherine the Great. It rests, as in 1783, not only on military power being exercised absolutely, but also in the supreme confidence that the distinctive Russian way – of governance, culture and heritage – will prevail against any hostile threats. In 2002 Bobo Lo claimed to identify a 'Potemkinization' of Russian external affairs in the post-Soviet era. He used this expression to contrast the Russian administration's 'use of major policy statements to convey an impression of unity and sincerity of purpose' with a situation 'fundamentally at odds with the real – fragmented and opportunistic – nature of foreign policy'.[23] Although it can be argued that there remains opportunism and incoherence in President Putin's thinking and action, annexed Crimea is no modern Potemkin village. For all of Potemkin's supposed false fronts lining the river Dnieper in 1787 to impress Catherine the Great and her retinue, the establishment of a strategically important naval base at Akhtiar harbour was real enough. Sevastopol, then as now, stands as a proud testament to Russian foreign and military policies that show much continuity over the last 230 years and more.

Russia's safeguarding (to most Western eyes, aggresive seizure) of Crimea and Sevastopol came at the expense of Ukraine and the post Cold War security settlement in Europe. International condemnation and economic sanctions resulted. For all Russia's burgeoning and demonstrable military capabilities, however, there remains intrinsic economic weakness. But it would be surely a mistake to regard her newfound strength and confidence on the world stage as a modern form of Potemkin bluff. It is deadly real and observable. Sevastopolians today proudly witness a steadily modernising Black Sea Fleet, which remains an unambiguous statement of Russian power projection. In each of the three 'defences' of their city, whether the Crimean War, the Second World War or late February 2014, the citizens of Sevastopol displayed a special 'spirit' – a combination of chauvinism, defiance and stoicism that has underpinned a fiercely patriotic Russian feeling. That feeling lives on: Sevastopol will not succumb.

We can only hope we have seen the last of Sevastopol's wars. Crimea from Potemkin to Putin has surely seen far too much blood spilt in successive conflicts and revolutions. If there is anything to be learned from Sevastopol's long history, then surely it can be simply put: we can ill afford to neglect the study of past conflicts if we wish to understand the present, let alone attempt to envisage the future. The nature of both politics and war, however, remains enduring. Therefore it remains prudent to recall *why* states and peoples go to war as much as *how* they do. Thucydides summed this matter up neatly a long time ago: people fight not only out of fear and self-interest, but also for honour.[24]

Although the latter approach may not always induce the most pragmatic course of action, it still plays a significant part in world affairs today. Whatever the declared grounds for going to war, miscalculation, particularly in the quest for a 'quick win', can abound, not least in the unintended consequences of such action. History is replete with 'popular' foreign wars being waged to assuage domestic political concerns.[25] Although Russia has spectacularly rebuilt its military capabilities since the early 2000s, its domestic economy has yet to experience such transformation. Therefore it appears advisable to examine Russia *internally* in an effort to understand how its structures (and associated strains) of power might affect or drive its *external* policies and actions.

No doubt many in the Kremlin now, and perhaps long into the future, would argue that Russia's honour was at stake in Sevastopol as much as its national interests. While the majority of Crimea's citizens certainly feel 'at home', reunited with Mother Russia, a dishonoured Ukraine has been dispossessed of the Crimean peninsula – one of its few crown jewels. Whether the two countries Russia and Ukraine will ever come to terms over this diamond-shaped patch of long-contested land remains a matter of speculation. Russia will surely seek to ride out the economic sanctions imposed as a result of its actions on Crimea, and hope for international acquiescence or acceptance of the status quo in the longer-term. It will be recalled that when Russia in 1870 repudiated the Treaty of Paris (1856), which had demilitarised the Black Sea, the Western Powers failed to oppose her. In the meantime, the main base of the Russian Black Sea Fleet remains secure today in 'Legendary Sevastopol'. History may never repeat itself, but in Sevastopol's case it certainly seems to chime.[26]

CHRONOLOGY

ANCIENT CHERSONESOS AND BYZANTINE CHERSON

422–421 BC	Founding of the Greek colony of Chersonesos.
350–275 BC	Chersonese rule over southwestern Crimea. Defence against Scythian raids.
63 BC	Chersonesos becomes a dependency of Rome.
44–36 BC	Chersonesos probably receives its first charter from Rome.
AD 50–200	Sarmatian tribes begin to displace Scythians throughout Crimea.
88–97	St Clement is exiled to Chersonesos.
c. 14–250	Vexillations (detachments of Roman legions) are stationed in Chersonesos and vicinity.
c. 250–270s	Goths move into Crimea, displacing Sarmatians.
330	The Roman Empire is split into West and East. Constantinople becomes the main capital of the East and subsequently becomes the centre of the Byzantine Empire.
c. 370	The Huns advance into Crimea.
527–565	Rule of Justinian I. Western Crimea and Chersonesos are fortified against various barbarians.
655	Pope Martin is exiled to Chersonesos, which is renamed Cherson.
695–711	Justinian II, exiled to Cherson, then regains temporarily the Byzantine throne.
860–861	St Cyril, translator of the Bible into Old Church Slavonic, visits Cherson.
988–989	Prince Vladimir of Kiev besieges Cherson; he is converted to Christianity.

13th Century (C.)	Genoa establishes strongholds on Crimea and dominates the Black Sea trade.
1223	First Mongol incursion into Crimea.
c. 1250	A major fire destroys much of Byzantine Cherson.
1347	The Black Death breaks out in Caffa (now Feodosiya), and spreads across Europe.
15th C.	Cherson declines further, leading to its eventual abandonment.

CRIMEAN KHANATE, MUSCOVY AND RUSSIAN EMPIRE TO 1853

1427	Establishment of the Crimean Tatar Khanate.
1453	The capture of Constantinople by the Ottoman Turks marks the end of the Byzantine Empire.
1475	The Ottomans conquer Crimea; Crimean Khanate becomes a vassal of the Turks.
16th–18th C.	Crimean Tatars raid into the area of modern southern Ukraine and Muscovy, notably reaching Moscow in 1521 and 1571.
1547–1584	Rule of Ivan IV (the Great), the first crowned tsar of Russia.
1559 and 1560	Russian forces threaten the Crimean Khanate.
1683	Ottoman troops, including Crimean Tatars, fail to capture Vienna.
1686–1700	Russo-Turkish War.
1687	The first expedition of Vasily Golitsyn to Crimea fails to reach the Perekop.
1688	A major Crimean Tatar raid threatens Kiev and Poltava.
1689	Second expedition of Golitsyn is blocked by Crimean Tatars at the Perekop.
1695	Peter the Great fails to capture the Ottoman fortress of Azov.
1696	Peter the Great seizes Azov and establishes a naval base at Taganrog.
1700	Peace of Constantinople: Russia retains Azov and Taganrog. The Russian tribute to the Crimean Khanate is abolished.
1710–11	Russo-Turkish War.
1711	Russian army under the Peter the Great is humiliated at the river Prut: Russia is forced to abandon the Sea of Azov.
1735–39	Russo-Turkish War.
1736	The Russian offensive into Crimea under command of Field Marshal Count Burkhard von Münnich is followed by withdrawal. Field Marshal Count Peter Lacy seizes Azov.

1737 and 1738	The second and third Russian offensives into Crimea, both under the command of Lacy, are followed by withdrawal.
1762	Accession of Catherine II ('the Great') as Empress of Russia.
1768–74	Russo-Turkish War, in which Grigory Potemkin distinguishes himself.
1770	Naval battle of Chesma, at which Thomas Mackenzie distinguishes himself.
1774	Treaty of Kuchuk Kainardzhi. Crimea is declared independent of Turkey. Russia regains Azov and parts of the Kuban and Kerch peninsulas, which are fortified.
1776	Potemkin is appointed commander-in-chief and governor-general of the newly established province of Novorossiya.
1777–83	Khan Shagin Giray nominally rules Crimea; series of Russian incursions.
1778	General Alexander Suvorov erects temporary Russian defences at Akhtiar (later named Sevastopol).
1783	Russia annexes of Crimea. Founding of Sevastopol by Rear Admiral Mackenzie and establishment of the Russian Black Sea Fleet.
1787	Triumphal visit of Catherine the Great and Potemkin to Sevastopol with Joseph II of Austria and other distinguished foreign guests.
1787–92	Russo-Turkish War. Admiral Fyodor Ushakov wins a series of naval victories.
1788	Field Marshal Pyotr Rumyantsev invades Moldovia. Potemkin storms the Turkish fortress of Ochakov guarding the mouth of the river Dnieper.
1801	Accession of Alexander I.
1806–12	Russo-Turkish War. Successful Russian operations at sea by Admiral Dimitry Senyavin and on land by Kutuzov.
1818	Completion of Sevastopol's North Fort, which falls into disrepair by the time of the Crimean War.
1820	Opening of the Inkerman lighthouses.
1822	Opening of the first Black Sea Fleet Library.
1824	Visit of Alexander I to Sevastopol.
1825	Accession of Nicholas I.
1827	British, French and Russian naval forces defeat an Ottoman and Egyptian combined fleet at the battle of Navarino, at which Mikhail Lazarev distinguishes himself. First excavations of the ancient city of Chersonesos.

1828–29	Russo-Turkish War. Naval fight involving the *Merkurii*.
1830	Plague and wide scale civil unrest in Sevastopol.
1831–52	Construction of Sevastopol's dry docks and its water supply (the aqueduct), designed and supervised by John Upton.
1833	Treaty of Unkiar-Skelessi between Russia and the Ottoman Empire.
1835	Construction of Sevastopol's southern (landward) defences starts slowly.
1837 and 1845	Visits of Nicholas I to Sevastopol.
1841	London Straits Convention regulates passage of the Turkish Straits.
1844 and 1849	Opening of the second and third buildings of theBlack Sea Fleet Library.
1852	Inspection of the Black Sea Fleet by Nicholas I.

THE CRIMEAN WAR

1853

2 July	Russian Army crosses the river Prut into Moldavia (present-day Romania).
5 October	Ottoman Empire declares war on Russia.
30 November	Turkish naval squadron destroyed at the battle of Sinope by a Russian fleet under command of Vice Admiral Pavel Nakhimov.

1854

4 January	Allied fleets enter the Black Sea.
28 March	Britain and France declare war on Russia.
14 September	Unopposed Allied landing at Kalamata Bay, south of Yevpatoriya, Crimea.
20 September	The battle of the river Alma: Allied victory. Russian withdrawal to Sevastopol.
23 September	Russian scuttling of ships of the Black Sea Fleet in Sevastopol harbour.
17 October	Opening of the first Allied bombardment of Sevastopol.
25 October	The battle of Balaklava: an inconclusive outcome.
26 October	The battle of Little Inkerman: Allied defensive success.
5 November	The battle of Inkerman: bloody Allied victory.
14 November	The Great Storm destroys Allied shipping.

December | Great suffering of Allied (particularly British) troops in their camps; conditions are not much better for the Russians defending Sevastopol.

1855

January–April | Construction of the Grand Crimean Central Railway from Balaklava to the British lines at Sevastopol, later extended to support the Sardinian positions.

17 January | The Russian attack on Yevpatoriya is defeated.

2 March | Death of Nicholas I. Accession of Alexander II.

9 April | Second bombardment of Sevastopol opens.

25 May | The Allies capture Kerch and dominate the Sea of Azov.

6 June | Third bombardment opens. The Allies capture the Mamelon and the Quarries.

17 June | Fourth bombardment opens.

18 June | Allied assaults on the Malakhov and Redan are repulsed with heavy losses.

16 August | Battle of the Chernaya River. The Russians are defeated by the French and Sardinians.

17 August | Fifth bombardment opens.

5 September | Sixth bombardment opens.

8 September | French seize the Malakhov; the British are repulsed again at the Redan.

9 September | Russian evacuation of the southern side of Sevastopol.

13 September | Allied demolitions of Sevastopol's naval infrastructure commence.

17 October | Allies capture Kinburn. Russian forces evacuate Ochakov.

1856

16 January | Alexander II accepts Austrian demands for peace.

26 February | Signing of an armistice between the Allies and Russia.

30 March | Signing of the Treaty of Paris; subsequent demilitarisation of the Black Sea.

12 July | Last Allied troops leave Crimea.

THE CRIMEAN WAR TO THE FIRST WORLD WAR

1857–62 | American salvage operation under John Gowen raises Sevastopol's sunken ships.

1860s | Limited reconstruction of Sevastopol.

1861	Visit of Alexander II to Sevastopol and Chersonesos, and laying of the foundation stone of St Vladimir Cathedral at Ancient Chersonesos.
1869	Opening of the Black Sea Fleet Museum, Sevastopol.
1870	Russia repudiates the demilitarisation of the Black Sea.
1875	Opening of the railway from Kharkov to Sevastopol. Reconstruction of the city gets into full swing and Sevastopol opens as an international port.
1878–79	Russo-Turkish War.
1881	Accession of Alexander III.
1880s	Construction of first armoured cruisers for the Black Sea Fleet in Sevastopol.
1894	Accession of Nicholas II; first telephone exchange in Sevastopol is opened.
1904	Unveiling of the monument to the Scuttled Ships in Sevastopol.
1904–05	Russo-Japanese War; construction of the Historic Boulevard in Sevastopol.

THE 1905 AND 1917 REVOLUTIONS, THE FIRST WORLD WAR AND THE CIVIL WAR

1905

22 January	Bloody Sunday in St Petersburg precipitates the 1905 Russian revolution.
27 May	Opening of the Panorama Museum, Sevastopol.
27 June – 8 July	*Potemkin* mutiny, Odessa, and Constanta, Romania.
30 October	Nicholas II's October Manifesto, which fails to quell revolutionary spirit.
24–29 November	The Schmidt mutiny in Sevastopol is severely suppressed.

1913

| 9–13 August | Nicholas II visits Sevastopol, including the flying school at Kacha. |

1914

16 August	The German battlecruiser *Goeben* anchors at Constantinople having evaded interception by the Royal Navy in the Mediterranean.
29 October	German/Turkish bombardment of Russian Black Sea ports: Odessa, Sevastopol, Yalta, Feodosiya and Novorossiysk.
2 November	Russia declares war on Turkey.

18 November	Inconclusive naval battle of Cape Sarych off southern coast of Crimea.
1915	
28 March and	Bombardments and minelaying by the Black Sea Fleet off the
25 April	Bosporus to support Western Allied operations in the Dardanelles.
30 April	Nicholas II inspects ships of the Black Sea Fleet at Sevastopol.
1916	
25–28 May	Final visit of Nicholas II to Sevastopol and the Black Sea Fleet.
August	Vice Admiral Aleksandr Kolchak assumes command of the Black Sea Fleet.
22 November	The battleship *Imperatritsa Mariya* is destroyed by a massive explosion in Sevastopol harbour.
1917	
Late February	Growing street protests in St Petersburg.
15 March	Abdication of Nicholas II. Formation of a provisional government.
22 April	Mass demonstrations in Sevastopol.
7 November	Bolsheviks under Vladimir Lenin seize power in the 'October' Revolution.
1918	
1 May	German troops under General Robert Kosch occupy Sevastopol unopposed.
24-26 November	Western Allied (Entente) ships enter Sevastopol. French forces occupy the city.
1919	
16–17 April	Fighting between Allied forces and the Red Army at Sevastopol takes place.
19–21 April	Mutiny breaks out aboard ships of the French Black Sea Squadron.
28 April	Completion of the Allied evacuation of Sevastopol, followed by Bolshevik control.
June	White forces under General Anton Denikin re-establish control over Crimea.
October	White offensive towards Moscow culminates at Oryol, followed by retreat.
1920	
March	Denikin's forces are evacuated by Allied ships from Novorossiysk to Crimea.
4 April	General Pyotr Wrangel assumes command of White forces in Crimea.

7 June	White offensive into southern Ukraine opens, but is blocked at the river Dnieper.
October	Red Army counter-offensive under Mikhail Frunze forces Whites back to Crimea.
7–16 November	Red Army's Southern *Front* assaults Crimea.
11–16 November	White forces and their dependants evacuate Crimea, marking the end of the Civil War in southern Russia.
15 November	Red forces occupy Sevastopol.

BETWEEN THE WARS

1920–21	Red Terror in Crimea.
1921	Establishment of the Crimean Autonomous Socialist Soviet Republic.
1922	Establishment of the Soviet Union.
1924	Stalin consolidates power.
1927	Strong earthquake strikes southern Crimea, including Sevastopol and Yalta.
1929	Stalin visits Sevastopol, including inspection of the new Coastal Battery No. 35.
1930s	Rapid growth of Sevastopol as an industrial city; new warships join the Black Sea Fleet; modernisation of shore defences.
1936	The Montreux Convention regulates passage of the Turkish Straits.
1940–41	Further upgrading of Sevastopol's defences against air and amphibious attack.

THE SECOND WORLD WAR

1941

22 June	Luftwaffe air attack on Sevastopol opens Germany's hostilities against the Soviet Union. Beginning of the Great Patriotic War.
July–October	Hasty construction of Sevastopol's defensive lines to counter an attack to landward.
24–28 September	German Eleventh Army under General Erich von Manstein assaults the Perekop.
15 October	Completion of the evacuation of Soviet forces, including the Coastal Army commanded by Major General Ivan Petrov, from Odessa to Crimea.

18–31 October	Germans break through the Soviet defences at Ishun and break out into Crimea.
1 November	Axis forces capture Simferopol. First Axis assault on Sevastopol begins.
4 November	Establishment of the Sevastopol Defence Region under the commander-in-chief of the Black Sea Fleet, Vice Admiral Filipp Oktyabrsky.
6–16 November	Axis seize Kerch peninsula.
16 November	Axis forces complete conquest of Crimean peninsula, less Sevastopol.
17 December	Second Axis assault on Sevastopol opens.
26 December	Soviet amphibious landings at Kerch.
29 December	Soviet amphibious landing at Feodosiya. German evacuation of the Kerch peninsula.
31 December	Suspension of the second Axis assault on Sevastopol; followed by partial withdrawal.

1942

5 January	Soviet amphibious landing at Yevpatoriya.
18 January	Axis forces recapture Feodosiya.
February–April	Repeated attempts by Soviet forces to break out of the Kerch peninsula.
8–19 May	Axis Operation BUSTARD HUNT defeats Soviet forces in Kerch peninsula.
2 June	Opening of air and artillery bombardment as the prelude to the third Axis assault (commencing on 7 June) on Sevastopol (Operation STURGEON CATCH).
29 June	Axis attack on the inner fortress zone of Sevastopol (Operation TORCH DANCE).
1 July	Capture of Sevastopol by Axis forces and start of its occupation. Soviet leaders, including Oktyabrsky and Petrov, escape. The remaining Soviet forces on the Chersonese peninsula are defeated on 4 July.
September	Deportations of Sevastopol's population begin.

1943

January	Soviet resistance to Axis occupation of Sevastopol established.
2 February	German surrender at Stalingrad, followed by Red Army advance into Ukraine.
9 October	Completion of German evacuation of the Kuban peninsula (Operation KRIMHILD).

30 October	Forces of the 4th Ukrainian *Front* block the Perekop, cutting off the Crimean peninsula and thereby trapping the German Seventeenth Army.
1 November	Soviet amphibious landings near Kerch (the Kerch–Eltigen operation).

1944

8 April	Opening of the Crimean strategic offensive operation by the 4th Ukrainian *Front* under General Fyodor Tolbukhin.
13 April	Liberation of Simferopol.
15 April – 12 May	Axis defence of the Sevastopol area, and evacuation of forces by air and sea.
7 May	Soviet forces storm the Sapun 'Mountain' (an escarpment).
9 May	Liberation of Sevastopol by Soviet forces.
12 May	Last surviving Axis soldiers lay down their arms at Cape Chersonese.
18 May	Expulsion of the Crimean Tatar population commences.

1945

7 February	Visit of Field Marshal Alanbrooke, British Chief of the Imperial General Staff to Sevastopol during the Yalta conference.
12–14 February	Visit of Winston Churchill to Sevastopol following the Yalta conference.
24 April	Visit of Clementine Churchill to Sevastopol.
1 May	Along with Leningrad, Stalingrad and Odessa, Sevastopol is named as a Hero City of the Soviet Union by Stalin.
9 May	Victory Day (commemorated by the Soviet Union and its successor states as marking the end of the war in Europe)
20 June	Crimea becomes an *oblast* of the Russian Soviet Federative Socialist Republic (RSFSR).
1 November	Under Decree No. 2722 of the Soviet government, Sevastopol is nominated as one of fifteen cities to be accorded first priority for reconstruction.

THE COLD WAR

1948	Visit of Stalin to Sevastopol. Reconstruction efforts are accelerated accordingly.
1953–54	Completion of the reconstruction of Sevastopol.
1954	Crimea transferred to Ukraine. Reopening of the Panorama Museum, Sevastopol. Sevastopol is awarded the Order of the Red Banner.

1959	Opening of the Diorama Museum at the Sapun 'Mountain'.
1965	Sevastopol awarded the Order of Lenin and the Gold Star Medal.
1967	Unveiling of the Memorial to the Heroes of the Defence of Sevastopol in 1941–42 at Nakhimov Square, including the plaques that list the names of the fifty-four Heroes of the Soviet Union who participated in the Second Defence and Liberation of the city.
1983	Bicentenary of the founding of Sevastopol. The city is awarded the Order of the October Revolution.

THE FORMER SOVIET UNION

1990

| 12 June | Declaration of the state sovereignty of the RSFSR. |
| 24 August | Declaration of Ukrainian independence. |

1991

August	Failed coup attempt against President Mikhail Gorbachev, his brief incarceration at Foros, Crimea.
8 December	Agreement by leaders of Belarus, Russia and Ukraine to establish the Commonwealth of Independent States.
25 December	RSFSR is renamed the Russian Federation. The Soviet Union is no more.

1992

| 5 May | Supreme Soviet of Crimea declares the independence of the 'Republic of Crimea', which is not recognised. |
| 29 June | First modern Tatar congress in Crimea, reflecting the return of the Tatar population. |

1994

| 8 February | Ukraine joins NATO's Partnership for Peace programme. |
| 5 December | Budapest agreement signed by Russia, Ukraine, the United States of America and the United Kingdom provides for Ukraine's nuclear disarmament and territorial integrity. |

1995

| 17 March | The Ukrainian parliament (the Verkhovna Rada) annuls the Crimean constitution of 1992. |

1996

| 28 June | Adoption of a new Ukrainian constitution, in which the Autonomous Republic of Crimea is recognised. |

1997

28 May   Signing of the Black Sea Fleet Agreement between Russia and
              Ukraine, which allows for a 20-year lease of Sevastopol as a
              base of the Black Sea Fleet for Russia.

31 May   Treaty on Friendship, Cooperation and Partnership signed
              between Russia and Ukraine.

2004

December   Orange revolution in Kiev.

2008

August   Russo-Georgian War.

2010

21 April   Kharkov accords between Russia and Ukraine extend the lease
              of Sevastopol as the main base of the Russian Black Sea Fleet
              for another 25 years from 2017.

15 July   President Viktor Yanukovych of Ukraine confirms his country's
              non-aligned status.

2013

21 November   Suspension of negotiations between Ukraine and the European
              Union over an association agreement, followed by the Maidan
              protest in Kiev.

December   Growing anti-government protests gather pace throughout
              Ukraine.

2014

January   Worsening violence takes place in central Kiev.

22 February   President Yanukovych is forced to flee from Kiev, following a
              'people's revolution' (Ukrainian nationalist perspective) or a
              coup d'état (majority Russian view).

22–25 February Concerns grow in Crimea about the future of the peninsula:
              protest demonstrations both for Ukraine and Russia take place
              in Simferopol.

23 February   A mass meeting in Sevastopol calls for the city's independence
              from Ukraine, followed by the recruitment of volunteers to
              defend Sevastopol and the establishment of a ring of
              checkpoints around the city.

26/27 February The Crimean parliament building is taken over by masked
              armed men; pro-Russian special riot policemen (*Berkut*) from
              Sevastopol block the Crimean border crossings with Ukraine at
              Perekop and Chongar.

March	Ukrainian armed forces offer passive resistance to Russian troops and local 'self-defence' groups, and then withdraw from Crimea.
16 March	Crimea, in an internationally disputed referendum, votes for a return to Russia.
18 March	Sevastopol and Crimea are incorporated into the Russia Federation.
20/21 March	The European Council strongly condemns the annexation of Crimea and Sevastopol to the Russian Federation, and refuses to recognise this act.
27 March	The United Nations General Assembly adopts a non-binding resolution calling upon states not to recognise changes in the status of Crimea.
9 May	President Vladimir Putin makes a triumphal visit to Sevastopol, marking the 70th anniversary of the liberation of Sevastopol.

ACKNOWLEDGEMENTS

The research and writing, let alone completion, of this book would not have been possible without the sustained interest and support of numerous friends and colleagues, residents of Crimea and Sevastopol, and, not least, family members over a six-year period. Notwithstanding the advice and assistance I have received from many people, I remain responsible for all opinions stated and for any errors of fact.

I thank the staff of several British institutions for their assistance, including the Royal Engineers Museum, Library and Archive, Chatham (notably its chief curator, Rebecca Nash); the Royal Military Academy, Sandhurst; the British Library; the Royal United Services Institute; and the Reform Club, London. The Club's librarian, Simon Blundell, has been particularly helpful in providing sources while I have been writing various parts of the book in the Club's fine Study Room.

I am most grateful for the wise counsel of all those who have kindly reviewed various parts of my manuscript. Foremost amongst this group is Charles Dick, former head of the Conflict Studies Research Centre of the Defence Academy, who has not only read all the chapters, but also provided much expert advice on Soviet military matters. Other peer reviewers (many drawn from the British Commission for Military History (BCMH) – starred*) include: Robin Brodhurst* and Neil Pattenden (who both provided invaluable advice on naval matters); Professors Beatrice Heuser*, Brian Holden Reid* and Neil Kent; Dr Megan Edwards; Dr Andrew Monaghan; Dr Andrew Stewart; Charles Messenger*; Eric Morris; Chris Donnelly; Major General David T. Zabecki* PhD; and Colonel Peter Knox*, a former president of the Crimean War Research Society. I would also like to thank Irina Isakova for providing me with a Russian bibliography of Sevastopol, which greatly assisted my early research.

I thank in particular Mr Nick Ogle, who very generously put at my disposal his extensive unpublished account of his forebear, Rear Admiral Thomas

Mackenzie, the founder of Sevastopol in 1783, from which I have extensively quoted. I also acknowledge the interest and support of his cousin, Allan Mackenzie, a direct descendant. Although we had planned to travel to Crimea together in May 2014 on a BCMH battlefield tour to Sevastopol, the Russian annexation of the peninsula in March 2014 caused the cancellation of that trip.

I am indebted to General Sir Richard Shirreff, author of the chilling fiction *War with Russia* (2016), for providing me with copies of the letters home of his ancestor, James Pattullo, who fought and died in the Crimean War. Chuck Veit has kindly given me permission to quote extensively from his published research into the raising of the sunken Russian ships following that conflict. I thank Anthony Dawson, who provided several French primary sources from the Crimean War, and Dr Peter Lieb, who gave me a copy of the private diary of the First World War German General Robert Kosch, extracts of which feature in this book. I acknowledge the expert advice of Antony Beevor, with whom I discussed matters relating to Sevastopol and Stalingrad; of Major General Peter Craig, Colonel Dr John Blair, Dr Emily Mayhew and Pete Starling on the history of medical science; and of Dr Roger Knight on naval affairs of the Napoleonic period. I am grateful to Dr Andrew Gordon, whose classic study of command, *The Rules of the Game* (1996), prompted my interest in the German battlecruiser *Goeben* and its role at Sevastopol in the opening weeks of the First World War. I also thank Richard M. Langworth for assisting me with several Churchill quotations.

In Germany, I am grateful to the staffs of the Federal German Military Archive in Freiburg, and of the Centre for Military History and Social Science of the Bundeswehr in Potsdam, and thank Colonel Karl-Heinz Frieser PhD for his interest in this project. I also thank Colonel Peter Uffelmann for providing me with a valuable source on Field Marshal Erich von Manstein's campaign in Crimea, 1941–42. I thank Manstein's surviving son, Rüdiger, for again granting me permission to draw on his father's personal war diary, which I first used in researching and writing *Manstein: Hitler's Greatest General* (2010).

In Russia, I thank the staff of the Research Institute (Military History) of the Military Academy of the General Staff of the Armed Forces in Moscow. In particular, I thank Captain First Rank Denis Kozlov, who kindly donated a copy of his monograph *Strange War in the Black Sea, August – October 1914* (2009). I would like to thank the staff of the British Embassy, Moscow, for facilitating this visit in September 2012.

In Ukraine, I am indebted to Oleksiy Melnyk of the Razumkov Centre, Kyiv, who provided very valuable public polling evidence and analysis relating to Crimea, and to Viktor Myroshnyk, who guided me around the Poltava battlefield museum in April 2015. I am also grateful to the staff of the National Pirogov

Museum Estate at Vishnya, near the city of Vinnytsya, who assisted my visit to the former home and memorial to the celebrated nineteenth-century Russian military surgeon at Sevastopol, Professor Dr Nikolay Pirogov.

In Crimea, my Yalta-based researcher and interpreter, Tanya Bukharina, accompanied me on several field trips to Sevastopol (2011–13) while I researched this book. She has delved most diligently into the city's archives and libraries, provided countless translations of Russian texts, and facilitated interviews with veterans. I thank her and the following individuals for their first-hand accounts of the Second World War, the Cold War and more recent events: Vasily Eliseev; Rear Admiral Alexsandr Glushakov; Captain First Rank Sergey Gorbachev; Alla Khanilo; Vladimir Kolesnikov; Mikhail Molenov (†); Colonel Viktor Potakov; Colonel Genady Ryzhenok; and Yevdokiya Sikorskaya (†).

I am very grateful to many Crimea and Sevastopol based historians, guides and residents who have variously assisted my research and supplied me with a wide range of primary and secondary sources, including Sergey Chennyk; Oleg Doskato; Olga Lazarchuk; Pavel Lyashuk; Eduard Rogovsky; Vladimir Savilov; Nikolay Skiba; Vladimir Usoltsev (†); and Tanya Zizak. Tanya Bukharina, Vladimir Zizak and Nikolay Skiba have all kindly provided a number of photographs of contemporary Sevastopol. So too has Sergey Gorbachev, who kindly sent me a copy of his book *From the Third Defence to the Russian Spring* (2015), together with a selection of associated images from 2014, many of which have found their way into this volume. I would also like to thank the staffs of the following organisations for their assistance: the State Historical and Archaeological Museum-Preserve of Chersonesos; the Simferopol and Sevastopol State Archives; the Russian Federation Black Sea Fleet Library, and the Black Sea Fleet Museum, Sevastopol; and the State Museum of the Heroic Defence and Liberation of Sevastopol (which includes the Panorama, Diorama and Resistance museums). I am particularly grateful to the latter's director, Nikolay Musieyenko, for supplying at short notice an image of Winston Churchill at the Panorama Museum.

Back in the United Kingdom, I have received the support of a number of further members of the BCMH, notably Mrs Barbara Taylor*, who has drawn the excellent colour maps for this volume, and from Dr John Peaty* and Lieutenant Colonel Matthew Whitchurch*. Lady Caroline Dalmeny has kindly hosted me at Rosebery House, Midlothian, on a number of occasions. In its delightful surroundings I have drafted or revised several sections of the book. I also thank the very helpful staff of the Summerhill Hotel, Paignton, Devon, where I have written various chapters. Donald Smith, a former British Army comrade-in-arms, has provided a set of most valuable translations of Russian sources, primarily from the diary of Vice Admiral Filipp Oktyabrsky, commander of the Soviet Black Sea Fleet during the Second World War. I also thank another former military colleague, Kingsley Donaldson, for his personal assistance during the early part of this book project.

I acknowledge the encouragement and support I have received from my agent, Robert Dudley, and from my editors at Osprey, Kate Moore, and more recently, Marcus Cowper. Marcus has accepted with great understanding and forbearance a number of long delays as this book steadily expanded in ambition and volume. Laura Callaghan of Osprey has assisted in the provision and selection of the pictures, and has been most patient with me during the final editing process. I am also grateful to Paul Skelton-Stroud and Mary Duffy of the Army and Navy Club, London, for kindly providing copies of William Simpson's famous prints of the Crimean War.

Finally, within my own family, I thank my younger daughter Stephanie for her painstaking reading of the entire manuscript, for advising on a number of classical sources and compiling the bibliography. My elder daughter Catharine has provided much encouragement and my son-in-law, Adam Lewitt, has commented helpfully on a number of chapters. My most profound thanks, however, go to my long-suffering wife Sigi, who, as ever, has made the greatest sacrifices of all during the long years of my research and writing of Sevastopol, all well beyond the call of duty.

Mungo Melvin
Chilmark, Wiltshire, November 2016

NOTES

Author's Note

1. Ялта and Юлия.
2. Евпатория and Чапаевская стрелковая дивизия.
3. Орёл.
4. A battalion (usually 500–1000 men) comprises a number of companies, each containing a number of platoons.
5. During the course of the First World War, the German Army dropped the brigade level. By the Second World War, the Soviet Army retained it for tank formations.
6. The traditional ranks of the Russian Imperial Army were reintroduced in 1940, replacing the functional Bolshevik system of Komdiv and Kombrig etc.
7. Rank linked to the parent arm (*Waffengattung*) of the recipient – another example would be General der Artillerie, General of Artillery.

Prologue

1. Alexander Dobry and Irina Borisova, *Welcome to Sevastopol. Guide-book* (Sevastopol: Art-Print, 2003), p. 1.
2. V. S. Usoltsev, *Foma Fomich Mekenzi* [Thomas son of Thomas Mackenzie] (Sevastopol: Art-Print, 2001).
3. Vladimir Putin, 'Speech at [the] gala concert to mark the 69th anniversary of Victory in the Great Patriotic War and 70th anniversary of the liberation of Sevastopol from Nazis', 9 May 2014, accessed at http://en.kremlin.ru/events/president/transcripts/20993 on 25 October 2016.
4. Vladimir Stepanovich Usoltsev (1926–2016) was born in the Russian 'federal subject' of Altai Krai in southern Siberia. His family moved to Crimea in 1938, where he continued his school studies. Joining the Red Army in October 1943, he served in the Caucasus as an artilleryman. Settling in Sevastopol in 1950, he was employed throughout his working life in the Sevastopol Marine Plant, serving as mechanic, controller, teacher of special technology and chief economist. On retirement in 1986, he devoted himself to veterans' affairs and writing local histories. For a comprehensive biography (in Russian), see http://sevastopol.su/person.php?id=297.
5. Leo Tolstoy, trans. Louise and Aylmer Maude, *Sevastopol* (London: Archibald Constable, 1905), p. 19.

6. Described in Chapter 4.

7. The present author is indebted to Charles Dick, former Head of the British Army's Soviet (later, Conflict) Studies Research Centre, Sandhurst, for recounting this amusing anecdote.

8. As a member of the 'State Emergency Committee', Yazov was implicated in the coup against President Mikhail Gorbachev in August 1991. The plotters placed Gorbachev and his wife Raisa under house arrest in their summer residence at Foros on the southern Crimean coast. For a time, the Gorbachevs feared for their lives when completely cut off from the outside world. Thanks largely to the counter-demonstrations and protests of Moscow's population, however, the coup failed. Yazov was tried for treason, imprisoned and then pardoned by President Boris Yeltsin of the Russian Federation. See David Pryce-Jones, *The War That Never Was. The Fall of the Soviet Empire 1985–1991* (London: Weidenfeld & Nicolson, 1995), pp. 404–13.

9. Manstein's campaign in Crimea (1941–42) is described and analysed in Mungo Melvin, *Manstein: Hitler's Greatest General* (London: Weidenfeld & Nicolson, 2010), Chapter 10.

10. Ilya Ehrenburg, 'City of Courage', *Sevastopol November, 1941 — July, 1942. Articles, Stories and Eye-Witness Accounts by Soviet War-Correspondents* (London: Hutchinson, 1942), p. 9. This publication was one of a series of 'Soviet War Books', published by authority of the press department of the Soviet Embassy in London. Hereafter referred to as *Sevastopol November 1941 – July 1942.*

11. This sustained effort was in stark contrast to the British Army's precipitate capitulation of Tobruk in North Africa in June 1942 and, even more shamefully, the devastating defeat of British Empire forces by Japanese at Singapore in February 1942. Although the Japanese were inferior in numbers in the battle for Singapore, they proved to be far superior to their opponents in operational art, tactics and in command.

12. Andrew Monaghan, *The New Politics of Russia. Interpreting Change* (Manchester: Manchester University Press, 2016), p. 18.

13. Interview with V. F. Eliseev on 21 December 2012 at the Sevastopol Veterans' House.

14. '*Ty zhivesh' v Sevastopole?*': '*Ya – russkaya*' – the question posed, and answer given, on 18 August 2012 at the Lenin statue in Sevastopol.

15. Sergey Gorbachev, *Ot tretyey oborony k Russkoy Vesne. K godovshchine vozvrashcheniya Sevastopolya i Kryma v sostav Rossii* [From the Third Defence to the Russian Spring. On the Anniversary of the Return of Sevastopol and Crimea to the Russian Federation] (Simferopol: Salta Ltd, 2015), pp. 17–18.

16. Following the Russian annexation of Crimea in 2014, it can be argued that the post-War settlement of Europe has been overturned, and that international boundaries 'are now up for grabs'. The history of the borders of the Soviet Union (and Russian Federation), however, remains relevant in any such analysis. The internal boundaries of the Soviet Union were often drawn in seemingly illogical places to divide rather than to unite peoples, and to hedge against the risk of secession. Large numbers were moved around to generate balance and integration. Local populations were reinforced with ethnic Russians to achieve this goal and to strengthen the workforce, so meeting the demands of Soviet industrial and agricultural policies. Eastern Ukraine and Crimea received large influxes of Russians following the Second World War for such reasons. A wider discussion of both precedent and outcome concerning Russia's external and internal boundaries lies beyond the scope of this book. For a detailed survey of the peoples of the former Soviet Union, see Vadim Medish, *The Soviet Union* (2nd revised ed.) (Englewood Cliffs, NJ: Prentice-Hall, 1985), Chapter 2.

Chapter 1: Crucible of Conflict

1. Alexander Pushkin, trans. and ed. Stanley Mitchell, *Eugene Onegin* (London: Penguin Classics, 2008), p. 201.

2. This geographical description, and some of the background history of Crimea, is drawn from Neal Ascherson, *Black Sea: The Birthplace of Civilisation and Barbarism* (London: Vintage, 2007), p. 6 et seq.

3. Crimea's longer, latitudinal, axis is approximately 300km in length; from north to south it is just short of 200km; its area is 26,100sq km, or nearly 70 times the size of the similarly proportioned Isle of Wight that lies off England's southern coast.

4. Ascherson, pp. 5–7.

5. The two rail links between the Crimean peninsula and Ukraine at Chongar and Perekop were severed in the autumn of 2014.

6. François, Baron de Tott, *Memoirs of the Baron de Tott on the Turks and the Tartars*, vol. ii (Dublin: White, Cash & Marchbank, 1785), pp. 118–19. Originally published in Paris in 1785 as *Mémoires du Baron de Tott, sur les Turcs et les Tartares*.

7. [Jean Racault, Baron de] Reuilly, *Travels in the Crimea, and along the Shores of the Black Sea, Performed during the Year 1803* (London: Richard Phillips, 1807), p. 29. Originally published in Paris by Bossange, Messon and Besson in 1806 as *Voyages en Crimée et sur les bords de la Mer Noire*.

8. De Tott, p. 116.

9. Mrs Kate Guthrie, *Through Russia: from St. Petersburg to Astrakhan and the Crimea*, vol. ii (London: Hurst and Blackett, 1874), p. 159.

10. To preserve the seclusion of the greater Yalta area, where the Russian royal family built their summer palaces, concluding with the construction of Livadia in 1910–11, Tsars Alexander III and Nicholas II had forbidden any extension of the railway from Simferopol other than to Sevastopol and to Feodosiya on Crimea's south-western and eastern coasts respectively.

11. Robert K. Massie, *Nicholas and Alexandra* (New York: Atheneum, 1967), pp. 170–71.

12. See M. Rostovtzeff, 'The Bosporan Kingdom' in (ed.) S. A. Cook, F. E. Adcock and M. P. Charlesworth, *The Cambridge Ancient History*, vol. viii, *Rome and the Mediterranean 218–133 B.C.* (Cambridge: University Press, 1930), pp. 561–62.

13. The Greek geographer Strabo described it thus: 'Then comes the Old Chersonesos, which has been razed to the ground; and after it comes a narrow-mouthed harbour, where, generally speaking, the Tauri, a Scythian tribe, used to assemble their bands of pirates in order to attack all who fled thither for refuge. It is called Symbolon Limen [Balaklava]. This harbour forms with another harbour called Ctenus Limen ['comb harbour', now the site of modern Sevastopol] an isthmus forty stadia in width; and this is the isthmus that encloses the Little Chersonesos, which ... is a part of the Great Chersonesos [Crimea] and has on it the city of Chersonesos, which bears the same name as the peninsula.' *Geography*, 7.4.2. English translation from Horace Leonard Jones, *The Geography of Strabo*, vol. iii (London: Heinemann, 1924), p. 233.

14. Although the Sapun Gora is commonly translated as the Sapun 'mountain', this is a most misleading description. The Sapun feature, marking the eastern edge of an area of high land (the Chersonese plateau), overlooks the valley of the river Chernaya and the 'valleys' of Balaklava. For this reason, this book adopts the term Sapun escarpment.

15. From the prefatory note of the English translator and editor, Gilbert Murray (1910), taken from http://www2.hn.psu.edu/faculty/jmanis/euripides/Euripides-Iphigenia.pdf accessed on 8 December 2014.

16. The city of Chersonesos was built on a promontory of the Heraklion peninsula on southwestern Crimea – itself a peninsula. Thus Chersonesos represented a 'Peninsular City' three times over.

17. The description of Chersonesos as a 'Peninsular City' and some details of its ancient history are taken from Norman Davies, *Europe: A History* (London: Bodley Head, 2014), pp. 105–06. First published by Oxford University Press in 1996.

18. Glenn R. Mack and Joseph Coleman Carter (ed.), *Crimean Chersonesos: City, Chora, Museum, and Environs* (Austin, Texas: Institute of Classical Archaeology, 2003), p. 7. This work is an indispensible, authoritative and detailed academic guide to ancient Chersonesos.

19. Ibid., p. 4.

20. Ibid., p. 18.

21. Ibid.

22. Ibid., pp. 59–80.

23. As recounted by Nikita Khrapunov and Dmitriy Prokhorov, *A Short History of the Crimea* (Simferopol: Dolya Publishing House, 2013), p. 195. This bilingual (Russian and English) text has provided an invaluable source of information on Crimea, Chersonesos and Sevastopol. Maxim Elovik kindly presented a copy to the present author.

24. Mack and Carter, p. 76.

25. As Mack and Carter explain (p. 19), the settlement of Chersonesos 'became a *polis* (a self-governing unit consisting of an *asty*, or urban centre, with an agricultural territory, *chora*) in its own right'.

26. From a translation by T. Lytle, quoted by Mack and Carter, p. 136. Noting that *demos* means the body of common people, there would appear to be some deliberate repetition in the translation in the expression 'the demos of the people of Chersonesos'. A check of the inscription by Stephanie Melvin, classics scholar, at http://epigraphy.packhum.org/text/184596, however, reveals 'damos' = 'demos' is only mentioned once.

27. Davies, *Europe*, p. 105.

28. Mack and Carter, p. 27.

29. Edward N. Luttwak, *The Grand Century of the Roman Empire from the First Century A.D. to the Third* (Baltimore and London: Johns Hopkins University Press, 1976), p. 169.

30. Edward Gibbon, *The History of the Decline and Fall of the Roman Empire*, vol. ii (London: Methuen, 1896) pp. 218–19.

31. Mack and Carter, p. 30.

32. Gibbon, v (1898), pp. 182–83.

33. Mack and Carter, p. 2.

34. Edward N. Luttwak, *The Grand Strategy of the Byzantine Empire* (Cambridge, Massachusetts and London: Belknap Press, 2009), pp. 5–6.

35. Mrs Maria Guthrie, *A Tour, Performed in the Years 1795–96, Through the Tauridia, or Crimea* (London: Cadell and Davies, 1802), p. 96.

36. This description is taken from Khrapunov and Prokhorov, pp. 172–74. As these authors point out, all the events associated with Vladimir could not have taken place in one year (988), which is the 'official' date of his conversion; a far more likely year for his baptism and marriage is 990, particularly if one is to give any credence to the appearance of Halley's comet in 989 during the siege.

37. P. J. Heather, *Empires and Barbarians* (London: Macmillan, 2009), pp. 517 and 520.

38. The formal title of the world heritage site is the 'Ancient City of Tauric Chersonese and its Chora'. A UNESCO report on its condition is at http://whc.unesco.org/archive/periodicreporting/EUR/cycle02/section2/groupb/1411.pdf.

39. Alan W. Fisher, *The Crimean Tatars* (Stanford, CA: Hoover Institution Press, 1978), p. 10. As Fisher describes (p. 11), however, Ottoman authority in Crimea was not firmly established until 1478 through the reinstatement of Khan Mengli Giray, who had been temporarily ousted by the Khan of the Golden Horde, Seyvid Ahmed. While other authors spell Giray as 'Girey', Fisher's usage is used throughout this book.

40. Martin Sixsmith, *Russia: A 1,000 Year Chronicle of the Wild East* (London: BBC and Random House, 2012), p. 121.

41. Major General J. F. C. Fuller, *The Decisive Battles of the Western World and their Influence upon History*, vol. 2, *From the Defeat of the Spanish Armada to the Battle of Waterloo* (London: Eyre & Spottiswoode, 1955), p. 157.

42. Carol B. Stevens, *Russia's Wars of Emergence 1460–1730* (Harlow: Pearson Education, 2007), p. 84.

43. Nicholas V. Riasanovsky, *A History of Russia*, 5th ed. (New York and Oxford: Oxford University Press, 1993), pp. 147 and 151–52.

44. Archer Jones, *The Art of War in the Western World* (New York: Barnes & Noble, 1987), pp. 142–43.

45. Heinrich von Staden, *The Land and Government of Muscovy: A Sixteenth-Century Account* (Stanford: University Press, 1967), p. 76.

46. The name Zaporizhia (Ukrainian: Запорíжжя, *Zaporizhzhya*; Russian: Запорóжье, *Zaporozhye*) is derived from '*za*' (beyond) '*poroža*' (the rapids).

47. Norman Davies, *Vanished Kingdoms: The History of Half-Forgotten Europe* (London: Allen Lane, 2012), p. 260.

48. New Russia (*Novorossiya*) was a historical term used in the Russian Empire in the late eighteenth and early nineteenth centuries denoting an area north of the Black Sea, which Russia had won in a series of Russo-Turkish wars. It was so named because this territory was not part of old Rus. Much of the area concerned lies now within the territory of modern Ukraine. Pro-Russian separatists in eastern Ukraine and nationalists in the Russian Federation have revived the term Novorossiya in the wake of the crisis of 2014 over Crimea and ongoing conflict in the Donets Basin (Donbas).

49. Simon Sebag Montefiore, *Catherine the Great and Potemkin: The Imperial Love Affair* (London: Phoenix, 2011), pp. 294–95. First published in 2000 by Weidenfeld & Nicolson as *Prince of Princes: The Life of Potemkin*.

50. Ibid., p. 271.

51. Robert K. Massie, *Peter the Great: His Life and World* (London: Head of Zeus, 2012), p. 85. Originally published in the United States of America by Alfred A. Knopf in 1980.

52. The fortifications of the so-called Belgorod *abattis* line (the *Belgorodskaya cherta*) stretched for 800km from Tambov (about 500km south-west of Moscow) through Voronezh of the middle Don to Belgorod and west to Akhtyrka (ceded by Poland to Muscovy in 1647). Constructing and manning this new frontier line not only consumed a vast proportion of Muscovite economic and military resources, but also represented a considerable organisational achievement, one which helped pave the way for the later modernisation and expansion of Russia. See Stevens, p. 134, for further details.

53. Massie, *Peter the Great*, p. 84.

54. Riasanovsky, p. 214.

55. Massie, *Peter the Great*, p. 87.

56. Ibid.

57. Ibid., pp. 88–89.

58. Ibid., p. 104.

59. This censure and banishment did not mean the end of the noble family Golitsyn. Prince Nikolay Dmitriyevich Golitsyn (1850–1925) served briefly as the last Prime Minister of imperial Russia in 1917.

60. Akdes N. Kurat and John S. Bromley, 'The Retreat of the Turks, 1683–1730', Chapter XIX in J. S. Bromley (ed.), *Cambridge New Modern History*, vol. vi, *The Rise of Great Britain and Russia* (Cambridge: University Press, 1970), p. 625.

61. Massie, *Peter the Great*, p. 137.

62. Ibid., pp. 140–41.

63. Riasanovsky, p. 219.

64. Peter's incognito guise was transparent. He merely wished his visit to be informal so as to achieve his educational objective and to avoid the suffocating court formalities that would stand in the way.

65. The present author is grateful to Viktor Myroshnyk, a battlefield museum guide, whom he met at Poltava on 10 April 2015, for his insights into the battle.

66. J. F. C. Fuller, p. 184.

67. Ibid., p. 183.

68. Riasanovsky, p. 229.

69. Quoted by Anatoli A. Razdolgin, *The Russian Navy* (St Petersburg: Maritime Publishing House, 2003), p. 11.

70. General Christopher Hermann von Manstein, ed. David Hume, *Contemporary Memoirs of Russia, from the Year 1727 to 1744* (London: Longman, Brown, Green and Longmans, 1856), p. 105. Republished as a Nabu Public Domain Reprint on demand.

71. Ibid., p. 107.

72. It is estimated that the campaign cost 30,000 Russian deaths from hunger, famine and disease and only 2,000 from battle. Statistics from Virginia H. Aksan, *Ottoman Wars 1700–1870* (Harlow: Pearson Education, 2007), p. 105.

73. Douglas Smith (ed. and trans.), *Love and Conquest: Personal Correspondence of Catherine the Great and Prince Grigory Potemkin* (Dekalb: Northern Illinois Press, 2004), p. xxxvii. Smith's translations are based on V. S. Lopatin, *Ekaterina II i G. A. Potemkin. Lichnaya perepiska, 1769–1791* [Catherine II and G. A. Potemkin. Personal Correspondence, 1769–1791] (Moscow: Nauka, 1997), available at http://az.lib.ru/e/ekaterina_w/text_0030.shtml. Readers should note that Smith numbers the letters between Catherine and Potemkin differently from Lopatin. As Smith's translation has been used for the most part, his letter numbering is given in the relevant endnotes.

74. Catherine's private secretary, 'Grand Chancellor' and principal foreign policy adviser, Count Alexander Bezborodko, had drawn up a proposal for the 'Greek project' on her behalf in 1780. It foresaw the 're-establishment of the ancient Greek empire', a matter she discussed with Joseph II of Austria in 1781 and developed in subsequent years through an exchange of letters. Whether it was ever a serious – let alone realisable – strategic goal remains in some doubt: see Orlando Figes, *Crimea: The Last Crusade* (London: Allen Lane, 2010), p. 13. According to Sebag Montefiore, moreover, Potemkin was the originator of the project, while Bezborodko was merely the scribe who documented it. For further details, see Sebag Montefiore, pp. 241–45.

75. Sebag Montefiore, p. 292.

76. Quoted by K. Osipov, trans. Edith Bone, *Alexander Suvorov* (London: Hutchinson, undated – 1941?), p. 74. Originally published in the Soviet Union in 1941.

77. For a more detailed description of Russia's foreign policy in this period and the importance of religion in driving it, see Figes, *Crimea*, pp. 9–17.

78. Ibid., p. 13. St Sophia is the Latin name for the Greek Hagia Sophia. The Turks called it Ayasofya. They called Constantinople Konstantiniyye until 1920, when they switched to the Greek popular expression 'to the city' – '*eis ten polin*' – Istanbul. The author is grateful to Professor Beatrice Heuser for her advice on this matter.

79. Fisher, p. 37.

80. This translation is directly derived from Lopatin, Letter #635, and differs slightly from Smith, Letter #259, Potemkin/Catherine, before 14 December 1782 [OS], p. 124: 'Kherson in the Tauride! From you piety flowed to us. Now watch how Catherine the Second introduces to you anew the meekness of Christian rule.'

81. Smith, Letter #259, Potemkin/Catherine, before 14 December 1782 [OS], pp. 123–24.

82. Looking back on the events of 2014 in relation to the Russian re-annexation of Crimea, it could be reasonably said that a combination of Ukrainian weakness and Western indecision emboldened Russian moves.

83. Fisher, p. 54.

84. Although Fisher uses the spelling Şahin, the alternative 'Shagin' is used in this book. Other authorities transliterate Tatar family names differently, Giray being spelt either Girey or Gerei, for example.

85. This point is also well made by Jeremy Black, *War and the World: Military Power and the Fate of Continents* (Yale: University Press, 1998), p. 108.

86. Ibid.

87. The Russians' tactical emphasis on speed, surprise and shock action, and Suvorov's cult of the bayonet ('*pulia duraka, no shtyk molodets*') is described in William C. Fuller, *Strategy and Power in Russia 1600–1914* (New York: The Free Press, 1992), pp. 165–66. Suvorov's legacy to Russian military thought and action was far more profound than his famous maxim about the bayonet might suggest. In the history of the Russian Imperial Army, Suvorov was noted as a moderniser and reformer. For a good summary of his legacy, and how it was subsequently distorted, see Lieutenant-Colonel Serge Andolenko, 'The Imperial Heritage' in B. H. Liddell Hart (ed.), *The History of the Red Army* (London: Weidenfeld and Nicolson, 1956), pp. 15–19.

88. Also commonly rendered in English as Kutchuk Kainardji.

89. Robert K. Massie, *Catherine the Great* (London: Head of Zeus, 2012), p. 383.

90. Sebag Montefiore, p. 273.

91. Fisher, p. 58.

92. Ibid., p 69.

93. This annexation was neatly reprised by the Russian Federation some 231 years later in wresting Crimea from Ukrainian control with hardly a shot fired in anger. Its tragic aftermath, a civil war in the Donbas region between pro-Russian separatists and Ukrainian armed forces, has proved most bloody. See Chapter 16 and the Epilogue of this book.

94. Quoted by D. Smith, pp. 123–24.

95. A. A. Lebedev, *U istokov Chernomorskogo flota Rossii* [Sources of the Russian Black Sea Fleet] (St Petersburg: Gangut, 2011), pp. 623–24.

96. G. A. Grebenshchikova, *Chernomorskiy flot v period pravleniya Yekateriny II* [The Black Sea Fleet during the Reign of Catherine II] (St Petersburg: Ostrov, 2012), pp. 428–29.

97. D. Smith, pp. 123–24.

Chapter 2: The Founding of Sevastopol

1. Inscribed in a monument standing on Nakhimov Square on the southern (city) side of Sevastopol, overlooking Sevastopol Bay and harbour.

2. The first of these unflattering views of Semple Lisle stems from James Grant, *The Scottish Soldiers of Fortune; Their Adventures and Achievements in the Armies of Europe* (London: Routledge, 1889), republished by Forgotten Books in 2012, p. 39. Grant censured him further, noting (p. 42): 'when in Russia, [Semple Lisle] was mixed up in a disreputable way with the famous Duchess of Kingston'. The second description is cited by Sebag Montefiore, p. 219, who mentions the title of a contemporaneous book published about Semple Lisle: *The Northern Hero – Surprising Adventures, Amorous Intrigues, Curious Devices, Unparalleled Hypocrisy, Remarkable Escapes, Internal Frauds, Deep-laid Projects and Villainous Projects*! Another edition of this very critical account (or a separate work altogether?) of Semple Lisle has recently been republished by Eighteenth Century Collections Online Print Editions – *The Northern Impostor; Being a faithful Narrative of the Life, Adventures, and Deceptions, of James George Semple, commonly called Major Semple* (London: printed for G. Kearsley, 1786).

3. J. G. Semple, *The Life of Major J. G. Semple Lisle Containing a Faithful Narrative of His Alternate Vicissitudes of Splendor and Misfortune* (London: W. Stewart, 1799), p. 10. There are grounds to suspect the reliability of Semple Lisle's memoirs, particularly in view of his highly dubious

background. He wrote his work while in prison, probably with the assistance of a ghostwriter. This autobiographical work does not focus on Semple Lisle's highly irregular (and mostly illegal) financial affairs.

4. In writing this chapter of the book, the present author has been greatly assisted by the detailed research of Mr Nick Ogle, who has spent many years investigating the naval career of Rear Admiral Thomas Mackenzie, with whom he is related on his mother's side. His unpublished manuscript *Rear Admiral Thomas Mackenzie: Life and Times with the Black Sea and Azov Sea Command 1783–1786*, based on primary Russian sources, has proved an indispensible source of reference. Mr Allan Mackenzie, a direct descendant, has also provided further insights. In addition, this chapter draws extensively on Usoltsev's Russian-language monograph on Mackenzie, previously cited.

5. In the manner of Peter the Great, Catherine the Great encouraged the employment of Royal Navy officers. As a result, a significant proportion of officers in the Russian Navy were British – several high-ranking such as Elphinstone, Greig and Sir Charles Knowles. The Russian Navy received assistance from Britain in two further ways: through the design, construction and maintenance of vessels; and through the training of Russian crews on British men-at-war. For further details, see M. S. Anderson, 'Great Britain and the Growth of the Russian Navy in the Eighteenth Century', *Mariner's Mirror*, 42 (1956), pp. 132–46; and Anthony Cross, *By the Banks of the Neva: Chapters from the Lives and Careers of the British in Eighteenth-Century Russia* (Cambridge: University Press, 1997), pp. 183–218. Cross (p. 205) believes that 'a figure well in excess of 150 British officers' joined the Russian Navy during the reign of Catherine the Great.

6. Grant, p. 43.

7. Aksan, *Ottoman Wars,* considers (p. 153) that the Morea revolt was a 'prelude to the arrival of the Russian fleet'; yet she also acknowledges that it 'compounded the problems of [Ottoman] mobilization'. Her interpretation raises a moot historical point: was the Greek revolt – from a Russian strategic perspective – the *supported* or a *supporting* line of operations in relation to the deployment of the Russian fleet?

8. This strategic move foreshadowed the redeployment of the Baltic Fleet in 1904–05 to the Far East to fight the Japanese.

9. The outstanding Russian maritime artist of the nineteenth century, Ivan Aivazovsky, depicted the night action of Chesma in one of his most famous works.

10. Lieutenant Thomas Mackenzie, letter of 29 July 1770, published in *Scots Magazine*, vol. XXXII, September 1770, p. 504. Naval experts, however, are divided over the role of the fire ships. John Tredea and Eduard Sozaev, for example, in *Russian Warships in the Age of Sail 1696–1860* (Barnsley: Seaforth Publishing, 2010), p. 85, state: 'The Russian success should be attributed to the successful use of explosive ordnance in conjunction with the use of the fire ships, along with the passivity and incompetence of the Turkish commanders.' A modern Russian source gives individual credit to Lieutenant Ilyin, who commanded another of the fire ships. See *The History of Russian Navy*, Chapter 3, 'Chesma and Patras', at http://www.neva.ru/EXPO96/book/chap3-4.html, accessed on 12 October 2013. The most balanced account, perhaps, is given by Cross (p. 188): 'By the time the fireships entered the fray around 2 a.m. on 25 June (6 July), their objective had already been in part fulfilled by a projectile from the *Grom* that had set fire to one of the Turkish battleships. Four volunteers commanded the fireships: two Russians, Lieutenant Dmitriy Ilyin and Midshipman Prince Vasiliy Gagarin, and two Britons, Lieutenant Thomas Mackenzie and Captain-Lieutenant Robert Dugdale. Dugdale's fireship was intercepted by the Turks, but Mackenzie managed to reach his target – a ship that was, however, already in flames. It was Ilyin who administered the coup de grâce by reaching the end of the Turkish line and setting it alight, leaving Gagarin with nothing to do.'

11. Another account of the Russian naval deployment to, and action at, Chesma is given by Robert K. Massie in *Catherine the Great*, pp. 376–77. Massie outlines the scope of British support, including the provision of 'facilities to the Russian fleet to rest, resupply, and carry out repairs in

the English naval harbours of Hull, Portsmouth, and again at Gibraltar and Minorca in the Mediterranean'.

12. Usoltsev, p. 20.

13. M. V. Makareyev and G. N. Rizhonok, *Chernomorskiy flot v biografiyakh komanduyushchikh 1783–2004* [Black Sea Fleet in the Biographies of its Commanders], vol. 1, 1783–1917 (Sevastopol: Mir, 2004), p. 18. Along with Thomas Mackenzie, Robert Dugdale was promoted to rear admiral.

14. Dobry and Borisova, p. 16.

15. Quoted by Usoltsev, p. 21.

16. The old Russian unit of measurement of distance, the *verst*, was 3,500ft, corresponding to 1.067km. Thus the length of the Sevastopol main bay is approximately 7.5km, and its width 1.5km.

17. Quoted by Ogle MS, p. 1; D. N. Senyavin, *Morskoy Sbornik* [Naval Journal], *1783–1786*, contained in S. I. Elagin and F. F. Veselago, *Materialy dlya istorii russkogo flota* [Materials concerning the History of the Russian Fleet], vol. 15, *Krym 1783–1785* [Crimea 1783–1785] (St Petersburg, 1885), pp. 128–129. Hereafter the volume is cited as *Materialy* and the specific journal as Senyavin.

18. Admiral V. P. Komoyedov et al, *Chernomorskiy Flot Rossii (Istoricheskiy ocherk)* [The Black Sea Fleet of Russia (Historical Review)] (Simferopol: Tavrida, 2002), p. 37; D. Smith, p. 118.

19. Makareyev and Rizhonok, pp. 18–19.

20. Usoltsev, p. 23.

21. Ogle MS, p. 3, quoting *Materialy*, Document 10, 6 May 1783 [OS].

22. Usoltsev, p. 23.

23. Ogle MS, p. 3, *Materialy*, Document 11, 6 May 1783 [OS].

24. Ibid., *Materialy*, Document 12, undated.

25. It is on Senyavin's memoirs that much of the early history of Akhtiar (to be renamed Sevastopol in 1784) rests, complemented by Usoltsev's research.

26. This description of the bays, and how they got their names, is developed from Usoltsev, p. 23, and Dobry and Borisova, pp. 103–07. Confusingly, up to the Second World War, Sevastopol's main bay (described in the 19th century as the 'Roadstead') was also known as the Northern (Severnaya).

27. Matyushenko Bay is named after Afansy Nikolayevich Matyushenko, one of the leading members of the Potemkin mutiny of 1905, described in Chapter 9.

28. Ogle MS, p. 4, *Materialy*, Document 15, 12 May 1783 [OS].

29. Frigates No. 8 *Ostorozhniy*, No. 9 *Pospevshniy*, No. 10 *Krym*, No. 11 *Khrabu* and No. 13 *Pobeda*.

30. Komoyedov, p. 38.

31. The foundation of Sevastopol is commemorated in a monument on Nakhimov Square, erected on 14 June 1983, which overlooks Sevastopol Bay. It is inscribed with the words: 'Here on 3 (14) June 1783 was founded the city of Sevastopol – the naval fortress of South Russia'. This date is officially remembered today not only as the birthday of Sevastopol, but also that of the Russian Black Sea Fleet.

32. Senyavin, pp. 130–31.

33. Ibid., p. 131.

34. Makareyev and Rizhonok, p. 19.

35. Quoted by G. V. Goncharov, *Admiral Senyavin. Biograficheskiy ocherk s prilozheniyem zapisok admirala D. N. Senyavina* [Admiral Senyavin. Biographical Sketch incorporating the Notes of Admiral D. N. Senyavin] (Moscow and Leningrad: NK VMF, 1945), p. 122.

36. Sebag Montefiore (*Catherine the Great and Potemkin*, p. 320) raises doubt as to whether Semple Lisle ever went to Crimea in 1783, stating that he left Russian service in the autumn of 1782.

This turn of events, however, seems unlikely in view of the detail of the Scotsman's descriptions of Akhtiar and of Thomas Mackenzie, noting that Sebag Montefiore does not quote Semple Lisle directly himself. On balance, therefore, the present author believes that Semple Lisle did indeed visit Crimea, and that his account provides valuable colour to the founding of Sevastopol. Furthermore, Semple Lisle might also have been acting for the British government in an unofficial capacity on account of his good relations with Sir James Harris, the British envoy at the court of Catherine the Great. As Harris was a close friend of Potemkin, one might well assume that Semple Lisle owed his introduction and subsequent employment to his British patron. Christina Backmann in her Internet article 'Major James George Semple Lisle and his wives' provides further biographical detail, including a description of Semple Lisle's dubious exploits in Paris, observing he 'was remarkable for all the travelling he did and there seems to be no doubt that he was indeed a secret agent or in fact a spy' – accessed at http://www.tufftuff.net/majorsemple.htm on 12 October 2013.

37. Semple, p. 37.
38. Ibid., pp. 37–38.
39. Ibid., p. 38.
40. Ibid., p. 25.
41. Ogle MS, p. 10, *Materialy*, Document 44, undated (probably early October 1783).
42. Smith, Letter #271, Catherine/Potemkin, 9 June 1783 [OS], p. 138.
43. Smith, Letter #272, Potemkin/Catherine, 13 June 1783 [OS], p. 139.
44. The Black Death – the bubonic plague – was introduced to Western Europe in 1347 by the Genoese from their Crimean port of Kaffa (now Feodosiya). It arrived in England in 1348.
45. Ogle MS, p. 10, *Materialy*, Document 46, 20 November 1783 [OS].
46. Smith, Letter #272, Potemkin/Catherine, 13 June 1783 [OS], p. 139
47. The text of President Putin's speech at the Duma on 18 March 2014 is at www.en.kremlin.ru/events/president/news/20603.
48. Dobry and Borisova, pp. 16–17.
49. Ibid., p. 7, which describes Sevastopol as a 'city, worthy of worship', an equally good translation of the Ancient Greek words *sebastos* (σεβαστός) and *polis (πόλις)*.
50. G. I. Vaneev, *Sevastopol: Stranisty, Istorii 1783–1983 Spravochnik* [Sevastopol: Pages of History, 1783–1983, A Companion] (Simferopol: Tavriya, 1983), p. 13.
51. Makareyev and Rizhonok, p. 20.
52. Komoyedov, pp. 37–38.
53. Documented by Anthony Cross, 'A Russian Engineer in Eighteenth-Century Britain: The Journal of N. I. Korsakov, 1776–7', *The Slavonic and East European Review*, Vol. 55, No. 1 (January 1977), pp. 1–20.
54. Smith, Letter #280, Potemkin/Catherine, 29 July 1783 [OS], p. 146.
55. N. Yu. Bolotina, *Glavnaya krepost' dolzhna byt' Sevastopol': Dokumenty o sozdanii bazy Chernomorskogo flota. 1784–1793gg* [The Main Fortress should be Sevastopol: Documents Concerning the Establishment of the Base of the Black Sea Fleet, 1784–1993]. Document 5: РГВИА. Ф. 52 оп. 1 Ч. 1 Д. 160 (Ч.3). Л. 57-58об. Подлинник. Accessed from http://www.vostlit.info/Texts/Dokumenty/Russ/XVIII/1780-1800/Osnov_Sevastopol/text.htm on 30 September 2014.
56. As noted by Smith, p. 147.
57. Cross, 'A Russian Engineer', p. 20.
58. Komoyedov, pp. 37–38.
59. Ogle MS, p. 11, *Materialy*, Document 53, 12 June 1784 [OS].
60. Sebag Montefiore, p. 287.
61. Usoltsev, p. 26.

62. Senyavin, pp. 135–36.

63. Ibid., p. 137.

64. Usoltsev, p. 26.

65. For example, Dobry and Borisova (p. 16) state that 'the construction of the naval base was supervised by Lieutenant D. Seniavin, later the well-known Russian sea captain'.

66. The omens, however, do not look good. Significantly, a modern Ukrainian naval monument on Nakhimov Square was removed in 2014 to make place for a new statue of Senyavin rather than one of Mackenzie, thus compounding the historic injustice.

67. Dmitry Fedosov, 'Under the Saltire: Scots and the Russian Navy, 1690s–1910s' in Murray Frame and Mark Cornwall (eds), *Scotland and the Slavs: Cultures in Contact 1500–2000* (Newtonville, Massachusetts and St Petersburg: Oriental Research Publishers, 2001), p. 38.

68. Letter from William Glen, executor of Rear Admiral Mackenzie's will, writing in St Petersburg, to Mrs Maria Bryne at Bristol [sic], dated 17 July 1786 [OS] – from the unpublished Albert Mackenzie family documents and letters (1980), cited in Ogle MS, pp. 14-15.

69. Ibid.

70. Fedosov, 'Under the Saltire', p. 38.

71. She was first married to the long-suffering William, 6th Baron Craven (1783–91), who built a long-since demolished house near the river Thames, Craven Cottage, the site of Fulham Football Club's London ground since 1896.

72. Sebag Montefiore, p. 320.

73. Elizabeth Lady Craven, *A Journey through the Crimea to Constantinople in a Series of Letters to his Serene Highness the Margrave of Brandebourg, Anspach and Bareith, Written in the Year M DCC LXXXVI* [1786] (London: G. G. J. and J. Robinson, 1789), p. 186.

74. *The Glory of Catherine*, the *Slava Ekateriny*, was the first in a class of 66-gun ships of the line constructed at Kherson for the new Black Sea Fleet. A large Soviet concrete and metal monument in Kherson, situated on the site of the former shipyard on the bank of the river Dnieper, commemorates her launch in 1783. In service, *The Glory of Catherine* was based at Sevastopol. She cruised and fought in the Black Sea from 1785 to her decommissioning in 1791. Catherine the Great visited the ship at Sevastopol in 1787. She was renamed *Prebrazhenie Gospodne* [The Transfiguration] in 1788. Further details are given by Tredea and Sozaev, pp. 268–69.

75. The pendant is an alternative name for the ship's pennant, flying on the tallest mast.

76. Craven, p. 187.

77. Ibid., pp. 156 and 158.

78. Ibid., pp. 156 and 158–59.

79. Massie, *Catherine the Great*, p. 490.

80. Mary Durant, 'Catherine's Boat Ride', *Horizon – A Magazine for the Arts*, vol. viii, no. 4 (Autumn 1966), p. 98.

81. Durant, op cit., states that 'Catherine's gold-plated tour lasted six months, entertained three thousand guests, covered more than a thousand miles, and cost seven million roubles, or roughly eighteen million dollars in present-day [1966] terms'.

82. Isabel de Madariaga, *The Travels of General Francisco de Miranda in Russia* (London, 28 March 1950), p. 5.

83. Massie, *Catherine the Great*, p. 491.

84. Anon, *Puteshestviye Yeyo Imperatorskogo Velichestva v poludennyy kray Rossii, predpriyemlemoye v 1787 godu* [Journey of Her Imperial Majesty to the Southern Part of Russia in 1787] (St Petersburg: Mining Institute, 1786) p. 73.

85. Ibid., p. 74.

86. Orlando Figes, *Crimea*, p. 14.

87.	A. Yu. Malenko, *'Byla pora: Yekaterinin vek'. Yekaterina II i Krym po stranitsam dokumentov* ['It was a high time: the Catherine Century'. Catherine II and Crimea through the pages of documents], (Simferopol: Biznes-Inform, 2013), p. 113. The milestones were erected following an order of Potemkin on 8 (19) September 1784. Malenko considers that the probable designer and supervisor of the project was Colonel of Engineers, N. I. Korsakov.

88.	*Archivo del General Miranda: Viajes [&] Diaros 1785–1787* [The Archive of General Miranda: Travels and Diaries, 1785–1787], Tomo [vol.] II (Caracas: Editorial Sur-America, 1929), p. 229.

89.	Durant, p. 100.

90.	Ibid., p. 102.

91.	Sean McMeekin, *The Russian Origins of the First World War* (Cambridge, Massachusetts and London: Harvard University Press, 2013) argues that the Russian quest for Constantinople and the Straits (and associated manipulation of Britain and France to obscure this ambition) was the prime cause of the First World War.

92.	Durant, p. 100.

93.	Massie, *Catherine the Great*, p. 499.

94.	Ibid., pp. 500–01.

95.	The poem captured the high drama of life and death in the Khan's harem.

96.	Trans. and quoted by D. Smith, pp. 178–79. He notes that Catherine 'showed her poem in praise of Potemkin to Khrapovitsky, her secretary, who corrected (and possibly rewrote) it'.

97.	The exact location of this event is disputed. Many sources give Inkerman at the eastern end of Sevastopol Bay. One eyewitness, Baron de Ségur, states indeed that the imperial party arrived for lunch at Inkerman, but he also describes it as Akhtiar as well, suggesting that he used 'Inkerman' as a general, and not as a specific, location. Noting that the last milestone to Catherine II stands at the north side of Sevastopol, opposite the historical centre of the city, perhaps a more likely location for Potemkin's theatrical is in the vicinity of the Red Army memorial to the Heroic Second Guards Army, commemorating its role in the liberation of Crimea and Sevastopol in April–May 1944. This accords with the view of local historian Vladimir Usoltsev who has investigated a number of competing locations.

98.	Ségur, pp. 66–67.

99.	As described by Dobry and Borisova, p. 17. There are many other accounts of this famous scene. Among the best is that by Massie, *Catherine the Great*, p. 501.

100.	Massie, Ibid.

101.	Ségur, p. 67.

102.	Vaneev, *Spravochnik*, pp. 10–11.

103.	Ibid.

104.	Ibid., p. 9.

105.	Smith, Letter #318, Catherine/Potemkin, 24 August 1787 [OS], p. 193.

106.	Ibid.

107.	Smith, Letter #319, Catherine/Potemkin, 29 August 1787 [OS], p. 195.

108.	Smith, Letter #323, Potemkin/Catherine, 24 September 1787 [OS], p. 199.

109.	Smith, Letter #327, Catherine/Potemkin, 2 October 1787 [OS], p. 205.

101.	Ibid. D. Smith, however, does not translate the original French wording of this section of Catherine's letter: '… *Vous êtes impatient comme un enfant de cinq ans*'.

111.	Maria Guthrie, p. 90.

112.	Ibid., pp. 93–94.

113.	Ibid., p. 94.

114.	De Reuilly, p. 70.

115.	Ibid, p. 69.

116.	Ibid.

Chapter 3: Bastion of Maritime Power

1. A. A. Chernousov, *Admiral M. P. Lazarev, Rol' lichnosti v istorii Rossii* [*Admiral M. P. Lazarev, The Role of Personality in the History of Russia*] (St Petersburg: Gangut, 2011), p. 90.

2. Le Baron Auguste de Haxthausen, *Les Forces Militaires de la Russie sous les Rapports Historiques, Statistiques, Ethnographiques et Politiques* (Berlin: Behr & Paris: d'Amyot, 1853), pp. 221–22.

3. Greig's contribution to Nikolayev was of great significance. Realising that an understanding of astronomy was vital to seafarers, he founded a naval observatory for the training of officers in navigation, which opened in 1829. It was to become a famous scientific research institution in its own right, which remains functioning today in modern Ukraine. In addition, Greig founded men's and women's colleges for the expanding city. In May 1873, Nikolayev's citizens erected dutifully a fine monument in Greig's memory. Sadly this was destroyed in early Soviet times in 1922, notwithstanding Lenin's decree for the protection of such monuments of the imperial era.

4. Lieutenant-Général E. de Todleben, *Défense de Sébastopol* [Defence of Sebastopol] (Saint-Petersbourg: N. Thieblin, 1863). Originally published in Russian with an official translation in French, two volumes, each of two parts. Hereafter referred to as Todleben, *Defence of Sevastopol*. There is no complete English translation available. The most comprehensive (but greatly summarised and annotated) is [Sir] William Howard Russell, *General Todleben's History of the Defence of Sevastopol. 1854–5. A Review* (London: Tinsley Brothers, 1865). This work is still available as a British Library Historical Print Edition. Hereafter referred to as Russell, *General Todleben's History*.

5. Hence the title of a classic study of 'joint' land and sea power, C. E. Callwell, *Military Operations and Maritime Preponderance: Their Relations and Interdependence* (Edinburgh and London; William Blackwood and Sons, 1905), republished with a new introduction and notes, ed. Colin Gray, 1996 by the United States Naval Institute, Annapolis, Maryland. All references in this book are to the 1996 edition.

6. A 'fleet in being' was described by Vice Admiral Philip Colomb in 1891 as 'a fleet which is able and willing to attack an enemy proposing a descent upon territory which that force has it in charge to protect'. Other writers, including Alfred T. Mahan, Julian Corbett and Geoffrey Till, have offered different interpretations. For a recent analysis, see the article by the distinguished naval historian John B. Hattendorf, 'The Idea of a "Fleet in Being" in Historical Perspective', *Naval War College Review* (Winter 2014), pp. 43–60; available at https://www.academia.edu/5367169/_The_Idea_of_a_Fleet_in_Being_in_Historical_Perspective_.

7. Lawrence Sondhaus, *Naval Warfare, 1815–1914* (London: Routledge, 2000), p. 17.

8. By way of comparison, a modern Royal Navy mine-hunter of the Sandown class displaces about 600 tonnes.

9. Tredea and Sozaev, p. 290.

10. Fred T. Jane, *The Imperial Russian Navy: Its Past, Present, and Future*, rev. ed. (London: W. Thacker, 1904), p. 133.

11. Sondhaus, *Naval Warfare, 1815–1914*, p. 17.

12. Callwell, pp. 257–58.

13. Sondhaus, *Naval Warfare, 1815–1914*, (p. 29) considers the Black Sea Fleet as a 'fleet in being' more by accident than by design.

14. Harold Temperley, *England and the Near East: The Crimea* (London: Longmans, Green, 1936), pp. 72–73.

15. The present author is grateful for the advice he has received on this point from Charles Dick.

16. Temperley, p. 73.

17. Ibid., pp. 73–74.

18. Harold N. Ingle, *Nesselrode and the Russian Rapprochement with Britain, 1836–1844* (Berkeley & London: University of California Press, 1976), p. 58.

19. For further details of the *Vixen* affair, see Ingle, pp. 63–65; and Peter Hopkirk, *The Great Game: On Secret Service in High Asia* (London: John Murray, 1990), pp. 156–59. An anonymous contemporary account by an 'Old Diplomatic Servant' (perhaps none other than the Turcophile David Urquhart, secretary to the British ambassador in Constantinople, who had instigated the voyage of the *Vixen* and had been recalled to London as a scapegoat) in *British Diplomacy Illustrated in the Affair of the "Vixen" Addressed to the Commercial Constituency of Great Britain*, 3rd. ed. (Newcastle: Currie and Bowman, 1839), p. ii, alleged that there was 'incontrovertible proof' of 'collusion of our Foreign Minister [Palmerston] with the Government of Russia'. Urquhart continued to criticise Palmerston for many years.

20. Henry Danby Seymour, *Russia on the Black Sea and Sea of Azof: being a Narrative of Travels in the Crimea and Bordering Provinces with Notices of the Naval, Military, and Commercial Resources of those Countries* (London: John Murray, 1855), p. 92.

21. A point made by Robin Brodhurst to the present author.

22. Cecil Woodham-Smith, *Queen Victoria. Her Life and Times*, vol. I: 1819–1861 (London: Cardinal, 1975), pp. 316–17. First published by Hamish Hamilton in 1972.

23. The charm worked both ways. The young queen, whose godfather had been Alexander I of Russia, was captivated by Nicholas I's 'striking good looks and graceful manners'. But she noted 'the expression of his eyes is formidable and unlike anything I ever saw before' (Hopkirk, p. 281).

24. Sir John Sinclair, *Thoughts on the Naval Strength of the British Empire* (1782), quoted by Roger Knight, *Britain Against Napoleon: The Organization of Victory 1793–1815* (London: Allen Lane, 2013), p. 21. I am grateful to the author for his permission to reuse this quote and for his advice on naval and strategic matters of the period.

25. In 1787, the Black Sea Fleet consisted of five ships of the line and 19 frigates (a total of 24); in 1788, the Baltic Fleet comprised 23 line of battle ships and no fewer than 130 frigates (a total of 153 vessels).

26. Tredea and Sozaev, p. 293.

27. Todleben, vol. i, pt 1, p. 22.

28. While the present author has found no evidence to support Fred T. Jane's claim (*The Russian Imperial Navy*, p. 709) that Lazarev was present at the battle of Trafalgar, it is perhaps significant that Seymour (p. 91) claims this also; of course, the earlier assertion could have led to the later one. Although Philip Longworth, *Russia's Empires. Their Rise and Fall from Prehistory to Putin* (London: John Murray, 2005), p. 209, states that Lazarev served as a midshipman on HMS *Victory*, his name is not to be found in Colonel Robert Holden Mackenzie, *The Trafalgar Roll* (London: George Allen, 1913). In this comprehensive work only two Russians are listed as serving as midshipmen – Nickolas Koravaeff on HMS *Belleisle* and Alexander Koolomsin on HMS *Euryalus*.

29. For the operational context and details of this naval engagement, see Tredea and Sozaev, pp. 71–72. Lazarev's participation, however, is not mentioned in this account.

30. In the expedition of 1819–21, which he had prepared, Lazarev served as deputy to Captain Fabian Gottlieb von Bellingshausen, a Baltic German in the service of the Imperial Russian Navy and famous cartographer and explorer. While Lazarev captained the sloop *Mirny*, von Bellingshausen commanded from the sloop *Vostok*. The ships circumnavigated the Antarctic continent.

31. This description of Admiral Lazarev and the Black Sea Fleet is based on Tredea and Sozaev, p. 105, augmented by biographical details from Chernousov, *Admiral M. P. Lazarev*.

32. Her larger sister, HMS *Cyclops* (1839), participated in the bombardment of Sevastopol of 17 October 1854.

33. Anon, *Sobor Svtatogo Ravnoaposolnogo kniazia Vladimira – usypalnitsa vydayushchikhsya admiralov Rossiiskogo Imperatorskogo Flota*, [Cathedral of Saint Equal to Apostles, Prince Vladimir – Burial Vault of Eminent Admirals of the Russian Imperial Navy] (Simferopol: Biznes-Inform, 2004), p. 120.

34. Tredea and Sozaev, pp. 296, 300–02, 304–05, 423–24.

35. Todleben, vol. i, pt 1, pp. 22–23.

36. This description owes much to Andrew Lambert, *Battleships in Transition* (London: Conway Maritime Press, 1984), pp. 37–38.

37. Ibid., p. 38.

38. There are contradictory views of the effectiveness of the Russian shell guns at the battle of Sinope. Whereas Fred Jane was of the opinion that the new weapon was important, Sondhaus, *Naval Warfare, 1815–1914* (p. 58), disagrees, observing that 'it took Nakhimov six hours to destroy the Turco-Egyptian squadron, despite the facts that he had six ships of the line with over 600 guns and that Oman Pasha's largest warships were frigates. Competent gunnery using solid shot alone would have achieved the same outcome'.

39. Reflecting the short lives of Black Sea vessels, the first ship of the line *Parizh*, which had featured at the sieges of Anapa and Varna in 1828, had been launched in 1826 and decommissioned in 1835. The second warship of that name, which Nicholas I inspected in 1852, was launched in 1849 and scuttled at Sevastopol in 1855.

40. This account of Nicholas I's inspection on board the ship of the line *Parizh* in 1852 draws from A. Zayonchkovskiy, *Nikolay I i Ego vremya* [Nicholas I and His Times] (Moscow: Olma-Press, 2000) vol. 2, pp. 371–74.

41. '*Zdraviya zhelayem*', literally, 'we wish you health', is a standard greeting in the Russian armed forces to this day from junior ranks to more senior ones.

42. Corresponding to the Third Class of the Order, roughly equivalent of a British Companion of Bath (CB).

43. Laurence Oliphant, *The Russian Shores of the Black Sea in the Autumn of 1852 with a Voyage down the Volga, and a Tour through the Country of the Don Cossacks* (Edinburgh and London: Blackwood, 1853), p. 258.

44. Ibid., pp. 259–60.

45. Ibid., p. 259.

46. Ibid., pp. 263–64.

47. In its worldwide corruptions perception index, Transparency International places (2015) the Russian Federation 119th out of 168 states listed; in comparison, the United Kingdom is measured as 10th and Ukraine is 130th. Data from http://www.transparency.org accessed on 2 November 2016.

48. Vaneev, *Spravochnik*, p. 16.

49. Ibid. p. 15.

50. 'By a Lady Resident Near the Alma' [catalogued by the British Library as Mrs Andrew Neilson], *The Crimea, Its Towns, Inhabitants and Customs* (London: Partridge, Oakey and Co., 1855), p. 76. There are indications that Mrs Neilson could have been the Edinburgh-born Anne Neilson, who married the Crimean Tatar, Katti Giray Sultan Kirim-Giray, who tried to convert the Muslim Tatars to Christianity. Although widowed in 1846, she remained in Crimea until her death in June 1855. Details of her husband's work are contained in Hakan Kirimli, 'Crimean Tatars, Nogays, and Scottish missionaries', *Cahiers du monde russe*, 45/1–2 (2004), pp. 61–07. URL: http:// monderusse.revues.org/2603 accessed on 23 September 2015.

51. Alexander William Kinglake, *The Invasion of the Crimea: its Origin, and an Account of its Progress down to the Death of Lord Raglan*, vol. iii (Edinburgh and London: Blackwood, 1868), p. 120.

52. Vaneev, *Spravochnik*, pp. 16–17.

53. Callwell, p. 65.

54. For details of this shipworm and the destructive effect it had on the scuttled warships of the Crimean War, see Chuck Veit, *The Yankee Expedition to Sebastopol: John Gowen and the Raising of the Russian Black Sea Fleet 1857–1862* (Lulu.com, 2014), pp. 95–96.

55. Maria Guthrie, p. 90.

56. A British visitor to Sevastopol in 1844 was informed that 'a cannon-ball, which would lodge in one side of an English ship, would go right through both sides of a Russian one'. Furthermore, 'for certain parts of all the ships', the Russians were 'obliged to import oak from England' as the 'Crimean oak' was 'very good, but not obtainable in large quantities'. (Seymour, p. 89.)

57. De Reuilly, p. 72.

58. Vaneev, *Spravochnik*, p. 14.

59. Tredea and Sozaev, pp. 39–40.

60. The Rev. Thos. Milner, *The Crimea, Its Ancient and Modern History; the Khans, the Sultans, and the Czars with Notices of its Scenery and Population* (London: Longman, Brown, Green and Longmans, 1855), p. 291.

61. Quoted by Chernousov, p. 47.

62. Research by Major Colin Robins and two Russian colleagues ('K/R') in *The War Correspondent*, vol. 28, no. 1 (April 2010), augmented by Michael Vanden Bosch (a descendant of John Upton) and Roger Bartlett, 'More Light on the Upton Family, Part Two, *The War Correspondent*, vol. 30, no. 1 (April 2012), p. 26, shows that Upton's replacement of Raucourt de Charleville was due to a combination of Admiral Greig's distrust of the French and other related objections by the governor-general of New Russia (which included Crimea), Count (later Prince and Field Marshal) Mikhail Vorontsov. Both men had been educated in Britain; the latter had been born in England when his father was serving as Russian ambassador to the Court of St James. Vorontsov's sister, Countess Catherine Semyonovna Vorontsova, married George Herbert, 11th Earl of Pembroke. Their son, Sidney Herbert, became the British Secretary at War in 1852. This largely administrative post was junior to the Secretary of State for War and the Colonies, which dealt with policy.

63. Milner, p. 297.

64. Seymour (p. 68) notes that Upton was the architect of Fort Nicholas on Sevastopol's southern shore.

65. The fate of John Upton's successors is described in Michael Vanden Bosch and Roger Bartlett, 'More Light on the Upton Family', Part Three, *The War Correspondent*, vol. 30, no. 3 (October 2012), pp. 10–19.

66. If Jesse was a British spy, as might be supposed, there is little evidence that the Allies made much use of his information when planning their expedition to Crimea in the summer of 1854.

67. Captain [William] Jesse, *Notes of a Half-Pay in Search of Health: or Russia, Circassia and the Crimea in 1839–40* (London: James Madden, 1841), p. 135. Jesse recycled much of this work in a later publication, *Russia and the War* (London: Longman, Brown, Green and Longmans, 1854), designed, no doubt, to cash in on the topicality of Crimea and Sevastopol.

68. Ibid., p. 136.

69. Ibid.

70. Charles Henry Scott, *The Baltic, the Black Sea and the Crimea: Comprising Travels in Russia, a Voyage down the Volga to Astrakhan, and a Tour through Krim Tartary* (London: Bentley, 1854), p. 263.

71. Seymour, p. 69.

72. Jesse, *Notes of a Half-Pay*, pp. 136–37.

73. Milner, p. 297.

74. Michael Vanden Bosch and Roger Bartlett, 'More Light on the Upton Family, *The War Correspondent*, vol. 30, no. 1 (April 2012), p. 27.

75. Jesse, *Notes of a Half-Pay*, pp. 136–37.

76. Of the six aqueducts built at Chorgun, Inkerman, St George's Ravine, Careening Bay, Ushakov Ravine and Apollo Ravine, the impressive stone arches of the last (the *Apollonova Balka*) can be seen today in the Nakhimov district of eastern Sevastopol.

77. Milner, p. 296.

78. Ibid.

79. Jesse, *Notes of a Half-Pay*, p. 139.

80. A known weakness in Upton's executed works for the dry docks and canal in comparison with the original French design was the lack of a guaranteed supply of water.

81. Milner, p. 297.

82. Oliphant, p. 265.

83. Chernousov, pp. 91–92.

84. Jesse, *Notes of a Half-Pay*, p. 141.

85. Chernousov, pp. 59–60.

86. According to James Wyld's 1854 map of the town and harbour of Sevastopol, the lower (elevation, 413ft or 126m above sea level) 'Inkerman West' light could be seen at 28 miles (45km) out to sea, while the upper (elevation 613½ft or 187m) 'Inkerman East' light was visible at 33 miles (53km). Both Inkerman lighthouses have been closely guarded military 'objects' since their construction. The Russian Navy never relinquished control of them following the break-up of the Soviet Union, causing from time to time serious diplomatic incidents with Ukraine until the Russian annexation of Crimea in March 2014.

87. Quoted by Chernousov, p. 57.

88. Being medals of the Second Class, these were hung on neck ribbons. Details from Michael Vanden Bosch and Roger Bartlett, 'More Light on the Upton Family', *The War Correspondent*, vol. 30, no. 1 (April 2012), p. 27.

89. Milner, p. 293. The French revolution that overthrew Charles X was in fact in 1830, not 1831 as Milner states.

90. For details of the Ochakov crisis, see Knight, pp. 17–19.

91. Quoted by Kinglake, vol. ii (London and Edinburgh: Blackwood, 1863), p. 69.

92. Quoted by Chernousov, p. 90.

93. Referred to by Kinglake, vol. iii, pp. 52–53, together with a facsimile of the sketch concerned facing p. 54.

94. Vernon John Puryear, *International Economics and Diplomacy in the Near East: A Study of British Commercial Policy in the Levant, 1834–1853* (Stanford: Stanford University Press, 1935), p. 23.

95. Lord de Ros, *Journal of a Tour in the Principalities, Crimea and Countries Adjacent to the Black Sea in the Years 1835–36* (London: Parker and Son, 1855), p. 112.

96. For further details, see Constantin Ardeleanu, 'A British Military Mission to the Near East, Russia and the Danubian Principalities (1835–1836)', *Anuarul Institutului de Istorie „A. D. Xenopol"*, t. XLVIII, 2011, pp. 101–16.

97. Seymour (p. 71) claims: 'after the discussions occasioned by the capture of the Vixen in 1837 [sic], when war was supposed imminent between Russia and England, the Cabinet of St Petersburg grew frightened at the possibility of the English in case of war making a descent upon some point of the Heracleotic Chersonese [the Chersonese peninsula], and defences were then ordered to be constructed on the land side of Sevastopol'.

98. Chernousov, p. 94.

99. Callwell, p. 99.

100. Jesse, *Notes of a Half-Pay*, p. 148.

101. Jesse, *Russia and the War*, p. 141.

102. De Reuilly, p. 71.

103. Todleben, vol i, pt 1, p. 89.

104. Ibid., p. 102.

105. Ibid., p. 111.

106. Captain R. Hodasevich, *A Voice from within the Walls of Sebastopol: a Narrative of the Campaign in the Crimea, and of the Events of the Siege* (London: John Murray, 1856), pp. 9–10.

107. Letter of April 25, 1856. Demetrius C. Boulger (ed.), *General Gordon's Letters from the Crimea, the Danube, and Armenia* (London: Chapman and Hall, 1884), p. 95. Hereafter referred to as the Gordon Letters.

108. De Ros, pp. 112–13.

109. Orlando Figes, *Crimea*, fn on pp. 222–23, claims that Nicholas I 'had dismissed the danger of an attack by the Turks or the Western Powers in the Black Sea. He had overlooked the huge significance of steamships, which made it possible to carry large armies by sea.' However, this assertion ignores the visits of Nicholas I to Sevastopol in 1837, 1845 and 1852 and the reinforcement of the city's shore defences prior to the Crimean War, and not least before the Allied invasion in September 1854. That Nicholas I travelled on the steam paddle-frigate, the *Vladimir*, when making his inspection of the Black Sea Fleet in the autumn of 1852, as narrated in this chapter, hardly suggests that Russian Emperor was entirely ignorant of steam power. What he missed was its strategic potential – as Figes correctly infers.

110. G. I. Vaneev, I. P. Kondranov, M. A. Korotkov and N. N. Fomina, *Sevastopolyu 200 let: 1783–1983. Sbornik dokumentov i materyalov.* [Sevastopol 200 Years: 1783–1983. A Collection of Documents and Materials] (Kiev: Naukova Dumka, 1983). Document 17. 'From the Report of the Military Inspector to Nicholas I concerning the results of the inspection of Sevastopol garrison artillery.'

111. Todleben, vol. i, pt 1, pp. 108 and 110.

112. Ibid., p. 113. The present author has not been able to explain the difference between that given by Todleben here and previously at p. 22.

113. Rather confusingly, Todleben lists the total numbers of guns of the Constantine Battery rising from 94 in September 1853 to 97 in May 1854. There must have been undisclosed losses as well as gains.

114. Vaneev, *Spravochnik*, p. 15.

115. Ibid., p. 21.

116. Seymour, Appendix E, 'Commerce of Ports of Crimea, 1852' (pp. 350–54), gives a detailed account of coasting and international trade during this period.

117. The account is drawn principally from Vaneev, *Spravochnik*, pp. 18–19.

118. Vaneev et al, *Sevastopol 200 Years*, Document 11, p. 35.

119. Neilson, p. 73.

120. Ibid.

121. Ibid., pp. 74–75.

122. Ibid., p. 76.

123. Ibid., pp. 74–75.

124. By way of comparison, it took nearly ten years to construct the ring of five forts on Portsdown Hill to defend Portsmouth, Britain's major naval base on the southern English coast, from landward attack. This vast undertaking was executed in response to the 1859 Royal Commission that reported on a perceived (and totally exaggerated, it turned out) threat of French invasion. Fort Nelson, the best preserved, was built between 1861 and 1870 at a cost of £78,649 – the 'economic cost' in 2012 would have been £142.6 million, according to Lawrence H. Officer and Samuel H. Williamson, "Five Ways to Compute the Relative Value of a UK Pound Amount, 1270 to Present", Measuring Worth, 2014, derived from: www.measuringworth.com/ukcompare/ accessed on 5 March 2014.

125. Quoted by John S. Curtiss, *Russia's Crimean War* (Durham, NC. Duke University Press, 1979), p. 304.

Chapter 4: The Eastern War

1. Lieutenant Colonel The Hon. George Wrottesley (ed.), *Life and Correspondence of Field Marshal Sir John Burgoyne*, vol. ii (London: Bentley & Son, 1873), p. 40.

2. In Waterloo Place, there are two other monuments with a Crimean War connection: the memorials to Lord Clyde (Sir Colin Campbell) and to Field Marshal Sir John Fox Burgoyne.

3. The largest, and arguably most impressive, monument to the Crimean War in the United Kingdom is the memorial arch erected by the Royal Engineers in Brompton Barracks, Chatham.

4. Jeremy Paxman, *The English: A Portrait of a People* (London: Penguin, 1999), p. 87, is only half right when he states 'It is not the victories at the Alma or Sebastopol that are recalled from the Crimean War, but the doomed charge of the Light Brigade'. Inkerman was the second victory after Alma; Sevastopol was more a French success than a British one.

5. An Internet search reveals the following in British towns: 'Alma' – nine avenues, 77 roads and 99 streets; 'Balaclava' – 17 roads and four streets; 'Inkerman' – 12 roads and 17 streets; 'Sebastopol/Sevastopol' – only three roads or streets. Data from www.streetmap.co.uk accessed on 9 September 2015.

6. Some maritime-minded authors disdain the use of the term 'Crimean War', pointing out (rightly) the much wider extent of the conflict, which, apart from the Black Sea theatre of operations, also took place in the Baltic and in the Far East. At the time, it was known in Britain as the 'Eastern War' or the 'War with Russia'; the term 'Crimean War' became more common by the close of the nineteenth century. See, by way of example, Peter Hore, *The World Encyclopedia of Battleships* (London: Hermes House, 2005), who states (p. 10): 'The Crimean War was in fact a campaign and part of a larger war, more accurately known as the Russian War 1854–56, which raged on a global scale, and heavily depended upon sea power ...'. Quite so, but the Russians also refer to the Crimean War, and this term has been the commonly accepted one since the end of the nineteenth century despite its inaccuracy. The naval actions in the Far East were minor, and little was accomplished in the Baltic, despite the considerable effort and expense.

7. The figure of 59 is taken from the regiments listed by C. B. Norman, *Battle Honours of the British Army* (Uckfield: Naval & Military Press, 2006) [Originally published in London in 1911], p. 306. 'Sebastopol', was one of five possible clasps to the Crimea Medal; the others were: Alma, Balaklava, Inkerman and Azoff – only members of the Royal Navy and Royal Marines were entitled to the latter.

8. Robert Rogers and Rhodri Walters, *How Parliament Works* (6th ed.) (Harlow: Pearson Education, 2006), pp. 345–46.

9. http://hansard.millbanksystems.com/commons/1855/jan/26/army-crimea#S3V0136P0_18550126_HOC_6 accessed on 15 December 2014.

10. This sacrificial aspect reinforces the religious importance of Sevastopol laid out in Chapter 1. In his annual speech to the Federal Assembly in Moscow on 4 December 2014, President Putin declared: 'All of this allows us to say that Crimea, the ancient Korsun or Chersonesus, and Sevastopol have invaluable civilisational and even sacral importance for Russia, like the Temple Mount in Jerusalem for the followers of Islam and Judaism.' From http://en.kremlin.ru/events/president/news/47173 – accessed 20 August 2015.

11. The phrase belongs to Cecil Woodham-Smith, *The Reason Why* (London: Constable, 1953).

12. This section of the chapter draws from Clive Ponting, *The Crimean War: The Truth Behind the Myth* (London: Pimlico, 2005) and Andrew Lambert, *The Crimean War: British Grand Strategy against Russia, 1853–56* (2nd ed.) (Farnham: Ashgate, 2011).

13. A detailed description of the 'Eastern Question' and the long, twisting road to the Crimean War is beyond the scope of this study. It is well covered in Chapters 1–3 of Curtiss, *Russia's Crimean War*; and, more recently, by Orlando Figes, *Crimea*, Chapters 1–4. See also Winfried Baumgart, *The Crimean War 1853–1856* (London: Oxford University Press, 1999) and David M. Goldfrank, *The Origins of the Crimean War* (New York: Longman, 1994).

14. In addition to Curtiss and Figes, see also Ann Pottinger Saab, *The Origins of the Crimean Alliance* (Charlottesville: University Press of Virginia, 1977).

15. Saab, p. 61.

16. Ponting, p. 29.

17. Memorandum by Graham, 22 January 1854, Graham Papers. Quoted by Hew Strachan, 'Soldiers, Strategy and Sebastopol', *The Historical Journal*, vol. 21, no. 2 (June, 1978), pp. 311–12.

18. Quoted by Lambert, *The Crimean War*, p. 114.

19. Wrottesley, p. 40.

20. Quoted by Strachan, 'Soldiers, Strategy and Sebastopol', p. 315.

21. Wrottesley, p. 56. Tylden died of cholera shortly after the Alma. Tragically, his son, Richard, also a Royal Engineer, died of his wounds and illness following distinguished service during the siege of Sevastopol.

22. See, for example, Lambert, *The Crimean War*, p. 146 and p. 153.

23. A parallel may be drawn with the First World War: many popular accounts of the battle of the Somme (July–November 1916), for example, confine the very significant contribution of the French to a paragraph or a page or two.

24. Apart from the many first-hand accounts such as Edward Hamley, *The Story of the Campaign of Sebastopol* (Edinburgh: Blackwood, 1855) and the semi-official history by Kinglake, a predominantly British view is given in a host of later works. These include (only a small selection can be given here): C. E. Vulliamy, *Crimea: The Campaign of 1854–56* (London: Jonathan Cape, 1939); Cecil Woodham-Smith, *The Reason Why: The Story of the Fatal Charge of the Light Brigade* (London: Penguin, 2000) [originally published in 1953]; W. Baring Pemberton, *Battles of the Crimean War* (London: Batsford, 1962); John Sweetman, *The Crimean War 1854–1856* (Oxford: Osprey, 2001); Alastair Massie, *The National Army Museum Book of the Crimean War* (London: Sidgwick & Jackson, 2004) [republished by Pan, 2005]; D. S. Richards, *Conflict in the Crimea: British Redcoats on the Soil of Russia* (Barnsley: Pen & Sword, 2006). Further comprehensive histories are provided by Clive Ponting: *The Crimean War: The Truth Behind the Myth* (London: Chatto & Windus, 2004; Pimlico, 2005); Trevor Royle, *Crimea: The Great Crimean War 1854–1856* (London: Little, Brown & Company, 1999; Abacus 2000). Two notable exceptions in giving a Russian perspective are: John Shelton Curtiss, *Russia's Crimean War* (Durham, NC: Duke University Press, 1979) and Orlando Figes, *Crimea: The Last Crusade* (London: Allen Lane, 2010). The final two chapters of John Shelton Curtiss's earlier work, *The Russian Army Under Nicholas I, 1825–1855* (Durham, NC: Duke University Press) are also useful. The most comprehensive Russian contemporary source, available in English, is Robert Adolf Hodasevich [Chodasiewicz], *A Voice from within the Walls of Sevastopol: a Narrative of the Campaign in the Crimea, and of the Events of the Siege* (London: John Murray, 1856), which is extensively quoted in this chapter, along with other Russian eyewitness accounts collated in Albert Seaton, *The Crimean War: A Russian Chronicle* (London: Batsford, 1977). The Crimean military author, Sergey Chennyk, has written a series of detailed volumes about the Crimean War. The present author is grateful to him for his kind permission to quote extensively from his work.

25. Quoted in the monograph *Thinking Strategically*, 3rd ed. (London: Royal College of Defence Studies, October 2010), edited by the present author.

26. The description of the 'Russian Clausewitz' is borrowed from Colin S. Gray, *The Future of Strategy* (Cambridge: Polity Press, 2015). Gray dedicates his book to the Russian, noting (p. 122) that 'in some parts', A. A. Svechin's *Strategy*, 2nd ed. (1927), is 'worthy of comparison with Clausewitz' *On War*'.

27. Quoted in David M. Glantz, *Soviet Military Operational Art: In Pursuit of the Deep Battle* (London: Routledge, 1991), p. 23. In *Strategy* [Strategiya] Svechin explores the relationship between the three levels of war (tactical, operational and strategic). He is generally credited with coining the term 'operational art'.

28. Quoted by Vulliamy, p. 191.

29. Ibid., p. 95.

30. Curtiss, *Russia's Crimean War* (p. 300), states that Menshikov requested the release of the '11th' Infantry Division, which was available for redeployment following the Russian evacuation of the Danubian Principalities. Hodasevich (p. 28), however, records the arrival of the 16th Division from Odessa on 30 August 1854.

31. Curtiss, *Russia's Crimean War*, p. 303.

32. The best English-language monograph on the battle is Ian Fletcher and Natalia Ishchenko, *The Battle of the Alma 1854: First Blood to the Allies in the Crimea* (Barnsley: Pen & Sword Military, 2008). The most detailed modern Russian account is Sergey Chennyk, *Alma* (Sevastopol: Gala, 2011).

33. The term 'space' here means the ground or terrain to be marched across, defended or attacked. In a military estimate of the situation, the factors to be considered include: terrain, enemy, friendly forces, time and space, surprise and security, administration/logistics and command.

34. Sweetman, *The Crimean* War, p. 37.

35. Ibid., p.39. Other sources indicate two naval battalions, which would mean a total of 43 infantry or equivalent battalions.

36. Many British descriptions of the battlefield exaggerate the height of the sea cliffs, the southern banks of the Alma, and the elevations of the ridges to the south of the river. A close inspection of the ground, armed with a modern topographic map, reveals that claims for the high ground to reach 150m in elevation, and the sea cliffs to be 105m high (c.f. Sweetman, *The Crimean War*, p. 37, an error replicated in several popular websites) are inaccurate. These sources are probably based on earlier, unverified, accounts of the battle without the benefit of any detailed mapping. The present author suspects that Lieutenant General Sir John Burgoyne's authoritative – but inaccurate – description of the Russian position has heavily influenced many writers and corrupted understanding of the terrain. Edward Hamley gives the best contemporary British description of the ground.

37. See Hamley, p. 36, for an alternative description of the terrain, noting that he does not use 'Telegraph Height'. Neither does he refer to 'Kourgane Hill', which appears to be a piece of tautology as the Russian word *kurgan*, a burial mound, is also used for a tumulus or small hill, as in the Malakhov Kurgan (Hill) at Sevastopol. Both Telegraph Height and Kourgane Hill were Allied rather than Russian names.

38. Sweetman, *The Crimean War*, p. 40.

39. Descriptions of the number of Russian guns positioned in these redoubts vary. Hamley (p. 36), for example, indicates that the Great Redoubt (which he describes as an 'epaulment') contained an 18-gun battery.

40. Forces deployed 'in echelon', whether in attack or defence, are not 'true' reserves. They form an integral part of a defensive or offensive scheme of manoeuvre and, as such, are given a specific task such as to support the attack or defence in a specified zone or sector respectively. 'True' reserves are normally allocated a *number* of potential tasks, the choice as to which is to be executed remaining dependent on the situation and the relevant commander's intentions and resulting decisions in battle.

41. In Russian, the titles of the regiments are adjectival such as *Volynskii*. Following earlier traditions of transliteration, these have been converted into proper nouns such as Volyn.

42. The track was probably regarded as immaterial by Russian officers used to the parade-ground manoeuvre of large bodies of men. In contrast, their French counterparts, particularly those who had experienced the irregular warfare of Algeria, sensed how to exploit this sort of difficult, and hence unexpected, avenue of approach. Yet Russia had been at war for many years in the Caucasus, and pertinent lessons from this theatre of war might have been applied wisely in Crimea.

43. Dr Cabrol, *Le Marechal de Saint Arnaud en Crimée* [Marshal de Saint Arnaud in Crimea] (Paris: Stock et Tresse et Co., 1895), p. 272. Translation kindly provided by Anthony Dawson.

44. Cabrol, p. 273.

45. Ibid., p. 280.

46. Wrottesley, p. 88.

47. From a letter to his mother of 22 September 1854 from a 'Bivouac Nr Alma'. Lieutenant Colonel James Brodie Patullo, ed. A. G. Shirreff, *Crimean Letters* [From the family archive of General Sir Richard Shirreff KCB CBE], p. 55. Hereafter referred to as the Pattullo Letters.

48. British military nomenclature departed from continental practice in that infantry 'regiments' were not a tactical formation of three or four battalions. Numbered regiments were battalions. Later (as part of the Cardwell reforms) regiments were given county names, and usually comprised two battalions, one for duty abroad and the other for home service and depot functions.

49. For example, see Saul David, p. 205: the facing map on p. 204 is very inaccurate.

50. Information from Anthony Dawson.

51. Hodasevich, pp. 66–67.

52. The British–Russian War of 1807–12 consisted of a number of skirmishes at sea.

53. The British Army first employed the rifled musket using the Minié ball (0.702-inch calibre), issued in 1851, during the Eighth Xhosa (Kaffir) War of 1852–53 in South Africa. It is believed that British troops at the Alma used this early model rather than the better-engineered and smaller calibre (0.577-inch) Enfield 1853 pattern rifle, which was being brought into service in 1854–55. Not all divisions in Crimea were initially equipped with rifled muskets: the 4th Division only received its Enfields in early 1855, having fought at the battle of Inkerman (5 November 1855) with the 1842 Pattern smooth-bore musket fitted with a percussion cap firing system. For further details of the Minié rifle (1851) and its successor, the Enfield of 1853, see Peter Smithurst, *The Pattern 1853 Enfield Rifle* (Oxford: Osprey, 2011).

54. A more detailed account of Codrington's brigade's failed attempt to capture the Great Redoubt and the Russians' robust response is given by Figes, Crimea, pp. 212–13.

55. Hamley, p. 29.

56. Quoted by Richards, pp. 28–29.

57. Figes, *Crimea*, pp. 214–17.

58. Hamley, p. 33.

59. Hodasevich, p. 72.

60. Ibid., p. 86.

61. Chennyk, *Alma*, p. 40.

62. Ibid., p. 41.

63. Hodasevich, p. 72.

64. Ibid., p. 86.

65. Chennyk, *Alma*, p, 41.

66. Russell/Todleben, pp. 52–53.

67. Pattullo Letters, 22 September 1854, p. 54.

68. Hodasevich (p. 85) gives Russian casualties as '1762 killed, 2315 wounded, and 405 "contused" [bruised or injured], making a total of 4482 *hors de combat*'.

69. Hodasevich, pp. 96–97.

70. This account draws on that given by Seaton, pp. 111–12, which, it must be stressed, diverges strongly from Hodasevich, who claims that it was Kornilov's original idea to sink the ships.

71. Russell/Todleben, p. 80.

72. Figures from Seaton, p. 112.

73. Quoted by Seaton, p. 113.

74. Hodasevich, p. 98.

75. Seaton, p. 113.

76. Hodasevich, p. 108.

77. Ibid., p. 115.

78. Seaton, p. 115.

Chapter 5: The First Defence of Sevastopol

1. Called to give evidence on 15 May 1855 to the Select Committee on the [British] Army before Sebastopol, the former Prime Minister, the Earl of Aberdeen, was asked: 'When the army landed in the Crimea, the government were under the impression, were they not, that Sebastopol would fall almost immediately by a *coup de main*?' His answer was unequivocal: 'That was the general belief'. [Parliamentary Papers, House of Commons], *Reports from Committees: Army Before Sebastopol*, Session 12 December – 14 August 1855, vol. IX, *Minutes of Evidence*, p. 290.

2. This subject is covered extensively in Andrew Lambert, *The Crimean War*, Chapter 9 – 'The Grand Raid', and particularly at pp. 145–46 and 151–54.

3. Ibid., p. 145.

4. Cecil Woodham-Smith, *The Reason Why*, p. 211.

5. Kinglake, vol. iii, pp. 49–50.

6. Ibid., pp. 50–52.

7. Ibid., pp. 55–56.

8. The intelligence about the state of Sevastopol's defences available to the Allies prior to the landing in Crimea was sketchy, disputed and open to contradiction. When Admiral Dundas gave evidence to the parliamentary Select Committee on 10 May 1855 it transpired that a certain Mr Yeames (most probably the same British consul in Odessa, whom Lieutenant Colonel de Ros had met in 1835) had written on 17 March 1854 to Lord Stratford de Redcliffe (the British ambassador in Constantinople) to the effect that 'French and English merchants were to quit' Sevastopol on 'March the 17th, 1854' and that it had been 'confirmed ... that works have been constructed at Sebastopol for defence on its land side'. Lord Stratford had communicated this information to Admiral Dundas in writing on 23 March 1854. It is not clear whether this intelligence was passed back to London either by Stratford or Dundas. (*Minutes of Evidence*, p. 208.) Dundas, however, went on to state, quoting from a private letter dated 10 May 1854 he had sent to Lord Raglan: 'Sebastopol is a second Gibraltar. We see many new works erecting, and from prisoners learn that the land side is equally being strengthened. An encampment is seen, of large size, close to the south of the town; and we are told that 120,000 men are in the Crim ea, 30,000 of whom are in Sebastopol'. (*Minutes of Evidence*, p. 211.) This evidence was completely at variance with Burgoyne's testimony of 1 May 1855. He had told the Committee when asked 'At that time, as I understand you, there was no knowledge whatever, on the part of any authorities with the British army, of the strength either of the Russian forces or of the fortress of Sebastopol?', he replied: 'I believe there was not; I had no knowledge of it.' (*Minutes of Evidence*, p. 339.)

9. In giving evidence to the Select Committee on 15 May 1855, Aberdeen was not of this opinion. When asked 'Did not the circumstance of the fortress being found to be much stronger than anticipated, and the fact that our army being compelled to lay a regular siege to it, alter the complexion of the expedition to the Crimea?', he replied curtly: 'No, I do not think that in the least.' (*Minutes of Evidence, p. 291.*)

10. The present author, a former Royal Engineer officer, although disagreeing with Burgoyne's fallacious assessment of the situation and associated arguments for the flank march, is not

entirely unsympathetic to him. Kinglake's criticism was perhaps underpinned by a prejudice against a figure who nowadays might be described as a typically clever but over-opinionated engineer.

11. Reproduced as Appendix No. 10 in Captain H. C. Elphinstone RE, *Journal of the Operations Conducted by the Corps of Royal Engineers*, Part I, *From the Invasion of the Crimea to the close of the Winter Campaign 1854–55*. (London: Eyre and Spottiswoode, 1859), pp. 107–08. Hereafter cited as Elphinstone.

12. Ibid., p. 108.

13. Major-General Whitworth Porter, *History of the Corps of Royal Engineers*, vol. i (Chatham: Institution of Royal Engineers, 1889; reprinted in 1977), pp. 421–22: 'On July 19th [1854], the commanding officers of Artillery and Engineers had been directed "To prepare for an operation of great importance in which a siege equipment will be required"; ... large parties were employed making gabions [baskets of stone] and fascines.'

14. Wrottesley, p. 69.

15. Ibid., p. 72. Burgoyne meant here the Star or North Fort rather than Fort Constantine. Kinglake, vol. iii, p. 67 notes: 'Fort Constantine was one of the sea-forts, but at this period of the invasion the name was often applied by mistake to the Star Fort.'

16. Porter, p. 426.

17. Ibid.

18. According to Wrottesley (p. 93, fn 2), based on information provided by Burgoyne, 'all the French staff officers present, including Trochu and General Bizot of the Engineers, strenuously opposed the project [the flank march] at this time, and brought forward one trivial objection after another, until Marshal St Arnaud broke up the conference by saying that he thought General Burgoyne was right; that difficulties which appeared great at a distance often disappeared on a nearer approach'.

19. Kinglake, vol. iii, p. 72.

20. Porter, p. 426.

21. The present author adopted this general definition when editing *Thinking Strategically*, a guide to strategy-making produced by the Royal College of Defence Studies, London, in 2010. For a detailed discussion on the definitions of strategy, see Colin S. Gray, *Modern Strategy* (Oxford: Oxford University Press, 1999), pp. 17–23. Gray (p. 17) describes strategy as the 'bridge that relates military power to political purpose; it is neither military power *per se* nor political purpose. By strategy I mean *the use that is made of force and the threat of force for the ends of policy*'. [Emphasis as in original.]

22. Pattullo Letters, 28 September 1854, p. 58.

23. Elphinstone, p. 12.

24. Ibid., p. 13.

25. Ibid.

26. Ibid., p. 14.

27. Porter, in his *History of the Corps of Royal Engineers* (p. 428), took the opposite view, loyally supporting Burgoyne: 'In after days, the Russians were fond of pointing out that [a *coup de main*] could and should have been [attempted]. No one, however, who studied the question without bias could form such an opinion. The hazard of a failure was extreme, and must have involved the sacrifice of the entire allied army, causing the ignominious termination of the enterprise.'

28. Wrottesley, p. 95.

29. Yu. G. Malis (ed.), *Sevastopol'skiye Pis'ma N. I. Pirogova 1854–1855* [Sevastopol Letters of N. I. Pirogov, 1854–1855] (St Petersburg: Merkushev, 1907; reprinted in 2010), p. 78. Hereafter referred to as the Pirogov Letters.

30. General Sir Howard Douglas, *Remarks on the Naval Operations in the Black Sea and the Siege of Sevastopol*, 2nd ed. (London: John Murray, 1855), p. 11. Douglas gave a light update of his

analysis of the siege of Sevastopol in Appendix C to the fifth edition of his main work, *A Treatise of Naval Gunnery* (London: John Murray, 1860).

31. Lambert, *The Crimean War*, p. 153.

32. Todleben, vol. i, pt 1, p. 257.

33. Quoted in Russell/Todleben, pp. 114–15, translated from Todleben, vol. i, pt 1, p. 280.

34. Indirectly quoted in Russell/Todleben, p. 110, based on Todleben, vol. i, pt 1, p. 259.

35. Captain W. Edmund M. Reilly, CB, *An Account of Artillery Operations conducted by the Royal Artillery and Royal Naval Brigade before Sebastopol in 1854 and 1855* (London: Eyre and Spottiswoode, 1859), p. 1.

36. It would appear that Peter Duckers, *The Crimean War at Sea: Naval Campaigns Against Russia, 1854–6* (Barnsley: Pen & Sword Maritime, 2011), p. 61, has got the British Left and Right Attacks mixed up.

37. Strictly speaking, the transliteration of the Russian should be Kadykoy, but the more usual spelling of Kadikoi in English-language texts is used in this volume. No village of that name survives: the former settlement (renamed Kadykovka)has long since been absorbed into Balaklava.

38. Reilly, p. 4.

39. Members of the Royal Artillery were quick to attest to this deficiency. Colonel E. C. Warde, Royal Horse Artillery, who commanded the siege train for a period of six months, for example, declared: 'No Siege Train ought ever, in my opinion, to leave this country during a time of war without full and adequate means of transport being sent out with it ... I have come to this conclusion in consequence of the great difficulties which occurred during operations before Sebastopol for want of this means of transport, from the utter ruin, and I may almost add annihilation, of our Field Artillery, owing to their being compelled to act as transport for the heavy siege *matériel* during inclement weather ...' (Reilly, p. 233).

40. Since the early 1990s, various impoverished British Army contingents have resorted to this dubious but pragmatic practice in various operations in the Balkans, Iraq and Afghanistan. Until governments decide to resource the Army and its supply chain adequately, this pattern of activity is likely to continue.

41. Reilly, pp. 3–4.

42. Duckers, p. 61.

43. Todleben, vol. i, pt 1, p. 264.

44. Pattullo Letters, 7 October 1854, p. 61.

45. Details of Russian and Allied artillery holdings at the commencement of the first bombardment on 17 October 1854 are taken from Todleben, vol. i, pt 1, pp. 313–15; Reilly, pp. 7–8; and Lieutenant-Colonel C. H. Owen, RA, *The Principles and Practice of Modern Artillery*, 2nd ed. (London: John Murray, 1873), p. 497.

46. The armament of the British batteries, for example, had increased to 207 guns and mortars by the final period of the siege in early September 1855. The French fielded no fewer than 605 in total during the campaign. (Statistics from Reilly, pp. 205 and 244).

47. Todleben, vol. i, pt 1, pp. 252, 270 and 274.

48. Wrottesley, pp. 98–99.

49. Ibid., p. 100.

50. The second siege of Badajoz in 1811; the sieges of Ciudad Rodrigo and Burgos in 1812; and the siege of San Sebastián in 1813.

51. Pattullo Letters, 7 October 1854, p. 61.

52. Russell/Todleben, p. 123.

53. Ibid., p. 129.

54. Reilly, pp. 8–9.

55. Ibid., p. 9.

56. Ibid.

57. Lambert, *Battleships in Transition*, p. 46.

58. The Royal Navy had fired such a lucky shot during the bombardment of Acre on 3 November 1840, which not only resulted in a massive explosion within the fortress magazine, causing many casualties, but also led to the almost immediate surrender of the Egyptian garrison. The Allied attackers and Russian defenders of Sevastopol, however, were made of stronger stuff. For a description of the action at Acre, see Andrew Lambert, *Admirals: The Naval Commanders who Made Britain Great* (London: Faber and Faber, 2008), pp. 248–49.

59. Lambert, *Battleships in Transition*, p. 46.

60. Duckers, p. 66.

61. Douglas, *Remarks*, pp. 19–24; Duckers, pp. 66–67; Lambert, *Battleships in Transition*, pp. 46–47; Todleben, vol. i, pt 2, pp. 331–36.

62. Todleben, vol. i, pt 2, p. 336.

63. Gordon Letters, April 25, 1856, p. 95.

64. Reilly, p. 12.

65. Russell/Todleben, pp. 128–29.

66. Ibid., pp. 129–30.

67. Quoted by Seaton, p. 137.

68. Lambert, *The Crimean War*, pp. 160–65.

69. Reilly, p. 13.

70. Pattullo Letters, 18 and 22 October 1854, p. 64.

71. Reilly, p. 17.

72. Ibid., p. 20.

73. Baring Pemberton, p. 121.

74. Feature films entitled 'The Charge of the Light Brigade' were made in 1936 and 1968. The former, a Hollywood production of Warner Brothers, starring Errol Flynn and Olivia de Havilland, had only a loose connection to history. The British production of 1968, starring Trevor Howard, Vanessa Redgrave, John Gielgud and Harry Andrews, was more authentic but still took great liberties with the true course of the battle of Balaklava, such as omitting the defence of the 93rd Highlanders and the charge of the Heavy Brigade.

75. Alfred Tennyson, 'The Charge of the Light Brigade', first published in *The Examiner*, 9 December 1854. Lines quoted in this book are taken from the *Poems of Tennyson* (Oxford: Oxford University Press, 1926), pp. 420–421.

76. Woodham-Smith, *The Reason Why*, p. 211.

77. Curtiss, *Russia's Crimean War*, p. 320. Seaton (p. 134) states that on 19 October 1854, 14,000 rounds had been fired; thereafter the daily expenditure rate 'varied from 10,000 to 12,000 shot and shell'.

78. Hodasevich, p. 163.

79. Ibid., pp. 167 and 182.

80. This description of Liprandi's initial and grander plan of attack, which was not executed, is based on Sergey Chennyk, *Ot Balaklavy k Inkermanu* [From Balaklava to Inkerman] (Simferopol: Gala, 2014), pp. 44–45.

81. Curtiss, *Russia's Crimean War*, p. 320.

82. Ibid., p. 321.

83. Quoted by Chennyk, *Ot Balaklavy k Inkermanu*, p. 51.

84. Curtiss, *Russia's Crimean War*, p. 321.

85. The numbers of cavalry squadrons/*sotni* and the distribution of guns within the total of 78 varies according to differing accounts. Most reliable, with some minor exceptions, is John Sweetman,

Balaklava 1854 (London: Osprey, 1990), augmented by Sergey Chennyk, *Ot Balaklavy k Inkermanu*.

86. Woodham-Smith, *The Reason Why*, p. 208.

87. A point made well by Baring Pemberton, p. 77.

88. Chennyk, *Ot Balaklavy k Inkermanu*, p. 96.

89. This description of the Russian deployment is taken primarily from the 'Report of Lieutenant General Liprandi, Commander of the Twelfth Division of Infantry, to Aide-de-Camp General Prince Menshikov', dated 14 October 1854 [OS] [No. 3076]. The translation used is from Tyrell, *History of the War with Russia*, augmented by Mark Conrad at http://www. marksrussianmilitaryhistory.info/Liprandi.htm accessed on 27 October 2016. Further information from Chennyk, *Ot Balaklavy k Inkermanu*, pp. 95–100.

90. Quoted by Seaton/Conrad. Ivan Ivanovich Ryzhov, 'O srazhenii pod Balaklave; Zapiska General-Leitenanta Iv. Iv. Ryzhova' [On the Battle of Balaklava; Notes of Lieutenant General Iv. Iv. Ryzhov], *Russkii Vestnik*, April 1870, Vol. 86, pp. 463–69. This translation is by Mark Conrad at http://www.marksrussianmilitaryhistory.info/Ryzhov.htm accessed on 23 December 2014.

91. Quoted by Seaton/Conrad. Stefan Kozhukhov, 'Iz Krymskikh Vospominanii o Polednei Voine' [Crimean Memoirs of the Last War], *Russkii Arkhiv*, 1869, vol. 7, pp. 381–84. This translation is by Mark Conrad from http://marksrussianmilitaryhistory.info/Kozhukhov.htm accessed on 23 December 2014.

92. Quoted by Seaton/Conrad. Lieutenant Koribut-Kubitovich, 'Vospominaniya o Balaklavskom dele 13-go Oktyabrya 1854 goda' [Recollections of the Balaklava Affair of 13 October, 1854], *Voennyi Sbornik*, 1859, No. 2. This translation is by Mark Conrad from http:// marksrussianmilitaryhistory.info/Kubitovich.htm accessed on 27 October 2016.

93. This author follows Sweetman, *Balaklava 1854*, in his listing of four retrospective phases of the battle: (1) 'Fall of the Redoubts'; (2) the 'Thin Red Line'; (3) the 'Charge of the Heavy Brigade'; (4) the 'Charge of the Light Brigade'; but adds (5) the relief attack by the Chasseurs d'Afrique. These five engagements are depicted at Map 7 of this book.

94. Ryzhov, 'On the Battle of Balaklava'.

95. Ibid.

96. Sir Colin Campbell, from his Despatch of the Battle of Balaklava, Camp, Battery No. 4, Balaklava, 27th October, 1854, reprinted in Lieutenant Colonel Anthony Sterling, *The Story of The Highland Brigade in the Crimea founded on Letters written during the Years 1854, 1855, and 1856* (London: Remington & Company, 1895), pp. 97–98.

97. Ibid.

98. Duckers, p. 69.

99. Lord Lucan's report published in *The Times*, Monday, November 13, 1854.

100. Ryzhov, 'On the Battle of Balaklava'.

101. Ibid.

102. Lord Lucan's report, op. cit.

103. There is a significant literature on the Charge of the Light Brigade: it is extensively if not exhaustively covered in most of the histories of the Crimean War. A valuable recent addition, however, is Anthony Dawson (ed.), *Letters from the Light Brigade: The British Cavalry in the Crimean War* (Barnsley: Pen & Sword Military, 2014), which gives a fresh set of sources (including both French and Russian) of the battle of Balaklava.

104. Baring Pemberton, p. 96.

105. Ibid.

106. Ibid., p. 97.

107. [British] Army Doctrine Publication Volume 2, *Command* (1995), Army Code No. 71564, p. 2–9, paragraph 0221. The present author, the principal researcher and writer of this military

publication, observed: 'for those who aspire to command or hold key operational staff jobs in the Army, there is no substitute for professional competence, including fluency in the language of command'. This homily echoed Woodham-Smith's (*The Reason Why*, p. 258) criticism: 'Above all the disaster [at Balaklava] was the fruit of the system under which the British Army was commanded. Untrained, untried officers were in charge of divisions and brigades in the field, the staff were ignorant of their duties and quite unable to translate the Commander-in-Chief's wishes into clear language, the Commander-in-Chief himself, Lord Raglan, unpractised and inexperienced in active command, was fatally ambiguous. To the trained staff officer of today the famous four orders of Balaclava are vague, obscure, the work of an amateur, and an invitation to disaster'.

108. Woodham-Smith, *The Reason Why*, p. 237, quotes the exchange between Cardigan and Lucan: '"Certainly, sir; but allow me to point out to you that the Russians have a battery in the valley on our front, and batteries and riflemen on both sides". Lord Lucan once more shrugged his shoulders. "I know it" he said; "but Lord Raglan will have it. We have no choice but to obey."'

109. Ibid., p. 242.

110. Liprandi, Report of 14 October 1854 [OS].

111. Stepan Kozhukhov, 'Neskol'ko slov po povodu zapiski General-Leitenanta Ryzhova o Balaklavsom strazhenii' [Some Words Regarding Lieutenant General Ryzhov's Account of the Battle of Balaklava], *Russkii Arkhiv*, 1870, Nos. 8 and 9, Year 8, pp. 1,668–76. This translation is by Mark Conrad from http://marksrussianmilitaryhistory.info/Kozhukhov.htm accessed on 25 December 2014.

112. Lord Raglan's Dispatch No. 85 addressed to his Grace the Duke of Newcastle. From *The Times*, Monday, November 13, 1854, as reprinted from the *London Gazette Extraordinary* of Sunday, November 12, 1854.

113. Ibid.

114. Ibid.

115. 'General-Adjutant Prince Menshikov's report on the offensive operation by Lieutenant-General Liprandi's force against the camp of the Allies who are covering the road from Sevastopol to Balaklava.' Originally published in *Russkii Invalid* No. 235, 1854, and *Severnaya Pchela* No. 236, 1854. This translation is by Mark Conrad from http://marksrussianmilitaryhistory.info/Mensh-Balaklava.htm accessed on 10 September 2015.

116. Liprandi, Report of 14 October 1854 [OS].

Chapter 6: Inkerman and the Spirit of Sevastopol

1. Letter to his brother, Count S. N. Tolstoy, 20 November 1854 [OS]; translation from R. F. Christian (ed.), *Tolstoy's Letters*, vol. i, *1828–1879* (London: Athlone Press, 1978), p. 45. Hereafter referred to as Tolstoy Letters.

2. Fletcher and Ishchenko, *The Crimean War: A Clash of Empires*, p. 159, quoting from N. F. Dubrovin, *Istoriya Krymskoy voiny i oborony Sevastopolya* [History of the Crimean War and the Defence of Sevastopol] (St Petersburg, 1900), vol ii, p. 114.

3. Seaton, pp. 157–59.

4. Ibid., p. 159.

5. Baring Pemberton, p. 127.

6. Curtiss, *The Russian Army under Nicholas I*, pp. 106–07 and 112. 7. Pirogov Letters, 24–28 November 1854 [OS], p. 82.

8. According to Seaton, p. 175, 'Dannenberg did not know the ground to the south of Sevastopol, although he said that he did. Nor were there *any* maps of the hinterland of Sevastopol, the Sapun or the Chernaia valley in Menshikov's headquarters; in St Petersburg itself there was only one set

of maps and these had not been copied, nor had Menshikov set his own cartographers to work.' This acute observation rather misses the point that Russian engineers were hardly able to reconnoitre, let alone survey, the area to the south of Inkerman as it was already in Allied hands.

9. See for example, Baring Pemberton, pp. 125–26, which provides a very good description of the ground, on which the one in this volume is largely modelled, supplemented by other sources, including Patrick Mercer, *Inkerman 1854: The Soldiers' Battle* (Oxford: Osprey, 1998), and by personal observation of the present author.

10. A valid point made by R. L. V. Ffrench Blake, *The Crimean War* (Barnsley: Pen & Sword Military, 2006), p. 82, who states that 'Home Ridge was 636 feet [194m] above sea level, Shell Hill 588 feet [179m]. Modern topographical maps, however, depict the summit of Shell Hill – now the *Gora Suzdalskaya* [Suzdal Hill] – as 183m in elevation with an unnamed spot height on Fore Ridge, a slightly more elevated extension of Home Ridge, as 207m.

11. The picquet system at Inkerman was based on each brigade of the 2nd Division providing four company-sized pickets of about 60 men. Each picquet would mount a temporary base, from which pairs of riflemen would be despatched forward towards the enemy to form a screen of static observation points. On observing the enemy, one soldier was meant to open fire while the other rushed back to the picquet base in order to call forward support. Picquets were not meant to stand and fight: they were designed to locate the axes of any enemy advance, to warn the main body of troops accordingly and to delay the enemy as much as possible. In many respects they formed an observation and skirmishing screen in defence.

12. This interpretation is disputed. For example, Fletcher and Ishchenko, *The Crimean War* (p. 192), consider it 'extremely unlikely' that the Russians ever intended to remain on Shell Hill.

13. This summarised account is drawn mainly from Mercer, pp. 37–40.

14. The Yekaterinburg, Tomsk, Kolyvansk, Vladimir, Suzdal, Uglitsk and Butyrsk Regiments.

15. The Selenghinsk, Yakutsk, Okhotsk, Borodino and Tarutin Regiments.

16. Seaton, p. 162.

17. Russell/Todleben, p. 174.

18. Hamley, p. 99.

19. Ibid, pp. 102–03.

20. Russell/Todleben, p. 184.

21. Hamley, p. 106.

22. For a detailed description, see Mercer, pp. 53–60.

23. Hodasevich, pp. 192–93.

24. Ibid., p. 193.

25. Ibid., p. 196.

26. Thereafter Cathcart soon came to an untimely end – he charged the Russian infantry in a defiant, suicidal, attack at about 0830 hours.

27. Seaton, p. 170.

28. Ibid., p. 171.

29. Hodasevich, p. 202.

30. Ibid.

31. Quoted by Vaneev, *Spravochnik*, p. 28.

32. Pattullo Letters, 7 November 1854, p. 70.

33. These casualty figures are taken from Mercer, p. 78. Seaton (p. 172), however, states that there were 2,610 British and 1,726 French casualties, which would change the percentages to 35% and 21% respectively.

34. Mercer, pp. 78–79.

35. Pattullo Letters, 7 November 1854, p. 71.

36. Mercer, p. 78.

37. Ffrench Blake, p. 100.

38. Ibid.

39. Ponting, p. 163.

40. Figures from Elphinstone, pp. 156–57. The proportion of sick continued to grow in the New Year. On 13 January 1855, for example, while the force total had climbed to 43,960 men, only 20,444 'sergeants, trumpeters and drummers and rank and file' were available to fight. No fewer than 16,176 were listed as 'sick', including both 'present' and 'absent', with 6,246 men 'detached on command, batmen and otherwise employed'.

41. Seaton, p. 173.

42. Ibid.

43. Russell/Todleben, p. 203.

44. Ibid., pp. 204–06.

45. Seaton, p. 176.

46. Curtiss, *The Russian Army under Nicholas I*, pp. 102–03.

47. Seaton, p. 176.

48. Ibid., p. 178.

49. Sweetman, *The Crimean War*, p. 27.

50. Pirogov Letters, 24–28 November 1854 [OS], pp. 80–81.

51. Ibid., 29 November [OS], pp. 84–85.

52. This phenomenon was amply demonstrated in the Allied campaign in north-west Europe in 1944–45, in which Eisenhower increasingly called the shots not only because he was the nominated 'supreme' commander-in-chief, but also because the United States Army predominated more and more over British and Canadian forces in the numbers of divisions it could field.

53. Elphinstone, p. 138.

54. Ibid., p. 139.

55. Ibid., p. 140–41.

56. Ibid., pp. 141–42.

57. Quoted by Wrottesley, p. 198.

58. Ibid., p. 200.

59. Niel (1802–1869) had successfully directed British–French land operations during the siege of Bomarsund in the Baltic (July–August 1854). He was very highly respected within the French Army. After the Crimean War, he was appointed as an army corps commander; was promoted to Marshal of France on the battlefield of Solferino in 1859; and later became a minister of war (1867–69).

60. Wrottesley, pp. 202–06.

61. Ibid., p. 210.

62. Ibid., pp. 217–18.

63. Porter, p. 444.

64. Hansard, House of Lords debate, 16 February 1855: http://hansard.millbanksystems.com/lords/1855/feb/16/army-reform-army-service-act-amendment#S3V0136P0_18550216_HOL_5 accessed on 13 September 2015.

65. Wrottesley, p. 239.

66. Ibid., p. 279.

67. Ibid., p. 275.

68. Porter, p. 448.

69. Curtiss, *Russia's Crimean War*, pp. 365–66.

70. Quoted by Seaton, p. 185.

71. Quoted by Vaneev, *Spravochnik*, p. 32.

72. Ibid.

73. Now more commonly referred to as Chişinău, the capital of Moldova – and of the former Russian province of Bessarabia.

74. Tolstoy Letters, 17/18 October 1854 [OS], p. 42.

75. Leo Tolstoy, trans. Louise and Aylmer Maude, *Sevastopol. Two Hussars* (London: Constable, 1905), pp. xi–xiii. Hereafter cited as Tolstoy, *Sevastopol*. Tolstoy's qualities as a correspondent did not go unnoticed. When the first of his *Sevastopol Sketches* was published in the St Petersburg *Contemporary* in April 1855, it attracted the attention of the new Emperor Alexander II, who issued direction to his army to 'take care of the life of that young writer'.

76. Ibid., pp. 2–3.

77. Ibid., pp. 3–4.

78. Ibid., pp. 9–10.

79. Ibid., pp. 13–14.

80. Ibid., pp. 14–15.

81. Ibid., p. 15.

82. Ibid., p. 16.

83. Ibid., pp. 16–17.

84. Ibid., p. 19.

85. Ibid., p. 20.

86. It will be recalled from Chapter 2 that Green Hill was the site of Rear Admiral Thomas Mackenzie's burial place. Reflecting typical soldiers' humour, a *mamelon* (from the French word for 'nipple') was the name given to this breast-shaped hillock. Confusingly, the British Army also called the same feature for a time Gordon's Hill.

87. Casualty figures from Ponting, p. 261.

88. Various sources, including Alexander Vostokov, 'Beneath the Mellow Sun of Taurus', pp. 89–90; accessed from http://www.taleon.net/taleonclub_ru/ProjectImages/2451/82-95.pdf on 17 February 2013.

89. Statistics from M. M. Frolow, *Défense de Sébastopol, Exposé de La Guerre Souterraine 1854–1855* [Defence of Sevastopol, Description of the Underground War] (Saint Petersburg: Nékludow, 1870), p. 211.

90. Gordon had become a Victorian national hero following his military exploits in China during the 1860s. Consequently known as 'Chinese Gordon', he was also famous for his philanthropic work amongst the working-class poor of Gravesend in England. Gordon's martial reputation was confirmed by his martyr's death in 1885 at Khartoum, Sudan. It is said that Queen Victoria wept on learning of the shocking news that he had been speared by the followers of the Mahdi, who had besieged the Sudanese city.

91. Gordon Letters, 12 December 1854, p. 4.

92. Ibid., 3 January 1855, p. 10.

93. Ibid., 8 January 1855, p. 11.

94. Henry Clifford, VC, *His Letters and Sketches from the Crimean War* (London: Michael Joseph, 1956), letter of 12 January 1855, pp. 144–145. Hereafter referred to as Clifford Letters.

95. Ibid., 19 January 1855, p. 145.

96. Gordon Letters, 3 January 1855, p. 10.

97. Brian Cooke, *The Grand Crimean Central Railway* (Knutsford: Cavalier House, 1990 and 1997), p. 20.

98. Ibid., pp. 23–24.

99.   Ibid., pp. 42–43.

100.   Clifford Letters, 12 February 1855, p. 171.

101.   Ibid., p. 64.

102.   Gordon Letters, 18 January 1855, pp. 12–13.

103.   Ibid., p. 13.

104.   Ibid., pp. 13–14.

105.   Ibid., 2 February 1855, p. 14.

106.   Ibid., 12 February 1855, p. 15.

107.   As explained, for example, in a recruiting and information wall poster depicting the history, life and work of the Royal Engineers published by the British government's Central Office of Information in 1983 on behalf of the Ministry of Defence (Army).

108.   Gordon Letters, 17 February 1855, p. 17.

109.   Ibid., 28 February 1855, pp. 21–22.

110.   Ibid., 23 March 1855, p. 27.

111.   Ibid., pp. 27–28.

112.   Ibid., 31 March 1855, pp. 30.

113.   Ibid., 20 April 20 1855, pp. 35.

Chapter 7: Defeat and Defiance

1.   Frederick Engels, 'The Battle of the Chernaya', *New York Daily Tribune*, No. 4494, September 14, 1855. Article sourced from Marx and Engels Collected Works, Volume 14 (Moscow: Progress Publishers, 1980), pp. 504–12; available at http://marxengels.public-archive.net/en/ME0947en. html and accessed on 30 November 2015.

2.   Gordon Letters, 13 and 20 April 1855, pp. 30–31 and 33 respectively.

3.   Pirogov Letters, 7 April 1855 [OS], p. 132.

4.   Ibid., 30 April 1855 [OS], pp. 143–44.

5.   Ibid., 7 May 1855 [OS], pp. 147–48.

6.   Ibid., 7 May 1855 [OS], p. 148.

7.   In Sofia, the Bulgarian national medical university bears Pirogov's name. A large monument to him stands in the Estonian city of Tartu, where he studied for a doctorate in anatomy at the German university there, then known as Dorpat within the former Russian province of Livonia. From 1840 until the Crimean War, excluding a break of three years of military service in the Caucasus, Pirogov held the chair of surgery at the academy of military medicine in St Petersburg. The Russian Academy of Sciences recognised his contribution to learning with the award of the prestigious Demidov Prize in 1844, 1851 and 1860. The greatest physical memorial to him, however, remains the Pirogov museum located at his former country home and medical clinic at Vishnya, near the Ukrainian city of Vinnytsia in Ukraine.

8.   Helen Rappaport, *No Place for Ladies: The Untold Story of Women in the Crimean War* (London: Aurum Press, 2007), p. 118.

9.   Pirogov Letters, 6 December 1854 [OS], p. 89.

10.   Ibid., 29 November 1854 [OS], p. 85.

11.   Rappaport, p. 77.

12.   Pirogov Letters, 29 November 1854 [OS], p. 85.

13.   Florence Nightingale's initiative in recruiting British nurses to care for the wounded faced much opposition from the British military medical establishment. Had it not been for the implacable support she received from Sidney Herbert, the British Secretary at War, it is highly unlikely that her mission would ever have got off the ground. The Russian Sisters of Mercy encountered many

similar challenges. There were, however, essential differences. Whereas Florence Nightingale's team was based at Scutari, near Constantinople, many of the Russian nurses served much closer to the fighting, not least in places under fire such as Sevastopol. They also probably suffered from more prejudice. As Helen Rappaport has explained (p. 116), 'old diehards in the Russian army' had put about 'wild stories ... that it was all bound to end in immorality: women's presence among the troops would inflame male sexuality and lead to mass rape and pregnancy among the sisters – and a corresponding increase in syphilis'. Of course, it was all nonsensical misogynist scaremongering. None the less, it is very much to Emperor Nicholas I's credit that he warmly supported Elena Pavlovna's initiative and issued a special decree recognising her mission of the Community of the Holy Cross. Moreover, the Grand Duchess generously helped to fund Pirogov's work and medical supplies.

14. N. Pirogoff [sic], *Grundzüge der Allgemeinen Kriegschirurgie nach Reminiscenzen aus den Kriegen in der Krim und im Kaucasus und aus der Hospitalpraxis* [Basics of General Military Surgery from Observations of the Wars in the Crimea and Caucasus and from Hospital Practice] (Leipzig: F. C. W. Vogel, 1864).

15. N. Pirogoff [sic], *Die Gemeinschaft der Schwestern* [The Community of Sisters of the Holy Cross for the Care of Wounded and Sick] (Berlin: Schneider, 1856), p. 33.

16. Pirogoff, *Grundzüge*, pp. 38–39.

17. Ibid., p. 44.

18. Following the Crimean War and a brief period working as an educational administrator in Kiev, Pirogov retired to his country estate to write and to run his local hospital and pharmacy, occasionally leaving to lecture at universities at home and abroad. When war in Europe broke out again his professional services remained in high demand. For example, as a representative of the Russian Red Cross, he inspected the field hospitals of the Franco-Prussian War of 1870–71. At the ripe old age of 67, the father of modern military medicine returned to service for the final time as a field surgeon during the Russo-Turkish War in 1877. For further biographical details of Pirogov, see [Colonel] Dr J. S. G. Blair, 'Nikolai Ivanovich Pirogov (1810–1881)', *Journal Royal Army Medical Corps* (2002), vol. 148, p. 303; and for his work on anaesthesia, see I. F. Hendriks, J. G. Bovill, F. Boer, E. S. Houwaart and P. C. W. Hogendoorn, 'Nikolay Ivanovich Pirogov: a surgeon's contribution to military and civilian anaesthesia', *Anaesthesia* (2015), vol. 70, pp. 219–227. The only biography is in Russian, Vladimir Il'ich Porudominsky, *Pirogov* (Moscow: Young Guard, 1969), a Russian-language volume in the series 'The Life of Notable People'. The present author thanks Pete Starling for giving him a photocopied chapter of this book (subsequently revealed to be Chapter VII, pp. 168–203) concerning Pirogov's time in Sevastopol, translated by Alexander Kennaway of the former Conflict Studies Research Centres, RMA Sandhurst (undated, but believed to be of the early 2000s).

19. Gordon Letters, 20 April 1855, pp. 35–36.

20. Troop numbers from Seaton, p. 189.

21. Baring Pemberton, p. 196.

22. Cheshire Archives and Local Studies, DHB – Letters and Papers of Colonel Hugh Robert Hibbert (1828–1895) mainly relating to service in the Crimean War, 1854–1855, DHB/57 – Camp before Sebastopol. Accessed at http://discovery.nationalarchives.gov.uk/details/rd/fe1d0b65-fc6d-4073-9c89-a072cd3f3198 on 27 November 2015.

23. John Pollock, *Gordon: the Man behind the Legend* (London: Constable, 1993), p. 304.

24. Tolstoy, *Private Diary*, 31 May 1855 [OS], p. 120. English translation from Aymer Maude (ed.), *The Private Diary of Leo Tolstoy 1853–1857* (London: Heinemann, 1927).

25. Ibid.

26. Baring Pemberton, p. 200.

27. Pattullo Letters, 11 June 1855, pp. 139–40.

28. Gordon Letters, 8 June 1855, p. 42.

29. Seaton, p. 190.

30. Quoted by Ponting, p. 276.

31. Seaton, p. 191.

32. Tolstoy, *Private Diary*, 6 June 1855 [OS], p. 122.

33. Gordon Letters, 21 June 1855, p. 47.

34. Pattullo Letters, 18 June 1855, pp. 145–46.

35. Ibid., 23 June 1855, p. 148.

36. Gordon Letters, 21 June 1855, p. 49.

37. Ponting, p. 281.

38. Gordon Letters, 30 June 1855, p. 51.

39. Pattullo Letters, 29 June 1855, p. 150.

40. Sterling, p. 316. Sterling had little faith in the appointments of general officers, and the associated patronage shown. In a letter dated 20th August 1855, he complained (p. 318) that there were now 'three Divisions (Bentinck, Rokeby, Codrington), and three Brigades ... commanded by officers from the Guards; which is pretty well, out of Six Divisions and Twelve Brigades, besides the Commander-in-Chief and the Chief of the Staff'.

41. Baring Pemberton, p. 218.

42. The complacent response to the 'warning' of the action of Little Inkerman demonstrated grave shortcomings in the British high command, a persistent problem that remained not only unaddressed throughout the campaign in Crimea, but also, in many respects, for long after. At least the Russians had an embryonic general staff – however limited in effectiveness – during the Crimean War: the British had none until one was established in 1905 following the poor showing of the army in the Boer War. Fifty years earlier, at the tactical level, there was plenty of initiative shown by field-grade and junior officers, non-commissioned officers and soldiers once battle was joined. In this respect, many of the British and French often demonstrated rather more enterprise than the majority of their Russian counterparts. The failed actions at the Redan on 18 June and 8 September 1855 displayed equal weaknesses in British tactical command and initiative.

43. Quoted by Seaton, p. 192.

44. Ibid.

45. Ibid., p. 194.

46. Ibid., p. 195. The habit of sending a senior officer forward to a theatre headquarters in order to supervise the work of a local commander was not unusual in the Russian imperial military system, and was to be continued in Soviet days. Stalin regularly employed '*Stavka* representatives' such as General (later Marshal of the Soviet Union) Georgy Konstantinovich Zhukov during the Second World War to co-ordinate (and to watch over) the work of more junior *front* and army commanders.

47. Ibid, pp. 195–96.

48. Ibid., p. 196.

49. Ibid., p. 198.

50. Sergey Chennyk, *Posledniy Shturm* [The Final Assault] (Simferopol: Gala, 2014), p. 79.

51. Reilly, p. 155.

52. Seaton, p. 202.

53. Ibid., p. 204.

54. Ibid., p. 205.

55. Chennyk, *Posledniy Shturm*, pp. 214–19.

56. This rough estimate is made from the following calculation. Assuming only 3.5 out of 6 divisions engaged, representing 7/12ths of the total Russian infantry force of roughly 48,000 men, the overall casualty rate of those engaged is derived from: $(8000/(7/12 \times 48,000)) \times 100$, or between

28% and 29%. Sergey Chennyk's (*Posledniy Shturm*, p. 215) rather more conservative estimate is 'a minimum of 20%, but perhaps 25%'. A more accurate figure could be derived from a more specific examination of the casualty records at regimental and battalion level, not available to the present author.

57. Tolstoy, *Private Diary*, 2–4 August 1855 [OS], p. 133.

58. Leo Tolstoy, trans. Louise and Aylmer Maude, *Sevastopol. Two Hussars* (London: Constable, 1905), Tolstoy, Sevastopol, pp. xi–xiii. Hereafter cited as Tolstoy, *Sevastopol.*

59. Chennyk, *Posledniy Shturm*, p. 234.

60. Although Reilly, *Artillery Operations*, makes no mention of any British artillery support at the battle of the Chernaya, Hamley (p. 266) mentions: 'A feeble attack on the Piedmontese in the valley of Tchergoum was also easily repulsed, with the co-operation of some 8-inch howitzers we had lent to the Sardinians, and an English battery of 32-pound howitzers, which compelled a Russian battery of lighter metal to withdraw'.

61. Sterling, pp. 315 and Pattullo, p. 174. Both letters concerned were dated 17 August 1855.

62. Giuseppe Francesco Ceresa di Bonvillaret, *Diario della campagna di Crimea dal 1. Aprile 1855 al 16. Giugno 1856* [Diary of the Crimean Campaign from 1 April 1855 to 16 June 1856] (Torino: L. Roux, 1894). Cited by Chennyk, *Posledniy Shturm*, pp. 220–21.

63. During the Second World War, the Germans called the Gasfort feature *Kapellberg* (Chapel Mount). Today a modern memorial to the Sardinians sits at its the western foot, overlooking Balaklava's North Valley and the Fedyukhin Heights – the area in which the Piedmont–Sardinian contingent engaged the Russians so effectively during the battle of Chernaya (16 August 1855).

64. Sterling, p. 317.

65. M. A. Vrochenskiy, *Sevastopolskiy razgrom. Vospominaniya uchastnika slavnoy oborony Sevastopolya.* [Sevastopol Debacle. Recollections of a member of the glorious defence of Sevastopol] (Moskva: 2011; originally published in Kiev in 1893). Cited by Chennyk, *Posledniy Shturm*, p. 220.

66. Sterling, p. 316.

67. Reilly, p. 170.

68. Curtiss, *Russia's Crimean War*, p. 446.

69. Woodham-Smith, *Queen Victoria*, p. 459.

70. Reilly, pp. 159–60.

71. On the British side, the Chief Royal Artillery was Major General Sir Richard Dacres and the Chief Royal Engineer was General Sir Henry (Harry) Jones; their French colleagues were Generals Thiry and Niel respectively.

72. Porter, p. 461; Reilly, pp. 179–80. According to Léon Guérin, *Histoire de la Dernière Guerre de Russe (1853–1856)* [History of the Last War of Russia] (Paris: Dufour, Mulat et Boulanger, 1858), *tome second* [vol. ii] (p. 380), however, Jones was the only Briton who attended this council of war, and that he represented General Simpson, 'possessing his full confidence'. The remainder present were all French generals: Pélissier, Bosquet, Martimprey, Thiry, Niel and Frossard.

73. Reilly, p. 180.

74. Ibid., pp. 178 and 181.

75. Seaton, pp. 209–10.

76. Anon., *A Complete History of the Final Bombardment and Fall of Sevastopol compiled from Authentic Correspondence, Reports of Eye-Witnesses and the Official Despatches* (London: J. Clayton & Son, 1855), p. 4.

77. Ibid., pp. 5–7.

78. Curtiss, *Russia's Crimean War*, pp. 450–51.

79. Pattullo Letters, 7 September 1855, pp. 182–83.

80. Seaton, p. 212.

81. Tolstoy, *Sevastopol*, p. 143.

82. Ibid., p. 144.

83. Gordon Letters, 16 September 1855, p. 68.

84. Quoted by Ponting, p. 296.

85. Seaton, p. 215.

86. The full list of the assaults given by Todleben, vol. ii, pt 2, p. 246: 'Second Bastion – 4; Curtain – 2; Malakhov and Gervais Battery – 1; Third Bastion and neighbouring batteries – 2; Schwartz [Svarts] Lunette – 1; Fifth Bastion – 1; Belkin Lunette – 1. 'Vrochenskiy, p. 188, gives the same statistics except listing – correctly – three rather than two Allied assaults of the Third Bastion (the Great Redan), thus making a total of 13 rather than Todleben's 12.

87. Seaton, p. 217.

88. Todleben, vol. ii, pt 2, p. 259.

89. Quoted by E. V. Tarle, *Krymskaya voyna* [Crimean War] vol. 2 (Moscow:, Leningrad, 1945), p. 500.

90. Tolstoy, *Sevastopol*, p. 153.

91. Todleben,vol. ii, *Pièces Justificatives* [Appendix of Supporting Documents], pp. 148–55.

92. Ibid., main text, p. 261.

93. Gordon Letters, 6 September 1855, p. 70.

94. Ibid., pp. 68–69.

95. Tolstoy, *Sevastopol*, p. 151.

96. Ibid., pp. 151–52.

97. Todleben, vol. ii, pt 2, p. 262.

98. Gordon Letters, 16 September 1855, p. 70.

99. Pirogov Letters, 31 August 1855 [OS], p. 151.

100. Todleben, vol. ii, pt 2, pp. 244–45, gives the following details of Russian losses, which totalled 12,913 men: 2,900 killed, 6,500 wounded, 1,250 'bruised', presumably injured, 1,838 missing or taken prisoner.

Chapter 8: Ruin, Peace and Recovery

1. Mark Twain, *The Innocents Abroad* (London: Penguin, 2002), p. 282. First published in the United States of America by the American Publishing Company in 1869.

2. Major Richard Delafield, US Army, *Report on the Art of War in Europe in 1854, 1855 and 1856* (Washington [DC]: George W. Bowman, 1860), p. 53.

3. Todleben, vol. ii, pt 2, p. 264.

4. Quoted by V. G. Shavshin, *Bastiony Sevastopolya* [Bastions of Sevastopol] (Sevastopol: Tavriya-Plus, 2000), p. 160.

5. Todleben, vol. ii, pt 2, pp. 265–66.

6. Ibid., p. 271.

7. Quoted by Tarle, p. 501. Seaton, p. 218, although offering a slightly different account, gives the same quote about the star.

8. Pirogov Letters, 8 September 1855 [OS], p. 153.

9. Tolstoy, *Sevastopol*, p. 153.

10. From *Sevastopol'skiye bastiony. Sbornik rukopisey predstavlennykh Ego Imperatorskomu Vysochestvu Gosudaryu Nasledniku Tsesarevichu o Sevastopol'skoy oborone sevastopoltsami* [Sevastopol Bastions. A Set of Manuscripts presented to His Imperial Highness, the Heir Apparent, about the Defence of Sevastopol by Sevastopol Residents] (Moskva: Voennoye Izdatelstvo, 1998), p. 468.

11. Quoted by Tarle, p. 500.
12. Todleben, vol. ii, pt 2, pp. 273–75.
13. Tolstoy, *Private Diary*, 2 September 1855 [OS], p. 135.
14. Sterling, pp. 333–34.
15. Todleben, vol. ii, pt 2, p. 271.
16. Sterling, p. 335.
17. Hamley, pp. 313–14.
18. Ibid., pp. 322–24.
19. Ibid., pp. 335–26.
20. Quoted by John Grehan and Martin Mace, (ed.), *Despatches from the Front. British Battles of the Crimean Wars 1854–1856* (Barnsley: Pen & Sword, 2014), pp. 243–45.
21. Ibid., p. 246–47.
22. Todleben, vol. ii, pt 2, pp. 308–09.
23. Further details can be found at as follows. For the plaque at Topoli, unveiled on 8 September 2015, see http://maxpark.com/community/5134/content/3682724; for the one at Zalesnoye, mounted on 11 November 2008, see http://www.shukach.com/ru/node/15143. Both sites accessed on 4 January 2016.
24. Todleben, vol. ii, pt 2, pp. 309–10.
25. Ibid., pp. 310–11.
26. Grehan and Mace, p. 248.
27. Ibid.
28. From the Report by Lieutenant Colonel Edward T. Lloyd dated 1 February 1855, quoted by Grehan and Mace, p. 289.
29. Deane's diving work at Sevastopol is documented extensively in John Bevan, *The Infernal Diver: the lives of John and Charles Deane, their invention of the diving helmet and its first application to salvage, treasure hunting, civil engineering and military uses* (London: Submex, 1996). This author, however, is mistaken in stating that Deane had overall responsibility for the demolitions. He did not: this was a military task – led by British and French engineers – in which Deane had an important, but none the less *supporting*, role.
30. Gordon Letters, 27 December 1855, pp. 83–84.
31. Ibid., p. 85.
32. Quoted by Bevan, p. 257.
33. Gordon Letters, 27 December 1855, p. 85.
34. Bevan, p. 259.
35. Gordon Letters, 3 February 1856, p. 86.
36. Ibid., pp. 86–87.
37. Pollock, pp. 37–38.
38. Gordon Letters, 3 February 1856, p. 88.
39. Ibid., p. 87.
40. Ibid., 22 February 1856, pp. 90–91.
41. The present author recalls one of his very first lessons of demolitions training as a young Royal Engineers officer in 1975 – *always* test a length of safety fuse by timing its burn rate before using it to initiate a high-explosive charge via a detonator.
42. Gordon Letters, 9 March 1856, pp. 91–92.
43. Bevan, p. 262.
44. Gordon Letters, 21 March 1856, p. 93.
45. Bevan, p. 263.

46. Grehan and Mace, p. 290.

47. R. H. Vetch, 'Gordon, Sir (John) William (1814–1870)', rev. James Lunt, *Oxford Dictionary of National Biography*, Oxford University Press, 2004 [http://www.oxforddnb.com/view/article/11069, accessed 21 December 2015].

48. Charles Chesney, 'Chinese Gordon', *Fraser's Magazine for Town and Country*, vol. LXXIX, No. CCCCLXX, February 1869, p. 144.

49. As summarised by Curtiss, *Russia's Crimean War*, p. 491.

50. Such a condition would, of course, also exclude Turkish naval power.

51. Curtiss, *Russia's Crimean War*, pp. 491–92.

52. Ibid., pp. 499–500.

53. Tarle, pp. 544–55.

54. Extracts of the Treaty of Paris are taken from Sir Augustus Oakes and R. B. Mowat (eds), *The Great European Treaties of the Nineteenth Century* (Oxford: Clarendon Press, 1918), pp. 176–78.

55. Ibid., pp. 178–79 and 184–85.

56. Undated 'A General Note on the Danubian Question by General Gordon', Gordon Letters, p. 103.

57. Tarle, pp. 546–47.

58. Ibid., p. 594.

59. Ship data are from Chuck Veit, *The Yankee Expedition to Sebastopol. John Gowen and the Raising of the Russian Black Sea Fleet 1857–1862* (Lulu.com: 2014), p. 36. This section of Chapter 8 draws heavily on this work with the author's kind permission and co-operation.

60. From an article of 3 March 1857, 'Raising of the Russian War Vessels at Sebastopol', quoted by Veit, p. 102.

61. Eufrosina Dvoichenko-Markov, 'Americans in the Crimean War', *Russian Review*, Vol. 13, No. 2 (April 1954), p. 141.

62. William Benton Whisenhunt, 'In Service to the Tsar: American Surgeons in the Crimean War, 1853–1856' in William Benton Whisenhunt and Norman E. Saul (eds), *New Perspectives on Russian-American Relations* (New York and Abingdon; Routledge, 2016), pp. 52 and 55–56.

63. Stephen W. Mears, *George McClellan: The Young Napoleon* (New York: Ticknor & Fields, 1988), pp. 45–46.

64. Delafield, p. x.

65. Ibid. Italics as in original.

66. Ibid., p. xi.

67. Mears, pp. 48–49, highlights the significant omissions of the study of high command (but not the lack of a general staff) and the rifled musket. This author, however, mistakenly refers to 'McClellan's' as opposed to Delafield's report.

68. To put this statement into perspective, the casualties on both sides (Union and Confederate) were American.

69. Tolstoy, *Sevastopol*, p. 137.

70. Dvoichenko-Markov, pp. 137–38.

71. Ibid., pp. 139–40.

72. Gordon Letters, 6 December 1856, p. 122.

73. Veit, pp. 99–101.

74. John Gadsby, *A Trip to Sebastopol, Out and Home, by Way of Vienna, the Danube, Odessa, Constantinople, and Athens*, 2nd ed. (London: Gadsby, 1858). This work represents an important contemporary source. First, he describes in detail the state of Sevastopol nearly two years after its fall; secondly, he provides an initial account of Gowen's work; and thirdly, he documents the war cemeteries and monuments left by the British. In contrast, the commentaries on the battles of the Crimean campaign interspersed within his narrative, although of interest, are less valuable.

75. Gadsby, p. 69.
76. Delafield, p. 47.
77. Gadsby, p. 70.
78. Quoted by Veit, p. 110.
79. Gadsby., p. 103.
80. Foreign visitors to Sevastopol today (or, for that matter, at any other military installation in either the Russia Federation, the United States of America or most other parts of the world) are advised not to repeat this trick – they are liable to be shot.
81. Gadsby, pp. 131–32.
82. Ibid., p. 106.
83. Veit, p. 116.
84. Ibid., p. 111.
85. Ibid.
86. Ibid., pp. 99–100.
87. Gadsby, pp. 70 and 140–41.
88. Veit, p. 132.
89. Ibid., p. 160.
90. Ibid., p. 186. Veit notes that the timing of the completion of the sixth caisson 'remains imprecise'. The two new caissons were considerably larger than the first four. Veit (p. 159) provides the technical details.
91. Ibid.
92. Ibid., p. 195.
93. Ibid., p. 202.
94. Ibid., p. 208, Fig. 53.
95. George C. Herring, *From Colony to Superpower: US Foreign Relations since 1776* (Oxford: University Press, 2008), pp. 228–29. The quotation is taken from Norman E. Saul, *Distant Friends: The United States and Russia, 1763–1867* (Kansas: Kansas University Press, 1991), p. 305.
96. Veit, pp. 212–18.
97. Ibid., p. 219.
98. Gordon Letters, 3 June 1858, pp. 187–88.
99. Ostrovskiy letters on-line at http://www.knigolubu.ru/translit/russian_classic/ostrovskiy_an/pisma_1842_-_1872_gg.10996/?page=17, accessed on 28 December 2015.
100. Twain, p. 282.
101. Russkoye obshchestvo parokhodstva i torgovli (ROPiT).
102. Anon, 'Iz istorii flota. Morskoy flot' [From the History of the Fleet. The Merchant Marine Fleet], *International Maritime Journal*, No. 3, 2007, p. 90. Accessed at http://www.morflot.su/archives/articles1499file.pdf on 26 January 2016.
103. As proudly recalled in the website of the Alexander Gorchakov Public Diplomacy Fund – accessed at http://gorchakovfund.ru/en/about/gorchakov/ on 26 January 2016.
104. Readers may note some parallels here with the resurgence of the Russian Federation following the dissolution of the Soviet Union, particularly under the leadership of Vladimir Putin since his election as President in 2000.
105. Oakes and Mowat, p. 317.
106. Ibid, p. 316.
107. Ibid, p. 318.
108. Riasanovsky, p. 387.
109. Respectively Kharkiv, Lozova and Zaporizhzhya in modern Ukraine.

110. Vaneev, *Spravochnik*, p, 44.

111. Quoted by Alla Golovacheva, *Chekhov and Crimea* (Simferopol: Dolya, 2008), p. 8.

112. Vaneev, *Spravochnik*, p, 45.

113. Fred T. Jane, *The Imperial Russian Navy: Its Past, Present and Future* (London: W. Thacker, 1904), pp. 403–04.

114. Vaneev, *Spravochnik*, p. 49.

115. Ibid.

Chapter 9: The 1905 Revolution

1. *Sevastopolskaya Gazeta*, No. 73, Thursday, 30 March (12 April) 1906, p. 3.

2. Tarle, vol. 2, p. 542.

3. Ibid.

4. This Mrs Kate Guthrie, as far as can be established, was no relation of the earlier Mrs Maria Guthrie who visited Sevastopol at the end of the eighteenth century. The date of her visit is unknown, but from her account it would appear to lie between 1862 and 1869.

5. Kate Guthrie, *Through Russia: from St. Petersburg to Astrakhan and the Crimea*, vol. ii (London: Hurst and Blackett, 1874) pp. 168–70.

6. Vaneev, *Spravochnik*, p. 42.

7. Dobry and Borisova, p. 50.

8. Kate Guthrie, p. 189.

9. Dobry and Borisova, p. 56.

10. Ibid., pp. 54–55.

11. *Krymskiy Vestnik*, No. 143, Wednesday, 8 (21) June 1905.

12. Dobry and Borisova, pp. 29–30.

13. Vaneev, *Spravochnik*, p. 43.

14. Orlando Figes, *A People's Tragedy: The Russian Revolution 1891–1924* (London: Jonathan Cape, 1996), p. 138.

15. Vaneev, *Spravochnik*, p. 46.

16. Ibid., pp. 59–60.

17. The Rossiyskaya sotsial-demokraticheskaya rabochaya partiya (RSDRP).

18. Figes, *A People's Tragedy*, pp. 151–52. The two terms are directly derived from the Russian, meaning 'Majoritarians' and 'Minoritarians'.

19. Vaneev, *Spravochnik*, p. 61.

20. Ibid.

21. The English translation is *Prince Potemkin of Tauris*. The other capital ships involved were: *Tri Svyatitelya, Rostislav, Dvenadtsat Apostolov, Georgii Pobedonosets, Sinop* and *Ekaterina II*.

22. Lawrence Sondhaus, *Navies of Europe* (London: Longman, 2002), pp. 128–29.

23. Arthur J. Marder, *From the Dreadnought to Scapa Flow*, vol. i, *The Road to War 1904–1914* (London: Oxford University Press, 1961), pp. 110–11.

24. Sondhaus, *Navies of Europe*, pp. 130–31.

25. Paul Bushkovitch, *A Concise History of Russia* (New York: Cambridge University Press, 2012), pp. 282–83.

26. Neal Bascomb, *Red Mutiny: The True Story of the Battleship Potemkin Mutiny* (New York: Houghton Mifflin, 2007), p. 32. The same point is made more generally by Orlando Figes, *A People's Tragedy*, pp. 57–58.

27. A number of references to this infamous sign 'Собакам и нижним чинам вход воспрещен' are listed at http://ru-history.livejournal.com/3396305.html, accessed on 22 January 2016.

28. Bascomb, Chapters 5 and 7.

29. Ibid., Chapters 12–18.

30. St Panteleimon is also rendered as St Pantaleon, the 'All-compassionate'. One of St Petersburg's earliest churches is dedicated to St Panteleimon, which reinforces the naval connection.

31. *Krymskiy Vestnik*, No. 246, Sunday, 16 (29) October 1905.

32. Riasanvsky, pp. 407–08.

33. *Krymskiy Vestnik*, No. 248, Wednesday, 18 (31) October 1905.

34. Vaneev, *Spravochnik*, p. 64.

35. Komoyedov, p. 120.

36. Ibid., p. 121.

37. Ibid.

38. Named after the city now known as Białystok in Poland.

39. Komoyedov, p. 120.

40. Ibid., p. 121.

41. *Sevastopolskaya Gazeta*, No. 70, Saturday, 25 March (7 April) 1906, p. 6.

42. Ibid, No. 73, Thursday, 30 March (12 April) 1906, p. 1.

43. Ibid., pp. 2–3.

44. Komoyedov, pp. 121–22.

45. Yevgeniy Shmidt-Ochakovskiy, *Leytenant Shmidt, 'Krasny Admiral': Vospominaniya Syna* [Lieutenant Schmidt, 'Red Admiral': Memories of [his] Son] (Odessa: KP OGT, 2006), p. 162. Accessed at http://museum-literature.odessa.ua/Krasny_Admiral.pdf on 25 January 2016.

46. Ibid., pp. 163–64 and 167.

47. Ibid., pp. 164–68.

48. Ibid., pp. 168–72.

49. *Sevastopolskaya Gazeta*, No. 73, Thursday, 30 March (12 April) 1906, p. 3.

50. Ibid.

51. Vaneev et al., *Sevastopol 200*, pp. 107–08.

52. Shmidt-Ochakovskiy, p. 286.

53. *Sevastopolskaya Gazeta*, No. 60, Tuesday, 14 (27) March 1906 and No. 65, Sunday, 19 March (1 April) 1906.

54. *Sevastopolskaya Gazeta*, No. 189, 20 August (2 September) 1906.

55. Komoyedov, p. 122. To be fair, the present author's comment rests on the translation of the word 'жестоко' as 'brutally' as opposed to the alternative 'severely'.

56. Figures for numbers executed and killed in relation to the Kronstadt mutiny are taken from Figes, *A People's Tragedy*, p. 767.

57. Komoyedov, p. 122.

58. Ibid., p. 123.

59. As reported in *Krymskiy Vestnik*, No. 270, Wednesday, 23 November (6 December) 1905, Chronicles, p. 3.

60. A point made by Bascomb, p. ix.

61. N. Lenin [pseudonym], 'The Armed Forces and the Revolution', *Novaya Zhizn*, No. 14, November 16, 1905, republished in V. I. Lenin, *Collected Works*, vol. 10, November 1905–June 1906 (Moscow: Progress Publishers, 1965), pp. 54–55. Accessed at http://www.marx2mao.com/PDFs/Lenin%20CW-Vol.%2010.pdf on 22 January 2016.

62. Dobry and Borisova, pp. 64–65.

63. Anna Geifman, *Thou Shalt Kill: Revolutionary Terrorism in Russia, 1894–1917* (Princeton, NJ: University Press, 1995), p. 69.

64. The Russian Mobilisation Plan 19A in its final form of the summer of 1914, immediately prior to the outbreak of the First World War, foresaw two armies of the Northwestern Front (the 1st and the 2nd) attacking German East Prussia while four armies of the Southwestern Front (3rd, 4th, 5th and 8th) would attack Austro-Hungarian Galicia. Four armies (6th, 7th and the newly constituted 9th and 10th) were to be held in general reserve in Polish Russia. The plan suffered from the fact that neither of the two wings was strong enough to be decisive.

65. Details from *Handbook of the Russian Army*, 6th ed. (London: General Staff, War Office, 1914), pp. 170–72 and 263.

66. Additional details of troops stationed in Sevastopol not contained in the *Handbook of the Russian Army* (1914) are taken from http://marksrussianmilitaryhistory.info/RUSS1914.html accessed on 16 January 2016. Mark Conrad cites his additional source as V. V. Zvegintsov, *Russkaya Armiya 1914 g. Podrobnaya dislokatsiya, formirovaniya 1914–1917, regalii i otlichiya*, [Russian Army in 1914, Detailed Deployment, Formations 1914–1917, Regalia and Insignia] (Paris: self-published, 1959).

67. Norman Stone, *The Eastern Front 1914–1917* (New York: Charles Scribner's Sons, 1975), pp. 18 and 28. Table 1 (p. 28) contains details of 'Ordinary Defence Expenditure over the period 1909–1913', from which data the overall increases in army and naval expenditure have been extracted.

68. Viscount Hythe and John Leyland, *The Naval Annual 1914* (London: William Clowes, 1914), p. 48. Cited hereafter as Hythe and Leyland.

69. Stone, *Eastern Front*, p. 29.

70. Ibid., p. 18.

71. George Nekrasov, *North of Gallipoli: The Black Sea at War 1914–1917* (New York: Columbia University Press, 1992), p. 12; Hore, p. 177.

72. Nekrasov, p. 15.

73. John Leyland, 'Foreign Navies' in Viscount Hythe (ed.), *The Navy Annual 1913* (Portsmouth: J. Griffin, 1913), p. 55. Cited hereafter as Leyland.

74. Laid down as *Ekaterina II*, this battleship was subsequently renamed *Imperatritsa Ekaterina Velikaya* [Empress Catherine the Great], and then *Svobodnaya Rossiya* [Free Russia].

75. *Imperatritsa Mariya* was launched on 1 November 1913; *Imperator Alexander III* on 22 April 1914; *Ekaterina II* on 6 June 1914. For further details of this class, see Hore, p. 178.

76. Completion dates are shown in parenthesis. Ships' data from Hythe and Leyland, pp. 244–47 and 278.

77. Leyland, p. 59.

78. Nekrasov, p. 15.

79. Vaneev, *Spravochnik*, p. 73.

80. From the reports contained in *Krymskiy Vestnik*, Nos. 203–208, Saturday–Thursday, 10–15 (23–28) August 1913.

81. Details from Nicholas II's private diary at http://emalkrest.narod.ru/txt/1913.htm, accessed on 17 February 2013.

Chapter 10: World War to Civil War

1. Winston Churchill, *The World Crisis 1911–1914* (London: Thornton Butterworth, 1923), p. 252.

2. There is an alternative historical analysis which undermines the narrative of German–Turkish provocation of Russia, and sees the latter as an injured party forced into declaring war. Russian

strategic planning before the First World War included options to capture Constantinople and to secure the Turkish Straits. Sean McMeekin argues (p. 112) that: 'Far from an accidental spillover from the European conflict, as most British and French accounts would have us believe, Turkey's entry in the war was just as inevitable as [the Russian ambassador to the Porte] Girs had foretold, given the presence of the *Goeben* in the Bosphorous.'

3. For a detailed consideration of Turkey's decision to join the Central Powers, see Hew Strachan, *The First World War*, vol. i, *To Arms* (Oxford: University Press, 2001), pp. 651–80.

4. For the technical specifications and construction history of the *Goeben*, see Gary Staff, *German Battlecruisers of World War One. Their Design, Construction and Operations* (Barnsley: Seaforth Publishing, 2014), pp. 108–14; for a comparison of British and German warships, see Mark Stille, *British Battlecruiser vs German Battlecruiser* (Oxford: Osprey, 2013).

5. Barbara W. Tuchman, *The Guns of August* (London: Penguin, 2014; originally published by Macmillan in 1962), p. 154.

6. The narrative of the voyage of the *Goeben* and *Breslau* from the Adriatic via the Mediterranean to Constantinople draws on: Tuchman, *The Guns of August*; Paul G. Halpern, *The Naval War in the Mediterranean 1914–1918* (London: Allen & Unwin, 1987); Andrew Gordon, *The Rules of the Game: Jutland and British Naval Command* (London: John Murray, 1996); Dan van der Vat, *The Ship that Changed the World*, 2nd ed. (Edinburgh: Birlinn, 2000); and Robert K. Massie, *Castles of Steel: Britain, Germany and the Winning of the Great War at Sea* (London: Jonathan Cape, 2004). Unsuspecting readers should note that the alluring title by Owen P. Hall, *The Last Battlecruiser: SMS Goeben Operations in the Mediterranean and the Black Sea 1914–1918* (Bennington, Vermont: Merriam Press, 2012), is a work of historical fiction.

7. Quoted by Massie, *Castles of Steel*, p. 37.

8. Nekrasov, p. 19.

9. Massie, *Castles of Steel*, p. 35.

10. Ibid., p. 39.

11. Ibid., pp. 39–40.

12. Ibid., pp. 41–45.

13. Gordon, pp. 389–90.

14. This expression has been borrowed from Colin S. Gray, *The Leverage of Seapower: The Strategic Advantage of Navies in War* (New York: The Free Press, 1992). Curiously, however, Gray omits the *Goeben* incident in his analysis.

15. Nekrasov, p. 23.

16. Details of the attacks by Souchon's force on 29 October 1914 are taken principally from D. Yu. Kozlov, *'Strannaya voyna' v Chernom more (avgust – oktyabr 1914 goda)* ['Strange War' in the Black Sea (August – October 1914)] (Moskva: Kvadriga, 2009).

17. Komoyedov, p. 128.

18. Kozlov, pp. 86–87.

19. Ibid., pp. 108–09.

20. Nekrasov, p. 24.

21. Kozlov, pp. 110–11.

22. Ibid., p. 113.

23. Ibid., p. 115.

24. Ibid., p. 117.

25. Ibid., p. 119. Further details (including a claim that a shell from the *Goeben* caused the Russian gun to explode rather than a misfire) are taken from the account of the action contained in the 'Report of the Commandant of the Sevastopol Fortress, Lieutenant General A. N. Ananin, to the Commander of Seventh Army, General of Artillery V. N. Nikitin, of 16 (29) December, No. 1001'. Reproduced by Koslov, p. 181.

26. During a refit in 1911, the main armament of 12-inch (305 mm) guns had been removed and replaced by additional 6-inch (152 mm) guns.

27. Nekrasov, pp. 24–25.

28. From the German original reproduced in Kozlov, pp. 190–91.

29. Hew Strachan, *First World War*, pp. 349 and 354.

30. An excellent analysis of this opening phase of the First World War in the East is given by Stephen Walsh, 'The Russian Army and the Conduct of Operations in 1914', *British Journal for Military History*, Volume 2, Issue 2, February 2016, pp. 59–88, accessed at http://bjmh.org.uk/index.php/bjmh/article/view/92 on 1 February 2016.

31. Nekrasov, pp. 27–28.

32. A detailed account is given by Stephen McLaughlin, 'Predreadnoughts vs. a Dreadnought: The Action off Cape Sarych, 18 November 1914' in Antony Preston, *Warship 2001–2002* (London: Conway Maritime Press, 2001), pp. 117–40.

33. Nekrasov, pp. 29–34. Quotation from p. 34.

34. Ibid., pp. 43 and 67.

35. Ibid., p. 68.

36. *Dnevniki Nikolaya Vtorogo* [Diaries of Nicholas II], Entries for 17 (30) April and 18 April (1 May) 1915, accessed at http://www.tsaarinikolai.com/tekstit/Dnevniki_Nikolaja.pdf on 1 February 2016.

37. *Krimskiy Vestnik*, No. 121 (8770), 13 (26) May 1916.

38. The children of Nicholas II were Olga, Tatiana, Maria, Anastasia and Alexey.

39. *Dnevniki Nikolaya Vtorogo* [Diary of Nicholas II], Entries for the period 12/25 – 15/28 May 1916, accessed at http://www.tsaarinikolai.com/tekstit/Dnevniki_Nilolaja.pdf on 1 February 2016.

40. Ibid.

41. Nekrasov, pp. 78–79.

42. Ibid., pp. 81–84.

43. Ibid., pp. 94–95.

44. Vaneev, *Spravochnik*, p. 74; Nekrasov, p. 110.

45. O. E. Ivitskaya, 'Odin god iz zhizni admirala (maloizvestnye fakti biografii admirala A.V. Kolchaka)' ['One Year in the Life of An Admiral (Lesser-known Facts of the Biography of Admiral A.V. Kolchak)'], in *Sevastopol – vzgliad v proshloye* [Sevastopol – a Glance in the Past] (Sevastopol: Arefyev, 2007), p. 241.

46. This summary is simplified. For more information and analysis, see, for example, Jonathan D. Smele, *The 'Russian' Civil Wars* (Oxford: University Press), pp. 14–15.

47. This overview of Russia in 1917 is drawn in the main from Sheila Fitzpatrick, *The Russian Revolution*, 3rd ed. (Oxford: University Press, 2008), pp. 38–52.

48. Ivitskaya, p. 246.

49. Vaneev, *Spravochnik*, p. 76.

50. Nekrasov, p. 124.

51. Quoted by Y. B. Altabayeva, *Smutnoe Vremya: Sevastopol' v 1917–1920 gg.* [Muddy Times: Sevastopol in 1917–1920] (Sevastopol: Teleskop, 2004), pp. 35–36.

52. Nekrasov, p. 127.

53. Ivitskaya, p. 248.

54. Altabayeva, pp. 35–36; *Dictionary of American Fighting Ships*, vol. 3 (Washington, DC: US Naval Historical Center, 1968), entry for 'Glennon' (a US Navy destroyer launched in 1942 was named after Rear Admiral James Henry Glennon).

55. Nekrasov, p. 127.

56. United States Department of State, *Papers relating to the Foreign Relations of the United States, 1918. Russia*, vol. I, *American and Russian Special Missions* (Washington, DC: US Government Printing Office, 1918), p. 125. Accessed at http://digital.library.wisc.edu/1711.dl/FRUS. FRUS1918v1 on 3 February 2016.

57. Altabayeva, p. 51.

58. Vaneev, *Spravochnik*, p. 78.

59. *Izvestiya Sevastopol'skogo Soveta Voyennykh i Rabochikh Deputatov* [News of the Sevastopol Soviet of Military and Workers Deputies], No. 148, 15 (28) November 1917.

60. *Izvestiya Sevastopol'skogo voyenno-revolyutsionnogo komiteta* [News of the Sevastopol Military-Revolutionary Committee], No. 1, 19 December 1917 (1 January 1918). Confusingly, the appearance of this publication meant that Sevastopol had two *Izvestiya* newspapers during this period.

61. Altabayeva, pp. 92–95; Nekrasov, pp. 129–30. Nekrasov suggests that the execution of the admirals and the murders of the officers of the *Gadzhibey* were separate incidents; contemporary newspaper reports, however, indicate that they were but one.

62. Vaneev, *Spravochnik*, p. 79. By the end of 1917, new elections took place in Sevastopol, resulting in a big victory for the Bolsheviks, who won 87 seats in a newly organised soviet. Of its presidium, there were four Bolsheviks and one Social Revolutionary.

63. Brian Glyn Williams, *The Crimean Tatars: From Soviet Genocide to Putin's Conquest* (London: Hurst & Company, 2015), pp. 62–64.

64. Altabayeva, pp. 125–26.

65. Alexis Wrangel, *General Wrangel 1878–1929. Russia's White Crusader* (London: Leo Cooper, 1990), pp. 59–60.

66. Dominic Lieven, *Towards the Flame: Empire, War and the End of Tsarist Russia* (London: Allen Lane, 2015), p. 358.

67. First published in serialised form in 1925, Mikhail Bulgakov's *Belaya Gvardiya* [The White Guard] describes the lives and fortunes of a Kiev middle-class family confronting the vicissitude and violence of short-lived Ukrainian independence, the Russian Civil War and the kaleidoscope of rapidly changing governments in Ukraine's capital city.

68. Quoted by Peter Lieb, 'The German Occupation of the Ukraine, 1918' in Matthias Strohn (ed.), *World War I Companion* (Oxford: Osprey, 2013), p. 210.

69. Quoted by Michael S. Neiberg and David Jordan, *The Eastern Front 1914–1920* (London: Amber Books, 2008), p. 163. [Fuller text: We are compelled to submit to a distressing peace. It will not stop revolution in Germany and Europe. We shall now begin to prepare a revolutionary army, not by phrases and exclamations, as did those who after January 10th did nothing even to attempt to stop our fleeing troops, but by organized work, by the creation of a serious national, mighty army. Their knees are on our chest, and our position is hopeless. This peace must be accepted as a respite enabling us to prepare a decisive resistance to the bourgeoisie and imperialists. The proletariat of the whole world will come to our aid. Then we shall renew the fight.]

70. John W. Wheeler-Bennett, *Hindenburg: The Wooden Titan* (London: Macmillan, 1967), pp. 132–33.

71. Lieb, p. 212.

72. BA/MA, N754/10, *Nachlass, General der Infanterie Robert Kosch. Kriegstagebuch, März 1918 – Mai 1918*. [Bequest of General of Infantry Robert Kosch. War Diary, March–May 1918.] The author is very grateful to Dr Peter Lieb for bringing his attention to the Kosch papers. Kosch's typewritten war diary was put together after the conflict, drawing very extensively on his contemporaneous letters home from the front, supplemented by various copies of the orders his headquarters issued. Hereafter simply termed as 'Kosch War Diary', with specific reference to either his letters or orders. The German abbreviation 'zbV', or z.b.V., means '*zur besonderen Verwendung*' (for special employment).

73. Details of German formations and initial tasks are taken from Kosch War Diary, Generalkommando (z.b.V.) Nr. 52, Ia Nr. 4904 dated 18.4.18, Korpsbefehl [Corps Operation Order]. Whereas the three infantry divisions had served under Kosch in Romania, the Bavarian Cavalry Division had been transferred from XXII Reserve Corps.

74. The rationale for the occupation of Crimea and seizure of Sevastopol is given in the official German military history: *Der Weltkrieg 1914 bis 1918*, vol. xiii, *Die Kriegführung im Sommer und Herbst 1917. Die Ereignisse außerhalb der Westfront bis November 1918* [The World War 1914 to 1918. The Conduct of War in the summer and autumn of 1917. Events excluding the Western Front until November 1918] (Berlin: Mittler und Sohn, 1942; republished by the Bundesarchiv in 1956), p. 383.

75. Professionally trained as a general staff officer, Kosch had spent the majority of his wartime service on the Eastern Front, commanding army corps successively in East Prussia, Galicia and the Balkans in 1914–15, during which period he had been decorated not only with the *Pour le Mérite*, but also, exceptionally, the oak leaves to go with it, signifying a second award. After six months' duty in the Verdun sector on the Western Front in 1916, he assumed command of Generalkommando zbV Nr. 52, leading it throughout the German campaign that defeated Romania.

76. Kosch War Diary, Letter 82, 17.4.18.

77. Ibid., Letter 83, 18.4.18.

78. Altabayeva, p. 145.

79. Kosch War Diary, Letter 86, 21.4.18.

80. Altabayeva, p. 147.

81. Kosch War Diary, Letter 87, 23.4.18.

82. Ibid., Continuation of Letter 87, 24.4.18.

83. Ibid.

84. Kosch War Diary, Letter 88, 25.4.18.

85. Tsentralnyi komitet Chernomorskogo flota.

86. Altabayeva, pp. 148–49.

87. Kosch War Diary, Letters 89, 27.4.18 and 90, 28.4.18.

88. Kosch War Diary, enclosed copy of Korpsbefehl [Corps Operation Order], Generalkommando (z.b.V.) Nr. 52, Ia Nr. 5047 dated 27.4.18.

89. Kosch War Diary, Letter 91, 29.4.18.

90. Ibid.

91. Altabayeva, p. 150.

92. Ibid., p. 151. The colours of the Russian Navy flag, returned into use at the end of the Soviet Union, are thus the opposite of the Scottish national flag – a white cross against a blue background.

93. Kosch War Diary, Letter 92, 30.4.18.

94. Plokhy, *The Gates of Europe*, p. 267.

95. Altabayeva, pp. 159–60.

96. Albert Hopman, diary entry for Wednesday, 1 May to Saturday, 4 May, in Winfried Baumgart (ed.), *Von Brest-Litovsk zur Deutschen Novemberrevolution: Aus den Tagebüchern, Breifen und Aufzeichnungen von Alfons Paquet, Wilhelm Groener und Albert Hopman, März bis November 1918* [From Brest-Litovsk to the German November Revolution: from the Diaries, Letters and Notes of Alfons Paquet, Wilhelm Groener and Albert Hopman, March to November 1918] (Göttingen: Vandenhoeck & Ruprecht, 1971), p. 484. Hereafter referred to as Hopman War Diary.

97. Altabayeva, p. 160.

98. Peter Kenz, *The Defeat of the Whites. Civil War in South Russia, 1919–1920* (Berkeley and Los Angeles: University of California, 1977), p. 192.

99.   Kosch War Diary, Continuation of Letter 92, 1.5.18.

100. Plokhy, p. 211.

101. Kosch War Diary, Letter 94, 3.5.18.

102. Ibid.

103. Altabayeva, p. 159. Hopman War Diary, Saturday, 5 May [1918], p. 486, lists the 'very large booty in Sevastopol' as 'all the old ships of the line, several cruisers, ten torpedo-boats [destroyers], ten large U-boats, 150 aircraft, 50,000 tonnes of coal etc'.

104. Hopman War Diary, Tuesday, 7 May [1918], p. 487.

105. V. I. Lenin, *Collected Works*, vol. 27, February–July 1918 (Moscow: Progress Publishers, 1965), pp. 358–59. Accessed at http://www.marx2mao.com/PDFs/Lenin%20CW-Vol.%2027.pdf on 12 February 2016.

106. Hopman War Diary, Thursday, 9 and Friday, 10 May [1918], p. 488.

107. Ibid., p. 503.

108. Ibid, pp. 522–23.

109. Nekrasov, p. 135.

110. Altabayeva, p, 164.

111. Following the Russian re-annexation of Crimea in 2014, groups of aggrieved Tatars started to blockade the peninsula economically, cutting off the supply of food and goods (and, most spectacularly, destroying electric power lines) – allegedly with tacit Ukrainian governmental support. Russian nationalists, recalling the Ukrainian blockade of 1918, now refer to this more recent action as the 'second blockade'.

112. Plokhy, p. 225.

113. Quoted by Williams, p. 67.

114. M. N. Guboglo and S. M. Chervonnaya, *Krymskotatarskoye natsionalnoye dvizhheniye* [Crimean Tatar National Movement], vol. ii (Moscow: TsIMO, 1992), pp. 175–76.

115. Vaneev, *Spravochnik*, p. 87; Altabayeva, p. 170.

116. Hopman War Diary, pp. 622–24.

Chapter 11: Allied Intervention and the Russian Civil War

1.   Alexis Wrangel, p. 210.

2.   Bruce Lincoln, *Red Victory: A history of the Russian Civil War* (London: Simon & Schuster, 1990), p. 11. Page references are to the Sphere Books paperback edition of 1991.

3.   Michael Jabara Carley, *Revolution and Intervention: the French Government and the Russian Civil War, 1917–1919* (Kingston, Ontario: McGill-Queen's University Press, 1983), p. 110.

4.   As suggested in the title of Ian C. D. Moffat, *The Allied Intervention in Russia, 1918–1920: The Diplomacy of Chaos* (Basingstoke: Palgrave Macmillan, 2015).

5.   This brief account is based on the more detailed analysis given by Peter Kenez in *The Defeat of the Whites. Civil War in South Russia, 1919–1920* (Berkeley/Los Angeles: University of California, 1977), pp. 178–80.

6.   Smele, p. 251.

7.   Carley, p. 112.

8.   The boycott by London dockers of the SS *Jolly George*, bound with weapons for Poland, in May 1920 was one notable example of the hostility and unrest. The present author is grateful to Charles Dick for bringing this aspect of the domestic opposition to intervention to hisattention.

9.   Paul Halpern (ed.), *The Mediterranean Fleet 1919–1929* (Farnham: Ashgate, 2011), p. 8 and fn 5.

10.   Paul G. Halpern (ed.), *The Royal Navy in the Mediterranean 1915–1918* (London: Temple Smith, 1987), p. 575. Both volumes of the Naval Records Society concerning the activities of the

Mediterranean Fleet in the First World War and subsequent decade of operations provide invaluable sources of Royal Naval documents pertaining to events in the Black Sea, Crimea and Sevastopol during the period 1918–20. The present author is grateful to Robin Brodhurst for loaning these volumes to him.

11. This is usually described as the 'Second Kuban Campaign'; the first (February–May 1918), the so-called 'Ice March', had ended in disaster for the Whites.

12. Smele, pp. 65–66.

13. Hopman War Diary, p. 654.

14. Ibid., pp. 650–51. Mariya Feodorovna, the wife of Alexander III, was the sister of Alexandra, Princess of Denmark, the queen consort of King Edward VII.

15. In her diary for 15 (28) November 1918, for example, Mariya Feodorovna wrote: 'At 12 o'clock, Captain Royds, commander of the 'Canterbury' arrived. I am so happy to see him again. He repeated the kind proposal from Georgie [King George V], and passed to me an invitation from the King of Italy to come to Rome. It is all extremely kind of them, but with their offers they will torture me to death. Now I will have to think about it all, but I will rely on God's will. He will definitely suggest to me what to do.' From: *Dnevniki Imperatritsy Mariyi Feodorovny* (1914–1920, 1923 gody) [Diaries of Empress Mariya Feodorovna] (Moscow: Vagrius, 2005), p. 278.

16. Hopman War Diary, pp. 652–54.

17. Altabayeva, p. 174.

18. Ibid., pp. 180–81.

19. Although Klochkovsky was appointed as a representative of Ukrainian Hetman Skoropadsky, by the time of this meeting he was serving on behalf of Denikin as the naval commander of Sevastopol, alongside de Bode as senior military representative. De Bode's daughter, the 21-year-old Sofiya Nikolaevna, had already been killed in action serving with the Volunteer Army during the first Kuban campaign in the spring of 1918.

20. Halpern, *1919–1929*, pp. 12–13.

21. As related by Kenez, p. 199, based on the memoir of V. Obolenskii, 'a liberal Crimean politician'.

22. Halpern, *1919–1929*, p. 16.

23. As related by McLaughlin, p. 323, on 21–22 December 1918, the *Volya* steamed to Ismid with a skeleton crew from the Royal Navy battleship HMS *Agamemnon*, which escorted the Russian warship.

24. Halpern, *1919–1929*, p. 17.

25. Ibid., p. 24.

26. Ibid.

27. Vaneev, *Spravochnik*, pp. 88–89; Kenez, pp. 197–99.

28. Kenez, pp. 200–01.

29. Halpern, *1919–1929*, pp. 26–27.

30. Carley, p. 161.

31. Halpern, *1919–1929*, pp. 28–29.

32. Kenez, p. 202.

33. Halpern, *1919–1929*, pp. 34–35.

34. Ibid., pp. 35–36.

35. Ibid., pp. 37–38.

36. Ibid., p. 39.

37. Carley, p. 174.w

38. Halpern, *1919–1929*, pp. 42–43. Further details of the French naval mutiny at Sevastopol are given in Jacques Raphael-Leygues and Jean-Luc Barré, *Les Mutins de la Mer Noire* [The Mutinies of the Black Sea] (Paris: Plon, 1981), pp. 25–32.

39.   Halpern, *1919–1929*, p. 44.

40.   Carley, p. 174.

41.   Halpern, *1919–1929*, p. 44.

42.   Carley, pp. 144–45.

43.   Halpern, *1919–1929*, pp. 45–46.

44.   Ibid., p. 46.

45.   Vaneev, *Spravochnik*, p. 90.

46.   Halpern, *1919–1929*, p. 50.

47.   Ibid., p. 75.

48.   Ibid., p. 85.

49.   Ibid., pp. 98–99.

50.   Ibid., p. 103.

51.   The following section draws on: Lincoln, *Red Victory*; Evan Mawdsley, *The Russian Civil War* (Edinburgh: Birlinn, 2008) [first published by Allen and Unwin in 1987]; and Clifford Kinvig, *Churchill's Crusade: The British Invasion of Russia 1918–1920* (London: Hambledon Continuum, 2006).

52.   Robert Rhodes James (ed.), *Winston S. Churchill: His Complete Speeches 1897–1963*, vol. iii (London and New York: Chelsea House Publishers & R.R. Bowker: 1974), p. 2671. The present author is grateful to Richard M. Langworth CBE for his assistance in providing this reference and his advice on other quotations by Churchill.

53.   James, pp. 372–73.

54.   Quoted by Smele, p. 174.

55.   Kinvig, pp. 224–30. A Royal Tank Corps detachment manned Whippet and Mk V tanks; 47 Squadron RAF was equipped with RE8 and DH9 aircraft. Britain supplied considerable quantities of tanks and aircraft to Denikin's forces, and provided instruction and training in their use.

56.   Alexis Wrangel, pp. 151–52.

57.   General P. N. Wrangel, trans. Sophie Goulston, *The Memoirs of General Wrangel. The Last Commander-in-Chief of The Russian National Army* (London: Williams & Norgate, 1929), p. 137. Hereafter referred to as Wrangel Memoirs.

58.   Wrangel Memoirs, pp. 141–46; Alexis Wrangel, pp. 153–54.

59.   Ashton Wade, *A Life on the Line* (Tunbridge Wells: D J Costello, 1988), p. 59.

60.   Alexis Wrangel, p. 153.

61.   Smele, pp. 166–67.

62.   Alexis Wrangel, p. 183.

63.   Halpern, *1919–1929*, pp. 227 and 229.

64.   James, pp. 386 and 389.

65.   Wrangel Memoirs, p. 153.

66.   Ashton Wade, pp. 59–60.

67.   Halpern, *1919–1929*, p. 229.

68.   Ibid., p. 235.

69.   This brief biographical sketch is derived from Walter Darnell Jacobs, *Frunze: The Soviet Clausewitz 1885–1925* (The Hague: Martinus Nijhoff, 1969), pp. 6–14.

70.   Ibid., pp. 197–202.

71.   Ibid., p. 209.

72.   Ibid., p. 215. *Glavkom* is an abbreviated form of *Glavnyy komandir* (principal commander).

73.   Ashton Wade, p. 61.

74. In illustration of the complexity of the Russian Civil War, Makhno's Black Army was an anarchist force that fought against all sides.

75. Wrangel Memoirs, p. 308.

76. Jacobs, p. 220, fn 37.

77. Quoted by Mawdsley, p. 371.

78. Wrangel Memoirs, pp. 307 and 309–10.

79. Anon, *Borba Trudyashchikhsya Kryma protiv Inostrannoy Voyennoy Interventsii Kontrrevolyutsii v gody Grazhdanskoy Voyny* [The Struggle of the Crimean Working Class against Foreign Military Interventionists and Counter-Revolutionaries in the Years of the Civil War], vol. ii, May 1918 – November 1920, (Simferopol: Krymizdat, 1961), p. 297, Document No. 333, 5 November 1920, 'Order by M.V. Frunze to the Troops of the Southern Front concerning the Delivery of a Decisive Blow to the Enemy in the Battles to Secure Crimea'. Hereafter referred to as *Borba Trudyashchikhsya Kryma*.

80. Some reports suggest that the western Syvash was at that time completely frozen over, and that this freak of nature (rather than the wind and the fords) accounts for the Red Army's crossing of the obstacle.

81. Wrangel Memoirs, pp. 313–14.

82. Ibid., p. 314.

83. Jacobs, pp. 221–22.

84. *Borba Trudyashchikhsya Kryma*, Document No. 341, 11 November 1920, 'Order of the Revolutionary Military Council of the Southern Front Concerning the Successful Advance of Red Army Troops into Crimea and the Treatment of Captives', p. 306.

85. Wrangel Memoirs, pp. 315–16.

86. Halpern, *1919–1929*, p. 281.

87. Lack of space precludes a description of the naval support in this account. Details of the French Navy's commitment are given in Marc Saibène, *La Flotte des Russes Blancs. Contribution de l'escadre française à l'évacuation des Russes blancs de Crimée, Novembre 1920* [The White Russian Fleet. Contribution of the French squadron to the evacuation of the White Russians from Crimea, November 1920] (Rennes: Marines editions, 2008). French warships that took part in the evacuation operation included (p. 86 refers): the cruisers *Waldeck-Rousseau* and *Provence*; the destroyers *Sénégalais*, *Algérien*, *Sakalave*; and the sloops and gunboats *Bar-le-Duc*, *Toul*, *Duchaffault* and *Dunkerque*.

88. Wrangel Memoirs, pp. 317–18.

89. Halpern, *1919–1929*, p. 284.

90. Wrangel Memoirs, pp. 318–19.

91. Jacobs, pp. 222–23.

92. Wrangel Memoirs, p. 319.

93. Ibid., p. 320.

94. Altabayeva, pp. 351–54.

95. Wrangel Memoirs, p. 323.

96. Altabayeva, p. 356.

97. Ibid.

98. Wrangel Memoirs, p. 324.

99. Ibid., pp. 324–26.

100. Lenin, Stalin, Frunze, Voroshilov, ed. R. M. VuP., *O Razgrome Vrangelya. Stati, Rechi, Dokumenty* [Concerning the Defeat of Wrangel. Articles, Speeches, Documents] (Simferopol: State Publishing House, Crimean ASSR, 1940), p. 133.

101. Wrangel Memoirs, pp. 324 and 326.

102. Jacobs, p. 223.

103. Wrangel Memoirs, p. 327.

104. Ibid.

Chapter 12: Red Terror to Patriotic War

1. Speech of 1 July 1921 'In Defence of the Tactics of the Communist International', V. I. Lenin, *Collected Works*, vol. 32, December 1920–August 1921 (Moscow: Progress Publishers, 1965), p. 468. Accessed at https://www.marxists.org/archive/lenin/works/cw/pdf/lenin-cw-vol-32.pdf on 29 May 2016.

2. Dmitry Sokolov, 'Mest' pobediteley. Krasnyy terror v Sevastopole v 1920–1921 gg.' [Revenge of the Winners. The Red Terror in Sevastopol of 1920–1921], *Russkaya Liniya*, 22.10.2007, accessed at http://rusk.ru/st.php?idar=112133 on 6 March 2016. Hereafter referred to as 'Revenge of the Winners'.

3. Lenin, Stalin, Frunze, Voroshilov, p. 133. The translation is also given by Mawdsley, p. 378.

4. Sokolov, 'Revenge of the Winners'.

5. *Borba Trudyashchikhsya Kryma*, Document No. 341, 11 November 1920, 'Order of the Revolutionary Military Council of the Southern Front Concerning the Successful Advance of Red Army Troops into Crimea and the Treatment of Captives', pp. 306–07.

6. The force ratio of 4.5:1 (186,068 to about 41,000) is taken from Colonel-General G. F. Krivosheev, *Soviet Casualties and Combat Losses in the Twentieth Century* (London: Greenhill Books, 1997), p. 14, extracted from Table 4, 'Numerical Strength of Red Army and Enemy Troops Engaged in Fighting at the Front, 1918–20'. This is a translation of the Russian-language original.

7. Dmitry Sokolov, 'Dva mesyatsa iz zhizni krasnogo Sevastopolya. Maloizvestnyye stranitsy istorii goroda v noyabre-dekabre 1920 g.' [Two Months in the Life of Red Sevastopol. Little-known Pages of History of the City in November–December 1920], *Russkaya Liniya*, 27.10.2015, accessed at http://rusk.ru/st.php?idar=72992 on 6 March 2016. Hereafter referred to as 'Two Months'.

8. Lenin, Stalin, Frunze, Voroshilov, pp. 134–35.

9. In 1918 the Russian Social Democratic Labour Party (Bolsheviks) changed its name to the Russian Communist Party (Bolsheviks), which in turn became the All-Union Communist Party (Bolsheviks) in 1925. This title was amended in 1952 to the Communist Party of the Soviet Union.

10. V. I. Lenin, *Collected Works*, vol. 31, April–December 1920 (Moscow: Progress Publishers, 1966), pp. 455–56. Accessed at http://www.marx2mao.com/PDFs/Lenin%20CW-Vol.%2031.pdf on 10 March 2016.

11. Cheka is the abbreviated form of Chrezvychaynaya Komissiya, or Emergency Commission.

12. NKVD stands for Narodnyi Komissariat Vnutrennikh Del – People's Commissariat for Internal Affairs. KGB is the abbreviated form of Komitet Gosudarstvennoy Bezopasnosti – Committee for State Security.

13. Sokolov, 'Revenge of the Winners'.

14. *Richtlinien für die Behandlung politischer Kommissare* (Guidelines for the Handling of Political Commissars).

15. Sokolov, 'Revenge of the Winners'.

16. The present author was made aware of this fact when lecturing about Field Marshal Erich von Manstein's campaign in Crimea (1941–42) at Taurida University in December 2011. His academic host asked him to look out of the first floor seminar room window, and pointed to where the executions of the Red Terror of 1920–21 had taken place.

17. Quoted by Lincoln, p. 385.

18. Ibid., p. 386.

19. Béla Kun was leader of the short-lived Soviet Hungarian republic of 1919, which lasted just over four months.

20. Lincoln, p. 386.

21. Khrapunov and Prokhorov, pp. 360–61, provide the following breakdown of the 1921 census: '298,666 (42.2%) Russians; 196,715 (26%) Crimean Tatars; 72,352 (9.5%) Ukrainians; 49,406 (6.9%) Jews; 42,350 (5.9%) Germans; 23,868 (3.4%) Greeks; 12,017 (1.7%) Armenians; 10,572 (1.5%) Bulgarians; 5,734 (0.9%) Poles and other nationalities', but leave 2% unaccounted for. Alexey V. Basov, *Krym v Velikoy Otechestvennoy Voyne 1941–1945* [Crimea in the Great Patriotic War 1941–1945] (Moscow: Nauka, 1987), p. 8, provides a different set of statistics, which do not reflect the census total of 719,331 [figures in thousands]: Russians, 274.9 (42.9%); Tatars, 164.2 (25.6%); Ukrainians, 45.7 (7.2%); Belorussians, 1 (0.2%); Greeks, Bulgars; Armenians and Germans, 154.5 (24.1%), giving a total population of 640,300. ,

22. A figure taken from B. P. Vologdin, 'Naseleniye Kryma' [The Population of Crimea], unpublished Taurida University thesis (recorded as 'last modified on 01-Dec-2008'), p. 1, accessed from elib. crimea.edu/krim/vologdin.pdf on 31 October 2016.

23. A. M. Chikin, *Sevastopol'. Istoriko-literaturnyy Spravochnik* [Sevastopol. Historical and Literary Guide] (Sevastopol: Veber, 2008), p. 612.

24. Khrapunov and Prokhorov, p. 353.

25. *Sovkhoz* is the abbreviated form of '*sovetskoye khozyaystvo*', Soviet (= state-owned) farm.

26. Williams, p. 70.

27. Khrapunov and Prokhorov, pp. 358–59.

28. Williams, p. 71; Khrapunov and Prokhorov, p. 360.

29. Williams, p. 70. Kolkhoz is the abbreviated form of '*kollektivnoye khozyaystvo*', collective (= cooperative-owned) farm.

30. At a speech given in Moscow on 21 November 1921 titled 'Our Foreign and Domestic Position and Party Tasks, Lenin had declared: 'There can be no question of rehabilitating the national economy or of communism unless Russia is put on a different and a higher technical basis than that which has existed up to now. Communism is Soviet power plus the electrification of the whole country, since industry cannot be developed without electrification'. V. I. Lenin, *Collected Works*, vol. 31, April– December 1920 (Moscow: Progress Publishers, 1966), p. 419. Accessed at https://www.marxists.org/archive/lenin/works/cw/pdf/lenin-cw-vol-31.pdf on 29 May 2016. The project became known as The State Commission for Electrification of Russia (GOELRO) Plan.

31. Examination of documents and photographs contained in Warwick University's digital collection 'The Russian Revolution and Britain, 1917–1928' indicates that a British railway workers' delegation in May 1926 to the USSR came from the Associated Society of Locomotive Engineers and Firemen (ASLEF). It is thus highly likely that this group visited Sevastopol, and that one of the delegates was ASLEF's assistant general secretary at the time and later Labour Party Member of Parliament, Percy Collick.

32. Vaneev, *Spravochnik*, p. 98.

33. Ibid., p. 100.

34. Ibid.

35. André Gide, *Retour de l'U.R.S.S.* [Back to the USSR] (Paris: Gallimard, 1936), p. 91.

36. G. I. Vaneev, *Sevastopol 1941–1942. Khronika Geroicheskoy Oborony* [Chronicle of a Heroic Defence], vol. 1. (Kyiv: Ukraina, 1995), p. 7. Hereafter referred to as Vaneev, *Khronika* to differentiate it from his earlier *Spravochnik* (1983)

37. The official title for the Soviet Navy 'Naval Forces of the Workers' and Peasants' Red Army' – Voenno-Morskikh Sil Raboche-Krestyanskoy Krasnoy Armi (VMS RKKA), also referred to as the 'Workers' and Peasants' Red Fleet' – Raboche-Krestyansky Krasny Flot (RKKF).

38. Data from 'The Formation of the Soviet Navy: Introduction', based on the articles of V. N. Krasnov and E. A. Shitikov, accessed at http://rusnavy.com/history/Refleet/formation.php on 13 March 2016.

39. McLaughlin, p. 323.

40. A. B. Shirokorad, *Chernomorskiy Flot v Tryokh Voynakh i Tryokh Revolyutsiyakh* [The Black Sea Fleet in Three Wars and Three Revolutions] (Moscow: Khranitel, 2007), p. 234.

41. Sokolov, 'Two Months'.

42. McLaughlin, p. 330.

43. Vaneev, *Spravochnik*, p. 96. Although Kalinin continued to serve as the purely nominal head of state of the Soviet Union under Stalin, his name is preserved in the Baltic port of Kaliningrad, the former East Prussian city of Königsberg, and in the associated Kaliningrad Oblast of the Russian Federation sandwiched between Lithuania and Poland.

44. Ibid.

45. McLaughlin, p. 330.

46. Ibid., p. 338. Emergency repairs were undertaken on both ships at Brest following the storm in the Bay of Biscay.

47. Hore, pp. 248–49. General Erich von Manstein recorded seeing a 'battleship of 35,000 tonnes' on the stocks when flying over the Nikolayev yard on 17 September 1941, the day he assumed command of the German Eleventh Army.

48. Data from Shirokorad, *Black Sea Fleet*, pp. 241–44. Slightly different figures are given in Komoyedov, p. 211, which lists 6 rather than 5 cruisers; 47 rather than 44 submarines; 15 rather than 12 (mine-sweeping) trawlers; 84 rather than 78 torpedo boats; 10 rather than 24 mine-hunters.

49. Details from Miroslav Morozov, *Vozdushnaya Bitva za Sevastopol 1941–1942* [Air Battle for Sevastopol 1941–1942 (Moscow: Yauza, 2007), pp. 11–13.

50. Gun data from http://www.navweaps.com/Weapons/WNRussian_12-52_m1907.htm accessed on 16 March 2016. Other sources suggest a range of up to 42km, but that distance would have only been achievable with a lighter shell introduced after the First World War. Aleksandr Shirokorad, *Bitva za Chernoye More* [Battle for the Black Sea] (Moscow: Tranzitkniga, 2005), p. 199, explains whereas a 470.9kg shell fired with a muzzle velocity of 762m/s in 1911 could achieve a range of 28.7km, a high explosive, long-range shell of 1928, weighing 314kg and fired at 950m/s, could achieve 44km.

51. This incident is mentioned by Robert Forczyk, *Where the Iron Crosses Grow. The Crimea 1941–44* (Oxford: Osprey, 2014), p. 33. He gives considerable further information about the history of the construction of Batteries 30 and 35. See also Clayton Donnell, *The Defence of Sevastopol 1941–1942. The Soviet Perspective* (Barnsley: Pen & Sword Military, 2016), pp. 32–38, which contains a detailed account of the development of Sevastopol's coastal defence batteries.

52. See Map 13.

53. Table based on General'nyy Shtab Krasnoy Armii Voenno-Istoricheskiy Otdel [General Staff of the Red Army Military Historical Department], *Oborona Sevastopolya, Operativno-Takticheskiy Ocherk* [Defence of Sevastopol. Operational-Tactical Report] (Moscow: 1943), p. 10; on P. A. Morgunov, *Geroycheskiy Sevastopol* [Heroic Sevastopol] (Moscow: Nauka, 1979), p. 42; and supplemented by information provided by local Sevastopol sources. The table is generalised in time: when the new guns of Battery No. 14 were being installed in early November 1941, Battery No. 54 was being overrun by German troops.

54. The numeration of Sevastopol's batteries is confusing: the numbers used before the First World War were not all retained in the 1920s–1930s and during the Second World War. For example, Battery 20 (Shishkova) became No. 16 and Battery 24 (Streletskaya) became No. 15. For details of these batteries see Gerhard Taube, *Festung Sewastopol* [Fortress Sevastopol] (Hamburg: E. S. Mittler & Sohn, 1995), pp. 15–16 and Donnell, pp. 32–42. To make things even more confusing, a new Battery 24 had been added to Battery No. 16 (Shishkov).

55. Three out of five marshals, 14 out of 16 army commanders; 60 out of 67 corps commanders; 130 of the 199 divisional commanders and another 35,000 or so more junior officers.

56. To associate himself with the October Revolution of 1917.

57. R. F. Oktyabrskaya (ed.), *Istoriku na zametku. Iz arkhiva admirala F. S. Oktyabrskogo* [Notes for the Historian. From the Archive of Admiral F. S. Oktyabrsky] (Sevastopol: Mistye, 2013), p. 11. This hybrid book contains both historical notes written by Oktyabrsky after the Second World War and his wartime diary (22 June 1941 – 30 June 1942, pp. 42–205). Hereafter referred to as 'Oktyabrsky', and where applicable, annotated with 'Diary'. Although we are fortunate in that Oktyabrsky left such a detailed diary of his wartime experiences, which this present account utilises, a degree of caution must be exercised in their interpretation.

58. For a good history of the Romanian Army in the Second World War, see Mark Axworthy, Cornel Scafes and Cristian Craciunoiu, *Third Axis. Fourth Ally. The Romanian Armed Forces in the European War, 1941–1945* (London: Arms and Armour Press, 1995).

59. This survey of Soviet defensive and German offensive plans prior to the outbreak of the German–Soviet war draws on an unpublished essay by C. J. Dick, 'Strategic Background to the Crimean Campaign of 1941–1942. The Soviet View', prepared for Exercise UNITED SHIELD 2007, a military staff ride to Crimea and Sevastopol organised and led by the present author, who is grateful to Charles Dick for permission to adapt this material.

60. English translation from H. R. Trevor-Roper (ed.), *Hitler's War Directives 1939–1945* [texts from Walter Hubatsch, *Hitlers Weisungen für die Kriegführung 1939–1945*] (London: Sidgwick and Jackson, 1964), p. 49.

61. Ibid., pp. 50–51.

62. Morgunov, p. 12.

63. Ibid., p. 24.

64. Ibid., p. 34.

65. The train that stands today near Sevastopol bus and railway stations displays a 180mm (TM-1-180) coastal defence railway artillery gun, which was employed in the defence of Tuapse from September to December 1942. Although this particular weapon was not used in the defence of Sevastopol, 1941–42, it commemorates the role of the Soviet coastal artillery during the Great Patriotic War.

66. Marek J. Murawski, *Luftwaffe over Sevastopol* (Lublin: Karego, 2008), p. 5.

67. Ibid., pp. 33–34.

68. Ibid., p. 6.

69. English text from Vladimir Karpov, *Russia at War 1941–45* (New York: Vendome Press, 1987), p. 37.

70. Shirokorad, *Black Sea Fleet*, pp. 252–54; V. B. Ivanov, *Sevastopolskaya Epopeya 1941–1944 v ofitsialnykh dokumentakh* [Sevastopol Epic 1941–1944 in official documents] (Sevastopol: Bibleks, 2004), pp. 13–14. Oktyabrsky (pp. 34–38) offers a rather different view of events.

71. Geoffrey Roberts (ed.), *Marshal of Victory. The Autobiography of General Georgy Zhukov* (Barnsley: Pen & Sword Military, 2013), p. 281. Originally published by the Agentstvo Pechati Novosti in Moscow in 1969 under the title *Vospominaniya i Razmyshleniya* [Memories and Reflections]. Note that the original Russian language version (p. 247) gives the time for the first telephone call on 22 June 1941 from Oktyabrsky as 0317 hours, rather than 0307 hours given in the English language text.

72. Georgy Zadorozhnikov, *Memuary Starogo Malchika* [Memories of an Old Boy] *(Sevastopol 1941–1945)* (Sevastopol: NPTS EKOSI-Gidrofizika, 2013), p. 29.

73. Ivanov, p. 13.

74. Zhukov, p. 46.

75. Oktyabrsky, pp. 29–33 and Diary, 22 June 1941, p. 42.

76.   Oktyabrsky, Diary, 13 July 1941, p. 53.

77.   Ivanov, p. 20.

78.   Oktyabrsky, Diary, 17 July 1941, p. 55.

79.   For a succinct description of the siege of Odessa from a Romanian viewpoint, see Axworthy et al., pp. 49–56.

80.   Oktyabrsky, Diary, 31 July 1941, p. 64.

81.   Ivanov, p. 22.

82.   Quoted by David Stahel, *Operation Barbarossa and Germany's Defeat in the East* (Cambridge: University Press, 2009), p. 425.

83.   Supplement to Hitler's Directive No. 34., Trevor-Roper, p. 93.

84.   Bernd Wegner, 'Die Kämpfe auf der Krim', *Der Globale Krieg: Die Ausweitung zum Weltkrieg und der Wechsel der Initiative 1941–1943* ['The Fighting in Crimea', The Global War: Expansion to World War and the Change of Initiative 1941–1943] [*Das deutsche Reich im Zweiten Weltkrieg*, vol. 4] (Stuttgart: Deutsche Verlags-Anstalt, 1990), p. 840.

85.   Norman Rich, *Hitler's War Aims: The Establishment of the New Order* (London: André Deutsch, 1974), p. 383.

86.   Also termed in translation as the 'Maritime Army'.

87.   This author's original title for his biography of Manstein was *Manstein: Hitler's Most Controversial General*. Reluctantly he was over-ruled by his publisher who considered that *Manstein: Hitler's Greatest General* was a better title.

88.   For a comprehensive account and analysis of Manstein's career, see Mungo Melvin, *Manstein: Hitler's Greatest General* (London: Weidenfeld & Nicolson, 2010). Other perspectives are to be found in Benoît Lemay, trans. Pierce Heyward, *Erich von Manstein: Hitler's Master Strategist* (Havertown, PA; Newbury, Berkshire: Casemate, 2010), originally published as *Erich von Manstein. Le stratège de Hitler* (Paris: Perrin, 2010); and Marcel Stein, *Field Marshal von Manstein. The Janus Head. A Portrait* (Solihull: Helion, 2007), originally published as *Der Januskopf – Feldmarschall von Manstein. Eine Neubewertung* (Bissendorf: Biblio Verlag, 2004). Manstein's wartime memoirs, *Verlorene Siege*, were published by the Athenäum Verlag in Bonn in 1955; the edited translation, *Lost Victories*, was published by Collins in London in 1958.

89.   Porter Randall Blakemore, *Manstein in the Crimea: The Eleventh Army Campaign, 1941–1942* (Ann Arbor, Mich: University Films Internation, 1989), p. 28.

90.   Basov, p. 34.

91.   Soviet dispositions are given in Basov, pp. 34–35. See also the biography of General I. E. Petrov by Vladimir Karpov, *Polkovodets* [Commander] (originally published in Moscow by Sov. Pisatel in 1988 and republished by Veche in 2014 under the title of *Polkovodets. Voyna generala Petrova*) – of which there are two translations: a considerably abridged version, *The Commander*, trans. Yuri S. Shirokov and Nicholas Louis (London: Brassey's, 1987); and a 'lightly shortened' version in German, *Der General und Ich*, trans. Peter Lobig and Dr Werner Tschoppe (Berlin: Militärverlag der Deutschen Demokratischen Republik, 1989).

92.   Basov, p. 50.

93.   Details of the LIV Corps attack are taken from Wilhelm Tieke, *Kampf um die Krim 1941–1944* [The Battle for the Crimea, 1941–1944] (Gummersbach: Selbstverlag Wilhelm Tieke, 1975), pp. 13–23.

94.   Basov, p. 52.

95.   Tieke, pp. 23 and 25.

96.   BA-MA, N/507-92. Der Oberbefehlshaber der 11. Armee, A.H.Qu., den 4.10.41.

97.   Oktyabrsky, Diary, 25 September 1941, p. 86.

98.   Ibid., 26 September, p. 86.

99.   Ibid., 28 September 1941, pp. 87–88.

100. Ibid., 30 September 1941, p. 88.

101. Ibid., 1 October 1941, p. 89.

102. Ibid., 5 October 1941, p. 90.

103. Ibid., 11 October 1941, p. 91.

104. Ibid., 18 October 1941, pp. 92–93.

105. Basov, p. 58.

106. BA-MA, N/507-92. Der Oberbefehlshaber der 11. Armee, A.H.Qu., den 15. Oktober 1941. Ia Nr. 4080/41 geh.Kdos. Betr.: Operationen Krim – Kertsch An Oberkommando der Heeresgruppe Süd.

107. Blakemore, pp. 62 and 72.

108. In this operational context, *Vorausabteilung* is best translated as a 'forward detachment' rather than as a 'vanguard'. The difference lies in the task allocated the force involved. A forward detachment can have a variety of offensive roles such as finding gaps in the enemy's defences, seizing vital crossings over obstacles and generally unhinging the enemy by appearing unexpectedly quickly in his depth. A 'vanguard', on the other hand, has a much more restricted role in guarding – as the name suggests – the main body of an advancing formation.

109. Karpov, *Der General und Ich*, p. 110. Blakemore (p. 70), however, asserts that the first of Petrov's troops entered the battle on 20 October 1941, the third day of Manstein's attack at Ishun.

110. Manstein, *Lost Victories*, p. 219.

111. Ibid., p. 220.

112. Dietrich von Choltitz, *Soldat unter Soldaten* [Soldier amongst Soldiers] (Zürich: Europa Verlag, 1951), p. 102.

113. Oktyabrsky, Diary, 21 October 1941 p. 93.

114. Ivanov, p. 24.

115. Ibid., p. 25.

116. Tieke, pp. 45–46.

117. Karpov, *Russia at War 1941–45*, p. 37.

Chapter 13: City of Courage: the Second Defence of Sevastopol

1. Ehrenburg, p. 9.

2. L. Solovyev and M. Kogut, 'Sevastopol Nights', *Sevastopol November 1941 – July 1942*, p. 17.

3. For example, see Morgunov pp. 48 and 107.

4. In covering the period 1 November – 16 December 1941, in the German original of *Verlorene Siege*, Manstein describes the pursuit (*Verfolgung*), following the break-out from the Perekop–Ishun isthmus, briefly in eight pages (pp. 227–35) whereas in the English translation (*Lost Victories*), the same section is reduced to just over two (pp. 220–22), with very scant details as to either intentions or dispositions. Likewise, the 'First Assault of Sevastopol', launched on 17 December 1941, also receives brief mention (pp. 235–40 in the German edition and pp. 222–25 in the English). In many ways, these cursory accounts represent some of the least satisfactory parts of his memoirs, whether in the German or English editions. Manstein's personal war diary, however, is full of detail for the months of November and December 1941, as is the official war diary of Headquarters Eleventh Army. Hence he had ample material on which to draw on in writing his memoirs. Therefore it seems reasonable to assume that Manstein wished to reduce the significance of his attempts to storm Sevastopol off the line of march in November 1941 (regarded by the Soviet defenders as the *First* Assault) and of the attacks mounted in December 1941 (the Germans' 'First' Assault, listed by the Soviets as the *Second*). There is much greater detail afforded to the 'Second' Assault of June 1942.

5. Oktyabrsky, Diary, 4 November 1941, pp. 96–97.

6. According to Shirokorad, *The Battle for the Black Sea* (p. 201), in the period 1–4 November 1941, 'Coastal Battery No. 30 fired 142 12-in. shells and Battery No. 10 276 10-in. shells. The fire of these batteries destroyed 30 tanks and 60 vehicles, and caused up to 650 casualties of the enemy infantry'.

7. Leninskiy Kommunisticheskiy Soyuz Molodozhi Ukrainy (LKSMU). The Communist Youth League is better known by its Russian abbreviated form of *Komsomol*.

8. Interviews conducted by the present author with Rear Admiral (retired) Professor A. R. Glushakov at the Veterans' House (*Dom Veteranov*) in Sevastopol on 16 May and 30 September 2011.

9. For details of the monument to the cadets, see www.memento-sevastopol.ru/necropol. php?code=28. A more detailed description of the cadets' action, see http://gazetam.ru/22-fevralya/kursantskiy-morskoy-batalon-voenno-morskogo-uchilischa-beregovoy-oboronyi-im.-lksmu-v-oborone-sevas.htm.

10. Karpov, *The Commander*, p. 63.

11. Ibid., pp. 63–64; more detail is given in Karpov, *Der General und Ich*, pp. 113–14. The English translation contains a significant error in that it describes the 'road to Simferopol through Bakhchisaray' as being 'probably cut'. From the context of Petrov's remarks (and from the German translation), it is quite clear that the road to Sevastopol is meant.

12. Karpov, *The Commander*, pp. 64–65.

13. Karpov, *Der General und Ich*, p. 120.

14. Oktyabrsky, Diary, 4 November 1941, p. 98.

15. Karpov, *Der General und Ich*, p. 122.

16. Oktyabrsky, Diary, 4 November 1941, p. 99.

17. Tieke, p. 65.

18. As recounted to Ms Tatyana Bukharina in a personal interview at Yalta in December 2011. Madame Sikorskaya died in Yalta in 2014 and is buried in her home town.

19. Oktyabrsky, Diary, 7 November 1941, pp. 100–101.

20. In a similar manner to the suppression of the news of the sinking of the British liner *Lancastria* off the French port of St Nazaire on 17 June 1940, the Soviet authorities hushed up the scale of losses on the *Armeniya*.

21. Manstein, Private War Diary, Entry for 7 November 1941. On 8 November 1941, the German *Wehrmachtsbericht* merely reported that the Luftwaffe had 'destroyed in the waters to the south of Yalta a transport ship of 8000 BRT'.

22. See Melvin, *Manstein*, p. 168.

23. Information on the Romanian Mountain Corps has been taken from Victor Nitu, 'The 3rd Army in the Ukraine and the Crimea – 1941', posted on the 'Romanian Armed Forces in the Second World War' website at http://www.worldwar2.ro/arr/?article=6, accessed on 17 April 2016; and from Axworthy et al., pp. 62–65. Comprising six infantry battalions of Vanatori de Munte (mountain hunters), supported by an artillery group and an engineer battalion, a fully equipped and manned Romanian mountain brigade contained considerable potential fighting power, particularly in combat over complex terrain such as that flanking Sevastopol to the east.

24. BA-MA, N/507-92. Der Oberbefehlshaber der 11. Armee, A.H.Qu., den 15. Oktober 1941, Ia Nr. 4080/41 geh. Kdos. Betr.: Operationen Krim – Kertsch An Oberkommando der Heeresgruppe Süd, p. 2, paragraph 2.

25. Manstein Personal War Diary entry for 18.9.1941: 'Estimation of the [Eleventh] Army HQ concerning the Romanians: Soldiers undemanding, willing and brave. Officers can and bring in the majority not much.'

26. Ivanov, pp. 31–32.

27. BA-MA, N/507-92. Armeeoberkommando 11. A.H.Qu., den 9. November 1941, I a (? OB) Betr.: Weiterführung Operation Krim. An Heeresgruppe Süd.

28. Ibid.

29. This table is a simplified version of that given in Morgunov, pp. 511–13.

30. From interviews conducted by the present author with V. F. Eliseev at the Veterans' House in Sevastopol on 14 September and 21 December 2012.

31. Manstein, Private War Diary, Entry for 16 November 1941.

32. Ibid.

33. Karpov, *Russia at War 1941–45*, p. 37.

34. Oktyabrsky, Diary, 25 November 1941, p. 109.

35. Tieke, p. 72.

36. Friedrich-August von Metzsch, *Die Geschichte der 22. Infanterie-Division* (Kiel: Verlag Hans-Henning Podzun, 1952), pp. 32–33.

37. Ibid., p. 7.

38. Ibid., p. 33.

39. Quoted by Karpov, *Der General und Ich*, p. 130.

40. Oktyabrsky, Diary, 23 November 1941, p. 107.

41. M. Rudny, 'Eight Months', *Sevastopol November 1941 – July 1942*, p. 11.

42. M. Turovsky, 'The Underground City', *Sevastopol November 1941 – July 1942*, pp. 52–54.

43. Vaneev, *Spravochnik*, p. 114.

44. Zadorozhnikov, p. 47.

45. BA-MA, RH 20-11/489, Eleventh Army War Diary. Entries for 20–22 November 1941.

46. Blakemore, p. 108.

47. Krivosheev, p. 107, Table 75, 'Casualty Figures for Selected Army Group Operations', No. 5.

48. Oktyabrsky, Diary, 23, 26 and 29 November and 5 December 1941, pp. 107–12.

49. Manstein, *Verlorene Siege* p. 237, states that the logistic lift was reduced to 50%.

50. Manstein, Private War Diary entries.

51. Quoted in German by Tieke, pp. 73–74; translation by the present author. Blakemore, p. 110, offers a slightly different interpretation.

52. Trevor-Roper, p. 108.

53. David M. Glantz, *Forgotten Battles of the German-Soviet War (1941–1945)*, vol. ii, *The Winter Campaign 5 December 1941–April 1942* (Carlisle, Pennsylvania: privately published, 1999), p. 9.

54. Manstein Personal War Diary, 1 December 1941.

55. Ibid., 17 December 1941.

56. Renamed Krepkoe in 1945, but the former village no longer exists – one of several vanished Tatar settlements on the Crimean peninsula.

57. Tieke, p. 78.

58. Ivanov, pp. 15–16.

59. Ibid., and Karpov, *The Commander*, pp. 78–79.

60. A good example is Field Marshal Sir Douglas Haig's famous 'Backs to the Wall' Special Order of the Day of 11 April 1918 to all ranks of the British Army in the face of the German offensive on the Western Front during the First World War.

61. Ivanov, pp. 15–16.

62. Oktyabrsky, Diary, 21 December 1941, p. 121.

63. Ibid., 22 December 1941, p. 122.

64. Quoted by Tieke, p. 85.

65. Metzsch, p. 34.

66.   Ibid.

67.   Oktyabrsky, Diary, 23–27 December 1941, pp. 123–24.

68.   Metzsch, p. 35

69.   Ibid.

70.   Manstein, *Lost Victories*, p. 226.

71.   Sponeck's subsequent fate – court martial resulting in death sentence, commuted to six years' fortress arrest, and execution in the wake of the 20 July 1944 plot against Hitler (a matter with which he had nothing to do) lies well beyond the scope of this book.

72.   Significantly, Manstein, *Verlorene Siege*, p. 246, described the Dzhankoy–Simferopol railway line as the '*Lebensader der Armee*' (the 'lifeline of the Army').

73.   Manstein, Personal War Diary, 29 December 1941.

74.   Oktyabrsky Diary entries for 28–30 December 1941, pp. 125–26.

75.   Manstein, *Verlorene Siege*, pp. 239–40.

76.   The historian of the German 22nd Infantry Division claimed: 'An intact regiment could have seized the Sevastopol Bay on the last day of the year [1941]'. (Metzsch, p. 35).

77.   Manstein, *Verlorene Siege*, p. 243.

78.   Glantz, *Forgotten Battles*, vol. ii, pp. 121–23.

79.   Leutnant Kolbe, '… ins Meer zurückzuwerfen', in *Wir Erobern die Krim. Soldaten der Krim-Armee berichten* [… 'To be Thrown back into the Sea'. We Conquer the Crimea. Soldiers of the Crimea-Army report] (Neustadt/Weinstrasse: Pfälzische Verlagsanstalt, 1943), pp. 88-100.

80.   Manstein, *Verlorene Siege*, p. 249.

81.   Blakemore, pp. 145–46.

82.   Manstein, Personal War Diary, 14 January 1942.

83.   Glantz, *Forgotten Battles*, vol. ii, p. 131.

84.   Ibid., pp. 137–38.

85.   General Staff of the Red Army Military Historical Department, *Oborona Sevastopolya*, p. 26.

86.   Solovyev and Kogut, *Sevastopol November 1941 – July 1942*, p. 19.

87.   As described by L. Oserov, 'The Girl With the Rifle', *Sevastopol November 1941 – July 1942*, p. 26. In fact, Pavlichenko had already achieved 187 kills in the defence of Odessa, so there is some literary license in Oserov's account of her activities in Sevastopol.

88.   Pavlichenko's memoirs have been republished: L. M. Pavlichenko, *Ya – Snayper v Boyakh za Sevastopol' i Odessy* [I am a Sniper in the Battles of Sevastopol and Odessa] (Moscow: Veche, 2015). A biographical Russian–Ukrainian film of Pavlichenko (titled *Bitva za Sevastopol'* [Battle of Sevastopol] in the Russian version and *Nezlamna* [Indestructible] in the Ukrainian) was released in 2015.

89.   Glantz, *Forgotten Battles*, vol. ii, pp. 141–42.

90.   Ibid., p. 144.

91.   Ibid., p. 149.

92.   Manstein, *Lost Victories*, p. 230.

93.   Glantz , *Forgotten Battles*, vol. ii, pp. 153–54.

94.   Trevor-Roper, pp. 117–18.

95.   Manstein, *Lost Victories*, p. 231.

96.   BA-MA, RH 20-11/464a, Armeeoberkommando 11, Abt. Ia Nr. 1833/42 geh. Kdos. A.H.Qu, den 30. April 1942, 24,00 Uhr. Armeebefehl für "Trappenjagd" [Army Order for Trappenjagd], paragraph 2.

97.   Oktyabrsky, Diary, 8 and 9 May 1942 at p. 163 and p. 164 respectively.

98.   Ibid., 2 May 1942, p. 165.

99.   Adapted from Moltke the Elder, who wrote 'Even a *single* error in the original assembly of the armies can hardly ever be made good again during the entire course of the campaign' – from

Daniel J. Hughes (ed.), *Moltke on the Art of War. Selected Writings* (New York: Ballantine Books, 1993), p. 91.

100.   Oktyabrsky, Diary, 14 May 1942, p. 166.

101.   Ibid., 17 May 1942, pp. 168–69.

102.   Karpov, *The Commander*, p. 83.

103.   Manstein, *Lost Victories*, p. 238.

104.   Karpov, *The Commander*, p. 85.

Chapter 14: The End of the Second Defence and Axis Occupation

1.   Vice-Admiral F. S. Oktyabrsky, 'The Defence of Sevastopol', *Sevastopol November 1941–July 1942*, p. 70.

2.   Trevor-Roper, p. 117.

3.   Manstein, *Lost Victories*, p. 239.

4.   Ibid., pp. 242–43.

5.   Karpov, *Der General und Ich*, p. 175.

6.   General Staff of the Red Army Military Historical Department, *Oborona Sevastopolya*, p. 47; Vaneev, *Khronika*, vol. 2, pp. 160–63.

7.   Supporting LIV Corps, Sturmgeschütz-Abteilungen 190 and 197 held 18 and 13 assault guns apiece respectively; supporting XXX Corps, Sturmgeschütz-Abteilung 249 fielded only 12 assault guns – making a grand total of 43 such armoured vehicles. Details from Tieke, pp. 156–57.

8.   The full unit title was Panzer-Abteilung 300 (FL) – FL meaning *Funk-Lenk* or radio-controlled.

9.   This is a direct translation of the German – 'heavy' in this case includes what other armies would have classified as 'medium' such as 150mm-calibre artillery pieces.

10.   BA-MA, RH 20-11/465a, 'Artillerie an SSewastopol-Front, Stand 6.6.42' [Artillerie on the Sevastopol Front. As at 6.6.42].

11.   Manstein, *Lost Victories*, p. 245.

12.   Ibid., pp. 245–46.

13.   BA-MA, RH 20-11/464a, Generalkommando VIII. Fliegerkorps I a, Nr. 7515/42 geh., Befehl für den vorbereitenden Angriff gegen Sewastopol, 1. Juni 1942 [Order for the attack to be prepared against Sevastopol, 1 June 1942].

14.   VIII Air Corps employed seven *Kampf* (bomber) groups; three *Stuka* (dive-bomber) groups; and four *Jagd* (fighter) groups. The medium bombers comprised two groups from Kampfgeschwader (KG) 27 (He 111); two groups from KG 51 (Ju 88); two groups of KG 100 (He 111) and II./KG 26 with He 111, which could also torpedo ship targets. Stukageschwader 77 provided the three groups of Ju 87 Stukas. Jagdgeschwader 52 and 77 each provided two groups of ME 109 fighters.

15.   Karpov, *Der General und Ich*, p. 177.

16.   Oktyabrsky, Diary, 1 June 1942, p. 176.

17.   I. A. Laskin, *Na puti k perelomu* [On the Way to the Turning Point] (Moscow: Voenizdat, 1977), pp. 108–09.

18.   Lenin adapted this maxim from the old Russian proverb 'Doveryat' doveryay, da pochashche proveryay'. ('Keep on trusting, but control often').

19.   Karpov, *Der General und Ich*, pp. 178–79.

20.   Oktyabrsky, Diary, 4 June 1942, p. 179.

21.   Ibid., 6 June 1942, p. 180.

22.   Boris Voyetekhov, trans. Ralph Parker and V. M. Genne, *The Last Days of Sevastopol* (London: Cassell, 1943), pp. 68–69.

23.   Karpov, *Der General und Ich*, p. 180.

24. Manstein, *Lost Victories*, p. 248.

25. Ibid.

26. Hitler cut Eleventh Army some slack on air support the next day. On 8 June the War Diary of OKW (the German Supreme Command) noted: 'In view of the strong enemy resistance at Sevastopol, the Luftwaffe employed there should no longer be withdrawn after 3 days, but rather remain there until a decisive success is achieved or is imminent'. Andreas Hillgruber (ed.), *Kriegestagebuch des Oberkommandos der Wehrmacht (Wehrmachtführungsstab)* [War Diary of the German Armed Forces High Command (Command Staff)], Band II: 1. January 1942 – 31. Dezember 1942 (Frankfurt am Main: Bernard & Graefe, 1963), p. 410. (However, as the battle dragged on, the quantity of air support diminished.)

27. Oktyabrsky, Diary, 7 June 1942, p. 181.

28. Ibid., 8 June 1942, pp. 181–82.

29. Zadorozhnikov, p. 56.

30. Oktyabrsky, Diary, 9 June 1942, pp. 182–83.

31. Ibid.

32. BA-MA, RH 20-11/34, Armeekommando 11, Abt. Ia Nr.2475/42 geh., Vorgesch.Gef.Stand, den 8.6.42. [Untitled letter signed by Manstein.]

33. BA-MA, RH 20-11/465b, Armeepionierführer b.A.O.K.11 (Pi.1), A.H.Qu., den 11.6.42, An OB/Chef/Ia, 'Erfahrungen der ersten 4 Tage des Angriffes auf SSevastopol (Nordfront) im Minenkampf' [Lessons from the First Four Days of the Attack on Sevastopol (North Front) in minewarfare].

34. BA-MA, RH 20-11/465b, [Brief] an Generaloberst Halder, Chef des Genst. des Heeres, 9.6.42.

35. Quoted by Vaneev, *Spravochnik*, pp. 124–25.

36. Metzsch, p. 42. Interestingly, Manstein narrates the same story and wording in *Verlorene Siege*, p. 274 and *Lost Victories*, p. 250, perhaps drawing on the divisional history.

37. Eugene Petrov, 'Under Fire', *Sevastopol November 1941 – July 1942*, p. 59.

38. From the article describing the history of the 'Cruiser Molotov' in the Russian-language website Chernomorskii Flot, http://flot.sevastopol.info/ship/cruiser/molotov.htm, accessed on 16 June 2016.

39. As recounted by Voyetekhov, pp. 64–65.

40. History of the 'Cruiser Molotov'.

41. Manstein, *Lost Victories*, p. 248.

42. Oktyabrsky, Diary, 14 and 17 June 1942, pp. 188 and 190 respectively.

43. Manstein, *Lost Victories*, p. 251.

44. Oktyabrsky, Diary, 22 June 1942, pp. 195–96.

45. The five German infantry regiments concerned were: the 57th, 116th, 318th, 360th and 420th.

46. Oktyabrsky, Diary, 17 June 1942, p. 190.

47. Leonid Sobolev, 'In the Old Fort', *Sevastopol November 1941 – July 1942*, p. 63.

48. Oktyabrsky, Diary, 18 June 1942, p. 191.

49. Voyetekhov, p. 113.

50. Oktyabrsky, Diary, 25–26 June 1942, pp. 199–200.

51. Manstein, *Lost Victories*, p. 253.

52. Ibid., pp. 253–254.

53. Ibid., p. 254.

54. Oktyabrsky, Diary, 25–26 June 1942, pp. 199–200.

55. Eye-witness account by Valentina Pavlovna Kutuzova in Irina Shpakova, 'A vy rosli vmeste s voynoy Inogo mira vy ne znali' [You grew up together with war. You did not know another world], *Sevastopol'skiye izvestiya*, #24 (1871), 25 June 2016, pp. 6–7, accessed at https://sevzakon.ru/view/pressa/gazeta/14032/14970/ on 30 October 2016.

56. Manstein, *Verlorene Siege*, pp. 278–79 and *Lost Victories*, p. 255. Note that the English edition incorrectly states that a '90-foot wall of rock fell in over a length of some 900 yards'. The correct length was 300m.

57. Manstein, *Lost Victories*, p. 257.

58. Quoted by Tieke, p. 216.

59. Voyetekhov, p. 146.

60. Oktyabrsky, Diary, 30 June 1942, pp. 204–05.

61. Quoted and translated by Alexander Werth, *Russia at War 1941–1945* (London: Pan Books, 1965), pp. 368–69.

62. Oktyabrsky, Diary, 30 June 1942, p. 205.

63. Oktyabrsky, pp. 208–09.

64. Karpov, *The Commander*, p. 94.

65. Ibid., p. 95; Karpov, *Der General und Ich*, p. 209–10; Ivanov, p. 113.

66. Manstein, *Lost Victories*, p. 257.

67. Zadorozhnikov, p. 58.

68. Manstein, *Lost Victories*, p. 257.

69. Zadorozhnikov, p. 59.

70. Manstein, *Lost Victories*, pp. 258–59.

71. Primary sources contradict themselves over the roles of the Romanian 4th Mountain and 18th Infantry Divisions on 1 July 1942. Whereas Manstein (*Verlorene Siege*, p. 281) writes that the former unit was committed to Balaklava, Headquarters Eleventh Army's war diary states that latter formation 'seized at 0545 hours the town, railway and harbour of Balaklava'. (BA-MA, RH 20-11/460, Kriegstagebuch, 1.7.1942.)

72. Axworthy, p. 70. He follows Manstein in stating that the Romanian 4th Division cleared Balaklava. This division, however, was subordinated to LIV Corps at the time.

73. From B. A. Borisov, *Sevastopoltsy ne sdayutsya* [Sevastopolians do not Surrender] (Simferopol, 1961), p. 176, as quoted and translated by Werth, p. 367.

74. Khrapunov and Prokhorov, p. 371.

75. Headquarters Eleventh Army War Diary, 4 July 1942.

76. Tieke, p. 223.

77. Krivosheev, Table 75, 'Casualty Figures for Selected Army Group Operations', No. 6, p. 107.

78. *Die Wehrmachtberichte 1939–1945*, Band 2, p. 194.

79. Axworthy, p. 70.

80. For a similar interpretation of the Axis casualties, see Tieke, p. 223.

81. Zadorozhnikov, pp. 60–62.

82. Ivanov, p. 268.

83. Tieke, p. 224.

84. From an article in *Sevastopol'skiye izvestiya*, #24 (1871), 25 June 2016, p. 7.

85. Ivanov, p. 268.

86. Ibid., p. 267.

87. Tieke, p. 224.

88. Manstein's hand was all over the programme for the late afternoon of 5 July 1942. It comprised a *Grosser Zapfenstreich* (beating retreat), followed by a reception and concert party. The musicians of the 16th and 102nd Infantry Regiments (from the 22nd and 24th Divisions respectively) formed a combined military band, who were joined by an engineer sub-unit (the 2nd Company, 70th Engineer Battalion) for the parade. Significantly, the event opened with the march of Manstein's very first unit prior to the First World War, the 3rd Foot Guards, 'the Brewer of Preston'. The programme included prayers to the fallen, the singing of the traditional lament '*Ich*

hatt' einen Kamaraden' ['I had a comrade'] and a rousing '*Sieg Heil*' to the Führer prior to the national hymns of Germany and Romania.

89. Manstein, *Verlorene Siege*, pp. 283–84 (the account of the event at Livadia on 5 July 1942 is missing from the English translation); details of the programme are from Oliver Richter, 'Unternehmen "Störfang" – Die Eroberung Sewastopols 1942' [Operation STURGEON CATCH – The Capture of Sevastopol 1942], *Militär und Geschichte: Bilder, Tatsachen, Hintergründe* (2008), Heft 42, p. 19; further information from Tieke, p. 222. The author is grateful to Colonel (GS) Peter Uffelmann, German Army, for providing a copy of Richter's article. ·

90. Quoted by Tieke, p. 222.

91. Manstein, *Verlorene Siege*, pp. 285–89.

92. Axworthy, p.70.

93. As reproduced in translated form at Vice-Admiral F. S. Oktyabrsky, 'The Defence of Sevastopol', *Sevastopol November 1941 – July 1942*, p. 63.

94. I. Petrov, in Al[eksandr] Khamadan, *Sevastopol'tsy. Zapiski voyennogo korrespondenta* [Sevastopolians. Notes of a Military Correspondent] (Moscow: Molodaya Gvardiya, 1942), p. 3. Petrov's introduction was dated 28 July 1942. This volume was republished by Git Pak of Sevastopol in 2014.

95. Vice-Admiral F. S. Oktyabrsky, 'The Defence of Sevastopol', *Sevastopol November 1941–July 1942*, p. 70.

96. Ivanov, p. 269.

97. An analysis of the relevant charges against Manstein and his resulting sentence is given in Melvin, *Manstein*, pp. 470–73 and 478.

98. Tieke, pp. 224–25.

99. Manstein, *Lost Victories*, pp. 260–61.

100. For further details, see Manstein, *Lost Victories*, pp. 264–67.

101. Tieke, p. 224.

102. Ivanov, p. 270.

103. Ibid., pp. 269–70.

104. Ibid., pp. 270–71.

105. Otto Dieter Pohl, *Die Herrschaft der Wehrmacht. Deutsche Militärbesatzung und einheimische Bevölkerung in der Sowjetunion 1941–1944* [The Rule of the *Wehrmacht*. German Military Occupation and Indigenous Peoples in the Soviet Union 1941–1944] (Munich: Oldenbourg, 2008), p. 193. For further details of the German occupation policy on Crimea, see Alexander Dallin, *German Rule in Russia 1941–1945. A Study of Occupation Policies* (London: Macmillan, 1957), pp. 253–66.

106. BA-MA, RH 20-11/424, Geheime Kommandosache! A.O.K.11/O.Qu., Betr.: Räumung der Krim [Clearance of Crimea], 3.6.42.

107. Ivanov, p. 269.

108. N. F. Zadorozhnaya, *Dom-muzey sevastopolskikh podpolshchikov 1942–1944* [Memorial House of the Sevastopol Resistance, 1942–44] (Sevastopol: Borisov, 2007), p. 19. The museum's website at http://www.sev-museum-panorama.com/ru/undergroundmembers gives a good overview of the resistance and its activities.

109. Ibid., p. 46. The acronym KPOVTN stands for 'Kommunistcheskaya podpolnaya organizatsiya v tylu nemtsev'.

110. According to Khrapunov and Prokhorov, p. 374, by 15 January 1944 'there were 3,733 partisans in Crimea, including 1,944 Russians, 348 Ukrainians, and 598 Tatars'. These authors did not explain the discrepancy in their figures – the missing 843 individuals.

111. Zadorozhnaya, p. 32.

112. Vaneev, *Spravochnik*, p. 127.

113. Zadorozhnaya, pp. 41–43.

114. Ibid., p. 47.

115. Ibid., p. 45.

116. Ibid., p. 44.

Chapter 15: Liberation and Reconstruction

1. The first turning point is generally regarded as the battle of Moscow (December 1941); the third the battle of Kursk (July 1943).

2. Paul Carell, *Scorched Earth: Hitler's War on Russia*, vol. 2 (London: Harrap, 1970), pp. 454–55.

3. Tieke, p. 230.

4. Manstein, *Lost Victories*, p. 486.

5. Tieke, pp. 244–45.

6. Ibid., p. 259.

7. Ibid., pp. 249–50.

8. Karpov, *Der General und Ich*, p. 413.

9. Weber, the commander of the Seventeenth Army's training school, since August 1943 had been serving as '*Kampfkommandant der Landenge von Perekop*' – Battle Commander of the Perekop Isthmus.

10. Walter Warlimont, trans. R. H. Barry, *Inside Hitler's Headquarters 1939–45* (Novato, CA: Presidio Press, 1994), pp. 394–95. First published in Germany by Bernard & Graefe in 1962 under the title *Im Hauptquartier der deutschen Wehrmacht 1939–45*.

11. Ibid., p. 395.

12. Described in a speech on 6 November 1944 given to commemorate the '27th anniversary of the Great October socialist revolution'.

13. The table had been adapted from that given by Klaus Schönherr, 'Der Rückzug der Heeresgruppe A über die Krim bis Rumänien', in Karl-Heinz Frieser (ed.), *Das Deutsche Reich und der Zweite Weltkrieg, Band 8, Die Ostfront 1943/1944* [The German Reich and the Second World War, Volume 8, The Eastern Front 1943/1944] (Munich: Deutsche Verlags-Anstalt, 2007), p. 467.

14. Tieke, p. 257.

15. Sea distances between the ports concerned were derived from http://www.sea-distances.org on 10 August 2016.

16. OKH Operations Order No. 7 dated 2 April 1944 – 'Directive for Further Operations by Army Group A, Army Group South and Army Group Centre'. From http://der-fuehrer.org/reden/english/wardirectives/54.html accessed on 9 July 2016.

17. Soviet armour had appeared phantom-like out of the Syvash. Striking through weaker Romanian forces, the attack turned the Perekop defences and threated the German rear position at Ishun. There was no magic in this surprising manoeuvre: Soviet sappers had built a series of causeways, which were laid in such a way that their tops remained just below the water surface. Such was the Soviet skill in camouflage and concealment that the Axis forces had failed to detect these underwater bridges. A Soviet breakthrough now developed. The operation illustrates the Soviet emphasis on surprise and reminds one that its enabler, *maskirovka*, was a mandatory element in every operational-level plan.

18. From interviews conducted by the author in Yalta on 30 March 2012 and 21 March 2013.

19. Carell, p. 461.

20. Excerpt from M. Gareis, *Kampf und Ende der 98. Infanteriedivision* [Fighting and End of the 98th Infantry Division] (1956), quoted by Alex Buchner, *Ostfront 1944. The Defensive Battles on the Russian Front 1944* (West Chester, PA: Schiffer Military History, 1991), p. 111.

21. The Germans had ordered the exploitation of large swathes of the native Crimean pine forest. The straight, tall and rotting-resistant timber was felled, cut and loaded on to barges for Romania, and thence by train to Germany for a variety of uses, notably as pit-props.

22. From a conversation conducted at the Chekhov museum, Yalta, on 17 December 2011.

23. Schönherr, p. 488.

24. Tieke, p. 280. Tieke gives the equivalent loss figures for the other four German infantry divisions as: 50th, 22%; 98th, 43%; 111th, 67%; and the 226th, 23%. The relatively low figure for the 50th Division, however, is surprising in view of its intense combat at Perekop at the beginning of the Soviet offensive.

25. Ibid.

26. Ivanov, p. 289, for instance, claims that the 'Germans had not only resurrected the old fortifications on which the defence had been conducted in 1941–42, but had also significantly strengthened them'.

27. Tieke, pp. 279–81.

28. Ibid., p. 281.

29. Table 15.2 is based on the Seventeenth Army's order of battle provided by Tieke, pp. 282–83.

30. Tieke, p. 286.

31. Müller was a controversial figure, having been responsible for the brutal clearance of Yevpatoriya in January 1942, and a bloody reprisal at Anogia in Crete in the late summer of 1944 when serving as a 'fortress commander'. The latter action caught up with him after the war. Arrested for war crimes, he was tried in Athens, sentenced to death and shot in 1947.

32. Tieke, pp. 286–87.

33. Much of the following narrative of operations over the period 5–9 May 1944 is taken from two Russian language sources: Museum of Heroic Defence and Liberation of Sevastopol, *Sapun Gora* (Simferopol, PolyPRESS, 2006); and 'Shturm Sapun-Gory', 27.02.2015, accessed from http://www.pomnivoinu.ru/home/reports/1751/ on 14 July 2016.

34. Ivanov, p. 290.

35. *Sapun Gora*, p. 86.

36. From an article in *Sevastopol'skiye izvestiya*, #24 (1871), 25 June 2016, p. 7.

37. From 'Shturm Sapun-Gory'.

38. Carell, p. 470.

39. Ivanov, p. 296.

40. These two armies took part in the Belorussian strategic offensive operation (Operation BAGRATION), 22 June – 19 August 1944, under command of the First Baltic Front.

41. Ivanov., pp. 472–73.

42. Carell, p. 477.

43. *Die Wehrmachtberichte 1939–1945*, Band 3, 1. Januar 1944 bis 9. Mai 1945, entries for 10 and 13 May 1944, pp. 100 and 102 respectively.

44. According to Werth, p. 756, Vasilevsky was awarded an honorary GBE (Grand Cross of the Order of the British Empire) on 10 May 1944 in Moscow.

45. Eddie Gilmore, 'Crimea Reborn', *The National Geographic Magazine*, vol. LXXXVII, no. 4, April 1945, p. 501.

46. This account is taken from interviews conducted by the present author on 30 March 2012 and 21 March 2013 at Yalta.

47. Krivosheev, p. 143: description of 'The Crimean Strategic Offensive, 8 April–12 May 1944'.

48. Schönherr, p. 490.

49. Krivosheev, p. 143.

50. Werth, pp. 749 and 751.

51. Gilmore, pp. 497–501.

52. Ibid., p. 510; Werth, p. 752.

53. Gilmore, p. 510.

54. Ibid., p. 509.

55. Werth, p. 753.

56. Soviet Government Decree No. 2722 of 1 November 1945, quoted by Dobry and Borisova, p. 39.

57. The 15 priority cities for reconstruction within the RSFSR were: Rostov-on-Don, Novgorod, Pskov, Smolensk, Voronezh, Kalinin, Novorossiysk, Sevastopol, Kursk, Orël, Velikiye Luki, Murmansk, Vyazma, Bryansk and Krasnodar. Listed by Karl D. Qualls, *From Ruins to Reconstruction. Urban Identity in Soviet Sevastopol after World War II* (Ithaca and London: Cornell University Press, 2009), p. 56, fn 25.

58. Werth, pp. 746–47.

59. Ibid., p. 753.

60. In accordance with Resolution No. GOKO-5859 of 11 May 1944 of the State Defence Committee of the USSR.

61. Aleksandr I. Solzhenitsyn, *The Gulag Archipelago 1918–1956. An Experiment in Literary Investigation V-VII* (New York: Harper & Row, 1977), p. 389.

62. The imperial Russian Tavricheskaya guberniya (the Taurida Governorate), whose capital was Simferopol, included not only the Crimean peninsula but also a wide stretch of land (now in southern Ukraine) from the lower Dnieper to the Black Sea and the Sea of Azov.

63. Khrapunov and Prokhorov, p. 377.

64. Fisher, p. 166, quoting from Ann Sheehy, *The Crimean Tatars and Volga Germans: Soviet Treatment of Two National Minorities* (London, 1971), pp. 10–11.

65. From USSR State Defence Committee (GKO) Resolution N5859ss dated 11 May 1944, quoted by J. Otto Pohl, 'The Deportation and Fate of the Crimean Tatars' (April 2000), a conference paper published by the International Committee for Crimea at http://www.iccrimea.org/scholarly/jopohl.html accessed on 11 June 2013. The secondary source quoted by Pohl is Svetlana Alieva, ed., *Tak eto bylo: Natsional'nye repressii v SSSR, 1919–1952 gody* [How it Was: National Repression in the USSR, 1919–1952] (Moscow: Russian International Cultural Fund, 1993), vol. iii, pp. 62–65.

66. Werth, p. 752.

67. Pohl, p. 5.

68. Khrapunov and Prokhorov, p. 379.

69. Ibid., p. 391.

70. Neil Kent, *Crimea. A History* (London: Hurst, 2016), p. 145.

71. Khrapunov and Prokhorov, p. 377.

72. Gilmore, p. 512.

73. Ibid., p. 511.

74. As quoted by Qualls, p. 18.

75. Statistics from Qualls, p. 17, and p. 20, Table 1, Population in Sevastopol.

76. Ibid., pp. 55–72.

77. Nakhimov Square has had a convoluted history. Named 'Labour' in 1921–28, it was called 'Third International' in 1928–32; in 1932–46 it became 'Lenin', and in 1946–51, 'Parade', ironically the German name.

78. Lazarev Square was originally called the 'Square with Chapel'. Its names changed successively over the years: during 1932–35, 'Red'; 1935–52, 'Tolstoy'; 1952, 'Nakhimov'; 1952–93, 'Revolution'.

79. It seems highly probable that this positive impression of Soviet fighting power influenced Alanbrooke's consideration of Operation UNTHINKABLE, Churchill's idea – more a flight of fantasy – to conduct military operations against the Soviet Union at the end of the Second World War. See Jonathan Walker, *Operation Unthinkable. The Third World War. British Plans to Attack the Soviet Empire, 1945* (Stroud: The History Press, 2013), pp. 102–03.

80. Alex Danchev and Daniel Todman (eds), *War Diaries 1939–1945 [of] Field Marshal Lord Alanbrooke* (London: Phoenix, 2002), pp. 658–59.

81. Department of State, Office of the Historian, Foreign Relations of the United States: Diplomatic Papers. Conferences at Malta and Yalta, 1945. White House Files. Log of the Trip, Sunday, February 11th – Monday, February 12th 1945. Accessed from https://history.state.gov/historicaldocuments/frus1945Malta/d322 on 23 July 2016.

82. Quoted by Ivanov, unnumbered lead-in page.

83. Winston Churchill, *The Second World War*, vol. vi, *Triumph and Tragedy* (London: Collins, 1954), pp. 345–46. The 'Russian admiral' in question was most probably Vice Admiral Nikolay Efremovich Basisty. From November 1944 to November 1948, he served as the chief of staff of the Black Sea Fleet, and from January to April 1945, its acting commander when Admiral Oktyabrsky was on the sick list.

84. From the transcript of a conversation between Oleg Glebovich Doskato and Olga Dmitrievna Lazarchuk held on 28 July 2013 at Sevastopol.

85. Clementine Churchill, *My Visit to Russia* (London: Hutchinson, 1945), pp. 37–38. To the present author's knowledge, no serving British premier, let alone a spouse, has since visited Sevastopol. The Duke and Duchess of Gloucester visited the Crimean War battlefields on 13–15 September 1994, as did the Duke of Edinburgh on 23-25 October 2004, coinciding with the 150th anniversary of the battle of Balaklava.

86. Victoria Avakyan, 'Clementine Churchill in Sevastopol', *International Affairs*, No. 5, May 2010. [Original in Russian.] Accessed from https://interaffairs.ru/jauthor/material/242 on 26 July 2016.

87. From the transcript of a conversation between Oleg Glebovich Doskato and Olga Dmitrievna Lazarchuk held on 28 July 2013 at Sevastopol.

88. The other hero-cities were Leningrad, Odessa and Stalingrad. The list subsequently expanded to embrace 13 cities.

89. From an internet post, 'Josef Stalin in Sevastopol', 22 January 2015, accessed from http://www.liveinternet.ru/users/4768613/post351007906/ on 21 July 2016.

90. The original Russian title was: *Upravleniye po vosstanovleniyu Sevastopolya* (UVS).

91. Qualls, pp. 70–71.

92. In the latter part of the Soviet period (1976–91), Inkerman was named 'Belokamensk' – White Stone Town – after its famous white limestone.

93. Based on an interview with the author at Yalta on 18 December 2011.

94. Vaneev, *Spravochnik*, p. 142.

95. Chikin, p. 613.

Chapter 16: Fraternal Conflict

1. Address by President of the Russian Federation, Kremlin, 18 March 2014, accessed at http://en.kremlin.ru/events/president/news/20603 on 11 August 2016.

2. In his work *Frontline Ukraine: Crisis in the Borderlands* (London: I. B. Tauris, 2015), p. 101, Richard Sakwa lends support to this interpretation of events: 'The transfer was voted for by the USSR Supreme Soviet without debate or consulting the people involved, allegedly prompted by a semi-inebriated Khrushchev, the General Secretary who had just a year earlier had taken over from Stalin.'

3. William Taubman, *Khrushchev. The Man and His Era* (London: Free Press, 2003), p. 186.

4. Kent, p. 141. For a more detailed description of the leading positions and personalities of the Soviet Union in 1954, see Roy Medvedev, trans. Brian Pearce, *Khrushchev* (Oxford: Basil Blackwell, 1992), pp. 57–58. He indicates that Khrushchev increasingly dominated the Soviet leadership by the end of 1954, not at the year's beginning when the decision over Crimea was taken. Taubman, however, disagrees, stating (p. 264) that, 'by the end of 1953, [Khrushchev's] approval was required for all major decisions. Until February 1954 Malenkov occupied the seat of honour when the Presidium gathered for ceremonial occasions in the Great Kremlin Palace; after that Khrushchev did'.

5. Following the Presidium of the Communist Party of the Soviet Union (CPSU) on 25 January 1954, the RSFSR Council of Ministers and the Presidium of its Supreme Soviet met on 5 February; and the UkSSR Supreme Soviet on 13 February 1954. For translations of the protocols of the meetings, see note 7 below.

6. Translation accessed from http://digitalarchive.wilsoncenter.org/document/119638 accessed on 25 July 2016.

7. This public narrative, however, failed to mention that the former imperial Russian Governorate of Taurida comprised Ukraine's Black Sea littoral and the Crimean peninsula; therefore there was a much more recent historical precedent.

8. Mark Kramer, 'Why Did Russia Give Away Crimea Sixty Years Ago?', Wilson Centre, Cold War International History Project e-Dossier No. 47, 19 March 2014, accessed from https://www.wilsoncenter.org/publication/why-did-russia-give-away-crimea-sixty-years-ago on 4 August 2016.

9. Kent, p. 141.

10. Jeremy Smith, 'Leadership and Nationalism in the Soviet Republics, 1951–1959', in Jeremy Smith and Melanie Ilic (eds), *Krushchev in the Kremlin. Policy and Government in the Soviet Union, 1953–1964* (London: Routledge, 2011), p. 79.

11. Details from 'Pivnichno-Kryms'kyy kanal. Istoriya budivnytstva' [North Crimean Canal. History of Building], dated 13/05/2014 in *Istorichna Pravda*, accessed from http://www.istpravda.com.ua/articles/2014/05/13/142692/ on 25 July 2016.

12. Sakwa, p. 68.

13. Gagarin was the first to receive the honour since 1916, following a break of 45 years. Surprisingly, Vice Admiral Oktyabrsky was only honoured in 1967, two years before his death. For a full list of Sevastopol's honorary citizens, see https://sevzakon.ru/view/istoriya_goroda_sevastopolya/2691/.

14. In 2014, statues of Catherine the Great and of Potemkin were placed at the bases of Sevastopol's triumphal arch.

15. The 'Soldier and Sailor' monument remains controversial as many Sevastopolians regard it as an eyesore, as opposed to a fitting tribute to the forces who fought in 1941–42 and liberated their city in 1944.

16. Interview of 21 December 2012 at the Sevastopol Veterans' House.

17. Ibid.

18. Andrew Monaghan, *A 'New Cold War'? Abusing History, Misunderstanding Russia*. Royal Institute of International Affairs, Research Paper, May 2015, accessed at https://www.chathamhouse.org/sites/files/chathamhouse/field/field_document/20150522ColdWarRussiaMonaghan.pdf on 11 August 2016. President Putin's remarks made during his address to the Federal Assembly of the Russian Federation on 25 April 2005 should be seen in their wider context and in the official English translation: 'Above all, we should acknowledge that the collapse of the Soviet Union was a *major geopolitical disaster* [emphasis added] of the century. As for the Russian nation, it became a genuine drama. Tens of millions of our co-citizens and compatriots found themselves outside Russian territory. Moreover, the epidemic of disintegration infected Russia itself.' Text accessed from http://en.kremlin.ru/events/president/transcripts/22931 on 11 August 2016.

19. Bobo Lo, *Russian Foreign Policy in the Post-Soviet Era* (Basingstoke: Palgrave Macmillan, 2002), p. 80.

20. Sakwa, p. 68.

21. Serhii Plokhy, *The Last Empire: The Final Days of the Soviet Union* (London: Oneworld, 2014), p. 310.

22. Ibid.

23. A similar point is made by Sakwa, p. 69.

24. Tor Bukkvoll, *Ukraine and European Security* (London: Pinter, 1997), p. 46; Sakwa, p. 101.

25. Bukkvoll, p. 48.

26. Razumkov Centre, 'Political Process in the Crimea: The Phases of Development and Basic Trends', *National Security and Defence* No. 4 (16), 2001, p. 4, accessed from http://razumkov.org.ua/eng/files/category_journal/NSD16_eng.pdf on 31 August 2016.

27. Bukkvoll, pp. 52–53.

28. An official English translation is at http://faolex.fao.org/docs/pdf/ukr127467E.pdf, accessed on 7 August 2016. The original Ukrainian version is at http://zakon5.rada.gov.ua/laws/show/254к/96-вр/page.

29. The Constitution of the Autonomous Republic of Crimea of 1998 is found at http://zakon3.rada.gov.ua/laws/show/350-14, accessed on 7 August 2016. An unofficial English translation is at https://en.wikisource.org/wiki/Constitution_of_Crimea,_1998.

30. As investigated in the OSCE Report, *The Integration of the Formerly Deported People in Crimea, Ukraine. Needs Assessment* (August 2013), accessed at http://www.osce.org/hcnm/104309?download=true on 13 August 2016.

31. Interview of 21 December 2012 at the Sevastopol Veterans' House.

32. Some of the following section concerning the crisis between the Russian Federation and Ukraine over the status of Sevastopol and division of Black Sea Fleet is drawn from the unpublished thesis, Dale B. Stewart, 'The Russian–Ukrainian Friendship Treaty and the Search for Regional Stability in Eastern Europe', Naval Postgraduate School, Monterey California (December, 1997) accessed at http://calhoun.nps.edu/bitstream/handle/10945/8939/russianukrainian00stew.pdf on 29 July 2016. However, the present author departs from Stewart's analysis in certain respects.

33. Significantly, this contribution to the Council's deliberations was omitted by Stewart, who misquotes the Security Council record to state that the Council 'condemned' the Supreme Soviet's action. The Minister for Foreign Affairs of Ukraine made the condemnation in his letter of protest. Hence the Security Council's statement (see the following note) was more nuanced.

34. United Nations Security Council, 'Complaint by Ukraine regarding the Decree of the Supreme Soviet of the Russian Federation concerning Sevastopol. Decision of 20 July 1993 (3256th meeting): statement by the President', accessed from http://www.un.org/en/sc/repertoire/93-95/Chapter%208/EUROPE/93-95_8-22-UKRAINE.pdf on 29 July 2016.

35. See http://www.aparchive.com/metadata/youtube/748a8dde8097e0333af2c16c68266d9f for a brief reportage on the meeting.

36. Quoted by Stewart, p. 25.

37. Quoted by Bukkvoll, p. 43.
38. Based on Stewart, pp. 37–42.
39. Ibid, pp. 51–52.
40. Ibid, p. 69.
41. The Ukrainian Rada's ratification is given at http://zakon5.rada.gov.ua/laws/show/13/98-вр, accessed on 30 July 2016.
42. Sakwa, pp. 69–70.
43. For a record of decision by the Russian State Duma and the Federation Council, see: http://archive.mid.ru//bdomp/dip_vest.nsf/99b2ddc4f717c733c32567370042ee43/551b02dbd01887acc325688700443754!OpenDocument, accessed on 30 July 2016.
44. Ibid.
45. Sakwa, p. 2.
46. Pryce-Jones, p. 437.
47. Anatole Kaletsky, 'Why Russia needs Communists', The Times, Tuesday, February 20, 1996, p. 14.
48. From http://www.nato.int/cps/en/natohq/official_texts_25468.htm, accessed on 31 July 2016.
49. From http://www.cfr.org/nonproliferation-arms-control-and-disarmament/budapest-memorandums-security-assurances-1994/p32484, accessed on 18 August 2016.
50. A transcript of Putin's speech is at http://www.washingtonpost.com/wp-dyn/content/article/2007/02/12/AR2007021200555_pf.html, accessed on 31 July 2016.
51. Perhaps the most egregious example in the United Kingdom was the shocking disbandment in 2010 of the Conflict Studies Centre (CSRC) – subsumed into the Advanced Research and Assessment Group (ARAG) – at the Defence Academy of the United Kingdom. There is now an independent CSRC that lies completely outside the UK's Ministry of Defence. Although the British Army has since established a Centre for Historical Analysis and Conflict Research (CHACR), it lacks the Russian historians and language specialists of the former CSRC.
52. Sakwa, pp. 72–73.
53. Ibid., p. 53.
54. Ibid., p. 54.
55. Nick Paton Walsh, 'Russia tells Ukraine to stay out of NATO', The Guardian, 8 June 2006, accessed from https://www.theguardian.com/world/2006/jun/08/russia.nickpatonwalsh on 3 August 2016.
56. Razumkov Centre, 'Attitude of the Crimean Residents to Probable Threats and Issues Bearing a Strong Conflict Potential', National Security and Defence, No. 4–5 (121–23), 2011, p. 33, accessed from http://razumkov.org.ua/eng/files/category_journal/NSD122-123_eng.pdf on 31 August 2016.
57. From the account of the rally on 19 April 2008 given by Andrey Yakimenko, 'The 225th Anniversary of the Reunification of the Crimea with Russia' accessed at http://www.ruscrimea.ru/cms/index.php?go=Pages&in=view&id=105 on 3 August 2016.
58. Details from Ariel Cohen and Robert E. Hamilton, The Russian Military and the Georgian War: Lessons and Implications (Carlisle, PA: Strategic Studies Institute, June 2011), pp. 41–42.
59. Ukrainian text at http://www.pravda.com.ua/articles/2010/04/22/4956018/ accessed on 18 August 2016.
60. Results from OSCE/ODIHR 'Ukraine Presidential Election 17 January and 7 February 2010 Election Mission Final Report', Annex 2, Turnout and Results by Region, accessed from http://www.osce.org/odihr/elections/ukraine/67844?download=true on 6 August 2016. Specifically, Yanukovych won 90.44% in Donetsk, 88.96% in Luhansk, 84.35% in Sevastopol and 78.24% in Crimea.

61. Text of the Medvedev–Yanukovych Kharkov agreement accessed from http://www.pravda.com. ua/articles/2010/04/22/4956018/ on 6 August 2010.

62. Sakwa, p. 59.

63. As reported by Miriam Elder, 'Ukrainians protest against Russian language law', *The Guardian*, 4 July 2012, accessed from https://www.theguardian.com/world/2012/jul/04/ukrainians-protest-russian-language-law on 9 August 2016.

64. Specifically, Article 11 of the Law 'On the Principles of Domestic and Foreign Policy' stated: 'Ukraine, being a European non-aligned state, exercises an open foreign policy and strives for cooperation with all interested partners, avoiding depending on specific states, groups of states or international structures', accessed at http://zakon3.rada.gov.ua/laws/anot/en/2411-17 on 11 August 2011.

65. Francis Fukuyama, 'The End of History?', *The National Interest* (Summer 1989). To be fair, Fukuyama has since modified his view in the light of subsequent events. The 'end of history' is an absurdity.

66. From http://www.eeas.europa.eu/ukraine/about/index_en.htm, accessed on 9 August 2016.

67. Text of the Association Agreement accessed at http://eeas.europa.eu/ukraine/pdf/3_ua_title_ii_pol_dialogue_reform_pol_assoc_coop_convergence_in_fsp_en.pdf on 9 August 2016.

68. Sakwa, p. 75.

69. L. N. Shishelina, 'Russia, the Visegrad Group and the Eastern Partnership Programme', in L. N. Shishelina et al., *Russia and the Visegrad Group: The Ukrainian Challenge,* Report 22/2015 (Moscow: Russian International Affairs Council, 2015) accessed at http://russiancouncil.ru/common/upload/RIAC-Visegrad-Report22-Eng.pdf on 14 August 2016.

70. Council of the European Union, Joint Declaration of the Eastern Partnership Summit, Vilnius, 28–29 November 2013, accessed at http://www.consilium.europa.eu/uedocs/cms_Data/docs/pressdata/EN/foraff/139765.pdf on 9 August 2016.

71. 'Euromaidan' is a slogan, based on a Twitter hashtag, derived from the words 'Europe' and the 'Maidan' – the latter referring to Kiev's Nezalezhnosti Maidan [Independence Square].

72. The events of Kiev's Euromaidan have been comprehensively documented in several works. For a comprehensive, but largely pro-Ukrainian view, see Andrew Wilson, *Ukraine Crisis. What it Means for the West* (New Haven and London: Yale University Press, 2014), pp. 66–98; Sakwa, pp. 81–99, is more critical of the West's actions in relation to the revolution of February 2014. Both books are well reviewed by David Edgar, 'What did Happen?', *London Review of Books*, Vol. 38, No. 2, 21 January 2016, pp. 9–12.

73. A partisan group derived from the Organisation of Ukrainian Nationalists led by Stepan Bandera (OUN-B) that fought Germans, Poles and the Red Army during the Second World War, and the Red Army into the early 1950s, in Western Ukraine, notably in the Carpathian Mountains.

74. Edgar, p. 10.

75. 'Polite people' is a Russian-generated term for the special forces who facilitated the annexation of Crimea, attributed to the Russian Federation Minister of Defence, Sergey Shoygu.

76. Kent, p. 155.

77. Alissa de Carbonnel, 'RPT-INSIGHT-How the Separatists delivered Crimea to Moscow', 13 March 2014, accessed from http://in.reuters.com/article/ukraine-crisis-russia-aksyonov-idINL6N0M93AH20140313 on 16 August 2016.

78. Ibid.

79. Gorbachev, p. 19.

80. The information given here is based on confidential Ukrainian military sources, who for obvious reasons, wish to remain anonymous.

81. Interview between Tanya Bukharina and Sergey Gorbachev on 16 August 2016 in Sevastopol.

82. BBC Report, 'Russian troops storm Ukrainian bases in Crimea', 22 March 2014, retrieved from http://www.bbc.co.uk/news/world-europe-26698754 on 18 August 2016.

83. Ibid.

84. From 'A brief course of UNA-UNSO's history', retrieved from http://una-unso.com/korysno-znaty/a-brief-course-of-una-unso-history.html on 18 August 2016.

85. Gorbachev, p. 18.

86. Sevastopolians' remarks as reported by Howard Amos, 'Ukraine crisis fuels secession calls in pro-Russian south', *The Guardian*, 23 February 2014, retrieved from https://www.theguardian.com/world/2014/feb/23/ukraine-crisis-secession-russian-crimea on 17 August 2016.

87. Gorbachev, pp. 18–19.

88. Chaly resigned in December 2015 and Menyaylo was relieved of his duties in July 2016.

89. Wilson, p. 113.

90. Ibid.

91. Address by President of the Russian Federation, Kremlin, 18 March 2014, accessed at http://en.kremlin.ru/events/president/news/20603 on 15 August 2016.

92. See Lukas I. Alpert, 'Crimean Tatar Leader Is Barred From Returning to Russia', *The Wall Street Journal*, 22 April 2014, http://www.wsj.com/articles/SB10001424052702304049904579517073656192990, and Alison Quinn, 'Leader of Crimean Tatars Labeled 'Extremist', Banned From Home', *The Moscow Times*, 6 July 2014, https://themoscowtimes.com/articles/leader-of-crimean-tatars-labeled-extremist-banned-from-home-37050, both accessed on 16 August 2016.

93. Agence France-Presse, 'Crimean court bans 'extremist' Tatar governing body', *The Guardian*, 16 April 2016, accessed at https://www.theguardian.com/world/2016/apr/26/court-bans-extremist-crimean-tatar-governing-body-mejlis-russia on 16 August 2016.

94. Address by President of the Russian Federation, Kremlin, 18 March 2014, accessed at http://en.kremlin.ru/events/president/news/20603 on 16 August 2016. For an analysis of this speech within a much wider historical context from the time of Tsar Ivan IV ('the Terrible') to the present and the struggle of Russia to overcome disorder and chaos, see Greg Carleton, 'Forever a Time of Troubles', *History Today*, February 2015, pp. 28–35.

Epilogue

1. Vladimir Putin, from his speech at the 'We're Together!' concert and meeting in Moscow celebrating the first anniversary of Crimea and Sevastopol's reunification [sic] with Russia. Text accessed from http://en.kremlin.ru/events/president/news/47878 on 25 September 2016.

2. Ibid.

3. The alternative history of White rule preserved in Crimea is explored in the fictional work by Aksyonov, Vassily, *The Island of Crimea* (London: Hutchinson, 1985). First published in Russian as *Ostrov Krym* by Ardis Publishers, 1981.

4. Alexei Tolstoy, 'The Flag of Sevastopol', *Sevastopol November 1941 – July 1942*, p 73.

5. The author expresses his special thanks to Charles Dick, Dr Megan Edwards, Dr Andrew Monaghan and Dr Andrew Stewart for their advice and insight offered in this section.

6. In contrast, following the events in Crimea and eastern Ukraine in 2014, there was an upsurge of interest in the subject of Hybrid War. See, for example, Guillaume Lasconjarias and Jeffrey A. Larsen (ed.), *NATO's Response to Hybrid Threats* (Rome: NATO Defense College, 2015), which contains a foreword by General Philip M. Breedlove, Supreme Allied Commander Europe, and 18 essays and case studies written by various subject matter experts.

7. Frank G. Hoffman, *Conflict in the 21st Century: The Rise of Hybrid Wars* (Arlington: Virginia: Potomac Institute for Policy Studies, December 2007), p. 8: 'Hybrid threats incorporate a full range of different modes of warfare, conventional capabilities, irregular tactics and formations,

terrorist acts including indiscriminate violence and coercion, and criminal disorder…. The effects can be gained at all levels of war.'

8. V. Gerasimov, 'Tsennost Nauki v Predvidennii', *Voyenno-promyshlennyy kur'yer*, No. 8(476), 27 February – 5 March 2013, accessed at http://www.vpk-news.ru/articles/14632 on 15 August 2016.

9. A distinction stressed to this author in most strident terms by a senior Ukrainian diplomat in May 2016.

10. See, for example, Igor Sutyakin, *Russian Forces in Ukraine*, Royal United Services Institute Briefing Paper, March 2015, at https://rusi.org/publication/briefing-papers/russian-forces-ukraine.

11. David Glantz, 'Vladimir the Terrible', *The Economist*, 20 September 2014, accessed at http://www.economist.com/news/letters/21618669-letters-editor on 25 September 2016.

12. James Sherr, 'Ukraine's Fightback', *The World Today*, August and September 2014, p. 50.

13. Sherr deals with hybrid warfare more fully in his Clingendael Report, 'The New East–West Discord. Russian Objectives, Western Interests', December 2015, pp. 57–60. Available at https://www.clingendael.nl/sites/default/files/The_New_East-West_Discord_JSherr.pdf

14. Monaghan, Andrew, 'Putin's Way of War. The "War" in Russia's "Hybrid Warfare"', *Parameters* 45 (4) (Winter 2015–16), pp. 65–74, http://strategicstudiesinstitute.army.mil/pubs/parameters/issues/Winter_2015-16/9_Monaghan.pdf, p. 68.

15. Gerasimov, op. cit.

16. Monaghan, 'Putin's Way of War', p. 67.

17. For a detailed historical examination of the subjext, see David M. Glantz, *Soviet Military Deception in the Second World War* (London and New York: Frank Cass, 1989). See also C. J. Dick, *Decisive and Indecisive Military Operations*, vol. 2, *From Defeat to Victory. The Eastern Front, Summer 1944* (Lawrence, Ka: University Press of Kansas, 2016), pp. 241–242; and for the contemporary importance of *maskirovka* in hybrid warfare, pp. 280–283.

18. Tim Judah, *In Wartime: Stories from Ukraine* (London: Allen Lane, 2015), pp. 156–57.

19. Conclusions of the European Council (20/21 March 2014), accessed at http://www.consilium.europa.eu/uedocs/cms_data/docs/pressdata/en/ec/141749.pdf on 11 August 2016.

20. See, for example, the EU External Action Fact Sheet, 'The EU non-recognition policy for Crimea and Sevastopol' (Brussels, March 2016) accessed at https://eeas.europa.eu/top_stories/pdf/the-eu-non-recognition-policy-for-crimea-and-sevastopol-fact-sheet.pdf on 11 August 2016.

21. In respect of a UN resolution entitled the 'Territorial Integrity of Ukraine', 100 votes were in favour to 11 against; with 58 abstentions. Result accessed from http://www.un.org/press/en/2014/ga11493.doc.htm on 4 August 2016.

22. As reported by http://www.unian.info/society/1467421-russia-deploys-s-400-anti-aircraft-missile-system-in-crimea.html, accessed on 18 August 2016.

23. Lo, p. 67.

24. Thucydides, *History of the Peloponnesian War*, I. LXXV.3–4 (London: Heinemann, 1956), pp. 127 and 129: 'It was under the compulsion of circumstances that we were driven at first to advance our empire to its present state, influenced chiefly by fear, then by honour also, and lastly by self-interest as well …'. For a discussion of this 'Athenian Thesis', see Laurie M. Johnson Bagby, 'The Use and Abuse of Thucydides in International Relations', *International Organization*, Vol. 48, No. 1 (Winter, 1994), p. 136.

25. Argentina's invasion of the Falkland Islands in 1982 is a case in point.

26. The chorus of the Sevastopol Hymn (full text at http://www.sevastopol.info/music/page01.htm) is:

> *Legendarnyy Sevastopol,*/Legendary Sevastopol,
>
> *Nepristupnyy dlya vragov,*/Impregnable to enemies,
>
> *Sevastopol, Sevastopol –*/Sevastopol, Sevastopol –
>
> *Gordost russkikh moryakov*/Pride of Russian sailors.

BIBLIOGRAPHY

A. Unpublished Documents and Manuscripts, including Archival Sources and Family Papers

Bundesarchiv/Militärarchiv, Freiburg im Breisgau, Germany (BA-MA)

a. *Nachlässe* **(N) [Bequests of documents]**

N754/10 General der Infanterie Robert Kosch. Kriegstagebuch, März 1918 – Mai 1918 [War Diary, March 1918 – May 1918]

N507 General-Feldmarschall Erich von Manstein

b. *Heeresdienststellen* **(RH) [Headquarters files of the *Reichsheer*]**

RH 20-11 Armeeoberkommando 11 [Headquarters, Eleventh Army], including:

RH 20-11/460 Kriegstagebuch [War Diary, 1941–1942]

In Private Possession

General'nyy Shtab Krasnoy Armii Voenno-Istoricheskiy Otdel [General Staff of the Red Army Military Historical Department], *Oborona Sevastopolya, Operativno-Takticheskiy Ocherk* [Defence of Sevastopol. Operational-Tactical Report] (Moscow: 1943)

Manstein, Erich von, *Privates Kriegstagebuch* [Private War Diary] in the Manstein family archive.

Ogle, Nicholas, *Rear Admiral Thomas Mackenzie: Life and Times with the Black Sea and Azov Sea Command 1783–1786* (December 2005). Personal manuscript.

Pattullo, [Lieutenant Colonel] James Brodie, ed. A.G. Shirreff, *Crimean Letters*. From the family archive of General Sir Richard Shirreff KCB CBE.

B. Unpublished Interviews

Interviews conducted by the present author in Sevastopol and Yalta

Vasily Federovich Eliseev, 14 September and 21 December 2012.

Rear Admiral (retired) Professor Aleksandr Romanovich Glushakov, 16 May and 30 September 2011.

Alla Vasilyevna Khanilo, 17 December 2011.
Vladimir Antonovich Kolesnikov, 30 March 2012 and 21 March 2013.
Mikhail Grigoryevich Molenov, 18 December 2011.
Colonel (retired) Viktor Alekseyevich Potapov, 21 December 2012.
Colonel (retired) Genady Nikolayevich Ryzhenok, 21 December 2012.

Interviews conducted on behalf of the present author by Ms Tatyana Bukharina in Sevastopol and Yalta

Yevdokiya Konstantinovna Sikorskaya, 30 December 2011.
Sergey Pavlovich Gorbachev, 16 August 2016.

C. Published Primary Sources, including War Diaries and Personal Memoirs

Anon, *A Complete History of the Final Bombardment and Fall of Sevastopol compiled from Authentic Correspondence, Reports of Eye-Witnesses and the Official Despatches* (London: J. Clayton & Son, 1855)

Anon [an 'Old Diplomatic Servant'], *British Diplomacy Illustrated in the Affair of the "Vixen" Addressed to the Commercial Constituency of Great Britain,* 3rd ed. (Newcastle: Currie and Bowman, 1839)

Anon, *Die Wehrmachtberichte 1939–1945, Band 3, 1. Januar 1944 bis 9. Mai 1945* [The *Wehrmacht* [Daily] Communiqués, vol. 3, 1 January 1944 – 9 May 1945] (Munich: Deutscher Taschenbuch Verlag, 1985)

Anon, *Borba Trudyashchikhsya Kryma protiv Inostrannoy Voyennoy Interventsii Kontrrevolyutsii v gody Grazhdanskoy Voyny* [The Struggle of the Crimean Working Class against Foreign Military Interventionists and Counter-Revolutionaries in the Years of the Civil War], vol. ii, May 1918 – November 1920 (Simferopol: Krymizdat, 1961)

Baumgart, Winfried (ed.), *Von Brest-Litovsk zur Deutschen Novemberrevolution: Aus den Tagebüchern, Briefen und Aufzeichnungen von Alfons Paquet, Wilhelm Groener und Albert Hopman, März bis November 1918* [From Brest-Litovsk to the German November Revolution: from the Diaries, Letters and Notes of Alfons Paquet, Wilhelm Groener and Albert Hopman, March to November 1918] (Göttingen: Vandenhoeck & Ruprecht, 1971)

di Bonvillaret, Giuseppe Francesco Ceresa, *Diario della campagna di Crimea dal 1. Aprile 1855 al 16. Giugno 1856* [Diary of the Crimean Campaign from 1 April 1855 to 16 June 1856] (Torino: L. Roux, 1894).

Boulger, Demetrius C. (ed.), *General Gordon's Letters from the Crimea, the Danube, and Armenia* (London: Chapman and Hall, 1884)

von Choltitz, Dietrich, *Soldat unter Soldaten* [Soldier amongst Soldiers] (Zürich: Europa Verlag, 1951)

Churchill, Clementine, *My Visit to Russia* (London: Hutchinson, 1945)

Churchill, Winston, *The Second World War,* vol. vi, *Triumph and Tragedy* (London: Collins, 1954)

Clifford, Henry, VC, *His Letters and Sketches from the Crimean War* (London: Michael Joseph 1956)

Craven, [Lady] Elizabeth, *A Journey through the Crimea to Constantinople in a Series of Letters to his Serene Highness the Margrave of Brandebourg, Anspach and Bareith, Written in the Year M DCC LXXXVI* [1786] (London: G. G. J. and J. Robinson, 1789)

Danchev, Alex, and Todman, Daniel (eds), *War Diaries 1939–1945 [of] Field Marshal Lord Alanbrooke* (London: Phoenix, 2002)

Delafield, [Major] Richard, *Report on the Art of War in Europe in 1854, 1855 & 1856* (Washington, DC: George W. Bowman, 1860)

Ehrenburg, Ilya, 'City of Courage', *Sevastopol November 1941–July 1942. Articles, Stories and Eye-Witness Accounts by Soviet War-Correspondents* (London: Hutchinson, 1942)

Elagin, S. I. and Veselago, F. F. *Materialy dlya istorii russkogo flota* [Materials concerning the history of the Russian fleet], vol. 15, *Krym 1783–1785* [Crimea 1783–1785] (St Petersburg, 1895)

Elphinstone, [Captain] Howard C., RE, *Journal of the Operations Conducted by the Corps of Royal Engineers*, Part I, *From the Invasion of the Crimea to the Close of the Winter Campaign 1854–55.* (London: Eyre and Spottiswoode, 1859)

Frolow, Mikhail M., *Défense de Sébastopol, Exposé de La Guerre Souterraine 1854–1855* [Defence of Sevastopol, Description of the Underground War] (Saint Petersburg: Nékludow, 1870)

Gadsby, John, *A Trip to Sebastopol, Out and Home, by Way of Vienna, the Danube, Odessa, Constantinople, and Athens*, 2nd ed. (London: Gadsby, 1858)

Gide, André, *Retour de l'U.R.S.S.* [Back to the USSR] (Paris: Gallimard, 1936)

Gilmore, Eddie, 'Crimea Reborn', *The National Geographic Magazine*, vol. LXXXVII, no. 4, April 1945

Goncharov, G. V., *Admiral Senyavin. Biograficheskiy ocherks prilozheniyem zapisok admirala D. N. Senyavina* [Admiral Senyavin. Biographical Sketch incorporating the Notes of Admiral D. N. Senyavin] (Moscow and Leningrad: NK VMF, 1945)

Guthrie, Maria, *A Tour, Performed in the Years 1795–96, Through the Tauridia, or Crimea* (London: Cadell and Davies, 1802)

Guthrie, Mrs Kate, *Through Russia: from St. Petersburg to Astrakhan and the Crimea*, vol. ii (London: Hurst and Blackett, 1874)

Hamley, Edward, *The Story of the Campaign of Sebastopol* (Edinburgh: Blackwood, 1855)

Hodasevich [Cbodasiewicz], [Captain] Robert A., *A Voice from within the Walls of Sebastopol: a Narrative of the Campaign in the Crimea, and of the Events of the Siege* (London: John Murray, 1856)

Jesse, [Captain] William, *Notes of a Half-Pay in Search of Health: or Russia, Circassia and the Crimea in 1839–40* (London: James Madden, 1841)

Jesse, [Captain] William, *Russia and the War* (London: Longman, Brown, Green and Longmans, 1854)

Khamadan, Al[eksandr], *Sevastopoltsy. Zapiski voyennogo korrespondenta* [Sevastopolians. Notes of a Military Correspondent] (Moscow: Molodaya Gvardiya, 1942). Republished by Git Pak of Sevastopol in 2014.

Kolbe, [Leutnant], '… ins Meer zurückzuwerfen', in *Wir Erobern die Krim. Soldaten der Krim-Armee berichten* ['… To be Thrown back into the Sea' in We Conquer the Crimea. Soldiers of the Crimea Army Report] (Neustadt/Weinstrasse: Pfälzische Verlagsanstalt, 1943)

Laskin, Ivan A., *Na puti k perelomu* [On the Way to the Turning Point] (Moscow: Voenizdat, 1977)

Lenin, Stalin, Frunze, Voroshilov, ed. R. M. VuP., *O Razgrome Vrangelya. Stati, Rechi, Dokumenty* [Concerning the Defeat of Wrangel. Articles, Speeches, Documents] (Simferopol: State Publishing House, Crimean ASSR, 1940)

Mackenzie, [Lieutenant] Thomas, letter of 29 July 1770, published in *Scots Magazine*, vol. XXXII, September 1770

Manstein, [General] Christopher Hermann von (ed. David Hume), *Contemporary Memoirs of Russia, from the Year 1727 to 1744* (London: Longman, Brown, Green and Longmans, 1856). Republished as a Nabu Public Domain Reprint.

Manstein, [Generalfeldmarschall] Erich von, *Verlorene Siege* (Bonn: Athenäum Verlag, 1955)

—, [Field Marshal] Erich von, *Lost Victories* (London: Collins, 1958)

Mariya Fyodorovna [Maria Fedorovna, Dowager Empress of Russia], *Dnevniki Imperatritsy Mariyi Fedorovny* (1914–1920, 1923) [Diaries of Empress Mariya Fyodorovna] (Moscow: Vagrius, 2005)

Menshikov [General-Adjutant Prince Aleksandr Sergeyevich], 'Report on the offensive operation by Lieutenant-General Liprandi's force against the camp of the Allies who are covering the road from Sevastopol to Balaklava', *Russkii Invalid* No. 235, 1854, and *Severnaya Pchela* No. 236, 1854

von Metzsch, Friedrich-August, *Die Geschichte der 22. Infanterie-Division* [The History of the 22nd Infantry Division] (Kiel: Verlag Hans-Henning Podzun, 1952)

Miranda, [General] Francisco, *Archivo del General Miranda: Viajes [&] Diaros 1785–1787* [The Archive of General Miranda: Travels and Diaries, 1785–1787] Tomo II (Caracas: Editorial Sur-America, 1929)

Neilson, Mrs. Andrew, ['By a Lady Resident Near the Alma'], *The Crimea, Its Towns, Inhabitants and Customs* (London: Partridge, Oakey and Co., 1855)

Oktyabrskaya, R. F. (ed.), *Istoriku na zametku. Iz arkhiva admirala F. S. Oktyabrskogo* [Notes for the Historian. From the Archive of Admiral F. S. Oktyabrsky] (Sevastopol: Mistye, 2013)

Oktyabrsky, Vice-Admiral F. S., 'The Defence of Sevastopol', *Sevastopol November 1941–July 1942*

Oliphant, Laurence, *The Russian Shores of the Black Sea in the Autumn of 1852 with a Voyage down the Volga, and a Tour through the Country of the Don Cossacks* (Edinburgh/London: Blackwood, 1853)

Oserov, L., 'The Girl With the Rifle', *Sevastopol November 1941 – July 1942*

Pavlichenko, Lyudmila M., *Ya – Snayper v Boyakh za Sevastopol' i Odessy* [I am a Sniper in the Battles of Sevastopol and Odessa] (Moscow: Veche, 2015)

Petrov, Eugene, 'Under Fire', *Sevastopol November 1941 – July 1942*

Pirogov, N. I., *Die Gemeinschaft der Schwestern zur Kreuzerhöhung zur Pflege der Verwundeten und Kranken* [The Community of Sisters of the Holy Cross for the Care of Wounded and Sick] (Berlin: Schneider, 1856)

—, *Grundzüge der Allgemeinen Kriegschirurgie nach Reminiscenzen aus den Kriegen in der Krim und im Kaucasus und aus der Hospitalpraxis* [Basics of General Military Surgery from Observations of the Wars in the Crimea and Caucasus and from Hospital Practice] (Leipzig: F. C. W. Vogel, 1864)

—, (ed.) Malis, Yu. G., *Sevastopol'skiye Pisma N. I. Pirogova 1854–1855* [Sevastopol Letters of N. I. Pirogov, 1854-1855] (S. Petersburg: Merkushev, 1907). Reprinted in 2010.

de Reuilly, [Baron] Jean Racault, *Travels in the Crimea, and along the Shores of the Black Sea, Performed during the Year 1803* (London: Richard Phillips, 1807). Originally published in Paris by Bossange, Messon and Besson in 1806 as *Voyages en Crimée et sur les bords de la Mer Noire*.

de Ros, [Lord] William L. L. F., *Journal of a Tour in the Principalities, Crimea and Countries Adjacent to the Black Sea in the Years 1835–36* (London: Parker and Son, 1855)

Rudny, M., 'Eight Months', *Sevastopol November 1941 – July 1942*

Scott, Charles H., *The Baltic, the Black Sea and the Crimea: Comprising Travels in Russia, a Voyage down the Volga to Astrakhan, and a Tour through Krim Tartary* (London: Bentley, 1854)

Semple, [Major] James G., *The Life of Major J. G. Semple Lisle Containing a Faithful Narrative of His Alternate Vicissitudes of Splendor and Misfortune* (London: W. Stewart, 1799)

Seymour, Henry D., *Russia on the Black Sea and Sea of Azof: being a Narrative of Travels in the Crimea and Bordering Provinces with Notices of the Naval, Military, and Commercial Resources of those Countries* (London: John Murray, 1855)

Smith, Douglas (trans. and ed.), *Love and Conquest: Personal Correspondence of Catherine the Great and Prince Grigory Potemkin* (Dekalb: Northern Illinois Press, 2004)

Sterling, [Lieutenant Colonel] Anthony, *The Story of The Highland Brigade in the Crimea founded on Letters written during the Years 1854, 1855, and 1856* (London: Remington & Company, 1895)

Sobolev, Leonid, 'In the Old Fort', *Sevastopol November 1941 – July 1942*

Solovyev, L. and Kogut, M., 'Sevastopol Nights', *Sevastopol November 1941 – July 1942*

de Todleben, [Lieutenant-Général] Eduard, *Défense de Sébastopol* [Defence of Sevastopol] (Saint-Petersbourg: N. Thieblin, 1863)

Tolstoy, [Count] Leo N., trans. Louise and Aylmer Maude, *Sevastopol* (London: Archibald Constable, 1905)

—, ed. Aylmer Maude, trans. Louise and Aylmer Maude, *The Private Diary of Leo Tolstoy 1853–1857* (London: Heinemann, 1927)

—, trans. and ed. R. F. Christian, *Tolstoy's Letters*, vol. i, *1828–1879* (London: Athlone Press, 1978)

Tolstoy, Alexei, 'The Flag of Sevastopol', *Sevastopol November 1941 – July 1942*

de Tott, [Baron] François, *Memoirs of the Baron de Tott on the Turks and the Tartars*, vol. ii (Dublin: White, Cash & Marchbank, 1785). Originally published in Paris in 1785 as *Mémoires du Baron de Tott, sur les Turcs et les Tartares.*

Turovsky, M., 'The Underground City', *Sevastopol November 1941 – July 1942*

Twain, Mark, *The Innocents Abroad* (London: Penguin, 2002). First published in the United States of America by the American Publishing Company in 1869.

Voyetekhov, Boris, trans. Ralph Parker and V. M. Genne, *The Last Days of Sevastopol* (London: Cassell, 1943)

Vrochenskiy, M. A., *Sevastopolskiy razgrom. Vospominaniya uchastnika slavnoy oborony Sevastopolya.* [Sevastopol Debacle. Recollections of a Member of the Glorious Defence of Sevastopol] (Moscow: State Public Historical Library of Russia, 2011). First published in Kiev in 1893.

Wade, Ashton, *A Life on the Line* (Tunbridge Wells: D J Costello, 1988)

Warlimont, Walter, *Inside Hitler's Headquarters 1939–45* (London: Weidenfeld & Nicolson, 1964). First published in Germany by Bernard & Graefe in 1962 under the title *Im Hauptquartier der deutschen Wehrmacht 1939–45.*

Wrangel, [General] Pietr N., trans. Sophie Goulston, *The Memoirs of General Wrangel. The Last Commander-in-Chief of The Russian National Army* (London: Williams & Norgate, 1929)

Wrottesley, [The Hon.] George (ed.), *Life and Correspondence of Field Marshal Sir John Burgoyne*, vol. ii (London: Bentley & Son, 1873)

Zadorozhnikov, Georgy, *Memuary Starogo Malchika (Sevastopol' 1941–1945 gg.)* [Memories of an Old Boy (Sevastopol 1941–1945)] (Sevastopol: NPTs EKOSI-Gidrofizika, 2011)

Zhukov, [Marshal of the Soviet Union] Georgy, *Vospominaniya i Razmyshleniya* [Memories and Reflections] (Moscow: Agentstvo Pechati Novosti, 1969).

Newspaper Articles (not online)

Krymskiy Vestnik, No. 246, Sunday, 16 (29) October 1905; No. 248, Wednesday, 18 (31) October 1905; & No. 270, Wednesday, 23 November (6 December) 1905

Sevastopolskaya Gazeta, No. 60, Tuesday, 14 (27) March 1906; No. 65, Sunday, 19 March (1 April) 1906; No. 70, Saturday, 25 March (7 April) 1906; No. 73, Thursday, 30 March (12 April) 1906); & No. 189, 20 August (2 September) 1906

Izvestiya Sevastopol'skogo Soveta Voyennykh i Rabochikh Deputatov [News of the Sevastopol Soviet of Military and Workers Deputies], No. 148, 15 (28) November 1917

Izvestiya Sevastopol'skogo voyenno-revolyutsionnogo komiteta [News of the Sevastopol Military-Revolutionary Committee], No. 1, 19 December 1917 (1 January) 1918

Bingham, [Field Marshal] George C., Third Earl of Lucan, report published in *The Times*, Monday, November 13, 1854, as reprinted from the *London Gazette* Extraordinary of Sunday, November 12, 1854

Engels, Frederick, 'The Battle of the Chernaya', *New York Daily Tribune*, No. 4494 (14 September 1855), reproduced in *Marx and Engels Collected Works*, Volume 14 (Moscow: Progress Publishers, 1980)

D. Other Published Works

Anon, *Puteshestviye Yeyo Imperatorskogo Velichestva v poludennyy kray Rossii, predpriyemlemoye v 1787 godu* [Journey of Her Imperial Majesty to the Southern Part of Russia in 1787] (St Petersburg: Mining Institute, 1786)

Anon [Believed to be David Urquhart], *British Diplomacy Illustrated in the Affair of the "Vixen" Addressed to the Commercial Constituency of Great Britain,* 3rd. ed. (Newcastle: Currie and Bowman, 1839)

Anon, *Sevastopol'skiye bastiony. Sbornik rukopisey predstavlennykh Ego Imperatorskomu Vysochestvu Gosudaryu Nasledniku Tsesarevichu o Sevastopol'skoy oborone sevastopoltsami* [Sevastopol Bastions. A Set of Manuscripts presented to His Imperial Highness, the Heir Apparent, about the Defence of Sevastopol by Sevastopol Residents] (Moscow: Voennoye Izdatelstvo, 1998)

Anon, *Sobor Sviatogo Ravnoapostolnogo kniazia Vladimira – usypalnitsa vydayushchikhsya admiralov Rossiiskogo Imperatorskogo Flota* [Cathedral of Saint Equal to Apostles, Prince Vladimir – Burial Vault of Eminent Admirals of the Russian Imperial Navy] (Simferopol: Biznes Inform, 2004)

Aksan, Virginia H., *Ottoman Wars 1700–1870* (Harlow: Pearson Education, 2007)

Aksyonov, Vassily, *The Island of Crimea* (London: Hutchinson, 1985). First published in Russian as *Ostrov Krym* by Ardis Publishers, 1981.

Alieva, Svetlana (ed.), *Tak eto bylo: Natsional'nye repressii v SSSR, 1919–1952 gody* [How it Was: National Repression in the USSR, 1919-1952] (Moscow: Russian International Cultural Fund, 1993)

Altabayeva, Yekaterina B., *Smutnoye Vremya: Sevastopol' v 1917–1920 gg.* [Muddy Times: Sevastopol in 1917–1920] (Sevastopol: Teleskop, 2004)

Anderson, Matthew S., 'Great Britain and the Growth of the Russian Navy in the Eighteenth Century', *Mariner's Mirror* 42 (1956)

Andolenko, Lieutenant-Colonel Serge, 'The Imperial Heritage' in B. H. Liddell Hart (ed.), *The History of the Red Army* (London: Weidenfeld and Nicolson, 1956)

Ardeleanu, Constantin, 'A British Military Mission to the Near East, Russia and the Danubian Principalities (1835–1836)', *Anuarul Institutului de Istorie „A. D. Xenopol"*, t. XLVIII, 2011

Ascherson, Neal, *Black Sea: The Birthplace of Civilisation and Barbarism* (London: Vintage, 2007)

Axworthy, Mark, Scafes, Cornel and Craciunoiu, Cristian, *Third Axis. Fourth Ally. The Romanian Armed Forces in the European War, 1941–1945* (London: Arms and Armour Press, 1995)

Bascomb, Neal, *Red Mutiny: The True Story of the Battleship Potemkin Mutiny* (New York: Houghton Mifflin, 2007)

Basov, Alexey V., *Krym v Velikoy Otechestvennoy Voyne 1941–1945* [Crimea in the Great Patriotic War 1941–1945] (Moscow: Nauka, 1987)

Baumgart, Winfried, *The Crimean War 1853–1856* (London: Oxford University Press, 1999)

Bevan, John, *The Infernal Diver: the lives of John and Charles Deane, their invention of the diving helmet and its first application to salvage, treasure hunting, civil engineering and military uses* (London: Submex, 1996)

Black, Jeremy, *War and the World: Military Power and the Fate of Continents* (Yale: University Press, 1998)

Blair, [Colonel] Dr J. S. G., 'Nikolai Ivanovich Pirogov (1810–1881)', *Journal of the Royal Army Medical Corps* (2002), vol. 148

Blakemore, Porter R., *Manstein in the Crimea: The Eleventh Army Campaign, 1941–1942* [dissertation] (Ann Arbor, Mich: University Microfilms International, 1979 and 1992)

Buchner, Alex, *Ostfront 1944. The Defensive Battles on the Russian Front 1944* (West Chester, PA: Schiffer Military History, 1991)

Bukkvoll, Tor, *Ukraine and European Security* (London: Pinter, 1997)

Bulgakov, Mikhail, *Belaya Guardiya* [The White Guard], trans. Marian Schwartz (New Haven, Connecticut: Yale University Press, 2008)

Bushkovitch, Paul, *A Concise History of Russia* (New York: Cambridge University Press, 2012)

Cabrol, Jean F. H. B., *Le Marechal de Saint Arnaud en Crimée* [Marshal de Saint Arnaud in Crimea] (Paris: Stock et Tresse et Co., 1895)

Callwell, [Major General] Charles E., *Military Operations and Maritime Preponderance: Their Relations and Interdependence* (Edinburgh and London; William Blackwood and Sons, 1905). Republished with a new introduction and notes by Colin Gray in 1996 by the United States Naval Institute, Annapolis, Maryland.

Carleton, Greg, 'Forever a Time of Troubles', *History Today*, February 2015

Carley, Michael J., *Revolution and Intervention: the French Government and the Russian Civil War, 1917–1919* (Kingston, Ontario: McGill-Queen's University Press, 1983)

Carell, Paul, *Scorched Earth: Hitler's War on Russia*, vol. 2 (London: Harrap, 1970)

Carter, Joseph C. and Mack, Glenn R. (eds), *Crimean Chersonesos: City, Chora, Museum, and Environs* (Austin, Texas: Institute of Classical Archaeology, 2003)

Chennyk, Sergey, *Krymskaya kampaniya 1854–1856 gg. Vostochnoy voyny 1853–1856 gg.* [The Crimean Campaign 1854–1856 [of] The Eastern War 1853–1856] in five parts (Simferopol: Gala, 2010–2014)

—, Part II, *Alma* (2011)

—, Part IV, *Ot Balaklavy k Inkermanu* [From Balaklava to Inkerman] (2014)

—, Part V, *Posledniy Shturm* [The Final Assault] (2014)

Chernousov, Andrey A., *Admiral M. P. Lazarev, Rol' lichnosti v istorii Rossii* [*Admiral M. P. Lazarev, The Role of Personality in the History of Russia*] (St Petersburg: Gangut, 2011)

Chesney, Charles, 'Chinese Gordon', *Fraser's Magazine for Town and Country*, vol. LXXIX, No. CCCCLXX, February 1869

Chikin, A. M., *Sevastopol'. Istoriko-literaturnyy Spravochnik* [Sevastopol. Historical and Literary Guide] (Sevastopol: Veber, 2008)

Churchill, Winston, *The World Crisis 1911–1914* (London: Thornton Butterworth, 1923)

Clark, Alan, *The Donkeys: A History of the British Expeditionary Force in 1915* (London: Hutchinson, 1961)

Cohen, Ariel, and Hamilton, Robert E., *The Russian Military and the Georgian War: Lessons and Implications* (Carlisle, PA: Strategic Studies Institute, June 2011)

Cook, Stanley A., Adcock, Frank E. and Charlesworth, Martin P., *The Cambridge Ancient History*, vol. viii, *Rome and the Mediterranean 218–133 BC.* (Cambridge: University Press, 1930)

Cooke, Brian, *The Grand Crimean Central Railway* (Knutsford: Cavalier House, 1990 and 1997)

Cross, Anthony, 'A Russian Engineer in Eighteenth-Century Britain: The Journal of N. I. Korsakov, 1776–7', *The Slavonic and East European Review*, Vol. 55, No. 1 (January 1977)

—, *By the Banks of the Neva: Chapters from the Lives and Careers of the British in Eighteenth-Century Russia* (Cambridge: University Press, 1997)

Curtiss, John S., *The Russian Army Under Nicholas I, 1825–1855* (Durham, NC: Duke University Press, 1965)

—, *Russia's Crimean War* (Durham, NC: Duke University Press, 1979)

David, Saul, *Victoria's Wars* (London: Penguin, 2007)

Dallin, Alexander, *German Rule in Russia 1941–1945. A Study of Occupation Policies* (London: Macmillan, 1957)

Davies, Norman, *Vanished Kingdoms: The History of Half-Forgotten Europe* (London: Allen Lane, 2012)

—, *Europe: A History* (London: Bodley Head, 2014)

Dawson, Anthony (ed.), *Letters from the Light Brigade: The British Cavalry in the Crimean War* (Barnsley: Pen & Sword Military, 2014)

Dick, C. J., *Decisive and Indecisive Military Operations*, vol. 2, *From Defeat to Victory. The Eastern Front, Summer 1944* (Lawrence, Ka: University Press of Kansas, 2016)

Dobry, Alexander and Borisova, Irina, *Welcome to Sevastopol: Guide-book* (Sevastopol: Art-Print, 2003)

Donnell, Clayton, *The Defence of Sevastopol 1941–1942. The Soviet Perspective* (Barnsley: Pen & Sword Military, 2016)

Douglas, [General Sir] Howard, *Remarks on the Naval Operations in the Black Sea and the Siege of Sevastopol*, 2nd ed. (London: John Murray, 1855)

—, *A Treatise of Naval Gunnery* (London: John Murray, 1860)

Duckers, Peter, *The Crimean War at Sea: Naval Campaigns Against Russia, 1854–6* (Barnsley: Pen & Sword Maritime, 2011)

Durant, Mary, 'Catherine's Boat Ride', *Horizon – A Magazine for the Arts*, vol. viii, no. 4 (Autumn 1966)

Dvoichenko-Markov, Eufrosina, 'Americans in the Crimean War', *Russian Review*, Vol. 13, No. 2 (April 1954)

Fedosov, Dmitry, 'Under the Saltire: Scots and the Russian Navy, 1690s–1910s' in Murray Frame and Mark Cornwall (eds), *Scotland and the Slavs: Cultures in Contact 1500–2000* (Newtonville, Massachusetts and Saint Petersburg: Oriental Research Publishers, 2001)

Ffrench Blake, Robert L. V. F., *The Crimean War* (Barnsley: Pen & Sword Military, 2006)

Figes, Orlando, *A People's Tragedy: The Russian Revolution 1891–1924* (London: Jonathan Cape, 1996)

—, *Crimea: The Last Crusade* (London: Allen Lane, 2010)

Fisher, Alan W., *The Crimean Tatars* (Stanford, CA: Hoover Institution Press, 1978)

Fitzpatrick, Sheila, *The Russian Revolution*, 3rd ed. (Oxford: Oxford University Press, 2008)

Fletcher, Ian and Ishchenko, Natalia, *The Battle of the Alma 1854: First Blood to the Allies in the Crimea* (Barnsley: Pen & Sword Military, 2008)

—, *The Crimean War. A Clash of Empires* (Staplehurst: Spellmount, 2004)

Forczyk, Robert, *Where the Iron Crosses Grow. The Crimea 1941–44* (Oxford: Osprey, 2014)

Freedman, Lawrence, *Strategy: A History* (Oxford: University Press, 2013)

Frieser, Karl-Heinz, *Das Deutsche Reich und der Zweite Weltkrieg, Band 8, Die Ostfront 1943/1944* [The German Reich and the Second World War, vol. 8, The Eastern Front 1943/1944] (Munich: Deutsche Verlags-Anstalt, 2007)

Fukuyama, Francis, 'The End of History?', *The National Interest* (Summer 1989)

Fuller, [Major General] J. F. C., *The Decisive Battles of the Western World and their Influence upon History*, vol. 2, *From the Defeat of the Spanish Armada to the Battle of Waterloo* (London: Eyre & Spottiswoode, 1955)

Fuller, William C., *Strategy and Power in Russia 1600–1914* (New York: The Free Press, 1992)

Geifman, Anna, *Thou Shalt Kill: Revolutionary Terrorism in Russia, 1894–1917* (Princeton, NJ: University Press, 1995)

Gibbon, Edward, *The History of the Decline and Fall of the Roman Empire*, vol. ii (London: Methuen, 1896)

—, vol. v (1898)

Glantz, David M., *Soviet Military Deception in the Second World War* (London and New York: Frank Cass, 1989)

—, *Soviet Military Operational Art: In Pursuit of the Deep Battle* (London: Routledge, 1991)

—, *Forgotten Battles of the German-Soviet War (1941–1945)*, vol ii, *The Winter Campaign (5 December 1941–April 1942* (Carlisle, PA: privately published, 1999)

Goldfrank, David M., *The Origins of the Crimean War* (New York: Longman, 1994)

Gorbachev, Sergey, *Ot tretyey oborony k Russkoy Vesne. K godovshchine vozvrashcheniya Sevastopolya i Kryma v sostav Rossii* [From the Third Defence to the Russian Spring. On the Anniversary of the Return of Sevastopol and Crimea to the Russian Federation] (Simferopol: Salta Ltd, 2015)

Gordon, Andrew, *The Rules of the Game: Jutland and British Naval Command* (London: John Murray, 1996)

Grant, James, *The Scottish Soldiers of Fortune; Their Adventures and Achievements in the Armies of Europe* (London: Routledge, 1889). Republished by Forgotten Books, London in 2012.

Gray, Colin S., *Modern Strategy* (Oxford: Oxford University Press, 1999)

—, *The Future of Strategy* (Cambridge: Polity Press, 2015)

Grebenshchikova, G. A., *Chernomorskiy flot v period pravleniya Yekateriny II* [The Black Sea Fleet during the Reign of Catherine II] (St Petersburg: Ostrov, 2012)

Grehan John and Mace, Martin (eds), *Despatches from the Front. British Battles of the Crimean Wars 1854–1856* (Barnsley: Pen & Sword, 2014)

Guboglo, M. N., and Chervonnaya, S. M., *Krymskotatarskoye natsionalnoye dvizhheniye* [Crimean Tatar National Movement] vol. ii (Moscow: TsIMO, 1992)

Halpern, Paul G., *The Naval War in the Mediterranean 1914–1918* (London: Allen & Unwin, 1987)

—, (ed.), *The Royal Navy in the Mediterranean 1915–1918* (London: Temple Smith, 1987)

—, (ed.), *The Mediterranean Fleet 1919–1929* (Farnham: Ashgate, 2011)

de Haxthausen, [Baron] Auguste, *Les Forces Militaires de la Russie sous les Rapports Historiques, Statistiques, Ethnographiques et Politiques* [The Armed Forces of Russia. Historical Reports, Statistics, Ethnography and Politics] (Berlin: Behr & Paris: d'Amyot, 1853)

Heather, Peter J., *Empires and Barbarians* (London: Macmillan, 2009)

Hendriks, I. F., Bovill J. G., Boer F., Houwaart E. S. and. Hogendoorn P. C. W., 'Nikolay Ivanovich Pirogov: a surgeon's contribution to military and civilian anaesthesia', *Anaesthesia* (2015), vol. 70

Herodotus, trans. A. D. Godley, *Histories,* vol. ii (London: Heinemann, 1921)

Herring, George C., *From Colony to Superpower: U.S. Foreign Relations since 1776* (Oxford: University Press, 2008)

Hillgruber, Andreas (ed.), *Kriegestagebuch des Oberkommandos der Wehrmacht (Wehrmachtführungsstab)*, Band II: 1. Januar 1942 – 31. Dezember 1942 [War Diary of the German Armed Forces High Command (Command Staff), vol. ii: 1 January 1942 – 31 December 1942] (Frankfurt am Main: Bernard & Graefe, 1963)

Homer, trans. E. V. Rieu, *The Odyssey* (London: Penguin, 1946)

Hopkirk, Peter, *The Great Game: On Secret Service in High Asia* (London: John Murray, 1990)

Hore, Peter, *The World Encyclopedia of Battleships* (London: Hermes House, 2005)

Hughes, Daniel J. (ed.), *Moltke on the Art of War. Selected Writings* (New York: Ballantine Books, 1993)

Hythe, Viscount, and Leyland, John (eds.) *The Navy Annual 1914* (London: William Clowes, 1914)

Ingle, Harold N., *Nesselrode and the Russian Rapprochement with Britain, 1836–1844* (Berkeley and London: University of California Press, 1976)

Ivanov, Valeriy B., *Sevastopolskaya Epopeya 1941–1944 v ofitsialnykh dokumentakh* [Sevastopol Epic 1941–1944 in official documents] (Sevastopol: Bibleks, 2004)

733

Ivitskaya, O. E., 'Odin god iz zhizni admirala (maloizvestnye fakty biografii admirala A.V. Kolchaka)' [One Year in the Life of an Admiral (Lesser-known Facts of the Biography of Admiral A.V. Kolchak)], in Sevastopol State Archives, *Sevastopol – vzgliad v proshloye* [Sevastopol – a Glance in the Past] (Sevastopol: Arefyev, 2007)

Jacobs, Walter Darnell, *Frunze: The Soviet Clausewitz 1885–1925* (The Hague: Martinus Nijhoff, 1969)

James, Robert R. (ed.), *Winston S. Churchill: His Complete Speeches 1897–1963*, vol. iii (London/New York: Chelsea House Publishers & R.R. Bowker, 1974)

—, *Churchill Speaks. Winston S. Churchill in Peace and War. Collected Speeches, 1897–1963* (Leicester: Windward, 1981)

Jane, Fred T., *The Imperial Russian Navy: Its Past, Present, and Future*, rev. ed. (London: W. Thacker, 1904)

Johnson Bagby, Laurie M., 'The Use and Abuse of Thucydides in International Relations', *International Organization*, Vol. 48. No. 1 (Winter, 1994)

Jones, Archer, *The Art of War in the Western World* (New York: Barnes & Noble, 1987)

Judah, Tim, *In Wartime. Stories from Ukraine* (London: Allen Lane, 2015)

Karpov, Vladimir, *Russia at War 1941–45* (New York: Vendome Press, 1987)

—, *The Commander,* trans. Yuri S. Shirokov and Nicholas Louis (London: Brassey's, 1987)

—, *Polkovodets* [Commander] (Moscow: Sov. Pisatel, 1988); 2nd ed. (Veche, 2014) under the title of '*Polkovodets. Voyna generala Petrova*'

—, trans. Peter Lobig and Dr Werner Tschoppe, *Der General und Ich* (Berlin: Militärverlag der Deutschen Demokratischen Republik, 1989)

Kent, Neil, *Crimea. A History* (London: Hurst, 2016)

Kenez, Peter, *The Defeat of the Whites. Civil War in South Russia, 1919–1920* (Berkeley/Los Angeles: University of California, 1977)

Khrapunov, Nikita and Prokhorov, Dmitriy, *A Short History of the Crimea* (Simferopol: Dolya Publishing House, 2013)

Kinglake, Alexander W., *The Invasion of the Crimea: its Origin, and an Account of its Progress down to the Death of Lord Raglan*, vols. ii and iii (Edinburgh and London: Blackwood, 1863 and 1868)

Kinvig, Clifford, *Churchill's Crusade: The British Invasion of Russia 1918–1920* (London: Hambledon Continuum, 2006)

Knight, Roger, *Britain Against Napoleon: The Organization of Victory 1793–1815* (London: Allen Lane, 2013)

Komoyedov, [Admiral] V. P. et al., *Chernomorskiy Flot Rossii: Istoricheskiy ocherk* [Russian Black Sea Fleet: Historical Review] (Simferopol: Tavrida, 2002)

Kozlov, D. Yu., '*Strannaya voyna' v Chernom more (avgust – oktyabr 1914 goda)* ['Strange War' in the Black Sea (August–October 1914)] (Moscow: Kvadriga, 2009)

Kriegsgeschichtliches Forschungsanstalt des Heeres [Army Military Research Institute into the History of War], *Der Weltkrieg 1914 bis 1918*, vol. xiii, *Die Kriegführung im Sommer und Herbst 1917.* [The World War 1914 to 1918. The Conduct of War in the Summer and Autumn of 1917] (Berlin: Mittler & Sohn, 1942)

Krivosheev, [Colonel-General] Grigori F., *Soviet Casualties and Combat Losses in the Twentieth Century* (London: Greenhill Books, 1997)

Kurat, Akdes N. and Bromley, John S., 'The Retreat of the Turks, 1683–1730', Chapter XIX in J. S. Bromley (ed.), *Cambridge New Modern History*, vol. vi, *The Rise of Great Britain and Russia* (Cambridge: University Press, 1970)

Lambert, Andrew, *Battleships in Transition* (London: Conway Maritime Press, 1984)

—, *Admirals: The Naval Commanders who Made Britain Great* (London: Faber and Faber, 2008)

—, *The Crimean War: British Grand Strategy against Russia, 1853–56* (2nd ed.) (Farnham: Ashgate, 2011)

Lasconjarias, Guillaume and Larsen, Jeffrey A. (ed.), *NATO's Response to Hybrid Threats* (Rome: NATO Defense College, 2015)

Lebedev, Aleksandr A., *U istokov Chernomorskogo flota Rossii* [Sources of the Russian Black Sea Fleet] (St Petersburg: Gangut, 2011)

Lemay, Benoît, trans. Pierce Heyward, *Erich von Manstein: Hitler's Master Strategist* (Havertown, PA; Newbury, Berkshire: Casemate, 2010). Originally published as *Erich von Manstein. Le stratège de Hitler* (Paris: Perrin, 2010).

Leyland, John, 'Foreign Navies' in Viscount Hythe (ed.), *The Navy Annual 1913* (Portsmouth: J. Griffin, 1913)

Lieb, Peter, 'The German Occupation of the Ukraine, 1918' in Matthias Strohn (ed.), *World War I Companion* (Oxford: Osprey, 2013)

Lieven, Dominic, *Towards the Flame: Empire, War and the End of Tsarist Russia* (London: Allen Lane, 2015)

Lincoln, Bruce, *Red Victory: A History of the Russian Civil War* (London: Simon & Schuster, 1990)

Lo, Bobo, *Russian Foreign Policy in the Post-Soviet Era* (Basingstoke: Palgrave Macmillan, 2002)

Longworth, Philip, *Russia's Empires. Their Rise and Fall from Prehistory to Putin* (London: John Murray, 2005)

Luttwak, Edward N., *The Grand Century of the Roman Empire from the First Century A.D. to the Third* (Baltimore and London: Johns Hopkins University Press, 1976)

—, *The Grand Strategy of the Byzantine Empire* (Cambridge, Massachusetts/London: Belknap Press, 2009)

de Madariaga, Isabel, *The Travels of General Francisco de Miranda in Russia* (London: Kitchen & Barratt, 1950)

Makareyev, M. V., and Rizhonok, G. N., *Chernomorskiy flot v biografiyakh komanduyushchikh 1783–2004* [The Black Sea Fleet in the Biographies of its Commanders], vol. 1, 1783–1917 (Sevastopol: Mir, 2004)

Marder, Arthur J., *From the Dreadnought to Scapa Flow*, vol. i, *The Road to War 1904–1914* (London: Oxford University Press, 1961)

Massie, Alastair, *The National Army Museum Book of the Crimean War* (London: Sidgwick & Jackson, 2004)

Massie, Robert K., *Nicholas and Alexandra* (New York: Atheneum, 1967)

—, *Castles of Steel: Britain, Germany and the Winning of the Great War at Sea* (London: Jonathan Cape, 2004)

—, *Peter the Great: His Life and World* (London: Head of Zeus, 2012)

—, *Catherine the Great* (London: Head of Zeus, 2012)

Mawdsley, Evan, *The Russian Civil War* (Edinburgh: Birlinn, 2008). First published by Allen and Unwin in 1987.

McLaughlin, Stephen 'Pre-dreadnoughts vs. a Dreadnought: The Action off Cape Sarych, 18 November 1914' in Preston, Antony (ed.), *Warship 2001–2002* (London: Conway Maritime Press, 2001)

McMeekin, Sean, *The Russian Origins of the First World War* (Cambridge, Massachusetts/London: Harvard University Press, 2013)

Mears, Stephen W., *George McClellan: The Young Napoleon* (New York: Ticknor & Fields, 1988)

Medvedev, Roy, trans. Brian Pearce, *Khrushchev* (Oxford. Basil Blackwell, 1992)

Melvin, [Major General] Mungo, *Manstein. Hitler's Greatest General* (London: Weidenfeld & Nicolson, 2010)

— (ed.), *Thinking Strategically*, 3rd ed. (London: Royal College of Defence Studies, October 2010)

—, 'Sevastopol: Crimean Citadel from Potemkin to Putin', *RUSI Journal*, vol. 159, no. 3, June/July 2014

Mercer, Patrick, *Inkerman 1854: The Soldiers' Battle* (Oxford: Osprey 1998)

Milner, [Rev] Thomas, *The Crimea, Its Ancient and Modern History; the Khans, the Sultans, and the Czars with Notices of its Scenery and Population* (London: Longman, Brown, Green and Longmans, 1855)

Moffat, Ian C. D., *The Allied Intervention in Russia, 1918–1920: The Diplomacy of Chaos* (Basingstoke: Palgrave Macmillan, 2015)

Monaghan, Andrew, *The New Politics of Russia* (Manchester: University Press, 2016)

Montefiore, Simon Sebag, *Catherine the Great and Potemkin: The Imperial Love Affair* (London: Phoenix, 2011). First published in 2000 by Weidenfeld & Nicolson as *Prince of Princes: The Life of Potemkin*.

Morgunov, P. A., *Geroycheskiy Sevastopol* [Heroic Sevastopol] (Moscow: Nauka, 1979)

Morozov, Miroslav, *Vozdushnaya Bitva za Sevastopol 1941–1942* [Air Battle for Sevastopol 1941–1942] (Moscow: Yauza, 2007)

Murawski, Marek J., *Luftwaffe over Sevastopol* (Lublin: Karego, 2008)

Museum of Heroic Defence and Liberation of Sevastopol, *Sapun Gora* (Simferopol: PolyPRESS, 2006)

Neiberg, Michael S., and Jordan, David, *The Eastern Front 1914–1920* (London: Amber Books, 2008)

Nekrasov, George, *North of Gallipoli: The Black Sea at War 1914–1917* (New York: Columbia University Press, 1992)

Norman, Charles B. *Battle Honours of the British Army* (Uckfield: Naval & Military Press, 2006). First published by Murray, London in 1911.

Oakes, [Sir] Augustus and Mowat, Robert B. (eds), *The Great European Treaties of the Nineteenth Century* (Oxford: Clarendon Press, 1918)

Osipov, K, trans. Edith Bone, *Alexander Suvorov* (London: Hutchinson, 1941?) While the edition in the author's possession is not dated, an identical title is listed in the British Library as being published in 1941, along with an undated edition.

Owen, [Lieutenant-Colonel] Charles H., RA, *The Principles and Practice of Modern Artillery*, 2nd ed. (London: John Murray, 1873)

Paxman, Jeremy, *The English: A Portrait of a People* (London: Penguin, 1999)

Pemberton, William Baring, *Battles of the Crimean War* (London: Batsford, 1962)

Plokhy, Serhii, *The Last Empire: The Final Days of the Soviet Union* (London: Oneworld, 2014)

—, *The Gates of Europe. A History of Ukraine* (New York: Basic Books, 2015)

Pohl, Dieter, *Die Herrschaft der Wehrmacht. Deutsche Militärbesatzung und einheimische Bevölkerung in der Sowjetunion 1941–1944* [The Rule of the Wehrmacht. German Military Occupation and Indigenous Peoples in the Soviet Union 1941–1944] (Munich: Oldenbourg, 2008)

Ponting, Clive, *The Crimean War: The Truth Behind the Myth* (London: Chatto & Windus, 2004; Pimlico, 2005)

Porter, [Major-General] Whitworth, *History of the Corps of Royal Engineers*, vol. i (Chatham: Institution of Royal Engineers, 1889). Reprinted in 1977.

Porudominsky, Vladimir Il'ich, *Pirogov* (Moscow: Young Guard, 1969)

Pryce-Jones, David, *The War That Never Was. The Fall of the Soviet Empire 1985–1991* (London: Weidenfeld & Nicolson, 1995)

Puryear, Vernon J., *International Economics and Diplomacy in the Near East: A Study of British Commercial Policy in the Levant, 1834–1853* (Stanford: University Press, 1935)

Pushkin, Alexander, trans. and ed. Stanley Mitchell, *Eugene Onegin* (London: Penguin Classics, 2008)

Qualls, Karl D., *From Ruins to Reconstruction. Urban Identity in Soviet Sevastopol after World War II* (Ithaca and London: Cornell University Press, 2009)

Raphael-Leygues, Jacques, and Barré, Jean-Luc, *Les Mutins de la Mer Noire* [The Mutinies of the Black Sea] (Paris: Plon, 1981)

Rappaport, Helen, *No Place for Ladies: The Untold Story of Women in the Crimean War* (London: Aurum Press, 2007)

Razdolgin, Anatoli A., *The Russian Navy* (St Petersburg: Maritime Publishing House, 2003)

Riasanovsky, Nicholas V., *A History of Russia*, 5th ed. (Oxford/New York: Oxford University Press, Hurst 1993)

Rich, Norman, *Hitler's War Aims: The Establishment of the New Order* (London: André Deutsch, 1974)

Richards, Don S., *Conflict in the Crimea: British Redcoats on the Soil of Russia* (Barnsley: Pen & Sword, 2006)

Richter, Oliver, 'Unternehmen "Störfang" – Die Eroberung Sewastopols 1942' [Operation STURGEON CATCH – The Capture of Sevastopol 1942], in *Militär und Geschichte: Bilder, Tatsachen, Hintergründe* (2008), Heft 42

Rogers, Robert, and Walters, Rhodri, *How Parliament Works*, 6th ed. (Harlow: Pearson Education, 2006)

Royle, Trevor, *Crimea: The Great Crimean War 1854–1856* (London: Little, Brown & Company, 1999; Abacus 2000)

Russell, [Sir] William H., *General Todleben's History of the Defence of Sebastopol. 1854–5. A Review.* (London: Tinsley Brothers, 1865)

Saab, Ann Pottinger, *The Origins of the Crimean Alliance* (Charlottesville: University Press of Virginia, 1977)

Saibène, Marc, *La Flotte des Russes Blancs. Contribution de l'escadre française à l'évacuation des Russes blancs de Crimée, Novembre 1920* [The White Russian Fleet. Contribution of the French squadron to the evacuation of the White Russians from Crimea, November 1920] (Rennes: Marines editions, 2008)

Sakwa, Richard, *Frontline Ukraine: Crisis in the Borderlands* (London: I. B. Tauris, 2015)

Saul, Norman E., *Distant Friends: The United States and Russia, 1763–1867* (Kansas: Kansas University Press, 1991)

Seaton, Albert, *The Crimean War: A Russian Chronicle* (London: Batsford, 1977)

Shavshin, V. G., *Bastiony Sevastopolya* [Bastions of Sevastopol] (Sevastopol: Tavriya-Plus, 2000)

Sheehy, Ann, *The Crimean Tatars and Volga Germans: Soviet Treatment of Two National Minorities* (London: Minority Rights Group, 1971)

Sherr, James, 'Ukraine's Fightback', *The World Today*, August and September 2014

—, 'The New East–West Discord. Russian Objectives, Western Interests', Clingendael Report, December 2015

Shirokorad, Aleksandr [B.], *Bitva za Chernoye More* [The Battle for the Black Sea] (Moscow: Tranzitkniga, 2005)

—, *Chernomorskiy Flot v Tryokh Voynakh i Tryokh Revolyutsiyakh* [The Black Sea Fleet in Three Wars and Three Revolutions] (Moscow: Khranitel, 2007)

Sixsmith, Martin, *Russia: A 1,000 Year Chronicle of the Wild East* (London: BBC and Random House, 2012)

Smele, Jonathan D., *The 'Russian' Civil Wars, 1916–1926: Ten Years that Shook the World* (Oxford/New York: Oxford University Press, 2016)

Smith, Jeremy, 'Leadership and Nationalism in the Soviet Republics, 1951–1959', in Smith, Jeremy and Ilic, Melanie (eds), *Khrushchev in the Kremlin. Policy and Government in the Soviet Union, 1953–1964* (London: Routledge, 2011)

Smithurst, Peter, *The Pattern 1853 Enfield Rifle* (Oxford: Osprey, 2011)

Solzhenitsyn, Aleksandr I., *The Gulag Archipelago 1918–1956. An Experiment in Literary Investigation V–VII* (New York: Harper & Row, 1977)

Sondhaus, Lawrence, *Naval Warfare, 1815–1914* (London: Routledge, 2000)

—, *Navies of Europe* (London: Longman, 2002)

von Staden, Heinrich, *The Land and Government of Muscovy: A Sixteenth-Century Account* (Stanford: University Press, 1967)

Staff, Gary, *German Battlecruisers of World War One. Their Design, Construction and Operations* (Barnsley: Seaforth Publishing, 2014)

Stahel, David, *Operation Barbarossa and Germany's Defeat in the East* (Cambridge: University Press, 2009)

Stein, Marcel, trans. Gwyneth Fairbank, *Field Marshal von Manstein. The Janus Head. A Portrait* (Solihull: Helion, 2007). Originally published in German as *Der Januskopf – Feldmarschall von Manstein. Eine Neubewertung* (Bissendorf: Biblio Verlag, 2004).

Stevens, Carol B., *Russia's Wars of Emergence 1460–1730* (Harlow: Pearson Education, 2007)

Stone, Norman, *The Eastern Front 1914–1917* (New York: Charles Scribner's Sons, 1975)

Strabo, trans. Horace L. Jones, *Geographica*, vol. iii (London: Heinemann, 1924)

Strachan, Hew, 'Soldiers, Strategy and Sebastopol', *The Historical Journal*, vol. 21, no. 2 (June, 1978)

—, *The First World War*, vol. i, *To Arms* (Oxford: University Press, 2001)

Stille, Mark, *British Battlecruiser vs. German Battlecruiser* (Oxford: Osprey, 2013)

Svechin, Aleksandr A., *Strategiya* [Strategy], 2nd ed. (Moscow: Voyennyy vestnik 1927). An English language translation, ed. Kent D. Lee, was published by East View Information Services, Minneapolis, Minnesota in 1992.

Sweetman, John, *Balaklava 1854* (London: Osprey, 1990)

—, *The Crimean War 1854–1856* (Oxford: Osprey, 2001)

Tarle, E. V., *Krymskaya voyna* [Crimean War] vol. 2 (Moscow and Leningrad, 1945)

Taube, Gerhard, *Festung Sewastopol* [Fortress Sevastopol] (Hamburg: E.S. Mittler & Sohn, 1995)

Taubman, William, *Khrushchev. The Man and His Era* (London: Free Press, 2003)

Temperley, Harold, *England and the Near East: The Crimea* (London: Longmans Green, 1936)

Tennyson, Alfred, 'The Charge of the Light Brigade', *Poems of Tennyson* (Oxford: Oxford University Press, 1926)

Thucydides, trans. Charles Forster Smith, *History of the Peloponnesian War* (London: Heinemann and Cambridge, Massachusetts: Harvard University Press, 1956)

Tieke, Wilhelm, *Kampf um die Krim 1941–1944* [The Battle for the Crimea, 1941–1944] (Gummersbach: Selbstverlag Wilhelm Tieke, 1975)

Tredea, John and Sozaev, Eduard, *Russian Warships in the Age of Sail 1696–1860* (Barnsley: Seaforth Publishing, 2010)

Trevor-Roper, Hugh R. (ed.), *Hitler's War Directives 1939–1945* [texts from Walter Hubatsch, *Hitlers Weisungen für die Kriegführung 1939–1945*] (London: Sidgwick and Jackson, 1964)

Tuchman, Barbara W., *The Guns of August* (London: Penguin, 2014). First published by Macmillan in 1962.

Tyrell, Henry, *History of the War with Russia: Giving Full Details of the Operations of the Allied Armies, in three volumes* (London: The London Printing & Publishing Company, 1855–58)

Usoltsev, Vladimir S., *Foma Fomich Mekenzi* [Thomas, son of Thomas Mackenzie] (Sevastopol: Art-Print, 2001)

Vanden Bosch, Michael and Bartlett, Roger, 'More light on the Upton Family', Parts One, Two, and Three, in *The War Correspondent*, vol. 30, no. 1 (April 2012) & no. 3 (October 2012)

Vaneev, Genady I., Kondranov, I. P., Korotkov, M. A., and Fomina, Natalia N., *Sevastopolyu 200 let: 1783–1983. Sbornik dokumentov i materyalov* [Sevastopol 200 Years: 1783–1983. A Collection of Documents and Materials] (Kiev: Naukova Dumka, 1983)

Vaneev, Genady I., *Sevastopol: Stranisty, Istorii 1783–1983 Spravochnik* [Sevastopol: Pages of History, 1783–1983, A Companion] (Simferopol: Tavriya, 1983)

—, *Sevastopol 1941–1942. Khronika Geroycheskoy Oborony* [Chronicle of a Heroic Defence], 2 vols. (Kyiv: Ukraina, 1995)

van der Vat, Dan, *The Ship that Changed the World*, 2nd ed. (Edinburgh: Birlinn, 2000)

Veit, Chuck, *The Yankee Expedition to Sebastopol: John Gowen and the Raising of the Russian Black Sea Fleet 1857–1862* (Lulu.com, 2014)

Vulliamy, Colwyn E., *Crimea: The Campaign of 1854–56* (London: Jonathan Cape, 1939)

Walker, Jonathan, *Operation Unthinkable. The Third World War. British Plans to Attack the Soviet Empire, 1945* (Stroud: The History Press, 2013)

War Office, Great Britain, *Handbook of the Russian Army*, 6th ed. (London: General Staff, War Office, 1914)

Wegner, Bernd, 'Die Kämpfe auf der Krim', *Der Globale Krieg: Die Ausweitung zum Weltkrieg und der Wechsel der Initiative 1941–1943* ['The Fighting in Crimea', The Global War: Expansion to World War and the Change of Initiative 1941–1943] *Das deutsche Reich im Zweiten Weltkrieg*, vol. 4 (Stuttgart: Deutsche Verlags-Anstalt, 1990)

Werth, Alexander, *Russia at War 1941–1945* (London: Pan Books, 1965)

Wheeler-Bennett, John W., *Hindenburg: The Wooden Titan* (London: Macmillan, 1967)

Whisenhunt, William B., and Saul, Norman E., *New Perspectives on Russian–American Relations* (New York and Abingdon: Routledge, 2016)

Williams, Brian G., *The Crimean Tatars: From Soviet Genocide to Putin's Conquest* (London: Hurst & Company, 2015)

Wilson, Andrew, *Ukraine Crisis. What it Means for the West* (New Haven and London: Yale University Press, 2014)

Wolmar, Christian, *Engines of War: How Wars Were Won and Lost on the Railways* (London: Atlantic Books, 2010)

Woodham-Smith, Cecil, *The Reason Why: The Story of the Fatal Charge of the Light Brigade* (London: Penguin, 2000). First published by Constable in 1953.

—, *Queen Victoria. Her Life and Times*, vol. i: 1819–1861 (London: Cardinal, 1975). First published by Hamish Hamilton in 1972.

Wrangel, Alexis, *General Wrangel 1878–1929. Russia's White Crusader* (London: Leo Cooper, 1990)

Zadorozhnaya, N. F., *Dom-muzey sevastopolskikh podpolshchikov 1942–1944* [Memorial House of the Sevastopol Resistance, 1942–44] (Sevastopol: Borisov, 2007)

Zayonchkovskiy, Petr A., *Nikolay I i Ego vremya* [Nicholas I and His Times] vol. 2 (Moscow: Olma-Press, 2000)

Zvegintsov, V. V., *Russkaya Armiya 1914 g. Podrobnaya dislokatsiya, formirovaniya 1914–1917, regalii i otlichiya,* [Russian Army in 1914, Detailed Deployment, Formations 1914–1917, Regalia and Insignia] (Paris: self-published, 1959)

Resources Accessible Online

Anon, *The History of Russian Navy*, Chapter 3, 'Chesma and Patras', http://www.neva.ru/EXPO96/book/chap3-4.html

Anon, 'Shturm Sapun-Gory' [Assault on the Sapun Gora], 27.02.2015, http://www.pomnivoinu.ru/home/reports/1751/

Anon, Kharkov agreement of 21 April 2010, text in Ukrainian, http://www.pravda.com.ua/articles/2010/04/22/4956018/

Anon, 'Russia deploys S-400 anti-aircraft missile system in Crimea', http://www.unian.info/society/1467421-russia-deploys-s-400-anti-aircraft-missile-system-in-crimea.html

Anon, 'Iz istorii flota. Morskoy flot' [From the History of the Fleet. The Merchant Marine Fleet], *International Maritime Journal*, No. 3, 2007, http://www.morflot.su/archives/articles1499file.pdf

Anon, 'Iosif Stalin v Sevastopole' [Josef Stalin in Sevastopol], 22 January 2015, http://www.liveinternet.ru/users/4768613/post351007906/

Agence France-Presse, 'Crimean court bans "extremist" Tatar governing body', *The Guardian* (16 April 2016), https://www.theguardian.com/world/2016/apr/26/court-bans-extremist-crimean-tatar-governing-body-mejlis-russia

Alpert, Lukas I., 'Crimean Tatar Leader Is Barred From Returning to Russia', *The Wall Street Journal* (22 April 2014), http://www.wsj.com/articles/SB100014240527023040499004579451707365 6192990

Amos, Howard, 'Ukraine crisis fuels secession calls in pro-Russian south', *The Guardian* (23 February 2014), https://www.theguardian.com/world/2014/feb/23/ukraine-crisis-secession-russian-crimea

Avakyan, Victoria, 'Clementine Churchill in Sevastopol', *International Affairs*, No. 5 (May 2010) [Original text in Russian], https://interaffairs.ru/jauthor/material/242

Backmann, Christina, 'Major James George Semple Lisle and his wives', http://www.tufftuff.net/majorsemple.htm

BBC Report, 'Russian troops storm Ukrainian bases in Crimea', 22 March 2014, http://www.bbc.co.uk/news/world-europe-26698754

Bolotina, N. Yu. (ed.), *Glavnaya krepost dolzhna byt Sevastopol: Dokumenty o sozdanii bazy Chernomorskogo flota. 1784–1793gg* [The Main Fortress should be Sevastopol: Documents concerning the Establishment of the Black Sea Fleet. 1784-1793], http://www.drevlit.ru/docs/russia/XVIII/1780-1800/Osnov_Sevastopol/text.php

Browne, Anthony M., 'Memories of Winston Churchill', *Finest Hour* 50 (Winter 1985–86), http://www.winstonchurchill.org/resources/reference/149-uncategorised/finest-hour-online/2655-qmemories-of-winston-churchillq-1

de Carbonnel, Alissa, 'RPT-INSIGHT-How the Separatists delivered Crimea to Moscow' (13 March 2014), http://in.reuters.com/article/ukraine-crisis-russia-aksyonov-idINL6N0M93AH20140313

Elder, Miriam, 'Ukrainians protest against Russian language law', *The Guardian* (4 July 2012), https://www.theguardian.com/world/2012/jul/04/ukrainians-protest-russian-language-law

European Council, *Conclusions of the European Council* (20/21 March 2014), http://www.consilium.europa.eu/uedocs/cms_data/docs/pressdata/en/ec/141749.pdf

EU Joint Declaration of the Eastern Partnership Summit, Vilnius, 28-29 November 2013, http://www.consilium.europa.eu/uedocs/cms_Data/docs/pressdata/EN/foraff/139765.pdf

EU External Action Fact Sheet, 'The EU non-recognition policy for Crimea and Sevastopol' (Brussels, March 2016), https://eeas.europa.eu/top_stories/pdf/the-eu-non-recognition-policy-for-crimea-and-sevastopol-fact-sheet.pdf

EU *Eastern Partnerships* (May 2009), http://www.eeas.europa.eu/ukraine/about/index_en.htm

EU Text of the [Ukrainian] *Association Agreement* (undated), http://www.eeas.europa.eu/ukraine/pdf/3_ua_title_ii_pol_dialogue_reform_pol_assoc_coop_convergence_in_fsp_en.pdf

Euripides, *Iphigenia among the Taurians*, http://www2.hn.psu.edu/faculty/jmanis/euripides/Euripides-Iphigenia.pdf.

Gerasimov, V., 'Tsennost Nauki v Predvidennii', *Voyenno-promyshlennyy kur'yer*, No. 8 (476), 27, February – 5 March 2013, http://www.vpk-news.ru/articles/14632

Glantz, David, 'Vladimir the Terrible', *The Economist*, 20 September 2014, http://www.economist.com/news/letters/21618669-letters-editor

Gorchakov, Alexander, *Public Diplomacy Fund*, http://gorchakovfund.ru/en/about/gorchakov/

Hansard, House of Lords debate, 16 February 1855, http://hansard.millbanksystems.com/lords/1855/feb/16/army-reform-army-service-act-amendment#S3V0136P0_18550216_HOL_5

Hattendorf, John B., 'The Idea of a "Fleet in Being" in Historical Perspective', *Naval War College Review* (Winter 2014), https://www.academia.edu/5367169/_The_Idea_of_a_Fleet_in_Being_in_Historical_Perspective_

Hibbert, Hugh R., *Letters and Papers of Colonel Hugh Robert Hibbert (1828–1895)*, mainly relating to service in the Crimean War, 1854-1855, http://discovery.nationalarchives.gov.uk/details/rd/fe1d0b65-fc6d-4073-9c89-a072cd3f3198

Hoffman, Frank G., *Conflict in the 21st Century: The Rise of Hybrid Wars* (Arlington: Virginia: Potomac Institute for Policy Studies, December 2007), http://www.potomacinstitute.org/images/stories/publications/potomac_hybridwar_0108.pdf

Kirimli, Hakan, 'Crimean Tatars, Nogays, and Scottish missionaries', *Cahiers du monde russe*, 45/1-2 (2004), pp. 61–107, http:// monderusse.revues.org/2603.

Koribut-Kubitovich [Lieutenant], 'Vospominaniya o Balaklavskom dele 13-go Oktyabrya 1854 goda' [Recollections of the Balaklava Affair of 13 October, 1854 [OS]], *Voennyi Sbornik*, 1859, No. 2. Translated text by Mark Conrad at http://marksrussianmilitaryhistory.info/Kubitovich.htm

Kozhukhov, Stefan, 'Iz Krymskikh Vospominanii o Polednei Voine' [Crimean Memoirs of the Last War], *Russkii Arkhiv*, 1869, vol. 7. Translated text at http://marksrussianmilitaryhistory.info/Kozhukhov.htm

Kramer, Mark, 'Why Did Russia Give Away Crimea Sixty Years Ago?', Wilson Centre, Cold War International History Project e-Dossier No. 47 (19 March 2014), https://www.wilsoncenter.org/publication/why-did-russia-give-away-crimea-sixty-years-ago

Krasnov, V. N., and Shitikov, E. A., 'The Formation of the Soviet Navy: An Introduction', http://rusnavy.com/history/Refleet/formation.php

Lenin [pseudonym], N. 'The Armed Forces and the Revolution', *Novaya Zhizn*, No. 14, November 16/29, 1905, republished in V. I. Lenin, *Collected Works*, vol. 10, November 1905–June 1906 (Moscow: Progress Publishers, 1965), http://www.marx2mao.com/PDFs/Lenin%20CW-Vol.%2010.pdf

Lenin, Vladimir, Speech of 1 July 1921 'In Defence of the Tactics of the Communist International', *Collected Works*, vol. 32, December 1920–August 1921 (Moscow: Progress Publishers, 1965), https://www.marxists.org/archive/lenin/works/cw/pdf/lenin cw-vol-32.pdf

[Liprandi, Lieutenant General P. P.], 'Report of Lieutenant General Liprandi, Commander of the Twelfth Division of Infantry, to Aide-de-Camp General Prince Menshikov', dated 14 (26) October 1854 [No. 3076]. Translated text by Mark Conrad at http://www.marksrussianmilitaryhistory.info/Liprandi.htm

Lopatin, V. S. (ed.), *Ekaterina II i G. A. Potemkin. Lichnaya perepiska, 1769–1791* [Catherine II and G. A. Potemkin. Personal Correspondence, 1769–1791] (Moscow: Nauka, 1997), http://az.lib.ru/e/ekaterina_w/text_0030.shtml.

Menshikov, [General-Adjutant Prince Aleksandr Sergeyevich], 'Report on the offensive operation by Lieutenant-General Liprandi's force against the camp of the Allies who are covering the road from Sevastopol to Balaklava', *Russkii Invalid* No. 235, 1854, and *Severnaya Pchela* No. 236, 1854. Translated text by Mark Conrad at http://marksrussianmilitaryhistory.info/Mensh-Balaklava.htm

Monaghan, Andrew, *A 'New Cold War'? Abusing History, Misunderstanding Russia*. Royal Institute of International Affairs, Research Paper (May 2015), https://www.chathamhouse.org/sites/files/chathamhouse/field/field_document/20150522ColdWarRussiaMonaghan.pdf

—, 'Putin's Way of War. The "War" in Russia's "Hybrid Warfare"', *Parameters* 45 (4) (Winter 2015–16), http://strategicstudiesinstitute.army.mil/pubs/parameters/issues/Winter_2015-16/9_Monaghan.pdf

Nicholas II, [Tsar], *Dnevniki Nikolaya Vtorogo* [Diaries of Nicholas II], http://www.tsaarinikolai.com/tekstit/Dnevniki_Nikolaja.pdf

Nicholas II, [Tsar], *Dnevnik Nikolaya II* [Diary of Nicholas II], http://emalkrest.narod.ru/txt/1913.htm

Nitu, Victor, 'The 3rd Army in the Ukraine and the Crimea – 1941', 'Romanian Armed Forces in the Second World War', http://www.worldwar2.ro/arr/?article=6

OKH Operations Order No. 7 dated 2 April 1944 – 'Directive for Further Operations by Army Group A, Army Group South and Army Group Centre', http://derfuehrer.org/reden/english/wardirectives/54.html

OSCE Report, *The Integration of the Formerly Deported People in Crimea, Ukraine. Needs Assessment* (August 2013), http://www.osce.org/hcnm/104309?download=true

OSCE/ODIHR 'Ukraine Presidential Election 17 January and 7 February 2010 Election Mission Final Report', Annex 2, Turnout and Results by Region, http://www.osce.org/odihr/elections/ukraine/67844?download=true

Ostrovskiy letters online, http://www.knigolubu.ru/translit/russian_classic/ostrovskiy_an/pisma_1842_-_1872_gg.10996/?page=17

Paton Walsh, Nick, 'Russia tells Ukraine to stay out of NATO', *The Guardian* (8 June 2006), https://www.theguardian.com/world/2006/jun/08/russia.nickpatonwalsh

Pohl, Otto J., 'The Deportation and Fate of the Crimean Tatars' (April 2000), a conference paper published by the International Committee for Crimea, http://www.iccrimea.org/scholarly/jopohl.html

Putin, Vladimir, Speech to the Federal Assembly of Russian Federation on 25 April 2005, http://en.kremlin.ru/events/president/transcripts/22931

—, Speech given at the Duma on 18 March 2014, www.en.kremlin.ru/events/president/news/20603

—, Speech at gala concert to mark the 69th anniversary of Victory in the Great Patriotic War and 70th anniversary of the liberation of Sevastopol from Nazis, 9 May 2014, http://en.kremlin.ru/events/president/transcripts/20993.

—, Speech at the 'We're Together!' concert in Moscow on 18 March 2015, http://en.kremlin.ru/events/president/news/47878

Quinn, Alison, 'Leader of Crimean Tatars Labelled 'Extremist', Banned From Home', *The Moscow Times* (6 July 2014), https://themoscowtimes.com/articles/leader-of-crimean-tatars-labeled-extremist-banned-from-home-37050

Razumkov Centre, 'Political Process in the Crimea: The Phases of Development and Basic Trends', *National Security and Defence* No. 4 (16), 2001, http://razumkov.org.ua/eng/files/category_journal/NSD16_eng.pdf

—, 'Attitude of the Crimean Residents to Probable Threats and Issues Bearing a Strong Conflict Potential', *National Security and Defence*, No. 4–5 (121–23), 2011, http://razumkov.org.ua/eng/files/category_journal/NSD122-123_eng.pdf

Republic of Crimea, *Constitution of the Autonomous Republic of Crimea* (1998), http://zakon3.rada.gov.ua/laws/show/350-14

Russian State Duma, *Ratification of Russian-Ukrainian Friendship Treaty of 1997* on 25 December 1998 (confirmed by Federation Council on 17 February 1999), http://archive.mid.ru//bdomp/dip_vest.nsf/99b2ddc4f717c733c32567370042ee43/551b02dbd01887acc325688700443754!OpenDocument

Ryzhov, Ivan Ivanovich, 'O srazhenii pod Balaklave; Zapiska General-Leitenanta Iv. Iv. Ryzhova' ['On the Battle of Balaklava; Notes of Lieutenant General Iv. Iv. Ryzhov'], *Russkii Vestnik*, April 1870, Vol. 86. Translated text by Mark Conrad at http://www.marksrussianmilitaryhistory.info/Ryzhov.htm

Shpakova, Irina, 'A vy rosli vmeste s voynoy Inogo mira vy ne znali' [You grew up together with war. You did not know another world], *Sevastopol'skiye izvestiya*, #24 (1871), 25 June 2016, https://sevzakon.ru/view/pressa/gazeta/14032/14970/

Sherr, James, 'The New East–West Discord. Russian Objectives, Western Interests', Clingendael Report, December 2015, https://www.clingendael.nl/sites/default/files/The_New_East-West_Discord_JSherr.pdf

Shishelina, L. N., 'Russia, the Visegrad Group and the Eastern Partnership Programme' in L. N. Shishelina et al., *Russia and the Visegrad Group: The Ukrainian Challenge*, Report 22/2015 (Moscow: Russian International Affairs Council, 2015), http://russiancouncil.ru/common/upload/RIAC-Visegrad-Report22-Eng.pdf

Shmidt-Ochakovskiy, Yevgeniy, *Leytenant Shmidt, 'Krasniy Admiral': Vospominaniya Syna* [Lieutenant Schmidt, 'Red Admiral': Memories of [his] Son] (Odessa: KP OGT, 2006), http://museum-literature.odessa.ua/Krasny_Admiral.pdf

Sokolov, Dmitry, 'Mest' pobediteley. Krasnyy terror v Sevastopole v 1920–1921 gg.' [Revenge of the Winners. The Red Terror in Sevastopol of 1920–1921], *Russkaya Liniya*, 22.10.2007, http://rusk.ru/st.php?idar=112133

—, 'Dva mesyatsa iz zhizni krasnogo Sevastopolya. Maloizvestnyye stranitsy istorii goroda v noyabre-dekabre 1920 g.' [Two Months in the Life of Red Sevastopol. Little-known Pages of History of the City in November-December 1920], *Russkaya Liniya*, 27.10.2015, http://rusk.ru/st.php?idar=72992

Stewart, Dale B., 'The Russian–Ukrainian Friendship Treaty and the Search for Regional Stability in Eastern Europe', Naval Postgraduate School, Monterey California (December 1997), http://calhoun.nps.edu/bitstream/handle/10945/8939/russianukrainian00stew.pdf

Sutyakin, Igor, *Russian Forces in Ukraine*, Royal United Services Institute Briefing Paper, March 2015, https://rusi.org/publication/briefing-papers/russian-forces-ukraine

Timchenko, Zinayida, 'Pivnichno-Kryms'kyy kanal. Istoriya budivnytstva' [The North Crimean Canal. History of Building], *Istorichna Pravda* (13/05/2014), http://www.istpravda.com.ua/articles/2014/05/13/142692/

Ukrainian Parliament [*Verkhovna Rada*], *National Constitution*, http://faolex.fao.org/docs/pdf/ukr127467E.pdf

—, *Ratification of Russian-Ukrainian Friendship Treaty of 1997* (14 January 1998), http://zakon5.rada.gov.ua/laws/show/13/98-вр

United Nations, *Resolution, 'Territorial Integrity of Ukraine'*, http://www.un.org/press/en/2014/ga11493.doc.htm

United Nations Security Council, 'Complaint by Ukraine regarding the Decree of the Supreme Soviet of the Russian Federation concerning Sevastopol. Decision of 20 July 1993 (3256th meeting): statement by the President', http://www.un.org/en/sc/repertoire/93 95/Chapter%208/EUROPE/93-95_8-22-UKRAINE.pdf

United States Department of State, *Papers relating to the Foreign Relations of the United States, 1918. Russia*, vol. I, *American and Russian Special Missions* (Washington, DC: US Government Printing Office, 1918), http://digital.library.wisc.edu/1711.dl/FRUS.FRUS1918v1

USSR Supreme Soviet Presidium (19 February 1954), translation at http://digitalarchive. wilsoncenter.org/document/119638

Vetch, R. H., 'Gordon, Sir (John) William (1814–1870)', rev. James Lunt, *Oxford Dictionary of National Biography* (Oxford: Oxford University Press, 2004) at http://www.oxforddnb.com/view/article/11069

Vologdin, B. P., 'Naseleniye Kryma' [The Population of Crimea], unpublished Taurida University thesis, elib.crimea.edu/krim/vologdin.pdf

Walsh, Stephen, 'The Russian Army and the Conduct of Operations in 1914', *British Journal for Military History*, Volume 2, Issue 2, February 2016, http://bjmh.org.uk/index.php/bjmh/article/view/92

Yakimenko, Andrey, 'The 225th Anniversary of the Reunification of the Crimea with Russia' (19.04.08), http://www.ruscrimea.ru/cms/index.php?go=Pages&in=view&id=105

INDEX